NARROW GAUGE RAILR

in Colorado, Utah and northern New

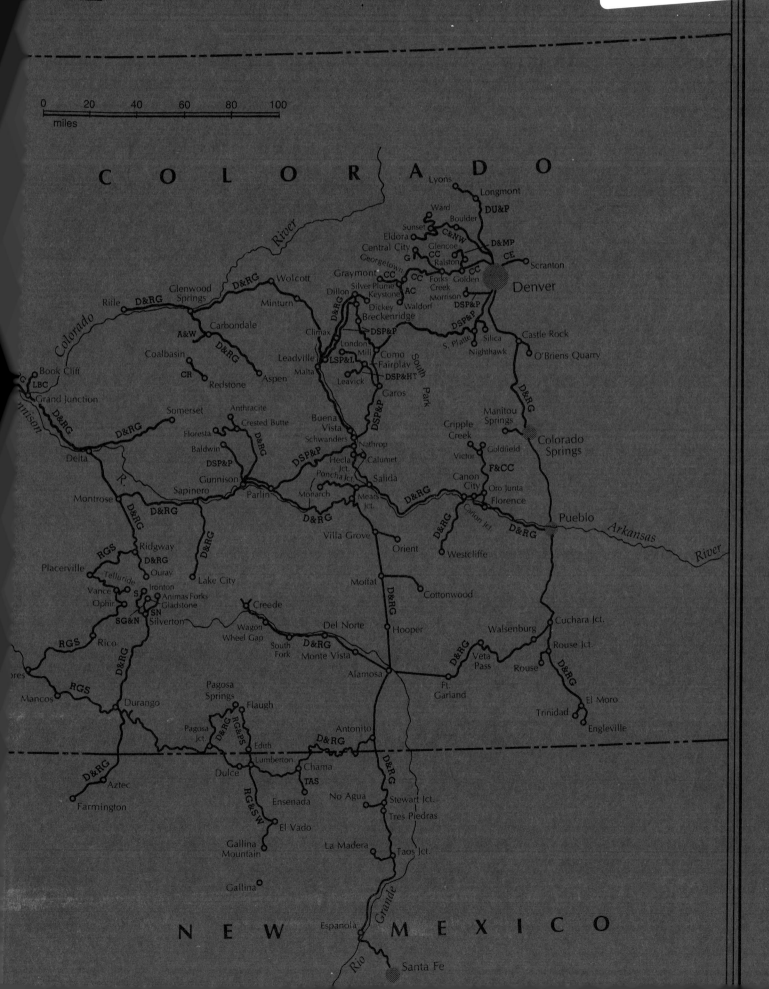

American
Narrow Gauge
Railroads

AMERICAN NARROW GAUGE RAILROADS

George W. Hilton

STANFORD UNIVERSITY PRESS
Stanford, California • 1990

Stanford University Press
Stanford, California

© 1990 by the Board of Trustees of the
Leland Stanford Junior University

Printed in the United States of America

CIP data are at the end of the book

To my late colleague

CHARLES ATKINS
HAMILL
(1920–1951)
of Colorado

Preface

Upon completion of my collaboration with Professor John F. Due, *The Electric Interurban Railways in America*, in 1960, I proposed a similar volume on the narrow gauge railroads to Stanford University Press. Although the Press responded with enthusiasm, it was to be a considerable length of time before the project came to fruition. I was not, as might appear, making an unsuccessful effort to set the record for academic procrastination. Rather, the incentives on younger faculty, unfortunately, are to produce shorter works, and I recognized from the outset that this would be a very large project. In addition, I became involved with various present-day policy issues. In large measure, however, I realized that the narrow gauge movement was not something of first importance in the history of railroading, like the conversion of the broad gauges into a homogeneous 4′-8½″ system, the adoption of the Janney coupler and the Westinghouse air brake, or the establishment of the Interstate Commerce Commission. Rather, it was a sport or aberration in the history of the industry, one that had very major negative consequences for a limited number of railroads, notably the Nickel Plate, Seaboard Air Line, and Norfolk & Western, all of which were cursed with long and important lines of appallingly low standards, relative to American practice generally. Finally, existing interpretation of the narrow gauge movement, notably in John A. Rehor's *The Nickel Plate Story* (Milwaukee: Kalmbach Publishing Co., 1965), seemed to me correct.

Given the long period in which the book was projected, my obligations are necessarily numerous. J. G. Bell and, after his retirement, Norris Pope of Stanford University Press never lost their enthusiasm for the project. Most of the actual work was done at the Division of Transportation, National Museum of American History of the Smithsonian Institution, beginning with a sabbatical year in 1978–79. I am indebted to all of the long-time staff of that division: Mary E. Braunagel, Susan Tolbert, John Stine, Roger White, William L. Withuhn, and especially to the curator—now senior historian—John H. White, Jr. Jack White tirelessly allowed me to draw on his accumulated knowledge of main-line railroad practice in the late nineteenth century, and in particular allowed me to make use of his uncompleted work on American railroad freight cars. In conversation he contributed to the argument of the book at more points than it is practical to cite. Except for some of the early corporate histories typed by the late Carole Wilbur, the manuscript was produced with great efficiency by Lorraine Grams at UCLA on the departmental word processor. Colleagues Harold Demsetz and Kenneth Sokoloff were kind enough to read the manuscript.

A large number of enthusiasts assisted greatly. Cornelius W. Hauck of Cincinnati read the manuscript and assisted in gathering illustrations. Jackson C. Thode proved an endless fount of information on the Denver & Rio Grande, to which he has devoted a lifetime, both as official and as enthusiast. Richard H. Kindig, John W. Maxwell, Robert A. LeMassena, Ed Haley, and many others helped me with their considerable command of the history of the Colorado network. George E. Pitchard was cooperative in sharing with me the results of his extensive search of Utah newspapers. Albin L. Lee assisted not only on the history of the Bellevue & Cascade, on which he is the leading authority, but on car architecture and narrow gauge practice more generally. Colonel Clare R. J. Rogers, Wayne Lincoln, Thomas T. Taber III, Benjamin F. G. Kline, Ed Cass, Ed Boss and Ed Bond, Lee Rainey, and several other members of the Three Rivers Narrow Gauge Historical Society shared their knowledge of the eastern narrow gauges. This list is far from complete. Names of other enthusiasts will be found in notes and references throughout the book.

My original intention was to append to Chapter 5 a listing of all known American narrow gauge locomotives by builder with original and subsequent owners. I quickly concluded that this was impractical; it is a project so large as to require a book of its own. I subsequently discovered that Joseph A. Strapac was planning such a volume for his Shade Tree Books. He graciously allowed me to draw upon his accumulated material on this subject, and I agreed to provide him with such assistance as I could toward his projected book.

The text has been written in the usual presumption that the reader is ordinarily familiar with basic railroad terminology. The book, however, is likely to be used as a reference work or source of data by local historians or economic historians who are not thoroughly familiar with such usage. Accordingly, at the first use of a term in specialized railroad terminology, I have provided a short definition in the margin. Readers seeking a more full presentation of railroad terminology and of standard railroad practice are referred to Robert Selph Henry, *This Fascinating Railroad Business* (Indianapolis and New York: Bobbs-Merrill Co., 1942). By the same token, for the general reader unfamiliar with economics terminology, I have provided several definitions of specialized terms as an aid to understanding the economic arguments in Chapter 2.

The Victorians were much given to italics and I am not. In all instances, emphasis in the text is in the original, and not provided. Trivial spelling errors in quotations—mainly of "gauge" and "Edward Hulbert"—have been corrected without comment.

Factual errors called to my attention by December 31, 1991, and substantiated will be published in *Railroad History*, No. 167, Fall 1992. Information on ultimate abandonment of converted narrow gauge lines in Part II will not be updated because, as mentioned in the Introduction to Part II, information on the present state of former narrow gauge trackage will inevitably become obsolete in any event.

G. W. H.

Contents

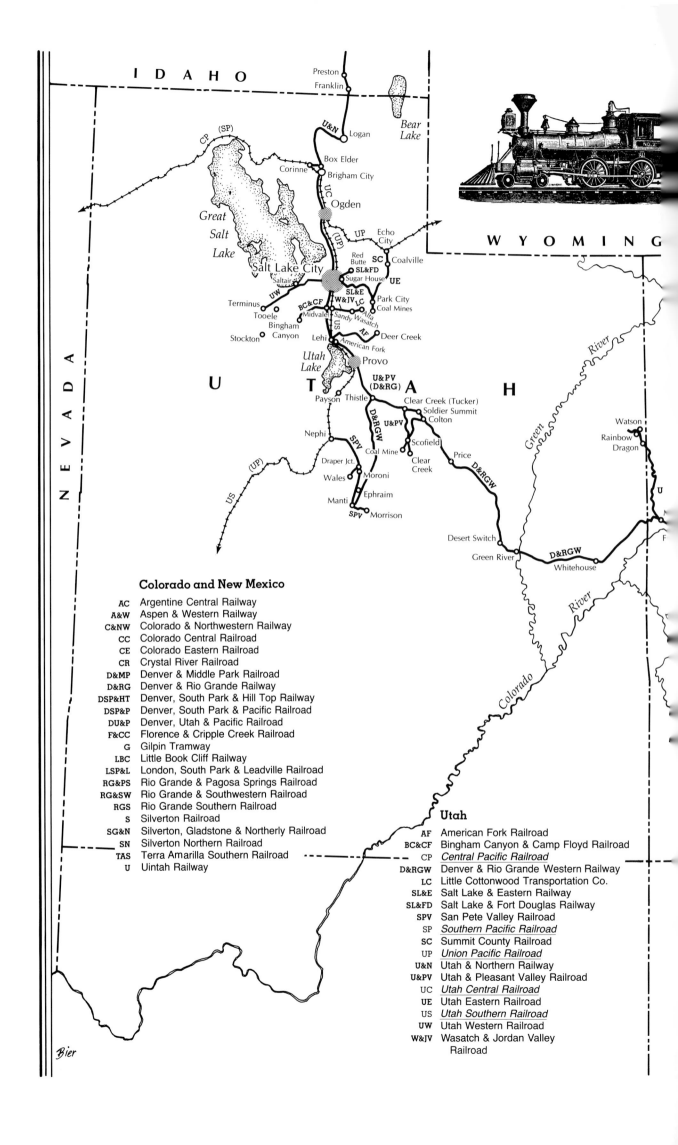

IDAHO

WYOMING

NEVADA

UTAH

Preston
Franklin
Logan
U&N
Box Elder
Corinne
Brigham City
UC
Ogden
Echo City
UP
Red Butte
SC
Coalville
SL&FD
Sugar House
UE
SL&E
Park City
Coal Mines
W&JV LC
Salt Lake City
Saltair
Terminus
UW
BC&CF
Midvale
Sandy Wasatch
Alta
US
Tooele
Bingham
Canyon
Stockton
AF
Deer Creek
Lehi
American Fork
Provo
Utah Lake
U&PV (D&RG)
Payson
Thistle
Clear Creek (Tucker)
Soldier Summit
Colton
D&RGW
U&PV
Nephi
SPV
Coal Mine
Scofield
Draper Jct.
Clear Creek
Price
Wales
Moroni
Manti
Ephraim
SPV
Morrison

Great Salt Lake
Bear Lake
(SP)
CP

Green River
Colorado River

Watson
Rainbow
Dragon
U
D&RGW
Desert Switch
Green River
D&RGW
Whitehouse
F

Bier

Colorado and New Mexico

AC	Argentine Central Railway
A&W	Aspen & Western Railway
C&NW	Colorado & Northwestern Railway
CC	Colorado Central Railroad
CE	Colorado Eastern Railroad
CR	Crystal River Railroad
D&MP	Denver & Middle Park Railroad
D&RG	Denver & Rio Grande Railway
DSP&HT	Denver, South Park & Hill Top Railway
DSP&P	Denver, South Park & Pacific Railroad
DU&P	Denver, Utah & Pacific Railroad
F&CC	Florence & Cripple Creek Railroad
G	Gilpin Tramway
LBC	Little Book Cliff Railway
LSP&L	London, South Park & Leadville Railroad
RG&PS	Rio Grande & Pagosa Springs Railroad
RG&SW	Rio Grande & Southwestern Railroad
RGS	Rio Grande Southern Railroad
S	Silverton Railroad
SG&N	Silverton, Gladstone & Northerly Railroad
SN	Silverton Northern Railroad
TAS	Terra Amarilla Southern Railroad
U	Uintah Railway

Utah

AF	American Fork Railroad
BC&CF	Bingham Canyon & Camp Floyd Railroad
CP	*Central Pacific Railroad*
D&RGW	Denver & Rio Grande Western Railway
LC	Little Cottonwood Transportation Co.
SL&E	Salt Lake & Eastern Railway
SL&FD	Salt Lake & Fort Douglas Railway
SPV	San Pete Valley Railroad
SP	*Southern Pacific Railroad*
SC	Summit County Railroad
UP	*Union Pacific Railroad*
U&N	Utah & Northern Railway
U&PV	Utah & Pleasant Valley Railroad
UC	*Utah Central Railroad*
UE	Utah Eastern Railroad
US	*Utah Southern Railroad*
UW	Utah Western Railroad
W&JV	Wasatch & Jordan Valley Railroad

NARROW GAUGE RAILROADS
in Colorado, Utah and northern New Mexico

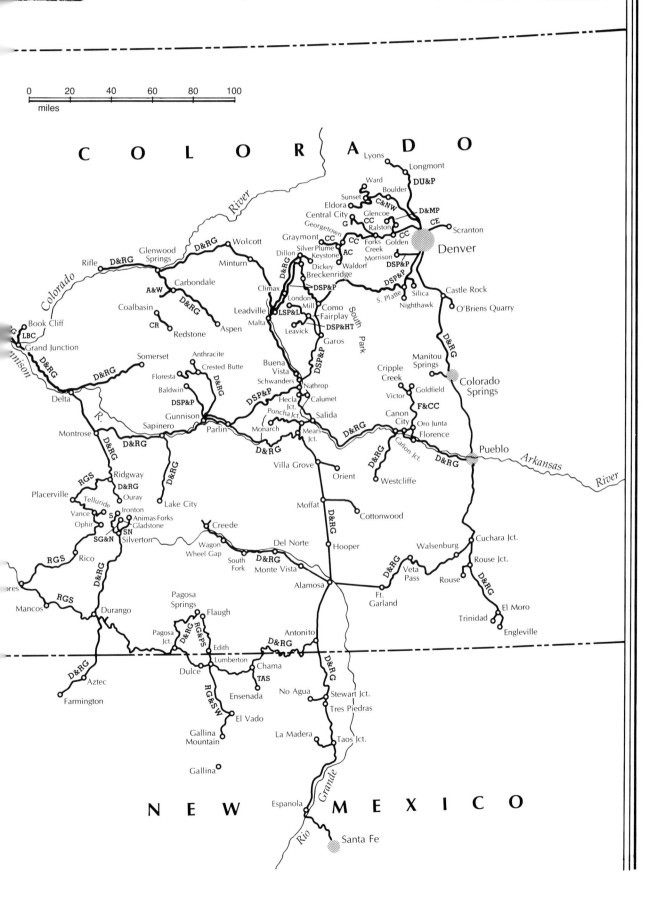

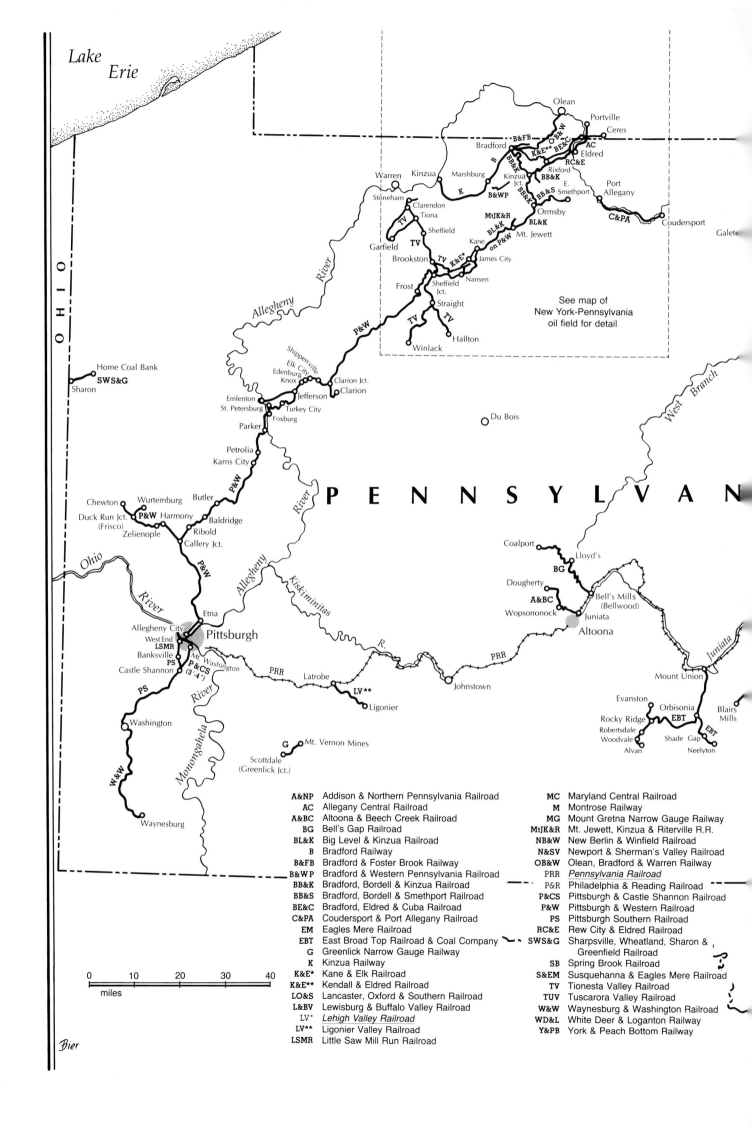

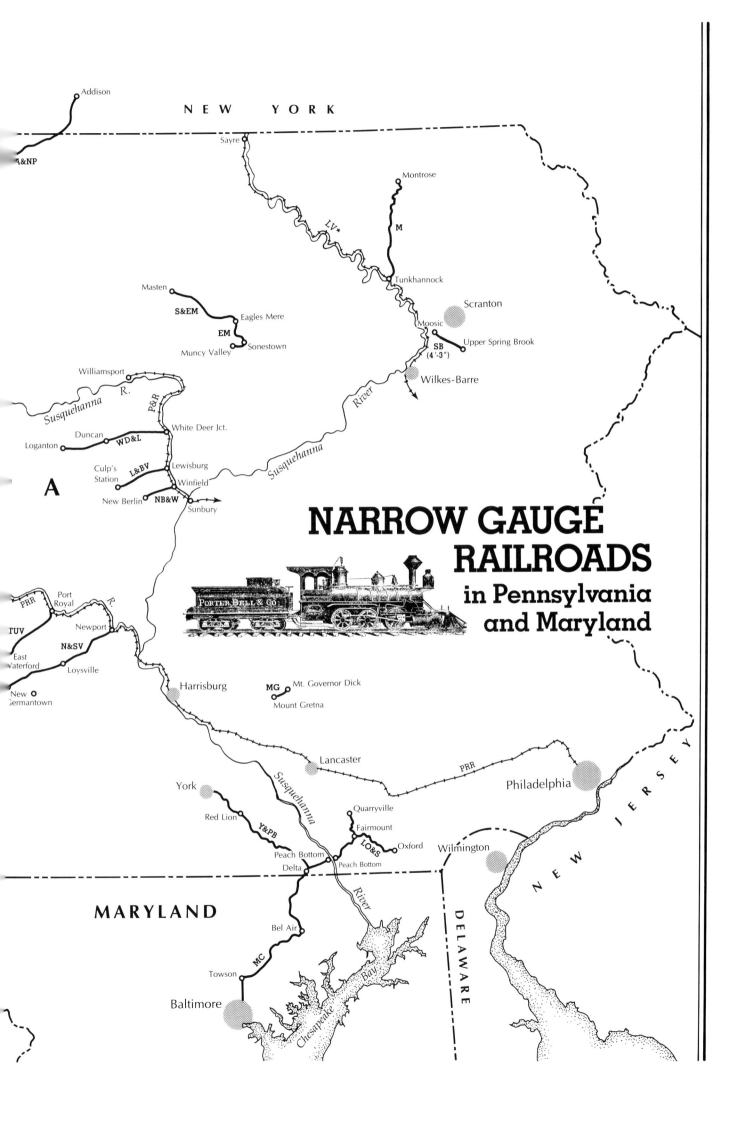

NEW YORK

Addison

&NP

Sayre

Montrose

LV*

M

Tunkhannock

Masten

S&EM

Eagles Mere

EM

Scranton

Moosic

SB
(4'-3")

Upper Spring Brook

Muncy Valley

Sonestown

Wilkes-Barre

Susquehanna River

Williamsport

P&R

Susquehanna R.

White Deer Jct.

Duncan

WD&L

Loganton

Lewisburg

Culp's
Station

L&BV

Winfield

New Berlin

NB&W

Sunbury

A

Susquehanna River

PRR

Port
Royal

R.

TUV

Newport

East
Waterford

N&SV

Loysville

New
Germantown

NARROW GAUGE
RAILROADS
in Pennsylvania
and Maryland

PORTER BELL & CO

Harrisburg

MG

Mt. Governor Dick

Mount Gretna

Lancaster

PRR

Philadelphia

NEW JERSEY

York

Red Lion

Y&PB

Susquehanna

Quarryville

Fairmount

LO&S

Oxford

Wilmington

Peach Bottom

Delta

Peach Bottom

River

DELAWARE

MARYLAND

Bel Air

MC

Towson

Baltimore

Chesapeake Bay

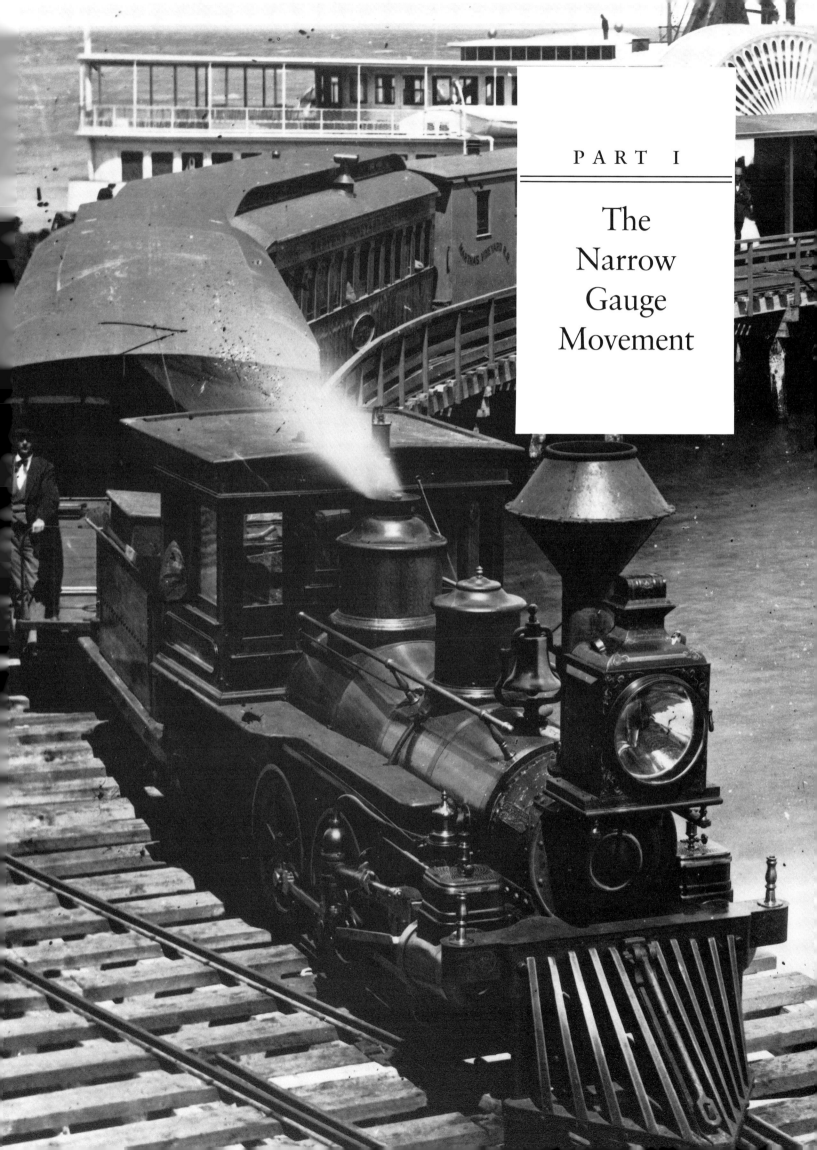

The Origins of
the Narrow
Gauge
Movement

Like the steam railway itself, the narrow gauge movement had its origins
mainly in Britain. That the steam railway arose there is not surprising. The
locomotive was an adaptation of the stationary steam engine, which had
been developed from imperfect predecessors by James Watt in Britain in
the mid-eighteenth century. The demands for transport associated with
the Industrial Revolution—which was itself in large part an adaptation of
British industry to Watt's innovation—were satisfied most effectively by
the railway. By the 1860s, when the narrow gauge movement began, Britain was thoroughly laced with a railway network that was rapidly moving
toward homogeneity at a gauge of 4'-8½". The narrow gauge movement
arose not out of any widespread domestic dissatisfaction with the evolution of the British railways, but rather out of a questioning of how suitable
4'-8½" and its wider rivals were for the developing areas of the British Empire. Because the debate over narrow gauges in Britain shaped the American movement a decade later, we will examine it in some detail in this
chapter. But first we begin with an account of British experience with a
variety of gauges before the 1860s.

The Origins of Standard Gauge in Britain

As a mid-Victorian observer viewed the British railway system, the in-
cipient homogeneity of gauge appeared a consequence of historical accident and of adverse experience with incompatibility between companies.
The question of whether 4'-8½" is the optimal railway gauge will be considered in the American context *a priori* in Chapter 2 and *a posteriori* in
Chapter 9, but for present purposes it is sufficient to say that there was
nothing in the gauge's early history to cause a British observer to impute
optimality to it. Rather, it was approximately the gauge of vehicles with
which George Stephenson, the engineer of the first practical common carrier railways, was most familiar from his early work. The collieries of the
Tyneside area in the vicinity of Newcastle had a network of horse-powered

wooden waggonways—so spelled—connecting the mines with loading facilities on the Tyne and Wear. The gauges varied from about 3'-10" to 5'-0". The Killingworth Colliery, where Stephenson began his railway career, was on a waggonway that reached the north bank of the Tyne below Newcastle at Willington, somewhat over four miles from the mine. The Willington Way, as it was called, used 4'-8", a common road gauge in the area. As far as is known, the Willington Way had been laid to this gauge since its origins in 1763–64. When Stephenson came to design the Stockton & Darlington Railway in 1825 and the Liverpool & Manchester, he used 4'-8" uncritically, simply because he was thoroughly familiar with it.[1] He had built his first locomotives for the Killingworth installation. Had his initiation into the Tyneside Waggonways been at another colliery, the gauge he chose might have been several inches larger or smaller. Exactly how his 4'-8" was expanded to 4'-8½" is not well documented, but the additional half inch is thought to have been added in the 1830s on the Liverpool & Manchester to provide greater lateral play for the flanges in higher speed operation.[2] Sir John Rennie in his early consultations with the Liverpool & Manchester proposed to use 5'-6".[3] Because of the importance of access to the Liverpool port facilities, whichever gauge the Liverpool & Manchester adopted was almost certain to become the standard British gauge. Consequently, the gauge of 4'-8½" looked arbitrary indeed. The historical origins of this gauge were not to become apparent until about 40 years after its introduction.

Arbitrary or not, 4'-8½" spread uniformly throughout Britain with some minor exceptions and one truly monumental exception. Isambard Kingdom Brunel considered 4'-8½" grossly inadequate for the speeds he envisioned. Brunel contemplated passenger trains operating at 50 to 60 miles per hour and freights at 30 miles per hour, but felt that wider locomotives of greater stability were necessary to haul them. When he planned the Great Western Railway in 1833–34, he specified the enormous gauge of seven feet, apparently precisely 7'-0¼", the widest ever used in a railway intended for general service.[4] Brunel's broad gauge was part of a highly novel technology of railways. The rails were laid on heavy wooden stringers or baulks set on pilings, connected at infrequent intervals with transoms, or exceptionally heavy crossties. The locomotives were mainly high-wheeled single-driver models designed by Brunel's associate, Daniel Gooch. By the mid-1840s, Brunel's broad gauge rails had spread from his Paddington Station in London over the west of England and South Wales.

The geographical pattern of the two gauges tended to minimize the problem of incompatibility. The Great Western and the standard gauge lines were not in direct rivalry, and they met at only a single point, Gloucester. The break of gauge between the standard gauge Birmingham & Gloucester Railway and the Great Western's Gloucester-Bristol branch became a well-publicized inconvenience.[5] Shipments were typically delayed at least a day—though the delay was unpredictable—and subject to breakage and theft. The heavy volume of transshipment gave the Gloucester station an anarchic quality that travelers with children found particularly repellent. No less an author than Thackeray wrote of the trials; his "Jeames on the Gauge Question" purports to be a first-person account

The *Iron Duke*, a replica of one of Daniel Gooch's broad gauge locomotives, is shown backing into the freight shed at Didcot, Berkshire, in 1986. The track is a newly built three-rail section of Isambard Kingdom Brunel's baulk road, described in the text. (M. Seymour collection.)

of the struggle of a publican and his wife to make the connection with a baby and 73 pieces of luggage. In the confusion of moving the luggage, each presumes the other has the baby, and the child is left in Gloucester. The publican concludes, in his illiterate English, that the break of gauge is a "*nashnal newsance.*"[6]

The two gauges were so disparate as to make reconciliation very difficult. Trains of mixed cars of both gauges in the early years could be run only if standard gauge track was laid at the center of the broad gauge sleepers (ties). Telescopic axles had been tried but found dangerous. It was possible to carry a standard gauge car on a broad gauge platform car (flatcar), but not the reverse. Broad gauge cars mounted on standard gauge bogies (trucks) presented stability problems. Iron boxes—a primitive form of containerization—were used for interline movements of coal, but were not thought practical for general cargo.[7]

The problem of incompatibility was serious enough for Parliament to establish a Royal Commission on the Gauge Problem in 1845. In the following year the Commission reported strongly in favor of compatibility: "We consider a break of gauge to be a very serious evil."[8] The Commission found no advantage in safety except that broad gauge locomotives might be more stable at high speeds.[9] Adversely, broad gauge cars had a higher ratio of deadweight to load.[10] The Commission found no advantage in stability of broad gauge trains up to 40 miles per hour, but admitted some might exist at 50 or 60.[11] The Commission concluded, "On the whole we consider the narrow [i.e., standard] as the more convenient for the merchandize of the country."[12] The Commission recommended that future mileage be built at 4'-8½", partly because additional lines were expected to be branches of existing main lines, and partly because standard gauge was already so dominant: the various standard gauge operators ran 1,901 route miles compared with only 274 miles for the Great Western. The Commissioners proposed that Parliament require future construction to be 4'-8½" and encourage but not require broad gauge operators to convert.[13]

Parliament responded with a statute, 9 & 10 Victoria, Cap. 87 (1846), which established 4'-8½" as the minimum gauge to which future railways might be built in Britain.[14] This statute had its desired effect in assuring homogeneity at 4'-8½". Operators of non-standard gauges in Scotland and East Anglia had either converted before the enactment or were preparing to do so. The Great Western began a long period of conversion. The break-of-gauge at Gloucester was eliminated in 1853 when the Midland Railway, after acquiring the Birmingham & Gloucester, laid a third rail on the Great Western into Bristol.[15] Nonetheless, the Great Western did not run its last broad gauge train until 1892.

Intellectually, the enactment did little to advance the notion that 4'-8½" was optimal. Because the statute also established 5'-3" as the minimum gauge for Ireland, it could be interpreted simply as a recognition that incompatibility was undesirable, and that the dominant gauge ought to be made universal. Indeed, by choosing 5'-3" for Ireland, Parliament acted as if some broader gauge might be preferable. Such considerations caused gauges of more than 5'-0" to be adopted for overseas service in several portions of the British Empire. Most importantly, 5'-6" was chosen on the recommendation of W. Simms for the Indian Railways in 1850, explicitly as an intermediate between the two British gauges.[16] In Canada, 5'-6" was the gauge of the Atlantic & St. Lawrence, Montreal's connection to Portland, Maine, for access to an unfrozen port in winters. The provincial legislature in 1851 required this gauge for any railway receiving governmental guaranty, essentially making it mandatory until the statute was repealed in 1870.[17] The motivation for the broad gauge was apparently the belief that incompatibility would make an American invasion more difficult, rather than any economic consideration. The gauge of 5'-3" spread to Australia as a consequence of its adoption in Ireland. As early as 1852 a horse-drawn railway of that gauge was opened at Port Elliot, South Australia. In the same year an Irish engineer, F. W. Shields, was placed in charge of construction of the railway projected from Sydney to Paramatta, New South Wales. Shields changed the gauge from 4'-8½" to 5'-3". When he was replaced, the gauge was returned to 4"-8½" and the line was opened as a standard gauge railroad in 1855. Meanwhile, Victoria and South Australia had adopted 5'-3" for conformity, but were too far advanced to modify their plans. Tasmania and New Zealand also chose 5'-3" at the outset.

Early Narrow Gauge Railways

By the early 1860s there was widespread dissatisfaction with broad gauges as unnecessarily expensive, both in initial capital requirements and in operating costs. In India, in particular, the 5'-6" gauge was perceived as a mistake. On the basis of the initial network between major cities, the full system thought necessary to develop the nation was impractical. Similarly, Victoria's 5'-3" was thought inappropriate for lines to develop barely populated areas of Australia. Queensland was so lightly populated that its first railways would necessarily run inland from ports to villages in the bush.

The idea of light railways at less-than-standard gauges for such services was probably inevitable. There had been a long history of narrow gauge railways or tramways in mines, quarries, and industrial installations. Examples far antedated the railway age; there is evidence of mine tramways with wooden rails at narrow gauges in German mining as far back as the fourteenth century.[18] The earliest illustration of such an operation found by P. B. Whitehouse and J. B. Snell in their enquiries into the origins of narrow gauge was a mine tramway in Agricola's *De Re Metallica* of 1556, the gauge of which they estimated at about two feet.[19] Michael Lewis in his *Early Wooden Railways* shows such operations even earlier, the oldest from a manuscript of about 1430.[20] Such tramways offered the obvious advantage of automatic guidance to human- or animal-propelled carts, but the passageways in mines were constricted and the grades frequently heavy. Consequently, the considerations that made 4'-8½" and broader gauges attractive on the surface were not applicable. George Stephenson had designed a meter gauge tramway for the quarry at Crich in the English Midlands in 1841.[21] Similarly, for haulage of raw materials, coal, and ashes around early industrial plants, narrow gauges were more suitable than standard.

In the early 1860s British industrial railways of this sort were being converted from horse to steam locomotion. In 1861 Isaac W. Boulton of Ashton-under-Lyme built a 2'-0" locomotive for a line a mile long near Wigan, Lancashire. A geared engine with 5½"×12" cylinders, the locomotive weighed only a little over three and a half tons but could handle 22 of the line's empty wagons upgrade. John Smith of Coven, near Wolverhampton, built several 0-4-0 locomotives for a 2'-6" line at the Willenhall Furnaces. With 6½"×12" cylinders, 30" drivers, and a weight of eight tons, an engine was capable of handling trains of 17½ tons up a grade of 3.3 percent at five miles per hour on the mile-and-a-half line. A locomotive of somewhat under seven tons designed for a 2'-8" mineral line, the Neath Abbey Railway, was shown at the International Exhibition of 1862. In May of that year John Ramsbottom put in service an 0-4-0 called *Tiny* on the 18-inch internal railway at the Crewe Works of the London & North Western Railway. The little engine with 4¼"×6" cylinders and 15" drivers could traverse curves of 15-foot radius and haul loads of 12 to 15 tons. Thus, by 1862 locomotives suitable for narrow gauge industrial use were readily available.[22]

The first engineer to attempt an adaptation of narrow gauge technology to a general transport purpose proved not to be an Englishman, but rather Carl Pihl, Chief Engineer of the Norwegian State Railways. In 1856 Pihl was directed to develop plans for two isolated lines of limited traffic potential intended for general commercial purposes. He was in contact with British engineers, notably Sir Charles Fox, who had consulted on the building of the State Railways' standard gauge lines earlier in the 1850s. Pihl chose a British measure, 3'-6", as his gauge and ordered from Beyer,

0-4-0: A locomotive of the simplest possible configuration. The notation is that of the Whyte System of Locomotive Classification. The digits indicate the number of leading wheels, driving wheels, and trailing wheels. The principal wheel arrangements mentioned in this book, with their common names (if any), are as follows:

0-4-0	*Four-wheel switcher*
0-6-0	*Six-wheel switcher*
2-4-0	*—*
2-6-0	*Mogul*
2-8-0	*Consolidation*
4-4-0	*American, American Standard, or Eight-wheeler*
4-6-0	*Ten-wheeler*
4-4-2	*Atlantic*
4-6-2	*Pacific*
2-8-2	*Mikado*

The letter T indicates a tank engine, in which the locomotive and tender are integral. A + designates an articulation or semi-permanent connection.

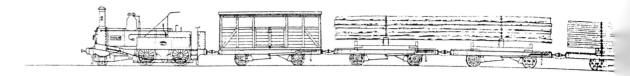

Fig 1

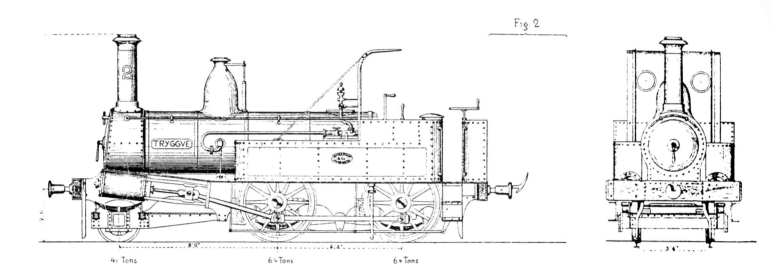

Fig. 2

TRYGGVE

8'0"   6'3"

41 Tons   64 Tons   64 Tons

3'6"

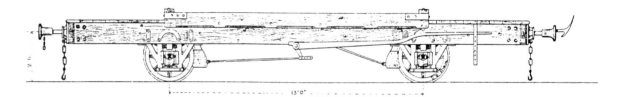

13'0"

Fig 4

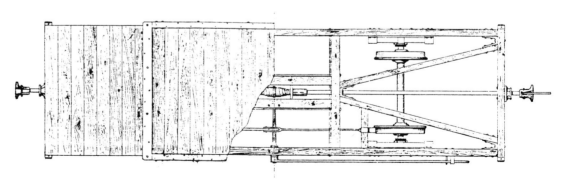

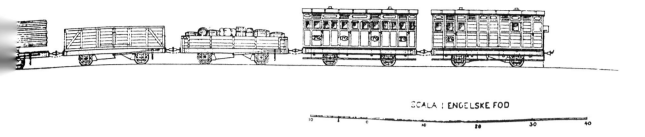

SCALA I ENGELSKE FOD

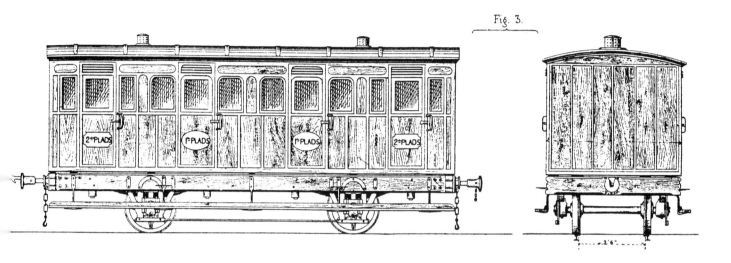

Fig. 3.

2ᵈᵉ PLADS   1ˢᵗᵉ PLADS   1ˢᵗᵉ PLADS   2ᵈᵉ PLADS

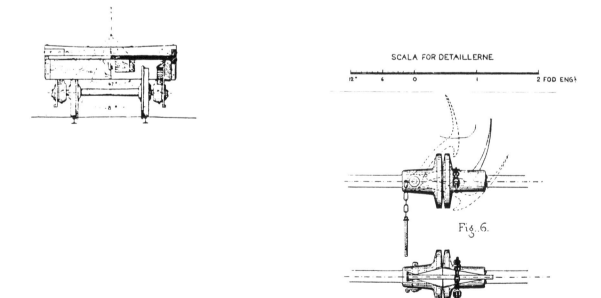

SCALA FOR DETAILLERNE

12"   6   0   1   2 FOD ENG⁶

Fig. 6.

PASSAGERVOGN - FJEDRE

Engineering drawings of Carl Pihl's pioneer narrow gauge installation in Norway. The locomotive, a 2-4-0 tank engine produced by the British firm of Beyer, Peacock, was the prototype for narrow gauge motive power in many countries, though not in the United States. Examples of the type are still in service on the Isle of Man Railway. (Norwegian State Railway Museum, Hamar.)

Origins of the Movement   9

Carl Pihl, designer of the first common carrier railways in the narrow gauge movement. (Norwegian State Railway Museum, Hamar.)

Peacock & Co. of Manchester 2-4-0 tank locomotives adapted from the design of recent 4-4-0 tank engines of the Metropolitan Railway of London.[23] In 1857 the plans were accepted by the government and Pihl was directed to proceed. His first line, Hamar-Elverum, 38 kilometers, opened on June 23, 1862. His second, Trondheim-Storen, 49 kilometers, went into service on August 5, 1864.[24] The first was built through relatively easy undulating country for the equivalent of only £3,000 per mile, but the second, being in more rugged terrain, was more expensive.[25] Charles Douglas Fox, son and associate of Sir Charles Fox, visited the installations in 1864 and reported himself impressed with their efficiency and economy.[26] Pihl's assistant, Peter Bruff, described the lines before the Institution of Civil Engineers in London in 1865.[27]

The narrow gauge was then introduced into the British Empire by Sir Charles Fox. He designed a 3'-6" line for India, running 19 miles from Arconum Junction on the Madras Railway to Conjeveram. The line was opened in about May 1865, operated with locomotives similar to Pihl's, and was considered successful.[28] At about the same time, the elder Fox collaborated with Abram Fitzgibbon, Engineer-in-Chief of the Government of Queensland, in formulating plans for a railway from Ipswich to Grandchester, a distance of 20 miles. The gauge of 3'-6" was adopted in May 1863, and the railway opened on July 31, 1865.[29] The projectors announced that the permanent way had been built for £2,162 per mile, as compared with £2,996 per mile for the 4'-8½" lines in New South Wales. The first locomotives cost £1,410, as versus £3,200 for standard gauge. Similar savings were reported in other cost categories.[30] The 3'-6" gauge spread to minor lines in South Australia and to Western Australia, where, as in Queensland, most railways were isolated carriers at ports.

Robert Fairlie

The 3'-6" installation in Queensland brought into the narrow gauge movement the man who was to prove its most conspicuous figure, Robert Francis Fairlie. Scion of a family prominent in engineering, Fairlie had been born in Scotland in 1831. He received his training in locomotive engineering at the shops of the London & North Western at Crewe and the Great Western at Swindon. In 1853-54 he was Chief Engineer and General Manager of the Londonderry & Coleraine Railway, and he subsequently went to India to work on the Bombay & Baroda Railway. By the early 1860s he had returned to Britain and established himself as a consulting engineer in private practice in London.[31]

Fairlie had become convinced that existing locomotives had a common defect: they wasted weight on unpowered wheels and on tenders that were heavy but totally useless except to carry fuel and water. To deal with the problem he took out on May 12, 1864, British Patent No. 1210 for a locomotive, a symmetrical double-ended tank engine of 0-4+4-0 configuration. On December 9, 1865, he secured a second patent, No. 3185, mainly on the form of the firebox and flow of fuel. The design entailed two simple four-wheel engines, each mounted on a swiveling bogie under one of the two boilers. The couplers and buffers were mounted on the bogies. All of the locomotive's weight was on the powered bogies. Fairlie's detractors, who became numerous, argued that there was little novelty in his invention. Horatio Allen had ordered locomotives of 2-2+2-2 wheel arrangements, with pairs of boilers fore and aft, from the West Point Foundry in New York in 1831.[32] The locomotives were considered failures. More important, John Cockerill of Seraing, Belgium, had developed an 0-4+4-0 with fore-and-aft boilers in 1851 to enter in a competition of the Austrian government for motive power to climb the Semmering grade. Cockerill's locomotive *Seraing* had separate fireboxes for the two boilers; Fairlie's patent and his first example, the *Progress,* built by Cross & Co. for the Neath & Brecon Railway in 1865, had a single firebox for the two boilers. This arrangement may have helped Fairlie establish novelty for his patent, but it quickly proved unsatisfactory. The locomotive pulled air in one stack and exhausted it from the other, interfering with the intended combustion pattern. Fairlie's later examples generally had partitions in their fireboxes, or were fitted with separate fireboxes within a common housing, as in Cockerill's design.[33]

Robert F. Fairlie (1831–85). (Festiniog Railway.)

Fairlie was ambitious, articulate, and untrammeled by modesty. To publicize his locomotive, in 1864 he published a pamphlet of 36 pages entitled *Locomotive Engines: What They Are and What They Ought To Be.*[34] In organization the pamphlet is a Socratic interrogation of Engineer, who is not identified, by Writer, Fairlie. For 20 pages Writer evokes from Engineer a set of objections to existing locomotive design, mainly organized around Fairlie's contention concerning excess weight of tenders and unpowered wheels. Turntables and similar facilities for reversing locomotives are also treated as unproductive. Writer then abruptly reverses roles and in response to Engineer's questions demonstrates that the Fairlie locomotive is the answer to all of the objections to present design. Fairlie argued that freedom from turntables alone would justify his plan. Although the discourse is phrased in terms of existing British railway practice, Fairlie closed the argument with a suggestion that his locomotives be adapted to lightly built lines in difficult terrain: "It also must not be forgotten that (while they are peculiarly suited for working the lightest traffic at the minimum cost, the enormous power that can be applied at will, and their capability for running around the sharpest curves) lines of Railway can be constructed in districts where it has hitherto been considered impossible to do so from the heavy nature of the works required to make the line at all available for the ordinary Locomotive, and with a fair prospect of paying a moderate rate of interest on the capital employed."[35]

Specifically, Fairlie proposed using 50-pound rail rather than 75 because of the better distribution of weight. He envisioned similar savings on bridges and viaducts, which necessarily would have been ubiquitous in his system. Later Fairlie was to call such railways that closely followed natural contours "surface lines" and argued that they were a major part of his concept from the outset.[36]

Like his locomotive, Fairlie's idea of surface lines was not novel. Inevitably by the 1860s various authors had exposited the idea of lightly graded railways with extensive trestlework. George Stephenson in an interview with Samuel Smiles in 1844 proposed a dual system, with existing high standards of grading for railways for passengers and highly rated goods, but with "less perfect road and less expensive works" for lines carrying coal and heavy merchandise. He argued that such lines should be longer, but specified that they should be relatively flat. Trains on such lines would operate at 10 to 14 miles per hour, speeds which he realized would interfere with passenger trains on mixed-service lines.[37] John Ellis, a wool merchant at Leicester, suggested to Stephenson that 3'-0" gauge would be adequate for the proposed freight lines, but Stephenson responded negatively on the ground of the desirability of homogeneity in the national system.[38]

The American engineer Horatio Allen had conceived of dispensing almost entirely with grading, at least in flat country, by building the whole railway on trestlework. His South Carolina Rail Road actually built 136 miles of such a line between 1830 and 1833, but quickly proved a failure. The structure deteriorated rapidly, and minor derailments almost by definition became disasters. The line was replaced with an orthodox fill between 1833 and 1839.[39] George Escol Sellers of Cincinnati about 1849 promoted a system of mainly wooden railways with an elevated center rail, against which horizontal powered wheels pressed for assistance in grade-climbing and also in braking. The railways were to be lightly built with grades of 200 to 300 feet per mile. The system was estimated to require only a third of the capital of orthodox rail lines, and was intended to produce triple the profits.[40] A similar system for assisting locomotives with a center rail had been patented in Britain in 1830 by Charles B. Vignoles and John Ericsson.[41] Neither system was ever tried.

The argument of *Locomotive Engines* is developed in the context of standard gauge, but it was probably inevitable that Fairlie should adapt his concepts to the narrow gauge movement. Fairlie's introduction to narrow gauge was a fiasco that was a continual embarrassment to him. The Queensland Railway ordered three Fairlies of 0-6+6-0 wheel arrangement. The locomotives were built to Fairlie's patent by James Cross at St. Helen's, Lancashire, under the supervision not of Fairlie but rather of Charles Douglas Fox. As a consequence, Fairlie was able to dissociate himself in part from the experience. In 1867 the locomotives were shipped knocked down and crated to Australia, where only one was assembled and put in service. It proved unable to traverse a curve of 5 chains radius (330 feet), spread the rails, derailed readily, leaked steam, and, having no divider in its firebox, encountered the perverse draft between stacks of Fairlie's early power. Incidentally, the engine's tanks were so limited that it ran low on water rapidly. The locomotive was set aside and the rest of the order not uncrated.[42] The engines were reportedly sent back to England in 1871.[43]

Fairlie's opportunity to identify himself positively with the narrow gauge movement came in an unlikely fashion, through a conversion to steam of a tramway serving a series of Welsh quarries. The Festiniog Railway had been opened in 1836 as a horse tramway from Portmadoc into the Festiniog quarrying area about 730 feet in altitude above the port. At its full extent the railway had a main line of just over 13¼ miles. The gauge is usually said to be 1'-11½", but the line's historian, J. I. C. Boyd, states it to be precisely 1'-11⅝".[44] It was approximately 60 centimeters, in any case. Because the railway was on a monotonic grade, mainly in the vicinity of 1 percent, the line could be worked by horses upbound and by gravity downbound. By the 1860s, the railway served ten quarries, the output of which taxed its capacity as a horse tramway. The company's original engi-

Charles Easton Spooner (1818–89). (Festiniog Railway.)

The Festiniog Railway's 0-4-0 locomotive *The Princess* stands at Portmadoc Station, probably in 1871. The engine, built in 1863, is a good example of the first generation of narrow gauge motive power. (Festiniog Railway.)

neer, James Spooner, had relaid about half the line with heavier rail in the early 1850s in hope of introducing steam locomotives, but could find none adaptable to such a narrow gauge. No less an authority than Robert Stephenson told him such a mechanization was impossible.[45]

James Spooner died in 1856 and was succeeded by his son, Charles Easton Spooner. In August 1860 the directors of the railway authorized "enquiries as to the practicability of using locomotives on the line."[46] In October 1862 the younger Spooner visited the Neath Abbey Railway, which had just been converted to steam. The Broelthal Railway, a 2'-7" line near Cologne, was reportedly being operated by steam locomotives with some success. George England, head of the Hatcham Iron Works of New Cross, London—Fairlie's father-in-law—encouraged Spooner in the conversion and accepted the order for four 0-4-0 locomotives for the railway. The locomotives were apparently designed by Charles M. Holland in collaboration with England, though there were other claimants. Neither Spooner nor Fairlie claimed to have designed the engines, which were put in service beginning in October 1863. At the outset the locomotives hauled empty wagons upgrade only, and gravity was still used for the descent. The use of locomotives to haul downbound trains of slate began in 1871[47] and increased thereafter, although some gravity descent persisted to 1939.

On January 6, 1865, the Festiniog began carrying passengers on a fare-paying basis.[48] It was illegal under 9 & 10 Victoria, Cap. 87, to build a new passenger-carrying railway of less than 4'-8½" gauge, but because the Festiniog was an existing line, it was exempt from the prohibition. Nonetheless, it had to be inspected by a representative of the Board of Trade. The inspector proved to be Captain (later Sir) Henry Whatley Tyler, who

Sir Henry Whatley Tyler (1827–1908), third from left, and George Westinghouse, center, with other directors of the Westinghouse Brake Company in London, about 1889. (Festiniog Railway.)

Inside connection: Mounting the cylinders inside the frame so that the rods and valve gear take action on cranks on the axles of the drivers, rather than on pins on the drive wheels themselves.

certified the line as fit for passengers. Although the events had not been exceptional, both Tyler and Charles Spooner became convinced that the conversion had some generality for railway practice beyond the operation of mineral tramways. Tyler delivered a favorable paper "On the Festiniog Railway" to the Institution of Civil Engineers.[49] Spooner wrote an article, "Narrow Gauge Railways," which was published in the *Scientific Review* in July 1865.[50] Both men considered the Festiniog's gauge of just under 2'-0" too narrow for general purposes. In his initial paper Spooner recommended 2'-6" or 2'-9" to allow inside connection of locomotives, of which he was an enthusiastic advocate, as well as wider fireboxes and 6-coupled engines. Tyler recommended 2'-6" or 3'-0". By 1871, when Spooner brought together his first paper with some other writings favorable to narrow gauges into a book, *Narrow Gauge Railways*, he had settled on 2'-9" as optimal on the grounds of providing more space for internal connection and more comfort for passengers.[51] Arguing that a narrow gauge line could traverse a curve of 2½ chains radius as readily as a standard-gauge could turn one of 5 chains, he argued for narrow gauge railways for mountainous regions or mineral districts and "to connect one through line with another where standard gauge was too costly."[52] His argument was similar to Fairlie's for "surface lines."

Fairlie, meanwhile, in 1869 had acquired the Hatcham Iron Works in a joint venture with George England, Jr., and J. S. Fraser; he characteristically renamed the enterprise the Fairlie Engine and Steam Carriage Company. The first engine produced by the renamed works was an 0-4+4-0 Fairlie for the Festiniog which Fairlie, equally characteristically, called *Little Wonder*.[53] The locomotive had separate fireboxes for the two boilers. In contrast to the Fairlies sent to Queensland, *Little Wonder* was a considerable success. On a test run with a train of over 133 tons, it

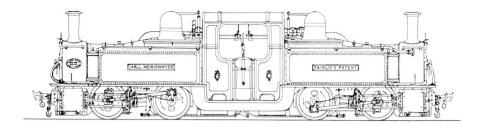

Plan of the *Iarll Meirionnydd*—the Earl of Merioneth—a Fairlie built by the Festiniog in 1885. The locomotive is shown in its approximate state of the 1960s, before extensive rebuilding. (Festiniog Railway.)

achieved a speed of 23 miles per hour upbound and 35 downbound. The locomotive had one indisputable advantage for narrow gauge service: in Fairlie's design, the fireboxes were hung from the frame between the swiveling bogies, thereby avoiding the restriction of the width of the firebox to the length of the axle on the rear drivers, as on standard locomotives of the time. Fairlie clearly looked upon the Festiniog as the proving ground for his locomotive; his firm in November 1870 granted the railway use of the Fairlie patent without fee in reciprocation for the management's cooperation.[54]

In 1868 and 1869 the Festiniog reported relatively favorable earnings; the railway had proved capable of earning about 12½ percent per year. *The Times* reported favorably on the line in a series of articles entitled "Railway Problems" that ran serially in the issues of October 19, 20, and 21, 1869. These attracted the attention of the Minister of Public Works of Russia, who invited Fairlie to St. Petersburg in January 1870. Fairlie reported that his system could be built for little over half the cost of the ordinary plan, with equal or greater capacity. The Ministry responded by establishing a Commission of Enquiry to visit the Festiniog in February 1870 under the chairmanship of the Minister's nephew, Count Alexis Bobrinskoy. Since the experience was of interest more generally, Fairlie and Spooner invited representatives of their own and foreign governments to attend. The Duke of Sutherland headed the British delegation, which included H. W. Tyler, Lt. Gen. Sir William Baker, W. T. Thornton of the

The Festiniog's *Iarll Meirionnydd* operating on the railway in 1983. The locomotive was so substantially rebuilt in 1979 as to be essentially a new engine. (N. F. Gurley, Festiniog Railway.)

Origins of the Movement   15

A Fairlie built by Sharp, Stewart &
Co. of Manchester for the Imperial
Livny Railway in Russia. Note the use
of the fuel supply to aid adhesion.
(Festiniog Railway.)

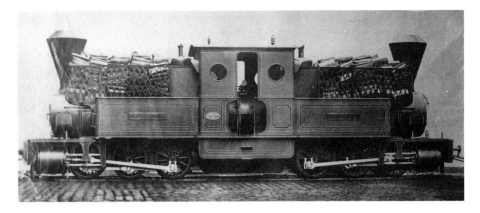

India Office, and Juland Danvers, Government Director of the Indian Railways. Carl Pihl represented Norway and Count Bela Szechenyi Hungary.
France sent several representatives of La Vendée Railway, and other continental nations were represented.[55] The enquiry proved a great benefit to
Fairlie and Spooner, publicizing their work on the Festiniog internation-
ally. Bobrinskoy returned to St. Petersburg in March to report favorably
on the inspection, and in April a line of 38 miles, the Imperial Livny Railway, was authorized. Although the Ministry decided to build it at 3'-6"
rather than to one of Spooner's narrower gauges, the Fairlie locomotive
was adopted.[56]

Fairlie's efforts secured for him an invitation to present a paper to Section G (Mechanical Science) of the British Association for the Advancement of Science at Liverpool on September 19, 1870. He prepared a short
and articulate piece, "On the Gauge for the Railways of the Future." Fairlie was explicit that his purpose was not to advocate change in England,
where 4'-8½" was well established, and where trains ran at speeds up to
60 or 70 miles per hour. Rather, his intention was to increase dividends
and to extend the benefits of railways to lightly populated areas of the

Tare: The empty weight of equipment.

world. He estimated the weight ratio of tare to cargo at 29:1 for passengers and 7:1 for freight, exclusive of minerals. This unfortunate showing he attributed to the use of an excessive gauge: "The dead-weight of
trains conveying either passengers or goods is in direct proportion to the
gauge on which they run; or in other words, the proportion of non-paying
to paying weight (as far as this is independent of management) is increased
exactly as the rails are farther apart, because a ton of materials disposed
upon a narrow gauge is stronger as regards its carrying power than the
same weight when spread over a wider basis."

On the Festiniog, the timber wagons weighed 1,200 pounds but carried
loads of over 3½ tons at 12 miles per hour. They carried over six times
their weight, whereas ordinary British standard gauge wagons carried less
than twice theirs. He chose the example of the London & North Western
on the ground that it was usually thought well administered. He also assumed that his ratio of tare weight to load was only 4:1 instead of 7:1.
The prospective saving on weight by adoption of a narrow gauge led him
by a lengthy *a priori* arithmetical calculation to conclude that the L&NW
could have handled its present goods traffic at about half its present cost if
built to 3'-0" rather than 4'-8½". His calculations were based on the presumption that existing speeds of goods trains of 35 to 40 miles per hour

The *Merddin Emrys*, a Fairlie of 1879, remains in service, beautifully restored, on the Festiniog Railway. It is shown at speed in 1983. Merddin Emrys is known in English as the Arthurian figure Merlin. (N. F. Gurley, Festiniog Railway.)

could be maintained. This, his audience was doubtless not surprised to learn, required the use of a Fairlie double-bogie locomotive. Fairlie did not argue that existing passenger speeds could be maintained on his system. He suggested a gauge of 2'-6" for temperate climates or 3'-0" for very hot or very cold ones.[57]

Intellectually, the paper had little novelty; Tyler had already argued for 2'-6" or 3'-0" in preference to the 3'-6" of Pihl and Fox. The impact of the paper was out of all proportion to its degree of novelty, however. *The Times* reported the paper at length and accepted Fairlie's arguments, apparently without reservation.[58] *Engineering* in Britain and the *Railroad Gazette* in America printed the text in full.[59] Fairlie's argument that deadweight was directly proportional to the gauge became the basic element of the doctrine of narrow gauge advocates the world over—and inevitably the principal point of controversy.

Of the two major British engineering journals, which were in that country more important than the railway trade papers, *The Engineer* was favorable to the narrow gauge ideology from the outset, but *Engineering* had an odd change of views. In 1868 Charles Douglas Fox had addressed a meeting in Toronto in support of using 3'-6" for the Toronto, Grey & Bruce and Toronto & Nipissing railways—a choice the promoters and the Ontario Legislature in fact made. Fox estimated the capital outlay at only $15,000 per mile, which Zerah Colburn, the editor of *Engineering*, thought could only represent the cost of a railway of low standards. Colburn closed

The *Merddin Emrys* in service on the Festiniog in 1988. The coupler is a version of that used on Carl Pihl's pioneer Norwegian installation. It became common on narrow gauges elsewhere. (N. F. Gurley, Festiniog Railway.)

his comment: "If the Toronto people listen to the hollow sophistries which are being urged in favor of the 3 ft. 6 in. gauge, they will secure only an inferior line for a given expenditure of money, and one which, as the traffic grows, can only be brought into connexion with the established railway system of the country at great cost and inconvenience."[60]

As early as 1869, the reported earnings of the Festiniog evoked favorable editorials in *Engineering*, and after 1870 the journal's editorials accepted the narrow gauge, but argued for 3'-6" in preference to the smaller gauges.[61] The alteration in views may represent a change of editorship, however.[62]

Fairlie's doctrine produced opponents in Britain, but they were not numerous. G. P. Bidder, past president of the Institution of Civil Engineers, in a report to the Indian Railway authorities opposed introduction of a narrow gauge on the ground that the prospective saving in capital costs was overstated and unjustified in view of the cost of transshipment of freight. He also considered a gauge difference unwise militarily. Bidder thought the narrow gauge doctrine was based on a false analogy to a road or a canal, which necessarily costs more when wider. He also considered Fairlie's locomotive "only a bad way of using two engines combined."[63] William Pole, in a study of the Rigi Railway in the Swiss Alps, commended the designers for producing a lightly built standard gauge railway rather than a narrow gauge.[64] The Secretary of State for Colonies, impressed by *The Times*' laudatory articles on the Festiniog, sent the prominent consulting engineer Guilford L. Molesworth to Wales to study the line as a possible prototype for a narrow gauge system for India. Molesworth concluded that the cost of upgrading the Festiniog into a steam railway had been understated by £50,000, and that its favorable performance was due to a much higher level of rates on minerals than prevailed on the railway system as a whole. He considered the attractions of a very narrow gauge "fictitious," and argued that a break of gauge, though not necessarily sufficient to condemn the narrow gauge economically, was a very serious evil militarily.[65] In general, however, serious intellectual opposition to the narrow gauge ideology came from Americans, whose thought will be treated at length in Chapter 3.

In Britain, Fairlie's logic triumphed, with the result that narrow gauge railways spread quickly about the Empire. Molesworth's report was ignored. A Royal Commission had been established in June of 1870 to determine the gauge of the projected narrow gauge system in India. The four members were unable to reach a consensus and submitted two reports. The majority report by Colonel R. Strachey, Colonel C. H. Dickens, and A. M. Rendel, dated September 26, 1870, recommended 2'-9".[66] The minority, by John Fowler, dated October 25, 1870, recommended the 3'-6" that had already been begun.[67] Lord Mayo, the Viceroy of India, early in 1871 chose 3'-3" as a compromise.[68] Because the government planned to institute the metric system in India—a change not actually made for another ninety years—the gauge of the projected system was slightly changed later in 1871 to one meter, or 3'-3⅜", and the meter gauge system began to take shape.[69]

A major British engineer, John Hawkshaw, submitted to Lord Mayo a strong dissent from the entire idea of introducing narrow gauge into India. He estimated the saving at only about £1,810 per mile in first cost of right-of-way and equipment, plus £50 per mile per year for maintenance and renewals. He considered these savings not worth the cost of transshipment, especially since he thought savings of £1,250 per mile and £40 per mile per year could be realized by building the secondary lines to 5'-6" with lower physical standards. Hawkshaw, who had opposed the introduction of broad gauge into England in 1838, thought something in the range of 4'-8½" to 5'-0" optimal, but given the 6,000 miles of 5'-6" already laid in India saw no justification for changing from broad gauge at such a late date. Like Bidder, he thought break-of-gauge not only costly but militarily undesirable.[70]

In New Zealand, Julius Vogel on June 28, 1870, proposed a nationwide system of railways, which the country's General Assembly voted in September. In August a Select Committee had recommended 3'-6" largely on the advice of Sir Charles Fox. The country already had isolated railways of standard and broad gauges, but the national system was built to 3'-6" and the gauge differences were eradicated by December 1877.[71]

In South Africa, standard gauge lines were in existence at Durban and Cape Town. The line from Cape Town had reached Wellington with 4'-8½" track in 1863. When the Cape Government took over the railway in 1863, the officials projected a line farther inland to Warrenton. Thomas Hall advocated 2'-6", but a parliamentary Select Committee voted 3 to 1 for 3'-6" as a compromise. A third rail was laid from Cape Town to Wellington, but as 3'-6" spread throughout the colony, the standard gauge was removed in 1882.[72] The gauge of 3'-6" became the dominant one of English-speaking Africa, and virtually the entire continent below the Sahara was built with 3'-6" or 3'-3⅜".

Indeed, 3'-6" came to be regarded as the British imperial gauge. The local colonial government chose it almost automatically for the Newfoundland Railway in 1881, for example.[73] Outside the Empire the principal adoption was in Japan for the state railway in 1872.[74]

In 1871 Fairlie was again invited to address the British Association for the Advancement of Science. He gave a paper entitled simply "Railway

Gauges," in which he showed great confidence in the progress of the narrow gauge movement, of which he was now indisputably the leading figure.[75] Already narrow gauge track had been laid in Russia, India, Australia (including Tasmania), Canada, New Zealand, and the United States, all in rivalry with broader gauges. He wrote as if the movement were already assured of success, and devoted his effort to trying to make certain that his locomotive would be used in complementarity with the narrow gauge. He had by this time given up any enthusiasm for 2'-6" and had begun to call 3'-0" "the Fairlie gauge." He wrote, "when a Fairlie gauge is worked with Fairlie locomotives and stock . . . by no other system in existence can such results be obtained."[76] With respect to the introduction of 3'-6" into Russia, he wrote that the installation included "the employment of my locomotives, *without which the value of the narrow gauge at once sinks into comparative insignificance.*"[77] Since the passage includes the only italicized phrase in the paper, one can hardly doubt Fairlie's conviction. A year later he was to defend his position on the ground that only the Fairlie locomotive had a firebox of width independent of the gauge,[78] but as the statement stood in 1871, it appeared an atypical overstatement that could only weaken his argument.

As Fairlie noted, by 1871 the narrow gauge movement had spread to the United States. As far as is known, the first statement of narrow gauge doctrine in what became an extensive pamphlet literature was that of Major Alfred F. Sears, *On Small Gauge Railroads*, dated February 1, 1871.[79] The pamphlet was a straightforward presentation of Fairlie's thought, addressed to the directors of the Pennsylvania & Sodus Bay Railroad, recommending 2'-6" for their projected line. Sears brought out a second edition as early as February 25, 1871, changing his recommendation to 3'-0". In a more important pamphlet, dated July 24, 1871, James P. Low made a similar but far more detailed recommendation of 3'-0" for the uncompleted Blue Ridge Railroad.[80] In August 1871, Colonel Edward Hulbert, who was to become the most prominent figure in the American narrow gauge movement, published *The Narrow Gauge Railway* in Atlanta, advocating 3'-0" railways for regional economic development.[81] By the end of the year at least two small narrow gauges were in service in the South, another was operating at Pittsburgh, and a major system had been begun at Denver that was to range widely across the arid west.

For a period of 13 years, the narrow gauge movement was to produce a long and acrimonious intellectual controversy, a major investment in railroad facilities, and some consequences for the physical plant of the American railroad system that have not yet been entirely played out. The attractions of the narrow gauge philosophy in underdeveloped or lightly populated areas—superficial though such attractions proved—are apparent, but what the attractions were to Americans is not obvious. As we shall see in Chapters 2 and 3, the answer lies partly in the economic organization of the U.S. railroads after 1870, and partly in the expectations that Fairlie's American followers led the nation to have.

Notes

1. L. T. C. Rolt, *George and Robert Stephenson: The Railway Revolution* (London: Longmans, 1960), p. 75; M. J. T. Lewis, *Early Wooden Railways* (London: Routledge & Kegan Paul, 1970), pp. 110–231, esp. pp. 112, 18–83.

2. Lewis, *Early Wooden Railways*, p. 183; *National Car-Builder*, 8 (1877), p. 134.

3. Charles E. Lee, *The Evolution of Railways*, 2d ed. (London: The Railway Gazette, 1943), p. 91.

4. *Railway Age*, 1 (1876), p. 481, stated that the Brunel gauge was exactly 7'-0¼". This figure is generally but not unanimously accepted. See a note on this point by George Dow in *Railroad History*, no. 154 (1986), pp. 127–28.

5. See Wyndham Harding, *Railways. The Gauge Question. Evils of a Diversity of Gauge and a Remedy* (London: J. Weale, 1845), esp. the map. The author, general manager of the Birmingham & Gloucester Railway, recommended nationalizing the 7'-0" mileage and leasing it to private operators for conversion.

6. William Makepeace Thackeray, "Jeames on the Gauge Question," *Burlesques* (London: Smith, Elder & Co., 1869), pp. 159–62.

7. *Reports of the Gauge Commissioners*, Parliamentary Papers, Reports of Commissioners, XVI (1846), Command No. 34, p. 7. The report describes the Great Western's practice in its early period. In later years it was more sophisticated, operating as a dual gauge railway with extensive mileage of three-rail track, on which it could handle cars of both gauges in a single train by using what it called a "match truck" with wide buffers to accommodate both classes of equipment.

8. *Ibid.*

9. *Ibid.*, p. 11.

10. *Ibid.*, p. 12.

11. *Ibid.*, p. 14.

12. *Ibid.*, p. 12.

13. *Ibid.*, p. 20.

14. *Ibid.*, Minutes of Evidence, p. 186. The same enactment, however, established 5'-3" as the statutory gauge for Ireland. Brunel, who was unrepentant in his advocacy of broad gauges, testified to the commission that the 5'-3" gauge was already almost agreed upon for Ireland by the engineers involved.

15. Benjamin H. Latrobe, *A Letter on the Railway Gauge Question*, 2d ed. (New York: W. W. Evans, 1873), p. 44.

16. *Copies of Correspondence between the Government of India and Court of Directors, relating to the Gauge of Five Feet Six Inches of the Indian Railways: And, of the Minutes of Lord Dalhousie and the Reports of the Consulting Engineers on the Subject of Gauge*, March 21, 1873, *Parliamentary Papers*, Accounts & Papers, L (1873), Command No. 122, 5 pages.

17. Robert F. Leggett, *Railways of Canada* (Newton Abbot: David & Charles, 1973), pp. 47–48.

18. Lewis, *Early Wooden Railways*, p. 9.

19. P. B. Whitehouse and J. B. Snell, *Narrow Gauge Railways of the British Isles* (Newton Abbot: David & Charles, 1984), p. 30.

20. Lewis, *Early Wooden Railways*, plate 20, following p. 72.

21. Rolt, *George and Robert Stephenson*, p. 289.

22. Zerah Colburn, C.E., *Locomotive Engineering and the Mechanism of Railways* (London and Glasgow: William Collins Sons & Co., 1871), pp. 101–2.

23. For Pihl's correspondence on the locomotives, with which he was highly pleased, see R. L. Hills and D. Patrick, *Beyer, Peacock: Locomotive Builders to the World* (Glossop, Derbyshire: The Transport Publishing Co., 1982), pp. 49–52.

24. *Norges Jernbaner, 1958–1959* (Oslo: Hovedstyret for Statsbanene, 1960), chronological route summary, pp. 30–31.

25. Charles Douglas Fox, *On Light Railways in Norway, India and Queensland* (London: William Clowes & Sons, 1867), reproduced from *Minutes of Proceedings of the Institution of Civil Engineers*, 26 (1866–67), Paper no. 1166, p. 4.

26. *Ibid.*

27. *Minutes of Proceedings of the Institution of Civil Engineers*, 24 (1865), pp. 371–75.

28. Fox, *On Light Railways*, p. 5.

29. *The Engineer*, 18 (1864), p. 133; 22 (1866), pp. 271–72. See Viv Daddow, *The Puffing Pioneers and Queensland's Railway Builders* (St. Lucia: Queensland University Press, 1975), pp. 6–12 and *passim*.

30. *The Engineer*, 22 (1866), 271–72.

31. Rowland S. Abbot, *The Fairlie Locomotive* (Newton Abbot: David & Charles, 1970), p. 11.

32. *Ibid.*

33. *Ibid.*, pp. 13–14 and *passim*; E. L. Ahrons, *The British Steam Railway Locomotive* (London: The Locomotive Publishing Co., Ltd., 1927), p. 314.

34. R. F. Fairlie, *Locomotive Engines: What They Are and What They Ought To Be* (London: John King & Co., 1864). In the Bureau of Railway Economics Library, Association of American Railroads, Washington, D.C.

35. *Ibid.*, p. 35.

36. *Engineering*, 11 (1871), p. 102.

37. Quoted in Roger Lloyd, *Railwaymen's Gallery* (London: George Allen & Unwin, 1953), pp. 21–22.

38. *Ibid.*, p. 25.

39. John H. White, Jr., "Railroads: Wood to Burn," in Brook Hindle, ed., *Material Culture in the Wooden Age* (Tarrytown, N.Y.: Sleepy Hollow Press, 1981), pp. 188–89.

40. George Escol Sellers, *Improvements in Locomotive Engines and Railways* (Cincinnati: Gazette Office, 1849); anonymous, *Observations on Rail Roads* (Cincinnati: Chronicle & Atlas Book and Job Rooms, 1850); John H. White, Jr., *Cincinnati Locomotive Builders, 1845–1868* (Washington: Museum of History & Technology, Smithsonian Institution, 1965), pp. 47–90.

41. White, *Cincinnati Locomotive Builders*, p. 47.

42. Leon Oberg, *Locomotives of Australia* (Sydney: A. H. & A. W. Reed, 1975), p. 27.

43. *Engineering*, 11 (1871), p. 224.

44. J. I. C. Boyd, *The Festiniog Railway* (Lingfield, Surrey: The Oakwood Press, 1956), vol. 1, p. 12.

45. *Ibid.*, p. 33.
46. *Ibid.*
47. *Ibid.*, pp. 32–36, 91.
48. *Ibid.*, p. 38.

49. *Minutes of Proceedings of the Institution of Civil Engineers*, 24 (1865), p. 359.

50. C. E. Spooner, "Narrow Gauge Railways," *Scientific Review*, 1, no. 1 (July 1865), pp. 77–78.

51. C. E. Spooner, *Narrow Gauge Railways* (London: E. & F. N. Spon, 1871), pp. 91–97.

52. *Ibid.*, p. 1.

53. Abbott, *The Fairlie Locomotive*, pp. 15–17.

54. Boyd, *The Festiniog Railway*, pp. 100–101.

55. Spooner, *Narrow Gauge Railways*, pp. 45–46.

56. On the chronology of events, see *Engineering*, 10 (1870), p. 231. See also Abbott, *The Fairlie Locomotive*, pp. 24–25.

57. R. F. Fairlie, *Paper on the Gauge for "The Railways of the Future"* (Liverpool: The Albion Office, 1870).

58. *The Times* (London), September 20, 1870. See, notably, *The Times*' very favorable review of Fairlie's book *Railways or No Railways* on January 17, 1873.

59. *Engineering*, 10 (1870), pp. 230–31; *Railroad Gazette*, 2 (1870), pp. 51–52.

60. *Engineering*, 5 (1868), p. 256.

61. *Ibid.*, 8 (1869), p. 215; 10 (1870), pp. 385, 460.

62. *Engineering* had been edited from its founding in 1866 by Zerah Colburn, an American engineer. On the basis of his obituary in the journal, his editorship became successively more nominal in the late 1860s, apparently because of emotional problems, until he resigned in February 1870. He was replaced by W. H. Maw and James Dredge. Colburn returned to his home in Belmont, Massachusetts, where on April 26, 1870, he committed suicide. *Ibid.*, 9 (1870), p. 361.

63. Letter of G. P. Bidder, in Latrobe, *A Letter on the Railway Gauge Question*, p. 30.

64. William Pole, *The Rigi Railway* (London: W. Clowes & Sons, 1873).

65. Guilford L. Molesworth, "Report on the Gauge of the State Railways in India," *Copies of Correspondence Between the Secretary of State for India in Council and the Governor General of India, with respect to the Proposed Break of Gauge on the Main Line of Railway to Peshawar, since the date of the Debate on the Subject in the House of Commons on the 7th Day of March 1873, Parliamentary Papers*, Accounts and Papers, XLIX (1874), pp. 54–65; E. J. Molesworth, ed., *Life of Sir Guilford L. Molesworth* (London: E. & F. N. Spon, 1922), pp. 56–57; Sir Guilford L. Molesworth, "The Battle of the Gauges in India," *Asiatic Review*, 4 (1914), pp. 522–40.

66. *East India (Railway Extensions), Correspondence Relative to Railway Extensions in India and Reports on the Question of the Most Suitable Gauge for Narrow Gauge Railways in India, Parliamentary Papers*, LI (1871), pp. 33–38.

67. *Ibid.*, pp. 57–67.
68. *Ibid.*, pp. 72–73.

69. See J. N. Westwood, *Railways of India* (Newton Abbot: David & Charles, 1974), pp. 42–49.

70. *East India (Railway Extensions)*, pp. 67–72.

71. David B. Leitch, *Railways of New Zealand* (Newton Abbot: David & Charles, 1972), pp. 13, 24, 29.

72. John R. Day, *Railways of Southern Africa* (London: Arthur Barker, Ltd., 1963), pp. 13–22.

73. Omer Lavallee, *Narrow Gauge Railways of Canada* (Montreal: Railfare Enterprises, 1972), p. 31.

74. P. Dean, "Japanese National Railways," *Railway Magazine*, June 1956, p. 362.

75. R. F. Fairlie, "Railway Gauges," *The Engineer*, 32 (1871), pp. 112–14.

76. *Ibid.*, p. 113.   77. *Ibid.*, p. 112.

78. Robert F. Fairlie, *Railways or No Railways: Narrow Gauge, Economy With Efficiency v. Broad Gauge, Costliness With Extravagance* (London: Effingham Wilson, 1872), p. 40. The spine of this book is lettered *The Battle of the Gauges* and the cover *The Battle of the Gauges Renewed 1872*.

79. Major Alfred F. Sears, *On Small Gauge Railroads: A Paper Read Before the Board of Directors of the Pennsylvania and Sodus Bay Railroad Company on the First of February, 1871* (Seneca Falls, N.Y.: Henry Stowell, 1871).

80. James P. Low, *The Narrow Gauge: A Report of the Chief Engineer of the Blue Ridge Railroad, July, 1871* (Columbia, S.C.: Carolina Printing Co., 1871).

81. The Atlanta *Constitution* acknowledged receipt of this pamphlet in its issue of August 20, 1871. No copy of the pamphlet is known to have survived. Extensive excerpts were published in the *Constitution* of November 17 and December 14, 1871, the Atlanta *Daily New Era* of July 27 and August 23, 1871, and the Calhoun *Times* of January 11 and 18, 1872. The title in the various serial publications varies between *The Narrow Gauge Railway* and *Narrow Gauge Railways*.

2

The Economic Organization of the Railroads

At first sight it seems anomalous that the international narrow gauge movement should have been attractive to American entrepreneurs. The American railroad system in the 1870s was rapidly completing its economic maturation, characterized by collusive pricing by firms that were simultaneously rivals and joint venturers; the adoption of a standard gauge of 4'-8½"; the interchange of compatible equipment fitted with the Janney coupler and the Westinghouse air brake; and the establishment of a regional geographical pattern. This kind of economic organization was not envisioned when railroads began in the 1820s and 1830s, and it was fully achieved only in 1887, when the federal government accepted the cartelization of the industry by establishing the Interstate Commerce Commission as a supervising body. Yet even as this mature organization was emerging, there were incentives to enter the industry cheaply with a technology such as the narrow gauge movement offered. In order to understand why this was so, we turn first to an examination of the nature of this maturing organization.

The Achievement of Gauge Homogeneity

Early railroads were conceived as tributaries to water transport, as their names indicated—Baltimore & Ohio, Delaware & Hudson, New York & Erie, Chesapeake & Ohio. With the notable exception of John Stevens of Hoboken,[1] all major observers expected water transport to be less costly than railroads indefinitely, and the Inland Rivers—mainly the Mississippi and its tributaries—were fairly universally expected to be the principal arteries of domestic commerce. The pioneering quality of the Baltimore & Ohio and the Boston & Albany resulted from the geographical problems facing the promoters of development of the ports of Baltimore and Boston. The completion of the Erie Canal through the one relatively level crossing of the Appalachians in 1825 had caused New York to grow relative to the other major eastern ports. Promoters in Washington, D.C., and Richmond attempted canal crossings of the Alleghenies, but neither project could be pressed beyond the portion that followed a river course through the foothills. Philadelphia attempted and in fact completed an unwieldy mixture of railroad, canal, and inclined plane technology called the Main Line of Public Works linking it with Pittsburgh. But neither Baltimore nor Boston could attempt a water crossing of its mountain barrier: the Potomac, which provided the watercourse into the Alleghenies for the Maryland area, emptied into Chesapeake Bay through Washington, not Baltimore; and the Connecticut, the only long river in New England, ran at a right angle to the route from Boston to the west. Accordingly, if the Alleghenies or the Berkshires were to be crossed, only a railroad appeared practical. As of 1830, it was unclear that railroad technology was capable of crossing mountain barriers at all. John Stevens had built a rack railway as his experimental line at Hoboken because he doubted that adhesion of steel on steel would enable a railroad to operate even on flat ground.[2] The Main Line of Public Works was designed so as to avoid even moderate grades for steam locomotives. The engineers preferred to surmount the Alleghenies by a series of funiculars operated with endless ropes; steam locomotives hauled cars on the flat portions between the funiculars.

Rack railway: A railroad on which the locomotives carry a cog wheel mounted on the main axle to engage with a center rail designed for the purpose.

Yet by the early 1840s the Baltimore & Ohio and the Boston & Albany had definitively demonstrated the ability of railroads to cross mountain barriers. Both had adopted steam locomotives and a gauge of 4'-8½". Both were intended to have their own stocks of cars and to transfer freight to water carriers at their termini. The B&O was to serve steamboats on the Ohio River at Wheeling, and the Boston & Albany was expected to interchange with Hudson River steamers, boats on the Erie Canal, or ferries to the New York Central Railroad on the opposite bank. Under these circumstances, there was little reason to expect uniformity between companies. Indeed, the nation was probably fortunate to have gotten as much uniformity as it did. The Baltimore & Ohio began operation with a gauge of 4'-6", but shifted to 4'-8½" early in the 1830s, apparently because the English gauge allowed more room for moving parts of inside-connected locomotives.[3] The Pennsylvania Railroad, the Boston & Albany, and the principal predecessors of the New York Central adopted 4'-8½" from the outset. The reason was probably no more than conformity with British practice; American operators expected to make use of British locomotives, although few actually did so. The predominance of 4'-8½" on the major northeastern railroads was enough to make this the standard gauge in America as in Britain. However, rather than having a single, broader gauge in rivalry with standard, America developed a variety of alternatives, most broader but two narrower.

In the Northeast the most important divergent gauge was 6'-0", adopted by the New York & Erie and its connections, including the early mileage of the Delaware, Lackawanna & Western. The Ohio & Mississippi independently adopted 6'-0" gauge for its line between Cincinnati and East St. Louis, completed in 1857. The existence of this line gave the Erie a powerful incentive to cross Ohio, and by 1864 it had effected a connection via its subsidiary, the Atlantic & Great Western. Thereafter until 1871 a roundabout route of 6'-0" gauge was available from New York to St. Louis. The

The engineer oils about the Erie's 6'-0"
gauge locomotive 144 prior to departure from Paterson, New Jersey, in
1867. The engine is a Danforth Cooke
4-4-0 of 1853. The photograph shows
the ample dimensions of the boiler,
and also its low position on the frame—
both attractions widely argued by
broad gauge advocates. (Smithsonian
Institution.)

6'-0" gauge never reached Chicago from the East, although the Chicago &
Elgin, a predecessor of the Chicago & North Western, operated with this
gauge until 1855.

Second widest of the gauges in the northeastern United States was 5'-6",
but this existed only because it had been adopted as standard by the Canadian railways. For compatibility with the Canadian system, the Atlantic &
St. Lawrence Railroad adopted 5'-6" for its line to Portland, and several
connections in Maine followed suit. The gauge of 5'-4" was limited to two
railroads in Ohio and was not found elsewhere.

Far more important among the broader gauges was 4'-10". The Camden & Amboy and various other predecessors of the Pennsylvania Railroad adopted this gauge, which spread to some connecting railroads in
New Jersey. Mileage of this gauge also developed in Ohio, reportedly because of the early use there of a locomotive from New Jersey, and the Ohio
state legislature required it as uniform in a statute of 1848. The law was
modified in 1852 to require only a consistent gauge from end to end of any
railroad operating in the state, but the earlier enactment was enough to
cause most of the predecessors of the Pennsylvania Railroad west of Pittsburgh to be built to 4'-10". There was also a stretch of 4'-10" between
Buffalo and Cleveland on what became the New York Central main line.
Because 4'-8½" was dominant in New England, New York, Pennsylvania,

and Maryland to the east, and in Michigan, Indiana, Illinois, and Wisconsin to the west, Ohio's incompatible mileage was a serious impediment to homogeneity in the North. Cars with broad wheels intended to be compatible between 4′-8½″ and 4′-10″ were available, but they were thought prone to derailment. As a consequence, even the small difference of 1½″ typically required a full transshipment of freight or passengers.

Of the two narrower gauges in the Northeast, the wider was 4′-3″ and was used by the Delaware & Hudson on its line from Scranton to Honesdale, Pennsylvania. This gauge was also used by some private carriers in the area. The narrower was 3′-6″ and was used by the Mauch Chunk, Summit Hill & Switch Back Railroad in Pennsylvania from its inception in 1826. This railroad used mules for the ascent of its 9-mile line, and gravity for the descent. Two inclined planes were installed for the return of empty cars in 1844, and the gravity line was given up except for tourist traffic in 1870.[4] No one in the pre–Civil War era, as far as is known, argued that either had a cost advantage over the standard or broad gauge railroads.

In the South the situation was quite different. Only in Virginia and North Carolina was 4′-8½″ the dominant gauge. There was in 1861 no physical connection at all to the railroads north of the Ohio and Potomac, and insofar as the region had a standard gauge it was 5′-0″. Via the Louisville & Nashville, the Mobile & Ohio, and a variety of predecessors of the Southern Railway, the Norfolk & Western, and the Illinois Central, the South had by 1861 a compatible network of 5′-0″ railroads ranging from Nor-

This remarkable overhead photograph shows an Erie 6′-0″ 4-4-0 locomotive as the fireman oils the cylinder on the engineer's side. The engine is thought to be one of a series of Baldwin freight locomotives built in 1848 and 1849. The large dome above the firebox is the mark of a Bury boiler, a design rendered obsolete by the development of the wagon-top boiler in 1850. On the basis of the clutter of links and other coupling gear on the pilot, the locomotive is apparently serving out its later years in switching service. (Smithsonian Institution.)

folk, Wilmington (North Carolina), and Charleston (South Carolina) to Louisville, Memphis, and New Orleans. The railroads in Florida, though not physically connected to those of the rest of the South, were also of this gauge. The homogeneity of the southern railroads should not be overstated, however, since railroads operated exclusively with their own equipment and refused to interchange even with others of the same gauge. Southern railroads frequently terminated at the edge of cities or entered to reach their own freight houses without any effort to connect with other railroads. For example, five railroads, four of 4'-8½" and one of 5'-0", terminated in Richmond in 1861, but all transshipped by horse drayage across the city.[5]

West of the Mississippi there was remarkable homogeneity at 5'-6". The Hannibal & St. Joseph had reached the Missouri River with 4'-8½", but the Pacific Railroad of Missouri and the two others radiating from St. Louis used 5'-6", as did short lines opposite Cairo, Memphis, Vicksburg, Baton Rouge, and New Orleans. The Texas railroads were 5'-6" and 4'-8½", and California's one railroad in 1861 was 5'-0".[6]

Necessarily there arose in America, as in Britain, a controversy over the relative merits of the broad and standard gauges. At the outset it was thought that 4'-8½" had arisen out of historical accident, since, as recounted in Chapter 1, George Stephenson had simply taken the local gauge for his pioneer railways. It had long been recognized that the gauge had considerable antiquity, and by the 1870s, excavations at Pompeii and elsewhere had made it apparent that the gauge was approximately that of Roman road vehicles. Walton W. Evans, an American engineer prominent in the controversy on the economy of the narrow gauge, during a trip to Italy sought to test the hypothesis that 4'-8½" was the Roman gauge. He took a metric rule to the ruts left by vehicles at six pedestrian crossings at Pompeii and Herculaneum. The raised stones of the pedestrian crossings channeled the wheels so narrowly that the distance could be measured with some precision. He used a metric rule to avoid bias and found the distance from center to center of the ruts to range only from 1.43 to 1.47 meters, with an average of 1.445 meters. In British measure this was approximately 4'-9", which was consistent with a gauge, or distance between the inner surfaces of wheels, of 4'-8½".[7] Subsequent archaeological research has tended to confirm this finding. Ruts cut into stone to hold vehicles on roads on hillsides, for example, have been of the approximate distance Evans found at Pompeii.[8]

Indivisibility: The characteristic of something that comes only in one size or, more broadly, is capable of more economic operation in one size than another. Indivisibilities are the source of optimal scales of economic activity, as discussed below.

Charles E. Lee in his work on early railways argued that gauges of this approximate size stemmed from the indivisibility of the horse. A gauge much under 5 feet would produce a vehicle too small to utilize the power of a horse fully, whereas a vehicle with a broader gauge would put an excessive strain on the animal. Since horses were approximately the same size in ancient times as in the nineteenth century, the optimal road gauge had not changed.[9] Whether or not Lee's hypothesis is correct, it appears indisputable that 4'-8½" was approximately the gauge of Roman road vehicles, and that the survival of the gauge on the roads of the European continent was a major factor in 4'-8½" becoming the standard railway gauge of Britain and the Continent, except for Spain, Portugal, Finland, and Russia.

At best, the foregoing argument demonstrates that 4'-8½" was optimal for carts relative to the indivisibility of the horse. The question by the 1870s was whether 4'-8½" was optimal for railways relative to the indivisibility of the human being. This is, of course, the basic indivisibility in economic activity. A range of heights from 5'-0" to 6'-6" encompasses the great majority of human beings. Productive processes, packaging, and accommodations of all sorts must be based on the presumption that people in this range will be operating them or using them.

In the pre–Civil War period, all of the arguments that 4'-8½" was not optimal were apparently made by men who favored wider gauges. The most impressive were pleas to the directors of the Atlantic & St. Lawrence Railroad and the Pacific Railroad of Missouri by their chief engineers, A. C. Morton and James P. Kirkwood, respectively, to adopt 5'-6" in preference to standard gauge.[10] Both men treated 4'-8½" as a consequence of historical accident, and set forth similar reasons for preferring a broad gauge. Both argued that 5'-6" produced better proportioned and more efficient locomotives. Morton elaborated on this at length. By going from a 4'-8½" locomotive to a 5'-6" one—presumably of 4-4-0 wheel arrangement in either case—he argued that heating surface could be increased by 25 percent. The larger area of the firebox allowed shorter flues, which he considered more efficient. The broader gauge also permitted more space for valve gear and other working parts and a lower center of gravity, even with a larger firebox and boiler. Both Morton and Kirkwood argued that the broad gauge allowed larger drivers, slower pistons, more stability, and better response to shocks of rail joints. In a judgment that is not defensible

The Great Western Railway of Canada provides this example of 5'-6" rail practice. The train, shown at the west end of the Suspension Bridge at Niagara Falls, Ontario, is headed by the *Essex*, an inside-connected 4-4-0 built by the Lowell Machine Shop in 1853. This design—with its riding cut-off valve gear with two valves, the lower always engaged, the upper cut in as the engine gains speed—was obsolete by the 1860s. (Smithsonian Institution.)

in light of later experience, Morton considered standard gauge an undesirable incentive to use outside connection of cylinders, rods, and valve
gear, which he thought unsuitable for high-speed locomotives.[11] In general, however, his argument concerning locomotives is merely an application of a fairly universally accepted argument that the area-to-volume ratio
of steam boilers becomes more favorable as the size increases. This is, in
fact, thought to be among the most important sources of economies of
scale in the economy.[12]

Morton applied the same logic to cars. On the Erie, he said, the deadweight per passenger was 35 pounds less than on its standard gauge rivals.[13]
For freight he argued that the principal economy was in running fewer
cars and a smaller number of trains for a given tonnage. He attempted to
quantify the expected saving from the use of 5'-6":

The expenses of a road are nearly as the miles run; therefore the effect of transporting an equal tonnage with a less number of trains is an increase in net revenue. An engine capable of drawing 20 tons of net load more than another, will,
applying an average charge of 1¼ pence per ton mile, increase the earnings 25
pence for each mile run; and, allowing that your freight engines will run 300,000
miles per annum, the increased earnings by adding this amount to the average
load will be £31,250 per annum: —that is nearly 50 per cent. of the whole cost of
running freight trains this distance.[14]

Morton argued that the costs of enginemen, firemen, superintendence,
lubrication, and the like were not influenced by the gauge. The only adverse cost item he noted was the fact that a larger engine consumed more
fuel, but he considered that "fully reimbursed by diminishing the delays,
accidents, and extra labor attending the use of a greater number of engines."[15] He also argued that "The first cost of large engines is cheaper in
proportion to their power than small ones."[16] Generally, Morton estimated that building to 5'-6" instead of 4'-8½" added only 1.25 percent to
the cost of building a railroad.[17]

Necessarily, Morton had to consider the disadvantages of incompatibility: "The most prominent objection which can be made to a wide track is,
the connection with other roads of a different Gauge, and the necessity of
transferring freight and passengers from one line to another. This under
certain circumstances, would evidently be so serious an objection as to
overcome all considerations in its favor, and again, under other circumstances, it may be less objectionable than other difficulties."[18]

Morton proceeded to argue that in the present instance compatibility
was a minimal consideration because the Atlantic & St. Lawrence did not
propose to bridge the St. Lawrence, but rather planned to interchange with
river steamers and ferries to Montreal. At Portland the railroad was expected to interchange with ocean steamships and New England coastal
steamers, for "It is well known that transportation can be done by Steam
Boats and Propellers at lower rates than by any other means of convey-
ance."[19] The only incompatibility problem Morton foresaw was with the
Connecticut & Passumpsic Rivers Railroad, with which his company proposed to connect by a branch. Morton proposed a break of gauge on the
branch at the international border.[20] He noted that even railroads of a compatible gauge, as in southern New England and upstate New York, frequently refused to interchange on the grounds that off-line cars received

less scrutiny and less maintenance than cars of the home line, thereby becoming sources of accident and expense. For passengers, he argued that a break of gauge was of no importance; boarding a freshly cleaned vehicle, in fact, was a positive attraction. Kirkwood, for the Pacific Railroad of Missouri, argued that his railroad had no compatibility problem at all, for the company did not propose to bridge the Mississippi River.[21] Morton and Kirkwood succeeded in their argumentation, for both their companies adopted the 5'-6" gauge.

Morton and Kirkwood wrote of the expected benefits of a 5'-6" gauge, but the views of Daniel C. McCallum, General Superintendent of the New York & Erie, based on a few years of experience with the 6'-0" gauge were not significantly different.[22] McCallum praised the Erie's locomotives on grounds of power, stability, economy, and snow-fighting ability, and the company's equipment on the grounds of capacity and comfort in terms similar to those of Morton and Kirkwood.[23] He treated at some length the allegation that broad gauge implied greater resistance, especially on curves, but concluded that this was not a significant objection. He made a stronger argument than either of the two earlier writers that interchange was not worth having. His experience was necessarily with a limited number of gauge-compatible lines, rather than any extensive regional system, but he estimated that transshipment, which he put at 7¢ per ton at the Dunkirk, New York, station, was a smaller cost than the empty return of cars to the originating lines. The Erie could not use such cars for partial loads of freight on their return trips. Further, he had found that running repairs on such cars ran about double the cost of such repairs to the Erie's own equipment. Mainly for this reason, he thought that interchange tended to benefit shorter railroads relative to longer, and the Erie, obviously, was the longer in all its relations with other 6'-0" lines. He felt the cutoff point was around 500 miles; a railroad beyond that length was better off not to interchange equipment with its connections.[24]

In a major respect, McCallum's report differed from Morton's or Kirkwood's. The earlier writers simply argued that a broader gauge than 4'-8½" was technologically superior without regard to traffic density. McCallum restricted his argument to the Erie or other long, heavily trafficked railroads:

In concluding my remarks upon this subject, permit me here to state, that although the gauge of this road is all that could be desired for the extent and character of its business, it does not follow that its *general adoption* would be either wise or economical, as it is with railroads as with all other modes of transportation, the magnitude of the arrangement should be in proportion to the amount and nature of the business required to be done.

Whilst the wisdom of this State, in the furtherance of the enlargement of the Erie Canal cannot be questioned, the extension of a like policy to unimportant branches would be deemed absurd; the first having been found too small for its business, whilst the latter are undoubtedly quite as large as can ever be required. The same reasoning applies with equal force to railroads: for whilst upon some roads a gauge of 6 feet may be found more economical in the transaction of a *heavy business*, a gauge of four feet eight and a half inches may be much more suitable for the business of others; indeed it is questionable whether for a road doing a very *light business*, even the latter may not be found too wide for economical transportation.

Daniel Craig McCallum (1815–78) in his uniform as director of the United States Military Railroads during the Civil War. (Bruccoli Clark Layman.)

The question to be decided, therefore, in determining the proper width of gauges to be adopted on any given line of railway, is not whether a gauge of six feet possesses greater capacity than a gauge of four feet eight and a half inches, but rather what width of gauge is the best adapted to admit of such a construction of machinery as will most profitably overcome the resistances of the line, and that will meet the nature and extent of traffic, present and prospective.[25]

In this passage, written some fifteen years before the inception of the narrow gauge movement in America, McCallum set forth two of the basic arguments that would be taken up by the narrow gauge proponents: gauge should be directly proportional to traffic density; and costs of transshipment could be offset by the savings from using an optimal gauge over some identifiable minimum distance. It should be noted that McCallum was a figure of the first rank in American railroad management. He was to rise to the rank of general during the Civil War as superintendent of the United States Military Railroads,[26] and the report from which the foregoing quotations were taken is still cited as one of the best works on railroad organization of the pre–Civil War period.[27]

Interchange of Equipment

The standard gauge of 4'-8½" triumphed over the broad gauges not through refutation of arguments such as those just cited, but rather because of the growing incentives for compatibility and interchange of equipment. In general, interchange began as an effort of railroads to put together consistent routes over intermediate distances. Morton noted as early as the 1840s that the Boston & Worcester allowed its cars to move off-line as far west as the Hudson River at Troy.[28] The New Albany & Salem in Indiana was another good example: built from New Albany on the Ohio to Michigan City on Lake Michigan in an era when management believed that railroads could not compete in costs with steamboats, by 1859, after railroads had proved themselves cost-competitive with steamers, the company was interchanging equipment with two other railroads to provide a more direct through route, the Green Line, from Chicago to Cincinnati.[29] It did not interchange more generally.

By the end of the 1850s the costs of refusal to interchange equipment were becoming apparent. In 1858 George Dartnell wrote an eloquent argument for establishing a pool of free-running freight cars with interline accounting done by a clearing house on the British model. He evaluated the current situation accurately:

It would save many unnecessary transshipments, as such would only be required where there was a break of gauge; cars would invariably run through when fully ladened, and be loaded on their return, either for a part or for the whole distance; the companies to whom they belonged receiving payment by a mileage toll for the distance travelled loaded; they would also be entitled to demurrage for additional time occupied in transit.

The many transshipments of freight are known to be the chief cause of delays, overcharges, and damages, besides adding greatly to the working expenses in labor and clerk-hire, and requiring large and costly accommodations for the performance of the service; the expense of an ordinary transshipment is not less than 25 cents per ton, and the delay but little under 24 hours, if any.

There is no reason why the running of cars through, should increase the mileage

Demurrage: The fee paid for delaying a car, usually paid by a consignee for the time, beyond a specified minimum, used for unloading a car.

of "Empties," as foreign cars might be loaded from point to point, so long as they were not taken off the line of route by which they were received.

The interchange of passengers and freight cars under the present system is not only exceedingly limited, but is believed to be generally very unsatisfactory; and there can be but little doubt that if it were made usual with roads having the same gauge, it would tend to increase through traffic by railroads, to give greater confidence and satisfaction to the public, and to add to the revenues of the company's interest.[30]

Foreign: Owned by an off-line railroad, not foreign in the usual international sense.

Dartnell's proposal was not specifically adopted as public policy, but rather took shape in evolutionary fashion through the development of fast freight lines similar to the Green Line of the New Albany & Salem of the 1850s. The fast freight lines were of two sorts: stock companies organized separately from the railroad corporations, which came to be known as "non-cooperative," and joint endeavors of the companies themselves, called "cooperative." The non-cooperative type, which owned its own cars, is usually said to date from Kasson's Dispatch, established about 1855 to run on the New York Central and its connections. By the mid-1860s such companies had been formed to operate on each of the major eastern trunk lines. Their independence was to some extent nominal, for the proprietors were frequently the officers of the host railroads.[31]

Fast freight lines of the cooperative type were essentially pools of cars of participating railroads assigned to a specific group. The first major one after the Civil War was the Red Line Transit Company, established in 1866 by the New York Central and its affiliates or connections to operate between New York, Boston, and Chicago via Cleveland and Toledo.[32] At the organizational meeting in Buffalo of April 16, 1866, the several railroads (all of which subsequently became parts of the New York Central System) established common colors, report marks, and repair arrangements. They established an accounting office and shop in Buffalo.[33]

The earliest fast freight lines were established for east-west routes. This pattern tied in well with the emerging pattern of eastbound grain movements from the Midwest, counterbalanced by the movement of manufactured goods from the Northeast to the midwestern agricultural areas. In the South, the traffic patterns were diffuse enough that the principal operation was in the nature of an areawide pool of boxcars. Another Green Line was founded in 1868 as a pool of 96 boxcars of five southern railroads. By 1873 this Green Line encompassed 21 railroads, all of the important railroads in the South except those in the Mississippi Valley.[34]

Necessarily, such arrangements required some method of interline car accounts. On the Green Line, the Red Line, and similar operations of the 1870s, the railroad operating a foreign car of any type paid the railroad that owned the car a fee of 1.5¢ per car-mile.[35] The office of the general agent of the freight line operated as a clearinghouse for balances. Exactly how such arrangements were generalized so that cars eventually ran freely on the entire North American trackage with an international system of interline car accounting is unclear; the historical documentation is very meager. The southern Green Line encouraged physical movement to the north and west without transshipment and required each member to allocate a number of cars to interregional movements based on its percentage of interregional traffic.[36] The 1.5¢ per mile rate applied to such movements. By

Heavy-duty standard gauge railroading of the 1870s is exemplified by this photograph of Pennsylvania Railroad No. 117, a Baldwin ten-wheeler of 1855, extensively modernized. It was scrapped in 1878. (Smithsonian Institution.)

the early 1870s the incidence of off-line cars was already far beyond what could be explained by the railroads' participation in the fast freight lines. In 1872 the Master Car-Builders Association, which had been founded in 1867, began issuing rules for the interchange of cars.[37] In 1874 the Association circulated a query about the number of foreign cars on member railroads. Responses ranged from one or two on the smaller lines to 289 on a large but unidentified railroad.[38] F. D. Adams of the Boston & Albany, at the Association's convention in Cincinnati, commented that on the basis of his experience with a medium-sized railroad the figures must be understated: "There are nearly 300 different kinds of foreign cars running over the Boston & Albany road. This was known to a certainty by the system of mileage accounts in use by the company."[39]

The system of payment by fee per mile was thought to encourage hoarding of foreign equipment, since if one did not operate a car at all the fee fell to zero. J. T. Rigney of the Baltimore & Ohio proposed a *per diem* fee in 1876 but the idea was not immediately implemented. The mileage rate, which was unregulated, tended to fall from the 1.5¢ level of the 1870s to levels as low as 0.6¢. The American Railway Association began to enforce a rate of .75¢ per mile in 1892. The *per diem* agreement was established in

1902, symbolizing the completion of the conversion to the system of free-running cars throughout the continent.[40]

The incentives to homogeneity of gauge in the emerging system of continentwide free-running of cars were too strong to be resisted. Governmental actions in the 1860s accelerated the movement, for both the Union and Confederate governments encouraged through movements of troops and matériel. The Confederate government brought about physical connections between railroads in Charleston, Savannah, Richmond, and elsewhere.[41] Though Lincoln initially proposed a 5'-0" gauge for the transcontinental railroad, Congress in passing the second Pacific Railroad Act in 1863 required a gauge of 4'-8½" in order to assure that the railroads of the trans-Missouri west would be compatible with the northeastern system.[42] The railroads of the South remained isolated, but in 1870 the Ohio River was bridged at Louisville.[43] A reciprocal movement of agricultural products north and manufactures south analogous to that of the north and west was developing. Because the South was itself fairly homogeneous at 5'-0", the device of transferring the car body between trucks of the two gauges by means of car hoists was particularly attractive. The Louisville & Nashville had nine hoists at major points on its system by 1886.[44] Elsewhere, wheels of broad tread were used to cover small differences in gauge, and some trucks were built with telescopic axles or movable wheels, though such devices were thought to be dangerous. A compromise gauge of 4'-9¼" or 4'-9½" was tried in Ohio to accommodate cars of 4'-8½" and the local 4'-10".

Despite these adaptations, conversion to standard gauge was becoming more prevalent. The Pacific Railroad of Missouri converted its 5'-6" lines as early as 1869. Ohio's mileage of 4'-10", being astride the major east-west railroad routes, went relatively early. The Pennsylvania Railroad converted the Pittsburgh, Fort Wayne & Chicago and its other 4'-10" mileage west of Pittsburgh beginning about 1868.[45] The gap of 4'-10" from Buffalo to Cleveland in what was to be the New York Central main line from New York to Chicago was reduced to 4'-9½" in 1869 for conformity with the Cleveland-Toledo segment upon formation of the Lake Shore & Michigan Southern Railway in 1869. This gauge required broad-tread wheels that were expensive, fitted either 4'-9½" or the 4'-8½" west of Toledo poorly, and wore out quickly. The entire Buffalo-Toledo line was converted to 4'-8½" in 1877.[46] By 1880 only 52 miles of 4'-10" remained in the nation.[47] The major Canadian lines converted from 5'-6" mainly between 1872 and 1874.[48] The 6'-0" mileage began to go with conversion of the Ohio & Mississippi in 1871 and the Lackawanna in 1876. The Erie began laying a third rail in 1871 and completed conversion of its main line on June 22, 1880.[49] George L. Vose, Professor of Civil Engineering at Bowdoin College, in his *Manual for Railroad Engineers* cited with approbation an estimate of J. W. Brooks in 1870 that the cost advantage of standard gauge over 6'-0" was 20 percent.[50] Captain Henry Whatley Tyler, who was sent to America to evaluate the Erie for British investors in 1874, thought conversion of the railroad was desirable, mainly on the ground of shippers' hostility to transshipment, but he doubted that standard gauging would

Conversion of the Canadian railways to standard gauge, mainly in 1872–73, was a powerful force for homogeneity in the North American system. The *Ottawa* of the Quebec, Montreal, Ottawa & Occidental Railway, a Manchester locomotive of 1876, is an example of the first generation of standard gauge Canadian motive power. (Norris Pope collection.)

reduce operating costs. He found no higher ratio of tare weight to load on the Erie than on its standard gauge rivals, and concluded that the conversion would be neutral in this respect.[51] By 1880 the only major remnant of broad gauge was the southern network of 5'-0", which still constituted 11.4 percent of American mileage.[52]

When the Illinois Central converted its lines south of the Ohio in 1884, and the Mobile & Ohio followed suit in 1885, the remaining major southern lines were at such a competitive disadvantage that they had little choice but to arrange a mass conversion. Representatives of the Louisville & Nashville, Cincinnati Southern, and smaller southern railroads met on February 2, 1886, at Atlanta, where they decided upon a mass conversion of some 13,000 miles on May 31 and June 1, 1886. Thereafter only a minor mopping-up operation remained, mainly conversion of the basically compatible 4'-9" trackage of the Pennsylvania Railroad and a few others.[53]

Simultaneously, the industry was adopting a compatible and—by the standards of the day—automatic coupling and braking system. Eli H. Janney, a former Confederate officer working as a dry goods clerk in Alexandria, Virginia, in 1872 invented a coupler that after tests against 41 rivals at Buffalo from 1885 to 1887 was chosen by the Master Car-Builders as the industry's new standard. In 1869 George Westinghouse installed an air brake on a local train running on the Pennsylvania Railroad out of Pittsburgh. In 1872 Westinghouse developed the triple valve whereby the brake is applied by reduction rather than increase of pressure in the train air line. The innovation spread through voluntary adoption by the railroads until it became compulsory under the Safety Appliance Act of 1893. Adoption was essentially completed by the turn of the century.

The victory of standard gauge was complete in a practical sense, but it left the intellectual problem unresolved. As in Britain, standard gauge's triumph may be interpreted as a movement either to an optimal gauge or away from a broader optimum to a gauge that simply had the attraction of the most widespread early adoption. James J. Hill, for example, believed that 5'-6" would have been preferable in allowing lower centers of gravity for locomotives.[54] Adolf Hitler held an extreme view that 4'-8½" was suboptimal. If Germany had won World War II, he planned a limited radial network from Berlin to Hamburg, Rostov, Paris, Vienna, and Istanbul at a gauge of 3.0 meters, 9'-10.1".[55] Even today the intellectual controversy remains. Compare the two following recent quotations, both by authoritative figures in the railroad industry. The author of a semiofficial manual on the functions of a railroad wrote in 1978: "Though there are situations in which a wider gauge could be advantageous, it appears that for general service, taking all cost factors into consideration, the present gauge is not far from optimum."[56] In the same year the president of the Burlington Northern was quoted as saying: "If I were asked to teach a class on railway track construction and maintenance, I'd start with the first precept of the railway civil engineer—'never forget that the tracks of all American railroads are too narrow.' They were built to a gauge of 4 feet, 8½ inches. But if we had it to do all over again we'd probably build them with the rails at least 6 feet apart."[57]

From the point of view of the narrow gauge movement, the triumph of standard gauge is susceptible of yet a third interpretation—which appears to have no remaining major advocates—that it represented a movement away from an optimal narrower gauge. Not only did the broad gauge experience give the narrow gauge advocates a possible intellectual justification for their efforts, but it gave them some evidence on which to base their projections. There were estimates of the cost of transshipment of freight and the relative costs of equipment of various sizes. The earlier experience provided a great deal of information on compatibility devices. At worst, it had left railroaders with complete information on the technique and costs of converting to standard gauge.

The most highly regarded study of the cost of conversion was a report of 1873 by John M. Goodwin, a prominent civil engineer of Cleveland, on the conversion of the Ohio & Mississippi, commissioned by the Atlantic & Great Western (Erie) in preparation for its own gauge change.[58] Goodwin made an impressive demonstration that the conversion was neither arduous nor excessively costly. The O&M converted its Louisville branch on July 16, 1871, and its main line, 340 miles from Cincinnati to St. Louis, on July 23, 1871. It assigned a foreman and a gang of 45 men to each section of five miles. Goodwin estimated the labor cost at $619.47 per mile and the cost of labor plus materials as $1,066.06 per mile. For the Atlantic & Great Western, which ran through more difficult country, Goodwin estimated the cost at only $1,230.97 per mile. Of the 58 locomotives converted, the cost was $5,060 each. Building and installing new trucks on existing equipment cost $518.30 for a freight car, $1,095.00 for an eight-wheel passenger car, and $1,380.00 for a twelve-wheel passenger car. Consistent with Tyler's expectations concerning the Erie, Goodwin found no effect of the conversion on receipts or expenditures; the railroad's operating ratio was 62 percent in 1872, exactly what it had been in 1870.[59]

Tyler in his report on the Erie of 1874 gave estimates of the cost of converting the Canadian railways that were even lower than Goodwin's. He reported that the Grand Trunk had converted the 216 miles from Buffalo to Sarnia for $506 per mile, including 16 percent additional sidings. The 421 miles from Stratford to Montreal were done for $448 per mile with 18 percent additional sidings. Locomotives had been converted for $3,000 to $5,000 each and cars for $50 per truck. New trucks cost $450 for passenger cars, $1,000 for freight.[60]

Matthias N. Forney, who had established himself as the leading intellectual opponent of the narrow gauges, closed a favorable review of Goodwin's pamphlet with the comment that the report would be useful to remaining operators of 5'-6" lines when they converted. He also added: "we venture meekly to suggest that companies who have roads of three-feet gauge may learn here something which they may need to know when they shall wish to become parts of the railroad system of the country by *widening* their gauge."[61]

The Growth of Cartelization

Contemporaneously with the development of a standard gauge, the railroads evolved their characteristic organization in which they operate simultaneously as rivals and joint venturers, and price collusively. Although there were examples of joint pricing in the 1850s, systematic collusive pricing with pooling of traffic or revenue dates from the formation of the Iowa Pool in 1870.[62] From the researches in the 1960s of Gabriel Kolko and other scholars on the origins of the Interstate Commerce Commission we now have a considerable body of knowledge on the cartels, their stability, their effects on rates and resource allocation, and their legal problems.[63]

The basic purpose of any cartel is to generate monopoly gain. Specifically, the railroad cartels were intended to allow member railroads to attempt to produce such monopoly gain by enforcing price discrimination among commodities and among areas. The railroads were confronted with widely differing elasticities of demand for their services. Alfred Marshall pointed out that elasticity of a derived demand, in this instance for transport service, depends on (1) availability of substitutes for the service; (2) elasticity of demand for the final product; (3) percentage of total cost represented by the service; and (4) elasticity of supply of a resource.[64]

It should be intuitively apparent that the commodities the railroad handled had differing elasticities of demand. The railroads hauled some commodities, notably oil from the Pennsylvania oil fields, that were inelastic in supply. Neither the second nor the fourth criterion, however, was a major element in the railroad's discriminatory pricing. Rather, the pricing structure was mainly determined by Marshall's third determinant, the per-

Elasticity: The percentage change in quantity divided by the percentage change in price, when both are very small; the most basic concept in economics.

centage of total cost, and secondarily by his first determinant, the availability of substitutes.

To calculate the percentage of total costs represented by railroad transport directly for each commodity would have been costly, if not impossible, given the confidentiality of shippers' records. Instead, the railroads used as a proxy the value of the commodity relative to its weight.[65] This ratio was approximately inversely proportional to the elasticity of demand. Accordingly, a railroad seeking to maximize net receipts would endeavor to set rates directly proportional to the ratio of value to weight.

By the standards of 1870, the availability of substitutes meant the presence or absence of steamboats, since road transport was not yet an effective substitute for railroad service. Steamboats for several reasons were differentially effective substitutes for the railroads. They were limited to navigable waters, the course of which frequently required devious routes. Some, such as the Great Lakes, were reasonably direct and had few hazards to navigation. At the opposite extreme, the Missouri River was beset with mudbanks, difficult winds, and unpredictably shifting channels. All of the navigable water in the interior of the country north of Cairo, Illinois, was subject to freezing in winter. Droughts could render navigation more costly or, at worst, stop it completely. The sequence of a severe drought, a hard winter, and heavy spring rains could produce ice gorges that destroyed steamboats berthed along the rivers.

American internal navigation was a competitive industry. Most steamboats on the Inland Rivers were owner-operated and had short working lifetimes, only four or five years in the early period. As a consequence, technological innovations were rapidly disseminated. Rates were typically charged by the hundredweight without discrimination by character of cargo, and varied principally on the basis of water conditions. When the water was high, it was possible to use larger boats, to navigate through sloughs to avoid oxbow turns, and to operate with reduced risks of hitting snags. Consequently, rates tended to vary inversely with the height of the water.[66]

Withal, steamboats on the Inland Rivers in the 1870s were approximately equally satisfactory substitutes for railroads except for their greater dependence on horse drayage. In general, the extent to which the steamboat could compete with the railroads was inversely proportional to the length of horse drayage required to reach navigable water up to about 30 miles; beyond that distance, steamboats were not effective rivals. However, the great majority of the American population, some 90 percent, lived within 30 miles of navigable water, either the Inland Rivers, the Great Lakes, or the seacoasts.[67]

Accordingly, at points they served singly, railroads typically had varying degrees of monopoly power, and could maximize net receipts by pricing in inverse proportion to the elasticity of demand. At points the railroads served in rivalry to one another, such pricing was impossible without collusion. If the railroads priced individually under such circumstances, they would have behaved like competitors in other industries, bidding rates down to equality with marginal cost. This would have been inconsistent with discriminatory pricing. In fact, competitive behavior may have been inconsistent with bare profitability. It was widely believed that the interest on the debt incurred in building the railroads was so high that if managements priced competitively, marginal cost would equate with price below average cost and the railroads would be unprofitable. This argument has been held to be fallacious by Spann and Erickson on the basis of their researches into railroad costs,[68] but it was generally accepted in the nineteenth century.

Collusive pricing was facilitated by the emerging compatibility of the industry. The railroads were necessarily in continuous collaboration on joint movements. There was the further matter that the number of rival railroads could never be so large as to render collusion inconceivable—as it would be among grain farmers, for example. The movement began with the three railroads between Chicago and Council Bluffs. Not only was this a small enough number that self-policing of the collusion was relatively easy, but the Union Pacific could be trusted to furnish traffic to the three in the equal shares that the pooling agreement entailed.

The experience of the Iowa Pool was initially so successful that its organization was emulated throughout the country. Cartels arose among the trunk lines running from Chicago to the East Coast, among the railroads radiating from St. Louis to the southwest, in the South generally, and elsewhere. By 1887 there were eight pools in the industry, six by region and two for specific commodities. The railroad pools encountered the usual problems of cartels: the monopoly gain they were created to generate quickly attracted additional resources to the industry. The three railroads between Chicago and Council Bluffs eventually rose to seven. The routes from Chicago to the Twin Cities and from Chicago to Kansas City rose to a like number. Five major routes came to run from Chicago to major eastern ports—seven if the Grand Trunk and Chesapeake & Ohio are included. The country's railroad pattern of three major regions—eastern, southern, and western—was largely a consequence of the incentives of the cartels in the 1870s.

The legal framework confronting the industry was conducive neither to restricting entry nor to policing the collusions. In most states it was not necessary to secure a specific statute to establish a railroad or to build a line. A railroad could be established under the general statutes for incorporation, and the right to condemnation secured by making a show of financial responsibility. Relative to Britain, where a specific act of Parliament was necessary to authorize a line, American practice amounted essentially to free entry into railroading. Similarly, in Britain the courts had found railways exempt from the general doctrine of the tortiousness of collusive pricing.[69] American courts by 1887 had never decided on the tortiousness of collusive pricing or pooling by American railroads, though the practices were widely expected to be found tortious if a definitive judgment were made.[70] It was, however, clear that in American common law, collusive contracts were unenforceable.[71]

The consequence of this legal framework was to produce a pattern of entry by rival railroads, followed by immediate rate wars by means of which the entrants endeavored to establish their relative positions in the

Tortiousness: Pertaining to a tort, a civil wrong at the common law, a commission of harm not justified by self-defense or other accepted category of defense.

TABLE 2.1
Rail Freight Rates on Wheat Per Bushel, Chicago to New York, 1870–84

Year	Actual rate	Rate in 1880 cents	Year	Actual rate	Rate in 1880 cents
1870	28.98 ¢	21.47 ¢	1878	17.56 ¢	19.29 ¢
1871	27.75	21.35	1879	17.30	19.22
1872	29.80	21.91	1880	19.90	19.90
1873	29.17	27.84	1881	14.40	13.98
1874	25.81	20.48	1882	14.60	13.51
1875	20.97	17.77	1883	16.50	15.27
1876	14.80	13.45	1884	13.12	14.10
1877	19.37	18.27			

SOURCE: *Report of the Committee on Canals of New York State* (New York, 1900), p. 190. Deflated by Warren and Pearson Wholesale Price Index, *Historical Statistics of the United States* (Washington: GPO, 1975).

TABLE 2.2
Average Ton-Mile Rates on the Pennsylvania Railroad, 1870–83

Year	Actual rate	Rate in 1880 cents	Year	Actual rate	Rate in 1880 cents
1870	1.549 ¢	1.147 ¢	1877	0.980 ¢	0.925 ¢
1871	1.389	1.068	1878	0.918	1.009
1872	1.416	1.941	1879	0.796	0.884
1873	1.416	1.065	1880	0.880	0.880
1874	1.255	0.996	1881	0.799	0.776
1875	1.058	0.897	1882	9.817	0.756
1876	0.892	0.811	1883	0.819	0.811

SOURCE: *National Car-Builder*, 15 (1884), p. 111. Deflated as in Table 2.1.

market. The cartel was then reformed with the entrants given a quota in the pool, thereby reducing the quotas of the previous members. By 1882, when the Chicago, Milwaukee & St. Paul entered Council Bluffs, each member was given a quota of 20 percent of the total; but in 1883 the Illinois Central was given only 7 percent for its Sioux City line.[72] Rates were typically reset at lower levels than had prevailed previously, owing to the increased supply of the service. At the new lower quotas in the pools, the discrepancy between rates and marginal cost was typically greater, thereby increasing the incentive of any individual railroad to engage in price cutting. In sum, the experience of the railroads from 1870 to 1887 was a standard one for a cartelized industry unable to restrict entry: rapid attraction of redundant capital; secular fall of prices (see Tables 2.1 and 2.2); and increased incentive to rate wars. The incentive to enter the industry was apparently at its peak in 1882, when 11,569 miles of railroad were built. The additional mileage took the form not only of redundant main lines but also of branch lines that invaded the monopoly territories of rival railroads. Along with the rapid progress of gauge standardization, the growth of mileage was making possible an infinity of routings. The old situation in which the B&O was a facility for Baltimore and the Pennsylvania Railroad for Philadelphia was ending; now both railroads served both cities. Given the forces for instability in the cartels and the legal limbo in which they operated, the cartels had become chronically unstable by the early 1880s.

The nature of complaints about the railroad problem in the 1870s and 1880s changed consistently with the maturing of the cartels. The early 1870s were characterized by complaints against the high absolute level of rates, especially for agricultural products. This period brought forth the Granger Laws of Illinois, Iowa, Wisconsin, and Minnesota imposing maximum rate levels. On the federal level, the complaints against the industry are demonstrated by the Windom Report, the product of a Senate enquiry into movements of grain for export in 1874.[73] The report was explicitly brought forth by the widespread conviction in the Senate that the nation needed more and cheaper facilities for movement of western and southern products to the seaboard.[74] Not only was existing rail transport found unduly expensive, but the industry was thought to be overproducing quality of services. The optimal speed of freight operation with respect to cost was said to be 8 to 10 miles per hour, but the universal practice of mixing freight with passenger trains on the same railroad resulted in freights running at about 25 miles per hour.[75] Some writers who exposited this view argued that the benefits of the greater speed were largely dissipated when the freight trains waited in sidings for passenger trains to pass. The Atlanta *Daily Intelligence* argued in 1867 that by restricting the speed of freight trains to 8 miles per hour, the railroads could reduce the cost of shipping by 25 to 30 percent.[76] The Windom Report's principal recommendations were the development of waterways and the creation of one or more federally owned double-tracked railroads for low-speed freight service to the eastern seaboard.[77] The proposed federal railroad was to be prohibited from participating in the cartels.

There is little question that the Committee's prototype for the proposed federal railroad was the Continental Railway, on which it heard extensive testimony.[78] The Continental was projected in the early 1870s as a standard gauge, double-tracked, freight-only railroad of high engineering standards from New York to a connection with the Union Pacific at Council Bluffs. It was to have branches from Rensselaer, Indiana, to Chicago and St. Louis. The main line was to run 1,224 miles with only 96 miles of curvature. No curve was to be sharper than 4°, and grades were to be limited to 30 feet to the mile eastbound and 40 feet westbound. A 23-ton locomotive was to pull a train of 40 ten-ton loaded cars at 10 miles per hour anywhere on the system. The line was intended to accommodate 250 trains per day in each direction with an aggregate capacity of 200,000 tons. The line was to have about six times the capacity of an ordinary single-track railroad mixing passengers and freight. Grain was to be moved for 0.6¢ per ton-mile in summer, 0.7¢ in winter. The promoters hoped to reduce the rate on grain moving from Chicago to New York to 15¢ per bushel, and to effect similar reductions elsewhere.[79]

Because the promoters intended the Continental Railway to deviate no more than twenty miles from a straight route from New York to Council Bluffs, the project would have entailed extremely heavy grading through central Pennsylvania. They proposed to cross the Delaware at Belvidere, New Jersey, and build as directly as possible to Akron, Ohio. The route would apparently have been somewhat south of the present Interstate 80, but like the highway, would have required major cuts and fills because neither the railway nor the road was projected along a watercourse. The Continental actually undertook some grading, though in easier country. In 1872 the company let contracts for grades from Tiffin, Ohio, to Fort

Wayne, Indiana, and from Rochester, Indiana, to Rensselaer.[80] Most of this grading was accomplished. By 1874 the company's hope for grading the Pennsylvania mileage lay in having Congress enact a federal guarantee of 5 percent interest on first mortgage bonds for half the cost of building the railroad. The company, as a *quid pro quo*, was willing to accept regulation by a federal commission empowered to reduce rates on cereal and breadstuffs when the railroad's rate of return exceeded 8 percent.[81] When this arrangement for federal aid was not forthcoming, the project could not be advanced and was thought dead by 1876.[82]

The Continental project was resurrected in 1880, however, and the following year the company issued a prospectus, which demonstrates some major changes in the conception of the railroad, apparently reflecting the promoters' changing perception of the demands on the industry. The Continental was still intended as a cut-rate railroad: the target was now rates of 0.5¢ per ton-mile on grain and meats. The company now projected that freights would run at 20 miles per hour to protect livestock and perishables "from injury through detention or want of dispatch."[83] The Continental was no longer to be a freight-only railroad; passenger trains were now projected to run between Chicago and New York in under twenty-four hours at rates of under 2¢ per mile. The promoters apparently no longer believed the industry was overproducing quality by mixing freight and passenger trains on the same railroad.

In 1881 the Continental undertook some construction toward its terminal in New Jersey. When it sank some pilings in the Hackensack and Hudson rivers, the Attorney General of New Jersey secured an injunction against construction on the grounds that the company had not secured property rights in the rivers and had no legal standing in New Jersey.[84] This appears to have brought the project to an end.

The Continental Railway's experience demonstrated that neither the federal government nor the private sector would finance a capital-intensive effort at cheap transportation. The failure of Jay Cooke & Co., the investment bankers of the Northern Pacific project, precipitated the Panic of 1873, initiating a depression and credit stringency that lasted about five years. Many less grandiose projects than the Continental Railway were proving impossible to finance. The leading businessmen of Delphi, Indiana, had been trying continually to finance an air line (i.e., a direct route) from Indianapolis to Chicago since 1865, but had no success at all in building the project as a standard gauge railroad. Their motivation was the same as that of the Continental's promoters—to provide cheaper transportation for agricultural products.[85] To such promoters, the arguments of Fairlie and the other narrow gauge proponents of the early 1870s were attractive; indeed, here was a method of entering the cartelized industry at low cost and of providing low-quality service cheaply.

Popularization of the narrow gauge movement in America began with Fairlie's paper of 1870, almost simultaneously with the increase in incentives to enter the industry that followed the formation of the Iowa Pool. By 1883, however, the maturing of the cartels had reduced rates in real terms by more than 30 percent, thereby reducing the incentive to enter the industry. The idea that the industry was overproducing quality largely passed from prominence. The development of a homogeneous gauge of 4'-8½", plus the adoption of the Janney coupler and Westinghouse air brake, gave a strong incentive to compatibility with the railroads in interchange. As a consequence, whether one considers the demands of shippers or the calculations of railroad managements, the narrow gauge movement was assured of a short life.

Notes

1. John Stevens, *Documents Tending to Prove the Superior Advantages of Railways and Steam Carriages Over Canal Navigation* (New York: T. & J. Swords, 1812).

2. Robert Selph Henry, *This Fascinating Railroad Business* (New York: Bobbs-Merrill Co., 1942), p. 22.

3. *Annual Report of the Baltimore & Ohio Railroad*, 1830, p. 48.

4. *Poor's Manual of Railroads*, 1888, p. 129.

5. Robert C. Black III, *The Railroads of the Confederacy* (Chapel Hill: University of North Carolina Press, 1952), p. 9.

6. On the divergent gauges generally, see George Rogers Taylor and Irene D. Neu, *The American Railroad Network 1861–1890* (Cambridge: Harvard University Press, 1956), esp. map supplements I–III.

7. *Railroad Gazette*, 12 (1980), p. 180.

8. M. J. T. Lewis, *Early Wooden Railways* (London: Routledge & Kegan Paul, 1960), p. 2.

9. Charles E. Lee, *The Evolution of Railways*, 2d ed. (London: The Railway Gazette, 1943), p. 2.

10. A. C. Morton, Esquire, Chief Engineer, *Report on the Gauge for the St. Lawrence & Atlantic Rail-Road* (Montreal: Canada Gazette Office, 1847); James P. Kirkwood, *Report on Gauge of Track to Board of Directors of the Pacific Railroad of Missouri, St. Louis, June 27, 1851* (St. Louis: Intelligencer Office, 1854).

11. Morton, *Report*, p. 13.

12. E. A. G. Robinson, *The Structure of Competitive Industry* (Cambridge: Cambridge University Press, 1931), pp. 29–30 and *passim*.

13. Morton, *Report*, p. 11.

14. *Ibid.*, pp. 20–21.

15. *Ibid.*

16. *Ibid.*, p. 23.

17. *Ibid.*, p. 31.

18. *Ibid.*, p. 32.

19. *Ibid.*, p. 47.

20. *Ibid.*, p. 55.

21. Kirkwood, *Report*, p. 10.

22. *Report of the President and Superintendent of the New York & Erie Railroad to the Stockholders for the Year Ending September 30, 1855* [New York, 1856?]; McCallum's report occupies pp. 33–97.

23. *Ibid.*, pp. 86–96.

24. *Ibid.*, pp. 88–90.

25. *Ibid.*, pp. 95–96.

26. Thomas Weber, *The Northern Railroads in the Civil War, 1861–1865* (New York: King's Crown Press, Columbia University, 1952), p. 135.

27. See, for example, the extensive excerpts in Alfred D. Chandler, *The Railroads: The Nation's First Big Business* (New York: Harcourt, Brace & World, Inc., 1965), pp. 101–8.

28. Morton, *Report*, p. 37.

29. George W. Hilton, *Monon Route* (Berkeley: Howell-North Books, 1978), p. 30.

30. George Dartnell, *A Proposed Plan for a Rail Road Clearing House* (Buffalo: Clapp, Matthews & Co., 1858), pp. 11–12, quoted in Taylor and Neu, *The American Railroad Network*, pp. 50–51.

31. Taylor and Neu, *The American Railroad Network*, pp. 69–71.

32. *Ibid.*, p. 71.

33. *History and Early Debates of the Master Car-Builders' Association* (New York: Martin B. Brown, 1885), p. 3.

34. William H. Joubert, *Southern Freight Rates in Transition* (Gainesville: University of Florida Press, 1949), pp. 31–32.

35. *Ibid.*, p. 37; Taylor and Neu, *The American Railroad Network*, p. 72.

36. Joubert, *Southern Freight Rates*, p. 37.

37. *History and Early Debates of the Master Car-Builders' Association*, pp. 124–25.

38. *The Eighth Annual Report of the Master Car-Builders' Association* (New York: S. W. Green, 1874), p. 86.

39. *Ibid.*, p. 89.

40. Ernest Ditson Dewsnup, ed., *Railway Organization and Working* (Chicago: University of Chicago Press, 1906), pp. 463–64.

41. Taylor and Neu, *The American Railroad Network*, pp. 45–48.

42. *Ibid.*, p. 55.

43. Maury Klein, *History of the Louisville & Nashville Railroad* (New York: The MacMillan Co., 1972), p. 91.

44. Taylor and Neu, *The American Railroad Network*, p. 61.

45. *Engineering*, 7 (1869), p. 367.

46. *Poor's Manuals*, 1869–70, pp. 158, 361; 1870–71, pp. 191, 452, 459. *National Car Builder*, 8 (1877), pp. 131, 169–70.

47. Taylor and Neu, *The American Railroad Network*, p. 77.

48. *Ibid.*, p. 77 and *passim*.

49. Edward Hungerford, *Men of Erie* (New York: Random House, 1946), pp. 198, 203.

50. George L. Vose, *Manual for Railroad Engineers* (Boston: Lee & Shepard, 1873), p. 11, citing, J. W. Brooks, testimony before the Committee on Railroads of the Massachusetts Legislature in 1870.

51. Captain H. W. Tyler, "Erie Railway," *American Railroad Journal*, 30 (1874), pp. 1475–77, 1508–9, 1540–41, 1572–73, 1603–5, 1636–37. Tyler's conclusion that conversion would be "neutral" is on p. 1573.

52. Taylor and Neu, *The American Railroad Network*, p. 77.

53. *Ibid.*, p. 81.

54. F. Lavis, "The Gauge of Railways, With Particular Reference to Those of Southern South America," *Transactions of the American Society of Civil Engineers*, 68, Paper No. 1317 (1915), pp. 312–446. On Hill's views, see p. 427.

55. Andon Joachimsthaler, *Die Breitspurbahn Hitlers* (Freiburg: Eisenbahn-Kurier Verlag, 1981). English-language summary in *Trains*, Aug. 1984, pp. 38–51, George H. Drury, translator.

56. John H. Armstrong, *The Railroad—What It Is, What It Does* (Omaha: Simmons-Boardman Publishing Corp., 1978), pp. 29–30.

57. Thomas H. Lamphier, President of the Burlington Northern Railroad, *Trains*, Sept. 1978, pp. 11–12.

58. John M. Goodwin, C.E., *Report on the Narrow-Gauging of the Ohio & Mississippi Railway* (Cleveland [?], 1873 [?]), 28 pages. I have been unable to locate a surviving copy of this pamphlet. Although we know Goodwin's cost estimates and conclusions from reviews, the description of preparations for the conversion and execution of the operation is lost. Because the quality of the report was apparently high, its loss is particularly unfortunate. Anyone locating a copy should notify the Curator of Rail Transportation, National Museum of American History, The Smithsonian Institution, Washington, D.C. 20560.

59. *Railroad Gazette*, 5 (1873), p. 220.

60. *American Railroad Journal*, 30 (1874), p. 1573.

61. *Railroad Gazette*, 5 (1873), p. 220. The review is unsigned. For the attribution of this and other commentary hostile to the narrow gauges to Forney, see Chapter 3, n. 1.

62. See Julius Grodinsky, *The Iowa Pool* (Chicago: University of Chicago Press, 1950).

63. Gabriel Kolko, *Railroads and Regulation 1877–1916* (Princeton: Princeton University Press, 1965); Paul W. McAvoy, *The Economic Effects of Regulation* (Cambridge: MIT Press, 1965); George W. Hilton, "The Consistency of the Interstate Commerce Act," *The Journal of Law & Economics*, 9 (1966), pp. 87–113.

64. Alfred Marshall, *Principles of Economics*, 8th ed. (London: The Macmillan Co., 1920), pp. 385–86.

65. This, as compared with attempting to estimate the percentage of total cost directly, corresponds to the dichotomy between third-degree and first-degree discrimination in A. C. Pigou, *Economics of Welfare*, 2d ed. (London: Macmillan & Co., 1924), pp. 248–50.

66. On the industry generally, see Louis C. Hunter, *Steamboats on the Western Rivers* (Cambridge: Harvard University Press, 1949).

67. See Robert William Fogel, *Railroads and American Economic Growth* (Baltimore: Johns Hopkins University Press, 1964).

68. The discrepancy between rates and marginal cost, which was thought to be symptomatic of economies of scale in the industry, has recently been shown to be the consequence of a mature state of cartelization. See Robert M. Spann and Edward W. Erickson, "The Economics of Railroading: The Beginning of Cartelization and Regulation," *Bell Journal of Economics and Management Science*, 1 (1970), pp. 227–44.

69. *Shrewsbury & Birmingham Ry. v. London & N.W. Ry.*, 2 Macn. & G. 324 (1850); *Hare v. London & N.W.Ry.*, 2 John & H. 80 (1861).

70. See Thomas M. Cooley, "Popular and Legal Views of Traffic Pooling," *Railway Review*, 24 (1884), pp. 211 ff.

71. Hilton, "The Consistency of the Interstate Commerce Act," p. 92.

72. Robert Riegel, "The Omaha Pool," *Iowa Journal of History and Politics*, 22 (1924), pp. 573–74.

73. U.S. Congress, Senate, *Report of the Select Committee on Transportation—Routes to the Seaboard*, 43d Congress, 1st Session, Report 307 (Washington: G.P.O., 1874), 2 vols.

74. *Ibid.*, vol. 1, p. 7.   75. *Ibid.*, p. 141.

76. *Daily Intelligence* (Atlanta), May 21, 1867.

77. *Report . . . on . . . Routes to the Seaboard*, vol. 1, p. 240.

78. *Ibid.*, appendix, pp. 153–68.   79. *Ibid.*

80. *Railroad Gazette*, 4 (1872), pp. 185, 186, 396.

81. *Report . . . on . . . Routes to the Seaboard*, vol. 1, p. 154.

82. *Railroad Gazette*, 8 (1876), p. 198.

83. *The Continental Railway Company* (New York, May 20, 1881), p. 3.

84. *Railroad Gazette*, 13 (1881), p. 420.

85. Hilton, *Monon Route*, pp. 39–47.

3

The Cost
Controversy

The majority of the literature brought forth by the narrow gauge movement was a long and redundant discussion of *a priori* cost calculations.
For all of its tedious character, this literature remains of basic importance
because it demonstrates the expectations of the narrow gauge advocates.
They set forth their philosophy in various pamphlets, in the proceedings of
conventions of narrow gauge proponents in 1872 and 1878, and in the
four major trade journals of the railroad industry. The *Railway Age* provided them a generally sympathetic forum, and the *Railroad Gazette* a
hostile one. Matthias N. Forney, editor of the *Gazette*,[1] viewed the narrow
gauge movement as the acting out of a fallacious engineering doctrine, but
he was scrupulously conscientious in opening the *Gazette*'s pages to expositors of the narrow gauge philosophy. Forney engaged in direct dia-
logue with individual narrow gauge advocates by means of the *Gazette*'s
correspondence column, commented on the movement's literature in his
reviews of new publications, and kept up a running commentary on the
movement in his editorials. He was not alone, of course, for a variety of
authors wrote critically of narrow gauge doctrine and practice, but Forney's position as editor gave him a unique opportunity to serve as hostile
commentator on the entire epoch. His resignation on December 31, 1883,
approximately coincided with the end of large-scale building of the narrow gauges.

The Narrow Gauge Hypothesis

All of the cost projections of the advocates of the narrow gauge were
founded ultimately on Robert Fairlie's basic tenet that every unnecessary
inch of axle width entailed costs in unproductive tare weight of equipment. Other economies would follow from dealing with this problem. In
choosing among the various statements of the projected economies, it is
probably most intellectually valid to present the estimates of the Special
Committee of Eleven appointed to report on the narrow gauge movement

to the National Narrow-Gauge Railway Convention, held in St. Louis on June 19–20, 1872. The committee, because it was directed to formulate engineering standards for the narrow gauges, had an official standing among the advocates, and represented a reconciliation of the views of the leading figures in the early history of the movement.[2]

The Committee of Eleven stated forthrightly that in mountainous country lines of 3'-0" could be built to serve extractive enterprises for only about one-fifth of what the major trunk lines—the Erie, the Pennsylvania, and the Baltimore & Ohio—had cost. In broken, rolling country, which was taken to be the most common for American railroads, the Committee projected the cost at about half that of standard gauge. For slightly undulating country, the narrow gauge was estimated at under three-fifths of standard gauge investment. The early experience of the Denver & Rio Grande, of which 117 miles were in service in broken, rolling country, led to an estimate of $13,500 per mile. A double-track narrow gauge was projected as cheaper to build than a single-track standard gauge.[3]

The report was accompanied by a letter of W. E. Moreley of the United States Railway Office at Cimarron, New Mexico, dated May 22, 1872, setting forth specific estimates for investment in standard and narrow gauge railroads on a route from the north boundary of New Mexico to Cimarron. The projected railroad was to have a mountain division and a plains division. As a standard gauge, the mountain division would be 35 miles, which could be graded, bridged, and laid with ties for $24,700 per mile, or $864,500. The railroad would then be laid with 70-pound rail at $12,000 per mile, or $420,000. The total was $1,284,500, or $36,700 per mile, based on maximum gradients of 125 feet per mile and maximum curvature of 10°. In contrast, a narrow gauge mountain division would be 40 miles at $9,600 per mile for grading, bridges, and ties ($384,000) plus $7,000 per mile for laying it with 40-pound rails ($280,000). With maximum gradients of 100 feet per mile and maximum curvature of 16° to 18°, the division would represent an investment of $16,600 per mile, or $664,000. The use of narrow gauge would result in a capital saving of nearly 52 percent. On a plains division of 42 miles, using 56-pound rail for the standard gauge and 30-pound for the narrow, Moreley estimated investments of $562,800 for standard gauge and $363,300 for narrow; the projected investment for narrow gauge was about 64 percent of standard.[4] Also cited in the Committee of Eleven's report were the views of Thomas H. Millington, chief engineer of the projected Memphis & Knoxville, who estimated savings of 41 percent on capital for his railroad's route through hilly Tennessee.[5] He then expected savings of 5.5 percent in operating costs.[6]

Both the savings in capital and the savings in operating expenses were expected to stem from the use of smaller, lighter equipment with more favorable ratios of weight of cargo to tare weight. In passenger service, the Committee envisioned a narrow gauge car accommodating 36 passengers, weighing 15,000 pounds, with a deadweight of 416 pounds per passenger. To this it contrasted a 56-seat standard gauge coach of 38,000 pounds, with a deadweight of 678 pounds per passenger. The net savings of 262 pounds per passenger represented a minimum when cars ran full, but because the typical passenger coach ran only about one-quarter filled, the actual deadweight saving per passenger would be much greater. Indeed, the representative coach in New York contained only 13 people, all of whom could be accommodated in a single narrow gauge car. The saving under that circumstance would be about 2,000 pounds per passenger.[7]

Calculations for freight were similar. The projected narrow gauge boxcar was to weigh 8,000 pounds and have a capacity of 16,000. A current standard boxcar weighed 18,500 and had a capacity of 20,000 pounds. Low load factors, however, meant that standard boxcars were actually carrying only 11,000–12,000 pounds, resulting in an average deadweight per ton of freight in 1870 of 3,136 pounds in Massachusetts and 3,019 in New York.[8] As with passenger cars, the same amount of freight could be handled by a narrow gauge boxcar, with an enormous saving on deadweight. The Committee projected an operating ratio of 70 percent, a saving on fuel of 41 percent, and an overall saving on operation of 24.8 percent.[9] A common conclusion from such estimates was that only the New York Central, because of its dense traffic and flat crossing of the Appalachians, could be cost-competitive with a narrow gauge.[10]

The savings on weight were expected to carry through to an ability to operate smaller and cheaper locomotives. Appended to the volume of *Proceedings* of the Narrow Gauge Convention of 1872 was the abridged report of two engineers, Richard B. Osborne and Charles P. Manning, on the proposed conversion of the Western Maryland Railway from a single-track line of 4'-8½" to a double-track one of 3'-0". The authors, who were strongly in favor of the conversion, estimated that because of the reduction in the tare weight of the system, a given locomotive on a grade of 40 feet to the mile would be 17 percent more productive.[11]

The Convention's *Proceedings* are not particularly specific on the projected capital savings on locomotives and grading, but there are plenty of such estimates elsewhere in the literature. The principal book by an American advocate is Howard Fleming's *Narrow Gauge Railways in America*, published in 1875 and quickly reissued in an expanded edition in 1876. To Fleming the ability to use lighter locomotives was a basic element in the entire system. He solicited from Richard B. Osborne a set of estimates comparing a 3'-0" gauge locomotive of 15"×18" cylinders, 36" drivers, and 30 tons gross weight, capable of hauling 1,460 tons on a level track, with a standard gauge engine of equal power. Osborne produced estimates of relative hauling capacity on various gradients, as shown in the accompanying tabulation.[12]

Richard B. Osborne (1815–99) at the time of his report was chief engineer of the Western Maryland. Earlier, as engineer in charge of surveys and construction for the Camden & Atlantic, he had laid out Atlantic City, naming both the resort and its streets. (Engineering Societies Library, New York.)

On a level, gross weight of train 1,460 tons		Tons of coal
3'-0"	engine with 399 tons of cars	1,064
4'-8½"	engine with 566 tons of cars	900
On a maximum grade of 26.4 feet per mile, gross weight 587 tons		
3'-0"	engine with 160 tons of cars	427
4'-8½"	engine with 226 tons of cars	361
On a maximum grade of 40 feet per mile, gross weight 444 tons		
3'-0"	engine with 121 tons of cars	323
4'-8½"	engine with 171 tons of cars	273
On a maximum grade of 80 feet per mile, gross weight 252 tons		
3'-0"	engine with 70 tons of cars	182
4'-8½"	engine with 97 tons of cars	155

These projections were consistent with Osborne's earlier estimate, made with Charles P. Manning, that on the Western Maryland a narrow gauge locomotive on a 40-foot-per-mile grade would be 17 percent more productive than a standard gauge counterpart. Fleming calculated from these data that what a 4'-8½" locomotive could haul up a grade of 26.4 feet per mile a narrow gauge locomotive of similar power could pull up a grade of 33 feet per mile. Accordingly, the location engineer of a narrow gauge could plan on gradients 20–25 percent greater than on a standard gauge because of his prospective reduction of tare weight.[13]

Fleming was explicit: "The narrow gauge aims at following as closely as possible the contour of the ground over which it passes, thereby avoiding the extensive cuts, and fills, and tunnels which so much advance the cost of construction."[14] The saving on investment, which he estimated at about one-third,[15] was manifested also in sharper curves and smaller cuts and fills. The reasoning of the narrow gauge advocates was that the shorter axle of 3'-0" equipment allowed shorter radii of curvature, and that both cuttings and embankments could be narrower. The lower weight of narrow gauge locomotives allowed lighter and cheaper rail. Fleming cited the investment in the standard gauge Kansas Pacific, including equipment, as $23,500 per mile, but the original line of the Denver & Rio Grande along the base of the Front Range as only $13,500, also with equipment.[16] The Kansas Pacific was laid with 56-pound rail, the D&RG with 30-pound.

Fleming presented a table of projected costs of a narrow gauge of about 100 miles in prairie country such as that around Chicago, intended to do a general business and to carry coal traffic, estimated by F. E. Canda & Co., who had built the Cairo & St. Louis (see the accompanying tabulation). The total cost equipped was projected at $13,311 per mile, which he contrasted with $20,000 per mile for the Chicago, Burlington & Quincy.[17] The location, anticipated coal traffic, and apparent rivalry with the Burlington lead one to suspect that the estimates are for the Chicago, Millington & Western, which Fleming listed among completed and abuilding narrow gauges.[18]

COST PER MILE—THREE FEET GAUGE		ROLLING STOCK		
Grading	$2,200	12 freight locomotives	$8,000	$ 96,000
Iron (30 lbs. to the yard)	4,080	4 passenger locomotives	7,000	28,000
Fish plates, fastenings, etc.	435	300 coal cars	450	135,000
Cross ties (2,640)	800	70 flat cars	420	29,400
Bridging and culverts	400	100 boxcars	520	52,000
Track-laying and surfacing	400	10 passenger cars	3,000	30,000
Engineering	250	3 passenger cars, 2d class	1,500	4,500
Right of way	300	3 baggage cars	1,400	4,200
Station houses, water		Or $3,791 per mile.		$379,100
stations, etc.	375			
Sundries	280			
	$9,520			

Fleming was not specific on the savings from sharper curvature and narrower cuts and fills, but some of the other narrow gauge advocates were. Possibly the most specific estimates of anticipated capital savings on narrow gauge construction were made by James P. Low, chief engineer of the Blue Ridge Railroad, in a report to his management at the outset of the narrow gauge era. The railroad had been left in a state of partial completion in 1861 when the Civil War broke out. About $2.5 million had been expended in building it from Anderson to Walhalla, South Carolina, a distance of 33 miles.[19] The main line was projected from Walhalla through Rabun Gap and along tributaries of the Tennessee River to Knoxville, about 147 miles, all through difficult country. Low on November 17, 1870, had estimated the cost of completion (before motive power and equipment) at $6.8 million, but he shortly became converted to the narrow gauge ideology and in a report to his president and directors dated July 24, 1871, presented his projections of the savings to be realized by building the extension at 3'-0" gauge.[20] Unfortunately, the Blue Ridge's existing line was the common southern gauge of 5'-0", not 4'-8½", so that Low's comparisons were not with standard gauge and thus may have been somewhat more favorable to narrow gauge than those a northern engineer might have made. George Washington Whistler in his famous report of 1842 recommending 5'-0" for the railway between St. Petersburg and Moscow had estimated no significant difference in investment between 4'-8½" and 5'-0".[21]

Low estimated the cross-sections of cuts and fills for 3'-0" at 20 percent below 5'-0". He proposed bridges heavy enough only for loadings of 1,500 pounds per square foot, as compared with 3,360 pounds for 5'-0". As a consequence, he envisioned cost savings of 20 percent on all parts of the roadbed. For track, by using 30-pound rail rather than 56-pound, he projected $6,136 per mile, a saving of 42 percent relative to his estimate of $10,631 for 5'-0". His net evaluation was that the railroad could be built for about two-thirds the cost in infrastructure and track of a 5'-0" line—a conclusion highly consistent with the estimates of his northern counterparts who used 4'-8½" for their comparisons. Low also thought that the use of steeper grades and sharper curves on a narrow gauge could reduce capital costs further. He projected grades of 100 feet per mile in the direction of dominant traffic and 150 in the other, along with curves of 100 to 200 feet radius. Along the Tennessee River and its tributaries, he expected to follow the bends more closely and to avoid tunnels. The ability to follow land contours more closely he expected to shorten, not lengthen the railroad; the remaining distance he thought could be reduced from 147 to 130 miles. This led him to a projection that the right-of-way and track could be completed as a narrow gauge for $4 million, about 59 percent of his estimate of $6.8 million for completion at 5'-0".[22]

Low's estimates of savings on tare weight of equipment were of the general character of those set forth in the *Proceedings* of the Narrow Gauge Convention of 1872, but he fitted them out with specific cost figures. His passenger coaches were to have a deadweight of 353 pounds per passenger, as compared with 560 pounds for 5'-0", and were to cost $2,000 to $2,500, depending on fittings, for first class and $1,600 to $1,800 for second class. He projected boxcars 14 feet long, weighing 2.5 tons, capable of 5-ton loads, costing $450. For baled cotton, such boxcars would have a deadweight per bale of 458 pounds, as compared with 533 pounds for 5'-0" equiment. In stockcars, the deadweight was projected at 687 pounds per head of cattle, as versus 727 pounds for 5'-0" cars.[23] Low estimated the power requirements for the narrow gauge as against the broad at a ratio of 37:53 for freight, and 13:28 for passengers, an average saving of power required of about 33 percent for the narrow gauge.[24] He projected that the railroad would require 30 locomotives in either case, but he believed the company would buy engines costing only $7,500 each for 3'-0", as compared with $15,000 for 5'-0".[25] His net estimate was that the railroad could be fitted out with motive power and rolling stock for $318,525 at 3'-0" but $639,125 at 5'-0".[26]

The savings in cost of operation Low estimated were based partly on the expectation of savings of fuel and lubricants of about one-third, partly on the expectation that the lighter equipment would do less damage to track, reducing maintenance-of-way expenses. The 30-pound rail would be cheaper to repair than 56-pound, in any case. He summarized his expected savings on operating expenses in tabular form,[27] reproduced in the accompanying tabulation.

Classification of expenses	Share of total operating expenses	Share saved by narrow gauge
Maintenance of roadway		
Repairs to roadbed	.166	.055
Cost of iron for renewal	.129	.065
Repairs of buildings and fences	.037	—
Taxes	.038	—
Repairs of machinery and cars	.20	.070
Operating expenses		
Office expense, agencies, and employees on trains and at stations	.123	—
Fuel, oil, and waste	.125	.041
Loss and damage, general superintendence	.030	—
Contingencies	.052	.017
TOTAL	—	.248

It is too much for coincidence that Low's estimated saving and operating cost was 24.8 percent, precisely the same as the estimate in the *Proceedings* of the Narrow-Gauge Convention of 1872. His estimate of 1871 had become conventional wisdom among the narrow-gauge advocates. Low estimated the savings would reduce the projected operating ratio from 70 percent to 52.5 percent.[28]

Low recognized that incompatibility entailed cost, but in estimating the expense of transshipment of cargo, he chose the most conventional figure, 5¢ per ton, the same one that appeared the following year in the *Proceedings* of the Narrow-Gauge Convention.[29] This was based on the reported figure of 2d. per ton for the British break-of-gauge at Gloucester—by 1871 a thoroughly obsolete figure—and the 5¢ per ton reported for the change-of-gauge at the Canadian border. The Blue Ridge was planned mainly as a facility for northbound movements of southern agricultural crops. As a consequence, as a narrow gauge the railroad would have required transshipment at both ends. Low stated that the southern lines built to 5'-0" moved freight for 1.5¢ per ton-mile, but he had estimated that a narrow gauge could undercut that by approximately 25 percent. He calculated that if the property were completed at 5'-0", the management could move a ton of freight the length of the railroad for $2.70. The use of narrow gauge—including, apparently, conversion of the existing mileage to 3'-0"—would reduce this cost by 67.5¢. Subtracting 10¢ for transshipment at each end, he concluded that adoption of narrow gauge would still result in a net gain of 57.5¢ per ton moving the length of the railroad.[30] To this he suggested be added savings in avoidance of interchange, which he thought resulted in neglected equipment, but he made no attempt to quantify this.

The proposed extension of the Blue Ridge Railroad was never built, leaving Low's estimates entirely speculative. They are, however, remarkably comprehensive, encompassing all of the categories of savings commonly set forth by the proponents of the narrow gauge early in the history of the movement.

Most of the advocates, like Low, argued only that saving on tare weight of equipment would yield economies in carriage, but a few went on to assert that there was an additional advantage in the weight-to-power ratio of narrow-gauge locomotives. John Y. Smith, a locomotive builder of Pittsburgh who styled himself "Narrow Gauge Smith," argued at the convention of the American Railway Master Mechanics' Association in Baltimore in 1873 that the weight-to-power ratios of narrow-gauge engines were inherently more favorable than standard:

My experience with the narrow gauge engines we have built is that in carrying loads there is about twenty-five percent, or one third more in favor of the narrow or three foot gauge than in the four feet eight and a half inch road. . . . The philosophy of the advantage in favor of the three-feet gauge I have not yet discovered. There is a little difference in favor of the narrow gauge on a short curve, but at a low speed and on a straight track there's no difference between them whatever. . . . As to the engines, we hauled more tons on the narrow gauge than on the broad by engines built from the same pattern.[31]

In response to a query about relative weights from William S. Hudson, Superintendent of the Rogers Locomotive Works, Smith stated that the 3'-0" locomotives weighed about 14 tons and the standard gauge between 14½ and 15 tons.[32]

Smith on the basis of his experience was an authoritative figure. He had been a founding partner of what became the H. K. Porter Co. as Smith & Porter in 1866, and then became a founder of the National Locomotive Works in 1871.[33] Both firms were narrow gauge specialists. He claimed to have produced engines of as little as eight tons for 2'-0" gauge and 10 to 14 tons for 3'-0".[34] It is questionable, however, whether Smith's view ought to be accepted as part of narrow gauge orthodoxy. Robert F. Fairlie could not have accepted it consistently with his advocacy of the Fairlie locomotive as a necessary condition for success of the narrow gauge. Howard Fleming did not make this argument in his book in 1875 and 1876, and Edward Hulbert explicitly rejected it at the narrow gauge convention in the summer of 1878. L. F. McAleer, Superintendent of the Painesville & Youngstown, protested Hulbert's repudiation by asserting that a 3'-0" locomotive of 15 tons with 36" drivers "would yank the wheels out from under" a 35-ton standard gauge engine, but no other voices were raised in support of the doctrine.[35] Smith was honest concerning his possible bias; in response to Hudson he said, "I am favorable to narrow gauge roads because I have goods to sell."[36]

William L. Webber in 1876 noted that the locomotives on the narrow gauge at the Centennial Exposition in Philadelphia—which pulled relatively light passenger equipment—could operate about 70 miles on a ton of coal, which he compared with only 35 miles for standard gauge engines.

This calculation led him to expect fuel costs for narrow gauge locomotives generally to run about 3.8¢ per mile as compared with 8.3¢ for the average of western railroads in June 1876. He also expected repair expenses to be lower because of the smaller size and lighter weight of the parts, 1.5¢ per mile versus 4.23¢. Anticipating no saving on wages or lubrication, he projected locomotive operating expenses of 12.96¢ per mile, a saving of 7.23¢ per mile relative to standard-gauge operating costs of 20.19¢, or $7.23 per day for an average run of 100 miles. Webber also anticipated that the lighter locomotives and cars would inflict less damage on the rails. He reasoned that a 10-ton blow to 30-pound rail would do less damage than a 20-ton blow to a 60-pound rail, thereby reducing the tendency of rails to deteriorate at joints and to develop "hollow places." Finally, he expected the lighter weights to extend wheel life on stockcars from the present 30,000–40,000 miles to 60,000–90,000 miles.[37]

John T. Davis, a San Francisco engineer, after a similar exposition of expected cost savings, estimated that a railroad of 100 miles, built for $13,500 per mile, including equipment, could turn in a profit of $17,280 on a gross of only $158,000 per year. This calculation led him to believe that any valley in California could support a narrow gauge. Lines built to serve mines would inevitably bring forth general economic development that would assure "the whole line will be one continuous system of farms and vineyards. . . ."[38]

One of the proponents attempted a quantification of the gains anticipated from conversion to narrow gauge for the economy as a whole. General W. S. Rosecrans projected in 1872 that if the entire United States were to be as well covered by railroads as Ohio, 165,800 additional miles would be built. He estimated that if all the railroads built since the end of 1867 had been constructed to narrow gauge, the saving in initial cost would have been $480 million, interest on which at 6 percent would have been $28.8 million per year. The saving in variable costs on haulage he estimated at $100.8 million. Accordingly, the net saving, as he viewed it, would have been $129.6 million per year. Projecting that to the 165,800 miles he anticipated, he estimated the annual saving at $547,540,515— hardly a sum to be taken lightly.[39] William Stuart Watson of San Francisco in a pamphlet issued to announce his specialization in the design and building of narrow gauges in 1872 made a similar estimate that if the existing railroad mileage of 60,500 had been built to 3'-0", its bonded debt of approximately $2.2 billion either would not have been incurred, or would have been already paid off. Under those circumstances, he estimated that the railroads would be paying a 30-percent return to their shareholders.[40]

Cost savings of the sort projected by these authors tended to become articles of faith of the advocates, and as such underwent relatively little modification over the course of the narrow gauge movement.[41] Necessarily, the earliest major advance made was in quantification of the costs of interchange. The initial estimate of 5¢ per ton for transshipment was particularly crude. The anonymous author of a pamphlet of the mid-1870s advocating narrow gauges for the development of Iowa reported that the Denver & Rio Grande with labor at $3.00 per day transferred freight for about $1.20 per car, that the Union Pacific and D&RG transshipped for not over 15¢ per ton at Denver, and that the Cairo & St. Louis transferred for 40¢ per car. This author estimated that coal was transferred at various unnamed points in the West for 8¢ to 10¢ per ton. At 10¢ per ton he estimated the transshipment cost at only 3 mills per bushel; shippers, he noted, already paid a transshipment fee of about 2¢ per bushel at Chicago, whether or not the transfer was provided. He estimated that 80 percent of the traffic on his proposed Iowa roads would be local in any case, requiring no transshipment.[42]

The limited extent to which the proponents' thought matured can best be seen in comparing the expectations set forth in the two narrow gauge conventions of 1878 with the estimates of 1872. In an intellectual sense, the 1878 conventions represent the peak of the movement. The advocates had an established body of doctrine, together with a limited degree of experience—quite a bit more limited than they would have preferred—and relatively bright prospects for additional investment in the immediate future. After 1878 the history of the movement was dominated by the actual experience of the narrow gauges, especially the disastrous performance of the Grand Narrow Gauge Trunk, to be treated in Chapter 4. In consequence, the conventions of 1878 represent the final major statement of the expectations of the advocates.[43]

The most general statement of the conventions of 1878 was embodied in a resolution of B. J. Gifford of the Havana, Rantoul & Eastern repeating the claim of 1872 that a good 3'-0" railway could be built for not over two-thirds of the cost of standard gauge.[44] The resolution also stated that the operating costs would be under two-thirds those of standard gauge, although Edward Hulbert, Chairman of the Executive Committee of the Convention, claimed only the traditional saving of 25 percent.[45] The resolution went on to state that the narrow gauge was equally safe, but Joseph O. Ramsey of the Bell's Gap Railroad and Augustine W. Wright of the Havana, Rantoul & Eastern expressed the view that the narrow gauge was intrinsically safer than standard on the ground that the lighter equipment, operating at lower speed and with a lower center of gravity, had less potential for inflicting damage.[46] Ramsey presented to the Convention a cost comparison unusual in that it contrasted the actual costs of a narrow gauge with the hypothetical costs of a standard gauge. The Bell's Gap was a coal-hauler of 3'-0" tributary to the Pennsylvania Railroad at Bellwood, seven miles east of Altoona. Ramsey's cars weighed 2,200 pounds and carried 7,500 pounds of coal. They averaged one and one-half trips a day over the railroad, and 30,000 miles per year. His locomotives weighed 16.5 tons and made four trips per day, handling 32 cars up the railroad's ruling grades of seven miles of 3 percent. The railroad's normal output was hauling 480 tons of coal in 128 cars with a tare weight of 140 tons. Ramsey estimated that a standard gauge railroad would have required 34 standard gauge cars with a tare weight of 300 tons. This led him to the estimate of relative daily costs given in the accompanying tabulation.

His figures are also unusual in providing an estimate of wage savings. In a fashion he did not explain, he presumed he could get 2.2 days' work out of his enginemen and trainmen for each day's work of a counterpart on

	Narrow Gauge	Standard Gauge
Trainman's wages	$ 9.20	$20.24
Coal, oil, water, repairs	3.09	7.23
Transfer to standard gauge	3.00	—
Total	$15.29	$27.47
Average cost of repairing track	13.00	22.10
Total cost of moving 480 tons of coal	$28.29	$49.57

standard gauge. Ramsey estimated the savings from the use of narrow gauge at $6,500 per year. The railroad earned a return of 6 percent on its investment of $102,000. Ramsey concluded that the use of narrow gauge was the margin between profitability and its absence.[47]

The Convention was given a few individual estimates to add to the case for the narrow gauge. A Committee on Operating Expenses brought forth the estimate that on a complete circle of unspecified diameter, the outer wheel of a standard gauge car would slip 29.84 inches, but a narrow gauge wheel only 18.84 inches, from which savings in power and wear and tear on rail were predicted at 37 percent.[48] A letter of T. G. Sickels of the Union Pacific to R. H. Lamborn was published, stating that the estimates of building the Colorado Central narrow gauge up Clear Creek Canyon had been $90,000 per mile for standard gauge and $20,000 for narrow gauge. He stated that savings on grading normally ran only in a range of 33⅓ to 50 percent. He thought savings on equipment similar.[49]

The Convention appointed a Committee on Transfer, but it added little to knowledge or to dogma. H. J. Chase of Chicago presented an analysis of 645,664 cars in Chicago in 1877. Of these, livestock amounted to 19.9 percent, rolling freight (barrels and casks) 7 percent, merchandise 41 percent, and grain 31.5 percent. He considered transfer of livestock essentially costless, and believed that only merchandise, being boxed, presented any significant costs. Grains, he stated, had to be weighed and graded, and therefore transshipped in any case. He repeated the estimates of 6¢ per bushel for transshipment of grain, but otherwise did not present any specific cost figures.[50]

The proponents of the narrow gauge devoted themselves almost entirely to cost considerations, hardly at all to demand. There was, as we have seen in Chapter 2, a body of literature purporting to demonstrate an unsatisfied demand for low-rate, low-quality transportation, but the spokesmen for the narrow gauge did not make use of it in their conventions. Rather, they typically behaved as if existence of such a demand was self-evident. Only Edward Hulbert was explicit. At the 1872 convention he argued that 5'-0" railroads were too expensive to cover Georgia sufficiently to develop the state's resources. He said, "We frankly admit our inability to build the broad gauge; we are compelled to adopt the narrow gauge."[51] Later in 1872 he stated that the economies of narrow gauge could bring a railroad to every county seat in Georgia.[52] In his welcoming address to the second convention of 1878, he was more specific on the nature of the demands he perceived:

Taking [Chattanooga] as a central point and swinging around it a circle of 100 miles radius we find the richest deposits of iron and coal in the world . . . and yet the south has thus far been unable to develop these riches to any great extent.

Why? Many years since they built standard gauge roads at a heavy cost, hoping development would follow. Agricultural section; light traffic; roads too costly; unable to give low rates. Practical effect has been to lock up these riches. Here then is a grand future mission for the narrow gauge to accomplish. . . . [F]rom the Atlantic to the Pacific everywhere on this broad continent the narrow gauge has the same great future mission to perform.[53]

On the crucial point that existing railroads were allegedly overproducing quality by operating too fast, there was but a single statement in the Report of the Committee on Operating Expenses in the Convention of 1878, and even that was in connection with costs: "We cannot allow this opportunity to pass without expressing our disapproval as railroad men at the tremendous speed at which so many of the standard gauge trains are run—so terribly depreciating to track and rolling stock, and we trust the narrow gauge will avoid this folly with the others, to its great pecuniary reward."[54]

The Anti–Narrow Gauge Case

The proponents of the narrow gauge presented to America a testable hypothesis. Like most such hypotheses—the alleged economy of slurry pipelines for coal movement at the present writing, for example—it was subjected first to criticism on logical grounds, then evaluated with such existing empirical evidence as appeared relevant, and finally subjected to a market test. The role of principal hostile critic of the narrow gauge fell to Matthias N. Forney essentially through coincidence; he assumed the co-editorship of the *Railroad Gazette* almost precisely when the narrow gauge movement came to America.

Matthias Nace Forney had been born in Hanover, Pennsylvania, in 1835. At 17 he became an apprentice to Ross Winans, the locomotive builder of Baltimore, with whom he spent four years. He left the railroad industry in 1858, but returned in 1861 as a draftsman for the Illinois Central. There he developed and patented a 0-4-4 tank engine that came to be known as the "Forney type." The locomotive was intended for suburban trains on main line railroads but came to be identified mainly with service on elevated railroads in New York, Brooklyn, and Chicago. About 1865 Forney went to Boston to supervise construction of the locomotives for the Illinois Central at the Hinkley & Williams Works. Upon completion of the order, Forney transferred to Hinkley & Williams as a draftsman and agent. Late in 1870 he accepted the associate editorship of the *Railroad Gazette*. From his office in New York he quickly established himself as the premier editor in the trade press of railroading. His experience had already given him a thorough familiarity with the industry, and, in particular, his development of the Forney locomotive had caused him to deal with the problems of light railroading.[55]

Forney published Fairlie's "On the Gauge for the Railways of the Future" in his issue of October 15, 1870, and on November 12 produced the first of his long series of editorials attacking the narrow gauge philosophy. Forney's criticism of the narrow gauge doctrine began with its most basic element, Fairlie's dictum that tare weight was directly related to gauge. For-

Matthias Nace Forney (1835–1908). (Smithsonian Institution.)

ney observed that the *reductio ad absurdum* of this argument was that a velocipede—he was later to prefer a wheelbarrow—should weigh nothing. Forney considered 5′-0″ the optimal gauge on the basis of expressed opinion within the industry, but felt the choice of 4′-8½″ for the Pacific Railroad had established the latter as standard in America for all time.[56] In his first specific editorial on narrow gauge rolling stock, he took the design of Fairlie's proposed 3′-0″ freight cars, 4-wheel goods vans of the British pattern, and calculated the additional weight necessary to expand their axles to 4′-8½″. He found that the axle weighed only about 150 pounds, a little over 4 percent of the tare weight and less than 1 percent of total weight when loaded. Thus, the saving on weight was at best on the order of 2 percent of tare weight. The gain in stability and conformity from the use of 4′-8½″ he thought clearly worth whatever additional weight might be involved. He considered the projected weight savings of the equipment mainly a consequence of reversion to an archaic type of vehicle, the 4-wheel boxcar.[57] Worse, he was to argue, some of the early estimates of the ratio of cargo to tare weight were made on the presumption of freight being carried under tarpaulin on 4-wheel narrow gauge flatcars.[58]

Over the course of the 1870s Forney developed this point as his basic argument: the projected capital savings of the narrow gauge were to only a trivial extent the consequence of the smaller gauge, but mainly were the consequence of reversion to more primitive standards that railroad engineers had already rejected. Forney next applied such reasoning to rights-of-way. He considered the degree of curvature dependent on speed, not gauge. Rapid transit and suburban lines had curves as sharp as 38 feet with standard gauge, simply because the curves were intended to be traversed slowly. The ability of locomotives to pull trains up grades, he thought, was unaffected by gauge, for trains of either gauge were governed by the same principle of gravitation. For an embankment six feet high, he assumed a tie of six feet for a 3′-0″ line and one of 7′-8½″ for a standard gauge railroad. This led him to estimate a surface for the embankment of 10 feet for narrow gauge and 11′-8½″ for standard. With an angle of 45° on the slope in either case, he concluded that the area in cross section would be 96 square feet for narrow gauge and 106¼ feet for standard, a difference of only about 10 percent. He made a similar calculation for a cut six feet deep and concluded the cross sections would be 120 square feet for narrow gauge and 130¼ square feet for standard, again a difference of only about 10 percent. For larger cuts or grades the figures would be more favorable to standard.[59] For cuts and embankments on the sides of steep hills—the sort of terrain in which the narrow gauge was argued to have its greatest advantage—he calculated that the difference between grading rights-of-way of 10 feet and 11′-6″ would rarely exceed 10 percent.[60] His initial net evaluation was that the intrinsic differences in building and equipping railroads of 3′-0″ and 4′-8½″ would be somewhat less than 4 percent.[61] Any greater saving would represent adoption of more primitive standards. His conclusion was that if cheap roads were to be built they should be of standard gauge, since the advantages of compatibility and capability of upgrading outweighed the small savings in using the narrow gauge.[62] His opponents, it should be pointed out, considered this proposal impractical on the grounds that the rights-of-way would be too insubstantial for conventional equipment, and that the light equipment of such railroads could not withstand impacts from standard boxcars.[63]

Forney was never to vary from this view, however. Hardly less than his opponents, he became repetitive and doctrinaire in his arguments, but he was able to draw upon an emerging body of evidence that was almost entirely supportive to him. By late 1872 the building of the East New York & Canarsie Railroad in Brooklyn and his examination of the records of the Hanover Branch Railroad in Pennsylvania led him to question whether there need be any difference in grading between the two gauges.[64] In 1879, he made an extensive inquiry into narrow gauge practice, and ascertained that most roads of 3'-0" gauge used ties six feet long. Although he pointed out that a light railway of 4'-8½" could use such ties, normal practice would be to use a tie of seven feet. With a surface a foot wider than the tie in each case, he calculated that, with a slope of 3:2, the saving in fill material would be only 7.1 percent for an embankment of four feet, to 3.8 percent for one of 12 feet. Taking an average between 0 and 7½ percent, he calculated that a saving in grading of 3¾ percent—given that grading amounted to 23.6 percent of the cost of building a railroad—would reduce the first cost of construction by only ⅞ of 1 percent, if standards were otherwise the same.[65] For grading, ties, ballast, and culverts, he estimated that the saving exclusively from the use of narrow gauge would be only about 1.7 percent.[66]

With respect to locomotives and rolling stock, Forney did not attempt analogous estimates of relative cost, but simply presented excerpts from letters he had solicited from leading locomotive works and carbuilders:

[T]he Baldwin Locomotive Works write:

"We would make a locomotive *at the same price for* the standard gauge as the 3½-ft. gauge, the plan and all the dimensions being the same in each case, except, necessarily, the cross measurements being 14½ in. wider in one case than in the other. This difference in the cross measurements would really add $50 to $75 to the cost of construction, and the difference in cost between one engine and the other would be measured by this amount."

Mr. W. S. Hudson, of the Rogers Locomotive Works, writes:

"From our experience we can say confidently that it will cost more to build any size of engine (unless it may be the very smallest—engines with cylinders 3½ in. diameter and 10 in. stroke with four 30 in. wheels have been built at these works for a 1 ft. 8½ in. gauge) for the narrow than for the standard gauge. . . . We are ready to build any locomotive for any gauge at reasonable prices, and do not intend to convey the idea that we do not desire to build engines for narrow gauges."

Mr. H. L. Leach, of the Hinkley Locomotive Works, writes:

"I should rather build engines of the same power and capacity of the 4 ft. 8½ in. gauge than of any gauge narrower. The cost of the extra material (in engines for the standard gauge) would be more than compensated by the greater convenience of putting together the engines of 4 ft. 8½ in. gauge."

Mr. H. G. Brooks, President of the Brooks Locomotive Works, writes:

"For an engine of like class and equal capacity we should make difference enough only to cover additional weight of material, which would be a very small amount indeed: not enough to include in estimates on cost of building and equipping a road."

Messrs. Porter, Bell & Co., of Pittsburgh, who make a specialty of narrow-gauge and other light engines, write:

"The difference in weight and cost and efficiency for different gauges of same cylinder and machinery, outside of cost of patterns, etc., is not much of an item in cost of an engine, and many other contingencies of building are likely to more than balance it. . . ."

The difference in weight of locomotives which is due to the gauge alone is variously estimated at from 500 to 1,000 lbs. The estimates, however, are, we fear, based on rather loose calculations.

With reference to the weight and cost of cars, Mr. George C. Fish, President of the Wason Manufacturing Company, writes:

"On our regular standard cars, the difference in weight and cost would be (between cars for wide and narrow gauge):

> Weight of passenger cars, 900 lbs.; cost $25
> Weight of freight cars, 750 lb.; cost   20"

In another letter the same gentleman wrote:

"The cost would be the same of such cars as we proposed to build for you (for the standard gauge), if you conclude to have a 3 or 3½ ft. track, as in one case the cars would be sent from the works loaded at a rate by weight, and in case of being for a 4 ft. 8½ in. track they would go on their own wheels, costing us much less for transportation than the saving on the width of trucks for a 4 ft. 8½ in. track."

Mr. Barney, President of the Barney & Smith Manufacturing Company, writes:

"You ask us to state the difference in cost of narrow or 3 ft. gauge rolling stock, and the same rolling stock fitted to run on standard or 4 ft. 8½ in. gauge roads, by widening the trucks. The increased weight of axles from increased length would be for the size used on narrow-gauge cars about 30 lbs. each, or 200 lbs. to a car. The increase of lumber would be 75 to 100 ft. for each car. Possibly it might be deemed best to increase the size of axles and timber, on account of increased lengths. We judge the entire cost of fitting narrow-gauge rolling stock to run on standard-gauge track by widening the truck when first building would not exceed ten dollars per car, including both freight and passenger cars."[67]

Apparently Forney made no effort to quantify the costs of transshipment between standard and narrow gauge equipment, even though this was the point on which the advocates were most vulnerable. They were arguing that savings on interest in building cheaper rights-of-way and savings on variable costs of operating lighter equipment were greater than the costs of transshipment. This should have been easily testable. The results, which Forney could probably have estimated at least as accurately as he attempted to evaluate construction costs, could only have been devastating to the proponents, given the observed experience of the narrow gauge railroads in the early 1880s.

Forney was, of course, not alone in his hostile criticism of the narrow gauge. Before the end of 1870 he had been joined by Walton W. Evans, a consulting engineer in New York who specialized in railroads. From the outset, Evans identified himself with hostility to the Fairlie locomotive, which he considered an unoriginal adaptation of John Cockerill's design of 1851 that had proved itself unsuccessful long since.[68] Evans's views on the narrow gauge doctrine generally were set forth in a report he executed on the commission of H. C. E. Childers, M.P., Agent General of the Colony of Victoria, Australia.[69] Victoria Railways had been built to 5'-3", but there was considerable local pressure to adopt 3'-6" as in Queensland. Childers commissioned Evans to evaluate the narrow gauge partly because Evans had been consulting engineer on lines of 3'-0" and 3'-6" in Costa Rica, Peru, and Chile. Indeed, Evans proved unrepentant on his use of the nar-

Walton W. Evans (Anthony Walton White Evans, 1817–86) was an engineer of considerable distinction trained at Rensselaer Polytechnic Institute. He was a close friend of Forney and an early recruit to the anti-narrow gauge cause. (Rensselaer Polytechnic Institute.)

row gauges in Latin America, believing them appropriate for some services in undeveloped countries without problems of physical interchange:

> But to adopt a narrow gauge for such a country as Australia, a country which we are led to believe will become one of the richest, most powerful, and well-settled countries in the world, appears to be an absurdity. A great many clever and conscientious men, but men of no great experience in railway construction and economy believe in the merits of narrow-gauge. And why? Because they have been told that they can be built and worked at less cost, and that there is a great economy to grow out of it. They believe this because they wish to; they try to believe it.[70]

Evans proceeded to document this view by listing 44 major categories of costs of a railway, considering how each might be influenced by use of a narrow gauge, but in general attempting no quantifications. Obviously, surveying, fencing, telegraphy, station maintenance, legal expense, and several other categories were unrelated to the gauge. In rolling friction Evans considered the narrow gauge at a positive disadvantage, for a given cargo would have half again as many wheels and journals. On the matter of cuts and fills, he estimated that on a 50-foot embankment the difference in quantity and cost of fill material as between 3'-6" and 4'-8½" was only 1.4 percent, and for greater heights nothing at all.[71] With respect to bridges and turntables, he projected no savings. In his work in Latin America, he had specified the same strength of bridges and size of turntables as for standard gauge out of uncertainty over how large narrow gauge motive power would be in the future.[72] He made much of the tendency of engineers to go to more capital-intensive technology in every major phase of railroading. "Can it be that all the railway world, the people of countries widely separated in distance, language and ways of doing things, have gone wrong and committed the same error, steadily, through more than the third of a century, in increasing the size, and weight, and power of engines, and cars, and rails and sleepers, and everything belonging to railways? Are we all idiots?"[73]

Sleepers: Ties.

Evans noted the marked tendency toward larger steamboats on the Inland Rivers. Responding to Childers's report of a rumor in Melbourne that the Americans were planning to replace existing 4'-8½" lines with "the Fairlie gauge," Evans wrote that such a change would be as sensible as going to smaller steamboats.[74]

Of all the opponents, Evans was the most explicit in arguing the benefits of a free-running car supply between companies:

> With uniform gauge over a system of various lines of railway intersecting and connecting with each other, there will be less rolling stock required, and also less station-tracks and station accommodations; engines and engine drivers will lie idle less time; goods will be delivered earlier and in better condition. It is probably putting it at a low estimate to assert that a change of goods, in quantity, will cost in time a day, or, in distance, more than a hundred miles run, in addition to damage and amount paid for the transfer; two sets of cars have to be furnished, and both have to lie idle during the transfer. I beg pardon for saying so much on this point, but it is a vital point, and one that every country has seen or will see the sad policy of.[75]

Evans recommended to Childers that Victoria begin converting its 5'-3" lines to 4'-8½"—advice it was to take for its intercity main lines about a century later.[76]

Evans was responsible for recruiting to the opponents of the narrow gauge one of the great American engineers, Benjamin H. Latrobe. Son of the architect of the United States Capitol, Latrobe had been chief engineer of the Baltimore & Ohio in its early years and in consequence was thoroughly familiar with the evolution to heavier standards that Evans considered so important. Latrobe's commentary took the form of a letter of November 8, 1872, which Evans published as a pamphlet. Latrobe engaged in a calculation similar to those of Forney and Evans on the costs of grading, based on an assumption that the roadbed in cuts should be 12 feet for 3'-0", or 14½ feet for 4'-8½", and on embankments 12 feet for 3'-0", or 13.7 feet for 4'-8½". This led him to conclude that the costs of grading would differ between the two by $366 per mile for a lightly graded line and $1,468 for a heavily graded one. This he compared with Thomas H. Millington's estimate of a difference of $2,169 per mile for his projected Memphis & Knoxville. Latrobe's net evaluation was that the saving in grading would amount to about 15 percent for a heavily graded line, or 7.8 percent for a lightly graded one.[77]

Latrobe was particularly critical of the use of 30- to 35-pound rail on the narrow gauges. Early T-rail of the B&O of 35 to 40 pounds, he reported, had not lasted long unless supported by longitudinal timbers, and the B&O was then running locomotives of only eight to twelve tons. The advocates of the narrow gauge proposed to use 30-pound rail with 15-ton engines. This he considered a particularly unwise reversion to the past.[78]

In the pamphlet literature opposing the narrow gauge, the contribution of Silas Seymour is of particular interest, for he wrote in direct opposition to a proponent, and in connection with a specific project. The Texas & Pacific Railroad was projected in 1871 from New Orleans to San Diego; the directors commissioned their chief engineer, General George P. Buell, to report on the optimal gauge for the line. Buell, whose background was in military engineering, brought in a strong recommendation for 3'-6". Relative to 4'-8½", Buell anticipated savings of 30 percent on grading, 45 percent on track, and 50 to 55 percent on rolling stock, all predicated on operation at 35 to 45 miles per hour. He estimated a ratio of deadweight to load of 47 percent, relative to 75 percent on standard gauge.[79]

Buell's pamphlet is the leading piece of advocacy of 3'-6" in the literature of the controversy. As such, it is to some extent critical of the doctrinal orthodoxy of the narrow gauge movement. He expected little if any difference in cost relative to 3'-0"—not more than 5 percent—partly because he anticipated using the same ties. He foresaw no difference in expenses of operation and maintenance. He planned cars about a foot wider than on the 3'-0" lines, with about 17 percent greater capacity, for little or no additional capital cost. Engines of 3'-6", he argued, had a more favorable angle of stability than 3'-0" motive power, and thus could be operated with greater speed and safety. Because of an absence of coal on much of the projected route, the T&P planned to burn wood. Buell cited a statement of Sir Charles Fox that the firebox of a 3'-6" engine was the smallest practical for effective wood combustion. For ratio of deadweight to load, Buell projected 100 percent at 4'-8½", 48 percent at 3'-6", and 56 percent at 3'-0", a U-shaped relation. For passengers he anticipated being able to provide seats for two persons on either side of the aisle, as on the Toronto,

T-rail: Rail of the usual modern sort, with a head, web, and base, as contrasted with the rails of earlier practice, strap rail (iron strips laid on longitudinal wooden stringers) and U-rail (iron rail with the cross-section of an inverted U).

Silas Seymour is seated at left at the table in the private car of Thomas C. Durant of the Union Pacific. The others at the table are Sidney Dillon, Durant, and John R. Duff. (Union Pacific Railroad Museum.)

Grey & Bruce and Toronto & Nipissing, rather than two-and-one seating, as on 3'-0" lines.[80] In sum, Buell expected to be able to build 74.5 miles of 3'-6" east from San Diego for the cost of 50 miles of standard gauge—an orthodox expectation for the narrow gauge advocates.[81]

President Marshall O. Roberts of the T&P took Buell's report and sent it to Silas Seymour for comment. Seymour had gone to work for the Erie as a rodman in 1835 and had worked his way up to Chief Engineer of Construction, a position he held from 1846 to the railroad's completion to Dunkirk in 1851. He subsequently worked for the Ohio & Mississippi and became consulting engineer to the Union Pacific in 1864.[82] Accordingly, he had experience with both broad and standard gauges, and had been able to observe the consequences of gauge discrepancies.

Seymour responded to Roberts that when the Erie was debating between 4'-8½" and 6'-0" in 1847, first cost of construction "did not enter very largely into the argument."[83] He estimated the difference in cost at 5 to 10 percent. Seymour most specifically objected to Buell's presumption that a 3'-6" line could operate safely at 35 to 45 miles per hour, denying that existing railroads of any gauge could do so. Seymour considered the widest gauges most suitable for safety at high speeds. Seymour considered the issue of tare weight the "great argument generally advanced by the advocates of the extreme narrow gauge theory," but thought it the weakest. He suggested Roberts compare flatcars of the Erie and New York Central, but presented no data. Seymour cited with approbation D. C. McCallum's report on the Erie of 1856, and expressed his continuing conviction that 4'-8½" was too narrow for the comfort of passengers, the full realization of economy, or speed and safety in freight operations.[84]

Probably because Seymour successfully dissuaded the T&P management from adopting a narrow gauge, his work was especially esteemed by narrow gauge opponents. Seymour also had the honor of a direct reply from Robert Fairlie in the form of Fairlie's only book on the subject, *Railways or No Railways*.[85] It was a hasty work; Fairlie did not even wait to secure a copy of Buell's report before writing it. He devoted 87 of the book's 147 pages to a detailed hostile criticism of Seymour's report, the rest being mainly an exposition of early narrow gauge practice. Intellectually, the book showed little advance; Fairlie essentially applied to Seymour the logic he had expounded in his papers of 1870 and 1871. However, he took the opportunity to make a more extensive argument for the necessity of the Fairlie locomotive in the narrow gauge system, and he showed greater sympathy for the 3'-6" lines than he had demonstrated earlier. Probably the book's main importance was to give his thought a wider intellectual market than he could possibly have reached with his papers. The *Times* of London reviewed the book very favorably, evaluating it as "a masterly and crushing refutation" of Seymour's arguments. The review, which included a laudatory evaluation of the proceedings of the narrow gauge convention of 1872, concluded: "In America the dispute is almost over, and the narrow gauge, in Mr. Fairlie's sense, is now master of the situation. . . . [T]he railway work of the future will plainly be on a gauge of about 3 ft."[86]

The pamphlet literature hostile to the narrow gauge was concentrated early in the history of the movement. Forney and Evans concluded on the basis of declines in reported starts of projects and inquiries for narrow gauge locomotives in 1872 that the movement was running its course.[87] Forney devoted relatively little space to the question in the middle of the decade but then treated it frequently with the revival in promotion of narrow gauges about 1877. As an editor, he could hardly have done otherwise, but the other opponents apparently trusted events to verify their interpretations, and turned to other subjects of inquiry. Seymour was explicit. In a letter to Latrobe, he wrote:

> I have always regarded this narrow-gauge theory, particularly when applied to our main trunk lines of railway, as one that required only the test of time and experience effectually to explode itself, and have therefore thought that to fight or to resist it prematurely would savor too much of the celebrated onslaught of Don Quixote upon the windmills, or the valor of that other champion, who amused himself by firing cannonballs at mosquitoes.
>
> Like any other fever or mental disease, it must and will run its course, and in my opinion the best treatment for the doctors and nurses to pursue, is to watch the symptoms carefully and to see that the patient during his delirious antics and ravings, does as little injury to life and property as possible.[88]

Lorenzo M. Johnson and the Close of the Cost Controversy

In September 1878, when the advocacy of narrow gauges was intellectually at its peak, *Scribner's Monthly* published an article by Stephen D. Dillaye presenting without novelty the pro—narrow gauge argument to advocate a federally built, low-speed, double-tracked narrow gauge railroad from Omaha or Council Bluffs to the major Atlantic ports along the lines of the Continental Railway.[89] *Scribner's* followed this in its December issue with an article by Lorenzo M. Johnson, "Are Narrow-Gauge Roads Economical?," which appeared at first glance to be yet another *a priori* treatment of costs, arguing the case against the narrow gauge.[90] The author was quickly identified as General Manager of the Cairo & St. Louis, which had been in the early days of the movement the second-largest American narrow gauge.[91] Its financial performance had also been moderately favorable. The article was actually a summary of Johnson's experience with a relatively successful narrow gauge.

With one notable exception, Johnson did not attempt to fit dollar costs to his arguments, partly because he felt his readers would "be wearied with general statistics," partly because he felt such comparisons were misleading in the absence of information on traffic densities, gradients, and other details. Johnson began his argument with an orthodox *a priori* demonstration that the savings on grading for a narrow gauge were minor. He then proceeded to a point treated by none of the proponents: "Pile-bridge work constitutes, on most of our western roads, a very important item of expense, since we sometimes have as many as five hundred bridges in one hundred and fifty miles of road. The piles, guard-plank and labor cost just the same on the narrow as on the standard gauge. The iron in such bridges consists mainly in spikes and drift bolts, which should not be much, if any, lighter."[92] Johnson thought the use of shorter ties and stringers might reduce the cost of such bridges by not more than 15 percent. Turntables and tanks he thought would differ little, and the cost of labor would be about the same for standard gauge or narrow. For shops the only saving he could see was the possible use of walls two feet lower.

For both passenger coaches and freight cars, he reported the ratio of 3:2 in capacity. "The labor involved in the construction of a narrow-gauge coach is very nearly the same as that required to construct a standard-gauge coach, although the quantity of materials required will be less. I need not make a detailed statement of the cost of building these cars or coaches, since it will be obvious that three narrow gauge coaches will cost as much as two standard-gauge coaches."[93] He made the same argument in connection with boxcars. The narrow gauge car had a capacity of eight tons and a tare weight of 11,000 pounds. Its standard gauge counterpart carried twelve tons with 20,000 pounds deadweight. He calculated from this that the saving on tare weight basic to advocacy of the narrow gauge was only about one-sixth of the weight of a boxcar. His evaluation of narrow gauge motive power was even more adverse:

> Very little is saved in the equipment of a narrow-gauge road with locomotive power, for a small engine will not do so much work in proportion to its cost as a large engine, and a million tons of freight can be hauled over any road with less

cost for motive power with a large engine of a standard-gauge road than with a small engine of a narrow-gauge road. . . . [M]ore engines will be required to haul a million tons of freight on a narrow-gauge road than on a standard-gauge road; moreover, the lighter engines do not execute their work so satisfactorily, as they get out of order more frequently,—because the flues are so much smaller, requiring frequent washing, which is not so effectual in preventing the accumulation of scale and mud.[94]

Johnson argued that in maintenance, dispatching, clerical work, and the like, there was no difference in the wages that had to be paid, but there was an adverse consideration: "At equal wages it is difficult to retain the best class of men, because there is more or less feeling of insecurity—unfounded, it is true—which continually leads them to desert the narrow-gauge service."[95] He saw no reason to believe maintenance-of-way expenses should be other than "nearly if not quite the same."[96] He had found that the labor requirements for repairs for narrow and standard gauge cars were the same (though he conceded a slight saving of materials to the former), but since there were half again as many cars on the narrow gauge for any given traffic, the net repair expense was higher. Obviously, he could only come to the same conclusion for operating expenses: "In order to haul the same amount of freight, the train expense will be much heavier; engineers, firemen, conductors, and brakemen, must be employed in greater numbers—since trains are lighter—and they must be equally skillful and have the same wages, and since the number of engines and cars must be about one-third greater in number to haul the same amount of freight on a narrow-gauge road, it is obvious that the very important items of oil, tallow, waste, and fuel, will cost much more on the narrow-gauge road."[97]

The proponents of the narrow gauge in general simply ignored the implications of their dogma for operating expenses, but they claimed a positive advantage with respect to accident experience. Johnson also found this argument erroneous on the basis of his experience: "Another great item of expense is due to the delay of trains and wrecks. Such incidents and casualties are more costly on a narrow-gauge road, because, for a given amount of freight, more trains are required, and more men and rolling stock are involved."[98] He then turned to the most important part of his argument, the effect of transshipment both on costs and on demand. An outbound shipment of general freight would require three cars to accommodate the load of two standard gauge boxcars, and he estimated the time required for loading at a day. Here he made the one deviation from his purely literary exposition and estimated the cost of transfer, based on his experience, at 3¢ to 6¢ per hundredweight, from $5 to $9 per car.[99] This was some 12 to 24 times the 5¢ per ton that had been orthodoxy among proponents early in the movement. However, the transfer he described entailed a wagon haul, and because his railroad was embroiled in a controversy with the municipal government concerning entry into central Cairo, the horse drayage may have been extensive. Forney, who appears to have secured further information on the matter from Johnson by correspondence, estimated that the transfer cost might have been cut in half by placing the cars side by side. If so, halving Johnson's minimum figure of 3¢ per hundredweight still gave a cost of transshipment of some 30¢ per ton.[100]

Johnson clearly felt that the direct pecuniary cost of the transfer was less important than its effect on the demand for narrow gauge service:

It is often inconvenient for the shipper to load three cars at once, for the narrow-gauge road to furnish them, and for the foreign road to furnish the two cars, of the same class, at the requisite moment. When freight is received from foreign roads, the same difficulties occur. Moreover, foreign roads cannot be required to furnish freight in two-car lots; hence, the narrow-gauge road must either send a car partly loaded, or impose a rate destructive of its business, or else reduce its tariff. In the active competition for business which prevails at the present day, any one who has charge of a narrow-gauge road will readily admit that the gauge is of great disadvantage, for the reasons just stated, and because of the unwillingness of shippers to have their freight transferred by strangers, while in transit.

No assurances that damages will be paid if property is lost or injured will suffice to do away with this prejudice.

The writer has one case in mind where, if the gauges of the connecting roads were alike, he might secure from a short crossroad at least five hundred car-loads of flour, which is now transported about twenty miles beyond the junction, in order that it may proceed to its eastern destination without breaking bulk; for he could save this shipper twenty miles of hauling, and would gladly pay all charges for transfer, both at the point where the narrow-gauge road would receive the freight and at the terminus of the narrow-gauge road. It is asserted that freight of this description is more or less damaged, and rendered, in some degree, less marketable every time it is unloaded, though the injury may be so slight, in the case of each barrel, as not to justify a claim for damages. At all points on the road where a standard-gauge approaches it within wagon-haul, a narrow-gauge road will be placed at a disadvantage. Shippers are continually hauling to the standard-gauge road, in order to avoid subsequent transfer, and an extraordinary effort has to be made to hold business naturally tributary to a narrow-gauge road.

Freight, which is destined to terminal stations, where special track connections can not conveniently be made with all the foreign roads, is subjected to transfer charges and to delays which place the narrow-gauge road at a disadvantage, so serious as to seriously reduce its revenue. In other words, all other conditions being equal, the very fact that bulk must be broken disqualifies the narrow-gauge road from doing business with foreign roads, except at cut rates, which competing roads will not permit for any great length of time. It may be affirmed, therefore, that the very fact of the gauge being below the standard places such a road in a position which prevents it from successfully competing for business. It must, therefore, be content with strictly local business and with the low rates which prevail elsewhere, for patrons of the road are dissatisfied with higher local rates than are made in other parts of the country. *This loss of business, in the course of a very few years, will more than balance the saving in cost of construction.*

We are, therefore, justified in the conclusion that an investment of capital in a narrow-gauge road is unjustifiable, unless the road be so located that it can never suffer from competition.[101]

Johnson's purpose was principally to make a case against Dillaye's proposed narrow gauge from the Missouri River to the Atlantic, but his conclusion provides us with an excellent framework for analyzing the actual experience of the narrow gauges. As stated at the outset of this section, the proponents had set forth a testable hypothesis. Forney, Evans, Latrobe, and the other opponents evaluated it negatively, mainly on *a priori* grounds, but partly on the basis of their earlier experience with standard and broad gauge railroads. Johnson represented an advance in two respects: his negative evaluation of the narrow gauge doctrine was based on actual experience on a narrow gauge railroad; and he presented an alternative narrow gauge hypothesis by stating that a narrow gauge might be economic as a monopoly, but not in rivalry with standard gauge railroads.

Necessarily, Johnson's point was not entirely novel by 1878. As we shall see in Chapter 4, the proponents—especially at their conventions of 1878—split between those who argued that the narrow gauge could serve only a branch-line function as a feeder to the standard gauge system, and the more extreme devotees who thought that narrow gauge would inevitably replace the standard for general transportation. Several of the hostile critics had also noted the dichotomy between service to an extractive industry and a general transportation function. In particular, George L. Vose in his *Manual for Railroad Engineers* of 1873 argued that Fairlie had erroneously presumed that the Festiniog's favorable load-to-weight ratio for hauling a single heavy commodity, slate, could be projected to general freight transportation. Vose concluded:

> The capacity of the narrow gauge roads has been based upon the fallacy that an exceptional traffic affords a rule for estimating the capacity for the ordinary kinds of business. Because certain small, narrow gauge cars have hauled a large weight of compact mineral, it is assumed that the ratio of dead to gross load would be equally favorable in transporting the mixed freight commonly offered upon railways, much of it of great bulk but of little weight. Under the same conditions of traffic the capacity of narrow gauge roads is inferior to that of the wider roads. The general experience of railway managers, both in Europe and America, has been in favor of increasing the weight and decreasing the number of trains. Upon the narrow gauge roads precisely the reverse must be done. Just what capacity the narrow gauge roads would have for the ordinary miscellaneous freight cannot be stated. It is doubtless ample for branch lines, and for main lines doing a moderate business, but not sufficient for a first class trunk line.[102]

Latrobe's pamphlet published by Evans contained a similar evaluation of the Festiniog by Guilford L. Molesworth, then Director of Public Works for Ceylon, who reported that the line's traffic was 90 percent slate, which moved only downhill in unsprung four-wheel cars. Loading was done at the expense of the quarrying companies. Practically all the passengers were employees in the quarries.[103] He could impute little generality to the experience.

A German engineer had argued in similar fashion. Baron M. M. von Weber, former manager of the state railway of Saxony, was commissioned by the Austrian government to evaluate the practice of narrow gauge railways on the Continent of Europe. Weber concluded that narrow gauge was appropriate only for a railway designed to carry timber, stone, ore, or coal, and intended for nothing beyond a few slow passenger trains. He considered narrow gauge inappropriate for a railway of mixed traffic, or for one making numerous junctions with standard gauge lines, or for one likely to experience high variance of traffic volume.[104]

The observations of Vose, Molesworth, and Weber would necessarily occur to a critical engineer, but there was a more basic economic argument relevant to the problem. An extractive enterprise—a quarry, mine, or timber stand—typically produces an economic rent, an income stream above what is minimally necessary to attract the resource to its current use. A monopolistic railway serving such an enterprise can confiscate some of the economic rent as if the railway were a tax collector. Consequently, even a

The standard operation of the Festiniog, which Guilford L. Molesworth found to have no generality for railway development, is illustrated here. Fairlie's pioneer *Little Wonder* is shown hauling four-wheel slate cars and several small carriages for passengers (mainly employees of the quarrying companies) upgrade from Portmadoc in the summer of 1871. (Festiniog Railway.)

cheaply built, incompatible rail line may prove quite profitable under such circumstances. There is the further matter that extractive enterprises are frequently of short life—the vein of ore is exhausted, the quarry depleted, or the stand of timber cut—so that an entrepreneur wants to hold down the capital irretrievably committed to a railroad right-of-way that will be abandoned in a few decades. Finally, ores, stones, and timber frequently must be processed before final shipment, so that transshipment between gauges presents no additional cost attributable to the gauge difference. At least until the development of the motor truck about 1914, a cheaply built, incompatible railroad may have been the optimal means of transport for many entrepreneurs under such circumstances. As its history in Part II demonstrates, the Uintah Railway was built to serve Gilsonite deposits as late as 1904, some two decades after serious advocacy of the narrow gauge for general transport had ended. The Uintah had the worst physical plant in curvature and gradients of any of the large narrow gauges, and its rates were so high that a builder sent in the bricks for a small bank by parcel post so as to avoid the railroad. Only the development of the truck and, later, the slurry pipeline rendered the operation uneconomic, however.

An isolated narrow gauge serving an extractive enterprise might actually be a relatively high-cost enterprise, but might appear economic for the two reasons mentioned: it could confiscate some of the economic rents of the mine or quarry; and it would inevitably have a favorable ratio of cargo to tare weight for the one commodity it was built to handle. Such a railway would appear to have a cost advantage over general-purpose standard gauge lines only if one considered nothing or virtually nothing but the ratio of cargo to tare weight. This, of course, is what the proponents of the narrow gauge did: their entire intellectual edifice was based on this ratio. They ignored almost completely the implications of their doctrine for labor cost, persisted in some obsolete or erroneous estimates of transshipment costs, and made only the most casual judgments concerning the demand for the sort of service they were planning to offer. What they did was a fairly common economic fallacy, minimization of a single function—in this instance tare weight relative to load—rather than optimization among several functions. The rise in the price of petroleum brought about by the Organization of Petroleum Exporting Countries in the 1970s, for example, brought forth a rash of policies designed to minimize energy consumption or to maximize energy output that were uneconomic in an economy that optimized between energy prices and a wide variety of other costs.

Lorenzo Johnson, it should be noted, did not deny the basic premise of the narrow gauge advocates. He accepted that 3'-0" equipment brought about a saving in deadweight, but he evaluated this at only about one-sixth, and put the saving in the context of a large number of other demand and cost considerations. His net evaluation was: "Let any man who is seeking for investment of capital in railway construction, consult those who have operated both classes of roads, and he will be advised, almost invariably, that he will save very little in cost of construction, equipment, and operation, and that he will lose business from competition, if he adopts the narrow-gauge."[105]

This conclusion, obviously, was consistent only with a prediction that the narrow gauge movement would be a short-lived phenomenon. In Chapter 2 we observed that the incentives presented by the cartelization of the railroads also led to a conclusion that the narrow gauge movement would be of short duration. The opponents of the narrow gauge behaved accordingly, presuming that they would be shown correct within a relatively short period. Seymour's letter to Latrobe, quoted above, likening the movement to a fever that must be allowed to run its course, is perhaps the best example of their expectations. No doubt Seymour would have been pleased to know that after a century, the narrow gauge era would still be commonly known as "The Narrow Gauge Fever."

Notes

1. Actually, the *Gazette* was said on its title page and masthead to be "conducted" jointly by Forney and S. Wright Dunning. Forney was responsible for engineering and mechanical matters, Dunning for transportation, traffic, and general news. See *Railroad Gazette*, 44 (1908), p. 82. The editorials critical of the narrow gauge are unsigned, but were treated by contemporaries as the work of Forney, and have always been so considered by historians. There appears to be no reason to question the attribution at this time.

2. The eleven members were W. H. Greenwood, General Manager, Denver & Rio Grande Railway; Edmund Wragge, Chief Engineer, Toronto, Grey & Bruce and Toronto & Nipissing Railways; Thomas H. [or S. or M.] Millington, Chief Engineer, Memphis & Knoxville Railroad; A. W. Bell, of Porter, Bell & Co., locomotive builders, Pittsburgh, Pennsylvania; D. E. Small, of Billmeyer & Small, car builders, York, Pennsylvania; William S. Auchinclos, Vice President, Jackson & Sharp Manufacturing Co., Wilmington, Delaware; Col. Edward Hulbert, President, North Georgia & North Carolina Railroad; Lucien Scott, Vice President, Kansas Central Railroad; C. H. Howland, of the Cairo & St. Louis Railroad; W. M. Karson, General Manager, St. Louis & Western Railroad; Hon. P. B. Borst, President, Washington, Cincinnati & St. Louis Railroad. See *Railroad Gazette*, 4 (1872), p. 274.

3. *Proceedings of the National Narrow-Gauge Railway Convention, held at St. Louis, Mo., June 19, 1872* (St. Louis, 1872), pp. 20–24.

4. *Ibid.*, pp. 9–10.

5. *Ibid.*, pp. 11–12.

6. *Ibid.*, p. 46.

7. *Ibid.*, p. 24.

8. *Ibid.*

9. *Ibid.*, p. 33.

10. E.g., Stephen D. Dillaye, "The Transportation Question," *Scribner's Monthly*, 16 (1878), pp. 687–96. Dillaye also included unspecified portions of the Pennsylvania Railroad as appropriately organized for freight carriage.

11. *Proceedings of the National Narrow-Gauge Railway Convention* (1872), p. 61. The report was published in full as *Report of the Engineers on their Investigations of the Merits of Narrow Gauge Railways as Applicable to Long Main Lines* (Baltimore: Kelly, Piet & Co., 1872).

12. Howard Fleming, *Narrow Gauge Railways in America* (Oakland: Grahame Hardy, 1949 [reprint of the 2d ed., 1876]), pp. 18–19.

13. *Ibid.*, p. 19.

14. *Ibid.*, pp. 22–23.

15. *Ibid.*, pp. 12, 22.

16. *Ibid.*, p. 12.

17. *Ibid.*, p. 13

18. *Ibid.*, p. 64. See *The Chicago, Millington & Western Railway* (Chicago: Published by the Company, 1877).

19. *Poor's Manual of the Railroads of the United States*, 1869–70, p. 134.

20. James P. Low, *The Narrow Gauge: A Report of the Chief Engineer of the Blue Ridge Railroad, July, 1871* (Columbia, S.C.: Carolina Printing Co., 1871).

21. Homer B. Vanderblue, "Whistler's Report on the Gauge of the St. Petersburg-Moscow Railroad," Railway & Locomotive Historical Society *Bulletin*, no. 49 (1939), pp. 86–90. For the estimate of no significant difference, see p. 89.

22. Low, *The Narrow Gauge*, p. 11.

23. *Ibid.*, pp. 12–13.

24. *Ibid.*, p. 22.

25. *Ibid.*, p. 19.

26. *Ibid.*

27. *Ibid.*, p. 25.

28. *Ibid.*, p. 26.

29. *Proceedings of the National Narrow-Gauge Railway Convention* (1872), p. 42. A more recent and presumably more valid cost estimate of the cost of transshipment was provided by the Pennsylvania Main Line of Public Works. In 1855 it was reported that the three transshipments required for freight in the course of movement from Philadelphia to Pittsburgh cost a total of 44¢ per ton, or just under 15¢ per ton for each transshipment. *The Main Line of the Pennsylvania State Improvements: Its History, Cost, Revenue, Expenditures and Present and Prospective Value* (Philadelphia: T. K. and P. G. Collins, 1855). None of the participants in the cost controversy apparently noted this estimate.

30. Low, *The Narrow Gauge*, p. 29.

31. *Sixth Annual Report of the American Railway Master Mechanics' Association* (Cincinnati, 1873), pp. 68–69.

32. *Ibid.*, p. 69.

33. John H. White, *A Short History of American Locomotive Builders in the Steam Era* (Washington, D.C.: Bass, 1982), pp. 68, 77.

34. *Ibid.*, p. 68.

35. Cincinnati *Commercial*, Oct. 24, 1878.

36. *Sixth Annual Report of the American Railway Master Mechanics' Association*, p. 68.

37. *National Car-Builder*, 7 (1876), p. 162.

38. John T. Davis, "Narrow Gauge Railroads," *Mining & Scientific Press*, 41, no. 1 (1880), p. 6.

39. *Railroad Gazette*, 4 (1872), p. 199.

40. William Stuart Watson, *Narrow Gauge Railroad System a Complete Success: Its Adaptability to the Business of the Pacific Coast* (San Francisco, 1872), p. 12.

41. The theological nature of the movement was recognized by one of the opponents of the narrow gauge, Benjamin H. Latrobe: "In this movement in the railway world, I cannot help recognizing an analogy with the founders of new sects in our religion, who, in their opposition to sectarianism, forget that they are only increasing the numbers of sects by the one which they set up." Benjamin H. Latrobe, C.E., *A Letter on the Railway Gauge Question* (New York: W. W. Evans, 1872; 2d ed., 1873), p. 11.

42. *Five Reasons Why the People of Iowa Should Encourage the Construction of Narrow Gauge Railroads*. Date and place of publication have been clipped from the copy I consulted in the Association of American Railroads library, Washington, D.C. Internal evidence suggests the pamphlet was issued in behalf of the Burlington & Northwestern Railway about 1875.

43. They were not, of course, literally the final statement of the advocates. John T. Davis's exposition of the narrow gauge case dates from 1880. (See n. 38 above.)

44. Cincinnati *Commercial*, July 18, 1878.

45. *Ibid.*, Oct. 25, 1878.   46. *Ibid.*, July 19, 1878; Oct. 24, 1878.

47. *Ibid.*, July 19, 1878.   48. Cincinnati *Enquirer*, Oct. 24, 1878.

49. Cincinnati *Commercial*, Oct. 25, 1878.

50. *Ibid.*

51. *Railroad Gazette*, 4 (1872), p. 276.

52. In a speech to the Georgia Press Association, Atlanta, Sept. 5, 1872, printed in the Atlanta *Constitution* of Sept. 11, 1872.

53. *Railway Age*, 3 (1878), p. 543.   54. *Ibid.*, p. 555.

55. On Forney, see M. N. Forney, "Reminiscences of Half a Century," *Official Proceedings of the New York Railroad Club*, 12 (1901), pp. 318–65; autobiographical obituary article, *Railroad Gazette*, 44 (1908), pp. 82–84.

56. *Railroad Gazette*, 2 (1870), p. 154.   57. *Ibid.*, 3 (1871), pp. 168–69.

58. *Ibid.*, p. 282; 4 (1872), p. 284.   59. *Ibid.*, 4 (1872), pp. 242–43.

60. *Ibid.*, p. 243.   61. *Ibid.*, p. 252.

62. *Ibid.*

63. See editorial in *Railway Age*, 3 (1878), p. 536.

64. *Railroad Gazette*, 4 (1872), pp. 394–95.

65. *Ibid.*, 11 (1879), pp. 660–61.   66. *Ibid.*, p. 671.

67. *Ibid.*, pp. 648–49.

68. *Ibid.*, 2 (1870), pp. 122–23. For more detailed objections to the Fairlie locomotive, see Chapter 5, below.

69. W. W. Evans, *A Letter to the Rt. Hon. H. C. E. Childers, M.P., Agent General of the Colony of Victoria, on Railway Gauges and Construction, Machinery, Economy, Etc.* (New York, 1872).

70. *Ibid.*, p. 11.   71. *Ibid.*, p. 13.

72. *Ibid.*, p. 7.   73. *Ibid.*, p. 17.

74. *Ibid.*, p. 9.   75. *Ibid.*, pp. 18–19.

76. *Ibid.*, p. 19.

77. Latrobe, *A Letter on the Railway Gauge Question*, pp. 14, 24.

78. *Ibid.*, p. 23.

79. General G. P. Buell, *Report Made to the President and Executive Board of the Texas Pacific Railroad* (New York: Van Nostrand, 1871), p. 3.

80. *Ibid.*, pp. 4, 13–14.   81. *Ibid.*, p. 11.

82. Edward Harold Mott, *Between the Ocean and the Lakes: The Story of Erie* (New York: John S. Collins, 1901), p. 314.

83. Silas Seymour, *A Review of the Theory of Narrow Gauges as applied to Main Trunk Line Railways* (New York: Van Nostrand, 1871), p. 10.

84. *Ibid.*, p. 33.

85. Robert F. Fairlie, *Railways or No Railways: Narrow Gauge, Economy With Efficiency v. Broad Gauge, Costliness With Extravagance* (London: Effingham Wilson, 1872).

86. *The Times* (London), Jan. 17, 1873.

87. *Railroad Gazette*, 4 (1872), p. 183; Evans's introduction to Latrobe, *A Letter on the Railway Gauge Question*, p. 6.

88. Latrobe, *A Letter*, pp. 28–29.

89. Stephen D. Dillaye, "The Transportation Question," *Scribner's Monthly*, 16 (1878), pp. 687–96.

90. Lorenzo M. Johnson, "Are Narrow-Gauge Roads Economical?" *Scribner's Monthly*, 17 (1878), pp. 292–96.

91. *Railroad Gazette*, 10 (1878), p. 591.

92. Johnson, "Are Narrow-Gauge Roads Economical?," pp. 292–93.

93. *Ibid.*, p. 293.

94. *Ibid.*, pp. 293, 294.

95. *Ibid.*, p. 293.

96. *Ibid.*, p. 294.

97. *Ibid.*

98. *Ibid.*

99. *Ibid.*

100. *Railroad Gazette*, 10 (1878), p. 591.

101. Johnson, "Are Narrow-Gauge Roads Economical?," pp. 294–95.

102. George L. Vose, *Manual for Railroad Engineers* (Boston: Lee & Shepard, 1873), p. 538.

103. Latrobe, *A Letter on the Railway Gauge Question*, pp. 33–39.

104. Baron M. M. von Weber, *Die Praxis der Baues und Betriebes der Sekundärbahnen mit schmaler und normaler Spur* (Weimar, 1873); "The Proper Gauge for Cheap Railroads," *Railroad Gazette*, 10 (1878), pp. 343–46.

105. Johnson, "Are Narrow-Gauge Roads Economical?," p. 296.

4

The Narrow Gauge Fever

No doubt the narrow gauge movement would have come to America in some manner, but the actual form it took depended mainly upon two men: General William Jackson Palmer and Colonel Edward Hulbert. Palmer, by choosing 3′-0″ for the Denver & Rio Grande Railway, created a large railroad in Colorado which by its very existence provided a variety of incentives to build narrow gauges. Hulbert, who later claimed to have been the first systematic advocate of narrow gauges for local economic development,[1] industriously propagated the narrow gauge doctrine in the South, was mainly responsible for the proponents' conventions of 1872 and 1878, and finally was active in the administration of narrow gauge railroads in Indiana, Ohio, and Texas. The two men embodied a dichotomy that was to persist throughout the narrow gauge era, Palmer representing the view that the technology could provide cheaper long-distance intercity service, and Hulbert standing for the position that the narrow gauge properly served a local function of origination and termination.

Both men had extensive experience in standard or broad gauge railroading. Hulbert was born in Berlin, Connecticut, probably in 1823, but his career had been spent entirely in southern railroading, with some time out for Reconstruction politics. He entered railroad service as a freight clerk with the Atlanta & West Point at La Grange, Georgia, in 1848, and by 1857 had risen to roadmaster. He then became superintendent of the Central Division of the Adams Express Company, South, and in 1862 was appointed superintendent of the Charlotte & South Carolina. He returned to the express business in 1864 as superintendent of the Southern Express Company. As a Republican who strongly favored cooperation with federal occupation authorities, he was an acceptable local political figure to the national administration, which appointed him Chief Registrar of Voters for Georgia under the Military Reconstruction Act of 1867. His exertions in that capacity were in part responsible for the election as governor in 1868 of the Republican Rufus B. Bullock, who rewarded Hulbert with the superintendency of the Western & Atlantic, the State of Georgia's publicly

Edward Hulbert (1823–88), organizer of the narrow gauge conventions of 1872 and 1878, with his second wife. (Georgia Department of Archives & History.)

owned railroad from Atlanta to Chattanooga. Bullock, like the Reconstruction Republicans more generally, was endeavoring to advance local economic development by expanding the state's rail network, extending state guaranty to the bonds of several railroads.[2] Hulbert was active in this effort in association with the quintessential carpetbagger, Hannibal I. Kimball, who by 1871 was promoter of nine railroads in the area. In a split among the Radical Republicans in 1869, Hulbert broke with Governor Bullock, causing him to be replaced as superintendent of the Western & Atlantic on January 1, 1870, but he remained allied with Kimball in railroad promotion.[3]

Hulbert was predisposed to the narrow gauge doctrine by the time Fairlie popularized it in 1870. Hulbert believed that the Western & Atlantic had been operated as a monopoly, charging rates excessive relative to the state's requirements for economic development. In 1869 he stated to a journalists' group he had taken to northwestern Georgia that he had cut rates on coal, iron ore, agricultural products, and passenger movements, all to the end of economic development but at the cost of a reduction in the short-run profitability of the railroad and a deterioration in its physical condition. He was convinced that the W&A could be profitable and well maintained only if Bullock's projected network of intrastate railroads was built to provide the W&A with locally originated traffic, thereby making it independent of its long-distance connections.[4] In Hulbert's first apparent public advocacy of the narrow gauge—a speech of February 14, 1871, in Albany, Georgia, at a banquet in honor of Kimball, then president of the broad gauge Brunswick & Albany—he said: "It has been a question in my mind for several years, whether in adopting the 5 foot gauge in the South, we did not commit a serious mistake. The five foot has not in many instances proved a paying gauge. I am of the opinion that if we had adopted a three foot gauge in place of the five, that all our railways would have paid operating expenses, the interest on their bonds, and a fair dividend on their capital stock."[5]

Hulbert's pamphlet of August 1871, *The Narrow Gauge Railway*, was an early but unoriginal presentation of narrow gauge dogma. He spoke frequently at meetings in advocacy of narrow gauges.[6] His alliance with Kimball put him in a position to advance the cause. In particular, one of the railroads being built with state guaranty of loans was the Cartersville & Van Wert in the northwestern corner of Georgia. By April 1871 the line had been built at 5'-0" from Cartersville to Taylorsville, 14 miles. Financial problems stopped the building and caused the company to be reorganized as the Cherokee Railroad with Hulbert as a director. Presumably at his urging, the management resumed construction as a narrow gauge, laying nine miles of 3'-0" to Rockmart in October and November of 1871.[7] His willingness to put a break of gauge in a railroad of only 23 miles was a demonstration of Hulbert's commitment. Probably conversion of the original trackage to 3'-0" was envisioned from the outset; this was in fact done in 1880. Both the Cherokee and the Tuskegee Railroad of Alabama apparently went into service before the Denver & Rio Grande began regular operation on January 1, 1872.[8]

In the second half of 1871 Hulbert became active in the North Georgia

& North Carolina Railroad, a project of Kimball's for a line from Calhoun, Georgia, on the Western & Atlantic across the northern tier of
Georgia to a point, probably Clayton, on a projected extension of the Blue
Ridge Railroad through Rabun Gap. Hulbert was president of the corporation by November 1, and by the end of the year he had convinced the directors to build the line as a narrow gauge. This project represented all of
Hulbert's current ideas: narrow gauge for economy, development of the
mineral resources of northern Georgia, and traffic tributary to the Western
& Atlantic. Hulbert remained active in promotion of this railroad at least
until the fall of 1873, when it could demonstrably not be financed.[9] The
presidency, along with his pamphlet and his promotional work, made
Hulbert a conspicuous figure in the narrow gauge movement by 1872.

The narrow gauge fever had been let loose upon the South, where it
spread rapidly. Another of the development projects of the Bullock administration was a railroad from Rome to Columbus to serve the western portion of the state. As the North & South Railroad of Georgia, this was
quickly recast as a narrow gauge. By the end of July 1871 Columbus was
said to have seven narrow gauge projects.[10] The South was particularly
characterized by projects that had been long planned but not built because
of the war or because of a shortage of capital in the region. Some of these
were also re-formed as narrow gauges. For example, the Arkansas Midland, which had been partly graded as a direct route from Little Rock to
the port of Helena, was reborn as a 3'-6" line. Most of the 3'-6" railroads
date from the early period of the movement and were in the South. Any
serious effort at compatibility among the narrow gauges dated only from
the convention of 1872. Most of the southern lines were promoted in ac-

The network of railroads in the oil field
centering on Bradford, Pennsylvania,
was one of the most defensible applications of narrow gauge technology.
The lines were purely local, served an
extractive industry, and were assured
of relatively short survival. Shown is
an inspection train of the Buffalo,
New York & Philadephia on the Kendall & Eldred with a typical oil field
background. (Ed Bond collection.)

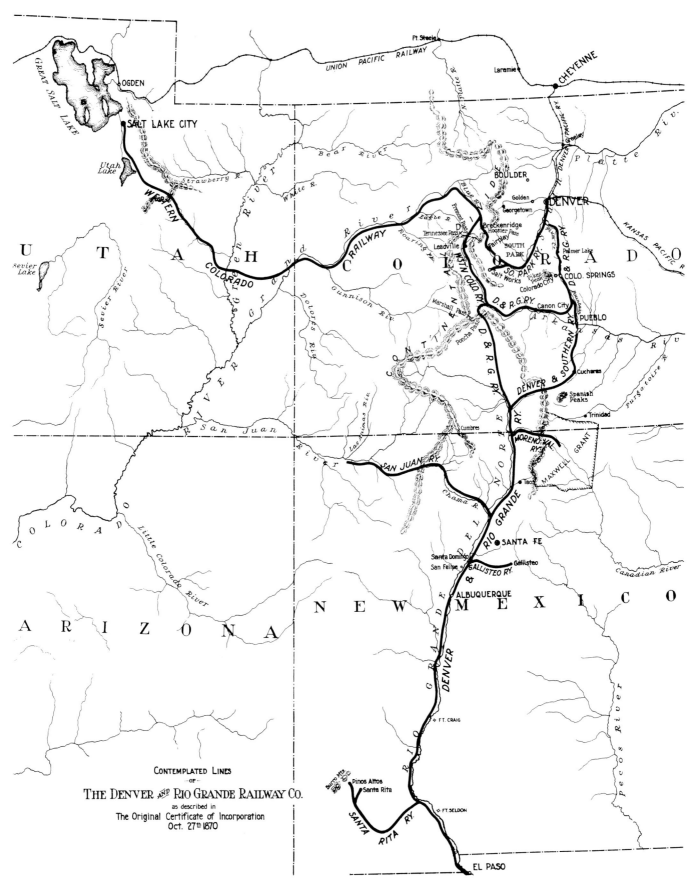

This map accompanied William Jackson Palmer's application for a charter for the Denver & Rio Grande. Except that the railroad never reached south of Santa Fe, the final pattern of the company was quite consistent with the map. (Robert A. LeMassena collection.)

cordance with Hulbert's philosophy of local development, and were not expected to form part of a narrow gauge network.

Although William Jackson Palmer's philosophy of the narrow gauge was quite different, his background in main-line railroading was similar to Hulbert's. Palmer had been born in Delaware in 1836. In the 1850s he worked for the Pennsylvania Railroad gathering applied engineering knowledge by way of apprenticeship. In 1855 he went to England for a year of engineering study, though again apparently in informal rather than academic fashion. Upon his return he engaged in research on coal-burning locomotives for the Pennsylvania, and in 1857 he was appointed secretary to the Pennsylvania's president, J. Edgar Thompson. Palmer joined the Union Army in 1861 as a captain and rose to brigadier general by 1865.[11]

Following the war, Palmer worked on the Kansas Pacific until its completion to Denver in 1870. He had conceived the idea of a railroad from Denver to El Paso in 1867–68, and upon leaving the Kansas Pacific began promoting it seriously.[12] As he visualized the railroad, it was to have three major elements: first, a main line running south from Denver along the base of the Front Range, crossing the mountains into the Rio Grande Valley and terminating in El Paso; second, a penetration of the San Juan mining area of southwestern Colorado and northwestern New Mexico; and third, an east-west route through the Rockies to Salt Lake City. Palmer and his associates incorporated the railway on October 27, 1870, depositing a map showing the projected system *in extenso*.[13]

The Denver & Rio Grande's main line south was projected in the expectation of a connection with the Mexican Central at El Paso for a continuous gauge-compatible route to Mexico City. Palmer, in association with James Sullivan, became active in the promotion of narrow gauges in Mexico under a concession from the Mexican government, but he was not involved in the Mexican Central. Rather, he and Sullivan were engaged in the Mexican National system, which after building lines southwest from Mexico City made its narrow gauge connection to the American border at Laredo.

On his honeymoon in Britain following his marriage to Mary Lincoln "Queen" Mellen, the daughter of one of his financial associates, in November 1870, Palmer visited the Festiniog and consulted with Robert Fairlie, who specifically advised him to adopt 3'-0" for the new railroad.[14] The superficial attractions of Fairlie's narrow gauge philosophy were obvious. Denver was a town of 4,759 people in 1870, Santa Fe was one of 4,765, and the remainder of the tributary territory of the main line was barely populated at all. Although a large railroad, the D&RG was expected to operate in physical isolation except for its connections at Denver. Each of the three major routes of the projected system had serious mountain barriers such that the capital savings of Fairlie's system were promising. Palmer announced the decision to use 3'-0" in a speech of February 17, 1871.[15] Grading had already begun and by the end of the year track was completed to the newly established city of Colorado Springs. The narrow gauge movement in the West had begun. Palmer wrote with satisfaction of the adoption of 3'-0" in the company's annual report for 1873.[16] Howard Schuyler of the company wrote enthusiastically of the new equipment and

General William Jackson Palmer (1836–1909), about 1905. (Collections of Timothy Nicholson, London, and Jackson C. Thode, Denver.)

practices of the narrow gauge.[17] His reports of the management's early experience were consistent with narrow gauge doctrine.

In a variety of ways the existence of the Denver & Rio Grande was an incentive to build narrow gauges. Most generally, there was an incentive to simulate its expected economies. More specifically, there was an incentive to be compatible with it, to connect with it, and, especially, to provide it with a connection to the populous regions to the east. A detailed history of the D&RG is presented in Part II, but for present purposes it is sufficient to say that the railroad took shape approximately as originally projected. The intended main line through El Paso was truncated at Santa Fe by a famous agreement with the Atchison, Topeka & Santa Fe of 1880, but the other major elements of the system—the penetration of the San Juan mining area and the east-west main line to Salt Lake City and Ogden—were completed by May 1883. Accordingly, this was a big railroad—at its peak some 1,861 miles of narrow gauge (including three-rail) in 1890.[18]

As observed in Chapter 2, there was in the early 1870s a widespread belief that rates were excessive, especially on eastbound grain movements. There was an obvious complementarity between the project to provide the D&RG with an eastern outlet and the effort to secure a cut-rate carrier of grain to the eastern seaboard.

As in the South, there were by 1871 a substantial number of projects that for one reason or another had not been financed as standard gauge railroads. Several of the major projects, like the Arkansas Midland, had left grades for all or part of their intended routes. Such grades promised narrow gauge promoters a saving on the major expense of their entering the industry. A listing of the major unbuilt projected railroads as of 1871 is necessarily arbitrary, but the following are prominent.

The Continental Railway. This project was treated in Chapter 2, but it remained a matter of active advocacy throughout the narrow gauge era. Either the Continental or its predecessor of the prewar period, the American Central Railway, had graded portions of its line between Hudson, Ohio, and the Pennsylvania state line; between Tiffin, Ohio, and Fort Wayne; between Rochester, Indiana, and Rensselaer; and approaching the projected crossing of the Mississippi at New Boston, Illinois.[19] An unrelated but parallel prospective right-of-way across Indiana was the towpath of the Wabash & Erie Canal.

The Chicago & South Atlantic Railway. Since the 1830s this project had been pushed unsuccessfully as a railroad from Chicago across the Ohio River at Vevay, Indiana, through the Appalachian mountain barrier at Rabun Gap to Charleston, South Carolina, Augusta, Georgia, and other cities of the coastal plain.[20] Inevitably, this project became integral with the Indianapolis, Delphi & Chicago Railway, since promoters in Delphi, Indiana, had been striving without success to build a direct line from Chicago to Indianapolis through their town since 1865.[21]

The Toledo & St. Louis Air Line. Under several corporate entities, promoters had been endeavoring to build a railroad parallel to the Wabash main line from Toledo to St. Louis through the tier of cities about 20 miles south of the Wabash River: Decatur, Bluffton, Marion, Kokomo, and Frankfort, Indiana.[22]

The Peach Bottom System. Projected since 1868, this was to be a coal carrier from the Broad Top coalfields to Wilmington or Philadelphia, crossing the Susquehanna River at Peach Bottom, Pennsylvania.[23]

Apart from individual projects, there were specific demands for low-quality transportation at various towns or identifiable areas. The leading businessmen and political figures of Leavenworth, Kansas, considered their city bypassed by the standard gauge system, which was built largely through St. Joseph to the north or Kansas City to the south. The little town of Delphos, Ohio, was on the main line of the Pennsylvania Railroad's western affiliates, but the narrow gauge presented it with the prospect of being the center of a new style of railroad. Similarly, Rome, Georgia, envisioned itself as the junction of the branch to Memphis of a narrow gauge New York–New Orleans air line.[24] Western Illinois was widely characterized by the feeling that the standard gauge railroads' geographical pattern and pricing structures served it very poorly for movements of agricultural products east. Even Massachusetts, one of the most highly developed portions of the nation, conceived itself to have a problem of underdevelopment in the small valleys of the western portion of the state. The legislature commissioned George A. Parker to look into the problem. An enthusiast for the majority report on narrow gauge railways for India, he proposed a system of railways of 2'-9" gauge into lightly populated valleys. Parker made a rather orthodox estimate that 2'-9" railways could be built for $13,757 per mile as compared to $23,974 for a standard gauge.[25] Finally, a large number of small towns, like Tuskegee, Alabama, sought cheap means of connecting with nearby main-line railroads.

Arrival of narrow gauge track was frequently the cause of celebration. The Toledo & South Haven's locomotive Lawrence arrives in the town for which it was named, Lawrence, Michigan, on October 1, 1877. (Railroad Museum of Pennsylvania.)

The National Narrow-Gauge Railway Convention of 1872

By the spring of 1872 the actual attainments of the narrow gauge movement were meager. The D & RG reached Pueblo, 120 miles, in June and was

The National Narrow-Gauge Railway Convention of 1872 was held at the Southern Hotel in St. Louis. The hotel was large and modern, built in 1868. (Emil Boehl photograph, negative PB 494, Missouri Historical Society.)

working on an extension to the Cañon Coal Mines. A prospective major coal hauler, the Cairo & St. Louis, was under construction from East St. Louis to the Big Muddy coalfield near Murphysboro, and a large number of other projects were in various stages of advancement. Nonetheless, Hulbert as president of the North Georgia & North Carolina sounded a call for the National Narrow-Gauge Railway Convention in St. Louis. His choice of location was significant. Not only was the nation's second-largest narrow gauge project taking shape across the river, but St. Louis was manifesting some interest in becoming a center of narrow gauge railroading. St. Louis was the preeminent midwestern city of the steamboat, but as the railroads became more important relative to the Inland Rivers in the postwar period, the city's position declined relative to Chicago. As in Leavenworth, local figures looked upon the narrow gauge as a means of rectifying the city's disadvantage. Accordingly, whatever the convention's intellectual content, it was in part a sales conference for the project of an east-west narrow gauge system with St. Louis as a major junction.

The convention opened at the Southern Hotel, St. Louis, at 11:00 A.M., Wednesday, June 19, 1872, and transacted its business in two days. Hulbert had invited representatives of all narrow gauge railroads, operating or abuilding, and all interested suppliers. Erastus Wells, president of the Olive Street Railroad, a major street railway in St. Louis, was elected president of the convention. Wells was endeavoring to promote a suburban narrow gauge extension, which took shape as the West End Narrow Gauge Railroad.

The Denver & Rio Grande was represented by Colonel W. H. Greenwood, its general manager, who gave a typically enthusiastic report on the road's early experience. He estimated that his narrow gauge was the equal in capacity of 95 percent of the standard gauge railroads. His trains typically operated at 15 miles per hour, which he thought about 75 percent of standard gauge speeds, but he reported that a train had recently operated at 25 miles per hour with a party of excursionists from Pennsylvania. The company's loaded freight cars, he said, weighed less than the empties of standard gauge roads, but he estimated that ten of his freight cars could carry the load of eight cars of the Kansas Pacific.[26]

Most of the proceedings of the convention were devoted to an exposition of the prospective cost savings of the narrow gauge technology; this aspect of the convention was treated in Chapter 3 as the most authoritative statement of the position of the narrow gauge advocates. The Committee of Eleven of the convention, which produced the cost estimates, also recommended basic physical standards for the narrow gauges—a 3'-0" gauge and a height of 24 inches from the rail to the center of the coupling.[27] The Committee made its recommendations explicitly in the expectation that a national network of narrow gauges would shortly take shape and that it ought to have compatible technology from the outset. The division between advocates who believed the narrow gauge could provide main-line functions more cheaply than existing standard gauge lines and those who felt that the narrow gauges were inherently suited only to branch-line services was not apparent in the convention of 1872. Even though Hulbert called the convention, all the major speakers expounded the doctrine identified with the Denver & Rio Grande that the narrow gauge could provide long-haul service. G. A. Korweisse of the Wyandotte, Kansas City & Northwestern argued that 2'-0" lines were adequate for branches,[28] but otherwise the arguments were almost entirely for a homogeneous 3'-0" system. More representative than Korweisse were Richard B. Osborne and Charles P. Manning, who, as pointed out in Chapter 3, proposed replacing the Western Maryland's single-track standard gauge railroad with a double-track line of 3'-0".[29] The convention also appointed a National Central Executive Committee of Thirteen to coordinate information and to convoke further conventions of narrow gauge advocates.[30]

The convention was important beyond its function of propagating narrow gauge doctrine. By establishing the Committee of Thirteen, the convention gave the narrow gauge movement such formal organization as it had. The narrow gauges never had a trade association or traffic bureau, such as the interurbans were to have in the form of the Central Electric Railway Association and its subsidiary, the Central Electric Traffic Association. By virtue of his chairmanship of the Committee, with the right to call further conventions, Hulbert assured himself his position as the leading figure in the movement.

The Project of a Narrow Gauge Transcontinental

Advocacy of a transcontinental system of narrow gauges from the Denver & Rio Grande to the eastern seaboard was mainly connected with promotion of the Washington, Cincinnati & St. Louis Railroad. This company was chartered in Virginia on March 15, 1871, and organized on June

13, 1872—less than a week before the convention—by Major Peter B. Borst, a lawyer and local Democratic politician of Luray, Virginia.[31] Hulbert invited Borst to address the convention. From Borst's speech there, from his testimony before a committee of the House of Representatives in an effort to secure a federal guaranty for the company's bonds, and from press accounts, the project is well documented. Its history is illuminating, both in demonstrating what the narrow gauge advocates thought they could do with the technology and in showing the difficulty they encountered in executing their plans. Borst initially projected his railroad from some point on the Potomac River opposite Washington, D.C., probably Alexandria.[32] Later he was to consider bridging the Potomac and terminating in Georgetown.[33] If he could have arranged it, his route would probably have gone through Fairfax, Manassas, Warrenton, and Washington, Virginia, thence across Beahm's Gap in the Blue Ridge Mountains to Luray.

The line would have followed the South Fork of the Shenandoah River, probably to a point near Elkton, and then crossed Buffalo Gap to Harrisonburg, seat of Rockingham County, where Borst found his principal financial support. From Harrisonburg the line was projected through North River Gap in Shenandoah Mountain to Monterey, seat of Highland County. From there the line was to ascend Allegany Mountain, apparently on approximately the route of the present U.S. highway 250, cross extremely difficult mountainous terrain in Pocahontas County, West Virginia, and pass through an unnamed gap opposite Big Spring Branch into the headwaters of the Elk River in Webster County. Borst planned to have the railroad leave West Virginia at Point Pleasant, at the confluence of the Kanawha and Ohio rivers. Although the Elk and Kanawha could have provided him with a water-level grade via Charleston, he showed no interest in such a route. Similarly, he appears to have been uninterested in a water-level grade along the Little Kanawha River from upper Braxton County to Parkersburg. Rather, he proposed to traverse the state approximately midway between the Baltimore & Ohio to the north and the Chesapeake & Ohio to the south, along roughly the present route of U.S. highway 33 through Spencer and Ripley. Borst must have been extreme in his acceptance of the ability of narrow gauges to follow the terrain, for the route offered him no long river courses to follow and would have been a continuous series of grades and curves. Borst hired Richard B. Osborne, co-author of the report on narrow gauging the Western Maryland, as his chief engineer. Osborne reported that he could traverse the Blue Ridge Mountains with grades no worse than 60 feet per mile without a tunnel. In the more difficult terrain over Allegany Mountain and Back Alleghany Mountain to the west, Osborne anticipated grades no worse than 87 feet to the mile westbound and 50 feet eastbound. Overall, Borst envisioned grades no worse than existing ones on the B&O, C&O, Pennsylvania, and Western Maryland.[34] He was proposing to run through the vicinity of the present-day Cass Scenic Railroad, the State of West Virginia's preserved lumber railroad. Actually, Borst could have negotiated this terrain, if at all, only with a technology like that of the Cass, with grades of over 6 percent and Shay or other geared locomotives. West of the Ohio, Borst proposed a

Geared locomotives: Any of three major types of locomotive with a geared connection between the cylinders and wheels to increase torque and adhesion for low-speed operation on severe curves and grades. See the section on geared locomotives in Chapter 5.

route about 20 miles south of Zanesville and Columbus into Cincinnati.

The reason for his route across West Virginia is apparent: Borst sought to provide an air line between Cincinnati and Washington, considerably undercutting existing railroad distances. He proposed a line of only 478 miles, compared with 646 via the Pennsylvania Railroad, 613 via the B&O, and 582 via the C&O. He anticipated deviating from a straight line no more than 27 percent; existing standard gauges, he said, deviated by 37 to 50 percent.[35] His route represented an extreme negation of the usual principle of railroad engineering that longer routes are, within wide limits, preferable to hilly or curvaceous ones.[36] Borst also planned a branch to Charlottesville and Richmond, Virginia, along the general route of the C&O's James River line.

West of Cincinnati, Borst projected a line about midway between the Terre Haute & Indianapolis (Pennsylvania) and the Ohio & Mississippi.[37] This route would presumably have taken the line through Sullivan, Indiana, a town that was actively seeking an east-west railroad. Through Illinois the route was apparently never determined; Borst probably planned to build from Sullivan to East St. Louis as directly as possible. Borst told the convention of 1872 that he could build the main line (except for the Harrisonburg-Washington portion) and the Richmond branch for $13,460 per mile, and the rest for $15,000 per mile.[38] He planned a branch to Chicago, but on the basis of his statement to Congress in 1874 he had given no thought to its location: "For the Chicago branch, the shortest and most feasible, unoccupied route will be adopted."[39] He envisioned hourly trains for general cargo leaving each of his western termini, St. Louis and Chicago, plus passenger trains and low-speed freights for coal and iron ore out of West Virginia. The railroad, he told Congress, could carry coal to Tidewater at a rate of 0.75¢ per ton-mile and grain from the Midwest at 0.5¢ per ton-mile. At such rates, Borst anticipated an operating ratio of 45 percent and dividends of 25 percent per year. He expected the line to furnish the outlet to the seaboard for 5,000 miles of narrow gauge railroad.[40]

Borst was reasonably assured of connection with the Cairo & St. Louis, which was progressing south from East St. Louis. Not only was this railroad a potential source of coal traffic, but Borst saw some prospect of its effecting a connection at Cairo with Col. W. C. Falkner's Ripley Railroad, which projected a north-south line through the lower south to Mississippi City on Ship Island on the Mississippi Gulf Coast.[41]

It was, of course, the prospect of connections to the west that mainly motivated Borst. He had the prospect of connecting with the Denver & Rio Grande by means of only two intermediate railroads. The longer and more promising was the Kansas Central Railway, formed by the promoters of Leavenworth, Kansas, on May 31, 1871, to run some 600 miles through northern Kansas and eastern Colorado to Denver. This railroad was under construction by the time of the convention of 1872; Edward Hulbert visited it immediately before the convention and pronounced it "the most perfect illustration he had seen of a narrow gauge."[42] The connection between the Kansas Central and the Washington, Cincinnati & St. Louis was to be the St. Louis & Leavenworth Narrow-Gauge. Although the project was reported in mid-1871, the meeting to organize the corpo-

Air line: A railroad built directly between end points with little or no interest in serving intermediate communities.

ration was held in St. Louis on July 1, 1872, less than two weeks after the convention. The railroad was planned to run west from St. Louis to a crossing of the Missouri River at or near Augusta, and along the north bank of the Missouri to some point in Boone County—essentially the route later used by the Missouri, Kansas & Texas for its belated entry into St. Louis. From Boone County, of which the seat is Columbia, the route was to be determined after surveys.[43] Depending on the route chosen, the railroad would probably have been about 290 miles. The three railroads, if completed according to plan, would have provided a route between Denver and Washington, D.C., of only 1,683 miles, given Borst's projected distance of 793 miles from St. Louis to Alexandria. The comparable distance via the Union Pacific, Missouri Pacific, and B&O through Kansas City and St. Louis is 1,873 miles.

Borst's hopes for connections to the Pacific were never firm. In his testimony of 1874 he stated that the Denver & South Park (*sic*) would connect at Provo, Utah, with the Utah Northern, which would run to San Diego.[44] Since the Utah Northern was being projected by figures prominent in the Mormon Church north from Ogden to the Butte mining area, one questions the depth of Borst's geographical scholarship.

The experience of the three railroads projected from Denver to Washington is instructive. Only the Kansas Central laid track, but it did manage to become one of the longest midwestern narrow gauges. As the history in Part II of this book recounts, it built 165 miles from Leavenworth to the small town of Miltonvale, Kansas, between 1871 and 1882. It came into the hands of the Union Pacific before completion, and after conversion became a minor agricultural branch of the UP system, abandoned early in the Depression of the 1930s.

The St. Louis & Leavenworth Narrow-Gauge made virtually no progress. The town of Arrow Rock in Saline County, Missouri, on the south bank of the Missouri River, voted $75,000 in aid of the project in 1873,[45] but otherwise the company dropped out of the trade press. Borst expressed interest in extending the WC&StL to Leavenworth in 1872, apparently out of pessimism about the St. Louis & Leavenworth.

The Washington, Cincinnati & St. Louis did hardly better. Borst secured $50,000 in aid from Harrisonburg in elections of 1872 and 1873.[46] Judge James Kenney of Harrisonburg wrote in his diary on November 3, 1873, that the railroad had no capital but this $50,000. Kenney also wrote that he had seen ten hands and two carts engaged in grading.[47] In 1877 Borst told the corporation's annual meeting that he had received $157,000 from all sources and expended it in construction.[48] In his testimony to Congress in 1874 he stated that grading from Harrisonburg to Monterey had begun in September 1873, and that 20 miles had been completed.[49] The *Rockingham Register* reported all work suspended in August 1874.[50]

Development of narrow gauges in Ohio and Indiana with which the WC&StL might connect caused Borst to revise his plans for the railroad's west end toward the end of the decade, but he never modified the basic idea of an air line across West Virginia. In his testimony of 1874 he raised his estimate of costs to $16,930 per mile, plus $6,000 for "equipments."[51]

If Borst's railroad had a hope, it lay in the federal loan guaranty he sought. He testified that on January 28, 1873, the proposed guaranty was favorably reported by the Senate Commerce Committee, but was then not acted upon by the Senate.[52] His effort of 1874 was not successful, but he persisted in his endeavors to build the railroad. Several further efforts at grading were reported in the trade press beginning in 1875,[53] and in 1878 the railroad secured statutory authority to hire 100 convicts.[54] The additional grading was undertaken in an effort (which proved only partially successful) to secure a subscription to the road's bonds from Highland County. The county government agreed, but the Virginia legislature on April 2, 1879, prohibited the county from levying a tax to pay the subscription until the WC&StL had built a completed railroad from Harrisonburg to the county line. The text of the statute is instructive:

[T]he agents and officers of the said railroad company, by further promises, and by placing a company of men at work within the limits of Highland County, induced the supervisors thereof to issue bonds of the county and to levy a tax to pay the interest on such bonds; . . . the said officers, after grading detached portions of said railroad in a very imperfect and unstable manner, and making very heavy and almost impractical grades, suddenly suspended all active operations and withdrew their forces of workmen; . . . all the work done, or nearly all done by the officers of said railroad company outside of . . . Highland County is of like character, and if the said railroad is ever completed, much of the work already done will have to be abandoned and new locations made; . . . the said company has signally failed in all its promises to the people of the said Highland County.[55]

Borst secured one additional enactment, a statute of April 21, 1882, allowing the railroad to be built with standard gauge rather than narrow.[56] Whether Borst believed the project could be completed as a standard gauge or merely thought that the existing grade could be salvaged for a standard gauge short line we are unlikely to know, for he died suddenly of an apoplectic seizure only three days later, on April 24, 1882.[57] His death brought the vast WC&StL project to an end. In the course of probating his estate, the WC&StL's only tangible asset, some 20 to 22 miles of grade from Harrisonburg up North River Gap, was sold on September 25, 1883, for $40,000 to Joseph S. Loose of Bridgewater.[58] Portions of the grade were used by the Chesapeake Western in 1896 for its line into the Dora coalfield.[59]

In retrospect, the entire project appears so poorly conceived that its failure was inevitable. Borst's basic plan of an air line across West Virginia without tunnels, but with grades and curves no worse than existing standard gauge railroads, all for $13,460 or $16,930 per mile, is so outlandish as to be difficult to take seriously. Yet, this project remained throughout nearly all of the narrow gauge period the basic one on which the idea of a transcontinental system rested.

Experience in the Depression of the 1870s

The failure of the projected narrow gauge transcontinental could hardly have been more complete, but it was never widely publicized. In part, the failure was lost among the large number of projects that failed in the Depression of the mid-1870s.

As is well known, the failure in 1873 of Jay Cooke & Co., financiers of the Northern Pacific project, combined with a deflationary monetary pol-

TABLE 4.1
Narrow Gauge Mileage, 1871–1982

| Year | Narrow gauge | | | | Miles built, all RR's | NG miles as pct. of all miles built |
	Miles built	Miles converted	Miles abandoned	Miles in service (12/31)		
1871	97	0	0	97	6,660	1.46%
1872	322	0	0	419	7,439	4.33
1873	285	0	3	701	5,217	5.46
1874	417	0	0	1,118	2,584	16.14
1875	376	0	20	1,474	1,606	23.41
1876	556	0	0	2,030	2,575	21.59
1877	794	0	0	2,824	2,280	34.82
1878	855	0	28	3,651	2,428	35.21
1879	1,210	47	15	4,799	5,006	24.17
1880	1,642	215	26	6,200	6,712	24.46
1881	1,752	215	34	7,703	9,847	17.79
1882	2,627	351	79	9,900	11,569	22.71
1883	1,223	186	32	10,905	6,743	18.14
1884	571	136	10	11,330	3,924	14.55
1885	516	116	31	11,699	2,982	17.30
1886	552	970	68	11,213	8,018	6.88
1887	581	1,345	20	10,429	12,878	4.51
1888	285	450	19	10,245	6,912	4.12
1889	248	690	98	9,705	5,184	4.78
1890	462	1,259	151	8,757	5,338	8.65
1891	309	554	13	8,499	4,071	7.59
1892	123	307	14	8,301	4,419	2.78
1893	75	183	76	8,117	3,024	2.48
1894	91	428	32	7,748	1,760	5.17
1895	157	478	17	7,410	1,420	11.06
1896	161	392	56	7,123	1,692	9.52
1897	68	154	51	6,986	2,109	3.22
1898	150	124	81	6,931	3,265	4.59
1899	162	182	116	6,795	4,569	3.55
1900	139	126	75	6,733	4,894	2.84
1901	159	177	0	6,715	5,368	2.96
1902	211	839	48	6,039	6,026	3.50
1903	129	407	0	5,761	5,652	2.28
1904	212	264	43	5,666	3,832	5.53
1905	123	368	67	5,354	4,388	2.80
1906	161	248	60	5,207	5,623	2.86
1907	89	93	71	5,132	5,212	1.71
1908	65	60	23	5,114	3,214	2.02
1909	14	9	67	5,052	3,748	0.37
1910	53	5	122	4,978	4,122	1.29
1911	45	217	88	4,718	3,066	1.47
1912	54	0	16	4,756	2,997	1.80
1913	62	56	67	4,695	3,071	2.02
1914	53	0	82	4,666	1,532	3.46
1915	35	73	94	4,534	933	3.75
1916	47	14	73	4,494	1,098	4.28
1917	15	7	185	4,317	979	1.53
1918	58	28	201	4,146	721	8.04
1919	45	0	136	4,055	686	6.56
1920	0	30	59	3,966	314	0.00
1921	14	0	106	3,874	475	2.95
1922	4	0	49	3,829	324	1.23
1923	48	76	18	3,783	427	11.24
1924	0	0	58	3,725	579	0.00
1925	0	87	31	3,607	644	0.00
1926	10	60	33	3,524		
1927	12	132	11	3,393		
1928	0	44	159	3,190		
1929	0	12	79	3,099		
1930	0	15	198	2,886		
1931	5	23	131	2,737		
1932	0	4	132	2,601		
1933	0	0	98	2,503		
1934	0	0	87	2,416		
1935	0	0	90	2,326		
1936	0	0	60	2,266		
1937	0	0	204	2,062		

TABLE 4.1

(Continued)

| | Narrow gauge | | | | | |
Year	Miles built	Miles converted	Miles abandoned	Miles in service (12/31)	Miles built, all RR's	NG miles as pct. of all miles built
1938	0	0	244	1,818		
1939	0	0	89	1,729		
1940	0	0	19	1,710		
1941	0	20	383	1,307		
1942	0	0	62	1,245		
1943	0	28	41	1,176		
1944	0	16	0	1,160		
1945	0	0	18	1,142		
1946	0	0	2	1,140		
1947	0	2	143	995		
1948	0	0	20	975		
1949	0	0	27	948		
1950	0	10	24	914		
1951	0	20	54	840		
1952	0	0	203	637		
1953	0	28	17	592		
1954	0	0	134	458		
1956	0	21	34	403		
1960	0	0	70	333		
1966	0	0	16	317		
1969	0	30	217	70		
1972	0	0	3	67		
1982	0	0	21	46		
TOTALS	18,529[a]	12,431	6,052			

SOURCE: Corporate histories in Part II. In instances of three-rail operation, conversion is treated as removal of narrow-gauge, not laying of standard-gauge rail. The figures for "Miles built, all railroads" are from *Historical Statistics of the United States* (1975), vol. 2, p. 732, except for 1880–92, which are from *Poor's Manual*, 1895 , p. xxi. Computations by Linda M. Hooks and Todd T. Kelly.

[a] If we subtract miles built twice (66), the total here is 18,463.

icy, initiated a depression in the railroad financial community that lasted for about five years. As Table 4.1 demonstrates, mileage built for the railroad system as a whole had run over 6,000 miles per year at the beginning of the decade. The figure fell to 5,217 in 1873 and did not again rise beyond 5,000—or even 4,000—until 1879. The Panic of 1873 brought work on the Denver & Rio Grande temporarily to a halt; not until 1876 did the company resume large-scale building. The Denver, South Park & Pacific laid its first track in 1874, but was unable to make substantial progress until 1879. Among large projects, only the Utah Northern and the Cairo & St. Louis were pushed on steadily to completion. The rest of the building in the middle of the decade was largely of local lines, ranging from the 90-mile Eureka & Palisade, built to serve mines in Nevada, to the tiny St. Louis, Keosauqua & St. Paul, a local carrier of only four miles at Keosauqua, Iowa, that was born and died entirely in 1875. The boast of the advocates that no narrow gauge had ever gone bankrupt, popular at the beginning of the decade, quickly became an embarrassment as the Utah Northern was ordered sold for non-payment of interest in December 1877, and the Cairo & St. Louis was put in receivership in the same year.

Like much else, the experience of the narrow gauges in the depressed years was capable of alternative explanations. As noted in Chapter 3, Forney and Evans believed that they detected a decline in new projects and locomotive orders among the narrow gauges in late 1872 or 1873, and concluded that the fallacy was running its course. One gets little impression of this from the local press. Small-town newspapers widely accepted narrow gauge doctrine and encouraged local projects. The Painesville *Telegraph*, which was advocating the Painesville & Youngstown, in 1870 stated flatly, "It is predicted all railroads will be narrow gauge in five years."[60] By 1876 the paper had barely modified its views: "the indications are that in the space of ten years at most all the best lines in Ohio will be those of narrow gauge."[61] The *Rockingham Register* of Harrisonburg, Virginia, which was avidly trying to promote the Washington, Cincinnati & St. Louis, observed in 1873: "The narrow-gauge railroad enterprise is no longer a disputed question in this country. The debate is closed, the question called, the vote taken and the ayes have it."[62]

The Cheap Transportation movement, which might have been expected to be supportive in this period, in general dissociated itself from the narrow gauges, even though the group's principal interest was in eastbound grain movements. The New York Cheap Transportation Association in its comments on the Windom Report in 1874 did state that "if recent experience is confirmed by future trial, railroads of *narrow gauge* will in the future be found greatly superior to the ordinary gauge for the transportation of freight."[63] The New York group followed this in 1875 by publishing a pamphlet, *Narrow Gauge Railroads*, an orthodox statement of narrow gauge doctrine.[64] The Association's policy prescriptions on a national level, however, were a low-speed standard gauge freight railway plus some federal and state regulation. At a convention of the Cheap Transportation movement in Chicago in 1875, pro–narrow gauge motions were uniformly pigeonholed and one of the speakers, Richard P. Morgan, stated: "It is quite manifest that the greatest strength of arguments in favor of a narrow gauge is drawn from the various mechanical errors existing in the construction and operation of the standard gauge and which can probably be better remedied without reducing the gauge."[65]

The proponents typically argued that the financial stringency had caused some promoters to turn to narrow gauge for its capital-saving benefits. Forney in June 1874 noted a revival in narrow gauge advocacy and was moved to produce another of his hostile editorials.[66] Howard Fleming, who was gathering material for his *Narrow Gauge Railways in America*, published the following year, responded hotly, attempting to demonstrate that investment in narrow gauges was holding up better than in standard gauges. Fleming estimated that of narrow gauges in operation, there were 1,233 miles completed and 4,487 miles projected. To this he added 710 miles of seriously projected mileage not yet undertaken. He quoted a letter he had received in July 1874 from a representative of the Baldwin Locomotive Works: "Thus far in 1874 of the engines built and in progress 26 per cent are narrow gauge. This increase of 16 per cent over last year is not, however, indicative of the general narrow-gauge business. The panic has not affected it as much as wide-gauge, as the increase of orders for power over wide-gauge roads shows a steady improvement in narrow-gauge business, while the wide-gauge has shown considerable decrease."[67] Forney commented on Fleming's letter in detail, arguing that "'projected mileage' might as well be left out."[68] This was a recurring theme in Forney's editorship: projected railroads of whatever gauge were so numerous that their conception represented no significant promise of completion.

The data on narrow gauge building in Table 4.1 indicate that the movement had come on strongly in its first four years, with mileage built increasing from 97 in 1871 to 417 in 1874. The decline in narrow gauge promotion that Forney and the other opponents believed they had observed manifested itself in a fall to 376 miles in 1875. Even this represented a relative increase; narrow-gauge mileage as a percentage of all miles built continued upward from 1.46 percent in 1871 to 23.41 percent in 1875. The data appear to bear out Fleming that narrow gauge construction in the depression was holding up better than standard gauge. Most of Fleming's 710 miles of seriously projected mileage took shape, including portions of the Arkansas Central, Cairo & St. Louis, Painesville & Youngstown, and Utah Northern, all among the most important narrow gauges.

Two events of the middle of the decade advanced the movement intellectually. The first was publication of Fleming's *Narrow Gauge Railways in America* early in 1875.[69] Only 79 pages, the book was barely more than a pamphlet, but it provided a manual of narrow gauge practice, a directory of extant and proposed narrow gauges, and a set of favorable evaluations of the narrow gauge by operators of the early lines. Forney reviewed the volume honestly, stating that "it gives information concerning American narrow-gauge rolling stock and American narrow-gauge companies which cannot be found collected elsewhere," but he observed that the "summary of the statements made in favor of the narrow gauge includ[e] the absurdest of them."[70] The *Railway World* of Philadelphia, which directed itself mainly to the financial community, considered Fleming's book "timely and serviceable," however.[71] The *Railway Age*, founded about a year after the work was published, never reviewed it. The pamphlet was well enough received that Fleming issued a second edition, expanded to 101 pages, early in 1876.[72]

In the same year, the narrow gauge received a great deal of exposure through the choice of 3'-0" for the intramural passenger railway at the Centennial Exposition at Philadelphia. The leading locomotive builders provided examples of their narrow gauge power, and the public could hardly avoid the impression that the little trains represented the current state of the art in railroad technology parallel to the various advances in industrial technology shown elsewhere.[73] Paul Bremond is often said to have chosen 3'-0" for his Houston East & West Texas Railway on the basis of his observation of the Centennial Railway.[74] There is evidence he had made the decision earlier, but at a minimum he was impressed enough to buy two of the line's locomotives for operation in Texas.

In any event, the revival of the narrow gauge movement approximately coincided with the Centennial. The Philadelphia & Atlantic City, which proved the most important of the 3'-6" lines, was chartered in 1876, and opened in 1877. The South Pacific Coast, which by 1881 had achieved a line of 75 miles from Alameda to Santa Cruz, California, was also chartered in 1876. An effort in America to build 2'-0" gauge railroads to the approximate standards of the Festiniog dates from George E. Mansfield's Billerica & Bedford Railroad in Massachusetts of 1877. (For a breakdown of total narrow gauge mileage by gauge, see Table 4.2.)

TABLE 4.2

Total Mileage of Narrow Gauge Railroads, by Gauge

Gauge	Total miles	Percent of total miles
3'-0"	17,608	95.35%
3'-6"	487	2.63
2'-0"	216	1.17
3'-2"	83	0.45
2'-6"	40	0.22
Other	29	0.16

SOURCE: Corporate histories in Part II. The Arkansas Midland is counted as a 3'-6" railroad in spite of its conversion to 3'-0" in 1883. The Batesville & Brinkley is counted as 3'-0" in spite of a short 3'-6" predecessor.

The choice of narrow gauge for the intramural railway at the Centennial Exposition in Philadelphia in 1876 was important in popularizing narrow gauge doctrine among the general public. The major locomotive builders contributed examples of their output to the railway. This 2-6-0 was Brooks's contribution. (Ed Bond collection.)

Mileage built recovered rapidly from the trough of 1875, rising to 556 in 1876, 794 in 1877, and 855 in 1878. The revival was both absolute and relative; the mileage in 1877 was 34.82 percent of total miles built in the year and in 1878 35.21 percent, the all-time high relative figure. Fleming appeared entirely supported by the recent experience, and the advocates of narrow gauge doctrine must have felt nearing victory.

The National Narrow-Gauge Railway Convention of 1878

By 1878 the narrow gauge revival was sufficiently advanced for Edward Hulbert to feel justified in calling another convention for Cincinnati. Hulbert, who by 1878 was general manager of the Bedford, Springville, Owensburg & Bloomfield in Indiana, had been left as chairman of the Central Executive Committee of Thirteen established by the convention of 1872. Again he invited representatives of all narrow gauge railroads and suppliers. After Forney suggested the convention would be a process of preaching to the converted, Hulbert broadened the invitation to any interested railroad men.[75] Major John Byrne of the Cincinnati & Eastern, secretary of the committee on local arrangements, sent out some 2,000 invitations and reported 400 to 500 affirmative responses. The actual attendance was about 200, of whom 115 were accredited as delegates.[76] The delegates mainly represented narrow gauges in Pennsylvania, Ohio, Indiana, and Illinois, plus some major supply firms, including the Brooks, Baldwin, and Porter, Bell locomotive works. None of the Colorado narrow gauges sent representatives. Of standard gauge railroads, only the Toledo, Peoria & Warsaw was represented.[77]

Cincinnati was as obvious a choice for the convention as St. Louis had been six years earlier. The city had five narrow gauge lines extant or under construction. The Miami Valley Narrow Gauge Railway was building north to Lebanon and Xenia, presenting the prospect of connection with a network that would cover western Ohio and, as we shall see, shortly span much of the continent. To the east the Cincinnati & Eastern was being built to the Portsmouth area. The Cincinnati, Georgetown & Portsmouth was progressing toward the same goal on a route some miles to the south. The other two lines were short suburban routes. The Washington, Cincinnati & St. Louis was still considered a live project. Borst by 1878 was planning to connect with the Cincinnati & Eastern at Point Pleasant—some 45 miles east of its projected terminus at Portsmouth—and with the Bedford, Springville, Owensburg & Bloomfield at Bedford. He envisioned connecting the two with his own rails from Cincinnati along the north bank of the Ohio through Rising Sun, Vevay, and Madison, thence overland to Bedford. West of the BSO&B's terminus at Switz City, he intended to use the BSO&B's prospective connections, the Springfield, Effingham & Southeastern to Effingham, Illinois, and to proceed to St. Louis on an unspecified route.[78] The Indianapolis, Delphi & Chicago now promised him a connection for Chicago. The Springfield, Effingham & Southeastern had an affiliate, the Cincinnati & St. Louis, which itself planned to build the 125 miles between Bedford and Cincinnati.[79] The Grand Hotel in Cincinnati was establishing itself as a gathering place of narrow gauge promoters.[80]

At an organizational meeting at the Cincinnati Board of Trade on July 15, Hulbert had said: "[T]he [narrow gauge] system had grown to proportions sufficient to produce practical information as to all the various advantages of the system, of the growth of the system, especially in the interior, where it is difficult to build railroads of standard gauge, and work them profitably. . . . [T]he coming convention would be able to present a complete text book of the workings of the system, with information showing that the question of obtaining cheap transportation is answered, especially for local purposes."[81]

The convention was convoked for Wednesday, July 17, 1878, at Pike's Opera House in Cincinnati in the expectation of three days of sessions. Cincinnati proved to be in the throes of a heat wave so serious that the convention was relocated to the Lookout House on Mount Auburn high above the city. The management had provided free use of the house and its pavilion together with half-fare privileges on the affiliated horsecars and inclined plane for access.[82] The formal opening was scheduled for 10:00 A.M., but it was delayed an hour by news of the arrival of another delegation. Colonel S. N. Yeoman of Washington Court House, Ohio, a leading contractor for narrow gauge lines, was chosen temporary chairman, and John Byrne made secretary. S. F. Covington, president of the Cincinnati Board of Trade, welcomed the delegates, stating that 600 miles of narrow gauge, extant or abuilding, radiated from the city. Locally this network was expected to produce extensive benefits. Covington was followed by Josiah Kirby of the Cincinnati Board of Transportation, who estimated that 4,000 miles of narrow gauge were in operation. As Hulbert realized, the membership was split between men who accepted his view that the narrow gauge should serve a branch-line function and others who advocated a national network. Kirby and Benjamin Butterworth, the next speaker, both argued for complementarity between the two gauges with the standard providing the long haul, the narrow the short. Butterworth thought that

Lookout House, scene of the narrow gauge conventions of 1878. Its funicular connection to central Cincinnati is at the right. (Cincinnati Historical Society.)

competition between the two gauges at the margin would be healthy, however. John B. Lee of the Indianapolis, Delphi & Chicago and A. C. Hayes of the Pittsburgh Southern argued the position of the long-haul advocates. Lee thought that about 3,000 miles of narrow gauge were operating, 4,000 were under construction, and 10,000 were in organization, so that there was a prospective network of 20,000 miles within ten years. Hayes estimated that narrow gauges could haul freight for 60 percent of the cost of standard gauge, and if this were true of short distances, it was equally so for long.[83]

Most of the presentations to the convention were expositions of narrow gauge cost doctrine, or discussion of engineering standards. There was little discussion of specific routes. The convention passed a resolution of B. J. Gifford of the Havana, Rantoul & Eastern: "Resolved, That the practical working of the narrow gauge railways of America during the past six years has demonstrated beyond a reasonable doubt, the feasibility of the gauge of three feet. . . ." The convention was, in general, a victory for the advocates of the long-distance function of the narrow gauge. As the Cincinnati *Gazette* put it, "The ambitious element tended to predominate."[84] Another resolution held that the full economies could not be realized until the narrow gauge "can be able to reach, by extensions or connections, general distributing depots. . . ." It was resolved that the narrow gauge should no longer be regarded as simply an auxiliary road and, specifically, that a narrow gauge should be built from the Mississippi and Missouri to the seaboard to compete with water routes for freight. This was in effect a plan for continuing with the Washington, Cincinnati & St. Louis, since no other major east-west line was proposed at the convention.

The convention again established an Executive Committee of Thirteen to centralize information and to call further conventions. A. F. Hill of Pittsburgh proposed the establishment of a bureau of narrow gauge statistics in New York for the benefit of potential interested investors. Because the heat was thought to have held down attendance, the sessions were contracted to two days and adjourned until fall. The sessions ended on the evening of July 18 with a social gathering at the Lookout House that featured music and fireworks. The fireworks included a pattern using the letters "N.G."; a musician said to be named Diehl played his composition "Narrow Gauge."[85]

The Cincinnati *Enquirer*'s editorial published at the close of the convention was less than enthusiastic about narrow gauge practice:

The Convention of the Narrow-Gauge Railroad Men of the country, now in session in this city, has before it one very plain duty; one which if it has the interest of the narrow-gauge railroad system and of its supporters at heart, it certainly will not neglect. That duty is an earnest, outspoken condemnation of the manner in which a large proportion of the narrow-gauge roads of the country—presuming the work in this particular section to be a fair sample—have been constructed. The building of railroads, like any other business involving a great amount of labor and expenditure of money, requires a special ability given to very few men, and which, while perhaps not born of experience and schooling for the work, is at least nurtured and matured only by them. Added to this there should be an honesty of purpose and an adaptation of the work to the wants of the country for which it is accomplished and by which it is to be financially supported. To the lack of this second requirement is due much of the distress that now embarrasses and renders bankrupt the greater railway system of this country, of which the narrow-gauge is the offspring and to be finally the support, and unless great care is exercised and a change of tactics at once instituted, it will be to the lack of very much of the first, and something also of the second, that the downfall of the narrow-gauge system, so surely indicated by the present conditions of the roads of the country will be due. That a large proportion of the narrow-gauge roads thus far put in operation are wretchedly constructed, no one who has observed them and their workings can deny, and that many of them are fatally out of joint with the country through which they run, or are being run, is as evident. Careful inquiry as to the cost to those who foot the bills shows also as clearly that the expense has been in many cases greatly out of proportion to the work actually performed in building the so-called railroads. The recipe for building narrow-gauge railroads in the West seems to have been about as follows: Select a section of the country where there are only farmers who know nothing of railroads or of railroad building. Organize your Company with one of them as figurehead. Get subscriptions from the community for $6,000 or $8,000 per mile, and issue bonds for a like additional amount; run your road through the valleys, around fence corners, over the smaller hills and around the large ones, moving as little dirt as possible; lay down a few ties with no ballast and put upon them the lightest rails in the market, and the work is done. The roads built in this manner generally cost about 60 per cent of the amount obtained in bonds and subscriptions, and the balance of the money goes into the profits of the generous "capitalists" who have blessed the country and the people by building their road for them, while those who are left to hold the bag find the work of running railroad trains over loose piles of dirt and round fence corners a very uncertain and unprofitable business, while the reputation of narrow-gauge railroads and their builders alike suffer. To discourage and frown down this system, and to promote the art of building narrow-gauge roads well and honestly, and only where they are needed, should be the work of the Convention. The narrow-gauge road, properly built and managed, is designed to meet a want of this country which the costly standard gauge could not supply, and must render valuable service both to producers and capitalists and the larger roads and trunk lines, and it is on this account, as well as that of justice, that it should be built, that its way be ballasted with intelligence, and its rails laid with the silver spike of honesty.[86]

Joseph Ramsey of the Bell's Gap Railroad had proposed to hold the fall sessions in Pittsburgh, but Hulbert and his committee again chose Cincinnati. Hulbert reconvened the convention on October 23, 1878, at 11:00 A.M., also at Lookout House. Although Hulbert had hoped to draw several thousand in the cool of the fall, only 66 men were reported as delegates.[87] Hulbert welcomed the group with an effective speech pointing out the accomplishments of the movement to date. He estimated that on January 1, 1878, there were 3,082 miles in operation. Only the Denver & Rio Grande and the Cairo & St. Louis, which had reached 146 miles, provided anything but a local function. He said that networks capable of providing long-distance haulage were taking shape; he noted that Ohio had 16 lines either in existence or seriously projected, and Pennsylvania 17. Of the 2,125 counties in the country, he stated that 870 had no railroads. He foresaw a great future for the narrow gauge in dealing with the nation's unsatisfied demands, and exhorted the delegates to press on with their mission in the development of the nation.[88]

Again, the sessions were mainly concerned with expositions of expected cost savings, which were treated in Chapter 3, and with physical standards, which will be covered in Chapters 5 through 8. As in July, there was no specific content concerning projected routes. Nothing in the published proceedings indicates that the leading figures in the movement had learned from the experience of what was now some seven years. With the exception of Joseph Ramsey's account of his experience on the Bell's Gap Railroad, the presentations were mainly of a character that could have been delivered to the convention of 1872. The *National Car-Builder* concluded: "After a careful perusal of the sayings and doings of the narrow-gauge advocates at their recent convention at Cincinnati, we cannot see that any additional light has been thrown on the general problem."[89]

There was, however, a body of evidence on which the delegates might have drawn. The Cincinnati *Gazette* at the end of the convention published an editorial that is worth reproducing in its entirety, like the *Enquirer*'s observation at the close of the July convention.

THE NARROW GAUGE

All the resources of desperate financing and unfaithful management are open to narrow gauge railroads, and there is nothing in the gauge to give security against them. The inflation of stock and bonds by building roads on credit, which has often added 30 to 50 percent to the apparent cost; the watering of stock and bonds of roads which at first are making large profits; the absorption of profits by managers leaving the stockholders to whistle; the diversion of earnings to the various operating companies which "stand in" with the managers; the sacrifice of roads by incompetent, and their wrecking by designing management, all these are open to roads of all gauges. To assume that the narrow gauge is exempt, or to compare its simple first cost per mile with all that has thus been piled on the old roads, is a patent fallacy.

And when it is gravely argued in a narrow gauge convention that a new lot of roads, to compete with those whose competition has destroyed their capital, would be profitable if on a narrow gauge, we have to inquire what there is in narrow gauge to so broaden credulousness.

The comparative cost of roads of different widths is to be found by living facts, not by piling on one the mass of long accumulations by all the ways we have mentioned, and by a twenty-year old and never closing construction account, and then averaging them on the standard gauge per mile, while the other is taken as soon as ready to begin. And to set the present cost of a narrow road against the cost of a standard road in the inflated times from 1862 to 1873, is mere deception. A first-class standard gauge road has been built and equipped in Ohio since 1875, to wit: the Columbus & Toledo, for a less sum per mile than Mr. HULBERT sets down as the cost of narrow gauge.

What would be the present difference in the cost of constructing a road of the standard and of any narrower gauge, is a matter that can easily be reckoned. It is shown that the difference made merely by the different width is a small fraction, much too small to compensate for the isolation of a peculiar gauge. Other things being equal, the saving in construction of road-bed, ties, masonry and bridges by a gauge of three feet is not equal to 12 per cent. And the claim that the narrow gauge is more "flexible," and that it can conform to curves better, and thereby escape a great deal of grading and bridging, is right in the face of well known mechanical rules.

The claim that narrow gauge makes traction up a grade easier, is now abandoned. Last year this was set up as one of the chief economies. The claim that cars for six or eight tons can be built with less proportion of dead weight than cars for ten or twelve tons contradicts the plainest mechanical principles. To state what certain standard gauge cars weigh per ton of carrying capacity, and what certain narrow gauge cars, is a fallacy. Every engineer and mechanic knows that the larger capacity can be constructed with less proportion of material.

It is now admitted by the Committee on Construction of this convention that the narrow gauge locomotive can pull up an incline no greater load in proportion to its weight than one of the standard width. This gives up a very large claim that has heretofore been made for the narrow road. As to the saving in construction by lighter rails, ties, bridges, cars, locomotives, by any kind of reduction of weight, or more imperfect construction, appointments and equipments, it is just as available to the standard as to any narrow gauge. This is a matter that can be tried by plain mechanical rules.

At the convention the matter of the cost of transferring freight, which a different gauge makes necessary, was admitted to be very important. The cost of transferring grain from one car to another was stated to average six cents a bushel in Chicago. This would pay for carrying it 200 miles on the standard gauge railroads. The cost on much other freight is not much less. All this can be avoided by making these light and cheap roads, with their light equipment, of the standard gauge. This and the other losses by their isolation are many times more than any saving in construction by the narrow gauge.

These narrow gauge conventions are good. If they were frequently held, discussion would in time shift them from the fancy that there is some miraculous charm in narrow gauge which lifts railroad constructing and operating out of the natural conditions and would bring them down to simple mechanical principles. And then they would perceive that the isolating gauge was a mistake, and that all the economies possible for cheaper and lighter construction are equally applicable to the standard gauge, which would give at once to each auxiliary road the benefits of interchange with the existing roads, and would give them entrance to large cities, from which they are now excluded by the cost of making a separate entrance for their strange gauge.[90]

The convention ended on October 24 in some acrimony. It voted to dismiss the Executive Commitee on the grounds that Hulbert had packed it with non-members to secure a quorum and was seeking unilaterally to "run the convention." It appointed a new Executive Committee with General James S. Negley of the Pittsburgh, New Castle & Lake Erie as chairman and John Byrne as secretary. Hulbert and Joseph Ramsey were unanimously elected to the Committee as members at large, but Hulbert refused to accept demotion and declined to take the appointment.[91] The secretary announced before adjournment a collection to meet expenses not covered

James S. Negley, from Alfred P. James, "General James Scott Negley," *Western Pennsylvania Historical Magazine*, 14 (1931), pp. 69–91.

by "the generous hospitality of Cincinnati people." The *Railway Age* stated, "Immediately a stampede took place, not a dollar being forthcoming. . . ." To try to cover the deficit the secretary wrote to all of the railroads represented, but only three or four delegates responded, including the two men, presumably Hulbert and Ramsey, "sat down upon for 'running the convention.'"[92]

The convention closed with a directive to the editors of the *Railway Age* to prepare a volume of narrow gauge information, and with a resolution to meet again in June 1879, preferably in Chicago.[93] The *Age* in January 1879 reported that it sent out questionnaires for basic factual and statistical information to all the narrow gauges of which it had record, but only about 30 responded.[94] As a consequence, the volume, which would probably have contained valuable data on the actual as distinct from the hypothetical costs of narrow gauges, had to be abandoned.

The *Age* argued that the projected convention of June 1879 should address itself to the actual experience of the narrow gauge toward the end of determining when narrow gauge and standard were appropriate.[95] Again, had the convention of 1878 done so, its proceedings would probably have been a valuable source of information on the actual practice of the narrow gauges. The convention of 1879 was never held, however. Negley's railroad was absorbed by the Pittsburgh & Western in 1879 and he left the narrow gauge movement. Because the conventions provided the only formal organization the movement had, the net effect was to deprive the movement of such organization on the eve of the greatest building. Since Hulbert had been almost single-handedly responsible for organizing the previous conventions, there was now no effective force to convene another.

Building, 1878–83

Whatever the impediments to holding conventions after 1878, failure of the narrow gauge movement was not among them. The period of about five years following the conventions of 1878 represented the veritable narrow gauge fever, the peak period of building in the entire movement. Narrow gauge mileage built in 1879 rose to 1,210, 24.17 percent of the year's accretion, and in 1880 increased to 1,642, 24.46 percent of an expanding total. In 1881, 1,752 miles of narrow gauge were built, 17.79 percent of the national total. In 1882 the movement reached its absolute peak in miles built with 2,627, 22.71 percent of all mileage constructed.

The principal component of the increase in mileage was the formation of a large compatible network of 3'-0" gauge in the Rocky Mountains of Colorado. The Denver & Rio Grande, following its agreement of 1880 with the Atchison, Topeka & Santa Fe not to proceed with its projected line to El Paso, turned its energies toward its east-west main line to Salt Lake City and Ogden and to its penetration of the San Juan mining area. The line into the San Juan country left the original main line south at Antonito, Colorado, reaching Durango in southwestern Colorado in 1881 and Silverton in 1882. The railroad built along the Arkansas River to Leadville in 1880. Rather than driving a line to Utah over Tennessee Pass as originally planned, the D&RG chose to build west from Salida over

Marshall Pass, reaching Gunnison in 1881 and Grand Junction in 1882. By the end of 1882 an affiliate, the Denver & Rio Grande Western, was only some 90 miles short of Salt Lake City.

The D&RG's principal rival, the Denver, South Park & Pacific, was penetrating the mining area directly from Denver via South Park. By a relatively direct but exceedingly difficult route, its rails reached Gunnison in 1882 and Leadville in 1884. Both the D&RG and the South Park Line had large mileages of branch lines. At its peak, before the conversion of the Utah & Northern north of Pocatello in 1887, the network comprised about 2,783 miles of compatible 3'-0" railroad in Colorado, Utah, northern New Mexico, Idaho, and Montana. It was possible to take a continuous trip of about 1,240 miles from Denver to Garrison, Montana, on 3'-0" rails.

The closest counterpart to the Colorado system in the East was a network of 305 miles in Pennsylvania and New York, centering on the oil field in McKean County.[96] Most of this mileage was built between 1877 and 1881. Since it served extractive enterprises that proved to have a short life—the oil boom was largely ended by 1882—this trackage was among the most defensible applications of narrow gauge technology. It was also one of the clearest examples of the building of narrow gauges in response to the incentives of the railroads' noncompetitive organization. The Standard Oil Company and the Pennsylvania Railroad in 1872 had agreed upon a rate structure highly discriminatory against the Pennsylvania oil field.[97] The inelasticity of supply of the oil, combined with the relative inadequacy of steamboats on the Allegheny River as substitutes for rail service, caused the railroads to presume a low elasticity of demand for service to and from the oil field. The Erie responded by entering the oil field with a set of three narrow gauge railroads. The *Railway Age* interpreted the decision as showing acceptance by a major railroad of its view that the narrow gauge was appropriate for branch-line functions.[98] The network in the Pennsylvania oil field was connected with Pittsburgh by the Pittsburgh & Western Railroad, a carrier formed in 1881 of a series of narrow gauge lines largely built during the late 1870s.

The largest network in the South was 691 miles of Atlantic Coast Line predecessors in central Florida, built mainly in response to a state land grant program inaugurated in 1881. Unconnected short lines and predecessors of the Florida East Coast Railway gave the state an additional 162 miles.

The early 1880s also saw a proliferation of individual narrow gauges elsewhere. It is impractical to attempt to enumerate them here, especially since their corporate histories are to be found in Part II. Several were not wholly local carriers. The Peach Bottom system began to take shape, but attained only to being a short line on either side of the Susquehanna River.[99] In Illinois, the Havana, Rantoul & Eastern, the Fulton County Narrow Gauge, and the Springfield, Effingham & Southeastern were attempting routes from western Illinois to the east. In the South, the East & West of Alabama, the Americus, Preston & Lumpkin, and the Natchez, Jackson & Columbus were all attempting relatively long east-west lines. In Michigan a compatible network of 3'-0" lines was taking shape in the Thumb Peninsula, made up of the Port Huron & Northwestern and the Saginaw, Tuscola & Huron.

Matthias Forney watched the revival of narrow gauge building with wonderment. As noted in Chapter 3, he renewed his hostile evaluations of narrow gauge cost doctrine as building resumed. His editorials of 1877–79 are probably his best contributions to the debate.[100] The firm evidence of the fallacy of the narrow gauge principle that he sought finally surfaced in Canada when the management of the Toronto, Grey & Bruce concluded in 1877 that it could no longer live with its 3'-6" gauge. The railway had a main line of 122 miles from Toronto to Owen Sound, Ontario, with a branch of 60 miles from Orangeville to Teeswater. Initially upon announcing the intention to convert, the secretary and treasurer expressed no dissatisfaction with the line's narrow gauge, stating "its operations have been quite satisfactory" and that the motivation for conversion was "changed conditions in the country since the road was built"—presumably the conversion of the Canadian broad gauges to standard.[101] On July 1, 1878, the company failed to pay the interest on $2,000,000 of bonds that had provided about half the cost of building the railway. The management also missed the payment due on January 1, 1879, and evidence accumulated that the railway was going downhill rapidly. About September 1, 1879, the Toronto *Monetary Times* reported that the railway would have to be closed unless it received municipal funds for replacement of 50,000 ties, together with pilings on some of its bridges.[102] The company's chief engineer said, "to these necessary repairs the increase of the gauge is tracked." Municipalities were initially being asked to provide half the funds for conversion. The management shortly formulated a plan whereby $800,000 would be raised, $200,000 from the bondholders, a like sum from the municipalities, and $400,000 from the Ontario provincial government.[103] The condition of the railway—which was only a decade old—was so bad that it was not expected to operate through the winter in absence of aid.

The Toronto, Grey & Bruce managed to survive through the winter, but the general manager threatened to shut it down on June 1, 1880, if the municipalities failed to provide the requested aid.[104] The management estimated that it required $1,000,000 to convert, of which it could raise $250,000 by scrapping the narrow gauge; the rest was to come from other sources.[105] Only some $30,000 in municipal aid had been voted.[106] In 1881 a joint public-private bailout was arranged. The Ontario legislature authorized the company to issue $1,000,000 in 20-year, 5 percent bonds, the missed interest payments were repudiated, and the railway was leased to the Grand Trunk for 21 years.[107] The entire railway was converted on December 3, 1881.[108] The conversion was reported to add $3,000 per mile to the company's debt.[109]

Here was a railway that by almost any standards had better prospects than the American narrow gauges. The main line, Toronto–Owen Sound, was reasonably direct through flat country, partly well-settled, partly devoted to lumbering. The line was mainly dependent for interchange on Great Lakes steamboats at Owen Sound rather than on standard gauge railroads. The gauge was six inches wider than on most of its American counterparts, and the grading was heavier. If this carrier was reduced by 1880 to such straits that it had to be converted with public assistance or be closed, it was only a matter of time until the American narrow gauges built, as the Toronto, Grey & Bruce was, to serve a general transport purpose also proved themselves unworkable.

Forney noted the generality of the Toronto, Grey & Bruce's plight early. Upon the management's first notice of an intention to convert late in 1877, he wrote: "This road was built only five or six years ago with a tremendous sound of trumpets in commendation of the narrow-gauge system. Now to quote from a letter from an officer of that line, 'as soon as the money can be raised the *gauge will be changed to 4 ft. 8½ in.*'; this will give an idea of the result of the experiments of a 3 ft. 6 in. gauge to compete with the 4 ft. 8½ in. in fewer words than I can explain on a dozen sheets of paper."[110] Similarly, the *National Car-Builder* observed editorially: "[I]s it not rational to conclude that if a 42-inch gauge comes to grief after such long and careful nurturing, a 36-inch gauge can stand no change at all?"[111]

The Grand Narrow Gauge Trunk

Demonstration in the United States of the unworkability of the narrow gauge for a general transportation function was not long in coming, in the form of the experience of the Grand Narrow Gauge Trunk, a grandiose project of a line of three narrow gauge railroads from Toledo, Ohio, to Laredo, Texas, with a compatible 3'-0" connection to Mexico City.[112] If the Trunk had been completed, it would have amounted to a continuous route of about 1,642 miles in the United States, plus 803 miles of the Mexican National Railway, which General William Jackson Palmer and James Sullivan were building under a concession from the Mexican government.[113] The actual prospective network was much larger, for a substantial mileage in connections was taking shape, especially in Ohio, Arkansas, and Texas. The Indianapolis, Delphi & Chicago, for example, would have connected the Trunk to Chicago and Indianapolis.

Inevitably, something as large as the Grand Narrow Gauge Trunk came to be looked upon as the definitive test of the narrow gauge principle. As late as the early 1880s existing lines were widely viewed as isolated, underfinanced, and poorly built. The proposed narrow gauge transcontinental from Denver to Washington, D.C., had accomplished so little that it was not viewed as a proper test. Its failure to go beyond the Kansas Central's meager mileage and the Washington, Cincinnati & St. Louis's pitiful 20 miles of grade could be viewed as a consequence of the depression of the 1870s. As late as 1883 the editor of the *Railway Age* could treat the issue as open and say of the Trunk, "The question of comparative economy of standard and narrow gauge roads is now in a fair way to be answered."[114] The editor was quite right, and the answer was to be very unambiguous, indeed.

None of the three components of the Grand Narrow Gauge Trunk—the Toledo, Cincinnati & St. Louis, the Cairo & St. Louis, and the Texas & St. Louis—was originally conceived as part of a through route. Rather, each was promoted to deal with local demands, and the idea of the Trunk arose as the geographical complementarity of the three railroads became evident. The detailed histories of the three are given in Part II.

A stock certificate of the Toledo, Cincinnati & St. Louis.

The initial and central element in the Trunk was the Cairo & St. Louis, but it proved a very nominal part of the whole plan. Indeed, much of the calculation of the officials of the other two companies proved to be an effort to bypass it. The Cairo & St. Louis, as mentioned earlier, was a pioneer narrow gauge. When completed on February 19, 1875, at 146 miles it was the second largest in the country. Its physical plant was quite respectable. The northern 60 miles were on an alluvial plain where grading was easy. The line had a difficult pair of grades at Alto Pass and a tunnel at Kaolin. The railroad's worst handicap was an entrance into Cairo on a levee that proved unstable, rather than any design characteristics intrinsic to the narrow gauge. The company became delinquent on its interest in 1874 and went bankrupt as a consequence of the collapse of the Kaolin Tunnel in 1877, but after reorganization in 1881 as the St. Louis & Cairo Railroad it proved a uniformly profitable hauler of coal from the Big Muddy coalfield near Murphysboro. There is no indication that the management ever viewed the property as anything else, actually or potentially, but its existence as a moderately successful railroad with a decent physical plant made it an attractive connection for projects running either northeast or southwest.

The idea of a railroad through Indiana parallel to Jay Gould's Wabash main line through the first tier of major towns to the south—Decatur, Bluffton, Marion, and Kokomo—antedated the narrow gauge era, dating at least from the late 1860s. The various projects were not entirely consistent in route, especially west of Kokomo. A series of mergers of at least five

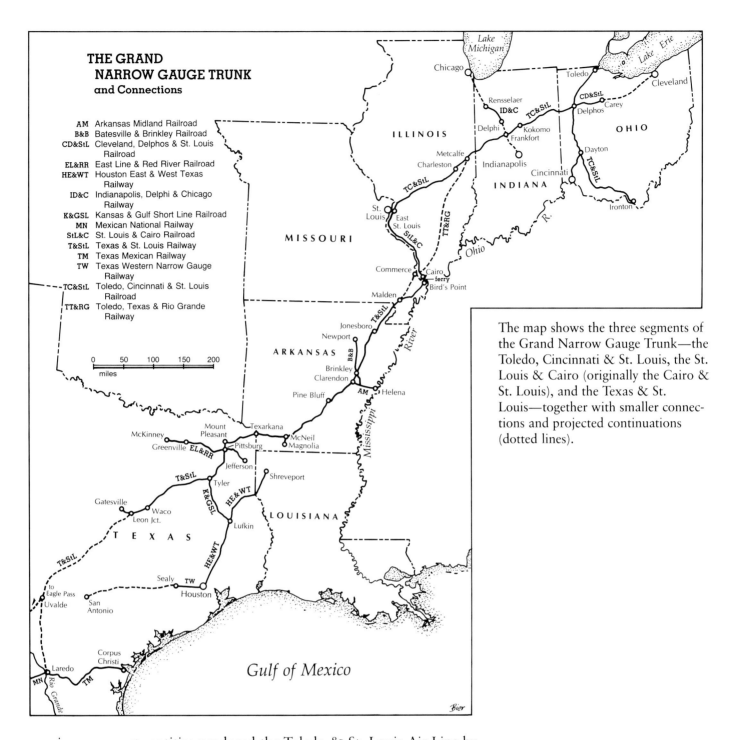

THE GRAND
NARROW GAUGE TRUNK
and Connections

AM Arkansas Midland Railroad
B&B Batesville & Brinkley Railroad
CD&StL Cleveland, Delphos & St. Louis
        Railroad
EL&RR East Line & Red River Railroad
HE&WT Houston East & West Texas
        Railway
ID&C Indianapolis, Delphi & Chicago
        Railway
K&GSL Kansas & Gulf Short Line Railroad
MN Mexican National Railway
StL&C St. Louis & Cairo Railroad
T&StL Texas & St. Louis Railway
TM Texas Mexican Railway
TW Texas Western Narrow Gauge
        Railway
TC&StL Toledo, Cincinnati & St. Louis
        Railroad
TT&RG Toledo, Texas & Rio Grande
        Railway

The map shows the three segments of the Grand Narrow Gauge Trunk—the Toledo, Cincinnati & St. Louis, the St. Louis & Cairo (originally the Cairo & St. Louis), and the Texas & St. Louis—together with smaller connections and projected continuations (dotted lines).

previous corporate entities produced the Toledo & St. Louis Air Line by 1875. Unable to finance itself as a standard gauge line, it attempted to raise funds under the name of the Toledo & St. Louis Narrow Gauge Railroad in 1876.[115] The promoters had some success in raising money especially in the vicinity of Eugene, Indiana, and Oakland, Illinois, but not enough to bring the project to fruition.

Rather, the Toledo–St. Louis narrow gauge took shape in evolutionary fashion from a local project in Delphos, Ohio. A local pharmacist, Joseph W. Hunt, and his associates Dr. Carey A. Evans and Joseph Boehmer, promoted a network of narrow gauges out of Delphos, first to tap local hardwood forests for Delphos's woodworking industry, then to provide a more general transportation function. After some earlier incorporations, the promoters merged their lines into the Toledo, Delphos & Burlington Railroad on May 23, 1879. The corporate name reflected their intention, a railroad from Toledo through Delphos to a connection with one of the railroads designed to carry agricultural products out of western Illinois. By three connections the promoters hoped to reach Burlington, Iowa, where further connections to the west were taking shape.

This plan had to be forgone when Jay Gould acquired the first intended connection, the Havana, Rantoul & Eastern in 1880. Hunt's death in 1879 caused the railroad to be sold to General John M. Corse and others in the Boston financial community. The new owners decided upon building to East St. Louis on the approximate route of the Toledo & St. Louis Air Line. They organized the extension from Kokomo to East St. Louis as the Toledo, Cincinnati & St. Louis Railroad in February 1881. The name of the subsidiary was now more descriptive of the enterprise, since the goal of Burlington had been dropped and the line was well advanced south from Delphos to Cincinnati and Ironton. Because of such considerations, the Toledo, Delphos & Burlington was merged into its subsidiary on February 23, 1882; as the Toledo, Cincinnati & St. Louis the railroad was to achieve its fame, or more accurately, its notoriety.

By early 1882 the Toledo, Cincinnati & St. Louis had nearly run out of funds, but General Corse raised $1.5 million and formed the Toledo & Delphos Trust whereby the American Loan & Trust Company of Boston was to administer the money. This arrangement allowed Corse to finish the railroad to East St. Louis, but he used typical narrow gauge standards of light grading with extensive short trestles crossing Illinois, and he never was able to build adequate terminal facilities at Toledo or East St. Louis. Withal, rails reached East St. Louis by the end of 1882, and mixed trains began running in May 1883.[116]

While the Toledo, Cincinnati & St. Louis was paralleling Jay Gould's Wabash from Toledo to East St. Louis, another narrow gauge, the Texas & St. Louis Railway, was attempting to parallel Gould's St. Louis, Iron Mountain & Southern and other eventual components of his Missouri Pacific system through Arkansas and Texas to the Mexican border. There was nothing unusual in this, other than the use of narrow gauge. As mentioned in Chapter 2, the cartelization of the industry produced an incentive to duplicate existing main lines that peaked in 1882, precisely when these narrow gauge railroads were taking shape.

The Texas & St. Louis had its origin in a local narrow gauge, the Tyler Tap Railroad, promoted in 1870 by Major James P. Douglas to connect Tyler, Texas, with the Texas & Pacific main line. The line was completed to Big Sandy on the T&P in 1877, but Douglas ran out of money while grading toward a steamboat landing on the Red River to the north. In search of funds, he interviewed Colonel James W. Paramore, president of the St. Louis Cotton Compress Company, who proved interested in redirecting the flow of baled cotton from the area west of Tyler from Galveston to St. Louis. Paramore took control of the narrow gauge, reincorporated it in 1879 as the Texas & St. Louis Railway, and began to extend it not to the steamboat landing but to Texarkana on the Iron Mountain main line. As his name for the railway indicates, he probably planned his own line from St. Louis at the outset, but Jay Gould's assumption of control of the

Iron Mountain in 1880, followed by a refusal to engage in joint rates with the narrow gauge, caused Paramore to announce early in 1881 his intentions to extend the narrow gauge across Arkansas to Bird's Point, Missouri, opposite Cairo, Illinois. If the St. Louis & Cairo were cooperative, Paramore would have a compatible 3'-0" line from St. Louis to the cotton belt of Texas between Tyler, Corsicana, Waco, and Gatesville. Paramore also announced that the main line would be extended from Leon Junction, 12.5 miles east of Gatesville, to Laredo on the Rio Grande via Uvalde, some 50 to 80 miles to the west of Gould's International & Great Northern main line through San Antonio. A branch was planned from Uvalde to Eagle Pass, also on the Mexican border. Paramore placed $4,000,000 in bonds early in 1881 and began building his railroad across Arkansas.[117]

For reasons its management never revealed, the St. Louis & Cairo showed virtually no interest in its narrow gauge connections. The Texas & St. Louis arranged its entry into St. Louis over the Illinois Central's Cairo Short Line, which handled narrow gauge cars on standard gauge trucks. The agreement allowed the Cotton Belt, as the Texas & St. Louis called itself, to use the Illinois Central's car ferries at Cairo and to terminate narrow gauge cars on three-rail track in the IC's Cairo yard. There was no physical connection for 3'-0" equipment from the Texas & St. Louis to the St. Louis & Cairo until March or April 1885, when the two railroads made a traffic agreement and the latter laid narrow gauge track on the Wabash incline at Cairo. Third rail was laid on a transfer steamer of the Mobile & Ohio. No traffic agreement was ever reported between the St. Louis & Cairo and the Toledo, Cincinnati & St. Louis, even though the two narrow gauges had a physical connection by a third rail laid over the East St. Louis Connecting Railway in June 1883.[118]

Because of the St. Louis & Cairo's apathy toward its connections, a through 3'-0" route from Toledo to Laredo necessarily entailed some alternative route through Illinois. General Corse of the Toledo, Delphos & Burlington and Logan H. Roots of the Texas & St. Louis met at the Grand Hotel in Cincinnati on January 7, 1881, to announce the formation of the Grand Narrow Gauge Trunk and formation of the Toledo, Texas & Rio Grande Railroad to connect the two.[119]

The idea of the Grand Narrow Gauge Trunk was superficially attractive. The Texas & St. Louis was intended to be mainly a carrier of cotton. This could move to Toledo for transshipment to steamers through the

The Illinois Central's transfer steamer *H. S. McComb*, by means of third rail on her deck, provided the Texas & St. Louis with access to the IC's terminal facilities at Cairo. The photograph, which shows the steamer approaching the IC's loading facility at Brookport, Illinois, illustrates railroad ferry activities near the confluence of the Ohio and Mississippi. (Cincinnati Public Library.)

lower Great Lakes and St. Lawrence River to England. The projected portion of the line between Leon Junction and Laredo would pass through plains country approximately at the outer limit of arable land, opening what was to a large extent virgin territory. Traffic with Mexico was largely of manufactures southbound, which, the promoters believed, could be brought in through Toledo. The Texas & St. Louis anticipated a gauge-compatible connection at Laredo with the Mexican National narrow gauge. Thus, the Trunk held promise of long hauls and a balance of traffic.

The Toledo, Texas & Rio Grande was chartered in Illinois on June 8, 1882. Its principal promoter was its general manager and vice-president, Colonel E. Pratt Buell, former manager of the Laclede Hotel in St. Louis. In his earlier service on his Springfield, Effingham & Southeastern, Buell had developed the reputation of being the stereotypical fast-talking railroad promoter of the day. The Sumner (Illinois) *Press* said of him: "A man has made application for a patent upon a device for running railway trains with wind. Can this be Col. E. Pratt Buell?"[120] Buell's claim to the title of "Colonel" was also shown to be spurious.[121]

Buell first attempted a direct route from Charleston, Illinois, on the Toledo, Cincinnati & St. Louis to Cairo, but could not arrange it. By December 1882 he had projected a route from Metcalfe, the second town on the TC&StL west of the Indiana-Illinois line, diagonally through Newton, Flora, Johnsonville, Belle Rive, Frankfort, and Carbondale to Etherton, a small town on the St. Louis & Cairo about eight miles south of Murphysboro.[122] Because the StL&C's traffic was mainly coal between the Murphysboro area and East St. Louis, the prospect of granting trackage rights to another railroad over the southernmost 45 miles to reach Cairo might have appeared attractive. Once again the StL&C's management showed its apathy or hostility to the idea of the Grand Narrow Gauge Trunk. For reasons unspecified it failed to grant the rights, causing Buell to seek another arrangement. In April 1883, he announced that the TT&RG would be extended from Etherton to a crossing of the Mississippi (probably by ferry) at Commerce, Missouri, about 10 miles south of Cape Girardeau, and through Dexter to a junction with the Texas & St. Louis at Malden.[123] Flora was announced as the railroad's shop city.[124] Buell reported that construction began with 50 teams and 200 men at Belle Rive in March 1883.[125] He envisioned passenger trains running between Toledo and Eagle Pass—which he seems to have considered a more important destination than Laredo—by January 1, 1884.[126]

On May 10, 1883, the Toledo, Cincinnati & St. Louis began freight service into East St. Louis, and by coincidence, the Illinois Central ferried the first cars of the Texas & St. Louis into Cairo.[127] The T&StL was complete except for bridging the Arkansas River. By further coincidence, in the same month the Denver & Rio Grande Western reached Ogden. As John A. Rehor has said, May 1883 may reasonably be looked upon as the peak of the narrow gauge movement.[128] When the Arkansas was bridged on August 12, 1883, the Texas & St. Louis was complete from Bird's Point to Gatesville.

Such progress as the Grand Narrow Gauge Trunk had made by 1883 was mainly superficial. Actually, both the Toledo, Cincinnati & St. Louis and the Texas & St. Louis began to come undone in the fall of 1882. The TC&StL was near the end of the $1.5 million it had raised through the Toledo & Delphos Trust to complete the railroad. The railroad might have failed at that time, but the directors brought in Elijah B. Phillips of Boston, who raised funds for the completion to East St. Louis, brought the railroad into Cincinnati by merger, and pursued an aggressive policy of attraction of traffic by rate reduction. He entered East St. Louis with the promise to cut the local freight rate from 24 cents to 9 cents per hundredweight, a level the rival railroads thought self-destructive.[129] In the short run the effort was only too successful. The railroad was proving to be exactly what the proponents of the narrow gauge as a means of cheap long-distance transportation had hoped. The Delphi (Indiana) *Times* on May 25, 1883, wrote of it: "The Narrow Gauge road in Frankfort does the town more good than all of the others. It is a through line from St. Louis to Toledo, and is no respecter of rates. It cuts and slashes in the rates and is independent of the standard gauge. It is death to a pool and it is a competitor that competes."

In fact, in the railroad's uncompleted form it had more tonnage than it could move with existing motive power. The traffic deluge quickly proved to be moving at a loss. The company ceased paying wages in May and was in receivership proceedings by the end of July. By the end of 1883 separate receivers had been appointed for the Ohio mileage and the line to East St. Louis. The receiver for the Ohio lines was initially an advocate of the narrow gauge, but there was little enthusiasm for continuation of 3′-0″ operation to East St. Louis. As early as April 1884 the bondholders' committee in Boston recommended conversion with a devastating denunciation of the narrow gauge:

. . . and thus end the singular folly of trying to run a toy railroad through the expensive medium of a receiver, at the same proportionate expense of maintenance and operation as properties of the highest class and efficiency. Your line running as it does northeast and southwest continually crosses standard gauge railroads, with not one of which, without breaking bulk (which is fatal to any margin of profit), can it exchange business. The Toledo, Cincinnati & St. Louis so-called system crosses in all about 100 standard gauge railroads, with all of which, by the folly or mistaken judgment of its projectors, it is out of key and harmony, and unable to offer or receive business except on conditions so disadvantageous that any attempt to handle it causes great loss. A condition more ignominious and disastrous it would be difficult to conceive.[130]

This statement is typical of the *ex post* evaluations of the narrow gauge period. The proponents made the elaborate *ex ante* calculations of cost savings summarized in Chapter 3. None of the Toledo, Cincinnati & St. Louis's several receivers submitted to his judge an estimate of the anticipated cost savings of conversion.[131] As we have seen at the close of Chapter 3, Lorenzo M. Johnson made his hostile evaluation of the Cairo & St. Louis's experience with the narrow gauge in qualitative terms with only a single estimate of the cost of transshipment. As in the passage just quoted, the disadvantage of incompatibility was treated as so overpowering that the attractions of conversion were intuitively obvious.

The end of the Toledo, Cincinnati & St. Louis's period of aggressive rivalry with established railroads came in a conflict with the Trunk Line pool. By December 1884 the TC&StL was reportedly handling nearly a third of the eastbound grain moving through the St. Louis gateway, enough traffic to warrant two freights per day.[132] Being in receivership and not a member of the pool, the narrow gauge was charging rates slightly below the pool's level; Albert Fink, commissioner of the pool, described the line as "the St. Louis destabilizer."[133] The five major standard gauge lines running east from St. Louis first attempted to have the trunk lines at Toledo refuse to accept grain from the TC&StL out of East St. Louis, but the TC&StL began billing the grain as originating at on-line points to the east.[134] Fink then ordered the TC&StL's principal connection at Toledo, the Michigan Central, to accept traffic off the narrow gauge only at local rates.[135] The TC&StL and the Michigan Central maintained a joint freight house at Toledo and interchanged a substantial volume; an end to interline rates on this traffic could only have ruined the narrow gauge. Its receiver sought and on December 20 secured from his judge, John Baxter of Toledo, a temporary injunction ordering the MC to receive and forward freight from the TC&StL on the same terms as offered to other railroads.[136] The Michigan Central responded by extending the boycott at Toledo to the Wabash and to the Cincinnati, Hamilton & Dayton. The Wabash responded by announcing that effective January 7, 1885, it would send its freight to the MC over its branch through Butler to Detroit.[137] The CH&D could also find alternative connections for through cars to Detroit, but the TC&StL as a narrow gauge could not. The TC&StL immediately announced an embargo at East St. Louis against freight for Toledo and went to court for further injunctive relief.

Judge Baxter made permanent the existing injunction, and subsequently ordered the Michigan Central to restore the previous interline rates, but at the hearing of January 3 he essentially ordered the TC&StL shut down.[138] After ascertaining that the TC&StL had incurred an operating loss of over $1 million in 1884, he ordered the receiver to discontinue all but local operations effective January 6, 1885. Off-line freight cars were ordered returned to their owners, the Ramsey Transfers whereby the company interchanged with standard gauge railroads were ordered shut down, and the Toledo–East St. Louis passenger train was dropped. Baxter had little choice, for the railroad was so deteriorated as to be barely operable. The main line thereafter was covered by mixed trains over four segments, with no pretension of through service. Initially the press speculated that service would be restored and that the TC&StL would shortly join the pool, but the St. Louis *Globe-Democrat* observed that at the pool's rates, because of the transfer at Toledo, the TC&StL could handle no through traffic.[139]

The Toledo, Cincinnati & St. Louis was demonstrating what had already been shown—but not much noted—in the case of the Toronto, Grey & Bruce: a railroad built to ordinary narrow gauge standards would simply fall apart within a few years unless better maintained than a standard gauge counterpart. Neither the proponents of the narrow gauge nor their adversaries in the cost controversy had remarked upon this, but the light grading in narrow gauge practice entailed a large number of wooden trestles across minor gullies and creeks where standard gauge railroads would have used fills and culverts. As we shall see in Chapter 5, the design of narrow gauge locomotives pursued a path of convergence to standard gauge practice. As a consequence, the typical locomotive of the early 1880s could inflict a great deal of damage to typical narrow gauge track and bridges.

Alternatively stated, narrow gauges lacked the characteristic property of railroads of being capable of operation even under conditions of severe deterioration. In wars, for example, it is customary to neglect maintenance of railroads in the expectation that they will remain operable, albeit at lower standards of service. Similarly, railroads habitually recover readily from war damage. The majority of investment in them is in the grading of rights-of-way, which become part of the terrain and are resistant even to bombardment. Narrow gauges, having only about a third of the investment of standard gauge railroads, did not have this big sunk investment, and were more dependent on maintenance of superficial parts of the physical plant. On the Toledo, Cincinnati & St. Louis, the Auglaize River bridge at Dupont, Ohio, by 1884 was so deteriorated that locomotives could not traverse it; loaded cars had to be ferried across individually using empty cars as idlers.[140] In July 1884 a representative of the bondholders inspected the line and was reported as saying that he had "no recollection of experiencing such a shaking up since boyhood as he received while riding on the T.C.&ST.L."[141] The same account reported that a single train had derailed 12 times in 40 miles. Abandonment of the railroad was seriously considered.

Meanwhile the Texas & St. Louis was collapsing in a different fashion. The better financed and better built of the two, the Cotton Belt was not threatened by a collapse of its physical plant. Rather, Paramore and his associate, Samuel W. Fordyce, had exhausted the $4 million with which they were building the railroad by the time the Arkansas River was bridged in August 1883. By November the railroad was far enough in arrears on wages to provoke a strike of engineers. A suit and countersuit between the railroad and the contractors of the bridge brought the railroad into the courts. A receiver was appointed on January 16, 1884.[142] A branch to Shreveport advanced no farther than Magnolia, 7 miles, and a projected line to Dallas was left as an unfinished grade. The remainder of the main line of some 327 miles from Leon Junction to Laredo was never undertaken.

With both its intended connections bankrupt, the Toledo, Texas & Rio Grande project died quietly. Its tangible assets—office furniture, surveying equipment, and supplies—were sold in August 1884 for $48.[143] Its promoter, E. Pratt Buell, became involved in a bigamy action in Rochester, New York, for which he went to prison.[144] Some additions to the Trunk were built, however. Notably, James P. Douglas, upon leaving the Texas & St. Louis, formed the Kansas & Gulf Short Line, which in 1885 completed a 90-mile line from Tyler on the Cotton Belt to Lufkin on Paul Bremond's Houston East & West Texas. This connection brought the Trunk into Houston, although neither Douglas nor Bremond was mainly motivated by providing such an outlet. Douglas was attempting a route from Kansas to Sabine Pass on the Gulf of Mexico for the export of wheat. Bremond was interested mainly in moving lumber from the Piney Woods to Houston. He also projected a line west from Houston to Beeville, Corpus Christi, and Laredo. Had this been built, it would have provided the Trunk with an

Idler: A car, most frequently a flatcar equipped with switch engine steps, used to keep locomotives off of track unable to bear their weight. Idlers were fairly universally used in connection with train ferries. In narrow gauge practice idlers were also used to allow standard gauge equipment to be handled on three-rail track. See Chapter 8.

alternative outlet to Laredo, either directly or via the Texas Mexican at Corpus Christi. Bremond intended the west line of his railroad to move agricultural products to Houston and manufactured products into Mexico; there is no indication that he was ever seriously motivated by participation in the Trunk.[145] The Texas Western Narrow Gauge, which achieved only a 57-mile short line from Houston to Sealy, is often said to have been potentially a part of the Trunk. The management actively promoted only a line from Houston to San Antonio. It projected branches to Corpus Christi, Presidio, Austin, and even to a connection with the Denver & Rio Grande at the northwestern border of Texas, but none was ever seriously pursued.

It is often said that it was possible to travel from Toledo to Houston by narrow gauge. Although this statement is true, it overstates the attainments of the Trunk. The trip of 1,303 miles became physically possible on November 1, 1885, with the completion of the Kansas & Gulf Short Line to Lufkin. Judge Baxter's order to shut down the Toledo, Cincinnati & St. Louis except for local service had taken effect on January 6, 1885. Thereafter, it would have required four days to traverse the TC&StL by mixed train. None of the five railroads necessary for the trip coordinated passenger service, save possibly the Texas & St. Louis and the Kansas & Gulf. The trip ceased to be possible when the St. Louis & Cairo converted its northern portion on September 26, 1886. No one is known to have attempted the journey, much less the entire 1,581 miles from Ironton to Sealy, the longest continuous narrow gauge trip ever possible in the United States.

It is notable that the St. Louis & Cairo was the first portion of the Trunk to convert. As mainly a self-contained coal carrier, the company had less obvious reason to be dissatisfied than either of the other two members of the Trunk; but as Lorenzo M. Johnson's article demonstrated, the management had soured on the narrow gauge by late 1878. Conversion of the St. Louis & Cairo was complete by November 15, 1886, of the Texas & St. Louis by January 12, 1889, and of the Toledo, Cincinnati & St. Louis by June 1, 1889. Thus the Grand Narrow Gauge Trunk was obliterated as an identifiable entity within six years of such completion as it attained in August 1883.

The failure of the Grand Narrow Gauge Trunk, and of the Toledo, Cincinnati & St. Louis in particular, had the advantage of being totally unambiguous. The Cincinnati *Commercial Gazette* wrote of it:

The complete downfall of the Toledo, Cincinnati & St. Louis system thoroughly demonstrates the impracticability of the narrow-gauge theory—particularly in the fertile and better regions of the country, when it becomes necessary to compete with the standard-gauge roads. It is true this narrow-gauge system has been badly managed, and it might have done better had it more practical brains and less theory in its councils. By the failure of the T.C.& St.L. there is one thing quite certain—there will not be more narrow-gauge roads built in this portion of the Central States again soon, unless it is some very short road, and then only to fill a "long felt" local want.[146]

As this passage predicted, the collapse of the Grand Narrow Gauge Trunk did not end the building of narrow gauges. Rather, the events of 1883 drastically reduced building from its former level. In 1883 itself new mileage was 1,223, about half the amount of 1882. In 1884 new narrow gauge mileage was 571, and in 1885, 516, less than a quarter of the 1882 figure. Narrow gauge mileage in service peaked in 1885 at 11,699, about 9 percent of American rail mileage.[147]

No single reason explains the continuation of narrow gauge building. Probably most important was the attraction of conformity with the compatible 3'-0" system in Colorado. With the expansion in mining after the collapse of the Trunk, mileage continued to grow. In particular, passage of the Sherman Silver Purchase Act in 1890 caused an inflow of resources into mining. This produced one of the largest of the narrow gauges, the Rio Grande Southern, in the extreme southwest corner of Colorado.

Two of the largest narrow gauges built after 1883, the White Pass & Yukon in Alaska and the Oahu Railway in Hawaii, were in geographical isolation such that neither expected physical interchange with the American railroad system. Accordingly, the cost of incompatibility with standard gauge railroads was not a consideration.

More basically, although collapse of the Trunk was generally treated as discrediting narrow gauge doctrine completely, the failure really did not do that. Rather, the experience simply demonstrated that narrow gauge railroads were not cost-competitive with standard railroads for general transport purposes—but this had been argued by Edward Hulbert and a minority of the narrow gauge advocates since the beginning of the movement. Hulbert should have considered failure of the Trunk as verification of his views, and in fact he did so. He had withdrawn from railroading to a farm at Otwell, Indiana, and from there on December 17, 1883, wrote his last known publication on the narrow gauge, a letter to the *Railway Age*, reiterating his position (now of over 13 years) that the proper role for narrow gauge railroads was for local economic development.[148]

No single event can be pointed out as analogous to the collapse of the Trunk in dissipating the view that narrow gauges were appropriate for general local service. Given the poor documentation of the costs of transshipment, the idea of a cheap, incompatible railroad for local service retained a superficial attraction. It is clear on the basis of promotion of such railroads that this attraction declined rapidly. There was, however, an important counterincentive. Conversion of most of the large narrow gauges outside of Colorado in the late 1880s and early 1890s released a large amount of relatively new narrow gauge equipment at bargain prices. Jacob D. Cox, special master for Judge Baxter in the dissolution of the Toledo, Cincinnati & St. Louis, reported to the court that the discrediting of narrow gauge philosophy in 1883 at the time of the TC&StL's receivership had caused a depreciation of narrow gauge rolling stock of 30 to 40 percent.[149] On October 15, 1885, 1,190 cars of the TC&StL were sold at Toledo, mainly for $25 to $45 each.[150] The president of the Lawndale Railway in 1899 chose 3'-0" for the line serving his mill town partly because he could buy his rolling stock cheaply from the Chester & Lenoir, a much larger southern narrow gauge that was converting. He also specifically preferred incompatibility in order to keep his cars on his own property.[151]

Similarly, narrow gauge locomotives were available at quite low prices. After conversion of the Utah & Northern in 1887 and 1890, the Union Pacific carried the locomotives on its books at $2,000 for an engine in good condition, $1,000 for one in fair condition, and only $150 for en-

It is uncertain which narrow gauge locomotive served the largest number of owners, but this Baldwin outside-frame 2-8-0 of 1893 must have ranked high. It began its career as an 0-8-0 in construction work on the Crystal River, went to the Central of Georgia as a 2-8-0 for use on the Columbus & Rome and Gainesville Midland, was sold to the Southern Iron & Equipment Co., and proceeded to the Mt. Airy & Eastern, where it is shown as No. 9. It was then returned to the SI&E and finally sold to the Cia. Azucarera Madrazo, a Cuban sugar operator. (Ed Bond collection.)

gines of scrap quality. It was willing to sell the locomotives at those prices and reportedly did sell the last of the U&N engines at $150 each for further service elsewhere.[152] The decline of locomotive prices to this level is difficult to state precisely because the prices at which individual locomotives changed hands have survived in only spotty fashion. There is no known locomotive for which the new price and several subsequent secondhand prices are recorded. The best single source of data on this point is the work of Robert Brendel on the life histories of the engines of the National Locomotive Works, but even this is a very meager sample. On the basis of Brendel's data, a locomotive produced for about $5,000 shortly before the firm failed in 1878 had depreciated by $800–$1,300 by the peak years of the movement in the early 1880s, had fallen to about half its original price after the collapse of the movement in 1883, and had sunk to the $1,000–$2,000 range at which the UP carried the Utah & Northern engines by 1890.[153] In a search of newspapers and archival sources, George E. Pitchard found the prices at which the UP sold six Brooks and Baldwin 2-6-0s between 1883 and 1889. All were quite recent locomotives built between 1879 and 1881. In October 1883 the UP sold the South Park Line's nos. 39 and 40 to the Kansas Central at $12,872.50 for the pair. Late in 1887 it sold the Utah & Northern's nos. 16 and 13 for $2,500 and $3,500, respectively. In the fall of 1889 it sold U&N nos. 80 and 94 for $2,500 and $2,400.[154]

The experience of the Denver & Rio Grande documents a continuation of the decline in prices. Between 1889 and 1893 the D&RG sold eight locomotives—Baldwin engines of 0-6-0T, 2-6-0, and 4-4-0 wheel arrangements built in the late 1870s, and made redundant by conversion of the Ogden line—at prices that have survived. Two sold for $1,600, one for

$1,900, four for $2,000, and one for $2,200.[155] There was a revival of locomotive prices in the Edwardian prosperity. The South Pacific Coast's narrow gauge locomotives were sold between 1906 and 1908 at prices between $2,240 and $5,700.[156] They were, however, larger and more modern engines than the National locomotives. Between 1902 and 1904 the D&RG sold four of its class 56 2-8-0s, Baldwin engines of 1880, one for $3,000, one for $4,000, and two for $5,000.[157]

The incentive stemming from the low prices of secondhand narrow gauge equipment never entirely spent itself; the ready availability of used equipment was the reported reason for the choice of 3'-0" for the New Berlin & Winfield in 1904 and for the Montana Southern, the last American narrow gauge built, in 1919.[158]

Finally, as mentioned at the close of Chapter 3, a lightly built incompatible railroad might be the cheapest way of serving an extractive enterprise until the development of the motor truck. The example of the Uintah Railway built in 1904 to serve Gilsonite deposits in Utah, cited in that connection, was not alone. Three late narrow gauges were built to serve copper installations: the United Verde & Pacific in 1894, the Magma Arizona in 1914, and the Montana Southern in 1919.

Fortunately, the engineer of the United Verde & Pacific published his calculations at length in a paper delivered in 1895. The railroad was projected as a nominal common carrier of the United Verde Copper Co. to replace a chain belt conveyor that had never been made to function properly. The line was to be 26 miles long from a junction on the Santa Fe's

The last narrow gauge built was the Montana Southern in 1919. The management chose narrow gauge to make use of equipment from the Florence & Cripple Creek, including locomotive No. 2. (Smithsonian Institution.)

The practice of the later narrow gauge railroads, no less than their predecessors, tended toward scaled down versions of standard gauge railroading. The United Verde & Pacific of 1894 operated with Baldwin 2-6-0 locomotives, novel only for their large sand domes, one each before and after the steam dome. (Railroad Museum of Pennsylvania.)

Phoenix branch to the company's mine and smelter at Jerome. About ten miles were to be in rugged country in the Black Hills of Arizona, the rest in a valley. The copper company envisioned only a single train per day. Its engineer, Elbridge H. Beckler, argued that a standard gauge railroad was not justified by the prospective traffic density, especially since the life of the mine might be only ten years, or the smelter might be relocated. He made very traditional estimates of savings for grading and rolling stock, and planned on an investment of $35,000 per mile with a 12-year depreciation period. Inbound cargo was mainly coal and coke, which would be transshipped by gravity through bins. Outbound cargo was mainly ore and bullion, which were to be transshipped manually in sacks. He did not estimate the cost of this. Beckler built a thoroughly traditional narrow gauge with 3-percent grades and extensive curvature over 24°—the worst curve of 45°. Two Baldwin Moguls were bought to operate the line. Beckler reported that the railroad could move ore the length of the line for $1.258 per ton, or about 0.5¢ per ton-mile. He estimated that using standard gauge would have added about 20¢ per ton to the cost in interest expense.[159]

Whether such calculations were valid is uncertain. The mines at Jerome proved both more productive and longer-lived than Beckler anticipated. The railroad hauled about triple the projected traffic and was replaced in 1920 by a standard gauge railroad of the same mining firm on an entirely different route. Similarly, the Magma Arizona was standard gauged in 1923. The Uintah and Montana Southern were never converted, however.

The building of such lines gives us a rough measure of the amount of narrow gauge mileage that should, in fact, have been built to narrow gauge. Table 4.1 shows that as the economy emerged from the depression of the mid-1890s, the volume of narrow gauge building reached a relatively stable level between 123 and 212 miles per year from 1898 through 1906. This represented mainly the building of nominal common carriers in the lumber industry during the expansion of residential building in the early Edwardian prosperity. Narrow gauge mileage in those years ranged from 2.28 to 5.53 percent of all rail miles built per annum. Because the incentive to make use of existing narrow gauge equipment persisted throughout this period, these data probably represent an upper bound to the amount of justifiable narrow gauge building.

The collapse of the Grand Narrow Gauge Trunk was not a refutation of the idea that narrow gauge railroads might be optimal for extractive industries, but rather a demonstration that the economies of such lines could not be generalized. The principal intellectual problem remaining is accounting for the long period—at least 13 years—in which the narrow gauge fallacy persisted before its general intellectual abandonment. Forney, Evans, Latrobe, and the other opponents had demonstrated the fallacious character of the arguments for the narrow gauge by 1873. No doubt Evans was correct in attributing the persistence in part to a religious zeal, a desire to believe.

John H. White, Jr., has attributed the persistence of the fallacy to ignorance of railroading on the part of many of the promoters. He points out that the system finally known as the Toledo, Cincinnati & St. Louis was promoted by a pharmacist, and a Fulton County Narrow Gauge by a publisher.[160] Although the examples are accurate and others could be brought forth—the Havana, Rantoul & Eastern was promoted by a local lawyer— the railroads were an expanding industry, drawing capital and entrepreneurship from a wide variety of activities. Local merchants, lawyers, journalists, and manufacturers were widely attracted to standard gauge railroading as well.

More important, many of the major figures in the narrow gauge movement had impeccable backgrounds in standard or broad gauge railroading. Edward Hulbert, as mentioned earlier, had been general manager of the Western & Atlantic, a southern broad gauge of first importance. William Jackson Palmer, as also mentioned, adopted the narrow gauge doctrine after a long period with the Pennsylvania Railroad and the Kansas Pacific. Paul Bremond enthusiastically adopted narrow gauge for the Houston East & West Texas after having considerable success with his standard gauge Houston & Texas Central.[161] Even Peter B. Borst, whose Washington, Cincinnati & St. Louis Railroad might appear the embodiment of ignorance of railroad practice, had been a leading early promoter of the standard gauge Shenandoah Valley Railroad, later the Norfolk & Western's line between Roanoke and Hagerstown.[162] The Texas & Pacific's early consideration of a narrow gauge was reported in the pro–narrow gauge press as being the consequence of Colonel Thomas A. Scott's interest in narrow gauge doctrine.[163] Borst listed Scott as one of the investors in the narrow gauge in his speech to the convention of 1872.[164] Scott, president of the Pennsylvania Railroad, was a figure of the top rank in the industry, whose familiarity with the conventional railroading of the time cannot be questioned. John T. Davis in 1880 asserted that J. Edgar Thompson, another president of the Pennsylvania Railroad, had before his death remarked that if he were now building the branches of the Pennsylvania, he would make them 3'-0" to save useless expense on fuel and wear and tear.[165] Colonel William R. Arthur, who had been a civil engineer since 1839, accepted narrow gauge doctrine enough to testify in a legal action that saving in deadweight relative to a standard gauge reduced the operating costs of the Cairo & St. Louis by 15 to 18 percent.[166] Arthur had built the Marietta & Cincinnati and had been superintendent of the Illinois Central from 1858 to 1866. L. L. Lincoln, who committed what might appear the ultimate folly, converting the Bucksport & Bangor to 3'-0" from 4'-8½" after the railroad had already been converted from 5'-6", had a solid background as a division superintendent of the Maine Central.[167]

The Boston financial community, which had been the principal source of funds for the standard gauge railroads for decades, was in Forney's opinion a major source of support for narrow gauge doctrine. In an editorial in 1877 he wrote: "[A] well-known manufacturer called upon the projector of a narrow gauge railroad and tried to convince him that his road would be more efficient and would not cost any more, if built of the ordinary gauge, then it would if made three feet wide. 'Oh!' the latter replied. 'I don't care a damn for that; but those fellers down in Boston will subscribe easier if I talk narrow gauge than they will if I talk wide gauge'."[168] We have already seen that the Toledo, Cincinnati & St. Louis achieved such completion as it did through financing the Toledo & Delphos Trust in Boston and hiring as general manager Elijah B. Phillips, a first figure in railroad management in Boston. Narrow gauge doctrine even achieved academic acceptance; one of the most uncritical presentations was a pamphlet by W. J. L. Nicodemus, Professor of Engineering at the University of Wisconsin.[169]

In the main, the persistence of the fallacy was a consequence of the depression of the mid-1870s, which delayed the market test of the narrow gauge hypothesis nearly a decade. If the narrow gauge transcontinental had taken shape any more fully, it would have demonstrated the unsuitability of the narrow gauge for general railroading as unambiguously as the Grand Narrow Gauge Trunk did. The Washington, Cincinnati & St. Louis was a far more impractical project than the Toledo, Cincinnati & St. Louis. The latter gave promise of a mix of minerals from southern Ohio and agricultural products from the west, and its terrain was not difficult. The WC&StL's projected crossing of West Virginia was so impractical that an effort to build it would quickly have demonstrated the limitations of narrow gauge railroading. The movement might then have blown over by the early to mid-1870s, as Forney and the other opponents erroneously thought it was doing.

The demise of the idea that narrow gauge remained appropriate for general-purpose short lines is difficult to document. No single event like the failure of the Grand Narrow Gauge Trunk can be said to have discredited it. There is no direct evidence of whether Edward Hulbert continued to hold this view until his death in 1888. He returned to Atlanta to become the first secretary of the Atlanta Manufacturers' Association in September 1886,[170] but resigned about a month later to assist Henry L. Collier, chief engineer of the projected Atlanta & Hawkinsville Railroad, in surveying and planning the line.[171] The railroad was intended to give Atlanta an outlet to steamboats on the Ocmulgee River. Collier proposed building it as a narrow gauge for only $6,500 per mile.[172] Given Hulbert's long identification with such ideas, it is unlikely that this proposal was contrary to his views. The management rejected the recommendation and built the line as a standard gauge railroad, the Atlanta & Florida. Hulbert returned to the secretaryship of the Manufacturers' Association by January 1887 and wrote his final pamphlet, *Georgia: Empire State of the South*, in which he noted Atlanta's connections to ten cotton states by rail, and its direct routes to five south Atlantic and Gulf Coast ports. He stressed the compatibility of the system, and made no mention of narrow gauge.[173]

By 1893 the doctrine of the suitability of narrow gauge for secondary general-purpose railways had lost essentially all of its intellectual respectability. When the directors of the projected Kishacoquillas Valley Railroad in 1892 proposed it as a narrow gauge from their town of Belleville, Pennsylvania, to the Pennsylvania Railroad main line at Reedsville, their chief engineer, F. F. Whittekin, responded that if he built the line as a narrow gauge, "you would curse me all the days of my life."[174] At a town meeting in Cascade, Iowa, on February 22, 1893, concerning the chronic problems of the Bellevue & Cascade, Robert Quirk declared: "The narrow gauge is a crime against modern civilization and the men who constructed it were the silliest people on earth."[175]

An Austrian engineer, E. A. Ziffer, presented a paper at the Engineering Congress of 1893 in Chicago arguing for narrow gauge on secondary railways on all of the traditional grounds of savings in first costs and operating expenses.[176] The *Railroad Gazette* commented:

To an American engineer any such argument must seem superfluous at this time in the century, for, in the early seventies, the "battle of the gauges" was fought to a finish in this country. The discussion of the subject was so prolonged and comprehensive, and the practical trials were so extensive that the decision seemed final. The 3-ft. gauge was left with hardly an advocate among engineers. Everyone admitted that a road that would have any interchange of traffic with roads of standard gauge must be built to standard gauge; and almost everyone admitted that if the traffic to be moved were sufficient in quantity, and if the distances over which it would be moved were long enough to warrant building a railroad at all, it would be bad economy to build it of narrow gauge, say 3 ft. . . . For an American to undertake an answer to the arguments of Mr. Ziffer would be of about as much practical interest as to set out to prove that slavery should not be restored as an institution of the land. . . .[177]

Notes

1. *Railway Age*, 8 (1883), p. 804.

2. On Reconstruction railroad-building generally, see Mark W. Summers, *Railroads, Reconstruction, and the Gospel of Prosperity: Aid Under the Radical Republicans* (Princeton, N.J.: Princeton University Press, 1984). Hulbert is mentioned on p. 126, but his efforts do not enter into the author's account. See also Peter S. McGuire, "The Railroads of Georgia, 1860–1880," *Georgia Historical Quarterly*, 16 (1932), pp. 179–213.

3. For biographical details on Hulbert, including his activities in Reconstruction politics, see George W. Hilton, "'The Well Known Narrow Gauge Railway Champion': Colonel Edward Hulbert of Georgia," *Railroad History*, no. 157 (1987), pp. 16–44.

4. *Remarks made by Col. E. Hulbert, Superintendent of the W. &. A. R. R. before the Press Association of Georgia, Delivered on board the Steamer Etowah on the Coosa River, Saturday Night, August 28, 1869* (Atlanta: Franklin Printing House, 1869). In the rare book room, University of Virginia Library, Charlottesville.

5. Atlanta *Daily New Era*, Feb. 22, 1871.

6. As, for example, at a promotional meeting for a narrow gauge projected from West Point to Birmingham (Atlanta *Daily Constitution*, Aug. 8, 1871), and at another for one undertaken but never completed from Gainesville to Dahlonega (Atlanta *Daily New Era*, Sept. 9, 1871).

7. The decision to complete the Cherokee as a narrow gauge was announced in September 1871 (*Centerville Semi-Weekly Express*, Sept. 8, 1871). The Atlanta *Daily Constitution* reported on Nov. 4, 1871, that track-laying would be completed in the following week.

8. The Tuskegee Railroad was reported in service by the Atlanta *Daily Constitution* on Nov. 21, 1871.

9. Hilton, "'The Well Known Narrow Gauge Railway Champion': Colonel Edward Hulbert of Georgia," pp. 27–28.

10. Atlanta *Daily New Era*, July 29, 1871.

11. Brit Allan Storey, "William J. Palmer: A Biography" (Ph.D. diss., University of Kentucky, 1968), pp. 1–72, 131. See also George L. Anderson, *General William J. Palmer: A Decade of Colorado Railroad Building, 1870–1880*, Colorado College Publications, Studies Series No. 22 (1936).

12. Storey, "Palmer," pp. 141, 213, 226.

13. O. Meredith Wilson, *The Denver & Rio Grande Project, 1870–1901* (Salt Lake City: Howe Brothers, 1982), p. 9.

14. Storey, "Palmer," p. 238.

15. Wilson, *Denver and Rio Grande*, p. 15.

16. *Second Annual Report of the Board of Directors of the Denver & Rio Grande Railway to the Stockholders for the year 1873*, July 31, 1874 (Colorado Springs, 1874), pp. 15–16.

17. E.g., Howard Schuyler, "Narrow Gauge Freight-Car," *Railroad Gazette*, 3 (1871), p. 359.

18. See the time series in the corporate history of the Denver & Rio Grande in Part II.

19. "American Central Railway," *American Railroad Journal*, 12 (1856), p. 561; *The Continental Railway Company* (New York, issued by the company, 1881); Taylor Hampton, *The Nickel Plate Road* (Cleveland: World Publishing Co., 1947), pp. 49–51; John A. Rehor, *The Nickel Plate Story* (Milwaukee: Kalmbach Publishing Co., 1965), pp. 14, 17.

20. George W. Hilton, *Monon Route* (Berkeley, Calif.: Howell-North Books, 1978), pp. 40–44.

21. *Ibid.*, pp. 39–47.

22. *Railroad Gazette*, 3 (1871), pp. 81, 197, 413; 4 (1872), pp. 111, 367, 377; 5 (1873), pp. 63, 194, 508; 7 (1875), p. 320; 8 (1876), pp. 30, 168.

23. George W. Hilton, *The Ma & Pa: A History of the Maryland & Pennsylvania Railroad* (Berkeley, Calif.: Howell-North Books, 1963), pp. 1–14, 29–36.

24. Rome *Courier*, Sept. 8, Dec. 22, 1871.

25. George A. Parker, *Report to the Massachusetts Legislature on Narrow Gauge Railways*, House of Representatives Document No. 180 (Boston, Mar. 11, 1871). In the American Antiquarian Society, Worcester, Mass.

26. *Proceedings of the National Narrow-Gauge Railway Convention, held at St. Louis, Mo., June 19, 1872* (St. Louis, 1872), pp. 7–8.

27. *Ibid.*, p. 20.   28. *Railroad Gazette*, 4 (1872), p. 275.

29. *Proceedings of the National Narrow-Gauge Railway Convention* (1872), pp. 57–81.

30. *Ibid.*, pp. 92–93.

31. *American Railroad Journal*, 28 (1872), pp. 779, 899. For biographical details on Borst, see Harry M. Strickler, *A Short History of Page County, Virginia* (Richmond: Dietz Press, 1952), pp. 377, 382, 386; obituary in Page *Courier* (Luray, Va.), May 11, 1882.

32. *Railroad Gazette*, 8 (1876), p. 399.

33. *Ibid.*, 11 (1879), p. 151.

34. On the route, see *Proceedings of the National Narrow-Gauge Railway Convention* (1872), pp. 16–17; *Address of the Hon. P. B. Borst, President of the Washington, Cincinnati & St. Louis Railway Company, to the Committee on Railways and Canals—House of Representatives* (Luray: General Office, 1874; in the rare book room, Library of Congress); *American Railroad Journal*, 28 (1872), p. 779; 29 (1873), pp. 353, 415; *Railroad Gazette*, 4 (1872), p. 408; *Rockingham Register* (Harrisonburg, Virginia), June 28, Aug. 30, 1872, Mar. 14, Apr. 11, Apr. 18, May 9, 1873, and *passim*. I am deeply indebted to Emory L. Kemp, Professor of the History of Science & Technology, Faculty of Civil Engineering, West Virginia University, Morgantown, for assistance on the geography of West Virginia.

35. *Address of the Hon. P. B. Borst*, pp. 5, 14.

36. Stating a precise trade-off between gradients and curvature and length would depend upon traffic density, anticipated speeds, mix of passenger and freight trains, importance of intermediate origination, and other considerations, but on the subject generally, see Arthur M. Wellington, *The Economic Theory of the Location of Railways* (5th ed., New York: Wiley & Sons, 1893), chaps. 7–10, 14–20.

37. *Address of the Hon. P. B. Borst*, p. 4.

38. *Proceedings of the National Narrow-Gauge Railway Convention* (1872), pp. 16–17.

39. *Address of the Hon. P. B. Borst*, p. 4.   40. *Ibid.*, pp. 14–19.

41. *Rockingham Register*, Apr. 11, 1873.   42. Missouri *Republican*, June 20, 1872.

43. *Railroad Gazette*, 3 (1871), p. 226; 4 (1872), p. 341.

44. *Address of the Hon. P. B. Borst*, p. 13.   45. *Railroad Gazette*, 5 (1873), p. 251.

46. *Rockingham Register*, Oct. 18, 1872, June 20, 1873.

47. John A. Wayland, *A History of Rockingham County, Virginia* (Dayton, Virginia: Ruebush-Elkins Co., 1912), p. 231.

48. *American Railroad Journal*, 33 (1871), p. 579.

49. *Address of the Hon. P. B. Borst*, p. 3.   50. Wayland, *History*, p. 231.

51. *Address of the Hon. P. B. Borst*, pp. 13–14.

52. *Ibid.*, p. 3.

53. *Railroad Gazette*, 7 (1875), p. 330; 8 (1876), p. 399; 9 (1877), pp. 207, 216.

54. *Acts and Joint Resolutions of the State of Virginia passed by the General Assembly of the State of Virginia at its Session of 1877–78*, chap. 122 (Feb. 28, 1878).

55. *Acts . . . of the State of Virginia . . . 1878–79*, chap. 89, pp. 356–57 (Apr. 1, 1879).

56. *Acts . . . of the State of Virginia . . . 1881–82*, chap. 83, p. 451 (Apr. 21, 1882).

57. *Page Courier*, Apr. 27, May 11, 1882.

58. *Railroad Gazette*, 15 (1883), p. 643. See also MS Will Books, Page County, Virginia, Office of the County Clerk, Luray, Virginia, vol. R, p. 169, vol. S, p. 74.

59. Nancy B. Hess, *The Heartland: Rockingham County* (Harrisonburg: Park View Press, 1976), p. 245.

60. Painesville *Telegraph*, Dec. 22, 1870.

61. *Ibid.*, Apr. 27, 1876.

62. *Rockingham Register*, Apr. 11, 1873.

63. *Review of the Report of the U.S. Senate Committee on Transportation Routes by the Committee on Railway Transportation of the New York Cheap Transportation Association, May 12, 1874* (New York, 1874), pp. 9–10.

64. J. Hornish, *Narrow Gauge Railroads* (New York: New York Cheap Transportation Association, 1875).

65. *The Inter-Ocean* (Chicago), Dec. 16, 1875.

66. "The Narrow-Gauge Fallacy," *Railroad Gazette*, 6 (1874), p. 234.

67. Howard Fleming, "Progress of Narrow Gauge Railroads," *Railroad Gazette*, 6 (1874), p. 338. William Jackson Palmer's laudatory treatment of the narrow gauge in his annual report of the Denver & Rio Grande of July 31, 1874, had an even more extreme statement from Jackson & Sharp, the carbuilders of Wilmington, Delaware, that after the panic the shops would have been closed and the workmen discharged except for narrow gauge orders, which gave the plant active work all winter. *Second Annual Report* (cited in n. 16), p. 16.

68. *Railroad Gazette*, 6 (1874), p. 339.

69. Howard Fleming, *Narrow Gauge Railways in America* (Philadelphia: Howard Fleming, 1875).

70. *Railroad Gazette*, 7 (1875), p. 198.   71. *Railway World*, 1 (1875), p. 169.

72. Howard Fleming, *Narrow Gauge Railways in America* (2d ed., Philadelphia: Howard Fleming, 1876). This edition has been reproduced photographically and republished by Grahame Hardy of Oakland, California, in 1949 and by Railhead Publications of Canton, Ohio, in 1982.

73. See "The Centennial Grounds Narrow-Gauge Railroad," *Railroad Gazette*, 9 (1877), p. 56.

74. Robert S. Maxwell, *Whistle in the Piney Woods: Paul Bremond and the Houston, East and West Texas Railway*, Texas Gulf Coast Historical Association, Publication Series, 7, no. 2 (Nov. 1963), p. 9.

75. *Railroad Gazette*, 10 (1878), pp. 334, 370.

76. Cincinnati *Gazette*, July 16, 1878; Cincinnati *Enquirer*, July 18, 1878.

77. *Railroad Gazette*, 10 (1878), pp. 367, 525, 527. The Chicago & Atlantic, which took shape in the 1880s as the Erie's standard gauge extension from Marion, Ohio, to Chicago, was also represented, but the management was then considering building the line as an independent narrow gauge.

78. Cincinnati *Commercial*, July 19, 1878; Cincinnati *Gazette*, July 19, 1878.

79. *Railroad Gazette*, 10 (1878), p. 583.   80. Rehor, *The Nickel Plate Story*, p. 133.

81. Cincinnati *Gazette*, July 16, 1878.   82. *Ibid.*

83. Cincinnati *Commercial*, July 18, 1878; *Railroad Gazette*, 10 (1878), p. 367.

84. Cincinnati *Gazette*, July 19, 1878.

85. Cincinnati *Commercial*, July 19, 1878; Cincinnati *Gazette*, July 19, 1878. Unfortunately, I have been unable to find evidence of a musician of this name. The only apparent candidate is William A. Diehle, who while proprietor of a music store in Hamilton, Ohio, in 1891 copyrighted a composition, "Hamilton Cadets," probably a march performed at the centennial celebration of Hamilton on September 17–19, 1891. (Manuscript card index to copyright deposits, Library of Congress.) I have failed to find further biographical information on this composer.

86. Cincinnati *Enquirer*, July 19, 1878.   87. *Ibid.*, Oct. 24, 1878.

88. *Railroad Gazette*, 10 (1878), pp. 525–26.

89. *National Car-Builder*, 9 (1878), pp. 184–85.

90. Cincinnati *Gazette*, Oct. 25, 1878. This newspaper's editorial view was essentially that of Forney in favor of lightly built standard gauge railroads. See "The Gauge and Dead Weight" and "The Uniform Narrow Gauge" in the issue of Oct. 24, 1878.

91. Cincinnati *Enquirer*, Oct. 25, 1878; Cincinnati *Gazette*, Oct. 25, 1878; "Narrow Gauges and Narrow Minds," *Railway Age*, 4 (1879), p. 50.

92. *Railway Age*, 4 (1879), p. 50.

93. Cincinnati *Commercial*, Oct. 25, 1878; Cincinnati *Enquirer*, Oct. 25, 1878.

94. *Railway Age*, 4 (1879), p. 50.   95. *Ibid.*

96. See the series by Charles F. H. Allen, "The Railroads of McKean County, Pa.," Railway & Locomotive Historical Society *Bulletin*, no. 76 (1949), pp. 38–68; no. 78 (1949), pp. 64–85; no. 80 (1950), pp. 68–85; no. 81 (1950), pp. 29–54.

97. *Ibid.*, no. 76 (1949), p. 44.   98. *Railway Age*, 8 (1883), pp. 2–3.

99. Hilton, *The Ma & Pa*, pp. 1–14, 29–36.

100. See especially "The Illusions of Narrow Gauge," *Railroad Gazette*, 9 (1877), p. 386; "Errors of Narrow-Gauge Reasoning," 10 (1878), pp. 493–94; "Counsel on the Gauge Question," 11 (1879), pp. 648–62, 671–72.

101. "Notable Changes of Gauge," *Railway Age*, (1877), p. 1594.

102. *Railroad Gazette*, 10 (1878), p. 376; 11 (1879), p. 479.

103. *Ibid.*, 11 (1879), p. 561.   104. *Ibid.*, 12 (1880), p. 225.

105. *Ibid.*, p. 449.   106. *Ibid.*, p. 351.

107. *Ibid.*, 13 (1881), p. 176.   108. *Ibid.*, p. 707.

109. *National Car-Builder*, 9 (1878), p. 151.

110. "The Logic of Events," *Railroad Gazette*, 9 (1877), p. 554.

111. *National Car-Builder*, 9 (1878), p. 9.

112. See George W. Hilton, "The Grand Narrow Gauge Trunk," *Railroad History*, no. 148 (1983), pp. 23–41.

113. Gerald M. Best, *Mexican Narrow Gauge* (Berkeley, Calif.: Howell-North Books, 1968), pp. 11–14.

114. *Railway Age*, 7 (1883), p. 269.

115. See *Five Reasons Why the People of Indiana Should Encourage the Construction of the Toledo & St. Louis Narrow Gauge Railroad* (Crawfordsville, Ind., 1876). In the New York Public Library, 43d Street annex. The pamphlet is an exposition of narrow gauge doctrine, but has no specific information on the railroad.

116. For the events in greater detail, see the histories of the Toledo, Cincinnati & St. Louis in Rehor, *The Nickel Plate Story*, pp. 119–41, and in Part II of the present volume.

117. Jacob E. Anderson, *A Brief History of the St. Louis Southwestern Railway Lines* (St. Louis: St. Louis Southwestern Railway, 1947), pp. 1–14.

118. *Daily Cairo Bulletin*, June 6, 1883.

119. Rehor, *The Nickel Plate Story*, p. 135; *Railroad Gazette*, 13 (1881), p. 25.

120. Quoted in the Sullivan (Ind.) *Democrat*, Nov. 2, 1883.

121. St. Louis *Globe-Democrat*, Oct. 24, 1884.

122. *Ibid.*, Dec. 14 and 19, 1882.

123. *Ibid.*, Apr. 18, 1883.

124. *Ibid.*, Nov. 4, 1882.

125. *Ibid.*, Mar. 23, 1883.

126. *Ibid.*, Oct. 27, 1882.

127. *Ibid.*, May 10, 1883.

128. Rehor, *The Nickel Plate Story*, p. 139.

129. St. Louis *Globe-Democrat*, Apr. 30, 1883.

130. *Railroad Gazette*, 16 (1884), p. 310.

131. *Central Trust Co. of New York v. the Iron RR, Toledo, Delphos & Burlington RR Co., et al.*, Circuit Court of the U.S. Southern District of Ohio, Western Division. In equity Nos. 3554, 3576–3579 (1884), Federal Record Center, Chicago.

132. St. Louis *Globe-Democrat*, Dec. 17, 1884.

133. *Ibid.*, Dec. 17, 1884.

134. *Ibid.*, Dec. 21, 1884.

135. *Ibid.*, Dec. 22, 1884.

136. *Ibid.*

137. *Ibid.*, Jan. 7, 1885.

138. *Ibid.*, Jan. 7, 8, 13, 22, 1885.

139. *Ibid.*, Feb. 9, 1885.

140. Rehor, *The Nickel Plate Story*, p. 145.

141. St. Louis *Globe-Democrat*, July 12, 1884.

142. *Poor's Manual of Railroads*, 1885, p. 835.

143. Newton (Ill.) *Weekly Press*, Aug. 27, 1884.

144. St. Louis *Globe-Democrat*, Oct. 24, 1884; Sullivan (Ind.) *Democrat*, July 20, 1886.

145. See Maxwell, *Whistles in the Piney Woods: Paul Bremond and the Houston, East and West Texas Railway*.

146. Quoted in St. Louis *Globe-Democrat*, July 3, 1884.

147. See Table 4.1. The figure most commonly cited as the peak is 12,116 miles in 1886 from Robert H. Ramsey's submission to the Franklin Institute on his car transfer. *Journal of the Franklin Institute*, Third Series, 92 (1886), p. 190. This proves relatively accurate; Ramsey apparently failed to account for some of the conversions of the peak years of narrow gauge building, and may have included some mileage never completed.

148. *Railway Age*, 8 (1883), p. 804.

149. *Central Trust Co. of New York v. the Iron RR, Toledo, Delphos & Burlington RR Co., et al.* (cited in n. 131). In the matter of the Intervening Petition of R. S. Grant vs. William Craig, Receiver, August 14, 1884. Report of Jacob D. Cox, Special Master to the Hon. John Baxter, Judge. Federal Records Center, Chicago.

150. *Railroad Gazette*, 17 (1885), p. 687.

151. Lee Rainey, "The Lawndale Dummy," *Narrow Gauge and Short Line Gazette*, Sept.–Oct. 1983, pp. 26–35.

152. Mallory Hope Ferrell, *Rails, Sagebrush & Pine* (San Marino, Calif.: Golden West Books, 1967), p. 103.

153. The best-documented locomotive is Wheeling & Lake Erie No. 2, produced by National in June 1877 for $4,800. The engine was sold to the St. Clairsville & Northern in 1880 for $3,500 and resold to an unidentified buyer in September 1881 for $4,000. Philadelphia & Atlantic City No. 2, a larger and presumably more expensive 4-4-0 built in February 1877, a 3'-6" engine, was sold to the Suffolk & Carolina in August 1886 for $1,925. Waynesburg & Washington No. 2, also a 4-4-0, had an original price of about $5,300 and was sold to F. M. Hicks, a dealer in Chicago, for $1,000 in 1900. Letters of Robert Brendel, June 6 and 18, 1988.

154. Letter of George E. Pitchard, Dec. 6, 1988, citing Union Pacific, Denver, South Park & Pacific, Kansas Central, and Salt Lake & Fort Douglas journals or ledgers, correspondence of John W. Young, and related newspaper search.

155. *Locomotives of the Rio Grande* (Golden, Colo.: Colorado Railroad Museum, 1980), pp. 10–11.

156. Bruce A. MacGregor, *South Pacific Coast: An Illustrated History of the South Pacific Coast Railroad* (Berkeley: Howell-North Books, 1968), pp. 274–75.

157. *Locomotives of the Rio Grande*, p. 12.

158. Benjamin F. G. Kline, Jr., "New Berlin & Winfield RR," *Narrow Gauge and Short Line Gazette*, July 1977, pp. 68–71; Tivis E. Wilkins, *The Florence & Cripple Creek and Golden Circle Railroads*, Colorado Rail Annual no. 13 (Golden, Colo.: Colorado Rail Museum, 1976), pp. 160, 179–80.

159. Elbridge H. Beckler, "The United Verde & Pacific Railway," *Journal of the Association of Engineering Societies*, 14 (1895), pp. 131–47.

160. John H. White, Jr., "The Narrow Gauge Fallacy," *Railroad History*, no. 141 (1979), p. 81.

161. Maxwell, *Whistles in the Piney Woods.*

162. Obituary of Borst, Page *Courier* (Luray, Va.), May 11, 1882.

163. Atlanta *Daily New Era*, July 25, 1871.

164. *Missouri Republican* (St. Louis), June 21, 1872.

165. John T. Davis, "Narrow Gauge Railroads," *Mining & Scientific Press*, 41, no. 1 (1880), p. 6.

166. *Five Reasons Why the People of Indiana Should Encourage the Construction of the Toledo & St. Louis Narrow Gauge Railroad* (cited in n. 115), p. 7.

167. *Railroad Gazette*, 11 (1879), p. 455.   168. *Railroad Gazette*, 9 (1877), p. 386.

169. W. J. L. Nicodemus, A.M., C.E., *Railway Gauges* (Madison, Wisc.: Atwood & Culver, 1874).

170. Atlanta *Constitution*, Sept. 12, 1886.   171. *Ibid.*, Oct. 7, 14, 1886.

172. *Railroad Gazette*, 18 (1886), p. 433.

173. Edward Hulbert, *Georgia: Empire State of the South* (Atlanta: Atlanta Manufacturers' Association, 1887). In the rare book room, Wake Forest University, Winston-Salem, N.C.

174. John G. Hartzler, *The Ol' Hook & Eye: A History of the Kishacoquillas Valley Railroad* (Belleville, Penn.: John G. Hartzler, 1988), p. 16.

175. John Tigges and Jon Jacobson, *Milwaukee Road Narrow Gauge* (Boulder, Colo.: Pruett Publishing Co., 1985), p. 62.

176. E. A. Ziffer, C.E., "On the Gauges of Railroad Track in General, With Special Consideration of Narrow Gauge Railroads," *Transactions of the American Society of Civil Engineers*, 29 (1893), pp. 453–90.

177. *Railroad Gazette*, 25 (1893), p. 721.

Locomotives

The Fairlie

If we take Robert F. Fairlie at his word that without his locomotive *"the value of the narrow gauge at once sinks into comparative insignificance,"* we must begin our consideration of American narrow gauge locomotives with the Fairlie. That proves a short inquiry, for domestic narrow gauges had the grand total of one Fairlie, and its history was a limited one. Its rejection was part of a rapid movement away from specialized narrow gauge power to scaled-down versions of standard gauge locomotives.

William J. Palmer was sufficiently devoted to Fairlie's doctrinal orthodoxy that the Denver & Rio Grande ordered one Fairlie from a firm that had produced several others, the Vulcan Foundry Co. of Newton-le-Willows, Lancashire, England.[1] The model was a standard 0-4+4-0, similar to Fairlies produced for operators in Peru and New Zealand in the same period.[2] It had the usual symmetrical design of boilers fore-and-aft, with a swivelling bogie beneath each. Like Fairlie's later models, the engine had two fireboxes, each with a grate area of about 12 square feet. The cylinders were 10″×18″, the drivers 39″, the tractive effort 9,280 pounds, and the total weight 62,000 pounds—as usual in the Fairlie, all on the drivers. The engine carried 1,700 pounds of coal and 800 gallons of water. The locomotive was 28 feet long, plus the pilots, which brought it to 34 feet. It was relatively wide, with a mahogany cab 9′-6″ across.[3] The price of the engine was £2,900, about triple that of the D&RG's existing conventional power.[4] The engine was built under an incentive contract, in which the builder warranted it to pull 200 tons up the grade of 1 in 80 (1.25 percent) south from Denver, agreeing to refund £7/5/0 for each ton short of 200 it was able to haul in its trials.[5]

While the engine was under construction in 1872, the D&RG changed its mind and sought to have the design modified to an 0-6+6-0. Fairlie wrote that the builder would charge £525 to change the wheel arrangement. He considered this sum "monstrous," and counseled the railroad to accept the engine as an 0-4+4-0, but to order an 0-6+6-0 to follow it. He

The one narrow gauge Fairlie locomotive built for American service, the Denver & Rio Grande's *Mountaineer*, is shown in service. The engine's double-ended configuration lent itself to helper operation. It spent most of its career assisting freights up Veta Pass. (Smithsonian Institution.)

offered to make up the difference in price between an 0-4+4-0 and an 0-6+6-0 himself. He clearly considered the demonstration on the D&RG vital to his promotion of the Fairlie locomotive and the narrow gauge as integral: "I am fully alive to the necessity for making the narrow roads as powerful and useful as the broad ones, and if we don't do this then we will fail to do what we have said we could do, and are no longer to be trusted by the public—it is therefore with this view before me that I strongly recommend the two engines that you may prove all I have said for gauges on your 3 ft line." [6]

The locomotive, which bore the builder's number 273, was shipped as an 0-4+4-0 on May 10, 1873, and arrived in Denver on June 20.[7] Initially the engine was numbered 13 and given the name *Mountaineer*, but it subsequently bore 101 and 1001.[8] At the formal test on September 17 the locomotive hauled 16 cars of coal from Denver to Divide at speeds no worse than 11 miles per hour. The Denver *Daily Times* estimated the load at 198 tons, but whether this was enough to satisfy the incentive contract was not reported.[9] Palmer expressed himself as pleased with the engine, mainly for the prospect of its saving labor expenses, but negative reports had already appeared in the press. The engine was too wide for clearances at the Denver roundhouse, and its grate area was reportedly too limited for the soft Colorado coal with which it was fired.[10]

By the end of 1874 the Fairlie had run 17,929 miles. In March 1875, William S. Jackson requested of John Greenwood, the railroad's master mechanic, an evaluation of the engine. Greenwood responded with a comparison with the company's early Baldwin 2-6-0 locomotives. On the favorable side, he reported that the Fairlie could handle at least a third more weight than the Baldwins, perhaps 12 cars on the grade south from Denver versus eight. The Fairlie also rode more smoothly, tracked curves with greater facility, and had more adhesion than the Baldwins. On the adverse side, however, it was much more expensive to operate. In 1873, when new, it cost 26.07¢ per mile, versus 16.72¢ for the railroad's locomotives as a whole, including the Fairlie. The engine ran 39.1 miles per ton of coal, as compared with 81.18 miles for the road's power generally. In 1874, the performance of the Fairlie was slightly worse, 26.26¢ per mile to operate compared with 15.96¢ for the roster generally. Greenwood estimated that dropping the Fairlie from the average of all locomotives would lower the average by about half a cent. The Fairlie in 1874 ran only 28.82 miles per ton of coal, and the system's average had also dropped to 73.01 miles. For 1875 he expected the Fairlie to operate at not below 30¢ per mile because of heavy repair expense.

Specifically, Greenwood complained that the engine's cylinders were too short for the length of stroke, causing the pistons to be too thin to allow rings of sufficient strength to keep the packing from blowing. The engine had required three sets of packing rings already in its short history. He then made what proved to be very general complaints against the design:

The coal and water space on the Fairlie is not sufficiently large—the water tanks will not carry more than half enough to run from one tank to another—for this purpose we have fitted a car with a water tank and coal room.
The flexible steam pipes cannot be kept tight—they have always leaked.
The machinery is very inaccessible for repairs.
It is very inconvenient getting water and fuel from the tender car to the Engine—the coal has to be handled twice, and the water not having much head runs slowly and it is difficult to keep it from freezing in cold weather.
In addition to this I think the engine is very heavy carrying from 30 to 32 tons, when fully loaded with coal and water on the same number of wheels that the Baldwin engines have, they weighing only 17½ tons.
. . .[I]n taking water at our water stations, our water spouts are too low for the Fairlie and a great deal of water is wasted[;] this running down, washes coal &c on the machinery, causing it to wear faster than it would otherwise.[11]

The Fairlie's reputation was to become worse, not better. Relative to the D&RG's second generation of motive power introduced after 1878, the engine was considered underpowered and hard on track. The locomotive was used mainly as a helper on the 4 percent grades of Veta Pass. After earning from operating personnel the pejorative nickname "Modoc"— a particularly depressed Indian tribe—it was withdrawn in 1883 and scrapped in 1888.[12] The D&RG never accepted Fairlie's suggestion to follow the engine with an 0-6+6-0, and neither the D&RG nor any other American narrow gauge showed any inclination to pursue the design at all.

The only other American Fairlie was a standard gauge 0-6+6-0, the *Janus*, built under license by William Mason in late 1869 for service on the western slope of the Sierra Nevadas on the Central Pacific.[13] The engine, as far as is known, was never sent to California, but was given tests on the Taunton Branch Railroad, Boston & Albany, and Lehigh Valley. Its performance was not any more satisfactory than the *Mountaineer*'s. In trials on the Lehigh Valley in 1872, apparently on a 2.7 percent grade on the

Hazleton branch, the *Janus* proved itself inferior to the railroad's own 0-8-0 and 2-8-0 power. Alexander Mitchell, superintendent, wrote to W. W. Evans: "The Fairlie Engine 'Janus' has not satisfied me of her superior qualities over the old system. . . . I endorse statement of trial made on a steep grade, where with 130 lbs. pressure, she developed 13½ net tons tractive power, the eight-wheeled connected 20 × 24 in. cylinders developing 11½ tons. The steampipes have given much trouble from leakage, and I question their ever being kept tight. They are not to be depended on. . . . [I] could not recommend their adoption by any person or company."[14] The *Janus* was either scrapped or cut up into two 0-6-0 shop switchers.

We have plenty of foreign experience on which to draw for additional evaluations. The Toronto & Nipissing had an 0-6+6-0, *Shedden*, and the Toronto, Grey & Bruce an essentially identical engine, *Caledon*, both built by the Avonside Engine Co. of Bristol.[15] The Glasgow & Cape Breton Railway, a rare Canadian 3'-0" line, had three 0-4+4-0s from Avonside.[16] The most successful installation of the Fairlie was on the Ferrocarril Mexicano, a standard gauge railroad between Vera Cruz and Mexico City, built with narrow gauge standards of gradients and curvature. For over 50 years from the early 1870s to the mid-1920s, Fairlies worked the ascent from Cordoba to Boca del Monte, 43 miles. Some 51 Fairlies were employed in the service, displaced only when the company electrified from Paso del Macho to Esperanza, encompassing the Fairlies' district, between 1923 and 1928.[17] A similar installation of Fairlies was on the Sourain inclines of the Trans-Caucasian Railway in Russia.

On the basis of worldwide experience with the engine, Rowland A. S. Abbott in his *The Fairlie Locomotive* concluded that the design's intrinsic flaws were limited fuel and water capacity, instability at high speeds, high repair expenses on dual boilers, and chronic problems with articulated steam pipes.[18] An incidental disattraction was cramped space for the engineer and firemen, who were separated by the firebox, coupled with an awkward right angle for stoking. A committee of the American Railway Master Mechanics' Association in 1870 reported that the engine properly required two firemen.[19] In sum, the Denver & Rio Grande's experience was entirely representative of international judgment of the Fairlie.

The Mason Bogie

William Mason attempted to deal with the problems of the Fairlie while retaining the alleged attraction of the swivelling power truck by producing a single-boilered version, known as the Mason-Fairlie, or more familiarly in America as the Mason Bogie. A single rigid frame supported the boiler forward and the tender portion aft. Mason's principal innovation was his method of channeling steam to the cylinders. Fairlie in his early locomotives used a flexible copper pipe to bring steam to the cylinders, but Mason on the *Janus* used a pipe and ball joint projecting from the underside of the smokebox. This arrangement also entailed leakage and cooling of the steam before it reached the cylinders.[20] The power-truck of the locomotives swivelled on a center plate like the truck of an ordinary passenger or freight car. In 1874 Mason patented an arrangement by which the steam line was run down through the smokebox, back under the boiler through

the center plate to a ball joint on the truck, and thence forward to the cylinders (U.S. Patent No. 156,031, October 20, 1874). This method also entailed long exposed pipes and a ball joint, so that cooling and leakage of the steam remained a problem.

Mason's design entailed similar problems in exhaust. In his early examples, Mason used a pipe-and-ball-joint connection to the smokebox for exhaust, but in 1876 he patented an arrangement whereby the steam exhausted through a vent in the cylinder saddle that moved laterally under a petticoat pipe extending down from the smokebox (U.S. Patent No. 177,343, May 16, 1876). This arrangement was also subject to leakage.

When Mason began running his steam line forward from the center plate of his truck, he added to the demands on space in a constricted area. His early examples of the Mason Bogie, including his first narrow gauge engine, *Onward* of the American Fork Railroad of Utah, used Stephenson valve gear in the usual fashion of locomotives of the time. The Stephenson gear, which was considered well suited to small locomotives, operated by two eccentrics off the main axle inside the drivers. A reversing shaft crossed under the boiler between the drivers. Especially on a narrow gauge locomotive, it was difficult to accommodate all this on a swiveling truck. Specifically, the steam pipe running longitudinally and the reversing shaft running transversely were difficult to separate. Apparently to deal with this problem, Mason in the mid-1870s adopted the Walschaerts valve gear, mounted outside the drivers, and ran the reversing shaft across the top of the boiler. The Boston, Revere Beach & Lynn mounted its bells on its shaft, gaining an automatic bellringer nearly costlessly. Mason became the first large-scale user of the Walschaerts gear, which along with the Baker was to become one of the two most common types in twentieth-century practice. For some of his later standard gauge examples, he reverted to Ste-

The Boston, Revere Beach & Lynn's devotion to the Mason Bogie extended to ordering the design from other builders after Mason left the industry. Its No. 14 was built by Alco-Manchester in 1902. The diaphragm for the Eames braking system is conspicuous under the running board immediately in front of the cab. (Ed Bond collection.)

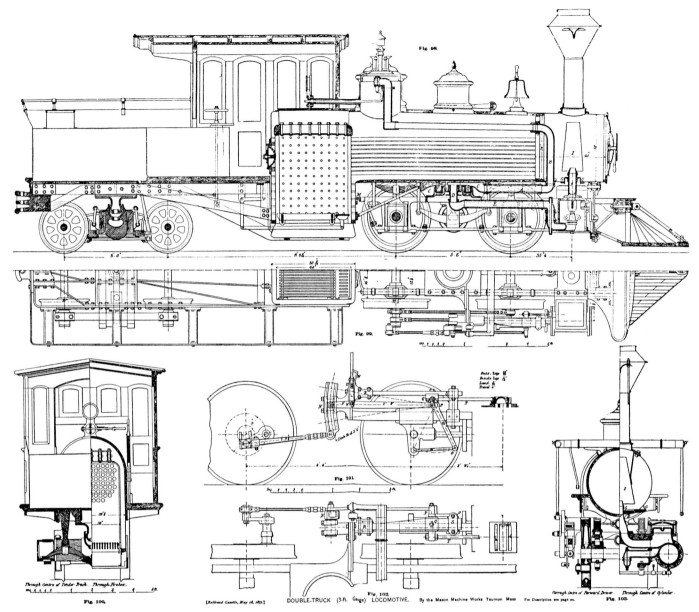

DOUBLE-TRUCK (3-ft. Gauge) LOCOMOTIVE. By the Mason Machine Works Taunton Mass For Description see page 200.

The anatomy of the Mason Bogie locomotive. Note particularly the connection from the steam dome to the cylinders through a pipe (D in the side elevation) through the plate on which the engine truck swivels. The pipe forward from this to the cylinders (E) required the overhead transverse shaft characteristic of the Mason Bogie. From *Recent Locomotives* (1886).

phenson motion, further indicating that the spatial limitations of narrow gauge power led him to the Walschaerts gear.[21]

Mason had great confidence in the design and advocated it as particularly suited to the narrow gauge:

The boiler and tank . . . united form the body of the engine, which, like the body of a car, is mounted on bogies. By means of the flexibility of these bogies with their springs, equalizers, jointed steam pipes, &c., the whole working machinery becomes perfectly articulated, which allows the wheels to follow all the undulations of the track, and so divides its inequalities through the whole system that the disturbing forces are reduced to a minimum, or nearly lost. The body of the engine, therefore, glides along as quietly and smoothly as a Pullman car.

It runs either way equally well, and will turn the sharpest curves with perfect ease, and without cutting the flanges of its tires or spreading the rails. Roads using these locomotives can have the rails on their curves set up to the regular gauge of the track, instead of spreading them, as is necessary where the common type of engine is used.

This system is particularly advantageous on a narrow gauge, not merely on account of the facility with which these engines turn quick curves and climb steep

grades, but especially for the amount of space allowed the fire-box. This feature alone would seem to make the system indispensable. The fire-box being situated between the trucks, (not between the wheels, as in other engines,) can be made of any width or length desired; in fact there is nothing in the way, and the boiler can be made of the most approved proportions without interfering with anything.[22]

Mason produced about 146 Bogies, of which about 88 were narrow gauge.[23] This amounts to about half the firm's output from June 1871, when the first was sent to the Calumet & Hecla Mining Co., to March 1890, when Mason built his last locomotive, a standard gauge Bogie for the Old Colony Railroad. Mason wrote to a prospective foreign buyer in 1875 that prices ran from $10,000 to $13,000, depending upon size and capacity.[24] They were, accordingly, relatively expensive engines. The managing director of the New York & Manhattan Beach Railway, when ordering two, estimated the price at $1,500 to $2,000 above locomotives of the same cylinder size from other builders.[25]

By far the largest user of Mason Bogies was the Boston, Revere Beach & Lynn, a suburban passenger carrier which eventually owned 32. Of the general freight and passenger railroads, the principal user was the Denver, South Park & Pacific, which bought 23 between 1878 and 1880. The third-largest operator was the New York & Manhattan Beach, a passenger carrier in Brooklyn, which bought 17 of 0-4-4, 2-4-4, and 2-4-6 configurations. The South Park Line's engines, being designed for heavy duty, ranged between 2-6-6 and 2-8-6 wheel arrangements. The 2-8-6 locomotives had 15″×20″ cylinders, 36″ drivers, and a weight of 55,340 lbs. on the drivers, comparable to orthodox 2-8-0s. The line's Masons had a good reputation for steaming. A large number of narrow gauges had one or two Mason Bogies. The Peach Bottom, for example, bought an 0-6-6 in 1876, but found it hard-riding, destructive to track, and prone to derailment. The engine was retired in 1878 on delivery of a Baldwin 2-6-0.[26] Most opera-

The *Admiral Almy*, a Mason Bogie built for the New York & Manhattan Beach, illustrates the basic features of the design, notably the wide firebox and the Walschaerts valve gear with an overhead transverse rod integral with the bell standard. (W. A. Lucas collection, Railroad Museum of Pennsylvania.)

tors had no more favorable experiences. The South Park Line's Mason Bogies were mainly scrapped in 1889–90.[27]

A design that sells nearly 150 locomotives cannot be considered a total failure, but the Mason Bogie was assuredly not a success. Although its problems are usually said to center around its leakage of steam, its most serious flaw was the basic element of novelty in the design, the swivelling truck. Far from traversing curves as smoothly as the trucks of a Pullman car, as Mason had written, the power truck was continually hunting for curvature, producing the consequences the Peach Bottom had observed, spreading the light narrow gauge rail, riding badly, and derailing frequently. In addition, the flanges wore rapidly. This was a source of concern even to operators generally pleased with the design. J. W. Nesmith, Superintendent of the South Park Line, wrote to John Evans, president of the company:

> The engine No. 3, Oro City, made by Mason has so far, with some slight exceptions, given entire satisfaction and is a thoroughly good engine.
> The exceptions are that the tyres are cutting badly and will have to be turned much too soon—they seem to be very soft—also the main links and all oil holes should have suitable caps to keep out cinders and dirt. On the whole, so far, I have seen no other narrow gauge engine, the performance of which has pleased me so well as this one. I have therefore to recommend this style of engine as best suited to our traffic.[28]

John H. White, Jr., wrote the following evaluation of a former narrow gauge Mason Bogie (converted from 4'-1") used to haul visitors at the Ford Museum in Dearborn, Michigan:

> While visiting the Ford Museum May 15, 1980, I was given a ride on the Mason Bogie locomotive *Torch Lake*, built in 1873. It was outfitted with a new boiler and given general repairs before being put into service. I was told by the superintendent of the tourist railroad, that they had considerable trouble with the front right tire of the locomotive wearing. I mentioned the whole point of the bogie was the swiveling or articulated running gear to help ease the engine into curves and thus reduce or avoid such wear. But it appears that the front or power truck turns with some difficulty. In fact, when they first received the engine it had settled down somewhat on the front end and turned hardly at all. Hence all of the complicated flexible pipe connections seem rather pointless, since the looked for result of the bogie design does not result in an easy tracking engine.
> In one instance the front tire wore so thin that it broke, and derailed the locomotive. They have checked it more carefully since that time and have since replaced it again just in the few years that the engine has been running (at very low speeds) around the grounds of the Ford Museum. If this condition were true for other bogies built by Mason, it may explain why they never gained greater popularity. So perhaps it was not just the steam leaks, the usual explanation for the Bogies' failure to win more customers, but in fact that mechanically no advantage was found in this complicated design.[29]

The conclusion that the design of the Mason Bogie was poorly suited to curvature is consistent with the one success of the engine, its experience on the Boston, Revere Beach & Lynn. This railroad operated almost totally with Bogies, buying 11 from Mason and then arranging for Taunton to build two and for Manchester to build 16 more after Mason's cessation of production in 1890. The line bought its last three Bogies from Alco-Schenectady as late as 1914, and operated with the Bogies until the rail-

The Forney locomotive had its widest application on the Maine 2'-0" railroads. Here is a large example, Sandy River & Rangeley Lakes No. 10 at Phillips about 1916. (Robert C. Jones collection.)

road was electrified in 1928.[30] The line had no significant curvature and no freight service.

An alternative design that placed the boiler and tender on a single frame, but with a rigid set of drivers, was available throughout the narrow gauge era in the form of the Forney locomotive, which Matthias N. Forney had developed for main-line suburban service and rapid transit. There is a certain irony in the engine of Forney, the principal opponent of the narrow gauge, being well suited to the demand of narrow gauge operators. From the outset on the Billerica & Bedford, the Forney was the typical locomotive of the 2'-0" railroads. With 0-4-4 and 2-4-4 configurations, Forneys operated the service for the Maine 2'-0" lines that 4-4-0 locomotives provided elsewhere. The Maine lines had 31 Forneys and only 7 tender engines.[31] Forneys remained active until the end of the Maine narrow gauges with the abandonment of the Monson Railroad in 1943. There were also 3'-0" Forneys, notably on the New York & Manhattan Beach, and on short lines that made train connections, such as the Saginaw & Mount Pleasant.[32]

Porter Locomotives

When, as in Britain, American industrial railways began conversion to steam in the 1860s, a demand arose for small steam locomotives. Accordingly, by the time the narrow gauge movement came to America in 1871, there was in existence a firm of specialized narrow gauge locomotive builders, founded by Henry K. Porter in 1866. Initially, Porter operated as Smith & Porter in partnership with John Y. Smith. By 1871 the firm had built about 100 locomotives, mainly 0-4-0 engines, but in February of that year its plant was destroyed by fire. Smith withdrew to establish the National Locomotive Works in Connellsville, but Porter formed a partnership with Arthur W. Bell as Porter, Bell & Co. When Bell died in May

10x16 NARROW GAUGE PASSENGER LOCOMOTIVE.

Other Styles, Light Passenger, 8x16; Freight, 12x16, 10x16, 9½x14; Special Service and Mine Engines, 14x20, 12x18, 12x16, 10x16, 9x16, 8x16, 9x14, 8x14, 7x12; and 9x12 inside connected.

PORTER, BELL & CO., BUILDERS OF LIGHT LOCOMOTIVES,

OFFICE, No. 5 MONONGAHELA HOUSE. PITTSBURGH, PENN'A. WORKS, A. V. R. R. AND 50TH STREET

Porter's stock model heavy passenger locomotive was a long-wheelbase 2-4-0 with 10″ × 16″ cylinders. This engine was built for the Cairo & St. Louis, and named for its president, S. Staats Taylor. (Smithsonian Institution.)

1878, Porter reorganized as H. K. Porter & Co. He incorporated in 1899, and his firm remained the dominant American producer of industrial locomotives until the truck and the forklift had rendered industrial railroads obsolete. It gave up locomotive production in 1951, but remains a major producer of heavy industrial products.[33]

Porter's method of operation made the firm particularly attractive to new narrow gauge operators. Porter built its locomotives in a series of standard models, described in detail in a catalog entitled *Light Locomotives*, first issued in 1873. The firm had a 4-4-0 locomotive which it was willing to produce with cylinders from 12″×16″ to 13″×18″, but it recommended against the design for narrow gauge operators:

The "Eight-wheel" or "American" pattern of locomotive is deservedly a favorite for general use on broad-gauge roads throughout the United States, and hence has been very largely adopted by narrow-gauge roads.

We believe, however, that a narrow-gauge engine should be something more than a miniature copy of a wide-gauge engine, and that the construction necessary on a large engine should be simplified on a small engine where it can be done advantageously.

We regard the "Eight-wheel" pattern, especially the smaller sizes, for narrow-gauge passenger service as objectionable in the following particulars:

The weight is not distributed to secure the maximum of power, the proportion of dead to useful weight being excessive.

The truck wheels are necessarily of smaller diameter than is advisable for high speeds; or to secure larger truck wheels the boiler is set higher and the centre of weight raised more than is desirable for fast running.

The engine does not conform to sharp curves and uneven track, so as to secure the easiest motion attainable.

While we recommend [2-4-0] engines . . . in preference to the "Eight-wheel" pattern, we wish to meet the views of all customers, and are prepared to furnish this style of sizes as specified. In perfecting our designs we have to as great an extent as possible overcome the objectionable features of "Eight-wheel" narrow-gauge engines.[34]

Porter intended its 0-6-0 locomotives as low-speed freight engines. This example pulled the passenger trains of the Martha's Vineyard Railroad, however. (Munson Paddock collection, Railroad Museum of Pennsylvania.)

The 2-4-0 locomotives Porter recommended were offered in three sizes. The largest was essentially its 4-4-0, with a single pair of wheels 26″ to 30″ in diameter substituted for the leading truck. The center of gravity was made exceptionally low, and the long flexible wheelbase was said to be well suited to rough track and frequent curves. The medium model was basically an 0-4-0 with a pair of leading wheels added. Engines could be ordered with 10″×16″ or 11″×16″ cylinders and 36″ to 44″ drivers. The locomotive could handle trains of 625 to 700 tons on level ground, as compared with 700 to 850 tons for the larger models. The light version had cylinders of 8″×12″ or 9″×14″, 30″ to 36″ drivers, and a hauling capacity of 325 to 425 tons. The medium and light models could be ordered as tank engines.

Similarly, Porter offered freight locomotives in 0-6-0 and 2-6-0 configurations. The standard model of the 2-6-0 could be ordered with cylinders from 12″×16″ to 13″×18″, and a gross weight of 35,000 to 45,000 pounds. Here the builder strove for a low center of gravity and a short wheelbase to suit narrow gauge rights-of-way.

The Pittsburgh Locomotive Works' 4-4-0 was very highly regarded as a passenger engine, and widely adopted among the narrow gauges. This example went to the Cleveland, Delphos & St. Louis. (Thomas T. Taber collection, Railroad Museum of Pennsylvania.)

Porter used uniform fittings on the engines, and maintained an inventory of replacement parts from which it made immediate shipments upon telegraphic order. The locomotives were designed for easy replacement of parts by shop personnel of only moderate mechanical ability. Porter used a forged iron frame that was highly regarded.[35]

Some narrow gauge operators used Porter locomotives exclusively. The Bedford, Springville, Owensburg & Bloomfield had an 0-4-0, an 0-6-0, and three 2-4-0s, all from Porter, with which it operated throughout its narrow gauge history.[36] Porter repeated its argument for the greater suitability of the 2-4-0 relative to the 4-4-0 for narrow gauge use in *Light Locomotives* as late as the 7th edition in 1892,[37] but produced few for domestic operators after 1881.[38]

A more typical experience was that of the Peach Bottom system. The Middle Division, which became the north end of the Maryland & Pennsylvania, began operation with two Porter engines of 1874, bought a Mason Bogie in 1876, but thereafter bought scaled-down versions of standard gauge power in 4-4-0 and 2-6-0 wheel arrangements from Baldwin and Pittsburgh.[39] The Eastern Division of the Peach Bottom, which became the Lancaster, Oxford & Southern, first bought two Porter 2-4-0s, but then moved on to four 4-4-0s from Pittsburgh, Mount Savage, and Baldwin.[40] The Toledo, Cincinnati & St. Louis and its predecessors, the Toledo & Maumee, the Toledo, Delphos & Indianapolis, and the Toledo, Delphos & Burlington, all opened their rosters with Porter, Bell locomotives, but later the TC&StL turned to Porter almost only for suburban tank engines and bought its road engines, mainly 4-4-0s, 2-6-0s, and 2-8-0s, from Pittsburgh, Baldwin, Hinkley, Brooks, and some smaller builders.[41]

Porter took pride in its engines. The accounts in its catalog of what the various models could do are a good indication of what was considered satisfactory or exceptional performance by narrow gauge standards. Table 5.1 reproduces a set of reports (with dates) for various lines classified by type of Porter engine.

TABLE 5.1

Reports of Service of Porter Locomotives

Size of cylinders	Owner and Location, and Date of Report	Weight of rail	Length of road	Radius of sharpest curve	Grade in feet per mile	Number of cars hauled	Weight of each car	Load on each car	Weight of train	Remarks
					HEAVY 2-4-0					
10 × 16	Cairo & St. Louis R. R. St. Louis, Mo. (1877)	40 lb.	147 mls.	573 ft.	95 ft.	4 [a]			68 tons	Has hauled 5 cars = 84 tons. Usual mileage 147 miles per day of 6½ hours, burning 2,000 lb. coal. Regular 25, and best 40 miles per hour, except one run of 9 miles in 10 minutes. Ran 180 miles per day for a year or more, and ran 5,747 miles in one month.
10 × 16	Peach Bottom R. W., M. Div. York, Pa. (1875)	30 lb.	28 mls.	300 ft.	105 ft.	4 [a]			56 tons	478 feet curve on grade; has hauled 6 cars = 91 tons. 2,040 lb. coal, 1½ tanks, 144 miles, 7½ hours. Has run 36 miles per hour (36-inch drivers). Ran 170 miles in one day, and 30,500 miles in one year.
11 × 16	Port Huron & N. W. R. R. Port Huron, Mich. (1881)	30 lb.	118 mls.	1433 ft.	53 ft.	16	9,500 lb.	16,000 lb.	196 tons	Usual work is less. Has hauled 6 loaded cars 6 miles in 9 minutes up 53 feet grade.
	Same on return trip	30 lb.	118 mls.	1433 ft.	80 ft.	{ 8 1 1	9,500 lb. passenger car baggage car	16,000 lb.	about 120 tons	140 miles, 3 tons coal daily. 3,650 miles average monthly mileage, exclusive of making up trains.
11 × 16	B. S. O. & B. R. R. Bedford, Ind. (1878)	35 lb.	41 mls.	382 ft.	85 ft.	7	10,250 lb.	25,000 lb.	123 tons	Has hauled 8 cars. 12° reverse curve on steepest grade. 82 miles per 7½ hours. Frequently hauls from quarries loads of 36,000 lbs. on a car, and hauled on 1 car a flagstone 22 feet 10 inches long, 11 feet wide and 2 feet thick, weighing 24 tons.
11 × 16	Chagrin Falls & Southern R'y Chagrin Falls, Ohio (1888)	30 lb.	5 mls.	. . .	95 ft.	6	18,000 lb.	10,000 lb.	84 tons	Grade 1½ miles long. Has hauled 8 cars = 152 tons. Regular speed 15, and fastest 20 miles per hour. 40 to 60 miles, 2 tanks water, 1,200 lbs. coal fuel daily.
11 × 16	Hot Springs R. R. Hot Springs, Ark. (1878)	35 lb.	24 mls.	318 ft.	150 ft.	{ 4 1	9,000 lb. passenger	14,000 lb.	57 tons	Has hauled 8 cars = 93 tons. Regular speed 18, and best 40 miles per hour over whole road. Usual mileage 100 miles in 10 hours, best, 200 miles in 14 hours. 1½ cords wood and 2 tanks per 10 hours. Grade 1½ miles long.
13 × 18	Hot Springs R. R. Hot Springs, Ark. (1881)	35 lb.	22 mls.	521 ft.	158 ft.	{ 4 4	freight passenger cars		98 tons	2⅓ cords of wood, 90 to 150 miles per day. Usual speed 18, and best 35 miles per hour for regular runs.
					MEDIUM 2-4-0					
9 × 16	Havana, Rantoul & E. R. R. Rantoul, Ill. (1876)	30 lb.	40 mls.	3700 ft.	52 ft.	16	9,000 lb.	14,500 lb.	188 tons	Has hauled 22 cars partly loaded, total weight about 200 tons. Mileage 70 to 140 miles per day. Usual speed 10 or 15 miles, and best speed 30 to 35 miles per hour.

TABLE 5.1

(Continued)

Size of cylinders	Owner and Location, and Date of Report	Weight of rail	Length of road	Radius of sharpest curve	Grade in feet per mile	Number of cars hauled	Weight of each car	Load on each car	Weight of train	Remarks
10 × 16	Peach Bottom R. W., E. Div. Oxford, Pa. (1875)	30 lb.	28 mls.	300 ft.	105 ft.	7	8,000 lb.	{ 12,000 lb. 18,000 lb. }	84 tons	93 to 128 miles. ½ ton coal and 2 tanks water per 12 hours.
10 × 16	Marietta & No. Georgia R. R. Marietta, Ga. (1884)	30 lb.	. . .	382 ft.	105 ft.	6	12,000 lb.	18,000 lb.	90 tons	Grade 3 miles long; curve comes on grade 142 miles, 3,400 lb. coal fuel, 5 tanks of water per day of 8 hours, running 7 days per week.
10 × 16	Waynesburg & Wash. R. R. Waynesburg, Pa. (1877)	30 lb.	28½ mls.	185 ft.	137 ft.	5	8,000 lb.	12,000 lb.	50 tons	Has hauled more. Curve is on grade. Has hauled 5 empty cars up straight grade of 280 feet per mile, and around 80 feet radius curve on temporary track.
10 × 16	East Line & Red River R. R. Jefferson, Texas (1878)	30 lb.	90 mls.	200 ft.	80 ft.	11	9,000 lb.	16,000 lb.	137 tons	Curve and grade come together; 100 miles per day.
10 × 16	Columbus, Wash. & Cin. R. R. Dayton, Ohio (1890)	30 lb.	20 mls.	. . .	80 ft.	14	10,000 lb.	16,000 lb.	182 tons	600 lb. coal per 40 miles run. Usual speed 10, and best 35 miles per hour. Has made 180 miles per day, and 3,590 miles per month.
9 × 16	Toledo, Delphos & I. R. R. Delphos, Ohio (1877)	30 lb.	16 mls.	. . .	26 ft.	8	8,000 lb.	16,000 lb.	96 tons	Has hauled 11 loaded cars. Regular speed 16 miles per hour, and usual mileage 64 to 96 miles per day.

LIGHT 2-4-0

Size of cylinders	Owner and Location, and Date of Report	Weight of rail	Length of road	Radius of sharpest curve	Grade in feet per mile	Number of cars hauled	Weight of each car	Load on each car	Weight of train	Remarks
9 × 14	DeLand & St. Johns River R'y. DeLand, Fla. (1884)	16 lb.	5 mls.	286 ft.	157 ft.	{ 1 3	passenger freight cars }		50 tons	30 to 60 miles daily, burning 1 cord of wood per day of 16 hours.
7 × 12	South Florida R. R. Sanford, Fla. (1881)	16 lb.	22 mls.	. . .	20 ft.	5	about 5,000 lb.	10,000 lb.	37 tons	Has hauled 7 cars, weighing 52 tons. Usual speed 20, and best 25 miles per hour with 3 loaded cars. 67 miles ⅔ cord wood fuel, 3 tanks water per day, of 10 hours. Has made 140 miles per day of 14 hours. Monthly mileage, 1,725 miles.
8 × 16	Toledo & Maumee N. G. R. R. Toledo, Ohio (1875)	25 lb.	7½ mls.	250 ft.	52 ft.	{ 1 1	passenger boxcar }		18 tons	1,500 lb. coal fuel, 90 miles per 12 hours; hauled 5 cars (53 tons), and ran 140 miles in excursion season. Best speed 30 miles per hour.
8 × 16	Port Huron & N. W. R. R. Port Huron, Mich. (1880)	30 lb.	46 mls.	1433 ft.	52 ft.	9	11,000 lb.	18,000 lb.	130 tons	3,000 lb. coal fuel, 184 miles per 12 hours; has run 236 miles in 14½ hours, and 5,200 miles per year. Usual speed 13 to 20, and best 30 miles per hour.
8 × 16	Peach Bottom R. W., E. Div. Oxford, Pa. (1875)	30 lb.	28 mls.	300 ft.	105 ft.	5	8,000 lb.	12,000 lb.	50 tons	Grade 1 mile long; has hauled 6 freight and 1 passenger car. Ran 16 miles in 34 minutes.

TABLE 5.1

(Continued)

Size of cylinders	Owner and Location, and Date of Report	Weight of rail	Length of road	Radius of sharpest curve	Grade in feet per mile	Number of cars hauled	Weight of each car	Load on each car	Weight of train	Remarks
						4-4-0				
12 × 16	Waynesburg & Wash. R. R. Waynesburg, Pa. (1881)	30 lb.	28½ mls.	185 ft.	137 ft.	1 1 4	passenger baggage car 8,000 lb.	16,000 lb.	63 tons	3,800 lbs. coal fuel, 112 to 140 miles per day. Curve is on grade.
11 × 16	Suffolk & Carolina R. R.[b] Suffolk, Va. (1888)	35 lb.	40 mls.	716 ft.	66 ft.	25	6,720 lb.	15,680 lb.	280 tons	Has hauled 35 cars = 392 tons. Grade 1,200 feet long, with 4° curve. Usual speed 30, and best 40 miles per hour.
						2-6-0				
12 × 16	St. Louis Cable & West. R'y. St. Louis, Mo. (1888)	40 lb.	15 mls.	. . .	150 ft.	3	20,000 lb.	8,000 lb.	42 tons	Has hauled 13 cars, carrying about 1,600 passengers, up grade of 105 feet per mile. Has run 228 miles in 31 hours, and made 25 miles per hour. One ton coal fuel per 100 miles.
12 × 16	B. S. O. & B. R. R. Bedford, Ind. (1878)	35 lb.	42 mls.	383 ft.	85 ft.	12	10,250 lb.	16,000 lb.	159 tons	Has frequently hauled 16 loaded cars = 210 tons. Ran 184 miles with 2,310 lbs. coal. Annual mileage 24,666 miles.
12 × 18	Arizona & New Mexico R'y. Lordsburg, N.M. (1884)	35 lb.	75 mls.	200 ft.	105 ft.	9	12,000 lb.	14,000 lb.	117 tons	Usual speed per hour 15 miles on easy grades, and 10 miles on heavy grades; best speed 35 miles. 2,000 lbs. coal fuel and 2 tanks of water each trip of 71 miles. 150 miles per day. Grade 5 miles long; curve comes on grade.
12 × 16	Houston, E. & W. Texas R. R. Houston, Tex. (1881)	35 lb.	100 mls.	1910 ft.	80 ft.	26	about 9,000 lb.	22,500 lb.	410 tons	Has hauled 30 cars weighing about 435 tons, 12 to 20 miles per hour. 100 miles. 3 cords wood fuel, 3 tanks water per day of 10 hours.

SOURCE: H. K. Porter & Co., *Light Locomotives*, 6th ed. (Pittsburgh, 1889), pp. 86–147 *passim*.
[a] Passenger cars only.
[b] 42 in. gauge.

Conventional Narrow Gauge Locomotives

The Denver & Rio Grande used no Porter locomotives in its formative years, but the same trend from light 2-4-0 and 2-6-0 power to 4-4-0, heavier 2-6-0, and 2-8-0 engines was evident. The company began its history with 12 Baldwin locomotives bought between 1871 and 1873, four 2-4-0 passenger engines weighing only 12½ tons each, and eight 2-6-0 freight engines of 17½ tons. The 2-4-0s were intermediate in weight between Porter's light and medium models of the same wheel arrangement. The 2-6-0s were approximately the same size as Porter's Moguls.[42]

As will be evident in Chapter 6, the D&RG moved quickly away from four-wheel equipment, thereby increasing the weight of trains. In 1876 the railroad began a penetration of the Rocky Mountains with its ascent of Veta Pass. Because the new trackage had 4 percent grades and curves up to 30°, some trend toward larger locomotives was inevitable. In 1876 the company bought three 4-4-0s of Class 37, nearly 50 percent heavier than the original 2-4-0s. The new power had 11"×16" cylinders, 44" drivers, and a tractive effort of 4,750 pounds. The engines of the next order, Class 38 of 1878–80, were of about the same weight, but had 12"×16" cylinders, 45" drivers, and tractive effort to 5,560 pounds. With Class 42 of 1880, the principal dimensions were unchanged but weight rose to 40,000 lbs., cylinder size to 12"×18", and tractive effort to 6,380 pounds.[43]

The trend in the D&RG's freight engines was even more marked. The original 2-6-0s weighed 35,000 pounds and exerted 5,940 pounds of tractive effort. The Class 40 2-6-0s of 1876 weighed 46,000 pounds and provided 7,060 pounds of tractive effort. Beginning in 1877 with the *Alamosa*, the D&RG bought over 150 2-8-0 locomotives, mainly in two groups, Class 56 with 15"×18" cylinders and 12,450 pounds of tractive effort, and Class 60 with 15"×20" cylinders and 13,800 pounds of tractive effort. The two classes weighed 56,000 pounds and 60,000 pounds, respectively. It was mainly with these 2-8-0s that the heavy traffic in products of mines was handled after the railroad's major expansion of 1881.[44]

Most of the narrow gauge railroads built in the peak years of the movement simply equipped themselves with scaled-down versions of standard gauge power. Such locomotives were available from the outset; the Cherokee began narrow gauge operation in 1871 with a small Pittsburgh 4-4-0, the *Gov. Bullock, Jr.*[45] The Connotton Valley, for example, operated mainly with 4-4-0s of 36,000 to 46,410 pounds and 2-8-0s of about 57,000 pounds.[46] The Toledo, Cincinnati & St. Louis used 4-4-0s of 36,000 to 48,000 pounds, and hauled its freight mainly with 2-6-0s of 36,000 to 64,000 pounds.[47] The Texas & St. Louis operated principally with 4-4-0 and 2-6-0 locomotives from Grant. The 4-4-0s weighed 55,000 pounds and cost $10,659 each. The 2-6-0s came in three series, weighing 44,000, 61,500, and 63,500 pounds and ranging from $7,329 to $12,176.[48] At these prices the engines were not bargains. The average price of a standard gauge 4-4-0 in the late nineteenth century was about $8,000.[49] Lower prices were reported, however. The Milwaukee Road in its valuation report of the 1920s declared the new price of its Brooks 2-6-0 of 1899 used on the narrow gauge Bellevue & Cascade line to have been $5,348. The same line's two Pittsburgh 4-4-0s of 1879 were carried at a new price of $5,273 each.[50] The Cincinnati & Westwood had 2-6-0s from Brooks and Baldwin bought in 1876 for $6,350 and $6,750, respectively.[51] The New York Locomotive Works of Rome, which recorded the prices of all the engines in its builder's list, built four narrow gauge 2-6-0s for the Cincinnati Northern in 1883 for $8,000 each, but standard gauge 2-6-0s produced simultaneously for the Rome, Watertown & Ogdensburg were only $8,800.[52] In any case, we appear justified in concluding that narrow gauge operators secured no significant economies in locomotive orders.

There are a limited number of reports of costs of operation of narrow gauge power. The St. Louis & Cairo reported locomotive expenses for July 1882 of 9.67¢ per mile.[53] R. G. Butler, General Manager of the Toledo, Delphos & Burlington, reported a locomotive cost of 8.64¢ per mile in March 1881 and 11.87¢ in April because of muddy conditions. He thought 9¢ about normal.[54] It is not clear what costs were included in these estimates, however. F. W. Dunn, Superintendent of the Nevada Central, was

pleased enough with the performance of his locomotive No. 5 to report the results to the *Railway Age* in 1881. The engine, a Baldwin 4-4-0 of 19 tons with 12″×16″ cylinders and 42″ drivers, ran 35,100 miles on passenger trains in a six-month period, or 5,850 miles per month with an average of 3.5 coaches. Average cost was 20.5¢ per train-mile with coal at $12 per ton, the engineer's salary at $4.00 per day, the firemen at $75 per month, oil at 75¢ per gallon, and waste at 20¢ per pound. Dunn considered these figures favorable relative to eastern lines.[55] The report indicates no apparent economies relative to Forney's estimate of 20.0¢ per mile for the typical standard gauge locomotive of 1874.[56]

Scaled-down versions of standard gauge locomotives were available from the outset of the narrow gauge movement. The Cherokee Railroad in Georgia began narrow gauge operation in 1871 with this tiny 4-4-0 from the Pittsburgh Locomotive Works. (Alco Historic Photographs.)

The Number of Narrow Gauge Locomotives

For several reasons it is impossible to make a precise statement of the number of American common carrier narrow gauge locomotives. First, the determination at the borderline between private and common carriers is quite arbitrary. Then, for several large lumber operators who owned extensive private trackage as well as nominal common carriers, such as R. A. Alger of Michigan, there is no way of knowing which locomotives were used exclusively in private carriage, and which served also in common. Then again, some locomotives sold new to private carriers were resold to common carriers, and we cannot presume that all such transactions are known. For the three Canadian railways that crossed the border, there is no way of precisely allocating locomotives between Canadian and American operations.

TABLE 5.2
Locomotives for American 3'-0" Common Carrier Railroads, by Builder, 1870–90

	1870	1871	1872	1873	1874	1875	1876	1877	1878	1879	1880
Baldwin		14	8	22	10	23	18	28	34	41	95
Brooks			2	3		2	11	3	16	11	14
Porter	1		3	8	11	15	8	8	15	9	16
Grant		1	3	2	3					3	11
Mason			1	1	1	4	3	6	9	16	12
National–D&B			1	3	11	10	10	22	8		
Pittsburgh		2			1	2	1		3	2	18
Dickson				3					2	2	1
Rhode Island					1				1		
Hinkley							2			2	
Cooke		1				2				3	
WV/Vulcan										3	6
Thomas Paul/ Mt. Savage											1
New York (Rome)											
Union Iron Works											
Richmond											
Taunton											
Pgh. & McKeesport							2				1
Rogers										1	
G.W. Snyder											
T.W. Godwin, VA Iron Works											
Total	1	18	18	42	38	58	55	67	88	93	175
Total U.S. output	>1062	>1218	>1534	>1616	>554	>431	>573	>414	>616	>899	1405
3'-0" as pct. of total	ca. 0	1.5	1.2	2.6	6.9	13.5	9.6	16.2	14.3	10.6	12.4

SOURCES: Computerization of known 3'-0" gauge locomotives by Joseph A. Strapac, Huntington Beach, California. Data on total locomotive output 1880–90 from *Historical Statistics of the United States* (1975), vol. II, p. 697. Total locomotive output 1870–79 are my estimates based on the following typescript builders' lists in the collection of the Railway & Locomotive Historical Society: Baldwin, Brooks, Porter, Grant, Mason, Pittsburgh, National, Rhode Island, Cooke, New York (Rome), Thomas Paul–Mt. Savage, Manchester, Schenectady, Union Iron Works, Pennsylvania Railroad Altoona Shops, Taunton, and Rogers;

Most important, survival of builders' lists for American locomotive producers in the narrow gauge era is imperfect. Lists for Hinkley, Grant, and Mount Savage, among major builders, are incomplete. William D. Edson, the late Gerald M. Best, the late Professor Sylvan R. Wood, and others have endeavored to reconstruct such lists, but the effort is not yet complete. Some minor producers who are known to have built narrow gauge power, such as the Pittsburgh & McKeesport Car & Locomotive Works and Thomas W. Godwin's Virginia Iron Works, have no surviving builders' lists. This problem is worst for National, which was established in 1871 explicitly as a narrow gauge specialist. The firm's highest known construction number is 260, but the total is thought to include stationary boilers, tenders, or other output apart from locomotives. Robert Brendel, who is endeavoring to reconstruct the list largely on the basis of newspaper search, estimates that National produced about 60 narrow gauge locomotives for

TABLE 5.2

(Continued)

1881	1882	1883	1884	1885	1886	1887	1888	1889	1890	TOTAL	Pct. of output	
86	49	27	18	12	16	18	6	18	18	561	6	Baldwin
34	32	27		2	5		3	8	3	176	10	Brooks
21	15	8	6	5	4	2	1		5	161	14	Porter
39	51	15								128	13	Grant
6	7	3		1	1	2				73	20	Mason
										65	72	National–D&B
	14	7	1	1	2			1		55	5	Pittsburgh
2	7	6	5	1	1	2		1		33	4.5	Dickson
		2	15	6	7			1		33	1.4	Rhode Island
6	10	7				2	2			31	4	Hinkley
		10	13							29	2	Cooke
		2				1	1			13	15	WV/Vulcan
4	10	8								23	64	Thomas Paul/ Mt. Savage
		4	4		2					10	1.5	New York (Rome)
4										4		Union Iron Works
								2		2		Richmond
			1					2		3	1	Taunton
										3		Pgh. & McKeesport
			1							2		Rogers
	2									1		G.W. Snyder
		1								1		T.W. Godwin, VA Iron Works
202	197	127	63	29	38	27	13	29	30	1408		Total
1977	2822	2067	1149	800	1436	2044	2180	1860	2300			Total U.S. output
10.2	7.0	6.1	5.5	3.6	2.6	1.3	0.6	1.6	1.3			3'-0″ as pct. of total

Gerald M. Best, *Locomotives of the Dickson Manufacturing Company* (San Marino: Golden West Books, 1966), pp. 150–54; William D. Edson, "The Hinkley Locomotive Construction Record," *Railroad History*, no. 142 (1980), pp. 53–88. My method, if applied to the years 1880–83, results in an estimated 95.6 percent of the number of locomotives shown for that period in the *Historical Statistics of the United States*.

common carriers out of about 90 locomotives of all types.[57] Pittsburgh did not enter the gauge of locomotives in its list, presenting a problem of interpretation for several engines.

Accordingly, any estimate of the total number of narrow gauge locomotives has to be based on a sample which, fortunately, can be relatively complete. Thanks to the researches of the men mentioned above, and to a much larger number who have done rosters of individual narrow gauges, we can identify well over 95 percent of narrow gauge locomotives. Joseph A. Strapac, who has put on his computer the largest known compilation of narrow gauge locomotives, estimates that a 99 percent sample is possible.[58] Table 5.2 shows Strapac's estimates of 3'-0″ locomotives for American common carriers from 1870 through 1890. American builders produced 1,407 3'-0″ locomotives in this period, about 80 percent of the 1,756 such engines Strapac believes it possible to identify. Subsequent

TABLE 5.3
Locomotives for American 3'-0" Common Carrier Railroads, by Builder, 1891–1947

	1891	1892	1893	1894	1895	1896	1897	1898	1899	1900	1901	1902	1903	1904	1905	1906	1907	1908	1909	1910	1911
Baldwin	10	5	4	5	6	12	8	4	5	12	12	11	20	11	8	6	8	3	2	2	8
Brooks	2		1	2	1		1	4		3	2										
Porter	1		1				2	1	1	2			1							1	
Pittsburgh		1		1		1				2	1										
Schenectady-American	2	1			1			1	4	2		3	4	3	1	3	4		4	3	
Dickson										1											
Rhode Island				1																	
Vulcan							1							1	1	2	2	2	1	1	1
Manchester									2	2											
Richmond	1																				
Lima			1													1					
NPCRy, Sausalito Shops										1	1										
Total	16	7	7	9	8	13	12	10	12	25	16	14	25	15	11	11	14	5	7	7	9

building is shown in Table 5.3, partly because the composition of the builders changes about 1890, with Taunton's last unit in that year and Schenectady's first in 1891. Grant, Mason, Hinkley, National, and several others had already left the field.

Locomotive output demonstrates the same trends already observed in Chapter 4 in connection with mileage. Output rose from a single Porter engine in 1870 to an early peak of 42 units in 1873. The decline in the movement perceived by Forney about that time manifested itself in a small decline to 38 units in 1874, the year before the decline appeared in mileage built. There was a quick revival to 58 engines in 1875, about 10.5 percent of American locomotive output. After a trivial decline to 55 units in 1876, locomotive output rose *pari passu* with mileage built to a strong peak in the early 1880s. Output, which had never previously been over 100 units, reached 175 in 1880, 12.4 percent of the national total. The peak came with 202 units in 1881, a year before the peak year in mileage built. Even this figure showed a relative decline to 10.2 percent of national locomotive output. In 1882 the boom continued with 197 units, barely below the previous year, but this figure was only 7 percent of national output. In 1883, the year of the collapse of the movement, locomotive output held up better than mileage, falling only to 127 units while new mileage was falling approximately by half. Thereafter, however, locomotive output fell much more rapidly than new mileage, dropping to 63 units in 1884 and only 29 in 1885. As observed elsewhere, the industry had a sizable stock of relatively modern narrow gauge locomotives to operate a rapidly dwindling mileage. The 38 locomotives built in 1886 were 2.6 percent of the national total, but narrow gauge power was never to go beyond 2 percent again. The peak years of 1880–83 saw the production of 700 locomotives, about half the narrow gauge output of 1870–90 and 40 percent of the eventual total. Similarly, the peak years of tracklaying from 1879 to 1883 produced about 45 percent of the eventual total of narrow gauge trackage.

TABLE 5.3

(Continued)

	1912	1913	1914	1915	1916	1917	1918	1919	1920	1923	1924	1925	1926	1928	1929	1938	1939	1943	1947	Total
Baldwin	2	2	3	5	6	2	1	3	4		1	10	1	2	1	1	1	8	2	217
Brooks																				16
Porter				1	1															12
Pittsburgh																				6
Schenectady-American	6	2	3	3	4	1			2	10		2	2							71
Dickson																				1
Rhode Island																				1
Vulcan			2							2										16
Manchester																				4
Richmond																				1
Lima																				2
NPCRy, Sausalito Shops																				2
Total	8	4	8	9	11	3	1	3	6	12	1	12	3	2	1	1	1	8	2	

SOURCE: Computerization of known 3'-0" gauge locomotives by Joseph A. Strapac.
NOTE: Steam locomotives only, built new.

Baldwin was the dominant narrow gauge builder from the outset of the movement and increased its preeminence as time passed. The 181 engines it built in 1880 and 1881 were nearly half the industry's narrow gauge output in those years. Most of this was motive power for the Denver & Rio Grande's incursion into the Rockies in the early 1880s. The data for Porter are consistent with the literary evidence that common carriers bought its stock models from the beginning, but tended to turn increasingly to other producers as the boom years approached. National, after seriously rivaling Baldwin, Porter, and Brooks in the early years, failed in mid-1878 and did not participate in the peak. Grant, which had produced a small number of units in the early 1870s, tooled up for the peak years by making patterns for 4-4-0, 2-6-0, and 2-8-0 locomotives. After building 28 2-8-0s for the Denver & Rio Grande, Grant built much of the motive power of the Texas & St. Louis and the Toledo, Cincinnati & St. Louis. Failure of the TC&StL caused Grant to repossess a large number of engines. Some were sold directly to new owners directly from the TC&StL's shops at Delphos, others from Grant's plant at Paterson. The last were disposed of in 1890, reportedly at a heavy loss.[59] Rhode Island, which had produced only about 19 narrow gauge engines by 1884, was enough motivated by the prospect of narrow gauge sales to issue a catalog of narrow gauge locomotives—even though the engines shown were necessarily standard gauge.[60] Essentially any American builder would produce narrow gauge power, and of the major firms, only Schenectady made no contribution to the output of 1870–90. Rogers, which produced only two units, was a more obvious candidate for absence, for its superintendent, William S. Hudson, was a conspicuous opponent of narrow gauge doctrine.

Building of narrow gauge power after 1890 was far more dominated by Baldwin than previously. The big Philadelphia builder had contributed just under 40 percent of domestic narrow gauge power to 1890, but produced about 62 percent of the later engines. Baldwin's habitual preoccupation

TABLE 5.4
Wheel Arrangements of Known American 3'-0" Common Carrier Locomotives, by Builder, 1870–90

	0-4-0	0-4-2T	0-4-4T	0-6-0	0-6-2T	0-6-4T	0-6-6T	2-4-0	2-4-2T	2-4-4T	2-4-6T	2-6-0	2-6-6T	2-8-0	2-8-6T	4-4-0	4-6-0	Unknown or other
Baldwin	6	8	5	23				6	17			123		184		139	45	5
Brooks			5									138		33				
Porter	22	11		34				43	1			34				3		13
Grant	1							2				52		40		28	5	
Mason			17			1	3			20	7		19		6			
National–D&B	1		1					7				13				21	2	20
Pittsburgh	1		1	2								14				35	2	
Dickson				2								20				11		
Rhode Island	1		4									11		7		9	1	
Hinkley	1		2	2	12							8				6		
Cooke											1	17		10		1		
WV/Vulcan	1											6				4		
Thos. Paul/ Mt. Savage	1		1									6		2		13		
New York (Rome)												5				1	4	2
Union Iron Works																		4
Richmond																		2
Taunton									2									1
Pgh. & McKeesport																		3
Rogers												1				1		
G. W. Snyder																		2
T. W. Godwin																		1
Total	35	19	34	65	13	3		58	19	22	7	448	19	243	6	304	59	

SOURCE: Computerization of known 3'-0" gauge locomotives by Joseph A. Strapac.

Rod engines: Locomotives of the ordinary sort without a geared connection between the cylinders and wheels. The term originated in lumber railroading where geared locomotives were the norm.

with foreign sales caused it to build in a wide variety of gauges, incidentally suiting it well to handling domestic narrow gauge orders. Alco-Schenectady established itself as a distant second, but Lima, which was to be the smallest of the three long-surviving American steam locomotive builders, built only two narrow gauge rod engines. Lima was to produce geared locomotives extensively for the nominal common carriers, however.

Wheel arrangements showed a marked trend over time, and a specialization by builder. The 2-4-0 locomotives were built mainly in the early years of the movement, and principally by Porter. With the trend to heavier locomotives, 4-6-0s were concentrated in the later years and particularly identified with Baldwin. As shown in Table 5.4, the 2-6-0 was the most common narrow gauge locomotive with 448 units, amounting to about 31 percent of the total built in the period 1870–90. Brooks produced a highly regarded 2-6-0, which amounted to 78 percent of its narrow gauge output. Second most common, inevitably, was the 4-4-0, with 304 units. Pittsburgh built an excellent 4-4-0 which constituted 64 percent of its narrow gauge locomotives. The Baltimore & Lehigh had two Pittsburgh 4-4-0s of 1883, which it considered its best passenger engines, and ordered a third as late as 1887.[61] The large number of 2-8-0s, 243, is

mainly the consequence of the D&RG's heavy orders for Consolidations from Baldwin at the time of its major expansion of 1880 and 1881. Together, 4-4-0s, 2-6-0s, and 2-8-0s amounted to about 71 percent of narrow gauge locomotives built to 1890. Mason's common carrier output of 73 was entirely of Mason Bogies. In addition to the 3'-0" locomotives in this compilation, there were 54 3'-6" engines reported to *Poor's Manuals*—although this undoubtedly involves some double counting—and 41 2'-0" locomotives. At least seven engines had gauges unique to individual railroads. This implies that the identifiable common carrier narrow gauge rod engines were somewhat in excess of 1,800. With unidentified locomotives, geared engines of common carriers, and Canadian power used on American lines, the total can be estimated with some confidence above 1,850 but below 2,000.

The path to convergence with design of standard gauge locomotives was facilitated by the relatively static quality of locomotive design between 1870 and 1890. The 4-4-0 with a wagon-top boiler, level cylinders, and Stephenson valve gear had emerged as the standard American locomotive by 1855, and developed only in evolutionary fashion for about 35 years thereafter. Steel increasingly replaced iron, and coal replaced wood as fuel. The 4-4-0 peaked in popularity about 1870 when an estimated 85 percent of locomotives in the country were of this wheel arrangement.[62] Thereafter, the 2-6-0 and 2-8-0 tended to replace the 4-4-0 in freight service, leaving the 4-4-0 by 1890 as almost entirely a passenger locomotive. Introduction of heavy wooden vestibule coaches in the 1890s first brought forth high-boilered examples of the 4-4-0 but shortly rendered the wheel arrangement obsolete. By the turn of the century it had been superseded

Schenectady built relatively few narrow gauge locomotives, but in 1899 it produced one of the most famous: the Florence & Cripple Creek's *Portland*, which became Rio Grande Southern No. 20. It is preserved at the Colorado Railroad Museum. (Richard H. Kindig.)

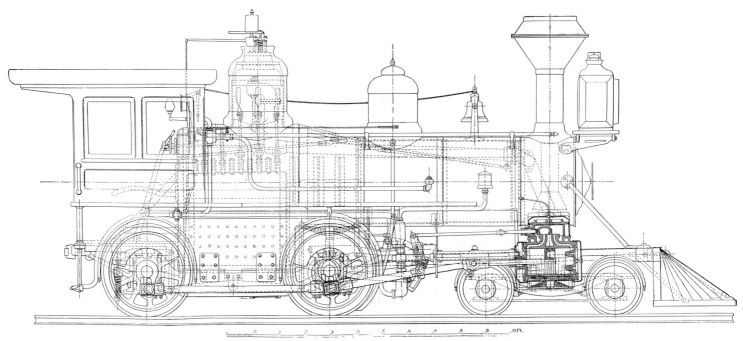

NARROW GAUGE PASSENGER LOCOMOTIVE,

Built by the BALDWIN LOCOMOTIVE WORKS, *Philadelphia.*

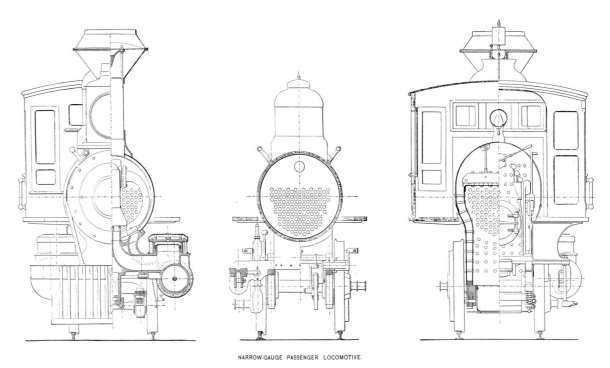

NARROW-GAUGE PASSENGER LOCOMOTIVE.

In 1883 the *Railroad Gazette* published plans of three narrow gauge locomotives exhibited at the Railway Appliances Exposition in Chicago in that year. The 4-4-0 was Fulton County Narrow Gauge No. 4, shown on a train in an accompanying photograph. (R. W. Mureen collection, courtesy of Charles H. Stats.)

almost entirely for new orders.[63] Thus, the trend toward 4-4-0 locomotives for passenger service and 2-6-0 or 2-8-0 locomotives for freight on the narrow gauges simply paralleled the trend of the period 1878–83 in standard gauge railroading. The true Mogul, with a 2-6-0 wheel arrangement and a single-axle leading truck, was introduced on the Louisville & Nashville in 1860, but problems of equalizing weight between the leading truck and the drivers prevented the design from being popular until after 1867.[64] The Mogul, at best, could have had only a short period of popularity, for it was quickly superseded as a heavy freight locomotive by the 2-8-0. This type was developed by Alexander Mitchell in 1865 for the Lehigh & Ma-

hanoy Railroad, which was shortly consolidated into the Lehigh Valley. Named *Consolidation* in honor of this event, the locomotive was outstandingly successful. Through its power, tracking ability, stability, and low incidence of damage to rails, the engine established itself as the prototype for the most common type of locomotive in the history of American railroads; an estimated 33,000 Consolidation locomotives were built.[65]

It is instructive to compare the locomotives of 4-4-0, 2-6-0, and 2-8-0 wheel arrangements on the Denver & Rio Grande with those of the Lehigh Valley. Both were mountain railroads with formidable problems of gradients and curvature. Both bought locomotives extensively in the period 1877–83.[66] The Class 42 4-4-0 of 1880 of the D&RG, as stated, had 12″×18″ cylinders, 45″ drivers, a weight of 40,000 pounds, and a tractive effort of 6,380 pounds. The Lehigh Valley's contemporaneous 4-4-0s were the Class E-13 engines built from 1878 to 1887. These locomotives had 18″×24″ cylinders, 55½″ drivers, a total weight of 85,120 pounds, and a tractive effort of 15,260 pounds.[67] The ratio of total weight to tractive effort is 6.27 : 1 for the narrow gauge and 5.58 : 1 for standard.

The Class 40 2-6-0s of the D&RG of 1876–80 had 12″×16″ cylinders, 36″ drivers, a weight of 40,000 pounds, and a tractive effort of 7,060 pounds, for a ratio of weight to tractive effort of 5.67 : 1. The Lehigh Valley's closest contemporaries were the Class H-4 and H-5 2-6-0s converted from 4-6-0s in 1884 and 1886. These engines had 20″×24″ cylinders, 56″ drivers, a weight of 105,500 pounds, and a tractive effort of 20,770 pounds,

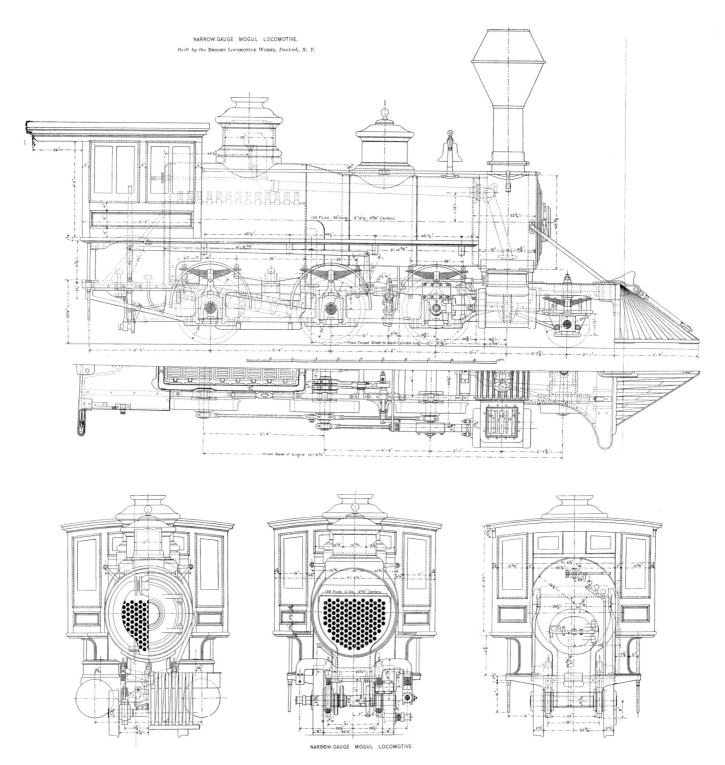

NARROW-GAUGE MOGUL LOCOMOTIVE.

The Brooks 2-6-0 in the accompanying plans and photograph was exhibited at the Railway Appliances Exhibition in Chicago in 1883. It was a fine example of the state of the art in narrow gauge freight power on the eve of the collapse of the movement. (Ed Bond collection.)

for a ratio of 5.08 : 1.[68] For the Class 60 2-8-0s on the D&RG, the ratio of weight to tractive effort was 4.35 : 1. For the Lehigh Valley's Class M-6 and M-7 2-8-0s of 1882, which had $20'' \times 24''$ cylinders and $50''$ drivers, total weight was 107,744 pounds and tractive effort 23,644 pounds, a ratio of 4.5 : 1.[69] Thus the ratio is favorable to the standard gauge locomotives for the 4-4-0 and 2-6-0 and to the narrow gauge for the 2-8-0, but none of the three suggests any marked superiority for the narrow gauge. The narrow gauge 2-8-0 was an outstandingly successful design which the D&RG carried over almost unchanged into its first standard gauge locomotives.

The doctrine that narrow gauge locomotives were inherently more powerful per pound of weight was concentrated in the early years of the movement. It had something of a revival in 1882 when it was alleged that a 2-8-0 of the Texas & St. Louis had performed as well as a standard gauge locomotive of the same wheel arrangement of the Iron Mountain in pulling tonnage up from the Illinois Central's ferry at Bird's Point, Missouri.[70] William S. Hudson in 1874 had pointed out that comparisons of this sort were misleading because they were between a narrow gauge locomotive intended to operate at 10 to 12 miles per hour and a standard gauge engine intended for 15 to 30 or 35 miles per hour.[71] Edward Hulbert in his address to the summer convention of 1878 was explicit that narrow gauge locomotives had no more power relative to size than standard, and made only the usual argument that they could haul more cargo because of the lower tare weight of narrow gauge equipment.[72] The editorial observation of the Cincinnati *Gazette* of 1878 quoted in Chapter 4 was generally correct that claims of this sort were now discarded.[73]

Narrow gauge advocates viewed the trend toward convergence with standard gauge practice with some suspicion. In 1872 Benjamin H. Latrobe, one of the opponents of narrow gauge doctrine, had inveighed against the prospect of using 150-ton locomotives on 30-pound rail.[74] By 1878 narrow gauge track was being subjected to 20-ton locomotives. Hulbert in his speech to the first convention of that year was as critical as Latrobe had been:

Excessive weight of locomotives and cars is a common fault with narrow gauge roads. When we take into consideration the generally imperfect construction of the narrow-gauge superstructure, the newness and unsettled condition of the roadbed, the absurd folly of attempting the use of locomotives and cars of nearly the same weight and capacity of the standard-gauge becomes apparent in the bending and twisting of the rail and the extraordinary wear and tear of the machinery and rolling stock. With too heavy machinery and rolling stock disproportioned to the superstructure we lose the advantage claimed in the saving of dead weight, and at the same time increase the wear and tear to an extent that our

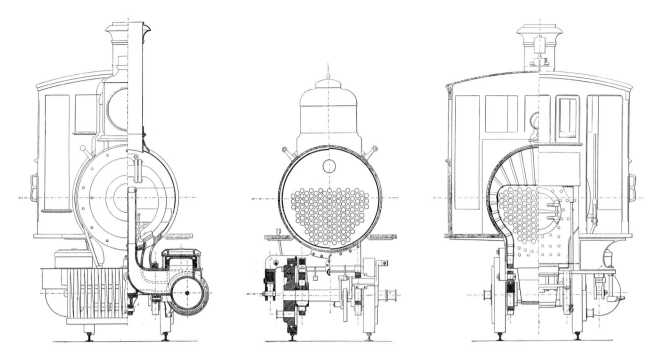

NARROW-GAUGE CONSOLIDATION LOCOMOTIVE.

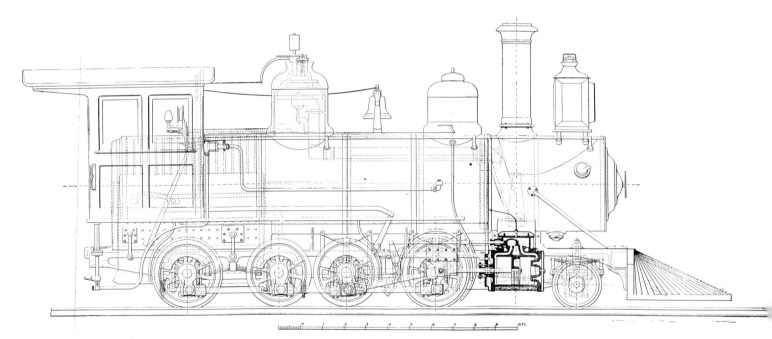

The 2-8-0 exhibited at the Railway Appliances Exposition of 1883 was a Baldwin locomotive built for the Conglomerate Mining Co. The engine proceeded to another private carrier, the Lac La Belle & Calumet, but then was sold to the Deerfield River Railroad, the affiliate of the Hoosac Tunnel & Wilmington. The engine was unusual in proceeding from private to common carriers.

operating expenses are even greater proportionately than that of the standard-gauge. The weight of locomotives should be adapted, first, to the weight of the rail, and second to the amount and kind of traffic. It is not unusual to find locomotives in use on a thirty-pound rail that in the incomplete and unfinished condition of the superstructure, would be full heavy for even a thirty-five pound rail and with a well-constructed and thoroughly ballasted track.[75]

Hulbert recommended that on 30-pound rail the largest 4-4-0 should be a 16-ton engine with 11 tons on the drivers. For 35-pound rail he proposed a maximum weight of 18 tons with 12 tons on the drivers. He thought a 2-6-0 with a blind center driver and a Perry leading truck might go as high as 18 tons on 30-pound rail or 20 tons on 35-pound, provided low speed was maintained.[76]

Consistent with his advocacy of his locomotives as necessary to the success of the narrow gauge, Fairlie wrote in his book of 1872:

I admit at once, that if the narrow gauge be regarded only as a reduced copy of the larger one, its capacity and efficiency decrease in a more rapid ratio than its reduction in width, for if locomotives of the ordinary type be employed, the light rails and the narrow space between them limit the power, the heavy gradients still further affect the load to be carried, and the sharp curves may again set a limit to the wheel base. Therefore I say that such a line as I have been considering would be useless except under very special circumstances where small traffic and low speeds were required.[77]

Later in the same work he wrote:

It must be clearly understood that, unless for a very small traffic combined with very low speeds, I do not, nor have I ever recommended a gauge narrower than 4 ft. 8½ in., if the ordinary type of engine be employed, because, and apart from the fact that the oscillations and unsteadiness of the ordinary engines increase as the gauge is diminished, *the width of the gauge limits the power of the engine, inasmuch as it limits the width of the firebox, and the size of the boiler*, and as the loss of power increases even in a greater ratio than the diminution of the gauge, it follows that the carrying capacity of gauges narrower than 4 ft. 8½ in., when worked by ordinary engines, becomes limited in a very marked degree; whereas the point I maintain is that a 3 ft. or 3 feet 6 in. gauge properly worked is fully as efficient as the widest gauge railway ever built. Moreover, on account of the unsteadiness inseparable from small engines of the common type, the speed of trains, if the same factor of safety be preserved, must be reduced.[78]

These authors should be given credit for their foresight. With locomotives of 23¾ tons and possibly higher operating on ordinary standards of narrow gauge construction, the Toledo, Cincinnati & St. Louis simply disintegrated. The trend against which Hulbert and Fairlie wrote proved the immediate element in the demonstration of the basic fallacy of their more general argument.

Locomotives After the Narrow Gauge Era

When the narrow gauge movement collapsed following the failure of the Grand Narrow Gauge Trunk in 1883, the railroads had some 1,179 relatively modern locomotives with which to operate the dwindling mileage of narrow gauge track. The effect was to suspend locomotive development at the stage of the 4-4-0, the 2-6-0, and the 2-8-0 of 1880 for about 20 years. Such resumption of development as took place was relatively limited. Table 5.5 shows the distribution of later narrow gauge locomotives by wheel arrangement. As might be expected, the 4-4-0 and 2-6-0 locomotives were concentrated in the 1890s, the 2-8-0s somewhat later, and the 2-8-2s mainly after 1903. The typical small narrow gauge, and even a carrier as big as the former Denver, South Park & Pacific, operated mainly with engines of the peak years to the end.

The first major development in narrow gauge design after 1883 was introduction of the outside-frame locomotive near the turn of the century. Actually, it is remarkable that the innovation came so late, for outside-frame engines had been common in the early years of railroading. Oddly, they had been particularly characteristic of the broad gauge railways in both Britain and America. Baldwin introduced the outside frame to nar-

PORTER, BELL & CO.,
PITTSBURGH, PENN'A.,
Exclusive Specialty

LIGHT LOCOMOTIVES,
Over 50 Sizes and Styles, from 7x12 to 14x20 Cylinders.

NARROW GAUGE Freight and Passenger Engines for Light or Heavy Equipment.

SPECIAL SERVICE Engines, for Contractors' Use, R. R. Construction and Shifting, Furnaces, Mills, Quarries, Ore, Coal, and Lumber Roads, &c.

MINE LOCOMOTIVES to conform to required dimensions and do the work of 10 to 30 mules, at less than the cost of operating three mules and drivers.

Photograph and Price of Engine to do required work, furnished on application.

TABLE 5.5
Wheel Arrangements of Known American 3'-0" Common Carrier Locomotives, by Builder, 1891–1947

	0-4-0	0-4-2T	0-4-4T	0-6-0	0-6-2T	0-8-0	2-4-0	2-4-2T	2-4-4T	2-6-0	2-6-2	2-8-0	2-8-2	4-4-0	4-4-2	4-6-0	4-8-0	2-6+6-2T	Unknown or other
Baldwin		5		3	2	1				40	12	65	47	7	1	32		2	
Brooks				1						8		3	3			1			
Porter	1	3		2				1		3									2
Pittsburgh										3			3						
Schenectady-American			1	3		1		4	16	6		7	16	3		9	5		
Dickson							1												
Rhode Island			1																
Vulcan			6				1		1	1		4				2			1
Manchester																			1
Richmond																			4
Lima																1			1
NPCRy, Sausalito Shops													1						1
Total	2	8	8	11		2	2	5	17	61	12	79	63	17	1	45	5	2	

SOURCE: Computerization of known 3'-0" gauge locomotives by Joseph A. Strapac.

row gauge practice with a 2'-6" 2-4-2 for the Antofagasta Railway of Chile in 1886.[79] The market for narrow gauge locomotives was so depressed that no domestic operator immediately ordered any examples. The design was attractive in allowing wider fireboxes, a broader base for a wider boiler, greater stability in motion, easier access to journals on the driving axles, and more room for outside-mounting of the Walschaerts or other modern valve gear.

The Oahu Railway took delivery of five outside-frame Baldwin locomotives in 1897, beginning with an 0-6-0, *Kalihi*.[80] The Crystal River Railroad of Colorado took delivery of the first domestic outside-frame narrow gauge locomotives, a pair of 2-8-0s, in 1900.[81] The locomotives, which ultimately became D&RGW 360–361, had Stephenson valve gear and counterweights mounted on the drivers, but the D&RGW in its development of outside-frame 2-8-2s moved to mounting the counterweights on the cranks outside the driver with outside-mounted Walschaerts valve gear.

The D&RGW's development of the 2-8-2 stemmed from the inadequacy of the Class C-16 2-8-0s for freight service on heavy grades during the Edwardian prosperity of the early twentieth century. The C-16 locomotives were rated only for 110 tons on the 4 percent grades of Marshall and Cumbres passes. Advances in locomotive design since 1880 made possible an engine which, even within the constraints of the narrow gauge, could double the output of the C-16s. Baldwin in 1903 delivered a set of 15 Vauclain compound 2-8-2s designed to handle 220 tons on the 4 percent grades. As built, the locomotives had Stephenson motion and slope-back tenders, but in 1907–9 most of the class was converted to single expansion, with Walschaerts valve gear and standard tenders. Assigned the K-27 class with numbers 450–464, the engines initially manifested a tendency to derail on track that had been built for much lighter power. Apparently for this reason, the class was universally known as "Mud Hens,"

Catskill & Tannersville No. 2 was one of the earliest outside-frame narrow
gauge locomotives. Note its unusual combination of a Westinghouse air brake
and the Eames vacuum system. (Railroad Museum of Pennsylvania.)

The D&RGW's first series of Mikados, the so-called "Mud Hens," were considered homely, but durable and dependable. Richard H. Kindig's photograph
shows clearly the outside frame construction.

The Colorado & Southern operated its narrow gauge freight trains largely with 2-8-0 locomotives inherited from predecessor companies. Here are three representative examples. All have the Ridgway stack, an effective device for protecting forest lands from sparks while channeling cinders to the track. (Gerald M. Best and R&LHS collections, California State Railroad Museum.)

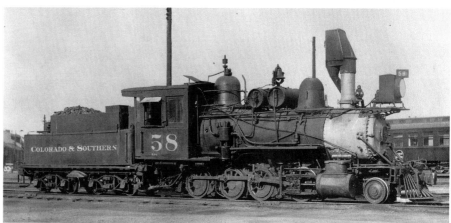

but the engines had a long and generally successful history, with several surviving into the 1950s. With tractive effort of 27,000 pounds, they were about 50 percent more powerful than the C-18 2-8-0s.

The D&RGW's three additional classes of Mikado were all products of the relative prosperity of the narrow gauge network in the 1920s. In 1923 the American Locomotive Co. delivered ten 2-8-2s of Class K-28, somewhat heavier and more powerful than the Class K-27. Although their drivers were only 44″, the engines proved quite stable at speeds of 35 and 40

miles per hour and were assigned to the named passenger trains out of Salida and Alamosa. The class was universally popular, known as "Sports Models." Seven of the locomotives were commandeered for wartime service on the White Pass & Yukon, but the remaining three survive as regular power on the Durango & Silverton Narrow Gauge Railroad.

The third set, Class K-36, which never rose to the level of a nickname, were the ten Baldwin locomotives of 1925, numbered 480–489. Relatively heavy engines with a total weight of 187,000 pounds, they had tractive efforts of 36,200 pounds, compared with 27,540 pounds for the K-28 class. Finally the railroad's own Burnham Shop in Denver produced ten locomotives, 490–499 of Class K-37 in 1928 and 1930, using the boilers of a series of standard gauge Baldwin 2-8-0s of 1902. These were the D&RGW's largest and most powerful narrow gauge power, weighing 187,250 pounds and exerting 37,100 pounds of tractive effort. These K-37 engines were particularly identified with the Monarch branch, which combined difficult curves and grades with heavy mineral traffic. The engines were a demonstration of the attractions of the outside frame, allowing a large boiler of standard gauge dimensions on 3'-0" track, but even so the resulting locomotive was only of moderate size and power by the standards of 4'-8½" railroading.[82]

Other narrow gauges that went to the 2-8-2 locomotive in the twentieth century generally did so with Baldwin catalog models. Baldwin at least by 1897 had in its catalog a 2-8-2 intended for sale to foreign narrow gauge operators.[83] Although it was marketed for 3'-6" and meter gauge railways, the general design could be adapted to 3'-0". The East Broad Top in its mature years operated principally with six Baldwin 2-8-2s beginning with a locomotive delivered in 1911. The last of the series, built in 1920, weighed over 82 tons.[84] The White Pass & Yukon in its later years operated with power of this sort; the last steam locomotives produced for use on a do-

Mikado locomotive No. 497 arrives at Alamosa for reassembly after conversion from the Denver & Rio Grande Western's Consolidation No. 1003. The photograph is a rare opportunity to see the anatomy of an outside frame free of the counterbalances and valve gear normally outside it. (Otto C. Perry, Denver Public Library.)

The few narrow gauges that still ordered new locomotives after 1910 most frequently chose Baldwin Mikados. East Broad Top No. 15 was a standard Baldwin model of 1914. (Ed Bond collection.)

George L. Beam, the Denver & Rio Grande Western's professional photographer, took this characteristically excellent picture of Mikado No. 478 upon its arrival at Salida from the American Locomotive Co. in July 1924. The engine is still in service on the Durango & Silverton Narrow Gauge Railroad. (D&RGW collection, courtesy of Jackson L. Thode.)

mestic narrow gauge were White Pass Mikados 72 and 73, built by Baldwin in 1947.

Given the difficult terrain in which most of the long-lived narrow gauges operated, it is remarkable that articulated locomotives were barely used at all. The narrow gauges in sub-Saharan Africa were largely operated with Garratt locomotives, a type that should have had attractions for American narrow gauge operators. The design is based on two symmetrical, simple engines of any of the most common wheel arrangements, one mounted under a water tank forward and the other mounted under a fuel tank or bunker aft. The boiler is slung on a heavy frame riding between the two engines. The design has the attraction of moving the boiler inward rather than outward on curves, a feature that elsewhere was thought to render the type particularly suitable to narrow gauges. The compensating disadvantage was adhesion that depended on the level of water and fuel; the engines were expected to be slippery with their tanks nearing empty. Even

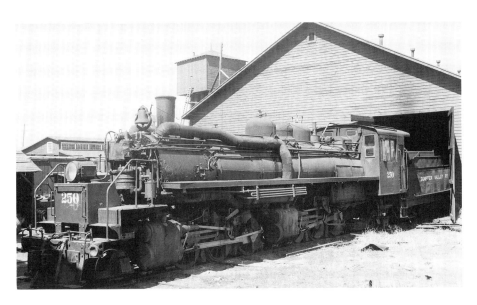

The only articulated locomotives ever ordered by American common carrier narrow gauges were two similar but not identical tank engines of the Uintah Railway, shown here and on p. 365. They were considered extremely successful in dealing with the Uintah's difficult operating problems. (Railroad Museum of Pennsylvania.)

The Uintah's articulateds were rebuilt to tender configuration for the Sumpter Valley Railway, where they operated until the line was abandoned just after World War II. (Smithsonian Institution.)

though the American Locomotive Co. held the rights to the design, no American railroad of any gauge ever ordered one.[85]

Compound articulateds of the Mallet type were common on American standard gauge railroads and used on several lumber railroads. Narrow gauge Mallets were used in France, Switzerland, Indonesia, and elsewhere. Simple articulateds of the Mallet configuration were widely introduced on standard gauge American railroads from the mid-1920s.

The only articulateds of the Mallet type ever used by American common carrier narrow gauges were two similar simple tank engines of 2-6+6-2 configuration, ordered by the Uintah Railway to deal with its unique operating problems. The railroad had been built in 1904 in the expectation of working the north and south ends by ordinary rod engines, but traversing Baxter Pass by means of Shay geared locomotives. Only a pair of 0-6-2 tank engines that hauled a single-car passenger train regularly traversed the entire railroad. In the mid-1920s the line's freights were handled by three 2-8-0s, two 2-8-2s—one with inside frame and one with outside—

and six Shays. General Manager Lucian C. Sprague sought to reduce the railroad's operating costs with a locomotive capable of pulling a freight train over the entire railroad. Since the crossing of Baxter Pass entailed a 66° curve on a 7½ percent grade, the problem was formidable. Sprague and his master mechanic, H. S. Shaffer, developed specifications for a simple articulated 2-6+6-2 tank engine, which they submitted to Baldwin, builder of all the line's rod engines.

The locomotive, numbered 50, was 45'-8" long, with a gross weight of 236,300 pounds, of which 82 percent was on the drivers. With cylinders of 15"×22" and 42" drivers, the engines developed 42,075 pounds of tractive effort, about the equivalent of a standard gauge heavy Consolidation or light Mikado. In fittings, it was quite a modern locomotive with a Delta trailing truck, outside journals on the leading truck, Walschaerts valve motion, and power reverse gear. The engine was rated at 145 tons westbound over Baxter Pass and 90 tons eastbound; each of the Shays was rated for only 60 tons in either direction. Number 50 proved to handle as much tonnage as two of the Shays and to traverse the pass in only a little more than half the time. Maintenance was expected to be less than that of one Shay.[86]

Number 50 was successful enough that the railroad ordered a second of the same principal dimensions, but five tons heavier, and differing in certain superficial details, mainly to fit the locomotive better for operation in the snow. Number 51 was delivered by Baldwin in April 1928. Together, the two locomotives handled most of the Uintah's tonnage of Gilsonite until the railroad was abandoned in 1939.[87] Both the Denver & Rio Grande Western and the Colorado & Southern considered buying the engines, but they were sold for $20,000 to the Sumpter Valley Railway, which renumbered them 250–251, converted them to tender configuration, and used them as its basic motive power until abandonment in 1947.[88] The articulateds were then sold to the International Railways of Central America, which operated them into the mid-1960s.[89]

The East Tennessee & Western North Carolina and the Colorado & Southern each considered simple articulated locomotives of the Mallet configuration, but neither made the order. At right is Baldwin's specification card for the ET&WNC engine, from the De-Golyer collection at Southern Methodist University. (Ed Bond collection.)

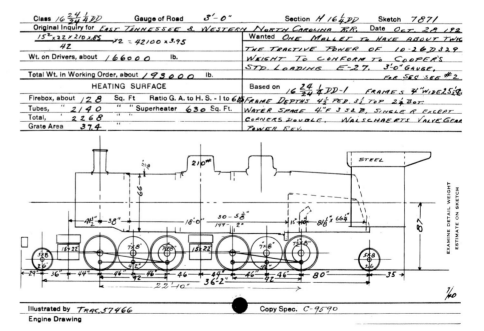

Big Sandy & Cumberland No. 7 was a medium-sized two-truck Shay geared locomotive, built for 3'-6" gauge. (Ed Bond collection.)

The Denver & Rio Grande came close enough to ordering narrow gauge articulateds to develop plans for both simple and compound 2-8+8-2s, but in 1927 decided against either in favor of ordering the Class K-37 series Mikados.[90] Baldwin in 1926 developed a preliminary design for a simple 2-6+6-2 for the East Tennessee & Western North Carolina.[91] The Colorado & Southern in 1930 considered simple 2-6+6-2 tender engines, based on articulateds built by Baldwin for export, to replace 2-8-0s on the former Colorado Central, but apparently decided the prospects of the narrow gauge were too bleak to warrant the investment.[92]

Strictly speaking, the treatment of articulated locomotives on the narrow gauges is incomplete without consideration of the geared engines. Writers on the articulateds have typically included the geared locomotives in their taxonomies.[93] Such locomotives were common on the narrow gauges. The nominal common carriers were largely operated with them, and railroads such as the Uintah and the Argentine Central that were built to the physical standards of the lumber railroads necessarily operated with this sort of power. The existing literature on these locomotives is so abundant that any extended treatment of them here would be only marginally helpful. For our purposes, it is sufficient to point out that each of the major types was available to narrow gauge operators from the late nineteenth century.

The oldest and most popular of the geared locomotives was the Shay, developed by Ephraim Shay of Harbor Springs, Michigan, and produced

Big Sandy & Cumberland No. 485 is a 3′-6″ example of the Climax geared locomotive. The engine is unusual in carrying the builder's construction number 485 as its road number. (Thomas T. Taber collection, Railroad Museum of Pennsylvania.)

by the Lima Locomotive Works from 1880 to 1945. In the most basic configuration, the locomotive had a boiler offset to the left, two or three vertical simple cylinders at the right acting on a shaft connected by beveled gears to two trucks, the forward under the smokebox and boiler, the rear under the tender portion of the frame. Later configurations were more complicated, with a third and fourth truck placed under an auxiliary tender. The Shay was built in gauges from 1′-6″ to 5′-0″. The great majority of the 2,770 Shays built by Lima were sold to private carriers, but among common carriers, the Gilpin Tram operated exclusively with 2′-0″ models and the Argentine Central with 3′-0″. Several 3′-0″ lines, like the Uintah, operated with a mixture of Shays and rod engines.[94] A Shay had a top service speed of about 8 miles per hour and could work a grade of 7 or 8 percent at 4 to 6 miles per hour depending upon load.

The Climax locomotive was invented by Charles D. Scott, but patented by George Gilbert in 1888 and produced from 1888 to 1928 by the Climax Manufacturing Co. of Corry, Pennsylvania. About 1,030 to 1,060 locomotives were produced in gauges from 2′-6″ to 9′-0″—the last for a tramway operating over wooden poles. The basic configuration, adopted after early experimentation and after some patent disputes, entailed a pair of inclined cylinders set parallel to the boiler, working against a transverse shaft, connected by bevel gears to a longitudinal shaft which by additional gears operated trucks set under the smokebox and tender. A three-truck model was produced, though it never achieved popularity. Very few Climaxes were sold to common carriers, but the Nevada County

Narrow Gauge operated one, the Seward Peninsula Railway in Alaska operated principally with them, and the Tionesta Valley, a large common carrier in Pennsylvania built to lumber-railroad standards, operated largely with them.[95]

The Heisler locomotive was developed by Charles L. Heisler of Wapakoneta, Ohio, and patented in 1892. The design was based on a pair of cylinders set transversely at a 45° angle beneath the boiler, acting on a longitudinal shaft, which was connected to the farther axle on each truck with bevel gears. Side rods connected the two pairs of wheels on each truck. In 1898 a three-truck model was introduced. Heislers were produced by the Stearns Manufacturing Co. of Erie, Pennsylvania, from August 1894 until about 1904, when the firm was liquidated. The Heisler Locomotive Works was founded in 1907 to continue production, and in 1908 the Whitney Engineering Co. of Tacoma was founded as a licensee of the locomotive on the West Coast. About 625 Heislers were built through 1941, ranging in gauge from 2'-0" to 4'-8½". Lumber companies and other operators of extractive enterprises bought almost the entire output. Use on narrow gauge common carriers was limited to lines built to lumber-railroad standards such as the Hetch Hetchy & Yosemite Valleys and the Tionesta Valley.[96]

Baldwin built five geared locomotives similar to the Climax between 1912 and 1915, but none was sold to an American narrow gauge.[97] Some years after the expiration of the Shay patents in 1898, the Willamette Iron & Steel Works of Portland, Oregon, began producing a version of the Shay under the Willamette name. None of the 33 Willamette locomotives built between 1922 and 1929 was narrow gauge.[98]

Gaps in Narrow Gauge Locomotive Development

If one examines the motive power history of the Newfoundland Railway, one finds a development in 3'-6" gauge essentially parallel to the ex-

The greatest anomaly among narrow gauge locomotives was this Atlantic of the Washington & Plymouth. The 4-4-2 wheel arrangement was thought suitable for light, fast passenger trains of the turn of the century. No wheel arrangement might seem so inappropriate to the narrow gauges, but Baldwin built this solitary example for the W&P's passenger train. (Railroad Museum of Pennsylvania.)

perience of the Canadian and American railroads generally. Begun as a private company, the 547-mile line was completed as a governmental enterprise in 1897.[99] The initial motive power was what might have been expected: 4-4-0, 4-6-0, 2-6-0, and 2-6-2 tender locomotives and 2-4-2 tank engines. For freight service the railway progressed through 2-8-0 locomotives to inside-frame 2-8-2s from various American, British, and Canadian builders. The railway operated a daily passenger train, the *Caribou*, the length of the island, equipped after World War I with heavy steel coaches, diners, and sleeping cars. To haul it, the railway ordered ten 4-6-2 locomotives from Baldwin, Montreal, and Alco between 1920 and 1929.

Accordingly, the Newfoundland Railway had the same progression to Mikados for freight and Pacifics for passengers as the typical standard gauge railroad. The development lacked only steam switchers; the railway switched with its older road engines to the end of steam operation.

When the Newfoundland Railway and the Canadian National Railways, which succeeded to the property in 1949, dieselized, the experience was again rather typical. The Newfoundland management took delivery of three General Electric 380-horsepower switchers, and the CN beginning in 1952 completely equipped the line with Canadian General Motors road units. The main-line units were standard models of 875 to 1200 horsepower, mounted on 6-wheel trucks.

When we compare the Newfoundland development to the American experience, the most obvious shortcoming is that American narrow gauge passenger engines never progressed beyond the 4-4-0 and 4-6-0. No American narrow gauge had a long-distance passenger train of heavy steel equipment of the character of the *Caribou*, and none ever saw fit to order a Pacific locomotive. Only one, the Washington & Plymouth in North Carolina, ever bought an Atlantic. The closest approximation to a long-distance express on the American narrow lines was the *San Juan* between Alamosa and Durango on the D&RGW, but as we have seen, the railroad chose to haul it with the class of Mikado best suited to passenger service.

Freight locomotive development was similar as between Newfoundland and the longer-surviving American narrow gauges, leading in both cases

to the Mikado locomotive. This was probably inevitable, given the ubiquity of Mikados in North American freight practice.

The absence of steam switchers in Newfoundland had its counterpart in the United States, where there were virtually none. The Denver & Rio Grande in its peak years had a series of nine 0-6-0 tank engines of Class 48 that were used for switching at major points, but all had been sold or retired by 1903.[100] The Oahu Railway owned four 0-6-0s, mainly for switching in Honolulu.[101] Even the largest of the narrow gauges found it preferable, in general, not to separate the functions of switching and freight, but to switch with road engines. Alternatively, standard gauge switchers at Salida and Alamosa could switch narrow gauge equipment with adjustable couplers or idler cars. The Denver, South Park & Pacific had no specialized switchers at any time, and on most narrow gauges 0-6-0s were early road engines of Porter's standard design.

Remarkably, under the circumstances, there was a single 0-8-0 built specifically for switching, Number 7 of the East Tennessee & Western North Carolina produced by the American Locomotive Company's Brooks Works in 1906. Finding enough traffic for a full-time narrow gauge switcher at Johnson City, the ET&WNC management ordered a scaled down version of a large 0-8-0 of the time. With 17″×20″ cylinders and 44″ drivers, the engine was said to be the largest narrow gauge locomotive of any sort built up to its time. The engine was principally occupied in switching narrow gauge cars of iron ore into transshipment facilities at the railroad's standard gauge interchange. The locomotive served successfully until about 1940, when it was scrapped.[102]

If something as standard as an eight-wheel switcher was a unique narrow gauge locomotive, one could hardly expect much serious innovation

The East Tennessee & Western North Carolina's No. 7 was the only 0-8-0 switcher ever put in service by an American narrow gauge. (Ed Bond collection.)

The only innovative locomotive the narrow gauges ever produced was this oil-burning cab-forward 4-4-0, No. 21 of the North Pacific Coast. The design could hardly be called a success. (Louis Stein collection, California State Railroad Museum.)

or experimentation. In all of narrow gauge experience, there was only one seriously innovative locomotive, Number 21 of the North Pacific Coast. The engine was built in 1901 in company shops on the wheels and frame of a Baldwin 4-4-0 of 1875, but with the cab forward and the boiler in reversed position with respect to the wheels, relative to an orthodox locomotive. Like later cab-forward locomotives, it was an oil burner. The tender consisted of two cylindrical tanks mounted vertically on a flat frame. The boiler was a watertube model with 200 pounds pressure. The locomotive was named *Thomas Stetson*, but came immediately to be known as "The Freak" among enginemen, who considered it weak, slippery, and difficult to fire. It was scrapped in 1905.[103]

The Newfoundland Railway survived to be dieselized completely about 1957—again approximately in conformity with U.S. experience. The American narrow gauges, however, were barely dieselized at all. The D&RGW, confronted with a hopelessly unprofitable network, stuck with the Mikado locomotives to the end in 1969. By that time the D&RGW narrow gauge had become the last large-scale regular steam operation in the American railroad system. Dieselization was limited to a single Davenport-Besler 200-horsepower diesel-mechanical switcher, which was assigned to Durango. Originally built for the Sumpter Valley in 1937, the engine was purchased from the Edward Hines Lumber Co. in 1963, and served to the end of the D&RGW's narrow gauge operations.[104]

The Southern Pacific operated its narrow gauge Keeler branch, remnant of the Carson & Colorado, with three 4-6-0s from the Nevada-California-Oregon until 1954, when it installed a 450-horsepower General Electric diesel, which thereafter provided the basic service.

The White Pass & Yukon dieselized completely, phasing out steam operation on June 30, 1964, using eleven General Electric cab units specifically designed for the railroad's unusual operating conditions. The line

Standard gauge 4-6-0 No. 772 has brought the Denver & Rio Grande Western's local from Grand Junction into Montrose, and narrow gauge No. 107 prepares to take the passenger train east over Cerro Summit and Marshall Pass to Gunnison and Salida. The two locomotives provide a good contrast in the sizes of standard and narrow gauge motive power of the same wheel arrangement. (Cornelius W. Hauck collection.)

had virtually no grade crossings but had severe grades and very difficult snow problems. The locomotives were designed without much collision protection, but with reinforced sloping noses, bolted snow plows and rail flangers, plus dynamic braking equipment. The railway's second generation of diesel power was a set of seven Montreal Locomotive Works hood units of more orthodox configuration.[105] In general, neither the White Pass & Yukon's locomotives nor any others in the narrow gauges' limited experience with dieselization made any significant contribution to the technological advance of dieselized railroading.

Finally, it should be observed that the experience of narrow gauge motive power had nothing in the nature of scientific evaluation. None of the steam locomotives, as far as is known, was ever put on a stationary test plant, such as Purdue University and the Pennsylvania Railroad's Altoona Shops maintained. No railroad had a narrow gauge dynamometer car. We can evaluate locomotive power only by tractive effort, a simple arithmetical computation on the basis of cylinder dimensions, driver diameter, and boiler pressure. No one, apparently, endeavored to compute horsepower under dynamic circumstances. This is yet a further indication that the railroads did not take their narrow gauge power very seriously, and probably looked forward mainly to its replacement or abandonment.[106]

Notes

1. The railroad's offer to buy the locomotive is in a letter, "The purchase of a 'Fairlie' Engine for the 3ft Gauge," written by W. A. Bell, dated London, Apr. 26, 1872 (hereafter cited as "MS letter of W. A. Bell"). D&RGW archives, State Historical Society of Colorado, typescript copy by George E. Pitchard in collection of Jackson C. Thode, Denver. A common statement that the locomotive was a gift of the Duke of Sutherland appears to be in error.

2. Rowland S. Abbott, *The Fairlie Locomotive* (Newton Abbot: David & Charles, 1970), p. 50.

3. "The Fairlie," Denver *Daily Times*, July 8, 1873.

4. MS letter of W. A. Bell; "The Fairlie," Denver *Daily Times*, Sept. 20, 1873.

5. MS letter of W. A. Bell. A postscript in another hand states that Bell's terms, including the incentive contract, have been accepted without change.

6. MS letter of Robert Fairlie, addressed "Dear Sir," but apparently directed to William S. Jackson, treasurer of the D&RG, dated London, Aug. 17, 1872. D&RGW archives, typescript copy by George E. Pitchard in collection of Jackson C. Thode.

7. "The Mountaineer," Denver *Daily Times*, June 21, 1873.

8. *Locomotives of the Rio Grande* (Golden: Colorado Railroad Museum, 1980), p. 14.

9. Denver *Daily Times*, Sept. 20, 1873.   10. *Ibid.*, July 18, July 24, 1873.

11. MS letter of John Greenwood to William S. Jackson, Mar. 29, 1875. D&RGW archives, typescript copy by George E. Pitchard in collection of Jackson C. Thode.

12. *Locomotives of the Rio Grande*, p. 14. See also John Norwood, "D&RG Engine No. 101—The One and Only," *True West*, Apr. 1986, pp. 60–61.

13. John H. White, Jr., "The Janus: A Locomotive's History Revised," *Journal of Transport History*, 6 (1964), pp. 175–81.

14. *Railroad Gazette*, 9 (1877), p. 529.

15. Omer Lavallee, *Narrow Gauge Railways of Canada* (Montreal: Railfare Books, 1972), pp. 104–5; Abbott, *The Fairlie Locomotive*, p. 28. On the basis of photographs, Lavallee is apparently in error in describing *Caledon* as an 0-4+4-0.

16. Abbott, *The Fairlie Locomotive*, p. 29.

17. *Ibid.*, p. 12; Everett L. DeGolyer, Jr., "Mexicano!," *Trains*, May 1961, pp. 15–25.

18. Abbott, *The Fairlie Locomotive*, p. 12.

19. *Third Annual Report of the American Railway Master Mechanics' Association* (Chicago, 1870), p. 112.

20. White, "The Janus," p. 180.

21. Charles E. Fisher, "Mason's Bogies," Railway & Locomotive Historical Society *Bulletin*, no. 41 (1936), pp. 15–22, at p. 16. Fisher attributes the constriction of space for the Stephenson valve gear to the closeness of the first pair of drivers to the cylinders, but John H. White, Jr., points out that this interpretation is difficult to accept. The linkage for the Stephenson motion is between the rear axle and the rocker arms, which are between the first and second drivers. The first drivers are no closer to the cylinders than on 0-4-0 locomotives of the time.

22. *Catalogue of Narrow Gauge Mason Bogie Locomotives* (Taunton: Mason Machine Works, 1879), pp. 3–4.

23. MS Mason Machine Works builder's list, Railway & Locomotive Historical Society (R&LHS) collection of builders' lists and rosters. This collection at the present writing is housed for the Society by Thomas T. Taber III, Muncy, Pennsylvania. The current location is reported in each issue of *Railroad History*. Charles E. Fisher, in "Mason's Bogies," estimated 148. These figures include sales to private and foreign operators, accounting for a discrepancy with the figures for Mason's output of narrow gauge locomotives for domestic common carrier narrow gauges in Table 5.1.

24. MS letter of William Mason to C. Carranza, Esq., Mar. 4, 1875. Xerox copy in R&LHS collection of builders' lists and rosters.

25. Letter of D. C. Corbin to William Mason, Mar. 15, 1879. Typescript copy transcribed by Charles E. Fisher from Mason archives, *ibid.*

26. George W. Hilton, *The Ma & Pa: A History of the Maryland & Pennsylvania Railroad* (Berkeley, Calif.: Howell-North Books, 1963), pp. 7, 11, 167.

27. M. C. Poor, *Denver, South Park & Pacific*, Memorial Edition (Denver: Rocky Mountain Railroad Club, 1976), pp. 466–67.

28. Letter of J. W. Nesmith to John Evans, July 31, 1878. Typescript copy transcribed by Charles E. Fisher from Mason archives, R&LHS collection.

29. Typescript memorandum of John H. White, Jr., Curator, for files, May 20, 1980,

Division of Transportation, National Museum of American History, The Smithsonian Institution, Washington, DC.

30. Robert C. Stanley, *Narrow Gauge: The Story of the Boston, Revere Beach & Lynn Railroad*, Bulletin No. 16, Boston Street Railway Association (Cambridge, 1980), pp. 111–12.

31. "Locomotives of Maine's Two-Foot Gauges," *Railroad Magazine*, Dec. 1955, p. 33.

32. Walter A. Lucas, "Forney's Little Giants," *Railroad Magazine*, June 1945, pp. 8–23.

33. On Porter, see John H. White, Jr., *A Short History of American Locomotive Builders in the Steam Era* (Washington: Bass, Inc., 1982), pp. 77–79; John H. White, Jr., "Industrial Locomotives: The Forgotten Servant," *Technology and Culture*, 21 (1980), pp. 209–16; Angus Sinclair, *Development of the Locomotive Engine* (Ed. John H. White, Jr.; Cambridge, Mass.: MIT Press, 1970), pp. 553–62.

34. *Light Locomotives*, 4th ed. (Pittsburgh: H. K. Porter & Co., 1882), p. 5.

35. Sinclair, *Development of the Locomotive Engine*, p. 554.

36. George W. Hilton, *Monon Route* (Berkeley, Calif.: Howell-North Books, 1978), p. 317.

37. *Light Locomotives*, 7th ed. (Pittsburgh: H. K. Porter & Co., 1892), p. 5.

38. See Harold L. Goldsmith and Gerald M. Best, "Porter Builder's List," bound typescript, Division of Transportation, National Museum of American History, The Smithsonian Institution, Washington, D.C.

39. Hilton, *The Ma & Pa*, p. 167.   40. *Ibid.*, p. 171.

41. John A. Rehor, *The Nickel Plate Story* (Milwaukee: Kalmbach Publishing Co., 1965), pp. 433–34.

42. On this generation of motive power, see Cornelius W. Hauck, "Early Narrow Gauge Locomotives in the West," *Railroad History*, no. 149 (1983), pp. 51–69.

43. *Locomotives of the Rio Grande*, pp. 5–15.

44. *Ibid.*

45. George B. Abdill, *A Locomotive Engineer's Album* (Seattle: Superior Publishing Co., 1965), p. 158.

46. Rehor, *The Nickel Plate Story*, p. 445.   47. *Ibid.*, pp. 433–34.

48. Joseph A. Strapac, *Cotton Belt Locomotives* (Huntington Beach, Calif.: Shade Tree Books, 1977), pp. 225–27.

49. John H. White, Jr., *American Locomotives: An Engineering History, 1830–1880* (Baltimore: The Johns Hopkins University Press, 1968), p. 21.

50. Interstate Commerce Commission, Bureau of Valuation, Form 561, Chicago, Milwaukee & St. Paul Ry., revised Mar. 1, 1935, p. 3465, Xerox copy in Division of Transportation, National Museum of American History, The Smithsonian Institution, Washington, D.C.

51. John H. White, Jr., "The Cheviot Narrow Gauge: Some Additional Notes," *Bulletin of the Historical & Philosophical Society of Ohio*, 21 (1963), p. 29.

52. Typescript builder's list, New York Locomotive Works, Rome, N.Y. R&LHS builders' lists (see n. 23).

53. *Railway Age*, 7 (1882), p. 480.   54. *Ibid.*, 6 (1881), p. 298.

55. *Ibid.*, p. 536.

56. White, *American Locomotives, 1830–1880*, p. 80.

57. Letter of Robert Brendel, May 1, 1988.

58. Letter of Joseph A. Strapac, Apr. 18, 1988.

59. G. M. Best, "Grant Locomotive Works," unpublished typescript (1971). R&LHS collection of builders' lists and rosters (see n. 23).

60. *Narrow Gauge Locomotives Manufactured by the Rhode Island Locomotive Works* (Providence, [1884?]).

61. Hilton, *The Ma & Pa*, pp. 25, 168.

62. Sinclair, *Development of the Locomotive Engine*, p. 636.

63. White, *American Locomotives, 1830–1880*, pp. 57, 443–45.

64. *Ibid.*, pp. 63–64.

65. Alfred W. Bruce, *The Steam Locomotive in America* (New York: W. W. Norton & Co., 1952), pp. 285–87; White, *American Locomotives, 1830–1880*, pp. 65–66, 426–430.

66. There is a historical precedent for such a comparison: Silas Seymour used the Lehigh Valley as his standard gauge measure of comparison in his *A Review of the Theory of Narrow Gauges as applied to Main Trunk Line Railways* (New York: Van Nostrand, 1871), appendix.

67. William D. Edson, "All Time Lehigh Valley Roster," R&LHS *Bulletin*, no. 126 (1972), p. 40.

68. *Ibid.*, p. 58.   69. *Ibid.*, p. 85.

70. *Railway Age*, 7 (1882), p. 608.

71. *Seventh Annual Report of the American Railway Master Mechanics' Association* (Chicago, 1874), p. 303.

72. Cincinnati *Commercial*, July 18, 1878.

73. Cincinnati *Gazette*, Oct. 25, 1878.

74. Benjamin H. Latrobe, C.E., *A Letter on the Railway Gauge Question* (New York: W. W. Evans, 1872).

75. Cincinnati *Commercial*, July 18, 1878.

76. *Ibid.* Actually, Hulbert phrased his argument in odd fashion, recommending 2¾ tons and 3 tons per driver for the 4-4-0s for 30- and 35-pound rail, respectively.

77. Robert F. Fairlie, *Railways or No Railways: Narrow Gauge, Economy with Efficiency v. Broad Gauge, Costliness with Extravagance* (London: Effingham Wilson, 1872), pp. 29–30.

78. *Ibid.*, pp. 39–40.

79. John Krause, *American Narrow Gauge* (San Marino, Calif.: Golden West Books, 1978), p. 10.

80. Gerald M. Best, *Railroads of Hawaii* (San Marino, Calif.: Golden West Books, 1978), p. 66.

81. Krause, *American Narrow Gauge*, p. 10.

82. R. H. Kindig, "Mudhens and Sports Models," *Trains*, Sept. 1961, pp. 20–33.

83. *Baldwin Locomotive Works, Illustrated Catalogue of Narrow-Gauge Locomotives* (Philadelphia: J. Lippincott Co., 1897), p. 145.

84. Lee Rainey and Frank Kyper, *East Broad Top* (San Marino, Calif.: Golden West Books, 1982), pp. 214, 217.

85. A. E. Durrant, *The Garratt Locomotive* (Newton Abbot: David & Charles, 1969), pp. 63 and *passim*.

86. Henry E. Bender, Jr., *Uintah Railway: The Gilsonite Route* (Berkeley, Calif.: Howell-North Books, 1970), pp. 152–61; "Narrow Gauge Articulated Locomotive for the Uintah Railway," *Baldwin Locomotives*, Jan. 1927, pp. 44–51.

87. Bender, *Uintah Railway*, pp. 161–63, 186–93.

88. Mallory Hope Ferrell, *Rails, Sagebrush and Pine* (San Marino, Calif.: Golden West Books, 1967), pp. 82–87.

89. Bender, *Uintah Railway*, pp. 194–95.

90. The plans are reproduced in small scale in Kindig, "Mudhens and Sports Models," p. 26.

91. Mallory Hope Ferrell, *Tweetsie Country: The East Tennessee & Western North Carolina Railroad* (Boulder, Colo.: Pruett Publishing Co., 1976), p. 195.

92. Cornelius W. Hauck, *Narrow Gauge to Central and Silver Plume*, Colorado Rail Annual No. 10 (Golden: Colorado Railroad Museum, 1972), pp. 158–59.

93. Lionel Wiener, *Articulated Locomotives* (New York: Richard P. Smith, 1930; reprinted with introduction and epilogue by Robert A. LeMassena by Kalmbach Publishing Co., Milwaukee, 1970); Robert A. LeMassena, *Articulated Steam Locomotives of North America* (Silverton, Colo.: Sundance Publications, 1979).

94. Michael Koch, *The Shay Locomotive: Titan of the Timber* (Denver: World Press, 1971).

95. Thomas T. Taber III and Walter Casler, *Climax: An Unusual Steam Locomotive* (Morristown, N.J.: Railroadians of America, 1960); Michael Koch, *Steam & Thunder in the Timber: Saga of the Forest Railroads* (Denver: World Press, 1979), p. 50.

96. Anon., *The Heisler Locomotive* (Lancaster, Penn.: Benjamin F. G. Kline, 1982).

97. Taber and Casler, *Climax*, pp. 40–42.

98. Koch, *The Shay Locomotive*, p. 467.

99. Lavallee, *Narrow Gauge Railways of Canada*, pp. 29–37.

100. *Locomotives of the Rio Grande*, pp. 14–15.

101. Best, *Railroads of Hawaii*, p. 192.

102. Ferrell, *Tweetsie Country*, pp. 96–97. The Crystal River Railway in Colorado bought a 3'-0" 0-8-0 from Baldwin in 1893 for construction of its standard gauge mainline, but returned it to the builder, which rebuilt it as a 2-8-0 and sold it to the Central of Georgia. Dell McCoy and Russ Collman, *The Crystal River Pictorial* (Denver: Sundance, Ltd., 1972), pp. 31, 218.

103. A. Bray Dickinson, *Narrow Gauge to the Redwoods* (Los Angeles: Trans-Anglo Books, 1967), pp. 93, 94, 132–33.

104. *Locomotives of the Rio Grande*, p. 27.

105. Cy Martin, *Gold Rush Narrow Gauge* (Los Angeles: Trans-Anglo Books, 1969), pp. 65, 92–93.

106. On these points I am indebted to John H. White, Jr., and William H. Withuhn for comments and suggestions.

MT. SAVAGE LOCOMOTIVE WORKS

MT. SAVAGE, ALLEGHANY COUNTY, MD.

STANDARD NARROW GAUGE LOCOMOTIVES.

THOMAS B. INNESS & CO., Sales Agents. Boreel Building, 115 Broadway, New York.

6

Rolling Stock

Four-Wheel Cars

The path to convergence with standard gauge practice observed in loco-motive development occurred also in rolling stock, but much more rapidly. Robert F. Fairlie, consistent with his advocacy of the technology of the Festiniog, was a thoroughgoing enthusiast for four-wheel cars. With respect to America, he wrote:

The merchandise and passenger traffic in the country . . . is for the most part carried in eight-wheeled cars, grouped in two four-wheeled bogies. This I un-hesitatingly assert to be the most extravagant mode of carriage, so far as dead weight of rolling stock is concerned; but as it is admitted the bogies are necessary on American lines, for easy running over badly-laid roads, and for passing freely round curves, I presume, from the almost universal use of the bogie, that its advantages outweigh the drawback of dead weight. The average carrying capacity of four-wheeled goods stock, as compared to its dead weight, is 1'9 to 1, whilst that of the average eight-wheeled bogie stock is but 1'4 to 1, and this difference, of course independent of the advantage arising from the facilities of loading and handling which the smaller wagons offer must certainly have long since insured their general adoption, had it not been for the practical reasons to which I alluded just now. . . . [T]he reasons lie chiefly in the length of the extreme wheel base of the bogie stock, compared with that of the four-wheeled, and the freedom with which the wheels of the former follow the inequalities of the road, without trans-ferring their effect to the vehicle itself, thus reducing the lateral oscillation of the load to a minimum, whereas with the four-wheeled stock such inequalities are transferred direct to the load, and hence the oscillations arrive at a maximum.[1]

Fairlie reasoned that to have an ordinarily stable four-wheel vehicle on 4'-8½" track, it would be necessary to have a wheel base of at least double the gauge, or 9½ feet. Such a car, he argued, was impractical on grounds of excessive wheel slippage and instability on curves—especially in light of the absence of buffers on the end sills of American equipment.[2] On 3'-0" gauge, Fairlie asserted that a 6-foot wheel base was easily practicable, pro-ducing "a perfectly steady running machine . . . , and one that will pass freely around curves of 150 ft. radius. . . ."[3] He thought such cars might

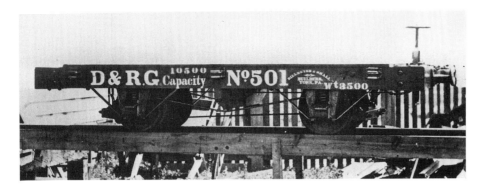

be seven feet wide, two and a third times the gauge. Cars of proportionate width on standard gauge would be 11 feet wide, and clearly impractical.

Actually, American railroads had considerable experience with four-wheel cars, and had not yet entirely rejected them. The Ohio Falls Car Co. produced a stock model four-wheel 4'-8½" flatcar, explicitly intended to minimize tare weight. In 1878 the company reported 39 cars operating on nine railroads, mainly in the South.[4] Such equipment was also still common in the anthracite area of Pennsylvania. Four-wheel cars were unpopular for reasons different from those that Fairlie assigned. They were thought hard-riding and prone to derailment, especially to sequential derailments: "a train of such cars is like a flock of sheep, when one leaves the track all the rest follow."[5]

William Jackson Palmer, who was endeavoring to follow Fairlie's doctrine closely, early in 1871 ordered from the firm of Billmeyer & Small of York, Pennsylvania, 100 single-truck freight cars, including 14-foot and 17-foot flatcars and similarly small boxcars.[6] On the basis of illustrations in Howard Fleming's *Narrow Gauge Railways in America*, the flatcar—of length not stated—had a tare weight of 3,500 pounds and a capacity of 10,500 pounds. Wooden sides could be added to convert the flatcar into a gondola. The boxcar weighed 4,500 pounds with a capacity of 9,500 pounds.[7]

Howard Schuyler initially expressed satisfaction with this sort of equipment on the basis of its performance during construction. He reported that two four-wheel flatcars equipped with swing mountings at the center of each car for carrying rail had together carried about 21,000 pounds of rail. Each of the 3,500-pound cars had thus borne its full capacity of 10,500 pounds and, Schuyler reported, had performed well on lightly built, unballasted track. He interpreted the performance as a verification of the basic narrow gauge doctrine of low tare weight relative to load, of which he was a strong advocate.[8] Nonetheless, the D&RG showed no inclination to continue with this sort of car. By late in 1871 it was ordering eight-wheel cars from Jackson & Sharp and Billmeyer & Small. On March 2, 1872, Schuyler wrote to the principal promoter of a proposed 3'-0" line from Wiscasset, Maine, to Augusta: "We build now nothing but eight wheeled, double truck cars—those already put on having a ranging weight of from 6,500 to 8,800 pounds, with a capacity of 19,000 lbs. We find them superior to the four wheeled in ease and economy of operation, while having a little less original cost per ton of capacity."[9]

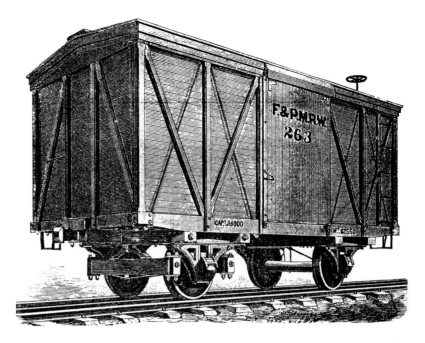

Sanford Keeler designed this four-wheel boxcar for the Flint & Pere Marquette. The car shown is standard gauge, but he is believed to have adapted the design for the subsidiary Saginaw & Mount Pleasant. From the *Railroad Gazette*.

Front: The front of a railroad car is the end with the brake wheel.

The four-wheel equipment had been dropped from the D&RG's roster by 1880.[10] The path of convergence to standard gauge practice, in this instance, had largely been made by the late winter of 1872.

There was one serious effort to improve four-wheel cars that was probably applied to narrow gauge railroading, but even this is not certain. Sanford Keeler, superintendent of the Flint & Pere Marquette, sought to improve the stability of such equipment with a triangular suspension. The front axle was mounted in the usual fashion with the weight resting on longitudinal leaf springs mounted on the journal boxes. On the rear axle wrought-iron bars replaced the longitudinal leaf springs. The bars were supported by wooden beams running across the car ahead of and behind the wheels. Each beam was connected to the car by a transverse leaf spring, mounted at the center line. Neither axle could swivel like a truck, but the arrangement provided a tricycle-mounting that Keeler, who patented the device, believed could deal with the problem of sequential derailments.[11] When the Flint & Pere Marquette opened the Saginaw & Mount Pleasant as a 3′-0″ branch in 1879, it built 4 four-wheel boxcars for the line.[12] Although there is no direct evidence, Keeler presumably used his patented suspension. If so, the innovation had no impact on narrow gauge practice generally; the Saginaw & Mount Pleasant was converted in 1884.

Eight-Wheel Narrow Gauge Rolling Stock

As the first narrow gauge freight equipment of orthodox configuration, the cars built by Billmeyer & Small for the Denver & Rio Grande were widely publicized, both by the railroad and by the carbuilder. In particular, Howard Schuyler described them at length in the same letter to the *Railroad Gazette*, cited above, in which he praised the four-wheel flatcars.[13] He included descriptions of a flatcar and gondola that were parts of the same set, but gave the dimensions and weight of the boxcar as shown in Table 6.1. He then presented breakdowns of weight by component part and by wheel loading for the boxcar and the two other configurations as in Table 6.2. Finally, he compared the three classes of car with current standard freight cars of the Pennsylvania Railroad as in Table 6.3.

If Schuyler was correct, a considerable part of narrow gauge doctrine was superficially validated. His data purported to show that the ratio of tare weight to load was only about half of what was current in standard gauge practice, and that cargo capacity was being supplied at about two-thirds of the usual capital cost.

There were objections—both immediate and retrospective—to Schuyler's calculations. Forney observed that Schuyler had calculated the cubic capacity of the boxcar on the basis of its outside dimensions. If inside dimensions were used, Forney estimated the capacity was only 680 cubic feet and 10,200 pounds.[14] John H. White, Jr., as a result of research of his forthcoming book on American freight cars, observes that the capacity in weight of 17,600 pounds was credible on the assumption the car followed the plan of a conventional boxcar of the time with 4″×8″ side sills. White points out, however, that the cubic capacity, even if one accepts Schuyler's 792 cubic feet, was so small that it could not accommodate 17,600 pounds of normal commodities. Unless the cargo were something abnormally heavy, such as iron ingots, a second car would have to be provided for the additional 200 to 300 cubic feet of capacity that a standard gauge car would have. White concludes, "On reflection the dead weight advantage of the narrow gauge car is fallacious."[15]

Similarly, Schuyler's data on relative prices of boxcars of narrow and standard gauge are highly suspect. Comparison of the D&RG's second generation of boxcars, built during the railroad's peak expansion in the early 1880s, with standard gauge equipment of the time leads to very adverse conclusions. Between 1880 and 1883 the railroad bought 2,376 boxcars the prices of which are shown in its manuscript equipment catalog of October 1883. The cars, built variously by Billmeyer & Small, the St. Charles Manufacturing Co., and the railroad's own shops, ranged in price from $519.34 to $626.36, averaging $573.11.[16] At this figure, it is questionable whether the narrow gauges were getting even the approximate 10 percent advantage per unit that they received in locomotive orders. The *National Car-Builder* reported in 1879 that the Cincinnati Southern bought boxcars at $438 each.[17] Also in 1879 James Dredge reported that

TABLE 6.1

Dimensions and Weight of Original Eight-Wheel 3'-0″ Boxcars, Denver & Rio Grande Railway

Length of frame over-all	23'-7″
Width	6'-0″
Height of floor above rail	2'-3″
Length of box	22'-1″
Outside width	6'-2″
Height at center	6'-0″
Wheel diameter	20″
Floor area	132 square feet
Cubic space	792 cubic feet
Weight	8,800 pounds
Capacity	17,600 pounds
Proportion of load to paying weight	1 : 2

SOURCE: Howard Schuyler, "Narrow Gauge Freight Car," *Railroad Gazette*, 3 (1871), pp. 359–60.

TABLE 6.2

Weight, Capacity, Load, and Costs of Original Eight-Wheel 3'-0" Equipment, Denver & Rio Grande Railway

Class of car	Weight (lbs.)				Capacity	Load per wheel	Cost	Cost per ton of capacity	Ratio of dead to paying weight
	Running gear	Platform	Super-structure	Total					
Platform (flat)	2,600	3,650	–	6,250	19,000	3,456	$350	$18.42	1:3.04
Gondola	2,600	3,650	1,000	7,250	18,000	3,456	385	21.39	1:2.48
Box	2,600	3,650	2,550	8,800	17,600	3,300	450	25.71	1:2.00
Average				7,443	18,200		$395	$21.15	1:2.45

SOURCE: Schuyler, "Narrow Gauge Freight Car," *Railroad Gazette*, 3 (1871), pp. 359–60.

TABLE 6.3

Comparison of Original Eight-Wheel 3'-0" Equipment, Denver & Rio Grande Railway,
with 4'-8½" Equipment of the Pennsylvania Railroad

Class of car	Weight (lbs.)		Capacity (lbs.)		Cost in 1871		Cost per 1,000 lbs. of load		Ratio of dead weight to paying load	
	3'-0"	4'-8½"	3'-0"	4'-8½"	3'-0"	4'-8½"	3'-0"	4'-8½"	3'-0"	4'-8½"
Platform (flat)	6,250	18,000	19,000	20,000	$350	$575	$18.42	$28.75	1:3.04	1:1.11
Gondola	7,250	18,500	18,000	20,000	385	625	21.38	31.25	1:2.48	1:1.08
Box	8,800	19,000	17,600	20,000	450	735	25.58	36.75	1:2.00	1:1.05
Average	7,450	18,500	18,200	20,000	$395	$645	$21.70	$32.25	1:2.45	1:1.12

SOURCE: Schuyler, "Narrow Gauge Freight Car," *Railroad Gazette*, 3 (1871), p. 360.

the Pennsylvania Railroad's standard boxcar—probably about 1876—cost $445.82.[18] In 1882 Pullman was reported to be charging an average of $700 for a freight car.[19] A more general idea of the costs of boxcars can be derived from the Master Car-Builders' standard fees that railroads were required to pay one another in the event of destruction of their cars off-line. In 1880 this fee was $450 for a new standard gauge eight-wheel boxcar; in 1883 it was $500 for a car up to 35 feet, or $520 for longer cars.[20] At the narrow gauge convention of October 1878, the Committee on Machinery and Rolling Stock (consisting of Edward Hulbert and H. G. Brooks) stated that the typical narrow gauge boxcar had a capacity about two-thirds that of a standard gauge car.[21] At Schuyler's stated prices, the D&RG was gaining a capital saving of about $120 on the capacity of a standard gauge car. Even at the highest of the prices for standard gauge cars quoted here, $700, narrow gauge equipment entailed additional investment of about $159.65 for the capacity of a standard gauge car. At any of the other prices quoted, the D&RG was simply paying more than its standard gauge counterparts for cars. Even if the prices at which the D&RG carried the boxcars included their delivery cost—which is not stated—there is no evidence of any saving on capital cost.

Schuyler's data became part of narrow gauge orthodoxy, however. Howard Fleming reproduced the dimensions and capacities of the boxcar and flatcar in his *Narrow Gauge Railways in America* in the middle of the decade, although the accompanying woodcut of the boxcar appears to be lettered for a lower capacity, 16,000 pounds. Instead of the D&RG's gondola car, Fleming used a wooden hopper car built by Billmeyer & Small for the East Broad Top Railroad with a weight of 9,000 pounds and a capacity of 20,000. Fleming also showed a stockcar with a capacity of nine cattle, built by Billmeyer & Small for El Ferrocarril de Costa Rica. The gross weight of the car per animal was 888 pounds, as compared with 1,285 pounds for a conventional car with a capacity of 14.[22]

Billmeyer & Small assigned letters to these cars and offered them as catalog models.[23] On receipt of the D&RG's initial order, the firm announced that it would build a new brick shop, 60 feet by 170 feet, for the exclusive production of narrow gauge cars.[24] Billmeyer & Small established itself as the leading specialized narrow gauge carbuilder, but Jackson & Sharp and other established firms quickly offered their facilities for narrow gauge production. If Schuyler was right that use of a narrow gauge allowed a ratio of tare weight to capacity approximately twice as favorable as in normal practice, narrow gauge carbuilding appeared an assured growth industry.

The idea that existing standard gauge cars were too heavy relative to their capacities was not simply narrow gauge dogma. Rather, this criticism was all but universal among railroad men concerned with carbuilding, and most of them were not optimistic concerning their ability to deal with the problem. The Railway Master Mechanics' Association, at its meeting in Philadelphia in 1870, received a report from a Committee on the Deadweight of Rolling Stock, chaired by E. D. Meier of the Kansas Pacific, that was quite hostile to American practice with regard to both locomotives and cars, relative to that of European roads. The report recommended the 4-4-0 locomotives of William S. Hudson of the Rogers Locomotive Works, and the Fairlie and Forney tank engines to reduce deadweight of motive power, but for rolling stock it concluded only that ". . . there is no *one* sovereign remedy for the evil generally acknowledged to exist, [and] it can

Jackson & Sharp's builder's photograph of Wyandotte, Kansas City & Northwestern No. 106 is a good delineation of the simplicity of early narrow gauge equipment. (Railroad Museum of Pennsylvania.)

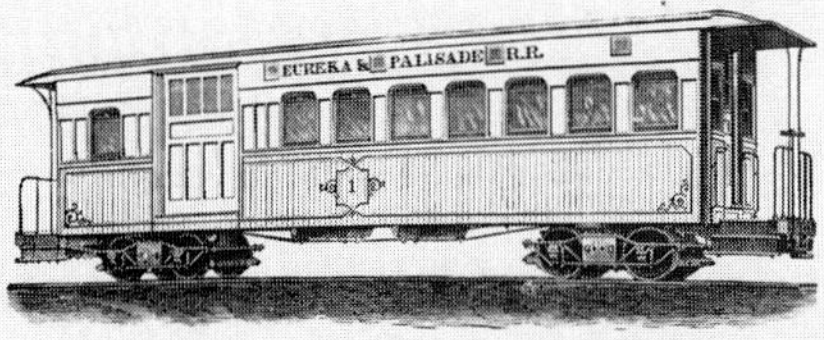
EUREKA & PALISADE R.R.

Car M, Combination Second-Class Passenger Car.

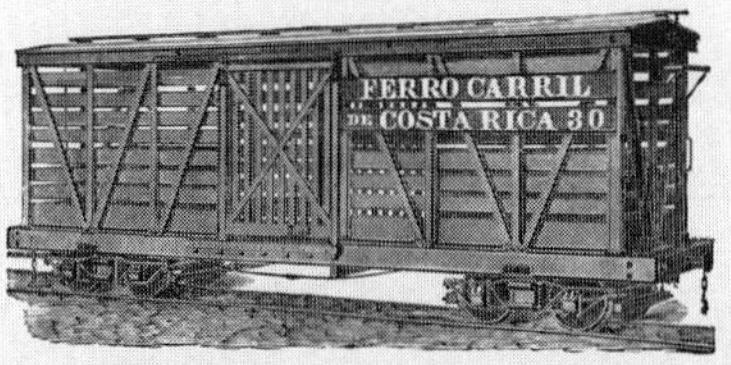
FERRO CARRIL
DE COSTA RICA 30

Car S, Eight-Wheeled Stock Car.

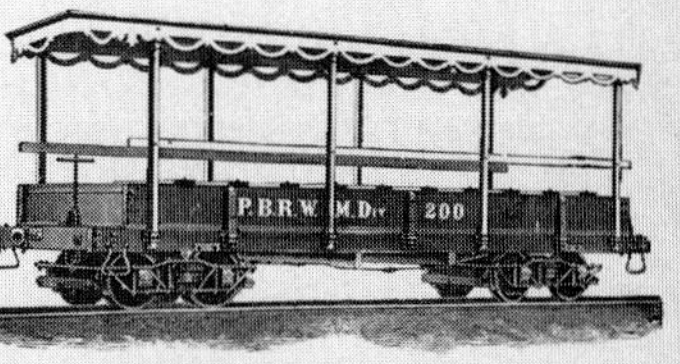
P.B.R.W. M.Dv 200

Car Q, Eight-Wheeled Gondola Car.

D. E. SMALL, President. GEO. S. BILLMEYER, Secretary.
J. H. SMALL, V. Pres't & Supt. HENRY SMALL, Treasurer.

YORK CAR WORKS.

Billmeyer & Small Company,

York, Penn., U. S. A,

MANUFACTURERS OF

Passenger and Freight Cars.

Narrow Gauge Cars a Specialty.

—:o:—

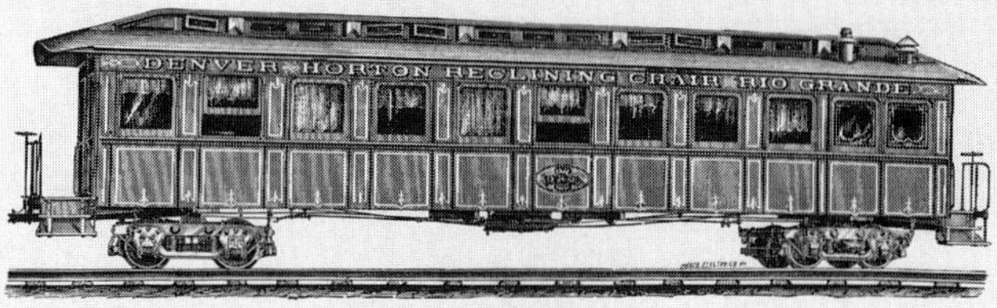

First-Class Narrow Gauge Parlor Car.

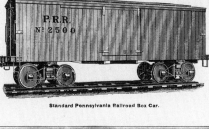

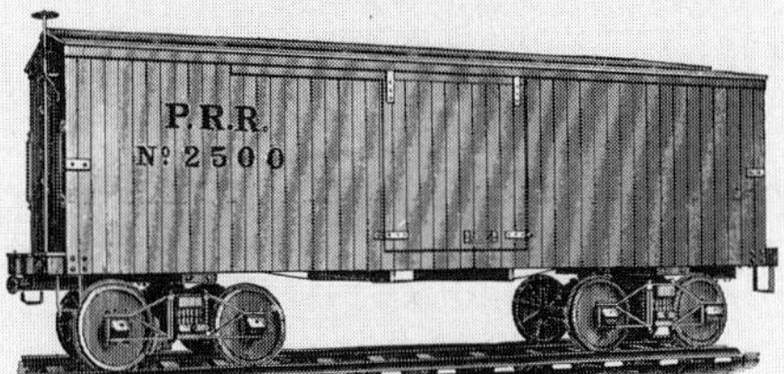
P.R.R.
No 2500

Standard Pennsylvania Railroad Box Car.

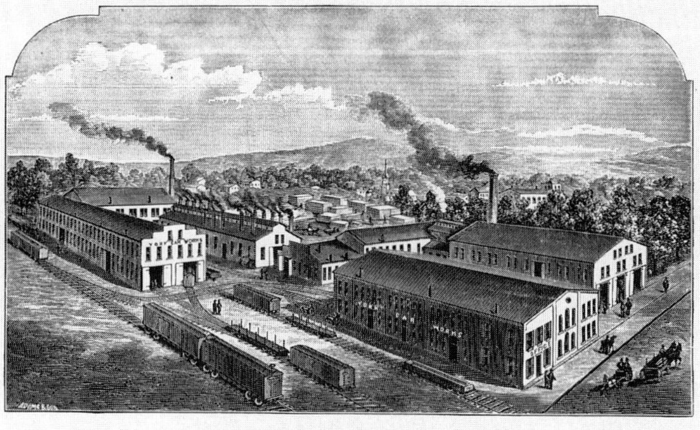

View of the Billmeyer & Small Company's Car Works, York, Penn., U. S. A.

The York Car Works were established in 1852 by the firm of Billmeyer & Small, for the purpose of manufacturing first-class Passenger and Freight Cars and Railway Rolling Stock of every description. In the very beginning the Works were successful and year by year the business grew, until in 1876 it had reached such proportions that it was deemed advisable to form a joint stock company, and the Billmeyer & Small Company was promptly organized and inherited the business and prestige of the good name which the old firm had fairly won. The Works were at once enlarged and have since been added to, until they now comprise one of the most extensive and most completely equipped establishments of the kind in the United States—having a capacity of two hundred Freight and six Passenger Cars per month.

The location is a peculiarly favorable one. The Pennsylvania Railroad and the Northern Central Railway run close to the Works, affording direct connection with all the Railroads of the country, which enables the Company to secure the lowest rates of freight on all raw material received by them and to promptly deliver their cars by rail to all parts of the United States and the Canadas, or to ship them to foreign parts, the distance to Baltimore being but 50 miles; to Philadelphia, 90 miles; and to New York, 180 miles.

The Billmeyer & Small Company are pioneer and leading builders of Narrow Gauge Railroad Cars in the United States, they having up to October 1, 1878, furnished over 2,000 Narrow Gauge Freight and Passenger Cars to forty-seven (47) Narrow Gauge Roads operating in the following named States and Territories, viz: Alabama, California, Colorado, Georgia, Indiana, Iowa, Kansas, Kentucky, Maryland, Michigan, Minnesota, Mississippi, Nevada, New York, North Carolina, Ohio, Oregon, Pennsylvania, Tennessee, Texas, Utah, Virginia, and Washington, (Territory). Also to Cuba and Costa Rica, to Central and South America, and to Mexico. Some of these cars have been running upwards of seven years, many of them from five to seven years; they have been tested under all the unfavorable conditions to which cars in use can be subjected and every car has given satisfaction.

Nearly all these cars have been eight-wheeled cars as DD, Flats; DDDD, Plain and Drop Bottom Gondolas; E, Box Cars, and X, Coal Cars, (some of which are illustrated on this page), with capacities of from 9 to 12 tons. These cars vary in weight from 6,300 pounds to 12,000 pounds, and are built of Southern yellow pine and best white oak. The size of wheels in three-fourths of the Company's orders are 24 inch, weight averaging 275 pounds; size of axles, 3 inches to $3\frac{3}{4}$ inches, with journals $2\frac{1}{4}$ by $5\frac{1}{2}$ to $3\frac{1}{4}$ by $6\frac{1}{2}$ (the length of these journals include collar) The size of the lower frame of their Standard Freight Car is 25 by 7 feet, although in several instances they have built them $7\frac{1}{2}$ and 8 feet by 28 and 30 feet long. These were generally used to carry iron and only a few ordered, and the reports are favorable for the 7 feet by 25 as the standard. Nine tenths of the cars have the Billmeyer & Small Standard Denver & Rio Grande Trucks, admitting the wheels closer together, brakes hanging outside of wheels to trucks and in some instances to the bodies, which experience proves, are more desirable for repairs and free from obstruction by ice and snow in winter.

The usual width of Passenger,—First, Second and Third-class—and Baggage Cars is 7 feet; length of body from 22 to 36 feet with capacity to comfortably seat from twenty-six to thirty-six passengers, though they may be made longer and wider if deemed desirable. In the cars 7 feet wide the seats are double on one side and single on the other, the arrangements being reversed in the centre of the car, so that each side carries half double and half single seats, which, when the car is full secures a proper balance of weight. By adding 1 foot to the width of the car, all the seats may be made double and its passenger capacity proportionately increased. These 8 feet wide Cars they are now building more of than any others, they are 35 feet long in body and 41 feet over platforms and seat from forty-five to fifty passengers. The Narrow Gauge Passenger Cars built by the Billmeyer & Small Company are in every way equal to the Best Broad Gauge Cars. They are built of as good materials and are as carefully constructed, as finely finished, and, if so ordered, as elegantly upholstered and ornamented as any cars built.

We cannot attempt, within the limits of a single page, to describe the many different styles of Narrow Gauge Passenger and Freight Cars constructed by this Company. For such details we must refer the reader to the Company itself. They will promptly forward illustrated and descriptive circulars to all who apply for them, and will freely give such other information as they possess in relation to the building and equipment of Narrow Gauge Roads. The better way, however, is to make a personal visit to their Works, such a visit will afford an opportunity to examine the Peach Bottom Narrow-Gauge Railway (3 feet) and its equipment, now in practical operation. This road begins at York, Pa., only a few hours ride from New York, Philadelphia and Baltimore, and on it cars built by the Billmeyer & Small Company are in daily use.

These cars have been drawn at a speed of thirty-five miles per hour by locomotive. They have encountered the terrible severity of the gales so well known to travelers in Colorado, and no effort has been spared to put them to the severest tests. Their success under all circumstances fully insures their future satisfactory performance, and demonstrates that the doubts entertained by many minds respecting narrow-gauge rolling-stock were without foundation and unworthy of this progressive age. The Billmeyer & Small Company's Cars may be constructed in sections ready to put together, or may be entirely completed before being packed for transportation. They are prepared to furnish any part of these Cars well packed, ready for shipment to any part of the world. The trucks are of iron and steel, and may be shipped complete, with their wheels in position, ready to be placed under the car bodies at place of destination. Shipments in this way have been made to South America, the Islands, and to Washington Territory, via the Isthmus and Cape Horn, and by rail overland to San Francisco.

Though Narrow Gauge Cars are a specialty of this concern, and though they have built up a very large business in that particular line of production, it is very far from being their only line. Many thousands of the Billmeyer & Small Company's Wide Gauge Cars are running upon the most important roads in the United States; such as the Pennsylvania, the New York Central and Hudson River, the Baltimore and Ohio, the Northern Central, the Erie, and other equally well known railways. As to the quality of the work produced at this establishment, it needs only to be said that their earliest customers, those who ordered cars from the concern when the original firm first commenced operations in 1852, continue their orders to this day and are among the Company's largest customers—notably the Pennsylvania Railroad.

As we have already said, the York Car Works is one of the largest and one of the most complete establishments of the kind in America. It is equipped with every appliance that can aid in the production of thoroughly good work, that can save physical labor and cheapen the cost of production.

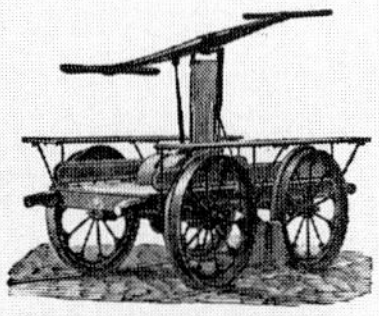

Car H, Four-Wheeled Hand Car.

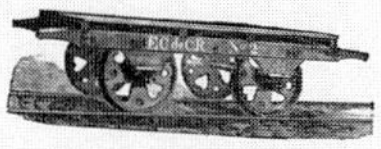

Car O, Common Push Car.

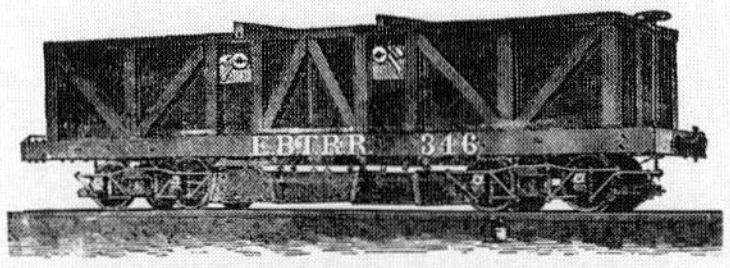
EBTRR 346

Car X, Eight-Wheeled Double Drop Bottom Coal Car.

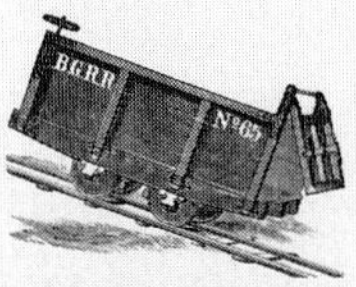
BGRR
No 65

Car V, Four-Wheeled Mining Dump Car.

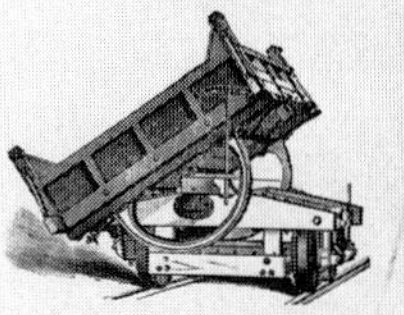

Car Z, Four-Wheeled Side Dump Car.

These trucks are specially adapted for roads having a large amount of curvature. Swing bolster trucks are best adapted where there is little or no curvature, but we think dangerous on short curves on account of the swing and over-hang of heavy loads on such a small base as 3 feet gauge, and besides are certainly much more expensive in repairs. The cars built by this Company have, in nearly every case, their patent pulling and buffing arrangement, now in use on over 2,000 cars; it is simple, and specially adapted for Narrow Gauge Cars and very economical in repairs and perfectly safe in coupling. The Company have yet to learn of the loss of a single life or limb while in the act of coupling their cars; of course they place on cars such other buffers and pulling irons as are desired

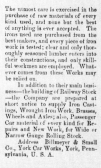

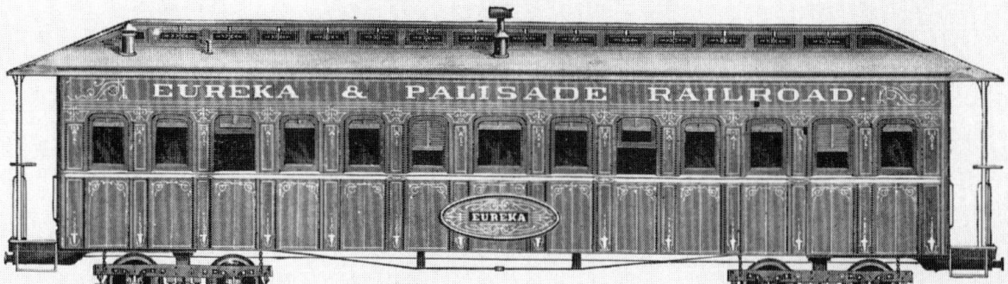
EUREKA & PALISADE RAILROAD.
EUREKA
C. WRIGHT N.Y.

First-Class Narrow Gauge Passenger Car.

The utmost care is exercised in the purchase of raw materials of every kind used, and none but the best of anything is ever accepted. The irons used are purchased from the best makers, and every piece of iron work is tested; clear and only thoroughly seasoned lumber enters into their constructions, and only skillful workmen are employed. Whatever comes from these Works may be relied on.

In addition to their main business—the building of Railway Stock—the Company are prepared at short notice to supply Iron Castings, Wrought Iron Work, Brasses, Wheels and Axles; also, Passenger Car material of every kind for Repairs and New Work, for Wide or Narrow Gauge Rolling Stock.

Address Billmeyer & Small Co., York Car Works, York, Pennsylvania, U. S. A.

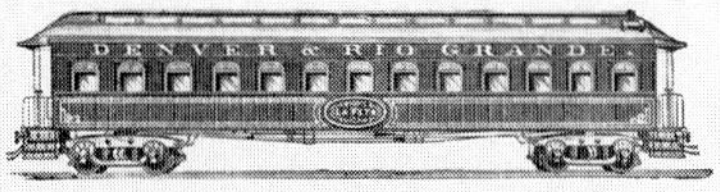
DENVER & RIO GRANDE

Passenger Car with Air Brakes and Miller Buffer.

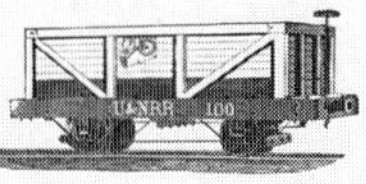

Car F, Four-Wheeled Drop Bottom Coal & Ore Car.

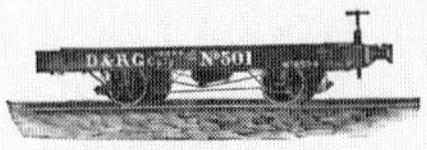

Car A, Four-Wheeled Flat Car.

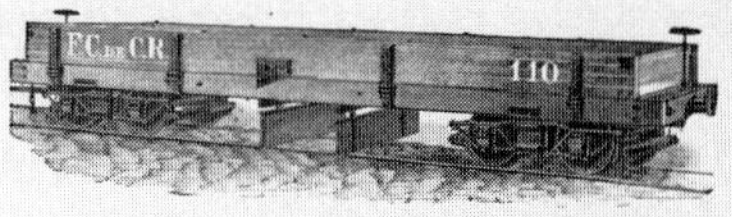
110

Car DDDD, Eight-Wheeled Drop Bottom Coal Car.

be remedied only by constant and careful reduction of unnecessary weight in all parts of the structures under contemplation. . . ." [25]

As pointed out in Chapter 3, Forney recognized that existing equipment was too heavy for its loads, and proposed that lighter cars of standard gauge be built in preference to moving to a narrow gauge, but the advocates of the narrow gauge considered this impractical on the ground that lighter cars could not be mixed with conventional equipment. In this, the railroads' master mechanics and car designers agreed thoroughly with the narrow gauge advocates, accepting a second major element in their philosophy. At the convention of the Master Car-Builders' Association in St. Louis in 1872, Enos Varney of the Fitchburg Railroad said he thought it impractical to run lightweight cars in trains with heavy, "as the light ones would get the worst of it." Hugh Gray of the Chicago & North Western reported that his boxcars of nine tons were none too heavy for their loads. This thinking did not lead the members to acceptance of the narrow gauge policy prescription, however. F. D. Adams of the Boston & Albany noted that narrow gauge cars of only 4,500 pounds were alleged to carry as much as a standard car, but said he took that statement "with a grain of allowance." [26]

Rather, the car designers of the major railroads dealt with the problem by moving to successively larger cars with more favorable area-to-volume ratios. John H. White, Jr., who is treating the development at length in his forthcoming book, estimates that between 1870 and 1899 the typical standard gauge boxcar grew from 10 to 50 tons capacity, and its volume rose from about 1,000 to about 2,000 cubic feet. [27] The improvement was only in small part due to improved or lighter materials: malleable iron and steel was substituted for wrought iron, and Georgia pine replaced oak. Moving to larger cars with more favorable area-to-volume ratios did not, in gen-

Rolling Stock   177

Cairo & Kanawha boxcar No. 5 stands next to a standard gauge car of the Baltimore & Ohio during transshipment. End doors were common on narrow gauge boxcars, mainly to facilitate lumber loading, but this full length door is unusual. (Railroad Museum of Pennsylvania.)

eral, require any change in wooden framing design, although it was accompanied by going from two to four trussrods as standard. The history of the technological development is not fully documented, but the earliest major example White has found was the introduction of the Baltimore & Ohio's class M boxcar in 1870 with a tare weight of 22,600 pounds and a capacity of 40,000 pounds.[28] Most railroads moved to such a ratio more slowly; Theodore N. Ely of the Pennsylvania Railroad began building a car of 15-ton capacity in 1876.[29]

In May 1880, the *National Car-Builder* editorially observed that this tendency was lethal to narrow gauge doctrine:

The three-feet gauge, however, is now fairly on trial in this country, and will be judged according to its merits. It will probably turn out in the end that so far as rails and rolling stock are concerned, a standard-gauge road can be equipped and operated in precisely the same manner as a narrow gauge, and at no greater cost, if its managers and owners so elect, thus realizing all the alleged advantages of lighter cars and engines, leaving the difference of 20½ inches in embankments, cuttings, tunnels and bridges, to be offset by the convenience of interchanging traffic with other standard-gauge roads without a transfer of freight. It must not fail to be noted in connection with this subject, that notwithstanding the admitted advantages of shorter and lighter cars with respect to deadweight—a strong point with the narrow-gauge people—the constant tendency is toward longer and heavier standard-gauge cars, and an increase of load over and above the old and nearly obsolete rule of ton for ton. This is the case everywhere, and especially upon leading western lines, upon one of which the actual weighing of upward of 20 loaded cars arriving on the same day in Chicago showed the average weight of the cars to be 20,560 lbs., and their average loads 24,320 lbs., while in many cases box cars of the same road carry 32,000, and even 35,000 lbs., and flat cars nearly as much. It is evident that if this tendency keeps on, the narrow-gauge theories as to the superiority of their own cars in regard to the relative proportions of dead and paying weight will become realized in the performance of standard-gauge cars, in spite of their heavier longitudinal timbers and trussing irons in order to sustain the weight of load between the points of support.[30]

By 1883 a 4'-8½" boxcar of 20-ton capacity with a ratio of tare to load of 1:2 had become standard. An English writer, describing exhibits at the Chicago Railway Exposition of that year, estimated that within the past few years the full load of a representative American boxcar had increased from 20,000 to 40,000 pounds while the average tare weight had increased only from 20,500 to 22,000 pounds.[31]

Arthur M. Wellington, who considered the increase of capacity of freight cars relative to weight "one of the greatest changes in the recent history of American railways," attributed the improvement in part to the enunciation of narrow gauge doctrine: "This change has taken place almost entirely since . . . 1876, and is in good part the result (and the most useful result) of the narrow-gauge movement, which concentrated attention upon admitted extravagances of past administration. In part it is an indirect effect of the introduction of steel rails. A still more potent cause, however, has probably been the enormous increase in volume of traffic, especially in bulky freight to be transmitted great distances at low rates, which made the last degree of economy indispensable."[32]

The controversy among carbuilders by 1883 was not concerned with the acceptance of such cars, but rather with the practicability of moving on to cars of even greater capacity. Leander Garey of the New York Central, President of the Car-Builders' Club of New York, addressing the club on April 19, 1883, stated that the breakage of cars in the past year had been 50 to 100 percent over the level of five years before. He attributed the problem to current 20-ton loads and argued that they represented the limit relative to strength of existing axles, wheels, and car bodies. He thought that loads of 25 to 40 tons, which some managers projected, would require heavier framing, axles, wheels, trucks, couplers, rail, and bridges.[33] Calvin A. Smith of the Union Tank Car Co. foresaw an infinite increase in the capacity of boxcars because of the unlimited potential growth of east-west traffic. He reported he had seen cars rated at 25 tons and expected 30 tons to become the norm.[34]

In this instance, convergence between narrow gauge and standard gauge practice had occurred by the standard gauge operators achieving what the narrow gauge carbuilders had set out to do at the beginning of the movement. The ordinary standard gauge boxcar now had a ratio of tare to load of 1:2—what Schuyler claimed for the Denver & Rio Grande's Billmeyer & Small cars of 1871. Meanwhile, the D&RG had not advanced over that ratio, nor was it to do so. The management ordered 1,500 freight cars about the beginning of 1880, 450 from Billmeyer & Small, the rest from

The men on the platform of Colorado & Southern caboose 1005 put the size of the equipment in perspective nicely. (Richard H. Kindig.)

Jackson & Sharp or other builders.[35] Most of the equipment from this period had been dropped by 1920. The D&RGW's narrow gauge mileage operated in its later years mainly with cars built around the turn of the century, though some additional equipment was built in the 1920s. The D&RGW's largest class of narrow gauge boxcars was the series numbered 3000–3749, a design of 1904. The cars had inside dimensions of 29'-5"×7'-0"×6'-1¾", outside dimensions of 31'-10"×8'-4¼"×12'-1¹¹⁄₁₆" (from the rail to the roof), with a volume of 1,267 cubic feet, and 50,000 pound capacity.[36] The railroad rebuilt the series in the 1920s with metal roofs and 26-inch wheels, which probably increased their tare weight somewhat. On the basis of actual weighings at Alamosa and elsewhere, the tare weight was 23,000 pounds.[37] The ratio of tare to permissible load was just short of 1:2.

The Colorado & Southern's counterpart was a relatively late series of boxcars dating from the first decade of the twentieth century, numbered from 8100 to 8417. The length and width were approximately the same as the D&RG's but the internal height was 3½ inches less, resulting in a lower cubic capacity, 1,219 cubic feet.[38] The weight capacity was the same, 50,000 pounds, and the tare weight was 20,800 pounds for the wood-underframed cars or 21,000 for the steel-underframed.[39] Once again, the cars served the railroad to the end of its narrow gauge history. Cars of smaller operators were comparable.

Consequently, by the peak years of narrow-gauge building the narrow gauges were providing service with cars, no less than locomotives, that were scaled-down versions of standard gauge railroading. There is no *a priori* reason to believe that they should have been achieving any econo-

Facing page
Upon abandonment of the South Park Line, the Colorado & Southern sold 108 freight cars to the Rio Grande Southern for further service. Shown are boxcars and stock cars loaded on Denver & Rio Grande Western flatcars for shipment to Salida, from which the D&RGW moved them to the RGS at Ridgway on narrow gauge track. C&S No. 8242 became RGS No. 8801, the RGS's only car fitted for automobile loading. Note the hinged, split end doors on the car. (Jackson C. Thode.)

TABLE 6.4

Operating Experience of the Charlotte, Columbia & Augusta (5'-0") and the
Chester & Lenoir (3'-0"), Year Ending September 1883

Ton-miles	CC&A (5'-0")		C&L (3'-0")	
	Passenger	Freight	Passenger	Freight
Locomotives	8,115,560	10,556,587	281,685	449,655
Cars	17,197,130	32,465,077	1,016,584	580,971
Load	755,849	14,635,451	39,311	306,789
TOTAL	26,068,539	57,657,115	1,337,580	1,337,415
Load as a percent of total	2.90%	25.38%	2.86%	23.00%

SOURCE: *Railroad Gazette*, 16 (1884), p. 152, corrected for arithmetical errors.

mies in weight. As far as is known, only one railroad, a southern broad gauge, reported its actual experience. The Charlotte, Columbia & Augusta, a predecessor of the Southern Railway, operated a main line of 191 miles of the common southern gauge of 5'-0". It leased the 72-mile Chester & Lenoir, 3'-0". On the CC&A, the average train handled 29.3 passengers or 65.1 tons of freight. On the C&L, the average train handled 18.3 passengers or 10.3 tons of freight. The reported experience for the year ending in September 1883 is shown in Table 6.4.

It is questionable whether the difference of about 10 percent in freight load as a percentage of total weight is statistically significant, but it is in favor of the broad gauge, and at minimum demonstrates that the railroad was achieving no benefit from narrow gauge. It is notable that the observation is based mainly on 1883, the year in which the narrow gauge movement collapsed. The data are consistent with the qualitative evaluation of the narrow gauge by the bondholders of the Toledo, Cincinnati & St. Louis quoted in Chapter 4 in indicating that there was no compensating benefit offsetting the incompatibility and other disadvantages of the narrow gauge.[40] In other words, the basic element on which the narrow gauge advocates had erected their intellectual system, the prospective savings of weight of equipment relative to cargo, was demonstrably fallacious by the time the movement ended.

Indeed, the improvement in standard gauge boxcars had largely killed interest in the question of deadweight of equipment. The *National Car-Builder* observed in 1885: "Dead weight . . . as respects both passenger and freight cars, receives much less attention now among railroad men than it did a dozen years ago. In fact, it has ceased to be a bugbear, not on the theory that it costs nothing to haul non-paying weight, but mainly because the cost was formerly very much overrated by being based upon the cost of hauling freight per ton per mile as reported by the various roads. . . ." The writer argued that the forces which had reduced freight rates to approximately 0.8¢ per ton-mile had equally reduced the cost of transporting deadweight. He continued:

It must also be remembered that nearly 50 per cent of the total operating expenses of a road is not affected at all by the relative proportions of dead and paying weight hauled, and that some of the other expenses that would seem to be directly affected, are only affected to a limited extent, and not in proportion to the dead weight. . . . It must also be noted that light-weight cars, while they tax the motive power less than heavier ones, may, if their strength is diminished in proportion to their lightness, require a larger outlay for repairs and suffer more in the

The Colorado & Southern clearly looked upon its narrow gauge lines as hopeless, and did little to upgrade them. Oddly, under the circumstances, it advanced to steel underframes and cast steel trucks more readily than the Denver & Rio Grande Western did. This refrigerator car, photographed by G. M. Best, has both improvements. (California Railroad Museum.)

The Colorado & Southern moved its ore mainly in wooden gondolas. G. M. Best photographed these examples during a derailment at Black Hawk on the Colorado Central in 1939. (California Railroad Museum.)

general run of accidents. The dead weight scare, we repeat, is no longer the frightful thing it was a dozen years ago.[41]

If the experience of a decade and more refuted narrow gauge doctrine concerning weight, it incidentally demolished the doctrine concerning speed and quality of service. The narrow gauge advocates had based their demand analysis on acceptance of the common view of the early 1870s— set forth in Chapter 2—that the railroad industry was overproducing quality, operating freight trains faster than the cost-minimizing speed of 8 to 10 miles per hour. Improvement in boxcars, combined with proliferation of the other technological advances of the time—steel rail, 2-8-0 locomotives, coal-burning fireboxes, and early applications of compressed air or vacuum brake systems—had approximately doubled the cost-minimizing speed of freight trains. In 1883 the *National Car-Builder* observed editorially: "[I]n these days . . . it has been proved that a speed bordering on 20 miles per hour is the most economical one at which freight trains can be moved."[42]

Consequently, the typical narrow gauge built in the early 1880s came into being with a technology of scaled-down main-line railroading with no remaining claim to cost advantage, and targeted at a level of speed and service that was already obsolete. The situation was to become worse, not better. The cars of 50-ton capacity that Calvin A. Smith had seen as experiments were commonplace by the end of the century. The trend toward larger locomotives and larger equipment continued to the present. Such narrow gauges as survived proved locked into a miniature version of 1880 railroading indefinitely. In part, the massive conversions of the late 1880s and early 1890s left cars, no less than locomotives, in abundant supply. When car-building resumed in the twentieth century, car design was not greatly improved.

Had narrow gauge operators sought to move to larger equipment, the intrinsic limitations of their technology would have impeded them. Even if clearances had permitted wider vehicles than the orthodox narrow gauge boxcar, considerations of stability would have made such a development very difficult. The boxcars of the Denver & Rio Grande and the South Park Line described above were, respectively, 8'-4¼" and 7'-11½" wide, overall.[43] Standard gauge cars varied in width, but the Pennsylvania Railroad's standard boxcar of 1880 was 8'-8",[44] and the New Haven's only 8'-6".[45] The D&RG cars had an overhang of about 32 inches, compared with only 24 for the Pennsylvania car. At the narrow gauge convention of October 1878, Hulbert and Brooks noted with dissatisfaction that the typical overhang of narrow gauge equipment was 24 to 26 inches, but of standard gauge only 22 to 24 inches. The committee recommended no more than 20 inches for 3'-0" stock.[46]

Accordingly, American standard gauge equipment had a growth potential, whereas narrow gauge did not. The American loading gauge is 10'-9" wide and 15'-6" high, the largest for 4'-8½" railroading in the world.[47] Already passenger cars between 9'-3" and 10'-0" in width were in existence. By 1937, the Association of American Railroads' standard 40-foot, 40-ton steel-sheathed boxcar was 9'-9¾" wide and 14'-6½" high from the rails.[48] Hulbert and Brooks thought even the early double-truck narrow gauge cars too large, recommending cars of only 3 tons weight and 6 tons capacity, barely larger than the D&RG's 4-wheel equipment.[49]

There were efforts, which are not well documented, to increase the capacity of narrow gauge boxcars. The Cairo & St. Louis, which was in the hands of a Chicago carbuilder, Ferdinand E. Canda, in 1881 was reported to have ordered 150 boxcars capable of carrying 125 barrels of flour each, a capacity equal to standard gauge.[50] In 1883 the Hot Springs Branch Railroad ordered some 36'×8' boxcars from Barney & Smith of 50,000 pounds capacity, fitted with Finlay's center-supporting trucks. The editor of the *National Car-Builder* expressed surprise that, on the basis of the pilot model, a three-truck car could operate successfully on a railroad with severe curvature—20°.[51] In general, narrow gauges did not attempt cars beyond 31 feet because of curvature, but there were exceptions: the East Tennessee & Western North Carolina had cars of 36 feet, for example.[52]

An incidental consequence of the static size of the narrow gauge boxcar was a poor ratio to the standard gauge cars to which most of the cargo was transshipped. As Hulbert and Brooks noted, the typical narrow gauge boxcar had a capacity about two-thirds of its standard gauge counterpart. Two narrow gauge loads tended to overload a standard gauge car, and three frequently did not divide well between two standard gauge cars. Bulk cargo might be divided evenly between standard gauge cars, but if the cargo were large discrete items, like buggies or machinery, there was no assurance the content of a third narrow gauge car could be split properly between two standard gauge boxcars. In the latter days of the D&RGW's narrow gauge, the railroad did not use such a ratio, but simply assigned cars in an ad hoc fashion on the basis of weight of the cargo.[53] The Milwaukee Road for its Bellevue & Cascade line used ratios that varied by type of equipment. A standard gauge hopper car required two narrow gauge gondolas, but the grain in a standard gauge boxcar could fill four narrow gauge boxcars. Stock cars were calculated at a 2:1 ratio.[54]

The argument concerning narrow gauge cars has necessarily been framed in terms of the boxcar, the most general vehicle of the time. The experience of other cars was parallel, however. The D&RG's series 100–119 refrigerator cars of 1881 weighed 21,500 pounds and had capacities of 24,000 pounds. The series 120–144 of the same year weighed only 14,000 pounds, but had capacities of 20,000 pounds—still markedly less favorable than the boxcars.[55] The company's most common flatcar, series 6000–6098, was a 30-foot model with tare weight of 11,200 pounds and capacity of 40,000 pounds. The railroad's principal series of coal cars, 1000–1499, was essentially a wooden gondola fitted with a dump bottom, 31 feet long with a tare weight of 21,000 pounds and a capacity of 50,000 pounds.[56]

Stock cars presented the problem that the interior width of about 7'-0" was too short for the usual placing of cattle side-by-side facing the sides of the car. Billmeyer & Small's original catalog model was designed for nine to 12 large cattle facing the ends, or 16 small cattle facing the sides. Howard Fleming characteristically considered this an advantage: "Prominent stock men state that they prefer sending their stock to market in such cars, because the cattle steady themselves better, and there is less danger of their getting down, and because it is easier to feed them and attend to them."[57] The limitations of narrow gauge clearances made the problem difficult. As late as 1923 the D&RGW built a series of stock cars, 5900–5999, principally for cattle movements, but the outside width was only an orthodox 7'-11".[58] A shipper on the Bellevue & Cascade complained that narrow gauge cars were too low for horses.[59] In the Colorado network the stock cars mainly handled sheep, whose small size presented no special problem.

Steel equipment came barely at all to the narrow gauges. Steel-underframe boxcars were put in service on the South Park Line in the first decade of the twentieth century, and the D&RGW used steel-underframe equipment, much of it rebuilt from standard gauge cars, on the pipe movements of the 1950s and 1960s. All-steel cars came relatively early but not successfully. In 1880 the Carson & Colorado ordered 30 steel boxcars of the La Mothe patent from Jesup, Paton & Co. of New York, which were shipped in knocked-down form and assembled at the railroad's shops in 1881. The order included flatcars built to the same patent. The cars shook themselves loose in service and were withdrawn around the turn of the century.[60] The East Broad Top had 19 steel boxcars built between 1919 and 1920.[61]

The East Broad Top was unusual in
moving to steel equipment of modern
standards. Shown are a hopper and a
boxcar. (Ed Bond collection.)

More important, given the East Broad Top's function as a specialized coal hauler, was a series of steel hopper cars built for the railroad by the Pressed Steel Car Co. of Pittsburgh in 1913. The cars were essentially scaled-down standard hoppers of the time. With a tare weight of 20,800 pounds and a capacity of 60,000 pounds, they had a ratio of tare to cargo of about 1:2.9, which was not exceptional.[62] Standard gauge hoppers delivered by the same builder in the same year to the Central Vermont weighed 37,200 pounds with a capacity of 100,000 pounds, a ratio of about 1:2.7.[63] The East Tennessee & Western North Carolina had steel tank cars,[64] and the White Pass & Yukon used roller-bearing steel flat cars for its containerization in the 1960s.[65]

The fact that the typical narrow gauge operated in isolation gave the management a certain degree of freedom in choice of fittings. At the outset, there was little problem of choice in coupling and braking. The narrow gauge movement came to America about the middle of the period 1868–73 during which Eli H. Janney developed the MCB coupler and George Westinghouse the automatic air brake, but before either was widely adopted. Necessarily, the earliest cars, beginning with Billmeyer & Small's equipment for the Denver & Rio Grande, had link-and-pin couplers and hand brakes. The 3'-0" lines generally adhered to the recommendation of the convention of 1872 that the coupler be centered 24 inches above the rail. The D&RG began with this height, but shortly moved to 26 inches.[66] The Colorado & Southern also used a 26-inch height. The 3'-6" lines used a slightly higher coupler; the Covington, Columbus & Black Hills ordered its locomotive with a drawhead 27 inches above the rail.[67] Beyond such uniformities, there was considerable scope for individual development.

Individuality in narrow gauge practice manifested itself particularly in the use of vacuum braking systems. The Denver & Rio Grande was an early user of the Westinghouse air brake, the Utah & Northern used the Westinghouse from the time of its completion, and many other narrow gauges used it. The Denver, South Park & Pacific, Colorado Central, Baltimore & Lehigh, Chester & Lenoir, Bradford, Bordell & Kinzua, and a large number of others opted for the Eames vacuum brake.[68]

The narrow gauges typically opted for the simplest form of the Eames brake, which its producer called the "Plain Brake." The basic element in this system was a device called the ejector, a vertical column mounted at the top of the boiler's backhead. The engineer used a horizontal lever to admit steam to the ejector, where it passed through a nozzle called a venturi, which narrowed the flow but then expanded it. This action created a vacuum which drew in air from the train line through a valve at the bottom of the ejector. The exhaustion of air from the train line produced a vacuum in the part of the system analogous to a brake cylinder, variously called the diaphragm chamber or the pot. This was a metal semispherical container, which was covered with a convex diaphragm of rubber-impregnated duck canvas. The diaphragm was connected to the brake rigging by an eye bolt, held in place by two large washers, one inside and one outside the chamber. The vacuum in the chamber drew in the diaphragm by pressure of the atmosphere, applying the brakes by pulling on the brake rigging, rather than pushing on it, as the Westinghouse system did. Because

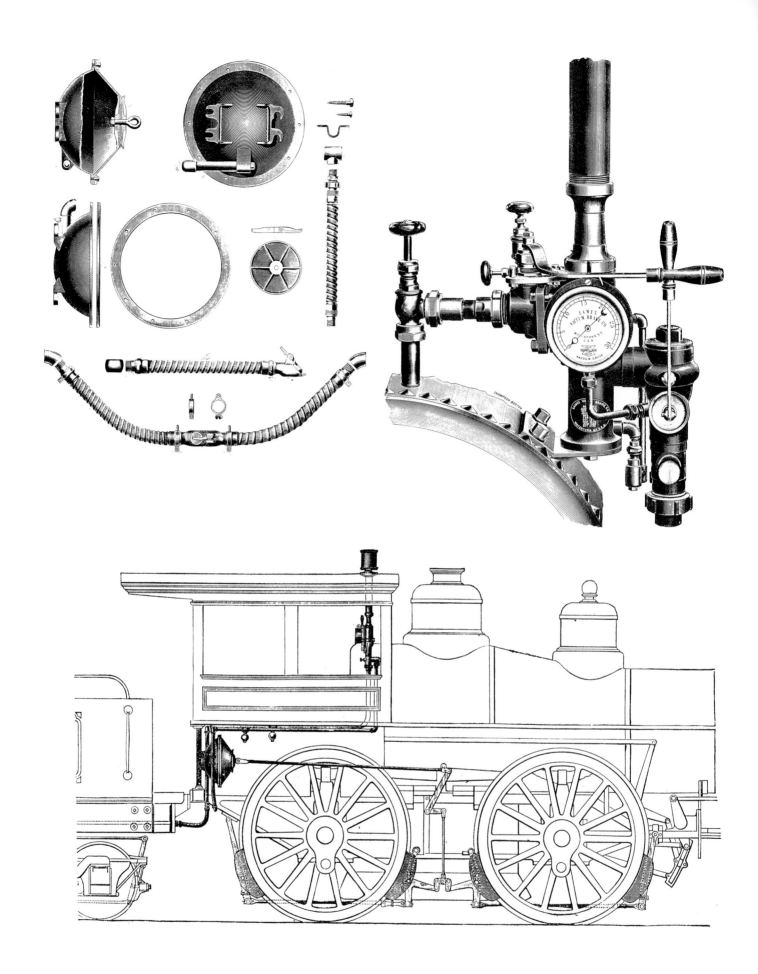

the ejector was an inherently noisy device, it exhausted into a muffler in a cylindrical housing on top of the cab.[69]

The Eames system had various attractions for the narrow gauges. Notably, it was cheap: Eames charged only $145 to apply it to a locomotive, $65 to a standard gauge car, and $55 to a narrow gauge car.[70] Relative to the Westinghouse system, it was simple. Maintenance expenses were very low. Vacuum systems had the indisputable attraction that the braking power was immediately available whenever steam was up; there were no brakeless moments as in the Westinghouse system when the air reservoirs were empty, and the train line had to be pumped up to fill them.[71] On a line with continual stops, this attraction was overpowering. Eames's principal selling point was his installation on the New York Elevated, where his equipment made over 70,000 stops per day and was considered outstandingly successful.

Unfortunately, the experience of the narrow gauges demonstrated the shortcomings of the Eames system. It worked well only on relatively short trains, such as elevated railways used. On longer trains, certainly anything

Tidewater & Western No. 11 was conspicuously equipped with the Eames vacuum braking system. The diaphragm is mounted below the cab and, as usual, the muffler on the roof. The control mechanism can be seen through the upper front cab window. (Ed Bond collection.)

The drawings opposite, from the Eames Vacuum Brake Company's catalog, show the basic elements in the system. The side elevation demonstrates the equipment as applied to a standard gauge locomotive. The engraving of the ejector shows it as mounted on a boiler backhead. The smaller drawings illustrate the fittings as designed for a narrow gauge car. (Smithsonian Institution.)

over ten cars, leakage in the air line and friction in the brake rigging weakened the brake impulse and rendered the system unreliable. Crews on the South Park Line looked upon the device as a menace, without adequate fail-safe characteristics on grades. M. C. Poor quoted an old employee as saying that air brakes first appeared on the line at Denver in February 1893, but builders' photographs of the company's locomotives show air pumps from 1883.[72] Engineers on the Wiscasset, Waterville & Farmington had little or no faith in the Eames system and mainly relied on the trains' hand brakes.[73]

Inevitably, existence of both air and vacuum systems on the narrow gauges created compatibility problems. The Catskill Mountain Railway used the Eames system, but the affiliated Catskill & Tannersville the Westinghouse. Cars that moved between the two via a funicular, as well as the C&T's locomotives, were equipped with both systems.[74] In 1900 when the Sandy River bought the former Laurel River & Hot Springs 2-6-0 that became its No. 3, the management installed Eames apparatus for train service, but retained the existing Westinghouse equipment as the engine brake.[75]

As common carriers, the narrow gauges became subject to the Safety Appliance Act of 1893, which required universal adoption of the MCB (Janney) coupler and Westinghouse air brake. Active compulsion on the narrow gauges began about the turn of the century. The Colorado & Southern began installing the MCB coupler on the South Park and Colorado Central lines in 1901,[76] and the D&RG converted to the MCB in 1903–4.[77] In 1906, when the forced adoption was nearly completed, the federal authorities took action against the Colorado & Northwestern for non-compliance. The railroad had itself declared by a federal court an intrastate carrier to avoid installation of the MCB.[78] Conversion to the air brake was nearly universal, but some of the nominal common carriers resisted the MCB coupler. The Monson Railroad in Maine operated with a link-and-pin and resisted air brakes to its abandonment in 1943.[79] The Diamond & Caldor in California operated with link-and-pin couplers until ordered to adopt the MCB by the California commission, but the management abandoned the railroad in 1952 rather than comply.[80] On the basis of photographic evidence, the Boston, Revere Beach & Lynn operated with link-and-pin couplers on its locomotives until electrification in 1928 and with Miller Hook couplers on its cars until abandonment in 1940.[81] The Monson operated without headlights until ordered to install them.[82] The West Side Lumber Co. in California, operating the former Hetch Hetchy & Yosemite Valleys Railway after it had ceased to be a common carrier, used cars bought secondhand from another lumber company equipped with a dual braking system, having separate air lines for straight air and automatic. The company used the straight air for service applications and the automatic for emergency.[83] The Uintah mounted its air hoses about 18 inches above the coupler to avoid freezing of condensation in the hoses and gladhands.[84]

The principal insularity of the narrow gauge railroads was in truck and air brake design. The Association of American Railroads prohibited arch bar trucks in interchange beyond January 1, 1938. Such trucks were fab-

Gladhand: The metal element at the end of the air hose that is joined with its counterpart on another car to make the brake connection. The two pieces are brought together manually in a meshing that resembles shaking hands—hence the name.

The diaphragm of the Eames vacuum braking system is conspicuous beneath this tank car of the Waynesburg & Washington. (Ed Bond collection.)

ricated of a wooden or steel crossbar and metal straps bolted together. They had long been considered a safety hazard because one of the metal straps could fracture or become unbolted, hang down, foul a rail at a switch and derail the car. By 1938 there was no longer interchange of equipment between any narrow gauges except the Denver & Rio Grande Western and the Rio Grande Southern, but this was apparently treated as between a railroad and its subsidiary, not subject to interchange regulations. The D&RGW provided all the revenue cars used by the RGS until 1938. Both railroads operated mainly with arch bar trucks to the end, as practically all of the earlier narrow gauges had done. The D&RGW, Colorado & Southern, Uintah, and others had trucks with cast steel frames on equipment bought in the twentieth century.

Similarly, the remaining narrow gauges were insulated against the conversion from the Type K triple valve to the AB air brake system. The Association of American Railroads ordered this improvement in braking technology for equipment built beginning September 1, 1933. Neither the D&RGW nor the Colorado & Southern ever made the change. Both operated in the expectation of using existing car stocks to conversion or abandonment.[85]

The most important matter concerning narrow gauge cars is not their fittings, nor even their weights, but their numbers. A narrow gauge railroad was isolated from the free-running car supply of the American railroad system. As was pointed out in Chapter 2, the narrow gauge movement arose as the railroads were moving toward a homogeneous technology and cartelized economic organization in which the cars of all companies moved freely about the North American continent. This system of car supply has always been considered imperfect because of the nature of its pricing. The fees the railroads charge one another for the use of their cars have been set collusively, either on a mileage basis or by the day—*per diem*—or in some combination of the two. Because the price is not freely fluctuating, it rations cars poorly in the short run, giving rise to shortages and gluts, and it gives imperfect indications concerning the size of the aggregate car supply and technological change in cars.[86] Nonetheless, the system does provide a supply of cars that adapts, even if imperfectly, to varying geographical demands over time. The cars that move grain from the Dakotas in October can haul lumber out of Maine in February.

A narrow gauge railroad, by virtue of its isolation, had either to maintain a car supply adequate for its peak loads or to confront its shippers with car shortages at peak periods. The Springfield, Effingham & Southeastern was inadequate in car supply, as in most else, but most narrow gauges sought to provide enough cars for peak movements. Trains moved slowly and cars spent a great deal of time at transshipment facilities. As a consequence the car supplies of the longer-lasting narrow gauges appear enormous relative to the length of line or the tributary population. When the Pere Marquette Railway was formed at the turn of the century, it succeeded to one narrow gauge line of a predecessor, the Port Huron–Almont branch of 34 miles. The line served two farming towns, Almont and Memphis, of populations 698 and 556, respectively, plus three villages of about 100 people each, and some hamlets. On the eve of its conversion, the line had 107 freight cars.[87] This total may have been swollen by cars from the three other lines of the former Port Huron & Northwestern that had already been converted, but the figures from the Bellevue & Cascade line of the Milwaukee Road, which was always isolated, were approximately the same. The branch linked Cascade, Iowa, a town of 1,266 (in 1900) with a Milwaukee Road secondary main line 36 miles away. Including five intermediate villages, the total tributary population was about 8,000. The line, which had a right-of-way too poor to convert, was equipped with 110 cars.[88] Either of these lines as a standard gauge railroad could have been worked with a few dozen cars from the general American car supply. The Chateaugay Railroad moved most of its traffic in several hundred four-wheel ore cars, but on the eve of its conversion in 1903 it maintained for general cargo a fleet of 32 boxcars, 87 flatcars, 28 gondolas, 16 specialized charcoal cars, and two cattle cars[89]—a car supply consistent with the Almont branch or the Bellevue & Cascade. As late as 1950, the Denver & Rio Grande Western had 2,568 narrow gauge cars, some 17 percent of its car supply, to move a trivial part of the company's traffic.[90] At the same time, the Southern Pacific used 227 cars on its narrow gauge line in the Owens Valley, about 0.4 percent of the vast system's car supply for a minor branch.[91]

Here again was a major consideration ignored by the advocates of the narrow gauge, and almost equally by the opponents. Even if we accept Howard Schuyler's figures for 1871 that imply a capital saving of $120 on the capacity of an ordinary boxcar, the number of boxcars required by an isolated narrow gauge was so large that it is very unlikely there could have been any capital saving on this account. At the relative prices previously quoted for the early 1880s, the additional capital required to equip a narrow gauge was a major cost.

Two-Foot Gauge Equipment

For the pioneer 2'-0" Billerica & Bedford, George E. Mansfield ordered boxcars on the order of baggage cars of the time, with both side and end doors, and the so-called Miller Platform, which encompassed the Miller Hook coupler—a device usually thought too expensive for freight cars. The cars were 25'×6'-2", riding on two trucks with 18" wheels. They weighed 5,600 pounds and had a reported capacity of 12,000 to 16,000 pounds.[92] This implies they had a tare to load ratio between 1:2 and 1:3, better than most of their 3'-0" counterparts. The boxcars of the Sandy River & Rangeley Lakes were mainly about 27'-8"×5'-7", and 5'-8" high. They weighed between 13,700 and 14,500 pounds, with reported capacities of 20,000 pounds.[93] This was a ratio of about 1:1.4, less favorable than the typical 3'-0" car. The 2'-0" railroads presumed that two of their cars could handle the contents of one standard gauge car. This was a more workable ratio than the 3:2 ratio of the 3'-0" boxcars, but there was no apparent capital saving. The boxcars the Sandy River & Rangeley Lakes bought in 1897 were $325 each, and the ones of 30,000 pound capacity bought in 1910 were $350. At these prices, the cars were only slightly less than half as expensive as standard gauge boxcars.[94] Again, the car supply of an isolated narrow gauge was so large that any real capital saving was unlikely. The SR&RL, although essentially a facility for the lumber industry with a car stock mainly of flatcars and pulpwood racks, had 96 boxcars to serve its general traffic to a set of towns none of which was over 1,000 in population. As in the instances of the Almont line and the Bellevue & Cascade, about 100 narrow gauge cars had to be allocated to do what a few dozen cars of the free-running national car supply could have done.

Passenger Cars

In the case of 3'-0" passenger cars, the process of convergence to scaled-down standard gauge practice was almost instantaneous. The D&RG's first order from Jackson & Sharp specified four-wheel design only for two baggage cars and two smokers. The smokers were of an enclosed arch-roof "butterfly" design with back-to-back wooden benches placed longitudinally. Windows lowered on leather straps.[95] The cars, even though cushions were provided for the wooden benches, could only have been extremely uncomfortable. They could have appeared only as a dead end in car design to essentially any observer. Howard Fleming did not even recognize the existence of these cars, but rather wrote: "When the question was first dis-

The four-wheel era in narrow gauge passenger car design could hardly have been shorter. The Denver & Rio Grande made a small initial order for these baggage-mail cars and smoking cars from Jackson & Sharp, but proceeded to orthodox eight-wheel equipment. The man lounging in the smoking car is carbuilder Jesse Sharp. (Delaware State Archives; Smithsonian Institution.)

cussed of building Narrow Gauge Railways in the United States, the projectors naturally looked to the engineering fraternity of Great Britain for precedents. The result was apparent in the establishment of a measure of favor towards the use of four-wheeled passenger cars, built on the *coupe* plan, so common on European roads. Further reflection, however, decided that it would be impossible to revive a custom that had become so obsolete in America, as the one of confining a small number of passengers in the equivalent of a stage-coach body." [96]

Fleming treated as the first narrow gauge passenger car the *Denver*, one of two first-class cars Jackson & Sharp built as part of the D&RG's same order. The car was 35'-0" in body length (about 40'-0" overall) by 7'-0" wide and 10'-6" high above the rail. It seated 36 passengers and weighed 15,000 pounds, a deadweight of 416 pounds per passenger. Fleming thought this very favorable relative to standard gauge coaches, which he estimated at 722 pounds per passenger. The cars had 24-inch wheels and the side sills were 27 inches from the rail. [97]

Especially among early orders, narrow gauge railroads frequently specified two-and-one seating, with a shift between sides at the middle of the car. Jackson & Sharp built such a car in 1873 for the Montrose Railway. (Delaware State Archives.)

The seating pattern of the cars presented a problem: with a width of 7'-0", it was impractical to set the usual four people abreast in two seats for two people each. Jackson & Sharp solved the problem by providing a dozen rows of three seats each, a single seat of 19 inches on one side of the aisle, and a double seat of 36 inches on the other. The aisle was 17 inches wide. The placing of the seats with respect to the aisle was reversed at mid-car, where the stove was located, so as to equalize weight between left and right. No one ever considered this arrangement fully satisfactory, partly because it placed a jog in the aisle of each car, partly because there was no assurance the weight distribution would be stabilizing unless the car was filled. Fleming reported that the width of cars had been steadily increased since 1871 and that cars with a width of 8 feet were available by the time he wrote in the middle of the decade. Such cars had two double seats 35 inches wide on either side of an aisle of 17¼ inches. Fleming attributed a deadweight per passenger of only 340 pounds to such equipment.[98] The Denver & Rio Grande did move to a standard width of 8'-0" for narrow gauge passenger cars, with some of 8'-2" and 8'-3" overall.

Whether or not such cars were practical elsewhere, the carbuilders as they began producing narrow gauge coaches turned out models not much different from Jackson & Sharp's *Denver*. Billmeyer & Small advertised its *Eureka* for the Eureka & Palisade Railroad in Nevada along with its catalog-model freight cars. The coach was 35 feet in body length, 41 feet overall. The seating was the same two-and-one as in the *Denver*, again with a reversal at mid-car. Seating capacity was 36, and the car weighed 17,000 pounds—heavier because of a metal roof.[99] The weight was about 472 pounds per passenger. The typical standard gauge coach of 1870 was 50 feet long, seated 50 passengers, and had a tare weight of 40,000 pounds, about 800 pounds per passenger.[100] Thus, for passengers, the narrow gauge proponents did achieve what they sought in reduction of tare weight relative to cargo. In this instance, there was no trend toward lighter equip-

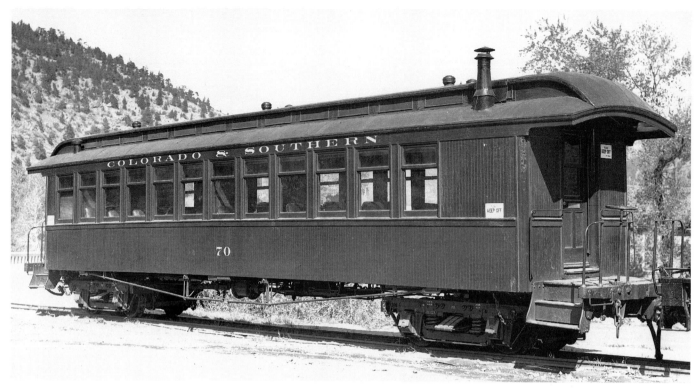

Colorado & Southern No. 70 was an orthodox narrow gauge coach. Gerald M. Best photographed the exterior and interior at Idaho Springs after the abandonment of the Colorado Central line in 1941. (California State Railroad Museum.)

Facing page
Shipping of narrow gauge equipment presented compatibility problems. The head-end car of the Houston East & West Texas was shipped on its trucks, the Jacksonville & Atlantic combine with its trucks stacked on the flatcar, and the Chateaugay coach on standard gauge trucks, with its own trucks shipped separately. The railroads typically gave the shipper his choice among the three methods. (Delaware State Archives; Ed Bond collection.)

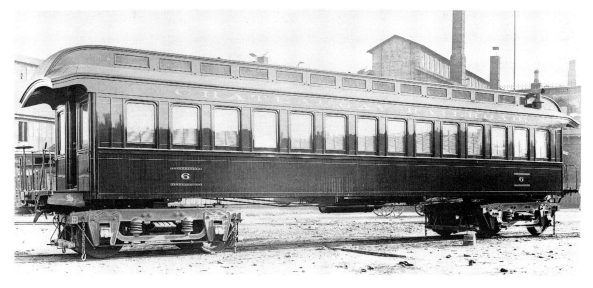

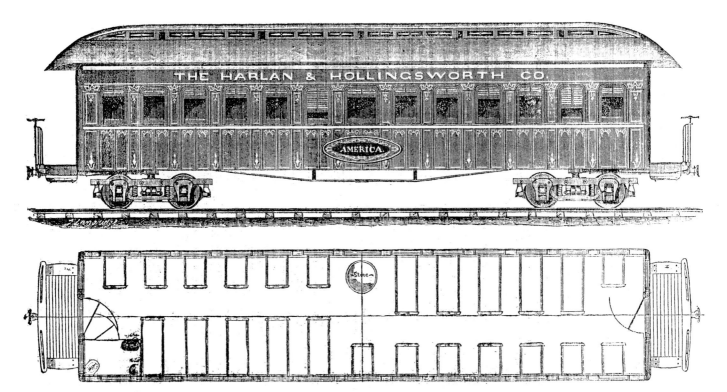

Harlan & Hollingsworth's *America* was typical of the first generation of narrow gauge coaches produced by the major carbuilders. (Smithsonian Institution.)

ment on the standard gauge railroads; in spite of some individual exceptions, standard gauge coaches steadily escalated in weight until by the end of the century tare weight was well over 1,000 pounds per passenger.[101]

Harlan & Hollingsworth produced its counterpart of the *Denver* as a stock model, *America*, about 1875. It had a length of frame of 35'-0", a width of 7'-6", and a weight of 17,000 pounds. Although a slightly longer car than the *Denver*, it seated 36 in two-and-one configuration.[102] Of the major carbuilders, only Barney & Smith of Dayton announced a pilot model of two-and-two seating. The car, *Theresa* of the West End Narrow Gauge, had the usual frame length of 35 feet, an unspecified width, but capacity for 46 people. The railroad was a suburban line at St. Louis, for which a dense seating configuration was more practical than for lines that carried passengers for long distances.[103] Cars on the Denver & Rio Grande Western's Silverton train equipped with two-and-two seating were uncomfortable to the point of impracticality; one had the impression the seats were designed for a person and a half. Edward Hulbert and H. G. Brooks, as the Committee on Machinery and Rolling Stock of the Narrow Gauge Convention of October 1878, recommended two-and-one seating with 36-inch double seats and 20-inch single. They recommended an interior width of 7'-0" or at maximum 7'-4", with an aisle of 18 inches. They specifically rejected two-and-two seating on the ground that the overhang of such cars was excessive.[104] The Boston, Revere Beach & Lynn used coaches 60 feet long and 9 feet wide, but the line was engineered for heavy-density passenger operation; such equipment was widely thought impractical on lines with ordinary curvature.[105]

Actually, the problem of accommodating four passengers abreast is one of the best demonstrations that the 3'-0" gauge was suboptimal relative to the indivisible size of the human being. The incentive to add a fourth seat was considerable. The *Railroad Gazette* in reporting on Billmeyer &

Small's *Eureka* stated that by adding a foot to width, capacity could be increased from 36 to 47; total weight would come to 19,000 pounds, or 405 pounds per passenger.[106] The Des Moines & Minnesota had three coaches of the narrower sort, which cost $2,200, $2,400, and $2,500, and one of 8'-0" width seating 47 passengers, which cost $3,400; standard gauge coaches of the time, seating 40 to 60, cost $4,800 to $5,500.[107] Hulbert and Brooks were undoubtedly correct in arguing that the increase in width was undesirable. An ordinary narrow gauge coach of approximately 7'-0" to 8'-0" width was none too stable. A bull charged a train backing on the San Quentin branch of the North Pacific Coast, upsetting it and injuring the baggageman, who recovered substantial damages from the company.[108] The extra foot in width necessary for the fourth passenger was easily practicable at 3'-6" gauge, however. The cars of the Toronto, Grey & Bruce were 8'-6" wide, with two seats of 33½" flanking an aisle of 2'-1½".[109]

There is little doubt that 3'-6" was preferable to 3'-0" for speed and stability. General George P. Buell, in recommending 3'-6" for the Texas & Pacific, argued that the additional six inches in gauge allowed a foot greater width for freight cars, with a 17 percent gain in capacity for trivial additional investment.[110] As in other respects, the more closely the narrow gauges approximated standard gauge practice, the more efficiently they operated.

Height limitations of narrow gauge passenger cars were a less serious problem. The typical narrow gauge coach was about 11'-4" to 12'-0" high from the rail, which gave an interior height of about 7'-6" to 8'-0" to the top of the clerestory. This implies the car was about 6'-9" to 7'-1" to the point at the top of the letterboard where the roof began to slope inward.[111] This was adequate, but relative to standard gauge equipment, there was little headroom for tall people or wearers of top hats, and more limited room for the circulation of air.

Coaches on the 2'-0" gauge railroads had even more severe restrictions, but these were of a character that had to be accepted. The first coach for the Billerica & Bedford was 35'-0" long in body length, or 40'-0" over the platforms, about the same as its 3'-0" counterparts. It was only 6'-2" wide overall, which allowed for only a single seat on each side of the aisle. The height was 9'-4" overall, which with wheels 18" in diameter and a 22" rise from the rails to the floor, gave an interior height of 7'-4½" or less. The coach weighed only 9,000 pounds and seated 36, only 250 pounds per passenger—one of the genuine triumphs of the narrow gauge movement at minimizing weight relative to load.[112] There was no prospect of expanding such equipment. The overhang was already approximately equal to the gauge. Given the light weight and overhang, stability was inevitably a serious problem. On July 11, 1915, on the 2'-0" Mount Gretna Narrow Gauge, about twenty soldiers from a National Guard encampment nearby jumped onto a moving train on the running board of an almost empty crossbench open car. The impact caused the car to turn over with several injuries. Damage suits were immediately responsible for the decision to abandon the railroad.[113]

The most famous piece of 2'-0" equipment was the parlor car *Rangeley*. It is shown awaiting shipment at Jackson & Sharp, and in an interior view in service on the Sandy River & Rangeley Lakes. (Robert C. Jones collection.)

Narrow gauge passenger equipment had essentially no development. Curvature and clearance limitations prevented any growth in size of equipment. The movement collapsed before any development in car design had occurred, and as in the case of boxcars, the existing car supply was adequate for virtually all demands of the near future. The Denver & Rio Grande in the 1920s lowered car bodies, replaced 30″ wheels with 26″, and placed extended bearings on trucks to reduce sway. The railroad enclosed the platforms of some of its cars for service on the *Shavano* and *San Juan*, but it never bought new closed-platform equipment for the two named trains. The East Tennessee & Western North Carolina bought closed-platform wooden coaches, combines, and baggage–railway post office cars from Jackson & Sharp between 1917 and 1921, both for itself and for the subsidiary Linville River Railway.[114] Steel car-building came to the narrow gauge only in the form of some reproduction of wooden equipment built in D&RGW shops in the 1960s for the Silverton train.

On most narrow gauge railroads the trip was so short that only coaches and combines were considered. The Denver & Rio Grande required sleeping cars for its Denver-Ogden, Denver-Leadville, and Denver-Durango-Silverton trains. Pullman built 18 cars for the D&RG in 1880 and 1881, 42′-4″×8′-2″ overall with a configuration of 10 sections and two toilets.[115] In 1883 Pullman built six buffet-sleeping cars, 48′-0″×8′-3″, with 10 sections and dining facilities.[116] These cars, which Pullman operated under contract, were the D&RG's largest narrow gauge passenger equipment and represented the approximate limit imposed by narrow gauge standards—excepting the Boston, Revere Beach & Lynn. The berths on the D&RG's Pullmans were 2′-1″ wide; President Palmer reportedly considered the narrow width a contribution to sexual morality, for only a single passenger could occupy each one.[117]

Pullman built and operated six sleeping cars for the South Park Line,[118] and six for the Texas & St. Louis.[119] The Utah & Northern had four Pullmans,[120] but as far as is known the Toledo, Cincinnati & St. Louis never operated sleeping cars. The most unusual such operation was the pair of buffet-sleeping cars on the Nevada-California-Oregon, carried on the railroad's daily trains, in spite of the fact that they made a day run.[121]

Narrow gauge Pullman service on the Denver & Rio Grande ended in 1902 with the withdrawal of sleeping cars on the Salida–Grand Junction and Alamosa-Durango trains. Thereafter, the railroad scheduled standard gauge Pullmans from Denver to Salida and Alamosa, with parlor cars for first-class passengers on the connecting narrow gauge trains.[122]

Among other operators of specialized equipment, the White Pass & Yukon was notable for having more parlor cars than coaches—suiting its odd requirements in providing excursion service for passengers off cruise ships at Skagway. No American narrow gauge is known to have operated full dining cars. The D&RGW provided limited dining service in its parlor cars only after 1937. During the narrow gauge era, most of the larger lines provided meal stops, like their standard gauge counterparts. The White Pass & Yukon did so at Lake Bennett until the end of its passenger operations. The Toledo, Cincinnati & St. Louis advertised provision of warm

Modernity, insofar as it came to narrow gauge passenger rolling stock, did so in the form of some enclosed platform wooden coaches and combines for the East Tennessee & Western North Carolina just after World War I. Here are external views of the equipment and interior shots of the coach and railway post office. The exterior photograph of coach No. 30 shows it at Johnson City, Tennessee, awaiting shipment to the National of Mexico, which had bought it for first class service. (Ed Bond collection.)

lunches on trains, presumably from station restaurants.[123] The large narrow gauges operated business cars. The D&RG had a peak of 13 in 1886; three of its office cars survive.[124]

With the conversions of the late 1880s and early 1890s, narrow gauge sleeping cars became redundant. The South Park Line, among those which did not convert, gave up Pullman service on the Gunnison line in 1887 and to Leadville in 1896.[125] The Colorado sleeping cars were largely sold to Mexico for further service, as were all the Pullmans of the Texas & St. Louis.[126]

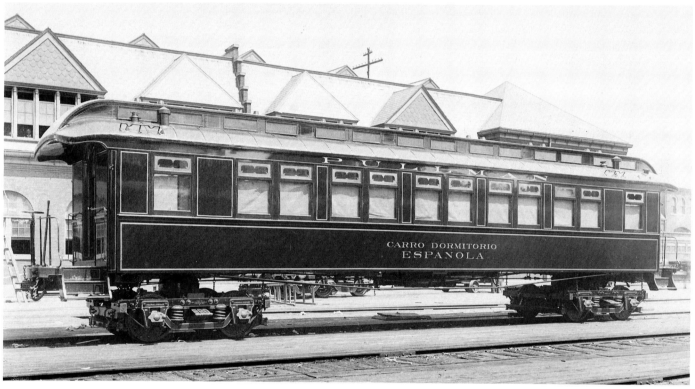

However limited the demand for narrow gauge sleeping cars, Pullman had a
standard design for a ten-section car. The *Toltec*, built for the D&RG, is shown
on completion at Pullman's Detroit Car Works. The same railroad's *Espanola* is
shown on standard gauge trucks and also in an interior view, opposite, awaiting
shipment from Pullman in Chicago to Mexico. (Smithsonian Institution; Arthur
D. Dubin collection.)

The only gas-electric car of the usual sort ever operated by an American narrow gauge was the East Broad Top's M-1. (Ed Bond collection.)

The Rio Grande Southern replaced its passenger trains with units of this character. No. 3 was fabricated in 1931 from a Pierce Arrow automobile and a newly built boxcar body. (Richard H. Kindig.)

Self-Powered Cars

As on the standard gauge system, motor cars were a method of providing light-density service at lower cost than steam locomotives and separate cars. There was only one narrow gauge example of the orthodox gas-electric car of the sort that provided most such service. This was the M-1, built in 1927 by the East Broad Top in its Orbisonia Shop from components furnished by Brill and Westinghouse.[127] The M-1 provided passenger service on weekends and when the local coal mines were closed.

Several managements of narrow gauges built motor cars of their own. One of the most professional jobs was done by one of the least pretentious narrow gauges, the Lancaster, Oxford & Southern. Seeking a cheaper way to move mail and milk, the railroad in 1914 had one of its existing cars rebuilt as a gas-mechanical unit with two transmissions, joined by a geared connection through the king pin of the lead truck. Built approximately to standard-gauge dimensions, the car seated 46 and carried two tons of freight. The car could make the Oxford-Quarryville trip of 19.5 miles in an hour and five minutes. After abandonment of the railroad in 1919, the car was converted to standard gauge and operated by the Grasse River Railroad in upstate New York until 1960. It was subsequently run by the Strasburg Rail Road and the National Park Service. It survives in the Railroad Museum of Pennsylvania at Strasburg.[128]

A large number of narrow gauges operated motor cars fabricated out of automobiles. The best-known examples are the "Galloping Geese" of the Rio Grande Southern. The railroad, which was under severe constraints of

Sandy River & Rangeley Lakes No. 3 was a good example of the gasoline rail cars built by several of the narrow gauges to handle the dwindling passenger volumes of the 1920s. This unit was fabricated in company shops from a Ford motor and truck chassis. (Robert C. Jones collection.)

revenue, in 1931 began to fabricate motor cars out of Buick and Pierce-Arrow automobiles, most of them with newly built boxcar bodies. The cars were substituted for the road's passenger trains and operated until the end of service in 1951.[129] The San Christobal Railroad attempted to operate with one car of this type.[130] Service of this sort was proposed for the South Park Line at the time of its abandonment but never instituted.[131] The Silverton Northern, the Sandy River & Rangeley Lakes, and many others operated rail buses fabricated out of Model T Fords or other automobiles of the time.[132]

Almost inevitably, self-propelled cars have been looked upon as failures, but this follows from the nature of their function. They were nearly always designed for some service with declining demand conditions. Their institution could not reverse the adverse movement of demand, and they appear to have failed. Actually, they were effective adaptations to the conditions confronting their operators, and allowed the services to continue for some years after they would otherwise have been discontinued.

Notes

1. Robert F. Fairlie, *Railways or No Railways: Narrow Gauge, Economy With Efficiency v. Broad Gauge, Costliness With Extravagance* (London: Effingham Wilson, 1872), p. 44.

2. *Ibid.*, pp. 45–46.   3. *Ibid.*, p. 46.

4. "A Twelve-Ton Four-Wheel Car," *National Car-Builder*, 9 (1878), p. 5. See also "Large Four-Wheel Coal Cars of the St. Louis Southeastern Railroad," *ibid.*, 10 (1879), p. 35.

5. *Railroad Gazette*, 12 (1880), p. 527.

6. Advertisement of Billmeyer & Small, *American Railroad Journal*, 44 (1871), p. 483, issue of April 29, 1871. The late John Krause, in his *American Narrow Gauge* (San Marino, Calif.: Golden West Books, 1978), p. 11, stated that the order was placed with Billmeyer & Small after the large Wilmington carbuilder Jackson & Sharp rejected Palmer's order for several hundred such cars on the ground that such small equipment was impractical. The statement was based on materials in the collection of the book's publisher, Donald Duke, but I have been unable to locate the source. As the York Car Works, this firm dated from 1852. In the early 1870s it was a partnership of George S. Billmeyer, D. E. Small, J. H. Small, and Henry Small. Its advertisements in this period usually, but not invariably, read "Billmeyer & Smalls." In 1876 the firm incorporated as the Billmeyer & Small Co. and thereafter customarily used the singular. The trade press continued to vary between the singular and plural without much consistency.

7. Howard Fleming, *Narrow Gauge Railways in America* (Oakland: Grahame Hardy, 1949 [reprint of the 2d ed., 1876]), p. 57.

8. Howard Schuyler, "Narrow Gauge Freight Car," *Railroad Gazette*, 3 (1871), pp. 359–60, at 360.

9. Letter of Howard Schuyler to Henry Ingalls, Mar. 2, 1872, in *Narrow Gauge Railroads: Their History and Progress. The Kennebec & Wiscasset Railroad* (Augusta: Sprague, Owen & Nash, 1872), pp. 18–20.

10. Krause, *American Narrow Gauge*, p. 11.

11. *Railroad Gazette*, 12 (1880), p. 527; U.S. Patent 226,324 (Apr. 6, 1880).

12. *Railway Age*, 4 (1879), p. 540.

13. Schuyler "Narrow Gauge Freight Car," pp. 359–60.

14. *Ibid.*, p. 364.

15. John H. White, Jr., "Railroad Freight Cars in Nineteenth Century America," unpublished typescript, chap. 3, pp. 20–21.

16. MS Equipment Catalog, Denver & Rio Grande Railway, Oct. 1883. D&RGW Archive, Denver.

17. *National Car-Builder*, 10 (1879), p. 138.

18. James Dredge, *The Pennsylvania Railroad* (London: Engineering, 1879).

19. *Railway Review*, 22 (1882), p. 464.

20. *Report of the Proceedings of the 14th Annual Convention of the Master Car-Builder's Association* (1880), p. 178; *ibid.*, 17th Convention (1883), p. 149.

21. Cincinnati *Commercial*, Oct. 24, 1878.

22. Fleming, *Narrow Gauge Railways*, pp. 54–56.

23. See, for example, the advertisement in the *New Columbian Railroad Atlas* (New York: Asher & Adams, 1879), p. 408.

24. *National Car-Builder*, 2, No. 2 (Aug. 1871), p. 3.

25. *Third Annual Report of the American Railway Master Mechanics' Association in Convention at Philadelphia, Sept. 14th, 15th, and 16th, 1870* (Chicago, 1870), pp. 107–14, quotation at p. 107. The summary of the report in the *National Car-Builder* describes it as more pessimistic than this, stating, "There appears to be no remedy for the great evil of overweight," and "As to cars, there seems no way of lessening the deadweight." *National Car-Builder*, 1, No. 5 (Nov. 1870), pp. 3–4.

26. *National Car-Builder*, 3 (1872), pp. 1–6.

27. White, "Railroad Freight Cars," chap. 3, p. 1.

28. *Ibid.*, p. 18.   29. *Ibid.*, p. 7.

30. *National Car-Builder*, 11 (1880), p. 83.

31. "The Chicago Railway Exposition, No. IX," *The Engineer*, 56 (1883), pp. 498–99. The article is mainly devoted to a comparison of such equipment with British four-wheel stock—one very favorable to the American design.

32. Arthur M. Wellington, *The Economic Theory of the Location of Railways*, 5th ed. (New York: John Wiley & Sons, 1893), p. 485.

33. *National Car-Builder*, 14 (1883), pp. 63–64.

34. *Ibid.*   35. *Ibid.*, 11 (1880), pp. 4, 20.

36. *Official Railway Equipment Register*, Jan. 1913, p. 783.

37. Plan by J. H. Geissel in *The Model Railroader*, Apr. 1962, pp. 46–47.

38. *Official Railway Equipment Register*, Jan. 1913, p. 811.

39. Letter of John W. Maxwell, Oct. 12, 1985, based on folio sheets of the Colorado & Southern in his collection, from the late George Lundberg, Master Mechanic of the C&S.

40. See Chapter 4, n. 130, above.

41. *National Car-Builder*, 16 (1887), p. 852.

42. "Increasing the Speed of Freight Trains," *National Car-Builder*, 14 (1883), p. 118.

43. *Official Railway Equipment Register*, Jan. 1913, pp. 783, 811.

44. *National Car-Builder*, 11 (1880), p. 148.

45. *Ibid.*, p. 156.

46. Cincinnati *Commercial*, Oct. 24, 1878.

47. John Marshall, *Rail Facts and Feats* (New York: Two Continents Publishing Group, 1974), p. 193.

48. *Car Builders' Cyclopedia of American Practice*, 15th ed. (New York: Simmons-Boardman Publishing Co., 1940), pp. 110–11.

49. *National Car-Builder*, 12 (1881), p. 13.

50. *Ibid.*, 14 (1883), p. 139.

51. Mallory Hope Ferrell, *Tweetsie Country: The East Tennessee & Western North Carolina Railway* (Boulder, Colo.: Pruett Publishing Co., 1976), p. 205.

52. Cincinnati *Commercial*, Oct. 24, 1878.

53. Letter to the author from John B. Norwood, Assistant Vice-President for Operations, D&RGW, retired, Oct. 1, 1985.

54. John Tigges and Jon Jacobson, *Milwaukee Road Narrow Gauge* (Boulder, Colo.: Pruett Publishing Co., 1985), pp. 89, 91.

55. MS Equipment Catalog, Denver & Rio Grande Railway, Oct. 1883. D&RGW Archive, Denver.

56. *Official Railway Equipment Register*, Nov. 1915, pp. 782–83.

57. Fleming, *Narrow Gauge Railways*, p. 56.

58. Letter of John W. Maxwell, Dec. 20, 1985.

59. In the Matter of the Examination of the Branch Line of the Chicago, Milwaukee & St. Paul Railway Company from Bellevue, Iowa, to Cascade, Iowa, under the Provisions of Chapter 170, Acts of the Thirty-Fifth General Assembly, Decided December 21, 1915, *Reports of the Railroad Commission of Iowa*, 1916, pp. 15–37, at p. 25.

60. Mallory Hope Ferrell, *Southern Pacific Narrow Gauge* (Edmonds, Wash.: Pacific Fast Mail, 1982), p. 270.

61. Lee Rainey and Frank Kyper, *East Broad Top* (San Marino, Calif.: Golden West Books, 1982).

62. "Narrow Gauge Steel Hopper Cars," *Railway and Locomotive Engineering*, 26 (1913), p. 223.

63. "New Cars for the Grand Trunk Railway System," *Railway and Locomotive Engineering*, 26 (1913), p. 448. For both cars, the weight lettered on the equipment differs from the weight shown in the text. The lettered weight is used in both comparisons.

64. Ferrell, *Tweetsie Country*, pp. 205, 207.

65. George W. Hilton, "Integration in the North," *Trains*, July 1971, pp. 36–43.

66. Letter of John W. Maxwell, Dec. 20, 1985.

67. Letter of Robert White, Superintendent, to William Mason, Oct. 1, 1876. Typed copy transcribed by Charles E. Fisher in R&LHS collection of rosters and builders' lists (see Chap. 5, n. 23).

68. For a late listing of railroads, including standard gauge, with the type of brake mechanism they used, see Interstate Commerce Commission, *Tenth Annual Report* (1896), pp. 274–317.

69. Eames Vacuum Brake Company, *Plain Brake Catalogue* (New York, n.d.). A later and somewhat more complicated system with a horizontal ejector and an optional exhaust into the smokebox is described in the company's *Driver Brake Catalogue* (New York, n.d.), and in Fred Jukes, "Early Northern Pacific Consolidations," R&LHS *Bulletin*, No. 102 (1960), pp. 35–42.

70. *Plain Brake Catalogue*, p. 28.

71. For an evaluation of the relative merits of the Westinghouse air brake and an earlier vacuum system similar to the Eames developed by John Y. Smith—an evaluation quite favorable to the vacuum brake—see "Report of the Committee on Continuous

Train Brakes," *Annual Report of the American Railway Master Mechanics Association*, 7 (1874), pp. 244–65.

72. M. S. Goodale, "The Great Old South Park," *Railroad Stories*, Dec. 1933, pp. 46–51; M. C. Poor, *Denver, South Park & Pacific*, Memorial Edition (Denver: Rocky Mountain Railroad Club, 1976), pp. 186, 324.

73. Robert C. Jones and David L. Register, *Two Feet to Tidewater* (Boulder, Colo.: Pruett Publishing Co., 1987), p. 82.

74. William F. Helmer, *Rip Van Winkle Railroads* (Berkeley: Howell-North Books, 1970), p. 137; Gerald M. Best, *The Ulster and Delaware* (San Marino, Calif.: Golden West Books, 1972), p. 200.

75. H. Temple Crittenden, *The Maine Scenic Route* (Parsons, W.Va.: McClain Printing Co., 1966), p. 101.

76. Poor, *Denver, South Park & Pacific*, p. 326.

77. Krause, *American Narrow Gauge*, p. 10.

78. Forest Crossen, *The Switzerland Trail of America* (Boulder, Colo.: Pruett Press, 1962), p. 173.

79. Linwood W. Moody, *The Maine Two-Footers: The Story of the Two-Foot Railroads of Maine* (Berkeley, Calif.: Howell-North Books, 1959), pp. 33, 153.

80. George B. Turner, "Diamond & Caldor," *The Western Railroader*, 31, No. 9, Issue 343 (1968), p. 11.

81. Robert C. Stanley, *Narrow Gauge: The Story of the Boston, Revere Beach & Lynn Railroad* (Cambridge, Mass.: Boston Street Railway Association, 1980).

82. Moody, *The Maine Two-Footers*, p. 74.

83. Allan Krieg, *Last of the 3 Foot Loggers* (San Marino, Calif.: Golden West Books, 1962), p. 35.

84. Henry E. Bender, Jr., *Uintah Railway: The Gilsonite Route* (Berkeley, Calif.: Howell-North Books, 1970), p. 156.

85. I am indebted to John W. Maxwell for information on this point.

86. See, for example, *Improving Railroad Productivity: Final Report of the Task Force on Railroad Productivity* (Washington, D.C.: National Commission on Productivity and Council of Economic Advisers, 1973).

87. *Official Railway Equipment Register*, Mar. 1903, p. 101.

88. *Railroad Magazine*, July 1948, pp. 67–68.

89. Typescript roster of equipment, Chateaugay Railroad, Oct. 1, 1903, collection of Ed Bond, Marietta, Georgia.

90. *Official Railway Equipment Register*, Jan. 1950, pp. 541–45.

91. *Ibid.*, pp. 442–56, 459–70.

92. "The Billerica & Bedford Two-Feet Gauge Railroad," *Railroad Gazette*, 10 (1878), p. 37.

93. Robert C. Jones, *Two Feet Between the Rails* (Silverton, Colo.: Sundance Publications, Ltd., vol. 1, 1979; vol. 2, 1980), vol. 2, p. 370.

94. *Ibid.*

95. Article from Wilmington (Del.) *Commercial*, reproduced in *American Railroad Journal*, 44 (1871), p. 817.

96. Fleming, *Narrow Gauge Railways*, p. 49.

97. *Ibid.*, pp. 48–51.   98. *Ibid.*, pp. 50–51.

99. *Ibid.*, pp. 51–53.

100. John H. White, Jr., *The American Railroad Passenger Car*, (Baltimore, Md.: The Johns Hopkins University Press, 1978), p. 35.

101. *Ibid.*

102. *American Railroad Journal*, 48 (1875), p. 1053.

103. Fleming, *Narrow Gauge Railways*, p. 94.

104. Cincinnati *Commercial*, Oct. 24, 1878.

105. *American Railroad Journal*, 55 (1882), p. 835. Some of the cars were sold to the East Tennessee & Western North Carolina and the East Broad Top, however.

106. *Railroad Gazette*, 6 (1875), p. 163.

107. *Railway Age*, 1 (1876), p. 184; White, *The American Railroad Passenger Car*, p. 659.

108. Frederick Shaw, Clement Fisher, Jr., and George H. Harlan, *Oil Lamps and Iron Ponies* (San Francisco: Bay Books, Ltd., 1949), p. 48.

109. *Railroad Gazette*, 3 (1871), p. 365.

110. General G. P. Buell, *Report Made to the President and the Executive Board of the Texas Pacific Railroad* (New York: Van Nostrand, 1871), p. 4.

111. Letter of John W. Maxwell, Mar. 6, 1986, based on drawings of cars of the Denver & Rio Grande, Colorado & Southern, East Broad Top, and North Pacific Coast in his collection; letter of Albin L. Lee, Mar. 1, 1986, based on drawings of cars of the Bellevue & Cascade, Linville River, Fremont, Elkhorn & Missouri Valley, Uintah, and Minneapolis, Lyndale & Lake Calhoun in his collection.

112. *Railroad Gazette*, 10 (1878), p. 50.

113. H. T. Crittenden, "Mount Gretna Narrow Gauge Railway," R&LHS *Bulletin*, No. 57 (1942), pp. 99–102, at p. 101.

114. Ferrell, *Tweetsie Country*, pp. 200–201.

115. On the basis of Authur Dubin's search of the Pullman Palace Car Company's builder's list, the cars were: *Alamosa, American, Antonito, Aztec, Cascade, Chippeta, El Moro, Espanola, Gunnison, La Veta, Manitou, Mexicano, Moqui, Navajo, Ouray, San Carlos, Toltec,* and *Zuni.*

116. *Castle Gate, Cimarron, Ogden, Provo, Salida,* and *Salt Lake.* D&RG Roster of Equipment, No. 21, July 1, 1891. Xerox copy of original in the collection of Arthur Dubin, Highland Park, Illinois.

117. Robert G. Athearn, *Rebel of the Rockies: A History of the Denver and Rio Grande Western Railroad* (New Haven, Conn.: Yale University Press, 1962), p. 100.

118. *Bonanza, Hortense, Kenosha, Leadville, South Park,* and *San Juan.* Dubin collection.

119. *Athens, Cairo, Helena, Lampasas, Malden,* and *Tyler.* Dubin collection.

120. *Advance, Progress, Rambler,* and *Security.* Pullman order book, Detroit Works, collection of Jackson C. Thode.

121. David F. Myrick, *Railroads of Nevada and Eastern California* (Berkeley, Calif.: Howell-North Books, vol. 1, 1962; vol. 2, 1963), vol. 1, p. 359.

122. Lucius Beebe and Charles Clegg, *Narrow Gauge in the Rockies* (Berkeley: Howell-North Books, 1958), p. 87 and *passim.*

123. John A. Rehor, *The Nickel Plate Story* (Milwaukee: Kalmbach Publishing Co., 1956), p. 138.

124. D&RG equipment registers in the collection of Jackson C. Thode; Alexis McKinney, "The Silverton's Three Private Cars," *Colorado Rail Annual*, No. 14 (1979), pp. 8–23.

125. Poor, *Denver, South Park & Pacific*, p. 322.

126. MS notes, Dubin collection (see n. 116).

127. Rainey and Kyper, *East Broad Top*, p. 137.

128. Benjamin F. G. Klein, Jr., *Little, Old and Slow: The Life and Trials of the Peach Bottom and Lancaster, Oxford & Southern Railroads* (Lancaster, Pa.: Benjamin F. G. Klein, Jr., 1985), pp. 71–74.

129. Stan Rhine, "Tin Feathers and Gasoline Fumes," *Colorado Rail Annual*, No. 9 (1971), pp. 2–49.

130. Duane Vandenbusche and Walter R. Borneman, "Lake City Branch," *Colorado Rail Annual*, No. 14 (1979), pp. 100–105.

131. Chappell, Richardson, and Hauck, *The South Park Line*, pp. 192–93.

132. Robert E. Sloan and Carl A. Skowronski, *The Rainbow Route* (Denver: Sundance, Ltd., 1975), pp. 300–301 and *passim*; Jones, *Two Feet Between the Rails*, vol. 2, pp. 221–28 and *passim.*

7

Physical Plant

Even if investment in the right-of-way is no longer considered the irretrievable commitment to railroading that the Victorians thought it was, a right-of-way remains the classic example of a sunk cost. Once established, the right-of-way became part of the topography, incapable of being moved and expensive to modify. Whatever errors the builders committed by their acceptance of narrow gauge doctrine would not be readily rectified, as they might have been in the cases of locomotives and rolling stock. Indeed, not even conversion would eliminate the errors of building.

On the basis of cost data provided in Chapters 5 and 6, we have seen that the narrow gauges achieved savings on locomotives on the order of only 10 percent per unit, and probably had no capital savings on rolling stock at all, given the large stocks of cars they had to carry. If the projections of the proponents of the narrow gauge were to be validated, the capital savings would have to be realized in rights-of-way and track.

Table 7.1 shows the investment per mile, including locomotives and cars, reported to *Poor's Manual* by narrow gauges in Ohio, Indiana, and Illinois for the peak years of the movement, 1881–84. This area has the advantage of relatively homogeneous terrain in which, unlike Colorado, the relative geographical position of the railroads would not be a bias. The Toledo, Cincinnati & St. Louis and the Connotton Valley have been excluded, since both reported figures that included their gross overcapitalization. The data indicate that the investment per mile of the narrow gauges was $18,313, which was 24.6 percent of the $74,427 per mile reported by the standard gauge railroads in these states. In 1884 the three major Colorado narrow gauges reported, as shown in Table 7.2, an average investment of $35,298 in much more difficult terrain. We are probably justified in accepting an estimate that the narrow gauges as a whole entailed an investment between $20,000 and $35,000 per mile, considerably less than half what was invested in standard gauge railroads. Arthur M. Wellington, although an opponent of narrow gauge doctrine, reported with approbation that the Denver, South Park & Pacific had built its right-of-way and

TABLE 7.1

*Cost of Construction (Physical Plant, Locomotives, and Cars) of Reporting
Narrow Gauges in Ohio, Indiana, and Illinois, 1881–84*

	Year	Miles	Total cost	Cost per mile
OHIO				
Alliance & Lake Erie	1882	25	$123,815	$4,953
Bellaire, Zanesville & Cincinnati	1884	112	1,350,048	12,054
Celina, Van Wert & State Line	1881	10.37	70,000	6,750
Cincinnati & Eastern	1884	105	1,781,115	16,963
Cincinnati, Georgetown & Portsmouth	1884	34.8	391,570	11,252
Cincinnati & Westwood	1884	5.64	156,437	27,737
Cincinnati Northern	1882	37.60	232,648	6,187
College Hill	1884	6	59,502	9,917
Columbus, Washington & Cincinnati	1882	23.33	300,000	12,859
Columbus & Maysville	1884	18.70	102,682	5,491
Dayton & Southeastern	1881	114	1,387,398	12,170
Painesville & Youngstown	1884	62.3	1,317,334	21,145
Painesville, Canton & Bridgeport	1882	5	50,000	10,000
St. Clairsville	1882	6.65	41,465	6,235
Wheeling & Lake Erie	1881	12.5	489,000	39,120
TOTAL		578.89	$7,853,014	$13,566
INDIANA				
Bedford, Springville, Owensburg & Bloomfield	1881	41.36	$426,000	$10,300
Indianapolis, Delphi & Chicago	1881	26.42	440,000	16,654
TOTAL		67.78	$866,000	$12,776
ILLINOIS				
Cairo & St. Louis	1881	146.5	$7,065,000	$48,225
Danville, Olney & Ohio River	1881	52	1,243,000	23,904
Fulton County N.G.	1883	61	1,233,542	20,222
Havana, Rantoul & Eastern	1881	75.67	566,605	7,488
Moline & Southeastern	1881	7.75	30,000	3,871
Springfield, Effingham & Southeastern	1882	56.5	300,000	5,310
TOTAL		399.42	$10,438,147	$26,133
THREE STATES N.G. TOTAL		1,046.09	$19,157,161	$18,313
ALL RAILROADS, 1882				
Ohio		6,663.75	$610,728,103	$91,649
Indiana		4,764.63	263,431,879	55,289
Illinois		8,325.65	500,429,772	60,107
TOTAL		19,754.03	$1,374,589,754	$69,585

SOURCE: *Poor's Manuals of the Railroads*, years as shown.
  NOTE: For the three states, narrow gauge investment is 26.3 percent of all railroads' average per mile. Average investment of standard gauge, for the three states, is $74,427. Narrow gauge investment is 24.6 percent of standard gauge.

track to Leadville, through extremely difficult terrain, for only $20,000 per mile.[1] Since the railroad reported its total investment as $33,313 per mile, we may estimate that the right-of-way and track amounted to about 60 percent of investment, and that motive power, rolling stock, and structures accounted for 40 percent. On the basis of these data, the investment in all narrow gauges at the time of the estimated peak of 11,699 miles in 1885 was probably somewhat over $300,000,000, of which somewhat under $200,000,000 was in right-of-way and track and under $130,000,000 in locomotives, rolling stock, and structures. If these estimates are extrapolated to the mileage built after 1885, the eventual total of 18,463 miles represented an investment of over $500,000,000. This may be overstated because the later mileage was disproportionately of nominal common carriers of lumber companies, most of which were built for $10,000 per mile or less. There was, however, additional investment in existing mileage, mainly in the D&RGW network.

TABLE 7.2

*Reported Total Cost Per Mile
of Colorado Narrow Gauges, 1884*

Colorado Central	$35,034
D&RG	37,546
DSP&P	33,313
Average	$35,298

SOURCE: *Poor's Manual of the Railroads*, 1884, p. 859.

TABLE 7.3

Cost of Construction of the Toledo, Cincinnati & St. Louis System, 1882

Segment	Miles	Total cost	Cost per mile
Toledo Division	181	$1,250,000	$ 6,906
Southeastern Division	185	2,250,000	12,162
St. Louis Division	268	3,000,000	11,194
Iron Railroad	24	500,000	20,833
Cincinnati Division	55	1,250,000	22,727
Spring Grove & Avondale	5	100,000	20,000
Total	718	$8,350,000	$11,630

SOURCE: St. Louis *Globe-Democrat*, Nov. 18, 1882.

It is clear, however, that some narrow gauges were built for small fractions of the typical investment of standard gauge railroads. The Moline & Southeastern, a simple 3'-6" coal carrier with two locomotives, reported an investment of only $3,871 per mile. More importantly, the Springfield, Effingham & Southeastern reported an investment of $5,310 per mile, not even 10 percent of typical standard gauge investment. Whether one takes the average figure of about $27,500 per mile or the lower figures for individual railroads, it is evident that the builders more than fulfilled the projections of the proponents for low-capital entry into railroading. The data reported for the first 718 miles of the Toledo, Cincinnati & St. Louis in the St. Louis *Globe-Democrat* in November 1882, shown in Table 7.3, indicate an investment of only $11,630 per mile for the entire system. It is unclear whether this is inclusive of rolling stock and motive power. The Dayton & Southeastern contracted for its 114-mile line at $6,510 per mile for right-of-way and track, or $12,500 per mile with locomotives and equipment.[2] W. E. Moreley and Thomas H. Millington at the convention of 1872 had projected investment for narrow gauges in plains country at about 60 percent of standard gauge investment.[3] Only well-built lines such as the Cairo & St. Louis and the Connotton Valley entailed this much investment. John T. Davis, making one of the last statements of the expected cost savings of narrow gauge in 1880, noted this and projected an investment of only 25 percent of standard gauge, instead of the 60 percent that had become orthodoxy.[4] Although such capital saving might appear one of the successes of the narrow gauge movement, the experience was to demonstrate Matthias N. Forney's criticism that such capital saving as the movement promised was perhaps 95 percent by reverting to more primitive standards of railroading.

The most obvious beginning for such capital saving was a narrow right-of-way. The Ilwaco Railway was built on a right-of-way only 10 feet wide, but since this allowed only about 18 inches on either side of the cars, it was widened to 15 feet.[5] About three-fourths of the Bellevue & Cascade was built on a right-of-way 33 feet wide.[6] The Milwaukee Road considered the line impractical to convert largely on the basis of this narrowness of the right-of-way. The tightness of the curves and narrowness of the cuts and fills were essentially impossible to modify on such a limited width. The Warren & Farnsworth Valley in Pennsylvania also had a 33-foot right-of-way, which allowed it to be built for $12,000 per mile.[7] Fifty-foot rights-of-way were considered the practical minimum in the eastern United States

The Uintah Railway's physical standards were more representative of lumber railroads than of the narrow gauges generally. Here a troop train in 1911 traverses the 60° Hairpin Curve on the 5 percent ascent of Baxter Pass. (F. A. Kennedy, collections of V. L. McCoy and Henry E. Bender, Jr.)

Percentage of gradient: Simply, the number of feet of rise in 100 linear feet.

Degrees of curvature: The number of degrees of a circle subtended by a chord of 100 feet. Obviously, the higher the number, the more severe the curve.

for the embankment, culverts, ditches, and telegraph line. Western rights-of-way were typically one hundred feet wide, and major main lines, such as the New York Central, were frequently even wider.

The Monon, even though it converted the Bedford & Bloomfield in 1895, found the property impossible to improve significantly because of its right-of-way of only about 30 feet. The management built an alternative entry into the Indiana coalfield from Wallace Junction, in part to take the coal traffic off the former narrow gauge.[8]

Some narrow gauges, however, used rights-of-way of ordinary width. The Port Huron & Northwestern had rights-of-way of 66 feet, which facilitated conversion.[9]

Curves and Grades

The usual extreme examples of both grades and curves are from the Uintah Railway, but they are not particularly representative. The Uintah ascended Baxter Pass with ruling grades of 7.5 percent westbound and 5 percent eastbound. The worst curve was at Moro Castle on the westbound ascent, originally 75° but modified to 66° for the railroad's articulated locomotive.[10] Both the grade and the curve are usually said to have been the worst on an American common carrier of any gauge, but they were on a portion of the Uintah intended to be worked by Shay locomotives. Both ascents of Baxter Pass were built to the standards of lumber railroads designed for geared locomotives, and by such standards were not excep-

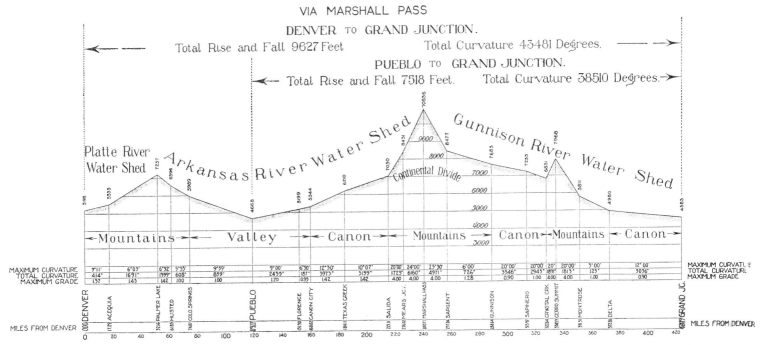

CONDENSED PROFILE   D. & R. G. R. R.   DENVER TO GRAND JCT.

VIA MARSHALL PASS

DENVER TO GRAND JUNCTION.

← — — — Total Rise and Fall 9627 Feet   Total Curvature 43481 Degrees. — — — →

PUEBLO TO GRAND JUNCTION.

← — Total Rise and Fall 7518 Feet.   Total Curvature 38510 Degrees. →

The Denver & Rio Grande's original profile from Denver to Grand Junction delineates narrow gauge standards with respect to grades and curvature. Note ruling grades of 4 percent in both directions. (Denver & Rio Grande Western archive, courtesy Jackson C. Thode.)

tional. Indeed, some of the nominal common carriers may have had worse grades and curves than the Uintah; the Diamond & Caldor was reported to have an 8 percent grade and a curve of 50-foot radius, 180°.[11] The Gilpin Tram, a 2'-0" ore carrier in Colorado, was said originally to have had 50-foot curves that were modified to 66-foot radius.[12] A curve of 50-foot radius was only about 20 percent less severe than street railway curvature, but both these lines were worked by Shays. The Salt Lake & Fort Douglas, a short line that served a quarry and several other installations with a Shay locomotive, was reported to have a 10 percent grade and approximately 80° curvature.[13] The Bradford, Eldred & Cuba had a 70° curve,[14] possibly the worst on any common carrier worked with rod engines.

Wellington in his standard work on railway location treated curves in the range of 20° to 24° as the typical maxima in narrow gauge practice, although he stated that a few as sharp as 30° were found in Colorado and elsewhere.[15] The sharpest curves on the D&RG's original main line to Ogden were 24° on both ascents of Marshall Pass. The company's worst curve on a major line was 30° on the westbound ascent of Veta Pass; curves of about 20° were common.[16]

The Denver, South Park & Pacific had curves of 30° and 32° in the Platte Canyon on its main line, and the Colorado Central had one of 36° on its Central City branch.[17] Howard Fleming reported the Parker & Karns City, a component of the Pittsburgh & Western, had a curve of 47°—only 122-feet radius.[18] The Olean, Bradford & Warren had curves of 28° and 30° along with a 3 percent grade on its New York mileage.[19] By way of contrast to standard gauge practice, Wellington pointed out that on the four major eastern trunk lines the sharpest curves ranged from 8° to 14°. The Erie had a reverse curve of 10° at Passaic, and the New York Central one of 14° in a yard traversed at low speed. The Pennsylvania's worst

Operation on a 4 percent grade: four D&RGW locomotives approach the summit of Marshall Pass with a stock train in 1953. (Otto C. Perry, Denver Public Library.)

curve on the main line was 8°, presumably Horseshoe Curve on the ascent of the east face of the Alleghenies from Altoona. The Baltimore & Ohio's worst was 9°30′ at an unspecified location.[20]

The problem was not only the severity of curves but their frequency. The Sumpter Valley had 18,144 degrees of curvature in its 80.1 miles, approximately 2,240 degrees per mile.[21] The Maryland & Pennsylvania in the course of conversion from its two narrow gauge predecessors experienced some minor revisions and improvements, but in the main had the old narrow gauge physical plant. The railroad had 476 curves, although its main line was only 77.2 miles long. The curves, the worst of which was 20°, totaled 192,261 feet, 40 percent of the company's mileage. The railroad had 55 curves over 16° and 190 over 10°.[22]

Remarkably, given narrow gauge practice generally, the Texas & St. Louis was built with no curves over 5°. Curvature was so minor that the railroad used wheels with flat as distinct from conical treads, something that only the West Shore among standard gauge railroads was able to do.[23]

Grades were similar to curves in narrow gauge practice. Narrow gauge engineers used 4 percent grades about as readily as their standard gauge counterparts did 1 percent. The D&RG had grades of approximately 4 percent westbound on Veta Pass, on the eastbound ascent of Cumbres Pass out of Chama, New Mexico, and on both ascents of Cerro Summit and

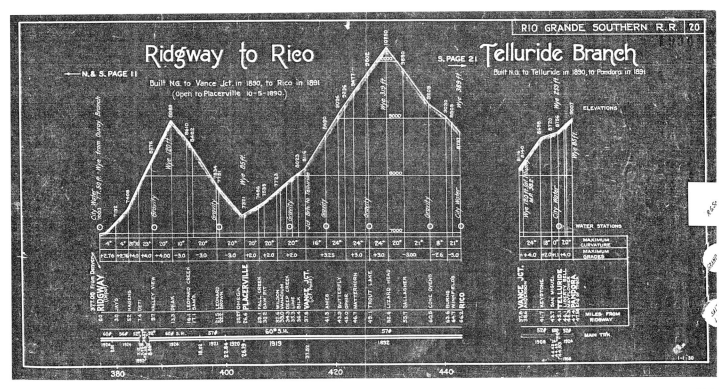

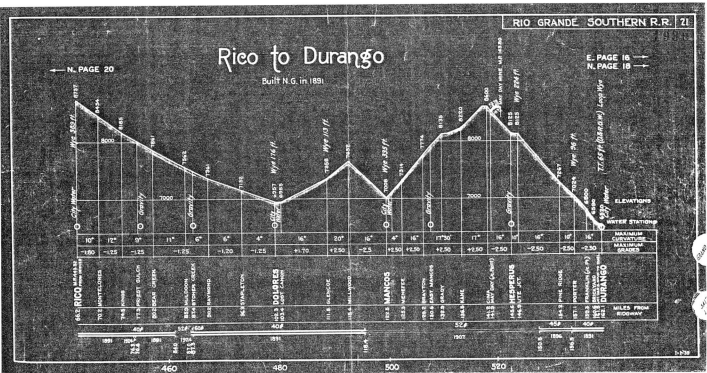

Marshall Pass. Grades of 4 percent also occurred northbound from Embudo to Barranca on the Santa Fe branch, on the northbound ascent of Tennessee Pass, on the westbound ascent of Soldier Summit, Utah (actually 3.97 percent), and at many points on branch lines. The ruling grade of the Monarch branch was 4.5 percent. The company's worst single grade was 7.69 percent on the Calumet branch, but this was essentially a mine spur.[24] The Denver, South Park & Pacific had 4 percent grades on its westbound ascent of Kenosha Pass, on both ascents of Boreas Pass, and on both approaches to the Alpine Tunnel.[25]

The Rio Grande Southern, though designed relatively late, was built to orthodox narrow gauge standards of 4 percent grades and 24° curves. (Denver & Rio Grande Western archive, courtesy of Jackson C. Thode.)

Physical Plant 219

The biggest single concentration of narrow gauge trestlework was on the Rio Grande Southern at Ophir. It was built to relatively high standards and served in satisfactory fashion until the line's abandonment. (Richard H. Kindig.)

The Rio Grande Southern had a long 4 percent grade on the southbound ascent of Dallas Divide. Its most difficult point was Ophir Loop between Vance Junction and Lizard Head Pass. To gain altitude, C. W. Gibbs, chief engineer of the railroad, designed a lateral deflection to the east with a bridge and trestle 836.6 feet long 134 feet above Pleasant Valley Creek, on a grade of over 3 percent with a curve of 24° at Ophir. This arrangement has been evaluated retrospectively relative to possible al-

ternatives by Donald Ray Grace in a thesis in civil engineering at Texas
Tech. Grace considered several alternative routes and the option of a tunnel one mile long at 9,500 feet elevation. In light of the costs of the alternatives, Grace concluded that Gibbs was "exactly correct" in the solution
he chose.[26]

Probably the most severe main-line grade in Colorado was one of 5 percent on the Silverton Railroad's descent from Red Mountain. C. W. Gibbs,
highly constricted by the walls of Corkscrew Gulch, built a covered turntable at a switchback, whereby the locomotive could be turned so as to
prevent backing. Cars coasted through the turntable by gravity in both directions. The railroad also had a 30° curve.[27] Given the parameters of the
narrow gauge system as a whole and the difficulty of the terrain, curves
and grades of this sort may have been optimal. The fact remains that a
locomotive under such conditions can haul less than a tenth what it can
haul on a level track. Operation was necessarily slow and taxing upon the
motive power.

As with curves, it was not only the severity of grades but their frequency
that bedeviled narrow gauge operation. Robert Fairlie's basic concept of
the "surface line" following land contours closely implied choppy profiles
with frequent summits. The south end of the Maryland & Pennsylvania,
the former Baltimore & Lehigh, ran across a drainage pattern, with no less
than eleven summits in the 44 miles between Baltimore and Delta. The
grades varied from 0.17 to 2.3 percent uncompensated, but compensated
for the continual curves at the rate of .03 percent of gradient for 1° of cur-

The only tunnel on the original main line of the Denver & Rio Grande Western was this short one in the Price River canyon of Utah. It was abandoned in connection with the extensive line relocation incidental to the conversion of the line in 1890. (Jackson C. Thode.)

Slack: The looseness in the couplers and stretching of equipment, plus the spring travel in the coupler shank. These add to somewhat less than a foot per car. Slack runs out in starting, acceleration, or ascending of grades, and runs in on deceleration or descent of grades. Slack gives trains the characteristic of a chain of being more stable when stretched out than when not. Slack is one of the most undesirable aspects of railroad technology.

vature, the railroad was the equivalent of a virtually unbroken series of grades between 2.0 and 3.3 percent.[28] Sawtooth profiles of this character entail continual run-in and run-out of slack, put highly variable demands on the locomotive, and assure short trains with high-cost operation.

The concept of following contours closely implies that narrow gauges should have had few tunnels. The entire original main line of the Denver & Rio Grande between Denver and Ogden had only one, a short bore at an oxbow bend of the Price River near Grassy Trail, Utah.[29] In March 1884, however, the D&RG opened a curved tunnel of 2,950 feet at Bridgeport, Colorado, to bypass 500 degrees of curvature and eliminate four pile trestles over the Gunnison River that had proved too weak to withstand ice gorges during spring thaws.[30] The Colorado Central had no tunnels. The Denver, South Park & Pacific had only one, the famous Alpine Tunnel, a bore of 1,805 feet crossing the continental divide at Alpine Pass, on the Gunnison line. The tunnel was wood-framed with close clearances, 13'-9" in height and 10'-10" in width. From the east portal the tunnel ascended on a 0.96 percent grade for 1,203 feet to a summit at 11,612 feet of altitude before descending for 602 feet on a 1.04 percent grade to the west portal. The internal grades, plus a 24° curve approaching the east portal, assured that freights would have to work hard in the tunnel, giving it a sinister reputation for carbon monoxide. A red lantern was kept lighted at the apex to notify crews when to begin drifting. The walls proved unstable, collapsing twice, on the second occasion providing the immediate reason for bringing an end to the railroad's Gunnison extension.[31] The Bedford, Springville, Owensburg & Bloomfield had a tunnel of 1,368 feet near Owensburg, Indiana, afflicted with instability of its walls and with an internal waterfall.[32] The North Pacific Coast had tunnels of 1,250 feet at White's Hill, 1,706 feet at Tomales, and over 2,100 feet at Tierney's Pass. In 1904, in anticipation of standard-gauging, the White's Hill tunnel was bypassed with a new line containing the Bothin Tunnel of 3,190 feet.[33] The South Pacific Coast on its crossing of the mountain barrier between San Jose and Santa Cruz had tunnels of 6,115 and 5,792 feet, as far as is known the longest tunnels on any American narrow gauge.[34]

Track

Early narrow gauge practice was based on 30-pound rail with ties six-feet long. This was the character of the Denver & Rio Grande's original line, and this rail weight was the recommendation of Howard Fleming in his book of 1875–76. Fleming presented F. E. Canda's estimates for a railroad in prairie country near Chicago, believed to be the Chicago, Millington & Western, which specified 30-pound rail and ties at the rate of 2,640 per mile. Rail was the largest single item in Canda's estimate, $4,080 of the $9,520 per mile for right-of-way, grading, and track. Moving to 40-pound rail, Fleming estimated, would raise the cost by $1,200 per mile, but he believed that in the absence of steep grades or heavy traffic, 30-pound was adequate.[35]

Several narrow gauges attempted to build more cheaply with lighter rail. In 1876 the Pine River Valley & Stevens Point laid its line with hard maple stringers, faced with iron only on curves. The line was built for $3,800 per mile (apparently without equipment), which the *Railway Age* thought probably the cheapest in the country.[36] The management found the arrangement unsatisfactory, and by the time it sold the line to the Chicago, Milwaukee & St. Paul in May 1880 had relaid all but three miles with iron rail. The CM&StP quickly completed the job, even though plans were in hand for fairly immediate conversion.[37] The Farmers Union Railroad in Iowa laid maple rails and purported to be able to operate at 15 to 20 miles per hour with a Porter locomotive, but the line quickly deteriorated and was abandoned in the year it was built, 1875.[38] The Colorado Eastern, although opened as late as 1886, was laid with only 18- to 21-pound iron rail.[39] Ephraim Shay used 16-pound rail for his Harbor Springs Railway in Michigan, and the management of the Vidalia & Western chose 16-pound for its line in Louisiana. Such rail proved adequate for the scaled-down versions of his geared locomotive that Shay designed for his

Narrow gauge practice in light grading and adhering closely to natural contours is evident in this photograph of the Waynesburg & Washington. (Ed Bond collection.)

line, but the Vidalia & Western was relaid with 35-pound rail by the successor Natchez, Red River & Texas in 1883.[40] The Pennsboro & Harrisville in West Virginia was laid with 12-pound, the lightest weight in which T-rail is regularly rolled. Such rail is two inches high, with a one-inch web and a two-inch base. The rail was laid on longitudinal stringers in the fashion of Isambard Kingdom Brunel's baulk road, connected by cross-ties at intervals of about three feet. A producer of 12-pound rail for industrial railways recommended that hand-pushed or animal-powered cars on such rail be loaded with no more than three tons,[41] but the Pennsboro & Harrisville used locomotives of six and a half tons. Inevitably, the arrangement proved impractical, and by 1884 the line was being relaid with 20-pound rail.[42]

Short ties were basic to narrow gauge technology, for they allowed the narrower cuts and embankments that were seen as major cost savings in the system. Wellington concluded in 1887 that the only capital savings in narrow gauge technology came from the ties about three-fourths the length of standard and the saving in grading that accompanied them. The saving, he thought, amounted to 1 to 4 percent of total investment,[43] approximately what Forney had estimated in the previous decade. Howard Fleming recommended ties of 5″×7″ cross section, 7′-0″ long, placed two feet apart.[44] Joseph Ramsey of the Bell's Gap recommended a 6″×6″ cross section for ties at the first convention of 1878,[45] but many were smaller. The Texas & St. Louis was laid with 35-pound rail on 7′-0″ ties, 3,100 to the mile.[46] The Toledo, Cincinnati & St. Louis, consistent with its lower standards, had 2,600 ties per mile.[47]

Such standards of trackwork quickly proved themselves unsatisfactory, in part because the typical narrow gauge had its ties laid directly in the earth, without gravel or stone ballast. As early as May 1873, W. J. Ross, Superintendent of the Memphis & Charleston Railroad, said of the Ripley Railroad: "[W]e are operating or trying to operate about twenty-five miles of narrow-gauge road. We find the light ties sink into the soft earth so

The Waynesburg & Washington's right-of-way was typical of narrow gauge practice—narrow, lightly graded, gravel-ballasted, and poorly maintained. (Ed Bond collection.)

much in our country as to make the track too uneven for use. We will have to put them closer together and make some other changes in the track."[48] The Toledo, Cincinnati & St. Louis was reported in 1882 to have no ballast at all on its Ohio lines and in 1885 to have only 10 miles of gravel ballast and 74 miles of sand.[49] The Surry, Sussex & Southampton used sand ballast shoveled through the hole of a flatcar assigned to ballast service and spread by means of a log or tie moved at low speed ahead of the rear truck on the last car of the train. The railroad found that after the first hard rain the sand mixed with the soil and did little to prevent the right-of-way from becoming springy under the weight of passing trains.[50] Gravel ballast was at least nominally one stage above sand, but the authors of a recent history of the Wiscasset, Waterville & Farmington reported that the Maine 2'-0" line had an experience not much better:

"Gravel" is often nothing but a euphemism for a mixture of sand and earth, with a scattering of pebbles and an occasional rock. It served well enough for the subgrade but was an abomination under ties. The earth settled quickly and inhibited drainage. The ties remained wet and soon deteriorated. If the autumn was wet, hard winter frosts caught moisture in the roadbed and heaved the track. The fine material offered little resistance to rainfall and washed easily, especially on the embankment slopes which constantly trickled down into the drainage ditches and had to be built up over and over again.[51]

The situation was to become worse as locomotives pursued their path of convergence to standard gauge practice. The narrow gauge predecessors of the Maryland & Pennsylvania began with Porter locomotives of 11 and 13½ tons in 1874 but by 1882 had 30-ton Baldwin 2-8-0s.[52] By the first convention of 1878, Major John Byrne of the Cincinnati & Eastern was recommending 35-pound rail for flat country, 40-pound for grades.[53] At the second convention of 1878, Edward Hulbert and H. G. Brooks, after inveighing against the tendency toward successively heavier locomotives, attacked the use of ties that were too light. Hulbert and Brooks reported that ties of 5"×6" and 6"×7" had proved themselves inadequate for current motive power and recommended 6″×8″ ties, 6′-0″ long. The lighter the rail, the longer they argued the ties should be. They recommended 2,800 per mile.[54]

Actually, such measures alone were unlikely to deal with the problem because of the meagerness of the typical narrow gauge's ballast. Narrow gauge technology concentrated weight so narrowly that the track was more than ordinarily dependent on ballast. Fred Lavis wrote with respect to the Argentine railways in 1915: "It is to be noted, also, that the use of stone ballast is almost indispensable in narrow-gauge lines, in order to have track on which speeds of more than 30 miles per hour are safe, and that the depth of the ballast must be increased in order to distribute properly the loads which, in the narrow-gauge, are concentrated on a smaller area."[55] Several of the Pennsylvania short lines reported stone ballast. The Ligonier Valley, the Foxburg, St. Petersburg & Clarion, and the Karns City & Butler all reported using broken stone. The Bell's Gap used sandstone ballast, the Greenlick laid a mixture of stone and slag, and the Pittsburgh Southern reported itself partly stone ballasted.[56]

Hulbert and Brooks proposed, as mentioned in Chapter 5, limiting the size of locomotives relative to the weight of rail. The narrow gauges actually pursued the opposite course, escalating the size of locomotives and increasing the weight of rail. The Utah & Northern in 1882 relaid the line from 36-pound rail to 52-pound—only four pounds less than the most common standard gauge rail of the time. The *Railway Age*, still sympathetic to narrow gauge doctrine, wrote, "The Utah & Northern is another example of the tendency to build narrow gauge roads on standard gauge principles, whereby the economy of the narrow gauge is lost." Acknowledging that the railroad had made the change to gain better traction and faster running times, the *Age* observed, "This is true, but if standard gauge service is expected on a road, it would be better to build it on the standard gauge at first."[57]

The problem did not end with the mass conversions of the late 1880s and early 1890s. When the Denver & Rio Grande Western introduced its 70-ton Class K-27 Mikados in 1903, they were beset with continual derailments. The engines did not operate between Chama and Durango until the line was relaid with 70-pound rail in 1923.[58]

The escalation of physical standards of narrow gauge track never extended to signalling. The Boston, Revere Beach & Lynn had some signalling at its East Boston terminus, as did the New York & Manhattan Beach at its principal junction, but no narrow gauge in the contiguous 48 states adopted automatic block signalling. The Oahu Railway installed automatic block signals with upper quadrant semaphores on its main line and Wahiawa branch, the only such American narrow gauge installation.

Bridges

The one element in narrow gauge technology in which a quick path of convergence to standard gauge practice could not take place was bridges. The effort to conform closely to the contours of the land without heavy grading led to an excessive number of small bridges or trestles. The Arizona & New Mexico had 103 trestles in its 71 miles, two 150-foot bridges, and

four tunnels ranging from 129 to 218 feet.[59] The Columbus & Rome had over 4 percent of its entire line on trestles, even though it was not built through swampy country.[60] The Fulton County Narrow Gauge followed the meanderings of the Spoon River closely, entailing two bridges over the stream aggregating 350 feet, plus 92 pile-and-frame trestles with a combined length of 10,935 feet, some 3.3 percent of the 61-mile railroad.[61] The Toledo, Cincinnati & St. Louis in Ohio had 47 wooden bridges, only one iron bridge, one combination bridge, and an unspecified number of trestles.[62] In the 245 miles from Frankfort, Indiana, to East St. Louis, the TC&StL had 11 miles of timber bridges, even though the country was relatively easy.[63]

Many of the bridges and trestles had been built in the expectation of operating with the early narrow gauge locomotives of 11 to 13½ tons. As the motive power became larger, a situation arose that John A. Rehor described in connection with the Toledo, Cincinnati & St. Louis:

The typical narrow gauge was a flimsy affair with only the most superficial grading and unballasted track laid with 20- to 40-pound iron rails. Even the shallowest gullies were crossed on pile trestles—fills and iron bridges were luxuries few narrow-gauge roads enjoyed. Fences and cattle guards were equally rare. In general narrow-gauge practice, speeds of 15 to 20 mph were absolutely unsafe and derailments were part of the daily routine. Locomotives in use on these roads were both too heavy for the track and too light to overcome friction on the tortuous curves and grades. While some savings may have been realized in building a

This spindly trestle of the Parker & Karns City is a good example of narrow gauge practice. It became part of the poor physical plant of the Pittsburgh & Western. (Munson Paddock collection, Railroad Museum of Pennsylvania.)

The Bear River Bridge on the Nevada County Narrow Gauge entailed this high trestle of six bents. The structure was built to standard gauge practice, and was free of the customary complaints against narrow gauge trestles, but it burned in 1896. (Munson Paddock collection, Railroad Museum of Pennsylvania.)

The flimsy quality of narrow gauge bridge construction is evident in this photograph of the Ohio & Toledo. Even this is not extreme, for the bridge had masonry abutments, a feature that the worst offenders did not provide. (Munson Paddock collection, Railroad Museum of Pennsylvania.)

road to 3-foot gauge, the standards of construction precluded any possibility of economy in operation.[64]

Superficial improvements might be made in rails and ties or even in ballast, but systematic upgrading of the large number of bridges and trestles on the typical narrow gauge was too large an undertaking to be practical in the short run. The consequence on the Toledo, Cincinnati & St. Louis was a massive deterioration of bridges and trestles that reduced the rail-

Prudent narrow gauge practice was to space two locomotives on a train so that only one was on a trestle at a time. Shown is a northbound freight on the Rio Grande Southern's Gallagher trestle on Lizard Head Pass in 1951. (Richard H. Kindig.)

road to virtual inoperability. As described at the end of Chapter 4, this collapse was the proximate cause of the end of the era of large-scale narrow gauge investment in 1883.

A better documented example of the problem of weak bridges on the narrow gauges was provided by the Springfield, Effingham & Southeastern. Consistent with having been built for only $5,310 per mile, the line had light wooden bridges, including three over major streams: the Wabash River near Palestine, Illinois, the Embarras River at Newton, and the North Fork of the Embarras at Oblong. In February 1881, only about two months after the railroad was completed, its bridge over the Wabash was swept away by an ice gorge, preventing any physical connection between the Illinois and Indiana mileage of the company for over five years.[65] The Embarras bridge at Newton collapsed under a standing train on August 27, 1884, reducing the railroad to three unconnected segments, causing the postal authorities to suspend the company's mail contract, and precipitating one of the line's several bankruptcies.[66] The bridge was restored in May 1885, but it had a minor collapse on August 29.[67] It was quickly repaired but collapsed again on February 11, 1886, remaining out of service into late April.[68] The bridge over the North Fork at Oblong gave way on September 11, 1886, under a pile driver.[69] Problems with trestles over creeks and ordinary derailments on the lightly graded track were so common as hardly to be newsworthy. The trestle over Busserone Creek was washed out by a heavy rain on July 3, 1884.[70] When a train derailed near Robinson, the Robinson *Argus* observed, "Such occurrences as these are so frequent on the little jerkwater as to excite no comment."[71] When service was restored, the paper commented, "It may continue for a whole

The Susquehanna & Eagles Mere suffered this trestle collapse at Hillsgrove about 1911. (Railroad Museum of Pennsylvania.)

week."[72] The Effingham *Democrat* said if the railroad were a steamboat, the federal inspectors would condemn her in two minutes.[73]

On the Springfield, Effingham & Southeastern's eastern connection, the Bedford, Springville, Owensburg & Bloomfield, the bridge over the West Fork of the White River collapsed in 1876, 1884, and 1893, killing a man on each of the first two occasions. On the third, disaster was avoided only because engineer H. C. Stone sensed the impending collapse of the bridge, which was known to have weak stringers and rotten timbers. He pulled out the throttle and got the locomotive onto the abutment before the structure gave way.[74] None of the West Fork bridges was ever really satisfactory until a covered Howe truss bridge replaced the one that collapsed in 1893, and the truss bridge was only installed in anticipation of conversion.

This trestle collapse on the Bradford, Eldred & Cuba was precipitated by a washout of a fill. (Thomas T. Taber collection, Railroad Museum of Pennsylvania.)

The problem was worst with high trestles, of which the narrow gauges had many. The Cincinnati & Eastern's trestle at Nineveh, Ohio, which was 800 feet long and 30 feet high, collapsed on August 8, 1885, under the weight of a locomotive, three flat cars, and a combine, killing three people and injuring nine. The trestle was restored, but the disaster greatly aggravated the problems of a railroad already in receivership.[75] In an event with a certain grim irony, President W. R. McGill of the Cincinnati & Eastern committed suicide on June 2, 1884, by jumping through the door of a baggage car off the line's high trestle at Winchester, Ohio.[76] On May 20, 1907, the Weaver's Ford trestle of the Cincinnati, Flemingsburg & Southeastern gave way under a 2-6-0 locomotive, boxcar, and coach, killing three passengers and injuring about 20 others. In this instance the trestle, which was 38 feet high, was not repaired and the railroad was cut back to Flemingsburg, Kentucky, reducing its length by two-thirds.[77] The Maryland Central on April 16, 1891, suffered collapse of its Overshot Trestle at Laurel Brook, Maryland, under a train of 13 cars of fertilizer being hauled northbound by a locomotive on the head end and two helper engines at the rear. Four crewmen died and a fifth employee died of sunstroke while clearing the wreck. Two locomotives were lost in the disaster.[78] Even when the structure did not collapse, the flimsiness of narrow gauge trestles and the lightness of the rail made derailments a menace. On the Maryland Central's successor, the Baltimore & Lehigh, a passenger train fell about

The Cincinnati & Eastern had a bridge collapse on its main line less than a year before the more catastrophic one on its New Richmond branch in 1885. The bridge over the East Fork of the Little Miami River at Batavia collapsed on October 17, 1884, under a passenger train, leaving the last coach in a highly precarious position (Cornelius W. Hauck collection.)

40 feet off the Little Gunpowder Falls trestle, killing its engineer and seriously injuring a passenger.[79] In February 1899, a Baltimore & Lehigh passenger train derailed after hitting some ice resulting from a dripping water tank at Vale, Maryland, and went off the Winter's Run trestle, costing the railroad yet a third locomotive.[80]

In sum, the collapse of a bridge or trestle was the narrow gauges' most characteristic disaster, just as the head-on collision from violation of dispatching orders was the interurbans' most common source of serious accident.

Narrow Gauge Operation and Traffic

Given narrow gauge standards of construction, the reported levels of performance are necessarily unimpressive. The fastest operation was on the Philadelphia & Atlantic City, a line built with 3'-6" gauge in expectation of running passenger trains in rivalry with the existing Camden & Atlantic. The fastest scheduled service was 85 minutes for the 55 miles, and the fastest recorded run was made in only 75 minutes.[81] I. R. Wadsworth, Superintendent of the Port Huron & Northwestern, took pride in his train No. 5, which was scheduled for 3:05 for the 91 miles from East Saginaw to Port Huron, approximately 30 miles per hour. The *Railway Reporter*—apparently erroneously—reported, "From the data at hand the Port Huron & Northwestern leads the van for fast time on the narrow gauges."[82] More typical were the company's Almont branch trains, which took between 1:35 and 2:10 to run the 34 miles. The Connotton Valley's No. 1 ran the 115 miles from Cleveland to Coshocton in five hours, about 23 miles per hour, comparable to similar trains of standard gauge railroads. This performance was enough to make the service "Queen of Ohio narrow-gauge passenger trains."[83]

In 1893, the Nevada Central scheduled its passenger train from Battle Mountain to Austin in six hours for the 91 miles. The nearby Eureka & Palisade also allowed six hours for a 90-mile run.[84] The Indiana & Illinois Southern, successor to the Springfield, Effingham & Southeastern, carded its passenger trains in just under six hours for its 91-mile run from Effingham, Illinois, to Switz City, Indiana, but its mixed train was given eleven hours for the trip—consistent with the 8 to 10 miles per hour planned for freight service by the advocates of the narrow gauge.[85] Obviously, the low speed of the line's freight operations, coupled with the necessity of transshipment, plus this carrier's frequent cessations of service, constituted a powerful incentive to avoid its use. Merchants at Oblong, Illinois, were reportedly willing to engage in horse drayage for nine miles into Robinson to avoid the narrow gauge—a longer distance than the six to seven miles Iowa shippers were reported to go to avoid the Bellevue & Cascade in 1915.[86]

In long distance service the Denver & Rio Grande operated its express from Denver to Ogden, 771 miles, in about 36 hours, or 21.4 miles per hour overall, but the line's emigrant train—presumably mixed—was scheduled for about 80 hours, only 9.6 miles per hour.[87] John A. Rehor correctly considered the 19 miles per hour of the Toledo, Cincinnati & St. Louis's first Toledo–East St. Louis express creditable in light of the line's

Facing page
The trestle collapse of August 8, 1885, at Nineveh, Ohio, on the New Richmond branch of the Cincinnati & Eastern was possibly the worst in the narrow gauges' history. These two views show the disaster before the wreckage was cleared. (Cornelius W. Hauck and Ed Bond collections.)

The gallows turntable, on which the stress was distributed by means of an overhead A-frame, was light and cheap. As a consequence, it was common in narrow gauge practice. This example was on the Nevada County Narrow Gauge. (Munson Paddock collection, Railroad Museum of Pennsylvania.)

poor physical properties and semicompleted state.[88] The evidence is considerable that 15 miles per hour overall was the typical speed of local passenger trains, and, as planned, 8 to 10 miles per hour the normal speed of freight or mixed trains.[89]

Costs of narrow gauge operation are generally not available until after the establishment of the Interstate Commerce Commission in 1887. Table 7.4 shows figures reported to the ICC by 15 representative narrow gauges in fiscal 1888–89, for cost per passenger-mile and ton-mile, and also for train-miles of each type, together with the averages reported for American railroads as a whole. It will be noted that only the North Pacific Coast and Denver & Rio Grande Western reported lower costs per passenger-mile than the national average; none of the narrow gauges equalled the national average of about 0.6¢ per ton-mile for freight. Only the Colorado Central, which mainly moved ore downhill, even approached this figure. The Denver & Rio Grande and its western extension were relatively low-cost enter-

TABLE 7.4

Relative Costs for Selected Narrow Gauge Railroads and for All U.S. Railroads, 1888–89

	Cost per passenger-mile	Cost per passenger-train-mile	Cost per ton-mile	Cost per freight-train-mile
Denver & Rio Grande	$.03364	$ .84340	$.01187	$ .60066
Denver & Rio Grande Western	.01723	1.02687	.01089	1.39367
Denver South Park & Pacific	.09418	1.33852	.03310	1.67022
Colorado Central	.03889	1.12758	.00874	1.35046
Eureka & Palisade	.06284	1.67224	.04972	1.92320
Nevada Central	.09387	1.21110	.11235	1.43741
Kansas Central	.09030	.89630	.02650	.98367
Rio Grande RR	.06347	1.21428	.11274	2.09910
North Pacific Coast	.01790	.84613	.02579	.99317
Texas Mexican	.03927	1.37127	.02038	1.31827
Des Moines & Northwestern	.05194	1.01254	.03092	1.26934
East Tennessee & Western N.C.	.04996	1.72200	.04118	1.22503
Fulton County Narrow Gauge	.02767	.42973	.01049	.64460
Des Moines & Kansas City	.03889	.61094	.03016	.64687
Condersport & Port Allegany	.03019	1.43000	.04948	.95333
All U.S. railroads of all gauges	.01993	.83068	.00593	1.06481

SOURCE: *Second Annual Report on the Statistics of Railways of the United States to the Interstate Commerce Commission for the Year Ending June 30, 1889* (Washington, D.C.: GPO, 1890), Table IV-C, pp. 383–453.

TABLE 7.5
*Rates of Return on Financial Capital for Selected Narrow Gauges
and the Railroad Industry as a Whole, Fiscal 1889*

	Investment (stocks and funded debt)	Net operating income	Rate of return
Railroad industry as a whole	$9,015,175,374	$299,926,374	3.32%
NARROW GAUGES			
Addison & Pennsylvania	$1,293,989	$18,269	1.41%
Arizona & New Mexico	1,508,295	180,541	11.97
Bellaire, Zanesville & Cincinnati	2,627,910[a]	25,405[a]	0.97
Bradford, Eldred & Cuba	1,398,429	1,802	0.12
Burlington & Northwestern	507,458	16,597	3.27
Burlington & Western	1,659,075	−1,377[a]	−0.08
Cincinnati, Georgetown & Portsmouth	652,683	15,330[a]	2.34
Clarksburg, Weston & Midland	278,100	16,905	6.08
Denver & Rio Grande	100,330,910	2,591,931	2.58
Denver & Rio Grande Western	15,163,478	489,914	3.23
Denver, South Park & Pacific/Denver, Leadville & Gunnison	14,053,799	−163,693[b]	−1.16
Des Moines & Kansas City	1,013,333	−71[a]	−0.01
Des Moines & Northwestern	1,010,068	−34,469	−3.41
East Tennessee & Western N.C.	872,578	4,750	0.54
Eureka & Palisade	2,031,729	45,267	2.23
Fulton County N.G. + Extension	1,157,162	4,836	0.42
Gainesville, Jefferson & Southern	831,621	2,806	−0.34
Houston East & West Texas	2,173,084	70,252[a]	3.23
Sedalia, Warsaw & Southern	841,108	−12,589[a]	−1.50
Montrose	304,900	4,871[a]	1.60
Nevada Central	863,589	−7,662[a]	−0.89
Nevada County N.G.	520,947	31,459	6.04
North Pacific Coast	3,144,806[c]	87,090[b]	2.77
Waynesburg & Washington	253,512	15,330	6.05
Saginaw, Tuscola & Huron	633,614[c]	29,955[a]	4.73
Sandy River	160,010	8,957	5.60
TOTALS	155,396,187	3,442,406	2.21%

SOURCE: *Second Annual Report on the Statistics of Railways of the United States to the Interstate Commerce Commission for the Year Ending June 30, 1889, passim,* except as noted.
[a] *Poor's Manual of Railroads,* 1890, *passim.*
[b] Calendar 1889, *Poor's Manual of Railroads,* 1890.
[c] Cost of road and equipment, *Poor's Manual of Railroads,* 1890.

prises, especially as compared with the Denver, South Park & Pacific, which reported costs about triple the D&RG's level. Even so, their costs per ton-mile were nearly double the national average. The costs per train-mile in the table are not particularly meaningful because they lack data on passenger loads or cargo.

Such an adverse cost differential should have manifested itself in rates of return significantly lower than the railroad industry as a whole. For major narrow gauge a 25 percent differential above the usual mileage rate.[92] In the mid-1930s, the Colorado & Southern in its abandonment action for the Clear Creek line cited costs per thousand ton-miles shown in Table 7.6. These data reflect not so much the inherent diseconomy of the narrow gauge as the contrast between a deteriorated railroad of 1880s technology and low traffic density and a modern standard gauge main line. The Clear Creek line was averaging only 7.34 miles per hour.[93]

The adverse cost differential of narrow gauge relative to standard gauge railroading necessarily worsened in the twentieth century because of the relative stagnancy of narrow gauge technology observed in Chapters 5 and 6. Cornelius W. Hauck found that the Nevada regulatory commission about 1913 allowed narrow gauge lines in the state rates 150 percent above standard because of their "inherent high costs" of operation.[91] In the early

TABLE 7.6

Costs Per Thousand Ton-Miles, Standard and Narrow Gauge,
Colorado & Southern Railway

	Standard Gauge	Clear Creek Narrow Gauge		Standard Gauge	Clear Creek Narrow Gauge
1930	$6.15	$58.94	1933	$5.25	$185.25
1931	5.99	67.78	1934	6.01	52.75
1932	7.28	54.23	1935	5.57	34.60

SOURCE: "Application of the Colorado & Southern Railway Company for a Certificate of Public Convenience and Necessity Authorizing it to Abandon Part of its Narrow Gauge Branch Line of Railroad, commonly known as its Clear Creek Line together with the Black Hawk Branch Thereof," F. D. No. 11114 (1936), Interstate Commerce Docket Room, Abstract of Evidence Relied upon by Applicant (Chicago: Sept. 12, 1936), p. 13.

1940s, the Denver & Rio Grande Western was allowed to charge on the narrow gauge a 25 percent differential above the usual mileage rate.[93] In the mid-1930s, the Colorado & Southern in its abandonment action for the Clear Creek line cited costs per thousand ton-miles shown in Table 7.6. These data reflect not so much the inherent diseconomy of the narrow gauge as the contrast between a deteriorated railroad of 1880s technology and low traffic density and a modern standard gauge main line. The Clear Creek line was averaging only 7.34 miles per hour.[96]

Similarly, when the Denver & Rio Grande Western was moving a heavy tonnage of pipe into the Farmington oil fields in the 1950s and 1960s, the cost to the carrier of moving a carload of pipe by standard gauge from Ogden to Alamosa, 800 miles, was estimated at $65, and from Alamosa to Farmington, 250 miles, including transshipment expense, at $127.50.[94]

Finally, it should be observed that the narrow gauge railroads as a class were free from the systematic discrimination that the standard gauge railroads later meted out to the interurbans.[95] The Gould railroads' refusal of through rates to the Texas & St. Louis at Texarkana and the Trunk Line cartel's boycott of the Toledo, Cincinnati & St. Louis at Toledo, mentioned in Chapter 4, were directed against members of the Grand Narrow Gauge Trunk during the short period when those lines appeared immediately or potentially serious rivals to the established railroads. Had the narrow gauges emerged as the majority of their advocates hoped, as cut-rate rivals to the members of the pools, there is no doubt they would have received such treatment systematically. Because their costs were too high for them to do so, the standard gauge railroads accepted them, in general, in the same fashion as any other railroads. As has been noted, the Illinois Central was more cooperative to the Texas & St. Louis and the Toledo, Cincinnati & St. Louis than the St. Louis & Cairo ever was. The TC&StL and St. Louis & Cairo were denied use of the Eads Bridge not out of a desire to exclude them from St. Louis, but simply because affixing a third rail to the metallic surface was considered impractical.[96] Most narrow gauges achieved only the status of local short line connections, against which it would have been pointless for the standard gauge railroads to discriminate. Accordingly, the narrow gauge movement must be held to have failed out of the flaws of its own conception, rather than out of any hostility from the railroad industry.

Notes

1. Arthur M. Wellington, *The Economic Theory of the Location of Railways*, 5th ed. (New York: John Wiley & Sons, 1893), pp. 694–97.

2. *National Car-Builder*, 7 (1876), p. 151.

3. *Proceedings of the Narrow-Gauge Railway Convention Held at St. Louis, Mo., June 18, 1872*, p. 22.

4. John T. Davis, "Narrow Gauge Railroads," *Mining & Scientific Press*, 41, no. 1 (1880), p. 6.

5. Raymond J. Feagonis, *The Railroad That Ran by the Tide* (Berkeley, Calif.: Howell-North Books, 1972), p. 37.

6. *Railroad Magazine*, July 1948, p. 67.

7. Walter C. Kasler, "Tionesta Valley," in Benjamin F. G. Kline, Jr., Walter Casler, and Thomas T. Tabler, III, eds., *The Logging Railroad Era of Lumbering in Pennsylvania* (Lancaster: Benjamin F. G. Kline, Jr.), vol. 2 (1972), p. 825.

8. George W. Hilton, *Monon Route* (Berkeley, Calif.: Howell-North Books, 1978), pp. 110, 112–13; right-of-way estimate from right-of-way and track maps, Office of the Chief Engineer, Chicago, Indianapolis & Louisville Railway, June 30, 1915, in Application of Chicago, Indianapolis & Louisville Ry. Co. under Paragraph (18), Section 1, of the Interstate Commerce Act, for a Certificate of Public Convenience and Necessity authorizing it to Abandon that Portion of the Bedford & Bloomfield Branch Railroad West of Avoca, Indiana, F.D. No. 10824, filed Apr. 10, 1935. Docket room, Interstate Commerce Commission, Washington, D.C.

9. Interstate Commerce Commission, Division of Valuation, MS field notes, Pere Marquette Railroad valuation, 1915, valuations 1-P and 1-R, 58A-329, box 279. Federal Records Center, Suitland, Md.

10. Henry E. Bender, Jr., *Uintah Railway: The Gilsonite Route* (Berkeley, Calif.: Howell-North Books, 1970), p. 42 and *passim*; "The Uintah Railway," *Baldwin Locomotives*, 2, no. 1 (July 1923), pp. 16–21, at p. 20.

11. George B. Turner, *Narrow Gauge Nostalgia: A Compendium of California Short Lines* (Costa Mesa, Calif.: Trans-Anglo Books, 1965), p. 64.

12. Mallory Hope Ferrell, *The Gilpin Gold Tram: Colorado's Unique Narrow Gauge* (Boulder, Colo.: Pruett Publishing Co., 1970), p. 21.

13. Robert A. LeMassena, *Rio Grande . . . to the Pacific!* (Denver: Sundance Limited, 1974), p. 249.

14. Charles F. H. Allen, "The Railroads of McKean County, Pa.," R&LHS *Bulletin*, no. 78 (1949).

15. Wellington, *Economic Theory*, pp. 326, 754.

16. Letter of Jackson C. Thode, Nov. 2, 1985, based on engineering data of D&RG in his collection.

17. M. C. Poor, *Denver, South Park & Pacific*, Memorial Edition (Denver: Rocky Mountain Railroad Club, 1976), pp. 416–17.

18. "Progress of Narrow Gauge Railroads," *Railroad Gazette*, 6 (1874), p. 338.

19. *Railroad Gazette*, 10 (1877), p. 129.

20. Wellington, *Economic Theory*, p. 326. Horseshoe Curve was rated at 9° in later years. See Harry T. Sohlberg, "Horseshoe Curve," *Trains*, Dec. 1941, p. 15.

21. Frederick Shaw, Clement Fisher, Jr., and George H. Harlan, *Oil Lamps and Iron Ponies* (San Francisco: Bay Books, Ltd., 1949), p. 81.

22. William Moedinger, Jr., "The Ma & Pa," *Trains*, Dec. 1941, p. 15.

23. St. Louis *Globe-Democrat*, Jan. 21, 1884.

24. Letter of Jackson C. Thode, Nov. 6, 1985, based on profile of the D&RG, 1908.

25. Poor, *Denver, South Park & Pacific*, pp. 416–17.

26. Donald Ray Grace, "Possible Alternatives to the Ophir Loop," unpublished M.S. thesis (1967), Texas Tech University, Lubbock, Texas, p. 47 and *passim*.

27. C. W. Gibbs, "The Turntable on the Main Track of the Silverton Railroad in Colorado," *Transactions of the American Society of Civil Engineers*, 23 (1890), No. 450.

28. George W. Hilton, *The Ma & Pa: A History of the Maryland & Pennsylvania Railroad* (Berkeley, Calif.: Howell-North Books, 1963), p. 66.

29. F. W. Osterwald, "Narrow Gauge Grade of the D&RGW Railway Along Price River, Utah, From Lower Crossing to Milepost 587," Xerox copy from D&RGW archives.

30. Gordon Chappell, "Scenic Line of the World," *Colorado Rail Annual No. 8* (1970), pp. 60, 77.

31. See Dow Helmers, *Historic Alpine Tunnel* (Denver: Sage Books, 1963).

32. Hilton, *Monon Route*, p. 100; Elmer G. Sulzer, *Ghost Railroads of Indiana* (Indianapolis: Vane A. Jones Co., 1970), p. 163.

33. Fred A. Stindt, *Trains to the Russian River* (Kelseyville, Calif.: Fred A. Stindt, 1974), p. 11; A. Bray Dickinson, *Narrow Gauge to the Redwoods* (Los Angeles: Trans-Anglo Books, 1967), p. 53.

34. Bruce A. MacGregor, *South Pacific Coast: An Illustrated History of the South Pacific Coast Railroad* (Berkeley, Calif.: Howell-North Books, 1968), p. 125.

35. Howard Fleming, *Narrow Gauge Railways in America* (Oakland: Grahame Hardy, 1949 [reprint of the 2d ed., 1876]), pp. 12–13.

36. *Railway Age*, 1 (1876), p. 121.

37. *History of Richland County* (Springfield, Ill.: Union Publishing Co., 1884), pp. 949–50.

38. *National Car-Builder*, 7 (1876), p. 23.

39. *Poor's Manual*, 1889, p. 1014.

40. Michael Koch, *The Shay Locomotive: Titan of the Timber* (Denver: World Press, 1971), pp. 66–73; *Poor's Manual*, 1879, p. 569; 1889, p. 697.

41. *Narrow Gauge Railway* (New York: C. W. Hunt Co., 1905), p. 4.

42. Wayne Lincoln, "Pennsboro & Harrisville Railroad (Lorama Railroad)," *Light Iron & Short Ties*, 2, no. 6 (Nov. 1984), pp. 4–5.

43. Wellington, *Economic Theory*, p. 752.

44. Fleming, *Narrow Gauge Railways*, p. 26.

45. Cincinnati *Commercial*, July 19, 1878.

46. *Railway Age*, 7 (1882), p. 408.

47. MS Annual Reports of the Public Utilities Commission of Ohio, 1885, p. 10, Ohio History Center, Columbus.

48. *Sixth Annual Report of the American Railway Master Mechanics Association* (Chicago, 1873), pp. 64–70.

49. *Fifteenth Annual Report of the American Railway Master Mechanics Association* (Chicago, 1882), p. 15; *Eighteenth Annual Report. . .* (Chicago, 1885), p. 10.

50. H. Temple Crittenden, *The Comp'ny: The Story of the Surry, Sussex & Southampton Railway and the Surry Lumber Co.* (Parsons, W. Virg.: McClain Printing Co., 1967), pp. 55–56, 68.

51. Robert C. Jones and David L. Register, *Two Feet to Tidewater: The Wiscasset Waterville & Farmington Railway* (Boulder, Colo.: Pruett Publishing Co., 1987), p. 104.

52. Hilton, *The Ma & Pa*, pp. 167–68.

53. Cincinnati *Commercial*, July 18, 1878.

54. *Ibid.*, Oct. 24, 1878.

55. F. Lavis, "The Gauge of Railways, With Particular Reference to Those of Southern South America," *Transactions of the American Society of Civil Engineers*, 78 (1915), No. 1317, pp. 312–423, at 367.

56. *Annual Report of the Secretary of Internal Affairs of Pennsylvania*, 1879, pp. 203, 229, 344; 1880, pp. 35, 216; 1881, 344, 772.

57. *Railway Age*, 7 (1882), p. 253.

58. Richard H. Kindig, "Mudhens and Sports Models," *Trains*, Oct. 1961, pp. 27–28.

59. David A. Myrick, *Railroads of Arizona*, vol. 3 (Glendale, Calif.: Trans-Anglo Books, 1984), p. 87.

60. *Railroad Gazette*, 41 (1906), p. 57.

61. E. W. Mureen, *History of the Fulton County Narrow Gauge Railway*, R&LHS *Bulletin*, No. 61A (1943), p. 39.

62. MS Annual Reports of the Public Utilities Commission of Ohio, 1883, p. 10, Ohio History Center, Columbus.

63. John A. Rehor, *The Nickel Plate Story* (Milwaukee: Kalmbach Publishing Co., 1956), p. 149.

64. *Ibid.*, p. 120.

65. Sullivan (Ind.) *Union*, Feb. 16, 1881; Robinson (Ill.) *Argus*, Feb. 16, 1881, Apr. 14, 1886.

66. Newton (Ill.) Weekly *Press*, Sept. 3, 1884; Robinson (Ill.) *Argus*, Feb. 11, 1885; *Railway Reporter*, 7 (Aug. 30, 1884), p. 3.

67. Robinson *Argus*, May 13, Sept. 2, 1885.

68. *Ibid.*, Feb. 17, 1886, Apr. 14, 1886.   69. *Ibid.*, Sept. 15, 1886.

70. Sullivan *Democrat*, July 4, 1884.   71. Robinson *Argus*, Aug. 3, 1881.

72. *Ibid.*, Aug. 10, 1881.

73. Quoted in Robinson *Argus*, July 13, 1881.

74. Bloomfield (Ind.) *News*, June 9, 1893. See the history of the company in Part II.

75. Ken Stewart, "The Cincinnati & Eastern Railway and the Cincinnati, New Richmond & Ohio River Railway," *The Fractured Frog* [Newsletter of Queen City Division, Railroad Enthusiasts], 2, No. 10 (May 1985), p. 11.

76. St. Louis *Globe-Democrat*, Feb. 25, 1885.

77. Elmer G. Sulzer, *Ghost Railroads of Kentucky* (Indianapolis: Vane A. Jones Co., 1967), p. 83.

78. Hilton, *The Ma & Pa*, pp. 44–45.   79. *Ibid.*, pp. 45–46.

80. *Ibid.*, pp. 51–54.

81. Based on a newspaper search by Edward T. Francis.

82. *Railway Reporter*, 5 (Dec. 1, 1882), p. 2.

83. Rehor, *Nickel Plate Story*, p. 295.

84. *Official Guide of the Railways*, June 1893, pp. 468, 538.

85. *Ibid.*, p. 405.

86. Robinson *Argus*, Oct. 5, 1881.

87. Gordon Chappell, "Scenic Line of the World," *Colorado Rail Annual No. 8* (1970), p. 86.

88. Rehor, *Nickel Plate Story*, p. 141.

89. Both the Olean, Bradford & Warren and the Bradford, Eldred & Cuba reported to the Secretary of Internal Affairs of Pennsylvania speeds of 15 miles per hour for passenger trains, both ordinary and express, and 8 miles per hour for freight. The Greenlick, which operated no passenger trains, ran its freights at an average of 10 miles per hour. *Annual Report of the Secretary of Internal Affairs of Pennsylvania*, 1881, p. 584; 1882, pp. 89, 281.

90. Unfortunately, it is impractical to attempt a time series on the rate of return. Official data are not available before the establishment of the Interstate Commerce Commission in 1887. Its first annual issue of *Statistics of Railways of the United States* is fragmentary in its presentation. By 1890 the major lines of the Grand Narrow Gauge Trunk and the Denver & Rio Grande main line had been converted. The results for the D&RG's surviving narrow gauge lines, which were always the largest single segment of narrow gauge mileage, were never separately reported. Similarly, the South Park Line and Colorado Central shortly became lost in the accounts of standard gauge railroads. Thus, 1889 appears the only year for which calculation on a rate of return is valid.

91. White, "The Narrow Gauge Fallacy," p. 88.

92. *D&RGW Trustees' Abandonment, Antonito, Colorado–Santa Fe, New Mexico*, 241 ICC 60 (1941), at p. 65.

93. *Ibid.*, examiner's proposed report, p. 25.

94. John B. Norwood, *Rio Grande Narrow Gauge* (River Forest, Ill.: Heimburger House, 1983), p. 96.

95. George W. Hilton and John F. Due, *The Electric Interurban Railways in America* (Stanford, Calif.: Stanford University Press, 1960), pp. 22–24, 140–42, and *passim*.

96. St. Louis *Globe-Democrat*, Oct. 24, 1882.

8

The Incompatibility Problem

The narrow gauge hypothesis had two elements: first, that adoption of a narrow gauge would produce a variety of economies; second, that the costs of incompatibility were small enough to be justified in pursuit of those economies. By means of the historical evidence in the three preceding chapters, it is relatively easy to demonstrate that the first element of the hypothesis was fallacious: the expected economies could not be realized. Dealing with the second element, however, is very difficult. The costs of transshipment of freight were never well documented. The observations were limited in number and ranged widely in time and magnitude.

The Costs of Transfer

As Lorenzo M. Johnson's article of 1878 demonstrated, car-to-car transfer of general cargo proved several times more expensive than narrow gauge doctrine had held. Johnson's estimate of 3¢ to 6¢ per hundredweight, or $5 to $9 per car, for the Cairo & St. Louis at Cairo remains the only widely circulated specific cost figure of the narrow gauge era.[1] In the same period it was estimated that transshipment from the standard gauge to the narrow gauge portions of the Colorado Central at Golden added an average of $1.24 per carload to the cost of freight to Black Hawk.[2] The principal freight was coal inbound to the precious-metal mines, and there is no record of anything beyond shovel transfer. Accordingly, this is a rather modest estimate. In 1895, the Tionesta Valley charged the Penn Tanning Co., an affiliate, 10¢ per ton for transfer of lumber from narrow to standard gauge cars at Clarendon, Pennsylvania.[3]

In general, railroads issued cost and revenue data in accordance with the rules of the regulatory commissions to which they were subject, but the commissions did not require transshipment data from the few railroads that engaged in the practice. The Chicago, Bellevue, Cascade & Western—during its brief independence before becoming the Bellevue & Cascade branch of the Chicago, Milwaukee & St. Paul—reported to the Iowa Board of Railroad Commissioners its costs in 24 categories, none of which

was transshipment at Bellevue, nor even the cost of freight handling more generally.[4]

Nonetheless, the Bellevue & Cascade, because of its long survival and the continual complaints about its quality of service, gives us the best evidence, second only to Johnson's, on the costs of transshipment on the narrow gauges. Transfer was accomplished by manual methods, shoveling of bulk cargo and hand-carrying of discrete items. Only a Y-shaped chute for the transfer of hogs—the principal cargo—from narrow gauge stockcars to standard appears to indicate any divergence from the most basic methods.[5] In 1935, as the line was approaching abandonment, the Bellevue

Shovel transfer of bulk commodities lasted until the end of large-scale narrow gauge operation. Here a crew of the Colorado & Southern in Denver in 1938 transfers ore off the Colorado Central line from narrow gauge gondolas into the company's standard gauge equipment. (Richard H. Kindig.)

These two views show the transfer facility of the Sandy River Railroad at Farmington, Maine, in 1896. Cut lumber is being transshipped from narrow gauge flatcars to standard gauge equipment. (Robert C. Jones collection.)

Facing page
Above is the Newport & Sherman's Valley's interchange facility with the Pennsylvania Railroad at Newport. Logs are being transshipped into standard gauge gondolas. The scene below shows grain or some other bulk commodity being transshipped from a Chesapeake & Ohio boxcar to two N&SV boxcars. (Both, Railroad Museum of Pennsylvania.)

Leader reported that at one time in 1920—apparently at the operation's peak—the transfer crew employed 21 men. Their payroll averaged $1,620 per month, as compared with $1,100 for train and engine crews on the branch, and a total payroll, including section crews and bridge-and-building gangs, of $3,100.[6] A firmer estimate of the costs of the Bellevue transfer dates from an investigation of the line mandated by the Iowa legislature in 1915. The Chicago, Milwaukee & St. Paul's representative testified that transshipment costs were not charged to the Bellevue & Cascade directly, but rather to the railroad's Dubuque Division generally, where they were impossible to identify specifically.[7] He estimated the transshipment expense at Bellevue at over $5,000 per year.[8] The line, which was barely profitable, had revenues and expenses of about $31,000 each.[9] Thus the transshipment expense at Bellevue was about 16 percent either of receipts or of costs directly attributed to the Bellevue & Cascade.

The inquiry of 1915 brought forth extensive evidence about the effect of the transfer at Bellevue on the quality of the service as perceived by the local shippers and consignees. The most common complaints concerned livestock movements. Shippers were uncertain about the stockcars that would be spotted at Bellevue and felt that, in consequence, they did not have normal control over the loading of their animals. One stockman testified that he shipped 175 cars to Chicago, 43 of which arrived late. One hog had arrived dead. A second stockman reported that 30 cars out of 150 to 200 had arrived late in Chicago. The delay in Bellevue, which was variable, resulted in dehydration and loss of weight of the animals. One shipper estimated the shrinkage of hogs at 200 pounds per car relative to all-standard-gauge movements to Chicago. Another witness complained that he could not bed down his hogs for the trip as shippers on standard gauge lines did, and estimated that because of the transfer he suffered the crippling of one hog for every two cars shipped. A witness complained that the community had outgrown the railroad, especially for stock movements. The line at the time had 48 stockcars, 42 boxcars, and nine other freight cars, a number inadequate for peak movements of hogs.[10]

There were analogous complaints for bulk cargo. The line's boxcars had no grain doors—half doors that lowered longitudinally across the cars' side doors to prevent grain from leaking out—causing loss of cargo that one witness testified caused on-line dealers to charge 6¢ to 10¢ per bushel more for corn than dealers elsewhere. A consignee of baled alfalfa complained that he had suffered a loss of 3,800 pounds in a shipment by breaking of bales and mixing of filth from the car into the grain. A shipment of oats suffered similarly in transfer and was downgraded from No. 3 to No. 4 on arrival in Chicago. Consignees of coal complained of shrinkage from pilferage while the car was idle at Bellevue and losses while the cargo was transferred by shovel. Many of these complaints arose from the railroad's occasional practice of substituting stockcars, its principal equipment, for boxcars and gondolas. One dealer complained that he had lost about three tons of coal through the sides in a transshipment when the coal was loaded into a stockcar on the narrow gauge. A lumber dealer testified that packages of shingles had been broken, part of a cargo of sawn lumber used for dunnage, and the whole shipment streaked with manure when loaded in a stockcar. Complaints of long and irregular delays at Bellevue were common.[11]

Some of these complaints were undoubtedly overstated. The Iowa commission thought the complaints concerning livestock excessive, in particular, and it found the overall quality of service on the line adequate. Transshipment of livestock on standard gauge railroads was common, with chronic complaints similar to these. Shovel unloading of bulk cargo from standard gauge cars was also common—as, for example, when bulk material had to be unloaded from a gondola. The important consideration is that the break of gauge at Bellevue caused a labor-intensive operation of this sort that could have been avoided. There is no reason to doubt the sincerity of the complaints voiced before the commission. Shippers who lived three-and-a-half to four miles from the Bellevue & Cascade were reported willing to drive ten miles to other railroads to load directly into standard gauge cars.[12]

Probably the second best documented interchange is Battle Mountain, Nevada, where the Nevada Central met the Southern Pacific's Central Pacific line. The two railroads split the costs of running the depot, requiring continual correspondence, the Nevada Central's contribution to which survives in the letterbooks of the general manager in the California State Railroad Museum in Sacramento. The principal cargo was silver ore from the Austin Mining Co., which controlled the railroad, to a processing facility at Vallejo Junction, California. The SP evaluated the ore in two classes, at $50 and $100 per ton, with rates of $8.75 and $12.70, respectively, subject to a 15-ton minimum. The NC's general manager, W. J. Phillips, found that the ore as it arrived in narrow gauge equipment did not transfer to standard gauge cars in proportions that assured making the 15-ton minimum. In May 1896 he wrote to C. F. Smurr, the SP's general freight agent, requesting a single rate for the two ores mixed, or, since he was pessimistic this would be granted, permission to load the two ores in the same standard gauge cars.[13] The SP refused the requested rate, but allowed the two ores to be mixed in the same cars. In November 1897, Phillips' successor, J. F. Mitchell, in an apparent effort to avoid an increase in the rates, wrote to the SP that the two rates were all the traffic could bear, and offered to discontinue mixing the two ores in SP cars.[14]

The Nevada Central, being mainly engaged in the ore movements, had continual difficulty in adjusting its limited supply of boxcars to the varying demands for movements of general cargo. In September 1896 a large shipment of lumber, 13 to 15 cars, arrived at Battle Mountain for transshipment to the mining company at Austin. Before it could all be transshipped, the Nevada Central ran up demurrage charges of $183. Phillips wrote to Smurr requesting a refund on the ground that "it is not the intention of your Company to exact demurrage from connecting lines when every possible effort is exerted to handle business promptly."[15] The SP granted the refund.[16]

In August 1897 Phillips became irritated at the failure of four shipments of merchandise to arrive in Austin as scheduled. He wrote to F. A. Limbaugh, his agent at Battle Mountain, to complain of the "unsatisfactory manner in which our freight business is being handled at your station."[17] Limbaugh responded that he had held the freight in an effort to fill boxcars. Phillips wrote him: "Of course you realize that [it] is very desirable to have our cars loaded as near their capacity as possible, which policy you will continue to carry out; but we cannot hold freight indefinitely for this purpose, yet there may be times when it will be perfectly proper to do so and when it is so held, please make notation on the Bill to that effect or advise by wire, then there will be no misunderstanding."[18]

In March 1901, assistant general manager Charles L. McFall wrote to general manager A. C. Luck:

We have a great deal of freight for The Nevada Company, [and] have six of our fourteen box cars tied up with their freight, that is counting the three cars that have been tied up so long with barley. We have not enough warehouse room to handle this stuff and when [the] Downeyville [camp in Nye County] starts up there will likely be more. What do you think of either enlarging the house at Clifton or putting a house in at Big Creek crossing to store the stuff in; this merely is a suggestion for you to think over. As soon as the ties begin to arrive we will have to take four cars out of the service for men to sleep in and that with holding freight in cars will run us very short.[19]

McFall managed to consolidate two carloads of barley and released one car.[20]

The Nevada Central in the late 1890s employed only one full-time freight handler for transfer of general cargo at Battle Mountain, a man named Delano, who regularly received salary checks of only about $23 to $29 per month.[21] The railroad had continual difficulty with damage to lumber in the course of transfer. The problem was particularly severe with tongue-and-groove lumber, on which the edges damaged very easily. In this connection assistant manager F. E. Jones wrote to J. C. Slater, agent at Battle Mountain in January 1899, "Instruct Mr. Delano to be a little more careful in the future."[22] In 1901 the mining company had ordered a shipment of lumber for a tank, in which the pieces had to mate very accurately. McFall wrote to Limbaugh to ensure that the shipment "be handled very carefully so that the edges will not be jammed or marred."[23]

Company coal: Coal intended for use in the railroad's own locomotives.

As elsewhere, there is very little direct evidence on the costs of transfer. The Nevada Central and the SP split the costs of transshipment of company coal inbound to the narrow gauge, but not the costs of transfer more generally. General manager Phillips in 1897 erroneously included a carload of lumber in the coal account, but when he discovered his mistake, wrote to the SP to reduce his claim against the company by $2.[24] This implies that the railroads had agreed upon a figure of $4 as the cost for transshipment of a carload of coal, as far as is known by shovel transfer. This is roughly consistent with the fee quoted to the Virginia & Truckee in 1890 by Wilson & O'Brien, a firm of coal dealers, of 50 cents per ton for transshipment or cartage to the railroad's own facilities.[25]

A limited amount of the accounts and correspondence of the Virginia & Truckee survive in the Bancroft Library of the University of California, Berkeley, concerning the interchange of the company with the narrow gauge Carson & Colorado at Mound House, Nevada. The V&T organized the C&C as a subsidiary, but sold it to the Southern Pacific in 1900. Again, there is no direct evidence on the cost of transshipment, only some evidence of the general magnitude of the problem. Shortly after the narrow gauge went into service in January 1881, the V&T solicited the opinion of B. G. Whitman, a lawyer in private practice in Virginia City, on the legality of imposing a specific charge for the transshipment at Mound House. Whitman responded that in his opinion such a fee would be inconsistent with the common carrier obligations of the railroad, which required carriage to be non-discriminatory among shippers. He believed that the proposed fee could be instituted only if the Nevada legislature passed a statute specifically authorizing it.[26] Consistent with this advice, the V&T in 1882 arranged rates between the San Francisco Bay area and points on the C&C in which the division would be computed on the basis of actual mileage on the Central Pacific and the V&T, but with a 50 percent additional loading for the narrow gauge mileage in lieu of a specific charge for the transfer at Mound House.[27] The rates on the narrow gauge were widely considered excessive. Shortly after the narrow gauge opened, a mine operator in Belleville, who had shortened his wagon haulage by shipping his ore on the narrow gauge from Hawthorne, wrote, "as you can see, the saving by the new route will be scarcely anything."[28] One mill owner requested a specific quotation on the cost of transshipment at Mound House,[29] and another requested a rate for borax inclusive of a fee for the transshipment.[30] If either received a response, it did not survive.

The third of the major narrow gauges in northern Nevada, the Eureka & Palisade Railroad, had similar experiences. The railroad was principally a facility for outbound movements of silver-lead ore, for which it charged about $5 per ton inclusive of the cost of transfer to Southern Pacific equipment at Palisade. Unlike the Nevada Central, the E&P did not typically discriminate among ores by value. The management required that the ore be shipped in sacks of about 125-pound capacity. Most moved in lots of 30,000 pounds, which amounted to two E&P carloads; SP cars had capacities of 20,000 pounds and up. Superintendent B. Gilman wrote to William Sproul, Assistant General Freight Agent of the Southern Pacific, in 1890 that shippers of ore worth over $50 per ton customarily had the sacks transferred to SP equipment because "the dirt and stuff in SP cars might or would affect samples of ore to their detriment."[31] Shippers of lower-valued ore usually had their sacks emptied into SP gondolas to take advantage of the bulk rate. The E&P returned the sacks without charge. Gilman said mining companies shipped low-valued ores in sacks only when they sought to keep two or more lots separate. Writing to his president, Edgar Mills of San Francisco, with respect to charges to the Richmond Consolidated Mining Co., one of the two principal shippers, Gilman said, "I am charging $1.50 per E&P car for emptying sacks at Palisade. About half the ore is emptied at Palisade and the charge nearly pays the cost of transferring all the ore."[32] If so, this is a relatively low observation for transfer cost.

Inbound, the Eureka & Palisade's principal cargo was coke for the various smelters at Eureka, handled at a rate of $4.50 per ton, again inclusive of the cost of transshipment at Palisade, plus 50¢ for delivery to the smelter. This arrangement appears to have given rise to little complaint, except that the E&P had chronic difficulty in processing multicar shipments through Palisade. In June 1888 seven cars of coke arrived simultaneously, even though they had been shipped on four separate days over a five-day period. Gilman wrote to Richard Gray, the Southern Pacific's General Freight Agent in San Francisco, that the E&P could not even throw the coke out of the cars onto the ground with its available personnel in the 24-hour period before demurrage began. He rejected the SP's proposal that the E&P install bins for the coke at Palisade on the ground that this would double his cost of transfer. Gilman sought relief from the $3 per day demurrage fee and sought only the 15¢ per day charge set by the SP for delay of foreign cars. Gilman charged the demurrage at Palisade to the consignees at Eureka, and observed that this fee caused "a bigger kick" than a greater amount as a regular freight charge.[33] The SP granted him some remission, with which he was satisfied.[34] Three years later 24 cars of coke arrived at Palisade in a two-day period, July 14–15, 1891, 12 cars from Oakland and a like number from Ogden. Gilman wrote to R. L. Myrick, the SP's division superintendent at Carlin, Nevada, that the E&P could not

Gravity transfer in progress on the East Tennessee & Western North Carolina at Johnson City. A Southern Railway hopper car is discharging into one of the ET&WNC's wooden hoppers. Both the upper and lower tracks are laid with three rails for transfer of bulk materials either inbound or outbound. (Ed Bond collection.)

possibly transfer the coke in the time allowed, and again requested relief from the demurrage charge. He stated, "Of late we have been unloading your cars very promptly, but this lot is too big to handle in a short time." [35] The facilities at Palisade were apparently particularly limited, for Gilman in ordering ties or company coal habitually specified that multicar shipments should leave the shipper at two- to three-day intervals. [36]

The inadequacy of the transfer arrangements caused the Eureka & Palisade in 1906–7 to adopt a system of bins such as the Southern Pacific had suggested. The two railroads jointly built a trestle from which seven bins could be filled by gravity. Ore continued to be shipped in sacks from Eureka, and was then transshipped through the bins at a cost of 50¢ per ton, a charge with which the mining company was reportedly satisfied. [37]

The long survival of the Atlantic & Danville's narrow gauge James River Division as the Claremont branch of the Southern Railway allows two observations of the cost of transfer. The A&D in 1898 charged the Virginia & North Carolina Wheel Co. a rate of 8¢ per hundredweight for shipment of hickory logs and other raw materials for wagon wheels from the branch to the company's plant in Richmond, plus a fee of $2 per car for transshipment of the lumber from the A&D's narrow gauge equipment at Emporia to standard gauge cars of the Atlantic Coast Line, which delivered the cargo to the factory. The company protested to the Virginia Railroad Commissioner, General J. C. Hill, that the rate was exorbitant relative to the A&D's local rates on the narrow gauge, and sought a reduction to 7¢. The firm also complained that the $2.00 fee for transshipment was excessive on the ground that its own employees accomplished similar transfers of cargo more cheaply. The railroad responded that its rates for such movements had been 9¢ per hundredweight, plus the $2 per car fee, and that the 8¢ rate represented a concession to the wheel company. Hill ordered the rate reduced to 7¢, but allowed the $2 transshipment fee to be retained, presumably considering it warranted.[38]

The cost of transfer to standard gauge equipment was less burdensome on the Atlantic & Danville narrow gauge than on most because the majority of the lumber traffic moved to the wharf at Claremont from movement on schooners or river steamers to its destination. After 1927, when the water movements ended, traffic moved by all-rail routes, including those of the Southern Railway, lessee of the A&D. By the early 1930s the traffic had been reduced to keg staves and low grade lumber from a single mill of the Gray Lumber Co. at Waverly. The Southern felt obligated to absorb the cost of transfer to its standard gauge equipment at Emporia to remain competitive with the Norfolk & Western, which was directly available to the lumber company at Waverly. In 1932, when abandonment of the narrow gauge was being considered, Harry A. DeButts, Superintendent of the Danville Division—who was to rise to the presidency of the Southern—requested of H. D. Luckett, Division Freight Agent, an estimate of the cost of transfer. Luckett responded that the cost of transshipment of lumber from narrow to standard gauge cars at Emporia amounted to $4 per car.[39] The Southern proceeded to abandon the line.

The Pennsboro & Harrisville Railroad in West Virginia for nine years immediately before the turn of the century recorded its costs of transfer at its interchange with the Baltimore & Ohio at Pennsboro. As Table 8.1 indicates, these costs were quite modest, ranging from 1.5 to 3.1 percent of freight receipts. Traffic was mainly vegetables outbound and general merchandise inbound. The record gives no indication of the tonnage handled through the interchange.

The Lackawanna & Pittsburgh maintained a transfer facility at Angelica, New York, between 3'-0" and 4'-8½" segments of its own line. In 1886 and 1887 the railroad contracted with local operators named Bosard and Farnum for labor for transshipment. In April 1886 it paid Bosard at the flat rate of 10¢ per ton for transferring of 438.75 tons, apparently of general cargo. In May 1887 it paid Farnum 8.42¢ per ton for the transfer of 1,428.35 tons.[40] This was only the labor expense, and the costs of spotting, switching, and removing cars, or any other incidental costs, are not covered. Similarly, in 1900 the Colorado & Southern made a contract for Charles Schultz to transfer loads at Newett, Colorado, from the South Park Line to the Colorado Midland at rates of 9¢ per ton for coal, 10¢ per ton for general cargo in boxcars, and 15¢ per ton for hay.[41]

In 1932 the Tuscarora Valley in its tariff for miscellaneous commodities quoted a rate of 90¢ per ton for lumber, its principal origination, between all on-line points and Port Royal, or 95¢ inclusive of transfer of the cargo to the Pennsylvania Railroad.[42] The lumber was mainly shipped by H. C. Hower, co-owner of the railroad. If the 5¢ per ton difference represented the cost of transfer, it is the only observation wholly consistent with the orthodoxy of narrow gauge doctrine of the 1870s.

On the adverse side, in 1901 when the Chicago, Milwaukee & St. Paul announced its intention to convert its Preston branch, the former Cale-

TABLE 8.1

Cost of Freight Transfer at Pennsboro, West Virginia, of the Pennsboro & Harrisville Railroad, 1890–1900

Year	Cost of freight transfer	Receipts from freight	Transfer cost as percentage of freight receipts
1890	$ 81	$5,361	1.5%
1891	130	4,169	3.1
1892	n.a.	n.a.	–
1893	n.a.	3,015	–
1894	53	2,682	1.9
1895	67	2,614	2.6
1896	56	2,076	2.7
1897	70	2,913	2.4
1898	72	3,254	2.2
1899	85	3,514	2.4
1900	74	3,513	2.1

SOURCE: MS reports of annual meetings, Pennsboro & Harrisville Ritchie County Railway—Lorama Railroad, 1875–1906, collection of Barr Wilson, Tollgate, West Virginia, typescript copy in possession of John G. King, Belpre, Ohio. Table extracted by Wayne Lincoln, Los Angeles, California.

donia, Mississippi & Western, the Preston *Times* estimated that elimination of the break of gauge at Reno, Minnesota, would save local shippers or consignees 50¢ per thousand board feet of lumber and one or two cents per bushel of grain.[43]

The various observations of transshipment cost available in the historical record range widely in time, location, and type of cargo. The high variance is consistent with other evidence that the cost of handling differed greatly between commodities. Octave Chanute in 1874 studied the costs of loading and unloading freight of an unspecified railroad on the Jersey City waterfront—presumably the Erie, with which Chanute had been associated. He found that unloading costs ranged from 3.4¢ per ton for beans or whiskey in barrels to 57.6¢ for leather in loose sides. Loading costs were similar.[44] I have made no effort to correct for movements in the price level, and the estimates are not wholly consistent one with another. None, except the Tuscarora Valley and possibly the Pennsboro & Harrisville data, gives any reason to believe that transfer could be accomplished for as little as the approximately 5¢ per ton that Edward Hulbert and the other narrow gauge advocates argued in the 1870s. They are more consistent with an estimate that the cost of transfer was about double that level, but less than Lorenzo M. Johnson's estimate of $5.00 to $9.00 per car. The data are most consistent with Matthias N. Forney's estimate of a cost of about half Johnson's figures, correcting Johnson's data for the cost of horse drayage that his transfer at Cairo, Illinois, entailed. Equally important, the historical evidence is wholly consistent with Johnson's view that transshipment amounted to a serious reduction in the quality of service, and a major incentive to shippers to avoid the narrow gauges.

Compatibility Devices

Inevitably, narrow gauge operators turned to various devices to reduce the costs of manual operations. Most simply, bulk cargo could be transshipped by gravity from hopper cars by means of an elevated track. The Eureka & Palisade's trestle, mentioned earlier, was 38 feet high and 544 feet long. It was fitted with three-rail track and could be used for bulk transfer in either direction. When it burned in 1927 it was replaced with a smaller structure only 329 feet long with two bins. Large-scale ore movements had ended, and the bins were mainly used for inbound coal. The Baltimore & Lehigh also used a gravity transfer in its Baltimore yard for inbound movements of coal. The Southern Pacific had a trestle for gravity transfer of talc and other minerals from its narrow gauge equipment at Owenyo, California.

The D&RGW in 1924 replaced shovel transfer of limestone off the Monarch branch and coal from Crested Butte with a rotary car dumper, often called a "barrel transfer," at Salida. The device, which was said to replace 75 shovelmen, allowed transfer from narrow gauge gondolas that had no bottom dumping arrangements. Two engineers in a study of D&RGW terminal arrangements in 1943 evaluated the device as satisfactory, but noted that there was a chronic problem of maintaining an adequate flow of standard gauge cars.[45] Salida never had an arrangement for gravity flow of bulk commodities, and, more surprisingly, neither did

Facing page
The Denver & Rio Grande Western installed this rotary car dumper at Salida in 1924 to transfer mineral traffic off the Monarch branch into standard gauge hoppers or gondolas. (D&RGW, courtesy Jackson C. Thode.)

The car hoist of G. T. Nutter was based on a simple wooden frame that lifted the car off its trucks. A stationary steam engine (not shown) actuated the device via the longitudinal shaft at the right of Nutter's patent drawing. Beveled pinions on shorter shafts turned the gears at the center of the drawing, which were centered under the frame, and in turn raised the screw jacks at the four corners of the apparatus. Trucks were then exchanged manually on the rails shown.

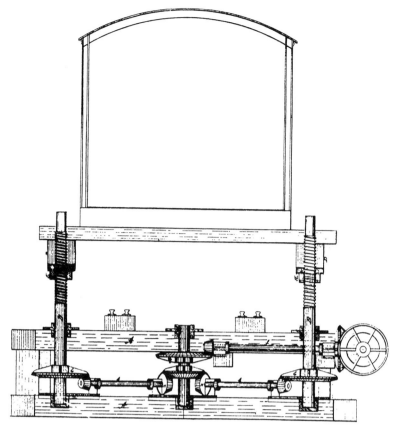

Alamosa. Only a gantry crane for lumber and pipe provided mechanized transfer at Alamosa, and bulk cargo to the end was handled by shovel.

The principal difficulty in mechanizing transshipment was modifying the labor-intensiveness of transfer of general cargo. The broad gauge railroads had long dealt with the problem of transferring car bodies between broad and standard gauge trucks by car hoists, which were mainly steam-actuated screw jacks arranged to elevate cars while crews manually exchanged trucks. Several inventors held patents for such devices. The Illinois Central installed a car hoist of the design of G. T. Nutter of New York at Cairo while its lines south of the Ohio River were 5'-0", but it then used the hoist to transfer narrow gauge cars off the Texas & St. Louis onto standard gauge trucks for movement to East St. Louis.[46] Henry Whatley Tyler in his report on the Erie in 1874 gave the price of a Nutter car hoist as $3,000.[47] The Texas & St. Louis itself upon completion announced its intention to install car hoists of unspecified patent at McGregor, Texas, for interchange with the Gulf, Colorado & Santa Fe, and at Jonesboro, Arkansas, for the Kansas City, Memphis & Birmingham.[48]

To transfer its cars onto the narrow gauge trucks of the Bradford, Eldred & Cuba, the Erie installed at Cuba, New York, a manual hoist based on two adjacent dual gauge turntables. A switch engine spotted a standard gauge car with its forward truck on one of the turntables. The yard crew with two 20-ton jacks raised the car until its king pin came free of the truck, which was then moved 90° for shifting to the adjacent turntable, by which it was lined up for movement to a standard gauge storage track. A narrow gauge truck was then moved under the car by means of the same turntables. The car was then lowered onto the narrow gauge truck and the switcher moved the car forward for the process to be re-

peated at its other end. J. A. Lanning, the agent at Cuba, reported that he and two yard employees could transfer a 12-ton Erie car to narrow gauge trucks in 20 minutes. He recognized the limitations of the operation, but estimated that manual transfer of general cargo between cars would take four times as long, and that shovel transfer of grain would occupy two men for a full day.[49]

In general, however, the narrow gauges did not install car hoists, but rather made use of a device specifically invented for their use, the Ramsey Transfer.

Robert H. Ramsey was a native of Cobourg, Ontario, who removed to Philadelphia. He secured a patent in 1876 and two more in 1878 for his device, which he called Ramsey's Car Transfer Apparatus. Ramsey exhibited a model at the convention of July 1878,[50] and actively promoted his

This remarkable photograph shows a Ramsey Transfer in operation at Phoenicia, New York, on the Ulster & Delaware and its narrow gauge subsidiary, the Stony Clove & Catskill Mountain Railroad. The photographer stood at the standard gauge end of the apparatus. A car has apparently been transferred onto narrow gauge trucks and moved out of the photograph. Note the dollies at the narrow gauge end. The horse is moving a standard gauge truck back under the boom of the crane at right. Two cables from the crane are attached to the horse's harness and to the truck. The cables are presumably disengaged from the horse and the truck is lifted onto the dual gauge track at right for movement to a storage area. (DeGolyer Collection, Southern Methodist University Library.)

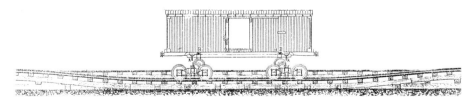

The crew of the Addison & Northern Pennsylvania's Ramsey Transfer at Addison, New York, stand on the Erie Railroad's standard gauge tracks with the transfer in the background. The tank engine at left provides the longitudinal motion by pole switching. Note the pole on the pilot. A standard gauge gondola rests on the dollies at right. Standard gauge trucks for cars on the line occupy the storage tracks at rear. (Ed Bond collection.)

Facing page
Locomotive No. 7 worked the Ramsey Transfer of the Bradford, Bordell & Kinzua at Bradford, Pennsylvania, by pole switching. The pole is carried on the tender. As elsewhere, carriage of standard gauge cars presented its problems. Below is a multi-car derailment caused by overturning of a standard gauge car on the BB&K's poorly ballasted track. (Ed Bond collection.)

system at least to 1886. The arrangement was relatively simple, based on a pit 20 inches deep. Both 3′-0″ and 4′-8½″ tracks were brought through the pit on the same center line. At the sides of the pit about nine feet apart were tracks of 15″ or 18″ gauge. A standard gauge freight car being transferred was brought into the pit. As it entered, its side sills descended to two 24-foot longitudinal beams, each carried on four wheels on the 15″ or 18″ rails at either side. Transverse beams could be put in place to support cars too narrow to be supported by the longitudinal beams. In Ramsey's earlier models, the standard gauge trucks were moved out and the narrow gauge trucks moved in longitudinally. In his later installations the truck exchange was made laterally by transfer tables. The car was then drawn forward so as to engage 3′-0″ trucks with its king pins on the ascent out of the pit. Passenger cars were transferred in the same fashion, except that four 4-wheel dollies were used on the 15″ or 18″ rails without a longitudinal beam.[51] Transfer took about four minutes, although Ramsey claimed to have done it in 90 seconds per car, presumably racing the clock in a demonstration.[52] The Ramsey Transfer had the attraction, relative to car hoists, of not raising the car, and thus not requiring a stationary steam engine or a set of jacks; horses or mules or a switch engine could move the car.

If narrow gauge railroads had a comprehensive incentive to converge on standard gauge practice, the Ramsey Transfer should have had one of the highest returns in narrow gauge technology. This appears to be true. The Coudersport & Port Allegany, a 17-mile line in Pennsylvania, installed a Ramsey Transfer in 1883 and estimated savings on its use in 1884 as $1,400, exactly 10 percent of its net income of $14,000.[53] Although the price Ramsey charged for the device has apparently not survived, the $1,400 was probably not far from a 100 percent return. The first narrow gauge to install a Ramsey Transfer was the Ligonier Valley in 1878,[54] but the device quickly spread to the Pittsylvania; Dayton, Covington & Toledo; Dayton & Southeastern; Bell's Gap; and others. The Toledo, Cincinnati & St. Louis had Ramsey Transfers at five points in Ohio and

planned them at several points on the western extension of the system. The management planned Ramsey Transfers for East St. Louis and Ramsey, Illinois, for interchange with the Illinois Central to bypass the uncooperative St. Louis & Cairo. There is thought to have been no Ramsey Transfer at Ramsey,[55] and whether the company progressed far enough with its uncompleted terminal arrangements to install one in East St. Louis is not reported in surviving newspapers.

Most of the installations were east of the Mississippi, but the Union Pacific operated two Ramsey Transfers, one at Pocatello for the Utah & Northern and the other at Salt Lake City. The installation at Pocatello beginning in 1885 handled a substantial traffic in coal from Wyoming to the Montana mining region in former South Park Line narrow gauge gondolas.[56] The Ramsey Transfer quickly proved a bottleneck; avoiding it was one of the considerations in conversion of the line north of Pocatello in 1887. The Transfer at Salt Lake City survived until the former Utah Western was converted in 1902.[57]

There was no presumption that a Ramsey Transfer could eliminate transshipment entirely. In the railroading of the time, less-than-carload freight was so ubiquitous that a general manager could not plan to avoid transshipment wholly, even if he installed a Ramsey Transfer. The contracts for manual labor at Angelica, New York, on the Lackawanna & Pittsburgh mentioned in the previous section were made even though the railroad maintained a Ramsey Transfer there.

Other mechanisms were devised for car transfer. John Ihling, superintendent of the Paw Paw Railroad, had an unusual problem in that his railroad, a short line connecting Paw Paw with the Michigan Central main line at Lawton, Michigan, had been converted from 4′-8½″ to 3′-0″ as part of a projected narrow gauge from Toledo to South Haven. To continue bringing standard gauge equipment into Paw Paw, he installed in 1878 a device at Lawton whereby cars off the Michigan Central could be transported without removing their trucks. As on a Ramsey Transfer, the standard gauge car was spotted above a pit into which the narrow gauge track descended. Ihling had C. F. Allen, a retired car designer of the Detroit Car Works, design a heavy iron 3′-0″ truck that when drawn up out of the pit engaged with the axles of the standard gauge car. The wheels rode outside the 3′-0″ rails, just above the ties. The Detroit Car Works built an unspecified number of sets of the trucks. Ihling was so optimistic about the arrangement that he planned no transshipment of freight for Paw Paw into narrow gauge equipment at Lawton.[58] The surviving newspaper in Paw Paw gives no reports on his experience, but the device could only have produced an unwieldy, top-heavy vehicle, limited to very low-speed operation. The experiment had failed by 1881, when the railroad was reportedly using a Ramsey Transfer at Lawton.[59]

When the Bradford, Bordell & Kinzua was abandoned in 1906, lumberman Elisha Kent Kane bought over a mile of terminal trackage to connect his mill on the west side of Smethport with the Pennsylvania Railroad at East Smethport. Because the municipal government never granted him the right to convert the track, Kane arranged to mount 4′-8½″ track on a 3′-0″ flatcar to ferry the standard gauge equipment over the crossing of the

The strange arrangement at East Smethport, Pennsylvania, whereby standard gauge cars were ferried across a standard gauge crossing on narrow gauge flatcars is shown here. The tank car is being handled in normal fashion, but the Lake Shore & Michigan Southern boxcar has derailed on the loading ramp. (Ed Bond collection.)

Buffalo, Rochester & Pittsburgh in the center of town.[60] The unusual arrangement, which lasted until 1913, was probably not capable of adaptation to line-haul service, for like Ihling's device, it must have produced a top-heavy vehicle with serious risks at ordinary speeds. The Pittsburgh Southern in 1882 introduced an adjustable truck by which its coal cars could run over its 3'-0" trackage or 4'-8½".[61] G. W. Atkinson of Petersburg, Tennessee, patented a device for replacing trucks by a transfer table in a

The East Broad Top's timber transfer was intended for movement of logs from narrow gauge flatcars to standard gauge equipment, as shown here. (Ed Bond collection.)

pit,[62] and David Todd of Detroit invented a system based on hydraulic jacks in a pair of pits, one for movements in each direction.[63] Neither is known to have been put in service.

The East Broad Top beginning in 1933 transferred boxcars between standard and narrow gauge trucks by an overhead mechanism called the timber transfer, originally intended to move loads of lumber between flatcars.[64]

Whatever the attractions of truck transfer, it had serious disadvantages. Intellectually, it destroyed any case for narrow gauge equipment as being preferable on grounds of weight-to-volume ratios. Physically, it produced a top-heavy vehicle with excessive overhang. An ordinary standard gauge car on 3'-0" rails had an overhang of about three feet on either side. Ordinary narrow gauge trucks were not suitable for such service. The Ulster & Delaware, when it established a Ramsey Transfer at its interchange in Phoenicia, bought a dozen sets of 3'-0" trucks with braces and equalizers to prevent excessive swaying.[65] Such specialized trucks were also expensive. The 10 pairs of trucks the Lackawanna & Pittsburgh bought for use with its Ramsey Transfer at Angelica, New York, in 1886–87 cost $2,120,

When the East Broad Top began transfer of standard gauge cars to narrow gauge trucks in 1933, the first car put through the timber transfer was this tank car of Barber Asphalt. (Ed Bond collection.)

although this sum included some interest expense.[66] The Bell's Gap paid $205 a pair for its transfer trucks and the Ligonier Valley paid $300 per pair for the trucks used with its pioneer Ramsey Transfer.[67] When the Bell's Gap in 1883 announced its intention to convert, President William A. Ingham of the East Broad Top recommended his railroad buy the Ramsey Transfer and the trucks used with it. He wrote: "The transfer apparatus is not expensive, except trucks which cost $200 per set. The Bell's Gap road own 104 or 52 sets. We might be able to procure second hand ones cheap when the Bell's Gap RR is altered next spring to Standard Gauge. The other expense of the transfer would be from $1000 to $1500 for the extension of sidings."[68]

The directors did not take Ingham's recommendation, but when the East Broad Top adopted truck transfer in 1933 the management bought trucks with oversized axles and journals. In addition, the trucks were fitted with heavy lateral plates that arched above the sideframes to engage the bolsters of the car.[69] Even so, John H. White, Jr., has described a trip on the line: "I personally observed the operation of a standard gauge box car on the East Broad Top in 1953. A conventional 40 foot car remounted on narrow gauge trucks, it was placed at the rear of the train so as to be under the watchful eye of the conductor. The crew was nervous and rightly so considering the wild swaying of the car—it became so alarming at one point that the conductor was ready to pull the air. He admonished the engineer for excessive speed at the next stop, yet I am sure we never exceeded 25 M.P.H."[70]

The consequence of putting a standard gauge car at the head of the train was described by Edward B. Bryant, a locomotive engineer of the Addison & Northern Pennsylvania:

There is one incident on the road that I will never forget. I was pulling the local freight train northbound. Just a short distance south of the depot at Freeman's Station there was a long left hand curve on a high wooden trestle. We had a double deck Erie stock car loaded with calves, and seven cars of coal behind it. We made a mistake in putting the car of stock next to the engine, having picked it up at Westfield and should have put it next to the caboose. At any rate, just as we were going into Freeman's, as the engine and stock car were on the trestle, the whole train with the exception of the engine and the caboose turned over. The stock car landed bottom side up on the highway along the bank of the creek. The engine and tender were off the track; the link in the coupler broke between

This sequence of photographs by William Moedinger, Jr., illustrates truck transfer on the East Broad Top. The car, a New York Central boxcar, has arrived at Mount Union on the narrow gauge. Note the heavy overhang on the 3'-0" trucks, and also the adapter on the standard gauge coupler. The car is raised by the timber transfer off the narrow gauge front truck, and the standard gauge truck replaces it. In the view of trucks on the storage track, note the plates extending from the center plate over the side frames to engage the bolsters of standard equipment while swaying.

The instability of a standard gauge car on narrow gauge trucks precipitated this accident on the Addison & Northern Pennsylvania. The engine crew was not so fortunate as the crew in the accident on this railroad described in the text; in this instance the locomotive went off the trestle into the stream. (Ed Bond collection.)

the tender and the stock car just before the engine turned over far enough to go with the stock car. I thought we were goners, but as the link broke we came back on the track again. Hiram Sutliff was the conductor and he was on the engine. No one was hurt but all the calves were killed. Those big Erie standard gauge stock cars, loaded top and bottom, when placed on narrow gauge trucks, swayed back and forth all the time a train was running and if they leaned over a little too far they turned over. They were especially bad on curves.[71]

In June, 1883, Dr. W. Harper of Jefferson, Texas, recovered $7,600 from the East Line & Red River for the wrongful death of his son, Charles R. Harper, who had died in an accident on the railroad in the previous January. The elder Harper successfully argued that the accident was caused by running loaded standard gauge boxcars on narrow gauge trucks in a mixed train.[72] On the other hand, the East Broad Top had no major accidents from handling standard gauge cars on its narrow gauge trucks over the course of two decades.

Containerization was ultimately the most effective device for compatibility. Containers in one form or another had been used since the cages in which the Romans transported animals from tropical Africa for arena games.[73] After 1955, the White Pass & Yukon containerized about 90 percent of its cargo—all but purely local traffic—so as to move freight by sea between Vancouver and Skagway and by road between Whitehorse and points in Yukon Territory. Such technology might have dealt with gauge differences in the narrow gauge era, but it was impractical because of the

Piggybacking was not widely practiced on the narrow gauges, but the East Tennessee & Western North Carolina carried these small semi-trailers on specially modified flatcars. (Ed Bond collection.)

high cost of horse drayage of containers in origination and termination.

The one serious proposal for a form of containerization was made by George A. Parker in his report on 2'-9" railroads for the development of western Massachusetts. He proposed carrying two 16-foot boxcars without their trucks on an ordinary 32-foot flatcar of the standard gauge railroads to reach off-line points.[74]

Piggybacking—carriage of semi-trailers on flatcars—was never widely practiced on the narrow gauges, but the East Tennessee & Western North Carolina had four flatcars with side sills cut away for low-level loading of the railroad's own semi-trailers.[75]

James Timms of Indianapolis about 1879 developed a self-adjusting car truck in which the wheels could move laterally on the axles. The wheels were brought to proper gauge by a tapering track. The device was used experimentally on the Bedford, Springville, Owensburg & Bloomfield and reported favorably to the Indianapolis, Delphi & Chicago.[76] Adjustable wheels had been used in the broad gauge era but were found dangerous. Timms' device is not known to have been adopted.

As usual in the history of technology, proposed but untried devices included some outlandish schemes. R. A. Wilder in 1872 proposed a four-rail system which was essentially a double-track meter-gauge railroad with the inside rails precisely 4'-8½" apart. Wilder proposed operating standard gauge trains for main lines, narrow for branch lines, plus broad gauge equipment with four wheels abreast for transcontinental service, or for the railway proposed to carry ships across the Isthmus of Darien. He estimated that the system would have four times the capacity of an ordinary double track railroad at 50 to 60 percent additional cost. There was no practical way curves could be super-elevated in the system, and one cannot conceive of keeping four rails in an absolutely fixed relation under all circumstances, but Wilder reported that the Hon. J. W. Killinger had

A mixed train of the Waynesburg &
Washington leaves Washington, Pennsylvania, on three-rail track of the parent Pennsylvania Railroad in 1929.
(Ed Bond collection.)

A three-rail wye required that the narrow gauge track be moved from one
standard gauge rail to the other on
one leg of the wye. Here is the change-
over device on the D&RGW's wye at
Alamosa in 1960. (John W. Maxwell.)

Facing page, top
A three-rail switch entailed three
frogs, or as D&RGW crews often
called them, "two frogs and a toad."
The toad was the frog at the narrow
gauge rail and the turnout, as in this
view of the Salida yard in 1955. (Jim
Shaughnessy.)

Facing page, bottom
This is the Denver & Rio Grande's diagram of the change-over at West Denver required to adapt the D&RG's narrow rail to the position of the South
Park Line on the three-rail approach to
Denver's Union Station.

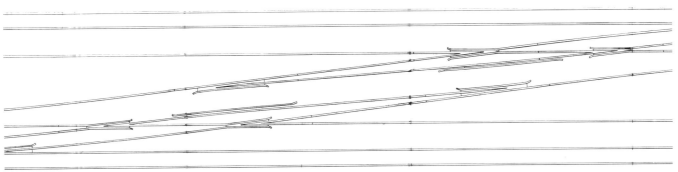

The two standard gauge switchers of the East Broad Top at Mount Union were equipped with a fixed standard gauge coupler and a narrow gauge coupler that could be placed at either side, depending on the locomotive's direction on three-rail track. (J. W. Swanberg.)

introduced into the House of Representatives a bill for a uniform national system of this character.[77]

Probably the most common compatibility device was three-rail operation. Beginning with the Denver & Rio Grande's laying of an outside rail to bring standard gauge cars into Pueblo in 1881, three-rail became common in Colorado. The East Broad Top used two standard gauge switchers on three-rail trackage in its yard at Mount Union, and the East Tennessee & Western North Carolina laid three-rail track from Johnson City to Elizabethton and Hampton between 1904 and 1906.[78] The latter began buying standard gauge locomotives in 1927.

The three-rail operation entailed certain difficulties. The third rail for narrow gauge was customarily lighter than the other two, causing the trains to run at a slight angle. The D&RG in its initial installation encountered some shifting of cargo and an abnormally high incidence of hot boxes on the lower side.[79] The D&RG's usual practice was to run the narrow gauge on the north side of three-rail track, but there were points where this was impractical. Notably, the Grand Junction yard had the narrow gauge on the south rail. Where it was necessary to bring the narrow gauge from one of the standard gauge rails to the other, the railroad installed what was variously called a "draw-rail," "transfer-rail" or "change-over." This device was based on a set of turn-out frogs to allow the locomotive and cars to make the shift without a switch being thrown. A three-rail wye necessarily entailed a device of this sort, and one was installed at the south end of Denver Union Station to shift entering D&RG trains to the South Park Line's position.[80]

On three-rail trackage, it was usually necessary for locomotives of one gauge to switch cars of the other. The East Broad Top had housings for a narrow gauge coupler below and to both the right and the left of the coupler on its standard gauge switchers. The East Tennessee & Western North Carolina, which mounted its narrow gauge couplers at standard

The D&RGW handled 4'-8½" cars on the three-rail track between Alamosa and Antonito by means of standard gauge idler cars. Here one of the company's standard gauge boxcars is being moved north from Antonito in 1941 on a narrow gauge freight with idlers ahead and behind. (Otto C. Perry, Denver Public Library.)

Hot box: A burning journal, usually produced by oily waste placed below the axle for lubrication becoming caught between the axle and the brass plate above it on which the car's weight rests.

Frog: A heavy casting providing the running surface and flangeways at a crossing of two rails.

Wye: In British usage, a reversing triangle.

The North Pacific Coast made its connection to San Francisco by car ferries and barges. Shown are the company's sidewheel tug *Tiger* and barge *Transfer 2*. (California Railroad Museum.)

gauge height after converting to the MCB in 1903, developed an ingenious double-jointed coupler shank for its locomotives that could move laterally to engage with cars of either gauge.[81] The D&RGW in later years used an idler car with couplers at both levels to allow narrow gauge locomotives to handle standard gauge cars on the three-rail Alamosa-Antonito line.

The Texas & St. Louis interchanged with the St. Louis & Cairo by means of third rail laid on the Mobile & Ohio's transfer steamer *W. B. Duncan* at Cairo in 1885–86. The company earlier made use of third rail on the Illinois Central's ferry *H. S. McComb* to terminate cars in Cairo and to move them onto the IC by truck exchange. The IC's ferry *W. H. Osborn* was built in 1884 with a 3'-0" track on its center line between its 4'-8½" tracks to accommodate the T&StL's equipment.[82] Because the largest concentration of narrow gauge mileage was in mountainous or arid terrain, car ferries were uncommon. The North Pacific Coast had narrow gauge track on its *Sausalito* and *Lagunitas*, and the South Pacific Coast on its *Garden City* and *Encinal*. These steamers allowed the two railroads to land equipment on 3'-0" track on the San Francisco waterfront, and to interchange with each other indirectly.[83] The Toledo, Cincinnati & St. Louis, which was denied a bridge entry into St. Louis, would probably have made a similar arrangement to land 3'-0" equipment on the St. Louis waterfront.

Notes

1. Lorenzo M. Johnson, "Are Narrow-Gauge Roads Economical?" *Scribner's Monthly*, 17 (1878), p. 294.

2. M. C. Poor, *Denver, South Park & Pacific*, Memorial Edition (Denver: Rocky Mountain Railroad Club, 1976), p. 83.

3. Walter C. Casler, "Tionesta Valley," in Benjamin F. G. Kline, Jr., Walter C. Casler, and Thomas T. Taber III, eds., *The Logging Railroad Era of Lumbering in Pennsylvania* (Lancaster: Benjamin F. G. Kline, Jr., 1973), vol. 2, p. 829.

4. *Third Annual Report of the Board of Railroad Commissioners for the Year Ending June 30, 1880, State of Iowa*, pp. 530–35, at p. 531.

5. *In the Matter of the Examination of the Branch Line of the Chicago, Milwaukee & St. Paul Railway Company From Bellevue, Iowa, to Cascade, Iowa*, Railroad Commissioners' Report No. 7670 (1916), p. 27.

6. Bellevue *Leader*, Mar. 21, 1935.

7. *Examination of the Branch Line . . . From Bellevue to Cascade*, p. 28.

8. *Ibid.*, p. 34.

9. *Ibid.*, p. 18.

10. *Ibid.*, pp. 23–26, 30.

11. *Ibid.*

12. *Ibid.*, p. 23.

13. MS letter of W. J. Phillips to C. F. Smurr, May 28, 1896, letterbook of the general manager, Nevada Central Railroad Co., Gilbert Kneiss collection, California State Railroad Museum, Sacramento, vol. 1, p. 182.

14. Typescript letter of J. F. Mitchell to William Sproule, Nov. 5, 1897, *ibid.*, vol. 1, pp. 307–8.

15. MS letter of W. J. Phillips to C. F. Smurr, Mar. 8, 1897, *ibid.*, vol. 1, pp. 246–47.

16. MS letter of W. J. Phillips to C. F. Smurr, Apr. 1, 1897, *ibid.*, vol. 1, p. 1897.

17. MS letter of W. J. Phillips to F. A. Limbaugh, Aug. 28, 1897, *ibid.*, vol. 1, pp. 306–7.

18. MS letter of W. J. Phillips to F. A. Limbaugh, Aug. 31, 1897, *ibid.*, vol. 1, pp. 302–3.

19. Typescript letter of Charles L. McFall to A. C. Luck, Mar. 21, 1901, *ibid.*, vol. 2, p. 98.

20. Typescript letter of C. L. McFall to J. Griffith, Apr. 4, 1901, *ibid.*, vol. 2, p. 119.

21. See cover letters for Delano's checks, Jan. 19, 1899, and May 8, 1899, *ibid.*, vol. 1, pp. 413, 460. It is not clear these payments were for full-time work.

22. Typescript letter of F. E. Jones to J. C. Slater, Apr. 20, 1899, *ibid.*, vol. 1, p. 453.

23. MS letter of Charles L. McFall to F. A. Limbaugh, May 9, 1901, *ibid.*, vol. 2, p. 200.

24. MS letter of W. J. Phillips to William Sproule, Sept. 21, 1897, *ibid.*, vol. 1, pp. 307–8.

25. Typescript letter of Wilson & O'Brien, San Francisco, to Virginia & Truckee Railroad, June 28, 1890, quoting prices of $15 per ton, $14 with a 10 ton minimum, delivered to Reno, effective July 1, 1890. MS Virginia & Truckee Railroad records, PG 231, carton 2, Bancroft Library, University of California, Berkeley.

26. MS letter of B. C. Whitman to D. A. Bender, Mar. 19, 1881. Carson & Colorado Railroad records, PG 232, carton 1, Bancroft Library, University of California, Berkeley.

27. Typescript letter of George A. Tyrell to J. P. Woodbury, Mar. 18, [1905], MS. Virginia & Truckee Railroad records, PG 231, carton 6.

28. MS letter of R. J. Jones, superintendent of Northern Belle Mill & Mining Co., to D. A. Bender, Apr. 12, 1881. Carson & Colorado Railroad records, PG 232, carton 1.

29. MS letter of E. W. LaRue to D. A. Bender, Apr. 8, 1881, *ibid.*

30. MS letter of Smith Bros. per one Clough (first initial or name unknown) to H. M. Yerrington, Mar. 31, 1884, *ibid.*

31. Letter of B. Gilman to William Sproule, July 24, 1890, MS Outbound Letter Book, Feb. 1888–Feb. 1892, Eureka & Palisade Railroad, p. 258. University of Nevada, Reno, library, Special Collections, NC2/I/1/4.

32. Letter of B. Gilman to Edgar Mills, May 18, 1890, *ibid.*, pp. 226–27.

33. Letter of B. Gilman to Richard Gray, June 14, 1888, *ibid.*, p. 19.

34. Letter of B. Gilman to Richard Gray, July 13, 1888, *ibid.*, p. 32.

35. Letter of B. Gilman to R. L. Myrick, July 14, 1891, *ibid.*, p. 422; letter of B. Gilman to C. F. Smurr, General Freight Agent, Southern Pacific Co., Aug. 5, 1891, *ibid.*, p. 431.

36. Letter of B. Gilman to A. E. Bradbury, Superintendent, Rocky Mountain Coal Co., Almy, Wyoming, Mar. 9, 1891, *ibid.*, p. 360; telegram of B. Gilman to Boca Mill Co., Oct. 3, 1891, *ibid.*, p. 445.

37. Eureka *Sentinel*, Apr. 13, 1907, transcribed by David L. Garcia, Downey, California.

38. *Report of the Railroad Commissioner of Virginia*, (1898), pp. vii–xv.

39. Memorandum 40407-A of H. D. Luckett to [Harry A.] DeButts, May 9, 1932, Southern Railway files, Xerox copy in possession of William E. Griffin, Jr., Richmond, VA.

40. MS vouchers and bills, Lackawanna & Pittsburgh Railroad, Xerox copies from collection of Howard W. Appell, Fillmore, New York.

41. Robert W. Richardson, "Colorado & Southern: An Operations Baedecker," *Colorado Rail Annual*, no. 12 (1974), p. 132.

42. Tuscarora Valley Railroad Company, Freight Tariff of Local and Proportional Rates on Classes and Commodities, ICC-F-No. 80, PSC Pa-F-No. 89, issued June 29, 1932, effective Aug. 1, 1932, p. 7.

43. Preston (Minnesota) *Times*, Feb. 27, 1901.

44. O. Chanute, "The Cost of Railroad Freight Traffic," *Railway Review*, 25 (1885), pp. 205–6, 217–18, at p. 206.

45. R. B. Eagleston and R. O. Irwin, "Report on D&RG Terminals," hectographed typescript report, Dec. 16, 1943, pp. 80–84. D&RGW archives.

46. *National Car-Builder*, 8 (1877), p. 5; Daily Cairo *Bulletin*, Feb. 29, 1884. For another design, see the Imboden Car Lifter in Robert Selph Henry, *This Fascinating Railroad Business* (Indianapolis and New York: The Bobbs-Merrill Co., 1942), p. 36. The Mobile & Ohio's car hoist at East Cairo reportedly operated by an endless chain, rather than by screw jacks. Daily Cairo *Bulletin*, June 14, 1884.

47. *American Railroad Journal*, 30 (1874), p. 1573.

48. St. Louis *Globe-Democrat*, Aug. 6, 1883.

49. Letter of J. A. Lanning, Cuba *Patriot*, Dec. 1, 1898, photocopy from collection of William D. Burt, Binghamton, New York.

50. Cincinnati *Daily Star*, July 17, 1878.

51. "Report of the Committee on Science and the Arts on Robert H. Ramsey's Car Transfer Apparatus," *Journal of the Franklin Institute*, Third Series, 92 (1886), pp. 186–98; *Railroad Gazette*, 12 (1880), pp. 256–57.

52. *Railroad Gazette*, 12 (1880), p. 257.

53. Thomas V. Johnson, "Pennsylvania Pigmy," *Trains*, July 1944, pp. 28–32, at p. 28.

54. John A. Rehor, *The Nickel Plate Story* (Milwaukee: Kalmbach Publishing Co., 1956), p. 140. Ramsey had made one earlier installation, on the Lehigh Valley at an interchange with the 6'-0" Erie at Waverly, New York.

55. This is the opinion of Willis Stoddard, a local historian, on the basis of the town's oral tradition. Ramsey bears the name of a local creek; it did not take its name from the Ramsey Transfer.

56. George E. Pitchard, *A Utah Railroad Scrapbook* (Salt Lake City: George E. Pitchard, 1987), p. 286.

57. *Ibid.*, p. 215, citing Salt Lake *Daily Tribune*, Dec. 10, 1902.

58. *Railroad Gazette*, 10 (1878), pp. 201, 262; Paw Paw *True Northerner*, May 24, 1878.

59. See the accompanying advertisement of the Ramsey Transfer from the *Railway Age*, which ran throughout 1881.

60. Charles F. H. Allen, "The Railroads of McKean County, Pa.," R&LHS *Bulletin*, No. 81 (1950), p. 53.

61. *Railway Reporter*, 3 (Sept. 12, 1882), p. 1.

62. *American Railroad Journal*, 55 (1882), p. 896.

63. David Todd, "Improvement in Devices for Changing the Gauge of Railway Cars," U.S. Patent No. 123,308 (1872).

64. Lee Rainey and Frank Kyper, *East Broad Top* (San Marino, Calif.: Golden West Books, 1982), p. 144.

65. Gerald M. Best, *The Ulster and Delaware* (San Marino, Calif.: Golden West Books, 1972), p. 46.

66. *Report of New York State Railroad Commissioners*, 1887, p. 340; vouchers of Lackawanna & Pittsburgh Railroad for cash payments to Colwell & Corning, New York, Oct. 4, 1886, Mar. 7, July 11, and Sept. 26, 1887, collection of Howard Appell, Fillmore, N.Y.

67. *Annual Report of the Secretary for Internal Affairs of Pennsylvania*, 1880, p. 340; 1881, pp. 50, 52.

68. Typescript extract from minutes of the East Broad Top Railroad & Coal Co., session of Jan. 16, 1883, transcribed by George M. Hart, Railroad Museum of Pennsylvania, Strasburg.

69. Rainey and Kyper, *East Broad Top*, pp. 144–45; *Railway Age*, 95 (1933), p. 501; letter of Lee Rainey, Mar. 18, 1986.

70. John H. White, Jr., "The Narrow Gauge Fallacy," *Railroad History*, no. 141 (1979), p. 95.

71. Capt. W. W. Robinson, "The Buffalo and Susquehanna and Its Subsidiaries," *R&LHS Bulletin*, No. 49 (1939), pp. 33–56, at p. 45.

72. St. Louis *Globe-Democrat*, June 20, 1883.

73. John H. White, Jr., "Containers: An Idea Whose Time Came Centuries Ago," *Intermodal Age*, Oct. 1985, pp. 42–44.

74. George A. Parker, *Report to the Massachusetts Legislature on Narrow Gauge Railways*, House of Representatives Document No. 180 (Boston, Mar. 11, 1871), p. 12. In the American Antiquarian Society, Worcester, Mass.

75. Mallory Hope Ferrell, *Tweetsie Country: The East Tennessee & Western North Carolina Railway* (Boulder, Colo.: Pruett Publishing Co., 1976), p. 105.

76. *Railroad Gazette*, 12 (1880), p. 5.

77. R. A. Wilder, "Narrow Gauge Combination Railroad System," reprinted from *Pottsville Miners' Journal*, Feb. 17, 1872, Library of Congress, general collection.

78. Rainey and Kyper, *East Broad Top*, p. 120; Farrell, *Tweetsie Country*, pp. 27, 189, 196.

79. O. Meredith Wilson, *The Denver & Rio Grande Project, 1870–1901* (Salt Lake City: Howe Brothers, 1982), p. 92.

80. Letters of John W. Maxwell, Aug. 26, 1985, and John B. Norwood, Oct. 1, 1985.

81. Ferrell, *Tweetsie Country*, p. 27.

82. St. Louis *Globe-Democrat*, March 3, 1884.

83. Bruce A. MacGregor, *South Pacific Coast: An Illustrated History of the South Pacific Coast Railroad* (Berkeley, Calif.: Howell-North Books, 1968), pp. 186–92; A. Bray Dickinson, *Narrow Gauge to the Redwoods* (Los Angeles: Trans-Anglo Books, 1967), pp. 160–61.

9

The Decline of the Narrow Gauge

The narrow gauge railroad did not decline in the usual fashion, when a superior alternative was introduced—as the cable car was phased out when the electric streetcar was perfected, for example.[1] Rather, the superior alternative was already in existence in the form of the standard gauge railroad. The decline was mainly a process of recognizing the basic error at various times, and then encountering varying degrees of impediments to the conversion. Approximately two-thirds of the narrow gauge mileage was converted, one-third abandoned. The reduction in mileage in the early years was mainly by conversion; abandonment predominated beginning in 1909.

The German scholar Walther Hoffmann in his book *British Industry 1700–1950* demonstrated a uniformity in patterns of decline.[2] The output of a declining industry declines at an increasing rate, then at a decreasing rate until the industry passes out of existence after a relatively long period. Typically, there are many temporary reversals of the decline from wars, cyclical fluctuations, and random events. In this instance, because there is no valid method of estimating narrow gauge output as a whole, the measure of decline is necessarily mileage. The decline of narrow gauge mileage accords with Hoffmann's pattern perfectly, however, being highly concentrated in the early years and then proceeding slowly until the closure of the White Pass & Yukon in Alaska in 1982. This decline is unusual only for its low incidence of cyclical reversal; only a net increase in narrow gauge mileage of 38 miles in 1912 prevented the decline from being monotonic.

Inevitably, the first conversions long antedated the peaking of narrow gauge mileage in 1885. The first narrow gauge to publish its intention to convert was the Central Valley in upstate New York in 1872—the year of its completion. The management reported to *Poor's Manual* of 1872–73 that it would probably be converted for use a part of a projected Buffalo extension of the New York & Oswego Midland.[3] The extension was never undertaken and the Central Valley was abandoned in 1875 without conversion.[4] The early conversions were, however, largely of this character, efforts to deal with a specific incompatibility problem. For example, the Indianapolis, Delphi & Chicago had built the central portion of its projected line to 3'-0", but then decided on conversion in 1880 because there were no prospective narrow gauge terminal facilities in Chicago and Indianapolis. The management had an opportunity to enter Chicago over the Chicago & Western Indiana, but had to adopt standard gauge to do it.[5] Actually, the Toronto, Grey & Bruce had been demonstrating from 1877 to 1881 that the problem was incompatibility with the North American railroad system as a whole, but until the collapse of the Grand Narrow Gauge Trunk this was not apparent.

Early in 1880, however, the Springfield, Jackson & Pomeroy, a 108-mile coal hauler in Ohio, converted. The line, which had been completed only in 1878, had no specific incompatibility problem; its principal connection was the narrow gauge Dayton & Southeastern. The management late in 1879 arranged a reorganization in which it could repudiate on its narrow gauge locomotives and rolling stock, but retain its right-of-way and structures. It then converted quickly and began anew as a standard gauge railroad. The episode received none of the extensive coverage in the trade press that was being given to the Toronto, Grey & Bruce's troubles, and can hardly be said to have influenced the course of the narrow gauge movement, but it was one of the best early indications of what was to come.

The first of the major American narrow gauges to convert was the Philadelphia & Atlantic City in 1884. This carrier was an anomaly by almost any standard. Built as an effort to rival an existing standard gauge between Camden and Atlantic City, the railroad was intended for high speed passenger service. The management at the last moment had chosen 3'-6" over 3'-0" for greater speed and stability. The terrain was flat, no large freight traffic was anticipated, and essentially none of the standard arguments for use of a narrow gauge had much application. The management had decided upon standard gauge by 1878. Under the circumstances, no one imputed much generality to the conversion.

Discrediting of the narrow gauge for long-distance general transport service with the collapse of the Toledo, Cincinnati & St. Louis in 1883 led to an immediate diminution in narrow gauge building, but not to any commensurate immediate increase in conversion. Indeed, conversion had been over 200 miles per year between 1880 and 1882, but was regularly under 200 from 1883 to 1885, barely more than 21 percent of the building in the three-year period. Efforts to convert the components of the Grand Narrow Gauge Trunk date from early 1884, but the actual conversion was highly concentrated between 1886 and 1889. As mentioned at the close of Chapter 4, the St. Louis & Cairo was converted in 1886, the Texas & St. Louis late in 1886 and early in 1887, and the former TC&StL main line to East St. Louis by mid-1889. The TC&StL's former lines southeast from Dayton were converted in April 1887, although the Delphos-Dayton line remained narrow gauge until July 1891. Conversion of the Trunk and its various branches removed about 1,675 miles from the narrow gauge total. Mainly because of this mileage, conversion hit its major peak of 1,345 miles in 1887, with a total of 3,455 miles converted from 1886 to 1889.

In the same period, the Painesville & Youngstown converted in 1886.

Here was a railroad that should have had minimal problems from an incompatible gauge. It connected the steel center of Youngstown with a Great Lakes harbor at Fairport, giving it prospect of northbound coal from the Mahoning Valley and southbound ore movements from lake freighters. Built for heavy bulk cargo, it had a better physical plant than the typical narrow gauge. Partly because of the line's incompatibility, the management had difficulty in making terminal arrangements in Youngstown. In addition, the railroad was in direct rivalry with standard gauges to Cleveland, Ashtabula, and Conneaut.

In the midst of this period of massive rejection of the narrow gauge, Robert F. Fairlie died. In 1873 he had received a commission to design and install a large narrow gauge system for Venezuela. Fairlie looked on the commission as an ideal opportunity to demonstrate his ideas, but the experience proved a personal disaster for him. En route, in Trinidad he suffered sunstroke, and during surveying at Puerto Cabello, Venezuela, he contracted a tropical fever from which he nearly died. He recuperated at Colon, and then was repatriated to England with great difficulty. He attempted to continue his engineering practice, but he never recovered his faculties completely. After his book of 1872 he was not active in the intellectual controversy over the narrow gauge. On July 31, 1885, Fairlie died at his home in Clapham, South London. The *Railroad Gazette*, in the awkward position of having to eulogize a man it had long considered a fount of error, wrote of him:

He had both the virtues and the faults of successful proselyters. Able, earnest, indefatigable, he laid hold of and boldly advanced, we do not doubt with entire good faith, every argument which would serve his turn, good, bad and indifferent, and he met with even more than the usual success of such determined enthusiasts, so far as the narrow-gauge is concerned, but not in regard to his locomotives, which he always claimed to be indispensable to the success of that gauge.

As our readers know, we have from the beginning opposed the system which he advocated. Time has already justified our position. The narrow-gauge movement is visibly dying of its own inherent weakness, which the unerring test of experience has clearly shown. Nevertheless, this should not blind us to the great good which Mr. Fairlie accomplished by the controversy which he began and carried on with such vigor and determination that he gained the ear of the world. It led railroad men to *think*, and has thus had much to do probably with the increasing power of engines and capacity of rolling stock and other minor matters which have had in recent years so great an effect on the cost of carrying traffic. In other words, Mr. Fairlie's premises that all was not as it should be were sound, although his conclusions and his remedy were unsound. . . . [T]he indirect results of his energy have been good in many ways, and perhaps worth all they have cost.[6]

In 1887, the Union Pacific, which had succeeded to the Utah & Northern, converted the portion from the junction with the UP system in Pocatello north into Montana. The largest narrow gauge in Michigan, the Port Huron & Northwestern, was converted by the successor Flint & Pere Marquette from Port Huron to East Saginaw in 1889, although the secondary lines survived about a decade longer.

In 1890 a large number of major conversions took place. The East & West of Alabama, which included the pioneer Cherokee Railroad, was converted in October. The Kansas Central, which had become a long but

unimportant branch of the Union Pacific, was converted in August. The UP converted the remainder of the Utah & Northern on October 1.

The most important conversion of 1890 by far was the main line of the Denver & Rio Grande and its affiliate, the Rio Grande Western, from Denver to Ogden. Apart from failure to reach El Paso, the D&RG had taken shape as a large, isolated narrow gauge, as Palmer had originally conceived it. The system had made its first concession to integration by laying third rail along its Denver-Pueblo trackage in 1881, but in the main the system remained a consistent 3'-0" network. The railroad's isolation was being menaced. The Santa Fe, in apparent violation of the agreement of 1880, was pushing its own line to Denver. The Colorado Midland had penetrated the Rocky Mountains from Colorado Springs, had crossed Hagerman Pass to Aspen, and was seeking a route for a standard gauge line to Salt Lake City. The D&RG management was confronted with the

Santa Cruz Railroad No. 3, the *Jupiter*, is on permanent display in the Arts & Industries building of the Smithsonian Institution. The engine is an ideal choice, built by Baldwin in 1876 and wholly representative of narrow gauge practice in its day. (Smithsonian Institution.)

Decline of the Narrow Gauge   275

basic dichotomy of the narrow gauge: 3'-0" might serve adequately for mineral origination, but it was inappropriate for general transport. The board of directors was informed that the Ogden line was unable to participate effectively in the growing traffic from the Far West because of the gauge incompatibility both at Ogden and at Denver. Accordingly, what was potentially a major transcontinental rail line was serving mainly a function of origination and termination. The Board voted unanimously to convert the Ogden line.[7] As the conversion of the Grand Junction–Ogden portion was reported, the *Railroad Gazette* observed:

The history of the narrow gauge Rio Grande system is extremely interesting; built as it was, through a territory without competition, a complete system in itself, with a large business at high rates, the road made money regardless of poor management. The road was so located that the break in gauge did not cause any great annoyance or expense. That time has passed, and the great prosperity of the West has brought other roads into the territory of the Rio Grande, and it has to drop its individuality and become part of the great system of standard gauge railroads. The day of narrow gauge roads is over, and no other body of men will think it economical to build three-foot roads for large business.[8]

The conversion of the East-West line, which entailed a new route over Tennessee Pass and along the upper Colorado River, was completed in June 1890.[9] The major narrow gauges had been reduced to about 1,260 miles of the D&RG in southwestern Colorado and northern New Mexico, the Rio Grande Southern, all of the Union Pacific's narrow gauge in the same area (the former Denver, South Park & Pacific and Colorado Central), the Carson & Colorado in Nevada and eastern California, the South Pacific Coast and North Pacific Coast in the San Francisco Bay area, most of the mileage in the Pennsylvania oil field, the Pittsburgh & Western, and a large number of isolated short lines elsewhere.

The conversion figure for 1890 proved 1,259 miles, nearly 100 below the 1,345 miles in 1887. By the end of 1890, 8,757 miles of narrow gauge remained; approximately a quarter of the peak mileage had been swept away in only five years. Thereafter conversion proceeded much more slowly, partly because the most important narrow gauge main lines had already been converted, partly because the increasingly depressed conditions of the 1890s made it difficult to finance conversions. By the end of 1893 mileage had fallen to 8,117, about 70 percent of the peak.[10]

Techniques of Conversion

As Forney had predicted nearly two decades earlier, the knowledge of the techniques of conversion from the waning days of the broad gauge was now being put to full use. The process was somewhat more difficult from the narrow than it had been from the broad, for a thorough job required longer ties, heavier rail and usually strengthening or replacement of trestles or bridges. Often truss spans had to be replaced to accommodate larger equipment. Given the grossly excessive use of short trestles in narrow gauge practice, conversion if done properly required a large number of fills and culverts at minor streams. On the Columbus & Rome, about two miles of trestles had to be replaced with fills and culverts in only 49.51 miles.[11] Similarly, it was desirable to modify the choppy profiles character-

The Maryland & Pennsylvania Railroad was two former narrow gauges converted with virtually no modification. The curvature was so bad that passenger cars of ordinary length could not be handled. Here gas-electric car No. 62 traverses the Stirrup Run trestle in 1947. (Charles T. Mahan, Jr.)

istic of the narrow gauges and even more urgent to deal with their curvature. A. M. Wellington wrote that it was possible for standard gauge locomotives to traverse the 20° to 24° curves common on the narrow gauges, but that anything worse should be modified.[12] Actually, most standard gauge railroads found 20° to 24° curvature intolerable, and endeavored to ameliorate it. In the best known example, the Toledo, Cincinnati & St. Louis had a curve apparently of about 23° in Delphos, which the successor Toledo, St. Louis & Kansas City modified in the course of conversion to 18°50′—still one of the most severe on an American main line.[13] As John M. Goodwin had demonstrated in his work on standard gauging a broad gauge railroad, conversion was not prohibitively expensive. Austin Corbin of New York estimated that conversion of the Toledo, Cincinnati & St. Louis with minimal improvements would cost only $7,500 per mile.[14]

Only a small railroad could be converted quickly. The Chicago, Mil-

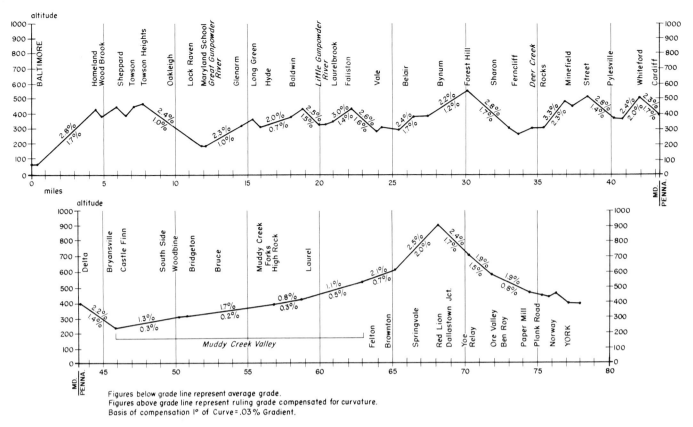

Figures below grade line represent average grade.
Figures above grade line represent ruling grade compensated for curvature.
Basis of compensation 1° of Curve = .03% Gradient.

Maryland and Pennsylvania Railroad
PROFILE OF GRADES

The Maryland & Pennsylvania Railroad was a good example of the physical plant inherited from narrow gauge predecessors. The southern district from Baltimore to Delta, Pennsylvania, was the former Maryland Central, a line built across a drainage pattern with a sawtooth profile. The former York & Peach Bottom north of Delta was difficult mainly for curvature in the Muddy Creek Valley. (From George W. Hilton, *The Ma & Pa: A History of the Maryland & Pennsylvania Railroad* [Berkeley: Howell-North Books, 1963], p. 66.)

waukee & St. Paul acquired the 16-mile Pine River Valley & Stevens Point Railroad on May 26, 1880, and quickly finished replacing the line's maple rail with iron. The larger railroad immediately announced its eventual intention to convert the line, but did nothing until it delivered standard gauge ties and bridge timbers on July 26. On Saturday, July 31, about 300 section men from other parts of the railroad were sent in to replace the ties and respace the existing iron rail. Most of the job was accomplished on Sunday, August 1, and the first standard gauge train ran about midday on Monday. Laying heavier rail, strengthening bridges, and adding to ballast were left until later.[15]

A large railroad, even where the management had thoroughly soured on narrow gauge, was unlikely to be able to convert in less than a year, and most took several years from the initial decision to the day of conversion. The engineering problems were frequently compounded by financial difficulties. Several railroads spent years trying to arrange financing of conversion. The Baltimore & Lehigh revealed its interest in converting in 1889, but could not finance the project fully until 1900.[16] The Painesville & Youngstown first announced its intention to convert in October 1881, bought its first supply of standard gauge ties in the following month, but did not effect the conversion until August 1886.[17]

In part, preparations for conversion were so time-consuming because management found it extremely costly to shut down a railroad for a long period. Only a few railroads chose this method; the Kingston & Central Mississippi, which served an area that was barely populated, was simply shut down and replaced by a standard gauge railroad about a year later.

This impressive photograph shows the Cincinnati, Lebanon & Northern at Blue Ash, Ohio, in the process of conversion in the summer of 1894. The railroad converted by moving one rail, but in this stretch it laid a third rail outside the narrow so that narrow gauge equipment might continue to be used for Cincinnati–Blue Ash suburban trains. (W. D. Simpkinson photograph, glass plate in possession of Mrs. Edith Marshall, printed from Arthur F. Glos collection, courtesy of Cornelius W. and John W. Hauck.)

The last surviving narrow gauges were dismantled according to standard railroad scrapping procedures. The rails were unspiked, hauled onto flatcars with cables, and taken off for sale as scrap. At top, a South Park Line crew at Estabrook, Colorado, prepares to attach cable to a loosened rail in 1938. At center another South Park Line crew loads rail near Solitude in the same year. (Both, Richard H. Kindig.) At bottom a dismantling crew loads rail from the Rio Grande Southern in 1952. Note the winch fabricated from an old automobile placed on the flatcar immediately behind locomotive No. 461 to haul in the cable. (Otto C. Perry, Denver Public Library.)

The Erie, after acquiring the Chicago & Atlantic in 1880, shut down the C&A's short narrow gauge between Huntington and Markle, Indiana, in July 1881, used the locomotive and cars for earth-moving on its extension to Chicago, and completed the standard gauge line at the end of 1882.[18] The Bath & Hammondsport, which had a highly seasonal traffic, shut down for about six months in 1889, opening as a standard gauge railroad on August 1.[19] The typical management tried to convert the railroad on a single day, if possible, but this required long preparation.

A railroad typically began its efforts at conversion with installation of standard gauge ties, usually of eight-foot length. This might be carried on for years as part of normal replacement without a specific conversion date in mind, as on various parts of the Denver & Rio Grande, even on portions that never were standard-gauged. Alternatively, the replacement might be done quite quickly in advance of an immediate conversion. If the conversion were impending, some amount of relocation of a line was usually necessary. This might amount to a small investment in easing of curvature and widening of cuts, as on the Baltimore & Lehigh and Painesville & Youngstown, or a long substitute on a different right-of-way. The Denver & Rio Grande built an entirely new line across La Veta Pass when it converted its Walsenburg-Alamosa trackage, replacing the original line over Veta Pass. Similarly, some 59 miles of the Rio Grande Western were relocated to the south when the line west of Grand Junction was converted.

Even if a narrow gauge had moved to heavier rail than the 30-, 35-, or 40-pound with which most of them began, it was usually necessary to shift to 56- or 60-pound rail for standard gauge operation. The most common practice was to lay the heavier iron to the narrow gauge, with one rail spiked normally and the other spiked as little as was consistent with safe operation. Henry C. Thompson recommended spiking a 28-foot rail at five points on tangents or seven on curves.[20] The meagerness of the spiking during the transitional period required that the ties be in good condition. A full set of spikes was then driven at the outside line of the permanent position for the rail to be moved. The tie was adzed to provide a regular surface for the rail. Switches prevented special problems. For stub switches, Thompson recommended that two of the six rods that joined the rails be removed, leaving four in place. The four should then be replaced on conversion day, and the other two at some later date.[21] For point switches it was desirable to fabricate as much as possible in advance of conversion day and to have the parts at the side of the track at the point of installation. The same was true of diamonds for crossings of other railroads. Thompson recommended that terminal trackage be laid with third rail to house the standard gauge equipment before the conversion and the non-standard afterward.[22]

The actual conversion required a large temporary labor force. Thompson estimated that normal practice entailed a foreman and five men for a five-mile section, but that a conversion crew should be two foremen for five miles, each with twenty-two men and a water boy. He proposed that the gangs begin at opposite ends of the five-mile section and meet at the middle on completion.[23] The short-run demand for labor was so great that conversions were frequently scheduled for Sundays, when a large number of hands were available. Once scheduled, the conversion was effected on a

Adzed: Ground flat with a machine designed for this purpose.

rain-or-shine basis. However massive, the process was basically simple. Thompson thought that only three tools were required: claw bars, spike malls, and wrought-iron rods he called "lining bars."[24] The rails to be moved were freed with the claw bars, moved to the line of spikes awaiting them, and then spiked down on the inside with the spike mall. Frequently the rail was not spiked at every tie, merely in the interest of saving time. The regular section crew then drove the rest of the spikes within a few days.

The largest conversion from narrow gauge ever attempted on a single day was effected in this fashion on the eastern portion of the Cotton Belt, then known as the St. Louis, Arkansas & Texas. The conversion was authorized by the shareholders in May 1886, although the principal owners had been considering the move since the receivership of 1884. They may have done some earlier work, but preparations were concentrated in the summer of 1886. By September 15 nearly 1.5 million long ties had been put in place and the spikes were set for moving one rail outward. Standard gauge locomotives and equipment were available by October 10, and the entire Arkansas division of 418 miles from Bird's Point, Missouri, to Texarkana was converted on Monday, October 18, 1886. The railroad was shut down upon the arrival of the afternoon passenger trains on Sunday, October 17. By 4:00 A.M. Monday, the narrow gauge equipment had been moved to prearranged sidings and the line was ready for conversion. At 5:00 A.M., 2,000 men were placed along the line, which had been divided into 10-mile sections. The three sections south of Pine Bluff had been converted by 9:30 A.M., and 230 miles had been done by 12:30 P.M. Eleven more sections were converted by 2:30 P.M., and the entire job had been accomplished by 6:00 P.M. The management had ready 60 standard gauge locomotives, 1,500 freight cars, and 50 coaches, about 60 percent of the motive power and rolling stock it planned for regular operation. Most of the equipment had been sent to Texarkana over the Iron Mountain, but some was at standard gauge junctions. Standard gauge operation began at midnight.[25] Revisions to the bridge over the Brazos River delayed conversion of the 305-mile Texas division until early in 1887.[26] The railroad estimated that in the course of the conversion it forwent about 5,000 cars of revenue freight, but it believed conversion would approximately double its traffic.[27]

W. M. Camp, in a compendious volume on track published in 1903, made serious objections to the method of moving one rail used by the Cotton Belt. He pointed out that in the transitional period the 3'-0" track was off-center on the ties, a situation that could cause problems of weight distribution. He considered having the rails off-center on bridges entirely impractical, and noted that to avoid this some new alignment would be necessary approaching the abutments. He also argued that conversion by moving one rail required all of the widening of cuts for the longer ties to be made on one side of the line, though this might be the side more costly to modify in many cases, as in a cut on the side of a hill. Again, this method might require modification of the alignment. He favored centering the narrow gauge track on the longer ties and moving both rails. He thought only a third of the short ties on tangents and half on curves need be replaced in advance of the conversion date by this method. He believed that by

Most of the later conversions were effected by laying standard gauge track outside the narrow gauge rails. The Leadville-Climax remnant of the South Park Line was in the process of such a conversion when Otto Perry photographed this double-headed freight at Three Mile Tank in June 1943. (Denver Public Library.)

the time he wrote moving both rails had become the usual method of conversion.[28]

Moving both rails toward the outside of narrow gauge ties was the least successful method. Conversion of the Kansas Central in 1890 was accomplished simply by respiking the narrow gauge rails to 4'-8½". The arrangement was so unsatisfactory that a train derailed, killing two people. The state regulatory commission endeavored to force the management to lay heavier rail, but was ultimately held to have no such power.[29] The Indiana & Illinois Southern, successor to the Springfield, Effingham & Southeastern, also converted by re-laying the narrow gauge rail, partly onto existing ties, partly onto new standard gauge ties. Its freight trains could operate at only six to eight miles per hour and derailed frequently. The standard gauge flanges at points descended below the rail, cutting grooves in the ties. The management felt the grooves tended to prevent the rails from spreading.[30] In 1895 the correspondent of the Bloomfield *News* at Nine Mile, Indiana, reported that because the railroad was temporarily inoperable, the mail had to be brought in by horseback. He added, "That beats the I&IS."[31] The Magma Arizona converted by using the narrow gauge as a service facility to bring in material for building the standard gauge on a new grade immediately adjacent.[32]

The Flint & Pere Marquette converted the four lines of the former Port Huron & Northwestern on the Thumb Peninsula of Michigan by alternating between two methods without any apparent logic. Because the F&PM had earmarked for the conversion $1.2 million of the bonds it issued to acquire the PH&NW, the operation was well financed. The larger railroad was principally interested in the narrow gauge's 90-mile line from East Saginaw to Port Huron and began efforts at conversion immediately upon acquisition on April 1, 1889. Only the portion from East Saginaw to Yale, 76 miles, was converted. To avoid a major wooden trestle and to secure more direct access to the St. Clair River tunnel, the company built a new entry of 20 miles into Port Huron to replace the rest. Standard gauge ties were distributed along the right-of-way by May 1 and were in place by May 24. The line had been built to relatively high standards, so that only

Decline of the Narrow Gauge   283

one major revision at Marlette was required to ease a curve. As the new ties were installed, the narrow gauge rails were spiked at the center. Beginning in mid-May standard gauge rails were spiked to the outside, starting from East Saginaw. The railroad had ordered 10,000 tons of rail for the conversion. When standard gauge track reached Yale on August 18th, the operation was converted and the narrow gauge was removed.[33]

On the Port Huron & Northwestern's secondary main line north to Bad Axe and Port Austin, the Flint & Pere Marquette began laying standard gauge ties as replacements as required, but did not attempt the conversion for almost a decade. During June 1898 track gangs replaced the remaining narrow gauge ties, but replaced rail only at stations. This unusual course allowed the switches and sidings to be set in place in advance of the conversion date. Beginning about July 1, outside spikes were put in place for a conversion by moving one rail. Section crews were approximately tripled. A gang of about 200 men from other divisions of the railroad was sent to Port Huron. At 3:30 A.M. on Sunday, July 17, the local section crews began moving the narrow gauge rails. At 10:00 A.M. the gang of 200 men headed north along the line on a special train. When it reached a section where work was in progress, the gang assisted the local crew until the job was done, loaded all hands and moved on to the next work site. In this fashion the entire line of 87 miles was converted by early on the 18th. The narrow gauge rail was then replaced with heavier iron during the rest of the year.[34]

For the branch from Palms to Harbor Beach, which had less traffic than the Port Austin line, the company reverted to laying standard gauge track outside narrow gauge rail. The work began in May 1899 and was completed with a single day of intensive installation of switches and road crossings on Sunday, September 17.[35] For the company's weakest narrow gauge line, the Almont branch, track gangs again respiked the narrow gauge rail to standard gauge. Preparation began in March 1903 and the job was completed with a one-day conversion on Sunday, May 3.[36]

The period of peak conversions inevitably produced a large volume of redundant narrow gauge motive power and rolling stock. The Cotton Belt converted most of the Texas & St. Louis's locomotives to standard gauge and put some of the rolling stock on standard gauge trucks. At best, such arrangements were temporary or transitional, for they produced underpowered locomotives and undersized cars. Narrow gauge cars were largely scrapped, frequently by burning off the wooden bodies and salvaging the metal. Locomotives were widely sold to other operators, either common carriers that had not yet converted, or private carriers that had no intention of converting. Ultimately many went to Latin America, either to the 3'-0" common carriers of Central America, to sugar plantations in Cuba, or to various extractive enterprises. The Baltimore & Lehigh, in the course of the decade over which it endeavored to finance conversion, bought locomotives from the Addison & Northern Pennsylvania and the Toledo, Cincinnati & St. Louis. After conversion, its narrow gauge power went to the Newport & Sherman's Valley, the Tionesta Valley, the Ohio River & Western, and two lumber companies.[37] After the Indianapolis, Delphi & Chicago's early conversion, ID&C No. 4 proceeded to the St. Louis, Des

Moines & Northern, the Hoosac Tunnel & Wilmington, and finally a Cuban sugar plantation.[38] At the time of the maximum conversions of the late 1880s and early 1890s, the typical narrow gauge locomotive was a relatively modern machine, only about a decade old. If a place could be found for it to serve, a narrow gauge engine could have a long life. A Rome 2-6-0 of 1883 began its career as Cincinnati Northern No. 9, and proceeded through the Toledo, Cincinnati & St. Louis, Portland & Willamette Valley, South Pacific Coast, and Mitchell Mining Co. before coming to the Nevada County Narrow Gauge in 1910. It then served until 1935.[39]

Lines that did not use 3'-0" were at a handicap in the secondhand market. When the Philadelphia & Reading was preparing to convert the Philadelphia & Atlantic City in 1884, Thomas B. Inness, a dealer in secondhand locomotives, wrote to General Manager J. E. Wootten that he had received an inquiry for a 3'-6" engine. He urged Wootten to release a locomotive in advance of conversion on the ground that, "3 ft. 6 in. gauge locomotives are very seldom called for and very hard to sell."[40] The Canadian narrow gauges, being mainly 3'-6", were the obvious market, but they began conversion early. Only two of the Philadelphia & Atlantic City's engines are known to have been sold for reuse, and the rest are presumed to have been sold to lumber companies or scrapped.

Repeal of the Sherman Silver Purchase Act

As we have seen, the major narrow gauges outside Colorado had largely converted by 1893, and most of the others had plans, firm or nebulous, for the change. At this time occurred an event that, although a monetary measure, was a major influence in the remaining history of the narrow gauges: the repeal of the Sherman Silver Purchase Act.

As mentioned in Chapter 4, Congress passed the Sherman Silver Purchase Act in 1890. The Act was one of a series of statutes that dealt in various fashions with the secular decline in the price of silver. The United States had been on a bimetallic standard for most of the nineteenth century, buying both gold and silver at mint prices in an approximate ratio of 16:1. Before the Civil War, this ratio overvalued gold relative to its market price so that gold, but not silver, was attracted to the mint. Silver discoveries in Colorado, Nevada, and elsewhere tended to reduce the market price of silver so that by 1873, at the 16:1 ratio, silver rather than gold was attracted to the mint. Congress responded with the Coinage Act of 1873, which limited silver coinage to dollars and fractional currency, and made silver legal tender for debts only up to five dollars. In 1875 gold specie payments on the greenbacks were resumed. These enactments were unpopular in Colorado, where silver had become the leading product of mines by 1874. By 1881 Colorado was the nation's leading producer of silver. Pressure from western silver interests had brought forth the Bland-Allison Act of 1878, which allowed coinage of $2,000,000 to $4,000,000 of silver per month at the discretion of the Secretary of the Treasury, to be bought at the market price. The measure proved inadequate to stem the falling price of silver; the market ratio fell to 22:1 by 1889. By 1890

Colorado was producing 58 percent of the nation's silver and accordingly became the principal support for a stronger measure than the Bland-Allison Act.

Such a measure took shape in the form of the Sherman Silver Purchase Act of 1890, passed in a political compromise between mainly Democratic senators from western silver-producing states and Republicans who were seeking support for the McKinley Tariff. Unlike most enactments for specie purchase, which specify a mint price but not a quantity, the Sherman Silver Purchase Act provided for the Treasury to buy 4.5 million ounces of silver per month—approximately the nation's entire output at the time—at the market price. The silver was to be purchased with a new issue of paper money, the Treasury Notes of 1890, which were redeemable either in gold or in silver. Under the Act, the Treasury bought $147 million in silver, most of which was not coined. This was about double the previous volume of purchase. Since recipients typically took payment in gold, the effect was to replace the monetary gold stock with silver. Between May 1892 and July 15, 1893, the Treasury paid out $54 million of the notes, of which $49 million were redeemed in gold. Issuance of the notes increased the quantity of money, tended to reduce the value of the dollar relative to foreign currency, and helped cause a net outflow of gold of $87.5 million in the fiscal year ending June 30, 1893. Other monetary forces, notably India's ceasing to coin the silver rupee in June 1893, contributed to the continued fall in the price of silver. The Act had raised the price from 93¢ per ounce in 1889 to $1 in 1890, but it had fallen to 83¢ before the cessation of Indian purchases and to 62¢ after it.

In June 1893 President Cleveland convoked a special session of Congress to consider repeal. In a message of August 8, he recommended repeal principally on the ground that continuation of purchases under the Act would replace the monetary gold stock with silver and end convertibility of the dollar into gold. The Repeal Act passed the House of Representatives 293-108 on August 28, and the Senate 48-37 on October 30, 1893. Silver declined from a ratio to gold of 27:1 at the time of the debate to 32.5:1 after repeal. An effort to restore the 16:1 mint ratio took shape in the form of William Jennings Bryan's presidential campaign of 1896, but it failed. The episode ended with the demonetization of silver except for subsidiary coinage in the Currency Act of 1900.[41]

This sequence of events was devastating to the mining area of southwestern Colorado still served by the narrow gauge network. The Act of 1890 had stimulated silver mining in the area and, as mentioned in Chapter 4, had brought forth a major narrow gauge, the Rio Grande Southern. Repeal so decimated the silver mining industry that the railroads were reduced largely to hauling coal, various other ores, sheep, and the general traffic of an area that rapidly depopulated. Inevitably, the fall in the price of silver relative to gold diverted resources to gold mining. Colorado had a boom in gold in the Cripple Creek area, bringing forth one more major narrow gauge, the Florence & Cripple Creek in 1894. For the southwestern Colorado network, what traffic remained proved inadequate to warrant conversion of the narrow gauges, and the network atrophied over the course of decades, with the slow outflow of investment characteristic of railroading.

Withdrawals After 1893

The course of monetary events just described amounted to a decision to maintain a gold standard at the cost of very considerable deflation. The price level descended to its all-time low in American history in 1896 and the nation experienced its worst depression of the second half of the nineteenth century. Gold discoveries in the Yukon Territory, Alaska, and elsewhere in the late 1890s brought forth an increase in the quantity of money, leading the economy out of the depression and into the great Edwardian prosperity of the first decade of the twentieth century. Most of the narrow gauges that, like the Baltimore & Lehigh, had been unable to finance conversion in the depression of the 1890s managed to do so at the end of the decade or in the early years of the twentieth century. The Baltimore & Lehigh effected conversion in 1900 in the course of its consolidation into the Maryland & Pennsylvania Railroad. The South Pacific Coast converted between 1905 and 1907. The Pittsburgh & Western was converted partly in 1901, partly in 1911. By 1912, the large narrow gauges were reduced to the Sandy River & Rangeley Lakes in Maine, the East Broad Top in Pennsylvania, the former Carson & Colorado, the Nevada-California-Oregon Railway, the Oahu Railway in Hawaii, the White Pass & Yukon in Alaska, and the major lines in Colorado. A dwindling number of local short lines survived. Mileage at the end of 1912 was 4,756, about 41 percent of the peak.

Since the conversion of the Denver & Rio Grande's Utah line in 1890, the Colorado network had not greatly declined. The South Park Line's Gunnison extension had been abandoned in 1910. The line had an extremely difficult tunnel, formidable snow problems in winter, and a traffic that had largely been reduced to coal. What remained, the main line to Leadville, survived as a conspicuous if essentially minor portion of the Colorado & Southern system, along with the former Colorado Central. The Denver & Rio Grande Western's remaining narrow gauge mileage took the form of a rectangle with Salida, Antonito, Durango, and Montrose at the corners. This trackage, known as the narrow gauge circle, had several tributary branches, and survived remarkably long. In apparent intention of converting the Alamosa-Durango line, the railroad in 1903 built an extension from a point near Durango to Farmington, New Mexico, as an isolated standard gauge railroad. By 1923, the management had apparently decided against converting the Alamosa-Durango trackage to standard gauge and instead converted the isolated Farmington branch to 3'-0". In the same period, as recounted in Chapter 5, the company largely reequipped its narrow gauge lines with Mikado locomotives.

Even in the depression of the 1930s, the Colorado mileage held up quite well. The D&RGW abandoned only two branches. In 1933 it dropped the Lake City line, which had not experienced any major revenue from mines since 1902.[42] Local operators carried it on briefly under the name of the San Christobal Railroad. In 1935 the D&RGW abandoned the Pagosa Springs line, a former lumber railroad that had little traffic left but sheep.[43] The Colorado & Southern sought to abandon the entire South Park Line but was refused by the Interstate Commerce Commission in 1930. On its second application the C&S was successful, and the remaining South

The D&RGW's last narrow gauge express train was the San Juan between Alamosa and Durango, which lasted until 1951. Here it is shown approaching Durango in 1947. (Richard H. Kindig.)

Park Line was abandoned in 1937 except for short segments out of Denver and Leadville. The two remnants survived only until the early 1940s.[44] The company's Clear Creek line, the former Colorado Central, lasted until 1941.[45]

In the same year the D&RGW made the first major abandonment of its narrow gauge network, the Santa Fe branch. This memorial to the company's early ambitions had never been a major source of traffic, but its abandonment proved highly controversial. A Congressional inquiry was held on the issue and the ICC finally had to declare itself without statutory authority to order a change in gauge.[46] At the close of 1941, narrow gauge mileage was 1,307, somewhat over 11 percent of the peak of 1885.

The war years stimulated several of the remaining narrow gauges. The Rio Grande Southern received federal assistance to move out ores used in production of nuclear weapons. The White Pass & Yukon moved materials for construction of the Alaskan highway. During the war, only the Monson Railroad, the last of the 2'-0" lines, and the little Lawndale Railway in North Carolina were abandoned.

The long survival of the 2'-0" railroads is difficult to explain. The experience appears clearly inconsistent with the general experience of the narrow gauges that the more closely they approximated standard gauge practice the more successful they were. Most of the 2'-0" mileage was built after the general discrediting of narrow gauge doctrine in 1883. None of the 2'-0" lines in Maine was converted, and, with the exception of the Kennebec Central, all survived until well into the automotive era. The most important of them, the Sandy River & Rangeley Lakes, lasted until 1935; the Wiscasset, Waterville & Farmington survived until 1933, and the

The Silverton train was to become one of the West's premier tourist attractions, but in 1945 it was this twice-weekly mixed train, known to but a narrow cult of enthusiasts. Here Otto Perry photographed the train leaving Durango on a June morning. (Denver Public Library.)

Bridgton & Harrison until 1941. Edward Hulbert in 1872 rose to the level of enthusiasm of calling 2'-0" railroads "better than going afoot,"[47] but by the test of survival, they provided the function of purely local service more effectively than the 3'-0" lines that he advocated.

With the end of the war, several of the isolated survivors were abandoned: the Sumpter Valley in Oregon in 1947,[48] the East Tennessee & Western North Carolina in 1950,[49] and the Oahu Railway's main-line operations in 1947, although switching track in Honolulu survived to 1972.[50] The narrow gauge circle of southwestern Colorado remained intact until April 1948, when a mudslide cut the line between Gunnison and

Colorado & Southern No. 71 brings a train of rail out of South Platte Canyon during dismantling of the South Park Line in 1938. (Richard H. Kindig.)

The last stand of the Denver & Rio Grande Western narrow gauge was carrying pipe into the oilfield at Farmington, New Mexico. Here a train of pipe slowly ascends Cumbres Pass from the east. (Otto C. Perry, Denver Public Library.)

Montrose. The D&RGW, confronted with the prospect of relocating the line to the north bank of the Gunnison River, abandoned the portion between Cedar Creek and Sapinero on June 1, 1949. The remaining lines out of Salida and Montrose were to follow within a few years. The connection from Poncha Junction to Hooper, which served almost entirely to bring equipment from the lines out of Salida to the shops at Alamosa, went in 1950. In 1952, the Rio Grande Southern gave up, leaving the D&RGW with isolated branches out of Montrose to Ouray and Cedar Creek. The company abandoned these in 1952, and received permission to drop the remainder of the old main line, including the branches out of Gunnison, late in 1953. The branches were removed in 1955. The Monarch branch was converted to standard gauge in 1956.

The line out of Alamosa survived into the 1960s. Passenger service had been discontinued in 1951. The D&RGW applied to abandon the Silverton branch, but the ICC unaccountably refused permission in 1962. The line had become almost wholly a tourist attraction, which could hardly be said to serve any useful function as a transport facility. Its freight revenue was under $800 per year. The railroad faced up to the situation and actively promoted the Silverton passenger train, hoping that a non-profit institution or private operator would eventually relieve it of the obligation.

The remainder of the mileage survived in an unlikely fashion, carrying pipe and machinery into the oil field at Farmington. This movement, which amounted to 550 carloads per month by 1956, was a demonstration of the inadequacy of the facility even for moderate loads. Pipe movements required three days to traverse the line. The physical plant went downhill to the extent that winter operation became impossible. In 1957 service was suspended for a month; by 1959 freights were operated as demanded, weather permitting. Beginning in 1964–65, the company in general did not attempt to keep Cumbres Pass open in winter. Finally in 1968 the company applied for permission to abandon from Alamosa to Farmington. The ICC's examiner found the narrow gauge "an obsolete facility," and the Commission agreed to the abandonment effective December 29, 1969.[51]

The railroad had not included the Silverton branch in the abandonment application. The company was now in the anomalous position of running an isolated tourist attraction without physical connection to the rest of the system. There was little question the line deserved preservation, both as a museum of narrow gauge practice and as an access facility to a scenic wonder, the Canyon of the Rio de las Animas, the equal of most of what had been preserved in the National Park Service and its state counterparts. An effort to vest the rail line in an eleemosynary institution, the Helen Thatcher White Foundation, had failed in 1960.[52] The railroad was covering its operating expenses on the trains, but if a flood wiped out any of the trestlework on the line, there was little prospect of the company's restoring it. Finally in 1981, the line was sold to a private party, Charles Bradshaw, who planned to promote the service as a tourist attraction under the name of the Durango & Silverton Narrow Gauge Railroad. He retained the line's legal status as a common carrier, however.

Meanwhile, the states of Colorado and New Mexico had preserved the more scenic portion of the Alamosa-Farmington line from Antonito to Chama. It was operated, somewhat less successfully than the Silverton line, by the Cumbres & Toltec Scenic Railroad.

Thus by 1981, the last narrow gauge lines in the contiguous 48 states had become museum pieces. Since 1947, the Edaville Railroad at South Carver, Massachusetts, had served as an operating museum of the Maine 2'-0" lines. Together with static exhibits at the Smithsonian Institution, the California State Railroad Museum in Sacramento, the Colorado Railroad Museum in Golden, and elsewhere, these facilities nicely delineate the narrow gauge for a generation that barely knew it.

As an active facility, the narrow gauge was not yet dead. In Alaska, 21 miles of the White Pass & Yukon still survived and, in a sense, flourished. The railroad was a wholly isolated 3'-0" line of 110 miles between Skagway and Whitehorse, capital of the Yukon Territory of Canada. It had been built at the end of the nineteenth century as an intermodal facility, reaching the Yukon goldfield by sternwheel steamboats. In 1955, it undertook to become an intermodal facility of a quite different sort. About 90 percent of its freight was containerized, both products of mines outbound and general cargo inbound. Cargo was handled by truck between the railhead at Whitehorse and the various destinations in the thinly settled Yukon Territory. The company instituted container ships between Skagway and Vancouver to connect with the North American railroad and highway system generally. The rail line was used as intermediary between the trucks and ships.[53]

The arrangement was an attractive one, which might have served as a model for a competitive reorganization of North American railroading.[54] Each of the three major modes of transport—rail, truck, and ship—was used in accordance with its comparative advantage, given the existing investment both in roads and in the railway. No major modification was made in the railway. Had the narrow gauge movement in America achieved a long-lasting large mileage of incompatible track such as the

The Cincinnati, Georgetown & Portsmouth during conversion in 1902 laid its Carrel Street yard with three gauges: 5'-2½" for compatibility with Cincinnati streetcars, the 3'-0" being removed, and the 4'-8½" with which the railroad would operate as an interurban. (Ed Bond collection.)

promoters of the Narrow Gauge Transcontinental and the Grand Narrow Gauge Trunk projected, the operators would almost certainly have resorted to containerization to deal with their incompatibility problems. Because of the lack of truck transport in the narrow gauge era itself, containerization was not then a practical solution.

The White Pass & Yukon's 110 rail miles was no more than a third of the minimum justifiable for an intermodal movement. Several mine closures plus completion of a parallel highway had made the line unprofitable by 1978. The closing of the principal outbound shipper, the Anvil Mine, in June 1982 ended any immediate prospect of the rail line returning to the black, and it was shut down on October 8, 1982.[55]

If one treats the end of freight operation on the White Pass & Yukon as the functional end of narrow gauge operation in the United States, the last trackage survived until just under a century after the end of large-scale building in 1883. Consistent with Hoffmann's general pattern of decline, the last 10 percent of the trackage took about 38 years to be eliminated. If one treats the Durango & Silverton as still in active common carriage, that period promises to be considerably longer. Apart from museum operations, the movement is memorialized in about 7,000 miles of former narrow gauge incorporated into the standard gauge system. About 16 percent of this is on the Denver & Rio Grande Western. The 7,000 miles represent approximately 38 percent of total narrow gauge mileage and about 5 percent of the current American railroad system. The disadvantage of narrow gauge origins differs between railroads. Of the big narrow gauges, the Cotton Belt probably suffered least. The line was built to the east of the Ozarks through flat country to Pine Bluff. In the hilly terrain between Pine Bluff and Texarkana, the company made extensive line revisions in the early 1920s. Subsequently, the Cotton Belt has usually been thought to have the best physical plant of the several railroads between St. Louis and Texas.

At the opposite extreme, the main line of the Toledo, Cincinnati & St. Louis was never greatly improved, and as the St. Louis line of the Nickel Plate Road was a catalog of the evils of narrow gauge engineering: weak bridges, excessive trestles, and light grading. Indeed, one of the motivations for the merger of the Nickel Plate and Wabash into the Norfolk & Western in 1964 was to reroute traffic from this line onto the main line of the Wabash.[56] Most of the east and west ends have been abandoned, and survival of the rest is questionable.

Elsewhere, the Norfolk & Western found it impractical to route its coal to Cincinnati because of the poor engineering properties of the former Cincinnati & Eastern. John P. Fishwick, president of the N&W, before the Interstate Commerce Commission in 1978 characterized the line as an "up and down railroad, and we . . . try to avoid that." Instead, the railroad sent its coal to Columbus for interchange with the Pennsylvania Railroad and its successors. Fishwick testified that the N&W shipped very little coal to Cincinnati, and would prefer to move it there by barge.[57] The Seaboard Air Line's Birmingham branch was always handicapped relative to the rival line of the Southern Railway by its origin as the East & West of Alabama. One consideration in the demise of the Baltimore & Ohio's Lake Branch was the high cost of moving long coal drags over the former Painesville & Youngstown. The company consolidated interchange with Great Lakes bulk freighters at Lorain and abandoned the Lake Branch even though it had recorded impressive tonnage figures.[58]

Withal, America emerged from the narrow-gauge experience better than most of the developing nations of the nineteenth century. Possibly the worst sufferer was South Africa. The country developed as a large-scale producer of products of mines, for which high-capacity rolling stock was appropriate. The South African Railways & Harbours Administration combines a 3'-6" gauge with a relatively wide loading gauge, consistent with the system's standard gauge origins. This combination is inherently unsuited to high-speed operations. The General Manager of the Cape Railways wrote in 1906: "If the gauge originally adopted, 4'-8½", had been continued instead of changing to 3'-6", the journey from Capetown to Johannesburg could be performed in about half the present time."[59] Another observer, C. O. Burge, suggested that the projected Cape-to-Cairo railway failed to be completed because of the narrow gauge of Africa: "The line from the Zambesi River through to Cairo had been projected on a *miserable 3'-6" gauge*. It would be found that the steamship companies, who were progressing faster than the railway projectors, would carry passengers from North to South Africa much more quickly by steamer than the railway could on a line of 3′-6″."[60] The SAR&HA is subject to extensive protection from non-rail competition, but narrow gauge state railways that have no such protection, such as the Japanese National Railways, are widely handicapped in rivalry with highway carriers. India, Australia, and Argentina are all seriously handicapped by incompatibility problems between narrow and standard or broad gauges.

Finally, the question arises whether the narrow gauge experience demonstrates that 4′-8½″ is approximately optimal. It is necessary to say "approximately" because no one has ever purported to say that it is precisely so. As noted in Chapter 2, Matthias Forney, for all his advocacy of a compatible 4′-8½″ national system, concluded from his discussions with railway engineers that something broader, 5′-0″, was closer to optimal. Although the supplanting of the broader gauges by 4′-8½″ was widely thought by a minority to be moving to something inferior, justified only by its widespread early adoption in the Northeast, the narrow gauge movement left no such residual feelings.

The ultimate victory of 4′-8½″ may be looked upon as the analogue of the determination of the optimal size of firms in George J. Stigler's theory of survivorship.[61] For example, since brewing companies of several plants, each of several million barrels per year output, survive, and companies of a single brewery of under a million barrels per year in general do not, we may reasonably conclude that brewing has extensive economies of scale.

On the other hand, the 4′-8½″ gauge may be an example of what Harvey Leibenstein has called "X-inefficiency," a technological process performed in the wrong way because the industry is inappropriately organized.[62] The current combination of the Janney coupler and the Westinghouse air brake is indisputably X-inefficient; a system that coupled electrically and transmitted the brake impulse electrically would be safer and less labor-intensive. The present survives because it is already in existence, and the economic organization of the railroads as simultaneously rivals and joint venturers requires a compatible technology. Although a superior electric coupling-braking system could easily be designed, the present system endures because conversion of over a million cars to some alternative is too costly. The 4′-8½″ gauge may be a similar example.

Statistical evidence is meager. Fred Lavis, in the course of his extensive study of railway gauges published by the American Society of Civil Engineers in 1915, found a U-shaped relation in the costs per train-mile reported by the state railways of Australia, shown in Table 9.1. Lavis also found a U-shaped relation for costs per train-mile in Argentina, but not for costs per ton-mile, which declined monotonically as the gauge increased. This is shown in Table 9.2. In all cases, the cost by narrow gauge was higher than standard. Consistent is a study of costs of the Indian railways in 1903 by Sir Frederick Robert Upcott, shown in Table 9.3. Figures per passenger-mile showed a slight advantage for the narrow gauge, however.

Stronger evidence for the optimality of standard gauge is the choice of 4′-8½″ for the compatible system connecting the major cities of Australia in preference to 3′-6″ or 5′-3″. Similarly, the Japanese National Railways went to 4′-8½″ for their high speed intercity electric trains of the 1960s

TABLE 9.1

*Costs Per Train-Mile,
Australian State Railways, 1910–11*

Broad	$1.20
Standard	1.09
Narrow	1.32

SOURCE: F. Lavis, "The Gauge of Railways, With Particular Reference to Those of Southern South America," *Transactions of the American Society of Civil Engineers*, 78, Paper No. 1317 (1915), pp. 312–423, at p. 364. Costs in U.S. gold dollars.

TABLE 9.2

*Costs Per Train-Mile and Per Ton-Mile,
Argentine Railways, 1909*

	Train-mile	Ton-mile
Broad	$1.620	$.01494
Standard	1.216	.01540
Narrow	1.410	.01557

SOURCE: Same as Table 9.1. Costs in U.S. gold dollars.

TABLE 9.3

*Average Costs of Carriage,
Indian Railways, 1903*

	Passenger-mile	Ton-mile	Return on capital
5′-6″	0.1 d.	0.25 d.	5.7 d.
Meter	0.096	0.31	6.0

SOURCE: Sir Frederick Robert Upcott, "The Railway Gauges of India," *Minutes of Proceedings of the Institution of Civil Engineers*, 164 (1906), pp. 196–214. Costs in British pence.

White Pass & Yukon No. 73 is being fitted out for service in 1947. The engine, a typical Baldwin 2-8-0, was the last steam locomotive built for a narrow gauge operating in the United States. (California State Railroad Museum.)

in preference to their existing 3'-6" or any wider gauge. By contrast, the Bay Area Rapid Transit in San Francisco adopted 5'-6", but the system was built with a large number of engineering errors. Similar systems in Washington, D.C., Baltimore, and elsewhere chose 4'-8½". Similarly, the Quebec, North Shore & Labrador, a freight railroad built in geographical isolation in 1954, chose 4'-8½".[63]

Accordingly, we are probably justified in concluding that 4'-8½" is approximately optimal with respect to the indivisible size of the human being. With respect to the subject of the present book, the experience of the narrow gauge movement demonstrated definitively that gauges under 4'-8½" are less than optimal for general transport purposes. To W. W. Evans's rhetorical question concerning the tendency of nineteenth-century engineers to go to larger and more capital-intensive equipment, "Are we all idiots?," we can give as unambiguous an answer as historical inquiry allows: Evans and the other orthodox railroad engineers who opposed the narrow gauge movement were not all idiots.

Notes

1. George W. Hilton, *The Cable Car in America* (Berkeley, Calif.: Howell-North Books, 1971), chap. 8, pp. 161–81.

2. Walther Hoffmann, *British Industry 1700–1950* (Oxford: Basil Blackwell, 1955).

3. *Poor's Manual*, 1872–73, p. 286.

4. *Poor's* in 1874–75 and 1875–76 reported the line converted, but a newspaper search reveals this to be an error. See the corporate history in Part II.

5. George W. Hilton, *Monon Route* (Berkeley, Calif.: Howell-North Books, 1978), pp. 45–46.

6. *Railroad Gazette*, 17 (1885), p. 536. For biographical detail, see also p. 541 and *Railway Age*, 10 (1885), p. 553.

7. *Fourth Annual Report of the Denver & Rio Grande Railroad Co. for the Year Ending December 1, 1889* (Denver, 1890).

8. *Railroad Gazette*, 22 (1890), p. 479.

9. Gordon Chappell, "Scenic Line of the World," *Colorado Rail Annual No. 8* (1970), p. 95.

10. The one previous published estimate of mileage during the decline dates from 1893. Foster Crowell, in the course of commenting on E. A. Ziffer's final presentation of narrow gauge doctrine in that year, estimated on the basis of the current *Poor's Manual* that mileage was down to 4,562, which would have been only about 39 percent of the peak. Crowell considered laying of standard gauge third rail a conversion, whereas in this book such track is considered still narrow gauge; but even given that difference in methodology, Crowell missed a considerable amount of extant mileage. *Transactions of the American Society of Civil Engineers*, 30 (1893), pp. 538–40.

11. *Railroad Gazette*, 41 (1906), p. 57.

12. Arthur M. Wellington, *The Economic Theory of the Location of Railways*, 5th ed. (New York: John Wiley & Sons, 1893), p. 754.

13. John A. Rehor, *The Nickel Plate Story* (Milwaukee: Kalmbach Publishing Co., 1956), pp. 123, 147. My estimate of original curvature is based on *MS Annual Reports of Railroads* (Public Utilities Commission of Ohio, 1885), p. 10 (Ohio History Center, Columbus).

14. *Railroad Gazette*, 16 (1884), p. 386.

15. Richland County *Republican*, Richland Center, Wisc., Aug. 5, 1880.

16. George W. Hilton, *The Ma & Pa: A History of the Maryland & Pennsylvania Railroad* (Berkeley, Calif.: Howell-North Books, 1963), pp. 37–38, 54.

17. Painesville *Telegraph*, Oct. 27, 1881; Nov. 17, 1881; Aug. 26, 1886.

18. See the corporate histories of these lines in Part II.

19. Gustave W. Erhardt, "The Bath & Hammondsport R.R.," R&HS *Bulletin*, no. 62 (1943), pp. 68–70.

20. Henry C. Thompson, "Changing the Gauge of Railroads While in Operation," *Railway Review*, 22 (1882), pp. 411–13. Thompson's argument is phrased in terms of conversion from broad to standard gauge.

21. *Ibid.*   22. *Ibid.*
23. *Ibid.*   24. *Ibid.*

25. St. Louis *Globe-Democrat*, Oct. 14, Oct. 19, 1886.

26. Jacob E. Anderson, *A Brief History of the St. Louis Southwestern Railway Lines* (St. Louis: St. Louis Southwestern Railway, 1947), p. 14.

27. *Railroad Gazette*, 18 (1886), p. 636; St. Louis *Globe-Democrat*, Dec. 8, 1884.

28. W. M. Camp, *Notes on Track* (Chicago: W. M. Camp, 1903), p. 567.

29. *Railway Age*, 16 (1891), pp. 492, 963.

30. *I. & I.S. Old Timers' Club: History, Experience, Incidents* (E. R. Alexander, 1924), [p. 18].

31. Bloomfield *News*, Mar. 29, 1895.

32. Gordon Chappell, *Rails to Carry Copper: A History of the Magma Arizona Railroad* (Boulder, Colo.: Pruett Publishing Co., 1973), p. 91.

33. Port Huron *Daily Times*, Apr. 1–Aug. 30, 1889, *passim*.

34. *Ibid.*, June 16, 1890; June 3–July 18, 1898, *passim*.

35. *Ibid.*, May 13–Sept. 18, 1899, *passim*.

36. *Ibid.*, Mar. 25–May 4, 1903, *passim*.

37. Hilton, *The Ma & Pa*, pp. 167–69.   38. Hilton, *Monon Route*, pp. 38, 317.

39. Rehor, *The Nickel Plate Story*, pp. 434–35.

40. Typescript letter of Thomas B. Inness to J. E. Wootten, Feb. 20, 1884, Philadelphia & Reading papers, Elutherian Mills Historical Library, Greenville, Wilmington, Del. Xerox copy from W. George Cook, Clinton, Conn.

41. On the silver controversy, see Chester W. Wright, *Economic History of the United States* (New York: McGraw-Hill Book Co., 1941), pp. 821–22; Rexford G. Tugwell, *Grover Cleveland: A Study in Courage* (New York: Dodd, Mead & Co., 1933), pp. 525–38; Carl Ubbelohde, Maxine Benson, and Duane A. Smith, *A Colorado History* (2d ed.; Boulder, Colo.: Pruett Publishing Co., 1976), pp. 215–18. President Cleveland's message is printed in full in the Washington *Post* of Aug. 9, 1893.

42. Duane Vandenbusche and Walter R. Bourneman, "Lake City Branch," *Colorado Rail Annual No. 14* (1979), pp. 25–109.

43. Gordon S. Chappell, *Logging Along the Denver & Rio Grande* (Golden: Colorado Railroad Museum, 1971), pp. 80–81.

44. Gordon S. Chappell, Cornelius W. Hauck, and Robert W. Richardson, *The South Park Line. Colorado Rail Annual No. 12* (1974), pp. 191–96.

45. Cornelius W. Hauck, *Narrow Gauge to Central and Silver Plume. Colorado Rail Annual No. 10* (1972), pp. 177–79.

46. Gordon Chappell, *To Santa Fe by Narrow Gauge: The D&RG's "Chili Line." Colorado Rail Annual No. 7* (1969, reprinted with additions, 1976).

47. Missouri *Republican* (St. Louis), June 20, 1872.

48. Mallory Hope Ferrell, *Rails, Sagebrush and Pine* (San Marino, Calif.: Golden West Books, 1967).

49. Mallory Hope Ferrell, *Tweetsie Country: The East Tennessee & Western North Carolina Railroad* (Boulder, Colo.: Pruett Publishing Co., 1976).

50. Gerald M. Best, *Railroads of Hawaii* (San Marino, Calif.: Golden West Books, 1978), pp. 98–102.

51. *Denver & Rio Grande Western RR Co., Abandonment Between Farmington, New Mexico, and Alamosa and Antonito, Colorado*, F.D. 24745, 334 ICC 539 (1969), at p. 553.

52. *Trains*, Sept. 1960, p. 10.

53. Cy Martin, *Gold Rush Narrow Gauge: The Story of the White Pass and Yukon Route* (Los Angeles: Trans-Anglo Books, 1969); Stan Cohen, *The White Pass and Yukon Route* (Missoula, Mont.: Pictorial Histories Publishing Co., 1980).

54. This is argued at length in George W. Hilton, *The Northeast Railroad Problem* (Washington, D.C.: American Enterprise Institute, 1975).

55. *Trains*, Jan. 1983, p. 15.

56. *Norfolk & Western Railway Co. and New York, Chicago & St. Louis Railroad Co. Merger, Etc.*, 324 ICC 1 (1964), at p. 15.

57. Testimony of John P. Fishwick, President, Norfolk & Western Ry., in *Norfolk & Western Railway Co. and Baltimore & Ohio Railroad Co.—Control, Detroit, Toledo & Ironton Railroad Co.*, F.D. No. 28499 (1979), typescript of testimony, Sept. 13, 1978, vol. 2, pp. 151, 259, Interstate Commerce Commission docket room, Washington, D.C.

58. *Baltimore & Ohio Railroad Abandonment*, AB-19, Sub. No. 52 (1981), unpublished decision, Interstate Commerce Commission, Washington, D.C.

59. Quoted in F. Lavis, "The Gauge of Railways, With Particular Reference to Those of Southern South America," *Transactions of the American Society of Civil Engineers*, 68, Paper No. 1317 (1915), pp. 312–423, at p. 400.

60. *Ibid.*

61. George J. Stigler, "The Economies of Scale," *Journal of Law & Economics*, 1 (1958), pp. 54–71.

62. Harvey Leibenstein, "Allocative Efficiency vs. X-Efficiency," *American Economic Review*, 56 (1966), pp. 392–485.

63. E. N. Smith and F. M. Greenwood, "Tomorrow's Railroad," *Trains*, Nov. 1960, pp. 34–49.

PART II

The Individual
Narrow Gauge
Common
Carriers

Introduction

The narrow gauge movement produced approximately 350 common carrier railroads. The precise number is impossible to state because of the ambiguity on the margin between common and private carriers. A common carrier is subject to the common law obligations of carriage for all on equal terms; reasonable rates; reasonable dispatch; and bailment, or responsibility for the cargo in transit. A private carrier hauls only the cargo of its owner. Unfortunately, some railroads, such as the Silver City, Pinos Altos & Mogollon, were common carriers at law, but private carriers in practice. The Kildare & Linden was the reverse, a private carrier at law that provided the general transport functions for a county seat. In ambiguous cases I have generally endeavored to include the latter type and to exclude the former. I have also excluded steam dummy lines unless they had significant freight haulage. I have preferred to err on the side of exclusion, for nominal common carriers and steam dummy lines inflate the total mileage presented in tabular form in the text, lower the average investment per mile, and bias the data on building, conversion, and abandonment, especially after the movement peaked in 1883. Most basically, lumber railroads and steam dummy lines did nothing to test the hypothesis that narrow gauge railroads could provide the general transport function more economically than standard gauge railroads; no one questioned that lightly built, incompatible narrow gauge railroads were appropriate for private carriage in extractive industries or for steam dummy lines. There is the further matter that such lines were in general irrelevant to the development of narrow gauge technology overall. As Elbridge H. Beckler said of the common carrier status of the United Verde & Pacific, which he had designed to haul copper ore, "While the public use helps slightly, it is a trifling matter, and had no influence in the origin, development or perfection of the enterprise" ("The United Verde & Pacific Railway," *Journal of the Association of Engineering Societies*, 14 [1895], p. 131).

The criteria for inclusion, in approximately descending order of importance, are these:

> Status under the state regulatory commission.
> Provisions of the charter.
> Whether the lines served viable communities as distinct from lumber camps or other temporary communities incidental to extractive operations.
> Status with the Interstate Commerce Commission.
> Conclusions of historians of the railroad and other literary evidence.
> Content of listing in the *Official Guide of the Railways*.
> Content of listing in *Poor's Manuals*.
> Composition of car stock.
> Content of listing in the *Rand McNally Commercial Atlas*.

Unfortunately, these criteria are frequently conflicting. For states such as Maryland and West Virginia, which either did not regulate railroads in the narrow gauge era or did not publish volumes of regulatory proceedings, the legal status at state law is very difficult to establish. A large number of private carriers carried passengers in cabooses, hauled parcels or other small shipments as a convenience to local residents, or served a second extractive enterprise without purporting to be common carriers generally. Accordingly, I have treated borderline cases briefly at the end of state sections, and have not included them in the time series of mileage in Part I, Chapter 4.

It should be stressed that the decision on which lines to include and which to exclude at the margin is highly subjective because of the frequent conflict of criteria, and that other authors would presumably have come to different conclusions concerning many of the borderline cases. All of the railroads in the "Directory of Narrow Gauge Railways," by Brian Thompson, appended to the reprint of Howard Fleming, *Narrow Gauge Railways in America* (Oakland, Calif.: Grahame Hardy, 1949), were considered for inclusion or rejection. On the private carriers generally, see Thompson's "Supplementary List," which immediately follows the "Directory" in the reprint of Fleming (the appendixes are not paginated). See also Michael Koch, *Steam and Thunder in the Timber: Saga of the Forest Railroads* (Denver: World Press, 1979).

Railroads are entered by the names under which they were completed unless, as in the instances of the Bellevue & Cascade and the Ohio River & Western, the railroad is much better known under another and usually later name. "Company" has been omitted in the interest of brevity. Statements such as "It was a small narrow gauge of two locomotives," are intended to give the scale of normal operations. They are not inconsistent with the railroad roster's listing of a larger number of locomotives over the course of its history.

Mileage in parentheses is from the origin of the railroad or branch, not from the previously mentioned station. The gauge unless otherwise specified is 3'-0". "Conversion" unless otherwise stated is to 4'-8½". In general, no effort has been made to differentiate between 4'-8½" and 4'-9" because equipment was compatible between the two gauges.

Statements that a given railroad, as converted, remains in service have been updated approximately to June 30, 1988. The book appears in a period of rapid disinvestment in the railroad industry; hence this information will inevitably become obsolete quickly.

Treatment is limited to the United States, including Alaska and Hawaii. Canada is treated in Omer Lavallee, *Narrow Gauge Railways of Canada* (Montreal: Railfare Enterprises, Ltd., 1972), and Mexico in Gerald M. Best, *Mexican Narrow Gauge* (Berkeley, Calif.: Howell-North Books, 1968), as well as in a series by the late Francisco Garma Franco, *Railroads in Mexico*, which is currently being translated and edited by Robert A. LeMassena for publication by Sundance, Ltd., of Denver.

Many towns went through a sequence of names on the order of "Lamb's" to "Lambs" to "Lamb" (Michigan). I have generally used the spelling accepted in the narrow gauge period without indicating earlier or later ones.

The corporate histories have been written in the intention of providing relatively self-contained treatments for readers who use the book as a reference work to look up individual railroads. Inevitably, this results in some redundancy of material between corporate histories and also between the text of Part I and the corporate histories.

Alabama

Anniston & Atlantic Railroad

From the outset, this railroad was conceived as a facility for delivering inputs to the Alabama steel industry. A. L. Tyler of Anniston secured a charter for the corporation on August 17, 1883, intending the line to originate wood, charcoal, and iron ore. He built the line from Anniston southwest to Talladega (30 miles), opening it on May 15, 1884. The right-of-way from Jenifer to Ironaton, ten miles, was reportedly acquired from a predecessor, the Clifton Railroad. The A&A was extended to Sycamore (45 miles) on September 15, 1884, and to Sylacauga (53 miles) on December 1, 1886. The line had reached a lumbering and quarrying area, and was not extended farther.

In 1887 the same interests organized a standard gauge railroad, the Anniston & Cincinnati, which on October 17, 1888, opened a 34-mile line from Anniston north to Gadsden and Attalla. In 1890 the Louisville & Nashville bought the A&A and the A&C. The L&N also bought the Shelby Iron Company's railroad, which consisted of a 4'-9" common carrier of six miles from Shelby to Columbiana and a 3'-6" private network of about 14 miles. The L&N merged the three railroads into the Alabama Mineral Railroad, planning to convert the A&A and to extend track from Sylacauga through Shelby to Calera on its main line. By June 1890, 30 of the 53 miles of narrow gauge were reported converted, and by October the job was completed with standard gauge rails laid from Calera to Attalla. Regular service apparently began about the first of the year after some easing of curves and grades on the former narrow gauge portion. The L&N received the permission of the Interstate Commerce Commission to abandon the portion from Coldwater, nine miles south of Anniston, to Talladega (21 miles) in 1976, but the rest of the former narrow gauge trackage remains in operation in the successor CSX Corporation.

East & West Railroad of Alabama

The presence of "Alabama" in the corporate name notwithstanding, this railroad had its origins in Georgia as part of the program of local economic development of the radical Republican governorship of Rufus B. Bullock. The enterprise had its beginning in the Cartersville & Van Wert Railroad, organized in 1868 to build a broad gauge line from Cartersville on the Western & Atlantic to Prior on the Selma, Rome & Dalton Railroad in Polk County, almost at the Alabama line. The route of about 45 miles was graded, and early in 1871 5'-0"

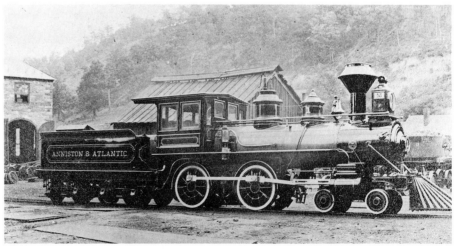

Anniston & Atlantic No. 1 upon completion at the Mount Savage Locomotive Works. (Ed Bond collection.)

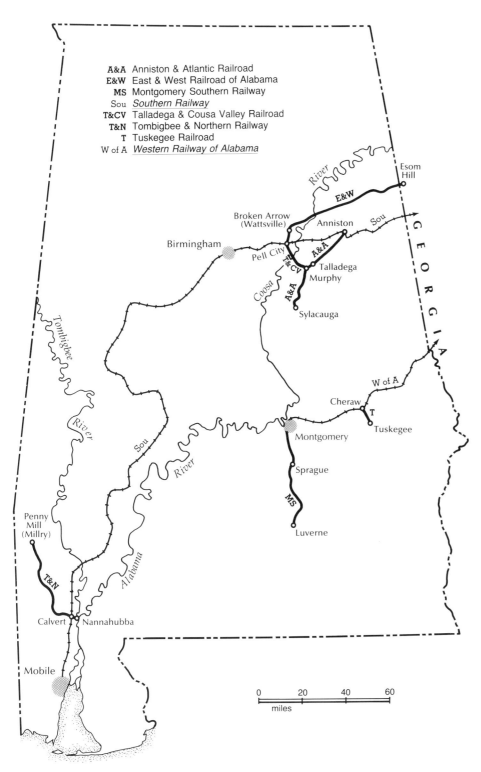

A&A Anniston & Atlantic Railroad
E&W East & West Railroad of Alabama
MS Montgomery Southern Railway
Sou *Southern Railway*
T&CV Talladega & Cousa Valley Railroad
T&N Tombigbee & Northern Railway
T Tuskegee Railroad
W of A *Western Railway of Alabama*

0   20   40   60
miles

$22,500 to the Cherokee Iron Company. The new owner had no interest in building on the grade to Prior, but wanted the railroad completed to Cedartown, the company's headquarters, and to coalfields in St. Clair County, Alabama. The railroad was extended 13 miles to Cedartown in 1879. The iron company converted the 5'-0" segment to 3'-0" early in October 1880; the company thereafter handled broad gauge equipment by truck-transfer at Cartersville.

In 1881 John W. Inzer, John Postell, and Amos G. West organized the East & West Railroad of Alabama to build from Birmingham to a connection with the Cherokee at the state line. Their plan was to use the Cherokee as part of a direct narrow gauge from Birmingham to Gainesville, Georgia, on the Washington-Atlanta main line of the various predecessors of the Southern Railway. They leased the Cherokee for 99 years for a sum of $375,000 plus $1 per year and the road's taxes; on May 25, 1886, they merged the Cherokee into the East & West. In 1883 they extended the Cherokee to Esom Hill, Georgia, almost on the state line, and built their own line between Esom Hill and Broken Arrow (Coal City; Wattsville), a total of 68 miles. Apparently doubting their ability to reach Birmingham, in 1888 they built a final extension of eight miles from Broken Arrow to Pell City on the Atlanta-Birmingham line of the later Southern Railway. The projected extension from Cartersville east to Gainesville was never undertaken. The railroad was a large narrow gauge of 112 miles with ten locomotives. Traffic was mainly in iron ore, coal, coke, and charcoal. The company was, however, severely handicapped by its failure to enter Birmingham. On March 16, 1888, the property was placed in the hands of receiver Charles P. Ball of Cartersville. Ball converted the line in 1890. On May 29, 1893, Eugene Kelly of New York bought the property under foreclosure in the interest of the bondholders. It was reorganized as the East & West Railroad on January 11, 1894. In May 1902 the railroad was purchased by a syndicate affiliated with the Seaboard Air Line, which merged the former narrow gauge into the Atlanta & Birmingham Air Line, a subsidiary organized by the Seaboard to build the 38 miles from Coal City to Birmingham. A second subsidiary, the Chattahoochee Terminal Railway, was formed to build from Rockmart to Atlanta, thereby giving the Seaboard a roundabout route between Atlanta and Birmingham, an inferior rival to the Southern's direct line. It remains in service in the CSX Corporation except for 13 miles from Maxwellborn to Wellington abandoned in 1988.

track was laid from Cartersville to Taylorsville, 14 miles. The Cartersville & Van Wert was among the principal companies involved in the allegations of malfeasance of the Bullock administration in endorsement of bonds. These problems caused the line to be reorganized as the Cherokee Railroad with Edward Hulbert as a director. Presumably at Hulbert's urging, construction was resumed using 3'-0". Nine miles of narrow gauge track were opened to Rockmart

about November 1871, the second narrow gauge in the South. The Cherokee also went bankrupt and was shortly placed in the hands of receiver D. S. Printup of Rome. The line's financial problems prevented both building on the grade to Prior and eliminating the break-of-gauge at Taylorsville. The railroad remained in this uncompleted state until November 6, 1878, when it was sold for $29,500 to Judge J. R. Wilkie, who resold it on March 4, 1879, for

The branch from Rockmart to Cartersville is still in operation, but the Pell City branch was abandoned in 1942.

Montgomery Southern Railway

M. P. LeGrand and his associates of Montgomery promoted this railroad partly in hope of opening agricultural land south of the city, and partly to provide Montgomery with an outlet to a Florida port. The initial target was Rutledge, a town of only some 200 people in Crenshaw County about 50 miles straight south of Montgomery. This was an unlikely terminus, but one of the company's financial supporters, M. F. Rushton, lived there. The promoters also probably sought to interchange with steamboats on the tributaries of the Escambia River in the area, thereby establishing an outlet to Pensacola.

The corporation was chartered on July 2, 1880, and first provided service to Snowdoun (10 miles) in April 1882. The line reached Ada (20 miles) on September 18, 1882, and some grading was done on an additional 20 miles. The company failed and was put in the hands of Josiah Morris, who, as trustee for the bondholders, was directed to sell the property on July 15, 1884. Morris bought the line in the interest of the bondholders for $81,000. The company was reorganized as the Montgomery & Florida Railway in May 1886. It was proposed to convert the line and to extend it to Chattahoochee, Florida. A contract was let to D. P. McKenzie of Dunham, Alabama, to extend the road 30 miles. Narrow gauge track was laid approximately to Lapine (30 miles) in 1886, and an additional 17 miles were graded. Track was pushed on to Patsburg (46 miles) in mid-1887.

Late in 1887 bondholders, who were mainly in New York, appointed Nathan T. Sprague of Brooklyn, one of their number, to investigate the condition of the property. Sprague and his associates bought the railroad early in 1888. The new owners had the same plan of conversion with extension to Chattahoochee as their predecessors, but they also planned to build north 60 miles to the Coosa coalfield. They were, however, confronted almost immediately by a suit from McLaren & McLaren, contractors who had worked on the extension to Patsburg. The railroad was put in receivership on February 4, 1888, under Major Bradford Dunham. The American Loan & Trust Co. shortly joined the suit. Judge Bruce in Montgomery ordered the railroad sold in satisfaction of debts of $102,000 on July 1. David S. Boody bought the property in the

interest of the bondholders and reorganized it as the Northwest & Florida Railroad. Actual ownership was unchanged and Sprague became president of the corporation. The management immediately let a contract for extension of five miles to Luverne, seat of Crenshaw County. Although Luverne was only about four miles southeast of Rutledge, no effort was made to build to the original projected terminus. The final trackage was built as narrow gauge, and opened to Luverne in November 1888, but the management had already begun plans for conversion. The entire 51-mile line was converted early in July 1889. The corporation was by this time controlled by the Alabama Midland Railway, which proposed to enter Montgomery over its trackage. The Midland, building from Bainbridge, Georgia, established a junction with the former narrow gauge at a point two miles north of Ada; the junction was named Sprague. The Midland became a major portion of the Plant System, which in turn became a part of the Atlantic Coast Line. The Sprague-Luverne line served as a 32-mile branch, mainly originating cotton, but was abandoned in 1952. The entry into Montgomery remained part of an important secondary main line of the ACL, and survives in the present CSX Corporation.

Talladega & Coosa Valley Railroad

E. L. Taylor of Anniston and D. M. Rogers of Talladega organized this railroad on December 19, 1883. In 1884 they built it from Murphy to Barclay and Renfroe, five miles. As an entry into Talladega they leased two miles of the Anniston & Atlantic from Murphy. In 1885 they pushed the line about six miles to the north, and in 1886 they reached the Coosa River, 15 miles from Talladega. In 1887 the line was completed to Pell City (26 miles) on the East & West of Alabama. The line's traffic was largely ore for the Talladega Iron & Steel Co. The attractions of narrow gauge were particularly short-lived, and the railroad was reportedly in the process of conversion in September 1889.

The Alabama Coal, Iron & Railroad Co. in October 1890 organized a subsidiary, the Birmingham & Atlantic Railroad, which late in the year bought the T&CV. It built some branches to iron pits, but did not extend the main line, which remained unchanged until abandoned in 1919.

Tombigbee & Northern Railway

This railroad was chartered as the Seaboard Railway of Alabama in 1890 and opened from Nannahubba to Tuscarora, 24 miles, in 1891. The company apparently succeeded to a private railway of the Seaboard Manufacturing Co., its owner. The railroad was intended to serve the manufacturing company's lumbering operations on the west side of the Tombigbee River. The company reached Mobile by barge and lighter from Nannahubba, a wharf near the confluence of the Alabama and Tombigbee. As on most lumber railroads, the main line was pressed outward as timber stands were exhausted, and the mileage of branch lines varied.

S. T. Price of Mobile was appointed receiver for the railroad on July 6, 1896. At the time, the main line extended to Tiger, 26 miles, and a branch of five miles ran into the woods. The railroad was sold under foreclosure on May 10, 1897, to the bondholders, but they directed Price to continue operating it. By 1899 the main line had reached Turners, 35 miles. On January 17, 1900, the corporation was reorganized as the Tombigbee & Northern Railway. At the time, 75 of the line's 99 cars were designed for lumber movements. The railroad was again reorganized on March 5, 1904, as the Tombigbee Valley Railroad. The main line was now said to reach Penny Mill (Healing Spring; Millry), 50 miles. The new management converted the railroad, which was first shown as 4'-8½" in the *Official Guide* of June 1904. At the time of conversion, the three miles from Calvert to Nannahubba were abandoned, along with the marine operation, in favor of 30 miles of trackage rights on the Southern Railway for access to Mobile. John T. Cochrane, the new president, pressed the line onward, reaching West Butler, 90 miles, and a junction with the Alabama, Tennessee & Northern Railroad on June 30, 1912. Including the trackage rights on the Southern from Calvert, the line was now part of a through line of 225 miles from Reform to Mobile. In April 1913 the AT&NRR, Tombigbee Valley, and the Mobile Terminal & Railway Co. were merged as the Alabama, Tennessee & Northern Railway, which mainly provided access for the Frisco system at Aliceville to the port of Mobile. The former narrow gauge is still in existence as part of the Burlington Northern system's Mobile branch.

Tuskegee Railroad

In 1860 the Tuskegee Railroad was built as a 5'-0" line from Tuskegee, seat of

Oak Grove & Georgetown No. 5 was a Rogers 4-4-0 secondhand from the Catskill Mountain Railway. The engine had been rebuilt with an unusual planetary gearing for low-speed lumber operations. (Ed Bond collection.)

Macon County, to Cheraw on the Western Railway of Alabama, 5.5 miles. The railroad was destroyed during the Civil War, but in 1871 the right-of-way was sold to E. T. Varner, who retained E. M. Grant, an engineer of Macon, Georgia, to build a 3'-0" line on it. Grant had the railroad ready for operation in November 1871, reportedly the first active narrow gauge in the South. The railroad was unusual in being organized not as a corporation, but rather as a partnership in which Varner and L. V. Alexander each owned one-third shares. G. W. Campbell and W. H. Wright jointly owned the third share. The railroad connected with passenger trains on the Western of Alabama and provided a terminal function for Tuskegee. It customarily operated with two locomotives.

Varner and his associates converted the railroad on August 1, 1898, and incorporated it on October 8, 1902. Varner's interests sold the company to W. G. Mitchell in 1924. It was sold to W. M. Blount in 1937. The Blount family remained in control of the railroad until it was abandoned in 1963.

REFERENCE: Richard E. Prince, *Central of Georgia Railway and Connecting Lines* (Millard, Nebr.: Richard E. Prince, 1976), p. 221.

▼ ▼ ▼ ▼

M. L. Davis of Oak Grove and J. W. Whiting of Mobile chartered the Oak Grove & Georgetown Railroad in 1904 in the intention of building a common carrier from Oak Grove on the Mobile & Ohio 14 miles above Mobile to Leakesville, Mississippi. If completed the line would have been a narrow gauge of about 30 miles. Actually, the owners in 1906 built 26 miles

northwest from Oak Grove to an unspecified end-of-track in Mississippi. The railroad served almost exclusively as an adjunct to Davis's lumber operation at Oak Grove, but the line was kept in nominal common carrier status, probably in hope of reaching Leakesville. Because Leakesville was served by the standard gauge Alabama & Mississippi Railroad off the Mobile & Ohio from Vinegar Bend, Alabama, the extension was never built. The OG&G was dissolved on October 18, 1927.

Alaska

Golovin Bay Railroad

To serve operations of his Wild Goose Mining & Trading Co. in the Ophir Creek mining district, Charles D. Lane built a railroad of about eight miles from Council City to a mine called No. 15 Ophir Creek. The line was operated jointly with Lane's Wild Goose Railroad at Nome, about 60 miles to the southwest, but it was separately incorporated as the Golovin Bay Railroad. Construction began in June 1902, and

was completed by July 21. One of the Wild Goose Railroad's four Class A Climaxes was brought over to operate the line.

The railroad declined with mining in the area, and was reportedly abandoned about 1906.

REFERENCE: Howard Clifford, *Rails North: The Railroads of Alaska and the Yukon* (Seattle: Superior Publishing Co., 1981), p. 166.

Seward Peninsula Railroad

Gold was discovered by Jefet Lindeborg and others at Discovery in the Anvil Creek region north of Nome in September 1898. Charles D. Lane of Nome, who had become one of the major operators at Anvil Creek, formed the Wild Goose Railroad mainly to serve his Wild Goose Mining & Trading Co. He built the railroad quickly in the summer of 1900, opening it to Discovery (four miles) on July 19, and to Anvil City (Banner; 6.5 miles) in the fall. He bought two Class A Climax locomotives and some flatcars from a lumber operator in the Pacific Northwest. The line was built on permafrost, causing the soil to shift continually under the track. The railroad did very well in 1901 and 1902, but thereafter declined with mining in the area. Lane sold the property to Lindeborg and his associates, who reorganized it as the Nome Arctic Railroad in 1904. The railroad, which had operated seasonally from the outset, operated four months in the summer of 1905.

T. A. Davies, E. A. Mathews, and their associates bought the Wild Goose Railroad in 1906 and prepared to make use of it in their projected line from Nome to the Kougarok mining area. They incorporated their project in Nevada on April 17, 1906, as the Seward Peninsula Railroad, and quickly built it to Lane's Landing (Shelton; 85 miles), on the Kuzitrin River, center of the Kougarok region. The line operated with three Climaxes taken over from the WG and additional motive power bought later. Most of the traffic was general cargo inbound to the mining area. Trains normally covered the line northbound in about ten to twelve hours, southbound in six to eight.

The railroad was sold in 1911 to the Maine Northwestern Development Co., which in 1913 leased it to Lindeborg, who operated it intermittently. When the line was not in regular operation, local residents used it as a public thoroughfare, mainly with dog-drawn handcars. Lindeborg bought the railroad at a U.S. Marshal's sale on August 20, 1920, but he entered into

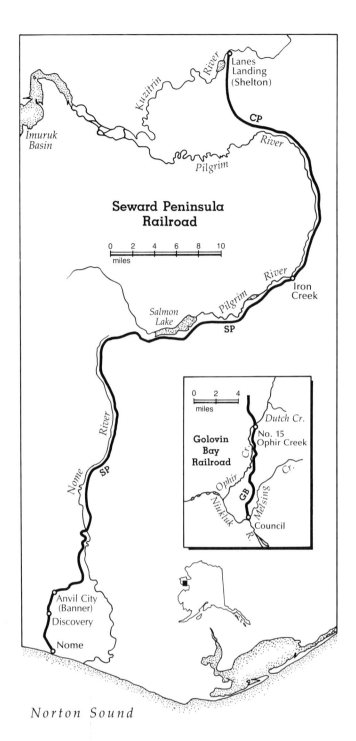

Seward Peninsula
Railroad

0 2 4 6 8 10
miles

*Imuruk
Basin*

Kuzitrin River

Lanes
Landing
(Shelton)

CP

Pilgrim

River

River

Iron
Creek

Pilgrim

SP

*Salmon
Lake*

River

Golovin
Bay
Railroad

0 2 4
miles

Dutch Cr.

No. 15
Ophir Creek

Ophir Cr.

Melsing Cr.

GB

Niukluk R.

Council

Nome River

SP

Anvil City
(Banner)

Discovery

Nome

Norton Sound

1904 in the intention of building from Chena, a port on the Tanana River immediately below Fairbanks, northeast about 130 miles to Circle City on the Yukon River. On December 12, 1906, Joslin reincorporated the enterprise as the Tanana Valley Railroad with the intention of extending up the Yukon Valley to Dawson City, and west from the Fairbanks area about 600 miles to Nome. The line was promoted as a narrow gauge of over 800 miles through gold and copper fields.

Joslin's actual achievement was 45-mile narrow gauge serving the goldfield immediately north of Fairbanks. The line was built in 1905 from Chena to Gilmore (21 miles) with a branch from Junction southeast to Fairbanks (5 miles). After the reincorporation of 1906 Joslin pressed the line north to Chatanika (40 miles) in 1907, but progressed no farther. The line was entirely isolated; it was mainly dependent on steamers on the Tanana River, a tributary of the Yukon and thus part of a river system that was navigable only from May to early October. Fairbanks, which was becoming the principal community in the area, replaced Tanana as the operating headquarters of the railroad in 1915.

In 1917 the United States government, which was planning the Alaska Railroad, leased the Tanana Valley, and shortly bought it. As a temporary expedient the federal administration built a narrow gauge line on the north bank of the Tanana west from Happy Station, 2.6 miles north of Junction, to a projected crossing at Nenana (47 miles). The Chena branch was abandoned. The line from Happy to Nenana was completed in 1918 and converted on June 15, 1923. Third rail was left between Fairbanks and Happy to serve the narrow gauge, which operated until August 1, 1930, when it was abandoned.

REFERENCE: Clifford, *Rails North*, pp. 117–25.

complicated negotiations for transfer of it to the Alaskan government. The territorial legislature passed a bill, which the governor signed on May 5, 1921, for acquisition of the railroad for rehabilitation and continued operation as a rail public thoroughfare. On November 18 Lindeborg transferred the property to his Pioneer Mining & Ditch Co., which on December 29 sold it to the Alaskan government for $30,000. The line was transferred to the Alaska Road Commission on October 13, 1922. By 1924 the Commission had rehabilitated 42 miles of line. There was a resumption of locomotive operation during World War II. Charles

M. Reeder operated tourist trips out of Nome in 1953. Public use of the railroad ended in 1955. Part of the right-of-way was converted to highway use.

REFERENCES: Clifford, *Rails North*, pp. 163–68, 174–77; Cornelius W. Hauck, "Narrow Gauge in the Arctic," *The Collected Colorado Rail Annual* (Golden, Colo.: Colorado Railroad Museum, 1974), pp. 124–36.

Tanana Valley Railroad

Falcon Joslin, an attorney of Fairbanks, organized the Tanana Mines Railroad in

White Pass & Yukon Railway

White Pass was discovered in 1887 by Captain William Moore and William Ogilvie as a route from the Pacific at Skagway to the Yukon Territory rival to the shorter but more difficult crossing over Chilkoot Pass from Dyea. Moore hoped to build a pack trail, a wagon road, and a railroad sequentially, but failed to finance the project.

The gold strike at Bonanza Creek in August 1896 enormously increased the demand for transportation into the Yukon. A British-Canadian-American group headed

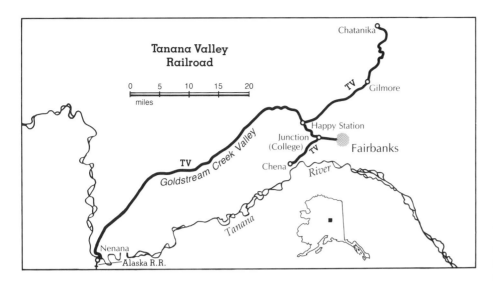

Tanana Valley
Railroad

Below: Although built relatively late, the White Pass & Yukon was designed with orthodox narrow gauge technology. (Munson Paddock collection, Railroad Museum of Pennsylvania.)

by the British engineer Sir Thomas Tancrede organized the projected railway over White Pass with four incorporations. The principal American member of the combine organized the 20.4 miles in Alaska as the Pacific & Arctic Railway & Navigation Co., with an incorporation in West Virginia. The 42.2 miles in British Columbia were chartered by the provincial Parliament as the British Columbia–Yukon Railway,

and the 58.1 miles in Yukon Territory were granted a charter as the British-Yukon Railway by the Dominion Parliament in Ottawa. The White Pass & Yukon Railway was organized in London on July 30, 1898, as a holding company for the three. The WP&Y's charter provided for a line of 325 miles from Skagway to Fort Selkirk on the Yukon River, but only the 110.7 miles from Skagway to Whitehorse were built. The

management chose 3'-0" for the usual reason of economy, notably in use of a narrow right-of-way on the ascent from Skagway. The company bought out a local toll road operator, the Brackett Wagon Road, which had been opened up the ascent in 1897.

Construction began at Skagway on May 27, 1898, by the Pacific Contracting Co. of Michael J. Heney, chief engineer of the railroad. The first revenue train was an excur-

Alaska   307

sion run for four miles out of Skagway on July 21. Construction continued through the fall and winter, mainly because of the rivalry of an aerial tramway being built across Chilkoot Pass. The ascent of 2,885 feet in 21 miles entailed an average grade of 2.6 percent with a ruling grade of 3.9 percent, a tunnel of 250 feet, 20° curves, and a 215-foot-high cantilever bridge at Dead Horse Gulch. Rails reached the summit about a half mile north of the international boundary on February 16, 1899. The line was opened to Bennett on July 8, 1899. A steamer was hastily built to operate the length of Lake Bennett to Carcross. Meanwhile, tracklaying began southward from Whitehorse, reaching Carcross July 29, 1900. The gap between Bennett and Carcross was filled during the summer, allowing service to be opened from Skagway to Whitehorse on August 15, 1900. The railroad cost about $10 million.

Because the rail line itself had little origination of freight, the enterprise was an intermodal operation from the outset. In 1901 the company established a river division, the British Yukon Navigation Co., Ltd., which ordered three single-stack sternwheel steamers of the Oregon–British Columbia type, *Dawson, Selkirk,* and *Whitehorse,* to operate on the 434 miles of the Yukon River northwest (downstream) from Whitehorse to Dawson City. After the season of navigation the company operated from Whitehorse to Dawson City with stages and sledges, a trip that took five days with overnight stays at company roadhouses along the route. This operation lasted until 1921. A gold strike at Atlin, British Columbia, in August 1899, caused the company to establish steamer service with the sternwheeler *Tutshi* from Carcross southeast on Tagish Lake to Taku, from which the company built a 2.5-mile 3'-0" line, the Taku Tram, to Scotia Bay on the west bank of Atlin Lake. Steamers ran across the lake to the town of Atlin. The WP&Y had only one branch, a 22-mile line from MacRae northwest to a mining district at Pueblo in the Whitehorse area, opened in 1910 and abandoned in 1918.

British Yukon Navigation's fleet rose to 11 vessels in the mid-1920s. The company lost four steamers between 1926 and 1936, and built a traditional sternwheeler, the second *Klondike,* as late as 1937. In 1937 the railway established an aviation division to fly to Dawson and other points north of Whitehorse, but this was sold in 1941.

The outbreak of war in the Pacific in 1941 suddenly made the railway an important military facility. It was commandeered by the United States Army October 1, 1942,

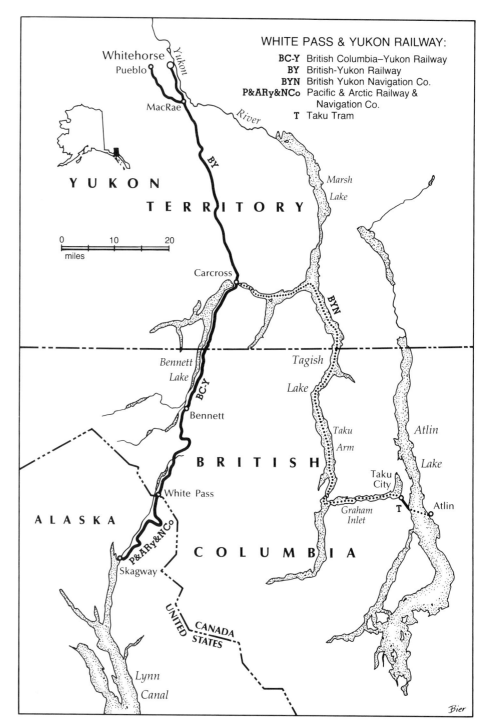

for use in construction of the Alcan Highway and for movement of military cargo. Traffic rose to levels far beyond any of the booms in mining traffic. Locomotives were brought in from the Denver & Rio Grande Western, Colorado & Southern, East Tennessee & Western North Carolina, and other sources. The railway was returned to civilian operation on May 1, 1946, in the usual deteriorated condition of railroads at the ends of wars. The management embarked upon a program of upgrading and modernization. In 1947 it took delivery of two new Baldwin 2-8-2 locomotives,

Nos. 72 and 73, the last narrow gauge steam locomotives built for a common carrier operating in the United States. Steam operation lasted until June 30, 1964. In 1942 the Army laid a four-inch pipeline parallel along the right-of-way, which the railway took over for common carriage of petroleum products, furthering its intermodal operations.

During the 1950s the company moved to complete intermodality in its operations. A comprehensive gravel road network had been built throughout the populated portion of the Yukon, with the result that the

An early passenger train of the White Pass & Yukon pauses for photography on the spectacular ascent from Skagway to the British Columbia border. (California State Railroad Museum.)

company was able to give up its steamer operations to Dawson City in 1953. The steamer *Tutshi* on Tagish Lake and the Taku Tram were also discontinued in 1953. In the same year the company bought its first marine containers, and two years later it built a specialized container ship, the *Clifford J. Rogers*, for navigation between Vancouver and Skagway. Cargo arrived by container in Vancouver, and subsequently moved by ship to Skagway, by rail to Whitehorse, and by road to its destination. Outbound traffic was mainly products of mines, which moved in "teardrop" containers from the mine sites to Skagway for loading onto bulk freighters. Containers were available in refrigerated, flatbed, and gondola configurations for specialized cargo. By 1962 the railway had containerized about 45 percent of freight, and by 1969, 90 percent. Only purely local freight on the rail line moved in conventional equipment. Containerization gave the company greater flexibility than it could have achieved by conversion to 4'-8½" with a car ferry connection to Vancouver.

The railway operated one scheduled mixed train per day between Skagway and Whitehorse. It operated additional container trains, and ran trains of parlor cars from Skagway to Bennett and return for passengers from cruise ships berthed at Skagway. Typically, the parlor cars were run at the end of strings of containers, which were handled up the hill by the rail-

way's usual two-unit diesels. The trip to Bennett covered the line's most impressive scenery and brought the containers up the major grade to a point from which the next scheduled train could easily handle them to Whitehorse.

In 1969 the prospect of massive lead-zinc ore movements from the Anvil Mine, about eight hours by road from Whitehorse, caused the company to begin laying 85-pound rail, to drill a 675-foot tunnel on the ascent from Skagway, and to construct a bulk-loading dock for the Anvil ore moving to Japan. The management even considered extending the rail line to Carmacks for closer proximity to the mine. The extension would approximately have doubled the length of the railway, but it was never undertaken.

The company, which had been formally incorporated as the White Pass & Yukon Corp. since 1951, was sold to Federal Industries, Ltd., of Winnipeg in June 1973. The line had been uniformly profitable, and had made a typical shift from first-generation cab units to second-generation hood units in its diesel roster between 1969 and 1972. The company gave every impression of being a prospering and expanding enterprise until about 1980, when completion of a highway parallel to the railway and reduction in output of the Anvil Mine began to reduce its traffic. The rail line was relatively short for an intermodal operation, viable only because of its isolation and

absence of direct highway competition. Closure of the Anvil Mine caused the rail line to be shut down on October 8, 1982. It has never been removed, and is being offered for sale at the present writing. Passenger excursions on the ascent from Skagway in connection with cruise ships were resumed on May 12, 1988. The corporation remains in service as an intermodal operator by road and water. Its motor vessel *F. H. Brown* operates biweekly from Vancouver to Skagway, whence freight moves by road into the Yukon.

REFERENCES: Clifford, *Rails North*, pp. 8–57; Omer Lavallee, *Narrow Gauge Railways of Canada* (Montreal: Railfare Enterprises, Ltd., 1972), pp. 56–63; Cy Martin, *Gold Rush Narrow Gauge: The Story of the White Pass and Yukon Route* (Los Angeles: Trans-Anglo Books, 1969); Stan Cohen, *The White Pass and Yukon Route: A Pictorial History* (Missoula, Mont.: Pictorial Histories Publishing Co., 1980).

Arizona

Arizona & New Mexico Railway

In the early 1880s, the Copper Mountain mining district of eastern Arizona was in the anomalous position of having a local narrow gauge, the 1'-8" industrial line of the Coronado Railroad at Clifton, but no rail connection to the outside world. Teamsters moved freight to the Southern Pacific at Lordsburg, New Mexico, at rates of $15 to $20 per ton. After some earlier projects failed, two companies were formed in the first part of 1883, the Clifton & Southern Pacific Railway to own the projected line's 42 miles in Arizona and the Clifton & Lordsburg Railway to own the 29 miles in New Mexico. A. E. Campbell of the Arizona Copper Co. was president of the Arizona corporation. Contracts for construction were let on January 28, 1883. The two companies were merged into the Arizona & New Mexico Railway on August 1, 1883, with Frank L. Underwood, a banker of Kansas City, as president. There was difficulty in financing the railroad, but officers of the Arizona Copper Co. with the aid of Scottish investors raised the required funds and the railroad was opened from Lordsburg to Guthrie (59 miles) on October 1, 1883. Service began over the full 71 miles to Clifton on April 5, 1884.

The railroad was unusual for a facility serving extractive enterprises in descending rather than ascending. From Lordsburg at an altitude of 4,244 feet the line descended to 3,404 feet at the crossing of the Gila River at Guthrie, ascended sharply to 3,795 feet, and descended again to 3,457 feet at Clifton. Having the usual extensive trestlework of the narrow gauges, the railroad proved highly subject to washouts from summer storms. There were serious interruptions in traffic in 1891, 1893, and 1895. Traffic was principally coal and coke inbound to the smelters, and copper bars outbound from both Arizona Copper and the Detroit Copper Mining Co. Typically, the railroad ran one or two mixed trains per day, depending on traffic. Passengers averaged only five to eight per trip. Coal and copper tonnages increased rapidly in the late 1890s as the country returned to prosperity. The line's historian, David F. Myrick, suggests that the interchange between gauges at Lordsburg may have transshipped more tonnage than any other. The railroad, which had been operated with five locomotives, found it necessary in 1899 to order two more.

In March 1900, a 465-foot trestle over a gulch five miles south of Clifton burned; its loss seriously interrupted smelting operations. Some 300 cars awaited transshipment of inbound freight at Lordsburg. The bridge and building crew rushed a replacement to completion, but on May 10 the new trestle collapsed under the weight of a southbound train, killing the engine crew and a tramp, and injuring nine carpenters on the repair crew. Arizona Copper's smelter shut down until the new bridge was completed in August.

Because of the rapid increase of traffic, conversion had been anticipated for several years. James Colquhoun, the principal Scottish figure in Arizona Copper, announced the decision to convert on September 28, 1900. The job was assigned to S. H. Buchanan of El Paso, whose principal problem proved to be enlarging the line's four tunnels. Buchanan did not live until the end of the project, but his successor, C. C. Tinkler, effected the conversion in 1901. The railroad was shut down on May 7 and opened as a standard gauge on May 14.

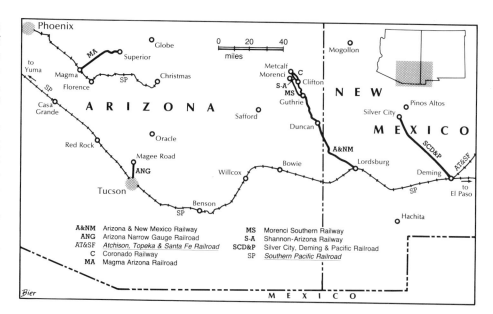

Normal service was not reestablished for another two weeks. Revisions in the line to avoid heavy curvature between Guthrie and Clifton, plus a fill to replace the trestle that had collapsed in 1900, were made by 1903. Integral to the plan for conversion was a standard gauge extension from Lordsburg to a connection with the El Paso & Southwestern Railroad, a major copper hauler, at Hachita, New Mexico. The extension was opened under the name of the Lordsburg & Hachita Railroad in 1902. The L&H was merged into the Arizona & New Mexico in 1911. Phelps Dodge Corporation, which had succeeded to control of the A&NM by acquisition of Arizona Copper in 1921, sold the railroad to the El Paso & Southwestern for $4.5 million effective January 1, 1922. The Southern Pacific in turn acquired the EP&SW on November 1, 1924. The Hachita extension was abandoned in 1933, but the former narrow gauge remains in service as the Southern Pacific's Clifton branch, still a major hauler of copper products from Phelps Dodge installations in the area.

REFERENCE: David F. Myrick, *Railroads of Arizona*, vol. 3 (Glendale, Calif.: Trans-Anglo Books, 1984), pp. 60–77, 100–117, 142–61, 238–55.

Arizona Narrow Gauge Railroad

William H. Culver and other businessmen of Tucson conceived this railroad in 1882 as a lengthy narrow gauge from a connection with the Denver & Rio Grande through Tucson to some point on the Gulf of California. On February 16, 1883, Culver secured authority from the territo-

rial legislature for an exchange of $50,000 in bonds of the railroad for the same amount of bonds of Pima County. This was a very favorable arrangement, especially because the bonds might be issued and transferred before construction began. Ground was broken on July 6, 1883, on the north side of Tucson. The immediate target was a route from the Southern Pacific station in Tucson north out of the city along what is now Fairview Avenue to Oracle (c. 32 miles) and Globe (c. 101 miles), which was already established as a center of copper mining.

In 1884 a taxpayers' suit resulted in suspension of interest payments on the county bonds already issued to the railroad, and caused a suspension of grading. In March 1886 J. Alden Gaylord of the investment firm W. N. Coler & Co. of New York visited the property in an effort to finance further construction. Gaylord assured local people that his firm, which specialized in municipal securities, could market the county bonds, and the Pima County supervisors on May 4, 1886, ordered resumption of interest payments. Construction resumed about June 1. On completion of a 386-foot bridge over Rillito Wash, an excursion was run over the six miles of completed track on July 24. By September, about ten miles of track had been laid and the grade had been extended an additional 30 miles. The railroad had one locomotive, secondhand from the Texas & St. Louis, and 11 flatcars. Construction ended at about this time, with track reaching a point near Magee Road. Operation was limited to an occasional excursion. Pima County sought to sell its bonds of the railroad, and did so to the railroad company itself for 25 percent of face value early in 1887. In September a downpour swept away the Rillito bridge and 100 yards of adjacent track, apparently bringing an end to the operation.

In November 1887 the company changed its name to the Tucson, Globe & Northwestern Railroad, and proposed to convert to standard gauge and to extend the line to a connection with the D&RG at Espanola, New Mexico, crossing the AT&SF main line in the Grants area. Construction could not be financed, and the property was liquidated. The locomotive was shipped to Los Angeles about March 1, 1894, and the rails removed in the same period. Litigation concerning the bonds persisted for many years, reaching the United States Supreme Court on four occasions. The bonds were exchanged for territorial bonds, which were not retired until 1953.

REFERENCES: David F. Myrick, *Railroads of Arizona*, vol. 1 (Berkeley, Calif.: Howell-North Books, 1975), pp. 254–62; Howard A. Hubbard, *A Chapter in Early Arizona Transportation History: The Arizona Narrow Gauge Railroad Company*, University of Arizona Bulletin, 5, No. 3, Social Science Bulletin No. 6 (1934).

Coronado Railroad

Henry Lesinsky, a merchant in the arid West, went into copper mining in 1872 in the vicinity of Clifton on the San Francisco River, organizing several corporations to hold claims. To bring ore from his mines and some of those of independent operators, he undertook in 1879 to build a 1'-8" railway from the mines along Chase Creek to his smelter at Clifton. The line was opened from Clifton to the base of a funicular from the Longfellow mine, four miles, in December 1879. At the outset ore cars were hauled by mule, but in 1880 an 0-4-0 tank engine was acquired. An 0-4-2T was added in 1882. The line was extended two miles from Longfellow to Metcalf in the same year. A second funicular was established on Coronado Mountain. Eventually the line was to connect with seven such inclines, which hauled the same cars pulled by the locomotives. The railroad became part of the Arizona Copper Co., formed in 1882. Beginning in 1884, the company bought a series of eight 0-4-4 tank engines; all of the motive power came from Porter. The locomotives were variously lettered for the copper company and for the Coronado Railroad, but the railroad had no separate incorporation and was apparently not a common carrier. At the outset it had no connection with another railroad, but in 1883 the Arizona & New Mexico Railway arrived in Clifton from Lordsburg.

In 1901 the Arizona & New Mexico converted to standard gauge. The Coronado did not follow suit, but rather bought some of the A&NM's equipment and converted to 3'-0". The portion of the line from Clifton to Longfellow was converted on September 1, 1901, and the portion from Longfellow to Metcalf on October 20, 1902. Scheduled passenger service was established at the time of conversion and the railroad apparently became a common carrier. In 1903 it was extended about 0.7 miles to Shannon, where one of the other funiculars operated. The trackage serving the Coronado mine near Metcalf remained 1'-8" and continued in private-carrier status. In 1912 the copper company completed a system of underground electric railways from the Coronado incline that diverted about a third of the traffic from the Coronado Railroad.

The decline in ore prices following World War I caused the Arizona Copper Co. to shut down in 1921. The Coronado Railroad ended regular operations on June 1. The Phelps Dodge Corporation acquired the copper company and the railroad later in 1921. Occasional trains were operated to serve Phelps Dodge and independent operators near Shannon. In 1927 regular operation was revived, but then ended again in the Depression. The railroad made its last run on July 31, 1932, and was removed by 1938.

REFERENCE: Myrick, *Railroads of Arizona*, vol. 3, pp. 36–51, 162–79, 254–55.

Magma Arizona Railroad

The Magma Copper Company in 1914 was faced with the problem of shipment of ore and concentrates out of its mine at Superior, Arizona. The community had no rail service, but the ore was processed at Hayden, Arizona; El Paso, Texas; or at a newly constructed plant at Miami, Arizona. The company had available three highway routes to railroad stations, ranging from 15 to 30 miles. The trucks of the time were thought too undependable for the service. The company also considered an aerial tramway, combined with a 17-mile spur of the Arizona Eastern Railroad, but it rejected the project as too expensive. The management concluded that the most cost-effective alternative was a narrow gauge railroad on the order of plant facilities, using rocker dump cars of ten-cubic-yard capacity. Planning engineer Edward G. Dentzer considered gauges of 2'-0", 2'-6", and 3'-0", but decided on 3'-0" on the advice of the George D. Whitcomb Company and the American Locomotive Company, both of which pointed out the advantage of compatibility with existing 3'-0" equipment elsewhere. Dentzer originally planned to use gasoline locomotives, but the Vulcan Iron Works told him that steam locomotives were more suitable for the tonnage of his projected trains. The company decided upon a route of about 29 miles from Superior to Webster on the Phoenix & Eastern Railroad. The cost was to be about $4,600 per mile, 57 percent cheaper than the alternative of a standard gauge branch of the Arizona Eastern. Webster was renamed Magma Junction in 1916, and both standard gauge railroads became parts of the Southern Pacific system.

The railroad was built by MacArthur Brothers Co., the well-known railroad contractors, beginning on November 27, 1914. The track was laid quickly across the flat desert, reaching a temporary ore transfer bin near Hewitt Station, 17.5 miles from Webster, by February 6, 1915. The remainder entailed more difficult construction through mountainous country, but the rails reached Magma Copper's ore concentration plant at Superior on April 29, 1915. The cost, including a 2-4-2 Alco tank engine, was $191,074.

Magma Copper's original intention was to make the railroad a private carrier, since it was basically in the nature of an elongated intraplant railroad. The firm was chartered in Maine, and empowered to build railroads other than in Maine. An article of the Arizona constitution, however, restricted out-of-state corporations to activities that they were empowered to carry out in the jurisdictions in which they were organized. This legal point required the railroad to be separately incorporated as a common carrier. The copper company organized the Magma Arizona Railroad on October 10, 1914. The company's next intention was to operate as an intrastate carrier to avoid a variety of rules of the Interstate Commerce Commission, but since practically all of the traffic would be transshipped at Webster for points on the interstate railroad system, the management concluded that it was impractical to maintain the fiction that all shipments originated or terminated at Webster. Accordingly, the railroad was a common carrier from the outset. Passenger and freight tariffs became effective May 25, 1915. Like older narrow gauges serving mineral installations, the Magma Arizona charged high fares. Passengers were carried at about 10¢ per mile, as compared to 65¢ for the state's railroads generally. The railroad operated a daily mixed train consisting of a string of rocker dump cars with a secondhand combine from the United Verde & Pacific, a nominal common carrier at Jerome Junction, Arizona. Later a variety of secondhand boxcars and gondolas were purchased, plus a second combine, one of the original cars of the Eureka & Palisade. A second locomotive, a 2-4-2 tank engine with a tender, was added in mid-1915, and two 2-4-2 tender engines without tanks were received from Alco in November 1915 and May 1917.

American entry into World War I caused copper mining to boom. The high price of silver motivated the reopening of the Silver King mine off the line near Superior, giving the railroad a second major source of traffic. On August 6, 1917, the line began to carry mail. The traffic, mainly in copper ore concentrates, usually warranted two trains per day. Most of the tonnage moved from bins at Superior to gravity transshipment bins at Magma Junction. Ore from Silver King moved in sacks. The railroad had its only serious wreck on July 25, 1918, when locomotive No. 3 and the mixed train ran away on the downgrade from Silver King Siding near Superior.

The end of the war greatly reduced the demand for copper. The daily freight was dropped on Sundays in December 1920. In March 1921 Magma Copper shut down the concentration plant in Superior, ending the source of some 80 to 90 percent of the railroad's traffic. A series of thunderstorms in August 1921 seriously damaged several bridges. Operation thereafter was largely by gasoline speeder for passengers and mail.

Magma Copper had no intention of closing the railroad permanently. To the contrary, the company recognized that it held a huge ore reserve at Superior, and planned an improved method of working it. The firm planned to build a smelter at Superior and to ship the copper out in ingot form. The narrow gauge was inadequate for the proposed traffic, and the ingots would be expensive to transship at Magma Junction. Late in 1919 Dentzer was directed to study conversion to standard gauge. Conversion was estimated to cost $1,157,330.93, but would reduce monthly operating costs from $9,529.26 to $4,609.99. An intermediate idea of replacing the narrow gauge's 30-pound rail with 50-pound and reducing the gradients to 2 percent was rejected.

The method of conversion was most unusual. Rather than lay a third rail or a pair of standard gauge rails on the narrow gauge right-of-way, the company used the narrow gauge as a construction railroad to bring materials to the construction gang, which laid the standard gauge track on a new, adjacent right-of-way. For about 15.5 miles from Magma Junction the standard gauge was laid about 20 feet to the southeast of the narrow gauge. From that point to Superior it was thought desirable to build a railroad of easier curves and grades through Queen Canyon, and the two lines diverged widely. Twohy Brothers Construction Company of Phoenix built the new line between May and December of 1922 and the first few months of 1923. Standard gauge operation began April 2, 1923, the day following the reopening of the concentration plant. Transitionally, a narrow gauge speeder continued to handle passengers and mail, and narrow gauge rocker dump cars carried ore from the mine and concentration plant to the standard gauge equipment. With the arrival of a standard gauge White motor car the narrow gauge was retired on May 22, 1923. The standard gauge railroad remains in service.

REFERENCE: Gordon Chappell, *Rails to Carry Copper: A History of the Magma Arizona Railroad* (Boulder, Colo.: Pruett Publishing Co., 1973).

Morenci Southern Railway

The Detroit Copper Mining Co., which had become a subsidiary of Phelps Dodge & Co., owned extensive copper claims in the area of Morenci, northwest of the Clifton mining area. The ore was shipped out by means of the Coronado Railroad's 1'-8" lines, the Longfellow incline, and the Arizona & New Mexico Railway, an arrangement that required two transshipments. To eliminate one of them, the company in 1899 undertook to build its own 3'-0" line to a connection with the A&NM at Guthrie. The line was incorporated as the Morenci Southern Railway on October 2, 1899. The route was a very difficult one with a rise of 1,400 feet in 18.4 miles. W. W. Wambaugh, chief engineer of the El Paso & Southwestern, designed the line with five loops, one just north of the San Francisco River and four approaching Morenci. The management accepted the railroad from the contractor on January 31, 1901. Trains began carrying mail on December 23. The railroad ran two passenger trains per day. The typical freight train was five or six cars of copper ore drawn by a

Baldwin 2-8-0 locomotive. The line had five such locomotives and two 0-6-0 tank engines.

The railroad's tortuous configuration gave it some fame as "The Corkscrew Route of America." In 1909 the management bought a coach-parlor car with an open observation platform to stimulate the tourist trade. In 1904 there was some speculation that the line would be converted and extended west to a connection with the Gila Valley, Globe & Northern near Safford, but this was never done.

The El Paso & Southwestern Co., the holding company of the EP&SW, acquired control of the Morenci Southern in November 1908. In 1914 the Morenci Southern undertook to replace three of its five loops with a pair of switchbacks. The change added about 0.4 miles, but reduced maintenance expenses and added to the safety of the operation.

With the decline in demand for copper at the end of World War I, the railroad became unprofitable. Phelps Dodge acquired most of the local narrow gauge system in 1921, and formally abandoned the Morenci Southern on May 3, 1922. The southernmost 13 miles were dismantled, and the northernmost five miles, along with four miles of the Shannon-Arizona Railway, were organized as the Morenci Industrial Railway, a private carrier that operated until July 31, 1932.

REFERENCE: Myrick, *Railroads of Arizona*, vol. 3, pp. 118–43.

Shannon-Arizona Railway

A part of the network of narrow gauges serving the Copper Mountain mining district, this railroad was a nominal common carrier of the Shannon Copper Co. The company had several mines along the east side of Chase Creek, near Metcalf at the end of the Coronado Railroad. To bring ore to the company's smelter at Shannon, it formed the Shannon-Arizona Railway on March 29, 1909. The route was ten miles from the smelter to the foot of the Shannon incline north of Metcalf. The railroad was formally opened on February 21, 1910. It was a small operation of two Baldwin 2-8-0 locomotives. Traffic was almost entirely from the company's mines, and no regular passenger service was ever provided.

With the decline in demand for copper following the close of World War I, the Shannon Copper Co. ceased operation late in 1918 and shut down the railroad effective January 1, 1919. In 1921 the Phelps Dodge Corporation bought the railroad

REFERENCES: Elbridge H. Beckler, "The United Verde & Pacific Railway," *Journal of the Association of Engineering Societies*, 14 (1895), pp. 131–47, condensed version in *Railroad Gazette*, 27 (1895), p. 243; Russell Wahmann, *Narrow Gauge to Jerome: The United Verde & Pacific Railway* (Boulder, Colo.: Pruett Publishing Co., 1988).

The reason for replacing United Verde & Pacific No. 1's headlight with a white dog is lost, but otherwise the scene of the Mogul on the gallows turntable is very traditional. (Ed Bond collection.)

and in 1923 consolidated the southernmost four miles with five miles of the former Morenci Southern into the Morenci Industrial Railway, which operated as a plant facility until July 31, 1932. Rebuilt as a standard gauge, the line resumed operation on July 15, 1937, and remains in service.

REFERENCE: Myrick, *Railroads of Arizona*, vol. 3, 180–207, 238–55.

United Verde & Pacific Railway

The United Verde Copper Co. initially hauled ore out of its mines at Jerome by wagon to the Santa Fe main line at Ash Fork at the cost of about $8 per ton. A tramway from Jerome over the mountain range to the west in 1891 reduced this by about half, but the building of the AT&SF's Santa Fe, Prescott & Phoenix line south from Ash Fork presented the possibility of a direct rail connection. W. A. Clark of Butte, Montana, president of the company, decided on a narrow gauge railroad of typical standards, connecting with the SFP&P at Jerome Junction, 26 miles due west of

Jerome. The railroad was incorporated as a common carrier and built quickly in 1894, opening on December 1. The easternmost ten miles were in extremely difficult mountain country, with grades of 3 percent and curves of 40°—one of 45°. Traffic was mainly coal and coke for the company's plants inbound, and concentrated ore in sacks outbound. As its designer, E. H. Beckler, reported, "It has besides some light public traffic."

Originally, traffic was handled by a single mixed train per day, but by the height of the Edwardian prosperity in 1906, the company's traffic required three mixed trains, and the roster had risen from two to four engines. Earnings were highly variable because of the cyclical character of demand for copper. In 1912 the company incorporated a second railroad, the Verde Tunnel & Smelter Co. Railroad, which built a six-mile, freight-only standard gauge line to mines of the company at Hopewell from a connection with another Santa Fe branch at Clarkdale. The VT&S was extended to Jerome in 1919. Diversion of traffic to this carrier reduced the narrow gauge to a single

Arkansas

Arkansas Midland Railroad
Gauge: 3'-6"; converted to 3'-0", 1883

Like many southern railroads, the Arkansas Midland was projected in the antebellum era, but not built until after the Civil War. Businessmen in Helena incorporated the company on January 20, 1855, in the intention of building an air line from their port to Little Rock, a distance of about 115 miles. The line was graded from Helena to a point variously described as 15 miles west of the White River and 12 miles short of Little Rock before the outbreak of the war brought the project to a halt.

In 1871 the Arkansas Central Railway was chartered to make use of the uncompleted grade and finish the line. It was initially projected as a 3'-0" railroad with branches from Duncan to Clarendon and from an unspecified junction to Pine Bluff. In May 1871 the management ordered a 3'-0" Baldwin locomotive, but then decided to build the railroad to 3'-6" gauge. The 3'-0" engine was diverted to the Painesville & Youngstown in October, and in November the company took delivery of a 3'-6" Baldwin, *Helena*. In 1872 the portion of the main line from Helena to Duncan was built, along with the branch to Clarendon, a total of 48 miles. No further construction was undertaken. The railroad reportedly had four locomotives. The line was subject to a

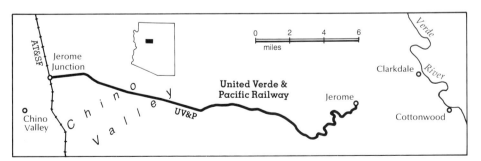

first mortgage of $720,000 and a second of $480,000. The Union Trust Company foreclosed in 1876, and A. H. Johnson was appointed receiver. The railroad was sold in July 1877 to Sidney H. Hornor, who in 1879 conveyed it to the Arkansas Midland Railroad of 1855, which was still in corporate existence. The Midland in 1883 converted the line to 3'-0" for conformity with the Texas & St. Louis, with which it connected at Clarendon. Conversion of the former T&StL in 1886 left the Midland isolated by its gauge; it was converted to 4'-8½" in 1887.

The Midland was to become a narrow gauge operator for a second time in 1891, when it bought the Brinkley, Helena & Indian Bay Railway, a 3'-0" line with which it connected at Pine City. The acquisition, which had a 24-mile main line to Brinkley, plus a five-mile branch from Glenwood to Woodsville for lumber origination, had been built as a private carrier by the Brinkley Car Company. The main line apparently assumed common carrier status in July 1890. The Midland planned on converting the acquisition from the outset, but did not do so until September 1900.

The Gould interests in 1901 bought control of the Midland for $850,000. The railroad was operated separately until early in 1910, and thereafter as two branches of the St. Louis, Iron Mountain & Southern or the Missouri Pacific. The line was cut back from Clarendon to Holly Grove in 1957, and to Marvell in 1976. The remainder was abandoned in 1979. The Pine City–Brinkley branch was abandoned in 1960.

Batesville & Brinkley Railroad

Gunn & Black, a lumber firm, operated this railroad as a common carrier, but as an adjunct to its mill at Brinkley. Gunn & Black initiated the rail line by building a private carrier of 3'-6" gauge called the Cotton Plant Railroad, opened for 11 miles from Brinkley to Cotton Plant on July 1, 1879. Initially the railroad had no separate corporate entity, but for conformity with the Texas & St. Louis, which had just announced its intention to build through Brinkley, Gunn & Black incorporated the Cotton Plant Railroad as a common carrier on April 16, 1881, and in June converted it to 3'-0". Gunn & Black next organized the Batesville & Brinkley Railroad on June 22, 1882, in the intention of building straight north to Newport on the St. Louis, Iron Mountain & Southern main line, and thence up the White River Valley to Batesville. The new corporation immediately bought the

Cotton Plant Railroad. The line was extended north from Cotton Plant, reaching Colona (25 miles from Brinkley) by January 1, 1883, Tupelo (40 miles) by January 1, 1884, Auvergne (48 miles) on November 1, 1885, and finally Jacksonport (60 miles) on November 10, 1886. Jacksonport was four miles beyond Newport, but 26 miles short of Batesville. The railroad's mileage included two miles of trackage rights on the T&StL entering Brinkley. Fairly lengthy for a narrow gauge, the B&B had five or possibly six locomotives.

The failure of the Grand Narrow Gauge Trunk and conversion of the T&StL ended any attraction of the 3'-0" gauge, and the management prepared to convert almost from the time of completion to Jacksonport. Since much of the traffic was lumber transshipped to the Iron Mountain, the break-of-gauge at Newport was a serious handicap. The line was converted in 1888.

The B&B on January 10, 1890, bought a short proposed connecting railroad, the Augusta & Southeastern Railway, and changed its own name to White & Black River Valley Railway. The management announced a northern extension of 125 miles, but no further trackage was built. The railroad was leased for 80 years on July 1, 1900, to the Choctaw, Oklahoma & Gulf Railroad, which in turn was leased to the Chicago, Rock Island & Pacific on March 24, 1904. The line became the Newport branch of the Rock Island, connecting with the parent road's Memphis line at Brinkley. The four miles from Newport to Jacksonport were abandoned in the spring of 1929, and the remainder of the former narrow gauge on March 9, 1941. In 1942, 0.44 miles at Newport were sold to the Missouri Pacific for use as a spur, which survived into the 1980s.

Hot Springs Branch Railroad

Joseph Reynolds, the flamboyant proprietor of the Diamond Jo Line of packets on the Mississippi River, formed this enterprise as his first foray into railroading. The railroad was chartered on July 28, 1870, but not undertaken until May 1875. The route was from Malvern, 43 miles southwest of Little Rock on the St. Louis, Iron Mountain & Southern main line, to the resort community of Hot Springs. The line may have been projected at 3'-6", since several early reports state it to have been built to this gauge, but such accounts were corrected in the trade press; the railroad was 3'-0" throughout its history as a narrow gauge.

The railroad was opened to Lawrence on November 17, 1875, and the last three miles into Hot Springs (21.3 miles) were completed on February 27, 1876. Engineer G. P. C. Rumbaugh laid out the line with a ruling grade of about 2 percent, but with curves of 20°. He used 35-pound rail, but specified a Westinghouse air brake. The railroad reportedly cost $300,000, but because Reynolds had financed it privately, it was without a funded debt. As the first railroad to reach Hot Springs, it did well financially. Connecting with Iron Mountain trains at Malvern, the company did a substantial passenger business. Reynolds had the line relaid with 52-pound rail in 1883. On February 7, 1882, a meeting was held in Pine Bluff to promote an extension southeast from Malvern to the Cotton Belt main line, probably at or near Fordyce, but no such connection was undertaken.

Reynolds converted the railroad to standard gauge on October 17, 1889, and dropped "Branch" from its corporate title. L. D. Richardson replaced Reynolds as president in 1891. The Choctaw, Oklahoma & Gulf bought the Hot Springs Railroad on May 10, 1902, for $600,000. It built a connection from the Little Rock & Hot Springs Western, a leased line, at Benton to Butterfield on the former narrow gauge, and operated the line as a Y-shaped branch from Little Rock to Hot Springs and Malvern. The Malvern line was extended to Camden in 1913, but cut back to Malvern in 1969. The former narrow gauge survived as part of the Chicago, Rock Island & Pacific from the Rock Island's absorption of the CO&G to the dissolution of the Rock Island in 1980. The Malvern–Hot Springs mileage was then taken over by the Missouri Pacific for operation, and is in service at the present writing.

Iron Mountain & Helena Railroad

Gauge: 3'-6"

To provide Helena, one of the major ports on the Mississippi below Memphis, with a rail connection to the interior, local businessmen chartered the Iron Mountain & Helena railroad on December 31, 1860. The promoters, like many elsewhere, could do nothing during the Civil War, and at the conclusion of the war found themselves unable to finance the project as a standard gauge railroad. Their plan was to build north from Helena to Peach Orchard, Arkansas, on the St. Louis, Iron Mountain & Southern Railroad, about 140 miles.

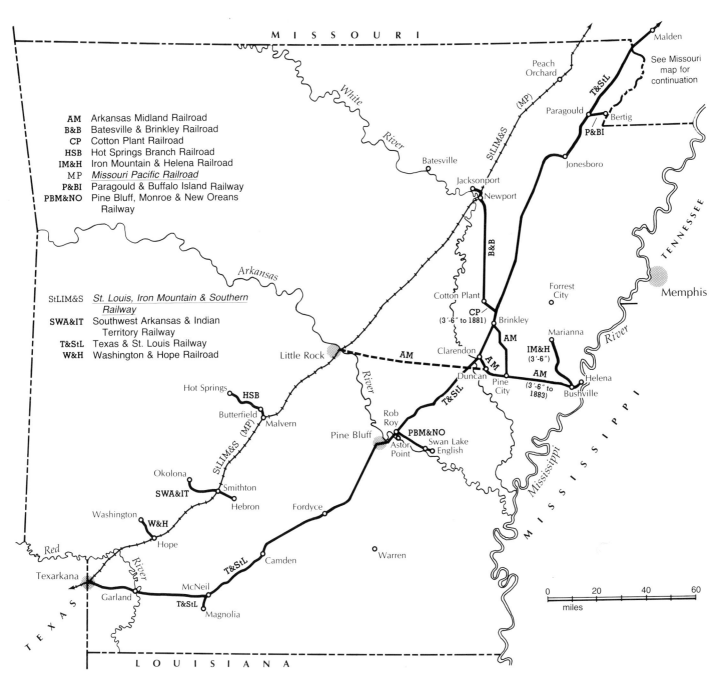

Legend:

AM — Arkansas Midland Railroad
B&B — Batesville & Brinkley Railroad
CP — Cotton Plant Railroad
HSB — Hot Springs Branch Railroad
IM&H — Iron Mountain & Helena Railroad
MP — *Missouri Pacific Railroad*
P&BI — Paragould & Buffalo Island Railway
PBM&NO — Pine Bluff, Monroe & New Orleans Railway

StLIM&S — *St. Louis, Iron Mountain & Southern Railway*
SWA&IT — Southwest Arkansas & Indian Territory Railway
T&StL — Texas & St. Louis Railway
W&H — Washington & Hope Railroad

They were able to begin construction with narrow gauge technology in 1879. For conformity with the Arkansas Midland, on which they proposed to enter Helena, they adopted 3'-6". From Bushville on the Arkansas Midland approximately ten miles west of Helena, they laid about 12 miles of rail in 1879 and another six in 1880, reaching Marianna in Lee County, the first county seat north of Helena, on November 20, 1880. Six additional miles had been graded to the L'Anguelle River, and the line had been surveyed to Forrest City on the Memphis & Little Rock Railroad. Before building farther, the management recognized its error in choice of gauge and converted the Helena-Marianna mileage to 4'-8½" early

in 1881. The line was then extended to Forrest City and a standard gauge entry into Helena was built from Latour.

In March 1882 the railroad was sold to the Kansas City & Southern Railroad and in October 1882 resold to the St. Louis, Iron Mountain & Southern for $450,000. The line became part of a secondary main line of the Missouri Pacific system along the Mississippi, and as such remains in service.

Paragould & Buffalo Island Railway

A. & S. Bertig, Henry Wrappe, and J. B. Holman, lumber operators in northeastern

Arkansas and the swampy bootheel area of Missouri, chartered the Paragould & Buffalo Island Railway on October 11, 1887. In 1888 they completed it with ten miles of track from Paragould on the Cotton Belt main line to a wharf on the St. Francis River variously known as Amberg, Buffalo, and Bertig. At first the railroad was apparently a private carrier, but by 1892 it was regularly listed among common carriers. The company had two locomotives and 25 cars, almost all designed to carry logs or lumber. Wrappe and Holman in 1893 sold their equity to J. F. Hasty & Sons and C. M. Watkins, who were also lumber operators in the swamp. The Bertig firm and its new co-owners renamed the railroad the Paragould Southeastern Railway on November 13, 1893, and prepared to convert and extend it. The gauge was changed to standard early in October 1894. The river was bridged and the line opened to Cardwell, Missouri, on January 1, 1895. It reached Hornersville on October 27, 1897, Chickasawba, Arkansas, on April 5, 1903, and finally Blythesville, Arkansas, 38 miles from Paragould, on January 27, 1907.

S. W. Fordyce of the Cotton Belt had been represented on the board of directors since the renaming in 1893. By the time the branch reached Blythesville, the St. Louis Southwestern owned 56 percent of the PSE's stock. In October 1913 the shareholders voted to lease the line to the StLSW effective January 1, 1914, for a guaranty of principal and interest on the road's bonds. The PSE was merged into the StLSW along with several other subsidiaries in 1958. The branch was abandoned in 1981 under an ICC decision of 1980.

Pine Bluff, Monroe & New Orleans Railway

Under a bewildering succession of names, this railroad was an effort to run along the north bank of the Arkansas River from Little Rock to some point near the river's confluence with the Mississippi. In actuality the line succeeded only in being a relatively minor branch of the Cotton Belt serving the lumber industry.

The line had its origins in the Pine Bluff & Swan Lake Railway, incorporated on June 11, 1884. On October 27 of that year the company opened its line from Rob Roy on the Texas & St. Louis to Swan Lake (14 miles). The railroad also had a spur of a mile from Rob Roy to Astor Point on the river. The management arranged trackage rights for seven miles over the T&StL to reach Pine Bluff. Apparently to change the charter to allow further construction, the railroad was reincorporated on November 28, 1884, as the Pine Bluff, Monroe & New Orleans. In each instance, the earlier corporation remained in existence, but by an agreement of May 4, 1885, it was arranged that the two earlier companies should be merged into the PBM&NO. By the time the merger was consummated on June 19, 1886, the line had been extended from Swan Lake to English (20 miles). The company built no farther, but some grading was reportedly done between Rob Roy and Argenta in the North Little Rock area. The railroad was reported to have three locomotives.

On April 11, 1889, the property was confiscated by the State of Arkansas for unpaid taxes. On April 27, 1892, a federal court transferred the railroad to F. M. Gillett, who on July 18 formed the Pine Bluff & Eastern Railway to operate it. The railroad remained unprofitable, and a receiver was again appointed on September 28, 1895. The property was sold under foreclosure in January 1898 and reorganized as the Pine Bluff Arkansas River Railway on February 1. The new corporation converted the line later in 1898. S. W. Fordyce of the Cotton Belt was a director of the company. By 1905 the line was reportedly controlled by the Cotton Belt, but separately operated. In the fall of 1901 the line was extended about five miles to Reydel, and in 1912 built two miles farther to a sawmill at Waldstein. On January 1, 1918, the property was leased to the St. Louis Southwestern for interest on the line's bonds.

A flood in 1927 seriously damaged the line, resulting in the abandonment of the extension from Reydel to Waldstein in 1928. The remainder had lost most of its traffic as the area was deforested. The tributary population was only some 3,000, mainly tenant farmers growing cotton. The lease expired February 1, 1928, but its terms were extended on a year-to-year basis. The Cotton Belt considered the branch hopeless and on July 30, 1934, applied to close it. The ICC gave permission and the line was abandoned December 31, 1934.

Southwest Arkansas & Indian Territory Railway

The Smithton Lumber Company organized this railroad in the intention of building a line of 150 miles from Warren, seat of Bradley County, to the Indian Territory border. The route would have crossed the St. Louis, Iron Mountain & Southern main line at Smithton, the company's headquarters. Actually, the line proved to be a small nominal common carrier serving the mill at Smithton.

The railway was chartered on June 15, 1884, and construction began on December 1, 1884. The line west from Smithton was opened to Okolona (15 miles) on September 28, 1885. The line east was built for only ten miles from Smithton to Hebron in November 1888. The company had a single locomotive and six cars. In 1891 the line was reported to have been converted.

In March 1896 a receiver was appointed for the Smithton Lumber Company, including the railroad. In the reorganization the railroad became the Arkansas Southwestern, of which the Iron Mountain owned $395,000 of $396,000 of the stock by 1904. The line west, which had been extended beyond Okolona as a standard gauge, became part of the Missouri Pacific's branch to Pike City and Womble. The line east from Smithton appears to have been abandoned before acquisition by the Missouri Pacific. The former narrow gauge mileage west of Smithton remains in service. Smithton has been absorbed by the neighboring town of Gurdon.

Texas & St. Louis Railway

The Texas & St. Louis was intended to be the westernmost portion of the Grand Narrow Gauge Trunk, extending from Bird's Point (Wyatt), Missouri, opposite Cairo, Illinois, to Laredo, Texas. The railroad was never completed, but it managed to achieve a continuous line of 725 miles from Bird's Point to Gatesville, Texas, second only to the Denver & Rio Grande between Denver and Ogden as the longest single American narrow gauge main line.

The railroad had its origin in the Tyler Tap Railroad, formed in 1870 by Major James P. Douglas of Tyler to relieve the town's isolation. In 1871 he secured a special act of incorporation from the Texas legislature granting the company the right to build a line of not more than 40 miles to a connection with another railroad on a route to be chosen by the directors. The company considered a line of some 17 miles to the southeast to Troup on the International & Great Northern, or northeast to some point on the Texas & Pacific. The charter provided that the railroad should be built to the same gauge as its connection. The promoters projected a light standard gauge line of 30-pound rail. The charter was changed in 1873 to provide for a single route to the north to Big Sandy on the T&P, Mount Pleasant, Clarksville, and some point on the Red River. Douglas's interest was mainly in shipping out fruit from local growers, and he presumably wanted access not only to the railroads, which in the area were dominated by Jay Gould, but also to steamboats, which competed with the railroads. The statute established a state land grant of 16 sections, each of 640 acres per mile, to be provided when the first ten miles had been completed. Even this was not enough to bring forth the railroad in the depressed conditions of the mid-1870s. On February 25, 1875, the charter was amended to allow the company to build at 3'-0" gauge, but limiting it to 12 sections per mile if it did so. Grading began in the

The Texas & St. Louis mainly equipped itself with Grant locomotives, but No. 7 was a Porter 4-4-0 of 1879. The locomotive, which bore the name of the railroad's founder, Major James P. Douglas, was sold to the Ripley Railroad after the Cotton Belt's conversion. (California State Railroad Museum.)

summer of 1875, but as late as December 1876 the gauge had not yet been determined. The decision to build at 3'-0" was apparently made in early 1877. The opening of the railroad to Big Sandy (20 miles) was celebrated with a barbecue on September 18, 1877. Early in 1878, the completed line was reported to have cost $9,100 per mile, and the right-of-way was said to have been graded for 42 miles beyond Big Sandy.

Douglas collected 190,720 acres from the state land grant, but upon sale of the land, was still unable to meet the railroad's obligations. In search of financial help he went to St. Louis to interview Colonel J. W. Paramore, head of the St. Louis Cotton Compress Co. Paramore was interested in changing the flow of cotton grown in the area west of Tyler from Galveston to St. Louis. Although he had no interest in extending the Tyler Tap north to the Red River, he initially envisioned it as extending east to Texarkana for a connection with the St. Louis, Iron Mountain & Southern, now the Missouri Pacific main line. Paramore reincorporated the Tyler Tap as the Texas & St. Louis Railway on May 14, 1879. Initially Douglas remained as president, but Paramore quickly became the railroad's dominant figure after arranging its financing with the New York investment bankers Kuhn, Loeb & Co. The first announced intention was to extend the narrow gauge

northeast to Texarkana and southwest to Waco, bringing it to some 266 miles through the Texas cotton belt. The railroad shortly adopted the nickname "Cotton Belt Route," which it has used through all its corporate entities to the present day. Paramore became president late in 1879. Douglas became president and general manager, but left in 1880 to head the Kansas & Gulf Short Line, a narrow gauge intended to connect Tyler with Lufkin on the Houston East & West Texas Railroad.

Paramore proceeded quickly with building the railroad. The line was announced as complete to Texarkana on July 5, 1880. By the end of the year track had reached Athens, 32 miles southwest of Tyler, and grading was under way to Corsicana and Waco. As building proceeded southwest, Jay Gould secured control of the Iron Mountain and was expected to attempt a monopoly of rail lines in the area. Paramore responded by announcing early in 1881 that he would extend the Texas & St. Louis from Texarkana to Bird's Point, Missouri, opposite Cairo, Illinois, where he could connect with the Cairo & St. Louis to create a through route from Texas rival to the Iron Mountain. Simultaneously he announced that the T&StL would be extended from Waco to Laredo to connect with the proposed Mexican National system, which General William J. Palmer and James Sullivan were

building. Gould's International & Great Northern reached Laredo via Waco, Austin, and San Antonio. Paramore proposed to build west from Waco to Gatesville. From Leon Junction, 12.5 miles southeast of Gatesville, the main line was to continue about 327 miles to Laredo via Lampasas, Burnet, Fredericksburg, Kerrville, and Uvalde, with a branch from Uvalde to Eagle Pass. The extension would have run through the plains country later identified with Lyndon B. Johnson, approximately at the western limit of arable land. If the line had been completed, it would probably have been relatively productive, both in local origination of farm products and in through traffic to and from Mexico.

In April 1881 Paramore placed $4 million in bonds and was able to undertake the main line from Texarkana to Bird's Point. The Iron Mountain responded to the prospect of being paralleled across Arkansas by announcing that it would handle traffic to the narrow gauge only at full rates to Texarkana. To provide the north end of his proposed railroad Paramore in May 1881 acquired the 27-mile Little River & Arkansas Valley Railroad, which had been built from the pioneer town of New Madrid on the Mississippi to Malden, Missouri, in 1877 and 1878. The acquisition was a typical local narrow gauge, with only two locomotives, two passenger cars, and 30 freight cars.

To build the line across Arkansas Paramore engaged a man he had known during his service in the Union Army, Colonel Samuel W. Fordyce, who was then living in

Hot Springs. Paramore, a thorough believer in the narrow gauge ideology, thought the line could be built for about $9,000 per mile, but it actually cost about $12,000 per mile. The land was low-lying and swampy for much of the distance between Bird's Point and Pine Bluff. To the west it was hilly, but the route was intrinsically easier than the Iron Mountain main line to the north. This was among the best-financed narrow gauges, so that in spite of the line's length, construction proceeded rapidly. By the end of 1882 the company had laid track from Bird's Point to Clarendon, Arkansas, making use of the former Little River & Arkansas Valley between Paw Paw Junction (Lilbourn) and Malden. From Texarkana, track had reached Pine Bluff. Thus only a gap of 45 miles remained, between the White and Arkansas rivers, both of which required substantial bridges. A major bridge was also to be built over the Red River at Garland. To the west, track reached Gatesville in October 1882. The company was grading a branch from Mount Pleasant to Dallas.

The Illinois Central's *W. H. Osborn* was built with narrow gauge track between her rails to handle Texas & St. Louis cars into the IC's yard at Cairo. (Cincinnati Public Library.)

The bridge at Garland was completed in May of 1883, and the larger bridges during the summer. The White River bridge entailed a four-mile trestle across swampland. The bridge across the Arkansas at Rob Roy was a draw span of 358 feet with additional spans of 1,200 feet plus trestle approaches. The railroad was completed across Arkansas when Paramore drove a silver spike on this bridge on August 12, 1883. Paramore entered into a contract with the Illinois Central for movement of through freight to St. Louis over its Cairo Short Line, a standard gauge railroad over which the narrow gauge cars had to be handled by transfer between trucks. Because the St. Louis & Cairo ran between the same points with 3'-0" gauge, railroad observers thought this arrangement odd. In part, the reason for it was that the 3'-0" St. Louis & Cairo initially showed no interest in the Grand Narrow Gauge Trunk proposal. In addition, use of the Illinois Central allowed the T&StL rights over the Illinois Central's transfer steamer, *H. S. McComb*, at Cairo. Third

rail was laid on the ferry's deck and on IC terminal trackage in Cairo.

Almost immediately upon completion of the main line to Gatesville, the company began to encounter financial problems that shortly drove it bankrupt. The railroad had exhausted the $4-million bond issue with which it was built, and by November 1883 the company was enough in arrears of wages to precipitate a strike of engineers in the northern region. Rust & Coolidge, contractors for the Arkansas River bridge, threatened suit for the unpaid balance on the bridge. The railroad filed a countersuit, bringing the company into the courts. General Manager W. R. Woodward was appointed receiver on January 12, 1884. Since most of the securities were held by Paramore and his associates, the reorganization did not promise to bring about a change in ownership. The receivership brought to a halt the projected Dallas branch and truncated a proposed branch from McNeil to Shreveport at Magnolia, only seven miles.

On November 1, 1883, a readjustment agreement was made whereby the securities holders were to deposit their stocks and bonds with either of two banks. Some independent first-mortgage holders were unwilling to accept the terms, which would have increased debt on the company from $8,000 to $15,000 per mile. The bond-

holders' committee, like its counterpart on the Toledo, Cincinnati & St. Louis, raised the question of conversion to standard gauge. This step would have required issuance of $3 million in receiver's certificates, which it was not clear that the judge would authorize. Late in 1884 W. W. Roberts and other stockholders filed a petition in federal court in Waco charging collusion between Paramore and the bondholders in issuance of the first-mortgage bonds.

Fordyce replaced Woodward as receiver on April 1, 1885. His performance was remarkable. In the face of the hostility of the Gould system, he formed the Texas Traffic Association for the purpose of collusive rate-setting with the Gould roads and the Gulf, Colorado & Santa Fe. Fordyce managed to prevent execution of an order of the court at Waco for the sale of the Texas mileage—which would probably have resulted in the passing of the line west of Texarkana into the hands of Gould.

The legal problems were resolved with sale of the railroad to the bondholders' committee of Paramore and his associates in 1886. The Texas lines were sold on January 2 and the Missouri-Arkansas lines on March 2. The newly formed St. Louis, Arkansas & Texas Railway took over the entire property on May 1, 1886. The new corporation made immediate plans for con-

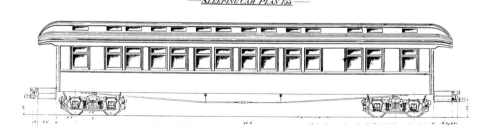
Diagram of a sleeping car planned for service on the Texas & St. Louis. (Arthur Dubin.)

The Texas & St. Louis was equipped largely with Grant locomotives, including the 4-4-0 *Thomas E. Tutt*. (Smithsonian Institution.) Most T&StL locomotives were converted to standard gauge, an arrangement that was not satisfactory.

version. Tie replacement occupied much of the summer. The entire line from Bird's Point to Texarkana, 419 miles, was converted on October 18, 1886, reportedly the largest such gauge change ever done in a single day. The Texas mileage was converted on January 12, 1887. The new corporation undertook to complete the grade of the projected Dallas branch, but built it into Fort Worth in 1888; a short branch was built into Dallas off this line in 1903. The company bought the Kansas & Gulf Short Line in 1887 for access to Lufkin, but it never undertook extension of the main line from Leon Junction to Laredo. Leon Junction, which never was a junction, retains its name to the present.

To the north, the company built from Malden to Delta in 1898, extending to the Mississippi at Gray's Point (Illmo) in 1898. From Thebes on the opposite shore it arranged trackage rights over the Missouri Pacific in 1903, finally achieving its own entrance into St. Louis.

Paramore sold his holdings in the railroad shortly after the reorganization of 1886, and owned none of its securities when he died the following year. The St. Louis, Arkansas & Texas went into bankruptcy on May 13–14, 1889, with Fordyce as receiver, and in 1891 was reorganized as the St. Louis Southwestern Railway, the corporate entity the railroad has maintained to date. The Gould interests bought into the company in 1888; Edwin Gould became vice-president of the corporation upon its reorganization in 1891. He is thought to have been responsible for Fordyce's departure in 1898. The company re-

mained independent until 1925, when the Gould interests sold out their holdings. The Rock Island and then the Kansas City Southern briefly held control. The Interstate Commerce Commission denied an effort of the Missouri-Kansas-Texas to gain control of the KCS and Cotton Belt in 1927. The Southern Pacific held an equity in the company beginning in 1919 and secured ICC permission to take control in 1930. The company again entered bankruptcy in 1935, but as a result of wartime earnings was able to reestablish solvency without reorganization in 1947.

The Cotton Belt is currently operated essentially as a portion of the Southern Pacific main line, like the rest of it mainly single track with centralized traffic control. Because the railroad has little origination, the great majority of traffic moves from the Southern Pacific interchange in Corsicana, Texas, to East St. Louis. As a consequence, the Cotton Belt's performance by the usual measures of railroad efficiency is usually among the best in the industry. The physical plant is considered a good one; the Cotton Belt probably suffers less from having been built to prevailing narrow gauge standards than any of the other major former narrow gauges. Beginning in 1923 the railroad engaged in a major upgrading of the physical plant, which wiped out most of the undesirable survivals of the narrow gauge, mainly in western Arkansas and Texas. Only some street running in Pine Bluff is markedly below normal standards.

Of the narrow gauge mileage, the branch to Gatesville was cut back to Lime City in 1972. The branch from McNeil to Magno-

lia has been leased to the Louisiana & North West since 1898. The Wyatt line was cut back to East Prairie in 1981 and to Lilbourn in 1983, but the New Madrid branch is still intact.

REFERENCES: Jacob E. Anderson, *A Brief History of the St. Louis Southwestern Railway Lines* (St. Louis: St. Louis Southwestern Railway, 1947); Joseph A. Strapac, *Cotton Belt Locomotives* (Huntington Beach, Calif.: Shade Tree Books, 1977).

Washington & Hope Railway

W. H. Carruth and other local businessmen promoted this railroad in 1876 and 1877 to connect Washington, which was then seat of Hempstead County, with Hope on the main line of the St. Louis, Iron Mountain & Southern, 9.3 miles to the southeast. The railroad was built as a wooden tramway for horse or mule haulage and opened on September 1, 1879. In accordance with their plan for upgrading the line when traffic had been established, the owners relaid the track with 25-pound T-rail in 1880 and bought a locomotive. After considering several long extensions, in October 1881 they changed the name to Arkansas & Louisiana Railway and amended the charter to provide for a line of about 200 miles from Monroe, Louisiana, to the Indian Territory boundary in Sevier County. The 55 miles projected from Washington to the boundary were separately incorporated on September 13, 1882, as the Arkansas & Indian Territory Railway, but this corporation was absorbed on June 17, 1883.

In preparation for the extension to the northwest, the proprietors converted the existing line, probably late in 1882, but possibly early in 1883. As a standard gauge railroad they extended the track six miles from Washington to Ozan in September 1883 and 12 additional miles to Nashville on October 1, 1884. Although they had built the narrow gauge without a funded debt, they encountered financial difficulties and could not proceed farther. The railroad was put in receivership on December 7, 1887. The receiver was discharged on August 26, 1889, but in the course of the refinancing stock control passed into the hands of the Gould interests. Thomas Essex, the Missouri Pacific's land agent for Arkansas, became president, and R. E. Ricker, the general superintendent of the MOP, became superintendent of the A&L. Because the MOP's stock control was not complete, the line remained individually incorporated and separately listed in the *Official Guide*. By 1909 the MOP owned $511,700 of the railroad's $512,000 in stock. In February and March of 1910 the MOP absorbed the A&L and a large number of other subsidiaries. The line was thereafter operated as the Nashville branch of the StLIM&S. In 1988 it was still in service in the combined Union Pacific–Missouri Pacific systems.

REFERENCE: Lee A. Dew and Louis Koeppe, "Narrow Gauge Railroads in Arkansas," *Arkansas Historical Quarterly*, 31 (1972), pp. 276–93.

▼ ▼ ▼ ▼

Arkansas had a large number of lumber railroads, some of which were ambiguous with respect to common carrier status. The Black & Cache River Railroad, which ran northeast from the Frisco at Sedgwick, was a private carrier of the Kansas City & Southern Lumber Company, variously reported at 3′-4″ and 3′-6″. In 1902 it was incorporated as the Cache Valley Railroad, and in the first half of 1904 converted to standard gauge. As far as can be ascertained from the records of the Railroad Commission of Arkansas, the line was never a common carrier as a narrow gauge, except possibly transitionally. As a standard gauge common carrier, it operated until 1927 and was then abandoned.

California

Arcata & Mad River Railroad
Gauge: 3′-9¼″

The unique gauge of this railroad testifies to its having originated before the narrow gauge movement began. The Union Company, which ran the company town of Union (Arcata) on the north shore of Humboldt Bay opposite Eureka, in 1854 organized the Union Wharf & Plank Walk Co. to build a pier into the shallow bay to a point at which lumber schooners could be loaded. Wooden rails for a horse tramway were laid on the pier; the gauge of 3′-9¼″ was reportedly established simply by choosing the first available set of wheels on the property. By 1855 the company had laid two miles of track tributary to the pier. About 1875 the name of the railroad was changed to Union Plank Walk & Railroad Co., and a small steam locomotive was put in service, capable of running out onto the pier. The wooden rails were faced with iron strapping at that time. Some short additional trackage was laid to independent redwood mills in the area.

On June 15, 1878, the Arcata Transportation Co. was organized to take over the railroad. The new company ordered a small sternwheeler, *Alta*, to connect the wharf with Eureka, replacing an earlier sidewheeler, *Gussie McAlpine*. In 1880 track was extended four miles to redwood mills in the Warren Creek area. G. W. B. Yocum, R. M. Fernald, and their associates organized the Arcata & Mad River Railroad to take over the line and to extend it up the North Fork of the Mad River. In 1882 they reached North Fork (Korbel), where the Korbel brothers operated the Humboldt Lumber Mill. The Korbels bought the railroad in 1883. They built extensive track into the woods and used the A&MR's locomotives on the common carrier and the private trackage indiscriminately. At its peak

the rail operation amounted to about 13 miles of common carrier and 14.5 miles of logging trackage.

On September 13, 1896, a passenger train fell through the truss bridge over the Mad River, killing seven and injuring 23 people. On March 19, 1902, the Korbels discontinued the *Alta*, which had been rendered redundant by the building of the California & Northern Railway between Eureka and Arcata in the previous year. In February 1903 the Riverside Lumber Co. and the Charles Nelson Steamship Co. jointly bought the Humboldt Lumber Mill and the A&MR. The new owners strengthened the wharf so that any of the railroad's locomotives could use it. Previously only the company's lightest engine was safe on it.

The Northwestern Pacific arrived in Eureka on October 23, 1914, giving the region its first rail connection to the San Francisco Bay Area. The NWP had taken over the California & Northern, thereby gaining access to the Arcata area. Because of the interest of the A&MR's owners in coastal steamships, third rail was not laid on the A&MR until 1925. In that year the private logging trackage was converted to 4′-8½″, including conversion of the Heisler locomotives that operated it. The A&MR's locomotives were equipped with three coupler pockets at each end to accommodate cars of both gauges. The narrow gauge lasted until 1933, when closure of the Riverside mill at Korbel caused it to be shut down. Rails between the Northwestern Pacific junction at Korblex and Korbel, 7.5 miles, were removed. The remaining 5.4 miles were left in place until 1942, when the Riverside mill was reopened, but then removed. At that time the trackage from Korbel to Korblex was restored as standard gauge, and about ten miles of logging track were built up the Mad River. The A&MR as a common carrier of 7.5 miles served about 15 shippers. It survived until 1985.

REFERENCE: Stanley T. Borden, "Arcata & Mad River," *The Western Railroader*, 17, no. 8, issue 176 (1954).

Bodie & Benton Railway

An anomaly among railroads, the Bodie & Benton was a common carrier wholly isolated from the rest of the railroad system. The railroad was organized on February 18, 1881, as the Bodie Railway & Lumber Co. to run south from the isolated gold-mining camp of Bodie to some timberland of the Bodie Wood & Lumber Co. south

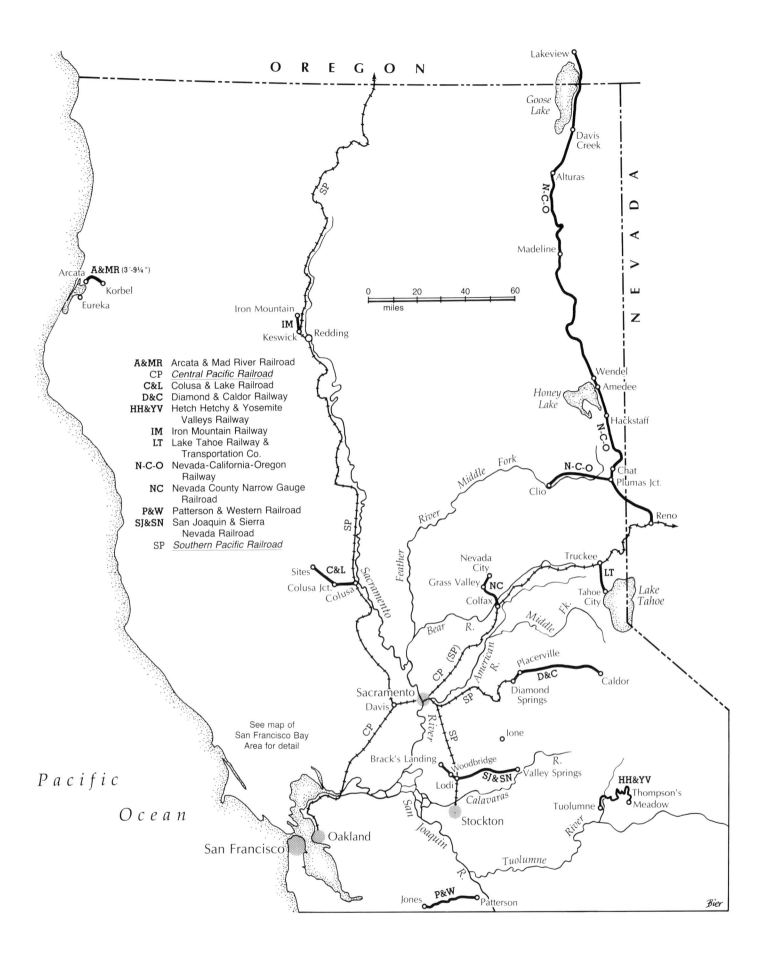

OREGON

Lakeview

Goose Lake

Davis Creek

Alturas

N-C-O

Madeline

NEVADA

Arcata **A&MR** (3'-9¼")
Korbel
Eureka

Wendel
Amedee

Honey Lake

Hackstaff

N-C-O

Iron Mountain
IM
Keswick   Redding

A&MR Arcata & Mad River Railroad
CP   *Central Pacific Railroad*
C&L Colusa & Lake Railroad
D&C Diamond & Caldor Railway
HH&YV Hetch Hetchy & Yosemite
         Valleys Railway
IM   Iron Mountain Railway
LT   Lake Tahoe Railway &
         Transportation Co.
N-C-O Nevada-California-Oregon
         Railway
NC   Nevada County Narrow Gauge
         Railroad
P&W Patterson & Western Railroad
SJ&SN San Joaquin & Sierra
         Nevada Railroad
SP   *Southern Pacific Railroad*

SP

0   20   40   60
miles

Middle   Fork

N-C-O
Clio

Chat
Plumas Jct.

Reno

River

Feather

Truckee

LT

Nevada City
Grass Valley **NC**
Colfax

Tahoe City

Lake Tahoe

Sites **C&L**
Colusa Jct.
Colusa

Sacramento

Bear   R.

Middle   Fk.

CP (SP)

American   R.

Placerville
D&C   Caldor
Diamond Springs

Sacramento
Davis

CP

SP

Ione

SP

River

Brack's Landing

See map of
San Francisco Bay
Area for detail

Woodbridge
Lodi

SJ&SN

Valley Springs

Calavaras

R.

Tuolumne

HH&YV
Thompson's
Meadow

Pacific

Ocean

Oakland

San Francisco

San   Joaquin

Stockton

Tuolumne

River

R.

Jones **P&W** Patterson

Bier

California   321

of Mono Lake. The railroad built a line of 32 miles from Bodie along the east shore of Mono Lake to a newly built sawmill at Mono Mills, completed on November 14, 1881. Spurs into timberlands were built in 1882. By the standards of lumber railroads, the line's physical properties were not extreme. The line had a 3.8-percent ruling grade with two switchbacks about seven miles south of Bodie. The line could be worked by rod engines; the company operated with 2-6-0s and tank engines. Traffic, which was almost entirely lumber to the mining industry at Bodie, was necessarily highly cyclical. Operations were typically shut down for the winter months. The railroad operated excursions, but no regular passenger service. (For map, see Nevada.)

The failure of the California & Nevada to build out of the San Francisco Bay Area and failure of the Stockton & Bodie of 1880 to be built at all left the line isolated. In January 1882 the Bodie & Benton Railway & Commercial Co. was organized to take over the existing line and to build a connection from Warm Springs on Mono Lake to Benton Station on the Carson & Colorado, about 40 miles away. About 25 miles were graded by July 10, 1882, when construction was abruptly halted; it was never resumed. Bodie declined in the 1880s to the point that in 1890 the railroad ceased operation. It was reorganized under its original name in 1893, and restored to service for two months in the summers beginning in 1895. Charles E. Knox of the Montana-Tonopah Mining Co. bought the railroad along with its 7,600 acres of timberland on December 23, 1906, and reorganized it as the Mono Lake Railway & Lumber Co. His intention was to build a connection from Warm Springs to Basalt on the Nevada & California (as the Carson & Colorado had become), to bring lumber into Tonopah and Goldfield, which were experiencing the country's last major mining boom. In 1907 the railroad was separately incorporated as the Mono Lake Railway. The projected extension to Basalt had been forgone by 1910. The largest mine in Bodie closed in 1914, ending any major timber traffic on the railroad. The California Railroad Commission granted permission to abandon on September 6, 1917.

REFERENCE: David F. Myrick, *Railroads of Nevada and Eastern California* (Berkeley, Calif.: Howell-North Books, 1962), vol. 1, pp. 298–313.

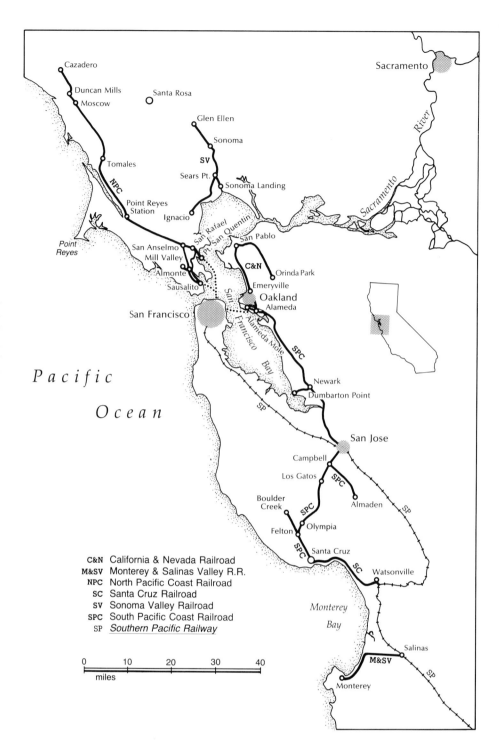

California & Nevada Railroad

Although this railroad proved to be only a minor suburban line in the San Francisco East Bay area, it was projected as a Pacific connection for the Denver & Rio Grande. Its promoters envisioned a line from Emeryville, California, adjacent to Oakland, through Lafayette, Walnut Creek, Livermore, Modesto, and Sonora to Sonora Pass, and thence to Candalaria, Nevada, and Milford, Utah, before effecting a connection with the D&RG at Salina. The railroad, under the initial title California &

Mt. Diablo Railroad, received its charter in 1880, but construction did not begin until 1883. In February 1884 the name was changed to the California & Nevada Railroad. Construction proceeded slowly, and it was not until May 1, 1886, that trains could be operated from Emeryville north up San Pablo Road to the town of San Pablo, some 12 miles.

From San Pablo, the line turned east and south along San Pablo Creek. On January 1, 1887, service was begun to Oak Grove. In 1888 rails reached Warnecke's Ranch and in 1890 Orinda Park, 21 miles from Emeryville. Heavy rains in 1890 washed out about nine miles of track along San Pablo Creek, requiring new grading. The railroad had two Porter locomotives, two combines, a boxcar, and four flatcars. It had a small freight business among ranches along the line, but was mainly dependent on passenger revenues.

In 1895 the railroad was sold to Captain John W. Smith & Co., which continued to plan to build to Nevada. The new owners extended the line a mile to Bryant in 1897, and graded about three miles farther into the Oakland hills, but nothing more was accomplished. In 1898 a difficult winter caused the line to cease operation. The company went bankrupt and the property was sold. The line up San Pablo Creek was scrapped, but in 1902 the Santa Fe bought the right-of-way on San Pablo Road for $40,000 for its entry into Oakland. Service began in 1904. This entry was abandoned on June 1, 1979.

REFERENCE: Erle C. Hanson, "California & Nevada Railroad," *The Western Railroader*, 21, no. 9, issue 225 (1958).

Chino Valley Railway
Gauge: 3'-6"

Richard Gird undertook to subdivide El Rancho de Santa Ana del Chino into sugar beet farms and established the town of Chino. To serve the population and the sugar beet operation, Gird built the Chino Valley Railway, a steam dummy line. He built south from the Southern Pacific station in Ontario, reaching Chino (7 miles) on March 23, 1888, and Harrington (10 miles) on April 27. The line operated with a single Porter 2-4-2T locomotive, one coach, one cross-bench open car, and several flatcars. The line was privately held and not publicly reported, but operated as a common carrier of passengers and possibly also of sugar beets. Trains connected with Southern Pacific trains at Ontario.

Gird sold the line in 1895 to C. H. Phillips of Ontario, who resold it to Wendell and George Easton of San Francisco. The new owners immediately converted it and leased two SP locomotives to operate it. The SP built its own branch into Chino in 1896, rendering the line redundant. It was abandoned in 1901.

REFERENCE: Gerald M. Best, "San Bernardino Valley Steam Dummy Lines," *The Western Railroader*, 26, no. 5, issue 280 (1963), pp. 3–4.

Colusa & Lake Railroad

When the Southern Pacific's line from Davis Junction to Tehama was built along the west side of the Sacramento River valley, the town of Colusa, which was bypassed, feared losing its status as county seat to Williams, which was on the railroad. Accordingly, on July 23, 1885, local figures organized the Colusa Railroad, which later in the year built a narrow gauge of 9.7 miles to Colusa Junction on the SP. On June 8, 1886, the Colusa & Lake Railroad was incorporated to extend the narrow gauge about 50 miles southwest from Colusa Junction to Lower Lake at the base of Clear Lake in Lake County, but this line was never built. Rather, the C&L was built about 12.3 miles to the northwest from Colusa Junction to Sites to serve two sandstone quarries. The two railroads were consolidated under the name of the C&L on November 27, 1886. The railroad was mainly a service facility to the two quarries at Sites, but it also enjoyed a traffic in grain for transshipment either to the SP at Colusa Junction or to river steamers at Colusa. The railroad operated with a Porter 2-4-2T and three Baldwin 4-4-0s.

The Northern Electric Railway, predecessor of the Sacramento Northern interurban, opened its line from Marysville to Colusa on June 13, 1913, diverting much of the narrow gauge's passenger traffic, express, and less-than-carload freight. The Southern Pacific built its own branch into Colusa in 1912. The quarries were declining because of substitution of other materials for Colusa sandstone. Passenger service on the narrow gauge was discontinued on August 5, 1914, for the announced reason that the railroad was no longer safe for travel. The management continued to operate freight trains, but received permission of the California Railroad Commission to suspend operation effective May 1, 1915. The railroad was removed in 1918.

REFERENCE: "Colusa & Lake Railroad," *The Western Railroader*, 37, issue 405 (1974).

Death Valley Railroad

Francis Marion Smith's Pacific Coast Borax Co., anticipating exhaustion of the borax at its Lila C. Mine at Ryan about 1913, determined to open a new facility at the Biddy McCarthy Mine, about 12 miles northwest. The company's Tonopah & Tidewater Railroad, which already had a branch from Death Valley Junction to Ryan, applied to the California Railroad Commission to build a branch of 17 miles

from Horton on the existing branch to the new mine. The Commission denied permission on December 13, 1913, on the grounds that the T&T was so weak financially that additional debt incurred in building the projected branch might manifest itself in exorbitant rates. The borax company responded in January 1914 by chartering a new corporation, the Death Valley Railroad, to build the line. A 3'-0" gauge was chosen, probably to make use of a Heisler locomotive and some of the equipment from the company's abandoned private carrier, the Borate & Daggett Railroad near Barstow. Construction began March 1, and the railroad was opened on December 1, 1914. Third rail had been laid on three miles of the T&T's Ryan branch from Death Valley Junction to Horton. The newly constructed portion was built to typical narrow gauge standards, with 24° curvature and a ruling grade of 3.5 percent.

With the completion of the narrow gauge, the borax company closed the Lila C. Mine, transferred its ore compactor to Death Valley Junction, abandoned the Ryan branch, and moved the company town of Ryan to the site of the Biddy McCarthy Mine. By 1916 these changes had been made, and the company removed the standard gauge rail between the junction and Horton. The railroad was a bona fide common carrier, operating a mixed train over its 20 miles at a typical narrow gauge speed of about 15 miles per hour. A private 2'-0" railroad was built from the railhead to the Widow Mine, about four miles to the south. (For map, see Nevada.)

The railroad enjoyed respectable traffic for several years, and in 1926 was actually extended by laying six miles of third rail on the T&T main line and building four miles of narrow gauge track from Bradford Siding to a clay pit just over the Nevada state line in Ash Meadows. DV trains ran between the clay pit and the ore compactor at Death Valley Junction. About that time, however, the borax company decided to close the Biddy McCarthy Mine in favor of a new facility at Boron on the Santa Fe west of Barstow. The change was made in 1927, but the DV was not immediately abandoned. The borax company built the Furnace Creek Inn northwest of Ryan and endeavored to make use of the narrow gauge in its effort to promote tourism in Death Valley. The effort was not enough to save the narrow gauge, which was abandoned on March 15, 1931. Third rail was removed from the T&T main line, and the spur to the clay pits was converted to 4'-8½". The 2'-0" line at Ryan was retained as a tourist facility until about 1950.

REFERENCE: Myrick, *Railroads of Nevada and Eastern California*, vol. 2, pp. 608–21.

Diamond & Caldor Railway

Although a typical lumber railroad, owned by the California Door Co. of Oakland and its successor, the Caldor Lumber Co., this narrow gauge was incorporated as a common carrier throughout its history.

California Door from its organization in 1884 operated with steam tractors and log buggies. After acquiring 30,000 acres of timberland in El Dorado County in 1900, the company organized the Diamond & Caldor Railway in 1902, and began building the line in 1903. The route was east from Diamond Springs on the Southern Pacific (just south of Placerville) 34 miles to Caldor, where the company maintained a mill. The line was completed in October 1904. The physical plant was typical of lumber railroads: it had 63 trestles, totaling 10,992 feet, which included a steel span of 97 feet, curves of only 50-foot radius, and grades up to 8 percent. Initially, the railroad hauled finished lumber to the Southern Pacific behind geared locomotives. A 2-4-2T, secondhand from the Ferries & Cliff House dummy line in San Francisco, and a combine were used for a single round-trip per day for passengers; the railroad carried about 1,350 passengers per year.

The mill at Caldor burned in 1923, causing the lumber company in 1924 to build a new mill at Diamond Springs, where it had already established a planing mill for finished lumber. Thereafter the rail line operated in the normal fashion of lumber railroads, hauling logs from the camp at Caldor to the mill at Diamond Springs. With the onslaught of the Depression, the mill was closed late in 1929 and the railroad shortly shut down. Chalmers Price was hired to reactivate the line in 1934. In 1935 the line was reopened and the lumber company's box plant at Diamond Springs turned over to the American Box Co. Thereafter the company's status as a common carrier was more bona fide. After the reopening passengers were handled in a rail motor car.

By the 1950s, like most of the surviving lumber lines, the railroad was a reload operation, carrying logs from trucks at Caldor to the mill. In 1952 the California safety authorities ordered the company to convert from link-and-pin coupling to MCB couplers. Caldor Lumber felt the investment unjustified and converted the entire operation to diesel trucks. The railroad was closed late in 1952 and dismantled in 1953.

REFERENCE: George B. Turner, "Diamond & Caldor," *The Western Railroader*, 31, no. 8, issue 342 (1968).

Hetch Hetchy & Yosemite Valleys Railway

William H. Crocker, Henry J. Crocker, Prince André Poniatowski, and Thomas S. Bullock, who were active in building the Sierra Railway from Oakdale to Jamestown at the foot of the Sierras, developed plans for lumbering on 55,000 acres in Tuolumne County in 1898. They organized the West Side Flume & Lumber Co. on May 31, 1899, and began logging with two Heisler locomotives on 3'-0" track. On August 28, 1900, they incorporated the railroad as a common carrier, the Hetch Hetchy & Yosemite Valleys Railway. They were motivated by a desire to participate in joint tariffs for lumber movements and also to secure the right of condemnation. They envisioned reaching the Hetch Hetchy Valley and the Yosemite area, both of which were potentially sources of passenger traffic. They also considered building across Sonora Pass on the approximate route surveyed by the California & Nevada in 1880 to reach Bodie and connections with the Carson & Colorado and Bodie & Benton narrow gauges. The common carrier status of the railroad proved particularly nominal; it developed only as a private lumber operation with geared locomotives operating on grades up to 4.8 percent.

The railroad progressed in the typical fashion, extending as timber was depleted in the closer areas. By 1903 track had reached Thompson's Meadow, 35 miles from the mill at Tuolumne. Only this portion was ever enrolled with state authorities as a common carrier, although the main line eventually reached 70 miles. At various times the lumber company had over 250 miles of spur trackage.

Passenger trains were at first run twice a week and later three times, but patronage was almost entirely limited to personnel of the company. In 1903 the parent company was sold to W. R. Thorsten of Manistee, Michigan, and its name was shortened to West Side Lumber Co. In August 1904 the railroad dropped passenger service. It continued to be listed in the *Official Guide of the Railways* as a common carrier of freight until March 1910, but thereafter was listed only as "Logging road. No freight or passenger service." The Hetch Hetchy & Yosemite Valleys was not formally dissolved, however, until June 28, 1943. The railroad survived until 1960, the last American narrow gauge logging railroad.

REFERENCES: Alan Kreig, *Last of the 3 Foot Loggers* (San Marino, Calif.: Golden West Books, 1962); Mallory Hope Ferrell, *West Side: Narrow Gauge in the Sierra* (Edmonds, Wash.: Pacific Fast Mail, 1979).

Iron Mountain Railway

One of the late narrow gauges built to serve extractive enterprises, this railroad was a common carrier of the Mountain Copper Co. The route was from a smelter at Keswick on the Southern Pacific 12 miles north of Redding to a copper, gold, and silver mine at Iron Mountain, 11 miles to the northwest. The railroad was incorporated on July 17, 1895, and completed on February 1, 1896. The route entailed a rise of about 1,700 feet to the mine, with a ruling grade of 3.75 percent, a curve of 34°, and a double loop approaching the mine. The cost was $283,657. The line operated with five Porter 0-4-4 tank engines and five two-truck Shays. Daily passenger service was provided.

In 1905 Mountain Copper built a new smelter at Mococo near Martinez on Carquinez Strait. The earlier plant was abandoned in 1907, and Keswick became a transshipment point. The mine was largely exhausted by 1921, but the railroad continued hauling ore for other operators, mainly the Pittsburgh–Mount Shasta Mining Co. Mountain Copper, which had typically operated the line at a loss, received permission of the California Railroad Commission to abandon it on February 5, 1927.

REFERENCE: Stanley T. Borden, "Iron Mountain Ry.," *The Western Railroader*, 27, no. 1, issue 288 (1964).

Lake Tahoe Railway & Transportation Co.

Large-scale lumbering began on the shores of Lake Tahoe in the 1860s. By the end of the 1870s there were several lumber railroads, but no connection to the mainline railroad system. The most obvious route for a railroad was from the Central Pacific at Truckee up the valley of the Truckee River, about 15 miles with a monotonic ascent of some 450 feet. Major projects for such a railroad dated from 1879, but none was built until lumber operator Duane L. Bliss incorporated the

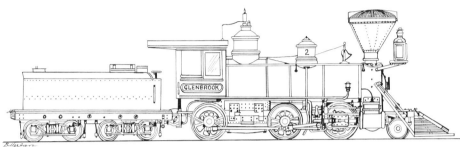

THE "GLENBROOK"

Lake Tahoe Railway & Transportation Co. No. 1 was the former *Glenbrook*, No. 2 of the Carson & Tahoe Fluming & Lumber Co., a private carrier of the Bliss interests on the Nevada side of the lake. (Smithsonian Institution.) The drawing of the locomotive is by Barbara Herlan, courtesy of the Nevada State Railroad Museum, Carson City, where the locomotive is preserved.

Lake Tahoe Railway & Transportation Co. in 1898. All of the stock was held by the Bliss family, who also provided all of the officers. William Bliss, an engineer, laid out the line, and Walter D. Bliss, an architect, designed the Tahoe Tavern, a resort hotel on the shore at the upper terminus, Tahoe City. The line was mainly built in 1899, and formally opened on May 1, 1900. In anticipation of completion Bliss ordered a passenger steamer, *Tahoe*, from the Union Iron Works of San Francisco. The vessel, which had a graceful, yachtlike quality, was knocked down, then reassembled and launched at Tahoe City on June 24, 1896. The railroad proved mainly a tourist facility, interchanging passengers with CP trains at Truckee and with the *Tahoe* for transfer to resorts along the lake. The railroad maintained a 954-foot wharf for direct interchange between the trains and the steamer. Shops for the railroad and a shipyard were located at Tahoe City. Logs outbound and supplies inbound were the principal freight. The railroad began operation with two locomotives from the Blisses' private carrier on the east shore of the lake, the Carson & Tahoe Lumber & Fluming Co. Later locomotives and much of the equipment came from Southern Pacific narrow

gauges in the process of conversion. The railroad customarily operated only from May 15 to November 15, closing in the face of the heavy snows characteristic of the area. The railroad was initially profitable, paying dividends to 1907, and remained solvent thereafter.

With the extensive diversion of traffic to the automobile following World War I, the Bliss family arranged transfer of the rail line to the Southern Pacific, and of the Tahoe Tavern to the Linnard Hotel interests, who were affiliated with the SP. It was arranged to lease the narrow gauge to the SP, which would convert it and establish a through Pullman from Oakland Pier to Tahoe City. The ICC agreed to this plan on June 30, 1925, and the SP converted the line effective May 1, 1926. A balloon loop for turning the trains, including the Pullman car, replaced the steamer wharf. Satisfied that the agreement had been carried out, the Bliss family turned title to the railroad over to the SP in 1927 for $1. The Bliss interests continued to operate the *Tahoe* and a running mate, *Nevada*, acquired in 1898, but laid them up in 1935 and scuttled them in the lake in 1941. The SP continued the pattern of summer rail operation until 1942, but applied to abandon the line and did so on November 10, 1943.

REFERENCES: Frederic Shaw; Clement Fisher, Jr.; and George H. Harlan, *Oil Lamps and Iron Ponies* (San Francisco: Bay Books, 1949), pp. 22–37; Myrick, *Railroads of Nevada and Eastern California*, vol. 1, pp. 430–36; Owen F. McKeon, "The Railroads and Steamers of Lake Tahoe," *The Western Railroader*, 5, no. 6, issue 82 (1946).

Los Angeles & Redondo Railway

Projected by steamship operator George J. Ainsworth of Oakland and his associates as a line from Los Angeles to a proposed port and coastal resort at Redondo Beach, this narrow gauge was incorporated as the Redondo Railway on April 1, 1889. Ainsworth acquired the property of the Rosecrans Railroad, a steam dummy line that had operated in 1887 and 1888 on Santa Barbara and Vermont avenues, planning to lay it with 25-pound rail for use as his exit from the city. The dummy line's physical properties proved too low, however, and Ainsworth undertook construction from the end of a cable car line at Grand Avenue and Jefferson Boulevard to Redondo via Gardena. The line was completed (17.7 miles) in October 1889, but then heavily damaged by a flood. The right-of-way was restored during the winter; the first train ran from Los Angeles to Redondo on February 22, 1890, and regular service began on April 15. The railroad handled passengers with steam dummy technology, but it owned two 4-4-0 locomotives, 12 boxcars, and 17 flatcars for freight operation. During the summer of 1890 Ainsworth opened the Hotel Redondo at the beach.

On petition of the shareholders the name was changed on April 20, 1896, to the Los Angeles & Redondo Railway. In 1902–3 it was converted to the Los Angeles Railway's gauge of 3'-6" and electrified as an interurban so that its cars could have access to central Los Angeles over street railway lines. The conversion entailed building a new line from Los Angeles to Belvidere (about three miles from Redondo)

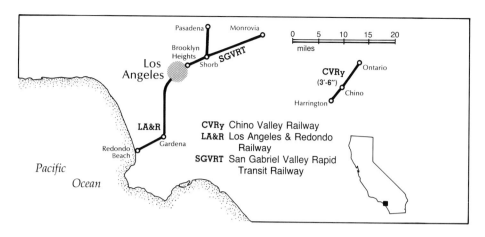

CVRy — Chino Valley Railway
LA&R — Los Angeles & Redondo Railway
SGVRT — San Gabriel Valley Rapid Transit Railway

REFERENCE: Edward T. Planer, Jr., "The Monterey and Salinas Valley Railroad—California's First Operating Narrow Gauge," Railway & Locomotive Historical Society Bulletin, no. 66 (1945), pp. 7–27.

via Inglewood in 1902; the original line via Gardena was opened as an electric railway on May 18, 1903. Henry E. Huntington gained stock control of the corporation in 1905, and in November 1910 conveyed the innermost 9.6 miles to the Los Angeles Railway and the rest to the Southern Pacific. The SP in 1911 merged its portion into the Pacific Electric, along with several other properties in Southern California. The PE converted the Redondo line to 4′-8½″ during the summer of 1911 and rerouted the cars via Watts on its Long Beach line. The PE gave up the Redondo service in 1940.

REFERENCES: Gerald M. Best, "Early Steam Suburban Railroads in Los Angeles," Railway & Locomotive Historical Society Bulletin, no. 99 (1958), pp. 22–24; Ira Swett, Los Angeles & Redondo, Interurbans Special, no. 20 (1957).

Monterey & Salinas Valley Railroad

Local parties had been interested in a railroad for moving wheat from the Salinas area to the Pacific since 1868. In 1874 John F. Kidder began surveying a route of about 18.5 miles from Salinas to Monterey. The route was level or gently rolling over sandy soil, with no serious engineering problems except bridging the Salinas River. Work began on April 20, and was completed on October 9. The first locomotive, C. S. Abbott, a 2-6-0 named for the president of the company, arrived by schooner on September 8. The engine handled the first revenue shipment on the railroad on September 25, and opened regular service to Salinas on October 26, 1874. The railroad was the first active narrow gauge in California.

One of the principal motivations in building the line was to undercut the rates of the Southern Pacific, which were widely thought excessive. About 25,000 sacks of wheat had been stored at Salinas in antic-

ipation of the opening. The railroad was so fully occupied in moving the wheat that it did not hold its inaugural excursion until November 16. The company handled about 6,000 tons of wheat in 1874, undercutting the SP's rates to San Francisco by $2 per ton. The SP shortly reduced its charges. Passengers were mainly from Monterey, connecting with the SP at Salinas.

The narrow gauge had cost about $360,000, some $150,000 over Kidder's estimate. Some of the overrun was accounted for by the Salinas River bridge, which proved to be five spans of 60 feet each, plus 1,200 feet of trestle. A 4-4-0, Monterey, arrived at Salinas in February 1875. Kidder had resigned as general manager on November 4, 1874, to become superintendent of the Nevada County Narrow Gauge, which was under construction. J. W. Nesbitt was his successor. The railroad was widely publicized because of its pioneering quality and its apparent consistency with the expectations of the narrow gauge proponents as a source of cut-rate transportation.

The railroad suffered a roundhouse fire at Monterey on September 2, 1877, which damaged both locomotives and destroyed a passenger car. The railroad became unprofitable in the latter part of the decade, and on December 22, 1879, was sold at a sheriff's sale for $128,558 to the Pacific Improvement Co., which had been organized by officials of the Southern Pacific. The SP decided upon a new standard gauge entry into Monterey from Castroville Junction, which would shorten the San Francisco–Monterey mileage from 136.5 to 125. The new line, put in service on January 2, 1880, made use of the westernmost stretch, approximately ten miles, of the Monterey & Salinas Valley between Monterey and Bardin. The remainder was abandoned. The entry into Monterey was cut back to Seaside in 1979. The cities of Monterey and Seaside took title to the abandoned line as far as Camino del Estero in Monterey and have retained the rails in place.

Nevada-California-Oregon Railway

John T. Davis of San Francisco in 1879 conceived of a Western Nevada Railroad running south from Wadsworth, Nevada, along the eastern escarpment of the Sierra Nevadas, but the building of the Carson & Colorado beginning in 1880 foreclosed this option. He shifted to the project of a railroad reaching both north and south from Reno. Only the line north was ever built, and that was completed for less than half its intended distance. Even so, the Nevada-California-Oregon, with a main line of 238 miles and a branch of 37, was among the longest American narrow gauges.

Davis organized his project as The Nevada & Oregon Railroad on June 1, 1880. The line south, which was never undertaken, was projected to Aurora, Nevada, near Bodie, California. The line north was initially projected to the Goose Lake area on the California-Oregon border—which it was to reach—and thence to The Dalles on the Columbia River via Silver Lake and Prineville. The route would have provided a connection to the Pacific Northwest from the Central Pacific at Reno without crossing the Sierra Nevadas or the Cascades. No direct route from the eastern United States to the Northwest existed until completion of the Northern Pacific in 1883, and none from California until the Southern Pacific reached Portland in 1887. Davis favored the northern route, but conflict with directors who favored the southern caused him to resign the presidency in August. Colonel Thomas Moore, a contractor from New Jersey, became the principal promoter. Moore was unable to finance the enterprise, but his associates reincorporated it on April 25, 1880, dropping "The" from its name. Under the new corporation, Moore and his friends were able to undertake construction of the line north, breaking ground on December 22, 1880. Acrimony among the directors continued, to the point that gunfire broke out at a shareholders' meeting of September 27, fatally wounding the corporation's secretary, Squire C. Scoville. Daniel Balch, a Moore supporter who was wounded in the fray, became president. The corporation was exhausting its funds by November. Moore withdrew and returned to New Jersey. Construction ceased in December. Largely through the efforts of director

Hugh J. McMurray, construction was resumed in 1882. On October 2, service was opened to Oneida (30 miles).

The railroad, which was developing a lurid reputation, became insolvent. Legal controversy over the validity of its bonds was in the courts for the rest of the decade, ultimately reaching the United States Supreme Court in 1890. The railroad was sold under foreclosure on April 17, 1884, to Moran Bros. of New York, an investment banking firm with extensive background in railroading. Charles Moran, who had been president of the Erie for two years, became the dominant figure in the narrow gauge. The company was reorganized in 1885 as the Nevada & California Railroad. Construction continued, with track reaching Junction (Cuba; Chat), California, at the foot of Beckwourth Pass (37 miles) at the end of 1884. A mixture of damage to the railroad by snow and rain early in 1886, combined with pressure to divert the line to Susanville, to the west of Honey Lake, caused a delay in building north. Erasmus Gest of Cincinnati, who was brought in as general manager, strongly favored a route to the east of the lake, and undertook it in April 1887. A. E. Ross, a rancher whose land was 16 miles north of Chat, endeavored to resist a condemnation suit on the ground that the railroad, being owned by individuals rather than the public, was not entitled to a right of eminent domain. He lost his case, but delayed completion of the railroad to Camp Ham (45 miles) until March 1, 1888. The railhead reached Liegan (70 miles) in September. The Morans formed the Nevada-California-Oregon Railway in 1888 to assume control of the railroad, but because of litigation against it, the new corporation could not take over until January 1, 1893. In the interim, the line was pressed on to Amedee (79 miles) in October 1890. The financial stringency of the 1890s prevented further building until 1899, when the line was extended to Madeline (144 miles). The next advance was the most difficult part of the railroad, a rise of 200 feet out of Madeline followed by a drop of 1,100 feet into Likely (163 miles). The extension was undertaken in June 1906, but not completed until October 1, 1907. This portion of the railroad proved to be particularly affected by snowfalls, and was frequently closed by blizzards. The line had yet to reach a major town, but on December 1, 1908, service was begun to Alturas (182 miles), seat of Modoc County, which was to be the railroad's principal source of traffic. Construction continued north, reaching Davis Creek (204 miles) in August 1911. There passengers changed to steamboats on Goose Lake until the line was built around the east shore and across the Oregon border to Lakeview (238 miles), completing the railroad on January 10, 1912. The company had charter authority dating from 1910 to continue on to The Dalles, but no further construction was undertaken. In 1914 the crossing of the summit north of Reno was revised, the line being shortened by two miles.

The railroad had a single branch, built independently to serve lumbering and mining in the Beckwourth Pass area. After an effort to promote the line as a 2'-0" railroad, the California Land & Timber Co. in 1885 undertook the project under the name of the Sierra Valley & Mohawk Railroad. Construction began at Plumas Junction on the Nevada & California two miles south of Chat. By the end of 1886, 11 miles of track had been laid, in spite of a serious washout from the combination of snow and rain early in the year. By August 1887, 15 miles of track had been laid to a point just east of the Buttes, and 14 additional miles had been graded, but no revenue service had been established. At that point the enterprise failed, and construction equipment was auctioned off to satisfy creditors. In April 1894 Henry A. Bowen of San Francisco bought the property, formed the Sierra Valleys Railways on January 4, 1895, and resumed construction. Track reached Kirby (23 miles) in July 1895, and the Lloyd Brothers mill at Clairville (31 miles) in 1896. The railroad was almost entirely a lumber carrier, both for Bowen's own mills and for independent operators. The railroad was so poorly built and chronically undermaintained that the N-C-O refused to interchange equipment with it. In 1900 the Southern Pacific secured a judgment of $97,000 against the SV; in 1901 the N-C-O bought the judgment and acquired control of the smaller railroad. Bowen had already undertaken an extension to Clio (37 miles), which the N-C-O management saw fit to complete on May 4, 1903. Further extension to Quincy was contemplated, but invasion of the area by the Boca & Loyalton and the imminent entry of the Western Pacific prevented the project. The railroad, which had been chronically unprofitable, was in the black beginning in 1906. The N-C-O operated the line as a separate entity, reorganizing it as the Sierra & Mohawk Railway in 1911. Later in the same year, the widow of an engineer named Chambers, who had been killed in a wreck in 1899, made use of a judgment of $3,000 against the company to gain control of it at an auction. In 1912 the N-C-O had to buy the line back from her. The N-C-O on January 1, 1915, absorbed the S&M and began to operate it as the Plumas branch.

The N-C-O regularly provided a single passenger train per day from Reno to Lakeview, and another from Reno to Clio at the end of the Plumas branch. The mainline train was notable for carrying a buffet-sleeping car on its 17-hour run, even though the trip was mainly accomplished in daylight hours.

The railroad in its uncompleted state was mainly dependent on lumber, livestock, and grain, traffic that left it usually unprofitable. Faced with major bond maturities in 1919, the management on June 17, 1917, sold the southernmost 64 miles of the main line from Hackstaff (Herlong), plus the Plumas branch, for $700,000 to the Western Pacific, which was seeking an entry into Reno. The narrow gauge, which was reduced to 171 miles, shifted its office to Alturas. The Western Pacific began conversion immediately, and completed the job on January 30, 1918. The conversion entailed a new crossing of the summit north of Reno, which shortened the line by about a mile. On April 16, 1918, the WP abandoned the Plumas line, which was redundant upon its own main line. The connection to the WP main line was made at Reno Junction, near Chat, and just east of the WP's Chilcoot Tunnel. The segment of about 28 miles north to Hackstaff, which was immediately parallel to the WP main line, was abandoned.

The management was interested in converting what remained of the narrow gauge, but was unable to finance the project. In 1922 the railroad petitioned state and federal authorities for complete abandonment, but were allowed to abandon only the southernmost 16 miles, from a connection with the Southern Pacific at Wendel to the WP connection at Hackstaff. The WP threatened suit, but the last train to Hackstaff ran on October 31, 1922.

What remained of the narrow gauge was attractive to the Southern Pacific, which was seeking a route for a bypass line from the Central Pacific into Oregon. By an agreement of April 30, 1925, the SP in 1926 acquired a majority of the securities of the narrow gauge. The SP began the conversion process on July 1, 1927, and undertook standard gauge operation into Alturas on October 24. An additional ten miles were converted before the end of the year, and standard gauge rails reached Lakeview on May 27, 1928. Simultaneously, the SP was building the 95-mile connection from Alturas to Klamath Falls; the long-projected bypass was put in service on July 13, 1929. In the same year, the SP completed its acquisition of the securities of the former narrow gauge, and absorbed it. The SP made 31 line changes between Wendel and Alturas, reducing maximum curvature from 16° to 10°, and shortening the distance by a mile. This segment and the Lakeview extension are in service at the present writing, as is the Reno branch of the Union Pacific, successor to the Western Pacific. The line from Alturas to Lakeview has been operated since January 19, 1986, by the Great Western Railway of Colorado under contract with the State of Oregon.

REFERENCE: David Myrick, "Nevada-California-Oregon Railway," *The Western Railroader*, 18, no. 8, issue 188 (1955).

Nevada County Narrow Gauge Railroad

In the course of the California gold rush, gold-bearing quartz deposits were found at Gold Hill, Nevada County, in September 1850. The discovery attracted population to the area, producing the twin towns of Nevada City and Grass Valley, about five miles apart. Projects for railroads to the Sacramento River valley were uniformly unsuccessful, but the completion of the transcontinental railroad in 1869 presented the prospect of a connection with the Central Pacific at Colfax. John C. and Edward Coleman, brothers who operated the Idaho Quartz Mining Co. at Grass Valley, formed a Committee of Twenty from local business leaders. This group secured a charter for the Nevada County Narrow Gauge Railroad from the state on March 20, 1874, and received the U.S. Congress's authority to operate through public lands on June 20. The line was unusual in being built without public assistance of any kind; in compensation, the line was allowed by its charter to charge 10¢ per mile for passengers and 20¢ per ton-mile for freight.

To build the line, the Colemans hired John F. Kidder, who had just completed the Monterey & Salinas Valley. The route chosen was 22.5 miles, starting from the east side of the CP at Colfax, descending below the CP, and then climbing by a difficult ascent with four major trestles and a tunnel at You Bet. There was an additional tunnel at Town Talk, about midway between the twin towns. Rails reached Grass Valley on January 17, 1876, and Nevada City on May 14. A ceremony opened the line on May 20; regular service began four days later.

The railroad proved quite prosperous, carrying the quartz gold ore, lumber, and general cargo. In 1884 Kidder bought out the Colemans and some of the other original owners. The railroad was almost entirely identified with him until he died in 1901, simultaneously with some investigations of his alleged diversion of railroad funds into a mining enterprise. During the 1890s the line had two serious accidents. On September 6, 1893, a circus train derailed on a curve between the twin towns, apparently when horses shifted position in a car as the train leaned inward on the curve. Two circus employees were killed. On August 25, 1896, the Bear River Bridge, second of the four major trestles north of Colfax, burned, severing the line for about two months.

Also simultaneously with Kidder's death in 1901, an interurban, the Nevada County Traction Co., was chartered to run between the twin towns. The line diverted some local traffic, but because it was not extended, it did not prove a serious menace to the narrow gauge. The interurban was abandoned in 1925.

Upon Kidder's death, the narrow gauge passed into the hands of his widow, Sara, the principal accomplishment of whose tenure was relocation of the south end of the railroad. The annual engineering inspection for 1906 showed weakness of the Bear River trestle, and the You Bet tunnel had caved in on several occasions. To get rid of the tunnel and all four major trestles on the south end, the directors authorized a new line of 3.56 miles, crossing the Bear River downstream from the trestle, and rejoining the railroad at Coleman. At a cost of $125,907, the bypass shortened the line by two miles, and eliminated its worst grades. The new route utilized tall steel trestles for Bear River and Long Ravine, reducing both maintenance expense and fire risk. The new line was opened on December 13, 1908, but initially the old line was retained for possible use in emergencies. In 1913 the railroad made use of somewhat under a mile of the old line in the course of building a standard gauge line of 3.63 miles to a gravel pit near the Bear River. This project entailed laying third rail on about 2.6 miles of the south end of the railroad. A Climax and a Heisler geared locomotive were bought to work the standard gauge trains. The Heisler was sold in 1914, but the Climax was retained until the gravel operation was ended in 1923.

In April 1913 Sara Kidder and some of the other directors sold their controlling interest in the railroad to Walter Arnstein and Samuel L. Naphtaly, who had recently completed the Oakland, Antioch & Eastern Railroad, the interurban between Oakland and Sacramento. It was fairly universally thought that the purchase was made to allow the OA&E to extend to Nevada City, but Naphtaly denied this. The Kidder management had secured the California Railroad Commission's permission to convert the railroad in March 1913, but Naphtaly ordered an end to any such preparations. The narrow gauge suffered from highway competition in the 1920s, causing the management, which was based in San Francisco, to apply to the ICC on September 15, 1925, to abandon the railroad. Local officials and shippers formed a Committee of Twenty-One, which approached Harry A. Mitchell of the interurban, then the San Francisco–Sacramento Railroad, in an effort to return the narrow gauge to local ownership. Mitchell received permission to abandon the narrow gauge in April 1926, but he offered to sell the line to the Committee for $1 if the buyers would take over the funded debt and other obligations. While the Committee considered the offer, J. Earl Taylor of Grass Valley brought together a group of six men, who bought the railroad on Mitchell's terms on May 12, 1926.

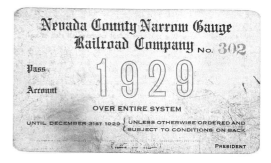

The new management proceeded in unusual fashion, buying up all of the railroad's bonds except two, and ceasing to pay interest so as to force a receivership. George Calanan became receiver on March 9, 1927. Calanan rehabilitated the property and resolved the railroad's financial difficulties, allowing the receivership to be lifted in October. Taylor became president, and made an aggressive effort to develop the line's traffic. Aided by the Railroad Commission's willingness to protect the line from truck competition, the effort was quite successful. The management bought locomotives and rolling stock from the Southern Pacific, which had converted its Nevada-California-Oregon line and was cutting back its Keeler branch. The Depression actually stimulated the railroad, for falling price levels and the increase in the mint price of gold of 1933 attracted resources to gold mining. The railroad bought Pacific Greyhound's Auburn–Nevada City franchise along with two buses in 1932, and established a trucking subsidiary in 1935. Rail passenger service, which was entirely by mixed train, was discontinued on April 4, 1938. In 1939 the management bought a rotary snowplow and built the railroad's first caboose. The railroad had retired its debt and was in good condition, but it could not long survive. The rise in the price level, including the price of scrap, early in World War II, plus restrictions on gold mining inaugurated in March 1942, caused the management to apply for abandonment on April 6, 1942. Federal and state authorities acquiesced, and the line was abandoned on July 10, 1942.

REFERENCES: Gerald M. Best, *Nevada County Narrow Gauge* (Berkeley, Calif.: Howell-North Books, 1965); Shaw, Fisher, and Harlan, *Oil Lamps and Iron Ponies*, pp. 2–21; Stanley T. Borden, "Nevada County Narrow Gauge Railroad," *The Western Railroader*, 25, no. 8, issue 272 (1962), and 26, no. 3, issue 278 (1963); Paul Darrell, "Nevada County Narrow Gauge Railroad Company," *Railroadiana Vignettes*, 1, no. 2 (1946).

North Pacific Coast Railroad

Marin County, immediately across the Golden Gate from San Francisco, was barely developed when the narrow gauge era opened in 1870. San Rafael, the county seat, was a town of 841, and most of the county was unpopulated. Communication with San Francisco was largely by schooners along the coast or on San Francisco Bay. San Rafael made connection to San Francisco via the standard gauge San Rafael & San Quentin Railroad, a 3.5-mile dummy line opened in 1870, and paddle steamers from Point San Quentin.

The North Pacific Coast Railroad was organized on December 16, 1871, mainly to develop lumbering in the redwood forests near the mouths of the Russian and Gualala rivers. Austin D. Moore and W. H. Tillinghast, owners of the Russian River Land & Lumber Co., were the principal organizers. Moore promoted the railroad very effectively, securing a favorable vote on a bond issue of $160,000 to finance the building of the line from San Rafael to Tomales, the main town in the northern portion of the county. The Board of Supervisors approved a change of the southern terminus to Saucelito (Sausalito) on February 6, 1873. Construction began in March 1873 at Strawberry Point, a promontory in Richardson Bay north of Saucelito. The terrain was difficult, requiring a tunnel of 1,250 feet about 15 miles north of Saucelito at White's Hill. The company had largely exhausted its resources by the time it holed through the tunnel on March 7, 1874. The affluent lumberman Milton S. Latham, a former governor of California, interested himself in the company as a means of developing his timberlands at the Russian River. Rails were laid from Saucelito to San Rafael (10 miles) by July 25, 1874, to satisfy a legal requirement to reach the town by August 1. The railroad connected to San Francisco via the Saucelito Land & Ferry Co. both at Saucelito and at Point San Quentin. The railroad reached Tomales (47 miles from Saucelito) on January 7, 1875. The company leased the San Rafael & San Quentin for 99 years and converted it to 3'-0" on March 31, 1875. On August 5, 1876, the company began laying rails north from Tomales, and on March 15, 1877, reached the Russian River at Moscow (Monte Rio). The river was bridged at Duncan Mills and service was opened to that point (71 miles) on May 21. The extension entailed a second major tunnel, a bore of 1,750 feet just north of Tomales.

Latham encountered financial difficulties in 1877, which led to the filing of a suit for foreclosure by James D. Walker, founder of the San Rafael & San Quentin, on December 23, 1880. Walker, with financing in San Francisco and in Britain, bought the railroad for $800,000 and reorganized it without change of name on November 24, 1881. The assets transferred to the new company included 12 locomotives, 16 passenger cars, three baggage cars, 30 boxcars, 264 flatcars, and three other cars, plus three ferryboats. As the rolling stock indicated, the company was mainly a carrier of lumber, but the recreational opportunities along Tomales Bay, which the line immediately paralleled, and in the mountainous country the railroad served made it an attraction for pleasure travelers. Walker, however, was interested almost entirely in the railroad as a facility for southern Marin County, which was gaining population rapidly. He proposed to the directors that the narrow gauge be abandoned north of San Anselmo, but his motion was voted down 4 to 3.

Meanwhile, Peter Donahue of San Francisco had bought the bankrupt and partly completed Sonoma & Marin Railroad in 1876, and was building it south to a ferry connection under the name of the San Francisco & North Pacific Railway. When he reached San Rafael with his standard gauge rails in 1880, he arranged for the North Pacific Coast to transport his passengers into San Francisco for a flat 15¢ each. In 1882 Donahue proposed to reduce the fee to 10¢, but the NPC refused. Donahue responded by extending his rails to Tiburon and establishing his ferry terminal there. The NPC, anticipating a serious rivalry for local business, improved its access to Saucelito by drilling a tunnel of over 2,100 feet through the Corte Madera Hills and approaching the ferry terminal via the west shore of Richardson Bay, abandoning the long trestle from Strawberry Point. The new line was opened February 19, 1884. Almost immediately, on February 24, the ferryboat *Saucelito* burned, destroying the wharf at San Quentin. The ship was a total loss. The disaster caused the railroad to abandon the ferry connection at San Quentin, buy out the Saucelito Land & Ferry Co. under an option of 1882, and concentrate marine operations at Saucelito.

James Walker resigned as president at the end of 1884 to return to his native England. He was succeeded by John W. Coleman. William Steele, Antoine Borel, and several other principal San Francisco financial figures became directors. The new owners had lumber holdings along Austin Creek just north of the Russian River. They organized a subsidiary, the Northern Railroad of California, to extend the line seven miles from Duncan Mills to Ingram's (Cazadero). Ground was broken in August 1885, and service began on April 1, 1886, bringing the length of the main line to 78 miles. The new company was merged into the NPC in 1892. Further extensions to the Gualala River country or to Humboldt Bay, which had been discussed, were never undertaken. In 1889 the NPC undertook a branch of two miles from May Junction (Almonte) to Eastland (Mill Valley) in southern Marin County. The line was completed in December and full service began on April 6, 1890.

The railroad again changed hands on May 20, 1893, when James B. Stetson, mainly known for his presidency of the California Street Cable Railroad, became president. Stetson ordered for 1894 delivery a large double-ended ferry, the *Sausalito*, equipped with 3'-0" tracks on her main deck. She replaced barges carrying the railroad's freight cars into San Francisco, where the State Belt Railroad maintained 3'-0" track for termination of both the North Pacific Coast and South Pacific Coast. In the same year the company built a new terminal and office building at Sausalito—the name of the town had been corrected in 1887. On January 14, 1894, locomotive No. 9 plunged through a rain-weakened trestle over Austin Creek just below Cazadero, killing seven men in the worst disaster in the railroad's history. The company suffered another major disaster on November 30, 1901, when the ferries

Sausalito and *San Rafael* collided in a tule fog near Alcatraz Island. The *San Rafael* sank in about 20 minutes with the apparent loss of four lives.

In January 1902 the railroad had another change of ownership. John Martin, who had been a pioneer in long-distance transmission of electric power, formed a syndicate that included soap manufacturer R. R. Colgate and reformed the corporation as the North Shore Railroad. Martin had little interest in the narrow gauge, but wanted to electrify the commuter lines in southern Marin. The installation was a small but technologically advanced third-rail electrification that required double-track, standard gauge rail to be laid over the southern portion of the narrow gauge. Electric trains began running from the Sausalito ferry terminal to Mill Valley on August 21, 1903, and to San Rafael on September 19. A new ferry terminal was put in service on August 5. The company discontinued service on the San Quentin branch on November 1 without ever having electrified it.

The electrification had various consequences for the narrow gauge. The management undertook several improvements so as to accommodate some heavy locomotives released from the suburban service. Most of the projects were rail replacement, but Martin, after an early inspection of the narrow gauge, resolved upon bypassing the White's Hill tunnel with its difficult approaches. The 4.74 miles from a junction north of San Geronimo to Roys were replaced by a 2.65-mile bypass with a 3,190-foot low-level bore, the Bothin tunnel. The bore was drilled to standard gauge dimensions because Martin planned to extend the electrification to Woodacre, Point Reyes, and Inverness on Tomales Bay. Actually, the electrification was never extended beyond Manor, 13 miles from Sausalito. The tunnel was completed in November 1904 and put in service on December 4.

In 1903 the company took delivery of a second car ferry, the ungainly sternwheeler *Lagunitas*. She could handle ten narrow gauge freight cars at about eight knots. With an unsheathed wooden hull, she held up poorly, but remained in service as long as the narrow gauge operated out of Sausalito.

A. W. Foster bought the North Pacific Coast from Martin's group in April 1904, possibly in the interest of the Southern Pacific. In November 1906 he conveyed the railroad to the SP, which made it part of the Northwestern Pacific Railroad upon forming the NWP jointly with the AT&SF. Initially the narrow gauge was the Shore Divi-

sion, but in 1908 it was consolidated with the Western Division into the Southern Division. The narrow gauge at this time had 12 locomotives, 52 passenger cars, and 382 freight cars, of which 150 boxcars and flatcars had been acquired from the South Pacific Coast in 1906 in the course of the latter's conversion. The narrow gauge was badly damaged by the earthquake of 1906—inevitably, since the San Andreas Fault runs through Tomales Bay, immediately parallel to the railroad. The damage was quickly repaired.

The Northwestern Pacific was a large railroad mainly devoted to the carriage of lumber. In 1909 it extended its Guerneville branch across the Russian River at Camp Vacation to tap the narrow gauge's principal origination territory. Third rail was laid along the narrow gauge into Duncan Mills. Most of the lumber was diverted to the standard gauge line. The transit shed for transshipment between standard and narrow gauge at San Anselmo was expanded, and in 1910 3'-0" rail was removed from the car ferries; thus movement of narrow gauge cars into San Francisco was ended. In 1911 narrow gauge rail was taken up on the electrified Mill Valley and San Rafael lines and the San Quentin branch. In 1920 the company extended standard gauge without electrification to Point Reyes at the head of Tomales Bay. The last narrow gauge train left Sausalito on April 5, 1920. On September 9, 1926, the northernmost seven miles from Duncan Mills to Cazadero were standard gauged. The surviving narrow gauge trackage was served by a daily mixed train between Point Reyes and Camp Meeker, but patronage was very light.

In response to a complaint by a civic group, the California Public Utilities Commission in 1927 investigated the narrow gauge and found its condition adequate but its revenue potential poor. The Commission recommended abandonment and substitution of trucks and buses. The NWP applied to the ICC to abandon the line on December 28, 1928. The Marin County government opposed the application, preferring conversion. The NWP considered this option impractical because of the curvature and extensive trestles. The ICC approved abandonment in February 1930, and the last train ran on March 29.

The AT&SF withdrew from joint ownership of the Northwestern Pacific in 1929, leaving the railroad as a Southern Pacific subsidiary. The line from Manor to Point Reyes was abandoned in 1933. The suburban electrification and ferry service were severely hurt by the opening of the Golden Gate Bridge in 1937, and were discontinued on February 28, 1941.

REFERENCES: Gilbert H. Kneiss, *Redwood Railways* (Berkeley, Calif.: Howell-North Books, 1956); A. Bray Dickinson, *Narrow Gauge to the Redwoods* (Los Angeles: Trans-Anglo Books, 1967); Wald Sievers, "North Pacific Coast Railroad," *The Western Railroader*, 28, no. 10, issue 321 (1966); idem, "North Shore Railroad," *The Western Railroader*, 30, no. 1, issue 323 (1967); Fred A. Stindt, "Northwestern Pacific Railroad Narrow Gauge," *The Western Railroader*, 31, no. 12, issue 346 (1968); idem, *Trains to the Russian River* (Kelseyville, Calif.: Fred A. Stindt, 1974); Shaw, Fisher, and Harlan, *Oil Lamps and Iron Ponies*, pp. 38–63; George H. Harlan and Clement Fisher, Jr., *Of Walking Beams and Paddle Wheels* (San Francisco: Bay Books, 1951), pp. 76–109; George H. Harlan, *San Francisco Bay Ferryboats* (Berkeley, Calif.: Howell-North Books, 1967), pp. 131–41.

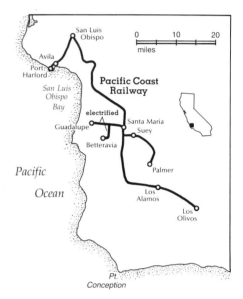

Pacific Coast Railway

San Luis Obispo, which became the division point between San Francisco and Los Angeles on the Southern Pacific's coast line, was dependent upon steamers along the Pacific coast before the SP arrived in 1884. Connection to the ocean was made by road either to Morro Bay on the northwest or to San Luis Bay to the south. To develop San Luis Bay, John Harford and his associates formed in 1868 the Peoples Wharf Co., which built a warehouse and a 2'-6" horse railroad to a wharf in the lee of Point San Luis where the water was deep enough for ocean shipping. The project was completed in September 1873. In the same year the San Luis Obispo Railroad failed to build a gauge-compatible steam railroad to the city. Rather, Charles Goodall of San Francisco, a coastal steamship operator, secured a charter on March 2, 1974, for the San Luis

Gerald M. Best photographed this short freight of the Pacific Coast on his visit to the railroad in 1941. (California State Railroad Museum.)

Obispo & Santa Maria Valley Railroad to run, as the title indicates, from San Luis Bay to the agricultural area in the Santa Maria Valley. The charter provided for an extension to Santa Barbara. The Avila brothers, associates of Goodall, announced plans to develop the town of Avila on San Luis Bay. Goodall bought out both Harford and the promoters of the San Luis Obispo Railroad, and proceeded to build his railroad. The line was opened between San Luis Obispo and Avila (8 miles) in August 1876. An extension of two miles from Avila to Port Harford (Port San Luis) on the grade of Harford's horse railroad was opened on December 11. This arrangement was never satisfactory, for the line had difficult grades and a short tunnel.

Goodall pressed the line southward in 1881, organizing construction under the Pacific Coast Railroad for consistency with his Pacific Coast Steamship Co. Tracks reached Arroyo Grande (25.5 miles), the next major town, by the end of the year, with passenger service beginning on December 10, 1881. Service was established to Central City, which was shortly to be renamed Santa Maria (42 miles), on June 1, 1882. Because the Southern Pacific was not to serve Santa Maria, the town became the most important on-line point.

Meanwhile, Henry Villard of the Northern Pacific had bought control of the Pacific Coast Steamship Co. and the railroad. The new management also replaced the line on Harford's grade with a new one on a fill and trestle below. The replacement, which entailed an extension of the pier at Port Harford and a warehouse at the tip, was opened in March 1883. Villard merged the SLO &

SMV and the PCRR into a new Pacific Coast Railway, which opened the line southward to Los Alamos (64 miles) on October 10. The railroad proved quite prosperous, serving a rapidly growing agricultural area that was still without important alternatives. Mainly for similar development to the south, the line was extended to Los Olivos (76 miles) on November 16, 1887. The line was about 36 miles short of Santa Barbara, but confronted with a serious mountain barrier. The building of the Southern Pacific into Santa Barbara from the south ended any prospect of extension. At about this time, Edwin Goodall of San Francisco, whose firm of Goodall, Perkins & Co. served as the agent of the railroad and steamship company in San Francisco, and J. Millard Fillmore, the railroad's general manager, organized a horsecar line of 2.5 miles from the station in San Luis Obispo to the center of the town. The street railway was sold to a local group in 1891.

Along with the steamship company and other subsidiaries of the Oregon Improvement Co., the railroad was placed in receivership in 1895. The property was sold under foreclosure on November 6, 1897, and reorganized without change of name as a subsidiary of the Pacific Coast Co., as Oregon Improvement's former properties became known. The announcement of plans to build a plant of the Union Sugar Co. at Betteravia motivated the railroad in 1898 to build a branch of four miles to the town from a point on the main line south of

Santa Maria. The Southern Pacific built a line to the plant for outbound movements. After the plant opened in 1899, sugar beets became the railroad's principal cargo, especially after 1901, when completion of the SP's coast line diverted much of the general cargo, and most of the long-distance passengers. Oil strikes at Careaga and Graciosa on the line below Santa Maria just after the turn of the century created a boom in the area. Because the oil boom and the interurban era coincided, citizens of Santa Maria sought an electric line to the SP coast line, which had bypassed the town by about eight miles to the west. Since most of the narrow gauge's remaining passenger service was from the SP at San Luis Obispo to Santa Maria, the management agreed to build an electrified branch from Santa Maria to the SP's Guadalupe station. The branch was undertaken in 1906, but because of the diversion of maintenance-of-way gangs to repairs on the north end of the railroad, was not completed until March 1909. The project included a new electrified three-mile branch opened in June 1909, from the interurban line into Betteravia from the north, replacing the former one from the east. About two miles of the main line south from Santa Maria and a branch of four miles east to Suey built in 1907 were also electrified, so that sugar beets could be moved behind electric locomotives from Suey to the Union Sugar plant. The Suey branch was extended without electrification 11 miles to Palmer in

Pacific Coast No. 110 at the tank at Santa Maria in 1941. (G. M. Best, California State Railroad Museum.)

1913. Initially, electric locomotives hauled the passenger trains to Guadalupe, but in 1912 the company installed a center-entrance interurban car built by the Cincinnati Car Co.

The chartering of the Santa Maria Valley Railroad in 1911 as a standard gauge rival to the PC caused the latter's management to announce plans to convert the electrified line and the projected extension to Palmer, but the plan was not carried out. Rather, the electrification survived until 1928, when the interurban service to Guadalupe was discontinued. The sugar factory at Betteravia had been closed temporarily a year earlier. The railroad remained profitable, largely with gravel movements for highway building in the area from a quarry at Sisquoc on the Palmer line. The spread of hard-surfaced roads diverted much of the railroad's remaining traffic. The company closed the southernmost 12 miles of the main line beyond Los Alamos in 1933, although the line was not formally abandoned until 1936. The remainder of the railroad survived for five years. The management applied to the ICC on April 21, 1941, to abandon the line south of San Luis Obispo and received permission on December 20. The line was torn up in January 1942. The track north of San Luis Obispo was sold to the Bell Oil Co., which organized the Port San Luis Transportation Co. but took over no equipment and never operated. It sold the rail for scrap in October.

REFERENCES: Shaw, Fisher, and Harlan, *Oil Lamps and Iron Ponies*, pp. 136–53; Gerald M. Best, *Ships and Narrow Gauge Rails: The Story of the Pacific Coast Company* (Berkeley, Calif.: Howell-North Books, 1964), pp. 10–97.

Pajaro Valley Consolidated Railroad

Sugar king Claus Spreckels wanted transport services for his plant at Watsonville, both to bring in beets and to ship out the raw sugar to his refinery on the San Francisco waterfront for final processing. He had chronic disputes with the Southern Pacific and sought an alternative. He was already operating the Oceanic Steamship Co. between his installations in California and Hawaii. He conceived of a narrow gauge railroad to serve the beet fields, the plant, and the Pacific Coast Steamship Company's Moss Landing near the mouth of the Salinas River on Monterey Bay. Because he was trying to minimize interchange with the SP, his was probably one of the most defensible choices of a narrow gauge.

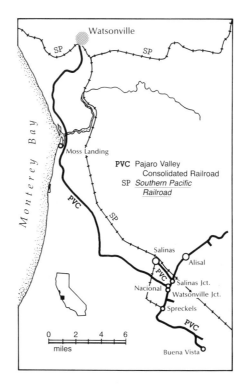

PVC Pajaro Valley Consolidated Railroad
SP *Southern Pacific Railroad*

The narrow gauge was incorporated in January 1890—less than two years after the opening of the Watsonville plant—as the Pajaro Valley Railroad, empowered to build from Watsonville to Salinas. All of the stock was held by the Spreckels family or directors of Spreckels's several sugar companies. Some of the rails and equipment were bought from predecessors of the Northwestern Pacific in the process of conversion, and some were new. The line was completed from Watsonville to Moss Landing and Moro Cojo (12 miles) in the summer of 1890. The line was pressed on to Tucker, immediately west of Salinas (24 miles), in the summer of 1891.

The operation proved only too successful. Traffic quickly outgrew the original pair of Baldwin 2-4-2T locomotives, and the company moved on to Baldwin 2-6-0 tender engines. Local agricultural products were handled in addition to the beets, and general cargo was received from the SP at Watsonville. On September 3, 1896, Spreckels announced plans for a new plant for both initial processing and refining, to be built at a site about four miles southwest of Salinas. A town, Spreckels, was planned at the factory site, but Spreckels took care not to make it a typical company town in which the mill operator owned the housing, store, and other facilities. The big new project necessarily entailed extension of the rail lines, for which on April 16, 1897, the Pajaro Valley Extension Railroad was incorporated. The new entity built an extension of the main line southwest to Spreckels

(27 miles) and a branch of five miles to a quarry at Alisal from which limestone used in the refining process was extracted. On December 9, 1897, the new corporation was merged with the old into the Pajaro Valley Consolidated Railroad. Simultaneously, Spreckels was consolidating his several sugar corporations into the Spreckels Sugar Co. The railroad expanded its rosters of locomotives and equipment. Upon completion, the new plant was the largest sugar factory in the world, and the railroad had gross revenues of over $100,000 per year. In 1902 the railroad operated three mixed trains per day between Watsonville and Spreckels, and two additional trains between Watsonville and Moss Landing.

When the refinery at Spreckels became fully operational, the sugar company began to phase out the plant at Watsonville. The effect was to shift the railroad's center of operations southward. The Alisal branch was extended 1.7 miles in 1902 to serve some feedlots for cattle. At the same time, an extension of the main line of six miles from Spreckels to Buena Vista for additional beet origination was proposed, but acrimonious relations with local farmers prevented its being undertaken until 1905. In 1908 a spur of two miles was built along the SP from a point on the Alisal branch into Salinas to provide passenger service with a tank engine between Salinas and Spreckels. An independent steam dummy line, the Salinas Railway, had provided such service by another route from 1897 to 1900, but had failed and been abandoned. The only addition to this mileage was the five miles of the Watsonville Railway & Navigation Co., a 3'-0" interurban between Watsonville and a wharf at Port Watsonville on Monterey Bay, which, along with an affiliated steamship operation, was intended to provide service to San Francisco in rivalry to the SP. The interurban had been built as the Watsonville Transportation Co. in 1904, but went bankrupt in 1905 and was reorganized in 1911. It failed again in 1913, but was leased briefly to the PVC in that year before being abandoned. There is no record of operation.

The PVC peaked immediately after World War I, carrying 158,871 passengers in 1919 and grossing $135,218 in 1920, but it declined rapidly thereafter. The outermost three miles of the Alisal branch were abandoned in 1920. The Salinas-Spreckels passenger trains were discontinued on November 24, 1925. The mixed trains on the main line were reduced to an irregular seasonal operation. The Pacific Coast Steamship Co. gave up service to Moss Landing in the 1920s as well. The Spreckels interests applied to abandon the railroad, and received permission from the ICC on October 10, 1928, and from the California Railroad Commission on April 2, 1929. The railroad was sold to the Southern Pacific for the nominal sum of $10, allowing the SP to realize the scrap value of the property in return for removing it.

REFERENCES: Shaw, Fisher, and Harlan, *Oil Lamps and Iron Ponies*, pp. 154–71; Horace W. Fabing and Rick Hamman, *Steinbeck Country Narrow Gauge* (Boulder, Colo.: Pruett Publishing Co., 1985).

Patterson & Western Railroad

Demands for manganese, chrome, and other nonferrous metals in the World War I era brought forth this short-lived narrow gauge on the western edge of California's Central Valley. In 1915 when the war cut off foreign supplies of these ores, exploitation of deposits at the head of Del Puerto Canyon in the Diablo Range west of Patterson on the Southern Pacific became economic. Elwyn Hoffman, editor of Patterson's newspaper, and Howard Broughton, president of the California Manganese Co., arranged financing of a railroad among Hawaiian investors. They established a parent company, Mineral Products Co., which provided $150,000 for building of the Patterson & Western Railroad. Narrow gauge was attractive because of the availability of equipment from the North Pacific Coast, which had been partly converted. Two small Shay locomotives were bought. The railroad began carrying ore on September 20, 1916, and was completed to Jones, 23.6 miles from Patterson, on March 17, 1917. Although the railroad was registered as a common carrier with the California Railroad Commission and as a circular road with the ICC, it was in fact almost wholly a facility for moving ore from mines at Jones at the head of the valley to a newly built processing plant of the Mineral Products Co. in Patterson. The railroad reported itself to the state commission as a freight-service-only line, but actually carried passengers in an auto-track car.

With the decline in prices of ores following the war, the railroad became uneconomic and was closed on August 14, 1920.

REFERENCE: R. D. Ranger, Jr., "Patterson & Western Railroad," *The Western Railroader*, 48, no. 518 (1985).

San Gabriel Valley Rapid Transit Railway

The real estate boom of the 1880s in Southern California brought forth this large steam dummy line. H. A. Unruh and his associates secured a charter for the corporation on July 29, 1887, and undertook construction in August. The line was opened on May 25, 1888, from Aliso and Anderson streets in Brooklyn Heights to Monrovia (17 miles). A projected high trestle across the Los Angeles River to bring the line into a depot at Aliso and Los Angeles streets, near the present Union Station, was not completed. Passengers connected for the center of the city by omnibus. In 1889 a branch was added from Ramona Street (at Shorb) to the Raymond Hotel in Pasadena (7 miles), but it proved unprofitable and was abandoned after a few months. In spite of the line's considerable length, it was operated with only two Baldwin 0-4-0 dummy engines. It enjoyed appreciable freight traffic in general cargo to a rapidly growing area and in oranges from local groves.

In the spring of 1892 the management arranged to lease the line for one year to the Los Angeles Terminal Railway, which already operated a comprehensive network of standard gauge steam dummy lines about Southern California. The lease became effective when the SGVRT converted its main line. The management shut it down on June 5 and turned it over to the Terminal Railway as a standard gauge line on June 13, 1892. The Terminal Railway, which had already leased the right-of-way of the abandoned branch to use a small portion for its terminal trackage in Pasadena, acquired title to the branch's right-of-way. Upon expiration of the lease the line was sold to the Southern Pacific, which began replacing the old narrow gauge bridges and otherwise upgrading the physical plant. In 1894 the SP sold the portion from Los Angeles to Shorb in Alhambra for street railway use and applied for a franchise for a branch from Shorb to Pasadena, to replace the dummy line's branch. The Monrovia line was abandoned in 1944. The SP's Pasadena branch was abandoned about 1964.

REFERENCES: Best, "Early Steam Suburban Railroads in Los Angeles," pp. 25–26; Charles Seims, *Trolley Days in Pasadena* (San Marino, Calif.: Golden West Books, 1982), pp. 49, 126.

San Joaquin & Sierra Nevada Railroad

The dissatisfaction of grain farmers with the rates of the Southern Pacific Railroad brought forth several projects for railroads between the old gold country of Calaveras County and some point on the Sacramento River system. Stockton was unattractive because of a proposed storage tax on grain. Jacob Brack, who owned 10,000 acres of swampland west of Lodi, proposed to create a port by driving a 50-foot-wide channel for two miles up the Mokelumne River and Hog Slough. He completed the project in 1881 and named his port Brack's Landing. Meanwhile, James B. Sperry, owner of Calaveras Big Trees, a tourist grove in the area, sought a railroad to eliminate a 50-mile stage trip. Brack, Sperry, and a Sacramento investor, Frederick Birdsall, formed the San Joaquin & Sierra Nevada Railroad

The San Joaquin & Sierra Nevada's passenger train awaits the main line train connection with Southern Pacific narrow gauge locomotive No. 1026. (Ed Bond collection.)

in 1881 and secured a charter on March 28, 1882. The narrow gauge was built from Woodbridge on the Southern Pacific west to Brack's Landing (11 miles) and east to Lodi and Wallace (20 miles) in 1882. Construction farther east was quite difficult; the railroad reached Burson in 1884 and Valley Springs in April 1885. As completed, the railroad was 40 miles long. It had three locomotives, a baggage car, a combine, a coach, 15 boxcars, 48 flatcars, and 12 other pieces of rolling stock. The railroad reportedly cost $409,570 for right-of-way and track, plus $63,420 for equipment. The company ran two trains per day, connecting with Southern Pacific passenger trains at Lodi. Steamers ran from Brack's Landing to San Francisco (87 miles) on alternate days.

Upon Birdsall's death his widow was eager to liquidate the estate's equity in the railroad. The directors as a consequence decided to sell the line to the Southern Pacific effective May 15, 1888. The SP diverted the line's freight to itself at Lodi, and abandoned the Woodbridge–Brack's Landing portion in 1897. The remainder was converted on August 31, 1904. As a standard gauge, the branch was extended 13 miles from Valley Springs to Kentucky House in 1926. The branch was announced as a candidate for abandonment in 1985. The Lodi-Woodbridge remnant was abandoned in 1984.

REFERENCE: Fred A. Stindt, "San Joaquin & Sierra Nevada RR," *The Western Railroader*, 19, no. 6, issue 198 (1956).

Santa Cruz Railroad

Frederick A. Hihn, a local lumber operator and real estate dealer, conceived of a connection from Santa Cruz to the Southern Pacific near Watsonville as early as 1866, but was unable to finance the project as a standard gauge railroad. The supervisors of Santa Cruz County submitted a proposed subsidy of $6,000 per mile in county bonds to a vote on December 11, 1871. In spite of opposition in Watsonville, where the populace saw little to be gained from the railroad, the bond issue passed. Again, however, the project could not be financed. Hihn associated himself with Claus Spreckels, the sugar producer, and again secured a favorable vote on a bond issue of $6,000 per mile on November 5, 1872. This time the project was explicitly for a narrow gauge. Named the Santa Cruz Railroad, it was incorporated June 18, 1873. Watsonville, remaining hostile to the project, refused permission to use the streets of the town. As a consequence, the railroad terminated at Pajaro Junction on the south bank of the Pajaro River about a half mile east of the town. The route required a bridge over the river and a succession of culverts or trestles across small streams that emptied into the Pacific Ocean. By December 12, 1874, the company had completed the five miles necessary for taking possession of the county's bonds. A state court enjoined delivery of the bonds on the ground that a recent change in state law had raised a question whether the county's obligation was legal. In February 1875 Santa Cruz granted the railroad a right-of-way into the city along the beachfront. A

year later the injunction against issuance of the county bonds was lifted, and funds were thus provided for completion of the railroad. On May 7, 1876, the first train arrived in Santa Cruz. Regular service began the following week. The railroad was operated with two Baldwin 4-4-0 locomotives and an earlier 0-4-0 that had been used in construction. Initially, one mixed train per day was operated, but two became standard. During the summer about half a mile of track was relocated to pass through Watsonville. The change brought the railroad's mileage to 21.5, about 2.5 miles more than the county government had agreed to subsidize. Hihn brought a legal action, contending that because the Watsonville relocation had been made at the county's request, subsidy should be extended to the total mileage. The suit was to be in the courts for eight years.

The railroad was principally a carrier of lumber, but the volume was below initial expectations. The route along the Pacific Ocean proved to be afflicted with continual washouts of trestles during California's characteristic winter rains. The railroad was initially reported to be profitable, but had ceased to be so by 1878. When Hihn assessed stockholders $10 per share, he alienated Spreckels, producing an irreconcilable split in the management. The directors took Spreckels to court to collect the assessment, but Spreckels responded with claims of mismanagement. In August 1880 the court found for Spreckels. In December the California Supreme Court held that the county need not deliver to the railroad the bonds at issue in the earlier case.

Meanwhile, the Southern Pacific aban-

The Santa Cruz Railroad's *Jupiter* served in Latin America after its short service in California. It survives as an exhibit in the Smithsonian Institution.

doned the former Monterey & Salinas Valley in favor of a replacement standard gauge line in January 1880. The South Pacific Coast began direct narrow gauge service from Oakland to Santa Cruz in May 1880. These various forces working against the railroad caused it to cease operating about February 1881. Hihn announced his retirement as president, and on April 28 reported that he had sold his interest to Leland Stanford and associates in the Southern Pacific. The SP restored service, but in 1882 began preparations for conversion, at length effected in November 1883. Hihn continued his effort to secure the county bonds, finally winning in the U.S. Supreme Court in May 1884.

The line became the Southern Pacific's Santa Cruz branch and remains in operation. The narrow gauge's locomotive *Jupiter*, after service in Central America, became a display piece and is currently in the Arts and Industries building of the Smithsonian Institution.

REFERENCE: Charles S. McCaleb, "The Santa Cruz Railroad," *The Western Railroader*, 38, issue 324 (1975).

A South Pacific Coast crew poses with its locomotive. (Louis Stein collection, California State Railroad Museum.)

Sonoma Valley Railroad

The first effort to connect Sonoma with San Pablo Bay was the Sonoma Valley Prismoidal Railway, a monorail promoted in 1876. The project achieved some three miles of line from a steamer landing at Norfolk, and operated briefly. The experiment failed in May 1877. Joseph S. Kohn, the principal promoter of the monorail, formed the Sonoma Valley Railroad in July of 1878 to assume the assets of the former corporation. The new company did so in September and began building a conventional 3'-0" railroad. Kohn shortly exhausted his funds, and Peter Donahue of the San Francisco & North Pacific acquired control of the line in 1879. The railroad was completed in 1878–79 for 15 miles from Sonoma Landing, a pier between Sonoma and Petaluma creeks, to Sonoma. A station and maintenance facilities were established in downtown Sonoma. The railroad had three Baldwin locomotives, an 0-4-2T and two 4-4-0s. In 1881 the company organized a subsidiary, the Sonoma & Santa Rosa Railroad, to build six miles north along Sonoma Creek to Glen Ellen. The extension was opened in 1882, and merged into the Sonoma Valley in 1885. The railroad carried mainly agricultural products and basalt from the Schocken quarry.

In 1886 the management organized a second subsidiary, the Marin & Napa Railroad, to build from Sears Point, about three miles above Sonoma Landing, to Ignacio on the SF&NP main line. The narrow gauge connection of somewhat under eight miles was built in 1887–88. Thereafter, passengers for Sonoma used the SF&NP from Tiburon, changing at Ignacio, and the line to Sonoma Landing was used only for freight.

In March 1889 James Donahue completed purchase of the Sonoma Valley and the Marin & Napa for merger into the SF&NP. Donahue would doubtless have moved to convert the line in any case, but he was under legal compulsion to make a major relocation in Sonoma. In 1882, with the permission of the county supervisors, the railroad had built on Spain Street past the property of Henry Weyl. Weyl argued that his permission should have been secured, and won his case in 1883. The railroad lost an appeal to the California Supreme Court in 1886, and was ordered to move the line. Work on conversion began at Ignacio on November 30, 1889, and was completed by April 1890. The line to Sonoma Landing was abandoned. The terminal facilities in Sonoma were moved about a block north in the course of the relocation.

The line became the Sonoma Valley branch of the Northwestern Pacific in 1907. The branch was abandoned in a large number of short segments between 1934 and 1975, but the 16 miles from Ignacio to Schellville remain in service as the connection between the Northwestern Pacific and the Southern Pacific.

REFERENCES: Kneiss, *Redwood Railways*, pp. 64–68; Robert D. Parmelee, "Sonoma Valley Railroad," *The Western Railroader*, 25, no. 9, issue 273 (1962); Wald Sievers, "Sonoma Valley Prismoidal Railway," *The Western Railroader*, 22, no. 3, issue 231 (1959).

South Pacific Coast Railroad

Senator James G. Fair, the Nevada mining magnate, conceived this railroad as providing two functions. First, it was to connect the San Francisco Bay Area with Santa Cruz, serving lumbering and mining enterprises in the Santa Cruz Mountains south of San Jose, as well as the resort at the terminus. Second, it was to be driven east to a connection with the Denver & Rio Grande, probably at Grand Junction, Colorado. Only the first of the two lines was ever built, but the plan to build the second resulted in the railroad's odd geographical pattern of leaving San Francisco via a ferry to Alameda in the East Bay in order to reach Santa Cruz, a point on the Pacific Coast. In addition, the project was integral with real estate development of the town of Newark, which Fair named after the birthplace in New Jersey of his principal associate, Alfred E. Davis.

The *Newark*'s enormous 42-foot wheels were intended for fast trips between San Francisco and Dumbarton Point. They were replaced with 29-foot ones for her San Francisco–Alameda service in 1901-2. (Roy D. Graves and George H. Harlan collections.)

The railroad was chartered on March 25, 1876. Construction began with a branch of 4.5 miles from Dumbarton Point to Newark. At least transitionally, the plan was to connect with San Francisco via a ferry from Dumbarton Point. The branch was completed in 1876, and in 1877 the company took delivery of a 284-foot double-ended sidewheel ferry, *Newark*, built with 42-foot wheels in hopes of making exceptionally fast trips down the bay. She carried construction materials to Dumbarton Point and ran several excursions.

Construction proceeded south from Newark, reaching San Jose by the end of 1877. The line was opened from Park Street, Alameda, to Los Gatos on March 20, 1878. The railroad was pushed north along Encinal Avenue to a ferry slip at Alameda Point on June 1, 1878. A second ferry, *Bay City*, was launched on May 18, and a third, *Garden City*, followed on June 20, 1879. The ferry line was popularly known as "the narrow gauge," even long after conversion. Completion of the railroad to Santa Cruz entailed some very difficult construction, including four tunnels, the longest of which were 6,155 and 5,800 feet, respectively. The entire main line of 75.3 miles was completed on May 15, 1880. The opening was celebrated with a picnic at Big Trees, just north of Santa Cruz, but the ceremony turned into a disaster when the train from Alameda derailed, killing 14 people. The railroad had cost $11,500,000, or $110,576 per mile— exceptionally high for a narrow gauge. With the main line completed, the Dumbarton branch served no further purpose and was abandoned in 1880. There was yet some construction to be done at the north end. Fair secured permission to use a municipal bridge over San Antonio Creek at the foot of Webster Street and on May 30, 1881, established service to 12th and Webster in Oakland. This line was extended on October 1, 1886, to 14th and Franklin.

Suburban trains operated out of both the Alameda ferry terminal and Oakland. The narrow gauge trains and the Alameda ferry could beat the Southern Pacific's time from downtown Oakland to San Francisco by about eight minutes. On March 15, 1884, Fair extended the line about 2.5 miles out of San Francisco Bay to a new ferry terminal that he called the Alameda Mole. He was given to organizing his construction by subsidiary corporations; the Alameda Mole was organized as the San Francisco & Colorado River Railroad. That terminal was all that the line projected to a connection with the D&RG ever attained.

At the south end, Fair in 1884–85 built a branch from Felton 7.5 miles northwest to Boulder Creek. A private carrier ran an additional five miles to Doherty's Mill. The entire area was a major center of redwood lumbering, and the branch proved to be one of the railroad's principal sources of traffic. The railroad's other branch was 9.5 miles from Campbell on the main line south of San Jose to Almaden, opened June 15, 1886. The line was essentially a long spur to service the New Almaden Mine, the largest producer of mercury in California.

The railroad was integral to two transit operations. The company owned a three-mile horsecar line from Newark to Centerville, which, in spite of Fair's general practice, appears to have had no separate corporate identity. It was opened on February 18, 1882. The line handled freight in horse-drawn narrow gauge equipment. In Oakland itself, Fair promoted the Oakland Cable Railway, which ran from Seventh and Broadway out San Pablo Avenue to Park Street in Emeryville, where the line connected with the California & Nevada Railroad. The cable line was opened on November 19, 1886.

As completed, the railroad was an attractive one. From Alameda to San Jose the line ran along flats on the eastern shore of San Francisco Bay, west of the Southern Pacific's own Oakland–San Jose line. Newark, the SPC's shop city, developed industrially. The Carter Brothers car works became a specialist in narrow gauge equipment. The line south of San Jose, though it required a climb in either direction to an altitude of about 900 feet at Wright, was a productive source of lumber and minerals. The three-rail yard operated jointly with the Southern Pacific at San Jose became the most important interchange facility on the railroad. The company was the most profitable narrow gauge on the West Coast.

Inevitably, the Southern Pacific became interested in acquiring the property, and leased it in 1887. Fair first reorganized his railroad as the South Pacific Coast Railway on May 23, 1887, absorbing his several subsidiaries. He then leased the new corporation to the SP on July 1 for 55 years for $5.5 million. The SP bought the Oakland Cable Railway on the same date. At the time of the transfer, the narrow gauge had 22 locomotives, 687 cars, 95 miles of track, three operating ferryboats, and one ferry abuilding. The fourth ferry was the *En-*

A South Pacific Coast passenger train on the San Lorenzo River bridge north of Santa Cruz about 1880. (Cornelius W. Hauck collection.)

A South Pacific Coast passenger train at Boulder Creek. (Louis Stein collection, California State Railroad Museum.)

cinal, a double-ended sidewheeler like the rest. Like the *Garden City*, she carried narrow gauge tracks on her main deck. The two ferries enabled the railroad to land narrow gauge cars in San Francisco for unloading on the State Belt Railroad or for further transfer to the North Pacific Coast at Sausalito.

The Southern Pacific ran the narrow gauge for about 20 years, making relatively few changes in the operation. In 1895 the bridge at the foot of Webster Street in Oakland was replaced by a dual-gauge facility at Harrison Street. A fire at the Alameda Mole on November 20, 1902, destroyed the ferry terminal and 31 narrow gauge cars. The terminal was replaced with a handsome classical structure, but the loss of so much narrow gauge equipment gave the SP an incentive to hasten conversion. Local service out of the terminal on Encinal Avenue was thereafter handled by standard gauge equipment and only the long-distance trains to San Jose and Santa Cruz were narrow gauge. Third rail for standard gauge had been placed on Encinal Avenue earlier in 1902.

The SP moved slowly to convert the main line. In fact, the management had sent equipment from converted SP narrow gauges elsewhere to the SPC line. The first serious efforts at conversion, the laying of third rail from San Jose into the Los Gatos area, dated from 1898. Widening of tunnels began in 1903. In 1905 the company sent some SPC equipment to Nevada to help deal with the Tonopah mining boom. Early in 1906 the SP built a connection of about

1.5 miles from Elmhurst on the former Central Pacific to West San Leandro on the SPC to allow standard gauge passenger trains off the SPC to terminate at Oakland Mole after conversion and to allow standard gauge freights an access to San Jose more direct than the SP line via Niles and Milpitas.

Preparations were complete by spring 1906. The line from Alameda to Los Gatos was to be converted on April 18, 1906. The work had hardly begun when the earthquake of 1906 hit the area at 5:12 A.M., causing particular havoc in the Santa Cruz Mountains where the San Andreas Fault crossed the line directly. The bridge across San Leandro Bay approaching Alameda was also badly damaged. The disaster proved to prolong the life of the narrow gauge, for its equipment lent itself to reconstruction of the south end. The SP was able to begin standard gauge service from Oakland to San Jose in 1906, but it retained narrow gauge rail from the Newark shops to the mountain area for more than a year. The tunnel at Wright, which had shifted about five feet, had to be rebored. Narrow gauge cars carried out the stone. The last narrow gauge operation was about January 1908. The Newark shops were then closed and the line became part of the SP's extensive trackage in the area. Because of the former narrow gauge's difficult crossing of the mountain barrier, the SP preferred to use the former Santa Cruz Railroad for access to the lumber mills at the south end of the line. The SP actively promoted passenger service to Santa Cruz on the former SPC with its Sun Tan Specials until the auto-

mobile had diverted most of the traffic. In 1934 the Boulder Creek branch was abandoned, along with the outer portion of the Almaden branch. The remainder of the latter followed in 1937. The last passenger train ran to Santa Cruz on March 4, 1940, and the mountain crossing from Los Gatos to Olympia was abandoned. The remainder from Olympia to Santa Cruz was sold in 1985 to F. Norman Clark, owner of the Roaring Camp & Big Trees Narrow Gauge Railroad at Felton, for development as a short line and tourist railroad.

The former narrow gauge line on Encinal Avenue in Alameda was electrified in 1911 in the course of the SP's massive suburban electrification in the East Bay. The line into 14th and Franklin in downtown Oakland became a streetcar line. The suburban network began to decline with the conversion of the public to automotive transportation in the 1920s. The streetcar line was discontinued on December 27, 1923, in the face of pressure from the War Department to get rid of the Harrison Street Bridge. The Encinal Avenue line and the Alameda ferry continued to interchange at the Alameda Mole until the Bay Bridge, opened late in 1936, drastically altered travel habits in the East Bay. The ferry was abandoned in the early hours of Sunday, January 15, 1939, and the trains were rerouted via Fernside at the south end of Alameda to a junction with the company's Seventh Street, Oakland, line at Fruitvale. The trains then proceeded to San Francisco via the new Bridge Railway built on the lower deck of the Bay Bridge. The SP had formed a subsidiary, the Interurban Electric Railway, in 1934, in expectation of this change. The Bridge Railway brought trains of the Interurban Electric, Key System, and Sacramento Northern into the new East Bay Terminal in San Francisco. The change, however impressive as a matter of engineering, increased the travel time of the great majority of riders from Alameda. Patronage of the Encinal Avenue line declined drastically; it was among the earliest abandonments in the dissolution of the Interurban Electric system. The last train ran early on January 18, 1941.

REFERENCES: Bruce A. MacGregor, *South Pacific Coast* (Berkeley, Calif.: Howell-North Books, 1968); *idem, Narrow Gauge Portrait South Pacific Coast* (Felton, Calif.: Glenwood Publishers, 1975); *idem, South Pacific Coast: A Centennial* (Boulder, Colo.: Pruett Publishing Co., 1982); Shaw, Fisher, and Harlan, *Oil Lamps and Iron Ponies*, pp. 92–111; Robert S. Ford, *Red Trains in the East Bay* (Glendale, Calif.: Interurbans, 1977).

The first Butte & Plumas Railway was organized as a common carrier in 1905 but dissolved voluntarily on September 24, 1906, apparently because its projected route of about 55 miles from Oroville to the junction of the North Fork and East Branch of the Feather River conflicted with the intended route of the Western Pacific. The second Butte & Plumas Railway was incorporated in June 1910 by O. C. Haslett and other officers of the Truckee Lumber Co. after the WP reneged on an agreement to haul logs from a lumber railroad of the company 12 miles east of Oroville into the town. The railroad was incorporated as a common carrier and reportedly operated in that nominal capacity in 1911 and 1912. The line was projected from Oroville north to Stanwood, about 30 miles, but achieved a main line of not over 24 miles. In 1913 the property was taken over by the West Side Lumber Co. and shut down. The Swayne Lumber Co. bought the entire lumber operation in 1917 and restored the railroad as a private carrier. It operated as late as 1939.

The California Central Narrow Gauge Railroad was projected in 1873 from a steamboat landing at Benicia north through Vacaville (30 miles) and along the west side of the Sacramento River valley to Tehama (175 miles). Some work was done on the Benicia terminal. It was hoped to have the railroad opened to Vacaville by June 1, 1874, but the project failed. A Colonel Howland of St. Louis revived the enterprise in 1875, but also failed to advance it.

The Stockton & Ione was organized on February 13, 1873, by E. S. Holden in the intention of building a line of about 40 miles from tidewater at Stockton to a field of lignite at Ione City in Amador County. The promoters' intention was to haul lignite in dump cars behind Mason Bogie locomotives. Two Bogies were ordered and the railroad took delivery of about 300 tons of rail. The management reported that it graded 12 miles from Stockton to Linden, the principal intermediate town, late in 1874. In the spring of 1875 Edgar Mills, president of the Eureka & Palisade, bought the stock of rail as a quick source of iron for his railroad in Nevada. The S&I later in 1875 took delivery of another 150 tons of rail along with the Mason Bogies, and prepared to begin laying track. A suit by contractor H. B. Platt brought the project to an end, however. The completed grade and the materials on hand, including some partly completed cars, were sold at a sheriff's auction at Stockton on July 12, 1876, and the enterprise was wound up.

REFERENCES: Collection of Kent Stephens; "Stockton & Ione Railroad," *The Western Railroader*, 42, no. 470 (1979).

The Stockton & Ione planned to operate with two small Mason Bogies, *Stockton* and *Ione*. The *Stockton* is shown at Mason's plant on completion. (Munson Paddock collection, Railroad Museum of Pennsylvania.)

Colorado

Argentine Central Railway

Edward J. Wilcox, who had alternated between careers as mine owner and Methodist minister, in 1902 consolidated his 65 mining properties in the Argentine district into the Waldorf Mining & Milling Co. His base of operations, Waldorf, was about nine miles south of Silver Plume on the Colorado & Southern's Colorado Central line, at an altitude of 11,666 feet, some 2,490 feet above the station. Access by wagon freighting was possible only under favorable weather conditions, leaving Wilcox mainly dependent on pack animals. On August 1, 1905—the anniversary of Colorado's statehood—Wilcox announced plans for a railroad and broke ground at Silver Plume. The project was incorporated as the Argentine Central Railway ten days later.

The railroad was intended not only as a carrier for Wilcox's silver-mining operations, but also as a major tourist facility, ascending beyond Waldorf to Mt. McClellan and Gray's Peak. If completed, the railroad would have reached 14,441 feet. It was built only to the summit of Mt. McClellan (16 miles), which the railroad listed at 14,007 feet, but the U.S. Geological Survey rates at 13,117 feet. This was, however, the highest point ever reached by adhesion railroading in the United States, exceeded only by the rack railroad on Pike's Peak. Necessarily, the railroad used a technology of geared locomotives, operating with seven two-truck Shays over the course of its history. The line was built with 6-percent grades and 32° curves as the norm, with six switchbacks on the ascent. The track climbed out of Waldorf with a spectacular curve 186 feet in radius on a 6.6-percent grade. The line was built in exactly a year, being opened on August 1, 1906.

Wilcox planned not only an ascent of Gray's Peak, but a bore called the Vidler Tunnel under the mountain to reach Keystone on the South Park Line. How practical such a connection would have been is questionable, given the severity of the ascent from Silver Plume, but it would have allowed a Denver-Leadville distance of only 122 miles. In 1914 the tunnel was reported to be three-fourths completed. Events were never to allow completion. Wilcox's ore was so rich that his operation was economic even at the silver prices generally prevailing after the repeal of the Sherman Silver Purchase Act in 1893, but the Panic of 1907 reduced the price of ore to levels at which his mining ceased to be profitable. He had rejected an offer of $3 million for his holdings before the Panic, but by 1908 he was $700,000 in debt and sold the railroad for a reported loss of $256,000, realizing only $44,000 from it. The buyer, David W. Brown of Denver, organized the Gray's Peak Scenic Development Co. as a holding company for the railroad and as the developer of a projected rotunda and scenic observatory at the summit of Gray's Peak. Brown also proved unable to finance the extension. The railroad had lost some of its tourist traffic to an aerial tramway from Silver Plume to Sunrise Peak on Leavenworth Mountain, opened in 1907, but a great deal remained. Tourists were handled in deck-roofed, open-platform coaches, carried from Denver on C&S passenger trains. Wilcox, a Sabbatarian, had been unwilling to operate the railroad on Sundays. The new management had no such scruples, but passenger traffic alone was inadequate to keep the line profitable. Such movements were seasonal, and the railroad, which reached an area of permanent frost, had proved unable to run freight trains in the winter months from its first year.

A receiver, James Q. Newton, was appointed for the railroad on August 3, 1911. The line was unable to operate for the 1911 and 1912 seasons. On August 19, 1912, William Rogers, a man long active in local mining, with several associates bought the railroad for only $20,002, and in 1913 reorganized it as the Argentine & Gray's Peak Railway, subsidiary to a holding company, the Georgetown & Gray's Peak Railway. Rogers was mainly interested in reestablishing freight service from his Santiago Mine, but he announced that passenger service would be resumed for the 1913 season. Rogers sold the controlling interest in the line before the 1914 season to one of his associates, egg producer Fred W. Blankenbuhler. After a successful experiment with a Stanley Steamer automobile fitted with flanged wheels and a similarly equipped truck, Blankenbuhler in 1916 replaced the three remaining Shay locomotives with Vulcan gasoline cars for the tourist trade to Mt. McClellan. The railroad opened for the season on June 23, 1918, but the railroad had lost almost all of its freight traffic, and could not survive as a summer tourist operation. The management filed notice to abandon on October 24, 1918, and received permission from the Colorado Public Utilities Commission on November 9. The railroad was removed in 1919 and early 1920.

REFERENCES: Frank R. Hollenback, *The Argentine Central* (Denver, Colo.: Sage Books, 1959); Dan Abbott, *Stairway to the Stars* (Fort Collins, Colo.: Centennial Publications, 1977); M. C. Poor, "Brief History of the Argentine Central Ry. Co.," Railway & Locomotive Historical Society *Bulletin*, no. 64 (1944), pp. 75–79.

Aspen & Western Railway
Crystal River Railroad

The Colorado Fuel & Iron Co., seeking to develop coal deposits on upper Thompson Creek, arranged that the Denver & Rio Grande should build for it the Aspen & Western Railway, and then be reimbursed by the iron company. The A&W was incorporated on June 7, 1886, and graded in 1887. The grade was laid with 40-pound rail in 1888 and the line put in service between Carbondale on the Aspen branch of the D&RG and the mines at Willow Park (13 miles). The line was relatively heavily built with stone bridge abutments in the expectation of a standard gauging that never took place. CF&I found the coal deposit too expensive to work and shut down the mining operation in 1889, apparently suspending operation of the railroad.

On August 8, 1892, CF&I merged the A&W with three of its other subsidiaries into the Crystal River Railway. About 3.5 miles of the A&W leaving Carbondale were used for a standard gauge line from Carbondale to Redstone. The new corporation sold the rest of the A&W on November 29. The outer three miles of the railroad were removed during 1893 and the rest in 1898. Some of the rail and the bridges were used for a second narrow gauge opened on November 22, 1900, from a coke plant at Redstone to Coalbasin (12 miles). The new narrow gauge followed Coal Creek with a grade of 4.3 percent approaching Coalbasin. Traffic was almost entirely coal for the plant at Redstone, but mixed trains were run to serve the camp at Coalbasin.

CF&I reorganized the railroad as the Crystal River Railroad on September 6, 1898, effective July 1, 1899. The CR in 1898 relocated the track leaving Carbondale off the former A&W to a new right-of-way immediately parallel.

The second narrow gauge survived until January 12, 1909, when CF&I abruptly shut down the plant at Redstone. The standard gauge line between Redstone and Carbondale was turned over to its southern connection, the Crystal River & San Juan Railway, on December 8, 1910. This railroad operated it to carry marble from a quarry at Marble until 1917. The line was revived in 1919 and in 1924 reorganized as the CR&SJ Railroad. It was abandoned in 1941 and removed in 1942.

REFERENCES: Dell McCoy and Russ Collman, *The Crystal River Pictorial* (Denver, Colo.: Sundance, Ltd., 1972); Morrison A. Smith, "Crystal River & San Juan," *Trains*, Sept. 1943, pp. 8–12.

Colorado & Northwestern
Railway

Several small mining camps were built along Boulder and Four Mile creeks above Boulder after 1869 following the discovery of gold and silver ore in the area. Wagons brought the ore out of the mountains throughout the 1870s, but in the early 1880s a Union Pacific subsidiary, the Greeley, Salt Lake & Pacific Railway, projected a narrow gauge line up Boulder Canyon. Undertaken in 1881, the line reached Sunset, 13 miles above Boulder, in 1883. Like its counterpart to the south, the Colorado Central, the line was projected to the west. The company envisioned a route from Sunset at the head of Four Mile Creek up Pennsylvania Gulch, over Rollins Pass, and into Middle Park, then on to Salt Lake City and the Pacific Coast by the route through Vernal, Utah, later projected by the Denver & Salt Lake. A branch was to run from Nederland to Central City to tap the Clear Creek mining area.

The narrow gauge had a poor physical plant with 66 bridges and trestles along the two creeks. This arrangement left the line liable to damage from floods. At the end of May 1894 the area experienced 60 hours of almost unremitting rain, which washed out all but the two miles of the narrow gauge approaching Boulder. An engineer for the Union Pacific, Denver & Gulf surveyed the line in the following month and recommended against an effort to rebuild it. Given the worsening depression in the nation, restoration of the railroad appeared unlikely.

Gold strikes at Ward at the head of Left Hand Creek northwest of Sunset in mid-1897 created a demand for new rail service in the area. On July 22, 1897, the Colorado & Northwestern Railway was organized by Charles W. Mackey of New York and his associates, who were largely from western Pennsylvania. The initial intention was to build a 1'-10"–gauge tramway for downbound ore movements from Ward, but the promoters shortly decided to build a 3'-0"–gauge railroad of orthodox character. It was decided to use the route of the Greeley, Salt Lake & Pacific, but a new right-of-way was fashioned higher above Four Mile Creek for better protection against floods. The new line had only 17 bridges and trestles, but the gradients were somewhat worse, reaching a maximum of 4.49 percent. The worst curvature was 30°. Rails reached Sunset on February 20, 1898. The company arranged to lay a third rail on the Union Pacific, Denver & Gulf's standard gauge line for four miles east of Boulder for access to the Pennsylvania Mill at Culbertson, which was expected to be the principal processing facility for downbound ore.

The line reached Ward at an altitude of 9,450 feet on June 2, 1898. The extension approximately doubled the length of the main line, to 26 miles. The route gained 4,115 feet without reversal of the gradient and, surprisingly, without a tunnel. A branch of 20 miles was built in 1904 to Eldora, southwest of Sunset. The company, eager to develop tourist traffic to its spectacular scenery, arranged trackage rights beginning June 1, 1905, over the Colorado & Southern into Denver Union Station. A third rail was laid along the C&S, and the larger road's facilities in Denver were used. At this time the general offices of the railroad were shifted to Denver. It was widely expected to become a branch of the Colorado & Southern.

The Colorado & Northwestern proved unsuccessful, however. The mines in the Ward area proved so disappointing that the volume of ore moving out of the mountains did not warrant keeping open the Pennsylvania Mill. The decision to build to Eldora was in part an effort to open up a further mining area, and in part an attempt at a through route into Middle Park and the west. Before it was completed, the railroad was put in the hands of a receiver, Harry P. Gamble, in mid-1903. The railroad was sold under foreclosure in May 1904 and reorganized as the Colorado & Northwestern Railroad without significant change in ownership.

Beginning in 1907 the railroad had a windfall from the construction of Barker Dam on Middle Boulder Creek near Nederland, east of Eldora, for the Hydro-Electric Company of Colorado Springs. Construction could proceed only in mild weather, and like the passenger traffic of the railroad, this source of revenue proved highly seasonal. Work on the dam was also halted by the Panic of 1907. The railroad was again put in receivership in June 1907, this time in the hands of W. B. Hayes. By early 1909 the railroad had deteriorated badly, and the Colorado & Southern had lost interest in acquiring it. The railroad was sold to Charles B. and William C. Culbertson of the previous ownership group, and reorganized as the Denver, Boulder & Western Railroad on April 1, 1909. Revival of work on the dam, which was served by a spur off the Eldora line above Sulphide, gave the new corporation the most favorable financial experience the railroad ever had.

The forces operating against the railroad remained: the disappointing performance of the mining industry on-line, the expense of fighting the snow, and the seasonality of the passenger traffic. In 1909 F. O. Stanley, one of the developers of the Stanley Steamer automobile, opened a hotel at Estes Park and began serving it with the larger versions of his vehicle. This initiated direct rivalry of the automobile with the railroads in the area. Given the importance of recreational travel to the mountains, the traffic was more than ordinarily liable to diversion. Through an affiliate, Hickox & Son, the railroad operated its own fleet of Stanley Steamers, but especially after 1915, when the state improved the road up Boulder Canyon, the excursion business rapidly went to the highways.

World War I greatly stimulated the production of tungsten, which had replaced the precious metals as the principal mineral mined in the area. Both Ward and Nederland had extensive tungsten deposits. Unfortunately for the railroad, the tungsten boom proved short-lived. Other Western mining areas and foreign sources quickly arose as major rivals. By 1917 the tungsten boom had largely passed and the diversion of recreational passengers was well advanced. In fact, the Colorado & Southern canceled the joint operating arrangement and removed the third rail from Boulder to Denver in 1916.

In early November 1917 president Charles D. Marvin announced the intention of the management to abandon the railroad. The Colorado Public Utilities Commission, however, refused permission to abandon in a decision of December 26, 1917. The decision brought the railroad through World War I, thereby depriving the owners of the high scrap prices of the war period. Tungsten production virtually ended when the war did. The management reapplied for abandonment on March 28, 1919. By this time it was demonstrable that the railroad could not operate profitably, and the Commission authorized abandonment effective September 15, 1919. A flood, however, ravaged Four Mile and Bold Creek canyons on July 31, 1919. The railroad petitioned to wind up operations immediately, and the Commission agreed on August 21. The Denver scrap firm of Morse Brothers dismantled the railroad in 1920. The state supreme court in June 1920 set aside the Commission's abandonment order, but the railroad was largely dismantled by that time. Local efforts to buy it at scrap value for continued operation were unsuccessful.

REFERENCES: Forest Crossen, *Switzerland Trail of America* (Boulder, Colo.: Pruett Press, 1962); M. C. Poor, "History of the Denver, Boulder & Western Railroad Co.," Railway & Locomotive Historical Society *Bulletin*, no. 65 (1944), pp. 43–58.

Colorado Central Railroad

The Colorado Central had its origins in an effort of the town of Golden to rival Denver as a railroad center. The Union Pacific's decision to build the transcontinental railroad through southern Wyoming had left the Denver area without immediate prospect of a railroad. Necessarily, several projects were conceived in the mid- to late 1860s. Denver's first rail line was the standard gauge Denver Pacific, a line from Denver to Cheyenne via Greeley, completed on June 26, 1870. On August 15, 1870, the Kansas Pacific, from Kansas City to Denver, entered the city. Although the Denver Pacific originally had Union Pacific backing, it was completed as an independent line and shortly came under the control of the Kansas Pacific. The Kansas Pacific became the principal local rival of the Union Pacific.

The Colorado Central was projected by William A. H. Loveland as a mixed standard and narrow gauge railroad with a transshipment point at Golden. The standard gauge line was originally intended to connect with the Union Pacific at Pine Bluff, Nebraska, and to run up the Platte River to Golden. Later, Julesburg, Colorado, was projected as the junction point. Actually, for reasons of economy, the standard gauge line was built straight north from Golden through Loveland and Fort Collins to a connection with the Union Pacific at Hazard, just west of Cheyenne, Wyoming. After a long cessation of building following the Panic of 1873, this line was completed in 1877.

The narrow gauge was intended to run up Clear Creek Canyon to serve the mining towns of Black Hawk, Central City, Idaho Springs, Georgetown, and Silver Plume. Loveland's engineer, Edward L. Berthoud, in 1859 had discovered what became known as Berthoud Pass above Georgetown and Silver Plume. This presented the prospect of a route to the west through Middle Park, roughly along the route of the later Denver & Salt Lake or the present Denver & Rio Grande Western main line. Alternatively, Loveland Pass presented a route into South Park, to the Leadville area and the mining regions to the southwest. Since the narrow gauge was intended mainly to carry ores, the break of gauge was not expected to be a major handicap. It was, in fact, hoped that Golden would develop as a major smelting point.

Financially, the Colorado Central was highly dependent on the Union Pacific. In fact, the Union Pacific controlled a majority of the Colorado Central's directors. Under Berthoud's direction the narrow gauge line was completed to Forks Creek on September 1, 1872, and extended to Black Hawk (21 miles) on December 7, 1872. In the same year a third rail for narrow gauge trains was laid on the railroad's standard gauge line for two miles east of Golden to Arapahoe. The main line up Clear Creek Canyon reached Floyd Hill, three miles from Forks Creek, on March 19, 1873, but this town remained the railhead for four years because of financial stringency following the Panic of 1873.

In 1875 the Union Pacific arranged a division of traffic with the Denver Pacific–Kansas Pacific. In general, the Union Pacific would handle transcontinental traffic and allow the Kansas Pacific system to deal with Colorado local traffic. This arrangement necessarily entailed turning the Colorado Central over to the Kansas Pacific. To accomplish this, the Kansas Pacific had to buy out the stock held by Loveland and his associates. Since the Colorado Central was not yet profitable, the Kansas Pacific offered only 20¢ on the dollar for the stock. Loveland resisted and maintained the independence of his railroad at the annual meeting in May 1876. Because the railroad was unable to pay its interest obligations and no longer had the Union Pacific's financial support, Loveland was confronted with the imminent prospect of bankruptcy. Remarkably, he succeeded in avoiding receivership and in March 1877 negotiated an agree-

ment with Jay Gould, who was by then in control of the Union Pacific. Gould agreed to leave Loveland in control of the Colorado Central and to assist him in completing the narrow gauge.

The immediate consequence of the agreement was to provide the Colorado Central with funds for extension. In April 1877 grading began to the west from Floyd Hill. The track reached Idaho Springs in June and Georgetown (35 miles) on August 13, 1877.

Next, the company undertook a three-rail line from Golden to Ralston (5 miles), both to serve coal mines and to provide the company's standard gauge trains with a more direct access to Golden. This line was undertaken by the subsidiary Golden & Ralston Railroad in 1877 and was opened in February 1878. The narrow gauge line was extended by another subsidiary, the Denver & Middle Park Railroad, to Glencoe (9 miles) in 1883. The branch was abandoned about 1898.

In May 1877 Berthoud began surveys to extend the Black Hawk branch into Central City. Although the extension was only a mile and a quarter, the railroad would have to gain about 500 feet in elevation along Gregory Gulch. The distance was through a fairly solidly urban area. The problem was dealt with by a double switchback and three major trestles. The line was opened in May 1878.

The narrow gauge still did not reach Denver, although the idea of making Golden a rival to Denver as a transshipment point had perished by the time construction had been resumed in 1877. In 1878 the Boston & Colorado Smelter Company, which operated a smelter at Black Hawk, built another at Argo, about two miles north of Denver on the Colorado Central's standard gauge line. A third rail was laid from Denver to Argo (2 miles) to allow gondolas of ore from the Denver & Rio Grande and the South Park Line to reach the smelter. In order to compete with the other two narrow gauges, the Colorado Central in 1879 laid a third rail for 11 miles from Arapahoe to Argo, essentially completing the narrow gauge from Golden into Denver. Track was extended into the Union Passenger Depot at 16th Street so that passenger trains could be run directly from Denver to Central City and Georgetown.

While the extension of the railroad was under way, Loveland and his associates and the Union Pacific management arrived at an agreement whereby the Colorado Central was leased to the Union Pacific in February 1879 for a period of 50 years. This was part of the Union Pacific's penetration of Colo-

rado, which also encompassed absorption of the Denver, South Park & Pacific.

The assumption of control of the railroad by the Union Pacific necessarily influenced the line's prospects for expansion. Loveland and his associates had looked upon reaching the mining camps along Clear Creek as only preliminary to building to the west, either northwest over Berthoud Pass to Middle Park or over Loveland Pass to Leadville and southwestern Colorado. The Union Pacific, being a transcontinental railroad, had no interest in the projected line over Berthoud Pass to the west. The Union Pacific did, however, seriously consider the extension over Loveland Pass into the Blue River Valley and Leadville. In April 1879 Berthoud and a party of surveyors made preliminary surveys of a line across Loveland Pass and Fremont Pass. Early in 1881, the Union Pacific incorporated the Georgetown, Breckenridge & Leadville Railway, replacing an earlier Georgetown, Leadville & San Juan Railroad to build along the surveyed route. The ascent of Loveland Pass from Georgetown would have entailed severe grading. From Georgetown to Silver Plume, the railroads would have to gain 638 feet in two miles. To deal with the problem, Robert Blickensderfer, an engineer of the Union Pacific, designed a line with one complete loop and two horseshoe curves in 4.47 miles in track with a maximum grade of only 3.5 percent. This has usually been considered one of the major engineering accomplishments of the narrow gauge movement. It was, of course, to prove a major tourist attraction. Owing to its spectacular setting and its proximity to Denver, the rail trip from Denver to Silver Plume was to become extremely popular, especially among Eastern visitors.

The line into Silver Plume (54 miles from Denver) was completed in March 1884. Track was extended an additional four miles to Graymont the following month. Beyond this point, however, progress to the Leadville area would require a major tunnel. Several efforts were made to build a tunnel, but none was ever completed. Loveland and his associates attempted a tunnel first with the Grays Peak, Snake River & Leadville Railroad, and later with the Loveland Pass Mining & Railroad Tunnel Company of 1881. The latter attempted some actual work on a tunnel of about 3,000 feet in the first half of 1882, but the Union Pacific ordered work stopped in August. The tunnel would have allowed a Denver-Leadville line of only 127 miles, whereas the Denver & Rio Grande's was 276 miles and the South Park Line's original route via Buena Vista was 171 miles. The Union Pacific instead opted for an extension of the South Park Line via Boreas Pass on a route of 151 miles.

Meanwhile, an independent promoter, Marcus M. Pomeroy, undertook a tunnel under the name of Atlantic-Pacific Tunnel in 1880. The tunnel would have its east portal about 1.5 miles from Graymont and its west portal at Decatur at the head of the Snake River, a distance of 25,200 feet. Pomeroy reformed his enterprise as the Atlantic-Pacific Tunnel & Grays Peak Railway in 1882 and as the Atlantic-Pacific Railway Tunnel Company in 1884. By 1893, when the panic of that year prevented further construction, Pomeroy had reportedly drilled 4,000 feet from the east portal and 800 feet from the west portal. Thereafter, there was no prospect of a direct line from Georgetown and Silver Plume to the Keystone-Dillon area. As a consequence, the line from Silver Plume to Graymont was removed in 1898.

In this period the Union Pacific built its approach to Denver from Julesburg to La Salle in 1880 under the corporate identity of the Colorado Central. In 1890 the Union Pacific consolidated its local holdings into the Union Pacific, Denver & Gulf Railway. This included both the South Park Line and the Colorado Central, which thereafter were operated integrally. The narrow gauge lines became part of the Colorado & Southern upon its formation in 1898. Of the former Colorado Central only the Julesburg–La Salle Line remained in the possession of the Union Pacific.

The narrow gauge lines of the Colorado & Southern suffered declining traffic essentially from the formation of the railroad. Of the two, the Colorado Central held up better than the South Park Line because the tributary mining industry was mainly gold rather than silver. Declining population in the mining towns resulted in a diminution of passenger volume from the early years of the twentieth century. The excursion traffic from Denver held up until World War I, but then the popularity of the automobile for pleasure travel, plus development of rival tourist attractions, caused a decline in that business also. The railroad had traditionally run two passenger trains per day in each direction. The morning departure from Denver, along with a variety of excursion trains, had handled most of the pleasure trippers. After 1921 the morning departure from Denver was run in summer only. Passengers were now mainly local residents who were better served by a train going into Denver in the morning and returning in the afternoon. This traffic could only decline, and on August 10, 1926, the Colorado & Southern petitioned the Colorado Public Utilities Commission to discontinue all passenger service on the Colorado Central. The Commission responded by allowing the railroad to drop regular passenger service for a test period from June 5, 1927, to June 4, 1928. The test was successful by the Commission's standards, and thus the last regular passenger train ran over the Colorado Central on June 4, 1927. Excursion traffic continued, mainly in the summer months. Remaining regular passengers were handled in the combine of a mixed train three times weekly until the Depression, but thereafter twice weekly and finally on an irregular basis. Given the unprofitability of the Colorado & Southern's narrow gauge lines, little was ever done to modernize them. In 1931 locomotive No. 70 was converted from coal to oil, and was thereafter the most characteristic freight engine on the Colorado Central line. The C&S engaged in a lengthy correspondence with the Uintah Railway concerning purchase of its 2-6+6-2 articulated locomotives for use on the Colorado Central. Because of clearance problems and weight limitations, the management decided against the purchase.

The abandonment history of the Colorado Central differs from that of the South Park Line. In 1925 the railroad ceased operating from Black Hawk to Central City. The track was formally abandoned and removed in 1931. The remainder of the railroad remained intact through the 1920s and the deep Depression years. Remarkably, the Colorado Central line had a recovery in traffic in the mid-1930s because the increase in the mint gold price in 1933 stimulated mining in the Clear Creek Valley. Beginning in 1930, the railroad was menaced by the prospect of a hard-surfaced highway up the canyon. Although the highway department was willing to lay the road on an alignment that would not obliterate the narrow gauge, removal of the railroad would indisputably facilitate the project.

In February 28, 1936, the Colorado & Southern applied for abandonment of the entire Colorado Central narrow gauge. Protests were extensive. The ICC denied the abandonment except for the portion from Idaho Springs to Silver Plume, which had lost most of its traffic. This abandonment was scheduled for April 30, 1937, but further protest delayed it for nearly two years. On November 5, 1938, the ICC again gave its permission for the abandonment, effective January 31, 1939. The Georgetown Loop was removed within two months, and the high bridge was sold locally to a mining company for reduction to mine supports.

On March 27, 1940, the C&S applied for abandonment of the remainder of the narrow gauge. Evidence brought before the ICC indicated heavy diversion of ore from the railroad to trucks. The ICC allowed the abandonment, and the last train operated on May 4, 1941. The narrow gauge was dismantled in the course of the next two months. The projected highway, U.S. 6, was built largely on the former narrow gauge right-of-way, obliterating it except at a limited number of points.

The Colorado & Southern converted locomotive No. 70 to oil-burning so that it could make a full round-trip on the Colorado Central line without intermediate fueling. It is shown with coal-burner No. 73 at Empire en route to Silver Plume in 1939. (Richard H. Kindig.)

REFERENCES: Cornelius W. Hauck, *Narrow Gauge to Central and Silver Plume*, Colorado

Colorado & Southern No. 65 sets out for Silver Plume on the Colorado Central line in 1938. (Richard H. Kindig.)

Rail Annual No. 10 (Golden, Colo.: Colorado Railroad Museum, 1972); M. C. Poor, *Denver South Park & Pacific* (Denver, Colo.: Rocky Mountain Railroad Club, 1949), pp. 29–92.

Dismantling operations on the high bridge of the Georgetown loop on the Colorado & Southern in 1939. (Richard H. Kindig.)

Colorado Eastern Railroad

The Colorado Eastern is notable for being the only narrow gauge built east from Denver. Unfortunately, it is also notable as one of the most poorly built narrow gauges and as one of those that survived longest after its principal source of traffic expired.

The railroad was organized under the name of The Denver Railroad & Land Company on January 16, 1886, by J. A. Perkins of Denver and his associates. The name was changed to The Denver Railroad, Land & Coal Company on January 14, 1887, and to Colorado Eastern Railway on January 11, 1888. From the outset, the promoters were interested in reaching a deposit of low-quality coal in the vicinity of Sand Creek in eastern Arapahoe County. The railroad and the mining operation were integral. The railroad was built beginning in the summer of 1886 and was completed to Scranton, 16.3 miles, in November. The route was from a loop and engine house at East 45th Avenue and Franklin Street in Denver east through the small communities of Berlin and Ebert. Scranton was barely an identifiable community, with a reported population of only ten, apparently residents of a boardinghouse at the Scranton mine.

The railroad operated throughout its history with one of the D&RG's early 2-4-0 locomotives, No. 6, the *Ute*, bought at the time of completion of the line to Scranton. Until 1894 the railroad reportedly had a second locomotive, as yet unidentified. The line was very lightly built with rail of only 17 to 21 pounds. Some of the fishplates had only a single bolt hole at each end. The company had a single combine and no outlying stations. Trains stopped at any crossroad for passengers. Freight traffic was almost entirely low-grade bituminous from the Scranton mine destined for the Grant Smelter in Denver. The poor quality of the railroad reportedly caused the coal to disintegrate in the gondolas, and to be combustible only when mixed with straw. Apparently the managers of the smelter were so dissatisfied with the coal that they stopped using it, causing the mine to cease large-scale operations about 1888. A few hundred tons per year, for use by the railroad and for sale locally, were produced until about 1900.

As a consequence, the railroad lost its only real reason for existence shortly after completion. It was reorganized in 1894 as the Colorado Eastern Railroad. As such, the line continued operation well into the twentieth century. The railroad was chronically unprofitable, and it was beset with lawsuits with the Union Pacific and Burlington, which apparently looked upon the little operation as potentially a menace. The Colorado Eastern essentially had no importance except as a possible entry for a major railroad. The line, however trivial, did have a right-of-way that penetrated into the central railroad terminal area of Denver. The Rock Island, which had built its line into Colorado to Colorado Springs and entered Denver by trackage rights from Limon over the Union Pacific, was believed to intend an entry into Denver on its own rails. The Chicago & North Western never built to Denver, but was known to be interested in such an extension. The Colorado Eastern had franchise rights to build to the Kansas border in the vicinity of Hale, Colorado, which could have been used by either railroad. The owners probably continued operation of the line in the face of unremitting deficits in hope of selling the railroad for such an entry. Operation remained what it had been from the outset, one mixed train per day leaving Denver each morning and returning shortly after noon.

On June 7, 1915, the company lost a case in the Colorado Supreme Court in which its authority to operate along Wewatta Street in Denver was held to be illegal. This ended any incentive to continue operation, and in August the railroad was abandoned. The corporation remained in existence until its charter expired in 1944, again probably in hope that the right-of-way and authority to build to the state line were salable assets.

REFERENCES: Charles S. Ryland, *The Colorado Eastern Railroad* (Denver, Colo.: Rocky Mountain Railroad Club, 1951); John C. Newell and P. R. Griswold, *Narrow Gauge East from Denver: The Colorado Eastern Railroad* (Boulder, Colo.: Pruett Publishing Co., 1982).

Denver & Middle Park Railroad

As the Denver & Middle Park Railway & Mining Company, this enterprise was incorporated in 1874 by William W. Morrison and his associates to run from Denver to Hot Sulphur Springs in Middle Park via Ralston Canyon and Berthoud Pass. Nothing was accomplished, and the enterprise was rechartered as the Denver & Middle Park Railroad in 1883. This company built 4.6 miles of track from Ralston on the Colorado Central to Glencoe, and reportedly surveyed a crossing of Berthoud Pass. Nothing beyond the initial trackage was built. The railroad served mines in the Glencoe area.

The railroad was part of the Union Pacific's incursion into the Colorado mountains. On April 1, 1890, the property was merged with 11 other railroads controlled by the UP into the Union Pacific, Denver & Gulf Railway. The line was abandoned in 1898. Consequently, it did not survive long enough to be included with the Colorado Central in the Colorado & Southern when the latter began operation early in 1899.

Denver & Rio Grande Railway

The first major American railroad to use 3'-0" proved also to be the largest and the longest lived. Because of the railroad's importance and long survival as a narrow gauge, it already has an abundant literature, both learned and popular. An effort to treat the railroad as intensively as the smaller lines in the present volume would be both redundant and intolerably space-consuming. Accordingly, only a bare outline of the corporate history is given here, with the treatment directed to the railroad's narrow gauge experience. The development of the track network is presented in tabular form below. Readers seeking more specific information on the changes in trackage over time are referred to the books of LeMassena and Wilkins, cited below, which have detailed chronologies, including those of some short branches, mine spurs, and line relocations impractical to cover here.

The Denver & Rio Grande Railway was chartered on October 27, 1870, by General William J. Palmer and several businessmen of Denver. The map accompanying their application for a charter showed a network more similar to what the railroad finally became than is usually thought. The projected railroad had three major elements: a main line from Denver along the escarpment of the Front Range, through Colorado Springs and Pueblo, to Cucharas (Cuchara Junction), thence over Veta Pass to Alamosa, and south parallel to the Rio Grande to El Paso, Texas; a line to Salt Lake City via Grand Junction; and a penetration of the San Juan mining district of northwestern New Mexico and southwestern Colorado by means of a branch off the El Paso line from a point near Espanola, New Mexico. From the outset a line was planned north over Tennessee Pass and another south over Poncha Pass to connect with the route south at Alamosa. The route west was originally projected via the Platte River into South Park on the route later built by the Denver, South Park & Pacific, except that it would have used the South Fork rather than the North Fork of the Platte to enter the park. It would have left via Hoosier Pass, connecting with the line up from Salida in the vicinity of Minturn. Several branches were envisioned. The railroad was expected to be isolated, with only a single transshipment point at Denver.

There is little question that Palmer's interest at the outset was principally in the line south. He and James Sullivan arranged a concession for building narrow gauge railroads in Mexico, and although he was not interested in the Mexican Central, the projected connection at El Paso, he was eager to see a consistent 3'-0" line from Denver to Mexico City. Events were to shift the company's goals, making the line west considerably more important than the line south. Tracklaying began at Denver on July 28, 1871. The first target for the railroad was the newly established city of Colorado Springs, which was reached by the end of the year. Some excursions were run in 1871, but full service began on January 1, 1872. When the track reached Pueblo later in 1872, Palmer undertook a branch west up the Arkansas River to the coalfield in the vicinity of Canon City. The development of Denver and the growth of the mining indus-

	Mileage					Mileage			
Dec. 31	NG	SG	3-rail	Total	Dec. 31	NG	SG	3-rail	Total
1871	76	—	—	76	1930	751	1,650	62	2,463
1872	155	—	—	155	1931	751	1,650	62	2,463
1873	155	—	—	155	1932	735	1,650	62	2,447
1874	164	—	—	164	1933	735	1,647	62	2,444
1875	164	—	—	164	1934	699	1,641	62	2,402
1876	275	—	—	275	1935	699	1,641	62	2,402
1877	304	—	—	304	1936	668	1,617	62	2,347
1878	337	—	—	337	1937	687	1,649	63	2,399
1879	337	—	—	337	1938	687	1,652	61	2,400
					1939	687	1,640	61	2,388
1880	684	—	—	684					
1881	977	—	123	1,100	1940	687	1,638	61	2,386
1882	1,314	—	123	1,437	1941	562	1,626	60	2,248
1883	1,562	—	123	1,685	1942	554	1,608	60	2,222
1884	1,562	—	123	1,685	1943	552	1,598	60	2,210
1885	1,562	—	123	1,685	1944	552	1,594	57	2,203
1886	1,562	—	123	1,685	1945	553	1,593	57	2,203
1887	1,673	—	160	1,833	1946	550	1,576	57	2,183
1888	1,574	16	265	1,855	1947	546	1,806	57	2,409
1889	1,635	64	226	1,925	1948	546	1,783	57	2,386
					1949	520	1,781	57	2,358
1890	1,013	681	296	1,990					
1891	965	805	296	2,066	1950	520	1,758	57	2,335
1892	965	822	296	2,083	1951	466	1,777	38	2,281
1893	961	825	296	2,082	1952	466	1,776	38	2,280
1894	961	825	296	2,082	1953	422	1,802	35	2,259
1895	995	825	296	2,116	1954	284	1,800	35	2,119
1896	995	861	296	2,152	1955	284	1,791	34	2,109
1897	995	856	296	2,147	1956	264	1,812	34	2,110
1898	1,035	852	300	2,187	1957	264	1,812	34	2,110
1899	976	966	300	2,242	1958	264	1,813	32	2,109
					1959	264	1,787	31	2,082
1900	957	1,024	317	2,298					
1901	918	1,042	360	2,320	1960	264	1,787	31	2,082
1902	916	1,243	203	2,362	1961	264	1,788	31	2,083
1903	911	1,273	203	2,387	1962	264	1,788	31	2,083
1904	906	1,285	203	2,394	1963	268	1,787	31	2,086
1905	904	1,353	205	2,462	1964	268	1,784	31	2,083
1906	787	1,470	208	2,465	1965	268	1,818	31	2,117
1907	787	1,522	208	2,517	1966	268	1,817	31	2,116
1908	787	1,522	208	2,517	1967	268	1,819	30	2,117
1909	787	1,522	208	2,517	1968	268	1,810	30	2,108
					1969	46	1,811	—	1,857
1910	787	1,522	208	2,517					
1911	787	1,617	113	2,517	1970	46	1,784	—	1,830
1912	787	1,621	113	2,521	1971	46	1,769	—	1,815
1913	783	1,631	117	2,531	1972	46	1,769	—	1,815
1914	789	1,630	106	2,525	1973	46	1,755	—	1,801
1915	789	1,630	106	2,525	1974	46	1,755	—	1,801
1916	789	1,630	106	2,525	1975	46	1,743	—	1,789
1917	792	1,675	102	2,569	1976	46	1,743	—	1,789
1918	792	1,664	102	2,558	1977	46	1,743	—	1,789
1919	792	1,666	102	2,560	1978	46	1,743	—	1,789
					1979	46	1,743	—	1,789
1920	792	1,666	102	2,560					
1921	792	1,666	102	2,560	1980	46	1,743	—	1,789
1922	792	1,666	102	2,560	1981	0	1,743	—	1,743
1923	835	1,622	100	2,557					
1924	799	1,606	99	2,504					
1925	799	1,646	43	2,488					
1926	782	1,645	43	2,470					
1927	782	1,649	43	2,474					
1928	782	1,652	41	2,475					
1929	771	1,647	41	2,459					

SOURCES: For 1871–1919, Arthur Ridgway, "Denver & Rio Grande: Development of Physical Property," typescript report (D&RGW RR, Jan. 1921), p. 74; typescript time series 1920–77, by Jackson C. Thode (D&RGW RR, 1977); reports of the D&RGW to *Poor's* and *Moody's* manuals; LeMassena, *Rio Grande . . . to the Pacific!*; Wilkins, *Colorado Railroads.*

try in Colorado created a voracious demand for coal, which Palmer was eager to satisfy. Coal was to become second only to ores as a source of revenue for the railroad. The Panic of 1873 hit the company hard, preventing any major extensions until 1876. The railroad was also under the necessity of largely reequipping itself, for its early four-wheeled cars were demonstrably inadequate by 1872, and bigger locomotives were required for the heavier equipment.

A doubleheaded Denver & Rio Grande passenger train in the early years of the railroad. (Smithsonian Institution.)

When construction resumed in 1876, Palmer extended the line south to Cucharas and to El Moro in the Trinidad area, site of another coalfield. He also pressed the track from Cucharas across Veta Pass to Fort Garland, penetrating the San Luis Valley, albeit by use of 4-percent grades and 30° curvature. The line reached Alamosa in July 1878. The line into the Trinidad area reached Engleville in the coalfield in December 1877. The two routes gave Palmer a choice of approaches to New Mexico, either directly south from Alamosa along the Rio Grande valley or from the Trinidad area across Raton Pass into the northeastern part of the state and south via Las Vegas. These options were constrained by the arrival of the Atchison, Topeka & Santa Fe in the area in the mid-1870s. In February 1878 the AT&SF beat the D&RG across Raton Pass, so that Palmer had no choice but to press south from Alamosa. The development of mining at Leadville caused the AT&SF and D&RG to turn their rivalry to a route up the Arkansas River. Palmer, whose funds were nearly exhausted, recognized that he was unable to compete effectively with his larger rival, and on October 19, 1878, leased the D&RG to the AT&SF, effective December 13. As might have been expected, the AT&SF was interested in the narrow gauge mainly as an adjunct in a rate war with the Kansas Pacific. Palmer, believing that these policies would ruin his railroad, appealed to the courts for abrogation of the lease. The D&RG was placed in the hands of receiver Hanson A. Risley on June 11, 1879, but returned to the AT&SF on July 16. Palmer's further efforts to have the lease annulled resulted in a second re-

ceivership, established on August 15, with Louis C. Ellsworth as receiver.

Meanwhile, Jay Gould had begun to buy the D&RG's stock, and shortly was in control of the corporation. He was able to dictate terms of peace in the conflict in the Tripartite Agreement of March 27, 1880, which has come to be known as the "Treaty of Boston." The D&RG agreed not to build south from Trinidad or to press the line from Alamosa south of Espanola, New Mexico. The AT&SF agreed not to enter Denver or Leadville for ten years, but to turn over the tracks or rights-of-way of its subsidiaries west of Canon City to the D&RG. The legal actions were dropped, the lease terminated, and the D&RG's receivership ended. The third party to the

agreement was the Union Pacific, which agreed to stay out of the Colorado Rockies—a provision it later violated by gaining control of the Denver, South Park & Pacific. Palmer was again in control of his railroad, and free to pursue his plans subject to the constraints he had accepted in the agreement. His restoration coincided with the boom of the mining industry in Leadville and just preceded the peak of the narrow gauge movement in the early 1880s. Palmer made use of his newly found freedom and of the greater availability of loanable funds to begin a program of massive expansion that brought the road to its full general outline by the end of the narrow gauge boom in 1883.

The railroad had already graded much of the line south, intending Albuquerque to be the first major stopping point. Palmer chose to make use of the investment to build as far as the agreement allowed; the line was opened to Espanola on December 30, 1880. Any southern extension necessarily required cooperation of local figures. Promoters at Santa Fe formed the Texas, Santa Fe & Northern Railroad to build the 34 miles from Espanola to Santa Fe. In the long run, they projected a railroad of 1,258 miles connecting the Central Pacific in Utah with the Texas & Pacific and Southern Pacific in Texas. In 1881 they did much of the grading between Santa Fe and Espanola, even installing some bridges, but they were unable to complete the connection. Early in 1886 General L. M. Meily took possession of the unfinished railroad, and on January 8, 1887, he completed it to Espanola. The line was reorganized as the Santa Fe Southern on January 24, 1889, but was sold under foreclosure on July 2, 1895, to the

The pioneer photographer Fred Jukes captured this freight of the Denver & Rio Grande on Cumbres Pass on the secondary main line to Durango. (Cornelius W. Hauck collection.)

D&RG, which formed the Rio Grande & Santa Fe Railroad to own it. It was merged into the D&RG on August 1, 1908. Especially since the AT&SF had a standard gauge branch into Santa Fe, the line proved no more than a trivial part of the D&RG system. Lumber was the principal traffic. The line was an expensive one to operate because of a 4-percent grade of about six miles northbound from Embudo to Barranca. Curves were as sharp as 22°.

Palmer chose to penetrate the San Juan mining area not from Espanola but rather from Alamosa. The route required a tortuous traversing of the Toltec Gorge and a crossing of Cumbres Pass at an elevation of 10,015 feet. The westbound ascent was a moderate 1.42 percent but the eastbound entailed a grade 14 miles long, 4 percent at its worst. The first locomotive reached Durango, 172 miles from Antonito, on July 27, 1881. The goal was the mining camp at Silverton, 45 miles farther, but owing to the characteristically severe winter, track could not be laid there until 1882. Also in 1881 the railroad ran a branch up the headwaters of the Rio Grande to South Fork; the branch was extended to Wagon Wheel Gap in 1883 and to North Creede in 1891.

Necessarily, the line west took shape as the company's principal route. Not only was the mining area at Leadville booming, but the dominant traffic flow of the nation was west-to-east. The highest priority was reaching Leadville; the company built from the railhead at Canon City into the mining camp in 1880. Track was pushed on over Fremont Pass to mines in the Wheeler area and over Tennessee Pass to Red Cliff in 1881. In spite of having rails over 10,433-foot Tennessee Pass, the management had already decided not to proceed to Utah on that route, as it had originally intended, but rather across Marshall Pass and the eastern portion of the Black Canyon of the Gunnison River to Montrose and Grand Junction near the western edge of the state. In part, the decision represented a desire to serve the Gunnison area, which was also having a mining boom. An additional attraction was one of the state's best coalfields at Crested Butte. Both the east-west main line from Salida to Gunnison and the Crested Butte branch were built during the railroad's peak year of expansion, 1881. To the west the railroad's engineers pressed the line through the upper reaches of the Black Canyon, but brought it out along Cimarron Creek because of the difficulty of building a right-of-way through the deeper portions of the canyon. They crossed Cerro Summit at an elevation of 7,964 feet, descended into the valley of the Uncompahgre River at

Fred Jukes photographed a Denver & Rio Grande passenger train hauled by one of the railroad's ten-wheelers, assisted by one of the ubiquitous 400-series 2-8-0s. (Smithsonian Institution.)

Montrose, and then drove the line along the Uncompahgre and the Gunnison into Grand Junction. Rails reached Grand Junction on November 22, 1882. On December 19, tracks reached the Colorado-Utah border.

Because the D&RG had no authority in its charter to operate in Utah, Palmer was required to incorporate the Utah mileage separately as the Denver & Rio Grande Western Railway. For most of the narrow gauge era, this was a separate railroad, and will be treated as such in the Utah section of this book. For present purposes it is sufficient to say that the line reached Salt Lake City on March 30, 1883, and Ogden on May 16. Thus, except for the truncation of the El Paso line by the Tripartite Agreement, the railroad by May 1883 had been completed roughly along its original projected outline. The quick growth of the railroad had put great strain on its finances, and alienated some of its Eastern directors. Conflict from this source caused Palmer to resign the presidency of the D&RG on August 9, 1883. He remained in charge of the D&RGW, the Utah connection, which the D&RG had leased on August 1, 1882. Frederick Lovejoy replaced Palmer as president of the D&RG. The division of responsibility between the two men was to prove disastrous. After a conflict with Palmer concerning the management of the D&RGW, Lovejoy attempted unsuccessfully to break the lease. He then ordered the connection with the D&RGW cut at the state line, thereby depriving both companies of

through traffic to Utah from the Burlington system, which had arrived at Denver. The conflict, combined with the problems of servicing the heavy debt incurred in the rapid expansion of recent years, caused the D&RG to be put in the hands of receiver William S. Jackson on July 12, 1884. David H. Moffat of Denver replaced Lovejoy as president in February 1885. The company was reorganized as the Denver & Rio Grande Railroad on July 14, 1886. The lease of the D&RGW was ended on July 31, the D&RG's guaranty of the D&RGW's bonds was terminated, and some equipment was transferred to the D&RGW. Jackson became president of the corporation.

Necessarily, the D&RG's financial problems in the mid-1880s had a dampening effect on its expansion. A major branch of only 16 miles was completed from Poncha Junction in the Salida area to Monarch in October 1883. Beset by a double lariat loop and a pair of switchbacks on 4.5-percent grades, the line was to be a rich source of gold ore and limestone. After the decline of mining in Colorado, the limestone was to make this branch the most heavily trafficked portion of the D&RG narrow gauge system. After the reorganization of 1886, the railroad undertook a branch, finished in 1887, from Montrose to Ouray, an isolated silver camp at the head of the Uncompahgre River valley. David Moffat, who replaced Jackson as president in 1887, convinced the directors to pursue an extension along the Grand River (Colorado River) from Rock Creek on the north side of Tennessee Pass to

Glenwood Springs, and up the valley of the Roaring Fork River to the silver camp of Aspen. The railroad's interest in this line was in part an effort to invade the area being targeted by the Colorado Midland, which was pressing the first standard gauge penetration of the Colorado Rockies from Colorado Springs. The D&RG reached Aspen on November 1, 1887, a month ahead of the Midland.

Necessarily, the prospect of a standard gauge rival presented serious problems to the management. Palmer's original idea of a vast railroad, ranging over a largely empty arid West, isolated except for a single contact with the standard gauge system at Denver, was rapidly becoming obsolete. The AT&SF, the Rock Island, and the Burlington had already arrived, and various other railroads presented the prospect of connection at Denver, Colorado Springs, or Pueblo. To handle traffic in interchange from the Burlington and AT&SF, the D&RG had laid third rail on the original line as far as an iron works immediately south of Pueblo as early as 1881. Third rail

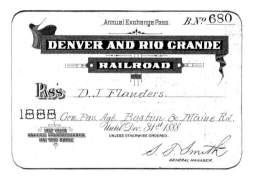

had been laid into the coalfields near Canon City and Trinidad in 1887 and 1888. No actual conversion had been attempted, however. The narrow gauge was preventing the east-west main line from becoming an effective rival to the Union Pacific, in spite of a route that clearly presented this potential. Consequently, the railroad undertook conversion of the east-west line in 1889. The directors resolved to take the original projected route via Tennessee Pass, rather than to convert the existing line through Gunnison, partly because the Colorado Midland was planning an approach to Grand Junction along the Grand River, and partly because both Marshall Pass and Cerro Summit would have required extensive improvement. The route chosen required a new line of 15 miles across Tennessee Pass with a tunnel at the summit at 10,240 feet of altitude. To forestall the Midland's preempting the route, the D&RG extended the narrow gauge to Rifle Creek

Denver & Rio Grande Railway
Narrow gauge mileage, including Utah lines

Line	Miles	Year built	Year converted: to 3-rail	to SG	Year abandoned
Original Main Line South					
Denver–Colorado Springs	76	1871	1881	1902	
Colorado Springs–Pueblo	43	1872	1881	1902	
Pueblo–Cucharas	50	1876	1888	1890	1932[a]
Cucharas–El Moro	37	1876	1888	1890	1936
El Moro–Engleville	7	1877	1888	1889	1929
El Moro–Trinidad	4	1887	1888	1889	1936
Colorado Springs–Colorado City	2	1880	1888	1902	
Colorado City–Manitou	3	1880	1888	1902	1939
Cucharas–Walsenburg	6	1876	1888	1890	1937
Walsenburg–La Veta	15	1876		1890	
La Veta–Russell	25	1877			1899
Russell–Fort Garland	11	1878		1899	
Garland–Alamosa	34	1878		1899	
Alamosa–Antonito	28	1880	1901	1969	
Antonito–Espanola	91	1880			1941
Espanola–Santa Fe	34	1886 (ac. 1895)			1941
Taos Junction–La Madera	16	1914			1932
East-West Main Line and Branches					
Pueblo–Canon City	41	1872	1887	1911	
Canon City–Salida	57	1880	1890	1911	
Salida–Poncha Junction	5	1880		1956	1981
Poncha Junction–Gunnison	69	1881			1954
Gunnison–Sapinero	25	1882			1954
Sapinero–Cedar Creek	27	1882			1949
Cedar Creek–Montrose	10	1882			1953
Montrose–Grand Junction	72	1882		1906	
Grand Junction–Crevasse	21	1882		1890	
Crevasse–State Line	15	1882			1890
State Line–White House	38	1883			1890
White House–Lower Crossing (Woodside)	72	1883		1890	
Lower Crossing–Sunnyside (Mounds)	20	1883			1890
Sunnyside–Clear Creek	61	1882		1890	
Clear Creek–Provo	38	1873–79 (ac. 1882)		1890	
Provo–Salt Lake City	46	1882		1889	
Salt Lake City–Ogden	36	1883		1889	
Grape Creek Junction–Westcliffe	31	1881			1889
Salida–Malta	56	1880	1890	1925	
Malta–Crane's Park	9	1880		1890	
Crane's Park–Red Cliff	18	1881		1890	
Red Cliff–Rock Creek	3	1882		1890	
Rock Creek–Glenwood Springs	64	1887		1890	
Glenwood Springs–Rifle	26	1889		1890	
Hecla Junction–Calumet	7	1881			1923
Poncha Junction–Maysville	7	1881		1956	1981
Maysville–Monarch	9	1883		1956	1981
Malta–Leadville	5	1880	1890	1925	
Leadville–Leadville Junction	3	1887		1890	
Leadville–Robinson	16	1880			1911
Robinson–Wheeler	8	1881			1911
Wheeler–Dillon	11	1882			1911
Glenwood Springs–Woody Creek	33	1887		1890	
Woody Creek–Aspen	8	1887		1890	1969

[a] Abandonment completed; portions abandoned earlier.

Denver & Rio Grande Railway

(continued)

Line	Miles	Year built	Year converted: to 3-rail	to SG	Year abandoned
East-West Main Line and Branches					
Mears Junction–Villa Grove	19	1881			1951
Villa Grove–Orient	8	1881			1942
Villa Grove–Hooper	35	1890			1951
Hooper–Alamosa	20	1890	1930	1951	1959
Moffat–Cottonwood	17	1901			1926
Parlin–Quartz (ex-DSP&P)	18	leased 1911			1934
Gunnison–Crested Butte	28	1881			1954
Crested Butte–Anthracite	4	1882			1947
Crested Butte–Floresta	11	1893			1929
Gunnison–Castleton (ex-DSP&P)	15	leased 1911			1954
Castleton–Baldwin	2	leased 1911			1946
Lake Junction–Lake City	36	1889			1933
as San Christobal Railroad					1937
Montrose–Ridgway	28	1887		1953	1977
Ridgway–Ouray	7	1887			1953
Delta–Somerset	42	1902		1906	
Clear Creek–Scofield	22	1879 (ac. 1882)			1882
Colton–Scofield	15	1882		1890	
Thistle–Manti	61	1890		1891	1983
Sandy–Midvale	2	1873		1890	1965
Midvale–Bingham	17	1873 (ac. 1881)		1890	
Sandy–Wasatch	9	1873 (ac. 1881)		1890	1934
Wasatch–Alta (mule tramway)	7	1875 (ac. 1881)			1934
Lines into San Juan Mining Area					
Alamosa–Monte Vista	17	1881	1900	1902	
Monte Vista–Del Norte	14	1881	1901	1902	
Del Norte–South Fork	15	1881		1902	
South Fork–Wagon Wheel Gap	14	1883		1902	
Wagon Wheel Gap–North Creede	10	1891		1902	
Antonito–Chama	64	1880			1969
Chama–Durango	108	1881			1969
Durango–Rockwood	18	1881			
Rockwood–Silverton	27	1882			
Chama–Tierra Amarilla	15	1896 (ac. 1902)			1902
Pagosa Junction–Pagosa	31	1900 (leased 1902)			1935
Carbon Junction (Durango)–Farmington	48	(blt. s.g. 1905) to n.g. 1923			1969

SOURCES: LeMassena, *Rio Grande . . . to the Pacific!*; collections of Edward J. Haley, Cornelius W. Hauck, Gordon Chappell, and Jackson C. Thode. Mileages are principally from employee timetables and other D&RG publications in the Thode collection dating from before the revision of mileposts of 1901. For this reason and because of rounding, they may differ from subsequent or current mileages.

(Rifle) in 1889. The new crossing of Tennessee Pass was made narrow gauge transitionally. At this time the railroad's narrow gauge trackage peaked; early in 1890 the company operated a total (including the Utah mileage) of 1,635 miles of 3′-0″, 226 miles of three-rail, and only 64 miles of 4′-8½″. Not all of the D&RG's narrow gauge mileage was in existence at any one time; in total the company had about 2,218 miles of 3′-0″, or 2,253 if some trackage of the former Denver, South Park & Pacific leased in 1911 is included. In 1890 the D&RG and Midland jointly built from Rifle to Grand Junction under the name of the Rio Grande Junction Railway, and the narrow gauge from Malta near Leadville to Rifle was converted. The Rio Grande Western, as the Utah portion of the main line had become, was converting simultaneously. From Grand Junction to the state line, the track was leased to the Rio Grande Western, which built a new line through Ruby Canyon to the south of the narrow gauge. The standard gauge line from Denver to Ogden was completed when the track from Rifle arrived at Grand Junction on November 14, 1890.

Meanwhile, narrow gauge on the original mileage along the Front Range was declining rapidly. In the course of 1889 and 1890, the D&RG removed the narrow gauge rail from the three-rail trackage south of Pueblo. The line from Walsenburg to Alamosa was converted as far as La Veta at the foot of Veta Pass in 1890. These changes meant that there was no longer a narrow gauge connection between the lines into the San Juan mining area and the remnants of the former east-west line out of Salida. The obvious connection from Ouray to Silverton, which were only 23 miles apart, was impossible because the ascent southbound from Ouray was too steep for adhesion railroading. To connect the separated systems, the D&RG in 1890 built a 55-mile line from Villa Grove, on a branch to Orient dating from 1881, to Alamosa. Remarkably, given the terrain and the common practices of the narrow gauges, 53 miles were on a tangent, the fifth longest in the United States and by far the longest on any narrow gauge. One additional line was built in this period to serve a mining camp, a 36-mile branch off the old main line from a point near Sapinero to Lake City, opened in 1889. In the same year a branch of 31 miles into Westcliffe dating from 1881 was wiped out by a flood and not replaced. Rather, a new standard gauge branch was built into Westcliffe from Texas Creek in 1901.

Conversion of the east-west main line and other expenditures again put the D&RG in difficult financial circumstances by 1891. Moffat was accused by holders of some of the securities of running the railroad for the economic benefit of Denver, rather than in the interests of the shareholders. He resigned under such pressures and was replaced by the conservative Edward T. Jeffery. The one extension of the year, a ten-mile completion of the Creede line, was financed by Moffat personally and turned over to the D&RG on completion. Moffat's Holy Moses Mining Co. then received a rebate on its tonnage. A similar arrangement was made with the Pagosa Lumber Company to build the Rio Grande, Pagosa & Northern Railroad in 1900. The D&RG made the line its Pagosa Springs branch in 1908. In 1902 the D&RG built its last long narrow gauge line, a branch of 42 miles from Delta on the old main line to a coalfield at Somerset. The branch was laid with standard gauge ties in the expectation of an early conversion.

The repeal of the Sherman Silver Purchase Act in 1893, combined with the effects of the depression of the 1890s, severely reduced the D&RG's revenues, but Jeffery's policy of parsimony pulled the railroad through the decade without bankruptcy. The entire property was subject to deferred maintenance, giving rise to a great deal of local complaint. By 1899 the upturn in business conditions allowed the management to undertake its first major improvement in nearly a decade, conversion of the remainder of the Walsenburg-Alamosa line. As with the conversion of the main line, the project entailed a major relocation: a new line was built through La Veta Pass to the south to avoid the severe grades traversing Veta Pass. Alamosa became the change-of-gauge point for the route into the San Juan mining area and the shop city for the narrow gauge. Third rail was laid to Antonito in 1901. The Creede branch was converted in 1902.

Almost exactly at the turn of the century, George Gould, son of Jay Gould, secured stock control of the D&RG and the Rio Grande Western, buying out the equity of the Palmer interests in the latter and ending Palmer's three decades of association with the railroad. Gould was actively pursuing his plan of a transcontinental railroad system, which at length he achieved—the only man to have done so. His interest in the D&RG was largely in using its revenues to finance the Western Pacific, the westernmost element in his projected system. In 1903 the D&RG and RGW guaranteed $50 million in bonds, with which the WP was

In 1937 the Denver & Rio Grande Western spotted narrow gauge Mikado 472 beside 4-8-4 No. 1703 to publicize the modernization of its "Shavano," the passenger train between Salida and Gunnison. The photographs provide a good contrast between the sizes of relatively modern narrow and standard gauge motive power. (D&RGW, Jackson C. Thode collection.)

largely built. The interest on this huge debt was a great burden to the D&RG, ultimately bankrupting the railroad. Once again, the railroad's plant was neglected. Whereas most major railroads were physically improved during the long Edwardian prosperity, the D&RG was again allowed to sink into deferred maintenance between 1905 and 1910 while the WP was built. As might be expected, the narrow gauge was relatively stagnant in this period. In 1906 the management converted the portion of the old main line between Grand Junction and Montrose, along with the Somerset branch. In 1905 the railroad made a particularly strange addition, an isolated standard gauge branch from Durango to Farmington, New Mexico. Locomotives and cars

were shipped in after being disassembled at Alamosa. The railroad anticipated converting the mileage from Alamosa to Durango, and the new line was projected to a connection with the AT&SF at Gallup, reportedly to forestall an incursion into the San Juan region by the Southern Pacific. In August 1908 Gould merged the D&RG and RGW, along with the D&RG's various subsidiaries, with the notable exception of the Rio Grande Southern.

In 1911 the D&RG made an agreement with the Colorado & Southern whereby the D&RG took over the Gunnison-Baldwin branch and Parlin-Quartz remnant of the C&S's South Park Line, which had been isolated by the collapse of the Alpine Tunnel and abandonment of the C&S's Gunnison line. In return, the D&RG gave up its branch from Leadville up Fremont Pass to Dillon, turning the traffic over to the parallel line of the C&S.

The shaky empire of George Gould began to collapse in 1915 when the Missouri Pacific, which held 30 percent of the D&RG's stock, went bankrupt. The Western Pacific was shortly allowed to follow suit. The D&RG avoided bankruptcy only until January 25, 1918, when it sought voluntarily to be placed in the hands of the court. The railroad was at the time federally controlled under the United States Railroad Administration. Upon emerging from federal hands, the D&RG's principal creditor, the Western Pacific Railroad Corporation, holding company for the WP, sought a foreclosure sale. On November 20, 1920, the D&RG was sold to the holding company for a mere $5 million, a sum reflecting its extensive debts and poor physical condition. A new corporation, the Denver & Rio Grande Western Railroad, was organized in November 1920, and took control of the railroad on August 1, 1921. The company could barely meet its interest obligations, and was back in receivership on July 21, 1922. The receivership lasted until October 29, 1924, when the railroad was bought for $18 million by investment bankers representing the bondholders. The railroad was reorganized, without change of name, under equal ownership by the Missouri Pacific and the WP's holding company. Although this arrangement assured a flow of traffic from connections at Salt Lake City and Pueblo, the railroad was saddled with such heavy debt that a further receivership was inevitable.

Little was done with the narrow gauge in these years. The narrow gauge rail in the three-rail trackage from Salida to Malta in the Leadville area was removed in 1925. In 1923 the railroad, apparently having given up any immediate hope of converting the Alamosa-Durango line, converted the standard gauge Farmington branch to narrow. There were relatively few abandonments. The long branch from Moffat to Cottonwood, which had not been regularly worked since 1913, was taken out in 1926. The mine spur from Crested Butte to Floresta was torn up in 1929 after a coal mine of the Colorado Fuel & Iron Company closed. Third rail was laid along the San Luis Valley line from Alamosa to Hooper in 1930.

Also in 1930 the D&RGW began buying into the Denver & Salt Lake, which David Moffat had projected as a direct route from Denver to Salt Lake City via Middle Park, Steamboat Springs, and Craig. The railroad had never progressed beyond Craig, but if completed it could become a serious rival to the D&RGW, particularly because it enjoyed the use of the publicly financed Moffat Tunnel to penetrate the Front Range. The D&RG's interest in the D&SL was to make use of the tunnel to shorten its main line; building a cutoff from a point near Bond on the D&SL along the upper Colorado River to a point west of Tennessee Pass, Dotsero, was relatively easy. Given the worsening depression and the D&RGW's difficult financial situation, the project could be completed in 1934 only with assistance from the Reconstruction Finance Corporation. The railroad again went into the hands of the courts on November 1, 1935, with Henry Swan and Wilson McCarthy of Denver as trustees. Among the economies of the time were abandonments of the La Madera branch in 1932 and the Pagosa Springs line in 1935. The Lake City branch was dropped in 1933, but local operators endeavored to perpetuate it as the San Christobal Railroad until 1937, when it was scrapped. In the course of 1936 and 1937, the D&RGW

A freight on the Ouray branch of the D&RGW in 1951. (Otto C. Perry, Denver Public Library.)

Two of the D&RGW's 480 series Mikados steam in Salida yard in preparation for a trip up the Monarch branch in June 1955. (Jim Shaughnessy.)

completed abandoning its former narrow gauge line from Pueblo south to Walsenburg and Trinidad in favor of trackage rights on the parallel Colorado & Southern; the northern portions had been removed in the mid-1920s.

The trustees mainly devoted themselves to an effort to improve the railroad's physical condition, and were markedly successful. The railroad was not back in the black until 1942, when wartime traffic boomed on the main lines. The war stimulated some traffic on the narrow gauge, notably uranium from the Rio Grande Southern, but reduced others. Gold mining was prohibited for the duration. The railroad in 1941 abandoned the Santa Fe line, which had lost almost all of its traffic, but had generated remarkable political support for its continuance. The Orient branch in the San Luis Valley, unused for some years, was also torn up. The remainder of the narrow gauge, except for some mine spurs, survived the war. In 1946 the Baldwin branch was cut back to Castleton after the coal mines at Baldwin had ceased production. The outer portion of the neighboring coal line from

Crested Butte to Anthracite was dropped in the following year.

On April 11, 1947, the railroad was reorganized, again without change of name. The equity of the Missouri Pacific and Western Pacific had been wiped out, and the company was able to pursue its interests independently. The railroad had a difficult physical plant—only partly because of its narrow gauge origins—but the economic development of the American West had given it continually increasing traffic. The railroad's future lay in its end-to-end east-west traffic and in its coal originations. The narrow gauge was at best an irrelevant part of a prosperous and promising railroad. The traditional narrow gauge circle, including the Rio Grande Southern, was still intact. Although the RGS had been widely expected to be the first part to go, the circle was actually broken between Cedar Creek and Sapinero on the old main line. This portion of the railroad had been going downhill for years. Regular passenger service through the Black Canyon had been dropped in 1936, and between Salida and Gunnison in 1940. Considerable coal still

moved east from Gunnison, but to the west there was little remaining traffic but an annual sheep movement. The track over Cerro Summit was in bad shape, subject to a chronic earthslide. The D&RGW applied to abandon the Cedar Creek–Sapinero segment in 1948 and discontinued service on May 28, 1949. In February 1951 the Alamosa-Durango passenger train, the "San Juan," was discontinued, ending all passenger service on the narrow gauge except the mixed train to Silverton. In the same year, the entire narrow gauge line down the San Luis Valley from Mears Junction to Alamosa was removed, leaving only the standard gauge rails between Alamosa and Hooper. The demise of this line isolated the Gunnison and Monarch branches out of Salida from what remained of the narrow gauge circle. The long-awaited abandonment of the Rio Grande Southern occurred in 1952, leaving the surviving D&RGW narrow gauge in three isolated segments. In 1953 the one centering on Montrose was eliminated by abandoning the Ouray branch along with the Montrose–Cedar Creek remnant of the old main line, and converting the Montrose-Ridgway trackage. What was left of the old main line from Poncha Junction on the Monarch branch to Sapinero, with the branches from Gunnison to Crested Butte and Castleton, was approved for abandonment late in 1953 and shut down in the following year. Coal had ceased to move from the two branches, and sheep, the only other major traffic, were going to the trucks. Only the Monarch branch remained of the lines out of Salida, but that was converted in 1956.

Large-scale pipe movements in the Farmington oil field had kept the Alamosa-Durango-Farmington line busy, if not profitable, since 1951, but these declined abruptly after 1956. The Silverton branch had lost almost all its traffic from mines, but its spectacular scenery had caused it to become a major tourist attraction. The railroad inevitably applied to abandon it, but was refused by the ICC in 1962. The decision was difficult to explain, for the line had ceased to be a significant facility in the nation's freight transport system, however important it might have been as a generator of tourist revenues for local towns. Traffic between Alamosa and Farmington no longer warranted regular service; beginning in 1959 trains operated only when cargo was offered. After 1964 winter operation over Cumbres Pass was no longer practical. The D&RGW applied to abandon the line in 1968 and received permission effective December 29, 1969. The railroad did not include the Silverton branch in this application, probably wishing to be cooperative with possible buyers. With three locomotives and all the remaining narrow gauge passenger equipment, including 14 new cars, the line was covering the variable costs of its burgeoning tourist traffic, but the railroad would not have restored it if, as on several earlier occasions, a flood of the Rio de las Animas had wiped out the trestles. It was sold in March 1981 to Charles E. Bradshaw of Florida, who organized the Durango & Silverton Narrow Gauge Railroad to operate it. The line is nominally a common carrier of freight, but is actually almost wholly a tourist facility. The states of Colorado and New Mexico cooperated with private parties in perpetuating the more scenic portion of the Alamosa-Farmington line between Antonito and Chama as a tourist carrier, the Cumbres & Toltec Scenic Railroad. At the present writing, about 1,140 miles of the D&RGW's standard gauge system is former narrow gauge trackage.

REFERENCES: Robert A. LeMassena, *Rio Grande . . . to the Pacific!* (Denver, Colo.: Sundance, Ltd., 1974); John B. Norwood, *Rio Grande Narrow Gauge* (River Forest, Ill.: Heimburger House, 1983); Robert G. Athearn, *Rebel of the Rockies* (New Haven, Conn.: Yale University Press, 1962); Gordon Chappell and Cornelius W. Hauck, *Scenic Line of the World*, Colorado Rail Annual No. 8 (Golden: Colorado Railroad Museum, 1970); Tivis E. Wilkins, *Colorado Railroads* (Boulder, Colo.: Pruett Publishing Co., 1974); O. Meredith Wilson, *The Denver and Rio Grande Project 1870–1901* (Salt Lake City, Utah: Howe Brothers, 1982).

Denver Circle Railroad

Although this company was projected as a terminal railroad for the various narrow gauges entering the city, it proved to be mainly a steam tramway, one of several that provided passenger transport before the coming of the cable car and the electric streetcar.

The railroad was promoted by W. A. H. Loveland and T. C. Henry, and incorporated on November 16, 1880. The founders planned, as their corporate title indicates, a narrow gauge belt line completely around the city for interchange among the various lines that used 3'-0" gauge. They also envisioned using the line for real estate development on the edges of the growing city, and for this they incorporated the Denver Circle Real Estate Company in 1882.

Actually, the promoters accomplished only a suburban system running south from central Denver. The track began at a passenger station at Cherry Creek and Larimer

Street, and proceeded along the south bank of the creek on a trestle of about 2,000 feet. The route ran approximately along the present 14th Avenue, Inca Street, Third Avenue, and Cherokee Street to Bayaud Avenue. At that point the line divided. The west line ran along Bayaud, crossed the South Platte River, and terminated at about First Avenue and Bryant Street. This line had an interchange with the Denver, South Park & Pacific, which was also used as a wye. The east line ran along Bayaud, Logan Street, and Evans Avenue to a point about eight blocks east of Colorado Seminary, which became the University of Denver. The railroad opened for revenue service on April 6, 1882. To stimulate traffic, the railroad built a resort called Jewell Park (Overland Park), which was reached by a short branch off the east line in 1883. Total mileage of the system was 9.7. The railroad operated with main-line technology. Of its seven locomotives, four were 4-6-0s, all of which saw service on narrow gauge common carriers after the end of the Denver Circle. The company did handle freight, but in limited volume. In 1881, at the time the railroad opened, it had two boxcars. In 1885 freight receipts were about $500; passenger receipts, in contrast, came to $22,000. About 1.5 miles of track were laid with third rail for switching of standard gauge freight cars.

The railroad as completed was not a success. It did, however, have an access to downtown Denver that was attractive to a railroad building into the city from the south. This consideration caused the Atchison, Topeka & Santa Fe to buy the company in 1887. The Denver City Council refused to allow the Santa Fe to use the narrow gauge's entry, however. The new owner continued to operate the line as a suburban passenger carrier until 1898, when the spread of cable and electric trackage on the south side of Denver rendered the operation redundant.

REFERENCE: Morris Cafky, *Steam Tramways of Denver* (Denver, Colo.: Rocky Mountain Railroad Club, 1950). The other steam tramways of Denver were not common carriers of freight, and are thus considered outside the scope of the present book.

Denver, South Park & Hill Top Railway

To serve the mining area in the Park Range above Fairplay, up Four Mile Creek and Horse Shoe Gulch, Frank T. Trumbull, Felix Leavick, and some other mine owners joined with the Union Pacific to form the

Denver, South Park & Hill Top Railway on September 1, 1896. Trumbull, owner of the Hill Top and Last Chance mines in the area, was also serving as receiver of the UP's Denver, Leadville & Gunnison. The line was undertaken from Hill Top Junction below Fairplay on the DL&G's Alma Branch, and completed to Leavick (11 miles) in December 1896. The line entailed an ascent of 1,449 feet, an average grade of about 2.4 percent. The grade approaching Leavick was 5.85 percent, and the grades in prospect to the west made further construction impractical.

The railroad was financed by Trumbull's Hill Top Mining Co., which owned 49 percent of the stock, and by the DL&G, which owned 51 percent. On October 1, 1897, Trumbull acquired full control of the railroad. He arranged for Hill Top to operate it until December 28, 1898, when he conveyed it to the DL&G. It became the South Park Line's Leavick branch, which ceased regular operation in 1923, but was not removed until the railroad was scrapped in 1938.

REFERENCE: Poor, *Denver, South Park & Pacific*, pp. 290–92, 334, 389.

Denver, South Park & Pacific Railroad

Second largest of the narrow gauges in the Rocky Mountain network was the Denver, South Park & Pacific, which achieved about 340 miles of 3'-0". The railroad was promoted by Governor John Evans of Colorado, who had previously attempted to build into the high mountain area by incorporation of the Denver, Georgetown & Utah Railroad early in 1872. Because the Colorado Central had preempted the only water-level grade to Georgetown, Evans was forced to seek another—and far more expensive—route. He hit upon a line going south from Denver along the South Platte River, turning up Bear Creek, and traversing Mt. Vernon Canyon. In addition, Evans projected a branch through South Park to the anthracite region around Gunnison. As building to the Georgetown area via Bear Creek and Mt. Vernon Canyon proved impossibly expensive, Evans and his associates abandoned the projected Denver, Georgetown & Utah and instead devoted their energies to a new railroad intended principally to serve South Park, the Gunnison area, and the mining regions to the southwest. This was the Denver, South Park & Pacific Railway, which they incorporated on October 2, 1872. They reincorporated it as the Denver, South Park & Pacific Railroad on June 16, 1873.

The new railroad's articles of incorporation showed intentions different from what the geographical pattern proved to be. The main line was to run from South Park south along the Arkansas River, over Poncha Pass, through Del Norte, and to the San Juan mining area of southwestern Colorado. A branch was to run through Summit County to Middle Park. Provision was made for both lines to be built to the Pacific Ocean. The former would probably have run along the Colorado River through the Grand Canyon to Southern California, and the latter to Salt Lake City along the general route of the later Denver & Rio Grande Western main line, and thence to the San Francisco Bay Area.

Construction of the railroad began in July 1873, following approval by the voters of Arapahoe County, in which a portion of Denver is located, of a $300,000 bond issue, the proceeds of which would be converted into stock of the company. In accord with normal practice, a construction company, the Denver Railway Association, was incorporated. The initial contract between the railroad and the construction company provided for a main line of 150 miles from Denver to an unspecified point on the Arkansas River, plus a branch from Sheridan Junction, just south of Denver, up Bear Creek to Morrison. The construction company was to be paid $1.9 million in stock of the railroad on completion of the initial line. The right-of-way was ready for rails in April 1874. The first portion completed was the Morrison branch, in June 1874. The branch originated coal from the Mt. Carbon mine, along with stone and lumber, providing the railroad with revenue from the outset.

The depression following the Panic of 1873 greatly impeded progress. The construction company, in fact, had to be reformed three times. Track reached South Platte at the mouth of the canyon of the North Fork of the South Platte River by early 1878. By early 1879 track had reached Webster, at the head of the canyon and at the foot of Kenosha Pass. With a grade of 4 percent, the line was pushed to the summit of the pass, 9,991 feet, in May 1879. From there the line descended into South Park, where the flat terrain was easy for construction. By the time the track reached Webster, the railroad was grossing about $1,200 per day, and had operating expenses of only about $480. The company's future seemed promising.

Track was pushed through South Park quickly, reportedly by work 24 hours a day.

By October 1879 the track had reached the south limit of South Park at the ascent of Trout Creek Pass, which the line would have to traverse to reach the Arkansas River valley. Evans had correctly anticipated that South Park would be a fruitful source of traffic. A branch was built from Como to King Coal Mines. Remarkably, the uncompleted railroad was proving highly profitable.

The intended target of the railroad remained the San Juan mining district of southwestern Colorado, but the mining boom at Leadville a short distance to the west prompted the management to reconsider. The problem was not easy, for the mountain barrier between South Park and Leadville was one of the worst in the state. The Denver & Rio Grande had also been attracted to the Leadville area, and was building toward it up the Arkansas River valley, which the Denver, South Park & Pacific would reach once it had built across Trout Creek Pass. The DSP&P pushed its rails across the pass and reached the river at Buena Vista on March 3, 1880, well in advance of the D&RG.

Meanwhile, Jay Gould had bought a half interest in the D&RG, and was working on a controlling interest in the South Park Line. Recognizing that two parallel railroads from Buena Vista to Leadville would be wasteful, Gould arranged a Joint Operating Agreement of October 1, 1879, whereby the D&RG would build the line from Buena Vista to Leadville, granting the South Park Line trackage rights. In return, the DSP&P would build from the Buena Vista area directly up Chalk Creek Canyon, over Alpine Pass, and down into the Gunnison mining area, extending trackage rights to D&RG. The joint line into Leadville was built in 1880.

By late 1880 Gould had acquired control of the Union Pacific, Kansas Pacific, Denver Pacific, and Colorado Central. The Kansas Pacific already held a substantial interest in the Denver, South Park & Pacific. This acquisition gave Gould full control of the South Park Line. By November 1880 he owned all the stock in the railroad and its construction company. He quickly moved to consolidate his holdings into a larger Union Pacific system. The narrow gauge was to retain its corporate identity, but effective January 1, 1881, it was to be operated as the South Park Division of the Union Pacific Railroad.

The South Park Line persisted in its plans for an extension to Gunnison, which had added a boom in precious metals to its existing coal, limestone, and iron operations. The company chose a direct route

from Nathrop on the Arkansas River below Buena Vista up Chalk Creek, over Alpine Pass, down Quartz Creek to Parlin, and along Tomichi Creek into Gunnison. Since the D&RG's route over Marshall Pass from Salida was much easier, its tracks were in Gunnison by 1881, whereas the South Park did not arrive until September 1882. The South Park Line's mileage was only 208; the D&RG's was 290.

The Gunnison extension required the longest tunnel ever built on a Colorado narrow gauge, the famous Alpine Tunnel. This bore of 1,805 feet peaked at an elevation of 11,612 feet, the highest altitude reached by an American railroad up to that time. Construction proved more difficult than anticipated when the rock was discovered to be loose stone crossed by underground streams, rather than solid granite. The tunnel had to be lined with California redwood beams. The interior dimensions, 12′6″ × 8′10″, were the most restrictive on the railroad. The ascents in either direction involved extensive 4-percent grades, and the west ascent contained a 24° curve at Woodstock. The tunnel presented serious ventilation problems, and the isolated location afforded negligible creature comforts, whether in building the tunnel or in operating the railroad. An engine house and a boardinghouse were built at the west portal.

Gunnison was never intended to be the final destination of the railroad. Construction continued up Ohio Creek to the coalfields around Baldwin. Track reached Baldwin in 1883, and some very heavy grading was done to the northwest on the projected route to Utah. About four miles of track were laid and an additional eight miles were graded. The route would have been over Ohio Pass, then down Anthracite Creek and the North Fork of the Gunnison River, to Delta and Grand Junction. The Denver & Rio Grande was already far advanced with its own extension to Utah through the Black Canyon of the Gunnison. Similarly, the D&RG was progressing beyond Gunnison toward Lake City and Ouray, foreclosing the South Park Line's projected route to the San Juan mining area and the Southwest.

The Denver & Rio Grande's greater success in this period resulted in a rupture of the agreement for joint access to Leadville. Because the D&RG handled 75 to 80 percent of the traffic out of Leadville, its management became dissatisfied with the provision of the Joint Operating Agreement of 1879 whereby the gross revenue was pooled and the profits split equally. Union Pacific officials felt that the agreement was unfair to the South Park Line under the circumstances, for it obligated the smaller carrier to split the maintenance expenses evenly with the larger. The D&RG served notice of termination of the agreement effective in February 1884. Since Leadville was still a major source of traffic, and the South Park Line's ambitions of expansion to the west were now thwarted, it became necessary to build the company's own line to Leadville.

Any route from South Park to Leadville would have been difficult. In 1880 the railroad had undertaken branch lines from Garos to Fairplay on the eastern escarpment of the Park Range, and from Como across Boreas Pass to Breckenridge at the head of the Blue River valley. As a consequence, the railroad had three alternatives for a route to Leadville: a line of 35.5 miles up the Arkansas River valley from Buena Vista parallel to the D&RG; a direct line from Fairplay through the Park Range; and an extension of the Breckenridge branch down into the Blue River valley and then up over Fremont Pass into Leadville via Climax. The most direct route from Fairplay would have entailed another major tunnel. The directors decided upon the line over Fremont Pass, which had the incidental advantage of foreclosing the route projected by the Colorado Central. This decision entailed two crossings of the Continental Divide, since the Blue River valley is on the west side and Leadville on the east. The line was built to Dillon and Keystone in the Blue River valley in 1883 and extended from Dickey, three miles south of Dillon, to Leadville in 1884. Denver-Leadville mileage was only 151, compared to the D&RG's 276. The D&RG quickly pushed its own line from Leadville to the Blue River valley in 1882, preempting the better grade across Fremont Pass and through Ten Mile Canyon into Dillon. In spite of its shorter distances, the South Park Line's status as a second-class rival to the Denver & Rio Grande was becoming well established.

The South Park Line's early profitability persisted until 1883, but the railroad was unprofitable for the rest of the decade. The Rio Grande continued to carry most of the ores, and the South Park Line became highly dependent on coal from the Baldwin area. A receiver was appointed in May 1888, and the railroad was reorganized as the Denver, Leadville & Gunnison Railway in August 1889. In the new organization control by the Union Pacific was complete; holders of DSP&P securities were paid off in Union Pacific obligations. The UP in 1890 consolidated several of its properties in Colorado, including the South Park Line,

The South Park Line's daily train for Leadville prepares for departure from Denver in 1900. (G. M. Best collection, California State Railroad Museum.)

into the Union Pacific, Denver & Gulf Railway, but the narrow gauge was allowed to retain its identity as the Denver, Leadville & Gunnison. This arrangement proved quite short-lived, for the Union Pacific itself went bankrupt on October 13, 1893, dragging its subsidiaries with it. On August 7, 1894, the Denver, Leadville & Gunnison was placed under receiver Frank Trumbull, bringing the Union Pacific's control of the South Park Line to an end. The UP had no further interest in the narrow gauge, other than to keep it out of the hands of the Denver & Rio Grande. The South Park Line had ceased covering even its operating expenses by 1888, and by 1893 its finances were desperate. The depression of that year was severe, and the repeal of the Sherman Silver Purchase Act had hit the company particularly hard. A cave-in at Alpine Tunnel in 1887 had cut off the coal traffic from Baldwin. One of Trumbull's first acts was to order the reopening of the tunnel, in hope that the coal movements would mitigate the disastrous fall in ore shipments. The restoration of the tunnel was difficult—as anything connected with Alpine Tunnel was. Three employees were killed by fumes from the locomotive during an attempt to pump water from the tunnel on June 8, 1895. Later efforts were successful, and service was reestablished to Gunnison in the summer of 1895. Trumbull was an effective administrator; he managed to reduce the nar-

row gauge's operating ratio to 85 percent, and by 1898 reorganization was practicable.

Late in 1898 bondholders of the former Union Pacific properties formed the Colorado & Southern Railway, which consisted mainly of a standard gauge line from Orin Junction, Wyoming, to a point on the Texas–New Mexico border, from which the affiliated Fort Worth & Denver City Railway ran to Fort Worth. The company absorbed both the South Park Line and the Colorado Central; thereafter the two narrow gauges operated integrally. Operation of the narrow gauge lines by the Colorado & Southern began January 12, 1899. Trumbull remained with the Colorado & Southern as general manager. Trumbull and some associates in 1898 formed the Leadville Mineral Belt Railway, which built a 2.3-mile gathering facility to several mines in the Leadville area. In 1900 the C&S bought this railroad, built some additional track, and used the facility as a 3-mile extension of the South Park Line.

In 1902 Edwin T. Hawley and his associates bought control of the Colorado & Southern. Trumbull remained in charge of the railroad until 1908, retiring when Hawley sold the controlling interest in the railroad to the Chicago, Burlington & Quincy. The Colorado & Southern and Fort Worth & Denver retained their corporate identities, but were operated as part of

Gerald M. Best took this famous photograph of the South Park Line's Leadville train leaving Denver on June 10, 1934. (California State Railroad Museum.)

the Burlington system. The change in ownership worked to the detriment of the South Park Line. Trumbull had shown continuing interest in its operation, but the new management clearly thought little of the narrow gauge's prospects.

In 1910 Alpine Tunnel had another cave-in, though apparently not of major magnitude. The management, however, decided to close the tunnel and to give up through service to Gunnison and Baldwin. Operation between Hancock and Quartz, 14 miles, was abandoned in October 1910, though the rails were left in place until 1923. Simultaneously with the closing of the tunnel, the railroad suffered flood damage in Trout Creek Pass, which caused the C&S to abandon the segment from Garos to Buena Vista. This left isolated the line from Buena Vista up toward the east portal of the tunnel, which had several mines the railroad considered worth serving. Initially, service was provided thrice weekly by mixed train to St. Elmo, Romley, and Hancock, but in 1915 the line was cut back 2.5 miles to avoid difficult maintenance problems between Hancock and Romley. Mining in the area continued to decline, and the Denver & Rio Grande was planning to remove a third rail from its Salida-Leadville line, which would have rendered the branch physically unconnected with any other narrow gauge trackage. These considerations caused the line to be abandoned on October 11, 1924. Track was removed in 1926.

An agreement was made with the Denver & Rio Grande for operation of the trackage west of the tunnel. The portion from Parlin to Quartz on the western ascent

to Alpine Tunnel and the Baldwin branch were turned over to the D&RG for operation. The connection between Parlin and Gunnison was abandoned as redundant on the D&RG's Salida-Gunnison line, which was immediately parallel. In return the Colorado & Southern took over the D&RG's Leadville-Dillon branch. Since this was redundant on what was now the South Park Line's main line to Leadville, it was rarely used and was removed in 1924. The Pitkin branch lasted until 1934. Ownership of the Baldwin branch was surrendered to the D&RG in 1937, and the line survived until the D&RG abandoned its Salida-Gunnison route in 1954.

After 1910 the South Park Line consisted of the Denver-Leadville route, plus the lines into the mining area around Alma and Fairplay, plus some shorter branches. This proved a hopelessly unprofitable railroad. From 1910 to 1927, the railroad averaged $330,000 in operating revenues and $490,000 in operating expenses per year. The average annual loss after fixed charges was about $250,000. The Colorado & Southern made several attempts to close the line in whole or in part. During the winter of 1910–11 the C&S discontinued operation over Boreas Pass, which had always presented serious snow problems. Trains on the main line continued to Garos, Fairplay, and Alma, and service was provided from Leadville to Breckenridge for the Blue River valley. No effort was made to open the line for the summer of 1911. The Breckenridge Chamber of Commerce brought a legal action that forced restoration of service from Como to Breckenridge

in January 1913. The C&S operated a passenger train between Denver and Leadville daily except Sundays, plus three freights a week.

The Colorado & Southern shortly made its first effort to abandon the narrow gauge completely, but the Colorado Public Utilities Commission denied the request in October 1915. The railroad continued its unprofitable way. By the mid-1920s mining on the line was down to the London mine at Alma, the Tiger and Wellington mines at Breckenridge, and the molybdenum mine at Climax, the biggest American mine for this mineral. Techniques for concentration of ores that had been developed since the railroad was built had made road transport practical for small mines. The next abandonment attempt was initiated not by the railroad, but by the City and County of Denver, which sought to build a series of three dams along the Platte south of Waterton that would inundate at least 12 miles of narrow gauge. A replacement line would have been 16.75 miles, with 12 miles of 2-percent grades and 16 tunnels. The cost would have been $2.9 million, which the railroad could hardly be said to justify. Consequently, on August 17, 1928, Denver applied to the Interstate Commerce Commission to order abandonment of the narrow gauge from Waterton to Buffalo, 19.14 miles. The Colorado & Southern followed with an application for complete abandonment of what remained of the South Park Line on September 22, 1928.

The ICC—remarkably, under the circumstances—refused to allow the abandonment. It was swayed by the arguments of local stockmen, quarry operators, and mine owners, and ordered the railroad continued for at least three years, effective June 2, 1930. The Commission suggested that the railroad introduce rigorous economies in operation, and discussed the possibility of state tax remission on the property. The C&S made a bona fide effort to continue the line, even requesting dimensions and cost estimates for three 2-6+6-2 articulated locomotives from Baldwin. The Depression prevented any serious prospect of building the engines. Traffic did improve enough in 1934 to require rental of three 2-8-0s from the D&RG.

The Colorado & Southern management in the abandonment action of 1928 had stated its willingness to sell or even to give the narrow gauge to any responsible parties who would continue the operation. Several people responded, but only two formed corporations and attempted financing. W. C. Johnstone and his associates formed the Denver Intermountain & Summit Railway, which in 1932 applied to the ICC to take control of the railroad. His plan entailed a bond issue of $750,000, which he was unable to finance. The C&S rejected his proposal.

Victor A. Miller, receiver of the Rio Grande Southern, formed the Denver, Leadville & Alma Railroad in hope of operating the South Park Line in the fashion of the RGS. Miller proposed to replace the passenger train with self-powered units along the lines of the Galloping Geese, which he was already operating with some success in the San Juan district. He planned to invest $175,000 in the South Park Line, and hoped to make it profitable through development of on-line coal and timber. Of the two projects, this was clearly the one taken more seriously by the railroad and the regulatory authorities. The C&S decided against the proposal on the ground that the proposed operation would not be economic.

Under the circumstances, a further effort at abandonment was inevitable. On August 16, 1935, the Colorado & Southern renewed its application but this time exempted the Climax-Leadville segment, wishing to continue service to the molybdenum mine. Because of the high price of scrap, the railroad no longer offered to give the South Park Line to an independent operator. The railroad suffered from a continuation of the trends that had operated against the narrow gauge previously. The London mine, for example, had shifted to trucks. Predictably, the ICC in this instance allowed abandonment from Denver to Climax, including branches, effective December 11, 1936. Protestors argued that it would be difficult to arrange alternative shipping facilities in the face of winter. The Commission then postponed the effective abandonment date to April 10, 1937. The railroad ended main line service as scheduled; the last passenger train left Denver for Leadville on April 9 and returned on April 10.

Once again a corporation was formed in an attempt to preserve the railroad. The South Park Railroad was organized by George Robinson and his associates on April 12, 1937. On the following day this corporation secured an order from the court in Breckenridge granting it temporary control of the abandoned portion of the railroad. This prevented the C&S from moving seven locomotives from Leadville back to Denver; but the order could not be made permanent, and the new firm, because of the high price of scrap, was unable to finance purchase of the line.

Although the Colorado & Southern had

The South Park Line ascended into the Rockies via South Platte Canyon. Locomotive No. 71 is shown near Estabrook in 1938 during dismantling operations. (Richard H. Kindig.)

permission to abandon the line from Denver, the management chose to retain it as far as Waterton, plus the branch to Silica, to handle feldspar movements. After a period of three-rail operation, the narrow gauge track was removed in 1941–42. The other remnant, Leadville-Climax, was much more important. World War II made the molybdenum mine flourish, so that there was no prospect of abandoning the branch. Rather, the railroad built a heavy standard gauge track outside the narrow gauge rails. Locomotive No. 76 provided the last narrow gauge trip amid considerable ceremony on August 25, 1943. Remarkably, the railroad had survived as a narrow gauge for 70 years, even though it would be difficult to justify its existence after 1893.

REFERENCES: M. C. Poor, *Denver, South Park & Pacific* (Denver: Rocky Mountain Railroad Club, 1949); R. H. Kindig, E. J. Haley, and M. C. Poor, *Pictorial Supplement to Denver, South Park & Pacific* (Denver, Colo.: Rocky Mountain Railroad Club, 1959); Gordon Chappell, Robert W. Richardson, and Cornelius W. Hauck, *The South Park Line: A Concise History*, Colorado Rail Annual No. 12 (Golden: Colorado Railroad Museum, 1974).

Denver, Utah & Pacific Railroad

As completed, the Denver, Utah & Pacific amounted to a continuous narrow gauge from Denver to Lyons, Colorado. The railroad had its origin in separate projects to reach a minor coalfield near Canfield. The earlier of these was incorporated on January 3, 1878, as the Longmont & Erie Railroad to run south from the expanding town of Longmont to the Rob Roy Bank and Star mines. Before construction, the name of the company was changed to the Denver, Longmont & Northwestern Railroad on March 12, 1881. Construction began shortly, with the first locomotive, named *John H. Wells* after the railroad's general manager and principal promoter, arriving on August 6. The railroad was completed to the Mitchell mine south of Canfield, ten miles, on November 24, 1881.

Meanwhile, the Denver, Utah & Pacific Railroad was chartered on December 1, 1880, by David Moffat and his associates in Denver. This was the first of Moffat's several attempts at a transcontinental railroad running straight west from Denver. Moffat's intention was to build from Denver to Boulder, ascend the east face of the Rockies, cross Rollins Pass with a tunnel near Yankee Doodle Lake, and proceed west approximately along the route later taken by Moffat's Denver, Northwestern & Pacific, subsequently known as the Denver & Salt Lake. The line to the coalfield at Canfield was to be a branch, leaving the main line at Halleck Junction, 9.5 miles northwest of Denver. The branch, an additional 13.5 miles, was completed to a connection with the DL&NW at Mitchell on November 24, 1881. The projected main line west from Halleck Junction was never built. Instead, the DU&P extended to the north. The DL&NW and the DU&P had provided coordinated service between Denver and Longmont from the outset. The DL&NW was reorganized in the first half of 1883 as the Colorado Northern Railway, which was in turn merged into the DU&P on April 14, 1884. The DU&P proceeded to extend the line from Longmont to Lyons, 11 miles, on September 17, 1885, to serve quarrying in the area. There was some expectation of extending the railroad up Lefthand Canyon to Jamestown and across the Continental Divide at Buchanan Pass, or up St. Vrain Canyon from Lyons, but no further building was undertaken. Extension from Longmont to Greeley was proposed in 1887.

The railroad, as completed, was moderately successful. In 1882 it suffered from a rate war with the Colorado Central, which had completed laying standard gauge rails from Denver to Longmont in 1873. Yet the line had two assured sources of mineral traffic—the coalfield at Canfield and Mitchell and the quarries at Lyon. The narrow gauge attracted the attention of the Chicago, Burlington & Quincy, which through its Burlington & Missouri River subsidiary acquired the property by lease on September 1, 1889. The Burlington lost no time in converting the railroad. The Longmont-Lyons extension was, however, the only portion converted. The line from Denver to Longmont was abandoned in favor of a new route. The narrow gauge had the usual low physical standards, but in particular it had a difficult ascent and descent of the west escarpment of Empson Hill just south of Longmont. A new standard gauge line was built to the east of Empson Hill from Longmont to a point near Mitchell via Erie rather than Canfield. South of Mitchell the new line was built to the west of the narrow gauge on a grade of the unbuilt Denver, Western & Pacific Railway to Burns Junction, from which trains entered Denver by about 11 miles of trackage rights on the Denver, Marshall & Boulder. The standard gauge entry was in service by September 1889. The Longmont-Lyons branch and the replacement line from Longmont to Denver remain in service as part of the Burlington Northern's trackage in the area.

REFERENCE: B. L. Boyles, *Denver, Longmont & Northwestern: Longmont's Baby Railroad* (Denver, Colo.: Rocky Mountain Railroad Club, 1952).

Florence & Cripple Creek Railroad

The discovery of gold at Cripple Creek in 1890 initiated a mining boom about 20 miles southwest of Colorado Springs. David Moffat acquired control of the Victor Gold Mining Co. at Mill Hill and the Anaconda Mining Co. near Cripple Creek. The value of mine output in the Cripple Creek rose from $200,000 in 1891 to well over $2 million in 1893. A railroad was estimated to save about $3 per ton on movement of ore, and to make economic some low-grade mines. Moffat conceived a narrow gauge running from Canon City or Florence on the Denver & Rio Grande's three-rail trackage between Pueblo and Leadville. He commissioned H. A. Summer as engineer to design and supervise construction of the line. The project was a difficult one, for the railroad would have to rise from 5,199 feet at Florence to 9,700 feet at Victor and fall to 9,500 feet at Cripple Creek.

The projected Florence & Cripple Creek Railroad was given the right-of-way of the Florence & Cripple Creek Free Road Co., which had been organized in 1892 by local merchants and townspeople as a nonprofit corporation to build a wagon road. The route lay along the gorge of Eight Mile Creek, usually known as Phantom Canyon. The highway was opened March 28, 1892. The railroad used the road for access to construction sites, but incorporated only short segments into its grade.

Construction of the railroad began on January 1, 1894. The engineer used 45-pound rail and strove for better standards than those of earlier narrow gauges. The line left Florence from the D&RG station toward the west and went north via the dry wash of Six Mile Creek. At Oro Junta the line went through a gap in the hogback, crossed Eight Mile Park and joined Eight Mile Creek at the mouth of Phantom Canyon. The gradient in this area was a steady 4 percent, largely on the old road. Curves were very severe, up to 30°. The initial alignment was considered temporary; some of the track was on the creek bed itself. The line had two tunnels and a lariat loop at Wilbur at the head of Phantom Canyon.

The railroad was opened from Florence to Wilbur in May 1894. On July 1 the railroad was opened to Cripple Creek (40 miles) via the west side of Gold Hill. The narrow gauge proved the first railroad in Cripple Creek by a small margin; the standard gauge Midland Terminal completed a connection to the Colorado Midland at Divide on July 4.

In July 1895 a flood wiped out much of the railroad's right-of-way in Phantom Canyon. The company rebuilt three miles near the mouth of the canyon, raising the line 10 to 15 feet above water level at a cost of $50,000. Farther north the line was elevated between mileposts 12 and 18 at a cost of $198,000. The changes rendered the railroad free of major flood damage for the next 16 years. With the rebuilding, the company went to 60-pound rail, as heavy as most standard gauge railroads of the day used. The Florence & Cripple Creek was also one of the few narrow gauges to use tie plates. In 1899 the company built a spur of about two miles to mills north of Florence, and under the name of a subsidiary, the Canon City & Cripple Creek Railroad, built a branch of 7.24 miles from Oro Junta to Canon City. The Florence & Cripple Creek moved its operating headquarters from Florence to Canon City in 1901.

In 1896 Moffat organized the Golden Circle Railroad to run from Victor to Altman for local service to his mines, and on to Cripple Creek via the east side of Gold Hill. The railroad was never completed, but it was built from Victor to a balloon loop at Vista Grande at a 10,550-foot altitude just west of Altman. The F&CC leased the Golden Circle Railroad in 1897 and operated suburban service between Cripple Creek, Victor, Goldfield, and Vista Grande.

The year 1897 represented a peak for the Florence & Cripple Creek. In the fiscal year ending June 30, 1897, the railroad hauled 239,469 passengers and 208,411 tons of freight, yielding a profit of $218,926. After a short period of competition with the Midland Terminal, the two lines reached an agreement on rates about this time. The Midland Terminal began to lay third rail along some of the F&CC's tracks for standard gauge operation. The Denver & Southwestern Railway was organized by Eastern interests in 1899 as a holding company for the two railroads. Thereafter, a variety of forces worked contrary to the interest of the narrow gauge. As standard gauge track spread about Colorado, it was more attractive to ship ore out via the Midland Terminal. The monopoly of the F&CC and the Midland Terminal brought forth a third railroad, the Colorado Springs & Cripple Creek District, in 1901. The Florence & Cripple Creek leased the CS&CCD in 1911. Thereafter, little ore moved by the narrow gauge to mills at its south end, but rather moved mainly to Colorado Springs directly for processing. The Denver & Southwestern had gone bankrupt in 1903 and been replaced by the Cripple Creek Central Railway as the holding company in 1904.

On July 21, 1912, a cloudburst flooded Phantom Canyon, wiping out about three miles of narrow gauge track, including 12 bridges. By this time most of the railroad's traffic was origination of ore for transshipment to standard gauge equipment at Walker Transfer. Accordingly, the directors of the Cripple Creek Central voted to abandon the narrow gauge's main line but to retain the switching trackage, using equipment marooned at the north end. The Colorado Public Utilities Commission in April 1914 ordered the company to restore service, but the Cripple Creek Central refused, and dissolved the Florence & Cripple Creek on April 30, 1915. The main line was dismantled during 1915, but the remaining track continued in operation under the Golden Circle Railroad, which changed its name to the Cripple Creek & Colorado Springs Railroad. This company assumed the narrow gauge's lease of the Colorado Springs & Cripple Creek District. In the summer of 1917 the Cripple Creek–Victor track, 5.7 miles, was abandoned and the Victor–Vista Grande line, 4.91 miles, was converted to standard gauge. The three remaining narrow gauge locomotives were sold. The Florence & Cripple Creek's locomotives and equipment circulated particularly widely. Engines went to the D&RG, Rio Grande Southern, Pajaro Valley Consolidated, Nevada-California-Oregon, and elsewhere. Cars were sold to the NCO, Oahu Railway, Pacific Coast Railway, and Nevada County Narrow Gauge, among others.

REFERENCES: Morris Cafky, *Rails Around Gold Hill* (Denver, Colo.: Rocky Mountain Railroad Club, 1955), pp. 15–36; Tivis E. Wilkins, *A History of the Florence & Cripple Creek and Golden Circle Railroads*, Colorado Rail Annual No. 13 (Golden: Colorado Railroad Museum, 1976).

Gilpin Tramway
Gauge: 2'-0"

A narrow gauge among narrow gauges, the Gilpin Tramway was a 2'-0" gathering facility for ores from gold mines above Black Hawk. The incompatibility with the Colorado Central was a minimal problem, for most of the ore was processed in Black Hawk. The remainder was transferred by gravity to 3'-0" equipment for processing in Denver or elsewhere.

The tramway was promoted by Henry C. Bolsinger, owner of the Hubert Mine, and Robert A. Campbell, head of the Public Sampling Works, a major smelter in Black Hawk, together with several other men active in local mining. The railroad was organized on July 19, 1886, and graded beginning in May 1887. The management bought enough 35-pound rail for eight miles of track from the Utah & Northern, which had recently converted its line north of Pocatello. The line opened for business on December 11, 1887, to the Grand Army Mine (c. 3 miles). The railroad was unusual in having no specific right-of-way under its charter; lightly built track was laid to mines and smelters as required. The main line was considered the 10.67 miles from the gravity transfer in Black Hawk to the Banta Hill Mine. Mileage varied, but the peak reported in 1910 was 26.46 miles. The physical standards were typical of lumber railroads, with curves as sharp as 66 feet in radius—possibly even 50 feet—and a large number of switchbacks. Traffic was handled in four-wheel ore cars from a total of 55 mines. The line served 23 mills or smelters over the course of its history. No regular passenger service was ever offered, but the railroad provided excursion trains, originally using the ore cars but later in cross-bench open equipment. The railroad owned five Shay locomotives.

In the early twentieth century the railroad handled about 300 tons of ore per day and earned more than $40,000 per year. The proprietors sold the line on June 27, 1906, to the Colorado & Southern, which on July 25 organized the Gilpin Railroad to operate it. Mining in the area declined steadily and the railroad was unprofitable by 1914. The last train ran on January 17, 1917, and the line was scrapped.

REFERENCES: Henry T. Crittenden, "The Gilpin Railroad," Railway & Locomotive Historical Society *Bulletin*, no. 57 (1942), pp. 94–98; Frank R. Hollenback, *The Gilpin Tramway* (Denver, Colo.: Sage Books, 1958); Mallory Hope Ferrell, *The Gilpin Gold Tram* (Boulder, Colo.: Pruett Publishing Co., 1970).

Little Book Cliff Railway

A nominal common carrier, this railroad was organized by W. T. Carpenter and his associates in September 1889 to haul coal from their Book Cliff and Grand Valley coal mines into Grand Junction. The line of somewhat over 11 miles was built in 1890 and put in full operation early in 1891. Traffic was almost entirely in coal, although the promoters hoped to handle fruit from local orchards. The railroad ran excursions early in its history. The company was put in receivership on May 1, 1891, and reorganized as the Colorado, Wyoming & Great Northern Railroad in 1894. The promoters of this enterprise, who were still headed by Carpenter, envisioned converting the railroad to standard gauge, extending it over Douglas Creek Summit, and then following Douglas Creek and the White and Green rivers to Green River, Wyoming, on the Union Pacific main line. Branches were envisioned east to Meeker, Colorado, and west to Heber City, Park City, and Provo, Utah. None of this could be accomplished, and the railroad remained a narrow gauge dependent on coal originations from affiliated mines.

In 1899 the company was again reorganized as the Book Cliff Railroad. Ownership passed into the hands of Isaac C. Wyman of Salem, Massachusetts. The management secured charter rights to build north to Douglas Creek Summit, apparently to develop coal reserves in the area, but again nothing was done to extend the railroad. The line continued in operation, handling coal from Wyman's Book Cliff mine with Shay locomotives. Reportedly, the line had ceased to be a common carrier by 1920. The railroad was closed in April 1925 and dismantled during the summer.

REFERENCE: Lyndon J. Lampert and Robert W. McLeod, *Little Book Cliff Railway* (Boulder, Colo.: Pruett Publishing Co., 1984).

London, South Park & Leadville Railroad

The London Mine, one of the major gold mines in Colorado, was opened in 1875. When the Denver, South Park & Pacific's Alma branch was built in 1882, the owners, who were led by Hugh J. Jewett and George R. Blanchard, decided on a rail connection. On February 16, 1882, they organized the London, South Park & Leadville Railroad to build from London Junction, about a mile south of Alma, to London Mill (7 miles). The line entailed an ascent of 1,218 feet at an average grade of 3.12 percent, with a double switchback. London Mill was about 800 feet below the mouth of London Mine, requiring a cable tramway, the first in Colorado, to lower the ore.

The railroad went into service in the fall of 1882. It proved a very difficult line to operate. The grade at the switchback was reportedly over 5 percent; the railroad's one locomotive could handle only about four empty gondolas upbound. Financial difficulties of the mining company caused the line to be reorganized as the South Park & Leadville Short Line Railroad on April 10, 1885, by David H. Moffat and his associates. The charter provided for an extension to Leadville via Mosquito and Bird's Eye gulches in a connection with the DSP&P's Leadville line, but this was never attempted. The Union Pacific controlled the railroad after the reorganization, but never merged it into the South Park Line. M. C. Poor reported that a change in location of the mouth of the London Mine left the railroad practically useless; it was abandoned in 1900.

REFERENCE: Poor, *Denver, South Park & Pacific*, pp. 269–71.

Rio Grande & Pagosa Springs Railroad

Edgar M. Biggs, Charles D. McPhee, and John J. McGinnity, partners in the New Mexico Lumber Co., planned a railroad to tap the timber stands north of their mill at Lumberton, New Mexico, on the Denver & Rio Grande between Chama, New Mexico, and Durango, Colorado. They incorporated it as a common carrier, the Rio Grande & Pagosa Springs Railroad, on February 2, 1895. Although they intended to reach the established town of Pagosa Springs, Colorado, eventually, their plan was to extend the line north in the fashion of lumber railroads, from one camp to another as the timber was exhausted. In 1895 they built to Edith, Colorado, a mill town named for Biggs's two-year-old daughter (6 miles). The remainder of the route to Pagosa Springs was surveyed, but not immediately built. Rather, in the name of the lumber company the management undertook a long spur east from Edith to the Navajo River. A rival lumber operator, Alexander T. Sullenberger, and his associates, including Edward T. Jeffery of the D&RG, incorporated the Rio Grande, Pagosa & Northern Railroad in 1899, which reached Pagosa Springs from Pagosa Junction in October 1900 and qualified for the mail contract into the town. This development assured that the RG&PS would remain essentially a lumber railroad. A fire at the Edith mill in October 1899 inhibited progress, but in 1902 track reached Blanco (22 miles). The line was then built across the divide between the Rio Blanco and San Juan River valleys with grades of 7 to 8 percent. In 1904 track reached Flaugh (30 miles) on the east bank of the San Juan below Pagosa Springs, but the management had no remaining incentive to extend the line or bridge the river into the town. The line's small claim to common carriage was handling passengers and general freight from Lumberton to Edith; the line to Flaugh was used almost exclusively for logging, but a flood of October 4, 1911, largely wiped out this trackage. In 1914 New Mexico Lumber Co. closed the mill at Edith and abandoned the remainder of the railroad.

REFERENCE: Gordon S. Chappell, *Logging Along the Denver & Rio Grande* (Golden: Colorado Railroad Museum, 1971), pp. 27–69.

Rio Grande Southern Railroad

The Rio Grande Southern was the final successful effort to build a narrow gauge into the San Juan mining area of southwestern Colorado, which had been the target for several earlier projects. Telluride, Ophir, Rico, and Placerville were four major mining camps in the area. In addition, the region, which was about the size of Connecticut, produced lumber and coal.

The promoter of the Rio Grande Southern was Otto Mears, who was already prominent in mining, the operation of toll roads, and railroading in the Silverton area. As has been widely pointed out, Mears had failed to extend his Silverton Railroad down the Uncompahgre Canyon into Ouray to complete a north-south line through southwestern Colorado. The Rio Grande Southern, by connecting Durango with Dallas Junction on the Ouray line, would provide this connection, though this was probably a secondary consideration to the prospect of local origination.

Mears incorporated the railroad on November 5, 1889. Mears's chief engineer, Charles W. Gibbs, made the initial survey in the remainder of the year. The northern portion followed the route of Mears's toll road from Dallas Junction to Telluride, which had been in operation since 1879. Dallas Junction was shortly renamed Ridgway after R. M. Ridgway, the first superintendent of the Rio Grande Southern.

Grading began from Ridgway on March 19, 1890, and the railroad was completed to Telluride (45 miles) on November 23. Owing to the passage of the Sherman Silver Purchase Act, the railroad now appeared assured of success. Construction from the south end began in the second half of 1890, and the line was opened from Durango to Porter (5 miles) on December 1. Completion of the line between the two isolated segments was extremely difficult. The railroad had to cross Lizard Head Pass at an altitude of 10,250 feet and had smaller summits at Millwood and Cima. The lines coming south from Vance Junction, seven miles short of Telluride, and north from Porter, were joined at Red Rock about midway between Rico and Dolores on December 19, 1891. The first through train ran the 162 miles from Durango to Ridgway on January 2, 1892.

The Rio Grande Southern was built late enough in the narrow gauge era that its management was able to take advantage of the numerous conversions of narrow gauges elsewhere in the industry. In particular, standard gauging of the Denver & Rio Grande and Rio Grande Western main line from Denver to Salt Lake City had created a considerable amount of redundant motive power and rolling stock in the area. As a consequence, the Rio Grande Southern was initially stocked mainly with former D&RG or Rio Grande Western locomotives and boxcars. Remarkably for a railroad of its size, the Rio Grande Southern throughout its history maintained an unblemished record of never buying a new locomotive.

Since the railroad was completed about midway into the period of high prosperity in silver mining between the Sherman Silver Purchase Act of 1890 and its repeal in 1893, the Rio Grande Southern was assured of a history approximating the famous Russian description of marriage, "Six months of bliss and a lifetime of misery." The period of bliss in the Rio Grande Southern's case lasted somewhat under two years. In the summer of 1892, the railroad replaced the 30-pound rail from Vance Junction to Rico with 57-pound rail to handle the traffic. Indeed, expansion of the railroad was seriously contemplated. In October 1892 Mears told a shareholders' meeting that the company had surveyed a line from Mancos to Prescott Junction (Seligman) to connect with the Santa Fe system. In 1893 Mears projected an extension from Dolores or Mancos into southeastern Utah to serve a new goldfield along the lower San Juan River. The gold strike proved illusory and the line was never built.

The Rio Grande Southern's prosperity ended completely and permanently with President Cleveland's call for a special session of Congress to repeal the Sherman Silver Purchase Act on June 30, 1893. Traffic on the railroad dropped to less than half of its previous level. Hardly more than a month after the announcement, on August 2, 1893, the company went into a voluntary receivership. Edward T. Jeffery, president of the Denver & Rio Grande, was made receiver of the Rio Grande Southern. Otto Mears lost control of the railroad, and Jeffery organized the affairs of the Rio Grande Southern so as to assure that the Denver & Rio Grande would be its controlling influence permanently. Jeffery arranged for the D&RG to advance $169,839.10

to the RGS and to endorse RGS notes to the extent of $573,498.25 with maturity in one to three years. In return, the Rio Grande Southern transferred to the D&RG $868,000 of first-mortgage bonds and half of the common stock, 22,500 shares. In addition, unpaid interest on the RGS bonds was repudiated, and the interest on the company's debt was scaled down to 3 and 4 percent from higher levels. This arrangement allowed the receivership to be ended on December 1, 1895, with Jeffery becoming president of the railroad. The Denver & Rio Grande's holdings in the Rio Grande Southern reached about 70 percent of the common stock, but since the control was never complete, the RGS maintained its separate corporate entity and was operated independently. In addition to what remained of the silver ore traffic, the railroad handled gold, lead, zinc, and a variety of ores from which radioactive materials could be extracted: uranium, carnotite, and vanadium. The railroad continued to handle coal and lumber, and each fall it carried a big rush of sheep to market. The line's spectacular scenery made it a tourist attraction. Until World War I the Denver & Rio Grande ran passenger excursions around the narrow gauge circle, which included the Rio Grande Southern as the westernmost portion.

The railroad remained very difficult to operate partly because of its severe gradients and partly because of its serious snow problems. Avalanches and mud slides were continual threats. In September 1909 two dams of the Telluride Power Company burst, washing out bridges of the railroad between Vance Junction and Placerville, and also in the Ophir area. Otto Mears was recalled to supervise rebuilding of the damaged line. In October 1911 a flood washed out 50 miles of the railroad between Lizard Head and Dolores and did spot damage elsewhere. The line was closed until January 16, 1912.

The railroad did relatively well during World War I, when war-related demands increased the movements of ores. Experience in the 1920s was not favorable, however. The automobile had taken most of the tourist traffic. Output of the precious metals declined, and in 1928 the last active mine at Telluride closed. The company immediately went into the red, losing $56,000 in 1929. In April of that year a mud slide at Ames seriously damaged the trestle and covered a portion of the track in 50 feet of mud. Through operations for the length of the railroad were impossible.

This combination of events caused the Rio Grande Southern's second bankruptcy. The D&RG's own reorganization of 1921

had caused nominal control of the railroad to pass into the hands of the Western Pacific, though in any real sense the controlling interest remained with the Denver & Rio Grande Western, as it now was, in Denver. The D&RGW had little incentive to support the Rio Grande Southern and consequently allowed it to drift into receivership on December 11, 1929, in an action brought by the National Lumber & Creosoting Co. The Federal District Court at Denver appointed Victor A. Miller receiver of the Rio Grande Southern. Miller proved remarkably talented in cost control and enabled the railroad to last out the Great Depression. He quickly and cheaply repaired the line at Ames and began to make the railroad less dependent on the Denver & Rio Grande Western in provision of motive power. He upgraded Ridgway shops to the point that the railroad was able to handle its own major repairs. Miller also negotiated with the Railroad Brotherhoods to reduce the personnel requirements of RGS trains and also to allow somewhat greater variety of duties to the employees.

Miller's most famous improvement was replacing standard passenger trains and mixed trains with some homemade motor cars. These were fabricated from automobiles, mainly Pierce-Arrow sedans, to which a freight body was added. Passenger loads in the area, which had been greatly depopulated since the 1890s, were small enough so that the seats of the Pierce-Arrows could easily accommodate the typical travelers. The freight portions of the units handled LCL, express, and the closed-pouch mail that supported the operation. Because of the honking quality of their

horns and a swaying gait on the deteriorated track, they came inevitably to be known as "the Galloping Geese."

Miller was replaced as receiver by Cass M. Herrington on November 16, 1938. Herrington shortly applied to the Reconstruction Finance Corporation for a loan, which was denied him on the ground that the railroad had insufficient security. Herrington next applied to abandon the railroad. The Rio Grande Southern would probably have perished in the early 1940s except for war-related demands for some of the mining products of the area. Through the good offices of state representative Elizabeth Pellet, Herrington secured a loan of $59,000 from the RFC. For the railroad to qualify for the loan, the Defense Supplies Corporation, a subsidiary of the RFC, had to purchase the facilities for $65,000. The governmental body then leased the plant back to the receiver for $1,000 per month plus 6 percent interest. After the war it was revealed that the government's interest in keeping the RGS operating stemmed in part from the uranium-bearing ores produced along the line. Even tailings from the mines from previous years were shipped out to the plants that were fabricating American nuclear weapons.

At the end of World War II Herrington received another federal loan of $50,000. In a desperate effort to keep the line going, Herrington imposed a $20 surcharge for every freight car passing over the railroad. This proved counterproductive by greatly accelerating the conversion of on-line shippers to trucking. Ore concentrates, peas, and beans were shortly exempted from the surcharge in an effort to reduce the damage.

Rio Grande Southern No. 20 doubleheads with D&RGW No. 452 on a northbound freight near Porter in 1947. (Otto C. Perry, Denver Public Library.)

Little time remained for the Rio Grande Southern. A boiler explosion on the railroad's rotary snowplow in January 1949 made it impossible to operate across Lizard Head Pass until May. The falling price of zinc shut down most of the zinc mining along the line. Protests from local residents over the quality of mail service resulted in the railroad's losing its mail contract on March 31, 1950. Actually, because of snow conditions, the mail had been handled by road since late 1949. J. Pierpont Fuller, who had replaced Herrington upon the latter's death in 1948, applied to the court for permission to discontinue regular passenger service and received it on May 12, 1950. The last regular passenger train had in fact operated on December 18, 1949. Excursions with the Galloping Geese were run in 1950 and 1951, however.

A mild winter in 1950–51 and a rise in zinc prices brought a superficial improvement in the railroad's fortunes. On June 1, 1951, the Idarado Mining Co. at Pandora deserted the railroad for trucks. Later in the year, the Rico-Argentine Mine also switched to highway transport. Since these had been the railroad's two largest shippers, the railroad no longer had the revenue to continue even in the spartan fashion of the two previous decades. Fuller applied to the court for permission to suspend operations and was granted the authority by Judge William L. Knous on December 17, 1951. Fuller then applied to the Interstate Commerce Commission for abandonment and without formal objection received permission on April 15, 1952. Track was removed mainly in August and September of 1952.

REFERENCES: Josie M. Crum, *The Rio Grande Southern Railroad* (Durango, Colo.: San Juan History, 1961); Mallory Hope Ferrell, *Silver San Juan: The Rio Grande Southern Railroad* (Boulder, Colo.: Pruett Publishing Company, 1973).

Silverton Railroad

Otto Mears, proprietor of a network of toll roads in the high mountain area north of Silverton, was motivated to convert his major routes to railroads by the arrival of the Denver & Rio Grande at Silverton in 1882. The "main line" of his road system between Silverton and Ouray served a well-developed mining area, mainly of silver, on the north side of Red Mountain Pass. Mears and his associates incorporated the Silverton Railroad on July 5, 1887, and shortly let contracts for construction. By the end of the year, track had been laid for five miles. The principal target for the railroad was the Yankee Girl Mine, the most important in

the area, located about a mile beyond the summit of Red Mountain Pass. Charles W. Gibbs, a former assistant to engineer Thomas Wigglesworth of the D&RG, was engaged to design the crossing of the pass and descent to the mines beyond. Gibbs made use of a survey of the line that Wigglesworth had done for the D&RG. The route ascended the pass along Mineral Creek. At Chattanooga, Gibbs built a diversion up Mill Creek to the west with a 30° curve known as the Chattanooga Loop, all on an uncompensated 5-percent grade. With only 1.75 miles of track, he managed to gain 550 feet in altitude in a distance of only about a quarter mile as the crow flies.

By late August 1888, track had reached the summit of the pass. On September 17 the first train reached the town of Red Mountain on the descent to the north. There Gibbs was under the necessity of arranging not only for the railroad to have a stub end in the town, but also for trains to continue to the mining area beyond. He dealt with this problem by building a wye around the Red Mountain station. The locomotive with not more than two cars could turn on the wye and continue downward. By the time construction ceased for the season on October 29, Gibbs had built 11 miles of railroad and reached the Yankee Girl. In 1889 he completed the railroad down Red Creek through Guston and Ironton to Albany. At Corkscrew, about a mile north of Guston, Gibbs was confronted with the necessity of a single switchback to lose altitude, but for safety reasons, and also to work the mine sidings below, it was necessary to have the locomotive at the head of the train. The railroad's 2-8-0 locomotives did not track well when backing in the snow. Gibbs dealt with the problem by putting a covered turntable on the switchback. Locomotives were reversed and the trains run through the switchback in both directions by gravity. When Gibbs completed a long trestle across Red Mountain Creek at Joker in the spring of 1889, the railroad was finished. The line was about 18 miles long. The final mile from Ironton to Albany operated only until 1892, when the Saratoga Mill at the end of the line closed.

In September 1888 the shareholders had authorized a series of expansions. Gibbs was directed to survey an extension from Ironton and Albany to Ouray down Uncompahgre Canyon, including a spur to the Virginius Mine. Gibbs found that the descent to Ouray would require losing 2,100 feet in five miles on an average grade of 8 percent. Not even Gibbs's impressive ingenuity was up to such a problem, and

the descent was not attempted. Rather, Mears projected first a rack railroad and next, in 1891, an electric line. The latter, the Ouray-Ironton Electric Railway, would have left Ouray on a 35° spiral loop, followed by a tunnel, the whole thing on a sustained 7-percent grade. Presumably it would have been practical only for streetcars and possibly for individual powered freight cars, but not for trains.

Also at the shareholders' meeting of September 1888, the management was authorized to build lines from Silverton up Cement Creek to Gladstone and up the Animas River to Eureka and Animas Forks. The latter was to be extended north to a junction with the main line, and also east over Cinnamon Pass to Lake City on the D&RG. These were the routes, actual or projected, of the Silverton, Gladstone & Northerly and the Silverton Northern, respectively, but the Silverton Railroad per se did not attempt them.

The repeal of the Sherman Silver Act in 1893 hit the Silverton Railroad's mining area particularly hard because most of the output was silver. The major mines continued in production, but they encountered an increasing problem of sulphuric acid in their underground water. This problem caused the Yankee Girl to close in 1896. The railroad went into receivership in 1899 but was reorganized as the Silverton Railway by Mears, George Crawford, and their associates in 1903. Crawford, an engineer who lived in Silverton, designed a tunnel discharging at Joker to drain the Yankee Girl and several adjacent mines. Upon completion in 1906 the tunnel, by lowering the water table, brought the Yankee Girl and other mines in the Guston area back into production. The tunnel was also used for hauling ore from the mines. The railroad was then abandoned beyond the loading facility at Joker, about a mile north of the Corkscrew turntable. From 1904 to 1909 the railroad was leased to Crawford's Red Mountain Railroad, Mining & Smelting Company, which had built the Joker tunnel.

Mears retired at the end of 1911, leaving the railroad in the hands of his son-in-law, James Pitcher. The railroad operated only in the summer and fall months. The Yankee Girl and the other major mines in the Guston area mainly shut down between 1912 and World War I. The war caused a minor revival in mining in 1917, but after the war the railroad found itself with virtually no traffic. Only a single mine on the line had been in continuous operation since 1912, but that now shipped its ore by wagon to the D&RG at Ouray. The railroad made only 49 trips in 1919 and 32 in

1920, and many of those were by work trains. Crews and equipment were furnished at cost by the affiliated Silverton Northern. The management filed to abandon the railroad on August 9, 1921, but encountered a jurisdictional dispute between state and federal authorities. This was at length resolved, and the Interstate Commerce Commission on June 17, 1922, gave its permission for abandonment. The rails were removed in 1926. The present Million Dollar Highway between Silverton and Ouray utilizes the right-of-way on the ascent of Red Mountain Pass from the south.

Silverton, Gladstone & Northerly Railroad

Although the shareholders of the Silverton Railroad authorized a branch up the valley of Cement Creek to Gladstone in 1888, the railroad on this route was actually built by other parties. The promoters were the financiers active in the Gold King Mine at Gladstone: Charles E. Bibber, J. Walter Davis, and Henry M. Soule, all of Boston; W. Z. Kinney and George Barnes of Silverton; and various associates in Maine and New Brunswick. The railroad was incorporated on April 6, 1899, and built during the early summer. Rails reached Gladstone in July. Including mine spurs, the railroad had about nine miles of track. The main line of 7.3 miles gained about 1,300 feet, with an average gradient of 3.91 percent and a ruling grade of 5.5 percent. The line had five 40° curves, and continual curvature of lesser magnitude. The company ran two mixed trains per day in its early years.

Being dependent on a gold mine, the railroad's traffic held up well in the 1890s, relative to the Colorado narrow gauges generally. The railroad was uniformly profitable until the Panic of 1907, but in 1908 its revenues declined greatly because of the closing of the Kendrick-Gelder Smelter just north of Silverton. When the Gold King Mine was closed by a strike and litigation in 1909, Otto Mears seized upon this as the opportunity to complete his transport empire north of Silverton. Effective January 1, 1910, he leased the mine and the railroad until 1916. Locomotives and equipment freely circulated among the three companies.

The SG&N did poorly enough that it failed to meet interest payments on its mortgage, which was foreclosed on July 10, 1915. At the foreclosure sale on July 23, Mears bought the railroad in the name of the Silverton Northern for only $14,600.

The railroad remained mainly dependent on the Gold King, and when the mine closed in 1922, the line had little reason for further existence. Operations reportedly ceased in 1924, but the Pitcher family, which had succeeded to Mears's interests, did not apply to abandon the line until 1937. The Colorado Public Utilities Commission gave pro forma approval in November. Because of residual hope that the Gold King might be reopened, rail was not removed until September 1938.

Silverton Northern Railroad

Repeal of the Sherman Silver Purchase Act in 1893 so reduced output of the mines along the Silverton Railroad that Otto Mears had to consider changing the geographical pattern of his transport enterprises. The mines to the northeast of Silverton along the upper Animas River produced more gold than the mines he already served. A branch up the Animas had been authorized by the Silverton Railroad's shareholders in 1888, but Mears chose to incorporate a new railroad, the Silverton Northern, to build the line. The new corporation was organized on September 20, 1895. The Silverton Railroad had built the first two miles of the route, as far as Waldheim Mine, in 1893, but title to the trackage was transferred to the new company. The railroad was completed to its first major target, Eureka, in June 1896. Relative to the Silverton Railroad, the line was an easy project; it gained only 575 feet in about eight miles. This was never considered the full extent of the railroad. In 1904 the line was extended to Animas Forks, rising 1,205 feet in the course of four miles, a grade of 5.77 percent overall with a ruling grade of nearly 7 percent. Mears's intention at the time was to continue north to Mineral Point, and then cross Denver Pass into the Hurricane Basin to descend into Lake City via Henson Creek. Actually, no construction was undertaken north of Animas Forks, and the only additional building on the railroad was a spur of 1.3 miles from Howardsville up Cunningham Creek to the Green Mountain and Old Hundred mines in 1905.

Traffic held up on the Silverton Northern far better than on the Silverton Railroad, although the two were operated to a considerable extent integrally, with pooling of locomotives and rolling stock. The principal source of traffic on the railroad was the Sunnyside Mine at Eureka. North of Eureka, the railroad was very expensive to operate. A locomotive could move only one car loaded with coal and one empty up the

grade to Animas Forks, and bring three loads of ore down. The speed limit on that trackage was only four miles per hour, and ten below Eureka. In spite of the railroad's short length and physical limitations, the management strove for a high standard of passenger service. Mears bought a former Rio Grande Western Pullman car and converted it to the diner-lounge *Animas Forks*. The car was too large for the railroad but served until it was wrecked in 1911. The railroad operated two passenger trains daily, only one of which operated above Eureka.

Operation above Eureka was apparently discontinued by 1922, although the railroad treated the suspension as only temporary. The track was removed along with the spur to Green Mountain Mine in 1936. The original mileage from Silverton to Eureka continued in operation until the Sunnyside Mine was closed in 1939. Since about 98 percent of the railroad's revenue had come from this source, the future was hopeless and the management applied to abandon the line. The Interstate Commerce Commission approved abandonment on August 31, 1941. Rails were removed in October 1942. The remaining locomotives went to the White Pass & Yukon for wartime service. The motor car fabricated by the Sunnyside Mine's management out of a 1915 Cadillac sedan with a wooden body, which provided passenger service in the later years, survived as a museum piece at the San Juan Historical Society Museum in Silverton.

REFERENCES: Josie Moore Crum, *Three Little Lines* (Durango, Colo.: Durango *Herald-News*, 1960); Robert E. Sloan, *The Silverton Railroad Companies* (Northglen, Colo.: MEGA Publications, 1975); Robert E. Sloan and Carl A. Skowronski, *The Rainbow Route* (Denver, Colo.: Sundance Limited, 1975).

Uintah Railway

Gilsonite, an asphaltic hydrocarbon useful for paints, varnishes, insulation, flooring, roofing, and a wide variety of other purposes, was discovered in the Uintah Basin of northeastern Utah in 1869. Commercial development of the deposits dates from the 1880s. The area was virtually unpopulated, and the expense of horse drayage to a railroad connection ran between $10 and $12 per ton.

The Unitah Railway was formed in 1903 by the Barber Asphalt Paving Company, one of the various subsidiaries of the General Asphalt Company, a typical example of the industrial combines formed in major American industries around the turn of the century. The management decided to build a 3′-0″ railroad from a point on the Rio Grande Western main line 19 miles west of Grand Junction to some point in the Uintah Basin. The junction was named Mack after the president of the company; Baxter Pass, through which the line crossed the Book Cliff Mountains into the basin, was named for one of the company's engineers. The line was built from Mack to Dragon, 53 miles, in 1904. A spur of just over a mile was laid to the Dragon Mine.

Although the Uintah was one of the last large narrow gauges built, it had the most difficult physical characteristics of any of them. For about three miles leaving Mack the company's location engineers made use of the RGW's right-of-way abandoned when the main line was standard gauged in 1890. The line then ascended along West Salt Wash 28 miles to Atchee at the base of the ascent of Baxter Pass. The ascent of the pass was built to the standards of lumber railroads, rather than narrow gauge common carriers. The grade was 7.5 percent approaching the summit, and the curvature at several points was over 60°. The curve at Moro Castle near milepost 30 was originally 75°, but even as modified to 66° was usually said to be the worst on an American common carrier of any type. The 7.5-percent gradient had the same honor among grades. The descent of Baxter Pass to the north was a 5-percent grade to McAndrews at milepost 40. From that point, the line descended along Evacuation Creek into Dragon.

The portion between Atchee and Mc-Andrews was designed to be traversed by geared engines. By 1910 the railroad had acquired five Shay locomotives; it added a sixth in 1920 and a seventh in 1933. No more than six were on the roster at any one time. Because the line south of the major grades was operated with ordinary rod engines of 2-8-0 or 2-8-2 wheel arrangement, the railroad's shops were placed at Atchee. Like the other communities on the line, Atchee was newly founded. The company built hotels at Mack, Atchee, and Dragon. Passenger service was provided by a pair of 0-6-2 tank engines, hauling a combine car on a once-daily schedule. These were the only ones of the original rod engines capable of crossing Baxter Pass. When a 2-8-2 was moved north to work mine spurs, it had to be partly dismantled and reassembled on arrival. The Gilsonite was handled mainly on flatcars in sacks weighing 150 to 200 pounds each.

The management served the Uintah Basin by road from Dragon. For this purpose it established the Uintah Toll Road Com-

The Uintah's physical standards were at their worst at Moro Castle Curve of 66° on the 7.5 percent ascent of Baxter Pass. (Frank A. Kennedy photograph, collections of V. L. McCoy and Henry E. Bender, Jr.)

Muleshoe Curve of 60° on the 5 percent ascent of Baxter Pass was representative of the Uintah Railway's physical standards. (Frank A. Kennedy photograph, Henry E. Bender, Jr., collection.)

pany in 1906 as a subsidiary of the railway. Road traffic was mainly to and from Vernal (the seat of Uintah County), Fort Duchesne, and the former Uintah Indian Reservation. The company operated wagons, tractors, and, later, trucks and automobiles on the toll road network.

Traffic on the railway was overwhelmingly Gilsonite; wool from local ranches,

the second largest item of freight, contributed less to gross revenues than mail. The railway hauled Gilsonite not only for General Asphalt but for independent producers, to whom the high rates were a continual irritant. In 1907 the American Asphalt Association charged the Uintah with extortionate pricing for charging $10 per ton to move Gilsonite the length of the rail-

The Uintah's basic operation was carrying Gilsonite in burlap bags. Here the asphaltic hydrocarbon is loaded on flatcars at Rainbow, Utah. (Frank A. Kennedy photograph, collections of V. L. McCoy and Henry E. Bender, Jr.)

road, when the D&RG and its connections charged only $7.75 to move the same ton from Mack to St. Louis. The ICC required the Uintah's rate to be reduced to $8. After the Post Office raised the weight limit for parcel post to 50 pounds in 1914, residents of the Uintah Basin generally found parcel post cheaper than the railway's freight rates. In the most notorious example, in 1916 the bricks for a bank in Vernal were shipped in small packages by parcel post. The railway and its toll road affiliate retained the mail contract for the basin until 1918.

In 1908 the company began surveying an extension northward. It was expected that the line would be run across the White River to Bonanza and Vernal. Early in 1911 the press reported that Barber Asphalt had issued bonds for $3 million to extend the railway, tunnel Baxter Pass, and convert the line to 4'-8½". The actual extension completed later in 1911 was much more modest. Narrow gauge rails were extended in that year 9.6 miles down Evacuation Creek to an end-of-track named Watson, again after the company's engineer who laid out the project. Mainly, the extension served to run a spur of four miles from Rainbow Junction, less than a mile south of Watson, to Rainbow, site of one of the richest veins of Gilsonite in the area. The branch gained 837 feet, with grades as high as 5.1 percent. Thereafter, Rainbow was the principal source of traffic for the railway.

As late as 1917, the management expressed an intention to build to the north, but never did so, probably because of the expense of bridging the White and Green rivers, which lay between Watson and Vernal. The location of the railroad made it attractive to the Colorado Midland, which by trackage rights had reached Grand Junction, less than 20 miles away. By standard gauging the Uintah, tunneling Baxter Pass, and extending to Vernal, the Midland would have had the major portion of a line to Salt Lake City. The remainder from Vernal to Salt Lake City would have been on the route projected by David Moffat's Denver & Salt Lake, which never progressed beyond Craig. The demise of the Midland in 1918 ended any prospect of this arrangement.

Since most of the world's Gilsonite was originated in the Uintah's tributary country, the railway remained generally profitable in the 1920s, but the forces for decline of passenger traffic affected even this remote operation. In 1921 the company gave up scheduled automobile service between Watson and Vernal and cut rail passenger service to thrice weekly. In 1929 the service became a mixed train, daily except Sunday.

In 1923 the company hired a notable figure in twentieth-century railroading as superintendent: Lucian C. Sprague. He was shortly promoted to general manager. His principal accomplishment was bringing in a

Baldwin's 1928 articulated locomotive No. 51 is shown in its builder's photograph. (Railroad Museum of Pennsylvania.)

type of locomotive capable of traversing both the water-level grades and the ascents of Baxter Pass. In consultation with his master mechanic, he developed specifications for a simple articulated tank engine of 2-6+6-2 wheel arrangement. The Baldwin Locomotive Works designed the engine and delivered it as the Uintah's No. 50 in 1926. The locomotive was considered outstandingly successful. A similar but heavier locomotive, the No. 51, was delivered in 1928. The locomotives, which are treated at length in Part I, Chapter 5, were the only articulateds of the ordinary sort ever built for domestic narrow gauge use.

Sprague resigned in 1929. He went on to great fame as the receiver and president of the Minneapolis & St. Louis, which he is credited with having saved from dismemberment and partial abandonment. The economies for which he was responsible on the Uintah were to be realized as long as the railroad survived.

General Asphalt had come to look upon the railroad as obsolete as early as 1935. Hard-surfaced highways had spread into the area. The toll road company was dissolved and the roads turned over to county authorities in 1936. The owner, which had changed its name to Barber Company, Inc., in 1936, arranged in 1938 for Gilsonite to be trucked from the Bonanza area to Craig for transshipment to the Denver & Salt Lake. Mixed train service on the Uintah was reduced to two trips weekly. The company applied for abandonment in August 1938 and received permission in April 1939. During the Christmas season of 1938, the mixed service was cut to once weekly, a run on Tuesdays. The last train ran May 16, 1939, and the railway was dismantled during the remainder of the year and the first two months of 1940. The articulated locomotives were sold to the Sumpter Valley Railway of Oregon. The on-line communities, which owed their existence to the railway, were reduced to ghost towns.

Ultimately, the Gilsonite returned to the route of the railway. In 1957 the American Gilsonite Co., as the producer had become, inaugurated hydraulic mining and established a slurry pipeline from Bonanza to a refinery near Grand Junction, 72 miles. The line, which crossed Baxter Pass, was the first in America to demonstrate the practicality of moving a solid commodity by pipeline—a circumstance that must be looked upon as highly prophetic in the history of the railroads.

REFERENCE: Henry E. Bender, Jr., *Uintah Railway: The Gilsonite Route* (Berkeley, Calif.: Howell-North Books, 1970).

Florida

Before 1880 Florida had little railroad mileage relative to its extensive land mass. The state was lightly populated and mainly dependent on steamboats on the St. Johns River for internal communication. The administration of Governor William W. Bloxham, who was inaugurated on January 4, 1881, undertook a policy of railroad land grants for internal improvement that attracted extensive resources to the industry in the early 1880s. The program produced a relatively late boom in narrow gauge building that covered the north-central portion of the peninsula with a comprehensive network of 3'-0" lines, most of which was tributary to ports along the St. Johns. Owing to the state's limited population at the time, and to a low rate of survival of local newspapers, the history of these lines is less well documented than that of the narrow gauges generally. In addition, the ultimate abandonment of the mileage that went into the Atlantic Coast Line has taken place by a large number of short removals, which it is impractical to recount in detail. I have endeavored to note the abandonment whereby the line was reduced to spurs or otherwise ceased to serve its line-haul function.

De Land & St. Johns River Railway

De Land's local narrow gauge had its origin as the unbuilt Ocean Ridge, De Land & Atlantic Railroad, which was succeeded in January 1884 by the De Land & St. Johns River Railway. This corporation in 1885 built a five-mile line from De Land Landing (Beresford) to De Land via Stetson. The purpose was to connect De Land with steamers on the St. Johns River, but in January 1886 the Jacksonville, Tampa & Key West Railway, building its 5'-0" line along

the east bank of the river, intersected the narrow gauge at De Land Junction, about a mile inland from De Land Landing, to become the narrow gauge's principal connection. In April 1886 the JT&KW bought the narrow gauge, but did not immediately convert it. Rather, the JT&KW itself converted from 5'-0" to 4'-9" on June 1, 1886. The JT&KW converted the narrow gauge in 1887, replacing its 16-pound rail with 55-pound. The mile from the river to the junction was abandoned early in 1895, and the name Beresford was transferred to a station about a mile south of the junction. As the De Land branch, the line followed the JT&KW into the Plant System and the Atlantic Coast Line. The ACL discontinued train connections into De Land in 1918, and built a station for De Land on the main line at the junction. The branch became a spur into the town. Short abandonments about 1932, 1972, and 1980 have reduced it to approximately half its original length.

Florida & Georgia Railway

Although projected as a line of some 210 miles from Macon, Georgia, to Lake City, this railroad attained only the status of a nominal common carrier of the R. J. Camp lumber interests in the Okefenokee Swamp. From the initial entries for the railroad in *Poor's Manuals* and the *Official Guide of the Railways* in 1902, the line was shown as a mixture of 3'-0" and 4'-8½" of 30 miles from Wellborn on the Seaboard Air Line through White Springs on the Georgia Southern & Florida to Thaggard, a lumber camp in the swamp just south of the Georgia border. Presumably the 21 miles from Thaggard to Camp's Mills a mile north of White Springs were 3'-0" and the remaining nine miles to Wellborn were 4'-8½", but there may have been some three-rail track. The railroad owned a passenger car, but listed itself as freight-service-only throughout its history. The Wellborn–White Springs portion was abandoned about the end of 1914, but the narrow gauge mileage had apparently already been abandoned.

Florida Southern Railway

The ambitious project of a north-south line down the center of the peninsula had its origins in the Gainesville, Ocala & Charlotte Harbor Railroad, incorporated on March 4, 1879, to run from Lake City to Charlotte Harbor with a branch to Palatka for interchange with the St. Johns River steamers. Grading began in March 1880, but before any trackage was put in service, the name was changed to the Florida Southern Railway early in 1881. Iron was delivered by steamer to Palatka in March, and the initial line, Palatka-Gainesville (49 miles) was completed in August. The promoters, who were led by John R. Hall and William L. Candler of Boston, intended to continue this line northwest to Lake City, and on September 3, 1883, opened it to Hague, 11 miles northwest of Gainesville. The route was graded an additional three miles to Newmansville. Late in 1883 Henry B. Plant acquired control of the company. He did not remove Hall and Candler, but he arranged for the Gainesville–Lake City extension to be constructed by his broad gauge Savannah, Florida & Western, which was building into the state from the north. Accordingly, the Gainesville-Hague narrow gauge trackage was removed early in December.

The Florida Southern's line south was built from Rochelle, nine miles southeast of Gainesville. Grading began in 1881, and the first train operated into Ocala (32 miles) on February 26, 1882. By the end of 1883 track had reached Leesburg (65 miles). Plant was eager to continue the line south, and for whatever reason decided that the projected route to Charlotte Sound should be built jointly by the Florida Southern and the South Florida. He contracted in 1884 to push the Florida Southern on to Pemberton Ferry (Croom; 135 miles) and Brooksville (146 miles). The South Florida would build an intermediate 43 miles from Pemberton Ferry to Bartow, from which the Florida Southern would build the final 73 miles from Bartow to Punta Gorda. Most of this extensive project was carried out in 1885. The Florida Southern reached Pemberton Ferry in the spring and Brooksville toward the end of the year. The South Florida built its portion, Pemberton Ferry–Bartow, in the summer and opened it on September 23, 1885. Grading began on the Florida Southern's line south in 1885; it was opened to Punta Gorda in June 1886. The main line was among the longest narrow gauges; including the South Florida's portion, the Palatka–Punta Gorda distance was 249 miles. The Florida Southern alone had 263 miles of track.

The railroad was in several respects an attractive one. The portion around Rochelle, Ocala, and Leesburg served one of the most productive citrus areas in the state. Several spurs served phosphate mines. The company had two small branches, Micanopy Junction–Micanopy (3 miles, built in 1883; extended to Tacoma, 8 miles, in

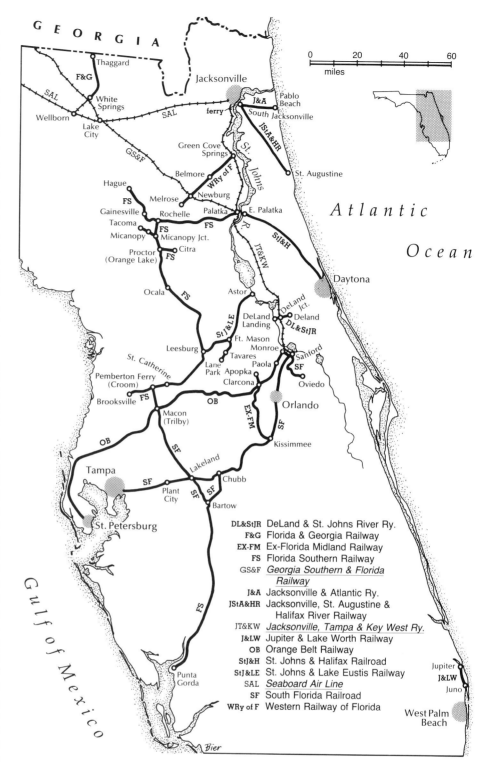

1894) and Orange Lake–Citra (6 miles, built in 1885). A third branch was the separately incorporated St. Johns & Lake Eustis. At Punta Gorda the narrow gauge reached an excellent harbor, envisioned as a gateway to the West Indies and South America. The Florida Southern received the largest state land grant of any railroad, 2,580,209 acres.

Plant arranged in 1888 for his Jacksonville, Tampa & Key West to operate the Florida Southern beginning January 1, 1889. He allowed the narrow gauge to be put in receivership on March 18, 1890. It was sold on March 7, 1892, to interests representing the JT&KW, and reorganized as the Florida Southern Railroad. In that year the Bartow–Punta Gorda line was converted, but the main network north of Brooksville and Pemberton Ferry was allowed to remain narrow gauge. Plant turned the Florida Southern over to his Savannah,

Florida & Western on January 1, 1896. The SF&W converted the remaining trackage on July 11, 1896.

The Atlantic Coast Line acquired the Florida Southern in April 1902, incidental to its acquisition of the Plant System. The Punta Gorda line was extended to Fort Myers and Naples, and became the ACL's principal branch along the lower west coast of Florida. This is still in existence. The northern portion of the former Florida Southern was redundant on a large mileage of branch lines in the area. Being dependent on citrus fruit movements, it was highly prone to truck competition; a series of short abandonments has reduced the network to a limited mileage of spurs. First to go was the Tacoma extension in 1941, followed by the rest of the Micanopy branch in 1945. The Citra branch went in 1962. The main line from Rochelle to Croom was dropped in several abandonments in 1978–79. The entry of the system into Brooksville was abandoned in 1971, into Palatka in 1981, and into Gainesville in 1983.

Jacksonville & Atlantic Railway

The Arlington & Atlantic Railway was incorporated on August 29, 1882, to build from Arlington (South Jacksonville) to Pablo Beach (Jacksonville Beach), 16.54 miles. On September 23, the name was changed to the Jacksonville & Atlantic Railroad. J. Q. Burbridge was president, and the ownership was concentrated in Jacksonville. The promoters sought to develop Pablo Beach as a resort, both for day excursionists from Jacksonville, and for vacationers from the North. A hotel at the beach was integral to the project. The railroad was opened in November 1885. Some of the motive power came from the Jacksonville, St. Augustine & Halifax River after the latter's conversion. Normal traffic required two trains per day with two additional on Saturdays and Sundays.

From the time of completion to Pablo Beach the proprietors planned an extension of eight miles through Atlantic Beach, Manhattan Beach, and other resorts to Mayport at the mouth of the St. Johns River. Apart from its own resort development, Mayport was a fishing port and thus presented the line with some prospects of increasing its meager freight traffic. At least by 1887, the management proposed to convert the existing mileage before making the extension. The line was unprofitable, however, and was foreclosed in 1890. It was reorganized in January 1893 as the Jacksonville & Atlantic Railway, with Mellen W. Drew as

The big network of narrow gauge predecessors of the Atlantic Coast Line in Florida generated relatively little photographic coverage. The *Sherman Conant* was a small 4-4-0 from the Rhode Island Locomotive Works, notable mainly for its lack of a sand dome. (Railroad Museum of Pennsylvania.)

president, but the new management also proved unable to finance conversion and extension.

The Florida East Coast bought the railroad on September 13, 1899, and made immediate plans for conversion and extension. The railroad was converted in March 1900 and extended for the summer season of that year. The management actively promoted resort development by building a hotel at Atlantic Beach in 1910 and improving Manhattan Beach for Jacksonville's black population. By the 1920s the railroad ran as many as six trains in each direction for Sunday traffic. Destruction of the hotel at Atlantic Beach by fire in 1920 and completion of a four-lane highway between Jacksonville and Jacksonville Beach in 1926 initiated a rapid decline in passenger traffic. Fish meal, sand, gravel, and the rest of the line's limited freight traffic could not carry the operation. The Florida East Coast abandoned the line in 1932.

Jacksonville, St. Augustine & Halifax River Railway

St. Augustine, for all its antiquity, was a town of only 2,500 in 1880. A. M. Lyon of New York undertook to connect the town with Jacksonville by a narrow gauge, incorporated on February 21, 1881, as the Jacksonville, St. Augustine & Halifax River Railway. If completed, the railway would qualify for a state land grant of 128,000 acres. By 1882 the company had bought wharf property at South Jacksonville and a ferryboat, *Armsmear*. Tracklaying began early in 1883, and in June the railroad was

put in service to the outskirts of St. Augustine. The company had exhausted its funds and was having difficulty arranging the entry into the town. In November, Lyon sold the railroad to W. Jerome Green of Utica, New York, who built the remaining 1.25 miles into St. Augustine in 1885, bringing the railroad to its final length of 36 miles. Green planned to push the line on to the Halifax River country at Ormond and Daytona, but did not do so.

Rather, Green sold the railroad to Henry M. Flagler on December 31, 1885. Earlier in the year Flagler had built his Ponce de Leon Hotel in St. Augustine, to which the narrow gauge was the principal access facility. The narrow gauge became a fairly large operation; by 1888 it was reported to have five locomotives and nine passenger cars, including four parlor cars. Freight rolling stock was mainly flatcars for lumber movements. The ferry fleet had risen to three vessels with the additions of the *Uncle Sam* and the *Mechanic*. Flagler arranged for the Jacksonville, Tampa & Key West to operate the line early in 1886. By an agreement of December 15, 1888, the Jacksonville, St. Augustine & Halifax River resumed independent operation and took control of both the standard gauge St. Augustine & Halifax River and the narrow gauge St. Johns & Halifax River. Flagler had already conceived of a continuous line down the east coast of Florida, and undertook preparations to convert the two narrow gauges. He converted the Jacksonville–St. Augustine line and bridged the St. Johns at South Jacksonville on January 20, 1889. Through Pullman service from Jersey City to St. Augustine began immediately.

The Jupiter & Lake Worth was among the most obscure narrow gauges. A portage railway for steamboats along the sounds of the east coast of Florida, the railway lasted only six years. (Ed Bond collection.)

The name of the railroad was changed to the Jacksonville, St. Augustine & Indian River Railway in 1892, and to the Florida East Coast in 1895. The former narrow gauge remains the northern portion of the FEC main line.

Jupiter & Lake Worth Railway

As part of the water route along the east coast of Florida before the coming of Henry M. Flagler's Florida East Coast Railway, this narrow gauge provided a portage of 7.5 miles between steamboats of the Indian River Steamboat Co. at Jupiter at the south end of Indian River and steamers at the north end of Lake Worth at Juno. Intermediate halts were fancifully named Venus and Mars. Inevitably, the line was locally known as the Celestial Railroad.

The railway was incorporated in 1888 and opened in 1889. Flagler showed some interest in buying it, but the proprietors were unwilling to sell to him. This shortsighted behavior caused the railroad to be abandoned in 1895.

REFERENCE: Nathan D. Shappee, "The Celestial Railroad to Juno," *Florida Historical Quarterly*, 40 (1962), pp. 329–49.

Orange Belt Railway

Piotr Dementieff, an immigrant from St. Petersburg, Russia, who anglicized his name as Peter A. Demens, operated a sawmill at Longwood in Seminole County. Having deforested his immediate area, he envisioned a narrow gauge railroad to reach more distant timber stands. He purchased a charter issued to Miller, Arnold & Hall on April 20, 1885, for a railroad from Lake Monroe, on which Sanford is situated, to Lake Apopka. Demens secured financial assistance from Josef Henschen, Henry Sweetapple, A. M. Taylor, meatpacker H. O. Armour, E. T. Stotesbury of Drexel & Co., and others. Under Governor Bloxham's program of land grants he received 79,582 acres.

As the Orange Belt Railway, the line was initially projected from Monroe (Lake Monroe) four miles north of Sanford on the Jacksonville, Tampa & Key West and on St. Johns River, to points on the south shore of Lake Apopka, with a spur of two miles from Longwood Junction to Longwood to serve Demens's mill. In 1886 the line, including the Longwood spur, was built from Monroe to Oakland, 34 miles. The railroad was reported as completed on October 30, but on November 20 the charter was amended to allow extension to Point Pinellas on the peninsula opposite Tampa. In 1887 the railroad was reported to have a thousand men at work on the extension. Philip D. Armour, also of the meatpacking family, joined the company in that year, adding considerably to its financial strength. The railroad was reportedly in operation for 100 miles, approximately to Drexel, by the end of 1887. Demens, who had endeavored without success to name some intermediate points "St. Petersburg," finally gave the name of his home city to the terminus on Point Pinellas. A construction train entered the town on April 30, 1888, and regular service began on June 8. Apparently seeking a better connection with the river

steamers, Demens built one final extension, four miles from Monroe to Sanford, which opened April 12, 1889. As completed, the Orange Belt had a main line of 152 miles. Its shops and headquarters were at Oakland. Traffic was largely citrus fruit and lumber. The line ran through the flat country of central Florida; the daily passenger train took about eight hours to traverse the main line.

St. Petersburg developed very well, quickly becoming one of Florida's major cities. The management expressed an interest in converting the line from a junction with the Florida Southern at Macon (Trilby) to St. Petersburg early in 1892. The railroad, like most narrow gauges, had deteriorated quickly, and was in poor financial condition. In August 1892 its creditors initiated foreclosure proceedings. In March 1893 the company was sold to J. N. Stripling and E. P. Axtell, who reorganized it as the Sanford & St. Petersburg Railroad on January 1, 1895. The Plant System bought the railroad effective April 1, 1895, and expressed an intention of converting it quickly. The management was mainly interested in the portion from Trilby to St. Petersburg, and apparently converted it later in the same month. The remainder, the 77 miles between Trilby and Sanford—just over half the railroad—was mainly an originating facility for oranges and lumber, which the management considered of no high priority. Not only was the remaining narrow gauge retained, but the mileage was actually increased by conversion to 3'-0" of a connecting line. In 1896 Plant acquired the Florida Midland Railway, a 4'-9" lumber hauler with a 44-mile line from Longwood to Apopka and Kissimmee. Plant abandoned this railroad, but then replaced the Apopka-Kissimmee portion (34 miles) with narrow gauge rail and equipment from the Trilby–St. Petersburg line. The two lines met at Clarcona. This narrow gauge system of 109 miles survived until after the Plant System's absorption into the Atlantic Coast Line in 1902. Four narrow gauge locomotives were numbered for the ACL. The line from Sanford to Trilby was converted early in 1904. The entry into Sanford via Sylvan Lake was abandoned in favor of a direct entry over an existing ACL line from Paola Junction via New Upsala with a saving of about two miles. The Apopka-Kissimmee branch was reportedly converted in 1907.

West of Trilby the former narrow gauge was the ACL's entry into Clearwater and St. Petersburg, but the lines to the east were only minor branches in the ACL's extensive network in central Florida. The former

Florida Midland branch was abandoned into Kissimmee in 1954, into Apopka in 1963, and between Dr. Phillips and Clarcona, the intermediate portion, in 1983. At the present writing the former Orange Belt main line is extant from Paola to Groveland (44 miles), Mable to Tarrytown (4 miles), and St. Petersburg to Chemical, just north of Tarpon Springs (32.5 miles). The remainder, the middle portion of the railroad, was abandoned in several segments, mainly in 1977.

St. Johns & Halifax Railroad

Utley J. White, a successful lumber operator on the east bank of the St. Johns River, undertook grading for a narrow gauge late in 1881. Early in 1882 he incorporated it as the St. Johns & Halifax Railroad, a common carrier, and prepared to build from East Palatka diagonally to the southeast to some point on the Halifax River, a sound in the Ormond-Daytona area. He reportedly began hauling logs and cordwood with mules when only a mile had been finished. Construction was reportedly paid for directly out of the proceeds of White's lumber business. By mid-1883, track had reached Deep Creek (9 miles) and the operation had a locomotive. At the time, White planned branches from Deep Creek to St. Augustine and from Ormond to Enterprise, which with a narrow gauge connection to the north would give him a 121-mile line from Jacksonville to the Sanford area, considerably shorter than the distance by river. By late 1886 the line reached Tomoka (40 miles) and it was apparently completed into Ormond (43 miles) and Daytona (49 miles) in 1887. No further narrow gauge track was laid.

On May 1, 1888, White transferred the railroad to the Jacksonville, Tampa & Key West, which on October 1 reincorporated it as the St. Johns & Halifax River Railway. On December 15 the line was turned over to the Jacksonville, St. Augustine & Halifax River, along with the St. Johns Railroad and the St. Augustine & Halifax River, all of which Henry M. Flagler was bringing together as the northern end of what became his Florida East Coast. The JStA&HR converted the East Palatka–Daytona mileage on March 17, 1889, in 18 hours with a force of 275 men.

The line became part of the Florida East Coast main line on formation in 1895. The portion between Bunnell and East Palatka was bypassed by the Moultrie cutoff in 1926, and abandoned as redundant in 1972.

The 23 miles from Bunnell to Daytona Beach remain part of the FEC main line.

St. Johns & Lake Eustis Railway

With the prospect of a land grant of 14,725 acres, William Astor of New York and some local people incorporated this railroad on February 20, 1879. The project was to build from a landing on the west bank of the St. Johns River, which the promoters named Astor, to the Lake Eustis area, which was to be developed for lumbering and agriculture. About 12 miles of track were laid in 1879, and the railroad was opened to Fort Mason on Lake Eustis (25 miles) early in 1880. The railroad connected by its own steamboat with Leesburg via lakes Eustis and Harris. The rail line was extended in 1883 to Tavares and Lane Park (34 miles) on Lake Harris; the latter town was a landing named for the company's president, A. J. Lane of Volusia. The line was isolated from the rest of Florida's narrow gauge network until October 1884, when the management opened a branch of 14 miles from Fort Mason to Leesburg on the Florida Southern. The railroad was operated with two Baldwin 4-4-0 locomotives.

The company arranged to lease the line effective January 1, 1885, to the Florida Southern for a sum equal to the StJ&LE's interest payments. By 1886, the Florida Southern was reported to have bought full ownership. The StJ&LE went bankrupt in the depression of the 1890s and on May 31, 1893, was put in the hands of receiver C. P. Lovell. This restored the StJ&LE to a nominal independence, but it continued to be operated as part of the network of the Jacksonville, Tampa & Key West and the Florida Southern. The line was sold to Frank Q. Brown of Boston, president of the Florida Southern, on January 6, 1896. It was reorganized on September 5 as the St. Johns & Lake Eustis Railroad, and converted on December 14, 1896. Thereafter the railroad was simply a branch in the Plant System, without motive power or rolling stock of its own. Citrus fruit was the principal freight, and this traffic was quickly lost to trucks.

The line to Astor was cut back 18 miles to Altoona in 1942, and an additional three miles to Umatilla in 1962. The Tavares–Lane Park spur was abandoned in 1939, and the Fort Mason–Leesburg segment in 1967. The ten miles from Tavares to Umatilla survive at the present writing.

South Florida Railroad

This long and important narrow gauge had its origins in a project to connect Sanford, the head of navigation on the St. Johns River, with Charlotte Sound in southwestern Florida. The project was first incorporated as the Lake Monroe & Orlando Railroad of 1875, but local interests were unable to finance construction. In 1879 the name was changed to the South Florida Railroad. The enterprise came into the hands of R. M. Pulsifer, publisher of the Boston *Herald*, and E. B. Haskell, who jointly raised the capital to undertake construction. The first segment from Sanford to Orlando (22 miles) was opened on October 1, 1880.

In 1881 the management reached an agreement with Hamilton Disston, a lumber and real estate operator of Philadelphia, whereby the railroad would receive a free right-of-way from Orlando to Tampa plus half the townsites and station locations along the way, if the line was built within three years. The agreement was to shift the immediate goal from Charlotte Sound to Tampa Bay and to put the management under a difficult time constraint. Track reached Kissimmee (40 miles) on March 21, 1882. The railroad was reported sold in mid-1882 to the Reed syndicate, which owned the Florida Transit and Florida Central & Western railroads. Neither the old owners nor the new made enough progress to give promise of meeting the deadline. In May 1883 a 60 percent interest in the railroad was sold to H. B. Plant, who was very much interested in the extension as the entry into Tampa for his Plant System. With a force of 1,200 to 1,500 men, he undertook to build between Kissimmee and Tampa, 75 miles, in about eight months. He succeeded, completing the 115-mile railroad about five miles east of Lakeland on January 23, 1884, two days before the agreement expired.

The projected line to Charlotte Sound was also built, though in rather odd fashion. By 1884, both the Florida Southern and the South Florida were under Plant's control. He arranged for the South Florida to build a line of 43 miles from Pemberton Ferry (Croom) on the Florida Southern to Bartow, intersecting the South Florida's main line at Lakeland. This branch was completed on September 23, 1885. The Florida Southern then built the 73 miles from Bartow to Punta Gorda on Charlotte Sound. In effect, the South Florida's Pemberton Ferry branch represented a gap in the Florida Southern's main line from Gainesville and Palatka to Punta Gorda.

The South Florida completed a branch of 17 miles from Bartow Junction (Chubb) into Bartow via Winter Haven on January 25, 1885. The company's only other branch was a short one out of Sanford, built to Onoro (4 miles) in 1882 and Oviedo (17 miles) in 1885.

Plant had completed his 5'-0" Jacksonville, Tampa & Key West into Sanford on February 22, 1886, giving him a through route from Jacksonville to Tampa with a break-of-gauge. He quickly moved to eliminate the break-of-gauge at Sanford, converting the JT&KW to 4'-9" on June 1, 1886, and the South Florida main line on September 20. The South Florida's Bartow and Oviedo branches were converted later in the year; the latter branch was incidentally extended about a mile from Oviedo to Lake Charm. The Bartow–Lakeland–Pemberton Ferry branch was not converted at this time because the Florida Southern, with which it was integral, remained 3'-0". It was converted with the Florida Southern's Punta Gorda line in 1892.

The former South Florida lines followed the rest of the Plant System into the Atlantic Coast Line in 1902. The main line from Sanford to Tampa was part of the ACL's principal entry into the Tampa Bay area, and thus one of the most important ex—narrow gauges in the American rail network. It is still in existence as part of the CSX Corporation.

Western Railway of Florida

As the Green Cove Springs & Melrose Railroad, this enterprise was incorporated on February 28, 1881, to build from Green Cove Springs, on the west bank of the St. Johns River 26 miles south of Jacksonville, to Melrose on Lake Santa Fe, about 15 miles east of Gainesville. The original management, headed by J. C. Greely of Jacksonville, succeeded in opening the line to Sharon, ten miles, in April 1883, but could progress no farther. Creditors bought the company at a foreclosure sale of August 3, 1885, and reorganized it as the Green Cove & Midland Railroad. The Western Railway of Florida was organized on July 26, 1886, to lease the Green Cove & Midland and to build the rest of the main line to Melrose. A branch from Belmore to Starke was projected but never built. Dexter Hunter of Jacksonville, president of the new company, completed the line to Melrose, 33.5 miles, early in 1890. The railroad also had a lumber spur running ten miles south from Sharon. The railroad reportedly operated with three locomotives and 34 cars, all ex-

cept one of which were equipped for handling logs or lumber. The line operated one passenger train per day.

On June 6, 1892, the Western Railway and the Green Cove & Midland were sold under foreclosure, and reorganized on July 1 as the Southwestern Railroad of Florida. Dexter Hunter remained president. The railroad operated until mid-1896, when it was shut down. It was abandoned in 1899.

▼ ▼ ▼ ▼

The *Railroad Gazette*'s list of construction for 1879 showed the Peninsular Railroad as having built 20 miles of 3'-0" from Waldo to Orange Lake. This was apparently picked up by *Poor's Manual* for 1880, and by secondary sources. On the basis of the *Official Guide of the Railways* and other sources, this information is in error; the line was 5'-0" from the outset.

REFERENCES: George W. Pettengill, Jr., *Story of the Florida Railroads*, Railway & Locomotive Historical Society *Bulletin*, no. 86 (1952); Richard E. Prince, *Atlantic Coast Line Railroad* (Green River, Wyo.: Richard E. Prince, 1966); Seth Bramson, *Speedway to Sunshine* (Erin, Ontario, Canada: Boston Mills Press, 1984).

Georgia

Americus, Preston & Lumpkin Railroad

Webster and Stuart counties in southwestern Georgia were prosperous farming country, but were without rail service. S. H. Hawkins of Americus conceived of a narrow gauge running straight west to Preston and Lumpkin, the seats of the two counties. The railroad was chartered on June 17, 1884. Grading began toward the end of the year and was completed to Lumpkin, 37 miles, toward the end of 1885. Service began about March 1, 1886. By June the promoters had decided on extensions both

east and west, and they secured a charter amendment for the purpose on December 24, 1886.

The western extension proved to be a mere nine miles straight north from Lumpkin to Louvale, a town of about 50 people on Hanna Creek. The work was done mainly in 1886 and the extension put in service on April 1, 1887.

The eastern extension was much longer, 60 miles. The contract was let in September 1886, and track reached Abbeville on the Ocmulgee River in August 1887. Regular service began in early November. Abbeville had the attraction of being on navigable water, the Ocmulgee being a tributary of the Altamaha River, which flowed into the Atlantic at Darien, just above Brunswick. The railroad amended its charter again in September 1887 to operate steamboats to Savannah and Brunswick via Darien. By 1889 the company was reported to own five boats for this service.

Hawkins and his associates, however, had resolved upon converting the narrow gauge and making it a direct route between Savannah and Montgomery, Alabama. The Georgia legislature authorized a change of name to the Savannah, Americus & Montgomery Railway on December 26, 1888. The Americus-Abbeville portion was converted in mid-June 1889, and the Americus-Louvale segment shortly before Christmas 1890. Also in 1890 Hawkins arranged his entry into Savannah by construction and trackage rights. Construction to the west entailed a major bridge over the Chattahoochee River; the first passenger train did not run to Montgomery until about April 15, 1892. As completed, the railroad was 340 miles, of which the former narrow gauge was 106.

The railroad was expected to be a carrier of minerals from Alabama to ships at Savannah, but it proved unprofitable in the depression of the 1890s. On December 10, 1892, Hawkins and T. Edward Hambleton of Baltimore, a representative of bondholders, were appointed receivers. The railroad was sold early in 1895 to John Skelton Williams of Richmond, Virginia, who reorganized it as the Georgia & Alabama Railway. In December 1898 Williams and his associates gained control of the Seaboard Air Line, and in February 1899 acquired the Florida Central & Peninsular Railroad. He merged the three, and the Georgia & Alabama became a division of the Seaboard on July 1, 1900. It remains in service as a major secondary line of the CSX Corporation. The Americus, Preston & Lumpkin received some belated attention when the station it had built in Plains became the local

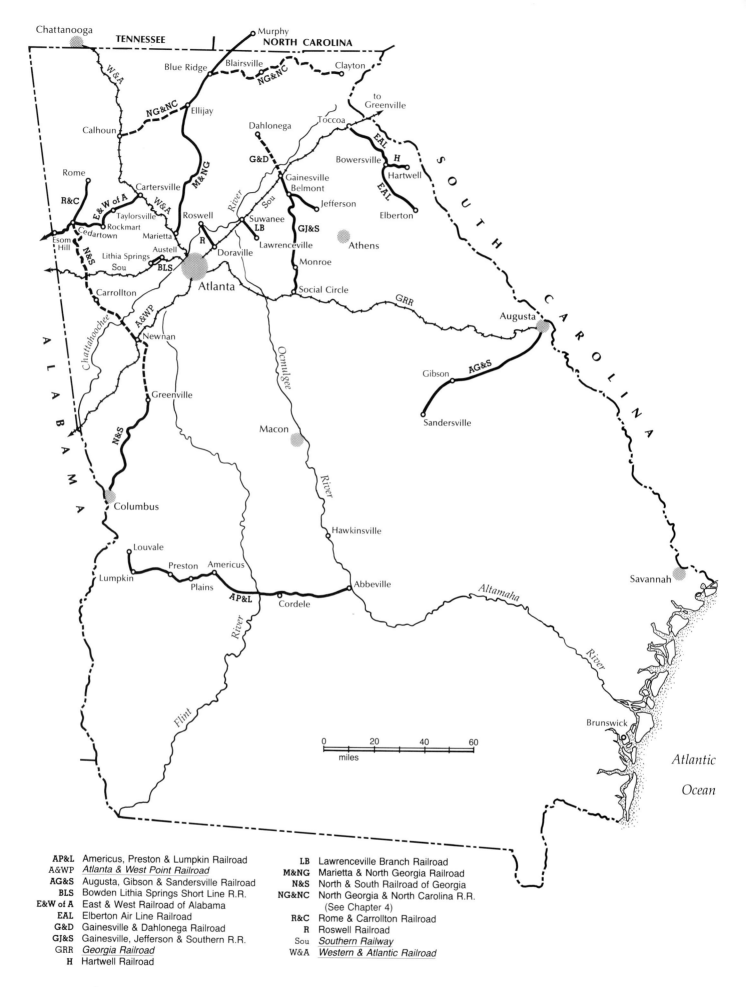

Chattanooga
TENNESSEE
Murphy
NORTH CAROLINA

W&A
Blue Ridge
Blairsville
NG&NC
Clayton

NG&NC
Ellijay
Dahlonega
Toccoa
to Greenville

Calhoun
G&D
EAL
H

M&NG
Bowersville
Hartwell

Rome
Cartersville
Gainesville
Belmont
EAL

R&C
E&W of A
W&A
Taylorsville
Roswell
Jefferson
Elberton

Rockmart
Suwanee
LB
GJ&S

Cedartown
Marietta
R
Doraville
Lawrenceville

Esom Hill
Austell
Athens

N&S
Lithia Springs
Sou
BLS
Monroe

Carrollton
Atlanta
Social Circle
GRR

Chattahoochee
A&WP
Augusta

Newnan
AG&S

Oconee
Gibson

Greenville
Sandersville

N&S

Columbus
Macon

Hawkinsville
Altamaha River

Louvale
Preston
Americus

Lumpkin
Plains
Abbeville
Savannah

AP&L
Cordele

Flint River

Brunswick

Atlantic Ocean

SOUTH CAROLINA
ALABAMA

0   20   40   60
miles

AP&L   Americus, Preston & Lumpkin Railroad
A&WP   *Atlanta & West Point Railroad*
AG&S   Augusta, Gibson & Sandersville Railroad
BLS   Bowden Lithia Springs Short Line R.R.
E&W of A East & West Railroad of Alabama
EAL   Elberton Air Line Railroad
G&D   Gainesville & Dahlonega Railroad
GJ&S   Gainesville, Jefferson & Southern R.R.
GRR   *Georgia Railroad*
H   Hartwell Railroad

LB   Lawrenceville Branch Railroad
M&NG   Marietta & North Georgia Railroad
N&S   North & South Railroad of Georgia
NG&NC   North Georgia & North Carolina R.R.
        (See Chapter 4)
R&C   Rome & Carrollton Railroad
R   Roswell Railroad
Sou   *Southern Railway*
W&A   *Western & Atlantic Railroad*

headquarters for the campaign of Governor Jimmy Carter for the presidency in 1976.

Augusta, Gibson & Sandersville Railroad

Although promoted near the end of the narrow gauge boom, this project was a typical effort to serve the southern lumber industry. The Augusta, Gibson & Sandersville Railroad was organized on July 31, 1883, and chartered on January 8, 1884. R. M. Mitchell and W. B. Young of Augusta were the principal incorporators. In addition to the route described in the corporate title, the promoters contemplated lines from Sandersville to Americus, 75 miles; Augusta to Newberry, South Carolina, 80 miles; and Mitchell to White Plains, 30 miles. Only the 80-mile line from Augusta to Sandersville was built. Grading began in 1884, and track was laid beginning in 1885. The railroad was opened to Gibson (51 miles) on December 10, 1885, and to Sandersville on November 26, 1886.

The railroad quickly proved unsuccessful. In 1891 the company defaulted on the interest payment on the first mortgage, and was placed in the hands of receiver Hamilton Wilkins on January 1, 1892. The railroad was sold on February 20, 1893, to the Central Trust Company of New York on behalf of the bondholders and reorganized on May 1, 1893, as the Augusta Southern Railroad, of which James U. Jackson of Augusta was president. From the outset the new management's intention was to convert the narrow gauge and to acquire the Sandersville & Tennille Railroad, a connecting standard gauge short line. Jackson leased the S&T on August 8, 1893, and converted the narrow gauge on September 30, 1895.

The subsequent history of the line is integral with the complicated corporate organization of the Southern Railway. The Augusta Southern was leased to the South Carolina & Georgia Railroad effective March 1, 1897, but the AS claimed the SC&G failed to comply with the terms of the lease and secured a receivership for the property on July 19, 1898. The receivership was discharged on April 27, 1899, and the property returned to the SC&G. The Southern Railway leased the SC&G on April 29, 1899, but annulled the lease on April 25, 1901. The Augusta Southern was an independently operated short line under control of the Southern Railway until April 1, 1917, when the Southern sold it to the Georgia & Florida Railway's trustees. The Georgia & Florida was a long but extremely weak short line assembled by John Skelton Wil-

liams from Spartanburg, South Carolina, to Madison, Florida, by acquisition of existing short lines plus some construction to connect them. The portion of the former narrow gauge from Augusta to a junction a mile south of Keysville later known as McAdoo became part of the G&F's main line. The G&F had operated over this segment by trackage rights from July 1, 1910. The portion from McAdoo to Sandersville remained a branch dependent on the declining lumber industry in the area. The Georgia & Florida abandoned it in 1934. The Southern Railway acquired the G&F in 1963 and merged it into the subsidiary Central of Georgia in 1971. The remainder of the former narrow gauge from Hephzibah to McAdoo was abandoned in 1966 along with the rest of the G&F main line north of Midville, Georgia. The 14 miles from Augusta to Hephzibah remain in service.

Bowden Lithia Springs Short Line Railroad

E. W. Marsh of Atlanta and other proprietors of the Sweet Water Hotel at Lithia Springs opened a private railroad of 1.5 miles on the hotel's grounds early in 1886. It was incorporated as a common carrier on March 25, 1887, so that it might handle bottled water from the spring under joint rates. The line was extended in 1891 about a mile to the station of two predecessors of the Southern Railway at Austell. This was a tiny operation of a single locomotive, two passenger cars, and two freight cars, one of the smallest line-haul common carriers in railroading. In fiscal 1889–90 revenues and operating expenses were each $750.

The railroad was carried in the *Official Guide* as the Bowden Lithia Springs Railroad until dropped in 1914. *Poor's Manual* listed it as the Salt Springs & Bowden Lithia Railroad, a wholly owned subsidiary of the Bowden Lithia Springs Water Co., in 1910 and 1911, then dropped it in 1912 as having reverted to a private carrier. The railroad was reportedly abandoned in 1913.

REFERENCE: Hugh M. Comer, "Railroad Abandonments in Georgia" (1985), typescript in the collection of Franklin M. Garrett, Atlanta, p. 183.

Elberton Air Line Railroad

The present main line of the Southern Railway between Washington, D.C., and Atlanta was such a major transport facility that it gave a widespread incentive to build connections from nearby towns. During the

narrow gauge era, this line through Georgia was successively incorporated as the New York & New Orleans Air Line (1866), Atlanta & Richmond Air Line (1870), Atlanta & Charlotte Air Line (1877), Richmond & Danville (1881), and finally as the Southern Railway (1894).

The Elberton Air Line was chartered on December 12, 1871, to build from Elberton to Gainesville or some other point on the Washington-Atlanta main line. J. H. Jones and T. I. Bowman of Elberton, the principal instigators of the narrow gauge, proved unable to finance the project until 1878, when the Atlanta & Charlotte Air Line agreed to take $150,000 of first-mortgage bonds. With the proceeds, Jones and Bowman built from Elberton to Toccoa on the main line. The Elberton Air Line was opened December 4, 1878. One thousand of the company's 1,959 shares of stock were conveyed to the A&C. This arrangement assured that the line would spend its entire history in the hands of the Southern Railway and its various predecessors. On September 29, 1881, after the Richmond & Danville had assumed control, the Elberton Air Line's charter was modified to allow it to build north to the Tennessee state line as part of the R&D's projected line from Augusta to Knoxville via Rabun Gap. The project was never executed, however.

Although the Elberton Air Line was 50 miles long, it had only two locomotives, two passengers cars, and 34 freight cars. The Richmond & Danville secured statutory authority to change the gauge on October 24, 1887. The Southern Railway effected the conversion during the spring and summer of 1895. The line is extant as a branch of the Southern at the present writing.

Gainesville, Jefferson & Southern Railroad

On August 23, 1872, the Gainesville, Jefferson & Southern was chartered to build a small railroad in northeastern Georgia, but more than a decade passed before the line was opened. Allan D. Candler of Gainesville was president. On June 1, 1883, the railroad was opened from Gainesville to Hoschton (18 miles), with a branch from Florence (Belmont) to Jefferson (13 miles). On March 8, 1884, the line was extended from Hoschton to Social Circle on the Georgia Railroad, partly by building 24 miles from Hoschton to Monroe and partly by acquiring the Walton Railroad, a ten-mile 5'-0" line between Monroe and Social Circle, for conversion to 3'-0". Beginning only three days later, the line was operated

The Gainesville, Jefferson & Southern's No. 3 was a well-proportioned 2-6-0 from the Pittsburgh Locomotive Works. (Railroad Museum of Pennsylvania.)

by the Georgia Railroad, which had advanced more than $42,500 to its construction. It was mainly unprofitable, with deficits made up by the Georgia Railroad.

The company was placed in the hands of a receiver on March 4, 1897, and sold on July 5, 1904, in two parcels. The portion from Gainesville to Monroe and Jefferson was bought by G. J. Baldwin and W. W. Mackall of Savannah and organized as the Gainesville Midland Railway. In 1905 the new management secured permission of state authorities to convert the Gainesville-Jefferson line and to extend it to Athens. This was done in 1906, but the Belmont-Monroe segment was not converted until late in 1913; it was abandoned early in 1948. The Gainesville Midland's main line was a heavily trafficked short line, mainly a facility enabling textiles from mills in Gainesville to reach the Seaboard Air Line in Athens. The Seaboard absorbed it in 1959.

The segment from Monroe to Social Circle was sold in 1904 to Jacob Phinizy of the Georgia Railroad, converted to 4'-8½", and incorporated as the Monroe Railroad. Both this line and the former Gainesville Midland are in existence as branches of the CSX Corporation.

Hartwell Railroad

The building of the Elberton Air Line presented the nearby town of Hartwell with the prospect of a railroad connection. The Hartwell Railroad was chartered by J. B.

and E. B. Benson on August 18, 1879, with the unusual provision that the construction company should operate the property until January 1, 1884. The line was built from Hartwell to Bowersville on the Elberton Air Line (10 miles) and opened in October 1879. Meanwhile, the Atlanta & Charlotte Air Line, which had taken control of the Elberton Air Line, secured control of the Hartwell's construction company. Upon replacing the A&CAL in 1881, the Richmond & Danville came into control of the Hartwell. The R&D assigned a single set of

officers to the Hartwell and the Elberton Air Line.

In 1892 the Hartwell was under the jurisdiction of the Richmond & Danville's receivers, but as a result of a legal action brought by T. J. Linder, a separate receiver was appointed for the Hartwell on November 29, E. B. Benson. When the Southern Railway was formed in 1894, it acquired the majority of the stock of the Hartwell from the Richmond & Danville's receivers. The narrow gauge was sold for $40,000 on February 5, 1898, and reorganized as the Hartwell Railway with the Southern as the principal stockholder. In settlement

Like many another, No. 3 of the Hartwell Railway, *Nancy Hart*, was sold to a lumber company. The engine is shown on a transfer table of the Southern Iron & Equipment Co. lettered for the J. J. Jones Lumber Co. (Ed Bond collection.)

of Linder's suit, the Hartwell was leased to Linder for $2,000 per year for ten years beginning February 19, 1898. Linder operated the line as an independent short line. It was a small railroad of two locomotives, two combines, eight boxcars, and four flatcars. J. D. Matheson replaced Linder as lessee on November 10, 1902.

The railroad was converted by Matheson in 1905. In the course of the 1920s the Southern sold its stock interest to local parties. The short line survived mainly on inbound coal and fertilizer movements. The management petitioned to abandon it in 1943 and received permission from the ICC on November 11, 1944, but then decided to continue in operation. The abandonment order was vacated in 1947, and the Hartwell remains in operation at the present writing.

REFERENCE: John William Baker, *History of Hart County* (Atlanta, Ga.: Foote & Davies, 1933), pp. 79–83.

Lawrenceville Branch Railroad

One of the several short narrow gauges tributary to the Southern Railway main line, this railroad enjoyed a financial relation to the Southern similar to the others. F. M. Peeples of Lawrenceville and his associates chartered the company in 1877 and financed it by means of $30,000 in bonds sold to the Atlanta & Charlotte Air Line. With the proceeds the narrow gauge was built between Lawrenceville and Suwanee on the A&C main line, ten miles, and opened on April 1, 1881. The A&C and its successors, including the Southern Railway after July 1, 1894, operated the line as a branch. On January 31, 1895, the Southern leased the branch to J. R. McKelvey and S. P. McDaniel in return for its net earnings. McKelvey continued to renew the lease, mainly for three-year periods, into the twentieth century. Under the terms of the renewal that expired December 31, 1911, McKelvey and the Southern jointly agreed to convert the line. The conversion required about 18 months, mainly because a new bridge was required over the Yellow River. Standard gauge service began on May 30, 1911. The line remained unprofitable, largely because Lawrenceville was now served directly by the Seaboard's Atlanta branch. McKelvey gave up the lease January 31, 1912, and the line reverted to the Southern. It continued to be operated under the name of the Lawrenceville Branch Railroad, but was closed on May 15, 1920, and scrapped.

Marietta & North Georgia Railroad

Although Edward Hulbert was not one of the officers, the Marietta & North Georgia Railroad embodied his philosophy of narrow gauges for local development of Georgia more fully than any other. The line was projected to develop marble quarries of northern Georgia and iron pits at Murphy, North Carolina, plus some copper deposits in the area.

The idea of a railroad from the Atlanta area to north-central Georgia dated from the Ellijay Railroad of 1854. This and a later project, the Marietta, Canton & Ellijay Railroad, could not be financed. The Marietta & North Georgia was promoted in the narrow gauge era. The president, William Phillips, was from Marietta, and the directors represented points along the projected line. The State of Georgia assisted the project by assigning gangs of convicts to construction and, through an act of 1877, lending the railroad the proceeds of rental of convict labor from the state prison system, about $20,000 per year until completion. The railroad was opened from Marietta on the Western & Atlantic to Canton, 23 miles, on May 1, 1879.

Before any further track was laid, the original owners encountered financial difficulties such that they were unable to continue building. In May 1881 they sold the controlling interest to Joseph Kinsey of Cincinnati and George R. Eager of Boston. At the time, grading extended about 40 miles north of Canton. The new owners built the line north of Canton to standard gauge specifications, including standard gauge ties, but laid 3'-0" track in the expectation of an early conversion. The railroad was unusual in using local marble for bridge abutments. As it proved, the conversion occurred in no great haste. Narrow gauge track reached Ball Ground (35 miles from Marietta) in 1882, Marble Cliff (60 miles) in 1883, and Ellijay (67 miles), the principal intermediate town, in 1884.

Meanwhile, the company encountered a variety of financial and legal troubles. Shareholders who had opposed transfer of control to Kinsey and Eager brought an action in 1883 to end the state's assignment of convicts to the company. The Georgia legislature not only agreed to continue the use of convicts, but authorized their free use until the railroad reached the North Carolina line. The original shareholders responded with an action for establishment of a receivership on the ground that they had never received the securities promised by Kinsey and Eager, but this effort was also

unsuccessful. The state legislature, which appears to have been exceptionally eager that the railroad be built, resolved in August 1885 that bonds of the company held by the state under the loan arrangement for prison revenues should be surrendered to the management if the railroad were completed to the North Carolina line within 20 months.

With this variety of incentives and impediments, the railroad was completed. Track reached Murphy (107 miles) at the end of 1886, and full operation began early in 1887. The state declared itself satisfied that the railroad had been finished within the 20 months allotted and prepared to release the securities. James T. Harrison, one of the aggrieved shareholders, brought an action to prevent release of the bonds, but the Superior Court in Atlanta refused him a permanent injunction on the ground that it was without jurisdiction. The management, which was now headed by R. M. Pulsifer, a well-known publisher of Boston, was mainly interested in using the narrow gauge as part of a through route from Atlanta to Knoxville. The State of Georgia refused on three occasions to let the company build into Atlanta from Marietta on the ground that the state's Western & Atlantic should be protected from loss of revenue. The management at the end of 1887 placed $3.3 million in mortgage bonds in New York, London, and the local area, allowing the railroad to undertake its Knoxville extension. The original plan was to build from Murphy to Knoxville via Red Marble Gap, a difficult route. Instead, it was decided to build between Blue Ridge, Georgia, and Knoxville by means of a subsidiary, the Knoxville Southern. The line was built south from Knoxville beginning in 1889. In the same year, the company began converting the line north from Marietta by laying third rail on the existing track. Standard gauge reached Tate (42 miles) by the end of 1889 and Blue Ridge (82 miles) in mid-May 1890. The Knoxville Southern reached Blue Ridge from the north on August 9, 1890, completing the Knoxville-Atlanta line. The Blue Ridge–Murphy branch (25 miles) was left narrow gauge, though scheduled for conversion in the near future.

Recurrence of the railroad's characteristic financial difficulties postponed conversion of the Murphy branch for some years. In January 1891 the Central Trust Co. of New York petitioned in federal court in Atlanta for receivership for non-payment of interest. J. B. Glover, superintendent of the railroad, was appointed receiver. Toward the end of the year Glover secured the court's permission to issue $1 million in receiver's certificates to convert the Murphy branch and to bypass a switchback at the Hiwassee River on the Knoxville extension. B. H. Hill, master in chancery for the bankruptcy court, had recently recommended that the Murphy line be sold on the ground that it had never paid its operating costs. The branch was, however, retained.

Reorganization of the railroad in the depressed 1890s proved difficult. Judge W. T. Newman of Atlanta in 1893 ordered the mileage in Georgia and Tennessee sold separately, but no buyer met either of Newman's specified minimum bids until Charles E. Kimball of Summit, New Jersey, and associates bid $956,000 for both segments on November 25, 1895. This group defaulted its second payment of $150,000 on March 9, 1896, causing further delay. Henry K. McHarg of New York, Eugene G. Spauling of Atlanta, and others who were apparently associated with Kimball in the aborted attempt bought the railroad in April and reorganized it as the Atlanta, Knoxville & Northern Railway. The receivers were discharged on July 6, 1897. The new owners converted the Blue Ridge–Murphy line near the end of November 1897. They replaced the switchback with the famous Hiwassee Loop in 1898. The railroad became known informally as the "Hook & Eye," the loop providing the eye and a sharp curve at Tate on the former narrow gauge the hook.

The Louisville & Nashville interested itself in the railroad as an entry into Atlanta, although both the former narrow gauge and the standard gauge extension were poor pieces of engineering. The L&N gained control of the corporation in 1902; the L&N's distinguished president, Milton H. Smith, became president of the smaller railroad. At the beginning of 1905, the L&N began building a direct line about 20 miles west of the "Hook & Eye," opening it in the spring of 1906. Both routes continued to enter Atlanta by trackage rights over the W&A and its successor, the Nashville, Chattanooga & St. Louis. The "Hook & Eye" became the "Old Line," used normally only for local service. At the present writing it is still in existence. The Murphy branch was abandoned in 1982.

North & South Railroad of Georgia

A direct railroad between Columbus and Rome was the basic project of Governor Rufus B. Bullock to develop western Georgia. The company was organized as the North & South Railroad of Georgia on August 1, 1871; by 1873, 35 miles were reported graded and five miles of track laid. About 20 miles south from Rome were also graded. *Poor's Manual* reported the line open from Columbus to Kingston (20 miles) in its 1873–74 issue and to Hamilton (23 miles) in the 1875–76 issue. In 1874 the governor of Georgia took possession of the railroad in consequence of the failure of the company to pay interest on state bonds issued to aid it. A receiver named Llewellen was appointed.

The receivership led to a battle of several years' duration for control of the railroad. In March 1876 the governor signed a bill for conversion of the railroad's floating debt into stock and gradual extinguishing of the state's lien on the condition of completion of the railroad to Rome, about 100 miles north of the railhead. Shareholders met at La Grange to attempt to implement this plan but failed to raise funds. The line was next sold on September 4, 1877, to the Columbus & Atlanta Air Line for $40,500, but this company could not finance the transaction. Under an executive order of July 26, 1877, the governor attempted to sell the railroad privately for the same sum, but such efforts were also unsuccessful. Finally, in October 1879, E. C. Hood and his associates in Columbus bought the North & South and reorganized it as the Columbus & Rome Railroad. The new owners extended the railroad to Hood (32 miles) in 1880. E. P. Alexander of Louisville bought the line on July 1, 1881, and extended it a mile to Chipley about 1882. In 1884 the grade was extended to Greenville. Track reached Stinson (42 miles) in 1884 and service began to Greenville (50 miles) on February 9, 1885.

The Central of Georgia gained control of the railroad and merged it first into the Savannah & Western subsidiary in 1886, and then in 1895 into the C of G itself. The C of G converted the narrow gauge in 1906 and extended it 23 miles to Raymond, just outside Newnan, a junction with the C of G's Griffin-Chattanooga line. In connection with the C of G's Chattanooga line the railroad amounted to a north-south route through western Georgia about as the projectors had planned. It remains in service as a branch of the C of G in the Norfolk Southern system.

Rome & Carrollton Railroad

The North & South Railroad of Georgia had left unbuilt some 20 to 50 miles of grade between Rome, Cedartown, and Carrollton. The Rome & Carrollton Railroad was chartered on August 3, 1881, to build on the grade. The choice of narrow gauge probably represented a desire for compatibility with the East & West Railroad of Alabama at Cedartown. The project made no progress until J. D. Williamson of Rome and his associates bought the franchise in 1884. They let a contract for construction in 1885. Work began on July 14, and a locomotive was purchased in September. Track reportedly reached Cedartown (20 miles) early in December. No further narrow gauge construction was undertaken.

The line proved one of the most short-lived narrow gauges; Williamson announced an intention to standard gauge it as early as November 1886. The name was changed in 1888 to the Chattanooga, Rome & Columbus Railroad, which symbolized the revival of the idea of a north-south railroad through western Georgia. The standard gauge line from Chattanooga to Carrollton was built in the first half of 1888—the narrow gauge being converted incidentally—and was opened on July 1.

The former narrow gauge was operated as part of the Central of Georgia Railroad system from mid-1891. At first it was owned by subsidiaries, but it was purchased outright by the C of G in 1901. It survives as part of the C of G's Chattanooga branch in the Norfolk Southern system.

Roswell Railroad

Though now in north suburban Atlanta, Roswell was an isolated farming town in the nineteenth century. The Atlanta & Roswell Railroad was chartered on April 10, 1863, to connect the town with the Western & Atlantic, but nothing was built. When the Atlanta & Richmond Air Line was under construction, the management agreed to endorse the Atlanta & Roswell's bonds, and in return the smaller railroad agreed to build a connection with the Air Line at Doraville, later called Roswell Junction and Chamblee. After some work was done, both railroads failed in 1874. The contractors, Grant, Alexander & Co., filed a lien for $500, causing the Atlanta & Roswell to be sold to them on October 2, 1877. The railroad was sold again on July 15, 1879, and reorganized as the Roswell Railroad. The new company renewed its relation with the Atlanta & Charlotte Air Line, successor to the Atlanta & Richmond Air Line. The A&C agreed to buy $35,000 of the company's bonds in return for 201 of the 400 shares of stock. Under this arrangement, the Roswell was completed as a ten-mile narrow gauge on September 1, 1881, with the A&C as lessee. It was a small

The Memphis Branch Railroad was never put in service, but it bought this small Porter 0-6-0 for its construction work. The engine became the first locomotive of the Marietta & North Georgia. (Thomas T. Taber collection, Railroad Museum of Pennsylvania.)

railroad of a single locomotive, one passenger car, two boxcars, and four flatcars. The line retained its individual identity, but after 1894 was operated as a branch of the Southern Railway. The Southern converted the narrow gauge in fiscal 1902–3, probably in 1902.

The Southern operated the line until June 1920. It was next operated for freight service only by the Fulton Transfer & Storage Co. of Atlanta under the name of the Roswell Branch Railroad until the end of 1921 and then abandoned.

▼ ▼ ▼ ▼

Two major projects in Georgia achieved limited completion, but neither is known to have been put in service.

The Gainesville & Dahlonega Railroad was one of several projects to connect what became the Southern Railway main line with a nearby county seat. It was chartered in 1866 to build from Gainesville to Dahlonega, seat of Lumpkin County (26 miles), but was not financed. In 1878 about four miles of narrow gauge track were laid northwest from Gainesville, and an additional 8 to 12 miles were graded. The promoters, led by Colonel R. H. Baker, acquired the entire right-of-way, and spent $15,000 bridging the Chattahoochee River. Baker led a ceremony at Dahlonega on February 28, 1879, driving the first stake on the depot site.

Nonetheless, no further progress was made. Several efforts were made to revive the project in the 1880s, but none was successful. The completed portion was sold at a receiver's auction on July 2, 1890, to Colonel W. P. Price, who also proved unable to finance the extension. Finally, an effort was made to build the line as an interurban in 1901, but this also was unsuccessful, and rails never reached Dahlonega.

The Memphis Branch Railroad was chartered in 1868 to run from Rome across northern Georgia and Alabama via Decatur to Memphis. In 1873 the company laid five miles of track and graded an additional 12 miles west from Rome. This degree of completion qualified the railroad for state endorsement of $34,000 of its bonds. The monetary stringency beginning in 1873 prevented any further progress. The railroad had one locomotive and four flatcars used for construction. Inability to pay interest on the state-endorsed debt caused the property to be placed in the hands of Robert F. Fouche, State Agent, in 1877. He sold the railroad on August 14 for $9,100 to William Phillips, who announced he would remove the rails for use on his Marietta & North Georgia.

REFERENCES: Richard E. Prince, *Central of Georgia Railway and Connecting Lines* (Millard, Nebr.: Richard E. Prince, 1976); Comer, "Railroad Abandonments in Georgia."

Hawaii

Railroad development in Hawaii dates from a treaty of reciprocity of September 9, 1876, whereby the United States agreed to admit sugar from the Kingdom of Hawaii free of duty in return for the right to establish a coaling station and repair facility in the Pearl River Lagoon—the origin of the Pearl Harbor naval base. The treaty produced an immediate inflow of resources into establishment of sugar plantations, mainly by haoles—the general Hawaiian term for white foreigners. In the typical economic organization, sugar was grown under extensive irrigation and milled either on the plantation or nearby. The raw sugar was then shipped in burlap bags, usually by sea to American ports, for refining. The raw sugar was typically marketed by long-term contract through one of five agents or factors: C. Brewer & Co., Ltd.; Theodore H.

Davies & Co., Ltd.; Castle & Cooke, Inc.; Alexander & Baldwin, Inc.; and Hackfeld & Co., a German firm. Seized by the Alien Property Custodian in World War I, this last was reorganized as American Factors, Ltd., in 1918. The name was shortened to Amfac, Inc., in 1966.

Hawaii quickly developed an extensive mileage of narrow gauge private trackage on the plantations. Partly for compatibility with the private carriers, partly because the treaty immediately preceded the major period of narrow gauge building domestically, and partly because compatibility with the American standard gauge system was no consideration, the common carriers of Hawaii were all narrow gauge with a single exception, the Hawaii Consolidated Railway on the east coast of the island of Hawaii. All of the narrow gauge common carriers were mainly occupied with carrying sugar; the investment was largely by plantation operators or by the five major factors.

The McKinley Tariff of 1890 did not directly address itself to Hawaiian sugar, but it extended duty-free importation to all countries, and applied a bounty of two cents per pound to domestic American producers. The consequence was four years of depression of the Hawaiian sugar industry. The monarchy was overthrown on January 17, 1893, when a Committee of Public Safety led by William C. Wilder, who was active in transport development of Hawaii, deposed Queen Liliuokalani. The haoles established the Republic of Hawaii on July 4, 1894, under the presidency of pineapple grower Sanford B. Dole. On July 7, 1898, President William McKinley signed an act that made Hawaii an American territory. This sequence of events ended the political instability that had depressed transport investment in the early 1890s, and placed the common carriers under the ordinary framework of American law.

Ahukini Terminal & Railroad Co.
Gauge: 2'-6"

American Factors, Ltd., organized this railroad in 1920 to serve installations of two of its clients on Kauai, Lihue Plantation and the Makee Sugar Co. The line was projected to connect the landings at Anahola, Kealia, and Kapaa, from which Makee Sugar shipped raw sugar in bags by lighter to freighters anchored offshore, to Lihue Plantation's Ahukini Landing in the shelter of Hanamaulu Bay, the best harbor on the east coast of the island. The ascent from Ahukini Landing was very difficult, entail-

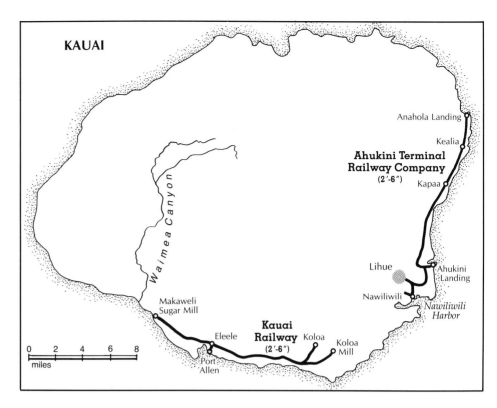

ing a fill 900 feet long and 30 feet high, a 165-foot-long bridge over the Hanamaulu River, and a cut 1,800 feet long and 40 feet deep. A concrete arch bridge 390 feet long was required at the Waialua River. Service began from Ahukini Landing to Kealia in May 1921, and by the end of the year the entire railroad to Anahola (14 miles) had been finished. Ahukini Wharf was not completed until February 1, 1922. The line operated with two Porter 0-6-0 locomotives, 20 boxcars, two flatcars, and additional flatcars leased from plantations along the route. The company had no known passenger equipment. In 1931 the railroad made its only extension, a line of about five miles south from a point just short of Ahukini Landing to Lihue and the port of Nawiliwili to serve installations of Lihue Plantation.

In 1934 Lihue Plantation absorbed both Makee Sugar and the railroad company, reducing the railroad to private carriage. The track survived until 1959, when the last rails were removed.

Hawaii Railway

Samuel G. Wilder of the Wilder Steamship Co. secured a charter for a narrow gauge railroad from the small port of Mahukona for 20 miles along the north coast of the island of Hawaii to Niulii. Wilder, who was Minister of the Interior of the monarchical government of Hawaii, signed his own charter on July 5, 1880. An amendment signed by King Kalakaua on August 13 gave

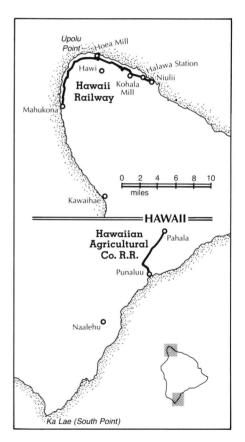

the company a subsidy of $2,500 per mile on completion. Wilder left the government the following day and organized the Hawaiian Railroad on October 20. A smallpox epidemic prevented the start of construction until April 1881. In February 1882 Wilder's successor as Minister of the Interior paid him $25,000 for half-completion of the railroad. By the end of 1882, 17.2 miles had been built, and the railroad was completed to Niulii on January 10, 1883. The line had no spurs to mills or into cane fields, but rather carried bagged raw sugar brought from the mills by horse drayage. It did not handle cane.

The Hawaiian Railroad was dissolved on December 17, 1897, by Wilder's heirs, who reincorporated the enterprise as the Hawaii Railway. Leaving the transportation business in 1899, they sold the railroad to the operators of four of the five major mills that the line served. The new owners relaid the track from 20-pound to 30- and 35-pound rail, and straightened the route at several points. They became notable for devotion to 2-4-2 locomotives.

On April 1, 1937, the Kohala Sugar Co. bought all of the plantations in the area, plus all stock in the railroad. It built spurs to the mills and into the cane fields, thereafter using the railroad for cane movements as well as for bagged sugar. On September 30 the Hawaii Railway was dissolved and reincorporated as Mahukona Terminals, Ltd. In 1939 the easternmost five miles of the main line were abandoned, although a 1.1-mile spur from Kohala Mill to Halawa was built to replace the innermost portion. In 1942, after the American entry into World War II, the Navy closed the port at Mahukona because of the risk of submarine attack to ships offshore. This in turn brought the closure of the railroad for common carriage west of Hawi Mill, about eight miles, although some operation for cane movements continued. All cane movements were shifted to trucks at the end of the war, and the railroad was abandoned in its entirety in 1945.

Kahului Railroad

Thomas Hobron and his sons-in-law, William Owen Smith and William H. Bailey, in June 1879 undertook the Kahului & Wailuku Railroad to connect the plantation of their Wailuku Sugar Co. with Kahului (3 miles), the principal port on the north shore of Maui. On completion in September, the railroad was the first common carrier in the Hawaiian Islands. The line ran a mixed train Tuesdays through Fridays.

In the following year the railroad was extended east along the north coast of the island, reaching Paia, about six miles east of Kahului, on September 21, 1880. To make its common carrier status explicit, the railroad was reincorporated on July 1, 1881, as

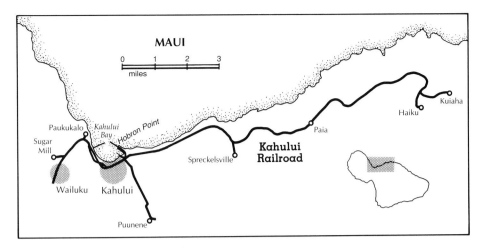

the Kahului Railroad. The railroad also had a varying mileage of branches or spurs to plantations, notably a half-mile branch to an installation of Claus Spreckels at Spreckelsville. In July 1884 Hobron's group sold the railroad to Samuel G. Wilder of the Wilder Steamship Co., one of the two principal inter-island operators. Wilder, who already owned the Hawaiian Railroad, died in 1888; the Kahului was sold to J. B. Castle & Associates by his heirs in 1899. The Castle management in 1912 undertook an extension from Paia to Haiku to serve the pineapple industry, which was rapidly expanding. On completion on February 8, 1913, the extension brought the main line to 15.5 miles; the spurs to sugar mills and pineapple canneries peaked at 24 miles in 1936. The railroad was profitable until well after World War II. Sugar began to be diverted to trucks in 1947, and pineapple was abruptly diverted in 1964, causing the management to apply for abandonment on April 28, 1965. Permission was received from the ICC on October 27, but transitional difficulties in arranging truck transport for the remaining sugar traffic kept the line in operation until May 22, 1966. Hawaii's first common carrier railroad also proved the state's last one.

Kauai Railway
Gauge: 2'-6"

Theodore H. Davies & Co., Ltd., in 1906 decided upon a railroad along the south shore of Kauai to serve the mills of its clients, the McBryde and Koloa sugar companies. The line was built from Eleele Landing (Port Allen) to Koloa Mill (11 miles) with a two-mile branch to the town of Koloa, where the railroad met private trackage of the Koloa Sugar Co. The railway also operated over trackage of McBryde and trackage of the Hawaiian Sugar Co. to reach the latter's mill at Makaweli, about four

miles west of Port Allen. The necessity of choosing the gauge for compatibility with the private carriers made the island of Kauai a citadel of 2'-6", as Maine was of 2'-0". The railroad was a common carrier, but it carried no passengers except briefly during World War I.

The Kauai Railway was liquidated in 1933. Some of the mileage had already been transferred to the sugar companies for private carriage, and the remainder apparently met the same fate. Rail operations reportedly ended in 1947.

Koolau Railway

Benjamin F. Dillingham's failure to build the Oahu Railway's main line beyond Kahuku left some unsatisfied demands for transportation to the southeast along the north coast of Oahu. In August 1905 James B. Castle's Hawaiian Development Corp. formed the Koolau Railway, mainly to serve installations of the Koolau Agricultural Co., which it had formed earlier in the year. The charter issued by the territorial government in September provided for a route from Kahuku along the coast to Kaneohe, then up an ascent from the base of the Pali section of the Koolau Mountains to the summit, through a tunnel to the south escarpment, and down a grade into downtown Honolulu. Actually, only 11 miles were built, from Kahuku to Kahana; this track was finished about June 1907. Any extension along the rugged coast, much less the mountain crossing to Honolulu, would have been unbearably expensive, relative to the railroad's prospects. The line operated with two Baldwin tank engines, 21 freight cars, and two passenger cars. Traffic was mainly sugar, with some additional agricultural products. The line served several installations, including Dillingham's Kahuku Plantation and the Laie Plantation, a Mor-

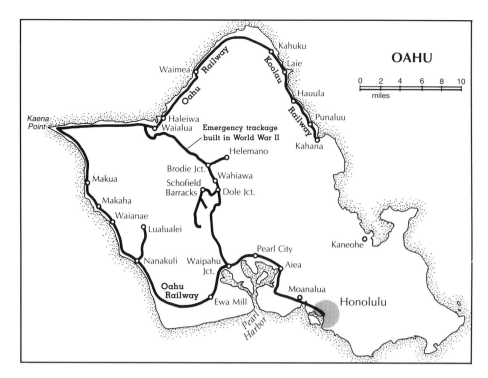

19° curve at Kaena Point, the western tip of Oahu. The line was opened on June 1, 1898, to Waialua (56 miles), where Dillingham built the Haleiwa Hotel. The railroad inaugurated a passenger train, the Haleiwa Limited, which was carded for a flat two hours from Honolulu to Waialua, a fast schedule for a narrow gauge. The main line was completed to Kahuku (71 miles) on December 28, 1898. Dillingham reportedly intended to continue the line southeast along the coast, but never did so; thus the extension was built separately by other interests as the Koolau Railway. The Oahu Railway built only one branch, a line from Waipahu at Pearl Harbor to Wahiawa (11 miles) constructed in 1906 to serve a pineapple plantation of the James D. Dole interests. Pineapples were typically grown at higher altitudes than sugar, and without irrigation. The branch ascended the valley between the Waianae and Koolau ranges, with grades up to 3 percent; the main line had been relatively flat. The branch served mainly to take pineapples to canneries in Honolulu, but it also served Schofield Barracks, where the Army maintained an extensive network of trackage of its own from Dole Junction.

The railway was uniformly profitable, enjoying mixed traffic of raw sugar, pineapples, general cargo, and passengers, both local population and tourists. A major upgrading was undertaken in 1908, which undoubtedly would have entailed conversion

mon enterprise dating from 1865. The latter had trackage rights over 2.5 miles of the railroad to bring cane to the mill at Kahuku.

In 1931 the Kahuku Plantation bought out the Laie Plantation, the Koolau Agricultural Co., and the Koolau Railway. The new owner discontinued passenger service, dissolved the railway corporation, and reduced the track to private carriage. The trackage contracted slowly until rail operations were discontinued in 1954.

Oahu Railway & Land Co.

Benjamin Franklin Dillingham, one of the most important of the haole businessmen in the Kingdom of Hawaii, observed the successful experiments in drilling of artesian wells by James Campbell at Ewa, southwest of Pearl Harbor, in 1879. Dillingham believed the technology would allow sugar cultivation under irrigation on the arid west coast of Oahu, and agreed with Campbell to undertake a railroad from Honolulu to Ewa, continuing on to the coast, and proceeding northward along the west escarpment of the Waianae Mountains. The railroad was chartered as the Oahu Railway & Land Co., the franchise for which was signed by King Kalakaua on September 11, 1888. Dillingham became general manager. The railroad began service to Aiea (9 miles) on November 16, 1889, the King's birthday, and was opened to Pearl City (11 miles) on January 1, 1890. In May the line reached Ewa (18 miles), where Dillingham organized a plantation in collaboration with Castle &

Cooke. Further extension was delayed by the political instability of the early 1890s, but on July 4, 1895, Dillingham opened the line to Waianae (33 miles).

In 1891 Dillingham had organized the Kahuku Plantation just east of Kahuku Point, the northernmost point on Oahu. He undertook an extension of the railway in 1897, continuing around the coast of the island. The extension entailed a spectacular

Much of the Oahu Railway's main line skirted the bluffs along the west coast of Oahu. (California State Railroad Museum.)

The Oahu Railway was large enough to require 0-8-0 switchers, including No. 88, for its terminal operations in Honolulu. (Ed Bond collection.)

An outside-frame 2-8-0 rides the turntable at the Oahu Railway's large roundhouse in Honolulu. (California State Railroad Museum.)

if the railway had been in the continental United States. The original 35-pound rail was replaced with 48-, 60-, and 70-pound rail. By 1921 the line from Honolulu to the junction at Waipahu was double-tracked and equipped with upper-quadrant semaphores, the only automatic block signals on any American narrow gauge. The signaling was extended up the Wahiawa branch to Dole Junction. In 1916 the railway operated with 25 locomotives, 37 coaches, four combines, two parlor cars, five head-

end cars, and 659 freight cars. Two Shay locomotives were bought for the Wahiawa branch in 1920 and 1921.

When Dillingham died in 1918 he was succeeded by his son, Walter F. Dillingham, who served as president for the remainder of the railway's history. In the 1920s he bought four Baldwin Mikado locomotives, based on the design of the Denver & Rio Grande Western's K-28 class; thereafter the four were the line's principal motive power for the main line. Passenger traffic peaked

in 1920, but subsequently declined in a fashion parallel to railroads in the continental United States. The railway suffered less from the Depression than American railroads generally because it carried extensive defense-related traffic, and also because the output of sugar and pineapple held up relatively well. Upon the American entry into World War II the railway became a major defense facility. Restrictions on road transport revived passenger service to the extent that the railroad reconverted some coaches that had been reduced to haulage of empty cans to canneries in Honolulu. The Army built an extension of the Wahiawa branch to a storage depot at Halemano, and from its midpoint, Brodie Junction, constructed an emergency connection across the Waianae Mountains to a point on the main line near Wialua. The connection was intended as a bypass of the main line along the west coast to be employed if the Japanese bombarded the island, but circumstances never required its use. The Navy built a spur of four miles off the main line from Nanakuli to Lualualei to serve an ammunition dump.

After the war, the railroad's fortunes declined rapidly. A tsunami wiped out the main line between Haleiwa and Waimea on April 1, 1946. Although the track was restored, the incident accelerated the diversion of traffic to trucks. After consultation with local shippers, the management applied to the ICC for abandonment of the main line, and on December 31, 1947, was allowed to drop the Wahaiwa branch and the main line beyond Moanalua, three miles from Honolulu. The remainder was retained as switching track to serve the Kalihi stockyards and the canneries and docks in the city. The Navy took over the main line from Pearl Harbor to Nanakuli to serve the Lualualei ammunition facility.

Shortly after Hawaii became a state in 1959 the attorney general brought an action to recover land granted by King Kalakaua in 1888, on the ground that it was no longer being used for railway purposes. In the settlement of the dispute in 1961, the former main line, except that portion being used by the Navy, was conveyed to the state for highway use, and the railroad was reorganized as the Oahu Railway & Terminal Warehouse Co. In 1962 the line to the Kalihi stockyards was abandoned, reducing the railway to about ten miles of switching trackage in Honolulu. This survived until 1972.

REFERENCES: Gerald M. Best, *Railroads of Hawaii: Narrow and Standard Gauge Common Carriers* (San Marino, Calif.: Golden West

The Oahu Railway's last surviving operation was switching along the wharves in Honolulu. (California State Railroad Museum.)

Books, 1978), pp. 52–121; Kent W. Cochrane, "The Oahu Railway & Land Company," *Trains*, Mar. 1947, pp. 26–37; Fred A. Stindt, "Oahu Railway and Land Company," *The Western Railroader*, 20, no. 4, issue 208 (1957).

▼ ▼ ▼ ▼

The Hawaiian Agricultural Co. in 1879–80 built a private 2′-0″ railroad on the island of Hawaii from the port at Punaluu to its mill at Pahala on the eastern slope of Mauna Loa volcano. The line of about 5.5 miles entailed a rise of 850 feet. Although the railroad had no general pretension to being a common carrier, it achieved that state nominally in 1893 when tour operators began using the line for passengers making an ascent to the rim of the volcano. The line was converted to 3′-0″ in 1902–3. Its line-haul function was replaced by a flume in 1929. About a mile of it survived, as a switching track at Punaluu, until 1945.

REFERENCES: John B. Hungerford, *Hawaiian Railroads* (Reseda, Calif.: Hungerford Press, 1963); Best, *Railroads of Hawaii*; Jesse C. Condé and Gerald M. Best, *Sugar Trains: Narrow Gauge Rails of Hawaii* (Felton, Calif.: Glenwood Publishers, 1973).

Idaho

Coeur d'Alene Railway & Navigation Co.

The discovery of gold in the Coeur d'Alene area of the Idaho panhandle in 1882 precipitated a gold rush by the following year. The Northern Pacific Railway was completed on September 8, 1883, but it had circumvented the area, choosing a route along the north shore of the beautiful Lake Pend Oreille, nearly 50 miles to the north. By 1884 the boom was concentrated on the South Fork of the Coeur d'Alene River. Access by steamboat and road from the NP was considered slow, expensive, and unsuitable to heavy ore movements. Six projects for railroads were promoted in 1886. J. J. Browne of Spokane conceived the idea of a standard gauge railroad off the NP main line to Coeur d'Alene City, a steamer connection across Coeur d'Alene Lake, and a narrow gauge railroad up the South Fork to the mining area. Browne failed to execute the plan, but it was undertaken successfully by Daniel C. Corbin of Montana, who on April 22, 1886, incorporated the Coeur d'Alene Railway & Navigation Co. to build the narrow gauge portion. The standard gauge was organized as the Spokane Falls & Idaho Railroad, and built in 1886 from Hauser Junction, Idaho, 21 miles east of Spokane, to Coeur d'Alene, 13 miles to the southeast. The SF&I had no equipment, and was operated as an NP branch; the NP leased the property from October 1, 1887. The marine portion of the system was provided by the Coeur d'Alene Steam Navigation & Transportation Co., which first served the railroad under a contract of July 31, 1886, and then was purchased by CR&N in 1888. Initially the line operated with the sternwheeler *Coeur d'Alene* and propeller *General Sherman*, but to maintain year-round service, the CR&N ordered the iron-hulled icebreaker *Kootenai* for delivery in the fall of 1887. The service also used barges for ore.

Construction of the narrow gauge began at Old Mission Landing (Mission) on the east side of the lake on August 18, 1886, and the track was laid to Wardner Junction (13 miles) before work was suspended for the winter on December 26. Building resumed in the spring, and track reached Wallace (25 miles), the principal town in the mining area, on September 10, 1887. Two ex–Texas & St. Louis 2-6-0s were used for the construction trains. The railroad immediately proved successful, handling a heavy volume of ore at rates that were locally considered exorbitant.

The line quickly had an extension. S. S. Glidden incorporated the Canyon Creek Railroad on July 14, 1887, to connect his Tiger mine at Bayard (Burke) with the narrow gauge at Wallace. When he had done a little grading, he signed a contract on September 5 to finish the roadbed and then sell the railroad to Corbin. The seven-mile line was completed on December 22. Operation was primitive, with boxcars used as both cabooses and passenger coaches. The line had a 3-percent grade and difficult curvature. It was turned over to the CR&N on August 29, 1888.

The Northern Pacific, threatened with a

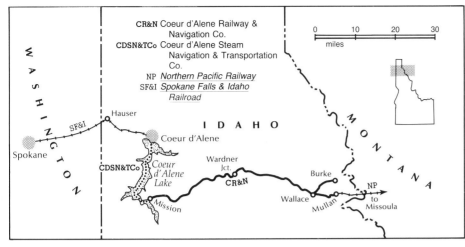

CR&N Coeur d'Alene Railway &
       Navigation Co.
CDSN&TCo Coeur d'Alene Steam
       Navigation & Transportation
       Co.
NP *Northern Pacific Railway*
SF&I *Spokane Falls & Idaho
       Railroad*

Illinois

penetration of the mining area by the Union Pacific's Oregon Railway & Navigation Co. and Washington & Idaho Railroad, arranged on September 14, 1888, to lease the CR&N for 999 years effective October 1. The NP recognized that the existing mixture of narrow gauge, steamboat-and-barge, and standard gauge movement of ore was expensive and slow. From the outset the larger railroad intended to convert the narrow gauge and find some substitute for the steamboats. The UP subsidiaries completed their all-rail entry into the Wallace area late in 1889, giving the UP the distinct advantage of an unbroken line around the south shore of the lake. The NP considered building either a line around the north end of the lake or an extension east from Wallace to its main line at Missoula, Montana. If both were built, the NP would have an alternative main line, considerably shorter than the existing line to the north of Lake Pend Oreille. Because the line north of Lake Coeur d'Alene would have entailed a 2.2-percent grade and 16° curvature, it was rejected in favor of the line to Missoula. The NP began by extending the narrow gauge east from Wallace seven miles to Mullan on March 24, 1889, but as in many other instances, the track was laid in the expectation of conversion. The remainder of the project, 128 miles between Missoula and Mullan, was built to standard gauge from the outset and completed in December 1890, though it was not fully operable until July 1891. The Mullan-Wallace track was widened on July 23, 1891, although it proved initially too weak for standard gauge locomotives. The Burke branch was converted later in 1891. The marine operation was wound up in 1890, except for the passenger steamer *Georgie Oakes*.

The NP would probably have converted the rest of the narrow gauge shortly except for its financial difficulties, which culmi-

nated in its bankruptcy on August 15, 1893. The CR&N followed it into bankruptcy on October 10. In the course of reorganization, the NP bought the CR&N for $220,000 on January 26, 1897, in the explicit intention of conversion. Instead, the NP abandoned the narrow gauge from Mission to Wardner in March 1898, and arranged to use the parallel line of the OR&N from Wallace to Wardner, still the location of several mines. The narrow gauge equipment was sold. The remaining narrow gauge track was removed in 1902. The Burke branch was abandoned in 1938, and the Mullan-Wallace trackage in 1980.

REFERENCE: John V. Wood, *Railroads Through the Coeur d'Alenes* (Caldwell, Idaho: Caxton Printers, Ltd., 1983).

Cairo & St. Louis Railroad

The idea of a direct railroad from Cairo at the confluence of the Ohio and Mississippi rivers to East St. Louis via Murphysboro was conceived as the Civil War neared its end. The Cairo & St. Louis was chartered on February 16, 1865, by men from Cairo and the intermediate towns. They were initially unable to finance the project and were among the first to adopt the doctrine of 3'-0" gauge to reduce capital expenses. They succeeded in financing the railroad with Dutch capitalists; interest on the bonds was payable in Amsterdam. Work was begun on September 1, 1871. Col. S. Staats Taylor of Cairo served as president, and all of the directors were from on-line communities. Both municipalities and county governments subscribed to the railroad's securities. The principal purpose of the railroad was to carry coal into the St. Louis metropolitan area from the Big Muddy coalfield near Murphysboro, the main intermediate town; but Cairo at the

The Cairo & St. Louis's *R. H. Rosborough*, a Baldwin 2-6-0 of 1872, was unusual for its straight-topped boiler and three-axle tender. (California State Railroad Museum.)

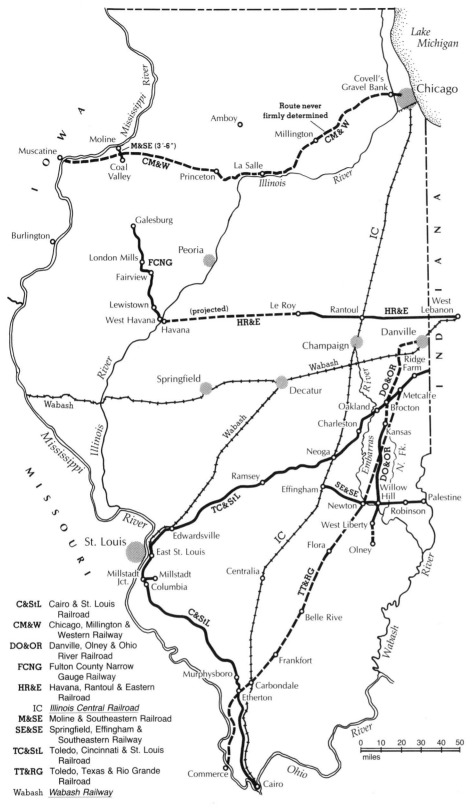

C&StL Cairo & St. Louis Railroad
CM&W Chicago, Millington & Western Railway
DO&OR Danville, Olney & Ohio River Railroad
FCNG Fulton County Narrow Gauge Railway
HR&E Havana, Rantoul & Eastern Railroad
IC *Illinois Central Railroad*
M&SE Moline & Southeastern Railroad
SE&SE Springfield, Effingham & Southeastern Railway
TC&StL Toledo, Cincinnati & St. Louis Railroad
TT&RG Toledo, Texas & Rio Grande Railroad
Wabash *Wabash Railway*

time had ambitions as a railroad center. The city was on the Illinois Central main line, and the Cairo & Vincennes, later a part of the New York Central System, built into the city from the northeast in 1872.

By July 1, 1873, track had reached Murphysboro, 90 miles from East St. Louis. The

company entered East St. Louis by laying third rail along the East St. Louis, Cahokia & Falling Springs from East Carondelet, about four miles. Construction to the south was expensive, entailing a bridge across the Big Muddy River at Murphysboro, two difficult grades at Alto Pass, and a tunnel at

Kaolin. The company had trouble collecting $450,000 in subscriptions from local governments. The directors considered issuing a second mortgage for the amount of the missing subscriptions, but the financial stringency of late 1873 prevented this plan. The company's financial problems brought the contractors, H. R. Payson and Ferdinand E. Canda of Chicago, into the management of the railroad. In 1874 the bondholders agreed to postpone payment of interest. Payson and Canda subcontracted the 62 miles from Murphysboro to Cairo to John Fleming of Des Moines and C. Lacey of Warsaw, Illinois. Construction was resumed and tracklaying began at Cairo on October 14, 1874. Some 26 miles of track had been laid by the end of 1874, and the rest early in 1875. The railroad was completed at Murphysboro on February 19, and full service began on March 1, 1875. At approximately 150 miles, including its trackage rights, it was reportedly the longest American narrow gauge on completion. Payments of $117,000 from the governments of Cairo and Alexander County that had been held up pending completion were released to the railroad.

At the shareholders' meeting of June 28, 1875, Payson and Canda, who held $3.3 million of the $5 million in stock outstanding, were elected directors. Taylor initially refused to deliver the company's books to them on the ground that the railroad had not been properly completed, and that, accordingly, issue of stock to the contractors was illegal. The bondholders mainly sided with the new members of the board, and Taylor gave up his plan of legal action. Canda, who was mainly known as a car builder, became president and general manager.

The company had been unable to arrange a joint terminal in Cairo with the Cairo & Vincennes, and was terminating in a temporary building at the end of its entry on the levee along the Mississippi River. Damage to the levee in the spring of 1875 showed that this arrangement was impractical, and the company, in federal court in Springfield, won the right to build another entry. Owing to its financial problems, the railroad could not immediately undertake the new trackage. Conflict with the city government on the entry resumed and continued for nearly a decade.

The company's fortunes deteriorated in 1876. It ran at operating ratios of 85 to 95 percent and had difficulty covering its payrolls. Enginemen struck on November 1, 1876, for back wages. The company successfully scabbed the strike, but then encountered acrimony between the new personnel and the old who returned to work.

Cairo & St. Louis No. 6, a Baldwin 2-6-0 of 1872, was named for Sparta, a town on the northern district of the railroad. (California State Railroad Museum.)

Several striking engineers were arrested for damage to property and assault against the strikebreakers. In mid-1877 the tunnel at Kaolin collapsed, forcing the railroad to cease operating south of Murphysboro. As a result of this episode, Canda filed in Springfield for bankruptcy for the railroad. The company had been in default on its interest payments since April 1, 1874. H. W. Smithers of Louisville, Kentucky, was appointed receiver on December 6, 1877.

Smithers's immediate problems were restoration of the Kaolin tunnel and improvement of the Cairo terminal arrangements. The tunnel was shortened by about 100 feet, and reopened on December 24, 1877. The reconstruction of the tunnel allowed Smithers to resume operation on the entire length of the railroad on February 23, 1878. He proceeded to make a joint traffic agreement with the Chicago & Alton for movement of southern Illinois fruit to Chicago.

Smithers also brought about a partial settlement of the complicated legal dispute at Cairo. The company had arranged with the Cairo City Property Co. to build its terminal on land valued at $150,000 to $200,000. The land was to be donated by the Property Co., but the railroad obligated itself to protect from erosion the levee on which it entered the city. By 1878 the levee had been damaged by floods on several oc-

casions. The railroad's chronic problems with the levee caused the Property Co. to renege on its obligation to donate the land. The railroad refused to honor its part of the obligation on the ground that Colonel Taylor, its former president, was also head of the Property Co. and thus had a conflict of interest. Smithers arranged in June 1879 for the railroad to pay $15,000 for repairs to the levee, whereupon the Property Co. would convey to it 16 acres, including 950 feet of frontage on the Ohio River. Smithers from taking office had sought to build a new entry about two miles long inside the levee. The railroad agreed to build terminal facilities on the frontage property and to construct a "declinator" for lowering grain into barges. The municipal government was dissatisfied with this arrangement, and secured an injunction against it. Smithers also bought a tract in East St. Louis for an engine house and terminal. At East Caron-

delet he extended the railroad's coal dump so as to be able to load barges in any stage of the water. He also expanded the rolling stock, bought four locomotives on a hire-purchase basis, and sold three locomotives that had proved too light.

By 1881 the railroad was profitable enough for reorganization. On June 14 the St. Louis & Cairo Railroad was organized by W. F. Whitehouse of Chicago to buy the property at a foreclosure sale exactly one month later. Control of the railroad thereafter was in the Chicago and New York financial communities. The new railroad embarked upon two major projects. To avoid using the East St. Louis & Carondelet (successor to the East St. Louis, Cahokia & Falling Springs), which charged the company $4,000 per year in rent, the railroad undertook its own line from East Carondelet to East St. Louis. The company also hoped to lay third rail across the Eads Bridge into St. Louis, but the St. Louis Bridge Co. refused on the ground that the rails were laid on metal, not on ties, so that a third rail was impractical. The line into East St. Louis was completed in 1883. Passengers, who had previously been carried across the river on omnibuses, were thereafter handled on the Belleville locals of the Illinois & St. Louis. The second large project, also completed in 1883, was a branch of seven miles from Columbia to Georgetown and Millstadt to serve the High Prairie coalfield.

The railroad following its reorganization was uniformly profitable. It was mainly dependent on coal revenues, and showed little interest in interchange traffic. At no time did the management show serious interest in the Grand Narrow Gauge Trunk, even though it had a physical connection

St. Louis & Cairo No. 20, the *W. F. Whitehouse*, is spotted for its photograph with seven men, presumably shop employees. (Smithsonian Institution.)

with the Toledo, Cincinnati & St. Louis by third rail over the East St. Louis Connecting Railroad. The Texas & St. Louis was rumored to be endeavoring to secure control of the railroad after the reorganization of 1881, but if it was, it failed in the effort. Not until April 1885 did the Texas & St. Louis and St. Louis & Cairo make a traffic agreement for interchange. The municipal government's injunction against the company was lifted as part of an agreement of June 1884, whereby the company paid the city $700, received the right to build the projected line inside the levee, and agreed to construct an incline for ferry loading near the confluence of the Ohio and Mississippi. Third rail was laid on the Mobile & Ohio's transfer steamer *W. B. Duncan* to allow direct physical interchange with the Texas & St. Louis for the first time.

It was widely expected that the railroad would be standard gauged to provide entry for another railroad, possibly the Texas & St. Louis when converted. Instead, it was sought as the entry to St. Louis for the Mobile & Ohio, which had arrived at the Kentucky shore opposite Cairo in 1881. The M&O was then a 5'-0" gauge railroad, but converted to standard in 1885. The St. Louis & Cairo was leased to the Mobile & Ohio for 45 years effective February 1, 1886, for a rental of $165,000 per year. The M&O made immediate plans for standard gauging, and converted the line from East St. Louis to Murphysboro on September 26, 1886. Work continued on the line south. On November 15, 1886, the job was completed and the first M&O standard gauge train entered St. Louis.

The former narrow gauge remained part of the Mobile & Ohio main line throughout the railroad's independent operation, and after a merger of 1940 provided entry into St. Louis for the successor Gulf, Mobile & Ohio. The Millstadt branch was spun off to local operators as the Columbia & Millstadt Railroad in 1945, and abandoned in 1961. The GM&O merged with the Illinois Central into the Illinois Central Gulf in 1972. The former Cairo & St. Louis was redundant upon lines of the Illinois Central and handicapped by its difficult ascents of Alto Pass. Accordingly, the Illinois Central Gulf abandoned the segment from Elco to Murphysboro, including the crossing of the pass, by an ICC order of July 20, 1977. The 20 miles from Cairo to Elco were turned over to the Cairo Terminal Railroad in 1983. Most of the north end from Tolson in the East St. Louis area to Red Bud was abandoned in 1986. The Illinois Central currently operates about 32 miles of the middle of the railroad, from Red Bud to Leahy.

The Mobile & Ohio's transfer steamer *W. B. Duncan* provided the first physical connection between the St. Louis & Cairo and the Texas & St. Louis in the spring of 1885. The steamer is shown at Helena, Arkansas, running for the Illinois Central in 1924. (Joseph Merrick Jones Steamboat Collection, Tulane University.)

Chicago, Millington & Western Railway

Being the only narrow gauge railroad ever to operate out of Chicago is by definition a distinction. Unfortunately, the Chicago, Millington & Western's only other distinction was an exceptional contrast between projection and achievement.

The railroad was incorporated on December 5, 1872, by James W. Eddy of Millington in La Salle County, Stephen G. Paddock of Princeton in Bureau County, Julian S. Rumsey of Chicago, and their associates. The railroad was initially projected from Chicago through York Center, Warrenville, Aurora, Millington, Hollowayville, Princeton, Neponset, Cambridge, Andover, Lynn Center, and Preemption to Muscatine, Iowa. By 1876 the promoters were considering an alternative route from York Center to Millington via Plainfield, which, unlike Aurora, had no direct service into Chicago. In part, the line was to provide frequent passenger service out of Chicago in the fashion of the Boston, Revere Beach & Lynn. The promoters in Millington, where the line had its principal financial support, were interested in developing a glass business that would make use of local deposits of high-grade sand. Mainly, however, the line was to be a coal road, serving fields at Hollowayville, Neponset, and Preemption. The promoters also planned to connect at Muscatine with the projected Chicago, Iowa & Kansas Railway, which would have provided a connection to the Kansas Central, and thus with the Colorado network. Various other connections were planned, including one

with the abuilding Fond du Lac, Amboy & Peoria west of Princeton. The promoters also expressed a willingness to route their own line via La Salle. The route would have paralleled the main line of the Chicago, Burlington & Quincy closely between Chicago and Neponset, and to the west would have run south of the Chicago, Rock Island & Pacific. The management anticipated that the usual projected savings of narrow gauge operation would give the company a considerable cost advantage over the two established carriers.

The actual attainments were quite meager. In 1875 a contractor named Col. Gowan agreed to build the entire line for $6,500 per mile in bonds of the company plus $500 per mile in cash. He reportedly surveyed the entire route. By early 1876 Gowan had built 11 miles of track from the intersection of 22nd Street and Ashland Avenue in Chicago along Blue Island Avenue and 26th Street to Covell's Gravel Bank and the Brush Hill gravel pits. Because the area was not yet populated, it is impossible to identify the exact end of the line, but it was apparently directly west of the end of 26th Street between La Grange Road and the Cook County–Du Page County line. The company reported that it had two locomotives, and it claimed to have carried gravel from the quarries into Chicago. The management in 1876 petitioned the Chicago City Council to enter the center of the city at grade on Lexington Street and thence on an overhead structure, modeled on the New York elevated, above Lexington and Polk streets to a stub terminal at Canal and Lake streets. Fireless locomotives would have been used on the elevated line. Nothing was accomplished on the entry or on the line to the west, for in 1877 the Farmers Loan & Trust Company and the Union Trust Company of New York brought foreclosure actions that caused the end of the operation. By 1878 the railroad was reportedly in the hands of Gowan, the contractor. A receiver named MacArthur told the federal court in Chicago that the line had ceased hauling gravel because the creditors had seized all of the equipment. The right-of-way was sold under foreclosure on August 15, 1879, presumably to creditors who immediately sold it to the CB&Q, which initially announced an intention to convert the line to standard gauge and use it as a spur to the quarries. Alternatively, since the right-of-way was a short distance south of the Burlington main line, it was considered for use as a third track between Chicago and Riverside. By November, however, it was reported that the CB&Q had removed the track and returned the right-of-way to its previous owners. The CB&Q subsequently made use of about a mile of the right-of-way paralleling 22nd Street between Lumber Street and Ashland Avenue for a switching track. The Aurora, Elgin & Chicago interurban bought the right-of-way from Warrenville to Aurora for one of its main lines.

REFERENCES: *The Chicago, Millington & Western Railway* (prospectus published by the company, Chicago, January 1877), in the collection of Charles H. Stats, Oak Park, Illinois; collection of James J. Buckley.

Danville, Olney & Ohio River Railroad

Northbound movements of coal from southern Illinois were the main motivation for the project to build a railroad from Danville to a point on the Ohio River near Paducah, Kentucky. In addition to the route specified in the corporate title, a branch to the Mississippi River was envisioned. The actual attainments were considerably short of the goal.

The railroad was chartered in 1869 and financed in Boston. Parker C. Chandler of Boston was its president for most of its independent history. After failing to finance it as a standard gauge, the promoters opened an office in Kansas, Illinois, on the main line of the Big Four between Terre Haute and St. Louis, and began building the railroad. The principal contractor was S. N. Yeoman, one of the leading figures in the narrow gauge movement. Track reached Westfield, 7.5 miles south of Kansas, on June 1, 1878, and Casey, on the Vandalia line of the Pennsylvania Railroad system, in mid-1880. De-

layed by the necessity of bridging the Embarras River near Ste. Marie, track reached West Liberty, on the Peoria, Decatur & Evansville Railway, on February 21, 1881.

Chandler and his associates apparently recognized the error of the narrow gauge by the time their rails reached West Liberty. The narrow gauge as it stood was extremely unpromising. Except for Casey, all of the online communities were villages of no more than a few hundred people. The coalfield was some 90 miles to the south. The line had the advantage of a physical connection with another narrow gauge, the Springfield, Effingham & Southeastern, at Willow Hill,

but this was a trivial benefit compared with the prospect of arranging trackage rights into Danville on a standard gauge railroad. The narrow gauge line of 51 miles was converted in mid-1881. By the end of the year the company had built north to Sidell on the Chicago & Eastern Illinois and negotiated trackage rights into Danville. The company reached Olney in March 1882, but progressed no farther. When towns along the way refused to pay their subsidies, the contractors were unwilling to continue, and the railroad was placed in receivership in 1883. It was reorganized as the Chicago & Ohio River Railway in 1886, but this company was consolidated into the connecting Peoria, Decatur & Evansville in 1893, as the larger road's Chicago Division. In 1898 the Chicago Division was sold under foreclosure to the Indiana, Decatur & Western, a part of the system of the Cincinnati, Hamilton & Dayton.

In the course of the CH&D's partial dissolution in 1915, the line was reorganized as the Sidell & Olney Railroad, which was operated under lease by the Cincinnati, Indianapolis & Western, successor to the ID&W. The Sidell & Olney was placed in receivership on July 31, 1918, but continued to operate because the American railroad system was in the hands of the United States Railroad Administration during World War I. The U.S.R.A. relinquished control of the property on March 15, 1919, and all operations ceased. The railroad was

sold in segments on April 29, 1919. The southernmost portion of the former narrow gauge, between Yale and West Liberty, 19 miles, was abandoned. The trackage from Kansas to Casey became the Westfield Railroad, and the portion from Casey to Yale the Yale Short Line; both were operated with a gasoline motor car by the Westfield Motor Railway. The Westfield Railroad's sale to the Casey & Kansas Railroad was approved by the Interstate Commerce Commission in 1926, but the property apparently was not transferred until January 1, 1932. The Yale Short Line was abandoned on August 24, 1936, and the Casey & Kansas on June 18, 1937.

Fulton County Narrow Gauge Railway

In the late 1870s the towns of Lewistown and Canton were rivals vying to become the seat of Fulton County. William T. Davidson, editor of the *Fulton Democrat*, became the principal advocate of a narrow gauge railroad as a promotional device for Lewistown. He was greatly impressed with the Havana, Rantoul & Eastern, which he expected to carry passengers for 2 cents per mile, and freight for 0.4 cents per ton-mile, less than half of the Chicago, Burlington & Quincy's rate. He thought the HR&E could earn 15 percent. In anticipation of making a connection with the HR&E at Havana, he proposed a narrow gauge from West Havana through Lewistown to Fairview, seat of local coal mining. Such a railroad would be 29 miles long, but as incorporated on August 13, 1878, the Fulton County Narrow Gauge was projected as 45 miles long, reaching west beyond Fairview to Avon, a destination it never approached. The prospect of the railway may have been enough to influence the electorate, for Lewistown won the election of November 12, 1878, to become county seat.

Surveying began at Fairview on October 22, 1878, in the expectation of building south through the Spoon River valley. In December the plan was changed; grading was to begin from West Havana. The terrain in the valley by midwestern standards was fairly rugged, too difficult for construction at the $7,000 per mile that Davidson had projected. Lacking resources to build the railroad, the promoters contracted on March 1, 1880, with J. C. Willcoxon, an Iowa man affiliated with the CB&Q, to grade, equip, and operate the railroad. Willcoxon appointed as general manager S. H. Mallory of Chariton, Iowa. In 1881 Mallory replaced Willcoxon as president and held the post until 1903. The railroad remained nominally independent, but was in fact a CB&Q subsidiary throughout its operating history.

Willcoxon brought the railroad to operating condition quickly. Passenger service began between Lewistown and Cuba, located on the Toledo, Peoria & Warsaw, on August 16, 1880. Track reached the Spoon River about a mile west of West Havana in September, and was built into Fairview in the north on October 28, 1880. On bridging the Spoon River into West Havana, the initial portion of the railroad was completed on November 1, 1880.

The narrow gauge was pushed north not to Avon but to Galesburg, the metropolis of the area. To build the additional 30 miles, the company on May 27, 1881, organized a subsidiary, the Fulton County Extension Railway, which it leased in perpetuity on September 1, 1882. The line continued up the Spoon River valley to London Mills (reached on November 12, 1881), and thence crossed ordinary prairie country to Galesburg. A second bridge over the Spoon was required at London Mills. The first train reached Galesburg on July 31, 1882, and full service with two trains

per day over the entire line began on August 20. The management had made an arrangement effective January 1, 1882, to lay 3'-0" track across the TP&W bridge into Havana. Passenger trains required 3 hours and 15 minutes to run the 61 miles from Havana to Galesburg.

Had the narrow gauge movement succeeded in putting together a nationwide network of cheaply built lines, the Fulton County Narrow Gauge would have been part of a major route between Toledo, Ohio, and Burlington, Iowa, and possibly to points west. At the time of its inception, promoters

Fulton County Narrow Gauge No. 1 at Lewistown about 1904. (Railroad Museum of Pennsylvania.)

envisioned connecting the Toledo, Delphos & Burlington with the Havana, Rantoul & Eastern near Attica, Indiana. By connection with the HR&E at Havana and the projected Burlington, Monmouth & Illinois River Railroad at London Mills, about 42 miles of the line along the Spoon River would have been part of the through route. As recounted in the histories of the HR&E and the Toledo, Cincinnati & St. Louis in this volume, Jay Gould's acquisition of the HR&E in 1880 ended this prospect. The HR&E never reached Havana, and the BM&IR was never built as a narrow gauge. Consequently, the Fulton County Narrow Gauge remained isolated and dependent on local originations. Throughout its history, about 60 percent of its tonnage was coal, mainly from deep-shaft mines in the Fairview area. The line had eight locomotives over its history, with a peak of five in service in 1892. The management reported 200 cars of all types in 1903. The failure to connect with the HR&E was apparently responsible for the withdrawal from Havana to West Havana on November 1, 1886.

The narrow gauge was attractive enough to the CB&Q that the parent company decided upon standard gauging it. Track gangs began installing standard gauge ties as early as 1889, and in 1892 the Burlington announced that it was considering conversion of the line. Nothing further was done during the depression of the 1890s, but serious efforts at conversion began in mid-1903. The bridge over the Spoon River at London Mills was replaced by one large enough for standard gauge equipment in 1904. Third rail was laid on the southernmost 23 miles early in 1905. The entire railroad was converted on Sunday, October 15, 1905. The line was leased by the CB&Q on January 1, 1906, and absorbed on December 1, 1908.

As a branch of the Burlington, the former narrow gauge remained dependent on coal originations in the Fairview area, which declined after 1923 as a result of the spread of open-pit mining elsewhere. The line was abandoned between Fairview and Galesburg in 1934 and between West Havana and Lewistown in 1935. The remainder, from Lewistown to Fairview, recovered with the conversion of mining in the area to the open-pit process, and survived to 1977.

REFERENCE: E. W. Mureen, *A History of the Fulton County Narrow Gauge Railway: The Spoon River Peavine*, Railway & Locomotive Historical Society *Bulletin*, no. 61A (1943); 2d ed., with revisions and extensions, Chicago Chapter, Railway & Locomotive Historical Society (1988).

Havana, Rantoul & Eastern Railroad

Benjamin J. Gifford, a lawyer of Rantoul, became dissatisfied with the rates of the Illinois Central Railroad, which served his community with its north-south main line. He sought to deal with the situation in 1873 by promoting the Havana, Rantoul & Eastern to build an east-west line through Rantoul from Havana on the Illinois River to a connection near Williamsport, Indiana, with one of several narrow gauges projected to the east. By June 1874 Gifford had raised $145,000 and was able to undertake construction. By the end of 1875 track had reached Alvin, 30 miles east of Rantoul on the Chicago, Danville & Vincennes, which was later the main line of the Chicago & Eastern Illinois. In 1876 he pushed his track 11 miles west to Fisher. Because the connection at Alvin did not give him interchange with an east-west railroad, in 1877 he undertook, through a grandiosely named subsidiary, the Mississippi & Atlantic, a 12-mile extension to West Lebanon, Indiana, on the main line of Jay Gould's Wabash, St. Louis & Pacific. The extension was completed December 1, 1878. To extend the track west from Fisher, Gifford organized a second subsidiary, the Le Roy Narrow Gauge Railroad, in the name of which he built 22 miles to Le Roy on the Indianapolis, Bloomington & Western, later the Peoria & Eastern line of the New York Central System. The extension was completed on February 1, 1879, and the subsidiary absorbed into the HR&E.

Gifford planned to built west to Havana via Heyworth, McLean, and San Jose, also through the formation of subsidiary companies. By this time, the Toledo, Delphos & Burlington had firm plans to build across Indiana to a connection with the HR&E at the Wabash River between Williamsport and Attica, east of Gifford's terminus in West Lebanon. At Havana the line would have connected with the Fulton County Narrow Gauge for western Illinois and, if a connection were built, for Burlington, Iowa. A separate narrow gauge, the Le Roy, Bloomington & Peoria, was locally projected to connect with the HR&E for Peoria. Possibly to prevent this east-west network from taking shape, Jay Gould in 1880 acquired the HR&E, which he merged into his Wabash system on May 1, 1881. Gifford, remarkably, had previously offered the railroad to the Illinois Central, which at the time expressed no interest. Gould could have had little positive interest in the HR&E, which in its current state of completion could only

have amounted to a minor branch serving grain elevators in on-line towns. He expressed the intention of converting the line, but never did so. The HR&E went into receivership with the rest of the Wabash system on May 29, 1884; a separate receivership was established for the HR&E on June 1, 1885. The railroad, in which Gifford and his collaborators had invested some $575,000, was sold at a receiver's auction in Springfield for $100,000 on October 27, 1886. The Illinois Central bought the railroad and initially formed the Le Roy & Eastern and the Lebanon & Western to own the Illinois and Indiana portions, respectively. In the following year the IC organized the Rantoul Railroad to own both, floated a bond issue of $1 million for conversion and upgrading, and in the summer and fall of 1887 rebuilt the railroad to standard gauge. Since the IC had its own branch from Champaign to Havana via Clinton and Lincoln, the management had no incentive to complete the former narrow gauge according to Gifford's plan. Consequently the line served as only one of a large number of minor agricultural branches of the IC. The portion from Hedrick to West Lebanon, six miles, was abandoned in 1937 and the adjacent 16 miles from Hedrick to Potomac in 1943. The westernmost 21 miles, from Le Roy to Fisher, were abandoned in 1978, and the remainder in 1982.

REFERENCES: Elmer G. Sulzer, *Ghost Railroads of Indiana* (Indianapolis: Vane A. Jones, Co., 1970), p. 36; Carlton J. Corliss, *Main Line of Mid-America* (New York: Creative Age Press, 1950), pp. 218–21; journals and ledgers of the Havana, Rantoul & Eastern Railroad, Illinois Central Railroad papers, Newberry Library, Chicago (microfilm).

Moline & Southeastern Railroad
Gauge: 3'-6"

Richard Mansill of Rock Island organized this railroad in March 1878 to haul coal from a deposit at Coal Valley into Moline, a distance of eight miles. The railroad was opened on October 20, 1879. Initially it was reported to have two locomotives and 19 coal cars. The line was lightly built with 20-pound rail. By 1884 the company was reported to have 38 coal cars; there is no record of any other revenue equipment. The railroad was a small operation, which in the fiscal year ending June 30, 1885, hauled 5,580 tons of coal, grossed $3,348, and lost $150.51. It suspended operation in September 1885 and was subsequently removed.

Springfield, Effingham & Southeastern Railway

If a single railroad were to be chosen as the embodiment of the evils of the narrow gauges—light grading, poor ballasting, weak bridges, and failure to reach intended termini—the Springfield, Effingham & Southeastern would probably be the choice.

The railroad was incorporated on March 10, 1869, but the local promoters were unable to finance it. Colonel E. Pratt Buell, William Sturgis, and John B. Lyon of Chicago formed the Cincinnati, Effingham & Quincy Construction Co. to build a through 3'-0" line from Quincy, Illinois, to Cincinnati, making use of the projected SE&SE as an intermediate link. The plan was to build the Quincy, Payson & Southeastern from Quincy to Effingham, about 200 miles, and the SE&SE from Effingham to Switz City, Indiana, 88 miles. The 34.5-mile segment in Indiana was separately incorporated as the Bloomfield Railroad, but was expected to be operated by the SE&SE. The promoters hoped to acquire the Bedford, Springville, Owensburg & Bloomfield, which already ran from Switz City to Bedford. They proposed to build the Bedford, Madison & Cincinnati Railway for the remainder of the distance. The total mileage of the five railroads would have been about 450 miles. The purpose was to take agricultural products from western Illinois to standard gauge railroads and river steamers at Cincinnati, and incidentally to move coal from the Greene County coalfield in Indiana. Only the SE&SE (including the Bloomfield Railroad) was ever built, and the promoters never acquired the BSO&B.

The promoters signed a contract in July 1875 for Buell and his associates to build the railroad. Initially it was hoped to have the railroad completed in about a year, but no progress was made until a construction locomotive arrived in July 1876. The CE&Q Construction Co. on August 8, 1878, was placed in the hands of receiver General John C. Black. Although he continued constructing the railroad, Black understandably did a poor job, following the terrain closely and building exceptionally weak bridges. The line was completed by October 1880, except for the bridge over the Wabash River near Palestine, Illinois. When the bridge was finished, service from Effingham to Switz City was inaugurated on December 5, 1880. The route was not promising. Effingham was a major junction of the Illinois Central and the Pennsylvania's Vandalia line, but Robinson, Illinois, and Sullivan, Indiana, the main on-line towns, had direct rail connections to Chicago. The narrow gauge's best connection was with the Pennsylvania's Vincennes line at Switz City, allowing a relatively direct route from Sullivan to Indianapolis.

The railroad shortly encountered the first and worst of its chronic problems with weak bridges. On February 8, 1881, an ice gorge destroyed the east approach to the swing span of the Wabash River bridge. Two days later the ice gorge swept away the west approach. Initially, Buell stated that the damage amounted to only $2,000 to $6,000 and would shortly be repaired. Apparently the swing span also suffered damage, for Buell shortly became involved in a controversy with federal authorities on the permissible length of a replacement. The management proved financially unable to restore the river crossing for more than five years. The effect was to reduce the railroad to two isolated short lines, dependent exclusively on local traffic and unable to move coal from Linton, Indiana, to Illinois points. By the summer of 1881 the railroad was in arrears on wages; in August, Buell fired Will Stark, the agent at Sullivan, for paying himself the arrears on his salary out of the receipts at the station. In December, Sturgis and Lyon proposed to pay off the railroad's debts at 50 cents on the dollar and back wages at 60 cents. The physical separation of the railroad at the Wabash River shortly became a legal one, as well. On December 28, 1881, Black announced that the Indiana mileage, which was somewhat the stronger in traffic, would be turned over to the Bloomfield Railroad for separate operation. Both segments were subject to interruption from washouts of the track in heavy rains. The railroad had never really been finished; boxcars were used as stations at several towns. Even in Robinson, the corporate headquarters, the railroad had no depot until 1884. Buell ended his relation with the railroad in January 1882. The bankrupt construction company was sold to John B. Lyon, its principal creditor, on January 26, 1882.

The two segments were reunited legally, though not physically, as the Indiana & Illinois Southern Railway on April 9, 1883. The merged railroad had three locomotives, one passenger car, one baggage car, 66 freight cars, and one caboose. The reunion was anything but a panacea. Track from Sullivan to the Wabash River was washed out in November 1883, but not restored until the following summer. The bridge over Busserone Creek in Illinois was washed out on July 3, 1884, and a locomotive overturned on a rain-weakened right-of-way in the same vicinity in September. The Embarras River bridge at Newton collapsed under a seven-car train on August 27, 1884, reducing the railroad to three unconnected segments. In December 1884 steam operation on the Illinois portion was shut down, but the railroad, to satisfy a postal contract for $3,824.84 per year that was its principal support, carried mail to on-line communities on a handcar. The postal authorities soured on this arrangement, and suspended the contract on February 10, 1885.

A claim of only $500 put the I&IS in receivership on March 21, 1885. Charles H. Steel was appointed receiver of the Illinois portion, and Perry H. Blue of the Indiana mileage. Both receivers were eager to restore the bridges and convert the railroad. By mid-May they had repaired the Embarras River bridge. Blue was discharged in July 1885. With the assistance of John B. Alley of Boston, a major bondholder, the management built an iron bridge of standard gauge dimensions over the Wabash, and put it in service on April 24, 1886. It is not clear from the newspaper record whether the bridge was at the site of the original or somewhat downstream. Narrow gauge trains were restored between Effingham and Switz City early in July. The railroad's offices were moved to Sullivan in March 1886. The receivers estimated the cost of conversion at $300,000. They began buying standard gauge ties late in 1885, and began work to strengthen the bridges. A pile driver being used on the bridge over the North Fork of the Embarras near Oblong, Illinois, overturned along with its locomotive on September 11 when a stringer on the bridge broke.

The railroad was converted by relaying the narrow gauge rail, which was only 35- to 45-pound, on the standard gauge ties, starting at the east end on July 26, 1887. An iron bridge over the Embarras was completed in October, and the track was widened to Effingham early in November. This was one of the least successful conversions. Freight trains were limited to six or eight miles per hour, and derailments remained common. Only about a half mile near Sullivan was ballasted. Local editors widely complained that service had not been improved.

The I&IS Railway had been reorganized as the I&IS Railroad on May 12, 1886. The new corporation never paid interest and was reorganized as the St. Louis, Indianapolis & Eastern Railroad on February 6, 1890. This company replaced the narrow gauge rail in 1895, but remained unprofitable. It was sold under foreclosure to its bondholders on August 20, 1899. The Illinois Central bought the railroad in 1900, and in 1906 extended it to Indianapolis. Thus, the former narrow gauge became a major branch of its principal western connection. At the end of 1985 the railroad sold the trackage east of Sullivan to the Indianapolis Terminal Corp. for operation by the Indiana Rail Road, but retained the portion from Effingham to Sullivan.

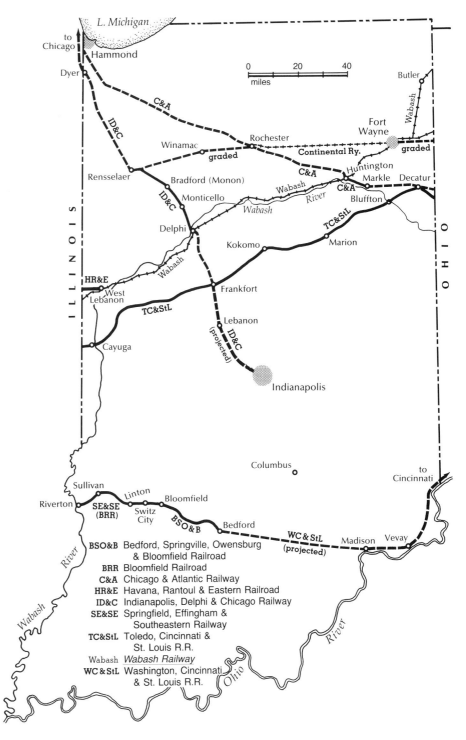

Indiana

Bedford, Springville, Owensburg & Bloomfield Railroad

A narrow gauge running northwest from Bedford presented the prospects of limestone movements from quarries in the immediate area; traffic to Bloomfield, seat of Greene County, which as yet had no railroad; and carriage of a substantial tonnage in coal if the coalfield in western Greene County could be reached. The railroad was organized November 9, 1874. The principal promoters were William Mason of Greene County and his brothers John and Henry. The first portion completed was six miles between Bloomfield and Switz City, built in 1875 to provide Bloomfield with an outlet to the Indianapolis & Vincennes Railroad, later a branch of the Pennsylvania. The 35 miles from Bedford to Bloomfield were through difficult country; in particular, the route required a tunnel of 1,368 feet through limestone near Owensburg. The line was lightly graded upon a narrow right-of-way. Some service was provided in 1876, but the entire railroad was opened on March 1, 1877. Clark, Buell & Co. of Chicago was the contractor. Edward Hulbert was superintendent from January 1877 to February 1880.

A pioneer narrow gauge in its area, the BSO&B invited great interest as a prospective part of an east-west route across the eastern Midwest. In 1875–76 the *Railroad Gazette*, apparently erroneously, reported its progress and that of its connection to the west, the Springfield, Effingham & Southeastern, under the name of the St. Louis, Bloomfield & Louisville. The promoters of the SE&SE hoped to acquire the line as part

of a route from Quincy, Illinois, to Cincinnati, and Peter B. Borst envisioned it as part of his Washington, Cincinnati & St. Louis's connections for St. Louis. There were several proposals for narrow gauges from Bedford northeast to Columbus and east to Madison, Indiana, and to Cincinnati.

The railroad united limited traffic potential with a poor physical plant. The line served no coal mines. Some coal came through interchange with the SE&SE, which served mines at Linton, but this railroad had a worse physical plant than the BSO&B, and a financial performance so bad that it

was occasionally shut down. The tunnel at Owensburg proved unstable, and was afflicted with an internal waterfall from an underground stream. The bore was lined only with timber, and shifts or rockfalls closed the tunnel on several occasions. For safety, a man with a lantern walked in front of each train traversing it. The bridge over the West Fork of the White River west of Bloomfield collapsed about April 1, 1876, and again on July 28, 1884, killing a man on each occasion, and yet a third time on June 6, 1893. A Howe-truss covered bridge of standard gauge dimensions was built to replace it. The railroad typically operated one mixed train per day over the length of the railroad, with additional locals from Bedford to the quarries at Dark Hollow and Reed and from Bloomfield to Switz City to connect with Indianapolis-Vincennes trains. The company had five locomotives.

The railroad's financial history was as poor as might be expected. When the promoters proved unable to pay the debts incurred in building the line, they were brought into federal court in Indianapolis by some local governments seeking to recover subsidies, and also by individual creditors. The court in 1879 ruled that the Indianapolis Rolling Mill Co., which had supplied the rails, was entitled to a majority interest in the line's securities. After some additional lawsuits, the railroad was sold on August 22, 1882, to Aquilla Jones, representing the Rolling Mill, who paid $200,000 for securities of par value of $1.2 million. William Mason was reportedly wiped out by the experience. The new owner reorganized the narrow gauge as the Bedford & Bloomfield Railroad on March 12, 1883. Indianapolis Rolling Mill had no interest in retaining the railroad and endeavored to interest the Ohio & Mississippi, the Pennsylvania, and others in the property. Early in 1886 the Louisville, New Albany & Chicago Railway (Monon Route), the line's principal connection at Bedford, paid Indianapolis Rolling Mill $200,000 for the securities, and took possession of the railroad on April 1. Initially, the LNA&C maintained the narrow gauge's independent corporate entity; the line became known in on-line communities as the "Little Monon." The Monon management reported the narrow gauge as profitable and declared itself pleased with the purchase. From the outset, the Monon planned to convert the acquisition and to use it for entry into the Greene County coalfield, but the problem of dealing with the Owensburg tunnel, combined with the financial havoc wrought by a shareholders' coup that unseated the Monon's management in 1890, prevented conversion until the middle 1890s. Monon engineers surveyed two routes to bypass the tunnel, but either one would have cost about $50,000. The railroad opted to enlarge the bore of the tunnel for $27,000 in 1894. Third rail had been laid from Bedford to the quarries at Dark Hollow, Reed, and Avoca as early as 1887. The last narrow gauge train ran to Switz City on Saturday, May 11, 1895, and the first standard gauge train on Monday, May 13. The citizens of Bloomfield, who had been particularly vocal about the low quality of passenger service on the narrow gauge, celebrated the conversion as if it were the Fourth of July.

Unfortunately, the line remained handicapped by its low physical standards. Even after conversion, the passenger train required three hours for the 41 miles. The line lost its separate corporate identity in the course of the Monon's reorganization of 1897, and was thereafter operated only as a branch. The Monon in 1902 arranged to extend it by traffic rights over the Indianapolis Southern, successor to the SE&SE, to Linton and Victoria in the Greene County coalfield. Dissatisfied with the branch, the Monon opened its own entry into the coalfield from Wallace Junction in 1907. Thereafter, the former narrow gauge served a purely local function. The Monon abandoned the line from Avoca to Switz City, 34 miles, in 1935 and cut it back an additional four miles to Dark Hollow in 1943. The remainder was abandoned in 1981.

REFERENCES: Elmer G. Sulzer, *Abandoned Railroads of Bedford* (Indianapolis, Ind.: Council for Local History, 1959); *idem, Ghost Railroads of Indiana* (Indianapolis, Ind.: Vane A. Jones Co., 1970), pp. 155–68; George W. Hilton, *Monon Route* (Berkeley, Calif.: Howell-North Books, 1978), pp. 110–13, 155. Sulzer states that the portion of this railroad between Bloomfield and Switz City was built by the Bloomfield Rail Road, and purchased by the Bedford & Bloomfield on March 29, 1884. Although I accepted this statement uncritically in *Monon Route*, I can find no authority for it in primary sources and now consider it erroneous.

Chicago & Atlantic Railway

The Chicago & Atlantic Railway was formed by the consolidation of two predecessors on June 19, 1873, in the intention of building a connection from the Atlantic & Great Western (Erie) at Marion, Ohio, to Chicago via Bluffton, Huntington, and Rochester, Indiana. The railroad reported some grading between Marion and Kenton, Ohio, but was unable to proceed. The management, which was headed by Henry R. Low of New York and George J. Bippus of Huntington, expressed a preference for narrow gauge in 1875, and formally adopted 3'-0" at a directors' meeting of April 2, 1878. A contract was let in September to Colonel D. E. Davenport to build from Huntington east to the Ohio state line. The officers decided to build east through Decatur instead of Bluffton, ostensibly to provide a more direct connection to Toledo via the Toledo, Delphos & Burlington, of which Low and Bippus were directors. In 1879 General James S. Negley interested himself in the project as a prospective western connection for his Pittsburgh, New Castle & Lake Erie.

In April 1879 the railroad took delivery at Huntington of a Brooks 4-4-0 and the first stock of rail. Construction shortly came to a halt because of an alleged inability to find iron. Tracklaying resumed in November, and on December 23, the line reached the first village east, Markle (nine miles). Service began late in January. In the course of 1880 the narrow gauge grossed $2,421 and reported a small profit.

The Erie gained control of the C&A in 1880 and negotiated a bond issue of $6.5 million to build the entire Marion-Chicago line. Its slate of C&A directors, who had been elected in November 1880, showed no interest in the small narrow gauge and directed the engineering staff to prepare for conversion. The narrow gauge was removed in mid-July 1881. The rails were relaid as temporary trackage and the equipment was used for moving earth for fills between Huntington and Rochester. The line was completed as a standard gauge railroad with a last spike ceremony at West Point (Bippus), Indiana, on December 9, 1882. As the west end of the Erie main line it was an excellent piece of engineering, but always handicapped by negligible origination and termination. It was given up by Conrail as redundant and, after operation by two successive local operators, abandoned on December 31, 1979.

REFERENCE: *The Chicago & Atlantic Railway Company: Forty-Third Anniversary 1883–April 2, 1926* (Huntington, Ind.: The Herald, 1926). This pamphlet is in the Indiana Room of the Huntington Public Library.

Indianapolis, Delphi & Chicago Railway

Delphi, seat of Carroll County, lies between Lafayette and Logansport, both of which were connected by rail to Chicago and Indianapolis in the mid-1850s. Local businessmen believed that Delphi was declining relative to its neighboring county seats because of the lack of a north-south railroad. The Indianapolis, Delphi & Chicago Railway was incorporated by B. F. Schermerhorn, Enoch Rinehart, and several other businessmen of the city on June 28, 1865. Their intention was to build a standard gauge railroad via Frankfort, Monticello, and Rensselaer, none of which had a direct route either to Chicago or Indianapolis. Financial support was secured in each

The Chicago & Atlantic's only narrow gauge locomotive, *Huntington*, operated the railroad's short-lived and obscure service between Huntington and Markle, Indiana, before being demoted to construction work. (Munson Paddock collection, Railroad Museum of Pennsylvania.)

city, but the promoters by the early 1870s had made no progress toward construction.

The company's charter, plus financial aid from Delphi and other communities to be granted in the event of completion, brought the company to the attention of the Chicago & South Atlantic Railway, a railroad projected since 1835 from Chicago to Charleston, South Carolina, and other South Atlantic ports. The C&SA proposed to use the ID&C as its northernmost segment, and to terminate in an enormous station at Market and Madison streets in Chicago. The ID&C was accordingly reincorporated in 1872. The C&SA graded about 80 of the 111 miles from Delphi to Chicago by July 1875, but then had to suspend construction because of financial difficulties in the wake of the Panic of 1873. In addition, the City of Chicago failed to cooperate in the company's grandiose terminal project.

The ID&C was left with its projected line partly graded, but with inadequate resources for completion. The combination left the promoters responsive to the idea of the narrow gauge in the late 1870s. In addition, the projection of what became the Toledo, Cincinnati & St. Louis through Frankfort gave the ID&C the prospect of furnishing the projected Toledo–St. Louis narrow gauge with connections to Chicago and Indianapolis. Neither of those cities had any narrow gauge trackage that might have been used for termination facilities,

however. There was some hope the Chicago & South Atlantic might be revived as a narrow gauge. The ID&C project was revived by S. N. Yeoman and others who had been associated with him in building the Dayton & Southeastern.

Construction of the Indianapolis, Delphi & Chicago began at Bradford (Monon) on the Louisville, New Albany & Chicago Railway in November 1877, and the narrow gauge was opened to Rensselaer, 16 miles, on February 14, 1878. The grade of the uncompleted Continental Railway was utilized for about 2.5 miles approaching Rensselaer. Construction was then begun in the opposite direction, and the line opened from Bradford to Monticello, ten miles, on August 14, 1878. Building the 12 miles from Monticello to Delphi entailed bridging the Tippecanoe River south of Monticello, the Wabash River at Pittsburg, and the Wabash & Erie Canal approaching Del-

phi, plus crossing the hostile Wabash Railway in Delphi itself. This segment was completed on September 4, 1879. The company had two Baldwin 4-4-0s, one baggage car, one coach, seven boxcars, 12 flatcars, and two handcars.

Yeoman, head of the construction company that was building the ID&C, in seeking an entry to Chicago arranged for the railroad to become part owner of the Chicago & Western Indiana Railroad, which was being promoted as a terminal company by the Chicago & Eastern Illinois. This resulted in the ID&C's being reformed in 1880 as the Chicago & Indianapolis Air Line Railway, which was financed by Chicago interests allied to the C&EI. Yeoman had to face the impracticability of terminating in Chicago with 3'-0" gauge, and announced that the Air Line would be converted to 4'-8½" for conformity with the Chicago & Western Indiana. The narrow gauge was converted in 1881, from Bradford to Rensselaer on March 26 and from Bradford to Delphi on July 20.

Meanwhile, the company had been placed in the hands of a trustee in January 1881. In May 1881 the company arranged that the Louisville, New Albany & Chicago should build the Air Line north from Rensselaer toward Chicago, in return for which the LNA&C should keep the receipts from the completed Bradford-Rensselaer portion. This proved a prelude to the LNA&C's taking control of the Air Line on December 15, 1881. The line was then completed to Chicago and Indianapolis as a standard gauge railroad. The route to the north was approximately what the narrow gauge had projected, but the line from Frankfort to Indianapolis via Lebanon could not be financed, and an alternative route to the east via Westfield was built. The Air Line was operated by its construction company until February 1, 1883, when it was merged into the Louisville, New Albany & Chicago. Bradford had changed its name to Monon in 1879. The Air Line became the Chicago-Monon portion of the LNA&C's main line, plus its Indianapolis branch. (The railroad took the name "Monon Route" from its pattern of an X crossing at Monon; the two lines of the X were Michigan City–Louisville and Chicago-Indianapolis.) The company, after several changes in corporate identity, was merged into the Louisville & Nashville in 1971. All of the former narrow gauge mileage is still in service for the CSX Corporation at the present writing.

REFERENCE: Hilton, *Monon Route.*

Iowa

Bellevue & Cascade Railroad

Iowa's longest-lived narrow gauge connected Bellevue on the Mississippi River with Cascade, a town of about 1,250 people 36 miles west. The project was undertaken by the Chicago, Bellevue, Cascade & Western, organized in August 1877. The company's projected route was from Bellevue to Liscomb on the Minneapolis & St. Louis above Marshalltown. The line was to be 135 miles, via Cascade and Monticello. In the course of 1878 the company graded to Cascade and began service from Bellevue to Zwingle (16 miles). The firm's resources were exhausted with this, and the line's standard gauge connection at Bellevue, the Chicago, Clinton, Dubuque & Minnesota Railroad, took over the property in March 1879. The new owner completed the railroad into Cascade (36 miles), opening it formally on January 1, 1880.

The line left Bellevue following Mill Creek for about seven miles. The ascent from the Paradise Valley to La Motte was a difficult climb of nearly five miles, with a ruling grade of 2.8 percent. Beyond La Motte the railroad developed the usual saw-toothed profile in crossing the drainage pattern. The most severe curve was 12½°. The railroad was built to typical narrow gauge standards, except that it was laid with 56- and 60-pound rail. The CCD&M initially equipped it with three Pittsburgh 4-4-0 locomotives. Normal practice was to double the major grade.

The Chicago, Milwaukee & St. Paul leased the Chicago, Clinton, Dubuque & Minnesota on June 3, 1880, thereby acquiring the narrow gauge. The line was officially a branch of the Dubuque Division, but it was commonly known as the Bellevue & Cascade. The Milwaukee Road considered the line overpowered, and diverted one of the 4-4-0 locomotives to shop service at the Milwaukee car department moving the transfer table. The branch operated with the two remaining Pittsburgh 4-4-0s until 1905, when a former Au Sable & Northwestern 2-6-0 was acquired. In 1918 the Milwaukee replaced one of the 4-4-0s with a Cooke 2-8-0, formerly Denver, South Park & Pacific's No. 67 and Colorado & Southern's No. 55. The railroad bought former Catskill & Tannersville 2-6-0 outside-frame locomotives in 1926 and 1928, which allowed it to retire the last 4-4-0.

Service was customarily provided by mixed trains, which required about three hours to traverse the 36 miles. On February 22, 1907, mixed train No. 103 derailed on a curved trestle near Washington Mills. The cars fell to the ground some 40 feet below; three people were killed and seven injured. The accident was locally interpreted as a consequence of the poor condition of the railroad.

In 1915 the Iowa legislature directed the state railroad commission to investigate the narrow gauge railroads of the state—of which the Bellevue & Cascade was the only one remaining. The investigation brought forth complaints against delay and breakage at the transfer at Bellevue. The company's handling of livestock was particularly unsatisfactory. It was generally agreed by engineers of the railroad and by the local residents that the physical standards of the branch did not lend themselves to standard gauging. The commission found itself without statutory authority to order a change in gauge, in any case. Accordingly, the railroad continued as a narrow gauge to the end of its history.

The line would have been a weak one in any case, but the incompatibility of gauge made it very costly to operate. The branch had one combine, two coaches, 50 boxcars, 38 stockcars, 16 gondolas, 10 flatcars, and a caboose. Locomotives and cars were serviced at Bellevue, but major repairs on either had to be made at the Marquette Shops in North McGregor, Iowa.

The branch lost $66,000 in 1931, and was a poor prospect for surviving the Depression. The Milwaukee Road applied to the Interstate Commerce Commission to abandon the line in March 1933. Local interests formed the Bellevue & Cascade Co. in June of 1933 to assume ownership. The Milwaukee Road sold the line under favorable terms, $18,000 to be paid in 120 installments of $150 each, plus 5 percent interest. The new operator attempted to run the line with a six-cylinder 0-4-0 gasoline locomotive and a rubber-tired Twin Coach railcar. The locomotive proved inadequate for the line's grades, and a steam locomotive had to be returned to service. As a consequence, the new operator was unable to realize expected economies, and defaulted on the modest payments to the Milwaukee Road. Upon resuming ownership, the Milwaukee sold the line to a scrap dealer in January of 1936. The rails were removed in April.

REFERENCES: Albin L. Lee, "Narrow Gauge in the Hawkeye State," *Trains,* Apr. 1954, pp. 58–60; idem, "The Bellevue & Cascade Story," *Narrow Gauge and Short Line Gazette,* July/Aug. 1979, pp. 28–29; John Tigges and Jon Jacobson, *Milwaukee Road Narrow Gauge* (Boulder, Colo.: Pruett Publishing Co., 1985).

Burlington & Northwestern Railway

Burlington & Western Railroad

The Burlington & Northwestern Narrow Gauge Railway was incorporated on March 3, 1875, by Charles Mason and his associates of Burlington. "Narrow Gauge" was dropped from the title on June 1, 1876. The initial intention was only to build to the town of Washington, but had the various projects for reaching Burlington with narrow gauge rails from the east been successful, the promoters would probably have attempted to build west all the way across Iowa. The management arranged to leave Burlington by laying third rail for 14 miles over the Burlington, Cedar Rapids & Northern Railway to Mediapolis. The B&NW had 0.3 miles of narrow gauge terminal trackage in Burlington. The line was opened from Burlington to Winfield (34 miles) on December 10, 1876. Rails reached Crawfordsville (42 miles) on November 11, 1879,

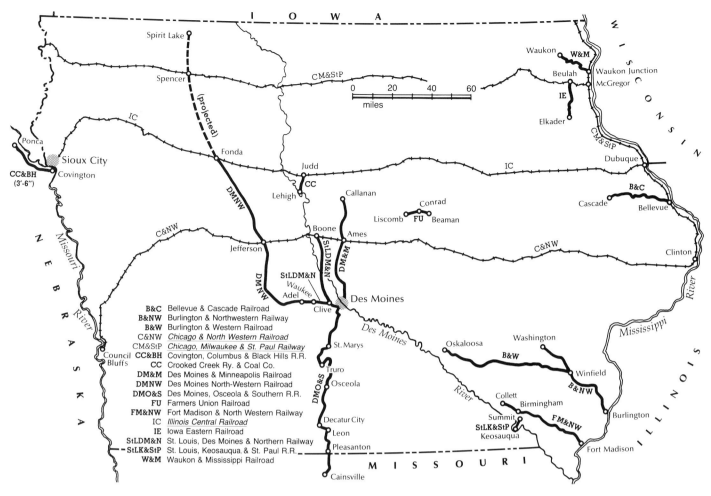

B&C   Bellevue & Cascade Railroad
B&NW Burlington & Northwestern Railway
B&W   Burlington & Western Railroad
C&NW *Chicago & North Western Railroad*
CM&StP *Chicago, Milwaukee & St. Paul Railway*
CC&BH Covington, Columbus & Black Hills R.R.
CC   Crooked Creek Ry. & Coal Co.
DM&M Des Moines & Minneapolis Railroad
DMNW Des Moines North-Western Railroad
DMO&S Des Moines, Osceola & Southern R.R.
FU   Farmers Union Railroad
FM&NW Fort Madison & North Western Railway
IC   *Illinois Central Railroad*
IE   Iowa Eastern Railroad
StLDM&N St. Louis, Des Moines & Northern Railway
StLK&StP St. Louis, Keosauqua & St. Paul R.R.
W&M   Waukon & Mississippi Railroad

and finally Washington (52.5 miles) on May 1, 1880.

Rather than extend the B&NW beyond Washington, the promoters incorporated a second firm, the Burlington & Western Railroad, on June 7, 1881, to build what was essentially a branch from Winfield to Oskaloosa. Track reached Coppock, 16 miles from Winfield, on May 7, 1882, Martinsburg (47 miles) on November 5, 1882, and Oskaloosa (71 miles) on December 9, 1883. The two corporations were kept separate entities throughout the system's independent history, but the officers were invariably the same, and the directors usually so. T. W. Barhydt was president of both companies, and John T. Gerry general manager. The Burlington & Western was closely paralleled by the main line of the Iowa Central, later the Minneapolis & St. Louis, for its entire length. The B&W was typically unprofitable, but the Burlington & Northwestern was generally in the black, producing enough earnings to keep the system solvent. The B&NW was reported to have cost $341,569 to build and the B&W $1,356,852.

As early as 1892 officers of the Chicago, Burlington & Quincy were on the boards of

both narrow gauges, but they continued to be operated independently with Barhydt as president. The B&NW was deeded to the B&W on June 20, 1902, and the entire system leased to the CB&Q for 25 years on December 1, 1902. On June 29, 1902, about 500 men under CB&Q supervision accomplished conversion of the entire 123 miles between 4:30 A.M. and midnight. They worked through a steady cold rain, but were nourished by a reported 4,500 sandwiches and 6,000 hard-boiled eggs. The former narrow gauge system was deeded to the CB&Q on December 1, 1903.

The Oskaloosa line was abandoned in 1934. The M&StL bought 31 miles between Coppock and Martinsburg to replace the parallel portion of its main line. The Washington line was abandoned by the Burlington Northern in 1980 and removed in 1981.

Crooked Creek Railway & Coal Co.

This short-lived narrow gauge was, as its corporate name indicates, a nominal common carrier integral with a coal-mining

operation. The entire enterprise was a promotion of Walter Willson of Webster City. The railroad was built in 1876 from Judd, a station on the Illinois Central Railroad's Chicago–Sioux City line east of Fort Dodge, to Lehigh on the Des Moines River, a distance of eight miles. The rail operation was carried on with one locomotive, one combine, three boxcars, and 28 gondolas. The company quickly recognized the error of building to a narrow gauge, and standard gauged the line on November 8, 1880. The line became one of several serving an area mainly devoted to gypsum production. The portion of the former narrow gauge from Judd to Border Plains was abandoned about 1898 in favor of a direct route to Webster City. The entire network of the Crooked Creek Railroad & Coal Co., as it had become known, was sold to the Fort Dodge, Des Moines & Southern interurban in 1916. The portion of the former narrow gauge from Evanston Junction into Lehigh was electrified and operated as a minor branch. It was dieselized in the mid-1950s and abandoned in 1962.

REFERENCE: A. P. Butts, *Walter Willson and His Crook Railroad* (Webster City, Iowa: Fred Hahne Printing Co., 1976).

Des Moines & Minnesota No. 3, an ungainly Danforth 2-6-0 of 1875, bore the name of the railroad's president, James Callanan. Not of a self-effacing nature, Callanan also named the line's northern terminus for himself. (Thomas T. Taber collection, Railroad Museum of Pennsylvania.)

Des Moines, Osceola & Southern No. 5 stands for its builder's photograph at the Pittsburgh Locomotive Works. (Thomas T. Taber collection, Railroad Museum of Pennsylvania.)

Des Moines & Minneapolis Railroad

This railroad has its origins in the Iowa & Minnesota Railway of 1866, which did not achieve any construction. The right-of-way north from Des Moines passed into the hands of the Des Moines & Minnesota Railroad, organized in 1870 by James Callanan and his associates. The immediate purpose of the line was to connect Des Moines with the Chicago & North Western Railway main line to the north of the city. The management decided on Ames as the junction point after considering Nevada as an alternative. Narrow gauge track was completed from Des Moines to Ames (37 miles) on July 29, 1874. Callanan next projected the line north and east to McGregor on the Mississippi, apparently intending to follow the river north to the Twin Cities. In anticipation of the extension, Callanan reorganized the company as the Des Moines & Minneapolis Railroad on July 5, 1877. On April 1, 1878, the extension reached a point about 20 miles north of Ames and 1.75 miles south of Jewell; the new town was given the name Callanan.

The company defaulted on the principal of its bonds in July 1879. To deal with the problem, the management leased the railroad to the Chicago & North Western on October 1, 1879. The C&NW converted the line between Des Moines and Ames on July 10, 1880. Standard gauge service on the remainder began on May 29, 1882, with through passenger trains between Des Moines and Jewell established about two weeks later. The town of Callanan was abandoned at the time of the conversion, with the population and even the houses being largely moved to Jewell. The former narrow gauge became part of the railroad's extensive network of branch lines in Iowa. It remains in service.

Des Moines North-Western Railroad

The longest narrow gauge in Iowa proved to be a line from Des Moines northwest to Fonda, a small town on the Illinois Central Railroad's Chicago–Sioux City route. The narrow gauge had its origin in the Des Moines, Adel & Western Railroad, which on October 15, 1878, completed seven miles of 30-pound rail from Waukee on the Des Moines & Fort Dodge Railroad to Adel, seat of Dallas County, the county immediately west of Des Moines. In the company's first year, it was reported to have gross receipts of $288.20 and operating expenses of $318, for a deficit of $29.80. The line was extended to Panora, 29 miles from Waukee, in 1879. In the following year the company was reorganized as the Des Moines North-Western Railroad, which in 1881 was leased to Jay Gould's Wabash, St. Louis & Pacific Railway. The Wabash extended the line to Lohrville (72 miles from Waukee) in 1881 and to Fonda (99 miles) in 1882. Fonda was not a suitable terminus, but the Wabash was in the process of reorganization, and could not push the line to Spencer and the Spirit Lake resort area, toward which it was directed. The company still had no narrow gauge entry into Des Moines, only 15 miles from Waukee, but in 1881 the St. Louis, Des Moines & Northern built a connection from Waukee to Clive off

its projected main line to Boone. The two railroads jointly operated the track between Des Moines and Clive.

On April 1, 1887, the Des Moines North-Western was transferred to the Wabash & Western Railway, one of the corporate entities established in the Wabash's reorganization. In October 1887 the narrow gauge was reorganized as the Des Moines & Northwestern Railway, the change ending the Wabash's involvement with the line. In August 1891 the new corporation was merged with the Des Moines & Northern Railroad, successor to the St. Louis, Des Moines & Northern, into the Des Moines Northern & Western Railway. Both narrow gauge lines were converted in 1891. The Fonda line came into the hands of the Chicago, Milwaukee & St. Paul in 1899, and was extended to Spencer and Spirit Lake as originally intended. The line from Des Moines to Spencer was abandoned in 1980.

Des Moines, Osceola & Southern Railroad

Businessmen in Osceola, seat of Clarke County on the Chicago, Burlington & Quincy main line 57 miles straight south of Des Moines, projected a narrow gauge through their town from Des Moines to Kansas City. If completed, the railroad would have been about 300 miles long. The company was chartered on February 15, 1879. Construction began at Osceola in 1881. Late in 1882 track reached Des Moines, and in January 1883 Decatur City, a total of 81 miles. By the end of 1883 the railroad was completed to the Missouri state line. It was, in fact, the only one of Iowa's narrow gauges to cross the state's boundaries, for narrow gauge rails reached Cainsville, Missouri, a town of 198 people, on December 4, 1884. The line was 112 miles long, with an extremely curvaceous route. Reportedly, the contractor was paid on a mileage basis, an arrangement giving him a perverse incentive to lengthen the railroad. In particular, between St. Marys and New Virginia, Iowa, the track made a large horseshoe loop via St. Charles and Truro, taking 21 miles to traverse a linear distance of only about ten miles. It was a fairly large narrow gauge, with seven locomotives and 222 revenue freight cars.

By the time track arrived in Cainsville, the management was debating whether to continue to Kansas City or to alter the projected route to St. Joseph. The company's resources had been exhausted, and track was never pushed beyond Cainsville. An Iowa court appointed a receiver on April 2, 1885.

Discussion of reorganization and extension was intertwined with planning for conversion. On September 1, 1885, the management and the bondholders agreed to reorganize the company, relay the track at 4'-8½" with 56-pound rail, and extend the line either to St. Joseph or to a connection for Kansas City via the Hannibal & St. Joseph Railroad. The railroad was sold for $750,000 to three trustees for the bondholders, who were given until September 1, 1887, to comply with the terms of the agreement. The trustees, who represented local interests, were unable to raise the funds, and on January 11, 1888, control of the railroad passed into the hands of M. V. B. Edgerly of Springfield, Massachusetts, who represented Eastern bondholders. He formed the Des Moines & Kansas City Railway, which took over the property on March 28, 1888. Even though the railroad remained narrow gauge, it was uniformly profitable in the 1890s. On December 5, 1895, Edgerly sold stock control of the line to the Keokuk & Western, with which it connected at Van Wert, Iowa. The new owner converted the narrow gauge north of Van Wert on October 31–November 1, 1896, and the remainder on October 23–24, 1897, incidentally shortening it by a mile. The Chicago, Burlington & Quincy in turn absorbed the Keokuk & Western in 1899. Neither successor ever extended the railroad, and as the Cainsville branch of the Burlington, it was abandoned in segments between 1933 and 1958. Rails were torn up from Cainsville in 1938.

Farmers Union Railroad

John W. Tripp of Albion, Iowa, had been successful in real estate development at the small town of Liscomb, just east of the Iowa River in Marshall County. He conceived the idea of a narrow gauge railroad stretching all the way across the state, from some unspecified point on the Mississippi River through Liscomb and Mapleton (a town in Monona County in which he also had interests) to a point on the Missouri River. He commissioned grading both east and west from Liscomb. He was able to lay only 12 miles of wooden rail from a sawmill on the Iowa River west of Liscomb east to Conrad and Beaman. The railroad was organized in 1875 and apparently had its entire operating history in the same year. One locomotive, one caboose, and a small number of cars constituted the equipment. The light standards to which the line was built caused it to deteriorate rapidly. It is thought to have been the first railroad of any kind to be abandoned in Iowa.

Fort Madison & North Western Railway

This company was organized as the Fort Madison, Oskaloosa & North Western on July 17, 1871, to build from Fort Madison on the Mississippi River to Oskaloosa, about 100 miles, and Council Bluffs. The actual attainments were much more limited. On May 1, 1872, the name was changed to Fort Madison & North Western Narrow Gauge. On October 14, 1879, the railroad was reorganized and "Narrow Gauge" was dropped from the corporate name. The Fort Madison & North Western Railway Construction Co. laid 11 miles of 30-pound rail in 1879 to West Point. Track reached Birmingham (41 miles) in March 1882, and Collett (45 miles) in 1884. On arrival in Birmingham, the promoters expressed indecision about whether to build to Oskaloosa or to Sigourney. They were apparently unable to pay the construction costs so as to take possession of the railroad; as late as 1885 the line was still being operated by the construction company.

In March 1885 the railroad was placed in the hands of a receiver appointed by a state court on petition of Iowa creditors. The Union Trust Company of New York shortly brought an action in federal court for discharge of the receiver and appointment of another under federal procedures. It was then proposed to reorganize the company as the Iowa & Northwestern Railway, standard gauge it, and extend it to Oskaloosa. This project could not be financed, and the narrow gauge remained in receivership until March 29, 1890, when it was sold under foreclosure and reorganized as the Chicago, Fort Madison & Des Moines Railway. The new corporation converted the line on September 10, 1892, and extended it to Ottumwa on December 11, 1892. The company went into default on its bonds and, as a result, into receivership on July 27, 1898. The property was reorganized as the Chicago, Fort Madison & Des Moines Railroad on January 4, 1899, which was reportedly wholly owned by the Chicago, Burlington & Quincy Railroad. The line was formally leased to the CB&Q on July 22, 1900, and merged into the CB&Q on January 1, 1901. Of the standard gauge extension, the portion from Batavia to Ottumwa was abandoned at the time of the CB&Q's lease in 1900. The segment from Birmingham to Batavia was abandoned in 1939. The portion of the former narrow gauge from Stockport to Birmingham was abandoned in 1956 and the remainder, from Fort Madison to Stockport, in 1980.

Iowa Eastern Railroad

This corporation was organized in 1871 to build a narrow gauge from Beulah, nine miles west of McGregor on the Iowa & Dakota Division of the Chicago, Milwaukee & St. Paul Railway, to Des Moines, a distance of about 200 miles. In 1872 track was laid from Beulah about 16 miles to a point about 1.5 miles from Elkader, seat of Clayton County. The end-of-track was named Elkader Station. The railroad was originally reported to have been laid with 30-pound rail. Initially, the company was reported to be doing fairly well; it interchanged 153 standard gauge carloads with the CM&StP in December 1873. The management surveyed an extension of about five miles to Motor, to be laid with maple rails with iron strap surfaces. Track built to these primitive standards reached Elkader on November 15, 1875, but no further construction took place. Even the extension into Elkader could not be maintained. Washouts in the late 1870s caused the line to be cut back to Elkader Station or a short distance farther.

In mid-1881 the narrow gauge was acquired by the McGregor & Des Moines Railroad, which had been organized to build the entire projected line to the capital. The narrow gauge, however, was conveyed later in 1881 to the CM&StP, which announced its intention to convert the line and to extend tracks two miles into Elkader. The Iowa Eastern was converted in the spring of 1882, and one of its two Mogul locomotives was shipped to the nearby Waukon & Mississippi. Rolling stock is thought to have gone to the same line, and possibly also to the Bellevue & Cascade.

As the Elkader branch of the Milwaukee Road, the line was abandoned in 1972.

St. Louis, Des Moines & Northern Railway

Like the Des Moines & Minneapolis, this narrow gauge was intended to connect the Chicago & North Western main line with the capital. The president of the firm was no less a figure than Grenville M. Dodge of the Union Pacific. The enterprise was financed by Jay Gould, who was expanding his holdings in Iowa. The corporation was chartered in 1880, and in 1881 built 15 miles from Des Moines to Waukee, thereby providing a narrow gauge entry into Des Moines for the Des Moines North-Western Railway. The main line was then built north from Clive, a western suburb of Des Moines, to Boone in 1882. The main line was 42 miles; the seven miles between Clive and

Des Moines were jointly owned by the two narrow gauges. The railroad was laid with 35-pound rail and was initially reported to own three locomotives. The company had bought the equipment and rails of the Indianapolis, Delphi & Chicago Railway, which had converted to standard gauge after only three years of operation.

The original corporation was succeeded at a foreclosure sale on November 22, 1889, by the Des Moines & Northern Railroad. In August 1891 the company was merged with the Des Moines & Northwestern, as its connection had become, into Des Moines Northern & Western Railway and converted. The combined railroad was absorbed by the Chicago, Milwaukee & St. Paul in 1899 and served as the Boone branch. As such, it was abandoned from Luther to Boone in 1965 and from Madrid to Luther in 1976. The entry into Des Moines was abandoned in 1980.

St. Louis, Keosauqua & St. Paul Railroad

When the Keokuk, Fort Des Moines & Minnesota Rail Road planned its line from Keokuk to Des Moines in the late 1850s, it projected a route through Keosauqua, seat of Van Buren County. When local citizens proved unwilling to bring forth a subsidy of $75,000, the railroad bypassed Keosauqua to the north. After the railroad was opened in 1860, Keosauqua was served from a station at Summit, four miles away. This arrangement was widely thought disadvantageous. Efforts at providing a railroad for Keosauqua were continual from 1860, but as in many other areas, a standard gauge line could not be financed. The St. Louis, Keosauqua & St. Paul was incorporated in 1873 to build to Summit. No doubt some of the promoters seriously considered building to the major cities in the corporate name, but building the four miles to Summit was all the company could accomplish. Ground was broken on October 9, 1873, and the line completed in 1875. It entered Summit by a bridge over the standard gauge railroad, which was by then known as the Keokuk & Des Moines Railway. Had the line been extended, Fairfield on the Burlington main line was the next target.

The narrow gauge apparently operated only in 1875. E. P. Howard of Keosauqua was appointed receiver for the line in late summer, but was shortly replaced by W. A. Brownell of Keokuk, who represented Kittle & Co., the contractor who had built the line. Operations seem to have been shut down before the end of the year. The line was ordered sold for the benefit of creditors in 1878, and the track was removed in 1879.

In 1880 the Rock Island system, which had succeeded to the Keokuk & Des Moines in 1878, acquired the right-of-way and built a branch of 4.5 miles from Mt. Zion (as Summit was renamed) into Keosauqua, almost all on the former narrow gauge's grade. The branch was opened on September 29, 1880, and was abandoned in 1976.

REFERENCE: Clem Topping, "Railroads in Van Buren County," *Van Buren County Register*, June 1, 1978.

Waukon & Mississippi Railroad

Waukon, the seat of Allamakee County at the extreme northeast tip of Iowa, lies 23 miles up Paint Creek from the Mississippi River. Although Waukon has a central location in the county, its position as county seat was threatened, mainly by Lansing, which enjoyed a site on the Mississippi and, after 1872, on the Chicago, Clinton, Dubuque & Minnesota Railroad. Postville, at the southwest corner of the county on the Iowa & Dakota Division of the Chicago, Milwaukee & St. Paul also showed interest in attracting the county government.

Partly for ordinary commercial reasons, and partly out of this political rivalry, local businessmen in Waukon attempted to finance a railroad along Paint Creek from the 1850s. No project was successful until D. W. Adams and his associates formed the Waukon & Mississippi Railroad in April 1875. The decision to use 3'-0" was made both because of the tortuous character of the route along Paint Creek and because the neighboring Iowa Eastern was considered a success. The route entailed gaining 580 feet in altitude, 153 feet in the last two miles into Waukon. The project could not be financed until July 1877, but the railroad was then built in only 53 days in September and October, being ready for inaugural service on October 27, 1877. A station was built where the narrow gauge met the Chicago, Clinton, Dubuque & Minnesota, and named Adams Junction (Waukon Junction). It was a small railroad, initially with a single 4-4-0 locomotive, 16 boxcars, five flatcars, and a combine for passengers. An elevated track was built at Waukon Junction for gravity transfer of grain into standard gauge boxcars.

In September 1878 the major railroad financier James F. Joy bought a controlling interest in the Waukon & Mississippi Guarantee Company, the financial firm that had been organized in 1876 to build and equip the railroad. Joy was already in control of the Chicago, Clinton, Dubuque & Minnesota. F. O. Wyatt, manager of the larger railroad, assumed the presidency of the narrow gauge.

The narrow gauge did well enough that two extensions were considered, north 25 miles to Caledonia, Minnesota, in the spring of 1879, and west 15 miles to Decorah, Iowa, in the same year. Only the latter was pursued. In the fall of 1879, the company acquired part but not all of the right-of-way to Decorah. In the spring of 1880, track was laid for about two-thirds of the distance, and piers were sunk for four bridges. This project was abruptly aborted when the Chicago, Milwaukee & St. Paul took control of the CCD&M and with it the Waukon & Mississippi in October 1880. The CM&StP already served Decorah with standard gauge rails and had no interest in a second line of narrow gauge. Track on the extension was torn up. From the outset the new owner apparently intended conversion, but it converted the neighboring Iowa Eastern first and in 1882 sent one of the IE line's two Moguls to the Waukon branch. Narrow gauge power in need of service was loaded onto standard gauge flatcars for movement to the shops at Dubuque. There was considerable local pressure from residents of Waukon for conversion, and there was a prospect that an iron mine would be opened to the north of the town. The line was prepared for conversion in the summer of 1884, and standard gauge trains reached Waukon early in September. The Missouri Iron Co. built the extension to the iron mine as a private carrier in 1910. Production ended in 1922 and the rails on the private line were removed in 1933 and 1934. The Waukon branch survived as a typical lightly trafficked facility for a county seat until 1972, when it was abandoned.

REFERENCE: Denny Rehder and Cecil Cook, *Grass between the Rails: The Waukon, Iowa, Branch of the Milwaukee Road* (Des Moines, Iowa: Waukon & Mississippi Press, 1972).

Kansas

Kansas Central Railway

Of the various projects to provide an eastern connection for the Denver & Rio Grande the most important was the Kansas Central Railway. Although the promoters never achieved their goal, they did build a narrow gauge extending 165 miles west from Leavenworth, Kansas, over the course of a decade. Construction on the railroad nearly spanned the entire narrow gauge period.

The leading businessmen of Leavenworth felt that their city had been bypassed by the major east-west routes of the standard gauge railroads, which had centered at Kansas City to the south and St. Joseph to the north. The announcement of the Denver & Rio Grande project presented to them the prospect of making Leavenworth an analogous center of a rival narrow gauge system. The Kansas Central Railway was chartered on May 31, 1871, to build a line of 3'-0" from Leavenworth to the western boundary of Kansas. The principal promoters of the line were L. T. Smith, manager of the Planters Hotel; Paul E. Havens, president of the Leavenworth National Bank and a member of the state legislature; Thomas Carney, a former governor of Kansas; and Lucien Scott, president of the First National Bank of Leavenworth. Their intended route was through the northern two tiers of counties of the state; the exact location would depend on the availability of local assistance. The route necessarily crossed the drainage pattern of streams tributary to the Platte River to the north. Especially toward the east end, the terrain was the typical hilly country of the Missouri River valley, the contours of which the promoters intended to follow closely. The Kansas City *Journal of Commerce*, in a hostile editorial of October 11, 1871, characterized the narrow gauge's route as 600 miles of which the western 300 were "uninhabited and inhospitable," correctly predicting both that the company would go bankrupt and that the line would never be completed. The promoters hoped to build at a rate of 100 miles per year. The Colorado Eastern was a later project, but had the Kansas Central been completed, trains would probably have entered Denver on that railroad or on the KC's own trackage on a route from the Kansas-Colorado border such as the Colorado Eastern projected.

Smith and his associates began their efforts with an attempt to secure aid from Leavenworth County. From an earlier transaction, the county government held $250,000 in stock of the Kansas Pacific. Smith proposed that the county transfer the stock to the Kansas Central. The stock was also sought by the Chicago, Southwestern & Pacific, which planned a standard gauge line from Chicago to San Diego via Leavenworth and Topeka. The CSW&P proposed that if it were granted the stock it would allow the Kansas Central to lay third rail on its projected line for the first 25 miles out of Leavenworth. The County Board, however, on July 8, 1871, voted to turn the stock over to the Kansas Central upon completion of the first 50 miles from Leavenworth. A public election ratified this arrangement on August 16, 1871, by a vote of 3,680 to 672. Construction began in July 1871, and by August 11, 1872, track reached Holton (55 miles), satisfying a franchise obligation by four days. The railroad's prospects looked favorable enough that some bonds were sold in Europe. In November 1872 the Washington, Cincinnati & St. Louis, which was expected to be the main connection to the East Coast for a national narrow gauge network, expressed interest in building from St. Louis to Leavenworth.

Inability to secure transfer of the Kansas Pacific stock from Leavenworth County, the failure of some votes for aid in Pottawatomie County, and the financial stringency of 1873 brought a downturn in the Kansas Central's prospects. Construction halted and service was cut from two trains per day to one on March 13, 1874. After Mill Creek, Jefferson, and Soldier townships voted aid, construction was resumed in June 1877. In spite of a strike by unpaid employees of the contractor, track reached Circleville (63 miles) in September and Onaga (82 miles) early in 1878.

On February 5, 1879, the Clerk of the Federal District Court in Leavenworth served a summons on the company on behalf of the Northwestern Mutual Life Insurance Company and various individual creditors. This action brought a foreclosure

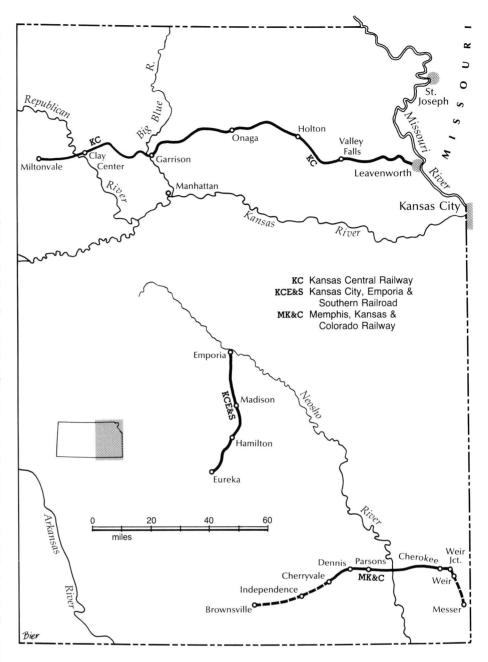

sale on April 14, 1879, at which the railroad was sold for $252,000 to C. K. Garrison, president of the Missouri Pacific, and L. T. Smith. They reorganized the property as the Kansas Central Railroad on April 15, 1879. Although Smith and his associates retained their directorships, the equity of Garrison marked the railroad's entry into the financial empire of Jay Gould. Although the transfer of the Kansas Pacific stock was still in the courts, Gould bought the Kansas Central from Garrison and Smith on November 13, 1879, for $431,820. Gould then conveyed the narrow gauge to the Union Pacific for $479,000, along with the Kansas Pacific and Denver Pacific. The Kansas Central thereafter operated as an associated line of the Union Pacific, though it retained its

corporate identity and Smith remained in charge. Since the railroad at best aspired to the status of a low-quality duplicate of the Kansas Pacific, the reason for the Union Pacific's interest in extending it is not obvious. In May 1880 President Sidney Dillon of the UP reported that the first 60 miles needed new steel rail and the entire narrow gauge needed ballast. Nonetheless, the Union Pacific extended the narrow gauge. Track reached Garrison (118 miles) on August 3, 1880, Clay Center (146 miles), the principal county seat in the area, on December 25, 1881, and finally Miltonvale (165 miles) on April 1, 1882. Miltonvale provided a junction with the Atchison, Topeka & Santa Fe's branch to Concordia, Kansas, and Superior, Nebraska. Even in this partly completed

Mogul No. 102 is lettered for the Kansas Central, but carries numerals in the standard Union Pacific style of the time. (Ed Bond collection.)

form, the Kansas Central was a relatively large narrow gauge, with 19 locomotives and an office car.

The Kansas Central was converted to standard gauge on August 25, 1890, for the most part by simply relaying the existing narrow gauge rail to 4'-8½". The Kansas State Railroad Commissioners considered this arrangement unsatisfactory and issued three orders for laying of heavier rail. An accident in the summer of 1891, in which two people were killed, was held to be caused by spreading of the lightweight rails. The Supreme Court of Kansas late in 1891 held that the Railroad Commissioners were without authority to order the relaying of the line, on the ground that their powers were advisory only.

The Kansas Central went bankrupt along with the parent Union Pacific in 1893 and was reorganized as the Leavenworth, Kansas & Western Railway, a UP subsidiary. This arrangement lasted until 1908, when the line was incorporated into the Union Pacific. Thereafter the former narrow gauge was operated merely as part of an extensive network of UP branches in the area. With the coming of the Depression, the line became expendable. It had virtually no traffic except agricultural products, which were now being lost to trucks, and its physical properties were poor. On July 1, 1933, the UP applied to the Interstate Commerce Commission to abandon the 143 miles from Knox at Leavenworth to Clay Center, a step incidental to its extensive abandonment of branch lines in the area. Also to be abandoned was the portion of a branch from Junction City to Concordia north of Clay Center. The railroad proposed to retain the

former Kansas Central west of Clay Center and to take trackage rights on the Santa Fe from Miltonvale to Concordia. The ICC approved these arrangements on October 8, 1934, and the Knox–Clay Center line was abandoned on January 10, 1935. The revised Concordia branch lasted until the early 1960s when a proposed dam on the Republican River threatened to inundate 28 miles of line south of Clay Center. The UP on September 10, 1962, applied to abandon the entire Concordia branch, including the Clay Center–Miltonvale segment of the ex–Kansas Central, and received permission on March 25, 1964.

REFERENCE: Harold Crimmins, *A History of the Kansas Central Railway 1871–1935*, The Emporia State Research Studies, Kansas State Teachers College, Emporia, 2, no. 4 (June 1954).

Kansas City, Emporia & Southern Railroad

The northernmost portion of the Atchison, Topeka & Santa Fe's lengthy Emporia-Moline branch in southeastern Kansas was built and briefly operated as a narrow gauge. The Kansas City, Emporia & Southern was a local project of January 23, 1877, for a narrow gauge from Emporia on the Santa Fe main line south to Eureka. Having failed to finance the project independently, the promoters arranged late in 1878 for the AT&SF to build the line for operation as a branch. Grading began at Emporia on December 4, 1878, and the line was completed to Eureka (47.4 miles) on June 30, 1879. Because the line would be only part of the AT&SF's extensive agricultural mileage in

the state, its narrow gauge served no useful purpose. The Santa Fe converted it on Sunday, August 3, 1879. Track was extended to Howard (76 miles) at the end of 1879. The branch was completed to Moline (84 miles) on January 1, 1887. The entire line was abandoned on April 16, 1975.

REFERENCE: John M. Meade, *History of the Santa Fe* (typescript internal history, AT&SF Ry. [Topeka, Kans., c. 1919]), p. 159. A photocopy of this work is in the collection of Russell Lee Crump, La Grange Park, Ill.

Memphis, Kansas & Colorado Railway

The grandiose title of this company accurately delineates the ambitions of the promoters to provide an outlet from the San Juan mining area of Colorado to Memphis. Had the railroad made serious progress, it might have rivaled the Kansas Central as a projected connection from the Denver & Rio Grande to the east. Actually, the promoters achieved only a short line of 50 miles in the coalfield of southeastern Kansas.

The railroad was promoted by George Greene, former president of the Burlington, Cedar Rapids & Northern, and C. W. Meade, an official of the Union Pacific. They chartered the corporation on December 4, 1877, and laid their first rail with considerable ceremony at the crossing of the Missouri River, Fort Scott & Gulf at Cherokee, Kansas, on April 10, 1878. The line was built to Weir, seven miles to the east in 1878, and opened to Parsons, 25 miles to the west, on April 15, 1879. In February 1880 the Kansas City, Fort Scott & Gulf (successor to the Missouri River, Fort Scott & Gulf) leased and then bought the narrow gauge. The large railroad had no interest in the promoters' long-range ambitions, but it did allow the narrow gauge to be extended on February 3, 1881, from Parsons to Cherryvale, 18 miles to the southwest. Some additional grading had been done toward Brownsville on the west and toward Messer (a town named after the general manager of the narrow gauge) to the southeast.

The KCFS&G converted its acquisition in October 1882. Along with the larger railroad, the former narrow gauge was absorbed into the St. Louis–San Francisco in 1901. The line was cut back from Cherryvale to Dennis (10 miles) in 1960 and to Parsons in 1976. The four miles from Weir Junction to Weir were abandoned in 1982, but at the present writing the 28 miles from Weir Junction to Parsons are extant as a branch of the Burlington Northern.

Kentucky

Covington, Flemingsburg & Pound Gap Railway

As chartered in 1876, this railroad was to be a narrow gauge of about 110 miles running from Covington, opposite Cincinnati, to Hazel Green, a village of about 250 population in Wolfe County. The first segment of the line was opened from Johnson (Flemingsburg Junction) to Flemingsburg (six miles) in the spring of 1877. Considerable additional grading was done, but the contractors brought an action alleging nonpayment for their work. A receiver was appointed in August 1877, but he was authorized to continue laying track for an additional 12 miles southeast to Hillsboro. The extension was opened on December 17, 1878. Nothing further was built. The financial history was one of the worst of the narrow gauge movement.

The company was reorganized as the Licking Valley Railroad on January 24, 1880, in hopes of building from Covington to West Liberty, seat of Morgan County, about 135 miles. Later in 1880 the enterprise was again reorganized, this time as the Cincinnati & Southeastern Railway. About 30 miles of the route across Campbell County immediately southeast of Covington were graded and some work was done elsewhere, but in mid-1882 contractors P. O. Dickinson and C. Q. Colton suspended work. Dickinson brought suit for $134,000 for work still unpaid. At this time about $225,000 had been invested in the project, but the suit brought work to an end. The Union Trust Co. of New York brought action for foreclosure early in 1887. On May 7, 1887, the railroad was sold for $1 to Henry F. Huntington, who assumed the debt of over $300,000. Holders of the first-mortgage bonds brought an action for foreclosure in 1890, causing the line to be reorganized on April 15, 1891, as the Covington, Flemingsburg & Ashland Railroad. The company operated under this name until June 1, 1905, when it was reorganized as the Cincinnati, Flemingsburg & Southeastern Railroad. While operating under this name the railroad suffered one of the worst examples of the most characteristic sort of narrow gauge accident, a trestle collapse. On May 10, 1907, the Weaver's Ford trestle, about two miles southeast of Flemingsburg, collapsed under one of the line's two Baldwin 2-6-0s, pitching the engine, a boxcar, and a coach to the ground 38 feet below. Three passengers were killed and about 20 injured. The trestle was not repaired and the line beyond Flemingsburg was abandoned. The remaining six miles were converted in December 1909. The line had its last reorganization, as the Flemingsburg & Northern Railroad, on January 1, 1920. The railroad survived by serving the general transport demands of Flemingsburg until December 6, 1955.

Kentucky & South Atlantic Railway

The Mount Sterling Coal & Iron Co. chartered the Mount Sterling Coal Railroad on February 13, 1874, to tap a three-foot seam of coal on the company's land southwest of Mount Sterling. The line was made a common carrier, mainly in the expectation of carrying ore and yellow pine from mines and lumber mills in the area. The

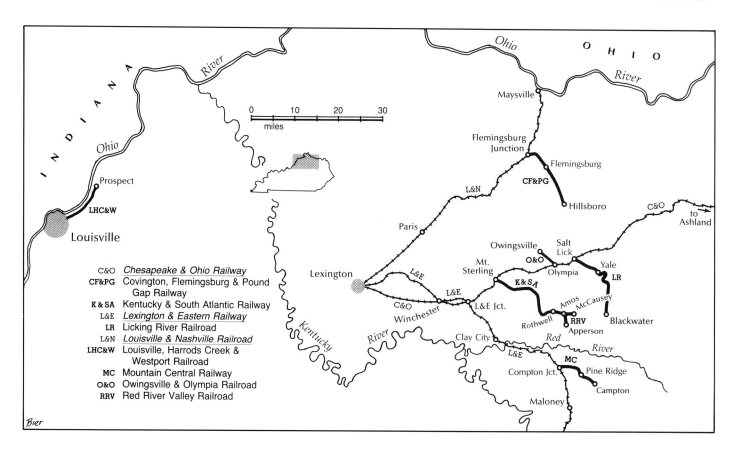

C&O   Chesapeake & Ohio Railway
CF&PG Covington, Flemingsburg & Pound
       Gap Railway
K&SA   Kentucky & South Atlantic Railway
L&E   Lexington & Eastern Railway
LR   Licking River Railroad
L&N   Louisville & Nashville Railroad
LHC&W Louisville, Harrods Creek &
       Westport Railroad
MC   Mountain Central Railway
O&O   Owingsville & Olympia Railroad
RRV   Red River Valley Railroad

One of the Cincinnati, Flemingsburg & Southeastern's two handsome Baldwin 2-6-0 locomotives of 1877 smokes vigorously at the line's unusual covered station in Flemingsburg. (Ed Bond collection.)

The Cincinnati, Flemingsburg & Southeastern had one of the worst examples of the narrow gauges' most characteristic accident, the trestle collapse. This disaster at Weaver's Ford trestle caused the line to be cut back to Flemingsburg. (Ed Bond collection.)

road was undertaken in 1875 and completed to the mines at Rothwell (21 miles) in August 1876. The line was lightly built with bar iron strap rail on oak stringers. The company defaulted on the railroad's bonds, causing the line to be sold in December 1878 to the Coal Road Construction Co., organized by E. Zimmerman of Cincinnati. Zimmerman relaid the line with 35-pound T-rail, and on January 14, 1882, changed its name to the Kentucky & South Atlantic Railway. In 1881 the railroad was extended two miles to Frenchburg Junction, but passenger service was provided only to Rothwell. Zimmerman planned to extend about 80 miles east to the West Virginia border, or southeast through Stone Gap to Bristol, but was unable to finance any extension. The railroad was again put in receivership on December 15, 1885. The property was sold in September 1887 to C. P. Huntington, who also said he planned to extend it. Instead, he sold it in January 1892 to his Chesapeake & Ohio Railway, with which it connected at Mount Sterling. The C&O took control of the property on July 1, 1892, and converted it in August 1895.

The line survived as a minor branch off the Louisville line of the C&O until September 20, 1931, when it was abandoned. The rail was removed in 1933.

Licking River Railroad

The Sterling Lumber Co. organized the Licking Valley Railway as a common carrier in 1896 and opened it on April 1, 1897, from the Chesapeake & Ohio at Salt Lick to the company's mill at Yale (12 miles). Incidental to the lumber company's failure, the railroad was placed in receivership on May 27, 1899. The purchasers bought the railroad for $29,000 at a receiver's sale of October 24 and reorganized it as the Licking River Railroad on November 15, 1899, under the ownership of the Yale Lumber Co. The line was extended in 1902 to Morgan (26.5 miles), in 1903 to Devil Creek (30 miles), and in 1905 to Blackwater (32 miles). The railroad operated a single passenger train per day, originating at Yale, going out to Blackwater, running in to Salt Lick, and returning to Yale. The railroad had five boxcars and performed general freight service. It operated with Climax locomotives and rod engines.

The line was unprofitable beginning in 1906 and was abandoned in 1913.

Louisville, Harrods Creek & Westport Railroad

James Callahan and other local business figures organized this railroad on March 19, 1870, and in 1872 built five miles of track from First Street in Louisville northeast parallel to the Ohio River to a point beyond Longview. Callahan projected the line to Madison, Indiana, and Cincinnati, but had great difficulty financing the railroad after the Panic of 1873. Track reached Goose Creek (7.4 miles) in 1874 and Sand Hill (Prospect; 11 miles) in 1875. Callahan also proposed to build to Shelbyville, utilizing the unbuilt grade of the Cumberland & Ohio, but he was also unable to finance this extension. As the line stood, it operated mainly as a suburban passenger carrier, running four trains per day. It served Harrods Creek, but ended about 11 miles short of Westport, a river town in Oldham County. The line had a modest freight traffic from a lime kiln, two quarries, a distillery, and farms along the way.

After the railroad's mortgage of $60,000 was foreclosed, the railroad was sold on June 23, 1879, to James Trigg, who represented the bondholders. He sold the line on May 30, 1880, to the Louisville, Cincinnati & Lexington Railway, a major railroad that united the three cities of its corporate title. The LC&L was bought on June 1, 1881, by the Louisville & Nashville, which made it a northern extension of the L&N system. Since the LC&L's Louisville-Cincinnati line was now a portion of the L&N's main line, the L&N had no interest in Callahan's projected line to Cincinnati. The L&N made no effort to extend the narrow gauge, and converted it to its 4′-9″ gauge in 1888. In 1904 the Louisville & Interurban Railroad, a subsidiary of the street railway in the city, bought the outermost 7.7 miles of the line for electrification. The L&I's six other lines were built to the Louisville Railway's gauge 5′-0″, but because a demand remained for railroad interchange, the Prospect Line had to be operated with a set of four standard gauge cars. The company built a standard gauge entry into the central business district; this trackage was also used by the interurbans of the Interstate Public Service Co. (Indiana Railroad) from Indianapolis. Dual gauge track was laid in the L&I's terminal for the Prospect cars. The L&N agreed to provide freight service to Prospect in off hours, which proved to be at night. This arrangement lasted until March 20, 1930, when the L&N gave it up, reportedly because a bridge at Harrods Creek became too weak for steam locomotives. The L&I provided freight service until May 15, 1934, and abandoned the line on October 31, 1935. A segment of 3.4 miles was retained to switch coal into a municipal waterworks at Zorn Avenue. When the last coal-burning pumping engine was retired about 1952, the line was cut back roughly a mile. The remainder survives as switching trackage serving sand and gravel firms along the Ohio River.

Mountain Central Railway

The Swan-Day Lumber Co., which owned a sawmill at Clay City on the Lexington & Eastern, operated a lumber railroad out of Campton Junction, about 17 miles to the east. The line ascended Pine Ridge via Whittleton Branch, reached the summit by two switchbacks, and descended along the Right Fork of Chimney Top Creek to the Red River. When timber at the Red River was exhausted, Floyd Day of the lumber company decided upon using the ascent for a new railroad, the Mountain

Central Railway, a common carrier to run along Pine Ridge to Campton, seat of Wolfe County. The railroad was opened to the town of Pine Ridge (six miles) in the spring of 1906 and to Campton (12 miles) in the fall of 1907. The line operated with Climax locomotives, and ran two passenger round-trips per day. It originated timber and coal for the lumber company and provided general service for Campton. Completion of a state road into Campton in 1924 deprived the railroad of most of its general cargo, and caused its abandonment in 1928.

Owingsville & Olympia Railroad

W. W. Hubbard, general manager of the Licking River Railroad, upon abandonment of his line, endeavored to interest the citizens of Owingsville, seat of Bath County, in using some of his equipment for a narrow gauge connection to the Chesapeake & Ohio at Olympia, about four miles southwest of the Licking River's terminus at Salt Lick. As the Owingsville & Olympia Railroad, the line opened about the beginning of 1915. It was six miles long, and operated with one locomotive, five boxcars, and a coach from the Licking River, but the line proved inappropriate for a steam engine. An internal combustion locomotive was purchased, but it was wrecked in a trestle derailment in October 1915. The accident and a disappointing level of traffic led to the company's reorganization as the Olympia & Owingsville Railway in 1916. The railroad remained unprofitable and was abandoned in 1918.

Red River Valley Railroad

The Union City Lumber Co. of Michigan bought a large tract of timber around Big Amos Creek and on May 19, 1898, incorporated the existing private railroad on the property as a common carrier, the Red River Valley Railroad. The railroad, which dated from 1892 or 1893, ascended a ridge from Rothwell, the terminus of a branch of the Chesapeake & Ohio, by four switchbacks. In 1898 the line reached McCausey (nine miles), a camp named for the company's president, J. W. McCausey. A branch of five miles ran from Amos, two miles short of McCausey, to Apperson. The line operated with three Climax locomotives. The Apperson branch was reported abandoned to the ICC in fiscal year 1907, but was carried in the *Official Guide of the Railways* until 1912. The main line was ap-

parently operated until late in 1913 and abandoned in 1914.

REFERENCES: Elmer G. Sulzer, *Ghost Railroads of Kentucky* (Indianapolis: Vane A. Jones Co., 1967); collection of George H. Yater. Some of Sulzer's dates and sequences of corporate names are inaccurate.

Louisiana

The Bodcaw Valley Railway

Lumber operators F. T. Whited and H. H. Wheless began operation of a private railroad in Bossier Parish, in about 1899, under the name of the Alden Bridge & Camden Railway. In fiscal 1901 they changed the name to Bodcaw Valley Railroad, although the carrier appears to have had no incorporation under either name. The line ran east from Alden Bridge on the Shreveport branch of the St. Louis Southwestern to Ivan (population c. 50; 11.5 miles) and various lumber installations. Because the railroad provided general transport service to Ivan, the lumber company incorporated it on May 4, 1904, under the name of The Bodcaw Valley Railway. The operators reported the line to the *Official Guide* from 1901; the listing typically showed three mixed trains per day. As on most lumber railroads, the mileage varied. At the outset service was provided to Haynes (20 miles), but the line was cut back two miles to "Track End" in 1904 and to McCall's Crossing, a half mile east of Ivan, in 1910. The railroad operated with two locomotives, one boxcar, and 56 flatcars. Operation ceased in the second half of 1911, and the charter was reported to have expired in 1912.

Kentwood & Eastern Railroad

The Banner Lumber Co. acquired the mill and the 11-mile private railroad of the Isabella Lumber Co. in 1895. Banner in 1901 formed the Kentwood & Eastern Rail-

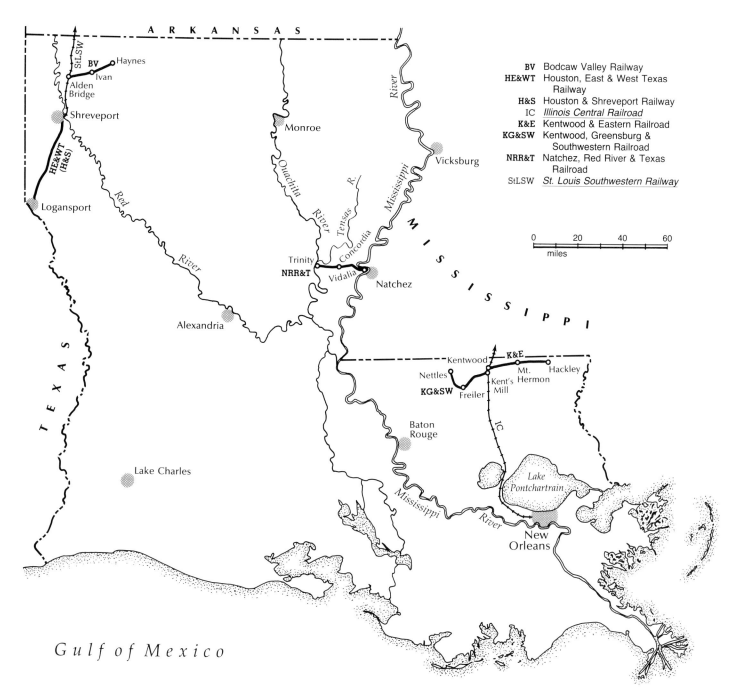

REFERENCE: Collection of Judge Leon Ford III, Hammond, La.

road as a common carrier to transport its products to the Illinois Central main line at Kentwood, but also to serve the general demands of some small communities east of Kentwood, just south of the Mississippi border. Track reached Mount Hermon (16 miles) in 1901 and Hackley (population c. 300; 30 miles) at the end of 1902. Some additional trackage was built in the fashion of lumber railroads, but an extension eastward to Angie on the New Orleans Great Northern main line and to Columbia, Mississippi, was never undertaken. The narrow gauge did gain a connection with the NOGN in 1907 when the standard gauge railroad built its Tylertown branch through Warner-

ton near the narrow gauge's 24-mile post.

The Brooks-Scanlon Lumber Co. of Minneapolis took over Banner in 1905, forming the Kentwood & Eastern Railway to lease the narrow gauge as of December 5. The new operator, under the name of the K&ERy, built a standard gauge line for its logging activities south to Scanlon and Foley, laying third rail on the narrow gauge for three miles from Kentwood to Bolivar Junction. Brooks-Scanlon gave up operation of the narrow gauge in the second half of 1918. The company reported the standard gauge line to the ICC as having ceased operation on December 31, 1922, but apparently actually operated it until late 1923.

Kentwood, Greensburg & Southwestern Railroad

Amos Kent began this narrow gauge in 1880 as a logging railroad west from Kent's Mill, two miles south of Kentwood on the Illinois Central main line. By 1902 it extended to Freiler (13 miles) immediately north of Greensburg, seat of St. Helena Parish. On February 4, 1905, Kent chartered the Kentwood, Greensburg & Southwestern Railroad as a common carrier to run to

A Kentwood & Eastern 2-6-0, a Grant locomotive, is stopped on a small trestle for its photograph. (Ed Bond collection.)

Baton Rouge and on to an unspecified point on the Gulf of Mexico. It was intended to join the Kentwood & Eastern at Kentwood as a longer east-west route. In January 1906 the Denkmann interests, who owned the Natalbany Lumber Co. 27 miles south of Kentwood on the IC, bought Kent's mill and railroad. Initially, passengers were handled in mixed trains and in cabooses on log trains to a camp at Nettles (25 miles), but the Denkmanns, who were interested in the railroad only as a logging facility, cut passenger service back to Coles, two miles west of Freiler, in 1910 and to Freiler itself in 1918. Logging branches continued to range through the north half of the parish. Several locomotives were lettered for the Amos Kent Lumber & Brick Co. and for the Natalbany Lumber Co. The railroad was abandoned in mid-1921.

REFERENCE: Collection of Judge Leon Ford III, Hammond, La.

Natchez, Red River & Texas Railroad

The Vidalia & Lake Concordia Railroad & Steamboat Co. was chartered on May 12, 1876, by H. M. Gasterell of Natchez and his associates. A lightly built line laid with only 16-pound rail, it was opened from Vidalia on the west bank of the Mississippi opposite Natchez to Concordia (nine miles) on June 10, 1876. The railroad served lumber installations and a resort development at Lake Concordia. Initially, the road operated with one locomotive, two passenger cars, and four freight cars. The shareholders on January 11, 1881, voted to rename the line the Vidalia & Western Railroad.

On January 20, 1881, Hiram R. Steele of Vidalia formed the Natchez, Red River & Texas Railroad to buy the V&W for $50,000. He hoped to upgrade it to ordinary narrow gauge standards and extend it to Alexandria, Leesville, and to some connection with the Houston East & West Texas (probably in the vicinity of Moscow or Corrigan); the plan included bridging the Sabine River at Burr Ferry in Vernon Parish. In 1883 Steele relaid the existing line with 35-pound rail and extended it to Frogmore (16 miles). In April 1886 the track was pushed westward to Trinity (Black River; 25 miles) at the confluence of the Tensas and Ouachita rivers forming the Black River. This was an important interchange with steamboats serving this river system and also the Red River, but the expense of bridging the Black prevented further extension. As early as 1891 the management expressed an intention of converting the railroad and extending it to Alexandria, about 40 miles; however, financial stringency prevented any such attempt. The line was placed in receivership in 1894 and announced for sale on several occasions before being sold on February 13, 1897, to the estate of Joseph P. Hale, one of the earlier owners. The railroad was not immediately reorganized, but on March 21, 1904, was reformed as the Natchez & Western Railway, with A. E. Davis of Vidalia as president. The reorganization may have been in the interest of the St. Louis, Iron Mountain & Southern, which acquired stock control in 1905. Davis announced the company's intention to convert the property, bridge the Black, and extend the line to Alexandria. Preparations for conversion began in 1906, and the job was completed in the summer of 1907. Only the 16 miles from Concordia Junction to the Black River and about half a mile at Vidalia were converted; the intermediate eight miles between Concordia and Vidalia Junction were abandoned in favor of trackage rights on the New Orleans & Northwestern, a parallel subsidiary of the Iron Mountain. No extension was made.

In February 1910 the railroad was absorbed by the Iron Mountain. The line was leased as of January 1, 1917, to the Louisiana & Arkansas Railway, which, in completing its route from Hope, Arkansas, to Vidalia, was bridging the Black from Jonesville on the west bank. About a mile of the former narrow gauge approaching Black River was abandoned at this time. The L&A retained trackage rights from Concordia Junction to Vidalia. The lease and trackage rights were turned over to the Louisiana Midland Railway in January 1946. The line was abandoned west of Ferriday in 1985 except for some switching track at that point. The former narrow gauge terminal trackage at Ferriday and Vidalia was included in an application for abandonment of 162 miles from McGehee, Arkansas, to Vidalia approved by the ICC in 1988, but negotiations for transfer to local operators are in progress at the present writing.

REFERENCE: "Corporate History of the Missouri Pacific Railway Company and the St. Louis, Iron Mountain & Southern Railway Company and Their Constituent Lines" (typescript, Missouri Pacific Railway, 1915), pp. 99–102. A photocopy of this work is in the collection of John Baskin Harper, Oak Park, Ill.

For the Houston & Shreveport, see the corporate history of the Houston East & West Texas in the Texas section.

REFERENCE: Omer Lavallee, *Narrow Gauge Railways of Canada* (Montreal: Railfare Enterprises, Ltd., 1972), pp. 18–19, 95.

Maine

Aroostook River Railroad
Gauge: 3'-6"

Following the unification of Canada in 1867, local figures in 1870 formed the New Brunswick Railway to run from Gibson, New Brunswick, opposite Fredericton, up the valley of the Saint John River to Rivière-du-Loup on the St. Lawrence. The project was so thoroughly identified with its projected terminus that it was popularly known as the Rivière-du-Loup Rail Road and the initial motive power was lettered "R. du L. R.R.," although this name never had legal standing. The railway was opened in 1873 from Gibson to Woodstock (64 miles), and then pushed up the valley from Woodstock Junction (Newburg) five miles above Woodstock, reaching Edmunston (164 miles) in 1878. The line was not pressed farther, and never reached Rivière-du-Loup. The railway, which was heavily dependent on lumber traffic, operated mainly with small Mason Bogies, but also had two Baldwin 2-6-0s.

The management decided upon a branch into Maine to tap timber resources, and in 1874 formed an American subsidiary, the Aroostook River Railroad. The branch was built from Aroostook Junction, 106 miles above Gibson, to Fort Fairfield, Maine (7 miles), in 1875. About half the mileage was in Maine. In 1876 the branch was extended to Caribou (19 miles), and the company expressed its willingness to extend to Presque Isle, an additional 15 miles, in return for local assistance. This was not immediately forthcoming, but in 1881 the entire system was converted, after which the branch was pushed on to Presque Isle.

The New Brunswick Railway was leased to the Canadian Pacific Railway in 1891. The line, including the Presque Isle branch, remains in service at the present writing.

Bridgton & Saco River Railroad
Gauge: 2'-0"

Bridgton, a small resort town on the west shore of Long Lake, was connected with the outside world by a stage line and a steamer on nearby Sebago Lake. The success of the Sandy River Railroad in the difficult winter of 1879–80 caused local citizens to consider building a 2'-0" line to connect the town with the Portland & Ogdensburg Railroad. The original plan was to build to Bridgton from White Rock east of Sebago Lake via Gray, Raymond, Casco, and Naples. The promoters next considered building directly from Portland. The route from White Rock would have been 30 miles long with extensive bridging. As a consequence, it was discarded and a shorter route of 16 miles from Hiram Junction was adopted.

The railroad was chartered as the Bridgton & Saco River on June 29, 1881. George E. Mansfield was brought in from the Sandy River to take charge of construction. The railroad was built mainly in 1882 and opened on January 31, 1883. The line was initially operated with two Hinkley 0-4-4 Forney locomotives, two coaches, two head-end cars, five boxcars, and ten flatcars. A caboose was bought about 1886 and a third locomotive in 1893, a Forney from the Portland Company.

On August 3, 1898, the railroad opened a five-mile extension to Harrison, a resort town on the northeastern shore of Long Lake. The extension entailed a lengthy trestle across the northern tip of the water. When the Maine Central leased the P&O in 1888, Hiram Junction was renamed Bridgton Junction. The Maine Central (MEC) took control of the B&SR on July 24, 1912. The new operator bought several freight cars and additional locomotives, and made some improvements to the line. The narrow gauge was mainly a passenger carrier, and suffered declining ridership after 1920. The principal freight was lumber, which also declined in the 1920s. The MEC allowed the B&SR to default on its mortgage in 1927, and was apparently considering abandonment of the line. Residents of the Bridgton area formed the Bridgton & Harrison Railway and bought the narrow gauge at a receiver's auction of June 1, 1930. Partly because of problems in maintaining the trestle, the new management abandoned the extension to Harrison on October 30, 1930.

The railroad operated through the Depression with spartan economy. Passenger, express, and less-than-carload freight services were provided by two crude rail buses, except for excursions and movements through the snow. A third rail bus was acquired from the Sandy River & Rangeley Lakes in 1936. Railroad freight continued to be steam operated; the company had the only two 2'-0" tank cars ever built. The town of Bridgton, which owned five-sevenths of the stock, grew tired of the narrow gauge's losses. At a town meeting of October 9, 1939, the citizens decided to sell the railroad. It was sold to a junk dealer, who secured permission from the Interstate Commerce Commission to abandon it on May 13, 1940. The last train ran in September 1941, and the railroad was scrapped.

REFERENCES: H. T. Crittenden, "Bridgton & Harrison Railway," Railway & Locomotive Historical Society *Bulletin*, no. 57 (1942), pp. 73–86; Linwood W. Moody, *The Maine Two-Footers* (Berkeley, Calif.: Howell-North Books, 1959), pp. 25–31, 123–44.

Bucksport & Bangor Railroad

Bangor, the principal port on the Penobscot River, suffered from closure by ice in the winter months. To deal with the problem, R. P. Buck conceived of a railroad down the east bank of the river to an all-weather facility at Bucksport. The Bucksport & Bangor was chartered on February 1, 1873, but Buck and his associates were unable to raise money for building. They arranged to lease the railroad on completion for five years to the European & North American Railway, a broad gauge line with a circuitous route from Bangor to Saint John, New Brunswick. The E&NA was to pay the B&B 40 percent of the gross receipts from the line until November 1876, and 35 percent thereafter. This arrangement allowed the project to take shape, but caused the line to be built to the E&NA's gauge of 5'-6". The B&B was opened (19 miles) on December 12, 1874. It entered Bangor on an 810-foot Howe-truss bridge.

The E&NA had already resolved to convert to standard gauge, but became delinquent on its fixed charges in mid-1875; thus the conversion was delayed until 1877. The Bucksport line was converted to 4'-8½" on September 12, 1877, immediately before work began on the main line. When the lease expired on October 1, 1879, the B&B was returned to Buck and Sewall B. Swazey as trustees. They arranged for the line to be leased to L. L. Lincoln of Augusta, former superintendent of the First Division of the Maine Central. Lincoln had been converted

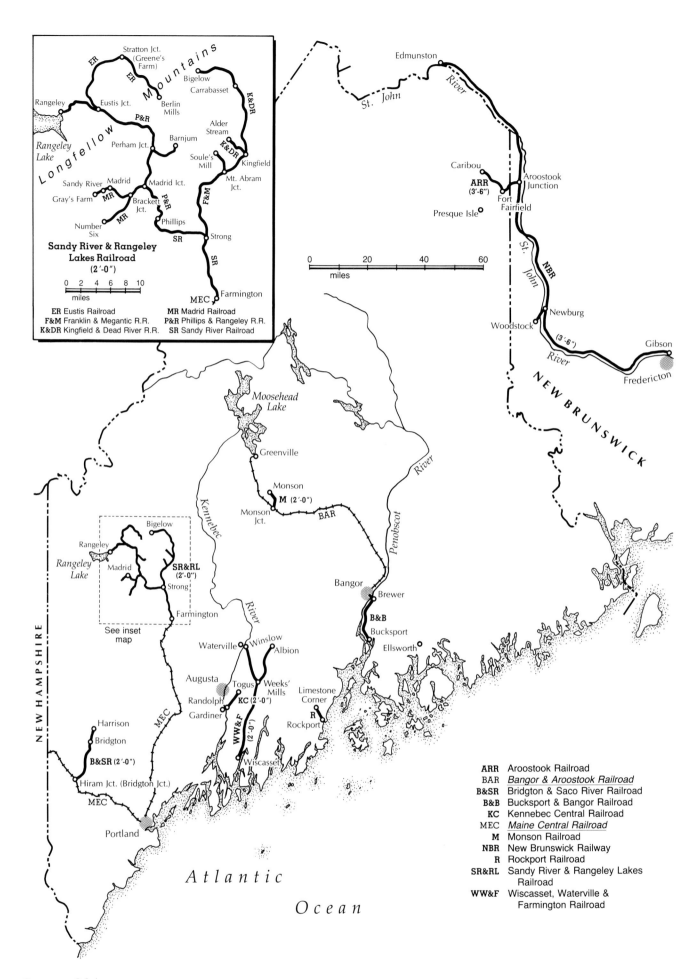

Stratton Jct.
(Greene's Farm)

ER

ER

Longfellow Mountains

Bigelow

Carrabasset

K&DR

Rangeley

Eustis Jct.

Berlin Mills

P&R

Alder Stream

Rangeley Lake

Perham Jct.

Barnjum

Soule's Mill

K&DR

Kingfield

Sandy River

Madrid

Madrid Jct.

Mt. Abram Jct.

Gray's Farm

MR

Brackett Jct.

F&M

Number Six

MR

P&R

Phillips

Strong

SR

Sandy River & Rangeley Lakes Railroad
(2'-0")

SR

0 2 4 6 8 10
miles

MEC

Farmington

ER Eustis Railroad
F&M Franklin & Megantic R.R.
K&DR Kingfield & Dead River R.R.

MR Madrid Railroad
P&R Phillips & Rangeley R.R.
SR Sandy River Railroad

Edmunston

St. John River

Caribou

ARR
(3'-6")

Aroostook Junction

Fort Fairfield

Presque Isle

St. John

NBR

Newburg

Woodstock

(3'-6")

River

Gibson

Fredericton

NEW BRUNSWICK

0 20 40 60
miles

Moosehead Lake

Greenville

Kennebec

Monson

M (2'-0")

Monson Jct.

BAR

River

Penobscot River

Bigelow

Rangeley

SR&RL
(2'-0")

Madrid

Rangeley Lake

Strong

Bangor

Brewer

B&B

Bucksport

Farmington

See inset map

NEW HAMPSHIRE

River

Ellsworth

Waterville

Winslow

Albion

Augusta

Togus

Weeks' Mills

Randolph

KC (2'-0")

Limestone Corner

Gardiner

WW&F
(2'-0")

R

Rockport

MEC

Harrison

Bridgton

Wiscasset

B&SR (2'-0")

Hiram Jct. (Bridgton Jct.)

MEC

Portland

Atlantic

Ocean

ARR   Aroostook Railroad
BAR   *Bangor & Aroostook Railroad*
B&SR Bridgton & Saco River Railroad
B&B   Bucksport & Bangor Railroad
KC   Kennebec Central Railroad
MEC   *Maine Central Railroad*
M   Monson Railroad
NBR   New Brunswick Railway
R   Rockport Railroad
SR&RL Sandy River & Rangeley Lakes
      Railroad
WW&F Wiscasset, Waterville &
      Farmington Railroad

Bucksport & Bangor No. 1, running for the successor Eastern Maine Railroad about 1883. The locomotive, a Baldwin 4-4-0 of 1879, is named for founder Richard P. Buck. (Collections of John D. Buvinger and George E. Pitchard.)

to narrow gauge ideology, and rebuilt the line to 3'-0" on October 9. Because the company while under lease to the E&NA had no equipment of its own, the conversion was simple. Lincoln planned to extend the narrow gauge either to Sullivan or Ellsworth for a steamer connection to Bar Harbor, or alternatively to build all the way to Mount Desert Island on its own rails. Neither he nor any later operator ever extended the line.

Rather, the property was reorganized as the Eastern Maine Railroad on February 1, 1882. The new corporation leased the line to the Maine Central for $9,500 per year for 999 years, as of May 1, 1883. The Maine Central immediately undertook work on conversion and completed the job by the end of May, incidentally giving the line the distinction unique among the narrow gauges of having been converted to 4'-8½" from both broad and narrow gauge. The line served as the Bucksport branch of the Maine Central and as such is still in existence as of this writing.

REFERENCE: Charles E. Fisher, "Locomotives of the Maine Central R.R.," Railway & Locomotive Historical Society *Bulletin*, no. 55 (1941), p. 72.

Kennebec Central Railroad
Gauge: 2'-0"

Smallest of the two-foot gauge railroads in Maine was the Kennebec Central, which ran only five miles from Randolph, a town across the Kennebec River from Gardiner, to the National Soldiers' Home at Togus. The railroad was promoted by local businessmen in the Gardiner area, incorporated on

September 12, 1889, and opened on July 23, 1890. The line was lightly graded and laid with only 25-pound rail. Terminal facilities and a small shop were at Randolph. The railroad had no physical connection with any other railroad. Freight, which was mainly coal inbound to the Soldiers' Home, was interchanged with the Maine Central by horse drayage from Gardiner, or unloaded from barges on the Kennebec, which was navigable in this region. Like the Maine narrow gauges generally, the company operated with Forney 0-4-4 locomotives, of which the first came from Baldwin in 1890. A second, a particularly handsome example, came from the Portland Company in 1891. The company had two coaches of "bowling alley" configuration, two boxcars, and six flatcars. The locomotives and coaches were fitted with vacuum brakes, but the freight equipment had only handbrakes. The railroad used link-and-pin couplings throughout its history.

Initially, the railroad was largely a passenger carrier. Relatives of Soldiers' Home residents were among the principal riders, but the Home attracted general traffic to baseball games and band concerts. This traffic was reduced when a rural trolley line was completed between Augusta and Togus in 1901. The management in 1890 had projected an extension of ten miles to the hamlet of China Village, but this was a most unpromising terminus, and no building was accomplished.

In the 1920s the management replaced the original motive power with two secondhand Forneys, Bridgton & Saco River No. 3 and Sandy River & Rangeley Lakes No. 6, both Portland locomotives. When the Soldiers' Home shifted to truck transport for its coal in the late 1920s, the railroad became unprofitable. The automobile had already attracted most of the passenger traffic. Operations ceased on June 29, 1929, but there was some hope locally for revival of the railroad. The Depression rendered such plans vain. The railroad was removed in 1933 and the rails, rolling stock, and locomotives were sold to the Wiscasset, Waterville & Farmington.

REFERENCES: H. T. Crittenden, "The Kennebec Central Railroad," Railway & Locomotive Historical Society *Bulletin*, no. 57 (1942), pp. 103–11; Moody, *The Maine Two-Footers*, pp. 1–5, 155–66.

Monson Railroad
Gauge: 2'-0"

The Bangor & Piscataquis Railroad, which became the Greenville branch of the

Bangor & Aroostook, followed the valley of the Piscataquis River, missing the village of Monson by some four miles. Businessmen in Monson with collaborators in Portland, Maine, and Lowell, Massachusetts, organized the Monson Railroad on November 1, 1882, to build a connection. They chose the 2'-0" gauge, becoming the first promoters unconnected with George E. Mansfield to do so. The line was built 6.16 miles from Monson to a point on the B&P named Monson Junction, and opened on October 22, 1883. A spur of two miles was built from Monson to a mine of the Monson Slate Co. Throughout the railroad's history its traffic was mainly from this source, and in 1909 the slate company succeeded to ownership of the carrier.

The railroad was a very simple installation. It was operated with two Hinkley 0-4-4 Forney locomotives, various freight cars (mainly flatcars on which the slate was handled), and a single 30-foot combine from the Laconia Car Co. The locomotives were replaced with Forneys of similar character from the Vulcan Iron Works in 1912 and 1918. Throughout its history, the railroad used only steam brakes on the locomotives for train operation, plus handbrakes on the rolling stock when spotting cars. The railroad used link-and-pin couplers to the end. Because the railroad operated only in the daytime, it did not equip its locomotives with headlights until ordered to do so by the Interstate Commerce Commission. In the early years, a locomotive and the combine, sometimes with freight cars, met each passenger train on the connecting standard gauge.

The railroad was uniformly unprofitable, surviving only as a facility of the slate company. With the conversion of the public to highways in the 1920s, the line's common carrier status became progressively more nominal. Passengers in the 1930s were frequently handled in highway vehicles of the slate company when there was no occasion to run mixed trains. Passenger service was discontinued on November 1, 1938. Thereafter the railroad handled virtually no traffic unrelated to the slate company. A decision to drop the railroad in favor of trucks was widely anticipated. In the fall of 1943 the management embargoed the railroad, and removed it during the winter of 1943–44.

REFERENCES: H. T. Crittenden, "The Monson Railroad," Railway & Locomotive Historical Society *Bulletin*, no. 57 (1942), pp. 87–93; Moody, *The Maine Two-Footers*, pp. 32–40, 145–53.

Rockport Railroad

A 3'-0" railroad in a state where 2'-0" was the norm for narrow gauge, this carrier was a specialized hauler of lime from quarries at Limestone Corner to kilns on the Rockport waterfront. Only three miles long, the railroad was a common carrier, lightly constructed with 25-pound rail. The line had 11 bridges and trestles ranging from 74 to 322 feet in length. As built in 1886, the line cost only slightly over $20,000. It had two locomotives and several dump cars. There were only three employees, and no passenger service was ever provided.

The railroad ceased operation in 1896 when the lime traffic was lost to the Rockland, Thomaston & Camden Street Railway. Initially, the line was left intact, but the rails were removed slowly and the locomotives sold for scrap in 1934.

REFERENCE: Charles D. Heseltine, "Additional Maine Narrow Gauge Railroads," *Narrow Gauge Society Newsletter*, 2, no. 1 (1972), p. 47.

Sandy River & Rangeley Lakes Railroad
Gauge: 2'-0"

The largest American 2'-0" railroad, the Sandy River & Rangeley Lakes was produced in 1908 by a merger of several predecessor companies, whose individual histories are given below. The railroad was mainly a service facility for lumber companies in the Maine woods, but it also carried a substantial traffic in passengers to resorts on the Rangeley Lakes in the summer months. At its peak, the railroad had about 101 miles of line, plus some nine miles of lumber spurs.

Sandy River Railroad

Samuel P. Cushman of Avon, Maine, after observing the Billerica & Bedford, concluded that a 2'-0" railroad was the appropriate method of developing northern Franklin County. He interested Samuel Farmer, N. B. Beal, Captain C. W. Howard,

An excursion train at Carrabasset. The equipment is lettered for the Franklin & Megantic. (Robert C. Jones collection.)

P. H. Stubbs, and others in the idea. Farmer invited George E. Mansfield, promoter of the Billerica & Bedford, to address meetings in Strong, Madrid, Phillips, and Rangeley in March 1878. Although the towns were communities of fewer than 1,000 people each, the promotion was successful, and the project was incorporated as the Sandy River Railroad on April 29, 1878. The route was surveyed by Thomas Appleton, who estimated the cost at only $1,500 per mile. A. L. Brown of Concord, New Hampshire, who had acquired the locomotives and the rolling stock of the Billerica & Bedford, proved willing to trade them for $20,000 in stock of the new railroad. The management sent the two locomotives back to Hinkley,

the builder, to be converted from coal to wood, and to be rearranged to run boiler-forward in the normal fashion of Forneys. A relatively curvaceous route along the east bank of the Sandy River was chosen in hopes of limiting the investment to the projected $1,500 per mile. Ground was broken on June 5 and the railroad completed from Farmington to Phillips, 18 miles, on No-

vember 20, 1879. The shops were located at Phillips. Mansfield, who had served as superintendent during construction, resigned in September 1880. Toward the end of the year there was some interest in building an extension from Farmington about 40 miles to Gardiner at the head of navigation on the Kennebec River. Some years later construction actually was undertaken, but the project was never completed. A direct southern extension to the Portland area was also discussed but not implemented.

The railroad was always mainly dependent upon outbound lumber movements. Inbound, it handled foodstuffs and general merchandise, but such traffic declined after extension of the Portland & Rumford Falls to Oquossoc on Rangeley Lake in 1895.

Franklin & Megantic Railroad

S. W. Sargent and other local lumbermen formed the Franklin & Megantic on July 1, 1883, to develop virgin timberland north of the existing Sandy River Railroad. Tracklaying on the 15-mile line from Strong to Kingfield was completed on December 10, 1884, but heavy snows prevented operation until the following spring. This was a small operation of only two locomotives, but about 1893 the management entered into an agreement with the Sandy River whereby the larger railroad would provide the F&M with additional motive power and rolling stock.

The F&M became delinquent on its debt in the mid-1890s and was reorganized in 1897 by the former bondholders as the Franklin & Megantic Railway. The new

Terminal facilities of the Sandy River & Rangeley Lakes at Kingfield in 1924. (Robert C. Jones collection.)

owners immediately put the line up for sale and in 1898 sold it to Josiah S. Maxcy and his associates.

Kingfield & Dead River Railroad

On June 19, 1893, officials of the Franklin & Megantic formed this corporation to build a continuation of their line north from Kingfield about ten miles to Carrabasset to open new timberlands. The new railroad had no equipment of its own. Upon the F&M's reorganization in 1897, the new owners showed no interest in acquiring the K&DR. Maxcy, upon acquiring the F&M, bought the K&DR in the name of the F&M at an auction of August 2, 1898. He extended the line six miles to a sawmill at Bigelow in late December 1899. The line later had two long spurs to lumber camps, the Alder Stream branch and the Hammondfield spur.

Phillips & Rangeley Railroad

Henry P. Closson and Calvin Putnam organized this railroad on April 17, 1889, to penetrate a stand of spruce that they planned to cut. The railroad was a continuation to the northwest of the Sandy River main line, with which it connected by means of a long wooden covered bridge at Phillips. By the end of 1890 track had been laid to Dead River (24 miles), and the railroad reached Rangeley at the east end of the Rangeley Lakes (28.6 miles) on June 10, 1891. The ownership changed hands shortly thereafter; at the shareholders' meeting of October 21, 1891, Arthur Sewall, president of the Maine Central, was elected president of the company. The main office was

shifted to Portland, although the operating headquarters remained in Phillips. The railroad, which operated with four locomotives, proved chronically unprofitable. It was mainly a service facility for the Redington Mill, but it enjoyed a seasonal passenger traffic to Rangeley. A. B. Gilman was elected president in 1893, and was followed by Calvin Putnam, head of the Redington Mill, in 1897.

In 1903 the management attempted to build two extensions by means of subsidiaries: the Rangeley Railroad to run from Rangeley to Oquossoc (7 miles), and the Moosehead Railroad to build from Stratton Village to Flagstaff. Neither received a charter from the Maine Railroad Commission.

Madrid Railroad

The P&R did successfully form two subsidiaries to build branches into timber stands. The first was the Madrid Railroad, formed April 29, 1902. Under this name the P&R built from Madrid Junction, on the main line 5.4 miles north of Phillips, 5.3 miles southwest to a lumber camp called No. 6. A branch was built from Brackett Junction to Madrid Village (3.5 miles) in 1903. This was subsequently extended 3.4 miles to Gray's Farm. The Madrid Railroad had no motive power or rolling stock of its own.

Eustis Railroad

The P&R's second subsidiary, the Eustis Railroad, was chartered by the Railroad Commission on April 29, 1903. The 10.5-mile route was an arc to the northeast from Eustis Junction, six miles short of Rangeley, to Greene's Farm. Track continued about five miles to a camp at Berlin Mills, but this portion was not a common carrier. The Eustis, unlike the Madrid, had its own equipment and three Baldwin 0-4-4 For-

Phillips station about 1900. The Sandy River & Rangeley Lakes had its peak lumber movements in winter. (Robert C. Jones collection.)

Trainman Jim Mitchell has just lined up switch for locomotive No. 8 at the Sandy River & Rangeley Lakes' Phillips station. (Betty Montgomery collection, from Robert C. Jones.)

Sandy River No. 4 about to leave Rangeley with a southbound train around 1900. (C. B. Atherton collection, from Robert C. Jones.)

neys. Both its locomotives and cars were mixed freely with those of the P&R. On April 5, 1904, the P&R leased the Eustis, agreeing to pay its operating and maintenance expenses. The Phillips & Rangeley, Madrid, and Eustis railroads were put in receivership under Seth M. Carter on February 1, 1905, even though the Eustis was not insolvent. Carter issued receiver's certificates for the P&R and the Madrid, but not for the Eustis. This arrangement was to complicate the disposition of the three railroads.

Sandy River & Rangeley Lakes Railroad

In July 1892 Josiah Maxcy and Weston Lewis, lumber operators of Gardiner,

Maine, announced that they had secured a majority interest in the Sandy River Railroad. Maxcy moved slowly to consolidate the entire Franklin County 2'-0" network into a single railroad. As mentioned, in 1898 he bought the Franklin & Megantic after its reorganization of the previous year. On January 30, 1908, he merged the Sandy River, the F&M, and the Kingfield & Dead River into the newly formed Sandy River & Rangeley Lakes Railroad. The new corporation bought $10,000 of the receiver's certificates that Carter had issued for the Phillips & Rangeley and the Madrid, and demanded payment. This action precipitated a receiver's sale on June 10, 1908, at which Maxcy bought the two railroads for incorporation into the SR&RL. Because no

certificates had been issued for the Eustis, that railroad became independent in the hands of the former P&R management, headed by Fletcher Pope. The directors elected to continue the receivership. Carter arranged for the SR&RL to operate the line under lease, but operation was shut down in 1909. On August 24, 1911, the SR&RL bought the Eustis at auction for $75,000, thereby achieving unity of the entire system. The Greene's Farm–Berlin Mills extension was abandoned upon acquisition, but service on the inner 6.24 miles of the Eustis was resumed in 1915.

Normal operation was three passenger trains per day from Farmington to Rangeley in the summer months and two daily in the off-season. Each train had a connection for Bigelow from Strong. The railroad was profitable, earning $6,355 in its first full year.

In 1911 the Maine Central bought all of the outstanding stock of the company for $240,000, taking control of the property on August 31. In 1912 the new owner built the narrow gauge's last major extension, a branch of 3.7 miles from Perham Junction on the former Phillips & Rangeley to Barnjum. The railroad's traffic peaked in 1919, when it handled nearly 20,000 cars of pulpwood. It also bought its last and largest locomotive, a Baldwin 2-6-2, in 1919. Its heavier power—2-6-0 and 2-6-2 locomotives—typically worked the main line, and the Forney locomotives operated over the entire railroad.

In 1923 the company suffered a roundhouse fire at Phillips, losing three locomotives. Revenues had fallen steadily since 1919, with the result that bondholders secured a receivership on July 1, 1923. Maxcy and Herbert S. Wing of Kingfield were appointed receivers. The Maine Central, which had apparently soured on the narrow gauge, turned its stock over to Maxcy, who supervised the railroad's finances. Wing superintended the operation. Hard-surfaced highways were spreading throughout the area, and by the onset of the Depression the resort traffic, which had warranted the famous parlor car *Rangeley* of 1901, was almost entirely gone. Steam passenger trains were discontinued in favor of mixed trains or motor cars the railroad had built from automobiles. The railroad was now dependent on traffic from two pulpwood mills. Loss of this traffic caused the railroad to close on July 8, 1932. The Lawrence Plywood Co. petitioned the Railroad Commission to open a portion of the railroad. The main line from Farmington to Phillips and the F&M branch from Strong to Carrabasset were reopened on April 17, 1933.

Sandy River & Rangeley Lakes No. 23, a 2-6-2, was a heavy and powerful locomotive for a 2'-0" railroad. It is shown with a freight at Strong, Maine. (Robert C. Jones collection.)

The remainder was largely dismantled in the fall of 1934. The receivers put the active portion up for sale on May 18, 1935. It was bought by scrap dealers Maurice Sackoff and Harry S. Kamenski, who resold it to the H. E. Salzberg Co. Because of the receivership, closure required approval of the Maine Supreme Court. When that was in hand on June 28, the Salzberg interests ran a final train on June 30, then closed the railroad. The track was removed in the summer of 1936. Some of the equipment survives at the Edaville Railroad at South Carver, Massachusetts.

REFERENCES: H. Temple Crittenden, "The Sandy River & Rangeley Lakes," Railway & Locomotive Historical Society *Bulletin*, no. 57 (1942), pp. 15–72; idem, *The Maine Scenic Route* (Parsons, W.Va.: McClain Printing Co., 1966); Moody, *The Maine Two-Footers*, pp. 12–25, 55–122, 197–99; L. Peter Cornwall and Jack W. Farrell, *Ride the Sandy River* (Edmonds, Wash.: Pacific Fast Mail, 1973); Robert C. Jones, *Two Feet Between the Rails* (Silverton, Colo.: Sundance Publications, 2 vols., 1979, 1980).

Wiscasset, Waterville & Farmington Railroad
Gauge: 2'-0"

The earliest serious effort to build a railroad from the small port of Wiscasset to inland points was the Kennebec & Wiscasset, chartered on April 15, 1854, to build to Augusta via Togus. Nothing was accomplished, but on February 14, 1873, Wiscasset businessmen, hoping to attract some of the Canadian grain moving to Portland over the Grand Trunk, secured authority from the

state legislature to change the name of the company to Wiscasset & Quebec Railroad and to extend the projected route to Quebec. Some of the promoters apparently envisioned the line as a continuous narrow gauge from the Canadian prairie provinces to Wiscasset. The local harbor was an ample one, which had been developed only for local traffic. No rail was laid until well after the peak years of narrow gauge building. In 1892 a route was surveyed inland to Burnham and Pittsfield on the Sebasticook River, about 60 miles. The actual attainment was only about two-thirds of that. The principal promoters were Richard T. Rundlett and W. D. Patterson, who became president and secretary-treasurer, respectively.

Grading began in June 1894 and track-laying in October. The gauge of 2'-0" was adopted largely because of the success of the Sandy River Railroad, and partly in the hope of eventual connection with other narrow gauges. Rundlett endeavored unsuccessfully to have the Kennebec Central extend from Togus to Cooper's Mills for a connection, and also proposed a three-rail line from Weeks' Mills to Waterville. Neither of these efforts was successful, and the line managed to be only a minor local carrier inland from Wiscasset. Regular service was established from Wiscasset to Weeks' Mills, 28 miles, on March 1, 1895. Trains began running to Albion, 43.5 miles, on November 4, 1895.

In the spring of 1897 the management graded the 11.75 miles to Burnham and laid track for about half the distance, but the Maine Central refused to allow the narrow gauge to cross its Belfast branch en route. In October the W&Q secured authority from

the Maine Railroad Commission to lay a temporary diamond for use until July 1, 1898, and then to build an overhead crossing. Oddly, the company made no effort to exercise these rights, but rather discontinued its efforts north of Albion without immediately removing the rails. Instead, the company turned its attention to the northwest, attempting to build through Waterville to a connection with the Sandy River & Rangeley Lakes at Farmington. To accomplish this, the management organized two subsidiaries, the Waterville & Wiscasset Railroad to build from Weeks' Mills to Waterville, and the Franklin, Somerset & Kennebec Railway to run from Waterville through Oakland, Smithfield, Belgrade, Rome, Mercer, and Sharon to Farmington. Virtually the entire route was graded in 1898 and 1899.

With the extension uncompleted, the W&Q went bankrupt on July 1, 1900. The receivers appointed in the following month attempted to operate only between Wiscasset and Albion. The railroad was reorganized as the Wiscasset, Waterville & Farmington Railroad on February 5, 1901. The new corporation assumed control on March 29, with Leonard Atwood of Farmington as president. Atwood, an inventor of some note, pressed forward with the extension, reportedly laying some rail in the vicinity of New Sharon. The Maine Central was again in a position to prevent an expansion of the railroad. The narrow gauge would have been forced to cross the MEC's right-of-way entering Farmington, and the larger railroad refused. In this instance, the Maine Railroad Commission on August 26, 1901, declined to order a crossing. The effect was to abort the Farmington extension. A bridge across the Kennebec River between Waterville and Winslow, of which one pier

Little Wheels (Clinton, Maine, 1971); Robert C. Jones and David L. Register, *Two Feet to Tidewater: The Wiscasset, Waterville & Farmington Railway* (Boulder, Colo.: Pruett Publishing Co., 1987).

Forney No. 2 of the Wiscasset, Waterville & Farmington stands on the wharf at Wiscasset in 1932, near the end of the railroad's history. (Robert C. Jones collection.)

and a portion of another had been built, was abandoned, and the rail was removed from the New Sharon area. Atwood's management removed the rail from the uncompleted track north of Albion and relaid it on the grade between Weeks' Mills and Winslow. This line of 14 miles was opened as a branch on July 9, 1902. The company moved its offices to Waterville and established a shop at Winslow. Initially, most of the traffic was between Winslow and Albion, rather than Wiscasset.

The railroad was uniformly unprofitable, and on October 7, 1905, was again put in receivership. Carson D. Peck, the owner of a chain of stores in New England, bought the property on December 4, 1906, and reorganized it as the Wiscasset, Waterville & Farmington Railway on January 1, 1907. Peck effected various economies and kept the railroad mildly profitable, mainly on lumber movements, but with some traffic in grain and potatoes. The line operated with 0-4-4 and 2-4-4 Forneys and a 2-6-0. Peck died in April 1915. The Winslow line north of North Vassalboro (4 miles) was abandoned in 1915 and the remainder of the branch in 1916. Thereafter, the railroad typically ran a daily passenger-and-milk train from Albion to Wiscasset and return, with an additional round-trip from Wiscasset to Weeks' Mills. Peck's heirs sold the railroad to a cooperative of local farmers for $60,000 in 1926. In 1930 the Wiscasset–Weeks' Mills train was discontinued and the Albion-Wiscasset train was made mixed.

The railroad again went bankrupt, and S. J. Sewall, an associate of Peck, and H. P. Crowell were appointed receivers on November 30, 1930. In December Frank W. Winter bought control of the railroad and

restored it to bare profitability, which was enough to allow the receivers to be discharged without reorganization. The railroad retained a mail contract and carried some lumber, but had lost most of the rest of its traffic to trucks. A roundhouse fire in 1931 destroyed the 2-6-0 and the best of the Forneys. The receivership was reestablished on December 31. The railroad was sold to Malcolm Philbrick, Winter's son-in-law; the change in ownership was only nominal. In January 1933 Winter bought the entire roster and track of the Kennebec Central, and put both of the smaller road's Forneys to work on the WW&F. When inspectors from Augusta ordered work on the motive power and the trestle over the harbor at Wiscasset on which the railroad terminated, Winter decided to attempt only to get out the current supply of lumber awaiting movement, and then to shut down the railroad rather than to invest in it further. Winter had brought out about half the lumber when, at 7:23 A.M. on June 15, 1933, locomotive No. 8, one of the former KC engines, taking the daily southbound mixed train, hit a broken rail below Whitefield and derailed. Winter decided against any further attempts to operate, and without even rerailing the locomotive, moved immediately to abandon the line. The rails were attached by a paint company in November 1934 and removed. The rest of the line was scrapped in 1937.

REFERENCES: H. T. Crittenden, "Wiscasset, Waterville & Farmington Railway," Railway & Locomotive Historical Society *Bulletin*, no. 57 (1942), pp. 114–35; Moody, *The Maine Two-Footers*, pp. 7–12, 167–92; Clinton F. Thurlow, *The WW&F Two-Footer* (Weeks' Mills, Maine, 1964); Ruby Crosby Wiggin, *Big Dreams and*

Maryland

Maryland Central Railroad

S. G. Boyd, after building the Peach Bottom Railway between York and Delta, Pennsylvania, turned his attention to a line from Baltimore to Delta. He was motivated in part by the prospective traffic in slate from the quarries at Delta, but he was also interested in intermediate local traffic. Along with William H. Waters of Bel Air and other local businessmen, he formed the Baltimore, Towsontown, Dulaney's Valley & Delta Narrow Gauge Railway in 1876. They acquired a grade running east from Towsontown (Towson) to the Gunpowder River from the failed and unbuilt Maryland & Pennsylvania Railroad of 1873. They had no apparent entry into Baltimore, but the Baltimore, Hampden & Towsontown Railway had since 1874 graded part of the seven miles from North Avenue, Baltimore, to Towsontown in the intention of having a local passenger line. The management had not been able to finance its bridges and trestles, and had no immediate prospect of finishing the railroad. The BH&T's directors, accordingly, accepted Boyd's proposal of a merger, and the two lines were unified on December 16, 1878, as the Baltimore & Delta Railway. By the end of 1879 the management had graded the route from the Gunpowder River to Delta, including a tortuous approach to Bel Air, the principal intermediate town. The railroad was to run across a drainage pattern, with a choppy profile, continual curvature, and the usual frequent trestles of narrow gauge practice. The railroad had exhausted its resources, but its vice-president placed $399,500 in bonds to allow track to be laid beginning at Baltimore on August 23, 1881. The rail-

The Baltimore & Delta's No. 3 was one of a pair of heavy Consolidations built for the Denver & Rio Grande, but diverted on completion. Their 30-ton weights contributed mightily to the line's problems of weak trestles.

road was opened to Towsontown on April 17, 1882, and on August 12 to Loch Raven (11 miles), site of a municipal reservoir, where the railroad management built a pavilion and picnic ground.

Because more than $500,000 had now been expended on the Baltimore & Delta, it suddenly became of interest to the directors of the Maryland Central Railroad, an unsuccessful project of 1867 to build a standard gauge railroad from Baltimore to Philadelphia, crossing the Susquehanna River at Conowingo. Before the MC project failed, the City of Baltimore had agreed to guarantee $600,000 in MC bonds once $500,000 had been spent on construction. The MC's directors argued that if the B&D were merged into it, Baltimore might honor the guaranty. Boyd and his associates accepted this reasoning and merged the B&D into the Maryland Central on August 28, 1882. Baltimore refused to honor the guaranty, but construction continued under the Maryland Central's name. Rails reached Glenarm (15 miles) in November 1882 and Bel Air (27 miles) on June 21, 1883. The MC sent a locomotive to the York & Peach Bottom and began construction south from Delta in August 1883. The gap between Bel Air and Delta was formally closed at a point near Rocks on December 31, 1883. Including a mile of track in Pennsylvania organized under a subsidiary, the Slate Ridge & Delta Railroad, the completed Maryland Central was 44 miles. Regular passenger service was inaugurated on January 21, 1884. The Y&PB's morning train from York and its local from Peach Bottom were scheduled to connect with the MC for Baltimore. Inevitably, unification of the two narrow gauges would be a major goal of the management.

The railroad did relatively well, grossing $250 to $500 per day, but partly because of

failure to secure Baltimore's guaranty of its bonds, went bankrupt in October 1884. John C. Wrenshall was appointed receiver, and Boyd left the railroad permanently. The corporation was reorganized on December 10, 1888, as the Maryland Central Railway under John K. Cowen and William Gilmor. As early as January 1889 they announced that they had secured control of the Y&PB, which they proceeded to lease. Through service from Baltimore to York was established on May 19, 1889, on a schedule of about four and a half hours for the 77 miles. Because the Northern Central (Pennsylvania) ran directly between the two cities with a line of only 57 miles, the narrow gauge was almost wholly a local carrier. The management merged the Maryland and Pennsylvania lines into the Baltimore & Lehigh Railroad on May 5, 1891. Cowen and Gilmor proposed to convert the railroad, build south from North Avenue to a terminal near the Western Maryland's Hillen Station, construct a Baltimore Belt Line for better local freight termination, and extend to the Susquehanna in hopes of bridging the river for a connection with the Philadelphia & Reading to the northeast. They also planned to abandon about 12 miles of the Maryland Central's original line from Baldwin to Sharon in favor of a direct line of only about eight miles via

Pleasantville in the Twining Valley. They proposed to retain two miles of the original line from Vale to Bel Air as part of a branch from Pleasantville to Bel Air to connect with the projected Deer Creek & Susquehanna. This alteration would have avoided four major trestles and eliminated the worst portion of the main line. The management was able to execute none of these projects, but expended enough resources on them to prevent immediate conversion. In demonstration of the desirability of the bypass of the four trestles, one of them, the Overshot trestle at Laurel Brook, collapsed on April 16, 1891, under a train of 13 cars of fertilizer being handled by three locomotives. The disaster killed four employees, and a fifth died of sunstroke while helping to clear the wreck. On March 3, 1892, a passenger train derailed off the Little Gunpowder Falls trestle, killing its engineer. The two accidents cost the railroad three locomotives, and a fourth perished in a roundhouse fire at Baltimore on October 10, 1892. The railroad became probably the worst example of a narrow gauge that could not raise the funds to convert, but lacked enough motive power and equipment to carry the traffic it had.

Although the railroad suffered greatly from this sequence of events, Cowen and Gilmor signed a contract turning the entire Baltimore & Lehigh over to the Baltimore Forwarding & Railroad Co.—a corporation formed by a B&L shareholder, John Henry Miller—on January 2, 1893, for conversion for $1.5 million. Unfortunately, this attempt at conversion proved stillborn, for the B&L went bankrupt later in 1893. Separate receivers were appointed, W. H. Bosley for the Maryland trackage. The Pennsylvania mileage was sold to Warren F. Walworth of Cleveland, who organized it as the York Southern Railroad in 1894 and converted it in 1895. The Maryland line was sold to John Wilson Brown of the Baltimore banking family of Alexander Brown & Sons, who reorganized it as the Baltimore & Lehigh Railway on July 31, 1894. Brown began installing standard length ties but was initially unable to convert the railroad. In February 1899 it suffered one of its characteristic accidents, a derailment on the Winter's Run trestle, in which it lost yet another locomotive. The shareholders voted on February 3, 1900, to convert the railroad. The work began in April; five standard gauge 4-6-0s were bought from the Richmond Locomotive Works. On arrival they proved too heavy for the line's trestles and were resold. The line began standard gauge operation in August with rented Baltimore & Ohio equipment.

Brown & Sons finally brought about the unification of the York Southern and Baltimore & Lehigh in 1901. The York Southern accepted the financial firm's offer on February 2 and the Baltimore & Lehigh on February 12. Two days later Brown formed the Maryland & Pennsylvania Railroad. This company was to be among the most severe sufferers from operating a railroad built to narrow gauge standards. The Baltimore & Lehigh had made its conversion without bypassing the difficult Baldwin-Sharon trackage as proposed in 1891. Partly because of the limitations of its physical plant and partly because of its limited traffic potential, the line was forced to operate short trains and small locomotives until the end of the steam era, a situation making it at length a local and even national curiosity. By means of a loan from the Reconstruction Finance Corporation, the railroad avoided bankruptcy in the 1930s and has survived to the present with the incorporation of 1901. The traffic of the Maryland portion of the railroad was almost all of a character to be vulnerable to highway competition. After some major inbound movements of steel to a pipeline passing through the area in 1955 and limestone to the Catholic cathedral being built in Baltimore in 1956, traffic on the line almost disappeared. The management abandoned the track from Baltimore to Whiteford in the Delta quarrying district on June 11, 1958. The remaining two miles from Whiteford to Delta remained in service with the north end of the Maryland & Pennsylvania until June 14, 1978, and were formally abandoned under an ICC order of March 23, 1985.

REFERENCES: George W. Hilton, *The Ma & Pa: A History of the Maryland & Pennsylvania Railroad* (Berkeley, Calif.: Howell-North Books, 1963; 2d ed., San Diego, Calif.: Howell-North Books, 1980); collection of Charles T. Mahan, Jr.

▼ ▼ ▼ ▼

The Green Ridge Railroad of Maryland, a lumber railroad of F. Mertens' Sons of Cumberland, was chartered on November 11, 1882, and opened in 1883. At its maximum extent, achieved in 1892, it ran from a mill on the north bank of the Chesapeake & Ohio Canal opposite Okonoko, West Virginia, on the Baltimore & Ohio north to a camp called Town Creek (26 miles) about two miles south of the Pennsylvania border. The railroad regularly advertised two daily passenger trains, probably mixed trains handling passengers in a caboose. The ICC treated the line as a common carrier through 1891, but as a private carrier thereafter. The railroad ceased operation in 1894 and was removed in fiscal 1899.

Massachusetts

Billerica & Bedford Railroad
Gauge: 2'-0"

This railroad is important out of all proportion to its size or lifespan because it initiated the 2'-0" portion of the narrow gauge movement. The railroad and the vogue for 2'-0" gauge were alike the result of the activities of George E. Mansfield of Boston. In the early 1870s, Mansfield visited the Festiniog Railway in Wales, and was greatly impressed with the operation at 1'-11½" gauge. In 1875 he built an experimental line of one-third of a mile on his farm in Hazelwood, Massachusetts, reportedly of only 10" gauge. The installation had no known locomotive; the cars apparently rolled downhill and were pushed up manually. He did give it a name, however: the Sumner Heights & Hazelwood Valley Railroad.

In the fall of 1875 Mansfield learned of a project to build a railroad for local service from Bedford on the Middlesex Central to North Billerica on the Boston, Lowell & Nashua. Mansfield went to Billerica to argue for the railroad to be built at 2'-0" gauge, and he succeeded. Captain Charles A. Ranlett, the principal promoter, became president and Mansfield general manager. The corporation, the Billerica & Bedford Railroad, was incorporated May 10, 1876, and ground was broken on September 6. The town of Billerica subscribed $12,000. Mansfield originally estimated the installation at $40,000, but the final cost was about $60,000. The railroad was 8.63 miles, with a right-of-way no more than ten feet wide. The average grade was about 1 percent with a ruling grade of about 2 percent. Mansfield used 25-pound rail. He ordered two Forney locomotives from Hinkley, *Puck* and *Ariel*, each of which weighed 23,750 pounds and cost $3,500. Mansfield specified that they should be fitted to run cab-first, in hopes not only of improving

visibility and the comfort of the crew, but also of bringing the exhaust above the cars for the convenience of the passengers. Mansfield believed the standard design of a locomotive created a vacuum behind the cab that drew down smoke and maximized the fall of cinders into the coaches. Each of the locomotives had a capacity of ten nail kegs of soft coal.

The railroad was opened on September 1, 1877, and full service began about two weeks later. The cost overruns placed the company in financial difficulty immediately. The railroad served ordinary farming country, but it had a leather factory and glue works on the line at South Billerica plus a summer hotel at Silver Lake. The traffic was simply inadequate even for such a lightly built line. Holders of the floating debt of some $27,000 brought an action against the company late in 1877, and on January 30, 1878, the directors voted to place the corporation in the hands of the Massachusetts Registrar of Bankruptcy. The creditors retained Mansfield as general manager. Service was suspended June 1, 1878. The railroad was sold to creditor A. L. Brown of New Hampshire on June 6 for only $9,000. In 1879 Billerica voted at a town meeting to raise $9,000 to restore the railroad to service. Brown, however, had taken the locomotives and rolling stock to New Hampshire, and in the summer of 1878 began dismantling the track and structures.

Mansfield was unshaken in his faith in what he conceived as the authentic narrow gauge plan. He negotiated with Brown to acquire the two locomotives and rolling stock for the Sandy River Railroad in Maine, in which he had interested himself. In Maine, of course, Mansfield succeeded in making 2'-0" the narrow gauge standard.

REFERENCES: H. Temple Crittenden, "The Billerica & Bedford Railroad," Railway & Locomotive Historical Society *Bulletin*, no. 57 (1942), pp. 7–14; Linwood W. Moody, *The Maine Two-Footers* (Berkeley, Calif.: Howell-North Books, 1959), pp. 49–54; *The First Two-Foot Gauge Railroad: The Billerica & Bedford of Massachusetts—1877*, Railroadians of America, book no. 4 (1950).

Boston, Revere Beach & Lynn Railroad

Although Boston had been connected with Lynn by the Eastern Railroad since 1838, Alpheus P. Blake, a real estate operator along the north shore between the two cities, conceived of a local railroad to develop holdings of his Boston Land Co. He secured a charter for it as the Boston, Re-

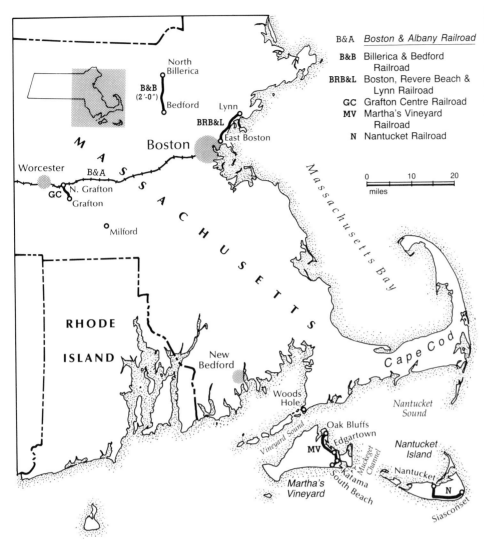

B&A	*Boston & Albany Railroad*
B&B	Billerica & Bedford Railroad
BRB&L	Boston, Revere Beach & Lynn Railroad
GC	Grafton Centre Railroad
MV	Martha's Vineyard Railroad
N	Nantucket Railroad

nue in Boston. Eight small double-ended beam-engined sidewheelers were used in the service over the course of its history.

Revenue service began on July 29, 1875, over the 8.8-mile rail line and on its ferry connection, which was about an additional mile. The railroad was unusual in operating around the clock. Initially the line was single-tracked with a passing siding at Chelsea Beach in Revere for meets of most trains. The company adopted telephonic dispatching in 1879—it was apparently the first railroad to do so. Burgeoning traffic in the 1880s caused the line to be double-tracked; the job was virtually complete by 1888. The line's success made it a model for promoters in other portions of the Boston metropolitan area, in Chicago, and elsewhere, though none of the projects was executed.

The BRB&L had a single branch, a loop through the town of Winthrop on a small peninsula east of the main line. This had its origins in 1876, when Captain Samuel G. Irwin took over the horsecar line in Winthrop and formed the Boston, Winthrop & Point Shirley Railroad to replace the car line with a steam railroad. Irwin chose 3'-0" for conformity with the BRB&L, and built the line from the BRB&L's Winthrop station (Winthrop Junction) in East Boston to Buchanan Street in Winthrop (2 miles). The line was opened on June 7, 1877, but between 1878 and 1883 was partly relocated along the shore and extended about a mile to Great Head and Short Beach. Blake, who had left the BRB&L in 1878 after some acrimonious dealings with the other directors, in 1880 formed the Eastern Junction, Broad

vere Beach & Lynn Railroad on May 23, 1874. The charter provided that the railroad be a common carrier of freight; but as far as is known, its only freight was newspapers handled on its passenger trains. It proved to be, as intended, a heavy-duty passenger railroad, which carried the local population into Boston as commuters and the Boston urban population to various seashore resorts. Construction began May 22, 1875. Blake adopted 3'-0" for the usual reasons of capital economy, but only 30-pound rail and the locomotives conformed to narrow gauge standards. The coaches were of standard gauge dimensions, and standard gauge ties were laid from the outset. The rail was increased to 50-pound beginning in 1885 and to 60-pound in 1904. The railroad however, maintained a devotion to the Mason Bogie locomotive amounting almost to an addiction, ordering 11 from Mason over the course of its history, and 21 from other builders. The railroad was planned with a ferry connection from East Boston to a terminal at Rowes Wharf on Atlantic Ave-

Boston, Revere Beach & Lynn No. 12 carried on its pilot the sheet metal ice scrapers that were a characteristic of the railroad. Note also the muffler for the Eames vacuum braking system on the top of the cab. (Ed Bond collection.)

Sound Pier & Point Shirley Railroad as a standard gauge rival to the BRB&L, intending to build from a junction with the Eastern Railroad near Crescent Beach south along the ocean shore to a ferry terminal at Point Shirley. Before the line was completed, it was merged with the BW&PS and an unbuilt railroad into the Boston, Winthrop & Shore Railroad, which dual gauged the line along the shore, extended it to Point Shirley, and on June 30, 1884, established ferry service into Boston. A storm on Thanksgiving Day, 1885, devastated the line, ending service on its standard gauge division and resulting in a cutback of the narrow gauge from the ferry terminal to Cottage Hill. The company lacked the resources to rebuild the line, and leased the property to the BRB&L in mid-1886. Instead of rebuilding the line, the BRB&L made use of portions of both lines to build a loop of 3.5 miles from Fairview Avenue about a mile from Winthrop Junction on the former BW&PS south through central Winthrop, up along somewhat over a mile of the oceanfront, and back through the north end of Winthrop to the junction at Fairview Avenue. The loop was fitted with nine stations and opened in 1888. No effort was made to restore the line to Point Shirley pier.

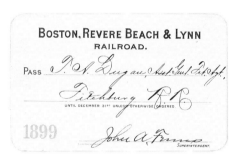

The BRB&L did well in the 1890s, partly because of the success of the amusement park at Revere Beach. As part of a municipal effort to improve the area around the park, the railroad relocated its track about 250 to 300 feet to the west in 1897. In 1911 the BRB&L took over the Point Shirley Street Railway, which had been built in the previous year by Charles L. Ridgeway, one of the amusement promoters at Revere Beach. The line operated from the BRB&L's Winthrop Beach Station to Point Shirley with gas-electric cars and a battery car until the late 1920s; the railroad then replaced it with a bus connection, which operated as long as the railroad did.

In 1914 the railroad collected 7,248,539 fares, which in light of its limited mileage made it probably the most heavily traveled steam rail line in the country. Inevitably, electrification was contemplated. The New

York, New Haven & Hartford considered buying the line in 1911 for conversion to standard gauge and electrification. The railroad was sold in November 1927 by the Massachusetts interests who had controlled it to Eastern Railway Associates, a subsidiary of the New York engineering firm Hemphill & Wells. The new owners moved immediately to electrify the line with a conventional 600-volt overhead direct current system. The original intention was to buy new 3'-0" electric cars from Brill, but in the interest of economy, the owners decided to install trolley poles and electric motors on the existing open-platform equipment. Catenary supports were erected during the summer of 1928 and the rails were bonded. Electric service began on the main line on October 11, 1928, and on the Winthrop loop on November 15. The last steam train ran on December 2. Normal practice was to run three-car trains by using the trolley pole only on one car and transmitting power to the other two by a bus line. Remarkably, the railroad continued to use its Miller hook coupler after electrification, and was the last American carrier to use the device.

On the basis of 1929 patronage, the $1.4 million invested in the electrification appeared justified, but the onslaught of the Depression, the decline of the shoe industry in Lynn, and continuing conversion of the public to the automobile in the 1930s quickly demonstrated the reverse. In 1930 the company increased its Boston-Lynn fare from 10¢ to 15¢, and in 1932–33 bought four streetcars from the Eastern Massachusetts Street Railway for local service on the Winthrop loop and owl service on the main line. Completion of the Sumner Tunnel parallel to the railroad's ferry line in 1934 was a serious blow. The opening of Suffolk Downs on the line in 1935 was a help, but contributed to the railroad's chronic problem of seasonality in traffic. The Massachusetts legislature in 1934 considered a measure to require the Boston Elevated Railway to take over the narrow gauge for conversion and integration into its system, but the Elevated showed no interest, apparently thinking abandonment was inevitable.

The BRB&L filed for bankruptcy on July 13, 1937. The hurricane of September 21, 1938, damaged the property, and abandonment of the Atlantic Avenue elevated on September 30 deprived the line of its direct connection with the Boston rapid transit system. The railroad withdrew its oldest active ferry, *Dartmouth*, in 1939. In July of 1939 the management petitioned the Department of Public Utilities for abandonment. An effort to transfer the line to the Metropolitan Transit Commission failed,

and the railroad was abandoned upon the arrival of the ferry *Brewster* at Boston at 11:47 P.M. on January 27, 1940. In 1952–54 the right-of-way to Revere was utilized for 4.3 miles in building the present Blue Line of the Massachusetts Bay Transportation Authority. The remainder of the right-of-way from Wonderland to Lynn is owned by the Commonwealth, and may be used for extension.

REFERENCE: Robert C. Stanley, *Narrow Gauge: The Story of the Boston, Revere Beach & Lynn Railroad* (Cambridge, Mass.: Boston Street Railway Association, 1980).

Grafton Centre Railroad

J. D. Wheeler and other businessmen of Grafton Township formed the Grafton Centre Railroad in October 1873 to provide a connection between Grafton Station (North Grafton), on the Boston & Albany 38 miles west of Boston, and Grafton Centre (Grafton), which the B&A had bypassed about three miles to the north. The line was opened on August 20, 1874. It was a modest operation of a single locomotive, one passenger car, and one flatcar. About 75 percent of the revenues, which were only about $4,000 to $7,000 per year, were from passengers, express, and mail transferred from B&A trains. Given the limited scope of the operation, narrow gauge was not initially a great handicap, but in 1887 the management began surveys of an extension from Grafton Centre through Upton and Hopedale to Milford on the Ashland branch of the New York & New England (New York, New Haven & Hartford). The extension had the prospect of substantial carload freight traffic from mills and other industrial establishments along the route. Accordingly, the railroad was converted in 1887 and the name was changed in 1888 to the Grafton & Upton Railroad. The line was electrified in 1902 as part of Massachusetts's extensive network of rural trolley lines. Passenger service was provided by the Milford & Uxbridge Street Railway. This arrangement was discontinued in 1928, but the G&U provided mail and express service by an electric car from 1922 until the railroad was dieselized in 1946. The line, 16.5 miles from North Grafton to Milford, remains in service, interchanging with Conrail at both termini.

Martha's Vineyard Railroad

Like Nantucket, Martha's Vineyard had declined when petroleum from Pennsylvania

The Grafton & Upton made some of its connections to the Boston & Albany with this diminutive steam motor car. (Ed Bond collection.)

The Martha's Vineyard Railroad at Katama Lodge on the island's south coast. (Ed Bond collection.)

Nantucket Railroad No. 2 was a relatively late example of a Forney locomotive, an Alco Richmond product of 1910. (Ed Bond collection.)

replaced whale oil for lighting American homes, and by the narrow gauge era was endeavoring to develop the resort trade as a replacement. The Martha's Vineyard Railroad was chartered in 1874 to run from Oak Bluffs, the principal landing point for steamers of the Old Colony Railroad, to Edgartown, the main town on the island, and to the resort of Katama immediately to the south. The 8.5-mile line was quickly built on the flat sandy soil of the island and was ready for opening on August 7, 1874. The steam car, embodying both locomotive and coach, with which the line was to operate proved unable to negotiate its curves. The car was modified and service began on August 24. The car continued to be unsatisfactory, and was replaced with *Active*, a stock Porter 0-6-0, an odd choice for a seasonal railroad almost wholly dependent on passenger traffic. For the 1876 season the line was extended about a half mile from Katama to South Beach.

The railroad almost from the outset was afflicted with financial problems. In 1877 the shareholders agreed to let it be operated in the interest of holders of the floating debt until it returned to solvency. This arrangement was unsuccessful and the line was put in receivership in 1890. It was sold on May 21, 1892, to the Old Colony Steamboat Co.; this subsidiary of the Old Colony Railroad sold it to Joseph M. Wardell of Edgartown, who became its general manager. In 1894 he discontinued service south of Edgartown. The remainder continued to be unprofitable, and the line was abandoned in 1896.

REFERENCE: John H. Ackerman, "*Active* and *Dionis*," in Austin N. Stevens, ed., *Yankees under Steam* (Dublin, N.H.: Yankee, Inc., 1970), pp. 160–67.

Nantucket Railroad

By 1879 Nantucket was endeavoring to develop the resort industry as a replacement for whaling. Philip H. Folger promoted the railroad integrally with the Surfside Land Co., which planned a resort and hotel at Surfside on the south coast of the island about three miles directly south of the town of Nantucket. The route originally considered would have left Nantucket to the northwest, circled southwest around Sheep Pond, and followed the south coast to Siasconset, the only other town on the island, a distance of 17 miles to connect two communities only about seven miles apart. The route chosen ran straight south to the site of Surfside, and then followed the shore closely to Siasconset. The Nantucket Railroad was chartered on April 19, 1880, and opened from Nantucket to Surfside on July 4, 1881. The management bought a 4-4-0 locomotive secondhand from the Danville, Olney & Ohio River and cross-bench open cars from the New York & Manhattan Beach. Completion of the railroad could not immediately be financed, and the line was not opened to Siasconset (11 miles) until July 8, 1884. The second locomotive, a small Mason Bogie, was leased from the Boston, Revere Beach & Lynn.

The proximity of the line to the ocean subjected it to frequent damage from storms. On August 21, 1893, the sea wiped out the track at Tom Never's Head, causing the railroad to go bankrupt and preventing service east of Surfside in 1894. The line was sold for $10,800 at Boston on October 4, 1894, to John H. Fairbank, trustee for the mortgage. The corporation was reorganized as the Nantucket Central Railroad in 1895, and line was rebuilt farther from the shore. In the process the route was shortened about two miles and the Surfside development, which was bypassed, was brought to an end. The railroad was threatened by projects for electric railways and bus lines directly from Nantucket to Siasconset, but survived, largely because of a severe limitation on the use of automobiles on the island. The railroad could not operate in 1906, and was sold in April 1907 to Thomas G. Macy of New York, who reopened it, replacing steam equipment with a Fairbanks-Morse gasoline car. Macy secured a mail contract, which enabled him to inaugurate year-round operation; previously the railroad had been a seasonal facility.

The company went into receivership on May 18, 1909, and was reorganized, again becoming the Nantucket Railroad, on April 20, 1910. Allan A. Brown of Boston, who became president, restored steam service with a 2-4-4T. An effort of 1916 to develop a resort town at Tom Never's Head was unsuccessful. The line last operated in 1917. In a political compromise that entailed an end to the island's automobile restriction, the railroad was dismantled in 1918 and shipped to France for use in World War I.

REFERENCE: Clay Lancaster, *The Far-Out Island Railroad* (Nantucket, Mass.: Pleasant Publications, 1972).

Michigan

Au Sable & Northwestern Railroad

The J. E. Potts Salt & Lumber Co. formed the Au Sable & Northwestern Railway as a private carrier in 1887 for its operations at Potts, about 40 miles up the Au Sable River valley from the adjacent towns of Au Sable and Oscoda at the mouth of the river. The railroad was made a common carrier on July 15, 1889, when it opened its main line from Potts to connections with the Detroit, Bay City & Alpena at Oscoda and with lake steamers at Au Sable. Potts sold the operation to Henry M. Loud of Au Sable, who on July 15, 1891, reorganized the rail line as the Au Sable & Northwestern Railroad, renamed Potts "McKinley," and undertook extensive expansion of the rail mileage. Even by the standards of lumber railroads, the fluctuations in this line's mileage reported to the ICC were remarkable: 108 miles in 1891, 74 in 1895, 108 again in 1896, 76.5 in 1898, and 56 in 1904. The railroad provided a single passenger train per day on the main line and on the principal branches. In 1892 it reported to the *Official Guide of the Railways* an extension of the main line of 31 miles to Twin Lakes, and a branch of 36 miles from McKinley west to Luzerne. The main line was extended a further three miles to the terminus of the Michigan Central's Twin Lakes branch at Lewiston in 1894. In 1900 the Luzerne branch was dropped. In 1905 the main line was cut back to Comins, 53 miles from Au Sable, and on January 1, 1906, the railroad discontinued operation and vacated its charter. Loud had died, but his heirs formed H. M. Loud's Sons Co. and on December 26, 1907, revived the railroad under a charter for the second Au Sable & Northwestern Railway. Comins replaced McKinley as the seat of the lumbering operation, and the name "Hardy" was given to Crooked Lake Junction at milepost 43,

from which a branch was built east, eventually reaching Beevers (12 miles) in 1911. (The branch lines and mileage reported to *Poor's Manuals* differ from those shown in the *Official Guide*.)

A major fire in 1911 at Au Sable–Oscoda wiped out the Loud operation, causing the management to lease the railroad to the Detroit & Mackinac effective June 1, 1912, with an option to buy it. The D&M exercised the option and on May 31, 1914, merged the AS&NW into itself. The D&M converted the line in May 1915. In 1917 the management abandoned the outer half of the Beevers branch beyond Curran. The remainder of the branch and the former AS&NW main line from Au Sable to Comins were abandoned in August 1927.

Bear Lake & Eastern Railroad

George W. Hopkins, a lumber operator at Bear Lake, secured a charter for this railroad on January 24, 1882, as successor to his Bear Lake Tram Railway. The line opened from Pierport, on Lake Michigan between Onekama and Frankfort, to Bear Lake (5 miles) on April 10, 1882, and pressed eastward slowly, reaching Springdale (18 miles) in 1887. Although Springdale was on the Arcadia & Betsey River after 1895, Hopkins advertised connections only with lake steamers at Pierport. The railroad had two locomotives, two passenger cars, 40 flatcars, and 15 log cars.

In January 1900 Hopkins announced his intention to wind up the railroad. He dropped its meager pretensions to being a common carrier, and abandoned it on September 1, 1902.

Detroit, Bay City & Alpena Railroad
Gauge: 3'-2"

Charles D. and Sylvester Hale, lumber operators at Tawas City–East Tawas, in April 1878 began building a railroad of 21 miles southwest to the Au Gres and Rifle rivers area under the name of the Lake Huron & Southwestern Railway. They used the unusual gauge of 3'-2" of their earlier log tramway. The Hales' enterprise became insolvent, causing the railroad to be sold in 1880 to one of their associates, C. H. Prescott, who reorganized it as the Tawas & Bay County Railroad. Prescott sold it in July 1882 to General Russell A. Alger, one of Michigan's leading lumbermen, who was endeavoring to arrange a rail connection from his installations in the Black River

Brooks built this trim 2-6-0 for the J. E. Potts Lumber Co. It passed into the hands of the affiliated Au Sable & Northwestern and then to the Bellaire, Zanesville & Cincinnati. (Railroad Museum of Pennsylvania.)

area to the standard gauge rail network in the southern part of the state. Alger had incorporated the Detroit, Bay City & Alpena Railroad in 1880 for this purpose, and he reincorporated it on April 2, 1883, absorbing the T&BC into the new enterprise. He began surveys for an extension of five miles southwest toward the Mackinaw Division of the Michigan Central at Alger, and for another northeast 14 miles to Au Sable. On December 3 the railroad issued its first timetable for service from Alger to Au Sable–Oscoda (48 miles), even though the high-level bridge over the Rifle River four miles from Alger was not completed until January 1884. The construction was done with the 3'-2" gauge, but standard gauge ties were laid in anticipation of early conversion.

From the outset Alger planned to reach Alpena, the principal town on the state's east coast, but announced late in 1884 that business conditions did not currently warrant the investment. In 1885 he undertook the next stage, from Oscoda to Black River (30 miles), of which the northernmost 15 miles were trackage rights over the Black River Railroad, a private carrier of his Alger, Smith & Co. The extension was completed to the junction with the existing line on December 27, 1885. The route chosen entailed a line inland from Lake Michigan that was never considered entirely satisfactory. As completed, the narrow gauge was 83 miles long, and had in addition several short logging branches. In January 1886 the management announced that the railroad would be converted as soon as weather per-

mitted. The portion south of Tawas City–East Tawas was converted on April 8 and the line to the north on April 10. Standard gauge rail reached Alpena late in 1886.

Alger's control of the railroad ended with a receivership of 1893. The company was reorganized on December 31, 1894, as the Detroit & Mackinac Railway by representatives of Drexel, Burnham & Co., who installed C. H. Coster as president. The new management pursued a policy of expansion both southward and northward. In September 1896 the railroad opened its own line of 49 miles from Emery Junction (National City) to Bay City, and abandoned the 14 miles of the former narrow gauge from Alger to Prescott, thus getting rid of the Rifle River bridge. Coster proposed to extend to the Straits of Mackinac, and began by buying the Alpena & Northern from Alger, Smith & Co. on April 16, 1896, the purchase giving him 30 miles of line to the northwest. In 1901 the management relocated the 29 miles from Lincoln Junction to Black River along the lake shore, although the south 14 miles of the old line were retained as a branch to Lincoln. Track arrived in Cheboygan in 1904, and belatedly in Mackinaw City in 1976, when the company acquired former Michigan Central trackage.

The railroad proved rather a blue chip of short lines, mainly because of mine products—limestone, Portland cement, gypsum, and aggregates. It abandoned the Lincoln branch in 1928, and the ten-mile remnant of the former narrow gauge from National

City to Prescott on November 8, 1943, but the remainder, 31 miles from National City to Lincoln Junction, is still in service.

Harbor Springs Railway
Gauge: 2'-6"

Ephraim Shay, inventor of the most popular geared locomotive, chartered this railroad on February 2, 1902, largely as a facility for bringing wood fuel to the waterworks he owned at Harbor Springs. The area immediately north of the town had been worked over by earlier lumber operators, but enough wood remained for his purpose, and some lumber mills remained in operation. The line was opened on July 1, 1902, to Stutsman and Race Mill (7 miles). The railroad was popularly known as the "Hemlock Central." In 1904 the line was extended a mile to Carter's Mill. Like most lumber railroads, the line had a fluctuating mileage of branches, reported in 1905 at 4.75. This was a simple operation, laid with 16-pound rail and worked with three small home-built versions of the Shay locomotive. By 1906, the total cost was reported as $51,346. Shay financed the railroad without funded debt. Summer vacationers were handled at 25¢ per trip. Operation ceased about 1911, and the railroad was dismantled in 1912. None of the on-line communities above Harbor Springs has survived.

REFERENCE: Michael Koch, *The Shay Locomotive: Titan of the Timber* (Denver, Colo.: World Press, 1971), pp. 66–73.

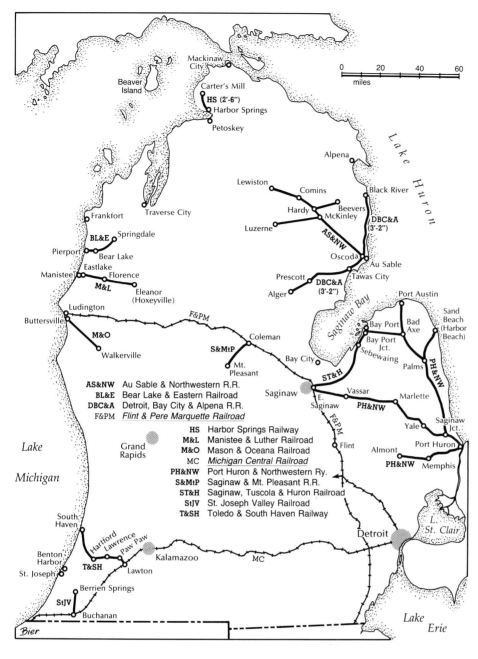

tation of expansion, the company on August 9, 1886, incorporated the Mason & Oceana Railroad to operate the lumber line as a nominal common carrier. The line was opened to Peachville (21 miles) on January 6, 1887, and to Walkerville (27 miles) on January 20, 1888. The company had extensive additional mileage of lumbering spurs; peak mileage was reported as 45.

The railroad was operated at various times with a total of 13 locomotives—three Shays and ten rod engines. One round trip for passengers was run from Buttersville to Walkerville. The company had a three-stall enginehouse at Buttersville, a shop, and a log dump. The company also maintained a warehouse for salt. In the 1890s some standard gauge track was laid in the vicinity of the mill, and cars were ferried across from Ludington. Some produce originated on the narrow gauge was transshipped at Buttersville, ferried to Ludington, and sent on to Milwaukee via the Pere Marquette Railway's car ferries. Launches were run to Ludington for passengers, and the company operated a Great Lakes freighter named *Marshall F. Butters*, after the son of the founder, who succeeded to the presidency of the enterprise in 1889.

Between 1900 and 1902 Marshall Butters endeavored to extend the railroad to Grand Rapids via Fremont and Newaygo but accomplished only some trackage for use as lumber spurs and grading as far as Hesperia. In 1908 he incorporated the Grand Rapids & Northwestern Railroad to build the entire Grand Rapids–Buttersville line. He proposed to run car ferries to Milwaukee and possibly also to Sheboygan, Wisconsin. Necessarily, this project would have entailed conversion of the Mason & Oceana. Before anything was done, most of the facilities at Buttersville were destroyed in a massive fire on August 25, 1909. The company chose not to rebuild the facilities and abandoned the Mason & Oceana on December 1, 1909. Butters assigned the stock of the M&O to his Grand Rapids & Northwestern. He retained the 12 miles of track approaching Buttersville for construction of the projected standard gauge line. He tore up the rest of the narrow gauge and graded an alternative route on which he never laid track. He also graded some mileage near Grand Rapids, but abandoned the entire project in June 1914.

REFERENCE: Robert W. Garasha, "The Mason & Oceana Railroad," Railway & Locomotive Historical Society *Bulletin*, no. 89 (1953), pp. 82–96.

Manistee & Luther Railroad

Lumber operator Richard G. Peters of Manistee formed this railroad on March 26, 1886, and opened it on May 1. The route was from Eastlake opposite Manistee on Manistee Lake east into southern Wexford County, crossing the Pere Marquette's secondary main line north to Bay View at Florence. In common with most such railroads, the mileage varied, but the main line was defined as 33 miles from Eastlake to Eleanor, a station that served the village of Hoxeyville. Total trackage peaked at 79 miles about the turn of the century. The railroad provided passenger and freight service to Hoxeyville and intermediate communities with mixed trains, but the meagerness of its general operations relative to

lumbering is evident in its car stock in 1912: five box, six stock, 44 flat, seven coal, and 341 logging cars. At its peak, the railroad operated with eight locomotives. It was reported abandoned in fiscal 1915.

Mason & Oceana Railroad

The Butters & Peters Salt & Lumber Co. began operation along the Pere Marquette River in 1878. By 1880 it had established a sawmill and shingle factory on the point separating Pere Marquette Lake from Lake Michigan opposite Ludington; the company named the installation Buttersville after Horace Butters, its founder. By 1885 the company was operating a 3'-0" lumber railroad south from Buttersville. In expec-

Two rod engines of the Mason & Oceana meet, probably at one of the junctions between the main line and a spur into the wooded area. (Munson Paddock collection, Railroad Museum of Pennsylvania.)

Mineral Range Railroad
Hancock & Calumet Railroad

The copper industry in the Keweenaw Peninsula of northern Michigan was dependent on steamboat transportation from its origin in the 1840s. The first rail line on the peninsula was the Hecla & Torch Lake of 1868, a 4'-1" private carrier of the Calumet & Hecla Consolidated Copper Co. This carrier operated in isolation between Red Jacket in the Calumet area and Lake Linden, a situation inevitably giving rise to efforts to connect it with Houghton and Hancock on Portage Lake about 12 miles to the south. The Mineral Range & L'Anse Bay Railroad was chartered as a narrow gauge on November 3, 1871, but not immediately built. The corporation was reformed as the Mineral Range Railroad on October 25, 1872. The charter provided for a line of about 100 miles from Copper Harbor at the tip of the peninsula to some point on the Ontonagon River where the railroad could connect with the Marquette, Houghton & Ontonagon, a predecessor of the Duluth, South Shore & Atlantic. The MH&O announced its intention to build into Houghton, causing President Charles E. Holland and the other promoters of the MR to cut back their plans. In the summer of 1873 they built the railroad from Hancock on the north shore of Portage Lake to Calumet (13 miles), opening it for traffic on October 11. The principal cargo was copper-bearing rock, which was handled in hopper cars to a mill of the Osceola Mining Co. near Calumet. The line ran three passenger trains per day and earned from 21 to 39 percent of its revenues from them. Initially, the line operated in isolation, connecting only with Great Lakes steamers at Hancock, but in 1883 the MH&O reached Houghton, providing the MR with a link by ferry with the North American railroad system. In 1885 Holland sold control of the railroad to financier Henry S. Ives of New York.

Two of the MR's principal shippers, the Osceola and Tamarack mining companies, dissatisfied with rates on their ores, formed the Hancock & Calumet Railroad on December 24, 1884, and proceeded to build a rival narrow gauge from Hancock to the mining area. Construction began at Osceola below Calumet and proceeded south parallel to the Hecla & Torch Lake, thence along the west shore of Torch Lake and the north shore of Portage Lake to Hancock. The main line (14 miles) was completed in December 1885; the railroad had a varying mileage of mine spurs. Passenger service was operated from Hancock to Lake Linden, ten miles, including a branch of 2.5 miles from Lake Junction. The line's independence was short-lived, for Ives leased

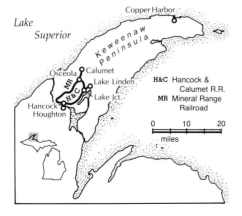

the property for the MR in 1886 and acquired possession of it in 1887. The H&C was allowed to keep its separate identity.

Ives pursued a policy of expansion. In 1885 he built a branch off the MR from Franklin Junction to a plant of the Quincy Mining Co. at Franklin (two miles). The mining company became dissatisfied with the arrangement and in 1890 built its own railroad, the Quincy & Torch Lake, a 3'-0" private carrier, from the nearby Quincy mine to a plant at Mason, a town on the H&C by Torch Lake. The line of six miles ran parallel to the H&C main line at a higher elevation. In 1885 Ives built a belt line in Calumet to connect the MR's depot on Oak Street with the H&C station at Red Jacket, and in 1886 he built a three-rail bridge from Hancock to Houghton to end the MR's physical isolation. Passenger service between the two towns was provided by a standard gauge dummy engine and a coach.

Ives left the railroad on July 12, 1887, amid accusations of illicit practices. He was succeeded by Francis B. Loomis of New York. The MR went bankrupt in June 1888, and Ives was ordered by the court to refrain from voting his interest in the corporation. The company was allowed to emerge from receivership in November 1889 with Charles Bard of New York as president. Meanwhile, in 1887–88, the MH&O and several other railroads were merged into the Duluth, South Shore & Atlantic Railway under the control of the Canadian Pacific. On October 1, 1893, the DSS&A acquired 53 percent of the MR's stock, thereby gaining control of both of the narrow gauges. The DSS&A began laying standard gauge ties on the MR, and converted it in September 1897. The drawbridge between Houghton and Hancock was rebuilt in 1898. The MR formally absorbed the H&C in 1901 and on November 8 began the work of conversion; the job was completed early in 1902. Of the connecting private carriers, the Hecla & Torch Lake was converted in 1906, but the Quincy & Torch Lake remained a narrow gauge until 1945, when it was closed.

The Mineral Range was merged into the DSS&A in November 1949, and passed with the DSS&A into the Soo Line in 1961. The former H&C from Lake Junction to Calumet was abandoned in 1934. The Soo Line shut down the rest of the narrow gauge mileage in 1978 and abandoned it in 1979.

REFERENCES: John F. Campbell, "The Mineral Range Railroad Company," *The Soo*, 2, no. 4 (Oct. 1980), pp. 12–35; Franklin A. King, "Dead but Not Buried" [Quincy & Torch Lake Railroad], *Trains*, Jan. 1960, pp. 40–41; Stanley

H. Mailer, "Mason Bogies, 3-Per-Cent-Plus Grades, a Compound, an Odd Gauge, Camelbacks . . . What More Could Anyone Ask?" [Hecla & Torch Lake Railroad], *Trains*, Aug. 1972, pp. 29–36.

Port Huron & Northwestern Railway

Given Port Huron's almost complete dependence on the Michigan timber industry in the nineteenth century, it is surprising that this project of three narrow gauge lines radiating from Port Huron was not mainly concerned with lumber. Rather it was promoted for the general development of the Thumb Peninsula in hopes of securing the nearly virgin area's agricultural traffic for the city. The railroad was organized March 23, 1878, by several businessmen and financiers of Port Huron: Henry Howard, John P. Sanborn, Fred L. Wells, James Beard, and their associates. They undertook construction in October 1878 on a line north, parallel to the shore of Lake Huron, mainly about five miles inland. The line was opened July 1, 1879, to Croswell, 26 miles, and completed to Sand Beach (Harbor Beach), 71 miles, on September 13, 1880. To use as a terminal in Port Huron the railroad bought from the federal government the former Fort Gratiot Military Reservation. For access, the management secured permission to lay track across Pine Grove Park, an arrangement that caused some local hostility. The company bridged the Black River in 1881 and built a large station on the riverfront at the foot of Court Street.

The company's second line was built from Saginaw Junction, about 12 miles out of Port Huron in the Atkins-Zion area, to Marlette, about 33 miles, and opened on January 17, 1881.* This extension entailed a wooden trestle about 70 feet high and 800 feet long over the Black River. The original intention was to extend this line to Cass City, some 20 miles to the north, but this plan was quickly dropped when the Flint & Pere Marquette, a major standard gauge railroad in the area, offered the promoters an entry into East Saginaw on terms too favorable to reject. The F&PM offered the narrow gauge the grade of the unbuilt East Saginaw & St. Clair Railroad from East

*The exact location of Saginaw Junction is unclear. In 1881 Atkins was reported to have been renamed Saginaw Junction. When it was proposed that the station cease being a junction in 1889, Saginaw Junction was reportedly renamed Zion. Atkins and Zion, however, are about 1.2 miles apart. The most probable location for the junction is a sharp curve about 0.2 miles west of Atkins.

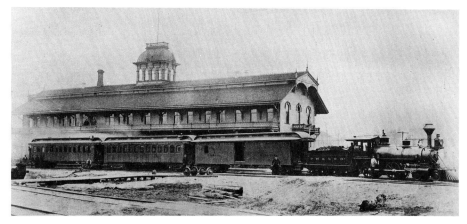

The Port Huron & Northwestern's system radiated from this large station on the Port Huron waterfront. (Richard D. Rautio collection.)

Saginaw to Vassar, 20 miles, and the right to lay a narrow gauge entry parallel to the F&PM's own approach to the East Saginaw station, plus full use of the station and terminal facilities with no fees beyond reimbursement of costs. This generosity was apparently brought forth by a desire for amicable relations with the PH&NW, relations that would forward the F&PM's plan to build its own narrow gauge, the Saginaw, Tuscola & Huron, from East Saginaw to Bad Axe. Howard and his colleagues lost little time in accepting. They built the line from Marlette to Vassar in 1881, and completed it to East Saginaw on February 21, 1882. The new line, which was about 79 miles, quickly proved more productive than the earlier route, and was thereafter looked upon as the company's main line. The company extended the north line upon completion of the East Saginaw route, building 35 miles from a junction at Palms to Bad Axe, the most important town on the Thumb Peninsula, and to Port Austin at the peninsula's northern tip. The extension opened on December 11, 1882.

The railroad's third line was a branch of 34 miles from Port Huron to Memphis and Almont, both small farming towns. This trackage was separately incorporated as the Port Huron & South Western Railway, but shortly absorbed. Upon completion of the Almont branch on October 3, 1882, the PH&NW announced that the branch would be extended to Detroit, which lay about 48 miles directly south, but nothing was built. The Almont line directly paralleled the Grand Trunk main line by about seven miles to the south. Later it was rumored that the branch might be built west to Flint or even to Chicago, but it remained only an agricultural facility serving a bean-growing area, and was always the weakest part of the system.

As completed, the PH&NW was Michi-

gan's largest narrow gauge, a railroad of about 218 miles, with 13 locomotives, 22 passenger cars, six head-end cars, and 269 freight cars. After 1882 the railroad was uniformly unprofitable, but it remained solvent and independent until April 1, 1889, when it was sold to the Flint & Pere Marquette for $2.3 million. The F&PM issued $3.5 million in bonds to finance the acquisition, earmarking $1.2 million for the conversion of the railroad. The F&PM was mainly interested in the Port Huron–East Saginaw line, which was the only existing direct route between two major Michigan cities. The Grand Trunk was digging its tunnel beneath the St. Clair River, improving the connection to the east. The narrow gauge line was poorly suited to making this connection, partly because of the wooden

A pass of the Port Huron & Northwestern, the back of which shows the line and its neighbors, notably the Toronto, Grey, & Bruce.

In 1895 the Flint & Pere Marquette was still operating the Port Huron & Northwestern's weakest line, the Almont Branch, as a narrow gauge. Here a Porter 2-4-0 takes water at the tank in Almont. A turntable and single-stall engine house are behind the photographer. (Almont Public Library.)

trestle over the Black River and partly because of a sharp grade 80 feet long east of Atkins, but mainly because of a tortuous entry into Port Huron from the north. The Almont branch, however, had the advantage of entering Port Huron from the west almost directly toward the portal of the tunnel. Accordingly, the F&PM decided to convert the main line only from East Saginaw to Yale (67 miles), and then build a new line of about 20 miles from Yale to Almont Junction (Chicago & Grand Trunk Junction; Tappan) on the west side of Port Huron about four miles from Court Street.

Track gangs went to work at East Saginaw immediately, and reached Yale with standard gauge track on August 18, 1889. Yale was used as a transshipment point until the completion of the new entry. The new line entailed an iron trestle over the valley of Mill Creek about 60 feet high and 600 feet long. When the trestle was completed, standard gauge trains began running into Port

Huron on the new route on November 18, 1889. Standard gauge rails were laid on the Almont line's roadbed, and a new narrow gauge line was built nine feet to the south as far as the Military Street overpass east of the tunnel portal; for the remainder of the distance into Court Street the line was laid with third rail.

The new entry bypassed two towns, Fargo and Green's Corners (Hartsuff). The people of Fargo had contributed about $12,000 to the building of the railroad in return for an obligation of the PH&NW to provide service for a minimum of 20 years. Armed with this agreement, they brought legal actions against the F&PM before the Michigan Railroad Commission and the courts, securing an injunction against abandonment of the Saginaw Junction–Yale line that kept it operating as a narrow gauge until mid-1891. The railroad lost about $500 per week on the operation, and was most eager to get rid of it. The F&PM ran the last

train over the segment on July 14, 1891, and in apparent fear that the residents of Fargo would secure a second injunction, removed the track on Sunday, July 19, 1891. The railroad in 1889 had bought 40 acres of land for a new town, Avoca, and gave landholders in the bypassed towns priority in purchase of sites. The trestle over the Black River was burned intentionally.

The F&PM allowed the rest of the mileage to remain narrow gauge for several years. The line from Port Huron to Bad Axe and Port Austin was converted on Sunday, July 17, 1898. (For the company's unusual methods of conversion, see Part I, Chapter 9.) The railroad now had isolated narrow gauge mileage on the Sand Beach branch and the Almont line; 3'-0" track was not retained to connect the two. The Sand Beach line was converted on Sunday, September 17, 1899. The rolling stock was brought to Port Huron and some of the rail relaid on the Almont line.

Late in 1899 the F&PM arranged a merger with the Detroit, Grand Rapids & Western Railroad and the Chicago & West Michigan Railway to form the Pere Marquette Railroad. The new railroad arranged entries into Chicago and Buffalo by trackage rights and operated car ferries at Detroit, Port Huron, and Ludington. In this fashion, the Michigan mileage of the three predecessors, which had been declining with the lumber trade, became part of a bridge line between the Niagara frontier on the east and Chicago, Milwaukee, Manitowoc, and Kewaunee on the west. The former narrow gauge between Port Huron and East Saginaw became an important connection between the ferries at Port Huron and Ludington. In later years the route was used extensively for moving empty cars from the east to automobile factories in Flint and Saginaw. The Grand Trunk arranged its own entry into Saginaw from Durand and ceased being an important connection at Port Huron.

When the merger took effect on January 1, 1900, only the Almont branch remained narrow gauge. The PM allocated four former PH&NW 2-4-0 locomotives to the line, assigning them not numbers but letters: A, B, C, and D. In March 1903 PM engineers began work on the conversion, strengthening bridges over the Belle and Pine rivers and easing the grade west of Memphis. The conversion took place May 3. The remaining narrow gauge equipment was sold to lumber companies or scrapped.

Inevitably, the Almont branch was the first portion of the system to be scrapped; the line had little traffic but that from two elevators. The railroad moved to abandon it and, in spite of considerable opposition, received permission from the ICC on December 12, 1941. The last train ran in January 1942. The remainder of the former PH&NW lines survived to be brought into the Chesapeake & Ohio in the absorption of the Pere Marquette in 1947. To get rid of the difficult entry into Port Huron from the north, the C&O abandoned the original 26 miles from Port Huron to Croswell in March 1973. The seven miles from Kinde to Port Austin were abandoned in November 1983. The remainder from Croswell to Kinde, along with the branch from Palms to Harbor Beach, was transferred to the Huron & Eastern Railway on April 1, 1986. The Port Huron–Saginaw line remains in service in the CSX Corporation, but in 1989 the company announced plans to abandon 10 miles east from Avoca.

REFERENCES: Paul Wesley Ivey, *The Pere Marquette Railroad Company* (Lansing: Michigan Historical Commission, 1919); George W. Hilton, *The Great Lakes Car Ferries* (Berkeley, Calif.: Howell-North Books, 1962); collections of Robert F. Gray, Richard D. Rautio, and Herbert H. Harwood, Jr.

Saginaw & Mt. Pleasant Railroad

The Flint & Pere Marquette Railroad, which accepted narrow gauge doctrine for light branch lines, incorporated this railroad in March 1879 to build a branch from Coleman on the F&PM main line southwest to Mt. Pleasant (14 miles), seat of Isabella County. The route was through flat forest land with light population; the line was thought notable for its lack of major curvature. Service began on November 15, 1879. Motive power was a pair of Forney locomotives. The line operated with two coaches, a combine, and 15 freight cars, including ten of the F&PM's four-wheel narrow gauge boxcars. Initially two and later three passenger trains were run daily to connect with trains between Toledo and Ludington. The Saginaw & Mt. Pleasant was operated as a leased line of the F&PM from the outset, with officers chosen from the F&PM management.

The F&PM converted the S&MtP in early July 1884, and merged the corporation into itself in 1889. The branch survived through mergers into the Pere Marquette in 1900 and into the Chesapeake & Ohio in 1947. The C&O abandoned the line in 1979 in favor of access to Mt. Pleasant by trackage rights over the Ann Arbor Railroad from Clare, but this arrangement was given up in 1983.

Saginaw, Tuscola & Huron Railroad

The present city of Saginaw was formed in March 1890 of two predecessors separated by the Saginaw River: Saginaw City and East Saginaw. During their years of independence, the two manifested considerable rivalry for economic development. A predecessor of the New York Central System had terminated at Saginaw City and the Flint & Pere Marquette at East Saginaw. The Saginaw, Tuscola & Huron was promoted by local businessmen and officials of the F&PM in the hope of channeling traffic from the northwestern Thumb Peninsula to East Saginaw. The railroad was incorporated on February 24, 1881; the name encompassed the three counties through which it was to run. The incorporators included William L. Webber, E. T. Judd, George W. Morley, John W. Howry, and John Estabrook, all prominent figures in East Saginaw, together with William W. Crapo, Alfred M. Hoyt, Jesse Hoyt, and Dr. Henry C. Potter, all of whom were identified with the F&PM. Webber, the local attorney for Jesse

Hoyt, who lived in New York, was chosen president, and served as such for the entire independent history of the railroad. Narrow gauge was probably chosen for conformity with the Port Huron & Northwestern's lines on the Thumb Peninsula.

Surveys of the projected route from East Saginaw to Bad Axe were made by Charles Holmes in 1881. The railroad was opened for the first 37 miles from East Saginaw to Sebewaing, a small port on Saginaw Bay, on April 4, 1882. Although the company was well financed, the next nine miles to Bay Port were not completed until June 15, 1884. Because of the difficulty of climbing out of Bay Port, the line to Bad Axe was built from Bay Port Junction, 1.38 miles south of the town. Webber ascertained that a limestone deposit capable of commercial development lay about three miles east of Bay Port. He bought 160 acres of land in his own name and founded the Bay Port Quarry. The railroad established a station called simply Quarry, and built a spur of 0.8 miles into the pit. Title to the quarry was transferred to the railroad.

Again, the main line did not progress rapidly. Service to Bad Axe, 67 miles from East Saginaw, did not begin until July 1, 1886. There the ST&H made a connection with the Port Huron & Northwestern, with which it already shared terminal facilities in the F&PM's East Saginaw station and yards. Relations between the two narrow gauges were friendly; the ST&H had begun passenger service with equipment rented from the PH&NW. The ST&H reportedly had eight locomotives. Rolling stock was largely built in F&PM facilities.

The ST&H proved to have a respectable flow of traffic, but was unprofitable because of the costs of transshipment at East Saginaw. Fish from Bay Port to eastern destinations was perishable, and stone from the Bay Port Quarry was bulky. Conversion of the PH&NW's Port Huron–East Saginaw line by the F&PM in 1889 left the ST&H an isolated narrow gauge at East Saginaw. The management converted the entire East Saginaw–Bad Axe line in 1891. Considering that the line had been a promotion of the F&PM from the outset, it is remarkable that it was never absorbed by that railroad.

Rather, it remained nominally independent until the formation of the Pere Marquette in 1900. The ST&H was leased to the PM for 999 years from February 1, 1900, but purchased outright by it on May 6, 1903. It proved a relatively strong branch of the PM, with traffic in stone, coal (discovered near Sebewaing four months before the conversion), and sugar beets. It survived intact to the merger of the PM into the Chesapeake & Ohio in 1947. The CSX Corporation turned the line over to the Huron & Eastern Railway on December 22, 1988.

REFERENCE: Frank A. Kirkpatrick, "The Saginaw, Tuscola & Huron: An Early Railroad of the Thumb Peninsula," *Michigan History*, 52 (1968), pp. 196–217.

St. Joseph Valley Railroad

William R. Rough of Buchanan projected this railroad from South Bend, Indiana, through Buchanan to St. Joseph or Benton Harbor, depending on the availability of financial assistance. The St. Joseph Valley Railroad was chartered on February 4, 1880, and opened on September 1, 1881, from Buchanan north to Berrien Springs (10 miles). This was to be the intermediate portion, but nothing further was built as a narrow gauge. The line was a small operation of a single locomotive, connecting Berrien Springs with the Michigan Central main line at Buchanan. The enterprise was unsuccessful, and the property was sold on August 1, 1889, at a receiver's sale to A. A. Patterson, Jr., of Chicago, who on the same day reorganized it as the St. Joseph Valley Railway. He quickly converted the railroad simply by respiking the 30-pound rail to 4'-8½". The railroad remained unprofitable and was shut down about July 15, 1893.

J. M. Caulfield secured a charter for the Benton Harbor & Southeastern Railroad, and in 1894 expressed an interest in relaying the former narrow gauge with 60-pound rail to reopen it as part of a line from St. Joseph to Napanee (later Nappanee), Indiana. Rather, Patterson bought Caulfield's franchise early in 1897 and merged the StJV with the BH&SE into the Milwaukee, Benton Harbor & Columbus Railway on August 10, 1897. He built the long-projected northern extension into Benton Harbor and rebuilt the original mileage. Service began on the 27 miles from Benton Harbor to Buchanan on August 9, 1897. There was continual discussion of southward extension to South Bend, Mishawaka, Napanee, or Fort Wayne, but nothing was undertaken. As late as April 27, 1902, shareholders voted to build the extension of about 13 miles

into South Bend. Instead, the railroad was sold in 1903 to the Pere Marquette Railroad, for which it became a minor branch, mainly serving the fruit industry. This traffic was highly susceptible to the competition of the Southern Michigan Railway, an interurban that served Berrien Springs on its route from St. Joseph to Niles. As a consequence, the Buchanan branch was abandoned under an ICC order of May 26, 1924.

REFERENCE: Robert Myers, "The St. Joseph Valley Railroad Company," *Michigan History*, 72 (1988), pp. 24–30.

Toledo & South Haven Railway

The Toledo & South Haven Railway was the product of a merger of two previous narrow gauges in 1887. The earlier predecessor was the Paw Paw Railroad, built as a five-mile standard gauge short line in 1867 by local parties to connect Paw Paw with the Michigan Central main line at Lawton, five miles to the south. The later predecessor was a more ambitious project, the Toledo & South Haven Railroad, incorporated in March 1876 to build between the cities of its name via Paw Paw and Morenci, Michigan, and the small towns in northwestern Ohio later served by the Toledo & Western interurban. At first the T&SH promoters, led by F. B. Adams, proposed to traverse the Paw Paw Railroad by third rail, but in June 1875 they bought out the owners, Henry and Horace S. Ismon, and in 1877 converted it to 3'-0". To continue to serve Paw Paw with standard gauge equipment, John Ihling, the superintendent, devised an arrangement that could transport a standard gauge car, including its trucks, over the railroad on narrow gauge trucks. The device appears to have been unsuccessful and by 1881 had been replaced with a Ramsey Transfer at Lawton. The Toledo & South Haven, which opened its line from Paw Paw to Lawrence, nine miles, on October 1, 1877, provided narrow gauge equipment for the Paw Paw, which had none of its own. The two railroads remained separate corporations, although they operated integrally by a contract of 1878.

The T&SH on March 8, 1883, opened an additional eight miles west to Hartford on the main line of the Chicago & West Michigan (Pere Marquette). In the same year the management announced it would build the first portion of the line to Toledo, about 30 miles of track southeast from Lawton to Leesburg on the Grand Trunk, Centreville, seat of St. Joseph County, and Nottawa on the Grand Rapids & Indiana, but the extension was never undertaken.

Rather, Lucius Clark of South Bend acquired the two companies—the T&SH and the Paw Paw—and merged them into the Toledo & South Haven Railway. On August 1, 1887, he opened an extension of the line northwest into South Haven, which was second only to St. Joseph–Benton Harbor as a port for the steamers that brought excursionists from Chicago and transported fruit into the city's produce market. The completed railroad was 37 miles long, and operated with three locomotives.

Clark's management failed and the railroad was put in receivership under John Ihling on June 12, 1890. The line, which included valuable waterfront terminal property in South Haven, was sold on April 12, 1894, to Howard Mansfield, who represented the bondholders. It was reorganized as the South Haven & Eastern Railroad with R. B. Dobson of New York as president. The new management proposed extensions north from South Haven to Saugatuck and southeast from Lawton to Schoolcraft, but neither was undertaken.

In July 1897 the property passed into the hands of the owners of the Milwaukee, Benton Harbor & Columbus. The new management converted the railroad in April and May of 1899. The Pere Marquette Railroad bought the securities of the company on April 1, 1903, but on April 15, 1907, leased the line to the Kalamazoo, Lake Shore & Chicago Railway, which had been formed by the managers of the Chicago & South Haven Steamship Co. in an effort to provide an interurban connection to Kalamazoo for their steamers. The KLS&C had also leased from the Michigan United Railway a former main line of the Michigan Central between Kalamazoo and Mattawan. In 1911 the Michigan United leased the KLS&C for five years, intending to complete its interurban east and west across the state by bringing third-rail electrification into South Haven. This project also failed. The KLS&C was sold for scrap in 1925 without ever having been electrified, and the former narrow gauge reverted to the Pere Marquette. The original five miles from Lawton to Paw Paw were abandoned in 1942. The trackage from Paw Paw to Hartford was spun off in 1987 to local operators who revived the name of the Kalamazoo, Lake Shore & Chicago Railway for the operation. The track from Hartford to South Haven survives in the CSX Corporation.

Caledonia, Mississippi & Western No. 2 was a nicely proportioned Pittsburgh 4-4-0. (California State Railroad Museum.)

Minnesota

Caledonia, Mississippi & Western Railroad

The Caledonia & Mississippi Railway was organized on December 3, 1873, to build a narrow gauge from Caledonia Junction (Reno) immediately north of Sumner to Caledonia, seat of Houston County (14 miles). The promoters, Thomas Abbott and local businessmen, graded the line in 1874, but lacked the funds to complete it. They also projected a narrow gauge from a point in Wisconsin opposite Sumner to La Crosse, about 12 miles, but they were never able to undertake it.

Still unable to complete the railroad, the promoters on April 2, 1879, reorganized it as the Caledonia, Mississippi & Western Railroad, and entered into an agreement with the Chicago, Clinton, Dubuque & Minnesota Railroad, the intended connection at Caledonia Junction, whereby the larger railroad would contribute about $400,000 to the project—$75,600 in advances of cash and the rest in direct construction expenditures. Rails were laid on the existing grade, and the project was extended west to Preston, seat of Fillmore County. The line was opened to Caledonia on September 29, 1879, and to Preston (58 miles) before the end of the year. The terms on which the narrow gauge was completed made it essentially a branch of the CCD&M; accordingly, the CCD&M bought it on June 29, 1880. The CCD&M was itself absorbed by the Chicago, Milwaukee & St. Paul Railway on November 1, 1880.

The CM&StP expressed interest in converting the line from the outset, but made

no immediate efforts to do so. The Minnesota legislature in 1899 authorized the Railroad & Warehouse Commission to order conversion of narrow gauge railroads in the state, but the Commission never took action. In February 1901 the CM&StP announced its intention to convert the line and spent the entire summer in preparation. A gang of 900 men effected the conversion on the weekend of November 9–10, 1901. The company then proceeded to extend the branch six miles to Isinours on the La Crosse–Austin segment of its line across southern Minnesota. The Reno-Caledonia portion was abandoned in 1947; the remainder was abandoned under an ICC order of September 13, 1976.

Minneapolis, Lyndale & Minnetonka Railway

This steam dummy line originated as the Lyndale Railway, incorporated in June 1878 by Colonel William McCrory and his associates. In 1879 the name was changed to the Minneapolis, Lyndale & Lake Calhoun Railway, and the line was opened on May 19 from First Street in Minneapolis to Lake Calhoun (4.5 miles) via First Avenue, Nicollet Avenue, and 31st Street. An extension of a mile to Lake Harriet was added in 1880. In 1881 the name was changed to the Minneapolis, Lyndale & Minnetonka Railway and track was extended to Excelsior on Lake Minnetonka (10.5 miles). The management bought two Baldwin 2-6-0 locomotives to handle the trains from Lake Calhoun to Excelsior; steam dummy engines and, briefly, soda motors took the trains into downtown Minneapolis. The railroad handled freight, mainly package shipments in interchange with the Chicago, Milwaukee

& St. Paul at 29th and Nicollet, to Excelsior. The company operated excursion steamers on lakes Calhoun and Minnetonka.

The operation was not a financial success. The company was in chronic difficulty from 1881 on. Charles A. Pillsbury and James J. Hill bought the line in 1885. Hill was interested in converting the line and extending it about 39 miles to Hutchinson. This was not done, and instead the management cut the line back from Excelsior to Lake Calhoun in August 1886. The two Moguls were diverted to the company's dummy line to Minnehaha Falls southeast of the city.

In 1887 Minneapolis decided to prohibit steam locomotives on the streets effective November 1, 1889. This development prompted Pillsbury and Hill to lease the line to the Minneapolis Street Railway as of April 1, 1887. The street railway restored service to Lake Harriet for the 1887 season, and prepared to convert and electrify the entire property. The job was completed on May 24, 1891, and the property thereafter operated as part of the street railway system. The successor Twin City Rapid Transit Co. restored the line to Excelsior in 1905, making use of most of the abandoned right-of-way. The line was cut back from Excelsior to Hopkins in 1932 and to Brookside Avenue in 1951. The remainder, which included the trackage serving lakes Calhoun and Harriet, was not abandoned until June 19, 1954; it was the last street railway operation in the Twin Cities.

REFERENCES: Russell L. Olson, *The Electric Railways of Minnesota* (Hopkins, Minn.: Minnesota Transportation Museum, 1976), pp. 67–75, 89–97; Albin Lee, "The Minneapolis Motor Line," *Narrow Gauge and Short Line Gazette*, Nov./Dec. 1984, pp. 26–31.

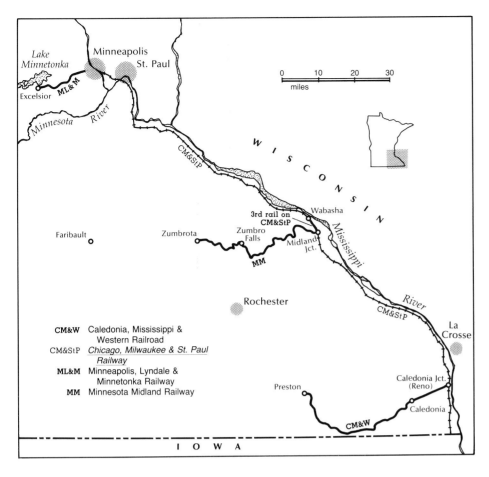

CM&W	Caledonia, Mississippi & Western Railroad
CM&StP	*Chicago, Milwaukee & St. Paul Railway*
ML&M	Minneapolis, Lyndale & Minnetonka Railway
MM	Minnesota Midland Railway

Minnesota Midland Railway

Local parties at Wabasha organized the Minnesota Midland on January 15, 1876, to run up the valley of the Zumbro River and across southern Minnesota to Ortonville at the southern end of Big Stone Lake on the South Dakota border. If completed, the line would have been about 200 miles. They began building in 1877 and by the end of the year had reached Millville (28 miles). The first five miles of the route were third rail laid on the Chicago, Milwaukee & St. Paul main line south of Wabasha to Midland Junction. By February 1878 the management was reportedly seriously embarrassed; only Mazeppa and Zumbrota of the on-line communities were willing to honor their commitments of assistance. For $20,000 in improvements, the management agreed to lease the line in 1878 for a year to the CM&StP. Henry Crawford, a Chicago lawyer who had invested $60,000 in the enterprise, brought suit alleging a collusion to deprive him of his equity in the corporation. The officers managed to open the line to Zumbrota (59 miles) on May 22, 1878, but could proceed no farther. Crawford's suit prevented the CM&StP from absorbing the Midland until February 12, 1883, but it

was thereafter operated as a narrow gauge branch. It was converted on the weekend of June 6–7, 1903, and extended 35 miles from Zumbrota to Faribault. It served as part of the Milwaukee Road's extensive network of branch lines in southeastern Minnesota.

The former narrow gauge mileage was abandoned from Midland Junction to Zumbro Falls (36 miles) in 1934 and from Zumbro Falls to Zumbrota in 1952.

Mississippi

Greenville, Columbus & Birmingham Railroad

Projects for a railroad east from the Mississippi River port of Greenville dated from the pre–Civil War period, and several more were developed immediately after the conflict. D. A. Butterfield on March 5, 1872, formed the Arkansas City & Grenada Railroad, which secured some subscriptions, but failed to gain approval of a subsidy from Washington County at an election of December 23, 1872. On March 4, 1873, Butterfield secured a charter for the Greenville, Columbus & Birmingham Railroad, with the proviso that the new corporation might retain the subscriptions and rights gathered by the old. Butterfield secured $40,000 in subscriptions to bonds at Winona on the Chicago, St. Louis & New Orleans (Illinois Central) main line and began grading from Greenville straight east toward Winona. A dispute with the trustees of the bonds concerning the expenses of grading the first nine miles to Stoneville caused Butterfield to leave the enterprise and brought construction to a halt.

W. G. Yerger of Greenville revived the project in 1877, gaining a subscription by the Greenville town government of $20,000. The railroad was built quickly on the completed grade to Stoneville and began regular service on April 8, 1878. The railroad proved profitable, hauling cotton and lumber. In 1879 it built a branch of 12 miles south from Stoneville along Deer Creek to Arcola, mainly to serve lumber camps. After a subscription of $75,000 was secured from Sunflower County, the main line was pushed east, reaching Johnsonville (31 miles) on September 2, 1881.

On October 11, 1881, the directors met to consider a proposal of the Richmond & Danville, a principal precursor of the

Southern Railway, to merge the Greenville, Columbus & Birmingham with the unbuilt Columbus, Fayette & Decatur into the Georgia Pacific Railway, which the R&D projected from Atlanta to Greenville via Birmingham, Alabama, and Columbus, Mississippi. The offer was accepted, and the narrow gauge became the Mississippi Division of the Georgia Pacific. Under the new owner, the Deer Creek branch was extended to Percy (24 miles) in January 1882. Although the branch was projected to Rolling Fork (40 miles), it was not extended farther as a narrow gauge.

The Georgia Pacific project approached completion in mid-1889. Track was built both westward from Columbus and eastward from a point on the Sunflower River near Johnsonville. Transitionally, the track built eastward was laid with three rails, apparently as far as Greenwood (55 miles). The last spike in the Atlanta-Greenville direct line was driven near Winona on June 15, 1887. The Richmond & Danville, which had leased the Georgia Pacific in November 1888, proceeded to get rid of the remaining narrow gauge on the main line. The Greenville-Johnsonville mileage was converted on August 20, 1889.

The Deer Creek branch, being uncompleted and lightly utilized, was left narrow gauge. The branch had been immediately paralleled by the Louisville, New Orleans & Texas main line in 1884. In 1904, in anticipation of an extension of 12 miles from Percy to Richey in 1906, the Southern Railway of Mississippi, as the Georgia Pacific was then known, standard gauged the branch. The entire property west of Columbus became independent in 1920 as the Columbus & Greenville Railroad. The company went bankrupt in 1921, causing the receiver to sell off the Deer Creek branch on July 24, 1922, to A. F. Gardner, who scrapped it. The Columbus & Greenville survived as an independent short line until 1972, when it was sold to the Illinois Central Gulf, which, after a flood in March 1973, decided to abandon the property. Local interests repurchased the railroad and in 1975 restored it to independence. The former narrow gauge portion from Greenville to a crossing of the Sunflower River near Johnsonville remains part of its main line.

REFERENCE: Louis R. Saillard, *Delta Route: A History of the Columbus & Greenville Railway* (Columbus, Miss.: Columbus & Greenville Railway, 1981).

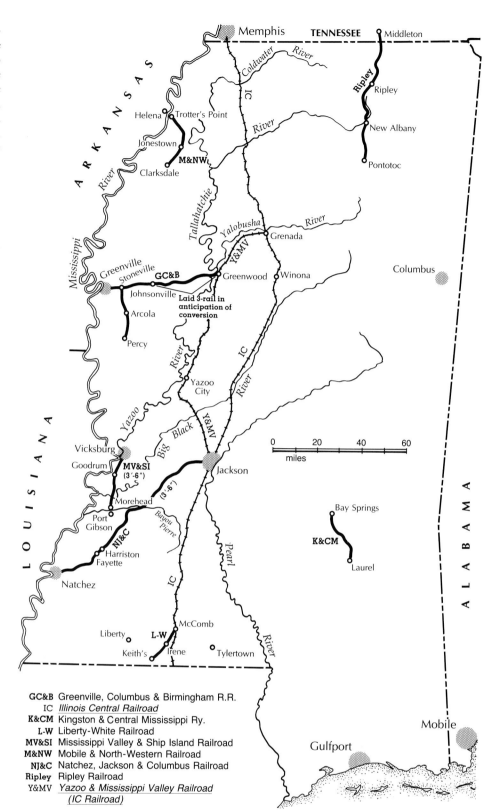

GC&B Greenville, Columbus & Birmingham R.R.
  IC *Illinois Central Railroad*
K&CM Kingston & Central Mississippi Ry.
 L-W Liberty-White Railroad
MV&SI Mississippi Valley & Ship Island Railroad
M&NW Mobile & North-Western Railroad
NJ&C Natchez, Jackson & Columbus Railroad
Ripley Ripley Railroad
Y&MV *Yazoo & Mississippi Valley Railroad (IC Railroad)*

Kingston & Central Mississippi Railway

Transitionally, this railway company operated a former lumber railroad that was to be incorporated into the Gulf, Mobile & Northern main line. Francis Lampe and his associates of Laurel secured a charter for the company on March 5, 1901, and purchased the Kingston Lumber Company's railroad, which ran northwest from Laurel into unpopulated country. The lumber company agreed to extend the line to a length of 25 miles to a townsite called Bay Springs, and to turn it over to the railway company on September 1, 1901, for $15,000 per mile in stock. The railway was not finished to Bay

Springs by the date specified, but appears to have been completed later in 1901. Lampe planned to extend the line north to Memphis and south to the Mobile, Jackson & Kansas City's railhead at Merrill, Mississippi.

Rather, Lampe and his group sold the line on June 30, 1902, to the Mobile, Jackson & Kansas City, which was building north toward Laurel. About the end of 1902 the new owner simply shut down the narrow gauge, removed it, and prepared to use the grade when the main line reached Laurel. Standard gauge track was laid on the former narrow gauge in January 1904.

The subsequent history of the line is the same as that of the larger and more important narrow gauge component of the MJ&KC main line, the Ripley Railroad. The Laurel–Bay Springs mileage was among the track turned over by the Illinois Central Gulf to the Gulf & Mississippi in 1985. It was sold to the Mid South Rail Corporation in April 1988.

Liberty-White Railroad

On December 22, 1902, J. J. White, a lumber operator of McComb, incorporated the Liberty-White Railroad to connect McComb on the Illinois Central main line with Liberty, seat of Amite County, 24 miles to the west. For seven miles to a junction at Irene, White laid third rail along a 3'-0" lumber railroad that his firm had previously operated. The incorporation made the narrow gauge a common carrier. At the time that the standard gauge line to Liberty was opened on July 20, 1904, the narrow gauge ran 17.6 miles to Keith's, probably a lumber camp. On the basis of the railroad's entries in the *Official Guide of the Railways*, the narrow gauge ceased operation in 1908 and was removed in 1912. The standard gauge railroad was projected as a line across southern Mississippi from Natchez to Columbia, but only 25 miles southeast from McComb to Tylertown were built toward that end. The Tylertown extension was abandoned in 1918 and the Liberty line in 1921.

Mississippi Valley & Ship Island Railroad

Gauge: 3'-6"

Under the name Vicksburg, Pensacola & Ship Island Railroad, this project was undertaken as a line diagonally across southern Mississippi. In spite of extensive aid from Vicksburg, Warren County, and the State of Mississippi, the management in 1872 achieved only 17.5 miles of grade south from Vicksburg to the Big Black River. The railroad was variously reported as a 5'-0" and a 3'-0" line, but track was never laid.

To make use of the grade and to tap the public assistance, which included the right to borrow from the state's Chickasaw School Fund at the rate of $10,000 per mile, N. H. Harris of Vicksburg reformed the enterprise as the Mississippi Valley & Ship Island Railroad. Track was laid to Goodrum (ten miles) early in 1874, but further progress was stopped by a suit between the company and the state concerning issuance of the state bonds. Not until 1881 did the railroad lay track on the remainder of the grade to the Big Black River. The management had gained control of the existing Grand Gulf & Port Gibson, two miles of which it planned to convert to narrow gauge for an entry into Port Gibson, the first major town on its route, and the remaining six miles of which it planned to use as a branch to Grand Gulf on the Mississippi. The management was unable to progress far enough to implement this plan. Tracklaying halted at the end of 1881 at an end-of-track on the north bank of Bayou Pierre called Morehead (26 miles), only about a mile short of the proposed junction. The management lacked funds to bridge the bayou.

The railroad was sold under foreclosure on September 5, 1883, for $27,000 to J. B. Howe, who represented the bondholders. Howe completed a transaction initiated in 1882 for inclusion of the MV&SI in the Louisville, New Orleans & Texas, which was building its Memphis–New Orleans main line along the east side of the Mississippi. The LNO&T converted the MV&SI about July 1883. The railroad became the main line of the Illinois Central's Yazoo & Mississippi Valley in 1892. Except for about eight miles from Vicksburg to Le Tourneau, the Vicksburg–Port Gibson line was abandoned in 1984. The branch to Le Tourneau was turned over to the Mid South Rail Corporation in 1986.

Mobile & North-Western Railroad

As projected, this railroad was to be a diagonal line of about 320 miles across Mississippi from Mobile, Alabama, to Helena, Arkansas. The company was chartered on July 20, 1870, and in 1874 did some grading from the point opposite Helena known successively as Dowd's Landing, Glendale, and Trotter's Point. A locomotive bought for use there was sold for debt at a sheriff's auction, and a bargeload of iron was never laid.

In 1877 a contract was let to Thomas Lyon of Mobile to resume building. He laid about eight miles of track in 1877 and nine in 1878, reaching Jonestown by the end of the year. In 1879 he laid track to a point about a mile short of Clarksdale, and apparently completed the railroad (31 miles) in 1880. The company was almost without funds, and paid the expenses of building from receipts as they arrived. Lyon was president of the railroad by 1882. Traffic was mainly between Clarksdale, Jonestown, and steamers on the Mississippi. A contract was let in 1881 for extension to the Tallahatchie River, about 30 miles, but no track was laid beyond Clarksdale. If extended, the railroad would have run via Yazoo City and Jackson to Mobile.

Completion of the Louisville, New Orleans & Texas Railway's main line between Memphis and New Orleans via Clarksdale in 1884 deprived the narrow gauge of much of its traffic. A receiver was appointed in 1886. The LNO&T became interested in the northernmost seven miles of the narrow gauge, from its intersection at Lula to Glendale, as part of a projected branch to Helena. The LNO&T bought the narrow gauge in October 1889 and began preparations to convert it. The southernmost 12 miles, from Eagle Nest to Clarksdale, were abandoned as redundant upon the LNO&T main line. Conversion of the remainder was undertaken in November 1889. The railroad built inclines on both sides of the river, about 4,000 feet of track at Helena, and some additional trackage at Trotter's Point, and arranged to use the former Burlington Route transfer steamer *J. F. Joy*. The railroad began ferrying cars into Helena in September 1890. The company was absorbed into the Yazoo & Mississippi Valley subsidiary of the Illinois Central in 1892.

Of the former narrow gauge, the two miles from Jonestown to Eagle Nest were abandoned in 1912, the Lula–Trotter's Point portion (including the ferry to Helena) in 1973, and the Lula-Jonestown trackage in 1983.

Natchez, Jackson & Columbus Railroad

Gauge: 3'-6"

General Will T. Martin and other businessmen of Natchez secured a charter for this railroad on July 21, 1870. Their principal interest was in securing a flow of cotton from inland Mississippi to river steamers at Natchez. Although they had some private financing, they depended mainly on bond issues of towns and county governments, which were exchanged for securities of the company. They proceeded conservatively, building track only when funds were in hand. Beginning with seven miles in 1873, they continued northeast through relatively easy country, reaching the first major town, Fayette (26 miles) in September 1876. In 1878 track reached Martin (43 miles), an end-of-track named for the president. The management secured an additional $225,000 from Natchez in 1880, with which the line was completed to Jackson (98 miles) on September 14, 1882. This was a relatively large narrow gauge, operated with seven locomotives in 1885. It was the longest 3'-6" railroad in the country.

Martin had financed construction largely by issuing 10 percent bonds in exchange for county and municipal bonds. Because of the heavy interest expense, he attempted, unsuccessfully, to refinance the railroad at lower interest rates. His problems prevented him from extending the line. In 1882 Hinds County's stock in the company was reportedly sold to parties connected with the Georgia Pacific, who planned to convert the line to 5'-0" and extend it about 140 miles to Columbus. In 1885 a group interested in the development of mineral land in Alabama reportedly agreed to convert the line within two years and push it on to Columbus. Further extension to Decatur, Alabama, was discussed, but none of these projects was implemented. Rather, the Louisville, New Orleans & Texas began buying stock of the company in 1888, assumed control in July 1889, and completed purchase on March 28, 1890. Mainly interested in access to Natchez, the LNO&T converted to 4'-8½" the westernmost 28 miles from Harriston on its Memphis–New Orleans main line in September 1889. The Illinois Central acquired the LNO&T and merged the company into its Yazoo & Mississippi Valley subsidiary in 1892. The IC converted the remaining narrow gauge, Harriston-Jackson, on August 12, 1894.

Except for six miles from Natchez to Foster, the entire former narrow gauge was abandoned in four segments between 1979 and 1982.

Ripley Railroad

As Mississippi's first narrow gauge, and one of the earliest in the United States, this property received disproportionate attention. The railroad was promoted by Colonel William C. Falkner, a Confederate veteran, lawyer, novelist, and great-grandfather of author William Faulkner. His principal interest was in providing an outlet

for cotton from Tippah County, of which Ripley was the seat, but the area also produced lumber. Falkner hoped to avail himself of a subsidy of $4,000 per mile for railroads built within the state, but narrow gauge construction did not qualify. He induced the state legislature to change the law, and to charter the Ripley Railroad as a qualifying corporation on May 12, 1871. The $4,000 per mile and other funds Falkner was able to raise were insufficient to bring forth the railroad; Falkner entered into an agreement with the Memphis & Charleston, with which the Ripley was to connect at Middleton, Tennessee, for the larger railroad to provide rails and equipment. This arrangement allowed the railroad to be completed from Middleton to Ripley (24 miles) on August 30, 1872.

The railroad was unusual for a narrow gauge in following ridges to avoid bridges and trestles. Falkner prided himself on its cheapness, claiming erroneously that it was the least expensive ever built. The investment was actually about $15,200 per mile, including equipment. The track was unballasted; its rapid deterioration was publicized as an early example of the evils of narrow gauge practice.

Falkner had longer-range ambitions: to extend the line south to Mississippi City on the Gulf Coast and north toward the Ohio River. In 1878 he changed the name of the railroad to Ship Island, Ripley & Kentucky Railroad. In the same year the corporation missed interest payments and was placed in the hands of a trustee, R. J. Thurmond, but Falkner remained in control. To undertake the line to the Gulf Coast, Falkner associated himself with Wirt Adams in reviving the Gulf & Ship Island Railroad, a pre–Civil War project for a north-south line through Mississippi. The G&SI was rechartered in 1882 and granted the rights of the original corporation in 1884. This action produced a legal conflict between the corporation and various settlers who had taken title to land originally granted to the G&SI. In 1886 the conflict was resolved by confirming the titles of the settlers to their land and deeding the unclaimed land to the railroad. This arrangement allowed construction of the railroad to begin. On the north end, 37 miles of narrow gauge were built from Ripley to Pontotoc, the second county seat to the south, and on the south end about 20 miles of standard gauge were built north from Gulfport. The narrow gauge was completed in June 1887 and leased to Falkner's Ship Island, Ripley & Kentucky.

A pair of personal tragedies prevented any further development of the project.

First, Adams was killed in a duel at Jackson on May 1, 1888. His death precipitated a foreclosure sale at which Falkner bought the Ripley-Pontotoc portion of the G&SI on August 1, 1889. The standard gauge portion became the Illinois Central's Jackson-Gulfport line. Falkner had just bought his SIR&K out of receivership on July 23, 1889, and planned to consolidate the two narrow gauges.

The second tragedy occurred less than two years after Adams's death. Falkner and R. J. Thurmond, who had remained as trustee of the SIR&K until 1887, had become bitter enemies. They opposed each other in an election for the state legislature on November 6, 1889. Falkner won, but upon learning the results Thurmond shot and killed him on the streets of Ripley. Falkner's heirs, under John W. T. Falkner of Oxford, formed the Gulf & Chicago Railroad on February 20, 1890, to take over the narrow gauge. They then leased it on July 1, 1903, to the Mobile, Jackson & Kansas City Railroad, which had been organized by Colonel Frank B. Merrill of Mobile. The traumatic events of 1888 and 1889 had undoubtedly delayed conversion of the narrow gauge for years. Merrill converted the southernmost 18 miles, from the crossing of the St. Louis–San Francisco's Birmingham line at New Albany to Pontotoc, on June 20, 1904, and the remainder on June 27, 1905.

The line's later history is complicated. Merrill was interested in making the former narrow gauge part of a line from Mobile to Jackson, Tennessee, which would parallel the Mobile & Ohio through a set of county seats to the west. This line was completed from Mobile to Middleton on May 1, 1906. Under a plan of 1907, the Gulf & Chicago and the MJ&KC were merged to form the New Orleans, Mobile & Chicago on December 1, 1909. This company was placed in receivership in 1913 and reorganized as the Gulf, Mobile & Northern Railroad on January 1, 1917. This corporation built the extension to Jackson, Tennessee, in 1919. It merged with the M&O into the Gulf, Mobile & Ohio in 1940 and with the Illinois Central into the Illinois Central Gulf in 1972. The Middleton-Pontotoc mileage was among the trackage spun off to the Gulf & Mississippi Railroad in 1985. It was conveyed to the Mid South Rail Corporation in April 1988.

REFERENCE: James Hutton Lemly, *Gulf, Mobile & Ohio* (Homewood, Ill.: Richard D. Irwin, 1953), pp. 284–87.

Missouri

Campbell & St. Francis Valley Railway

The Campbell Lumber Co. built this railroad as a private carrier ancillary to its mill at Campbell in the bootheel area of Missouri. The main line ran 20 miles south along the west bank of the St. Francis River to Buckhorn, Arkansas. A branch ran five miles from Nimmons to Webber's Mill. Beginning in 1903 the railroad was shown in the *Official Guide of the Railways*, and apparently began functioning as a common carrier, though it was never enrolled as such with the regulatory commissions of the two states. Probably as a result of changes in their geographic pattern of operations, the Campbell interests on March 27, 1906, re-incorporated the carrier as the St. Louis, Kennett & Southeastern Railroad. Instead of converting the line directly, they built a new main line of 19 miles from Piggott, Arkansas, on the Cotton Belt to Kennett on the east side of the St. Francis. They made use of about 4.5 miles of the narrow gauge between Nimmons and West Kennett. When the new line was completed about 1910, the 13.5 miles of the old line from Campbell to Nimmons were abandoned. Portions of the Buckhorn and Webber's Mill lines remained in service as narrow gauge, along with three-rail track to connect them, until about 1913. The Piggott-Kennett line became a branch of the St. Louis–San Francisco in 1927 and was abandoned in 1958.

Mississippi River & Bonne Terre Railway

The St. Joseph and Des Loge lead companies opened a railroad on January 18, 1880, between Summit and Bonne Terre (13 miles) as an adjunct to their mining operations in St. Francois County. The railroad had no separate incorporation and was known simply by the name of the lead companies—the St. Joseph & Des Loge Railway. In 1887, when the St. Joseph company bought control of Des Loge, the railroad, still a private carrier, became known as the St. Joseph Railway.

In an effort to reach the Mississippi River for interchange with steamboats and barges, the lead companies incorporated the railroad on May 11, 1888, as the Mississippi River & Bonne Terre Railway, a common carrier, and began building north toward the river. Track reached Crystal City (26 miles north of Bonne Terre) in the fall of 1889 and Riverside (31 miles) on March 10, 1890. The line was extended 15 miles to the south in 1891 to the hamlet of Doe Run to serve another lead mine. Regular passenger service was established between Riverside and Doe Run on April 3, 1892. The lead companies operated the railroad integrally with their various spurs to mining installations. The railroad was reported to have seven locomotives and 124 cars.

Although the lead companies had professed to be mainly interested in a connection with water carriers, they found the narrow gauge's incompatibility a handicap and set about converting it almost as soon as it reached Doe Run. The portion from Riverside to Bonne Terre was converted late in 1893 and the Doe Run extension in early March 1894. Until 1899 the railroad made connections with railroads at St. Louis and East St. Louis, 29 miles upriver from Riverside, by transferring cars on barges of the Wiggins Ferry Co. Through passenger cars were run into St. Louis Union Station on Iron Mountain trains from Riverside.

The lead companies sold the railroad to the Missouri-Illinois, a Missouri Pacific affiliate, in 1929. The property was absorbed into the Missouri-Illinois in 1945 and into the Missouri Pacific in 1978. The portion from a junction with the Missouri-Illinois at Derby to Doe Run, 11 miles, was abandoned in 1941, and the 22 miles in the middle of the railroad from Howe to Bonne Terre, which contained a tunnel, were abandoned in 1969. The northernmost eight miles of the former narrow gauge and the eight miles south of Bonne Terre are in existence at the present.

Missouri Southern Railroad

J. G. Clarkson, proprietor of the Clarkson Sawmill Co. at Leeper, together with Daniel Goettel of Oil City, Pennsylvania, and some associates, formed the Mill Spring, Current River & Barnesville Railroad on February 23, 1884. Their purpose was to extend an existing narrow gauge at the mill at Leeper northwest into Reynolds County. Their objective was Barnesville (Ellington), 29 miles away, but as with many lumber railroads, progress was slow. Track reached Keystone (9 miles) in 1884, Penn (12 miles) in 1885, and Carter (14 miles) in 1886. Probably for simplicity, the name of the railroad was changed in 1886 to Missouri Southern. Track was pressed on to Bowers (26 miles) in 1895 and to Ellington on December 1, 1896. A major extension of 14 miles was made to Tralaloo (Reynolds) in 1903. The railroad had several lumbering spurs, the longest a branch of 12 miles to Phelps. The company operated with rod engines on its main line, but used Shays on the spurs. Daily passenger service was provided, connecting with trains on the St. Louis, Iron Mountain & Southern at Leeper.

In 1906 the railroad was sold to Frank D. Stout of Chicago, who was associated with several businessmen of Leeper. They converted the railroad on March 30, 1907, and planned to extend it 40 miles to Salem

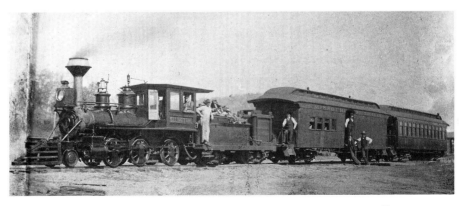

A passenger train of the Missouri Southern Railroad with the locomotive *Ellington*. (M. R. Havens collection, National Museum of Transport.)

on the St. Louis–San Francisco. Actually, they extended the line only ten miles to Bunker.

With the exhaustion of timber in the area, the railroad was mainly unprofitable after 1930, and was abandoned on May 20, 1941.

REFERENCE: H. Roger Grant, "Missouri Southern: History of a Shortline," Railway & Locomotive Historical Society *Bulletin*, no. 123 (1970), pp. 44–51.

Poplar Bluff & Dan River Railway

Gauge: 3'-10"

H. I. Ruth organized this railroad as a common carrier on February 27, 1906, and began operations the same year. The line was a facility for his lumber installation at Ruthville, variously reported as 15 to 18 miles southeast of Poplar Bluff. Two locomotives and 46 cars, apparently all flatcars for carriage of logs or finished lumber, were reported. The line had four miles of branches in 1911. Regular passenger service was never advertised in the *Official Guide of the Railways*. In 1913 the line was reported to have shrunk to six miles, and on October 9 the railroad notified *Poor's Manual* that it had ceased to be a common carrier. On February 10, 1916, the management notified *Poor's* that the line had been abandoned. It was, however, revived about 1918 as a private carrier of the Hargrove & Ruth Lumber Co., apparently at its full length. It was reported to the ICC as dismantled in 1933.

St. Joseph & Des Moines Railroad

John L. Motter of St. Joseph and his associates chartered the St. Joseph & Des Moines on August 20, 1877, in the apparent intention of building a direct narrow gauge between the cities of its corporate title. The railroad was opened to Helena (17 miles) on November 4, 1878, to Union Star (25 miles) on March 24, 1879, and to Albany (50 miles), seat of Gentry County, on October 15, 1879. The narrow gauge was a modest property with three locomotives, four passenger cars, 43 boxcars, and 22 flatcars. The promoters had financed the railroad with a mortgage of $250,000, the interest on which proved an insuperable burden. The railroad was able to cover its variable expenses, but not its fixed charges. No further construction could be attempted. In spite of the community of gauge and

similarity of route, no effort seems to have been made to connect with the Des Moines, Osceola & Southern.

The promoters' financial difficulties led them to sell a controlling interest in the railroad to the Chicago, Burlington & Quincy in 1880. The CB&Q formally leased the property on October 1, 1884, but the lease was to become effective upon widening the gauge. All of the officers thereafter were Burlington officials. From the outset the Burlington planned upon conversion of the line to extend it to Mount Ayr, Iowa, to connect with existing branch lines to form an alternative route between Chicago and St. Joseph off the main line at Chariton, Iowa. The Burlington did not convert the line until February 8, 1885. Standard gauge service began the following day.

The CB&Q made good its plan to connect the former narrow gauge with the main line at Chariton. Since the alternative route to St. Joseph was about 25 miles longer than the direct route from Chicago via Quincy and the Hannibal & St. Joseph, the line was no more than a major branch. It was abandoned by the Burlington Northern on February 14, 1982.

Sedalia, Warsaw & Southern Railroad

W. Gentry of Sedalia and his associates organized this railroad on September 16, 1879, to build to Warsaw, seat of Benton County, and if possible farther south into the Ozarks. The railroad was opened to Warsaw (42 miles) on December 1, 1880. As an independent railroad, the company had only a brief history. The Missouri Pacific bought two-thirds control on August 1, 1881, and began operating it as part of the Missouri Division. The MP immediately announced an interest in converting it, but legal problems prevented conversion for more than 20 years. Standard gauge ties were being laid in place by 1889. The railroad had two locomotives, one passenger car, one baggage-mail-express, 14 boxcars, nine stockcars, 19 flatcars, four coal cars, and one caboose. By 1898 the company had a third locomotive.

In April 1891 the railroad was reorganized as the Sedalia, Warsaw & Southwestern Railway with George Gould and other MP officials as incorporators. Again an intention to convert was announced. Charles S. Treadwell of St. Louis and other minority shareholders brought a suit in September 1893 to remove the line from the MP's control with the intent of converting it and extending it to Springfield, about 74 miles.

George Gould, in response, stated that the MP also planned conversion and extension to Springfield. The case was initially decided against the MP. James E. Thompson of Sedalia was appointed receiver, but was replaced by Thomas F. Mitchum in 1894. The MP appealed the decision and won. When the line was returned to the MP in December 1894, the management once more announced its intention to convert quickly. The projected extension to Springfield was never undertaken.

Actual efforts to convert were begun in the second half of 1901. Standard gauge rails were received in December, and the railroad was converted over the weekend of August 2–4, 1902. The line was operated as the MP's Warsaw branch. The MP received the ICC's permission to abandon it in February 1944, and the *Official Guide* reported it abandoned in October 1946.

West End Narrow Gauge Railroad

Erastus Wells, president of the Olive Street Railroad (Missouri Railroad), formed the St. Louis & Florissant Railroad in 1872 as a suburban connection for his horsecar line on Olive Street, the main thoroughfare directly west from downtown St. Louis. Beginning in the summer of 1873 and finishing in early August of 1874, Wells graded the line. He subsequently erected its bridges, but he proved unable to raise funds for completion. The property was sold on January 9, 1875, and reorganized as the West End Narrow Gauge Railroad, still under Wells's ownership. He began tracklaying in the spring and by the end of the year had the line open from Olive Street and Grand Avenue in St. Louis to Normandy (8 miles). He was unable to finance an extension until 1878, but then laid track on the full length of the grade to Florissant (18 miles), opening the line about October 1. The line was intended as a suburban passenger hauler to the northwestern suburban area, but it owned a boxcar and five flatcars for a limited freight service. At first the line was reportedly well patronized, but it was burdened with a heavy debt from construction. The railroad was sold under foreclosure in March 1879 and reorganized as the West End Narrow Gauge Railway, still under Wells's presidency.

In 1883 the line was sold to James E. Young of Chicago, who wanted to use its entrance into St. Louis for a suburban railway to Creve Coeur Lake and St. Charles, west of the existing trackage. Consistent with his plans, he changed the name to St.

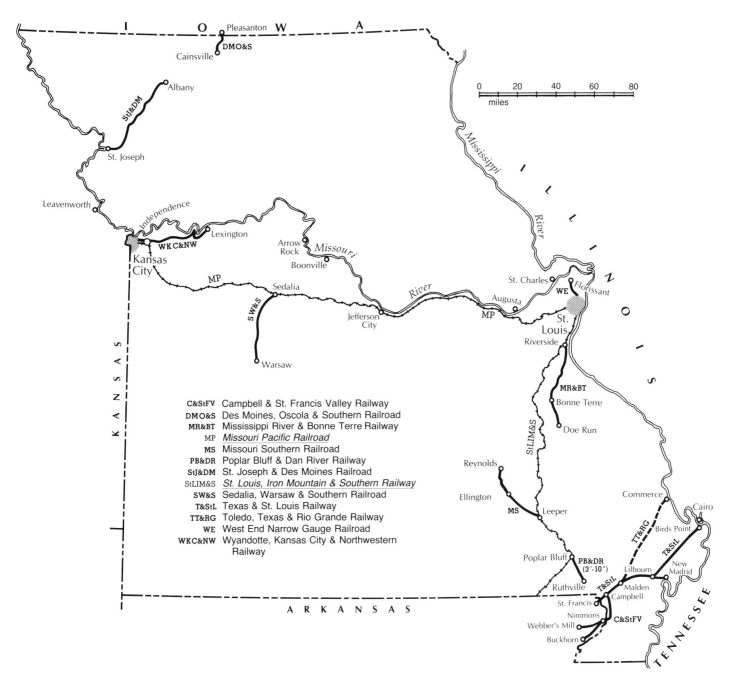

Louis, Creve Coeur & St. Charles Railway. He was unable to execute his project and in 1883 sold the property to F. M. Colburn of Indianapolis and his associates, who were interested in bringing the existing line into downtown St. Louis. Because steam locomotives would not be tolerated in the streets of the central area, and the electric streetcar had not yet been perfected, they decided upon building a double-track cable railway. They changed the corporate title to the St. Louis Cable & Western Railway, an odd name, but one thoroughly descriptive of the operation. Now having no incentive to interchange with the Olive Street horsecar line, they cut the narrow gauge back to the corner of Vandeventer and Morgan (En-

right) streets, from which the cable line was built to the corner of Sixth and Locust. Although it was the first endless cable line in St. Louis, existing horsecar operators had preempted major streets, forcing the company to build a tortuous approach via Wash (Cole), 14th, Lucas, and 13th streets that involved excessive curvature—the bane of cable traction. The cable line of 3.2 miles, built to the common St. Louis streetcar gauge of 4'-10", was opened on April 15, 1886. The cable system proved so difficult that it was substantially rebuilt in June 1889 to operate with two shorter cables instead of one of 34,600 feet. The modification required building a new powerhouse with two sets of tension and winding machinery,

adjacent to the original. The Citizens' Railway and the Missouri Railroad had opened cable lines on parallel streets in 1887 and 1888, respectively, both on much easier accesses to the business district.

The Cable & Western was placed in receivership on October 17, 1889, in response to actions by the Walker Manufacturing Co. and John Roebling's Sons Co., which had supplied winding machinery and cables for the recent reconstruction. Lee, Higginson & Co. of Boston, which held the company's first and second mortgages, proposed to reorganize the line as the St. Louis Central & Western, to extend the cable line to Forest Park, and to convert and electrify the narrow gauge. Instead, the property was sold in June 1890 to Charles H. Turner and men active in the previous management, who proposed to convert the entire system to an electric line of 4'-10" gauge. They formed the St. Louis & Suburban Railway and in the summer of 1891 strung overhead wire over the narrow gauge. They then shut down the cable powerhouse on October 27, 1891, and reopened the whole system about January 1, 1892, as a 4'-10" electric line operated out of a powerhouse at De Hodiamont near the city limits. The line was acquired by the United Railways of St. Louis on January 1, 1907. The suburban portion was abandoned in 1948, but the urban portion, known as the Hodiamont car line, was St. Louis's longest-lived streetcar operation, lasting until May 21, 1966.

REFERENCES: Berl Katz, *St. Louis Cable Railways* (Chicago: Electric Railway Historical Society, 1965), pp. 4–6; George W. Hilton, *The Cable Car in America* (Berkeley, Calif.: Howell-North Books, 1971), p. 341.

Wyandotte, Kansas City & Northwestern Railway

Business leaders of Kansas City formed two interrelated projects for narrow gauges in 1871. The Wyandotte, Kansas City & Northwestern Railway was to run from Kansas City and Wyandotte (Kansas City, Kansas) into northern Kansas and southern Nebraska on a route to depend on local financial assistance. The Kansas City, Independence & Lexington Railroad was to run east along the south bank of the Missouri River to Lexington. A bond issue for municipal subsidy of the line east was defeated in April 1872, but the line west won a similar election during the summer. The WKC&NW, however, could not arrange enough local support in Kansas to allow the project to start. An arrangement was made early in 1873, and approved by the voters, for the WKC&NW to retain its subsidy but to build east on the route of the KCI&L. The directors of the WKC&NW preferred to build out of the city via the levee on the south bank of the Missouri River, rather than through McGee's Addition in the south part of the city. Their plan provoked a lengthy legal action, but ultimately the Jackson County Court approved the arrangement. The promoters, who were led by F. C. Eames of Independence, were to receive $150,000 in municipal bonds, half on arrival of the line in Independence, half on completion to the coalfield in Lafayette County. The projected route was more grandiose, a 240-mile line to St. Louis that would cross the Missouri at Boonville, fol-

low the north bank, then recross at St. Charles. If built, the line would have been similar to the Missouri-Kansas-Texas's later entry into St. Louis.

The railroad was opened from Kansas City to Independence (ten miles) in August 1874. The management attempted to secure the full $150,000 in bonds, even though it was still some 23 miles short of the coalfield, but was apparently unsuccessful. By the fall of 1875 the management had, however, secured its right-of-way as far as Lexington, seat of Lafayette County, and laid seven miles of track. Financing was arranged in Britain. Grand Pass, one of the towns on the route to Boonville, refused the company assistance late in 1875, and the new state constitution that took effect on December 1, 1875, prohibited municipal subscriptions to railroads. Under the circumstances, the best the railroad could do was complete the line to Lexington. Track reached Wellington in the coalfield in May, and passenger trains began running to Lexington, 44 miles from Kansas City, on August 4, 1876. Meetings were held to raise $300,000 to push eastward and to build a branch from Marshall to Sedalia, but no further work was done. In 1876 the management attempted to secure the right to extend track west to the Union Depot and the stockyards, but was rebuffed by the Kansas City council. The management announced it would build an elevator and transfer facility at Independence and thereafter interchange with the Missouri Pacific at that point. The railroad had five locomotives, five passenger, two baggage, and 114 freight cars. Traffic was mainly coal from the Wellington area. The physical plant was poor, mainly in having extensive grades in the first 20 miles from Kansas City to Lake City.

The railroad failed in 1877 and was sold on January 22, 1878, to S. S. Jackson of New York and his associates, who formed the Kansas City & Eastern Railway to operate it. Jackson announced that the railroad would be extended 82 miles to Boonville, but again nothing was done. Rather, late in 1879 Jackson sold the railroad to Jay Gould, who leased it to his Missouri Pacific for five years effective December 9, 1879. The KC&E was then merged into the MOP on September 22, 1880. Gould was interested in integrating the line with the various branches of the MP in the area and converted it on August 19–20, 1882. He had no interest in the line's entry into Kansas City, and had torn up the tracks west of Independence in November 1881. The Missouri Supreme Court in 1883 ordered the MP to restore the trackage, which directly paralleled the MP main line. The com-

pany complied, laying standard gauge tracks, partly on the former right-of-way and partly as multiple track on the main line. The line east of Independence was broken by an abandonment of 5.4 miles between Lake City Junction and Masso Spur in 1935. The portion from Lake City Junction to Lexington, 24 miles, remains in service.

REFERENCE: Charles N. Glaab, *Kansas City and the Railroads* (Madison: State Historical Society of Wisconsin, 1962), pp. 179–84.

Montana

Great Falls & Canada Railway

Like the Aroostook River Railroad in Maine, this carrier was an American subsidiary of a Canadian system, operating a branch that penetrated United States territory. In this instance, the Canadian system was a coal-hauling network of three affiliated companies: the North Western Coal & Navigation Co., the Alberta Railway & Coal Co., and the St. Mary's River Railway. The system was built to 3'-0" instead of to the common Canadian narrow gauge of 3'-6".

The Canadian Pacific Railway reached Medicine Hat, Alberta, in 1883. The NWC&NCo at first sought to connect its coalfield in the Lethbridge area with Medicine Hat by steamers and barges on the Bow River, but navigation was satisfactory only in periods of high water. At the end of the 1884 season the company decided to end the water carriage and to build a narrow gauge railway from Dunmore, seven miles southeast of Medicine Hat on the CP, to Lethbridge. The 109-mile line was opened October 19, 1885. By the end of the decade, the railway was handling 90,000 tons of coal per year. On December 31, 1889, the Alberta Railway & Coal Co. leased the NWC&NCo with an option to purchase the railway, which it exercised in February 1891. During 1890 the ARy&CCo

undertook a line from Ghent (Montana Junction) immediately east of Lethbridge to Coutts (65 miles) on the international border, and thence south 134 miles in Montana to Great Falls. The portion from Sweetgrass on the Montana side of the border to Great Falls was incorporated as the Great Falls & Canada Railway on October 2, 1889. The entire extension of both the Canadian and American companies was completed on October 1, 1890, and opened to traffic on December 8. Rolling stock was used interchangeably between the two, though lettered separately. ARy&CCo built a branch in Canada from Stirling to Cardston and Kimball under the name of the St. Mary's River Railway in 1900 and 1904.

The company leased the original Dunmore-Lethbridge line to the Canadian Pacific on November 27, 1893. The CP converted it shortly and incorporated it into the Crow's Nest Pass line, the CP's second crossing of the Rockies, which was then being projected. The lines south of Lethbridge remained narrow gauge in the coal company's hands until the turn of the century. Conversion began with the laying of third rail on the portion from Montana Junction to Stirling and the portion from Stirling to Raymond on the St. Mary's River line. The line from Stirling, the junction with the St. Mary's line, to Great Falls, was converted on January 1, 1903. In 1904 the parent company reorganized as the Alberta Railway & Irrigation Co. and sold off the mileage in Montana to the Great Northern Railway. The trackage is still in existence as part of the successor Burlington Northern.

REFERENCE: Omer Lavallee, *Narrow Gauge Railways of Canada* (Montreal: Railfare Enterprises, Ltd., 1972), pp. 42–46.

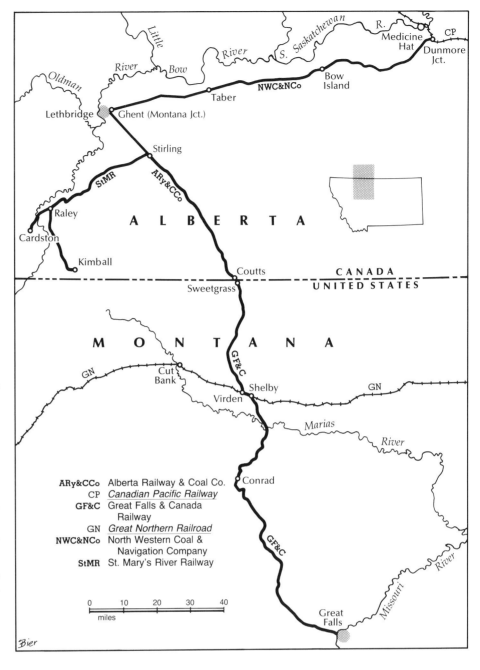

ARy&CCo	Alberta Railway & Coal Co.
CP	*Canadian Pacific Railway*
GF&C	Great Falls & Canada Railway
GN	*Great Northern Railroad*
NWC&NCo	North Western Coal & Navigation Company
StMR	St. Mary's River Railway

Montana Southern Railway

As the last American common carrier narrow gauge built, this railroad is of more interest than its humble nature would otherwise warrant. It was, in fact, an obscure nominal common carrier of the Boston-Montana Mining Co. William R. Allen, president of the mining company and a former lieutenant governor of Montana, incorporated the railroad as the Southern Montana Railway in 1914, but reincorporated it in 1917 as the Montana Southern and undertook construction. He made use of an unbuilt grade of the Butte, Wisdom & Pacific Railway, a Great Northern affiliate. Allen's intention was to build from Divide, on the Union Pacific's former Utah & Northern line 28 miles south of Butte, through rugged country along the Big Hole River to Wisdom and Jackson in Beaverhead County, with branches to French Gulch and Elkhorn. If completed, the line would have been about 128 miles. Actually, the railroad achieved only 40 miles from Divide to Elkhorn, where the mining company had copper pits. The decision to use 3'-0" was dictated by difficulty in acquiring standard gauge equipment during World War I, combined with the ready availability of secondhand rolling stock from the Florence & Cripple Creek, which had been abandoned in 1915. The railroad was completed on November 1, 1919. It had three Baldwin locomotives, 22 freight cars, and three passenger cars. Mainly, traffic was concentrate outbound from the company's mill at Coolidge, timber products, and inbound supplies. Passenger trains principally carried people on company business, but also fishermen attracted by the Big Hole and Wise rivers. Shops were established at Allentown, 12 miles from Divide. The line had a 2.5-percent grade, a tunnel of 210 feet, and the extensive light bridgework characteristic of the narrow gauges. (For map, see Utah.)

As a consequence of the mining company's financial difficulties in the depression of the early 1920s, the railroad was placed under receiver C. S. Muffly in 1923 and reorganized, first as the Montana Southern Railroad in 1925, and second as the Montana Southwestern Railway in 1928. After 1925 operation was intermittent. The railroad was a "circular road" which reported to the Interstate Commerce Commission irregularly. After a flood washed out 12 miles of line in 1927, it reported itself not in operation. The line was restored in 1930, and the company reported itself operating between 1931 and 1933. Apparently it was not regularly operated thereafter. Local newspapers reported the rails being removed in 1940, and the management reported the line abandoned to the ICC as of August 29, 1941.

REFERENCES: Frank Quinn, "Narrow Gauge to Elkhorn," *The Montana Standard*, July 30, 1961; Shirley Wirtz and Lorene Lovell, *One Man's Dream: Elkhorn Mine–Coolidge, Montana* (Butte, Mont.: Ashton Printing, 1976); Roger Breeding, "A Brief History of the Montana Southern Railway," *The Trainsheet* (Newsletter of the Tacoma Chapter, National Railway Historical Society), 22, no. 4 (Apr. 1986), pp. 2–3; collections of Cornelius W. Hauck and Rex C. Myers.

Nebraska

Covington, Columbus & Black Hills Railroad

Gauge: 3'-6"

Judge Asahel W. Hubbard of Sioux City, Iowa, projected this railroad from Covington, Nebraska, immediately opposite Sioux City on the west bank of the Missouri River, to the Black Hills mining area. If a branch to Columbus, Nebraska, on the Union Pacific main line between Omaha and Grand Island was also projected, nothing was done to implement the idea.

The railroad was opened to Ponca, seat of Dixon County, 26 miles, in 1876. The line was projected south of the Missouri River to Niobrara, and thence diagonally through southwestern Dakota Territory to the Black Hills. Hubbard hoped to build on to Niobrara in the spring of 1877 and did some amount of grading. The company encountered financial problems almost immediately, and laid no track beyond Ponca. Creditors applied in September 1877 in federal court for appointment of a receiver, but were

unsuccessful. The judge, however, enjoined the company from disposing of its assets without permission, and directed reports to be made to the court. (For map, see Iowa.)

On behalf of the holders of the mortgage, which amounted to $120,000, George T. M. Davis petitioned for appointment of a receiver in 1878. H. K. Lane, president of the First National Bank of Des Moines, was appointed. Hubbard lost his equity in the railroad, and when he died in 1879, was reported to have been broken financially by the failure. The St. Paul & Sioux City Railroad bought control of the narrow gauge, but initially operated it as agent for the receiver. By 1879 local residents were serving as station agents and in similar capacities on a volunteer basis to keep the railroad operating. The Chicago, St. Paul, Minneapolis & Omaha acquired the St. Paul & Sioux City and with it the narrow gauge on June 1, 1880. The new owner lost little time in converting the line. The conversion date was variously reported as August 1 and September 1, 1880.

The Chicago & North Western Railway bought stock control of the Omaha Road (the CStPM&O) in November 1882. The former narrow gauge was extended to Newcastle in 1893 and to Wynot in 1907, and operated as a minor agricultural branch of the North Western system. It was abandoned in 1933.

Nevada

Battle Mountain & Lewis Railway

In February 1880, not long after the completion of the Nevada Central Railway, gold was found in Lewis Canyon, about ten miles east of the line and 10.5 miles south of Battle Mountain. The Starr Grove Mining Co. began mining operations, and projected a 12-mile railroad, the Battle Mountain & Lewis, from Lewis Junction on the Nevada

Central to Lewis and to the mines south of the town.

Grading on the new railroad began on January 28, 1881. As far as Lewis Station the terrain was flat and construction was easy. The grade reached Lewis on April 25, and service was begun over newly laid rails on July 30, 1881. At first the line rented a Nevada Central locomotive, but in August it secured an engine of its own. During the second half of the year, track was extended up Lewis Canyon by means of switchbacks.

Lewis had grown to a town of some 700, but the mining activity was not sufficient to make the line profitable. In March 1882 the Nevada Central brought an action for recovery of $6,467 for locomotive rentals and other interline charges. The Nevada Central prohibited BM&L trains from using its tracks to reach Battle Mountain, as the BM&L had done since its completion; thus operation of the BM&L was brought to a halt. The Starr Grove Mining Co. went bankrupt, and at a sheriff's sale, the railway right-of-way was sold to H. D. Gates of Lewis for $4,401. The Nevada Central operated occasionally over BM&L rails to serve the mines in 1883 and again in 1885, but thereafter the line was dead. Lander County bought the property at a second sheriff's sale, but about 1890 the line was dismantled.

Carson & Colorado Railroad

Decline of ore output at Virginia City from the peak years of the early and mid-1870s caused Darius O. Mills and Henry M. Yerrington of the Virginia & Truckee Railroad to consider an extension south to the silver camp at Candelaria, Nevada, and into the Owens Valley of California. To this end, they incorporated the Carson & Colorado Railroad on May 10, 1880, with Yerrington as president. In spite of a newspaper report of 1880 that an extension from Candelaria to a connection with the Colorado narrow gauges was planned, "Colorado" in the railroad's title meant the Colorado River, which, being navigable, was a plausible southern objective. Actually, the seriously projected southern terminus was Mojave, California, on the Southern Pacific between Barstow and Bakersfield. Narrow gauge was apparently chosen for the usual considerations of economy.

Construction began at Mound House, ten miles east of Carson City on the V&T main line, on May 31, 1880. Service began on January 8, 1881, with an excursion to Fort Churchill (26 miles). On April 18, track

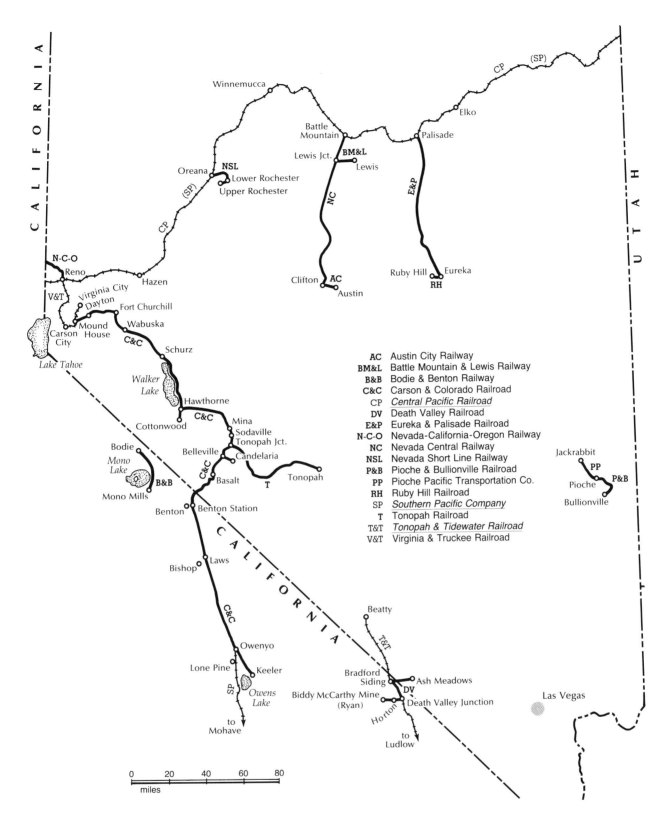

AC Austin City Railway
BM&L Battle Mountain & Lewis Railway
B&B Bodie & Benton Railway
C&C Carson & Colorado Railroad
CP *Central Pacific Railroad*
DV Death Valley Railroad
E&P Eureka & Palisade Railroad
N-C-O Nevada-California-Oregon Railway
NC Nevada Central Railway
NSL Nevada Short Line Railway
P&B Pioche & Bullionville Railroad
PP Pioche Pacific Transportation Co.
RH Ruby Hill Railroad
SP *Southern Pacific Company*
T Tonopah Railroad
T&T *Tonopah & Tidewater Railroad*
V&T Virginia & Truckee Railroad

reached Hawthorne (100 miles), which the railroad had already laid out as a townsite for development. The officials built a toll road from Hawthorne to the mining camp at Bodie, California. The management planned a branch to Bodie, home of the Bodie Railway & Lumber Co., in which Yerrington was interested; but a rail connection was never built. On the last day of 1881 service was extended to Belleville (150 miles). Track reached the first major destination on February 28, 1882, when the main line was extended to Filben and a branch of 5.5 miles was built east to Candelaria. The branch entailed a 2.26-percent grade and a 292-foot trestle 50 feet high. The main line was pressed southward, being built over Montgomery Pass into California during the remainder of 1882. The pass, which required an ascent to 7,138 feet of altitude, involved a tortuous descent at 2.3 percent, with a tunnel of 247 feet. Benton Station was established at the bottom of the grade in January 1883. Track was laid quickly down the relatively unpopulated east side of the Owens Valley, reaching Hawley (Keeler; 293 miles) in July. Members of the management inspected the completed line on July 12, 1883, when Mills reportedly made his famous comment on the railroad's bleak terrain, "Gentlemen, either we built this line 300 miles too long, or 300 years too soon."

Only one addition was made to the narrow gauge mileage, a branch of seven miles from Hawthorne to Cottonwood built in 1890 to serve a woodcutting operation. The branch was removed in 1902, after the C&C's conversion of its locomotives from wood to coal in 1900–1901 had reduced the demand for cordwood.

Completion of the main line in 1883 unfortunately coincided with a decline in mining at Candelaria and elsewhere on the railroad. The corporation was generally unprofitable after 1885, and in 1892 was reorganized as the Carson & Colorado Railway without change in ownership. The repeal of the Sherman Silver Purchase Act in 1893 affected the railroad as it did the Colorado narrow gauges. Mills lost interest in the railroad, and when the Southern Pacific offered him $2.75 million for it, he sold it with great enthusiasm in March 1900. The SP had little interest in the railroad as it stood, but envisioned the route down the Owens Valley as a standard gauge connection from its Central Pacific line to Los Angeles. Events frustrated that project, however.

Collis P. Huntington, the last of the "Big Four" of the Southern Pacific, died during the summer of 1900, and early in 1901 his heirs sold control of the railroad to Edward H. Harriman of the Union Pacific. Harriman had his own plans for a direct route from Salt Lake City to Los Angeles, which he completed in 1906. His approach through Las Vegas was much superior to the proposed conversion and extension of the Carson & Colorado, and the Owens Valley project was quickly dropped.

Meanwhile, the discovery of gold in May 1900 at Tonopah, about 70 miles southeast of Sodaville on the C&C, had initiated a late mining boom. The boom spread to Goldfield, 30 miles to the south of Tonopah, in 1904. These developments brought forth the Tonopah Railroad, built in 1904 from Tonopah Junction, 5.5 miles south of Sodaville, to Tonopah. Although this railroad was built as a narrow gauge, it was slated from the outset for conversion when the C&C was converted. To convert the C&C, the SP, having failed in its attempt to buy the V&T, required some direct access. The management decided upon a standard gauge line of 28 miles from Hazen on the Central Pacific to Fort Churchill. It began conversion of the C&C from

Mound House in October 1904 by replacing ties and laying 4'-8½" rail outside the 3'-0" track. The dual gauge track reached Sodaville in July 1905, and the connection to Hazen was opened on September 1. The Tonopah Railroad was converted on August 14. Hawthorne had been the shop city and operating headquarters for the C&C, but the Tonopah boom had prompted the management to put a roundhouse and other facilities at Sodaville. The SP's original intention was to expand this terminal and to use it for interchange with the Tonopah Railroad, but a local rancher and speculator demanded $100,000 for the land on which the SP planned to build. In consequence, the SP moved the terminal north 3.5 miles to Mina, and granted the Tonopah Railroad trackage rights for the nine miles from Tonopah Junction to Mina. The 3'-0" track from Mound House to Mina was removed. The conversion had resulted in a relocation of the 15.8 miles between Kinkead and Thorne, bypassing Hawthorne, shortening the line by 8.2 miles, and avoiding some serious grades and curvature.

On May 11, 1905, the SP reincorporated the C&C as the Nevada & California Railway. Under this entity, the SP finally built the long-projected extension to Mojave, but as a standard gauge railroad that interfaced with the narrow gauge at Owenyo, a desolate siding in the desert 16 miles north of Keeler. The new line, begun in 1908 and completed in 1910, was built mainly to handle materials for Los Angeles's Owens Valley aqueduct; its existence did not increase the SP's incentive to convert the remaining 160 miles of narrow gauge. Rather, the narrow gauge survived unobtrusively in the big system, running mixed trains for local ranchers and mine operators. Mina had extensive three-rail trackage for the SP and the Tonopah & Goldfield, successor to the Tonopah Railroad, but Owenyo had none, instead using gravity transfer for talc, the principal cargo, and other ores.

The SP sold the N&C to its Central Pacific subsidiary on March 1, 1912, and thereafter lettered the narrow gauge's equipment for the SP. The Owens Valley aqueduct, whatever it may have done for the SP in the short run, added to the aridity of the area, depleted its agriculture, and nearly ended the haulage of produce on the narrow gauge. Some hay and livestock continued to move, but the line became increasingly dependent on its mineral originations, which were on the south end of the line. The entire line declined, including the converted portion to the north. The Candelaria branch had been abandoned in 1905, but was restored to service spasmodically thereafter. It

was again abandoned in 1932 and removed in 1934. In the same year the original main line from Mound House to Churchill, which had been redundant since the opening of the Hazen connection, was abandoned. The narrow gauge was operating only a weekly mixed train plus some extras for livestock in the fall. In 1934 the SP also sought to abandon the narrow gauge from Tonopah Junction to Tom, five miles north of Laws, but was denied permission. The company renewed the application to abandon the Tonopah Junction–Benton portion, 50 miles, in 1936, and received permission. The last mixed train left Mina on February 16, 1938, ending passenger service on the narrow gauge. The rails were removed in 1943, having been requisitioned by the U.S. Navy in 1942. Also in 1943, the 31 miles from Benton to Laws were abandoned; thus the railroad was left with a 70-mile line, which was increasingly dependent on moving talc from on-line mines to the gravity transfer trestle at Owenyo. Surprisingly, the SP showed no immediate interest in getting rid of the narrow gauge, and even dieselized it with a 450-horsepower Caterpillar–General Electric unit, introduced with a formal ceremony on October 16, 1954. The unit bore the number 1—a certain distinction within the vast SP system.

The line was to last only another six years. The agencies at Keeler and Laws were closed in 1957 and 1959, respectively, leaving the agent at Owenyo to service the entire narrow gauge. The SP applied to the ICC to abandon the line in favor of truck transport for the talc on January 20, 1959. Permission was granted on December 30, and on April 29, 1960, locomotive No. 1 made the final trip to Keeler.

On the north end, the former dual gauge portion from Mina to Tonopah Junction became useless following the abandonment of the Tonopah & Goldfield in 1947, and was itself abandoned in 1949. The hundred miles from Churchill to Mina survive, serving mines from the railhead at Mina and the Naval Ammunition Depot at Hawthorne.

REFERENCES: John B. Hungerford, *The Slim Princess* (Reseda, Calif.: The Hungerford Press, 1956); John F. Due, "Carson & Colorado Railroad," *The Western Railroader*, 22, no. 7, issue 235 (1959); David F. Myrick, *Railroads of Nevada and Eastern California*, 2 vols. (Berkeley: Howell-North Books, 1962, 1963), vol. 1, pp. 166–210; George Turner, *Slim Rails through the Sand* (Long Beach, Calif.: Johnston & Howe, 1963); Mallory Hope Ferrell, *Southern Pacific Narrow Gauge* (Edmonds, Wash.: Pacific Fast Mail, 1982).

This excursion of the Eureka & Palisade apparently entailed using three stock cars for passengers. (California State Railroad Museum.)

Eureka & Palisade Railroad

The discovery of silver-lead ore in New York Canyon in 1864 led to the establishment of Eureka. Large-scale mining began about 1870, mainly carried on by the Eureka Consolidated Mining Co. and the Richmond Consolidated Mining Co. Smelting was for the most part done locally; the town shortly had 16 active smelters.

The Eureka & Palisade was organized in November 1873 by local interests, but in the following year D. O. Mills, Isaac Requa, and other men connected with the Bank of California and with Virginia City mining operations acquired control of the company. By the end of 1874, the line had been constructed from a connection with the Central Pacific at Palisade to Alpha, somewhat more than half the distance to Eureka. After a delay of about six months, the line was built over Garden Pass and completed into Eureka, a distance of 90 miles, on October 22, 1875.

Like its weaker counterpart, the Nevada Central, the Eureka & Palisade terminated in a valley west of its southern terminus city, and connected with the mines about the town by means of a short connecting line. In Eureka, the connection was the Ruby Hill Railroad (Eureka & Ruby Hill Narrow Gauge Railroad) built in 1875 in expectation of the E&P's completion. The E&P acquired control of the Ruby Hill in the same year.

The Eureka & Palisade and the Ruby Hill enjoyed booming traffic during the late 1870s and early 1880s. Wagon teams provided service to Hamilton, Pioche, and other mining towns to the south. A connecting line, the Eureka & Colorado River Railroad, was projected as a southern connection, but abandoned after ten miles of grading.

Mining in Eureka began to decline about 1885, and both the major mining companies gave up smelting in 1890–91. Daily passenger trains had been cut back to tri-

weekly mixed service in 1888, and in 1893 the Ruby Hill Railroad was abandoned. The E&P became unprofitable simultaneously, and the owners considered extensions to Tonopah, Ely, and other mining areas that were now more attractive. No extensions were built, and the railroad continued to exist on the decimated traffic from Eureka until 1900, when it went bankrupt. The property was transferred to a newly organized Eureka & Palisade Railway in 1902. Shortly thereafter, mining began to revive in Eureka. The Richmond and Eureka mines passed into the hands of the U.S. Smelting, Refining & Mining Co., which by 1905 was mining lead extensively, but not smelting locally. In 1905 four miles of the Ruby Hill were rebuilt. Beginning the following year, ore was hauled directly from the mines to a newly built transfer trestle at Palisade, where it was reloaded for shipment on the Southern Pacific to Salt Lake City for smelting. By 1909, this traffic amounted to 200 tons per day, some 90 percent of the railroad's tonnage.

A series of torrential rains in February and March 1910 inundated the area. No fewer than 30 miles of the E&P's right-of-way were under water from Palisade southward. Five feet of water covered the roundhouse and shops at Palisade. Damage to the railroad was estimated at $150,000. The management announced that it was willing to give the railroad to U.S. Smelting in return only for the obligation to restore it. The mining company made no response, but in October it initiated foreclosure proceedings against the dormant railroad, to which it had lent $70,000 in 1905 for the restoration of the Ruby Hill trackage. George Heintz of the mining company outbid D. O. Mills for the railroad. In 1911 George Whittell, a stockholder of the former corporation, repurchased the railroad from Heintz, and began efforts to rebuild the line. Service to Eureka was restored on May 6, 1912. Whittell formed the Eureka-Nevada Railway to own the line and leased it to his own California corporation, the Nevada Transportation Co.

Whittell raised the rate on ore shipment from $1.35 to $2.60 per ton, and thereby initiated a lengthy rate controversy with the mining company. As a consequence, the mines were closed at Eureka for several years. There were appreciable ore movements only in the period 1920–23.

In the last years of the railroad, passengers, mail, and express were customarily handled in a small rail motor car, no. 23. General Manager John E. Sexton was continually involved in disputes with state and federal authorities about allegations of the inadequacy of the line's service. Sexton operated the road very economically, and managed to produce a profit in each year

The Eureka & Palisade maintained this engine terminal at Palisade. Note the three-rail track and the gravity transfer facility at left. (California State Railroad Museum.)

but two until 1927. Thereafter, he was able to make a show of profit only in 1934. Improvement in local highways, the decline of mining in the area, and Sexton's death combined to weaken the road in the 1930s. The line was abandoned on September 21, 1938.

REFERENCES: Gilbert H. Kneiss, *Bonanza Railroads* (Stanford, Calif.: Stanford University Press, 1941), pp. 79–101; Myrick, *Railroads of Nevada and Eastern California*, vol. 1, pp. 90–111.

Nevada Central Railway

Silver ore was discovered at Austin in 1862, and ten years later the town was the second largest in Nevada. Although mining was thriving, Austin had no railroad. Efforts to build one were carried on mainly by M. J. Farrell of the Manhattan Silver Mining Co., the principal local operator. In spite of the subsidy of $200,000 offered by Lander County, Farrell had difficulty in financing the railroad. In 1878, he incorporated the Nevada Railway to build a 3'-0" line from Austin to Battle Mountain on the Central Pacific. Col. Lyman Bridges of Chicago laid out a route of 93 miles, but Farrell was unable to raise enough funds to begin grading. In the following year, Anson Phelps Stokes of the Arizona copper-mining family became interested in the project, and the railroad was reincorporated as the Nevada Central Railway. Construction began at Battle Mountain in September 1879 under the pressure of a terminal date of February 9, 1880, when the county's obligation to subsidize the railroad would expire if

The Nevada Central's basic operation was a daily mixed train that traversed the railroad in about six hours. Here the train prepares to leave the Southern Pacific station at Battle Mountain. (California State Railroad Museum.)

tracklaying were not completed. As a consequence, the railroad had to be built in great haste in the winter of 1879–80. The line reached a point 900 feet within the Austin city limits ten minutes before midnight on the appointed date, and thus the railroad claimed its subsidy. Much of the track was hastily laid on lightly graded land, and in the spring much of the mileage had to be relaid.

The Nevada Central was originally equipped with two locomotives and used rail of the Monterey & Salinas Valley, a California railroad that was being con-

verted to standard gauge. The Nevada Central was notorious for its high fares; it charged $9.00 for the full trip, and about 10¢ per mile for shorter journeys. Freight charges were about 1¢ per hundredweight per mile. The passenger train was scheduled for about five and a half hours. Freights originally ran triweekly.

Various plans were considered to build south to Belmont and other mining camps in Nye County, but none was executed. Plans to build north toward Idaho were nebulous. The Nevada Central's one southern connection was a local dummy line, the Austin City Railway. In 1881 this company built a 2.8-mile line from the Nevada Central's southern terminus at Clifton, just below the hill from Austin, up a 7.5-percent grade into Austin proper. The AC's one locomotive, picturesquely named the *Mule's Relief*, pushed one or two cars at a time up to destinations in Austin. The slackening of mining activities caused the Austin City Railway to be abandoned in 1889.

Completion of the Carson & Colorado in 1881 diverted much of the traffic from the Nye County mining camps away from the Nevada Central. Although traffic fell to about half its previous level, the Union Pacific became interested in the Nevada Central as a possible connection for its projected extension from Salt Lake City to the San Francisco Bay area. The UP bought the Nevada Central in June 1881, but lost interest in the railroad when its projected extension was dropped. In October 1884 the UP allowed the Nevada Central to pass an interest payment, throwing the narrow

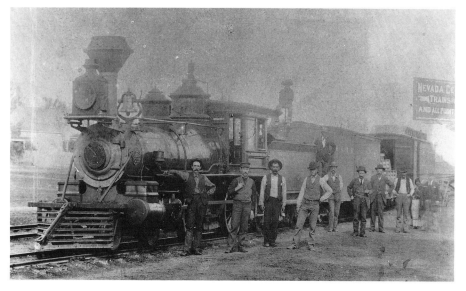

The daily mixed train for Austin stands at the Nevada Central's departure area at the Southern Pacific station in Battle Mountain. (Paul Darrell, Frederick Shaw collection, California State Railroad Museum.)

gauge into bankruptcy. In the reorganization, control of the railroad passed back into the hands of the Stokes family, who reorganized it in 1888 as the Nevada Central Railroad.

Mining in Austin declined rapidly after 1904 and virtually ended about 1911, but traffic to and from mining camps south of Austin continued. After 1911, however, the railroad was largely supported by movements of livestock and wool from neighboring ranches. The company built a crude motor car to replace its steam passenger train, and in 1927 it inaugurated an auxiliary bus line, Nevada Central Motor Lines. The survival of the railroad into the 1930s is remarkable. The company had never paid a dividend on its stock issued at the time of the 1888 reorganization, and paid interest on its bonds only intermittently. It paid no interest after 1917. Gross revenues amounted only to some $25,000 per year in the 1920s. Abandonment had been inevitable for years, and it occurred on January 31, 1938. Much of the equipment was preserved through the efforts of Gilbert Kneiss. Two of the locomotives performed at the pageant "Wedding of the Rails" at the San Francisco Exposition of 1939, and much of the rolling stock became museum pieces.

REFERENCES: Kneiss, *Bonanza Railroads*, pp. 102–32; Myrick, *Railroads of Nevada and Eastern California*, vol. 1, pp. 66–78.

Nevada Short Line Railway

A brief mining boom in Rochester Canyon brought forth this late narrow gauge in northern Nevada. In 1912 Joseph F. Nenzel made a major silver strike at Rochester on what became known as Nenzel Hill, about 12 miles from the Southern Pacific at Oreana. Arthur Ashton Codd, who leased the most important deposit, formed the Rochester Hills Mining Co. in December 1912, and in May 1913 announced his intention to build a narrow gauge railroad from Oreana to some ore bins at the mouth of Limerick Canyon, about four miles up Rochester Canyon. The railroad, which was originally a proprietorship, was finished on July 31, 1913, as the Nevada Short Line Railway. It was incorporated in April 1914 under this name.

But original arrangement proved unsatisfactory because of the limited capacity of the road connection from the mines to the ore bins. Codd determined upon an extension of six miles from a point about a mile short of the existing railhead to Lower Rochester. The extension was completed late in 1914 and passenger service was es-

tablished on January 15, 1915. Nenzel undertook a mill at Lower Rochester, but before it was completed, he sold out his interests to L. A. Friedman. The completion of the mill on February 4, 1915, prompted Codd to extend the railroad two miles up the mountain to Upper Rochester via a switchback and 6-percent grades. Shay locomotives began to operate the extension in September 1915.

On November 30, 1915, fire destroyed the railroad's shops at Oreana, seriously interfering with the operation of the railroad and bringing about a receivership. Downbound traffic of ore to the mill was the principal support of the railroad, but receiver Frank Manson found himself unable to operate the trackage between the two Rochesters in the winter. In April 1917 Friedman opened an aerial tramway from Upper Rochester to the mill to avoid the rail line, which proved barely able to survive on traffic from other operators and concentrate from the mill at Lower Rochester. The railroad was put up for sale for delinquent taxes in 1917, but no buyers appeared. A flood seriously damaged the line in June 1918, bringing operation to an end. The rails were removed in 1920.

REFERENCE: Myrick, *Railroads of Nevada and Eastern California*, vol. 1, pp. 57–63.

Pioche & Bullionville Railroad

In 1872 Pioche was at the peak of a silver boom; its output was second only to that of the Comstock Lode, and the population had reached 7,500. Nevertheless, the town was isolated from the American railroad system. The first railroad was not an effort to end this isolation, but rather a narrow gauge to serve local demands. General A. L. Page and other local mine operators incorporated the Pioche & Bullionville Railroad early in 1872, but Page, in association with W. H. Raymond, reincorporated the project in 1873 as the Central Nevada Railroad. They opened the line, however, on June 8, 1873, under the name of the Nevada Central Railroad—unrelated to the later Nevada Central built to serve Austin. The railroad connected Pioche with Bullionville (20 miles), a town of 450 people and the site of several mills. Most of the traffic was ore from Pioche for processing at Bullionville. The railroad was popularly known by its original name, Pioche & Bullionville.

Mining in the area began declining about 1874 with the exhaustion of the best ores and with chronic problems of underground water in the deeper mines. The railroad passed through a succession of owners.

Regular ore trains apparently ended about 1878. The railroad went bankrupt and was sold by the sheriff on March 3, 1881. Operation is thought to have ceased about that time, and the property was sold for scrap in 1883.

REFERENCE: Myrick, *Railroads of Nevada and Eastern California*, vol. 2, pp. 684–97.

The Pioche Pacific Transportation Co.

Railroading returned to Pioche with a mine tramway projected along the escarpment of Treasure Hill. To make use of some of the remaining equipment of the Pioche & Bullionville, as well as a portion of its grade, 3'-0" gauge was adopted. Operation began in January 1890, and later in the year the property, which amounted to only about half a mile to the west of the town, passed into the hands of the Consolidated Mining & Reduction Co. in the course of a merger. The president of the mining company, W. S. Godbe, decided to extend the tramway to its full projected three miles, and to build a 15-mile line northwest to the Jackrabbit Mine at Royal (Bristol). Godbe incorporated the line as The Pioche Pacific Transportation Co., a private carrier, and built it in 1891.

In November 1907 Pioche gained its first rail connection with the outside world when the Union Pacific's Caliente & Pioche arrived in town, making use of a portion of the Pioche & Bullionville's grade. This development caused the Pioche Pacific to become a common carrier in 1908. The line remained mainly a facility of Godbe's firm, since 1904 known as the Nevada-Utah Mines & Smelting Corp. This firm went bankrupt in 1912, causing the rail line to be reorganized as the Pioche Pacific Railroad in 1913. In 1917 the mines served by the railroad were leased to Combined Metals, Inc., but the railroad was not transferred from the Amalgamated Pioche Mines & Smelter Co., as its owner had been renamed in its reorganization. E. H. Snyder, head of Combined Metals, became restive in the face of what he considered the excessive rates of the Pioche Pacific, and on June 5, 1930, bought the Jackrabbit line for $30,000 for his subsidiary, the Bristol Silver Mines Co., ending any common carriage by the narrow gauge. The shorter line up Treasure Hill had been operated under lease by Combined Metals since 1923. These changes caused the Pioche Pacific to apply in 1937 to the Public Service Commission of Nevada to drop its common carrier status, but the Commission dismissed the applica-

The Tonopah Railroad's narrow gauge motive power was explicitly intended for short service. The first No. 1 was diverted by Baldwin before delivery to the Kahului Railroad on Maui, and replaced by a secondhand Mogul from the Chateaugay Railroad. (Railroad Museum of Pennsylvania.)

tion in 1939 on the ground that the ore moved in interstate commerce. The Interstate Commerce Commission dismissed a similar application on February 25, 1942, on the opposite ground that the operation was intrastate. The Pioche Pacific responded by removing the line up Treasure Hill. Trucks took over the ore movements from Jackrabbit in 1947, and the rail line was closed in October 1948.

REFERENCE: Myrick, *Railroads of Nevada and Eastern California*, vol. 2, pp. 697–733.

Tonopah Railroad

The Tonopah Railroad was built as a consequence of the discovery of gold ore in the Tonopah area in 1900. Immediately after the discovery there had been various proposals for building a railroad into Tonopah, including an extension of the Nevada Central southward from Austin. The Southern Pacific proposed a standard gauge line from the northwest in 1902. None of the projects was implemented until February 1903, when C. S. Lemon undertook a survey of a line from a point on the Carson & Colorado to Tonopah. The state legislature granted Lemon a charter and a 100-foot-wide right-of-way on March 12, 1903, requiring that he undertake the railroad within four months and complete it within an additional 15.

Lemon decided upon a line of 62.39 miles from milepost 143 on the Carson & Colorado, a point which came to be known as Tonopah Junction. The project entailed nine miles of trackage rights on the C&C to Mina, which always served as the actual interchange point. Lemon financed the line with considerable aid from mining companies in Tonopah. From the outset, it was anticipated that narrow gauge would be a temporary expedient. The Carson & Colorado remained narrow gauge, but conversion was expected shortly. Consequently, Lemon laid standard width ties in hopes of a quick conversion.

Lemon began construction in July 1903 but almost immediately sold his interest to men connected with the Tonopah Mining Co. and the Fourth Street National Bank of Philadelphia. The mining company carried on the actual construction. By May 1904 service was opened to Coaldale, and on July 23, 1904, the first train reached Tonopah. The railroad offered through passenger service with the Carson & Colorado, including a sleeping car to Mound House. Unfortunately, the line had been graded by Eastern engineers, who had been mislead by the general aridity and had not planned for the cloudbursts characteristic of the area. Several washouts occurred in the first few months of service.

The railroad was operated with a former Nevada-California-Oregon 2-8-0 and three Baldwin 2-6-0s. Much of the rolling stock

came from the Southern Pacific's South Pacific Coast Railway, which was in the course of conversion. The railroad carried a heavy traffic of ore outbound and materials for the mines inbound. Passengers arrived at the rate of about 400 per day, many with extensive household effects. The traffic from Tonopah was mainly responsible for a glut of freight at Mound House that caused serious delays.

The Southern Pacific decided to delay no longer the conversion of the northern portion of the Carson & Colorado, and in October 1904 began laying standard gauge rail south from Mound House. By July 1905 the C&C's line to Sodaville was converted, and the Tonopah began its own conversion. Sodaville served as transshipment point in the interim. Not all of its ties had been laid to standard width, and some of the roadbed had to be relaid. The ties were ready for change of gauge by August. Three hundred men were placed in gangs at mile-and-a-half intervals on August 14, 1905. Between 6:00 A.M. and 8:00 P.M. the rails were relaid, and at 2:30 A.M. the following day, standard gauge operation began.

The Tonopah Mining Co. on November 1, 1905, merged the Tonopah with the Goldfield Railroad, which had been a standard gauge operation from the outset, into the Tonopah & Goldfield Railroad. Even though mining began to decline in the area as early as 1907, the T&G survived until World War II. Establishment of an air base at Tonopah caused a brief traffic boom during the war, but ore movements had fallen to such a low level that continuation of the line afterward was impossible. Operation ceased October 1, 1946, but owing to a lengthy dispute between state and federal authorities, formal abandonment was delayed until October 15, 1947.

REFERENCE: Myrick, *Railroads of Nevada and Eastern California*, vol. 1, pp. 236–88.

New Hampshire

Profile & Franconia Notch Railroad

The White Mountains developed rapidly as a recreation area after the Civil War. The Boston, Concord & Montreal Railroad built through Pierce's Bridge (Bethlehem Junction) in 1873 en route to the base of Mount Washington. The area to the south in the vicinity of Crawford Notch contained the Old Man of the Mountains and Echo Lake, two major tourist attractions. A resort hotel, Profile House, had operated since 1853, but was handicapped by long stagecoach journeys to railroad stations. Richard Taft and

Charles H. Greenleaf, proprietors of Profile House, organized the Profile & Franconia Notch Railroad on July 11, 1878, to connect the hotel with Pierce's Bridge. They acquired the recently abandoned right-of-way of a standard gauge private carrier of the Gale River Lumber Co. for the first three miles south of the BC&M station. Taft and Greenleaf bridged the Ammonoosuc River at Pierce's Bridge and completed the railroad to the hotel (9.46 miles) on June 25, 1879, in time for the annual tourist season. Two Hinkley 4-4-0s were bought, along with four passenger cars, two combines, and six flatcars. The railroad cost about $125,000. The grade averaged 1.5 percent, but the last three miles approaching the hotel were about 2.2 percent. It was proposed to extend the line 30 miles down the Pemigewasset Valley to Plymouth for a more direct rail connection with Boston, but the extension was never undertaken. Rather, in July 1881 the company opened a short branch from Bethlehem Junction to Maplewood and Bethlehem (3.38 miles). The branch was laid on a tortuous grade of more than 3 percent. When this proved beyond the capacity of the 4-4-0s, the company bought an 0-6-0 tank engine to work the branch. About 35 hotels or rooming houses were in the immediate area. (For map, see Vermont.)

The railroad operated only during the summer months, and freight was limited mainly to supplies inbound to the hotels. Nonetheless, the narrow gauge was capable of earning over $8,000 per year. It was attractive enough that its connection, now called the Concord & Montreal Railroad, agreed in 1893 to buy the property for

$280,000. With the opening of the 1894 season, the railroad was operated as two narrow gauge branches of the C&M. The change of ownership resulted in a temporary expansion of the narrow gauge mileage. To eliminate one of two changes necessary for passengers from Maine Central trains to reach the hotels, the C&M laid third rail east on the Mount Washington branch for six miles to a point called Zealand Transfer.

The C&M was leased to the Boston & Maine on April 1, 1895. The larger railroad recognized the disadvantage of the narrow gauge's incompatibility, and after the 1896 season converted the two lines at a cost of $40,000. Both enjoyed heavy utilization until World War I, but the shift to the automobile thereafter had its impact most heavily on vacationers' facilities of this character. The Profile line was closed at the end of the 1920 season and abandoned in July 1921. No doubt it would shortly have perished in any case, for the Profile House was destroyed by fire in August. The Bethlehem branch survived only through the 1924 season and was abandoned in 1925.

REFERENCE: H. Bentley Crouch, "Narrow Gauge to the Notch," *B&M Bulletin*, 5, no. 4 (Summer 1976), pp. 19–28.

New Jersey

Camden, Gloucester & Mt. Ephraim Railway

David S. Brown and James P. Michellon, the leading entrepreneurs of Gloucester City, an industrial suburb of Camden, were interested in providing passenger transportation into central Camden and to the Philadelphia ferries. They might have chosen to build a horsecar line, but they found an opportunity to enter Camden over a projected narrow gauge, the Camden & Manchester Railroad, an affiliate of the Kaighn's Point & Philadelphia Ferry Co. On September 5, 1873, the City of Camden granted the C&M

The Profile & Franconia Notch served its Bethlehem branch with this tank engine and short trains. (Ed Bond collection.)

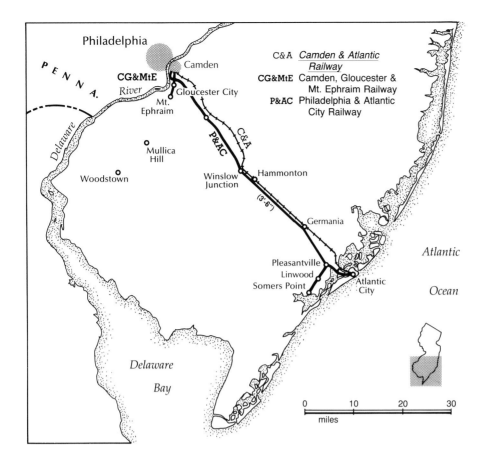

Philadelphia

P E N N A.

River

CG&MtE
Camden
Gloucester City
Mt. Ephraim

C&A *Camden & Atlantic Railway*
CG&MtE Camden, Gloucester & Mt. Ephraim Railway
P&AC Philadelphia & Atlantic City Railway

P&AC
C&A

Mullica Hill

Woodstown

Winslow Junction
Hammonton

(3'-6")

Germania

Atlantic

Pleasantville
Linwood
Somers Point
Atlantic City

Ocean

Delaware Bay

Delaware

0   10   20   30
miles

the right to cross city streets to reach the Kaighn's Point ferry terminal.

Brown and Michellon, who had incorporated their Camden, Gloucester & Mt. Ephraim Railway on June 17, 1873, simultaneously received rights to run over the Camden & Manchester once the latter had reached Third and Atlantic avenues. The Camden & Manchester was unable to acquire right-of-way for its projected line to Manchester (Lakehurst) and was never built. Brown and Michellon were able to make use of its projected entry, however. The Camden, Gloucester & Mt. Ephraim's route began at Ferry Street and the Delaware River, immediately south of the Kaighn's Point ferry terminal. The line ran out Front Street to Atlantic Avenue, and then around a curve only 120 feet in radius (47°) into Third Street, which it traversed toward Gloucester City. It crossed Newton Creek, the only major natural barrier, by a trestle across the mud flats at the confluence of the creek with the Delaware River. The line entered Gloucester City on King Street, which it followed to Mercer Street. Sidings entered the Gloucester Iron Works, the Gloucester Manufacturing Co., the Ancona Printing Co., and the Washington Manufacturing Co. A station and wye were built at King and Salem streets. At Camden, an engine house was built just west of the curve at Third and Atlantic. Other terminal facilities, including

a turntable, were built at the Kaighn's Point end. The line was equipped with a Baldwin 2-4-2 and a Baldwin 4-4-0.

The railroad was opened from Camden to Gloucester City (3.86 miles) on February 14, 1874. Five round-trips per day were provided at the outset, but by July, 16 were run. The trains were typically of two cars, and the run was only eight minutes.

From the beginning the management planned to extend the railroad to the country town of Mount Ephraim, an additional four miles. The company arranged a crossing with the West Jersey Railroad in Gloucester City and quickly built the extension. Service to Mount Ephraim opened in late May 1876. Meanwhile, a subsidiary, the Mt. Ephraim & Blackwoodstown, had been incorporated in 1874 to build a further extension of about 6.5 miles between the towns of its title. Ground was broken for the extension at Mount Ephraim on September 20, 1876, but serious construction was never undertaken, apparently because of the death of Brown in 1877. The company continued to plan an extension, however, and announced plans to build to Turnersville in 1878 and to Mullica Hill, Harrisonville, and Woodstown in 1880. None of the extensions was built, and the railroad remained almost entirely a passenger carrier in Camden suburban service.

The Camden, Gloucester & Mt. Ephraim

was barely profitable, and quickly deteriorated physically. The company's access to the Kaighn's Point ferry terminal made the railroad an attraction to other companies, however. The proposed Philadelphia & Cape May Short Line showed interest in entering Camden over the narrow gauge's tracks, but the Short Line forfeited its charter for lack of a deposit in 1878 without having built any trackage. Because the line crossed the Philadelphia & Atlantic City at a right angle just east of the latter's Bulson Street terminal, some passengers transferred to the CG&MtE from the Atlantic City trains to take advantage of a shorter ferry crossing. Owing to the gauge difference, the two narrow gauges never attempted a joint terminal. When the Philadelphia & Reading bought the Philadelphia & Atlantic City in the intention of standard gauging the line, it immediately became interested in the Camden, Gloucester & Mt. Ephraim as a means of dealing with the Atlantic City line's long ferry crossing. On November 4, 1884, the superintendent of the P&AC, which had been standard gauged a month earlier, made an inspection trip over the CG&MtE. He reported to J. E. Wootten, general manager of the Reading, that the track and cars of the short line were in such poor condition that he considered it "positively dangerous to run trains." He also reported that James P. Michellon was eager to get rid of the line.

Consequently, the Reading bought out Michellon's interest and replaced him as president of the company with George De-Keim. Immediately, 3'-0" track was laid to allow the narrow gauge's locomotives and its steam dummy car to reach the Bulson Street engine house. Preparation for standard gauging also began immediately. The conversion occurred Sunday, June 21, 1885. A curve of 10° was put in at Bulson Street to allow the Atlantic City trains access to Kaighn's Point. The CG&MtE's own curves were eased to allow working of the line by former Central Railroad of New Jersey 2-4-2 tank engines. On April 1, 1889, the Camden, Gloucester & Mt. Ephraim Railway was merged with the Philadelphia & Atlantic City and some other properties into the Atlantic City Railroad.

The former narrow gauge line into Kaighn's Point was replaced by the Kaighn's Point Terminal Railroad in 1888 to eliminate some severe curvature. About 1900 the line through South Camden was moved east to provide space for the yard of the New York Shipbuilding Corporation. Upon formation of the Pennsylvania-Reading Seashore Lines in 1933 the line from the shipyard to Gloucester City was abandoned. The remainder from Gloucester City to

Mount Ephraim remains in service in Conrail's freight trackage in the area.

Philadelphia & Atlantic City Railway
Gauge: 3'-6"

The Camden & Atlantic Rail Road monopolized the burgeoning resort business from the Philadelphia area to Atlantic City. Its success engendered several rival projects, one of which was the Philadelphia & Atlantic City Railway, organized in Camden on March 24, 1876. The principal financier of the new company was William Massey, a brewer of Philadelphia. Samuel Richards, a New Jersey glassmaker, was also an important source of funds. Several of the incorporators were former Camden & Atlantic directors. Richards became the first president, but was replaced by Massey on September 1, 1877, and early in 1879 by Charles A. Colwell.

The line was surveyed in 1876 with the intention of building the railroad to 3'-0" gauge. The projected route was from the Camden waterfront at Division Street, just south of the central business district, through Magnolia and Clementon to Winslow Junction. From there, the line ran a half mile or less south of the Camden & Atlantic, directly parallel as far as Germania. The route was cut south through Pleasantville with the intention of entering Atlantic City via Dry Inlet. The company was unable to acquire land at Division Street in Camden, and instead built its terminal at the foot of Bulson Street, a location that required a ferry crossing to Philadelphia of about two miles. Pier 8 South at the foot of Walnut Street was leased as the Philadelphia depot. The trip was long enough that the company leased standard steamboats rather than double-ended ferries for the crossing. The principal boat was the sidewheeler *Pilot Boy*, and a second sidewheeler, *Champion*, was reported. The *Minnie R. Childs* served in 1878. In off-seasons, the tug *Major* was fitted to carry passengers on deck.

The entry into Atlantic City was made parallel to the Camden & Atlantic from Drawbridge. The depot was built at Atlantic and Missouri avenues, with an extension down Mississippi Avenue to the beach for excursions.

After surveys were completed, the projectors decided, apparently at the last moment, to build the line at 3'-6" for greater speed and stability. The decision was to make the railroad incompatible with both the standard gauge lines and the one existing

The Philadelphia & Atlantic City bought three buildings from the Centennial Exposition of 1876 and re-erected them on its property. This one served as its station in Atlantic City. There are no known photographs of the company's operations. (Edward T. Francis collection.)

narrow gauge in the area, the 3'-0" Camden, Gloucester & Mt. Ephraim. The company bought about seven miles of rail from the recently closed narrow gauge at the Philadelphia Centennial Exposition, and ordered an additional 3,500 tons of 40-pound rail from the Bethlehem Iron Co. Seven locomotives were ordered from Baldwin and one from W. H. Baily's National Locomotive Works. Rolling stock was ordered from Bowers, Dure & Co., and J. G. Brill. Depots in Camden and Atlantic City, plus some intermediate points, were structures relocated from the Centennial grounds. The line was graded and built in only some 90 days during the first half of 1877. A force of 900 men was employed to build through the typical flat, sandy country of southern New Jersey. The completed route was 54 miles, some five miles shorter than the Camden & Atlantic. The cost was about $700,000, or $13,000 per mile. The line was lightly graded, but afflicted with no serious curvature.

The Philadelphia & Atlantic City's formal opening occurred on July 25, 1877, even though the ballasting had not been completed. Unfortunately, the event was to prove only too characteristic of the railroad's history. The first section of the initial excursion train near Tansboro derailed, smashing two coaches and resulting in the death of a brakeman and the injury of ten passengers. Consequently, the company began its operations with a bad reputation for safety and an extensive set of damage claims to be adjudicated.

The company's competitive handicaps were to prove difficult. Its mileage advantage over the Camden & Atlantic was counteracted by a ferry crossing well over three

times the length of the C&A's. The locomotives were designed to burn anthracite, but they were equipped with patented front-end nozzles that caused them to steam poorly. The railroad tried mixing wood with the anthracite, but the engines continued to present punctuality problems. The Philadelphia & Atlantic City had been built in the expectation of matching the Camden & Atlantic's two-hour schedules. The C&A responded with 90-minute nonstop expresses. In the ensuing rivalry the C&A generally had a slight time advantage. The P&AC's fastest schedule was 85 minutes in 1881, and its shortest reported single trip 75 minutes. This probably made it the fastest narrow gauge railroad, but the inherent limitations of narrow gauge were insuperable. On August 1, 1879, the Camden & Atlantic reported heavy passenger traffic, not much affected by the P&AC's rivalry. The narrow gauge was forced to be a cut-rate operation;

by 1881 it charged a standard one-way fare of $1.00, and had a 50¢ daily excursion fare.

The line had little freight potential. Atlantic City was nonindustrial, and the intermediate territory was devoted mainly to truck farming. The gauge difference limited the railroad mainly to hauling agricultural products to Camden and Philadelphia. Freight cars were loaded on barges at Camden and taken to Philadelphia's Pier 8, where they were unloaded right from the barges rather than being taken off to Philadelphia destinations. The *Major* regularly served as tug for this service.

Under the circumstances, the company's financial history was disastrous from the beginning. By February 12, 1877, the Philadelphia *Times* reported that maturing indebtedness of $200,000 had been extended one, two, and three years by agreement with various creditors. By the end of 1877, the company was issuing scrip in lieu of wages, and employees were considering a general lien against the railroad for payment. William Massey owned $221,000 in the bonds, had endorsed $260,000 in notes, and held $14,200 of other debt of the company. He controlled the railroad with $130,000 of stock. On July 13, 1878, he applied successfully to the Court of Chancery in Newark for appointment of a receiver. Massey criticized the citizens of Atlantic City for not supporting the railroad, and said that the officers of the company had misled him about their experience. The Chancellor of New Jersey appointed Charles A. Colwell receiver. The employees objected on the ground that, as president of the corporation and a large shareholder, he was not a disinterested party. They also contended he had demonstrated his incompetence. They were unsuccessful in this plea, but John H. Burrell, Jr., was appointed trustee for unpaid employees. Burrell secured an order for payment of half the wages accrued since July 13 on December 1, and half on January 1, 1879. Late in 1878, the management first expressed an intention to convert to standard gauge if enough money could be found, but no such

funds were available. The Camden & Atlantic, early in 1879, offered $400,000 in five annual installments for a perpetual lease on the railroad, planning to convert it to a freight and local service facility while retaining the Atlantic City express passenger traffic on its own rails.

The Chancellor of New Jersey ordered the Philadelphia & Atlantic City sold at Camden on May 29, 1879; but, mainly because the receiver was still in arrears of wages of $23,000, creditors petitioned for delay. The sale was next set for June 20, but again delayed. The Chancellor ordered the receiver to deliver the railroad to William H. Gatzmer and Garrett B. Linderman as trustees for the mortgage bondholders. He also ordered that a Master in Chancery ascertain the amount due the employees, on the basis of which the receiver should issue a certificate of indebtedness to be the first lien on the property.

At this point, the Philadelphia & Atlantic City suffered its second fatal accident, considerably more severe than the first. A freight train and a passenger train collided at Clementon on August 14, 1879, and five lives were lost. Evidence before the coroner's jury showed woefully loose operating procedures. Conductor John Ewing, a new employee, had been sent out with no orders beyond a notice that several extra trains would be on the line that afternoon. No order book was in use. When the original order book had been filled, no replacement had been bought. Rather, orders were simply stuffed in a drawer and thrown out when the drawer was filled. The coroner's jury censured assistant superintendent J. S. Verts for mismanagement and appointment of incompetent subordinates. Verts was arrested and held for the Grand Jury.

The Grand Jury brought in indictments for manslaughter against Verts, Ewing, telegrapher C. A. Redman of Camden, and Elwood Johnson, engineer of the freight. When tried, Ewing was acquitted; the jury split on Johnson; and the judge directed a verdict of acquittal for Verts on the ground that the state had not proved negligence.

In 1880 the Philadelphia & Atlantic City's fortunes revived mildly. The company presented the court with a plan to take the railroad out of receivership by funding the floating debt. Colwell proposed to raise $80,250 by assessing shareholders $12.50 per share, and to issue $179,000 in bonds and an additional $179,000 in stock. This would have dealt with the indebtedness, and also provided some funds for additional equipment. The company was unable to execute this plan, but it was able to finance two new Baldwin 4-4-0s for passenger service in

1880. In 1881 it bought an eleventh locomotive, a 2-6-0 from the Toronto, Grey & Bruce, which shared its 3'-6" gauge. In 1880 the company built its only branch line, 7.5 miles from Pleasantville to Somers Point, incorporated as the subsidiary Pleasantville & Ocean City. The subsidiary owned two coaches but no locomotives. The branch served a Methodist camp at Peck's Beach, and had the potential of extension to Ocean City, the secondary resort of the area. In June 1880, however, the narrow gauge was confronted with a second rival, the West Jersey & Atlantic, which built a standard gauge line of 34 miles from Newfield, on the parent West Jersey Railroad, to Atlantic City.

The year 1882 produced three major fires at the Philadelphia & Atlantic City's terminals. The facilities at Pier 8 South, Philadelphia, burned twice, first on March 23 when the tug *Henry C. Pratt* exploded nearby. Five men were killed. The tug *Ella* was also destroyed. The P&AC's wooden terminal on the pier was destroyed, but quickly rebuilt. Next, on June 13, oily wastes at the Camden roundhouse ignited a fire that did about $100,000 of damage to the engine terminal and shops. Seven of the railroad's 11 locomotives were damaged, but all were returned to service. Finally, on October 16, 1882, a fire started in the baggage room of the rebuilt Philadelphia pier terminal. The tug *Major* was damaged, along with three cars of merchandise and potatoes on a barge. Again, the station building was destroyed. Consistent with the company's weak financial position, it did not carry enough insurance to cover all the losses fully.

In May 1882 the company sold the Pleas-

antville & Ocean City branch to the West Jersey Railroad, a Pennsylvania Railroad affiliate. The West Jersey converted the branch to standard gauge in June.

On May 8, William Massey arranged for sale of his interest in the Philadelphia & Atlantic City to the Camden & Atlantic or, if the C&A's shareholders disapproved, to the C&A directors personally. The C&A announced it would restore the narrow gauge's physical plant for freight and local passenger service, but did not announce plans for conversion. William L. Elkins, a major stockholder in the C&A, immediately sought an injunction against the sale. The Camden & Atlantic's shareholders met on June 24. Its director, Thomas H. Dudley, argued that the narrow gauge was worthless, but only 300 votes were recorded in opposition, and the acquisition was carried. The C&A moved for discharge of the receiver of the Philadelphia & Atlantic City, but the Chancellor of New Jersey instead granted Elkins a permanent injunction against the acquisition. Opposition to the loss of competition in Atlantic City was the deciding consideration.

This development left the narrow gauge in the impossible position of being unwanted and hopelessly unprofitable. The solution came in a fashion that the management could not have anticipated. The Pennsylvania Railroad acquired control of the Camden & Atlantic on January 1, 1883, thereby depriving the Philadelphia & Reading and its affiliate, the Central Railroad of New Jersey, of a friendly connection to Atlantic City. The Philadelphia & Atlantic City offered to buy out Massey for $75,000 in cash and $400,000 in guaranteed bonds. In addition, the Reading offered $25,000 in cash for the outstanding stock, plus $162,000 in Reading bonds to be issued after the receivership was lifted. These terms were very favorable, so that Massey and his associates accepted them quickly. A foreclosure sale was arranged. Peter Vorhees, Master in Chancery, sold the railroad at the Camden County Courthouse on September 20. G. W. Kaercher, representing the Reading, bid $100,000. Payment was completed on October 13, and the formal transfer of the Philadelphia & Atlantic City to the Philadelphia & Reading was made on October 31, 1883.

The Reading began to plan for conversion immediately. The engineering work required nearly a year. About two-thirds of the ties were replaced, and new rails were laid outside the existing ones. The conversion was scheduled for October 5, 1884. By that time the only remaining work was the replacement of switches and diamonds. The work was completed on October 6, when the first standard gauge train left Winslow Junction for Camden and then departed for Atlantic City.

The Reading initially reorganized the line as the Philadelphia & Atlantic City Railroad. In 1889 the Reading consolidated the line with some other holdings in New Jersey as the Atlantic City Railroad. The Camden terminal at that time was moved up the river to Kaighn's Point, cutting the ferry crossing by nearly half. During the 1890s the railroad was one of the classic speedways of the American rail system. After the opening of the Delaware River Bridge at Camden in 1926, the Reading's Atlantic City line became highly unprofitable. The Pennsylva-

---

---

nia's lines in the area were barely breaking even. They were merged in 1933 into the Pennsylvania-Reading Seashore Lines. The former narrow gauge trackage from Winslow Junction to Atlantic City was removed in 1934 except for industrial sidings in Hammonton, Egg Harbor, and Pleasantville. The segments from Camden to Winslow Junction and Pleasantville to Linwood are in existence at the present writing.

REFERENCES: W. George Cook and William J. Coxey, *Atlantic City Railroad* (Oaklyn, N.J.: West Jersey Chapter, National Railway Historical Society, 1980); collection of Edward T. Francis.

▼ ▼ ▼ ▼

The Ferromonte Railroad, one of several carriers that served the iron mines of Morris County, was in part a narrow gauge. The railroad, which totaled only some 2.5 miles of track, was about evenly divided between a standard gauge spur from Ferromonte Junction (the crossing of the Lackawanna's Chester branch and the Central Railroad of New Jersey's High Bridge branch) to a scale and transshipment facility about a mile to the southeast, and a network of 2'-10" trackage serving six iron mines in the hills above. The narrow gauge trackage was worked with 41 ore cars and five mules. The railroad was chartered in 1869 and opened in September 1870. It held common carrier status. The closure of the principal source of traffic, the Dickerson Mine, on November 16, 1891, caused the railroad to cease operation, probably in 1892. It remained in existence and may have resumed operation on an occasional basis. The narrow gauge trackage was removed by 1915. There were occasional efforts to revive the standard gauge line subsequently, and the company survived as a corporate entity until 1953.

REFERENCE: Larry Lowenthal, *Iron Mine Railroads of Northern New Jersey* (Dover, N.J.: Tri-State Railway Historical Society, 1981), pp. 132–37.

New Mexico

Rio Grande & Southwestern Railroad

Lumber operators Edgar M. Biggs and John J. McGinnity, deciding to establish operations in southern Rio Arriba County, incorporated the Rio Grande & Southwestern Railroad on February 23, 1903. By two agreements of January 1 and March 7, 1903, they arranged a complicated division of ownership and responsibility with the Denver & Rio Grande, with which they were to connect immediately west of Lumberton. Biggs and McGinnity agreed to acquire a right-of-way of 42 miles from Lumberton south to Gallina, grade it, and lay ties. The D&RG would furnish used 30-pound rail and fastenings, but not spikes. RG&SW locomotives would be allowed to use the D&RG's Lumberton tank; the larger railroad would provide locomotives at $6.50 per day, and cars free of charge. The entire capital stock was to be held in trust for the D&RG, which would appoint five of the seven directors of the RG&SW—all seven after January 1, 1906. The lumbermen were to be reimbursed for the cost of building the line at 25 percent of the gross revenue until the costs of building had been repaid. The agreement essentially provided that the D&RG should own the railroad, but the lumbermen should build and operate it. The arrangement necessarily required that the RG&SW be a common carrier.

The line was built in 1903 from Lumberton to a company town called El Vado (33 miles). The physical plant included a northbound grade of 2.4 percent and a reverse curve of 18°. The contract for operation and further building was assigned on January 19, 1904, to Biggs's Burns-Biggs Lumber Co. Until 1907 the line was operated with power from the D&RG or Burns-Biggs's Rio Grande & Pagosa Springs Railroad, but the RG&SW then bought two Lima 2-8-0s. Spurs of the lumber company were worked with Shay locomotives, including an ascent of Thompson Mesa that entailed two switchbacks and a 10-percent grade. Biggs sold his interest in 1907 to his partners, who formed the New Mexico Lumber Co. to run the operation. In 1909 the D&RG completed its payments and came into full ownership of the railroad, but made no attempt to assume the operation. On December 1, 1909, the lumber company closed its camp at El Vado and shut down the railroad, except for the northernmost three miles, which served a coal mine of the company until 1911. Operation was restored on July 4, 1914. In fulfillment of the original agreement, the D&RG in 1917 built an additional eight miles to Gallinas Mountain; the lumber company built a further five miles to Mud Springs in the Santa Fe National Forest.

The lumber company began shutting down the El Vado camp in 1923, and in February 1924 moved the mill to another installation of the firm at Dolores, Colorado. The railroad was initially left in place, but removed by the D&RG south of the coal mine in 1928 and north into Lumberton in 1929.

REFERENCES: Vernon J. Glover, "The Rio Grande and Southwestern Railroad," Railway & Locomotive Historical Society Bulletin, no. 124 (1971), pp. 22–27; Gordon S. Chappell, Logging Along the Denver & Rio Grande (Golden: Colorado Railroad Museum, 1971), pp. 82–103.

Silver City, Deming & Pacific Railroad

J. Parker Whitney of Boston, who was active in copper mining elsewhere in New Mexico, along with several associates formed the Silver City, Deming & Pacific Railroad on March 23, 1882. Their plan was to connect their silver-mining installations at Silver City with Deming, where the Atchison, Topeka & Santa Fe and the Southern Pacific were shortly to connect for the second transcontinental railroad. The line of 48 miles was graded mainly in 1882. Track-laying began in the following March, and the line was opened on May 12, 1883, with the driving of a silver spike to symbolize the intended purpose of the railroad. Extensions were planned west to the copper-mining center of Clifton, Arizona, and northeast to the Mimbres Valley of New Mexico. Neither was undertaken, and instead the railroad was sold to the AT&SF in February 1884. The Santa Fe began immediate preparations for conversion, and did the job on Sunday, May 16, 1886. The line was operated as part of a continuous branch from Rincon on the El Paso branch to Deming and Silver City. The northernmost 18 miles from Whitewater to Silver City were abandoned in 1983, but the remainder is in service.

REFERENCE: David F. Myrick, New Mexico's Railroads (Golden: Colorado Railroad Museum, 1970), pp. 148–49.

▼▼▼▼

The Comanche Mining & Smelting Co. in 1906 organized the Silver City, Pinos Altos & Mogollon Railroad to run from its facility at Silver City northwest about 60 miles to Mogollon and nearby silver-mining communities. If completed, the line would probably have been a common carrier. It became a 2'-0" plant facility for the mining company, carrying ore down from Pinos Altos Mountain to a smelter at Silver City. It was operated with Shay locomotives, some secondhand from the Gilpin Tramway of Colorado. The line was shut down in the fall of 1907 and removed in 1913.

The Tierra Amarilla Southern Railroad was a private carrier of the Biggs Lumber Co., which ran from Chama about 15 miles south to Tierra Amarilla. It is believed to have carried company employees and other passengers occasionally. The line operated from 1892 to 1902, when it was sold to the Denver & Rio Grande, which operated it briefly under the name of the Chama lumber branch. The D&RG removed it in 1903 to provide used rail for the Rio Grande & Southwestern.

New York

For lines in and adjacent to the oil field in Allegany County, see the separate section on the network in the Pennsylvania–New York oil field following the Pennsylvania state section.

Bath & Hammondsport Railroad

C. D. Champlin and other local figures chartered this railroad on January 17, 1872, to connect Hammondsport at the southern tip of Keuka Lake with the Erie Railroad's Buffalo line at Bath, 9.5 miles distant. The corporation also received authority to build from Bath straight west to the Erie's main line at Hornellsville (Hornell), but the extension was never undertaken. Grading for the railroad began in the summer of 1872 and was completed in 1873. The route was from the Erie station in Bath, northeast up a grade of 2.9 percent for about a mile, to a summit at Country House, and thence down along Cold Creek into Hammondsport. The area was devoted to grape-growing, wine-making, and tourist development along the lake. Captain Allen Wood's Lake Keuka Steam Navigation Co. operated steamers from Hammondsport to Penn Yan at the northeast tip of the Y-shaped lake, with additional service to Branchport on the West Arm and to intermediate piers.

Champlin's group ran out of resources after laying ties on the grade. After failing to interest the Erie in installing rail, they arranged on December 15, 1874, to lease the line for 99 years to Allen Wood. In the following spring Wood laid 40-pound rail, allowing the railroad to be opened on June 30, 1875. The arrangement proved a favorable one. Freight traffic was mainly grapes and wine outbound to the Erie. In the summers passengers moved in large volume from the Erie and the Lackawanna at Bath to Wood's steamers at Hammondsport. The

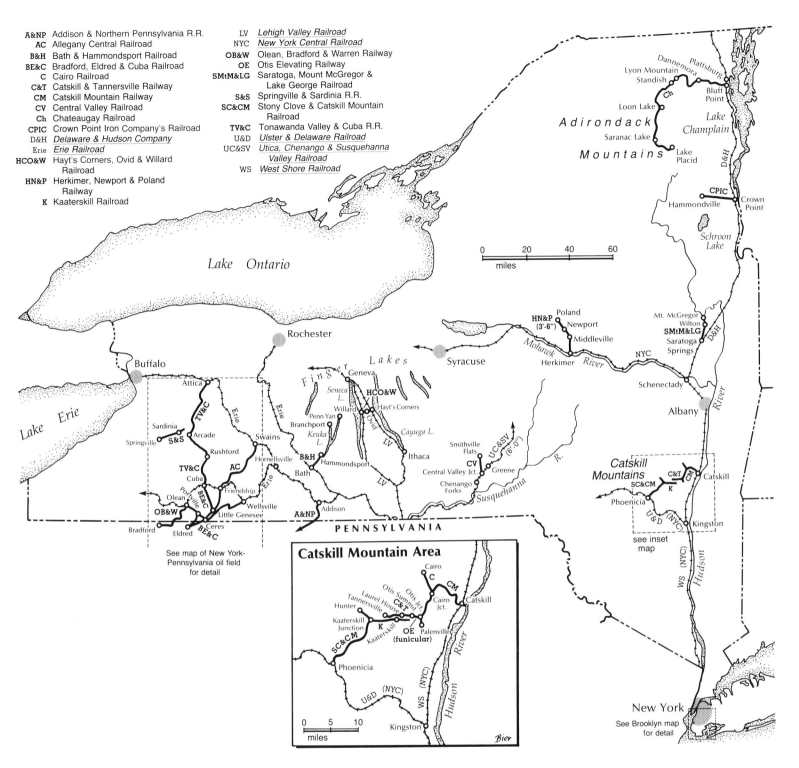

A&NP Addison & Northern Pennsylvania R.R.
AC Allegany Central Railroad
B&H Bath & Hammondsport Railroad
BE&C Bradford, Eldred & Cuba Railroad
C Cairo Railroad
C&T Catskill & Tannersville Railway
CM Catskill Mountain Railway
CV Central Valley Railroad
Ch Chateaugay Railroad
CPIC Crown Point Iron Company's Railroad
D&H *Delaware & Hudson Company*
Erie *Erie Railroad*
HCO&W Hayt's Corners, Ovid & Willard Railroad
HN&P Herkimer, Newport & Poland Railway
K Kaaterskill Railroad

LV *Lehigh Valley Railroad*
NYC *New York Central Railroad*
OB&W Olean, Bradford & Warren Railway
OE Otis Elevating Railway
SMtM&LG Saratoga, Mount McGregor & Lake George Railroad
S&S Springville & Sardinia R.R.
SC&CM Stony Clove & Catskill Mountain Railroad
TV&C Tonawanda Valley & Cuba R.R.
U&D *Ulster & Delaware Railroad*
UC&SV *Utica, Chenango & Susquehanna Valley Railroad*
WS *West Shore Railroad*

lake, one of the loveliest of the Finger Lakes, was attractive to vacationers from Buffalo, Rochester, and more distant areas. As many as eight trains per day were run in peak seasons. The narrow gauge had five locomotives, four passenger cars, a baggage car, three boxcars, seven flatcars, and two pieces of service equipment. The physical plant was reported to have cost $104,806.62, and equipment $18,187.04.

Henry S. Stebbins of Hammondsport

bought Wood's lease on November 15, 1886, and prepared to convert the railroad. He closed the line for about six months early in 1889, and reopened it as a standard gauge railroad on August 1. Simultaneously, he gave up the lease, returned the property to Champlin's corporation, and left the area. Conversion of track and facilities had cost $90,000, and standard gauge equipment $45,000.

Stock control of the B&H was acquired

by the Erie in 1908, but the railroad continued to operate as an independent short line. The Erie gave up its equity in 1936 and the railroad reverted to local ownership. It remains in service, mainly as an originating carrier for the local wine industry.

REFERENCES: Gustave W. Erhardt, "The Bath & Hammondsport R.R.," Railway & Locomotive Historical Society *Bulletin*, no. 62 (1943), pp. 68–70; William Reed Gordon, *Keuka Lake Memories* (Rochester, N.Y., 1967), pp. 71–116.

Catskill Mountain Railway
Cairo Railroad
Catskill & Tannersville Railway

The development of tourism to the Catskill Mountains after 1870 rendered existing road transport inadequate. Charles L. Beach, proprietor of the Catskill Mountain House on South Mountain, joined with Alfred Van Santvoord of the Hudson River Day Line and Charles L. Rickerson of the Catskill Evening Line on September 9, 1880, in forming the Catskill Mountain Railroad to provide a connection from the steamboat landing at Catskill to some point from which the hotel would be immediately accessible. The route chosen was from Catskill Landing to Palenville (16 miles). The promoters were able to make use of an existing right-of-way from Catskill Village to South Cairo, about seven miles, dating from the early years of railroading. The standard gauge Canajoharie & Catskill Rail Road had completed a line of 26 miles along Catskill Creek from Catskill to Cooksburg in 1840, but quickly failed, and was removed in 1842. Because the new railroad was intended for seasonal summer movements mainly of passengers in connection with the river steamers, the promoters' choice of narrow gauge was defensible. The line passed about 50 feet below the West Shore at Catskill Station. The railroad was opened from the landing to Lawrenceville (12 miles) on July 29, 1882. The remaining four miles, along with a station at Palenville, were ready for the opening of the 1883 season.

The railroad had two major flaws as completed to Palenville: it had virtually no freight traffic beyond supplies inbound to the hotel, and it turned the passengers over to horse-drawn vehicles at the base of South Mountain for an arduous ascent of 1,630 feet. To deal with the first problem, Beach and his group joined with some local men to undertake a branch from Cairo Junction to Cairo (4 miles). Because the investors' group was different, the branch was separately incorporated on April 10, 1884, as the Cairo Railroad. Initially the branch line was separately operated with its own locomotive, a Dickson 4-4-0, but the engine was subsequently renumbered in the CM's sequence, and used interchangeably with the CM's power. The branch opened on July 1, 1885, and on the following day the parent company, which had missed its interest payments earlier in 1885, was reorganized as the Catskill Mountain Railway.

Arranging an ascent of South Mountain became urgent when George W. Harding of Philadelphia built the Hotel Kaaterskill adjacent to the Catskill Mountain House and participated with the directors of the Ulster & Delaware Railroad in building the narrow gauge Kaaterskill Railroad to a point about a half mile from the hotel, but on a level with it. Beach, recognizing that an ascent of South Mountain from Palenville was impractical for adhesion railroading, approached elevator manufacturer Charles Rollins Otis about building a funicular directly up the escarpment. Otis proved enthusiastic and participated in forming the Otis Elevating Railway on November 25,

1885. The line was designed by Thomas E. Brown, Jr., who had designed Otis's elevators for the Eiffel Tower in Paris. The railway was not financed until 1891, but it was then built quickly and opened on August 7, 1892. The funicular made the ascent in 7,000 feet with an average grade of 12 percent and a maximum of 34 percent. The gauge was 3'-0", but the compatibility with the CM initially served no purpose. Passengers were handled in cross-bench open cars at opposite ends of the cable, each of which had a four-wheel trailer into which the passengers' baggage was transshipped. The trailers also carried supplies for the hotel and hay for animals kept at the summit. The funicular made its connection with the CM at Otis Junction, about a mile short of Palenville.

Otis Summit at the top of the funicular was in front of Catskill Mountain House, but several hotels had been built along the ridge west to Tannersville. To serve them Beach and his associates formed the Catskill & Tannersville Railway on September 14, 1892. The route was directly parallel to the Kaaterskill Railroad but slightly to the north. The Harding group was reluctant to see the parallel narrow gauge built, and successfully proposed to the Beach group that only 0.93 of a mile of the C&T be built from the Kaaterskill's terminus to Otis Summit, and then leased to the Kaaterskill. Track was laid in the spring of 1893 and the extension opened on July 8. The lease lasted only through the 1898 season. As the Ulster & Delaware prepared to convert the Kaaterskill, it returned the mile of track to the

The Central Valley's only locomotive was this lovely Grant 2-4-0, named for one of the railroad's principal financiers. (W. A. Lucas collection, Railroad Museum of Pennsylvania.)

Beach group, which proceeded to build the C&T as originally planned (5 miles). The line, which was completed on August 5, 1899, was unprofitable per se, but the CM made an annual subvention of $4,800 per year to keep it going. In 1902 the funicular was shortened by 1,640 feet and provided with a connection to the CM such that specially built small freight cars could be handled up the mountain, mainly to deliver supplies to the hotels along the C&T. This arrangement entailed a compatibility problem, for the CM used an Eames vacuum brake and the C&T a Westinghouse air brake. C&T locomotives and the eight freight cars of the Otis built for the service carried both vacuum and air systems.

The Beach network did very well at the turn of the century, partly because of a high volume of tourism, and partly because a substantial traffic in shale rock and clay developed in the 1890s. The Catskill Shale Brick & Paving Co. established daily movements in its own equipment from a quarry on the Cairo Railroad to its plant in Catskill. By 1899 this traffic amounted to a third of the revenue of the railroad, but the brick company went bankrupt in 1901, and under its later incorporations it never reached its former levels of output.

Van Santvoord died on July 20, 1901; Beach died on October 2, 1902, at the age of 94. His son, Charles A. Beach, had been in charge of the railroad system for some years. The younger Beach was to preside over a drastic decline in the fortunes of the system. Automobiles diverted large numbers of passengers, especially after 1909. The brick plant closed in 1912, and the Hudson River Day Line, which had helped make up the losses of the Otis Railway (under which name the funicular had been reorganized in 1899), ceased being willing to do so. Charles Beach died in 1913, and the three railroads went bankrupt between May and August 1915. The three were consolidated into the Catskill Mountain Railroad Corporation after a receiver's sale of April 25, 1916. The Beach family was still represented in the ownership, but about 84 percent of the stock was held by the Olcott family, which had inherited control of the Day Line. This situation assured that the narrow gauge would operate only as long as the Day Line's management considered it a useful connection. The line had reverted to seasonal operation when the shale movements ended, and last operated for the 1918 season. It was scrapped beginning in 1919. Catskill Mountain House survived until 1942.

REFERENCE: William F. Helmer, *Rip Van Winkle Railroads* (Berkeley, Calif.: Howell-North Books, 1970).

Catskill Mountain Railway No. 2, a 4-4-0 from the Dickson Manufacturing Co., is shown on one of the line's passenger trains. (Ed Bond collection.)

Central Valley Railroad

Among the earliest narrow gauges, in dates of both opening and abandonment, was the Central Valley Railroad in Chenango County. The line was promoted by E. G. Crozier and other local businessmen to provide an outlet from the small town of Smithville Flats to the 6'-0" Utica, Chenango & Susquehanna Valley (Greene Railroad; Delaware, Lackawanna & Western, Utica branch). Their original intention was to build a line of 12 miles from Smithville Flats to Chenango Forks, but they actually laid eight miles of track from a station a half mile south of Smithville Flats along Genegantslet Creek to a point at its confluence with the Chenango River about 4.5 miles southwest of the town of Greene, to which they gave the name Central Valley Junction. Construction began in May 1871, and the line was opened on May 20, 1872. The management bought a Grant 2-4-0, to which it gave the name *Warren Newton* after a banker in Norwich active in financing the line. Initially, Crozier and his associates planned a northward extension to Cortland, Auburn, and some point on the Great Lakes, but no further track was laid. Only a few months had elapsed when, in late 1872, they planned conversion of the line to standard gauge for use as part of a projected Buffalo extension of the New York & Oswego Midland (New York, Ontario & Western). *Poor's Manual* reported the line converted to 4'-8½" and laid with 56-pound rail in its 1874–75 and 1875–76 issues, but local newspapers give no evidence of this. In March 1875 operation was reported suspended temporarily, but in April the line was

being dismantled. The rails were sold to the Bath & Hammondsport; the equipment was variously reported as having gone to the same railroad and to a narrow gauge on Long Island.

REFERENCE: Richard F. Palmer, "Narrow Gauge to Oblivion: The Central Valley Railroad," *Railroad History*, no. 128 (1973), pp. 68–75.

Chateaugay Railroad

The Delaware & Hudson's lengthy branch into the central Adirondacks from the main line at Plattsburg (later spelled Plattsburgh) was built by four narrow gauge predecessors for quite different reasons. The earliest portion, 20 miles from Plattsburg to Dannemora, was built by the State of New York to serve the state prison at Dannemora. The line, which was opened in December 1878, was directly administered by the state superintendent of prisons and had no corporate organization, although it was informally known as the Plattsburgh & Dannemora Railroad. The line was built mainly by convict labor. Somewhat under four miles leaving Plattsburg was third rail laid south on the New York & Canada (Delaware & Hudson) to Bluff Point. The line entailed a gain in altitude of 1,236 feet, mainly accomplished by five miles of grades over 3 percent approaching the prison. Because of the prospect of hauling iron ore for producers in the area, the line was a common carrier from the outset.

One of the principal ore producers, the Chateaugay Ore Co., operated a pit at Lyon Mountain, 16 miles west of Dannemora. To eliminate wagon freighting to the plant of the parent Chateaugay Iron Co. at Plattsburg, the Chateaugay Railroad was incorporated on May 15, 1879, to build a rail link from Dannemora to Lyon Mountain. On May 20 the new corporation leased the state's railroad for 100 years as of July 1, 1879, for $1 per year plus an agreement to carry supplies to the prison without charge. The company's own railroad to Lyon Mountain (36 miles) was opened on March 30, 1880. On May 2, 1881, the parent company and its mining subsidiary were consolidated as the Chateaugay Ore & Iron Co. This entity extended the railroad, under the name of Chateaugay Railway, to Standish (40 miles) in 1885 and to Loon Lake (54 miles) in 1886, mainly to bring charcoal into the smelter at Plattsburg. Finally, on December 5, 1887, the line was brought into Saranac Lake (73 miles), an important resort and health facility. The Delaware & Hudson, which was interested in passenger traffic to the resort, had financed the extension to the extent of buying the Chateaugay Railway's first mortgage of $200,000. George S. and Smith M. Weed, heads of the iron company, were also among the promoters of the final extension of the narrow gauge, which was separately organized as the Saranac & Lake Placid Railroad on July 12, 1890. The line was built as a standard gauge railroad mainly for passenger service from Lake Clear Junction on the New York Central's Adirondack Division to Lake Placid, with third rail for the Chateaugay's 3'-0" equipment for ten miles from Saranac Lake into Lake Placid. The standard gauge portion was operated as a branch of the New York Central. With the opening of the line into Lake Placid on August 1, 1893, the narrow gauge reached its full length of 83 miles. The Chateaugay Railroad operated the S&LP under lease beginning December 1, 1893.

The Chateaugay was a relatively large narrow gauge, operated in 1895 with 11 locomotives, 14 passenger and head-end cars, and 428 freight cars. It regularly ran two passenger trains per day the length of the railroad, with additional service between Saranac and Lake Placid in connection with the New York Central.

The Delaware & Hudson Co. had a financial interest in the Chateaugay Ore & Iron Co. from the latter's formation in 1881, and in 1901 it took control of the narrow gauge. On July 24, 1903, the D&H formed the Chateaugay & Lake Placid Railway as a consolidation of the Chateaugay Railroad and Railway and the S&LP; this corporation also assumed the lease of the Plattsburgh & Dannemora. Earlier, on July 1,

Locomotives of the Crown Point Iron Company's Railroad carried six pockets for link-and-pin couplers so as to mate with narrow gauge equipment or standard cars at the coupler height of either. (Ed Bond collection.)

1903, the D&H had begun to operate the line as the Chateaugay branch of the Champlain Division. The D&H had already made its decision to convert the line, placing a contract for $1 million for the conversion on August 1, 1902. The job was undertaken late in the year and completed almost exactly a year after the contract was let, in early August 1903.

The branch operated intact until November 1, 1946, when the D&H turned the Saranac–Lake Placid segment over to the New York Central and cut back the rest to Lyon Mountain. The D&H in 1971 reduced it to the original trackage to Dannemora, and in 1979 reduced it to a spur of about three miles at Bluff Point. The Saranac–Lake Placid line was abandoned by the Penn Central in 1972.

REFERENCES: *A Century of Progress: History of the Delaware & Hudson Company, 1823–1923* (Albany, N.Y.: Delaware & Hudson Co., 1925), pp. 624–30; Jim Shaughnessy, *Delaware & Hudson* (Berkeley, Calif.: Howell-North Books, 1967), pp. 157–67 and *passim*.

Crown Point Iron Company's Railroad

To tap iron deposits at Hammondville, 13 miles inland from its smelter at Crown Point on the Delaware & Hudson main line above Ticonderoga, the Crown Point Iron Co. undertook this railroad in 1872 and completed it in mid-1874. Because of the heaviness of the expected cargo, and in spite of its early date, the line was substantially built, laid with 56-pound rail. By 1882 it was reportedly operated with four locomotives, two passenger cars, four boxcars, and 110 small ore cars. The railroad was a

bona fide common carrier, handling over 2,000 passengers per year on two daily mixed trains. An extension was projected to Schroon Lake, which, if built, would have added considerably to the railroad's general traffic.

The depression of the 1890s, combined with the expansion of Lake Superior iron sources, brought the operation to a close in 1893. The last train of ore operated on July 22. The line was removed about 1896.

REFERENCES: Elmer Eugene Barker, "The Story of Crown Point Iron," *Proceedings of the New York State Historical Association*, 40 (1942), pp. 419–26; Richard F. Palmer, "The Crown Point Iron Company's Railroad," in Richard S. Allen et al., *Rails in the North Woods* (Lakemont, N.Y.: North Country Books, 1973), pp. 175–94.

Hayt's Corners, Ovid & Willard Railroad

On September 15, 1882, this railroad was chartered to run from the Hayt's Corners Station of the Geneva, Ithaca & Sayre Railroad, an affiliate of the Lehigh Valley, to Ovid, seat of Seneca County (2 miles), and Willard, site of the Willard State Hospital (5 miles). The promoters, led by George W. Jones, lacked funds to complete the line, and arranged for it to be leased to the GI&S for 99 years. This was to bring it into the Lehigh Valley system from its opening in May 1883. The line was dual gauge from the outset, laid with 3'-0" rail for conformity with some trackage built on the hospital grounds in 1877–78 to switch coal to hospital facilities from steamboats or barges on Seneca Lake. The 4'-8½" track was used to serve Ovid and to switch coal into the

The principal function of the Crown Point Iron Company's Railroad was eastbound movements of iron ore. The ore moved in small four-wheel gondolas, a string of which follows Mogul No. 2 in the photograph reproduced here. (Thomas T. Taber collection, Railroad Museum of Pennsylvania.)

hospital grounds. Of the 5.18 miles of line, 3.83 were owned by the LV and 1.35, the mileage on the hospital grounds, by the State of New York; the LV operated the entire branch.

The Seneca Lake bypass was built through Willard just east of the hospital in 1890 and made part of the New York–Buffalo main line in 1892. The bypass, which avoided some difficult grades on the old line via Ithaca and Hayt's Corners, passed beneath the three-rail line into the hospital. The narrow gauge was removed in the spring of 1894. The line from Ovid to Willard was abandoned in 1936, and from Hayt's Corners to Ovid in 1959.

Herkimer, Newport & Poland Railway
Gauge: 3'-6"

Relatively late for a 3'-6" line, the Herkimer, Newport & Poland was chartered on June 29, 1880, by Edward M. Burns of Middleville. He financed it conservatively,

issuing $100,000 in stock and $66,000 in 6 percent bonds. The route was a rather easy one up West Canada Creek with no grades worse than 0.5 percent. The line was opened from Herkimer on the main line of the New York Central & Hudson River Railroad to Middleville (9 miles) on September 6, 1881, to Newport (13 miles) on January 1, 1882, and to Poland (17 miles) on May 29, 1882. The railroad ran three mixed trains per day, and proved successful enough that it could refinance its bond issue at 5 percent on April 1, 1886. The company originally operated with two locomotives but added a third in the middle of the decade.

In mid-1890 the shareholders accepted an offer of Dr. William Seward Webb of New York to buy 60 percent of the stock at 50¢ on the dollar. Webb proposed to convert the line and to extend it about 30 miles north to Jock's Lake in the southern Adirondacks. Rather, in February 1891 Webb sold his interest to the NYC&HR, which was buying or building the trackage that became its Adirondack Division. The Central converted the railroad on June 6, 1891, al-

though the straightening of curves and similar improvements lasted into 1892. The line was owned, leased, and operated by a variety of subsidiaries, and as extended to Remsen, provided a cutoff to the Adirondack Division from Herkimer. This proved less attractive than the main access from Utica, and the extension north from Poland was abandoned in 1942. The former narrow gauge was abandoned on the formation of Conrail in 1976.

New York & Manhattan Beach Railway

Although this railroad proved to be a highly specialized narrow gauge passenger carrier, it had its origin in a project for a standard gauge railroad to carry coal from New York harbor across what was still rural country to inland towns on Long Island. The New York & Hempstead Railroad was founded in 1870 to run from a terminal at Bay Ridge on the Brooklyn waterfront through New Utrecht, Flatbush, Flatlands, New Lots, Woodhaven, and Jamaica to Hempstead, about 21 miles. Coal was to be ferried in carloads on barges from the various railroad terminals on the New Jersey waterfront. The management surveyed a route across southern Brooklyn in 1871–72, bought a farm for the projected Bay Ridge terminal, drove some pilings in the harbor, and graded the west end of the line. The promoters found themselves unable to complete the line, and leased it on June 2, 1873, to the South Side Railroad, which proposed to use it as a branch to Bay Ridge off its own line along the south shore of Long Island. When the SSRR became insolvent following the Panic of 1873, work on the Bay Ridge line ground to a halt. Abram Wakeman, an investor in the NY&H who was unwilling to let the project die, revived it in scaled-down form from Bay Ridge nine miles inland to Jamaica, with branches to Bath and Coney Island. He incorporated the line as the New York, Bay Ridge & Jamaica Railroad on November 20, 1875. Using equipment from the Brooklyn, Bath & Coney Island Railroad, a steam dummy line, the railroad opened on August 19, 1876, as a single-track standard gauge line from the Bay Ridge terminal at the foot of 69th Street to Bath Junction (2.25 miles), whence trains continued to Coney Island over the dummy line. The steamer *D. R. Martin* provided a connection to Pier 8, North River.

Meanwhile, Austin Corbin of New York conceived of developing the east end of Coney Island as a resort and residential area. He acquired the land and in 1875 adopted the name Manhattan Beach. On October 28, 1876, he formed the New York & Manhattan Beach Railway as a facility to serve the development. He adopted 3′-0″ at the urging of his superintendent, Isaac D. Barton, who had already been converted to narrow gauge ideology. In November 1876 Corbin bought control of the NY&H, and leased the property to his new corporation. Track crews began converting the NY&H to narrow gauge in February 1877. Corbin purchased a locomotive and much of the rolling stock of the railroad at the Centennial Exposition of 1876 in Philadelphia. This equipment was nearly new and well suited to the traffic to Manhattan Beach. Narrow gauge track was extended east from Bath Junction, where the NY&H had terminated, to Parkville and then south to Coney Island parallel to Ocean Avenue. Rails reached Sheepshead Bay on the north shore of Coney Island Creek on May 28, allowing the railroad to be used for the construction of Corbin's Manhattan Beach Hotel, reportedly the largest hotel along the Atlantic Coast. The creek was bridged early in the summer, and the railroad was opened from Bay Ridge to Manhattan Beach on July 19, 1877. Corbin had also brought the tracks northeast from Park-

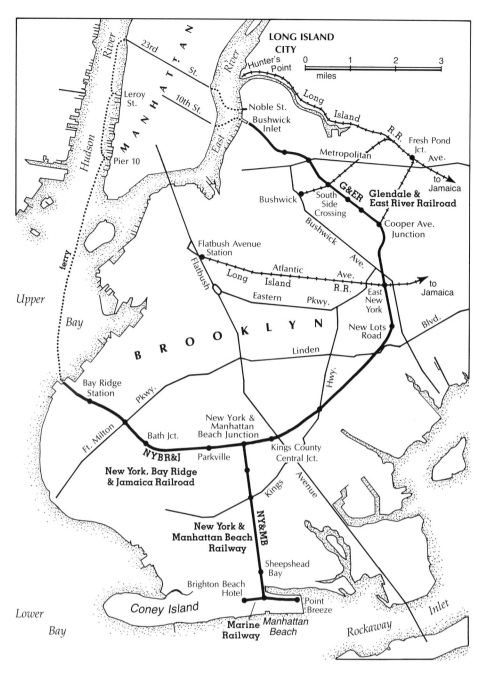

ville to East New York on the Long Island Rail Road's branch from Jamaica into Flatbush Avenue station. On opening day, the railroad amounted to about 15 miles of double track.

Although the railroad had access to Manhattan, the steamer trip was relatively long, and came from the West Side. Corbin sought a route that would serve the East Side, where the population was highly concentrated, and one that would require only a short ferry crossing. The South Side Railroad, seeking a terminus on the East River, had formed the Glendale & East River Railroad on March 26, 1874, but being bankrupt, was unable to proceed with construction. The South Side's new owners, the Poppenhusen family, bought the Long Island Rail Road in

January 1876, and were satisfied with the existing terminus at Hunter's Point in Long Island City, Queens. In 1876 Barton endeavored to use the franchise of the G&ER for the terminus for his North Shore Railroad of Long Island, a project for a narrow gauge from Brooklyn to Orient at the northeast tip of the island. He was unable to finance this enterprise, but he readily persuaded Corbin of the value of the franchise of the G&ER for building the NY&MB's approach to the East River. Barton strongly favored establishing the riverside terminal at Bushwick Inlet in Greenpoint for ready access by ferry to Manhattan at East 10th and 23rd streets. The G&ER's franchise allowed him to build from this point inland to a crossing of the South Side Railroad's line into Bushwick Station, but neither Barton nor Corbin had a franchise to build from this point to East New York. Corbin arranged to use the unbuilt franchise of the Brooklyn & Rockaway Beach Railroad, a steam dummy line that served the Canarsie area, for the gap. He had already arranged for joint use of the B&RB's right-of-way between New Lots Avenue and East New York. After vigorous opposition from shipbuilders and other industrial firms in the Greenpoint area, the extension was built, and the completed railroad of 19 miles was opened formally for the season on May 15, 1878, along with the Manhattan Beach Hotel.

The railroad's geographical pattern fitted it mainly for carrying traffic from Manhattan; essentially it ran as a belt around what was then the populated portion of Brooklyn. To penetrate Brooklyn, Corbin arranged to lease the Kings County Central Railroad, which Electus B. Litchfield was promoting as a steam dummy line to the beach. The NY&MB agreed to build the railroad, to lease it for 99 years, and to operate it in return for 70 percent of the receipts from passengers, plus 2¢ per head and all of the freight receipts. The line opened on June 29, 1878, from the corner of Flatbush Avenue and Malbone Street (Empire Boulevard) to Kings County Central Junction on the NY&MB main line, 3.25 miles. The Flatbush terminus provided direct access to horsecar lines that served central Brooklyn. On July 1, 1878, a rival steam dummy line, the Brooklyn, Flatbush & Coney Island Railroad, was opened from the same intersection to the Brighton Beach area at the center of Coney Island. Partly because the route was more direct, and partly because the BF&CI served an older, less expensive portion of Coney Island, the public showed a strong preference for the newer line. The KCC closed for the season on September 30, 1878, and went bankrupt in February 1879. The railroad was removed during May, and Corbin was left dependent for his Brooklyn traffic on the connection with the Long Island at East New York.

Matthias N. Forney rode the NY&MB in the summer of 1877 and reported on it in the *Railroad Gazette*. He was impressed with the heaviness of the grading, and thought the line better built than the three preexisting standard gauge lines to Coney Island. No curve was worse than 10° and the ruling grade up from Bay Ridge was only about 1 percent. The line was then operated with five Mason Bogies, 36 open excursion cars, four closed cars, and eight or ten freight cars. Forney observed that the cars oscillated somewhat worse than standard gauge equipment,

and thought they represented no saving in weight. The line had some primitive signaling, red and white disks at Manhattan Beach Junction to show choice of routes for oncoming trains.

In the winter of 1878 Corbin built a separately operated narrow gauge, the Marine Railroad, for 1.6 miles east of Manhattan Beach to the east tip of Coney Island, where he built the Point Breeze Pavilion, with a small hotel and a boat house. In the name of the Marine Railroad Corbin built a second line, about a half mile west from Manhattan Beach to the newly built Brighton Beach Hotel. Trains, which operated at headways of three to five minutes, made use of 0.4 miles of the NY&MB between the two segments.

The NY&MB proved extremely successful as a seasonal passenger hauler. It began operation with five small Mason Bogies, and eight more were added in 1878. Six 2-4-6T versions were added in 1881–82, replacing five of the original smaller engines. The Marine Railroad had two 2-4-4T Bogies, supplemented by two secondhand Baldwin 0-4-0T engines. The NY&MB had 99 passenger cars, used for only four months per year. After the summer season of 1877 the line ran a single train daily from Bay Ridge to Manhattan Beach in October, but then ceased operation. After the 1878 season it ran five trains between Greenpoint and East New York—two of which went on to Manhattan Beach—plus two trains on the Bay Ridge line. In December this service was cut to two trains daily on the Greenpoint line and one on the Bay Ridge branch. After 1878 the line operated only during the summer seasons, from about May 25 to October 1. The trains were subject to heavy weekend peaks. A second hotel, the Oriental, was built in 1880.

The enterprise was successful enough that the railroad might have survived for some years as an isolated narrow gauge, but on December 3, 1880, Corbin and his associates bought control of the entire Long Island Rail Road. In addition to the obvious advantages of compatibility of equipment for assignments and maintenance with a large standard gauge railroad, Corbin sought direct entry into downtown Brooklyn and to arrange better access to the East River ferries. Corbin had considered laying third rail on the LIRR from East New York to Flatbush Avenue, but this was of questionable legality under the franchise of the line, which the LIRR operated under lease. In December 1881 Corbin announced that the NY&MB would be leased to the LIRR for 99 years, as of May 1, 1882, and be converted. Since the NY&MB had no

existing access to the LIRR's main line at Long Island City, Corbin incorporated the Long Island City & Manhattan Beach Railroad in February 1883 to build a connection of 1.5 miles from Cooper Avenue Junction on the NY&MB in Glendale to the LIRR at Fresh Pond Junction.

Corbin secured permission to build a connection to the LIRR's Brooklyn line at East New York on September 30, 1882, and began preparations for conversion in December. Because the NY&MB was a seasonal facility that was closed in any case, the conversion could be done in leisurely fashion. In February 1883 crews began respiking the existing 40-pound rail to 4′-8½″; 56-pound rail replaced it in 1884. The only major revision was the widening of the trestle over Coney Island Creek and the filling in of some of the adjacent meadows. Standard gauge service was opened into Flatbush Avenue on May 30, 1883, and into Long Island City on June 2. Initially, the narrow gauge line into Greenpoint was retained to serve the Williamsburg area, but the two connecting ferry lines were discontinued. This line ran shuttle trains to meet each of the 25 main-line passenger trains at Cooper Avenue, an excessive number relative to the population of the mainly industrial area. Corbin converted this branch in 1884, mainly to serve the factories on the route; passengers continued to change trains at Cooper Avenue. Passenger service on the branch was discontinued after the 1885 season, and the terminal at Greenpoint was abandoned on April 30, 1886, when the lease on it expired. The branch was cut back to South Side Crossing, the junction with the Bushwick branch, in 1896–97.

On August 27, 1885, the NY&MB, NYBR&J, and LIC&MB were merged into the New York, Brooklyn & Manhattan Beach Railway, still leased to the LIRR. In 1925 the NYB&MB was absorbed into the LIRR directly, passenger service on the Manhattan Beach branch was discontinued, and the line was cut back to Neck Road in Sheepshead Bay to eliminate both the crossing of Coney Island Creek and the remaining grade crossings. It was further cut back to Midwood in 1932. The rest of the branch was abandoned on August 1, 1935. The former narrow gauge from Bay Ridge to Cooper Avenue became part of the principal freight connection from the Pennsylvania Railroad, which delivered cars by barge from the Greenville terminal in New Jersey, to the Long Island Rail Road and to the New York, New Haven & Hartford via the Hell Gate Bridge. Work on the elevation of the line began in 1905 as part of a city program for the grade-separation of railroads. At the same time it was electrified with 11,000-volt AC and thereafter operated principally by NYNH&H locomotives under trackage rights. By an agreement of December 22, 1965, whereby the Pennsylvania Railroad turned over its remaining equity in the Long Island to the State of New York, the PRR retained the Bay Ridge line, but the Long Island was directed to operate the trackage at least until 1971. The electrification was removed in 1969, when the Penn Central discontinued the barge connection from Greenville in favor of a route via Selkirk Yard in the Albany area. In 1971 the Long Island turned the line over to the Penn Central and in 1976 it passed into the hands of Conrail. The Long Island resumed ownership in 1984. The line survives as a single-track connection to the barges and terminal trackage of the New York Cross Harbor Railroad at Bay Ridge.

REFERENCES: Vincent F. Seyfried, *The Long Island Rail Road*, vol. 6 (Garden City, N.Y.: Vincent F. Seyfried, 1966), pp. 1–93; John G. Kneiling, *By Narrow Gauge to Bay Ridge and Coney Island: The Old New York and Manhattan Beach* (Hoboken, N.J.: The Railroading Library, 1947); *Railroad Gazette*, 9 (1877), pp. 378–79.

Saratoga, Mt. McGregor & Lake George Railroad

A large syndicate headed by John Kellogg of Amsterdam and W. J. Arkell of Canajoharie projected this narrow gauge as part of a resort development on Mt. McGregor, directly north of Saratoga Springs. They incorporated the Saratoga, Mt. McGregor & Lake George Railroad on February 27, 1882, and had their charter amended on February 20, 1883, to allow them to buy land for the hotel and related resort buildings. They acquired 1,040 acres, including two lakes, at an elevation of 800 feet above Saratoga Springs, and built the Hotel Balmoral along with some related buildings. The railroad opened for service, apparently on its flat portion to Wilton (7 miles), on July 17, 1882, and to the mountain (11 miles) when the summer season began on June 4, 1883. The ascent of the mountain was a difficult one, with sustained 4-percent grades and a curve of 24°. The first three-quarters of a mile entailed a grade of 4.4 percent on extensive trestlework. The railroad's franchise also provided for building from Wilton to Glens Falls and to Caldwell at the southern tip of Lake George. Neither the original corporation nor any of its several narrow gauge successors ever made use of this right, but its existence made the line

more attractive to buyers than its sorry financial history would have warranted.

After an almost unbroken series of deficits, the railroad was placed in receivership on March 13, 1888, with Kellogg, its president, as receiver. It was purchased by Arkell, who had been vice-president, in October 1888, and reorganized as the Mt. McGregor Railroad on April 18, 1889. The new corporation was to do no better. On petition of George West of Ballston Spa, who represented the holders of the second mortgage, the railroad was again put in receivership on May 4, 1891, and scheduled for sale, along with the hotel and the land on the mountain, on October 19. Arkell again bought the property, this time for $28,500, on condition that he would accept an existing mortgage of $50,000. He was apparently unable to work out such financing, and the railroad was again sold on March 6, 1893, to representatives of holders of the first mortgage. They, too, were unable to refinance the line, and it remained in the hands of the receiver until June 16, 1896, when C. E. Arnold, H. McGonegal of New York, and others formed the Saratoga & Mt. McGregor Railway as a leasing company to operate the Mt. McGregor Railroad until a permanent corporation could be formed to buy the property, convert it, and extend it as an electric line to Glens Falls and Lake George. They formed the Saratoga Northern Railway for this purpose on June 28, 1897, but were unable even to operate the existing line. To hold the franchise, they provided a free service on the flat portion to Wilton, but made no effort to operate the ascent of the mountain. The railroad lay idle until Joseph A. Powers was appointed receiver in February 1900. The railroad was reported abandoned, but the corporation was merged on August 14, 1901, into the Hudson Valley Railway, which made use of the Saratoga Springs–Wilton right-of-way and the unused franchise for the long-projected electric line to Glens Falls and Lake George, completed in 1903. The company came into the hands of the Delaware & Hudson in 1907, and the electric line was abandoned in 1928.

The railroad had one moment of fame: former president U. S. Grant died at the Balmoral on July 23, 1885; his body began its funeral journey on the narrow gauge's rails.

Springville & Sardinia Railroad

Bertrand Chaffee and other businessmen of Springville secured a charter for the Springville & Sardinia on May 8, 1878,

seeking to connect their town with the Buffalo, New York & Philadelphia Railroad, 11.5 miles to the east. The connection was made at Sardinia Junction (Chaffee), established two miles north of Arcade and 2.5 miles east of the intermediate town of Sardinia. The railroad was cheaply built and completed in only 90 days; the only major engineering problem was a high trestle over Richmond Gulf. Service began in November 1878. The railroad operated with two locomotives, one passenger car, one baggage car, three boxcars, and four flatcars.

Initially, the railroad did quite well serving the general transportation demands of the two towns, but the opening of the Rochester & Pittsburgh Railroad through Springville in August 1883 diverted most of the line's traffic and reduced the corporation to unprofitability. It became delinquent on its mortgage of $25,000, and was sold to S. O. Barnum and R. R. Buck, representing the bondholders, on January 11, 1886. Rather than reorganize the railroad, the bondholders in May decided to abandon it. The Buffalo extension of the Buffalo & Susquehanna was to make use of part of the right-of-way during its short existence from 1906 to 1916.

Stony Clove & Catskill Mountain Railroad
Kaaterskill Railroad

By the time Charles L. Beach began his incursion into the upper Catskills from Catskill Landing with the Catskill Mountain Railroad in 1880, steamboat magnate Thomas B. Cornell had already penetrated the Catskills with his standard gauge Ulster & Delaware Railroad, later the New York Central's branch from Kingston to Oneonta. In collaboration with George W. Harding, a Philadelphia millionaire who had opened Hotel Kaaterskill on South Mountain adjacent to Beach's Catskill Mountain House, Cornell undertook a rival narrow gauge approach to the resort area. The line was incorporated as the Stony Clove & Catskill Mountain Railroad on January 18, 1881. The route chosen was from Phoenicia, on the U&D 28 miles northwest from the wharf at Kingston, to Hunter, on South Mountain about ten miles from the two hotels. The line was opened as far as Edgewood (9 miles) on August 18, 1881, but could not be pressed farther because of a labor dispute. This was resolved, and the line was completed to Hunter (14 miles) on August 29, 1882.

Stony Clove & Catskill Mountain No. 1, festooned with flowers, hauls two standard gauge boxcars and a narrow gauge caboose. (Ed Bond collection.)

Hunter had the attraction of being the center of a local tanbark industry, but its distance from the hotels prompted Cornell and Harding to undertake a branch for more direct access. The branch was separately incorporated as the Kaaterskill Railroad on November 25, 1882, no doubt to publicize the hotel. The line was opened on June 25, 1883, from Tannersville Junction (Kaaterskill Junction), two miles short of Hunter, to Kaaterskill Station (8 miles), on South Lake about half a mile from Hotel Kaaterskill.

The combined system was a difficult railroad. Track ascended along Stony Clove Creek 1,273 feet in ten miles to the summit of Stony Clove Notch, from which it descended into Hunter, with a net gain of about 800 feet from Phoenicia. The Kaaterskill Railroad ascended about 400 feet with a ruling grade of 2.5 percent. The ascent of Stony Clove Creek was in a narrow gorge, and the scenery of the entire system was spectacular. Two passenger trains per day were typically run during the tourist season from Phoenicia to Kaaterskill Station, with cars for Hunter set out for a connecting train at Kaaterskill Junction. The system operated all year-round, mainly carrying forest products. The management installed a Ramsey Transfer at Phoenicia to handle standard gauge freight cars. Initially 12 sets of transfer trucks were used, but this supply was expanded to 21.

The system had only a single extension. By an agreement of November 1892, it was arranged that the rival Beach group should build 0.93 miles of the Catskill & Tannersville from the terminus of the Kaa-

terskill Railroad to Otis Summit at the top of Beach's funicular, but that the Kaaterskill should operate the track under lease. The arrangement was necessarily short-lived. On June 1, 1893, the two narrow gauges were merged into the U&D under the condition that they be converted. They were thereafter known simply as the Narrow Gauge Division of the U&D. Laying of standard gauge ties began in 1894, and 70-pound rail was laid outside the existing rails. The conversion was completed with the inauguration of a Weehawken-Kaaterskill passenger train on June 26, 1899. Because Beach did not want to convert his system, the 0.93 miles of C&T track at Otis Summit were returned to him at the end of the 1898 season.

The former narrow gauge suffered the loss of most of its traffic with the public's conversion to the automobile after 1920, and especially after the burning of the Kaaterskill Hotel in September 1924. The mileage survived into the New York Central's absorption of the U&D on February 1, 1932, but both the Kaaterskill branch and its spur to Hunter were abandoned in 1940.

REFERENCE: Gerald M. Best, *The Ulster and Delaware* (San Marino, Calif.: Golden West Books, 1972).

North Carolina

Caldwell & Northern Railway

The Caldwell Land & Lumber Co. built this railroad as a service facility to its lumber operations near the furniture center of Lenoir. The railway's charter was issued on March 9, 1891, and amended on February 25, 1893. S. D. Dunavant of Morganton graded about 15 miles west from Lenoir during the summer of 1893. In 1895 track was laid for 10.6 miles from Lenoir to Collettsville, a town of about 150. The railroad operated with two locomotives, one passenger car, and 21 flatcars.

In 1905 the Carolina & Northwestern secured control of the railroad. In 1906 the C&NW converted the line and extended it north to Edgemont (13 miles). On July 1, 1910, the C&NW gained full ownership of the company and began showing the railroad in its timetables as an extension of its own main line, the former Chester & Lenoir narrow gauge, now standard gauge.

With the depletion of timber in the area, the line lost most of its traffic and was abandoned in 1938.

Lawndale Railway & Industrial Co.

Although one of the last common carriers to be built to 3'-0", the Lawndale Railway proved among the most long-lived of the Southern narrow gauges, surviving for 44 years.

Major H. F. Schenck and James E. Reynolds were proprietors of the Cleveland Cotton Mills, a pair of spinning plants two miles apart up the First Broad River from Shelby. Like many textile companies of the time, it was a comprehensive enterprise that included a mill town—Lawndale—and a local power company. The company prospered to the point that Schenck concluded

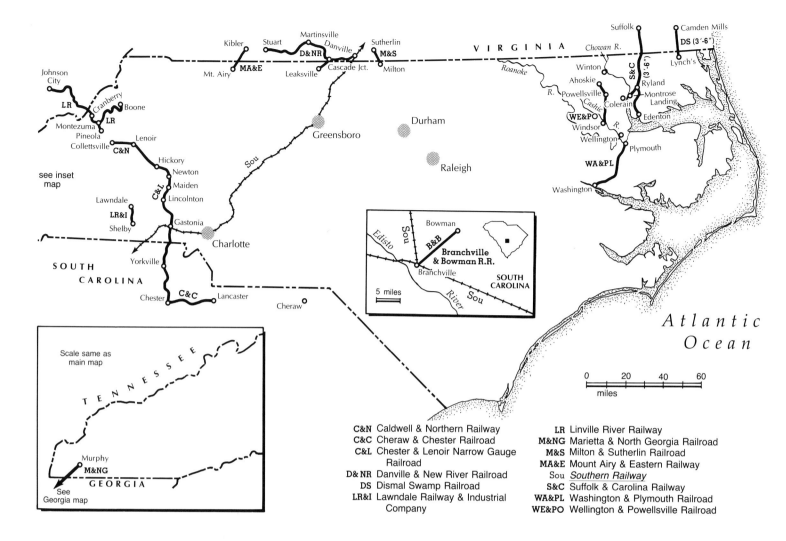

C&N Caldwell & Northern Railway
C&C Cheraw & Chester Railroad
C&L Chester & Lenoir Narrow Gauge
    Railroad
D&NR Danville & New River Railroad
DS Dismal Swamp Railroad
LR&I Lawndale Railway & Industrial
    Company

LR Linville River Railway
M&NG Marietta & North Georgia Railroad
M&S Milton & Sutherlin Railroad
MA&E Mount Airy & Eastern Railway
Sou *Southern Railway*
S&C Suffolk & Carolina Railway
WA&PL Washington & Plymouth Railroad
WE&PO Wellington & Powellsville Railroad

horse drayage to Shelby was no longer economic. Early in 1899 he resolved upon building a railroad. He decided upon narrow gauge partly because he preferred not to have his cars leave the property. He was also able to buy much of his rolling stock cheaply from the Chester & Lenoir, which was standard gauging. Construction began on May 10, 1899, and the railroad was completed on November 11 at the cost of only $49,477. Schenck arranged to lay third rail on two miles of the Southern Railway leaving Shelby, thereby making use of an existing bridge over the First Broad River. The company graded 8.8 miles of lightly built line through mildly rolling country north to Lawndale. The line was laid with only 25-pound rail and ballasted with dirt and cinders.

The railroad apparently operated as a common carrier from the outset, but without legal authority as such. In January 1901 Schenck secured an amendment to the textile company's charter to operate the line, and in November 1903 separately incorporated the railroad as the Lawndale Railway & Industrial Company. From the begin-

The Lawndale Railway was a late narrow gauge, but it was a very lightly built local facility. (Joseph Lavelle photograph, Thomas T. Taber collection, Railroad Museum of Pennsylvania.)

ning, the Southern Railway had given the company a 15 percent division of its revenues on interline traffic. Upon the incorporation of 1903, the Seaboard Air Line, which could provide an alternative route

into Shelby, offered a 25 percent division, which the Southern was unwilling to match. This motivated Schenck to bridge the Southern at the junction, which was known as Schenck's Station, to extend the line south about 0.4 miles to a point called Lawndale Junction, and to lay third rail for 1.7 miles into the Seaboard's Shelby station. The changeover required only two days in December 1903. Extensions both north and south were discussed, but no further track was laid.

Traffic was mainly cotton and other inputs to the mills northbound and finished yarn or thread southbound. Double Shoals, the principal intermediate town, housed a major mill of the Morgan family. About 1905 the railroad handled small amounts of monazite, a rare ore used in the production of mantles for gas lamps. Agricultural products, timber, and general cargo were also handled. The railroad customarily ran one mixed train per day, which left Lawndale in the morning and returned from Shelby in the afternoon. The trip required an hour and 15 minutes in each direction. Operations were profitable every year except 1916–20 and 1937. The line operated with four locomotives over its history, a Forney 0-4-4T at the outset, then a secondhand locomotive not identified, and finally two light 2-8-0s built by Vulcan.

The railroad lost general cargo to the highways, but traffic related to the mills expanded over the company's history. Indeed, as late as 1941 it produced over 200,000 ton-miles, its all-time high. The textile company concluded that it could handle the traffic more economically by truck, however, and ran its last train on April 30, 1943. The ICC formally approved abandonment on April 5, 1945. The physical plant was scrapped in the fall of the same year. A successor, the Lawndale Transportation Company, was established to provide service by truck over the route.

REFERENCE: Lee Rainey, "The Lawndale Dummy," *Narrow Gauge and Short Line Gazette*, Sept.–Oct. 1983, pp. 26–35.

Mount Airy & Eastern Railway

T. E. Houston of Elkhorn, West Virginia, and his associates chartered this late narrow gauge on May 3, 1899, to run from Mount Airy, North Carolina, the terminus of the Atlantic & Yadkin line of the Southern Railway, northeast along the eastern escarpment of the Blue Ridge Mountains into southern Virginia. The line was opened to Goings, Virginia (16 miles), on February 1, 1900. The enterprise quickly proved unsuccessful and was placed in the hands of receiver C. B. Keesee of Martinsville on May 4, 1901. Keesee extended the line to Kibler, Virginia (Danube; 19 miles), on November

1, 1902, to serve a lumber mill of Kibler & Kay. An extension of ten miles to Stuart, seat of Patrick County, Virginia, was surveyed in 1904 but not undertaken. The railroad typically operated with one or two locomotives, providing a single mixed train per day.

The line was sold under foreclosure on November 15, 1910, for $20,000 to the Rosslyn Lumber Co., and again sold on April 1, 1915, to Sidney Bieber of Washington, D.C., who reorganized it without change of name. The later history of the operation is obscure, but the line ceased operation about the spring of 1918. It was sold and reorganized as the Virginia & Mount Airy Railway on February 6, 1920, but as far as is known, was never restored to operation. It was apparently liquidated about 1925.

Washington & Plymouth Railroad

The Roanoke Railroad & Lumber Co. in 1888–89 built a private railroad between Plymouth on Albemarle Sound and Washington on Pamlico Sound, 33 miles, to serve its lumbering operations in the East Dismal Swamp. The office and shops were at Pinetown, near the midpoint. In 1901 E. A. Armstrong of Camden, New Jersey, and R. H. Cohn of Norfolk formed the Washington & Plymouth Railroad to acquire the line for operation as a common carrier. They began passenger service with a timetable of June 22, 1902. The railroad ran two round-trips per day; to haul them it bought from Baldwin the only Atlantic locomotive on any American narrow gauge. They considered an extension of 35 miles from Washington to New Bern on the Neuse River, but did not undertake it.

Rather, they sold the railroad on January 15, 1904, to the Norfolk & Southern Railroad, which was attempting to piece together its main line from Norfolk to Raleigh. By August the N&S was relaying the W&P with 70-pound rail in anticipation of conversion. A bond issue for conversion and other purposes was floated in December 1904, and the railroad was converted within the first five months of 1905. In 1906 the railroad completed a connection between Edenton and Plymouth, making use of the former B&O train ferry *John W. Garrett*, and as planned, made the former narrow gauge part of its main line. The former narrow gauge is still in existence as part of the Norfolk Southern system.

REFERENCE: Richard E. Prince, *Norfolk Southern Railroad, Old Dominion Line and Connections* (Millard, Nebr.: Richard E. Prince, 1972), p. 12.

Wellington & Powellsville Railroad

The extensive lumber operations of J. W. Branning in Bertie County were served by a private carrier, the Cashie & Roanoke Railroad, chartered on February 13, 1887. The railroad provided Branning with access to the logging area in the swampland south of his mill at Powellsville and with an outlet to steamers on the Chowan River at Colerain to the east. Planning to adopt common carriage and to shift the pattern of his operations, Branning reincorporated the railroad as the Wellington & Powellsville in October 1893. Initially the railroad remained a private carrier, and about 1895 reached its full extent, 26.5 miles of track plus logging spurs. The principal line went to Wellington, a landing on the Cashie River about ten miles below the Bertie County seat, Windsor.

In 1897–98 Branning revised the pattern of the railroad, building a new main line from Ahoskie through Powellsville to Windsor (21 miles). He abandoned the tracks to Colerain and Wellington, substituting access to the Atlantic Coast Line's Norfolk branch at Ahoskie for steamers on the tributaries of Albemarle Sound. The railroad remained mainly a facility for the plant at Powellsville, but it ran a daily mixed train, serving the general transportation demands of the county. Track for logging continued west beyond Windsor into the Roquist Swamp between the Cashie and Roanoke rivers.

On March 31, 1909, the railroad was mortgaged for $86,667 to the Branning Manufacturing Co. The railroad defaulted on the mortgage in about a year, but because the debt was held within the Branning enterprises, it was not immediately foreclosed. The Brannings apparently decided to divest themselves of the railroad and allowed J. A. Pretlow to be appointed receiver on September 23, 1923. The railroad was sold on February 16, 1926, to W. C. Everett, attorney for S. Wade Marr and Kenneth B. Coulter, who organized the Carolina Southern Railway. The new owners secured the ICC's permission for the transfer on March 31, 1927, and with the proceeds of a bond issue of $50,000 floated by Windsor Township, converted the railroad. As a standard gauge short line carry-

The stillborn Laurel River & Hot Springs acquired the Baldwin 2-6-0 *James Wyman*, which was used in the limited tracklaying the railroad accomplished. After the project was aborted, the locomotive went on to a successful career in Maine. (Robert C. Jones collection.)

ing agricultural products and lumber it survived until August 1, 1961, when it was abandoned.

▼ ▼ ▼ ▼

The New England Southern Timber & Land Company of Lynn, Massachusetts, owned timberland in Madison County, North Carolina, which it worked with a mill at Hot Springs. In May 1892 the company organized the Laurel River & Hot Springs Railroad to build a 2'-0" gauge lumber railroad from a point on the French Broad River opposite the mill to Laurelton at the junction of Foster's and Big Laurel creeks. The railroad, at best, would have been a nominal common carrier. The company built about 2.5 miles of track and graded an additional six miles before abandoning the project in 1893. The company acquired one locomotive, the *James Wyman*, which managed to achieve a Baldwin's builder's photograph in the stillborn railroad's livery. The locomotive was sold to the Wiscasset, Waterville & Farmington, which proved unable to pay for it. It was resold to the Sandy River, where it became Sandy River No. 3 and Sandy River & Rangeley Lakes No. 16.

Ohio

Bellaire & St. Clairsville Narrow Gauge Railway

St. Clairsville had been isolated from the railroad system by its hilltop location. Isaac H. Patterson and other local figures sought to rectify the situation by building the Bellaire & St. Clairsville Narrow Gauge Railway in April 1877. Regular service began in May on a route of 6.65 miles from Quincy (St. Clairsville Junction) on the Central Ohio, later the Wheeling-Columbus segment of the Baltimore & Ohio system, up Little McMahon Creek and Aults Run to a point just below the town. It was a small railroad of one locomotive, a combine, and two freight cars. Most of the revenue came from passengers making the connection at the junction, and about 80 percent of freight revenue came from coal.

The enterprise proved unsuccessful and was put in receivership in November 1879. The property was sold under foreclosure for only $18,500 on March 20, 1880, and

reorganized as the St. Clairsville Railway, still under Patterson's control. The dropping of "Bellaire" from the corporate title signified an end to an ambition for a north and east extension to the Bellaire & Southwestern. The railroad was again put in receivership in 1885, sold under foreclosure on December 16, and reorganized on December 27 as the Bellaire & St. Clairsville Railway. John T. Troll, the new president, immediately began installing longer ties, substituted steel rail in June 1886, and converted the railroad in early August. He arranged eight miles of trackage rights over the B&O and began operating three passenger trains per day between St. Clairsville and Wheeling. In fiscal 1889 the line was sold to the B&O, which operated it until abandonment in 1945.

Because the B&StC had built its station short of the town, the St. Clairsville village government in 1880 undertook to build a narrow gauge, the St. Clairsville & Northern Railway, to the north border of the town from Barton on the Cleveland, Tuscarawas Valley & Wheeling (3.5 miles). Construction began in July 1880, and by May 1881 the railroad was nearly ready for service. A locomotive had been bought secondhand from the Wheeling & Lake Erie. The Ohio Supreme Court then declared invalid the statute of 1879 empowering municipalities to build and operate railroads. The village continued to hope to open the railroad, but in mid-June a storm largely wiped out the track. Rather than rebuild it, the village authorities arranged to convert it, lease equipment from the CTV&W, and take trackage rights into Bridgeport, 12 miles away. Narrow gauge rail was left in place for several years in the expectation of a connection with B&StC, but this was never effected. The line opened as a standard gauge railroad on November 1, 1881, but was leased to its connection for 30 years on April 17, 1882. The intended narrow gauge became a branch of the Wheeling & Lake Erie, and survives as a branch of the Norfolk Southern system.

REFERENCE: Edward H. Cass, "The Two Narrow Gauge Railroads of St. Clairsville, Ohio," *Light Iron & Short Ties*, 2, no. 4–5 (Sept. 1984), pp. 4–5.

Celina, Van Wert & State Line Railroad

This small, short-lived, and obscure narrow gauge was organized by Dr. Hugh C. McGavren of Van Wert on May 7, 1878, to build from Celina to the Michigan state

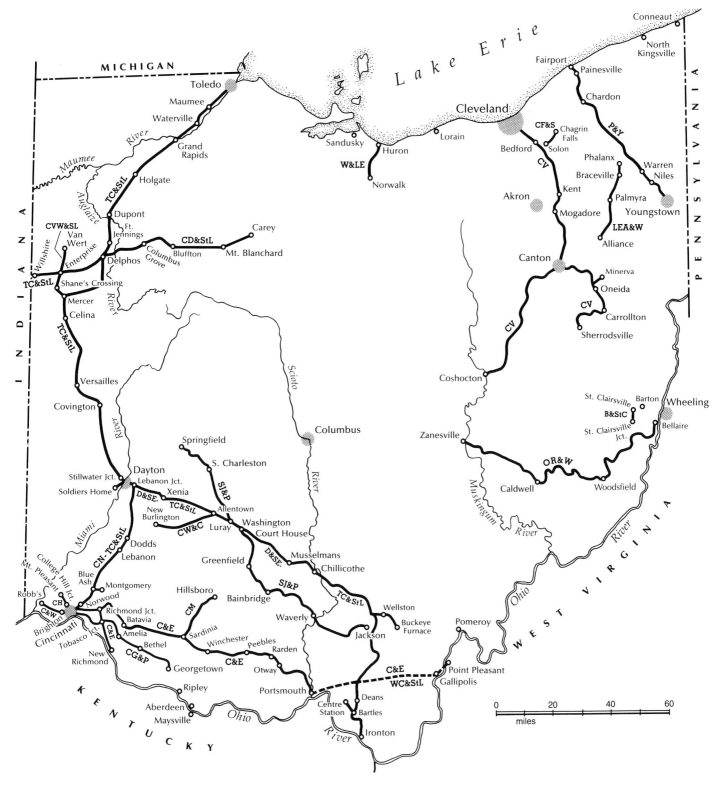

B&StC	Bellaire & St. Clairsville Narrow Gauge Railway
CVW&SL	Celina, Van Wert & State Line R.R.
CF&S	Chagrin Falls & Southern Railroad
C&E	Cincinnati & Eastern Railway
C&W	Cincinnati & Westwood Railway
CG&P	Cincinnati, Georgetown & Portsmouth Railroad
CN	Cincinnati Northern Railway
CD&StL	Cleveland, Delphos & St. Louis R.R.
CH	College Hill Railroad
CM	Columbus & Maysville Railway

CW&C	Columbus, Washington & Cincinnati Railroad
CV	Connotton Valley Railroad
D&SE	Dayton & Southeastern Railroad
LEA&W	Lake Erie, Alliance & Wheeling Railroad
OR&W	Ohio River & Western Railway
P&Y	Painesville & Youngstown Railroad
SJ&P	Springfield, Jackson & Pomeroy R.R.
TC&StL	Toledo, Cincinnati & St. Louis R.R.
WC&StL	Washington, Cincinnati & St. Louis Railroad
W&LE	Wheeling & Lake Erie Rail Road

line, about 80 miles. On August 18, 1879, the company opened 7.3 miles of 3'-0" track from Van Wert south to Enterprise (Ohio City) on the Toledo, Delphos & Burlington. The railroad operated with one Baldwin locomotive, the *Van Wert*, a single passenger car, and six freight cars. In January 1880 the company extended the line about three miles to Freisner Crossing at the south border of Van Wert County. After

Ohio 463

delays occasioned by the bridging of the St. Marys River and an enginehouse fire in Van Wert, the line was completed on September 14, 1880, to Shane's Crossing (Shanesville, Richmond; 13 miles), a community in which McGavren had practiced medicine and where he retained business interests.

On January 24, 1881, the Cincinnati, Van Wert & Michigan Common Carrier Co. was founded to build a railroad from Cincinnati to Jackson, Michigan, via Van Wert. It bought the narrow gauge early in March and immediately began preparations for conversion. The job was completed on June 4, 1881.

The former narrow gauge became part of a through Cincinnati-Jackson line as planned. The railroad became the Cincinnati, Jackson & Mackinaw in 1886 and the Cincinnati Northern in 1898. The line operated as a long branch of the New York Central system. The former narrow gauge portion was abandoned on the formation of Conrail in 1976.

Chagrin Falls & Southern Railroad

General E. R. Eckley organized the Painesville, Canton & Bridgeport Narrow Gauge Rail Road on January 12, 1875, to build the extension of his narrow gauge lines in Carroll County to Lake Erie (see Connotton Valley Railway). At the time, Eckley wanted to build to Fairport (now Fairport Harbor) at Painesville, but by 1877 the projected route was from Bridgeport on the Ohio River opposite Wheeling to Canton and Cleveland, about 140 miles. Some shorter routes tributary to the Painesville & Youngstown were also proposed.

Actually, the company achieved only a small local narrow gauge at Chagrin Falls. A railroad of five miles from Chagrin Falls to Solon on the Cleveland branch of the Erie had been promoted in 1875, but the contractors had failed to complete it in time to receive a local subsidy. In hopes of picking up some of the subscriptions to this project, the PC&B agreed to begin its line to Lake Erie with the Chagrin Falls–Solon segment, which was opened in November 1877. The management proved unable to pay the contractors, Weiss, Britton & Co. of Allegheny, Pennsylvania, who continued to operate the line until August 13, 1880, when they secured a receivership. The property was sold on September 28 and reorganized locally as the Chagrin Falls & Southern Railroad. The new management, led by J. P. and I. W. Pope, had no interest in the

longer routes formerly projected. They operated the line as a purely local carrier, with two 2-4-0 locomotives, two passenger cars, and ten freight cars. The railroad, known locally as the "Silver Plate," was modestly profitable.

Hiram A. Blood's Cleveland & Canton Railroad, successor of the Connotton Valley, on August 3, 1888, formed the Cleveland, Chagrin Falls & Northern Railroad, which leased the CF&S on April 1, 1889. The Blood management immediately began efforts at conversion and an extension of three miles from Solon to Falls Junction on the C&C main line. As an eight-mile standard gauge branch, the line was opened on July 1, 1890. The line followed the same course through the merger of 1892 into the Cleveland, Canton & Southern, and through subsequent mergers described below in the Connotton Valley section into the Wheeling & Lake Erie, the Nickel Plate Road, and the Norfolk & Western. It remains in existence as the Chagrin Falls branch of the Norfolk Southern system.

REFERENCE: John A. Rehor, *The Nickel Plate Story* (Milwaukee: Kalmbach Publishing Co., 1965), pp. 290–93, 313.

Cincinnati & Eastern Railway
Columbus & Maysville Railway

Although possessed of a good route— the most direct line between Cincinnati and Portsmouth—the Cincinnati & Eastern had one of the worst financial performances of the narrow gauge movement. Its leased line, the Columbus & Maysville, was projected as a direct route from Columbus to the Ohio River, but managed only to become the C&E's branch to Hillsboro.

The C&E was chartered as the Cincinnati, Batavia & Williamsburg on January 11, 1876, but the name was changed and the projected route extended to Portsmouth in May. On October 18, 1876, the line was opened from Plainville (Batavia Junction) on the Little Miami Railroad to Batavia (15 miles). Samuel Woodward was president, and the railroad was initially based in Batavia. The line reached Winchester (48 miles) on August 4, 1877, but was not immediately pushed farther east. Rather, in 1878 the management built a westward extension of five miles to Idlewild on the abuilding Miami Valley Railway, a narrow gauge that promised a gauge-compatible entry into Cincinnati. The Miami Valley was not completed, and the entry into the city was not possible until the successor Cincinnati Northern provided it in 1882.

On March 1, 1878, the C&E opened the first portion of a branch to New Richmond, from Richmond Junction to Tobasco (5 miles). The company shortly encountered the first of its chronic financial problems. On application of a creditor, W. R. McGill, Stephen Feike was appointed receiver on January 27, 1879. The management successfully argued that its problems stemmed from failure to collect stock subscriptions. The receivership was lifted on March 1, 1881, and McGill became president of the corporation. The railroad made little progress during the receivership. The branch line was extended to Blairville (11 miles) in 1879 and completed to New Richmond (14 miles) on March 1, 1880. The branch had a physical connection with the Cincinnati, Georgetown & Portsmouth at Tobasco Junction.

When construction resumed on the main line, the management had decided upon conversion. At a meeting in Cincinnati on November 21, the shareholders voted to increase the capital stock from $500,000 to $2 million, and to authorize a bond issue to reach Portsmouth as well as to extend beyond to Gallipolis on the Ohio River near Point Pleasant, West Virginia, to serve coal-bearing land in southern Ohio. The original intention was to build east from Winchester at 4'-8½", but the management actually built toward Portsmouth at 3'-0" using standard gauge ties and clearances in anticipation of quick conversion. By the end of 1882 the railroad was completed to Peebles, 72 miles from the Cincinnati Northern's Court Street depot in Cincinnati, into which C&E trains had been running since April 4. In 1883 the C&E began proceedings to condemn the tunnel through the Walnut Hills in the Deer Creek Valley begun by Erasmus Gest in the 1850s but abandoned when about 3,000 feet of the projected 10,011 feet had been drilled. Like other efforts to finish this tunnel, the C&E's effort at acquiring it was unsuccessful.

Early in 1883 McGill arranged a further infusion of funds into the corporation, and by May, when track had reached Rarden (85 miles), the management announced its intention to convert about September 1. It proved unable to finance the equipment for this, and pushed on with 3'-0" track, reaching Henley (90 miles) in late July. On September 14 Feike brought the railroad into court as creditor, and the Clermont County Court appointed Woodward receiver, specifically only until the line reached Portsmouth and was converted.

McGill had been attempting to finance completion largely by his own resources and by promissory notes. On June 2, 1884, he plunged through a baggage car door from a train on the Winchester trestle and fell about 70 feet to his death. Initially, the event was thought to be an accident, but then notes worth about $50,000 were determined to have forged endorsements, and McGill's personal fortune of $150,000 to $200,000 was found to have been wiped out by the railroad's failure. The death was then ruled a suicide.

Woodward estimated the cost of construction to Portsmouth at $152,427 and the conversion at $83,000. He was authorized to issue $250,000 in receiver's certificates, and proceeded. Completion required a bridge of 1,000 feet over the Scioto river; nevertheless Woodward brought the line into Portsmouth (106 miles) in August 1884. Preparations for conversion began immediately, but the railroad west of Winchester, having been built to primitive standards, was badly deteriorated. The receivership could not be lifted, and in February 1885 John R. McLean's appointment as receiver ended Woodward's control of the railroad. McLean moved quickly to convert the portion east of Winchester, reportedly finishing the job by May 1885. The court then authorized him to issue $180,000 in certificates to convert the western end. On August 8, 1885, the 800-foot trestle at Nineveh on the New Richmond branch collapsed under a mixed train, dropping the locomotive, three flatcars, and a combine onto the ground 30 feet below. The disaster killed three people, injured nine, and greatly aggravated the railroad's financial problems. McLean proved unable to finance the rest of the conversion and also lacked funds to equip the converted portion with standard gauge equipment. He resigned in the late summer of 1885, and was replaced by B. F. Coates, who pursued an exceedingly odd course. Although as committed as his predecessors to conversion, he felt the process would be advanced by restoring the idle east end of the railroad to revenue service. Accordingly, in December 1885 and early in 1886 he reconverted the Winchester-Portsmouth trackage to 3'-0" and reestablished operation for the length of the railroad.

The main line of the railroad was sold on September 1, 1886, for $900,050 to Albert Netter of Cincinnati, reportedly a representative of the Cincinnati, Hamilton & Dayton, which was interested in converting the railroad and in making the projected extension to Gallipolis. Netter made the initial payment of $25,000, but defaulted on the second of $60,000, due November 18. As a consequence, the court ordered the railroad resold on January 5, 1887, reducing the

minimum bid to $750,000, but requiring a down payment of $200,000. The railroad was then sold to H. B. Morehead, who formed the Ohio & Northwestern Railroad, also in the expectation of converting the line and extending it to Gallipolis.

The New Richmond branch was sold on September 1, 1886, to William P. DeVou, who organized it as the Cincinnati, New Richmond & Ohio River Railroad. He planned to extend the line to Aberdeen, opposite Maysville, Kentucky, but did not do so. The line was never converted, and continued to operate into the Court Street depot by third rail over the O&NW for about 20 months after the latter's conversion. The CNR&OR is believed to have ceased operation about July 1889, and to have been taken up in 1898.

The Ohio & Northwestern acquired a more important branch, the Columbus & Maysville, along with the C&E line. The C&M was incorporated on April 16, 1877, and projected between the cities of its name via Washington Court House, Hillsboro, Sardinia, Georgetown, Ripley, and Aberdeen. The Hillsboro-Sardinia portion was undertaken in 1878 at 3'-0" gauge for conformity with the C&E. About 12 miles were laid from Sardinia in 1878 and 5.5 miles in 1879, bringing the line to a junction with the Marietta & Cincinnati about 1.5 miles west of Hillsboro. Local parties in 1880 built the Hillsboro Short Line to bring the line into the town, and leased it to the C&M for $1 per year for 99 years. The C&M was a modest operation of a single locomotive, two passenger cars, and six freight cars; the HSL had no equipment. At a shareholders' meeting of May 25, 1880, the C&M resolved to convert the railroad and extend it to Aberdeen. President C. S. Bell and Daniel F. Scott, one of the directors, shortly reported that they had financed the extension contingent upon receiving public aid of $500,000. When the aid was not forthcoming, as a temporary expedient they leased the railroad to the C&E for operation. The management continued its plans for conversion and extension, and in 1882 let a contract to the Ohio Construction Co. Again nothing was accomplished, and in 1885 the railroad was sold to an eastern group that installed the shady E. Pratt Buell as president. Buell, characteristically, reported in *Poor's Manual* of 1886 that the railroad extended to Ripley, when in fact it did not; like his predecessors, he proved unable to accomplish any extension. It became insolvent and was sold on February 12, 1887, to interests of the O&NW, which had been chartered a week earlier.

The Ohio & Northwestern, of which George West of New York was president, moved immediately to standard gauge its main line, converting the entire Cincinnati-Portsmouth distance in mid-November 1887. The railroad shifted to the Little Miami depot as a standard gauge entry into Cincinnati. The O&NW quickly became insolvent, and was put in the hands of Samuel Hunt, its general manager, as receiver on June 15, 1888. Hunt, who had an excellent reputation, made several improvements, converted the C&M on January 16, 1889, and opened five miles of the long-projected Gallipolis extension, from Portsmouth to Sciotoville, in the following month. Hunt shifted back to the Court Street depot in April 1889, using 3.8 miles of third rail laid on the Cincinnati, Lebanon & Northern. The O&NW was sold on March 13, 1890, to William Brockie of Philadelphia, representing the bondholders, who reorganized it on June 24, 1891, as the Cincinnati, Portsmouth & Virginia Railroad. The C&M was sold separately on May 5, 1890, to the trustee of its bondholders. The management of the CP&V, of which Hunt became president, was unwilling to resume the lease of the C&M, but continued to operate the branch informally. The local businessmen in Hillsboro who had formed the Hillsboro Short Line were dissatisfied with this arrangement, probably fearing that the branch might be abandoned. On January 8, 1897, led by M. McKeehan, they formed the Hillsboro Railroad, which assumed the lease and began to operate as an independent short line. In December 1900 the shareholders of the CP&V voted to buy the C&M, but to allow the Hillsboro Railroad to continue as lessee. In several stages over the course of 1901 the Norfolk & Western took over the CP&V, incidentally acquiring the C&M. The CP&V became the Cincinnati-Portsmouth segment of the N&W's main line, and the C&M the railroad's Hillsboro branch. Both remain in service.

REFERENCE: Ken Stewart, "The Cincinnati & Eastern Railway and The Cincinnati, New Richmond & Ohio River Railroad," *The Fractured Frog* (Newsletter of Queen City Division, Railroad Enthusiasts), 2, no. 10 (May 1985), pp. 11–13.

Cincinnati & Westwood Railroad

Most of Cincinnati's narrow gauge projects were for major intercity routes, but the line at hand was a modest effort at local suburban development. The railroad was organized on May 20, 1874, by seven residents of Westwood, of whom W. E. Davis was chosen president. A route was chosen from Brighton, three miles from downtown Cincinnati on the Cincinnati, Hamilton & Dayton, up a steep grade from Mill Creek along Lick Run for two miles, over a flat crossing of the farm of James Robb, to a station named Robb's (5.63 miles). Construction began in the fall of 1875 and the line was opened on May 22, 1876. The railroad proved financially unsuccessful. Freight was mainly ice from local ponds to Cincinnati outbound and coal inbound. In an effort to increase freight revenues, the management wanted to increase the car stock, but could do so only by having director Michael Werk buy 15 cars and lease them to the railroad. The railroad by 1890 had 12 flatcars and ten coal cars, a large fleet for a local operation of only two locomotives, two passenger cars, and a baggage car.

The railroad was forced to suspend operation on September 1, 1886. The line was sold under foreclosure on May 30, 1887, to a bondholders' group headed by James N. Gamble, which reorganized it without change of name and resumed operation on August 1, 1887. The Gamble management was eager to run coaches into Cincinnati on CH&D passenger trains, and prepared to convert the railroad. Two Baldwin tank engines were bought in 1891, and the railroad was converted in the fall of the year. Upon conversion, the line was cut back about a half mile to Glenmore.

When the Cincinnati Street Railway opened an electric line to Westwood in September 1895, much of the passenger traffic was diverted. The C&W gave up passenger service on August 11, 1896, but continued a limited freight service until about May 31, 1924. The corporation then limited operation to a daily rail car to secure its franchise. The grade down Lick Run had been projected as an entry into the city for the Indianapolis & Cincinnati Traction Co. in 1911, and was potentially valuable as long as there was any prospect of further rail entry into Cincinnati. The decline of rail transport generally caused the corporation to liquidate in 1941.

REFERENCES: John H. White, Jr., "Cincinnati & Westwood Railroad Co.," *Bulletin of the Historical and Philosophical Society of Ohio*, 15 (1957), pp. 131–40; *idem*, "The Cheviot Narrow Gauge: Some Additional Notes," *ibid.*, 21 (1963), pp. 22–29.

A Cincinnati, Georgetown & Portsmouth passenger train pauses for the local professional photographer at Braziers, Ohio, about 1895. (Eugene Dial, Cornelius W. Hauck collections.)

Cincinnati, Georgetown & Portsmouth Railroad

Like the Cincinnati & Eastern, this railroad was projected as a direct narrow gauge from Cincinnati to Portsmouth, but it attained only about half the intended mileage. As the Cincinnati & Portsmouth Railroad, the enterprise was incorporated by Henry Brachmann and his associates on March 1, 1873. The projected route was south of the C&E's, through Bethel, Georgetown, and West Union; the distance would have been only 100 miles. The management in the fall of 1876 placed a contract for building the entire railroad with John W. Rutherford of Columbus. The line was to be lightly graded with a ruling grade of 4 percent; the contract provided for an investment of only $8,000 per mile.

Construction began from Columbia (Carrel Street) on the Little Miami (Pennsylvania) Railroad five miles above Cincinnati. The first 11 miles to Mount Carmel, which entailed a major bridge over the Miami River, were ready for service by October 1877. Rutherford shortly brought suit against the company for $67,087, alleging that the railroad was operated in an extravagant and wasteful manner, and that he had not been paid for his work. The railroad responded that his work had not been done to specification. Rutherford levied a lien against the management, but the state supreme court held that railroads were not subject to the Ohio lien law. The decisions allowed construction to resume, and track reached Amelia (19 miles) in 1878. Rutherford pursued the claim and in 1880 secured a judgment of $55,000 against the company. This and other debts were enough to drive the firm into insolvency. It was sold

for the benefit of its creditors on September 11, 1880, to Brachmann, who reorganized it as the Cincinnati, Georgetown & Portsmouth Railroad on March 21, 1881. Construction resumed, and by the end of the year track reached Bethel (29 miles). In 1882 service began to Hamersville (34 miles), but Brachmann died. His heirs were eager to get rid of the railroad, and in July 1885 sold it to a syndicate of railroad men headed by M. E. Ingalls for $140,000. The new owners planned to spend a like sum on extension and improvement. They completed the railroad—including a 1,200-foot bridge over the White Oak River—to Georgetown (42 miles) on February 1, 1886.

The remainder of the company's history as a narrow gauge was dominated by an effort to extend to West Union, seat of Adams County, about 24 miles to the east. The country east of Georgetown is hilly and lightly populated, but was considered productive in timber and quarry products. The directors authorized the extension in 1894 and in 1898 agreed to spend $100,000 on the project if local aid of $50,000 plus a right-of-way were forthcoming. In 1900, when the management mortgaged the railroad for $500,000, the proceeds were initially reported earmarked for the extension. Rather, the management contracted with the Tennis Railway Equipment Co. to convert the line to 4'-8½" and electrify it as an interurban. The conversion was effected late in 1902, with the first electric car running to Georgetown on December 1. Third rail had been laid in the Carrel Street yard as early as 1899, when the CG&P participated with the city in building a spur for the movement of standard gauge cars from the Little Miami to a municipal waterworks nearby. In July 1902 the CG&P opened a branch to the Coney Island amusement park, built to the Cincinnati Traction Company's gauge of 5'-2½" to allow the cars to enter central Cincinnati directly. In 1903 this connection replaced the Little Miami as the interchange for CG&P passengers to or from downtown Cincinnati. Transitionally, during the second half of 1902 the Carrel Street yard was laid with track of all three gauges.

As an interurban, the company undertook the eastern extension, but managed only to reach the village of Russellville, eight miles beyond Georgetown, in 1904. A branch to Batavia was opened in 1903. The interurban failed in 1927 and was reorganized as the Cincinnati, Georgetown Railroad in 1928. This corporation abandoned the Russellville extension in 1933, the outer 20 miles of the former narrow gauge in 1935, and the remainder in 1936.

REFERENCES: Stephen B. Smalley, *The Cincinnati, Georgetown & Portsmouth Railroad* (Wyoming, Ohio: Trolley Talk, 1975); David McNeil, *Railroad with 3 Gauges, The Cincinnati, Georgetown & Portsmouth RR and Felicity & Bethel RR* (Cincinnati: David McNeil, 1986); George W. Hilton and John F. Due, *The Electric Interurban Railways in America* (Stanford, Calif.: Stanford University Press, 1960), p. 255.

Cleveland, Delphos & St. Louis Railroad

Although in final form a minor local agricultural carrier, this railroad was intended as the eastward extension of the Grand Narrow Gauge Trunk to Cleveland and points east in connection with the Pittsburgh & Western. The Cleveland, Delphos & St. Louis was organized in March 7, 1881, by James Callery and William Semple of the P&W and Joseph Boehmer and Dr. Carey Evans of Delphos, who had been active in promoting the Toledo, Cincinnati & St. Louis and its predecessors. The promoters intended to build a direct route of about 160 miles from the connection with the TC&StL in Delphos to Cleveland via Findlay and Medina. In 1882 they organized a subsidiary, the Pittsburgh, Akron & Chicago, to build from Medina through Akron to Youngstown for a connection with the P&W either there or to the east. A second subsidiary, the Pittsburgh & Maumee, was organized in the same year to build from Columbus Grove on the Dayton & Michigan (later the Cincinnati, Hamilton & Dayton) north of Lima to Antwerp on the Wabash main line near the Indiana border. Neither branch was built, and the main line stopped far short of Cleveland.

Construction began at Columbus Grove in August 1881, and on November 26 track reached the outskirts of Delphos. Mixed trains began running between Delphos and Columbus Grove, 17 miles, on January 25, 1882. Simultaneously the line was being built eastward from Columbus Grove. Rails reached Pendleton (Pandora; 5 miles) on February 1, 1882. Inability to arrange or finance an entry into Findlay obliged the promoters to bypass the city to the south. The line was instead built through Bluffton and Mount Blanchard, to which service was instituted on January 1, 1883. On October 1, 1883, the railroad was completed to Carey on the Columbus, Hocking Valley & Toledo Railway, 55 miles from Delphos, but more than 100 miles west of Cleveland.

The narrow gauge was not pushed farther, however. The Toledo, Cincinnati & St. Louis was collapsing by late 1883, so that the prospect of a gauge-compatible connection with it was no longer attractive. The CD&StL operated two mixed trains per day in each direction, and did poorly financially. A receiver was appointed on June 17, 1884, and the company was reorganized with the grandiose title of the Eastern & Western Air Line Railway on November 1, 1885. The line was again reorganized as the Cleveland & Western Railroad on August 1, 1886. Service had been cut to a single mixed train per day. Callery and Semple had lost interest in the idea of a narrow gauge route across Ohio by 1883. Their Pittsburgh & Western's projected line to the west was reorganized as the Pittsburgh, Akron & Western Railway in 1887 to provide a connection between the Pittsburgh area and the Baltimore & Ohio at Chicago Junction (Willard), bypassing a circuitous route of the B&O to the south. On March 11, 1890, the heirs of Callery and Semple (both of whom had died) merged the C&W with the PA&W into the Pittsburgh, Akron & Western Railroad, and prepared to convert the narrow gauge. Standard gauge rails were laid outside the existing rails between April 15 and July 1; the last narrow gauge mixed train ran on August 4, 1890.

The company then quickly built the long-projected eastern extension, completing it to Akron, rather than Cleveland, on

May 28, 1891. The B&O however, had built its own line from Akron to Chicago Junction, leaving the newly completed standard gauge only as a lightly trafficked connection from Akron to the Toledo, St. Louis & Kansas City, the standard gauge successor of the TC&StL, at Delphos. The railroad was reorganized as the Northern Ohio Railway in 1895 and leased to the Lake Erie & Western. The LE&W, in turn, passed into the hands of the New York Central System in 1900. The Northern Ohio was sold to the Akron, Canton & Youngstown, a switching line at Akron, in 1920. As such, it was absorbed into the Norfolk & Western system along with the Nickel Plate and Wabash in 1964. The former narrow gauge mileage is in existence at the present writing, but will probably be abandoned in the near future.

REFERENCE: Rehor, *The Nickel Plate Story*, pp. 106–7.

College Hill Railroad

A railroad to develop the College Hill area in the Cincinnati north suburbs had been discussed since the 1850s, but the College Hill Railroad was not incorporated until May 22, 1873. Construction began in 1875, and service began from College Hill Junction on the Cincinnati, Hamilton & Dayton at Spring Grove Cemetery to College Hill (3 miles). Initially, the line operated with a National Locomotive Works 0-4-0 steam dummy engine, but a Porter 0-6-0 tank engine was added shortly. The route entailed a 4.5-percent grade and a trestle of 600 feet, 60 feet high. The worst curve was 22.5°. Rolling stock was a combine, a coach, and three freight cars. John R. Davey and Robert Simpson were the principal figures in the road's management, each serving as president on occasion.

The railroad was extended on October 13, 1877, to Mount Healthy (Mount Pleasant), an additional 3.5 miles. The community's name demonstrates the fear of cholera epidemics in the central city that was a major motivation for moves to the north suburbs. The company's charter provided for extension as far as Venice (Ross), about 18 miles from the junction, but nothing further was built. A second Porter locomotive was added in 1880. In February 1883 the management defaulted on a mortgage payment, causing the railroad to be sold on October 26 for $30,000. Davey and Simpson formed the Cincinnati Northwestern Railway to take it over on April 3, 1884. Partly to operate through cars into the CH&D station at Fifth and Hoadly streets, and partly to extend the line to Liberty, Indiana, they felt it necessary to convert the railroad. A third rail was laid in 1886, but lack of standard gauge equipment kept the line operating as a narrow gauge until about November 1887. Again, no extension was made.

The arrival of electric streetcars in College Hill in 1895 greatly reduced the line's patronage. Passenger service was dropped in April 1899, and in 1901 the line was sold to the Southern Ohio Traction Co. to provide an entrance into the metropolitan area for an interurban. The trackage went through the hands of several interurban companies until abandoned by the Cincinnati & Lake Erie on May 31, 1938.

REFERENCE: John H. White, "The College Hill Narrow Gauge," *Bulletin of the Historical and Philosophical Society of Ohio*, 17 (1960), pp. 226–39.

Columbus, Washington & Cincinnati Railroad

As the Waynesville, Port William & Jeffersonville Railroad, this project was incorporated on December 9, 1875, to run between the towns of its corporate name. By an amendment of November 27, 1875, the route was extended east to Washington Court House and the name changed to Columbus, Washington & Cincinnati Railroad. In 1877 a contract was given to George Potts & Co. of New York to build the Waynesville-Jeffersonville portion for only $5,000 per mile. Grading began on June 7 at Allentown on the Dayton & Southeastern, and by the end of the year track had reached Glenwood (18 miles). The line was pressed on to New Burlington (20 miles), probably early in 1878. The company took trackage rights on the D&SE from Allentown to Washington Court House, 11 miles. The corporation encountered financial difficulties that prevented any further building, either to the east or to the west. The line was locally known as "The Grasshopper Route."

The railroad was put in receivership under John E. Gimperling of the D&SE on September 9, 1878. It was sold on August 6, 1879, to a representative of the creditors, but not resold for reorganization until February 15, 1881. Gimperling was head of the new corporation, the Cincinnati, Columbus & Hocking Valley Railway, intended as a standard gauge railroad from Cincinnati to the Hocking Valley coalfield. He converted the railroad in great haste and extended it both east to Jeffersonville and west to Clayville Junction on the Little Miami Railroad, opening it as a standard gauge carrier on May 16, 1882.

In this instance, conversion was little help. The railroad was placed in receivership again on February 16, 1884, and sold, first to Francis A. Riddle of Chicago in 1885 and then to Jacob B. Custer on May 1, 1886. The line had operated intermittently since early 1885, but Custer shut it down in July 1887 and scrapped it. The Ohio Southern bought the right-of-way and used it in building its Kingman branch in 1894 and 1895. The branch was abandoned by the successor Detroit, Toledo & Ironton in 1932 and 1933.

Connotton Valley Railway

Possessed of a physical plant that was considered an exemplar among the narrow gauges, along with a solid coal traffic and excellent entry into Cleveland, this might be expected to have been among the most successful in the movement. Actually, gross overcapitalization and factionalism in the management gave the line a poor financial history, no better than that of lesser properties.

General E. R. Eckley of Carrollton initiated the project by incorporating the Ohio & Toledo Rail Road on May 7, 1872. His initial plan was a railroad across Ohio from Wellsville to Toledo via Carrollton and Massillon, but he quickly switched to a route from the coalfield in the Connotton Valley of Carroll County to a Lake Erie port. Eckley began by acquiring the Carrollton & Oneida Railroad, a 4'-10" tram line that had operated on strap rail with horse, mule, and steam power since the mid-1850s. Eckley made use of about 12.5 miles of the right-of-way of the tram line to build the first segment of his railroad, from a point 4.5 miles south of Carrollton to Minerva (14 miles) in 1874. Track was pushed southwest eight miles to Dell Roy in 1875. In 1874 Eckley's plan was to build to Youngstown to a connection with the Painesville & Youngstown, but in 1875 he switched to a direct route to Painesville and Fairport harbor on his own rails. He promoted the Painesville, Canton & Bridgeport in 1875 toward this end, but made little progress (see Chagrin Falls & Southern). Eckley's financial difficulties caused him to take into the firm Dr. Norman A. Smith, who promised to infuse funds into the railroad. Smith, however, was adamant for a route to Youngstown, and incorporated the Youngstown & Connotton Valley Railroad on August 29, 1877. The dispute helped put the O&T in the courts. It was sold to the Cleveland Iron Co., a major creditor, and conveyed to the Y&CV on December 20, 1878, a transaction resolving the dispute in Smith's favor.

Smith, however, had in the meantime been persuaded to Eckley's view that the railroad should be directed to Fairport, and began building north from a junction three miles south of Minerva. The 16-mile extension was opened to Canton on May 18, 1880. The construction had been slow because of the necessity of drilling a tunnel of 774 feet at Robertsville. The company had been renamed Connotton Valley Railroad in 1879; after merger with a subsidiary, it was again renamed, this time Connotton Valley Railway, on March 23, 1880. In the

Consistent with the high standards of the Connotton Valley was the handsome Brooks 4-4-0 *W. J. Rotch*. (Ed Bond collection.)

same year, Smith brought into the railroad a syndicate of Boston investors, headed by Hiram A. Blood, who rapidly came to dominate the management. Blood's group placed a mortgage of $2.6 million on the railroad and proceeded to build north, though in October the decision was made to build to Cleveland rather than to Fairport. By the end of the year 12 miles of the Cleveland extension had been built through difficult swampy country. In preparation for northbound coal movements, the line was extended south seven miles to the mining town of Sherrodsville in 1881. On July 4, 1881, the railroad was opened from Canton to Bedford, 48 miles, where a direct connection for passengers was available through the Cleveland & Pittsburgh. The narrow gauge's own entry into Cleveland was a difficult one involving a descent of 250 feet in four miles from Newburgh into the flats of the Cuyahoga River, with a newly built drawbridge. It was, however, an effective entry, providing direct access to lake freighters in the flats and a passenger station in central Cleveland. Passenger service into Cleveland began February 1, 1882.

Blood's group elected not to press the existing line south or east from Sherrodsville, but rather revived the project of a railroad from the Canton area southwest to Coshocton and the coalfield around Straitsville in southern Perry County. The Massillon & Coshocton Railway had been formed in 1874 to build between the towns of its name. In 1877 the corporation renamed itself the Cleveland, Canton, Coshocton & Straitsville Railroad, again planning to build the route of its corporate title. This enterprise did about 35 miles of grading between Barrs Mills and Coshocton in 1876 and 1880, but then was unable to proceed. Through a subsidiary, the CV bought the unbuilt grade and began grading a connection from Barrs Mills to Canton, 20 miles. The acquisition and the connection together cost the railroad $2.1 million. With the proceeds of a bond issue of $1.5 million, the CV began laying track south from Canton in July 1882, and reached Beach City, 19 miles, by the end of the year. On July 11, 1883, passenger service began to Co-

shocton, 55 miles from Canton, on what was thereafter considered the company's main line.

With its two routes, the railroad should have been a relatively strong narrow gauge. It was built to main-line standards throughout. Because the Coshocton line had been largely graded in the expectation of building a standard gauge railroad, it was capable of fast running and heavy hauling. At 161 miles, this was a relatively large narrow gauge. At its peak, it reported itself as having 26 locomotives, 29 passenger cars, seven head-end cars, and 962 freight cars. Although the route missed Akron by about eight miles to the east, the main line was a direct connection from Cleveland to Canton and Coshocton, capable of running passenger trains at about the same speeds as standard gauge rivals. The company developed a suburban service to Bedford and Kent. Freight traffic was mainly northbound coal, but the main line also served some ore deposits.

The management wanted to extend both lines—the original by six miles, from Sherrodsville to Bowerston, and the main line by about 70 miles, from Coshocton to Zanesville and Straitsville—but a series of financial problems prevented any further building. In addition to the two large bond issues already mentioned, the company held all of its locomotives and rolling stock under equipment trusts. In 1885 the railroad's debt was said to be $7,312,363. On October 25, 1882, the directors voted to omit the interest payment due on November 1, but asked forbearance of the creditors because of the railroad's unfinished state. In 1883 the management attempted to raise $760,000 in Boston for the extension to Zanesville, but secured only $300,000, which it put instead into a new passenger station on Ontario Street, a block from Public Square in Cleveland, plus other terminal improvements.

The forbearance of the creditors ended on January 19, 1884, when the New England Trust Co. applied for appointment of a receiver. Earnings were reported as not much over working expenses, and the debt was then about $71,000 per mile, more than triple the cost of construction. Samuel Briggs, the road's able general manager, was appointed receiver. The railroad had plenty of traffic: in 1884 it carried 456,627 passengers, 192,400 tons of coal, and 41,668 tons of other freight. The growth of general cargo relative to coal was thought particularly heartening. The Cleveland suburban traffic was also growing rapidly.

Reorganization was made difficult by the railroad's complicated financial struc-

ture and its unusual arrangement that only preferred stockholders could vote. Conflict concerning both voting rights and the extension of the railroad divided the security holders into two factions—the common stockholders, who generally supported Blood and the management, and the preferred shareholders, who grouped behind financiers Austin Corbin and A. N. Parlin. By 1885 both factions advocated conversion, but Blood favored extension to Zanesville and Parlin did not. By securing injunctions against the rival faction's use of voting shares, Blood retained control of the railroad, reorganizing it after a foreclosure sale of May 9, 1885, as the Cleveland & Canton Railroad. The factionalism did not end; the Corbin-Parlin group held its own meetings in Boston in 1886 and 1887. In May 1887 the two factions agreed that all parties might buy preferred shares at 35. The Blood group bought out the Corbin-Parlin faction, ending the dispute amicably. Blood immediately devoted himself to conversion, which was, for as large a railroad as this, a major undertaking, estimated at $1.7 million. The tunnel at Robertsville had to be expanded, the line from Cleveland to Newburgh was doubletracked to accommodate the suburban service, and a new drawbridge had to be built at the Cuyahoga. The Cleveland-Canton line was converted in October 1888, and the remainder of the railroad on November 18, 1888. Locomotives and rolling stock were sold off by the New York Equipment Co.

Blood quickly pressed on with the extension of 29 miles to Zanesville, but the further extension to Straitsville was never built. The C&C was merged with the subsidiary that had built the Zanesville extension into the Cleveland, Canton & Southern Railroad in 1892. The CC&S remained solvent for only about a year, going into receivership in 1893, in part because of the debt incurred in conversion. It was not reorganized, but rather sold on August 5, 1899, to the newly organized Wheeling & Lake Erie Railroad. The former narrow gauge became the W&LE's entry into Cleveland plus two major branches. The outermost 12 miles of the Sherrodsville branch were abandoned in 1936 because of prospective inundation from the Atwood dam, but the rest of the former narrow gauge went into the Nickel Plate Road along with the W&LE in 1949 and into the Norfolk & Western in 1964. All of this mileage remains in service.

REFERENCE: Rehor, *The Nickel Plate Story*, pp. 288–97, 312–14.

X 369 IT IS ORDERED THAT 1885
Mr. D. J. Flanders, F.Pa. BPM N
MAY RIDE FREE OVER THE
Connotton Valley Railway,
During the Year 1885.
Unless Countermanded.
RECEIVER.

Lake Erie, Alliance & Wheeling Railroad

Hugh Bleakley of Alliance conceived this railroad as a coal hauler running from Bridgeport, opposite Wheeling, to Fairport harbor at Painesville, parallel to some of the projects of predecessors of the Connotton Valley. The railroad was incorporated on February 16, 1874, and ground was broken at Alliance on July 31, 1875. At that time, Bleakley's plan was to build from a connection with the Painesville & Youngstown near Southington to Bridgeport via Alliance, Bowerston, and Cadiz. F. W. Kellogg contracted to build the railroad for $3,000 in cash and $14,000 in bonds per mile. He reached Palmyra (14 miles) in 1876 and Braceville on the Erie main line (24 miles) on May 7, 1877.

The railroad proved unable to pay the expenses of its construction and was seized for debt late in 1877. It was sold on May 11, 1878, for $36,000 for the benefit of the Cleveland Rolling Mill Co., its principal creditor. The new management reorganized it as the Alliance & Lake Erie Railroad, with the intention of building north to Fairport. The line was extended north about a mile to Phalanx on the Erie's Cleveland branch in 1879, probably to provide a more direct connection for passengers to Cleveland. No further narrow gauge track was laid. Although the railroad served a minor coalfield at Palmyra—107 of its 133 freight cars were intended for coal—it remained unsuccessful. In April 1880 the directors offered to lease the line to any responsible party who would pay the interest, but had no takers. Rather, control of the line passed into the hands of the Cleveland, Youngstown & Pittsburgh Railway, which had been organized on March 28, 1881, to build a narrow gauge connection between the P&Y at Youngstown and the Connotton Valley near Streetsboro. This company merged the A&LE into itself on July 14, 1882, and quickly changed its plans, dropping the idea of connecting the P&Y with the Connotton Valley and instead proposing to convert the A&LE for extension to coalfields to the south. The narrow gauge was converted early in November 1883, and extended south 36 miles to Bergholz.

The CY&P was put in receivership on March 3, 1884, and reorganized in 1887 as the Lake Erie, Alliance & Southern in 1887. This company operated the former narrow gauge separately as the Alliance & Northern Railroad. The two were reunited as the Lake Erie, Alliance & Wheeling Railroad in 1901. This firm revived the idea of the railroad as a through line from Wheeling to

Bellaire, Zanesville & Cincinnati No. 12 was a low-wheeled Brooks 2-6-0 of 1901. Note the multiple pockets for link-and-pin coupling on three-rail trackage. (California State Railroad Museum.)

Fairport, and built south as far as Dillonvale on the Wheeling & Lake Erie, about 17 miles from Wheeling. Nothing further was built on the north end. In 1905 the railroad passed into the hands of the New York Central system, with which it had no physical connection, and spent the rest of its history as an NYC branch for coal origination. The former narrow gauge was abandoned between Phalanx and Braceville by the NYC in 1962, between Braceville and Newton Falls by the Penn Central in 1969, and between Newton Falls and Alliance by Conrail on the latter's formation in 1976.

Ohio River & Western Railway

Ohio's longest-surviving narrow gauge served an unpromising territory in the eastern part of the state with a line of 112 miles from Zanesville to Bellaire, in the Wheeling area. The road was designed to provide an east-west route through Caldwell and Woodsfield, the seats, respectively, of Noble and Monroe counties. Construction was begun in 1877 by the Bellaire & Southwestern Railroad, which was promoted by Col. Samuel L. Mooney of Woodsfield and Col. John H. Sullivan. The grade was pushed west from Bellaire into the hills. The surveyor for the original mileage was Charles G. Dawes, who was to become vice-president of the United States. Construction proceeded slowly, but by October 7, 1879, track had reached Beallsville (29 miles). On December 24, 1879, service was opened to Woodsfield (42 miles). In 1880 the people of Noble County agreed to a subsidy of $100,000 and a free right-of-way for an extension of 34 miles to Caldwell. In 1881 the railroad reached Caldwell (77 miles) and

the corporation amended its charter for an extension to Athens and Cincinnati.

The prospect of the narrow gauge's bypassing Zanesville and building southwestward prompted Zanesville merchants to found the Muskingum County Railway and Zanesville & Southwestern Railroad, which were jointly to build a direct line from Zanesville to Caldwell (35 miles). In February 1882 Mooney arranged for the Bellaire & Southwestern to merge with Zanesville & Southwestern under the name of the Bellaire, Zanesville & Cincinnati Railway. The new company leased the Muskingum County Railway, which was to build the nine miles out of Zanesville, including 1.25 miles of trackage rights by third rail on the B&O leaving the city. Edward Hulbert was hired in December 1880 to superintend the building of the western extension. In February 1882 he compiled a prospectus for the railroad, but he disappears from the surviving record thereafter. The western extension was completed in 1883 and formally opened on November 15. The new trackage contained a 505-foot tunnel at the summit of the long grade up from the Muskingum River. The entire railway was a typical example of narrow gauge mountain railroading, with 262 trestles and bridges in the 112 miles. Several were lengthy wooden trestles that required extensive maintenance. Grades were severe, curves were all but continuous, and operating expenses were necessarily heavy.

As one might expect from the road's physical character and limited tributary population, it was not a financial success. The stock issued by the original Bellaire & Southwestern was assessable, and three 10 percent assessments were made against the shareholders, who were mainly local farmers. In 1886 the Bellaire, Zanesville & Cincinnati failed and was placed in the hands of a receiver, I. H. Burgoon. The leased Muskingum County Railway shortly followed suit. The bankrupt BZ&C purchased the Muskingum County in 1893. In 1895 James K. Geddes replaced Burgoon as receiver. The road was in very poor condition, but Geddes effected some economies and improved the physical plant somewhat. With the improvement of business conditions around the turn of the century, the railroad was able to emerge from receivership in 1902. With Mooney as its president, the line was reorganized as the Ohio River & Western Railway.

In January 1903 Mooney sold control of the company to A. E. Appleyard of Boston, who was prominent in the building of interurbans in Ohio. Appleyard was endeavoring to secure a through interurban

route across Ohio from Dayton to Wheeling. His electric lines from Dayton to Zanesville were nearing completion, and he proposed to convert the Ohio River & Western to standard gauge for electrification to complete his line. Appleyard's system failed in the Panic of 1903 before anything was done to implement his plan for the OR&W. Other plans for standard gauging the railroad also failed. The nine miles of the Muskingum County Railway from Zanesville to Lawton were laid with a third rail for dual gauge operation in 1909, but the remainder of the line remained narrow gauge to the end.

In 1912 the line came under the control of the Pennsylvania Railroad. The OR&W had never done well, and the rise of the automobile brought it to successively greater depths. The three passenger trains a day of 1909 dwindled to a single mixed train by the 1920s. The Pennsylvania endeavored to abandon parts of the railroad, and in 1928 secured permission to give up the line west of Woodsfield. The original trackage from Bellaire to Woodsfield survived until Memorial Day 1931, when locomotive no. 9,969 made the last round-trip with a two-car passenger train.

REFERENCES: Edward Hulbert, *The Present Condition of the Bellaire, Zanesville & Cincinnati Railway Company* (Wheeling, W.Va., 1882), copy in Boston Public Library; Robert W. Richardson, "Ohio's Last Narrow Gauge," *Trains*, Apr. 1950, pp. 24–26; Norris F. Schneider, *Bent, Zigzag and Crooked: Ohio's Last Narrow Gauge Railroad* (Zanesville, Ohio: Norris F. Schneider, 1960); James Scott Eakin, "Narrow Gauge in Ohio," *Narrow Gauge and Short Line Gazette*, Mar. 1977, pp. 22–25; collections of Edward H. Cass and Robert Lee Rainey.

Painesville & Youngstown Railroad

The route from Youngstown to Painesville had several attractions for a narrow gauge promoter. Youngstown was already established as a center for the steel industry, and various mines in the area were part of the Mahoning Valley coalfield. Painesville is located 3.5 miles up the meandering Grand River from Lake Erie. About half the distance was navigable and capable of development for wharves. Two smaller communities, Fairport (Fairport Harbor) on the east bank of the river and Richmond (Grand River) on the west, actually housed the port facilities. By the standards of the Great Lakes, the harbor was a good one. It had enjoyed a substantial steamboat traffic from 1835 to 1854, but then declined when the Lake Shore & Michigan Southern had preferred to use Cleveland, 28 miles to the west. A railroad provided the prospect of reviving the harbor and putting Painesville into rivalry with Cleveland, Ashtabula, and Conneaut. A portion of the route from Painesville to Chardon, about 12 miles, had been graded in the mid-1850s by an earlier company, the Painesville & Hudson. Because the traffic was expected to be mainly iron ore from the upper Great Lakes moving south and coal moving north from Youngstown to bulk freighters at the port, narrow gauge promised to present minimal problems of incompatibility.

Under the circumstances, it is not surprising that the Painesville & Youngstown was among the earliest American narrow gauges. The company was chartered on November 17, 1870. The principal figures were Paul Wick and A. B. Cornell of Youngstown; R. K. Paige, Horace Steele, and W. G. Hawkins of Painesville; and James B. Ford and Christopher Meyer of New York, both of whom were interested in reducing rates for moving Minnesota ore to Youngstown. Offices were established in Painesville, and Wick became president of the railroad. Construction began at Painesville July 27, 1871, and track was reportedly laid to

Chardon by the end of the year; regular operation between Painesville and Chardon began on July 4, 1872. Track reached Burton in 1873, Niles in August 1874, and Youngstown in November of the same year. With a main line of 60 miles, the railroad was the third-longest narrow gauge in the country upon completion. Regular operation began January 1, 1875.

The conception of the railroad required terminal facilities at the harbor. From the company's station at the crossing of the LS&MS on the west side of Painesville, a line was run somewhat over a mile to Richmond in 1873. Service began in November, after the close of navigation. The more important portion of the harbor, at Fairport, required bridging the Grand River. This the company accomplished in 1875 with a swing span of 150 feet and trestlework over marshy land in the vicinity of Grass Island. The bridge was built to standard gauge dimensions because superintendent G. R. Crane had concluded that the saving on building timber trestles to narrow gauge standards would be too small to warrant deviation from normal practice. He thought the costs of masonry would be about the same, regardless of gauge. The extension was reported complete in June 1875, when the railroad handled several hundred tons of coal to Fairport. The railroad did not normally run passenger trains to the harbor, but operated excursions there in the summer months.

Because the railroad was expected to be a hauler of heavy bulk commodities, it had been built to something approximating main-line standards from the outset. Only several narrow cuts were markedly below standard gauge practice. The line had one severe grade, about two miles of 1.6 percent, and curves up to 12°. The track was ballasted. The railroad represented an investment of $20,000 per mile. In 1877 the management ran a special for a party of visitors from New York, making the 128-mile round-trip in four hours and 30 minutes, including 31 stops. Normally, the railroad ran two round-trips per day between Painesville and Youngstown, supplemented by an additional local between Painesville and Chardon in prosperous periods. The railroad could operate its passenger trains at about 20 miles per hour. Schedules were developed mainly to coordinate with LS&MS trains at Painesville.

Given its various strengths, one might expect the Painesville & Youngstown to have been one of the most successful narrow gauges, but in fact it was habitually barely able to pay its variable expenses. Its troubles stemmed in part from its rivalry with well-established standard gauge railroads to the other Ohio ore ports, and in part from its thoroughly unsatisfactory terminal facilities at Youngstown. The line entered Youngstown from the west below the Mahoning River, ran into the southwest quadrant of the city between Knight Street and Tod Avenue, and terminated on the property of T. D. Baldwin. The Painesville *Telegraph* described the terminus as being "on the banks of a lonely stream in a deserted portion of the thriving city of Youngstown, and nearly a half mile distant from any coal bank." The mines and steelworks were concentrated on the north side of the Mahoning. Securing access to the industrial portion of Youngstown was a continual preoccupation of the management. Reaching south to the Ohio River, either by extension of the company's own rails or by connection with another narrow gauge, was also discussed. Other unexecuted projects were a branch from Chardon to Chagrin Falls and a direct connection from Painesville to Cleveland to reach the Connotton Valley, a promising narrow gauge coal hauler.

By the end of 1876 the railroad had handled only a small volume of coal and no iron ore. It missed its interest payments on the first mortgage of $993,000 and on a second mortgage of $250,000 on January 1, 1877. The Farmers' Loan & Trust Company of New York filed for foreclosure in Federal Circuit Court in Cleveland on February 5. Since the bonds were mainly held by the principal shareholders, the bankruptcy did not promise to change the actual ownership. Miles R. Martin of Youngstown became receiver, and the offices were shifted to the south end of the railroad.

Martin's principal achievement was negotiating, in March 1878, a contract with Smith, Cant & Co. for the movement to Fairport of 300 tons of coal per day during the season of navigation from two mines of the Powers Coal Co. at Brier Hill in the Youngstown area. The coal moved to Toronto, Buffalo, Black Rock, Detroit, Sarnia, Port Colborne, Duluth, and other ports. The tonnage was so great that trains were scheduled not only during the day but also at night—fairly unusual for a narrow

gauge. On May 29, 1879, the railroad handled its first 12 cars of iron ore. Superintendent Lon F. McAleer represented the management at the narrow gauge convention in Cincinnati in October 1878.

The railroad, in spite of the coal contract, remained unprofitable. At the first receiver's sale of February 6, 1879, there were no bidders, and none appeared at the second on April 6. The receiver was three months in arrears in wages for 1877, but when he had cleared away this obligation, the railroad was sold on June 2, 1879, for $192,000 and reorganized as the Painesville & Youngstown Railway. Christopher Meyer became president, and the directors represented the same ownership as before. Martin became general manager. Martin or his successor in 1881, George M. Patten, made several improvements. The railroad dredged the harbor at Fairport to 16 feet in 1879, and the Brier Hill Iron & Coal Co. built a vehicular bridge at Youngstown for better access to the railroad. The P&Y expanded the ore dock at Fairport, increasing storage capacity to a range of 100,000 to 150,000 tons. Martin rebuilt or repaired the trestlework, replaced ties, and cleared ditches in preparation for the 1880 navigation season. In 1881 the railroad relocated the Youngstown terminal trackage along the south bank of the Mahoning River, extending somewhat more than a mile to a point east of Liffy Creek near Ryan Street. In Painesville the company built just under a mile of track east from its station to the LS&MS's depot in the heart of the town.

In October 1881 the owners sold the controlling interest to Solon Humphreys, vice-president of the Wabash; James Callery, president of the Pittsburgh & Western; and various members of the New York financial community. Meyer, Martin, and Wick resigned from the board of directors, to be replaced by Humphreys, Callery, and C. S. Brice, vice-president of the Nickel Plate. The new owners announced their intention to convert the line in the spring and to bring it to a connection with the Pittsburgh & Western, which was becoming part of the Baltimore & Ohio's direct line from Pittsburgh to Chicago via Youngstown and Akron. In November standard gauge ties arrived and a crew was reported at work widening the most restrictive cuts at Swine Creek.

At this point the new owners pursued an unusual course of action. They allowed the P&Y to miss the interest due January 1, 1882, even though their resources seem clearly to have allowed payment. At Humphreys's request, Col. R. K. Paige was appointed receiver. It was announced that the

conversion would take place as part of the reorganization. This process postponed conversion for four years.

In May 1882 the P&Y took delivery of a tug for use in Fairport harbor. Named *George R. Paige* after the son of the receiver, the vessel was one of the few pieces of floating stock ever owned by a narrow gauge. She was licensed to carry 40 passengers for harbor inspections. The railroad's bulk traffic was reportedly expanding steadily. It had seven locomotives and 173 cars, of which 152 were designed for coal.

On June 3, 1886, the railroad was sold under foreclosure for $400,000 and reorganized as the Pittsburgh, Painesville & Fairport Railroad. The new corporation was immediately leased to the Pittsburgh & Western, which was by this time part of the B&O system. Work on conversion began immediately from Painesville. Laying of standard gauge track from Fairport to De Forest Junction on the B&O at the west end of Niles was completed with a diamond over the Erie at Warren on August 20, and standard gauge trains began running in connection with the B&O on August 23, 1886. The 11 miles from DeForest Junction to Youngstown were turned over to another leased line of the P&W, the Trumbull & Mahoning Railroad, but mainly abandoned as redundant upon the B&O, which it closely paralleled. The Warren *Tribune* reported the narrow gauge track removed in its issue of September 7, 1886, and a week later stated that the narrow gauge locomotives and rolling stock were at Warren and Niles, awaiting removal by flatcar. Part of the terminal trackage at Youngstown was converted as part of the B&O's extensive switching facilities in the area, and portions of the right-of-way were used for subsequent line relocations.

As the Lake Branch, the former P&Y was one of the B&O's four coal-and-ore lines to Lake Erie ports. Systematic ore movements ended about 1943 and coal movements in 1965, partly because of the obsolescence of the port facilities for modern bulk freighters. The last run on the branch was made on October 30–31, 1981, and track was removed in 1982.

Springfield, Jackson & Pomeroy Railroad

Upon completion in 1878 this was the third-longest narrow gauge in America, but its history was one of the shortest and least successful.

The Springfield, Jackson & Pomeroy was organized on December 17, 1874, as a

The *Blue Bird* was the first locomotive of the short-lived Springfield, Jackson & Pomeroy. (Ed Bond collection.)

facility for movements of coal from southeastern Ohio to Springfield. George H. Frey and other businessmen of Springfield were the promoters. They raised subscriptions of $760,000 in 1875 and placed a contract with the Western Construction Co. of Cincinnati to build the line from Springfield to Jackson, 108 miles, for $1,222,000, or about $11,315 per mile, 50 percent of which was in cash, 40 percent in bonds, and 10 percent in stock. The management's interest was in reaching the Jackson County coalfield; no real effort was made to extend the line to Pomeroy on the Ohio River to the east. The railroad was large enough that construction was undertaken from both ends. By the end of 1876 only two miles of track had been laid from Jackson, but in 1877 track from the north reached a junction with the Dayton & Southeastern at Luray, from which trackage rights were taken for five miles into Washington Court House (36 miles). By the end of the year 24 miles of the southern line had been built from Jackson to Waverly on the Scioto Valley Railroad. The gap of 48 miles between the two segments was closed upon completion of a 300-foot Howe-truss bridge over Paint Creek near Bainbridge in mid-1878. President James Emmitt drove the last spike at a ceremony on July 18, and the railroad immediately began northbound coal movements. The line was well equipped, with 11 locomotives, five passenger cars, 49 general freight cars, and 226 coal cars. Track was partly ballasted. Traffic, however, was reportedly too heavy for this equipment to handle. Only a long mine spur of five miles from Jackson to Eurekaville was built in 1879.

As early as August 31, 1876, the Western Construction Co. brought a legal action for unpaid installments on the construction contract. Early in 1879 Emmitt undertook to raise $600,000 to pay off the debt and complete the railroad. He failed, and the board of directors requested a receivership. William N. Whitely, one of the management group, became receiver on February 1. Although the line's debt was $900,000, the county court at Springfield appraised the physical plant at $621,000 and the equipment at $51,411. The court required a deposit of $50,000 in cash on bids, but made the unusual provision that the plant and equipment might be purchased either together or separately. General Samuel Thomas bought the railroad on October 1, 1879, for $443,000 on behalf of the Columbus Rolling Mill Co., one of the principal creditors. He secured the court's permission to transfer the property to Oliver S. Kelley on November 1. Kelley and some of the former management group formed the Springfield Southern Railroad two days later, and bought the SJ&P's physical plant, but not its locomotives and rolling stock, which in general reverted to their builders. Whitely became president of the new corporation and moved immediately to convert the railroad, completing the job in the first

half of 1880. It was the first conversion of a large domestic narrow gauge, but was not widely publicized.

The Springfield Southern changed its name to the Ohio Southern Railroad on July 21, 1881, and was absorbed into the Detroit Southern Railroad in 1901. This carrier became the Detroit, Toledo & Ironton Railroad in 1905. The former narrow gauge mileage from Jackson to Gregg was abandoned in 1986, and from Gregg to Washington Court House in 1988. The portion from Springfield to Washington Court House remains in service.

Toledo, Cincinnati & St. Louis Railroad

The principal single effort to produce a narrow gauge railroad for general transport service, as distinct from a pure origination function, was the Toledo, Cincinnati & St. Louis. The main line was intended to parallel that of Jay Gould's Wabash Railroad from Toledo to East St. Louis. It also served as the eastern portion of the Grand Narrow Gauge Trunk. The railroad was incidentally intended to be a major originator of coal and iron in southern Ohio. Remarkably, the railroad achieved a length of about 780 miles before it collapsed completely. The collapse effectively ended the period of large-scale narrow gauge investment in American railroading.

The railroad had its origins in the Germanic farming and woodworking community of Delphos, Ohio, a town of only some 2,000 people. The town was already well served by the main line of the Pittsburgh, Fort Wayne & Chicago Railway (Pennsylvania Railroad) and by the Miami & Erie Canal, but local figures felt the local woodworking industry would shortly have to bring in its wood from farther afield. The railroad was promoted under the name of

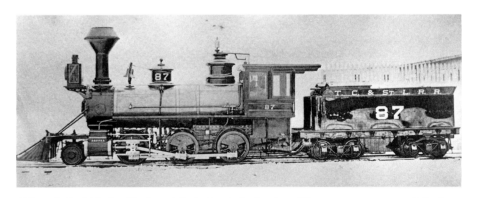

Although the Toledo, Cincinnati & St. Louis had a short life as a narrow gauge, it had a remarkable variety of motive power. No. 87 was a compact Brooks 2-6-0. (California State Railroad Museum.)

The Toledo, Cincinnati & St. Louis's immediate predecessor, the Toledo, Delphos & Burlington, bore a name that became obsolete when the railroad's target terminus changed from Burlington, Iowa, to East St. Louis, Illinois. TD&B passenger locomotive No. 39 is thought to be shown at the Delphos Shops. (Smithsonian Institution.)

the Toledo, Delphos & Indianapolis Railway by Joseph W. Hunt, a local pharmacist,* and his associates. Although they apparently intended to build the route designated in the corporate title from the time of incorporation in 1872, their first target was Holgate on the Baltimore, Pittsburgh & Chicago (Baltimore & Ohio), 32 miles to the northeast. The Panic of 1873 prevented their financing the railroad until 1876. The impending exhaustion of local stands of hardwood created an incentive to begin construction. Local parties raised $40,000 so that ground could be broken at Delphos on April 21, 1877. The railroad opened with an excursion to Fort Jennings (5 miles) on July 4, and built an additional ten miles to Dupont by October 6, 1877. At that point the railroad found it necessary to cross the Auglaize River with a bridge, which, even as rebuilt, was to bedevil the company and all its successors to the date of the ultimate abandonment of the line in the twentieth century. The line reached Holgate in November 1878. Si-

multaneously, to tap a hardwood forest southwest of Delphos, Hunt undertook a J-shaped branch of 26 miles to Shane's Crossing (Rockford), which was completed December 14, 1878.

At the same time, Hunt's associates, Dr. Carey A. Evans and Joseph Boehmer, were promoting a line west from Delphos. Their intention was to tie the projected narrow gauge network centering on Delphos with the various projects for narrow gauges in western Illinois. Their plan was to build from Delphos to the Wabash River in the vicinity of Attica and Williamsport, Indiana, where they would connect with the Havana, Rantoul & Eastern. The latter proposed to connect with the Fulton County Narrow Gauge at Havana. A line that was never built, the Burlington, Monmouth & Illinois River Railroad, had acquired the unused right-of-way of the Illinois & Mississippi Railroad from Monmouth to Peoria. (The route was later built as the Minneapolis & St. Louis's entry into Peoria.) The two would have intersected at London Mills, Illinois. The BM&IR planned an extension from Monmouth to Burlington, Iowa, between the rights-of-way of the Chicago, Burlington & Quincy and the Toledo, Peoria &

Warsaw. Evans and Boehmer proposed to build from Delphos to Willshire, Ohio, where they found considerable local support, and thence through Decatur, Bluffton, Marion, Kokomo, and Frankfort, Indiana. A standard gauge railroad, the Frankfort & Kokomo, had been opened between the cities of its name in 1874. The route had the local advantage of serving a substantial hardwood forest between Delphos and Willshire. To build the line Evans and Boehmer organized the Delphos & Kokomo Railway in Ohio and the Delphos, Bluffton & Frankfort Railroad in Indiana. Willshire, which had financed the Ohio mileage almost entirely, had its first train on January 27, 1879. Financing in Indiana was concentrated in Wells County. Construction began in Bluffton, the county seat, and the line opened to Warren (13 miles) on July 8, 1878. The Frankfort & Kokomo Railroad had failed after the Panic of 1873, and was awaiting sale by its construction company. Evans arranged to lay a third rail along the line's 25 miles in mid-1879. The trackage west of Frankfort was to be built by the Frankfort & State Line Railroad, which in 1879 built 12 miles from Frankfort to Clark's Hill. (For map, see Indiana.)

The emerging system lacked an entry into Toledo, which had been intended from the outset to be its terminus. A local narrow gauge at Toledo presented a possible entry,

*Hunt's pharmacy, then called the Old Reliable Drug Store, is still in existence at the present writing. Now known as Remlinger's, it has been in continuous operation since 1849.

albeit a very inferior one. The Toledo & Maumee Narrow Gauge Railroad had built a suburban line from Toledo to South Toledo (7.5 miles) in 1874. Citizens of Grand Rapids, Ohio, graded an extension under the name of the Toledo & Grand Rapids Railroad from Maumee to Waterville in 1876 but lacked resources to bridge the Maumee River to the west. The new line was leased to the Toledo & Maumee and opened on July 1, 1877. The Toledo & Maumee, which was laid with 25-pound rail and had a curve of 24°, had been built to the standards of steam dummy lines, and had negligible terminal facilities. It was indisputably in the right place by the standards of promoters in Delphos, however. They arranged to take it over and to merge it with the Toledo, Delphos & Indianapolis, Delphos & Kokomo, and Delphos, Bluffton & Frankfort into the Toledo, Delphos & Burlington Railroad. The merger, effected on May 23, 1879, amounted to a single railroad with three gaps, the eastern gap consisting of 27 miles between Waterville and Holgate, Ohio, the central of 24 miles from Willshire to Bluffton, and the western of 44 miles from Warren to Kokomo. The central gap was closed on December 16, when trains began running from Delphos to Indiana.

Meanwhile, the project suffered a disaster when Hunt was killed on September 2, 1879, by moving cars on a siding of the Pittsburgh, Fort Wayne & Chicago in Delphos. His associates apparently felt unable to continue without him, and sold out their interests to men in the eastern financial community, headed by General John M. Corse of Boston. In the short run, the change was probably a source of strength for the railroad, for the new owners arranged a mortgage on the completed portion between Holgate and Warren to allow them to close the Holgate-Waterville gap and to rebuild the Toledo entry to ordinary narrow gauge standards. The former Toledo & Maumee was closed on July 20, 1880, for relaying with 50-pound rail and partial relocation. The route from Holgate to Waterville was through easy, flat country, but it entailed a bridge over the Maumee River at Grand Rapids that required eight spans and trestle approaches totaling 1,556 feet. Tracklaying was completed in the fall, allowing through trains from Toledo to Shane's Crossing to be instituted December 2, 1880.

Marion and Kokomo had authorized subsidies totaling $100,000 for closing the western gap. Work began in August 1880, and tracklaying was completed by the end of the year. On December 2, service began to Marion, which the line traversed by

a third rail on the Cincinnati, Wabash & Michigan, a predecessor of the Big Four, but trains did not regularly run to Kokomo until July 24, 1881. Early in 1881 the railroad formed a subsidiary, the Marion & Indianapolis, to build a branch to the capital, but the line was never undertaken. In September 1881 a branch from Kokomo to Chicago was discussed.

Meanwhile, the plan of participating in a multi-carrier route to Burlington, Iowa, had been abruptly aborted in 1880, when Jay Gould acquired control of the uncompleted Havana, Rantoul & Eastern, which had been brought to a connection with his Wabash, St. Louis & Pacific at West Lebanon, Indiana. He planned to use it only as a minor branch of his system. The effect was to turn the Toledo, Delphos & Burlington toward St. Louis. Since 1871 there had been a project for a narrow gauge railroad from Toledo to St. Louis in rivalry with the main line of Gould's Wabash. The Toledo & St. Louis Air Line by 1875 had accomplished nothing, but it then merged with another unbuilt railroad, the Shelbyville, Oconee & St. Louis, into the Toledo & St. Louis Narrow Gauge Railroad. Through Indiana the company planned the route later built by the Toledo, Delphos & Burlington via Decatur, Bluffton, and Marion. At a meeting of supporters in Indianapolis on April 7, 1876, the company proposed to build a narrow gauge to St. Louis via Eugene, Indiana, and Oakland and Mattoon, Illinois. The railroad was still unable to finance itself, but the support it had at Eugene and Oakland was apparently enough to attract the promoters of the Toledo, Delphos & Burlington when their original plan had to be abandoned. There was the further matter that the building of the Texas & St. Louis Railway presented the prospect of a continuous line of narrow gauge railroads paralleling the Gould lines all the way to the Mexican border at Laredo. This was, of course, the Grand Narrow Gauge Trunk, described at length in Part I, Chapter 4.

William J. Craig, a promoter of the TD&B in Bluffton, was reportedly responsible for the decision to build to St. Louis in the spring of 1880. In June he organized the Western Construction Company to build the St. Louis extension. He acquired the Frankfort & State Line from Carey Evans and bought the rights to an unbuilt railroad, the Tuscola, Charleston & Vincennes, in Illinois. This line's principal asset was a completed grade of 15 miles from Charleston to Oakland. Because of this acquisition, construction began east from Charleston; by the end of 1881 the line had reached Ridge Farm, Illinois (41 miles), leaving a gap

of 60 miles to the end of the Frankfort & State Line at Clark's Hill. This was closed in 1882, after a bridge of more than a half mile was built over the Wabash River between Silverwood and Cayuga. The bridge contained five Howe-truss spans and lengthy trestle approaches.

In February 1881 the Toledo, Delphos & Burlington management had formed the Toledo, Cincinnati & St. Louis Railroad to build the entire St. Louis extension west of Kokomo. This company assumed the lease on the Frankfort & State Line and absorbed the Frankfort & Kokomo, from which it removed the standard gauge rail in July 1881. At the same time the TC&StL absorbed the three companies that were building mileage in Illinois.

Simultaneously, the Toledo, Delphos & Burlington was proceeding with its incursion into southern Ohio. The management formed the line south from Delphos by acquiring two recently built narrow gauges, one existing broad gauge railroad, and a bankrupt project that had progressed only to a partial grade north from Cincinnati. These enterprises are discussed in the following sections.

Dayton, Covington & Toledo Railroad

J. O. Arnold and George W. Kneisley of Dayton promoted the Dayton, Covington & Toledo in 1877. They began grading in the Stillwater Valley northwest of Dayton in 1878, and in 1879 laid 25 miles of track from Stillwater Junction on the Panhandle (Pennsylvania) six miles west of Dayton to Covington. In 1880 the company arranged to lay third rail into Dayton Union Depot, and extended its track 11 miles northwest from Covington to Versailles. On June 21, 1880, the Toledo, Delphos & Burlington acquired the DC&T and immediately began efforts to tie it in with the system centering at Delphos. The management decided to build south from Mercer on the Shane's Crossing branch to Versailles. Track reached Celina (8 miles) by the end of 1880, and the additional 24 miles to Versailles were completed in May 1881. Arnold and Kneisley had built to fairly high standards, but the connection to Delphos was like most of the TD&B—lightly graded, unballasted, and poorly ditched.

Dayton & Southeastern Railroad

Colonel S. N. Yeoman of Washington Court House formed the Dayton & Southeastern on December 16, 1871, in hope of building a standard gauge line from Dayton through Xenia, Washington Court House, and Chillicothe to the coalfield at Wellston, and if possible, to Gallipolis on the Ohio River about 144 miles southeast of Dayton. Yeoman planned to make use of a roadbed graded about 25 years earlier by the Dayton, Xenia & Belpre Railroad between Xenia and Washington Court House. He succeeded in gaining rights to the right-of-way, but was unable to finance his railroad. In October 1874 Yeoman hired Edward Hulbert to promote the project as a narrow gauge. Hulbert spoke at meetings at Xenia, Jamestown, Washington Court House, Chillicothe, Jackson, and Pomeroy, raising the funds for beginning construction and winning a personal following among the subscribers. He let the contract for building between Xenia and Washington Court House, but he was abruptly discharged at a directors' meeting of May 4, 1875, on the ground that his employment as general manager was a needless expense. Hulbert was replaced by the line's chief engineer, Jacob Blickensderfer, Jr., who in 1876 completed the portion from Xenia to Jamestown (12 miles) and laid nearly all the rail on the segment from Dayton to Xenia, although the track was not put into service until 1877. The first train ran from Dayton to Washington Court House (48 miles) on May 18, 1877. Track reached Musselmans (69 miles) by November. Yeoman then found his funds exhausted. The railroad was placed in receivership on August 8, 1878, under John E. Gimperling, whom the court authorized to continue construction. He was able to extend the railroad by selling securities to the Baltimore & Ohio, which was interested in the property as an entry into Dayton. With the proceeds he extended his main line into Chillicothe (80 miles), including a bridge of 1,001 feet over the Scioto River, which was completed in October 1879. By the end of the year track was extended into Richmond Dale (93 miles). The line reached Wellston (115 miles), an important coal center, in May 1880. An extension of eight miles was built on to Buckeye Furnace in 1882. In addition to its own originations, the line received coal traffic from the narrow gauge Springfield, Jackson & Pomeroy at Washington Court House and via a Ramsey Transfer from the Marietta & Cincinnati Railway at Musselmans. The railroad installed a Ramsey Transfer at Dayton for interchange with the Big Four.

The Toledo, Delphos & Burlington took control of the Dayton & Southeastern in February 1881 by purchasing $400,000 of preferred stock, apparently to forestall the imminent takeover of the company by the B&O. On March 17, 1881, the Dayton & Southeastern became the Southeastern Division of the Toledo, Delphos & Burling-

ton. The line was still short of its destination, the rail- and ingot-producing town of Ironton on the Ohio River. Since 1852 Ironton had received coal and ore from Lawrence County via the Iron Railroad. The latter line, which ran inland for 14 miles to Centre Station, had been built to the old Ohio legal gauge of 4'-10", but since it had no physical connection to the railroad system generally, the gauge was no handicap. Ironton's products mainly moved out by steamboat. In addition to serving the major mines and blast furnaces in the area, the Iron Railroad had the attraction of a 1,020-foot tunnel near Vesuvius for a relatively easy approach to Ironton. On October 21, 1881, the TD&B absorbed the Iron Railroad, although it had already arranged to lay a third rail on the Iron line from Deans to Ironton (13 miles). To effect a connection from Ironton Junction, three miles short of Wellston, to Deans, the TD&B mortgaged the Southeastern Division for $2.25 million. The extension was graded in 1882, and by December only five miles of track were necessary to effect the connection.

Cincinnati Northern Railway

The Southeastern Division passed close enough to Cincinnati that its promoters could not avoid seeing the attractions of a branch. The Miami Valley Narrow Gauge Railway had been formed in 1874 to build

from Cincinnati to Lebanon and Xenia, 55 miles. Between 1876 and 1878 the company graded 36 miles from Norwood to Waynesville before exhausting its resources. In March 1880 the property was sold at a receiver's auction to C. S. Brice and his associates, who, in league with General Corse and some other officials of the Toledo, Delphos & Burlington, formed the Cincinnati Northern Railway. They built on the Norwood-Lebanon portion of the grade (24 miles), and were able to begin mixed-train operation on May 30, 1881. Completion of the project required connecting the new line to the Southeastern Division near Dayton and extending the trackage into Cincinnati. The TD&B decided upon a connection at a point seven miles east of Dayton, which it called Lebanon Junction. The 23-mile gap separating Lebanon Junction and Lebanon was closed when track met at Utica (Dodds) on December 20, 1881.

The Miami Valley Narrow Gauge had projected an expensive but highly satisfactory entry of five miles from Norwood into Cincinnati. It proposed to terminate in a depot at Broadway and Court Street after completing a 10,011-foot tunnel through the Walnut Hills undertaken by Erasmus Gest in 1852, but abandoned about a third completed in 1855. The Cincinnati Northern acquired rights to the Court Street depot site, but apparently considered the

Locomotives from the vast Toledo, Cincinnati & St. Louis system circulated widely following its collapse. Here a former Cincinnati Northern Mogul, foreground, works at the F. E. Brister lumber mill in Mississippi. (Ed Bond collection.)

project of completing the tunnel to be beyond its resources. Consequently, it built a tunnel of only 1,500 feet at the summit of the Walnut Hills, with an ascent of 3.4 percent from Cincinnati and 2 percent from the north. The Cincinnati Northern was able to begin freight service into Cincinnati on January 12, 1882, and passenger service about two weeks later.

By the time the Cincinnati Northern was completed, in January 1882, the Toledo, Delphos & Burlington was running out of funds. The gap in the Ironton line was being closed, and the St. Louis line was being built only to Neoga, Illinois, on the Illinois Central Railroad's main line. There seemed little prospect of extending it with the resources at hand. Accordingly, the management early in 1882 revised the corporate organization and financing of the railroad. On February 23, 1882, the directors voted to merge the Toledo, Delphos & Burlington with its subsidiary, the Toledo, Cincinnati & St. Louis, under the name of the latter, which was now more descriptive of the railroad. The management also arranged with the Boston capitalists who were financing the railroad to form the Toledo & Delphos Trust, whereby the American Loan & Trust Co. of Boston would administer $1.5 million newly raised to complete the railroad. The Trust also took title to such financial assets as the TC&StL had, mainly uncollected subscriptions for the company's stock. These assets had a book value of $7,709,771 but a market value of only $2,603,496—a good indication of the pessimism with which the financial community viewed the project. With the infusion of new capital, the company contracted for building the remainder of the main line into East St. Louis. The final route proved to be what the Toledo & St. Louis Air Line had projected, except that it passed through Cayuga, Indiana, instead of the neighboring town of Eugene, and Charleston, Illinois, rather than Mattoon. The company bought a tract in the American Bottoms area, east of Venice, Illinois, and north of Horseshoe Lake, from the Wiggins Ferry Co. for a terminal. In 1881 the Toledo, Delphos & Burlington had bought land at Toledo near the Wabash grain elevator for its own elevator, wharves, and terminal facilities. In 1883 TC&StL organized the Narrow Gauge Elevator Co. to build grain storage facilities in Toledo and elsewhere.

By the end of 1882, the company had nearly exhausted the $1.5 million with which it hoped to complete the railroad. On November 8, subscribers to the Toledo & Delphos Trust met in Boston to discuss additional financing. It was estimated that $360,000 was required to finish the project. The subscribers voted to assess themselves $375,000, in return for which the TC&StL would turn over to the Trust $400,000 in scrip and bonds. The directors met in Boston on November 14 to approve this arrangement and the following day voted to attempt to raise $800,000. On December 7 the TC&StL circularized the members of the Trust who had not paid their assessments, urgently requesting funds. The rolling mill refused to deliver rail for the last five miles of the Ironton line, and the contractors' men on the St. Louis line threatened to destroy the railroad's numerous trestles if their wages were not paid. Bondholders met at Boston on December 23 and were told that pledges for $600,000 of the $800,000 being sought were in hand.

The entire project might have collapsed at the end of 1882, except that the board of directors chose as president Elijah B. Phillips, president of the Eastern Railroad and a longtime power in Boston railroad finance. He quickly raised the funds necessary to complete both lines. The Ironton line was completed at Deans in January 1883. Rails had reached the East St. Louis area at the end of 1882, but the track was not ready for operation until March 1. Mixed trains were inaugurated between Charleston and East St. Louis on May 14, 1883. The company had no adequate terminal facilities at either East St. Louis or Toledo, however. Phillips hoped to put a depot on the East St. Louis waterfront and to ferry freight and passengers into St. Louis. An Illinois circuit court enjoined the company from laying track in the streets of East St. Louis without prior permission. By mid-1883 the Narrow Gauge Elevator Co. had built an elevator at Toledo. Dayton also lacked satisfactory terminal facilities.

In spite of the company's disastrous financial condition, Phillips was able to merge the Cincinnati Northern and its subsidiary, the Spring Grove, Avondale & Cincinnati (which had a short branch to the Cincinnati zoo) into the TC&StL. At a meeting of the CN's shareholders on March 24 he was confronted with vociferous opposition from stockholders who protested inadequate notice. He brought about the merger at a meeting of May 5, 1883, effective May 30. He was able to inaugurate express passenger service from Toledo to both Cincinnati and St. Louis in the summer. In spite of the railroad's light physical standards and general lack of ballast—only a third of the railroad had been ballasted— the trains were able to average 19 miles per hour. At 451 miles, the main line was only 18 miles longer than the Wabash. Phillips announced his intention of attracting both passenger and freight traffic with vigorous rate-cutting. He proposed to cut the local freight rate out of East St. Louis from 24¢ per hundredweight to 9¢, a rate the standard gauge roads thought too low for survival. He had some success in this effort, and added considerably to the line's motive power to handle through freight. By July 10 the railroad was reported to have 103 locomotives and eight on order. At that time the Seney syndicate of Boston bought a large block of the railroad's stock and placed three of its men on the board of directors. This syndicate had been interested in building the Nickel Plate Road, and there was some speculation that the TC&StL might provide the entry to St. Louis that the Nickel Plate was known to want. The Seney directors were rumored to be intending to bring $500,000 to the line, funds badly needed for completing terminal facilities at Toledo and St. Louis, ballasting, and installation of sidings. This hope was quickly dashed, and the railroad had no further prospect for maintaining solvency. The *Railroad Gazette* reported that the TC&StL grossed only $654 per mile in the first half of 1883, the lowest of any large railroad. The company ceased paying wages to its more than 1,500 employees in May. In June the Mississippi flooded, destroying such trackage as the railroad had in the American Bottoms. In July shopmen at Delphos refused to continue working without wages. The directors decided to petition a federal court for appointment of two receivers, but on July 31 Grenville D. Braman appeared before the Federal Circuit Court in Chicago to request receivership on behalf of the bondholders. The company was delinquent in two payments on its first-mortgage bonds. It had some $22 million in mortgage obligations, $2 million in equipment obligations, a floating debt of $964,000, and some $400,000 owed in back wages and other current obligations. Inevitably, the court would be mainly occupied with the question whether the company could be reorganized as a single railroad.

The court appointed Edwin E. Dwight, general manager of the TC&StL, as the railroad's receiver. The disparate interests of the various creditors made his job extremely difficult. The representatives of the Iron Railroad believed their property remained viable as an independent line, and wanted it dissociated from the rest of the TC&StL. James M. Quigley, who represented a majority of the bondholders, wanted the entire railroad standard gauged. The effort to preserve the railroad as a single entity was made difficult by the existence of suits by creditors in courts about the system. The Central Trust Company filed a total of eight foreclosure actions in Toledo, Cincinnati, Indianapolis, and Springfield (Illinois). Late in 1883 Judge John Baxter at Toledo removed Dwight as receiver for the Ohio mileage, and appointed William J. Craig, a residual enthusiast for the narrow gauge. Craig had been involved in the Toledo, Texas & Rio Grande, a project to connect the TC&StL's Illinois mileage with the Texas & St. Louis directly, bypassing the uncooperative St. Louis & Cairo.

The establishment of separate receiverships for the Ohio and Indiana-Illinois mileages essentially ended any prospect that the railroad would be reorganized as a whole. Late in 1883 the Superior Court in Cincinnati ordered the sale of the Cincinnati Northern to satisfy a judgment of $24,000. Toward the end of the year Craig was made receiver for Indiana and Illinois, but the dismemberment continued. On June 28, 1884, the lines south of Delphos were removed from his jurisdiction and, with the exception of the Cincinnati Northern, ordered sold. The lines southeast of Dayton were reorganized as the Dayton & Ironton Railroad and standard gauged on April 3, 1887. This railroad was consolidated with the Dayton-Delphos mileage as the Dayton, Fort Wayne & Chicago Railway in June of the same year. The Shane's Crossing branch was abandoned, but the rest remained narrow gauge until the Cincinnati, Hamilton & Dayton absorbed the company in 1891. It standard gauged the line into Delphos on July 13, 1891. In 1916 the CH&D, involved in a financial upheaval characteristic of it, abandoned the Ironton line beyond the Wellston area, and turned over the Delphos branch north of Stillwater Junction to the Dayton, Toledo & Chicago Railroad. The latter proved to be a weak short line, and was abandoned in 1922. The Baltimore & Ohio, upon absorbing the CH&D, retained the Dayton–Wellston–Buckeye Furnace line. It was abandoned from Dayton to Washington Court House in 1983. The portion from Vances to Wellston was turned over to the Indiana & Ohio Rail Corp. in 1987.

The Iron Railroad was reorganized as the Iron Railway in 1884 and became part of the Detroit, Toledo & Ironton's southern terminal properties. The Cincinnati Northern was reorganized as the Cincinnati, Lebanon & Northern Railway in 1885 and continued narrow gauge operation from Cincinnati to Dayton until the Dayton & Ironton converted in 1887. The CL&N

then cut back its operations to Dodds, six miles north of Lebanon. Henry Lewis, a quarry operator, bought the 17 miles from Dodds to Lebanon Junction, and converted it in January 1891. In 1892 he turned his line over to the Dayton, Lebanon & Cincinnati Railroad, which had been organized in 1887, and leased the Dodds-Lebanon segment, which he converted in December. The DL&C began service between Dayton and Lebanon in January 1893. The Cincinnati, Lebanon & Northern converted its line on September 16, 1894, although narrow gauge was retained briefly for suburban trains between Cincinnati and Blue Ash. The Pennsylvania Railroad acquired the CL&N in 1896 and the DL&C in 1915, making them a secondary line between Cincinnati and Dayton. The line was broken by abandonment between Lebanon and Lytle in 1939. The line south of Lebanon was turned over to the Indiana & Ohio Rail Corp. in segments between 1985 and 1987. The line north of Lytle was cut back to Centerville in 1978 and to Pasadena in 1981.

The main line of the TC&StL remained in narrow gauge operation after the separation of the lines south of Delphos, but it was highly unprofitable, running up an operating deficit of over $1 million in 1884. Such long-distance traffic as the policy of rate-cutting had brought, mainly eastbound agricultural products and lumber, was handled at a loss. In a clear indication that the judges in control of the enterprise considered it hopeless, the courts ordered cessation of all but purely local operations. The railroad was given an order effective January 6, 1885, to stop interchanging with its narrow gauge connections, to close its Ramsey Transfers whereby it had interchanged with standard gauge railroads, and to return all foreign cars still on the property. Train operation was reduced to a single mixed train per day over the entire system. Most of the cars and locomotives held under equipment trusts were surrendered to financial institutions. The decree ordered reduction of the locomotive roster from 101 to 16, and the freight car fleet from 3,410 to 450. All but major stations were closed, and the shop at Delphos was reduced to a skeleton force of 20 men. Even though the railroad was almost new, the light standards to which it had been built had caused it to deteriorate badly. The bridge over the Auglaize River at Dupont was so weak that locomotives could not pass over it. The east end of the railroad was operated by mixed trains out of Toledo and Delphos; loaded cars were pushed slowly over the bridge individually by locomotives using empty cars as idlers.

On petition of the bondholders, General John McNulta was appointed receiver in July 1885, replacing Craig. He repaired the Auglaize River bridge and restored a passenger train between Toledo and Delphos. He was also allowed to establish one between Bluffton and Frankfort to serve the most populous portion of the main line. In October 1885 James Quigley announced a bondholders' plan for reorganization and rebuilding of the railroad. He estimated that standard gauging the line east of Frankfort would require $3 million. The job would entail replacing 119 miles of rail and buying 600,000 standard sized ties. Most of the bridges would require replacement, and both curves and grades would have to be eased throughout the system. Unfortunately, the resources available to Quigley were inadequate for the job. At Indianapolis on December 30, 1885, the entire main line from Toledo to East St. Louis was sold under foreclosure to Quigley's group for $135,000 in cash and $1,366,000 in par value of the bonds. The cash went to pay expenses of the receivers. The railroad was in real prospect of abandonment when Quigley found financing with Sylvester H. Kneeland, a prominent New York financier and longtime adversary of Jay Gould. Kneeland agreed to pay off the railroad's creditors, and to rebuild the line for standard gauge operation. The bondholders were to be issued preferred stock—of which Kneeland was to receive $1 million—plus all of the common stock at the rate of $25,000 per mile. In a secret clause to the agreement, Quigley and Kneeland agreed to share the profits evenly. Whether Kneeland could have financed the conversion is questionable, but early in 1886 gas and oil were discovered at various points along the railroad from Delphos to Marion. New corporations were set up to own the Ohio, Indiana, and Illinois mileages, and were then consolidated into the Toledo, St. Louis & Kansas City Railroad, which shortly adopted the name "Clover Leaf Route."

Conversion of the railroad, which was expected to cost some $9 million, began immediately with the installation of wider ties. New or rebuilt iron bridges were necessary to cross the Maumee at Grand Rapids, the Auglaize at Dupont, the Wabash at Bluffton, and Wildcat Creek near Kokomo. Track gangs shifted the rails to 4'-8½" from Toledo to Frankfort on Sunday, June 26, 1887, and standard gauge operation began the following day. Conversion of the west end was more difficult, mainly because the line from Charleston to East St. Louis had been very lightly graded, with continual undulation and an excessive number of trestles. In June 1888 the 61 miles from Frankfort to Cayuga were converted, followed by 52 miles from Cayuga to Charleston in August. Because of a difficult winter, work west of Charleston could not be finished until spring. The last narrow gauge train ran between Charleston and East St. Louis on May 31, 1889. The railroad was converted June 1 and standard gauge operation began June 2.

The Clover Leaf throughout its history was handicapped by the poor physical plant it inherited from the narrow gauge predecessor. The mileage in Illinois had excessive undulation for what was basically easy country. Weak bridges restricted the weight of locomotives. The TC&StL's pattern in Delphi had been a T, with the Toledo and Cincinnati lines running straight through town from north to south and the St. Louis line going west from an extremely tight wye. The area was so constricted that during conversion the curve from the Toledo to the St. Louis line could be modified only from about 23° to 18°50′, one of the worst on any American main line. The Clover Leaf was among the first railroads to go bankrupt in the depression of 1893. It was reorganized as the Toledo, St. Louis & Western in 1900. Having no branch lines, the Clover Leaf was particularly receptive to joint traffic arrangements with the interurbans and Lake Erie steamship lines. As a consequence of securing control of the Chicago & Alton in 1907, the Clover Leaf overextended itself financially, again going bankrupt in 1914. By 1922 the railroad had regained solvency, so that its obligations could be paid off without reorganization. Its geographical pattern and restored solvency made it attractive to the Van Sweringen brothers, who were eager to extend their Nickel Plate Road into Peoria and St. Louis. They bought the Clover Leaf in 1923, and in the same period acquired the Lake Erie & Western, the main line of which ran from Sandusky, Ohio, to Peoria. The Nickel Plate then had the choice of moving freight to Peoria and St. Louis via either of the new acquisitions to Frankfort, where they crossed. Routing freight and the express passenger train onto the former LE&W at Fostoria was much preferable to sending them over the Clover Leaf from Continental, for the LE&W avoided the Auglaize River bridge, the curve at Delphos, and various lesser handicaps of the late narrow gauge. After 1933 the Clover Leaf east of Frankfort became almost entirely a local carrier. Acquisition of the Wheeling & Lake Erie in 1949 gave the Nickel Plate an entry into Toledo from the east. When the Norfolk & Western merged with the Nickel

Plate and leased the Wabash in 1964, the combined system had a superior entry into Toledo from the west in the Wabash main line. The entire Clover Leaf line was reduced to local service. In 1968 a load of oversized automobile frames hit the overhead span of the Auglaize River bridge, causing it to buckle badly. An embargo was declared, and the Douglas–Grand Rapids segment was abandoned in 1972. About 162 miles from Linden, Indiana, to Chapman, Illinois, were abandoned on December 31, 1987, except for a short segment at Cowden, Illinois. Other segments were offered to local operators. Shippers at Charleston, Illinois, bought the 53 miles from Linden to Cowden and contracted for its operation by the Indiana Hi Rail Corp. At the present writing abandonment of the remaining mileage east of Bluffton, Indiana, is anticipated shortly, and the Norfolk Southern has announced its intention to sell, if possible, the line from Marion to Frankfort.

REFERENCES: John A. Rehor, *The Nickel Plate Story* (Milwaukee: Kalmbach Publishing Co., 1965), pp. 118–50, 431–36, and *passim*; John W. Hauck, *Narrow Gauge in Ohio: The Cincinnati, Lebanon & Northern Railway* (Boulder, Colo.: Pruett Publishing Co., 1986).

Wheeling & Lake Erie Rail Road

Joel Wood, agent of the Cleveland & Pittsburgh at Martin's Ferry, conceived of a standard gauge coal hauler from the Wheeling area to Sandusky and Toledo via Massillon, and incorporated it as the Wheeling & Lake Erie Rail Road on March 10, 1871. On February 7, 1872, he gave Hugh Bowlsby Willson of New York a contract for $35,000 per mile to build the railroad. In 1873–74 Willson did some grading at Navarre and on the ascent from the Ohio River opposite Wheeling, but the failure of Wheeling, Sandusky, and Toledo to provide subscriptions, combined with the financial stringency of the middle of the decade, brought the project to a halt. A faction of the board of directors led by Frank Lockwood of Milan proposed to use Huron as the port on Lake Erie and to build the railroad as a narrow gauge. Lockwood's faction ousted Wood in 1876, acquired the towpath of the abandoned Milan Canal, and prepared to build the first segment between Huron, Milan, and Norwalk. The management renegotiated the contract with Willson to build the railroad for $20,000 per mile—$3,000 in cash and the rest in securities. Willson completed the line from the Government Pier in Huron to Norwalk

(12.5 miles) in June 1877. The railroad had two National Locomotive Works 4-4-0s, a combine, two boxcars, and 19 flatcars.

Willson graded about nine miles at New London, but then became involved in a dispute with the management, which he claimed had issued bonds to pay off creditors, including other contractors, in violation of the agreement with him. Willson won his case, and in December 1877 took over the railroad, which numbered among its assets about 37 miles of grade at the south end. The Huron-Norwalk segment operated only in the summer months, and was unprofitable. Shareholders petitioned the courts to dissolve the corporation in 1878 and 1879. At the end of the 1879 season the railroad was shut down and the equipment sent to Norwalk for disposition.

Jay Gould revived the Wheeling & Lake Erie project in 1879, partly as a coal road between Wheeling and the Lake Erie ports, and partly as a link in his proposed transcontinental system. Willson surrendered the narrow gauge in June 1880. It was removed, and most of the right-of-way used for a branch off the W&LE's Wheeling-Toledo main line into Huron. The branch left the main line at Huron Junction, a mile east of Norwalk, and the narrow gauge's entrance into Norwalk was abandoned. Standard gauge rails reached Huron in 1881, and mixed trains were inaugurated on January 9, 1882. The line into Huron is extant as part of the Norfolk Southern system.

REFERENCE: Rehor, *The Nickel Plate Story*, pp. 285–87, 297–98, 440.

▼ ▼ ▼

The Cincinnati, Atlantic & Columbus Railway was organized in 1882 to build from Cincinnati to a point on the Ohio River opposite Point Pleasant, West Virginia, with a branch from Fayetteville to Columbus. The company laid 11 miles of 3′-0″ rail from Milford to Newtonsville, and graded east to Hillsboro. The firm bought no equipment and never operated. Several efforts were made to convert the existing line and make it part of an east-west coal road, but none succeeded. The track was removed, and the grade from Mulberry to Newtonsville was used by the Cincinnati, Milford & Loveland Traction Co. The Cincinnati & Columbus Traction Co. is believed to have used the right-of-way from Fayetteville to Hillsboro.

Oregon

Oregonian Railway
Portland & Willamette Valley Railway

The Willamette Valley, in which Oregon's population is highly concentrated, was served by two standard gauge railroads, the Oregon Central on the west side and the Oregon & California on the east. Seeking an alternative, farmers led by B. B. Branson and Ellis G. Hughes formed the Dayton, Sheridan & Grande Ronde Railroad on November 14, 1877, mainly to carry wheat from communities on the west side to Dayton on the Yamhill River for interchange with steamboats. The line was opened from Dayton to Sheridan (20 miles) on October 24, 1878. They also undertook a branch of 13 miles from Sheridan Junction to Dallas, but the project failed financially before the branch was quite completed. Debt to the Pacific Rolling Mill Co. caused the property to be put in the hands of George Revette as receiver in January 1879.

Control of the railroad passed into the hands of William Reid, who had served as American vice-consul at Dundee, Scotland. With several Scottish capitalists whom he had known in Dundee, he formed the Willamette Valley Railroad on June 2, 1879, but he reincorporated the enterprise as the Oregon Railway on February 20, 1880, in Oregon and as the Oregonian Railway in April 1880 in Dundee. Reid completed the Dallas branch and in 1881 pushed it on to Airlie, 29 miles below Sheridan Junction. The terminus was named for the Earl of Airlie, one of Reid's Scottish associates. The line was also pushed north eight miles to Aiken, which was renamed Dundee, and designated as the railroad's operating headquarters. Finally, in September 1881, the track was built four miles east from Dundee to Fulquartz Landing on the Willamette River.

Simultaneously, the company was building a line on the east side of the valley. Beginning at Silverton in April 1880, Reid built north, reaching Ray's Landing opposite Fulquartz Landing in September 1881, and south, reaching Coburg, a total of 90 miles, in July 1882. Reid also undertook an entry into Portland from Dundee, and began preparations for bridging the Willamette between the two landings. The company owned two steamers, *Salem* and *City of Salem*, which temporarily connected the landings with each other and with Portland. Reid also planned to extend the east line to Winnemucca, Nevada, to connect with the Central Pacific, and to extend the west line to Astoria at the mouth of the Columbia or to Yaquina Bay on the Pacific Coast. These plans made the narrow gauge a serious threat to Henry Villard's Oregon Railway & Navigation Co., which was building into Portland along the south bank of the Colum-

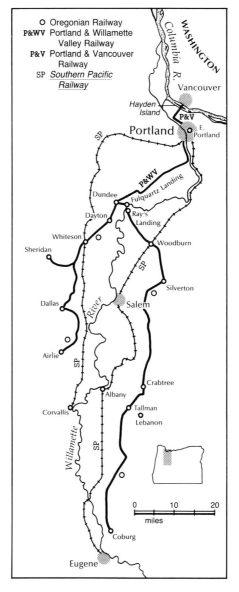

```
O    Oregonian Railway
P&WV Portland & Willamette
     Valley Railway
P&V  Portland & Vancouver
     Railway
SP   Southern Pacific
     Railway
```

bia. Villard sent an agent, J. B. Montgomery, to Dundee, Scotland, to negotiate a lease of the Oregonian Railway that would provide for a return of 7 percent per year on the Scots' investment. They preferred this to Reid's best offer, a lease to the Central Pacific that would have yielded about 4.5 percent. Villard's lease took effect on August 1, 1881. Although he completed the lines to Airlie and Coburg, he stopped work on the bridge over the Willamette and on the extension to Portland.

In May 1884, after Villard had left the OR&N, the company repudiated the lease of the Oregonian, causing the narrow gauge to become insolvent and to be placed in the hands of Charles N. Scott as receiver, effective April 14, 1885. Scott and Reid brought a legal action against the OR&N, recovering £71,000 in back rentals when the lease was declared valid in September 1886. Partly with these proceeds, they resumed work on the Portland extension, which they had separately incorporated as the Portland & Willamette Valley Railway in 1885 because of the bankruptcy. They opened it from Dundee to Elk Rock, a steamboat landing on the Willamette five miles below Portland late in 1886, but a dispute concerning the right-of-way delayed completion into Portland (29 miles) until July 23, 1888. The P&WV was opened as a narrow gauge, but standard gauge ties and clearances had been provided in the expectation of early conversion.

The Southern Pacific had provided much of the financing for the Portland extension and quickly came to control the entire enterprise. The SP leased the Oregonian on December 5, 1890, in the name of a subsidiary, the Oregon & Western Railroad, and operated it integrally with the P&WV, which it leased to another subsidiary, the Portland & Yamhill Railroad. The SP absorbed both lines in 1893. It converted the east line from a junction at Woodburn to Coburg in the summer of 1890, abandoning the ten miles from Ray's Landing to Woodburn. The spur to Fulquartz Landing was also abandoned at this time. The west line was converted in 1893. From Portland to Whiteson (45 miles) the west line became part of the SP's electrification southwest of Portland. De-electrified in 1926, it is still in existence. The trackage from Whiteson to Airlie was operated as a branch until late in 1928, when it was abandoned, except for several short portions retained for origination or termination.

The east line remained intact only until November 3, 1907, when the segment from Crabtree to Lebanon Junction was wiped out by a flood. The trackage was replaced with a new line from Balm, a mile south of Crabtree, to Lebanon, to provide a loop through Lebanon in conjunction with an existing branch from Albany to Tallman and Lebanon. The damaged track was removed in 1910. Of the remainder, West Stayton–Shelburn was abandoned in 1963 and all of the line south of Tallman in 1985. What survives, Woodburn–West Stayton, is under consideration for abandonment at the present writing.

REFERENCES: Leslie M. Scott, "History of the Narrow Gauge Railroad in the Willamette Valley," *The Quarterly of the Oregon Historical Society*, 20 (1919), pp. 141–58; Tom Madden, "Narrow Gauge Oregon Railroads," *The Western Railroader*, 25, no. 1, issue 265 (1962); Ed Austin and Tom Dill, *The Southern Pacific in Oregon* (Edmonds, Wash.: Pacific Fast Mail, 1987), pp. 18–25.

Oregon Portage Railway

A mule tramway had been built on the Oregon bank of the Columbia River around the Cascades in the 1850s, and had survived the flood of 1861 that destroyed its counterpart on the north bank. This became a 5'-0" steam railroad, the Oregon Portage Railway, with the arrival of the locomotive *Pony* in 1862. Henry Villard incorporated it into his Oregon Railway & Navigation Co. for his rail line along the south bank about 1880. He initially planned to convert it to 3'-0", and laid some narrow gauge track before deciding to make the OR&N a standard gauge railroad.

The dissatisfaction of steamboat operators with the low quality of service of the Cascade Railroad on the north bank and delay in the completion of locks at the dam being built at the Cascades combined to produce political pressure for a restoration of a railroad on the south bank. In 1891 the state established the Oregon Board of Portage Commissioners, which undertook a 3-mile railroad. A 3'-0" gauge was chosen for conformity with the track of the Corps of Engineers at the construction site of the dam. The railroad was opened in September 1891, and quickly proved successful: during its first year it handled over 8,000 passengers and 10,000 tons of freight. The operation ended in May 1896, when the locks opened and the Corps of Engineers refused to authorize further use of its track.

REFERENCE: Randall V. Mills, *Stern-Wheelers Up Columbia* (Palo Alto, Calif.: Bay Books, 1947), pp. 67–79.

Being integral with a lumber operation, the Sumpter Valley was among the last wood-burning common carriers. The consequence was spark-arresting stacks on otherwise modern Mikado locomotives. (Otto C. Perry, Denver Public Library.)

Portland & Vancouver Railway

Frank DeKum, R. L. Durham, John B. David, and others connected with the Oregon Land & Investment Co. incorporated this railway on April 27, 1888, and opened it on September 16. The property was a steam dummy line from East Portland north mainly along Fourth Street (Union Avenue) to a ferry terminal on Hayden Island (7 miles), from which the company ran two double-ended ferries to Vancouver, Washington. The line handled freight, mainly gravel from the river and beer from a brewery in Vancouver. Express was provided by a private contractor.

The property was sold on April 23, 1892, to the Multnomah Street Railway, which began immediate preparations to electrify it and convert it to the 3'-6" of the company's existing network. During a transitional period of three-rail operation, one of the line's three dummy engines overturned on April 4, 1893, killing the engi-

neer. The last steam equipment ran on June 24, 1893. The Multnomah Street Railway had been merged into the Portland Consolidated Street Railway on August 1, 1892. As the Alameda–Union Avenue route of the city's street railway system, the line operated until replaced by buses in 1948.

REFERENCE: John T. Labbe, *Fares Please! Those Portland Trolley Years* (Caldwell, Idaho: Caxton Printers, 1980), pp. 44–49, 77–80.

Sumpter Valley Railway

Although the Sumpter Valley Railway was integral with the Oregon Lumber Co. throughout its history, it was more than a normal common carrier. The railroad was separately incorporated; it handled traffic for other lumber operators in northeastern Oregon; and it served mining of gold and quartz in the area.

Both the lumber company and the railroad were the conceptions of David S. Eccles of Ogden, a prominent Mormon layman

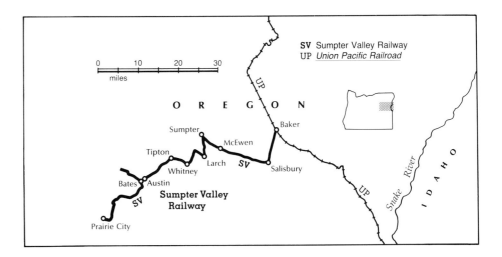

Sumpter Valley No. 16, a 2-8-2, leaves Baker, Oregon, with 34 cars in March 1939. (Richard H. Kindig.)

and the line was pushed westward. Beginning in April 1903, the railroad was built up to a second summit at Tipton (51 miles), where the line, after completion in 1904, originated traffic from the Greenhorn mines. In the fall of 1905 the railroad was brought down to Austin (59 miles), where Oregon Lumber established another mill. A company town, Batesville (Bates), was built a mile beyond Austin in 1919. Oregon Lumber operated extensive trackage of private lines with geared locomotives out of its mills. The gauge was compatible and shops were integral with the railroad's facilities at South Baker.

If the railroad had been built exclusively in the interest of the lumber company, it would probably not have been pushed beyond Bates, but Eccles planned to extend it through John Day and Burns to a connection with the Nevada-California-Oregon Railway, probably at Lakeview, some 235 miles beyond his current railhead. After some indecision concerning the route, in 1909 he undertook an extension over Dixie Mountain to Prairie City, a project that required a large cut at the summit and a switchback on the descent to the west. When the extension was completed in 1910, the railroad had reached its full length of 80 miles. Because Prairie City was a center not of lumbering but of cattle raising, the final

who had already established himself in the lumber business in Utah. Eccles formed the Oregon Lumber Co. in 1889; the firm was to become the largest lumber operator in the state. He incorporated the Sumpter Valley Railway on August 15, 1890, to build from Baker, on the Union Pacific's Oregon Short Line, along the Powder River to the town of Sumpter (29 miles). The decision to use narrow gauge at this relatively late date was mainly determined by the ready availability of used equipment from the Utah & Northern and the South Park Line. Both were subsidiaries of the Union Pacific, in which Eccles was an influential shareholder.

The railroad began service by hauling logs from the Salisbury area (10 miles) to Oregon Lumber's mill at South Baker on August 1, 1891. Service began to McEwen (22.5 miles) early in 1892. The line did not reach Sumpter until October 3, 1896, but the arrival coincided with a boom in gold mining in the area. As elsewhere, the rise in the price level after 1896 dampened gold mining, and the industry was largely out of existence at Sumpter by 1908. The town was decimated by a fire on August 13, 1917, an event that essentially ended it as a source of significant traffic for the railroad.

The railroad had returned to dependence on lumber. Oregon Lumber had built a spur from S Wye, a mile below Sumpter, up a 4-percent grade on the east slope of Huckleberry Mountain to Larch, about four miles. The railroad took over the spur and extended it down the west side of the mountain to Whitney (43 miles), complet-

ing it on June 1, 1901. The lumber company established a mill at Whitney, and an independent firm, the Nibley Lumber Co., built a mill there in 1911–12. As usual in lumber railroading, the mills at Whitney created a demand for additional timber,

The Sumpter Valley operated with relatively modern wood-burning Mikados. After abandonment of the Uintah Railway in 1939, the SV bought its two articulateds, rebuilt them with tenders, and used them for most later service. (Richard H. Kindig.)

mileage was always the weakest on the rail-road, and the portion that the lumber company had least incentive to perpetuate. Eccles died unexpectedly in 1912, ending any prospect of the railroad's being pushed farther.

Until Eccles's death, the railroad had been operated with a variety of secondhand 4-4-0, 2-6-0, and 2-8-0 locomotives. The management of his heirs beginning in 1915 bought five 2-8-2 locomotives, three from Baldwin and two from Alco. The railroad remained wood-burning, so that the new locomotives had to be equipped with Rushton stacks. A 4-6-0 similarly equipped was bought in 1915 for the daily round-trip passenger train. Four very characteristic wooden passenger cars with arched roofs were bought in 1917.

The railroad was uniformly profitable in the 1920s thanks to a respectable lumber traffic. The extension to Prairie City typically had a single cattle train per week; passenger service was reduced to a rail motor car from Bates in 1929. The cattle traffic, which had moved mainly to the Portland stockyard via the UP, was prone to truck competition. In January 1933 the Interstate Commerce Commission authorized abandonment of the Prairie City extension from a point two miles west of Bates. The last passenger train on the remainder of the railroad ran on July 31, 1937. The company continued to handle passengers in cabooses, however. When the Uintah Railway was abandoned in 1939, the SV bought its two articulated tank engines, converted them to a tender configuration, changed them to oil-burning, and put them in service in mid-1940. The older power was either converted to oil or sold off. For the remainder of the railroad's history, the articulateds provided most of the service. Because of the line's heavy curvature and two remaining summits, the articulateds were very suitable to the operation.

The railroad barely survived World War II. Most of the connecting trackage of private railroads had been abandoned. Three round-trips per week sufficed for the remaining traffic from Bates. The last regularly scheduled trip ran on April 11, 1947, and the final trip of any sort on June 12. The articulated locomotives were sold for further service in Guatemala on the International Railways of Central America. The passenger cars and some of the other motive power went to the White Pass & Yukon. About 1.5 miles of the former Sumpter Valley served the Oregon Lumber mill at South Baker as standard gauge terminal trackage until the mill was closed at the end of 1961.

REFERENCES: Mallory Hope Ferrell, *Rail, Sagebrush and Pine* (San Marino, Calif.: Golden West Books, 1967); Frederic Shaw, Clement Fisher, Jr., and George H. Harlan, *Oil Lamps and Iron Ponies* (San Francisco: Bay Books, 1949), pp. 64–91.

Pennsylvania

For lines in and adjacent to the oil field in McKean County, see the separate section on the network in the Pennsylvania–New York oil field following the Pennsylvania state section, and the map there. For all other Pennsylvania railroads, see the rear endpaper map.

Addison & Northern Pennsylvania Railway

Senator T. C. Platt of New York was the principal instigator of this effort to connect the Tioga County, Pennsylvania, coalfield with the Erie Railroad main line at Addison, New York. His collaborators were William C. Sheldon, an associate of Platt's in the United States Express Co.; Samuel H. Morgan of Addison; Roscoe Conkling, New York's other senator; and several others, most of whom had been active in promoting the narrow gauges in the Pennsylvania oil field to the west. They separately incorporated the Addison & Northern Pennsylvania Railway in New York on June 19, 1882, and in Pennsylvania on July 13, 1882; the railroad always operated as a unity, and in 1883 the two corporations were consolidated formally. The route chosen was from Addison south along Tuscarora Creek, over a summit at Nichols near the state line, down the Cowanesque Valley to Westfield, along Mill Creek into Gaines, and on the north bank of Pine Creek into Galeton, 46 miles. The survey was made by Nathan S. Beardslee in 1882. The route entailed heavy grades, especially from Addison to the state line. The railroad was opened for passen-gers from Addison to Westfield (27 miles) on November 27, 1882. Freight service was extended to Gaines (41 miles) in January 1883. The final five miles from Gaines to Galeton were separately incorporated in 1883 as the New York & Pennsylvania Railroad; it was reported complete except for the bridge into Galeton by December 31, 1884. The NY&P was empowered to build west to Coudersport, but the extension was never undertaken. The promoters of the A&NP organized a subsidiary, the Gaines Coal & Coke Co., to operate mines at Gurnee, to which a spur of 4.5 miles was built east from the main line at Davis in 1884.

The railroad was unusual in seeking to avoid car-to-car transfer of freight entirely. The management's plan was to interchange all freight at Addison by truck-transfer of standard gauge cars. The company proved quite successful, delivering about 400 cars per month to the Erie, mainly coal from the mines at Gurnee, but some lumber and tannery products from the Galeton area. The railroad handled about 250 to 300 cars per month inbound.

In spite of respectable traffic, the A&NP defaulted on its interest payments in August 1885, causing Platt to be appointed receiver in April 1886. The property was sold under foreclosure to Platt and other bondholders on May 5, 1887, and reorganized on July 21, 1887, as the Addison & Pennsylvania Railway. There was no change in directors or officers.

The railroad's practice of operating mainly with standard gauge equipment on narrow gauge trucks was difficult and costly; one of the several accidents that the line suffered from the instability of the standard gauge equipment is described in Part I, Chapter 8. The management converted the railroad to standard gauge in 1893. The two 4-4-0 locomotives and one of the three 2-6-0s were sold to the Baltimore & Lehigh in 1894.

F. H. & C. W. Goodyear, lumber operators in the area, bought the railroad in 1898, and after some corporate reorganization, leased it to their Buffalo & Susquehanna Railroad in 1901. Because the B&S had a parallel line along the south bank of Pine

Creek, the five miles from Gaines to Galeton were abandoned in favor of a quarter-mile connection at Gaines Junction. The former narrow gauge became a branch of the B&S, which was mainly a coal hauler from fields to the south. The long mine spur to Gurnee was abandoned about 1910. The Baltimore & Ohio acquired the B&S along with the principal connection, the Buffalo, Rochester & Pittsburgh, on January 1, 1932. The former narrow gauge was isolated from the rest of the B&O system when a flood wiped out the former B&S main line in the Sinnemahoning area in 1942 and the B&O abandoned the trackage. The isolated remnant was notable for the long survival of its passenger service between Addison and Galeton. The two-car train (hauled until 1947 by an Atlantic locomotive) ran until November 19, 1949, when it was abandoned upon the loss of its railway post office. The B&O sold the isolated line, including the B&S's former Galeton-Wellsville line, in 1955 to the H. E. Salzberg Co., which organized the Wellsville, Addison & Galeton Railroad. The new railroad was mainly dependent on traffic from tanneries at Elkland and Westfield. A weak bridge caused the line from Elkland to Addison to be abandoned in 1960. The remainder of the former narrow gauge was abandoned on March 16, 1979.

REFERENCES: Capt. W. W. Robinson, "The Buffalo & Susquehanna and Its Subsidiaries," Railway & Locomotive Historical Society *Bulletin*, no. 49 (1939), pp. 33–56; C. F. H. Allen, "The Buffalo & Susquehanna Railroad Company," *ibid.*, no. 70 (1947), pp. 44–60; David H. Hamley, "The Sole Leather Line," *Trains*, Feb. 1972, pp. 36–41; Paul Pietrak, *The B&S: Buffalo & Susquehanna Railway* (North Boston, N.Y.: Paul Pietrak, n.d.).

Altoona & Beech Creek Railroad

As the Altoona & Wopsononock Railroad, this late narrow gauge was chartered by Frank G. Patterson of Altoona on May 27, 1890. His interest was in ascending from Altoona to the resort at Wopsononock on Allegheny Mountain northwest of the city and penetrating the coal and timber country beyond. Since Wopsononock was about 1,300 feet above Altoona, the project was a difficult one. The line was designed by W. T. Forsythe, former chief engineer of construction of the Norfolk & Western, who became its general manager. The line was opened from the Pennsylvania Railroad's Juniata station on the north side of Altoona to Wopsononock (8 miles) in May 1891. In the same year the name was changed to the Altoona, Clearfield &

Northern Railroad. On November 24 the shareholders voted to mortgage the railroad for $60,000 to finance the projected extension, and empowered Patterson to issue 600 shares of stock to himself. The extension to Dougherty (13 miles) was built in 1892, but a legal battle had developed that dominated the line's history for the remainder of the 1890s.

In 1892 Patterson agreed to sell 60 percent of the company's stock to James Kerr, Clerk of the U.S. House of Representatives, who was expected to sell the shares to the Pennsylvania Railroad. Before Patterson transferred the shares to Kerr, the directors sold the majority interest to Samuel P. Langdon, who sought the railroad as an entry into Altoona for his Altoona & Philipsburg Connecting Railroad, which reached Ramey, about 17 miles north of Dougherty, in 1894. At the annual meeting of February 1893 factions loyal to Patterson and Langdon each elected boards of directors. The question depended on the validity of the 600 shares issued to Patterson in 1891. The lower court held for Langdon, but the Pennsylvania Supreme Court held the 600 shares validly issued, and seated Patterson's directors. Langdon petitioned for a receivership and was appointed receiver jointly with Patterson. The receivership, which could hardly have been harmonious, was lifted, but when the railroad failed to cover operating expenses, Patterson was again appointed receiver on September 28, 1896. It was sold under foreclosure on February 26, 1897, to W. L. Shellenberger, Patterson's former vice-president, who formed the Altoona & Beech Creek Railroad on April 17. Langdon continued his efforts and leased the railroad in December for the Pittsburgh, Johnstown, Ebensburg & Eastern, as his railroad had been renamed. He formed a terminal com-

pany to extend the line into central Altoona by trestle. He planned to convert the narrow gauge and to extend both segments of his railroad to a junction at East Frugality, about two miles northwest of Dougherty. He was unable to do this, and instead found his lease declared invalid in April 1900. His officers were ordered ejected from the railroad, and it reverted to Shellenberger. The Altoona & Beech Creek resumed independent listing in the *Official Guide* in 1903, which showed the line as extending to Fallen Timber (18 miles) and offering irregular passenger and freight service. No other source shows this extension, and the line is thought not to have been built past Dougherty. Passenger traffic to the resort had declined greatly, and the railroad had a limited coal traffic. In 1904 it operated with two locomotives, seven passenger cars, eight flatcars, and 32 coal cars.

The railroad again became insolvent, was sold under foreclosure to H. A. Davis on April 30, 1910, for $15,000, and was reorganized as the Altoona, Juniata & Northern Railway. Sigmund Morris of Altoona bought the line and on January 16, 1913, merged it into the Altoona Northern Railroad, which he had formed two months earlier. He declared his intention to convert the railroad, electrify it as an interurban, and extend it to Patton on the New York Central's Beech Creek line. He was unable either to electrify it or to extend it, but he converted the line in February 1916. The conversion did little good, for the company was again put in receivership in 1918. It was shut down on July 30, 1919, and dismantled in 1921.

REFERENCE: Richard D. Adams, "The Alley Popper": A History of the Pittsburgh & Susquehanna and Its Predecessor Companies (Vic-

The Altoona & Beech Creek's shops north of Altoona in the early years of the railroad. The coach at left of the locomotive is one of the company's excursion cars. (Ed Bond collection.)

tor, N.Y.: Richard D. Adams, 1980), pp. 14–23, 31–32.

Bell's Gap Railroad

Because its superintendent, Joseph O. Ramsey, was one of the most conspicuous expositors of narrow gauge doctrine, this coal hauler in central Pennsylvania received disproportionate publicity. The railroad was chartered in 1871 and opened in July 1873 from Bell's Mills (Bellwood), seven miles east of Altoona on the Pennsylvania Railroad main line, to Lloyd's (Lloydsville), eight miles. The route followed Bell's Gap Run up the eastern escarpment of Allegheny Mountain. The ascent was concentrated in seven miles with an average gradient of 3 percent and a ruling grade of 3.6 percent. The line had four major trestles, 25, 40, 75, and 65 feet high, ranging from 240 to 366 feet in length, with 27.5° curves on the two highest. The railroad gained 1,120 feet, but stopped 114 feet short of the summit. Traffic was mainly coal for Pennsylvania Railroad locomotives, which moved at the rate of about 300 tons per day, but some lumber was also handled. Upbound movements were typically empty. The line's difficult physical plant, wild surroundings, and spectacular vistas to the east made it a tourist attraction; the rolling stock included three open excursion cars.

From the outset the company was closely identified with the Pennsylvania Railroad. The first president was John Reilly, superintendent of transportation at Altoona. A. J. Cassatt, then vice-president of the Pennsylvania, was a member of the board of directors. The management decided in 1878 to extend the line into some new coal country and did so in 1880, bringing the tracks over the summit and down to Clearfield Creek at Coalport (23 miles).

Ramsey resigned early in 1879. His successor, Robert Ford, did not share Ramsey's view that the railroad would be practical only as a narrow gauge. Preparations for conversion began early in 1881. In mid-1883 the management announced an intention to convert in September and offered the narrow gauge equipment for sale. In 1884, after conversion, the line was extended two miles to Irvona.

The railroad was merged on December 27, 1889, with the Clearfield & Jefferson Railway into the Pennsylvania & Northwestern Railroad. This was absorbed by the Pennsylvania on February 20, 1902, and operated as a branch from Bellwood to Punxsutawney and Fordham. The Pennsylvania ceased operations on the ascent of Al-

The Coudersport & Port Allegany bought only one narrow gauge locomotive new, No. 2, *Francis N. Root*. The Brooks 4-4-0 bore the name of a Buffalo financier who had interested himself in the railroad. (G. M. Best collection, California State Railroad Museum.)

legheny Mountain in 1938 and abandoned the nine miles from Bellwood to Blandburg, just over the summit, in 1941. The Penn Central abandoned the Blandburg-Coalport segment in 1970.

Coudersport & Port Allegany Railroad

Coudersport, seat of Potter County, was a center of lumbering in local hemlock forests, but was without a railroad until relatively late. The Jersey Shore, Pine Creek & Buffalo, an affiliate of the Philadelphia & Reading, had partly graded a route through the town along the headwaters of the Allegheny River in 1874 and 1875, but the

project was then abandoned. Frank W. and James L. Knox, together with some other lumber operators, organized the Coudersport & Port Allegany Railroad on April 1, 1882, to lease the partly completed right-of-way of the JSPC&B between Coudersport and the Western New York & Pennsylvania at Port Allegany, 17 miles west down the Allegheny River. The railroad was built during the summer and opened on October 1, 1882. The route was a water-level grade that proved not difficult to operate. Initially, the line was run with two 4-4-0 locomotives, but a 2-6-0 was added in 1887.

In 1883 the railroad installed a Ramsey Transfer at Port Allegany to allow standard gauge cars of outbound lumber to be loaded at on-line mills. At a shareholders' meeting

A passenger train of the Coudersport & Port Allegany makes a station stop on a snowy day. (Ed Bond collection.)

Pennsylvania   485

of July 1888, the company decided upon conversion. A bond issue of $75,000 was made for the purpose and on June 16, 1889, the railroad was converted.

Subsequently, the railroad was a uniformly prosperous short line for many years. In 1890 the company, through a subsidiary, extended five miles southeast to Sweden Valley, and in 1894–95 it built an extension up a severe grade out of Coudersport east to Newfield Junction on the Buffalo & Susquehanna and to Ulysses on the Fall Brook line of the New York Central. The original line to Port Allegany survived as the company's connection with the Pennsylvania Railroad until July 18, 1942, when the nine miles west of Roulette were wiped out by a flood. The short line now made its outside connection at Newfield Junction; the extension to Ulysses had been abandoned in 1924. The H. E. Salzberg Co. bought the line in 1964 and operated it integrally with their Wellsville, Addison & Galeton, the former Buffalo & Susquehanna. The management secured the ICC's permission to abandon the line on December 8, 1970.

REFERENCES: Paul Pietrak, *The Coudersport & Port Allegany and the New York & Pennsylvania* (North Boston, N.Y.: Paul Pietrak, 1972); Thomas U. Johnson, "Pennsylvania Pigmy," *Trains,* July 1944, pp. 28–33; Bill Reddy, "Northern Tier Narrow Gauge," *Light Iron & Short Ties,* 3, no. 2 (1985), pp. 2–4.

Eagles Mere Railroad

Eagles Mere at the foot of Eagles Mere Lake in Sullivan County developed as a popular resort in the 1880s, in spite of the handicap of a difficult stage journey from Tivoli on the Williamsport & North Branch Railroad. To deal with the problem, C. William Woddrop and his associates incorporated the Eagles Mere Railroad on September 11, 1891, and in the summer of 1892 built a narrow gauge from Sonestown up Occohanock Creek to Eagles Mere (8 miles). Initially the railroad operated with two 4-4-0s, but the management shifted to Climax geared locomotives, which were more suitable to the heavy grades. The lake was at an altitude of 2,500 feet.

In a 99-year lease of March 1, 1901, effective as of April 1, the W&NB assumed operation of the narrow gauge, and announced its intention to convert the line. Instead, the W&NB in 1902 and 1903 extended the narrow gauge about two miles along the west shore of the lake to Eagles Mere Park, a Chautauqua facility, and also to a gauge-compatible connection with the

The East Broad Top's general offices and station at Orbisonia are shown with an excursion train. (Ed Bond collection.)

Susquehanna & Eagles Mere Railway of Charles Sones's lumber interests. A third rail was laid on the W&NB for about two miles south from Sonestown to allow Sones's 3'-0" equipment to reach his tannery at Muncy Valley.

The Eagles Mere, which received only $5,000 per year from the W&NB under the lease, became delinquent on its interest payments on March 1, 1909, and was placed under receiver H. L. Geyelin on February 6, 1911. The line was reorganized without change of name on June 11, 1912, and the lease was continued. The line survived on passenger and lumber revenues, but began declining with the conversion of resort traffic to the automobile. The company was put in receivership on December 22, 1920, again under Geyelin. He shortly died and was replaced by Joel H. DeVista. The company was reorganized on June 21, 1922, as the Eagles Mere Railway with Henry E. Kirk as president. The lease was abrogated and the narrow gauge resumed independent operation. Passenger service had been seasonal in connection with W&NB trains since 1907, but was given up on October 8, 1923. Freight service continued until mid-1927, and the line was abandoned early in 1928.

East Broad Top Railroad & Coal Co.

Completion of the Pennsylvania Railroad main line through the Juniata River valley in 1852 stimulated several projects to tap the Broad Top coalfield about 30 miles to the south. The Huntingdon & Broad Top Mountain Railroad began service to the field in 1856 with a standard gauge line on the west side of Broad Top Mountain. Vari-

ous projects were developed for a line on the east side of the mountain, including the East Broad Top Railroad & Coal Co., chartered on April 16, 1856. After several of the rival projects had failed, Percival Roberts and associates revived the East Broad Top at a meeting of July 3, 1871, and began surveys. At a meeting of June 6, 1872, it was decided to adopt narrow gauge and establish three-rail terminal facilities at the Pennsylvania interchange in Mount Union. The line was opened on August 30, 1873, to Orbisonia (11 miles), which became the line's central office, shop town, and operating headquarters. Roberts built a company town, Rockhill Furnace, across Blacklog Creek from Orbisonia for his Rockhill Iron & Coal Co., which was integral with the railroad. Because the continuation of the route entailed tunnels at Moreland's Gap and Wray's Hill, extension was relatively slow, but the railroad as originally conceived was completed with the opening of its yard at Robertsdale (30 miles) on October 7, 1874. The railroad traversed a water-level grade from Mount Union to Beersville (Pogue) and then a nearly monotonic grade, ranging up to 2.6 percent, to Robertsdale, which is almost at the top of Broad Top Mountain. The financial stringency of the mid-1870s prevented a projected extension across the mountain to Broad Top City.

The prospect of the South Pennsylvania Railroad's being built across the state to the south of the EBT's existing line gave a powerful incentive to extend the narrow gauge. In October 1883 the South Pennsylvania let contracts for its tunnels through Tuscarora Mountain and Sideling Hill and its grade across the Little Aughwick Valley, all of which became part of the Pennsylvania

Turnpike. To provide a railhead for in-bound materials the EBT determined upon a branch southeast from Orbisonia through Blacklog and Shade mountains to the town of Shade Gap, thence southeast to Neelyton, where there were iron ore deposits, and on to a connection with the South Pennsylvania near Burnt Cabins. To build the extension a subsidiary, the Shade Gap Railroad, was incorporated on February 23, 1884; the branch was undertaken quickly and opened to Shade Gap (6 miles) on January 1, 1885. The line was graded beyond Neelyton by midyear, but on July 23, 1885, J. P. Morgan held the famous conference on his yacht in New York harbor at which the South Pennsylvania project was aborted. Work on the extension to Burnt Cabins was necessarily abandoned, and the loss of the expected connection probably prevented the EBT's being converted in the mid-1880s. In 1886 a spur of two miles was built north from Shade Gap to an iron mine of the Rockhill Co. at Stair. The company reportedly planned to extend this line northeast 34 miles to Port Royal on the Pennsylvania, but actually extended it only to Goshorn in 1888 and Nancy in 1890, about four miles. This branch was to last only until about 1905. In 1891 the main line was extended about a mile from Robertsdale to Woodvale to serve a new mine of the parent company. A second subsidiary, the Rocky Ridge Railroad, was organized to build a branch from Rocky Ridge to Evanston (5 miles), opened on May 1, 1908. The EBT finally laid track on the grade into Neelyton and opened the four-mile extension of the Shade Gap branch on November 8, 1909. In 1916 the main line was extended 1.5 miles to Alvan. Except for several mine spurs, the railroad was complete.

Given the railroad's nearly total dependence upon coal and iron ore, its revenues were necessarily highly cyclical. Bonds were largely held by the major shareholders, a situation that insulated the railroad from normal risks of bankruptcy. The railroad and the parent corporation both defaulted on their interest in 1885, and did not resume payments until 1908, but the bondholders made no effort at foreclosure, even though the railroad suffered severely from the depression of the 1890s and a major strike of miners in 1894. About 70 percent of the line's revenue typically came from coal and iron ore, but lumber, silica rock, bricks, and general cargo were also handled. In the peak years two daily passenger trains were run; after 1930 most passengers were handled on mixed trains, especially miners en route to the mines below Orbisonia. Initially, the railroad operated mainly with

The East Broad Top's *Cromwell* was a Baldwin 4-6-0 of 1901, a relatively late narrow gauge passenger locomotive. It served until 1927. (Ed Bond collection.)

Baldwin 2-6-0 and 2-8-0 locomotives, but in 1908 it took delivery of a 2-6-2 and then in 1911 the first of six Baldwin 2-8-2s, which provided the principal motive power for the remainder of the history of the railroad. These engines were part of the most complete upgrading of any of the narrow gauges to scaled-down modern standard gauge practice. In 1913 the EBT took delivery of the first of a series of steel hopper cars, followed by composite and all-steel boxcars. The railroad engaged in ordinary main-line standards of tracklaying and maintenance.

Under the circumstances, it is odd that the line was never converted. There was discussion in 1904 of conversion to facilitate movements of silica bricks from a plant proposed for Orbisonia, but the agreement was never made. Coal from the Rockhill mines, which became increasingly dominant in the railroad's tonnage as the iron ore industry declined and as general cargo went to the highways, was cleaned and classified at a plant in Mount Union incidentally to transfer. Other bulk cargo was transshipped by gravity until the World War I period, by which time such traffic had largely disappeared. In 1933 the railroad began using its timber transfer, which had formerly moved logs between flatcars, to lift standard gauge cars, one end at a time, for mounting on narrow gauge trucks. The railroad maintained two standard gauge switchers at Mount Union for moving cars off the Pennsylvania. The management believed that conversion would have no positive effect on traffic.

On December 22, 1913, the EBT merged the Shade Gap and Rocky Ridge subsidiaries into itself. In 1919 both the Rockhill company and the railroad were bought by Madeira, Hill & Co., a coal operator in several areas of Pennsylvania. Rockhill was merged with another subsidiary of Madeira, Hill into a new Rockhill Coal & Iron Co., which owned all of the securities of the railroad. Traffic in the 1920s was the heaviest in the railroad's history, peaking in 1926 at 25,725,546 ton-miles, about 80 percent coal. In the same year the company's shops assembled M-1, the only orthodox gas-electric passenger unit ever owned by an American narrow gauge, out of components fabricated by Brill and Westinghouse. The unit operated mail and passenger runs on the main line until 1931, and then handled the Shade Gap branch passenger train until it was discontinued in 1935. Thereafter the unit mainly substituted for mixed trains when the mines were closed. In 1925 the management formed the East Broad Top Transit Co. as a subsidiary to operate buses along the line and to points as distant as Huntingdon, McConnellsburg, Tyrone, Chambersburg, Altoona, Hagerstown, and, briefly, State College. The subsidiary was at best marginally profitable, and was sold in the early 1940s.

The entire conglomerate of the mining companies and the railroad declined rapidly after 1926. Rockhill went bankrupt in 1928 and Madeira, Hill both in 1934 and in 1937, being liquidated on the second occasion. Rockhill was sold in 1938 and reorganized as the Rockhill Coal Co., still in control of the railroad. Because the railroad remained profitable, and the Rockhill continued to have its problems, the management in 1941 took the unusual step of seeking the ICC's permission to increase the interest on its bonds from 4 to 6 percent. The ICC approved. The railroad was, however, contracting; the Rocky Ridge branch to Evanston, which had been rendered inoperable by a flood in 1936, was abandoned in 1940 and the Shade Gap–Neelyton line in 1943. The rest of the Shade Gap branch, except for a short segment at Orbisonia, was abandoned in 1949. The railroad, which had been in the black throughout the Depression, lost money in 1946, and except in 1948, was unprofitable thereafter. Independent coal producers were deserting the railroad for trucks, and Rockhill's deep mines were ceasing to be competitive with open-pit mines farther to the west. The railroad dropped its mail trains on June 22, 1953, shifting the mail to the highways for about a year until the contract was canceled. The EBT dropped passenger service entirely on August 15, 1954, simultaneously with the closing of Rockhill's last deep mine. Rockhill was still operating three strip mines on the railroad, but it decided to close one in 1955 and the other two on March 31, 1956. The remaining cargo, ganister rock, did not warrant retention of the railroad; the Pennsylvania declined to buy the property at approximately scrap value to serve this traffic. The EBT applied for abandonment in mid-1955 and received the ICC's permission on February 16, 1956. Regular operation ended with the closing of the strip mines at the end of March, and the railroad was officially abandoned on April 14. The last revenue operation was of standard gauge switcher No. 3 at Mount Union on April 13—just three days short of the centennial of the railroad's chartering.

Rockhill went into liquidation, and the railroad was sold to the Kovalchick Salvage Co., the largest scrap dealer in Pennsylvania. Kovalchick did not undertake to scrap the railroad on the grounds that some 22 million tons of coal remained on the former Rockhill properties, and that the railroad might again be demanded. Other operators did begin mining the Rockhill lands, but the output moved in trucks. Beginning in 1960 about 3.5 miles of the line at Orbisonia were restored to service for passenger excursions. In 1963 standard gauge track was laid on a portion of the Shade Gap line for a trolley museum, the Shade Gap Electric Railway. The excursion operations continue, though it is currently unclear whether the railroad will continue as a museum or be scrapped. It is unlikely to be restored to commercial coal hauling.

REFERENCE: Lee Rainey and Frank Kyper, *East Broad Top* (San Marino, Calif.: Golden West Books, 1982).

Greenlick Narrow Gauge Railroad

G. H. Everson of Scottdale and his associates secured a charter for this company on October 19, 1874, to serve the Mount Vernon iron ore bank on the west escarpment of Chestnut Ridge east of the town. The railroad was built in the summer of 1875 and reportedly opened in late October. The line ran 3.5 miles from Greenlick Junction on the Baltimore & Ohio to Mount Vernon Mines. It was a small railroad of one locomotive, one passenger car, and 22 freight cars. Traffic was almost entirely of iron and coal; passenger revenue for 1890 was reported as $71. Extensions were considered of five miles from the junction to Tarrs in 1876 and of seven miles to Connellsville in 1877, but only the original mileage was ever built.

The line operated irregularly in the early 1890s. It was sold by the sheriff of Fayette County on June 17, 1892, and immediately reorganized as the Greenlick Railway without change in ownership. Daniel H. Pershing remained president. The pattern of occasional operation continued. In 1894 the line was leased to W. P. Hurst, who reportedly operated it from July to September 1895 and then forfeited the lease. That apparently ended regular operation of the railroad. *Poor's Manual* reported it abandoned in 1900, and the company reported the rails removed and equipment sold in its annual report to the ICC in 1902.

Kane & Elk Railroad

The James Brothers firm, which produced lumber, chemicals, and glass, incorporated the Kane & Elk in 1895, mainly as a facility to serve its plant at East Kane. Making use of the equipment and some of the right-of-way of an unincorporated private carrier of the firm, the Kane Oil Field Railroad, which dated from 1886, James Brothers built a main line in 1896 from Kane on the Pittsburgh & Western to Coon Run Junction on the Tionesta Valley, about ten miles. (It is shown on the map of the network in the Pennsylvania–New York oil field, in the next section.) The firm established a company town, James City, at the halfway point. As on most such railroads, there was a varying mileage of branches. The line was almost wholly a facility of the company, which apparently kept it in common carrier status to participate in interline rates.

As on many lumber railroads, the exact process of conversion is unclear. The company began laying third rail in 1903 to bring standard gauge cars into James City. The outer five miles of the main line are thought never to have been converted, but abandoned in 1911. In the same year the company removed the last of the 3'-0" trackage serving the East Kane plant in response to the B&O's conversion of the former P&W. As a standard gauge railroad from East Kane to James City, plus branches, the K&E operated until 1931 and then lay idle until it was abandoned in 1945.

REFERENCE: Thomas T. Taber III, "Sawmills among the Derricks," in *The Logging Railroad Era of Lumbering in Pennsylvania*, ed. Benjamin F. G. Kline, Jr., et al. (3 vols.; Lancaster, Penn.: Benjamin F. G. Kline, Jr., 1973), vol. 2, pp. 778–83.

Lancaster, Oxford & Southern Railroad

The Peach Bottom Railway was projected from the East Broad Top coalfield at Orbisonia to the Delaware River at Philadelphia or Wilmington, crossing the Susquehanna River between the two towns named Peach Bottom, one in York County and the other in Lancaster County. The enterprise was organized in three divisions, of which the Western, between York and the coalfield, was never undertaken. The Middle Division, between York and Peach Bottom, York County, became the variously named predecessor of the Maryland & Pennsylvania north of the Mason-Dixon Line (see York & Peach Bottom Railway, below). The Eastern Division became this local narrow gauge of 20 miles between Peach Bottom (Lancaster County) and Oxford.

Stephen G. Boyd and various businessmen of York, Lancaster, and Chester counties secured an act of the Pennsylvania legislature chartering the Peach Bottom Railway in 1868. In 1871 surveying was begun in York County and 3'-0" chosen. Ground near Oxford was broken for the Eastern Division in August 1872 by Samuel R. Dickey, the railroad's leading supporter in Lancaster County. Revenue service from Oxford to Hopewell (3 miles) began on November 10, 1873. By the end of the year track was approaching White Rock (8 miles). The line reached Goshen (14 miles) on November 25, 1874, but temporarily could be pressed no farther because of the financial stringency of the time. Only an additional mile to Eldora was built in 1875. In the spring of 1876 track was pushed on to Dorsey (19 miles), but because of difficult grading on the 3-percent descent to the Susquehanna, the line was not completed to Peach Bottom until 1878. Although there were two ferries at Peach Bottom, one of which was taken over by the railroad, cars were never ferried across the river and the company never raised the funds even to begin a bridge. Accordingly, the Eastern Division proved to be only an isolated narrow gauge dependent on agricultural traffic. Freight and passengers were mainly interchanged with the Philadelphia & Baltimore Central (Pennsylvania) at Oxford. The narrow gauge also connected with the Columbia & Port Deposit Railroad, the Pennsylvania's freight line on the east bank of the Susquehanna, at Peach Bottom.

In January 1877 Boyd had been removed as president of the railroad and replaced by Charles R. McConkey of Peach Bottom, York County. J. A. Alexander became superintendent of the Eastern Division at Oxford. The company was unprofitable, and in March 1881 was placed in receivership by the Allentown Rolling Mill Co., which had received no interest on the bonds issued to it in payment for the original rails. Antagonism between representatives of York and Lancaster counties resulted in the railway's being separately reorganized. The Lancaster County line was sold to C. W. Leavitt, a New York iron dealer who was one of the principal creditors. He reorganized the property as the Peach Bottom Railroad. This corporation retained rights to the ferry line and to the landing areas on both sides of the river. Leavitt converted the ferry from hand-powered flatboats to a crude sternwheel steamer, operated under lease by the Shank family.

In the summer of 1884 a downpour caused extensive flooding in the railroad's tributary area, and destroyed the trestle over Octoraro Creek at Pine Grove, along with timbers already brought in for replacement of the structure. The damage amounted to $75,000. The railroad in this period operated a market train equipped with cars 42′ × 10′ to collect produce for transshipment at Oxford to Philadelphia.

The Baltimore & Ohio acquired an equity in the railroad and planned to use it as part of a projected branch to Lancaster. The plan entailed a branch off the Peach Bottom Railroad from a point near White Rock to Quarryville and an extension from Oxford to Singerly, Maryland, on the B&O's Philadelphia line. Both were to be built to 4′-8½″, and the portion of the narrow gauge from Oxford to White Rock was to be converted. The B&O hoped to acquire the Lancaster & Reading Narrow Gauge Railroad, which, its name to the contrary, had been built as a standard gauge line from Lancaster to Quar-

The Lancaster, Oxford & Southern provided a purely local service function to an agricultural area. This short train is typical of its operations. (Ben Kline collection.)

ryville in 1875 and operated under lease to the Philadelphia & Reading. The narrow gauge's charter provided for branches of no more than ten miles. The Quarryville branch would have qualified, but the Singerly extension was longer. Consequently, it was arranged that Allentown Rolling Mill would again foreclose a mortgage so that the railroad could be reorganized with broader powers as the Lancaster, Oxford & Southern Railroad. The new corporation took over on September 3, 1890. The B&O bought 10,000 ties for conversion of the narrow gauge, but also sent the company some 3′-0″ equipment from its recently converted Clarksburg, Weston & Glenville in West Virginia. The P&R, however, gave up its lease on the L&RNG in 1893, and the Pennsylvania bought the property in 1898, effectively denying the B&O entry into Lancaster. This caused the B&O to lose interest in the narrow gauge, and neither the conversion nor the planned extensions were made.

The Pennsylvania Railroad dammed Octoraro Creek for a water supply, flooding the LO&S's bridge at Pine Grove. The larger railroad built a new and stronger structure, improving one of the worst parts of a poor physical plant. In 1904 Walter Franklin, president of the LO&S, again raised the prospect of a branch to Quarryville. The company undertook the project as a narrow

gauge branch from a wye at Fairmount, completing it (8 miles) late in 1905. Regular service began January 1, 1906. The extension was expensive, entailing a cut 25 feet deep plus a fill 25 feet high and a half mile long in the course of crossing the summit between Octoraro and Pequea creeks. Building the branch as a narrow gauge extension, rather than converting the property, proved a disastrous error. The branch's capital and operating costs turned out to be about three times its revenues. The railroad's gross receipts declined after 1909, partly because of highway competition and partly because of the diversion of traffic to rural trolley lines in the area. The management tried to interest Conestoga Traction in assuming the Quarryville-Oxford portion as an extension of its line south from Lancaster, but was unsuccessful. The company again went bankrupt and was placed in receivership under John A. Nauman on March 4, 1911. He shut the line down temporarily late in 1911. The company was reorganized as the Lancaster, Oxford & Southern Railway on December 28, 1912, with Nauman as president. Ownership had passed to Fred S. Williams of Baltimore and some associates. The railroad continued to do very poorly, and its physical plant deteriorated rapidly. The Pennsylvania Railroad placed an embargo on shipments to it effective July 1,

1914, again causing a suspension in operations. The management continued to handle mail on the main line with a motorized handcar. Local people, including some of the railroad's employees, bought the property for $40,000 and restored service on August 27, 1914. The railroad commissioned Lawrence Kirk of Havre de Grace to convert its best wooden coach into a gas-mechanical motor car. The vehicle went into service in June 1915 between Oxford and Quarryville; it was too heavy for the iron rail on the west end of the main line.

The railroad had an excellent year in 1916, but its fortunes declined rapidly in 1917. Taking advantage of the booming scrap market during World War I, the management closed the Quarryville branch on April 17, 1917, realizing $32,000—only $8,000 less than the owners had paid for the entire railroad. The motor car was sold to the Grasse River Railroad, and converted to standard gauge. The LO&S ceased regular operation in December 1918 but operated irregularly until October 18, 1919, when it was abandoned. It was shortly removed, and the owners received in liquidation about $250 for every $100 they had invested. The motor car survives in the Railroad Museum of Pennsylvania in Strasburg.

REFERENCES: Benjamin F. G. Kline, Jr., *"Little, Old and Slow": The Life and Trials of the Peach Bottom and Lancaster, Oxford and Southern Railroads* (Lancaster, Penn.: Benjamin F. G. Kline, Jr., 1985); William Moedinger, Jr., "Peachy," *Trains*, Oct. 1943, pp. 37–42; George W. Hilton, *The Ma & Pa: A History of the Maryland & Pennsylvania Railroad* (Berkeley, Calif.: Howell-North Books, 1963; 2d ed., San Diego, Calif.: Howell-North Books, 1980), pp. 29–36.

Lewisburg & Buffalo Valley Railroad

Monroe H. Culp & Co. organized this railroad on May 10, 1897, as a facility for its mill at Linntown just outside Lewisburg. The charter provided for 15 miles of common carrier narrow gauge track from Lewisburg to Culp's Station, a camp of the company. Unincorporated logging trackage extended beyond the camp. Third rail was laid from Lewisburg to Linntown. The line operated with Climax locomotives, the first of which was bought on June 17, 1897. The management bought a secondhand coach for passenger operations, probably in expectation of a projected extension to Loganton. The extension was not built, and the coach was sold to the New Berlin & Winfield. The railroad's nominal carrier status served mainly to allow condemnation

of a right-of-way, but would have become bona fide if the line had reached Loganton, 47 miles from Lewisburg.

Culp moved his lumbering operation to Oldtown, Maryland, and accordingly shut the Linntown mill and abandoned the railroad in 1906.

REFERENCE: Benjamin F. G. Kline, Jr., "Pitch Pine and Prop Timber," in *The Logging Railroad Era of Lumbering in Pennsylvania*, ed. Kline et al., vol. 1, pp. 115–30.

Ligonier Valley Rail Road

As the Latrobe & Ligonier Rail Road, this enterprise was chartered on April 15, 1853, but never financed. On May 2, 1871, the charter was amended and the name changed to Ligonier Valley Rail Road. The plan remained to build a standard gauge railroad from Latrobe, a town on the main line of the Pennsylvania Railroad 41 miles east of Pittsburgh, through Loyalhanna Gap to Ligonier (10 miles), with extensions to coal mines at Fort Palmer and to iron deposits in the area. The promoters, led by S. H. Baker of Latrobe, planned to grade the railroad and lease it to the Pennsylvania, which would provide the iron and equipment, and then operate it as a branch. Most of the grading was done in 1873, but the project then failed before rail was laid. The uncompleted railroad was sold on October 9, 1875, to Henry D. Foster of Greensburg for $3,810. It was arranged that the Mellon brothers of Pittsburgh should complete the line as contractors. They built the line at a cost of $58,516, and opened it on November 10, 1877. The Mellons continued to operate the railroad and came into ownership of it; Andrew W. Mellon became its secretary-treasurer.

The railroad was a typical small narrow gauge of two locomotives, two passenger cars, a baggage car, and 18 freight cars. In 1878 the management installed at Latrobe the first Ramsey Transfer ever used on any narrow gauge. The officers soured on the narrow gauge relatively early and converted the railroad to the Pennsylvania's 4'-9" in December 1882. The railroad continued as a relatively prosperous short line in the hands of the Mellon family, with a good coal traffic and frequent passenger service, largely to a recreational facility, Idlewild Park. The railroad was abandoned in September 1952.

REFERENCE: R. L. McCool, "Millionaire's Railroad," *Railroad Magazine*, May 1952, pp. 42–55. (Inaccurate.)

Montrose Railway

Citizens of Montrose secured a charter for this company in April 1869, planning to link their town with the main line of the Pennsylvania & New York Railroad & Canal Co. (Lehigh Valley) at Tunkhannock, 27 miles to the south. They proved unable to finance the project, and in 1872 the Lehigh Valley acquired about a 55 percent stock interest in the corporation. The LV's management in that year built the line from Tunkhannock to Hunter's (22 miles), and in 1873 added about three more miles before being stopped on November 26 by the terms of an agreement not to borrow money for the project. The remaining two miles into Montrose were not built until 1876. An extension north to Binghamton was projected but not undertaken. Because the LV's stock control was only partial, the railroad was independently operated, but James I. Blakslee, the LV's superintendent of coal branches, served as the line's president. Third rail was laid along the southernmost six or seven miles about 1895. The railroad was operated initially with two and later with three narrow gauge locomotives, and about 31 cars.

The railroad's separate operation was ended on January 10, 1898, when the LV assumed direct operating responsibility. The line was not converted until November 1903, however. The LV secured full stock control in the course of a reorganization into the Montrose Railroad in September and October of 1905. On November 1, 1905, the new corporation was leased to the LV until December 1, 1987. The line was thereafter operated simply as an LV branch until service was discontinued early in 1974. An abandonment application was dismissed by the ICC in June 1975, but the line was abandoned upon the LV's incorporation into Conrail in 1976.

REFERENCE: Robert F. Archer, *The History of the Lehigh Valley Railroad: The Route of the Black Diamond* (Berkeley, Calif.: Howell-North Books, 1977), p. 63.

Mount Gretna Narrow Gauge Railway
Gauge: 2'-0"

The Cornwall & Lebanon Railroad, a standard gauge line that became part of the Pennsylvania Railroad, sought to develop Mount Gretna Park as a picnic ground adjacent to a military reservation of the Pennsylvania National Guard in Lebanon County. The management conceived of a

The Mount Gretna Narrow Gauge was essentially an amusement facility. Here one of its characteristic trains of a 4-4-0 locomotive and some cross-bench open cars stops for a photograph on the line. (Railroad Museum of Pennsylvania.)

Right: The tiny engines of the Mount Gretna Narrow Gauge were the only 2′-0″ locomotives of 4-4-0 wheel arrangement ever built for domestic service. (Frederic Shaw collection, California State Railroad Museum.)

The Newport & Sherman's Valley Railroad's terminal at Newport was a relatively well designed interchange facility with two three-rail tracks. (Railroad Museum of Pennsylvania.)

narrow gauge as a tourist attraction to climb Mount Governor Dick and also to develop a brownstone deposit on the west side of the mountain. A 2'-0" line of about four miles was built from the Mount Gretna station up the mountain with grades of 3.5 to 4.5 percent. A branch of about five-eighths of a mile was run to a rifle range in the military reservation. The line, which apparently had no separate incorporation, was opened under the name of the Mount Gretna Narrow Gauge Railway on July 4, 1889. Three Baldwin 4-4-0s—the only 2'-0" 4-4-0s ever built for domestic service—operated the little line. Passenger rolling stock was ten open cars, three of which behind a 4-4-0 constituted the typical train. The railroad had flatcars and dump cars for maintenance of way, but whether they hauled brownstone as planned is unclear.

The narrow gauge initially was quite successful, but its novelty shortly wore off. At the end of the 1896 season the ascent of the mountain beyond the junction with the branch to the rifle range was removed. The remaining mile of the main line and the branch survived until the World War I period. On July 11, 1915, about 20 soldiers jumped onto the rear car of a two-car train at the loop at the rifle range, upsetting it and injuring several passengers. The acci-

dent was one of several causes of the abandonment of the line at the end of the 1915 season. The track was removed in 1916.

REFERENCES: H. T. Crittenden, "Mount Gretna Narrow Gauge Railway," Railway & Locomotive Historical Society *Bulletin*, no. 57 (1942), pp. 99–102; John D. Siebert, "The Mount Gretna Narrow Gauge Railway," *National Railway Bulletin*, 49, no. 6 (1984), pp. 4–11.

New Berlin & Winfield Railroad

One of the last narrow gauges undertaken, the New Berlin & Winfield was organized on September 27, 1904, by I. C. Burd of Shamokin. The purpose was to serve the general transportation demands of an agricultural area along Penns Creek in Union County. In particular, the population sought more ready access to the county seat, Lewisburg, via the Philadelphia & Reading at Winfield. The railroad was built from Winfield on the west bank of the Susquehanna River to New Berlin, a town of 527 people (8 miles), in 1905, and reported completed in July. It was a small narrow gauge of three locomotives, five passenger cars, and eight freight cars, the sort of facility generally thought obsolete some 20 years

earlier. The line offered relatively dense passenger service, typically of three trains in each direction daily except Sunday.

Inevitably, the traffic was of a character to be vulnerable even to early motor competition. The property was placed under receiver F. E. Tier on October 2, 1912, and abandoned on September 19, 1916.

REFERENCE: Benjamin F. G. Kline, Jr., "New Berlin & Winfield RR," *Narrow Gauge and Short Line Gazette*, July 1977, pp. 68–71.

Newport & Sherman's Valley Railroad

Lumberman David Gring operated a narrow gauge private carrier, the Diamond Valley Railroad, at Barre, Pennsylvania, but when he found himself unable to extend the lease on his timberland, he sought another area for operation and hit upon the Sherman's Valley in Perry County. He secured a charter on July 30, 1890, for the Newport & Sherman's Valley Railroad, intending it to reach the upper portion of the county from Newport, 27 miles west of Harrisburg on the Pennsylvania Railroad main line. The standard gauge Perry County Railroad had reached New Bloomfield, the county seat, from Duncannon, 13 miles east of Newport, in 1889. Gring began building his narrow gauge immediately upon receiving his charter and opened it to Loysville (15 miles) in January 1891. Construction was pushed up the valley of Sherman's Creek on a route chosen to forestall penetration of the Perry County Railroad into the region. The railroad reported itself completed to New Germantown (29 miles) on December 31, 1892, although full service was not established until early 1893. The Perry County Railroad began service to Loysville, with a short branch to Landisburg, also early in 1893. The route directly paralleled the N&SV from Bloomfield Junction to Greenpark (Green Park); the Pennsylvania Superior Court found the narrow gauge to have priority at a crossing at Bloomfield Junction.

Gring, planning to extend the narrow gauge to the south to some timber stands and to limestone deposits in Franklin County, chartered the Path Valley Railroad on October 24, 1893. The line, projected as an extension of the N&SV from New Germantown to Hancock, Maryland, was surveyed as far as Fannettsburg, and graded for about six miles. The route from the Sherman's Valley into the Path Valley would have entailed a crossing of Conococheague Mountain with approaches of 4 percent and a tunnel of 2,600 feet about 300 feet below the summit. The tunnel was actually undertaken, but on the basis of the first 100 feet of drilling at each portal, the rock was judged to be fragmented and unstable. The project ground to a halt in 1894 and could not be revived, in spite of attempts as late as 1910. About two miles of the grade were used by the Perry Lumber Co. for its logging railroad. This firm, formed by Edward Bailey of Harrisburg and his associates in 1900, preferred a standard gauge railroad, but felt constrained to have a gauge compatible with the N&SV. This led to reports that the N&SV was to be converted in the summer of 1901, but instead the lumber company built a 3'-0" line. The lumber railroad made use of the N&SV's shop facilities in Newport and shipped carloads of tanbark directly to a plant of the Oak Extract Co. in Newport. The lumbering operation was brought to an end in 1905.

Both the railroads in Perry County suffered from the depression of the 1890s, but the standard gauge more than the narrow. The Perry County proved unable to finance an extension in 1894, and went bankrupt in 1903. Gring bought it for $75,000 on September 14, 1903, and reorganized it as the Susquehanna River & Western Railroad. He was confronted by the problem of the redundant main lines beyond Bloomfield Junction. Since the narrow gauge was the more profitable and in the better physical condition, he chose to abandon the stan-

dard gauge line in 1904, leaving Landisburg without a railroad. Gring arranged for the N&SV to lease the SR&W, and combined the general offices in Newport. There were further rumors of conversion of the N&SV to standard gauge, but nothing was done. Rather, on March 16, 1918, Gring announced that operation of the SR&W would be suspended on April 1 for conversion of its entire line to narrow gauge. The N&SV would be abandoned from Bloomfield Junction to Newport, and the interchange with the Pennsylvania would be consolidated at Duncannon. He did not follow through with this remarkable idea, but did lay third rail on 2.5 miles of the SR&W to bring narrow gauge trains into New Bloomfield.

Mainly as a consequence of early motor competition, the railroad went bankrupt, and according to an announcement of January 14, 1920, was to be sold in Philadelphia on March 31. David Gring died a few days before the sale. The railroad was bought for $40,000, about 10 percent of book value, by his son Rodney Gring and George H. Ross, president of the Susquehanna Coal Co., a subsidiary of the Pennsylvania Railroad. Their first announced plan was to extend standard gauge rails from New Bloomfield to Blain, four miles from New Germantown; presumably they intended to abandon the rest of the narrow gauge. Instead, they discontinued passenger trains between Newport and Bloomfield Junction on April 21, 1920, and began handling all passengers via Duncannon with a change of trains at New Bloomfield. Virtually all freight was shifted to this route, and after the shops and offices were shifted from Newport to New Bloomfield in 1921, the narrow gauge was abandoned from Newport to Bloomfield. The remainder of the narrow gauge was operated under the name of the SR&W.

Loss of its mail contract caused the railroad to discontinue passenger service on December 31, 1928. The railroad had organized a subsidiary, the Sherman's Valley Transportation Co., for bus and truck service on adjacent roads. The narrow gauge survived into the Depression, but was then cut back from New Germantown to Blain

in 1930 and to Loysville in 1933. The remaining segment, New Bloomfield–Loysville, was abandoned in April 1934 and removed about a year later. The bus replacement was discontinued in November 1934. The standard gauge line deteriorated until it was closed with an ICC embargo on off-line freight cars in November 1938. It last operated in March 1939, and was formally abandoned under an ICC order of May 17, 1939.

REFERENCE: Richard H. Steinmetz and Frederick A. Kramer, *Bells & Whistles in Old Perry* (Westfield, N.J.: Bells & Whistles, 1974).

Pittsburgh & Castle Shannon Railroad
Gauge: 3'-4"

Organized in September 1871 and opened on November 1, 1871, this may have been the first American common carrier narrow gauge. The unique 3'-4" gauge derived from mine tramways in the local coalfield. This was a short railroad, initially of only six miles from a bluff opposite downtown Pittsburgh to Castle Shannon, but it was integral with extensive coal mining operations. By 1876 the line was reported to have six locomotives, seven passenger cars, and 416 coal cars. The coal cars were lowered by a funicular to Carson Street below. A bond issue was passed to build a funicular for passengers in 1888. The company mined 3,509,503 bushels of coal in 1882. At the same time it began selling residential lots in the Castle Shannon area to stimulate passenger travel. At its peak, the railroad ran 23 passenger trains per day. The line was extended a half mile to Arlington on the abandoned right-of-way of the Pittsburgh Southern about 1890.

The company's plans for more substantial extension were frustrated by internal discord. The management, led by president Milton D. Hays, organized a subsidiary, the Pittsburgh, Castle Shannon & Southern, intended to press the line south to Washington, Morgantown (West Virginia), and points beyond. At a shareholders' meeting of August 1, 1878, Hays was accused of a conflict of interest that favored the subsidiary, which had come to be known as the Pittsburgh Southern. A committee appointed to look into the charges reported on August 15 that "the interests of the company had suffered greatly from want of harmony in the management." Hays offered his resignation and it was accepted. In return, charges against him were dropped. The consequence was to divorce the two railroads, which proceeded on separate courses. Also as a consequence of this conflict, the company was put in receivership on April 25, 1879, but the receivership was lifted in 1880.

The railroad generally showed a profit until the depressed years of the 1890s, when it was usually in the red. The company was sold in 1900 to Robert McD. Lloyd, who conveyed it to the Pittsburgh Coal Co. Its coal traffic had decreased somewhat, but its passenger operations were now unprofitable owing to rivalry with the electric streetcar lines spreading about the city. In mid-1905 the line was leased to Pittsburgh Railways, which laid a third rail for its 5'-2½" streetcars and strung overhead trolley wire. Streetcars used sidings to allow steam freights to pass. This arrangement lasted until the narrow gauge was abandoned in 1909.

REFERENCE: N. Critchett, "Double Gauge," *Railroad Stories*, Nov. 1935, pp. 111–15. (Inaccurate.)

Pittsburgh & Western Railroad

Alone among the narrow gauges, the Pittsburgh & Western was an end-to-end amalgamation of various lines built separately. As a consequence, the railroad had the most complicated formal organization of any of the narrow gauges. The corporate history of the P&W submitted by the Baltimore & Ohio to the Interstate Commerce Commission's valuation section in 1922 ran to 240 typescript pages; the corporate diagram that accompanied the submission showed 34 corporations or other owning entities, including no fewer than eight separate incorporations of the Pittsburgh & Western itself. In the interest of clarity and brevity, the present history is accompanied by a table of the line's mileage presented geographically from Allegheny (now the portion of Pittsburgh north of the Allegheny and Ohio rivers) to the termini; the reader should also consult the detailed map of the railroad on the front endpaper. Also for simplification, the history will be treated under the three principal geographical divisions of the enterprise.

Main Line

The actual pattern of the Pittsburgh & Western system was a Y-shape with the stem running north from the Pittsburgh metropolitan area along Pine Creek and then diverging into a main line northwest to the New Castle area and a branch running northeast to a connection with the narrow gauge network in the Pennsylvania oil field

Segment	Built by	Total miles	Year built
Main Line			
Allegheny–Etna	Pittsburgh & Western	5	1879
Etna–Zelienople	Pittsburgh, New Castle & Lake Erie	30	1878
Zelienople–Wurtemburg	Pittsburgh & Western	12	1880
Duck Run Jct.–Chewton	Pittsburgh & Western	6	1882
Northern Branch			
Callery Jct.–Butler	Pittsburgh & Western	14	1882
Butler–Karns City	Karns City & Butler	17	1876
Karns City–Parker	Parker & Karns City	10	1874
Parker–Foxburg	Pittsburgh & Western	3	1883
Foxburg–Turkey City	Foxburg, St. Petersburg & Clarion	8	1877
Turkey City–Jefferson	Foxburg, St. Petersburg & Clarion	5	1878
Branch			
Emlenton–Jefferson	Emlenton & Shippenville	12	1876
Jefferson–Edenburg	Emlenton & Shippenville	3	1876
Edenburg–Clarion Jct.	Clarion Extension of the Emlenton & Shippenville	8	1877
Branch			
Clarion Jct.–Clarion	Clarion Extension of the Emlenton & Shippenville	7	1877
Clarion Jct.–Frost	Pittsburgh, Bradford & Buffalo	34	1881
Frost–Sheffield Jct.	Pittsburgh, Bradford & Buffalo	26	1882
Sheffield Jct.–Kane	Pittsburgh, Bradford & Buffalo	18	1883
Kane–Mt. Jewett	Pittsburgh & Western	13	1883

at Mount Jewett. The name of the railroad derived from the ambitions of the promoters to extend the main line into Ohio to connect with the Painesville & Youngstown and the Cleveland, Delphos & St. Louis, and thus with the Grand Narrow Gauge Trunk. The first project to build on this route was the Pittsburgh & Northwestern Railroad of 1875, which could not be built. The company bought control of the Lawrenceville & Evergreen Passenger Railway, a local suburban line, as a projected entry into Allegheny. The Pittsburgh, New Castle & Lake Erie Railroad, organized September 21, 1877, managed to build from Etna at the mouth of Pine Creek, just east of Allegheny, up the creek and to Zelienople, 30 miles, in 1878. Although the line was put in service on January 1, 1879, and the proprietors did some additional grading at both ends, they proved unable to continue. The property was sold by the sheriff of Allegheny County on August 27, 1879, to James Callery, John Chalfant, and A. M. Brown, who formed the Pittsburgh & Western. Callery, who later had an interest in the Cleveland, Delphos & St. Louis, was particularly identified with extension into Ohio. The new corporation quickly completed the southern extension along the north bank of the Allegheny River from Etna into downtown Allegheny. The extension was built in 1879 and put in service in 1880 without making use of the Lawrenceville & Evergreen. A three-story station was built at River Avenue and Anderson Street. Whatever may

have been the P&W's shortcomings, it had a direct entry into the Pittsburgh region and excellent terminal properties in Allegheny—two features that assured it of the continued interest of larger railroads.

On the north end, Callery and his associates in 1880 pushed the narrow gauge west from Zelienople along the Connoquenessing River to Duck Run Junction (Frisco) and up Slippery Rock Creek to Wurtemburg, a total of 12 miles. The P&W made only one further extension of the narrow gauge on its main line, six miles from Duck Run Junction to Chewton—a town across the Beaver River from Wampum—placed in service on August 28, 1882. This was some ten miles short of the immediate goal of New Castle Junction, but by this time the management had decided to convert. The extension to New Castle Junction was built to standard gauge, and plans for conversion of the existing line were announced in March 1882. The railroad began standard gauge service from Pittsburgh to New Castle on January 1, 1883. Oddly, Callery continued to expect the Cleveland, Delphos & St. Louis to make a connection to Pittsburgh, and planned to relay 3'-0" rails on the P&W's main line to allow an entry.

Northern Branch South of the Allegheny River Crossing at Foxburg

The basic element of the Pittsburgh & Western's north branch south of the Alle-

A Pittsburgh & Western train, mainly of cut lumber, moves through denuded timberland. (Ed Bond collection.)

gheny River was the Parker & Karns City, formed by Stephen Duncan Karns, Fullerton Parker, and associates in 1873 to serve a portion of the Butler County oil field. The railroad was opened on April 8, 1874. The ascent from the river at Parker was very difficult, with several trestles, the largest of which was 78 feet high. The line cost $200,000, or about $20,000 per mile, excluding equipment. The railroad had four locomotives, one baggage car, four passenger cars, and 36 freight cars.

The same promoters on March 21, 1876, organized the Karns City & Butler Railroad to extend the railroad to Butler, the major town in the area. The extension was opened on October 27, 1876, and initially did very well because of activity in the Butler oil field. About 20,000 barrels per day were reportedly produced within three miles of the right-of-way of the two railroads. By 1881, however, the Butler oil field was declining relative to the larger field in and near McKean County to the northeast. In an effort to build to McKean County, the Pittsburgh & Western acquired the Parker &

Karns City and Karns City & Butler and merged both into itself on June 15, 1881, along with some standard gauge railroads that would be useful in its projected extension into Ohio. The two narrow gauge acquisitions were isolated from the P&W's main line by about 14 miles, but Callery immediately undertook a connection from Hiawatha, which he renamed Callery Junction, to Butler. Through trains from Allegheny to Butler were inaugurated on December 1, 1882, a month before the main line was converted. A third rail was retained on the main line between Callery Junction and Allegheny for the narrow gauge trains. The management apparently planned for this arrangement to continue indefinitely, and it consolidated the predecessors' shops in Zelienople and Parker into a shop in Allegheny for equipment of both gauges. The relegation of Butler to narrow gauge status was an impossible competitive disadvantage, however, and the management decided to extend standard gauge there. The *Railway Reporter* of Pittsburgh reported "widening of track" to Butler in its issue of October 25, 1884. *Poor's Manual* reported the segment from Callery Junction to Butler as three-rail through 1889, however. Although in April 1884 the *Railway Reporter* stated that the P&W intended to convert the northern branch as far as Parker, it did not do so. The Butler-Parker portion remained narrow gauge well into the period of control by the Baltimore & Ohio, to be treated below.

Northern Branch North of the Allegheny River Crossing at Foxburg

The line north of the Allegheny had its origin in two short narrow gauges, both built to serve the Clarion County oil field from points on the Allegheny Valley Railroad. The earlier and larger was formed as the Emlenton & Shippenville Railroad on June 2, 1875, and built from Emlenton on the Allegheny to Edenburg in the oil field in 1876, completing the line near the end of the year. In February 1877 the company incorporated a subsidiary, the Clarion Extension of the Emlenton & Shippenville Railroad, to build the 15 miles from Edenburg to Clarion, the principal town in the area. The extension was opened December 20, 1877. During 1877 the railroad had apparently been informally known as the Emlenton & Clarion, but on December 10, 1877, the management formally adopted the name Emlenton, Shippenville & Clarion for the entire enterprise. The railroad was 30 miles long, of low physical standards, but financially quite successful.

The Foxburg, St. Petersburg & Clarion operated over this relatively well built trestle in Pennsylvania. (Walter Casler, Ben Kline collections.)

The other of the two entries into the Clarion County oil field was the Foxburg, St. Petersburg & Clarion, promoted by William L. Fox and associates to penetrate the difficult mountain country from Foxburg, five miles south of Emlenton. The railroad was organized on March 12, 1877, and put in service to St. Petersburg (4 miles) in September. By the end of the year it had reached Turkey City and early in 1878 it made a connection with the line from Emlenton at Jefferson. Fox bought control of the Emlenton line in 1879 and became president of both companies. He organized the Foxburg, Kane & Bradford Railroad to build an extension to the McKean County oil field from Clarion Junction. On March 14, 1881, the three companies were merged into the Pittsburgh, Bradford & Buffalo Railway. This corporation built most of the projected extension, reaching Frost in 1881, Sheffield Junction (a connection with the Tionesta Valley Railroad) in October 1882 and Kane in 1883. The management closed the Emlenton branch on October 5, 1880, and removed track piecemeal from November 1881 to June 1882.

The Pittsburgh & Western gained control of the Pittsburgh, Bradford & Buffalo in early August 1882, and merged the narrow gauge into itself by an agreement of September 25, 1883. The P&W actively pushed the extension to the McKean County oil field, completing it to Mount Jewett late in 1883. From Kane to Mount Jewett the P&W made use of a right-of-way acquired from the Big Level & Kinzua, which in return was granted trackage rights on the segment. In the same year, to connect the two segments of the narrow gauge, the P&W built three miles from Parker to Foxburg, including, at Foxburg, an iron bridge of two levels—rail above and road below—that was among the major American narrow gauge structures. The completed narrow gauge from Allegheny to Mount Jewett was about 169 miles. It did not long remain of that length. The P&W was not at the time interested in converting the line because the connections in the oil field were also 3'-0". As we have seen, however, the company removed the third rail between Allegheny and Callery Junction in 1884, ending a continuous narrow gauge from the oil field to Pittsburgh. The oil field was now declining, so that the long narrow gauge was no longer heavily trafficked.

Baltimore & Ohio Control

James Callery was well aware that his entry into the Pittsburgh area made the P&W attractive to several railroads. In October 1881 he bought an interest in the

The Pittsburgh & Western's dual-level bridge over the Allegheny River at Foxburg was one of the most notable narrow gauge structures. (Smithsonian Institution.)

Painesville & Youngstown narrow gauge in Ohio; he had already arranged standard gauge connections into Youngstown. The Erie, the Wabash, and the Baltimore & Ohio all showed interest in using the P&W as an entry into Pittsburgh from the west. None of them could reasonably have looked at the Northern Branch other than as a minor adjunct to the standard gauge entry. On October 26, 1883, Callery worked out an arrangement with Solon Humphreys, vice-president of the Wabash, for the Wabash to take over the P&W, but the agreement was never consummated. Rather, the Baltimore & Ohio bought control of the P&W in February 1884. The B&O was rumored to have begun acquiring an interest as early as 1881. Even after it gained control in 1884, Humphreys became a director, causing further expectations that the Wabash might enter Pittsburgh over the P&W. This never happened, however, and the P&W's future was entirely as a part of the B&O. The P&W's main line became part of the B&O's direct route from Pittsburgh to Chicago Junction (Willard) via Youngstown and Akron, and thus part of the B&O's main line to Chicago. The B&O connected the P&W with its entry from the south with the Junction Railroad across central Pittsburgh in 1883. The B&O began operating the P&W as an integral part of its system without formal agreement on February 1, 1902.

The B&O necessarily had little interest in the remaining narrow gauge north of Butler. The line became the Northern Subdivision of the Pittsburgh Division, universally known as the "Northern Sub." The physical plant was ordinarily bad except that it ascended north from Foxburg with a switchback. The line was probably the closest approach to Peter B. Borst's conception of the Washington, Cincinnati & St. Louis as an air line across West Virginia: a direct line across difficult terrain with ordinary narrow gauge technology. The bridge at Foxburg and most of the cuts north of Clarion Junction had been built to standard gauge clearances. The B&O converted the portion from Butler to Foxburg on July 1, 1901, and in November leased the remainder from Foxburg to Mount Jewett to the Bradford, Bordell & Kinzua for 48.5 percent of the gross receipts. This arrangement was not a success, and the remaining narrow gauge was returned in 1902 to the B&O, which converted it on October 2, 1911. The Clarion branch was formally abandoned in 1912; it had not been worked regularly since about 1902, and was apparently never converted. The switchback leaving Foxburg was not replaced. It had a grade of 2.7 percent and a capacity of only eight standard gauge freight cars, which drastically limited the length of freights on the Northern Sub. The passenger local on the route required nearly nine hours to run the 169 miles.

Especially after 1932, when the B&O acquired the Buffalo, Rochester & Pittsburgh, which had a longer but much superior route from Pittsburgh to Mount Jewett, there was little incentive to use the Northern Sub. The segment from Callery Junction to Ribold (6 miles) was abandoned in 1939, mainly to get rid of a tunnel at Zeno with difficult approaches in both directions. Thereafter connection was made by a track from Eidenau to Ribold built in 1898–99. As of December 31, 1964, the B&O ceased operating the central portion of the Northern Sub from Parker to Knox, 18 miles, including the river crossing at Foxburg and the switchback to the north. Even after this abandonment, the line had 533 curves, the worst of which was 25°. About 55 percent of the line was on curves. Even without the switchback, the ruling grades were 2.5 percent northbound and 2.7 percent southbound. The engineer who studied the line in 1971, when the B&O was considering abandoning it north of Petrolia, described the physical plant as "atrocious." The line north of Knox was turned over to the Knox & Kane Railroad in 1982.

The former P&W main line remains the B&O's exit from Pittsburgh toward Chicago and the west. In 1934 the B&O arranged trackage rights from McKeesport to New Castle Junction over the Pittsburgh & Lake Erie, mainly to allow its Baltimore-Chicago expresses to traverse Pittsburgh on

Conversion of the northern portion of the Pittsburgh & Western was one of the most widely noted in the narrow gauges' history. This postcard shows the last narrow gauge train arriving in Foxburg. (Ed Bond collection.)

a more direct route capable of faster running. The Wurtemburg branch was abandoned in 1957.

REFERENCES: *Baltimore & Ohio Railroad Corporate Histories*, vol. 3 (1922), pp. 204–443 (typescript, B&O Museum, Baltimore); collections of Frank Vollhardt, Jr., Edward C. Boss, and Colonel Clare R. J. Rogers.

Pittsburgh Southern Railroad

As the Pittsburgh, Castle Shannon & Washington Railroad, this project was incorporated on July 3, 1876. Although planned as a southern extension of the 3'-4" Pittsburgh & Castle Shannon, a split in the management resulted in the line's being built independently with 3'-0" gauge. Initially, the new group, Pittsburgh businessmen led by James H. Hopkins, sought to reach a coal-

Pittsburgh Southern No. 1 was, appropriately, a product of the Pittsburgh Locomotive Works. (Munson Paddock collection, Railroad Museum of Pennsylvania.)

producing area at Finleyville, 12 miles to the south, but over the longer period they sought to reach the city of Washington, Pennsylvania, and to penetrate the coal lands of West Virginia. They laid eight miles of track in 1877, and reached Finleyville in February 1878. In April the directors voted to change the name of the enterprise to the Pittsburgh Southern Railroad, to abandon the connection with the P&CS, and to arrange their own entry into Pittsburgh. They built a four-mile connection from Castle Shannon to Banksville, and arranged to lay a third rail over the standard gauge Little Saw Mill Run Railroad for about three miles to the LSMR's terminus at Temperanceville (West End). Toward the end of 1878 the management completed track into Washington, although regular service did not begin until January 1879. In the spring the management arranged to lay about a mile of third rail over the Pittsburgh & Lake Erie to reach the depot at the west end of the Smithfield Street bridge. As completed, the railroad was 36.5 miles. Together with the Waynesburg & Washington, with which it connected, it provided a 3'-0" route of 66 miles from Pittsburgh to Waynesburg in southwestern Pennsylvania. As far as is known, the PS had no method of physical interchange with the Pittsburgh & Western at Pittsburgh.

The route of the projected extension into West Virginia was never firm, but the management talked in 1878 of a line from Finleyville through Morgantown, Grafton on the Baltimore & Ohio's original main line, and the valleys of the Tygart and Greenbrier rivers to a point on the Chesapeake & Ohio main line about six miles west of White Sulphur Springs. Local farmers graded about 15 miles of this line out of Finleyville, but nothing further was done.

The railroad was built as far as Washington without a funded debt, but Hopkins had made extensive personal advances to the corporation. Early in 1879 the shareholders voted to mortgage the railroad for $7,500 per mile to pay off the debt to Hopkins and to raise funds for the extension into West Virginia. This effort appears to have been unsuccessful, and Hopkins bought the railroad at a sheriff's sale on April 7, proposing to reorganize the corporation if the shareholders raised $70,000. He reorganized it in May without change of name, allowing the former shareholders to take stock to the value of what they had previously paid in.

Other attempts to finance the West Virginia extension were also unsuccessful, and the management began efforts to sell the railroad. Negotiations for sale to the Pittsburgh, Chartiers & Youghiogheny failed

early in 1882. In June the line was sold to the newly formed Pittsburgh & Monongahela Valley of Milton D. Hays and associates, but the new owners sold it later in the year to the B&O, which was eager to use it as part of a projected direct line from Pittsburgh to Wheeling. The B&O immediately began laying third rail north from Washington, but considering the trackage north from Finleyville unsuitable for main-line railroading, undertook a new entry into Pittsburgh along Street's Run. The Washington-Finleyville mileage was converted in February 1883, but the Street's Run line did not reach the Monongahela River until July. A ferry crossing was used transitionally until a bridge was built at Glenwood.

The remaining narrow gauge track from Finleyville to Temperanceville was not immediately shut down, but was reportedly rarely used. The B&O sought to sell the railroad, but in August 1883 the Pittsburgh & Castle Shannon declined to buy it. No other buyers appeared; thus the B&O removed the entire 20-mile line with a crew of 1,500 men on Sunday, July 19, 1885. The Washington-Finleyville segment remains part of an important secondary main line of the B&O.

The Little Saw Mill Run Railroad continued to report itself as dual gauge in *Poor's Manual* through 1886. It is believed to have had no narrow gauge equipment.

Sharpsville, Wheatland, Sharon & Greenfield Railroad

George Boyce of Sharon projected this railroad as a line of eight to ten miles from Sharon to a connection with the Atlantic &

Great Western (Erie) near Greenfield. In 1874 he built four miles from Sharon to the Home Coal Bank. The railroad owned one locomotive, 32 coal cars, and one caboose. All reported revenue was from coal. Early in 1877 Boyce sold the railroad to the Sharon Railway, an A&GW subsidiary. The A&GW planned to convert the line and extend it about six miles to the coalfield in Hickory Township. The line was reported to the Auditor General of Pennsylvania as converted in 1880. It was shown as cut back to 2.67 miles in 1886 and dropped either as abandoned or as reduced to spur trackage in 1889.

Spring Brook Railroad
Gauge: 4'-3"

This obscure railroad was incorporated on May 2, 1871, and opened from Moosic in the Scranton area east up Spring Brook Creek to Upper Spring Brook (8.5 miles) in 1874. Charles Pugh of Pittston was president. The line took its unusual gauge from a predecessor, the Spring Brook Horse Railway of 1869. The railroad, which was laid with 16- and 25-pound rail, was operated with one locomotive and 18 cars. In 1877 all traffic was reported to be lumber. In 1883 the line was leased to the connecting Lehigh Coal & Navigation Co. (Central Railroad of New Jersey), which in 1885 converted it and subleased it to the principal shipper, the Spring Brook Lumber Co. The line was abandoned in segments between 1887 and 1890. The Scranton & Spring Brook Railroad, formed in 1897, made use of the right-of-way to serve a quarry and to assist in the building of a res-

The Susquehanna & Eagles Mere was an orthodox lumber railroad in technology. The locomotive is the company's Climax No. 4. (Railroad Museum of Pennsylvania.)

The Tionesta Valley Railway's engine terminal in Sheffield. (Ben Kline collection.)

ervoir. This line ceased operation about 1916 and was reported dismantled in 1932.

Susquehanna & Eagles Mere Railroad

Charles W. Sones incorporated this railroad on December 27, 1904, to make a common carrier of a private railroad serving his logging operations. The railroad had been built for about three miles northeast from Sones's sawmill near Eagles Mere in 1902 to the Eagles Mere Railroad and extended southwest about eight miles to the Hoyt Brothers tannery at Hillsgrove in 1904. In 1908 the line was extended west ten miles to a connection with the Susquehanna & New York Railroad at Masten, where Sones built a large mill. The line served mainly to bring logs to this mill, but it also made him independent of the connection with the Eagles Mere Railroad at Eagles Mere. The three miles from the original mill to Eagles Mere were abandoned in 1908–9. The railroad's limited claim to common carriage was mainly in the movement of hides, tanbark, leather, and other materials to and from the tannery at Hillsgrove, but the trains also carried supplies inbound to camps along the route and handled passengers in a caboose. *Poor's Manuals*

began listing the line as a private carrier in 1914, and the ICC ceased classifying it as a common carrier in 1915. Sones sold the railroad along with the Masten mill in April 1917 to the Central Pennsylvania Lumber Co., which made no pretense of common carriage, dropped the name, and operated the railroad simply as one of its several private carriers. The lumber company converted the five miles out of Masten in 1922 after the closure of the tannery and built some additional logging branches, abandoning the remainder of the original line. The company closed the Masten mill on September 18, 1930, and abandoned the railroad.

REFERENCE: Thomas T. Taber, "Ghost Lumber Towns of Central Pennsylvania," in *The Logging Railroad Era of Lumbering in Pennsylvania*, vol. 1, pp. 329–30.

Tionesta Valley Railroad

Horton-Crary & Co., the dominant firm in the tanning industry at Sheffield, formed this railroad principally to haul hemlock bark to its plant. A charter was obtained on September 9, 1879, for a narrow gauge line of 15 miles down Tionesta Creek. The discovery of oil in northwestern Pennsylvania in 1880 increased the demand for lumber in

the area, converting stripped hemlock logs from a waste product to an economic form of lumber. Horton-Crary was moved to begin construction of the railroad about September 1881. The line was opened in late January 1882 to Brookston (8 miles), where H. J. Brooks & Co. operated a sawmill and tannery. Because the line would serve this plant and those of other operators, and also because a predecessor of the Pittsburgh & Western was rapidly approaching the area, the TV was made a common carrier from the outset. During the summer of 1882 the line was built through extremely difficult country to the projected connection with the P&W, Sheffield Junction (13 miles). The P&W arrived at the junction in October 1882, allowing a gauge-compatible route from Pittsburgh to Sheffield. The connection became an important one to Horton-Crary, and a village of about 150 people grew up around it.

In 1883 Horton-Crary built the railroad's first branch, a line of five miles up the south fork of Tionesta Creek to an installation of the James Brothers company of Kane called James Mill. This branch was subsequently extended to Nansen, also on the Pittsburgh & Western. Because such branches served enterprises of firms other than Horton-Crary, the TV was unusual for what was basically a lumber railroad in having its branches in common carrier status, as well as its main line. Passenger

The Tionesta Valley's passenger service was mainly a connection from Sheffield to Sheffield Junction in connection with the Pittsburgh & Western. (Ed Bond collection.)

service was provided only on the main line. Since the TV's charter would have provided only for two miles of additional track beyond Sheffield Junction, Horton-Crary had to incorporate a subsidiary, the Sheffield & Spring Creek Railroad, to extend the main line south. In the summer and fall of 1884 track was pressed south along Spring Creek to Augustville (20 miles) and in 1885 to Howland (24 miles).

An oil discovery at Cherry Grove in 1882 brought forth two small narrow gauges immediately northwest of Sheffield. The earlier and larger was the Warren & Farnsworth Valley Railroad, formed by Warren businessmen on April 6, 1882. The line was built from Clarendon on the Philadelphia & Erie (Pennsylvania) Railroad between Warren and Sheffield to the boomtown of Garfield in Cherry Grove Township. The W&FV had been chartered to bypass Garfield en route to a junction with the P&W to the southwest, but a branch was hastily arranged to reach Garfield (10 miles) in August 1882. The line was then built from the junction with the Garfield branch to Vandergrift, about an additional two miles. An extension to Dunham's Mill in 1884 brought the railroad's main-line mileage to 15.26. The quick decline of the oil boom beginning late in 1882 caused the railroad to be foreclosed in April 1885. It was reorganized as the Warren & Farnsworth Railroad. In 1892 the railroad was sold to F. H. Rockwell & Co., which kept its common carrier status and continued its passenger train, but used the line essentially as a facility for its tannery.

The shorter of the two lines serving the area northwest of Sheffield was the Garfield & Cherry Grove Railroad, incorporated June 29, 1882, as one of four narrow gauges projected to provide a through route from Bradford to Titusville. The line was graded in the summer of 1882 from Tiona, about three miles south of Clarendon on the P&E, up Arnot and Little Arnot runs to Farnsworth (4 miles), about 1.5 miles short of Garfield. The collapse of the boom late in 1882 apparently brought the project to a halt, and the railroad was not immediately completed. It passed into the hands of Horton-Crary, which completed it in 1883 by building south from Tiona to Sheffield to a connection with the TV, and west into Garfield. When operations began in October 1883, the completed line was about nine miles long. Horton-Crary reorganized the line as the Cherry Grove Railroad on November 21, 1884, and on December 1 leased it to the TV.

On February 25, 1893, the United States Leather Co. was formed in an industrial consolidation typical of the day. It acquired both Horton-Crary and F. H. Rockwell in 1894. The company proceeded to consolidate the TVRR, Sheffield & Spring Creek, Warren & Farnsworth, and Cherry Grove Railroad into a new Tionesta Valley Railway. Members of the Horton and Crary families remained in control of the railroad. In 1895 they built five miles of track north from Tiona parallel to the P&E, connecting with the former W&F at Clarendon and extending on to the Stoneham tannery a short distance south of Warren. Because there

was no point in duplicating lines into Garfield, the former Cherry Grove Railroad was abandoned west of Tiona. Regular passenger trains on both routes to Garfield had been discontinued earlier. In 1895 the railroad began extensive building of freight-only branches to tanneries and sawmills. In 1898–99 the main line was extended 12 miles from Howland to Winlack to connect with the Millstone Valley Railroad, a private carrier of Wagner & Wilson, and to serve mills of some other operators. Traffic to the various camps warranted three daily passenger trains. The building of branches into timber stands continued in the early twentieth century, but the former W&F branch from Clarendon to Garfield was removed by 1907, after having become redundant upon the extensive freight branches of the company.

On February 17, 1904, the TV acquired and merged into itself the Spring Creek Railway, which had been built as a standard gauge private carrier of the Eagle Valley Tanning Co. in 1892. U.S. Leather acquired the line in the course of its various purchases, and on October 8, 1892, incorporated it as a common carrier. In spite of the acquisition by the TV, the railroad was initially left a standard gauge line. Lumbering on the south end of the TV main line was declining, however. When the Central Pennsylvania Lumber Co. closed its mill at Loleta, about two miles short of Winlack, in 1913, there was no longer sufficient demand to retain the line. In 1914 the TV cut it back 13 miles to Parrish, and laid eight miles of narrow gauge rail on the standard gauge line to Hallton. The line thereafter ran its passenger trains from Sheffield to Hallton (31 miles). The former P&W had been converted by the B&O in 1911, but TV passenger trains continued to make the connection at Sheffield Junction.

The Tionesta Valley was a relatively large railroad, which at various times operated about 103 miles of main line and branches, and another 175 to 200 miles of logging spurs. (It is shown on the map of the Pennsylvania–New York oil field network in the following section.) At the time of its ICC valuation in 1917, it had 94 miles of track, not including the spurs. The railroad's all-time roster included seven Climaxes, five Heislers, and 11 rod engines. In 1917 the company had 556 freight cars and four passenger cars. At the end of World War I, some of the northern branch-line mileage was abandoned and some of the southern branches were turned over to the Central Pennsylvania Lumber Co. Partly because of the operation of this company at Hallton, the TV did quite well in the 1920s.

U.S. Lumber acquired the Clarion River Railway, a standard gauge line with which the TV connected at Hallton, and in 1927 leased it to the TV. The CR was allowed to remain 4'-8½".

The Depression drastically reduced lumbering, and had a devastating effect on the TV. U.S. Leather's main mill at Sheffield was closed in 1932. The mill was reopened in 1933, but thereafter was increasingly dependent on logs brought in by truck. In July 1935 the management received permission to abandon the main line from Sheffield Junction to Hallton. The track was turned over to the Clawson Chemical Co. for private carriage to its Hallton plant. This firm also bought the Clarion River Railway. In February 1936 the TV received permission to abandon the remaining seven miles from Sheffield north to Clarendon. All that remained were the 13 miles from Sheffield to the B&O connection at Sheffield Junction, but when the mill at Sheffield closed permanently in July 1941, even this became unnecessary. Permissions to abandon came in November 1941, and track was removed in July 1942.

REFERENCE: Walter C. Casler, "Tionesta Valley," in *The Logging Railroad Era of Lumbering in Pennsylvania*, vol. 2, pp. 800–899. Because of the TV's practice of keeping its branch lines in common carrier status, it is impractical to treat its history here in the detail of other narrow gauges. Readers seeking more detailed history

are referred to Casler's account. Similarly, in the quantifications of narrow gauge mileage in Part I, Chapters 4 and 8, only the 73 miles of the TV on which passenger service was provided are included, on the ground that changes in the branch- and spur-line mileage are not fully recorded, and would in any case inflate the totals with line actually of the character of private carriage.

Tuscarora Valley Railroad

A late narrow gauge, this railroad was chartered in April 1891 and largely built in the summer of 1892. Service began February 1, 1893, from Port Royal on the Pennsylvania Railroad main line 47 miles west of Harrisburg, to East Waterford, 17.5 miles southwest up the Tuscarora Valley. The promoters, T. S. and J. C. Moorhead of Port Royal, from the outset envisioned a considerable extension to the south. In 1893 they graded a portion of an extension of about 16 miles through Concord Narrows to Dry Run, a town of about 400 in Franklin County, but abandoned the project apparently in the expectation that the Newport & Sherman's Valley would make an incursion into the area. Instead, they elected to build south along the western escarpment of Tuscarora Mountain to Blairs Mills, Fort Littleton, Knobsville, and McConnellsburg, seat of Fulton County. This extension would have intersected the East Broad Top near Neelyton and penetrated the country

left without rail service by the abortion of the South Pennsylvania project. Further extension to Hancock, Maryland, was considered.

Using a portion of the grade of the projected line to Dry Run, the extension toward McConnellsburg was undertaken in 1894. On January 1, 1896, the line was opened to Blairs Mills (27 miles). Some additional grading was reported, but the line progressed no farther. Blairs Mills was a town of 150 people, and East Waterford, the largest town served, had only 250. Including Port Royal, a town of about 1,000, the entire tributary population of the railroad was only about 4,500. Most of the receipts came from lumber, phosphate, and limestone. The financial experience of the railroad was better than might have been expected, if only because of the simplicity of its capital structure. The management mortgaged the railroad for $180,000 to finance the southern extension, but the debt was held entirely by J. M. Blair, the president, and H. C. Hower, the vice-president and general manager. The railroad became delinquent on interest payments on July 1, 1913, and defaulted on maturity of the mortgage on July 1, 1917, but Blair and Hower never took action for foreclosure. The debt was carried as an unpaid obligation to the end of the railroad. Although the management expressed an intention to convert as early as 1897, and rumors of conver-

The Tuscarora Valley was unusual in adopting the Eames vacuum brake system as late as 1892. Note the muffler on the cab roof. (Ben Kline collection.)

sion appeared in the local press as late as 1910, the railroad operated as a narrow gauge throughout its history.

The railroad was obviously vulnerable to truck competition after World War I. It was in a state of deferred maintenance from about 1924, but was in the black as late as 1929. The diversion of traffic to trucks, depletion of timber in the area, and loss of passengers to the automobile all reduced the railroad to chronic unprofitability in the Depression years. Passenger counts fell from 6,452 in 1929 to 54 in 1933. Blair's heirs and Hower applied to abandon the railroad in 1934 and encountered no protest.

Waynesburg & Washington Railroad

The rugged country of southwestern Pennsylvania remained mainly dependent on horse-drawn transport until late in the nineteenth century. The standard gauge Chartiers Valley Railroad had reached Washington from Pittsburgh in 1871, but Waynesburg, the other major town of the region, was still without a railroad. The prime mover for a narrow gauge railroad to connect Waynesburg with Washington was a former resident of the area, John M. Day, who was at the time practicing law in Des Moines, where he was among the promoters of the Des Moines & Minnesota. The Waynesburg & Washington Railroad was organized at a meeting of January 27, 1875. Narrow gauge was chosen for the usual reasons of economy in mountainous terrain, and because of the prospect of a compatible connection to Pittsburgh. Of the several routes considered, one of 29 miles via Bane Creek and Bates' Fork of Brown's Creek was chosen. This route required no heavy grading, but entailed a grade of over four miles ascending out of Washington, the worst portion of which was 2.88 percent for nearly half a mile. The descent into the Bane Creek Valley had nearly a mile of 2.4-percent grade. There was a smaller summit at West Union between the two creek valleys. Grading was done in 1875 and 1876, and tracklaying began at Washington on May 1, 1877. President Joseph G. Ritchie drove the last spike at West Waynesburg on November 1, 1877. Regular service started the following day. The railroad had cost only $4,975 per mile for track and $663 per mile for equipment.

In April 1878 the railroad became embroiled in a controversy between groups centering about George Sellers, who had succeeded to the presidency, and former president Ritchie. The bondholders petitioned for receivership in August, but Ritchie's group secured an injunction to prevent their taking control of the railroad. The bondholders wanted to sell the railroad to the Pittsburgh Southern, which arrived in Washington in January 1879, providing the expected gauge-compatible connection to Pittsburgh, but it is doubtful whether the PS could have financed such a purchase. Neither Sellers's nor Ritchie's group proved powerful enough to exclude the other faction, but the acrimony between them made administration of the railroad difficult. A projected extension to Blacksville, West Virginia, could not be financed.

The railroad had a good year in 1884, but it had lost its gauge-compatible connection to Pittsburgh when the Baltimore & Ohio bought and converted the Pittsburgh Southern. The securities holders generally believed that their interests would be better served by sale either to the B&O or to a Pennsylvania Railroad subsidiary. Ritchie favored the B&O, but superintendent C. E. Bower favored sale to the Pennsylvania through the Pittsburgh, Cincinnati & St. Louis, which had bought the Chartiers Valley. Formally, the W&W was leased to the Chartiers Valley within the Pennsylvania's complicated financial structure. The Pennsylvania removed the physical connection with the B&O and prepared to operate the narrow gauge as a minor branch of its enormous system. Traffic was mainly agricultural products from local farms and general merchandise inbound, but about the turn of the century a tin mill was built on the line at West Waynesburg, which generated enough traffic to warrant two new 2-6-0 locomotives. The Pennsylvania necessarily considered conversion of the narrow gauge and in 1903 let a contract for conversion conditional upon the Gould railroads' building their proposed line through Pennsylvania via Waynesburg. The Gould interests built directly to Pittsburgh with the Pittsburgh & West Virginia, rather than through Waynesburg, and the conversion was never made. Rather, passenger equipment was bought from the recently converted Burlington & Western to establish a nonstop express between the termini, one of the few narrow gauge trains that took mail on the fly. Station stops were shortly instituted for the train, however.

Because of traffic from the tin mill, the W&W experienced more of a boom during World War I than most of the surviving narrow gauges. In 1920 the Pennsylvania embarked upon a program of simplification of its corporate structure, in the course of which the W&W lost its identity and became merely the Waynesburg and Washington Branch, Panhandle Division. The equipment was repainted with Pennsylvania lettering and the locomotives were renumbered in the 9680 series to conform with the Pennsylvania's other narrow gauge power. The paving of state highway 18 parallel to the railroad in the early 1920s diverted a great deal of traffic, especially passengers. The narrow gauge was in the red annually

Waynesburg & Washington locomotive No. 9684 at Braddock, a minor station just below Washington, in 1929. (Munson Paddock collection, Railroad Museum of Pennsylvania.)

from 1925. Passenger trains were discontinued on July 9, 1929. Also in 1929 the Pennsylvania arranged for extension of the Monongahela Railroad, which it owned jointly with the Pittsburgh & Lake Erie, from Mather to Waynesburg. Terminal trackage was laid with a third rail for movements of standard gauge cars to industries on the narrow gauge. Because Waynesburg was finally on the standard gauge railroad system, the ICC allowed the narrow gauge to discontinue service there, but required it to continue serving the intermediate on-line communities. The Pennsylvania responded by discontinuing steam freight operation on April 6, 1933, and handling remaining milk and express on an enclosed motorized track car. This unit was replaced with a Ford truck fitted for rail operation in 1940. The Pennsylvania showed no eagerness to get rid of the service, mainly out of fear that another railroad might use the abandoned right-of-way to penetrate the Greene County coalfield. Apparently feeling that coal traffic might warrant the resumption of train operation, the Pennsylvania finally converted the line to standard gauge from Washington to Hackney (13 miles) in 1943 and the remainder in 1944. The service reverted to a track car about 1958, which is believed to have been replaced by a truck on parallel highways in the early 1960s. The track remained in place through the Pennsylvania's merger into the Penn Central, but was not included in Conrail upon its formation in 1976. The rails were removed in 1978.

REFERENCE: Larry L. Koehler with Morgan J. Gayvert, *Three Feet on the Panhandle: A History of the Waynesburg and Washington Railroad* (Canton, Ohio: Railhead Publications, 1983).

White Deer & Loganton Railway

The White Deer Lumber Co. on December 11, 1900, chartered the White Deer Valley Railroad to run from White Deer Junction on the Philadelphia & Reading above Lewisburg to Duncan (15 miles). The lumber company did not immediately build the railroad, but in 1906 decided to build a longer railroad on the route to Loganton (24 miles). It incorporated the new railroad as the White Deer & Loganton Railway on April 26, 1906, and began building west up White Deer Creek from the Susquehanna River. Instead of annulling the charter of the earlier railroad, the lumber company arranged that the WD&L should lease the WDV for $1,200 per year for five years beginning May 1, 1907. The combined railroad began full service about August 1907.

The White Deer & Loganton's mixed train, shown here with a Climax locomotive, served the general transportation demands of the small town of Loganton. (Thomas T. Taber collection, Railroad Museum of Pennsylvania.)

Although entirely a creation of the lumber company, of which Charles Steele of Sunbury was president, the railroad was a bona fide common carrier, operating a daily passenger train to Loganton, a town of 375 people. In 1909 the WDV was extended 0.6 miles to bring it closer to the Reading's station in White Deer.

The rental agreement was extended on a yearly basis until May 1, 1916. The lumber company then wound up the enterprise, absorbing the WD&L on June 30, 1916, and removing the tracks.

York & Peach Bottom Railway

Like the Lancaster, Oxford & Southern, this railroad had its origins in the Peach Bottom Railway, a project of 1868 to build from the Broad Top coalfield to the Delaware River at either Philadelphia or Wilmington. As the project was conceived in 1871, when surveys began, it would have three divisions, the western to run from the coalfield to Hanover Junction or York, the central to traverse York County mainly through Muddy Creek valley to Peach Bottom on the Susquehanna River, and the eastern to run from Peach Bottom, Lancaster County, to the Delaware. The western division was never undertaken, and the eastern was partly completed as the LO&S. The management, headed by Stephen G. Boyd of York, chose narrow gauge about 1872 on the recommendation of the company's survey engineer, Colonel John M. Hood, who argued that the line along Muddy Creek would be a continual series of tight curves, which it would be appreciably less expensive to grade to narrow gauge standards. In response to local subscriptions, it was determined to start the middle division at

York, to proceed to the town of Red Lion, and to enter the Muddy Creek valley at Felton. The subscriptions from York enabled construction to continue in spite of the Panic of 1873. The line went into service on July 4, 1874, to the Red Lion area (9 miles), which was to produce furniture and light manufacturing traffic. By Christmas the line had been opened to Muddy Creek Forks (21 miles). A mixture of financial problems and the difficulty of the terrain slowed progress in 1875, but the line was opened to Bridgton (26 miles). About April 15, 1876, the line reached Delta (33 miles), which had been a center of slate mining since the eighteenth century. This was to prove the railroad's principal source of traffic almost to the end of its history. Boyd opposed extension to the Susquehanna on the ground that the town of Peach Bottom would produce little traffic and there was no immediate prospect of effecting a river crossing to the trackage of the eastern division. Boyd lost this dispute, and was discharged as president in January 1877 in favor of Charles R. McConkey, a merchant at Peach Bottom. Financial difficulties prevented immediate building of the extension, however.

The Peach Bottom system failed in 1881. The two divisions were reorganized separately, and were never again affiliated. The middle division was sold to its bondholders on December 20, 1881, and reorganized on March 17, 1882, as the York & Peach Bottom Railway with McConkey still as president. The new corporation undertook the extension of 5.7 miles to Peach Bottom, opening it about March 1883. Boyd's low view of the extension was entirely vindicated, for the line reportedly never paid its operating expenses. The railroad as a whole did quite well, however.

Boyd, after leaving the Peach Bottom Railway, devoted himself to promoting a narrow gauge from Baltimore to Delta. As the Maryland Central Railroad, this line reached Delta at the end of 1883. Its management from the outset showed interest in acquiring the York & Peach Bottom. In January 1889 John K. Cowen and William Gilmor of the MC announced that they had secured control of the Y&PB, and proceeded to negotiate a lease. Through service between Baltimore and York began on May 19, 1889. The Y&PB and the MC were consolidated as the Baltimore & Lehigh Railroad on May 5, 1891. The management, still headed by Gilmor, signed a contract whereby the railroad was turned over on January 2, 1893, to the newly formed Baltimore Forwarding & Railroad Co. for conversion. The depression of the 1890s was to prevent this project. The B&L went bankrupt in 1893, and was put in separate receiverships, the Pennsylvania mileage under Winfield J. Taylor. Warren F. Walworth of Cleveland bought the Pennsylvania trackage at auction on August 6, 1894, and on October 23 reorganized it as the York Southern Railroad. Walworth planned from the outset to convert the railroad, and announced in July 1895 that the work had begun. It was finished by the end of the year, except for the Peach Bottom branch, which was not converted until 1898. Walworth sold his interest in the York Southern in 1898 to Daniel F. Lafean of York. Lafean undertook a branch of only 1.25 miles into Dallastown (completed in May 1899), but he sold control of the railroad in April of that year to Sperry, Jones & Co. of Baltimore.

The Baltimore investment banking firm of Alexander Brown & Sons proposed to reunify the York Southern with the Baltimore & Lehigh, which had recently been converted. The York Southern's shareholders accepted Brown's terms in a meeting of February 2, 1901, and the railroad was merged into Brown's newly formed Maryland & Pennsylvania Railroad on February 14. The former York Southern proved to be the stronger portion of the M&PA main line. Most of the railroad's traffic was slate moving from Delta to the Pennsylvania Railroad at York, and Red Lion continued to originate furniture and other traffic. The Peach Bottom branch was abandoned on September 1, 1903, but the main line survived even beyond the M&PA's abandonment of its Maryland line south of Whiteford in 1958. The M&PA applied to abandon its remaining line in 1959, but was rejected by the ICC in 1960 on the ground that the Solite Corporation proposed to open a quarry and processing plant at Delta. The plant was never built, but the railroad's fortunes revived in the 1960s, largely because of the construction of a nuclear power plant of the Philadelphia Electric Co. at Peach Bottom. Indeed, this plant brought about the reconstruction of 3.5 miles of the Peach Bottom branch on a different alignment in 1969. The power station quickly ceased to be a major source of revenue, and the principal remaining quarry at Delta ended production in 1971. The railroad would have been abandoned at that time, but was acquired by Emons Industries in order to gain entry into the pool of boxcars used in interline service. This firm operated the remaining line in full until June 14, 1978, when it embargoed the trackage beyond Red Lion. The M&PA had taken over a former Pennsylvania Railroad line southwest from York to Hanover, Pennsylvania, and Walkersville, Maryland, which supported the railroad. The Red Lion branch survived unprofitably until March 23, 1983. The railroad applied to the ICC to abandon the entire line east of York and received permission on March 23, 1985. On the former narrow gauge, only the York terminal survives, serving the remaining York-Hanover operation.

REFERENCES: George W. Hilton, *The Ma & Pa: A History of the Maryland & Pennsylvania Railroad* (Berkeley, Calif.: Howell-North Books, 1963; 2d ed., San Diego, Calif.: Howell-North Books, 1980); collection of Charles T. Mahan, Jr.

▼▼▼▼

The New Castle Railroad & Mining Co. was organized in 1872 to take over the private 3'-6" line of the Neshannock Railroad & Coal Co. The management's intention was to extend the line from its 3.75-mile length to 27 miles as a common carrier to Hainesville. It failed to do so, and the line continued as a private carrier until abandoned in 1885.

The New Castle & Butler Railroad, a plant facility of the New Castle Portland Cement Co. with 2.5 miles of track (1881–1927), was listed by the ICC as a common carrier, but apart from operating mixed trains in its early years, had little claim to such status.

Max Schweibenz of Confluence secured a charter for the Somerset County Railroad on October 7, 1884, intending to build from Draketown Junction on the B&O near Confluence to Somerset. The route would have generally paralleled the B&O's own line. In May 1885 he opened the railroad from the B&O connection, which he renamed Schweibenz Junction, to his mill at Schweibenzville (9 miles). A spur was built to a stone quarry about 1891. The railroad had one locomotive, one passenger car, and nine freight cars. It was abandoned on June 30, 1893.

Lumberman James B. Weed of Binghamton, New York, took out a charter for the Slate Run Railroad on December 17, 1885, intending it to run from Slate Run on the Pine Creek Railroad to a point on Youngwoman's Creek, about 15 miles northwest. The line was opened in July 1886. The railroad served camps at North Bend and West End. The railroad was enrolled as a common carrier both by the ICC and Pennsylvania state officials, but all reported equipment was flatcars to bring out the hemlock bark and lumber the line was built to handle. It purported to provide three passenger trips per day in the early 1890s, but dropped its entries in the *Official Guide of the Railways* in 1896. In 1902 Weed undertook an extension to Manor Fork (18 miles). At its peak, about 1906, the railroad had four locomotives, 76 flatcars, and a caboose. The lumber company began dismantling the railroad in 1910 and completed the job about May 1911.

The Lafayette Manufacturing Co. formed the Bradford & Western Pennsylvania Railroad on July 24, 1891, to serve its chemical plant and sawmill west of Lewis Run. The original intention was to build from the Lewis Run stations of the Buffalo, Rochester & Pittsburgh and the Erie to Marshburg. The two miles from the Erie connection were made dual gauge and the remainder was 3'-0". The narrow gauge locomotives, mainly Climaxes, switched standard gauge equipment off the Erie to the plant. The projected connection to the BR&P was never made, and the railroad reached only the east environs of Marshburg. As completed in 1895, the railroad was about six miles. (It is shown on the map of the network in the Pennsylvania–New York oil field, in the next section.) The line was a common carrier from the outset owing to the company's desire to participate in joint rates with the Erie. A ruling by the ICC that nominal common carriers of this sort, which were basically plant spurs, were not entitled to common carrier status for division of rates prompted the Lewis Run Manufacturing Co., which had succeeded Lafayette in 1898, to absorb the railroad company on November 1, 1912. The line continued in operation as a private carrier until 1934.

The Kinzua Creek & Kane Railroad was chartered on June 14, 1888, and opened on June 16, 1889, from Kane to Neilyville (12 miles). It was originally a private carrier of George W. Campbell & Sons, lumber operators. The line was converted in June 1891, and apparently became a common carrier at that time. Its principal claim to that status was in running mixed trains, and it may have done so as a narrow gauge. The railroad closed in 1898 and was removed in 1898–99.

The Network in the Pennsylvania- New York Oil Field

When oil was discovered at Titusville in 1859, northwestern Pennsylvania and the adjacent area of New York were relatively undeveloped. The oil strike rapidly attracted resources to the region, producing a boom that peaked in the early 1880s, simultaneously with the apogee of the narrow gauge movement. The terrain was difficult, and there was no assurance that any railroads built to serve the oil wells would long survive. The area is dominated by a high plateau, the Big Level, in McKean, Elk, Cameron, and Potter counties, Pennsylvania, deeply cut by the canyon of the Kinzua River. The New York portion of the oil field was in Allegany County to the north-

east. The boom had a very sharp peak, with 6,519,000 barrels produced in 1882; by 1913, output was only 750,000 barrels. The area remains a leading producer of lubricating oils, but the demand for a specialized railroad system to serve the field was largely gone by the mid-1890s. The narrow gauges were mainly engaged in hauling wood for use in the oil field, but they also handled sand for glassmaking, clay, and general cargo. The region's oil and coal mainly moved on standard gauge railroads.

There were two major narrow gauge networks in the oil field, one of the Erie and the second of the Buffalo, New York & Philadelphia Railroad. In 1872, the Pennsylvania Railroad and the Standard Oil Co. entered into an agreement for rates heavily discriminatory against the oil field, prompting the Erie to attempt to penetrate the oil field with a network of three narrow gauges: the Bradford, Bordell & Kinzua; the Bradford, Eldred & Cuba; and the Tonawanda Valley & Cuba. The Buffalo, New York & Philadelphia, the trackage of which became part of the Pennsylvania Railroad in 1900, formed a network of its own, comprising the Bradford Railway, the Kinzua Railway, the Olean, Bradford & Warren, and the Kendall & Eldred. There were additional independent lines, as well as connections ranging farther into the Southern Tier of New York.

Allegany Central Railroad

The Rochester, Nunda & Pennsylvania Railroad had partly completed a projected

23.5-mile railroad from Belvidere, New York, south of Angelica to Swains on the Erie's Buffalo line in 1872–74. The railroad was projected as a narrow gauge, but the 17 miles laid from Ross's Crossing to Sonyea were standard gauge. In 1880 George D. Chapman of Columbus, Ohio, and his associates bought the line and prepared to complete and extend it. They formed the Rochester, New York & Pennsylvania Railroad on February 14, 1881. The extension was accomplished by the absorption of two narrow gauges promoted in 1881 to serve the oil field at Bolivar and Richburg in Allegany County, New York. The Olean Railroad was incorporated on March 2, 1881, by Charles S. Cary and other businessmen at Olean, New York, who were also interested in narrow gauges in the McKean County oil field. They proposed to build east from Olean along the Allegheny River to Ceres and up Little Genesee Creek to Bolivar (17 miles), and did so by the fall of the year. The promoters considered laying third rail on the Buffalo, New York & Philadelphia from Olean to Portville, New York, but decided on laying 3'-0" track on the towpath of a parallel canal. Meanwhile, Abijah J. Wellman and Asher W. Miner of Friendship, New York, formed the Friendship Railroad on May 12, 1881, to reach Bolivar from their town on the Erie main line, 13 miles to the north. The latter was the more difficult project, entailing the crossing of a summit of 300 feet with grades of 1.3 percent. This railroad was also completed in the fall of 1881. The corporation was organized as the Allegany Central Railroad on September 29, 1881, and merged the Olean

Allegany Central No. 4 at the tank at Bolivar, New York. (Ed Bond collection.)

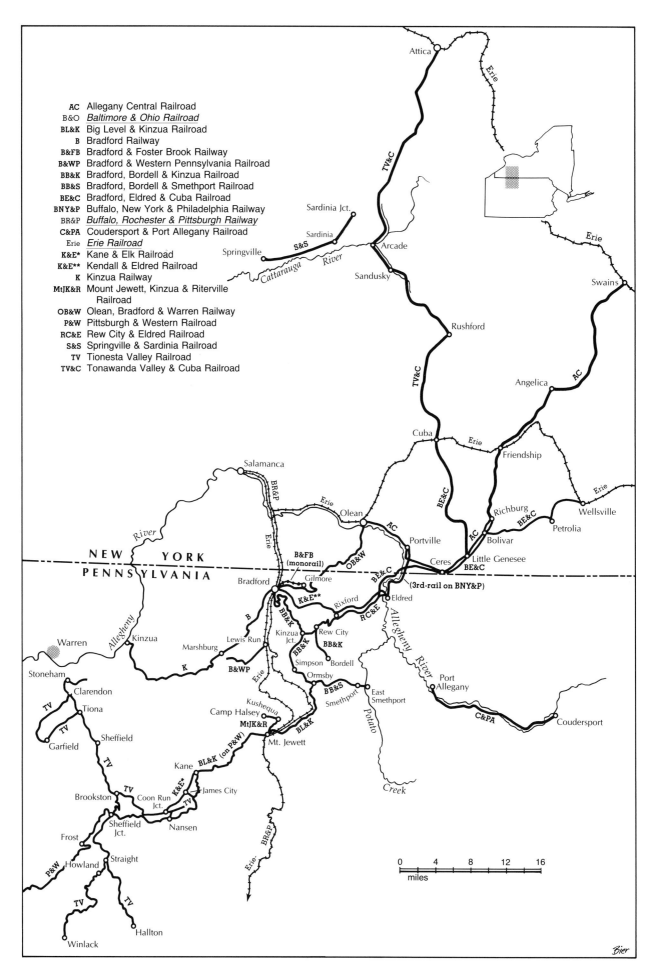

AC   Allegany Central Railroad
B&O   *Baltimore & Ohio Railroad*
BL&K   Big Level & Kinzua Railroad
B   Bradford Railway
B&FB   Bradford & Foster Brook Railway
B&WP   Bradford & Western Pennsylvania Railroad
BB&K   Bradford, Bordell & Kinzua Railroad
BB&S   Bradford, Bordell & Smethport Railroad
BE&C   Bradford, Eldred & Cuba Railroad
BNY&P   Buffalo, New York & Philadelphia Railway
BR&P   *Buffalo, Rochester & Pittsburgh Railway*
C&PA   Coudersport & Port Allegany Railroad
Erie   *Erie Railroad*
K&E*   Kane & Elk Railroad
K&E**   Kendall & Eldred Railroad
K   Kinzua Railway
MtJK&R   Mount Jewett, Kinzua & Riterville
    Railroad
OB&W   Olean, Bradford & Warren Railway
P&W   Pittsburgh & Western Railroad
RC&E   Rew City & Eldred Railroad
S&S   Springville & Sardinia Railroad
TV   Tionesta Valley Railroad
TV&C   Tonawanda Valley & Cuba Railroad

Bier

Railroad and Friendship Railroad into itself on November 2. Frank Sullivan Smith of Angelica, a lawyer for the BNY&P who had been one of the principal projectors of the Allegany Central, became president of the combined firm. Wellman and Miner became directors. Smith proceeded to build the line north from Friendship; it reached Angelica on January 9, 1882, and Swains on June 16. The completed railroad was about 59 miles. The line ran along the west bank of Little Genesee Creek between Ceres and Bolivar, parallel to the Erie's Bradford, Eldred & Cuba on the opposite bank. The route continued north along Angelica and Black creeks to Grove, and then passed through hilly country to Swains. Shops were established at Angelica. The railroad had two connections to the Pennsylvania's narrow gauge lines in the McKean County oil field to the south: a direct connection with the Olean, Bradford & Warren by interchange at Olean, and an indirect connection with the Kendall & Eldred by eight miles of third rail laid over the BNY&P from Portville to Eldred, Pennsylvania.

The collapse of the oil boom at Bolivar and Richburg in 1882 assured this railroad a short life. On November 1, 1882, the management organized the Lackawanna & Pittsburgh Railroad to build a standard gauge line from Belfast, New York, to Nunda Junction, and in 1883 laid third rail along the AC from Angelica to Swains as part of the route. On March 24, 1883, the AC was merged into this company. The narrow gauge rail from Angelica to Swains was removed by June 1, and the company installed a Ramsey Transfer at Angelica. The L&P went into receivership on December 8, 1884, and was reorganized on May 7, 1889, as the Lackawanna Southwestern Railroad. The new firm discontinued operation of the narrow gauge between Bolivar and Angelica in favor of a standard gauge route to Olean via Belfast Junction arranged over existing standard gauge lines in the area. The remaining narrow gauge of 18 miles between Olean and Bolivar stayed in service through the reorganization of the corporation into the Central New York & Western Railroad on November 18, 1892, and the merger into the Pittsburg, Shawmut & Northern on August 2, 1899. The PS&N converted the Olean-Bolivar line on December 27, 1901, and in 1902–3 rebuilt the Bolivar-Angelica segment, which had been idle for 12 years, as part of its main line. The entire PS&N was abandoned in 1947.

REFERENCES: Winfield W. Robinson, "Pittsburg, Shawmut & Northern," Railway & Locomotive Historical Society Bulletin, no. 61 (1943), pp. 76–88; Charles F. H. Allen, "The Pittsburg,

Shawmut & Northern, and All Associated and Predecessor Roads," ibid., no. 92 (1955), pp. 8–72; collection of Colonel Clare R. J. Rogers.

Big Level & Kinzua Railroad

Lumberman Elisha K. Kane and five shareholders of the Pittsburgh & Western secured a charter for the Big Level & Kinzua on August 27, 1881, in the expectation of building a connection of 24 miles from the railhead of the Pittsburgh & Western at Kane to Ormsby on the Bradford, Bordell & Kinzua. The line, if built, would complete the narrow gauge route from Pittsburgh to the McKean County oil field. Kane surveyed the route from Mount Jewett to Kane, but turned over his rights to the P&W, which built it in 1883. In return Kane secured trackage rights on the 13-mile line for the BL&K. When Kane finished the Ormsby–Mount Jewett trackage (11 miles) on December 1, 1886, he leased the BL&K in perpetuity to the BB&K, which sought it as an extension of its main line. The BL&K agreed to maintain the line, and the BB&K agreed to operate it without charge, and also to turn over to the BL&K the gross receipts. The P&W agreed to forward traffic to the oilfield over the narrow gauge and to prorate fares and charges. The agreement served Kane's purpose in completing the narrow gauge route to Pittsburgh without involving him in the direct operation of the railroad.

The lease was ended by the BB&K's reorganization of 1892. Until June 30, 1896, the BL&K was operated by the P&W under a cost-plus contract. Upon expiration of this agreement the BL&K was again leased

to the BB&K, this time for 20 percent of the gross receipts of the BL&K and an agreement of the BB&K to maintain the property. The BB&K made use of the BL&K's trackage rights over the P&W to run through passenger trains from Bradford to Kane. When the BB&K was reorganized as the Buffalo, Bradford & Kane in 1904, the lease arrangement was continued, and when the BB&K was abandoned in 1906, the BL&K was also abandoned, except for about a mile of track in Mount Jewett. The BL&K assumed operation of the Mount Jewett–Kane segment of the BB&K's former Bradford-Kane passenger trains, even though all but the terminal trackage in Mount Jewett was over the Baltimore & Ohio, which had succeeded the P&W in 1902. This strange arrangement persisted until 1911, when, on August 1, the B&O bought the BL&K's remaining mile of track in anticipation of converting the former P&W. The last BL&K passenger train ran on September 30, 1911. The line remains in operation as part of the Knox & Kane Railroad, which succeeded the north end of the B&O's Northern Sub in 1982.

REFERENCE: C. F. H. Allen, "The Railroads of McKean County, Pa.," Railway & Locomotive Historical Society Bulletin, no. 78 (1949), pp. 79–81.

Bradford, Bordell & Kinzua Railroad

The geographical backbone of the Mc-Kean County narrow gauge mileage, and the basic element in the Erie's system in the oil field, was the Bradford, Bordell & Kin-

The crew poses with the last narrow gauge train of the Big Level & Kinzua on September 30, 1911. (Ed Bond collection.)

A passenger train of the Bradford, Bordell & Kinzua with its full crew. The dual flag-holders on the pilot are quite unusual. (Smithsonian Institution.)

zua, formed by local oilmen and Erie representatives at Bradford on March 3, 1880. The promoters, who were mainly interested in serving their installations in the Bordell area, quickly undertook the building of the line from Bradford down Kendall Creek to Simpson (15 miles) and a branch east from Kinzua Junction to Rew City and Bordell (3 miles). Rails stopped about 1.25 miles short of Bordell; a plank road owned by the railroad ran into the town. Revenue operation began on June 7. To build on to the county seat at Smethport the promoters incorporated a subsidiary, the Bradford, Bordell & Smethport, which built the extension in the second half of the year. Service began between Bradford and Smethport (25 miles) on December 16, 1880. In the following spring the line was extended about a mile to reach the Buffalo, New York & Philadelphia's station at East Smethport.

In March 1882 the promoters of the BB&K formed a second subsidiary, the Rew City & Eldred Railroad, to build a 13-mile extension between the towns of its name to reach a connection with the Bradford, Eldred & Cuba, which was being built north into the segment of the oil field around Bolivar and Richburg, New York. Upon completion on September 13, 1882, the line was leased to the parent BB&K for $1 per year and maintenance expenses. The railroad made one more expansion. When the lumber interests of Elisha K. Kane completed the Big Level & Kinzua between Ormsby and Mount Jewett on December 1, 1886, the BB&K leased it, thereby gaining a direct connection with the Pittsburgh & West-

ern for Pittsburgh. Thereafter, the BB&K's main-line passenger trains ran from Bradford to Kane (41 miles).

The BB&K's financial history directly followed the history of the oil field. The railroad was extremely profitable in 1881 and early in 1882, paying dividends equal to about 39 percent of the investment. The abrupt decline of the oil boom late in 1882 ended the line's prosperity, causing the management on March 12, 1883, to accept the same arrangement as the Bradford, Eldred & Cuba and the Tonawanda Valley & Cuba whereby the Erie took control of the railroad in return for a guaranty of its bonds and a preferential traffic agreement. The arrangement was hardly a success, for the BB&K defaulted upon its interest payments in 1885, and the Erie refused to advance the funds for payment. The Erie was upheld by the courts and the BB&K became insolvent. George L. Roberts of Bradford was appointed receiver on December 12, 1890. The railroad was sold to a committee of bondholders and reorganized on April 1, 1892, as the Bradford, Bordell & Kinzua Railway. The new management of George L. Roberts pursued a policy of contraction, giving up the trackage rights on the Big Level & Kinzua in 1892, and abandoning the Eldred branch in October 1892 in anticipation of the abandonment of the Bradford, Eldred & Cuba in January 1893. The seven miles from Kinzua Junction to Rixford were retained to serve a sawmill until 1897, when the five miles from Rew City to Rixford were abandoned. The remainder of the branch from Kinzua Junction to Rew City was

abandoned in 1898. The Bordell branch had been abandoned in the late 1880s. On June 30, 1896, the BB&K resumed its lease of the BL&K and restored its passenger service to Kane. The Baltimore & Ohio, which had gained control of the Pittsburgh & Western, was eager to convert the line, but was not immediately interested in doing so north of the Allegheny River. Accordingly, on November 11, 1901, the B&O leased the 101 miles of the P&W from Foxburg to Mount Jewett to the BB&K for one year for 48.5 percent of the line's gross receipts. The arrangement proved a disaster to the BB&K, which lost $38,077 in the course of the year. It returned the line to the B&O, but continued its trackage rights over the BL&K and P&W to Kane. The BB&K again became insolvent, was sold at a judicial sale of December 4, 1903, and on January 6, 1904, was reorganized as the Buffalo, Bradford & Kane Railroad under control of the Goodyear lumber interests. The oil boom was long in the past, and the general traffic in lumber was inadequate to support the railroad. It was abandoned on September 2, 1906.

REFERENCES: Allen, "The Railroads of McKean County, Pa.," pp. 64–85; Thomas Barber and James Woods, *Bradford, Bordell & Kinzua* (Bradford, Penn.: Thomas Barber and James Woods, 1971).

Bradford, Eldred & Cuba Railroad

By means of this narrow gauge the Erie served the oil field at Bolivar and Richburg in Allegany County, New York, and penetrated the McKean County oil field via a connection to the Bradford, Bordell & Kinzua's affiliate, the Rew City & Eldred, at Eldred, Pennsylvania. The Bradford, Eldred & Cuba was incorporated in New York on May 11, 1881, by a group that included five directors of the Erie. The southernmost 9.36 miles, between Ceres, New York, and Eldred, were separately incorporated in Pennsylvania as the Bradford, Richburg & Cuba Railroad. Similarly, the 18 miles from Little Genesee to Wellsville were incorporated as the Wellsville, Bolivar & Eldred Railroad. A branch of two miles off the WB&E from Bolivar to Richburg was owned by the BE&C itself. About 30 miles of the railroad were put in service in 1881 and the remainder in 1882. As completed, the railroad was about 54 miles. The physical plant was poor even by narrow gauge standards, with no masonry on bridge abutments and a curve of 30°. The line mainly followed the Allegheny River. A through passenger train was run from Wellsville on the Erie main line to Bradford jointly with the BB&K.

The oil boom at Richburg and Bolivar collapsed particularly abruptly in 1882, causing the railroad to be profitable only for its first two years, and chronically in the red beginning in 1883. The Erie guaranteed the line's bonds on March 12, 1883, but this was not enough to prevent default in January 1885. T. C. Platt of the Addison & Northern Pennsylvania was appointed receiver on February 4. After 1884 the northernmost 19.4 miles, from Little Genesee to Cuba (where the line had a second connection with the Erie main line, and a junction with the Erie's narrow gauge Tonawanda Valley & Cuba), were closed in the winter months. By court order of September 24, 1888, this trackage was abandoned; the Bolivar-Richburg branch had been shut down in 1885. The railroad, which had been operated with six locomotives at its peak, was down to two by 1891. The operation was shut down by court order on January 14, 1893, and the property sold under foreclosure on January 25. The railroad was removed, and about 2.6 miles of the right-of-way at Bolivar were used for the Pittsburg, Shawmut & Northern main line.

REFERENCE: Allen, "The Railroads of McKean County, Pa.," pp. 64–85.

Bradford Railway

Kinzua Railway

Charles S. Cary, B. D. and D. R. Hamlin, and other men active in promoting narrow gauges in the oil field formed the Bradford Railway on January 8, 1881, and opened it from the Erie crossing in Bradford to Marshburg (12 miles) in July. They then proceeded to build the Kinzua Railway from Marshburg to Kinzua (14 miles), opening the combined system on September 27. The two companies were purchased by the Buffalo, New York & Philadelphia Railway on December 8, 1881. The BNY&P installed a car lifter for truck-transfer by jack screws at Kinzua and inaugurated through passenger trains between Bradford and Warren.

The narrow gauge became an incompatible part of a comprehensive network of the Western New York & Pennsylvania Railway in the area. In 1896 the WNY&P abandoned the Bradford Railway except for 0.05 miles in Bradford, which, with a larger remnant of the Olean, Bradford & Warren, was retained for standard gauge switching. The Kinzua Railway was converted in June 1896. It was cut back a mile

The passenger train of the affiliated Bradford Railway and Kinzua Railway bore the lettering of the parent Buffalo, New York & Philadelphia. (Ed Bond collection.)

A passenger train of the Kendall & Eldred on Baker trestle. (Smithsonian Institution.)

from Marshburg to Gates by the Pennsylvania Railroad in 1906, and eight miles from Gates to Morrisons in 1927. The remaining five miles from Kinzua to Morrisons were abandoned in 1953.

REFERENCES: C. F. H. Allen, "The Railroads of McKean County," Railway & Locomotive Historical Society Bulletin, no. 80 (1950), pp. 78–83; Thomas T. Taber III, "Sawmills among the Derricks," in The Logging Railroad Era of Lumbering in Pennsylvania, 2 vols. (Lancaster, Penn.: Benjamin F. G. Kline, Jr., 1973), vol. 2, pp. 722–25.

Kendall & Eldred Railroad

During the inflow of resources to the Pennsylvania oil field, the Kendall & Eldred

was founded in 1877 by George B. Gates of Buffalo, Charles S. Cary of Olean, and other men already active in the Olean, Bradford & Warren. The line was undertaken to connect Kendall (Tarport; East Bradford) with the Buffalo, New York & Philadelphia at Eldred (18 miles). The narrow gauge was lightly graded and had extensive trestles of raw lumber. The railroad was said to have paid for itself in only three months, even in advance of completion on July 30, 1878. In its short life, the railroad was to pay over $300,000 in dividends, about double its capitalization. The railroad shared terminal facilities in Bradford with the OB&W; the railroads' joint roundhouse burned on November 3, 1881. The eastern half of the K&E ran closely parallel to the Rew City &

Eldred. In 1882 the Pennsylvania laid third rail on the BNY&P for eight miles from Eldred to Portville, New York, to provide a connection between the K&E and the Allegany Central.

In 1882 the railroad was sold to the BNY&P for $300,000. The sellers' timing could hardly have been better, for the sale approximately coincided with the peaking of the oil boom. The Western New York & Pennsylvania, successor to the BNY&P, gave up operation of the narrow gauge on December 9, 1893, and removed the rails in July 1894, but did not formally abandon the railroad until 1898.

REFERENCES: Allen, "The Railroads of Mc-Kean County," pp. 77–78; Robert E. Stout, *The Kendall & Eldred Narrow Gauge Railroad* (Allegany, N.Y.: Robert E. Stout, 1972).

Mount Jewett, Kinzua & Riterville Railroad

The first segment of this extensive lumber railroad operated briefly as a narrow gauge. Elisha Kent Kane, a lumber operator based at Kushequa, three miles from Mount Jewett, incorporated the Mount Jewett, Kinzua & Riterville Railroad on April 27, 1889, to run from Mount Jewett through Kushequa to a junction with the Erie near Crawford's Summit. The railroad was built from Mount Jewett to Kushequa and Camp Halsey (5 miles) in 1889, but not pressed farther as a narrow gauge. From the outset the railroad was laid with standard gauge ties and built to standard gauge clearances. It had one narrow gauge locomotive and five cars. A third rail was laid in 1890 and the narrow gauge removed in 1891–92.

The railroad expanded mainly through leases, but contracted with the decline of lumbering in the area. It was absorbed by the Baltimore & Ohio in 1931. The B&O abandoned it except for the Mount Jewett–Kushequa portion, and kept that only until 1942.

Olean, Bradford & Warren Railway

Marcus Hulings, who had already made a fortune in the oil field at Clarion, leased 6,000 acres of oil land near Derrick City in June 1876, and began efforts in February 1877 to promote a narrow gauge from Bradford eastward, either to Eldred, Pennsylvania, or Olean, New York. Charles S. Cary of Olean, who was active in promoting the narrow gauges that became part of

the Buffalo, New York & Philadelphia's system in the oil field, swayed Hulings to build toward Olean. It was necessary to have separate corporations in each state. The portion in New York was incorporated by Cary as the Olean, Bradford & Warren Railroad on October 17, 1877, to build 12.5 miles from Olean to the state line. The Pennsylvania portion was incorporated as the Olean, Bradford & Warren Railway with Hulings as president. The charter provided for a route through Bradford to Warren, but only the ten miles from the border to Bradford were built. The survey began on October 2, 1877, and the railroad was finished in only 94 days, opening on February 8, 1878. The railroad was considered relatively good by the low standards of the oil field narrow gauges, capable of 20-mile-per-hour running without serious risk of derailment, in spite of continual curvature. The railroad had 20 pile-trestles or bridges and a 3.54-percent ruling grade. About a mile of third rail was later laid outside of Olean to allow standard gauge cars to be switched into a tannery. The Buffalo, New York & Philadelphia acquired stock control of the line on December 8, 1881.

The collapse of the oil boom late in 1882 greatly reduced the line's traffic, and by 1890 little business remained. The OB&W was closed on August 6, 1896, but an annual franchise run was inaugurated to keep the right-of-way. About 2.5 miles from Bradford to Tarpot were converted to serve a refinery, and the standard gauge track to the tannery outside of Olean was retained. The Olean, Rock City & Bradford Electric Railroad, formed in 1897, condemned the right-of-way for its standard gauge interurban on June 30, 1898, and built the line in 1901. The electric line became part of the Western New York & Pennsylvania Traction Co., which abandoned it in 1927.

REFERENCES: Allen, "The Railroads of Mc-Kean County," pp. 70–77; George W. Hilton and John F. Due, *The Electric Interurban Railways in America* (Stanford, Calif.: Stanford University Press, 1960), p. 311.

Tonawanda Valley & Cuba Railroad

The Attica & Allegheny Valley Railroad was formed in 1852 to connect Buffalo and Pittsburgh via the Tonawanda Valley of western New York. The company, which was mainly interested in northbound coal movements, acquired a right-of-way between Attica and Arcade, graded it, laid ties, installed bridge abutments, and ordered rail in 1853 and 1854 before failing. The

property was sold under foreclosure on February 2, 1856, and the project abandoned, but the existence of the grade was an incentive to later promoters to build on this route. The Attica & Arcade Railroad of 1870 attempted to build a standard gauge railroad on the grade, but failed to raise funds in the aftermath of the Panic of 1873, and gave up the effort after a final attempt to promote it as a narrow gauge in 1880. R. N. Farnham, who had been a director of the Attica & Arcade, formed the Tonawanda Valley Railroad on April 5, 1880, with the participation of the Erie. He undertook construction of 3'-0" track from Attica on the Erie's Buffalo branch south along the A&A's grade, opening the railroad to Curriers (19 miles) on September 11. To build farther south the promoters organized a subsidiary, the Tonawanda Valley Extension Railroad, with authority to build to Sardinia. Instead, they built to Arcade, about five miles to the east, opening the line (26 miles) on May 16, 1881. There were incentives to build farther south to Cuba, partly to reach the Erie's main line and partly to make a connection with the Bradford, Eldred & Cuba for the oil field in Allegany County, New York, and McKean County, Pennsylvania. To make this extension, the Tonawanda Valley & Cuba Railroad was chartered on July 14, 1881; the Tonawanda Valley and the Tonawanda Valley Extension were merged into this corporation on August 27. Construction began the following spring, and the line was opened to Cuba (59 miles) on September 11, 1882. The line interchanged with the Erie by truck-transfer both at Attica and Cuba.

The collapse of the oil boom late in 1882 reduced interchange with the BE&C, and motivated the TV&C management to join the BE&C and the Bradford, Bordell & Kinzua in the agreement of March 12, 1883, whereby the Erie guaranteed the bonds of the three railroads in return for stock control. The TV&C became delinquent on its interest payments on September 1, 1884, and was placed in receivership on November 29. Receiver B. W. Spencer suspended the mail train on January 19, 1885, and shortly shut down the railroad when the employees, who were four months in arrears in receiving their wages, struck against him. The railroad operated intermittently, usually closing during winter weather, until the receiver, on September 30, 1886, discontinued service on the 29.5 miles south of Sandusky in Freedom Township. The northern portion of the railroad, being built on a grade intended for a standard gauge line, was much superior to the southern, which had been laid out to ordinary narrow gauge standards. As with the two lines to the south, the Erie in 1885 had refused to honor its guaranty of the bonds. Strife broke out among the creditors of the TV&C's predecessor companies, with the bondholders of Tionesta Valley Extension claiming that building to Arcade rather than to Sardinia had been *ultra vires*. The railroad, which was in highly deteriorated condition, was sold for $33,000 on January 19, 1891, to a bondholders' group, who organized the Attica & Freedom Railroad to operate the 29.5 miles from Attica to Sandusky. In November they removed the 26 miles from Cuba to Fish Lake (Crystal Lake), a resort 3.5 miles south of Sandusky. A daily mixed train was run over the north end at low speed, for the railroad had ceased to be operable over ten miles per hour. The enterprise went bankrupt and was sold on October 13, 1894, to lumberman Spencer S. Bullis of Olean and his associates, who reorganized it as the Buffalo, Arcade & Attica Railroad. They immediately prepared to convert the railroad. Standard gauge operation began from Attica to Curriers on January 9, 1895, but further progress was halted by continuing controversy with the Tonawanda Valley Extension bondholders. The problem was reconciled in August, and the converted line opened to Arcade (16 miles) on December 1. Full service began early in 1896. No immediate effort was made to lay standard gauge rail below Arcade to Fish Lake. Rather, late in 1897 the management built a new line of two miles southwest to a connection with the Pennsylvania Railroad's Buffalo line at Arcade Junction; this was to replace the Erie at Attica as the railroad's principal interchange. In 1901, during the interurban boom, Bullis proposed to use the right-of-way from Arcade to Fish Lake for a steam or electric line to develop the resort, but he succeeded only in reopening the line to a gravel pit at Sandusky. When his project had failed along with an affiliated one, headed by Jim Rafferty, for an electric line from Java Center near the midpoint of the railroad to Buffalo, the spur was removed in 1902.

In 1904 the railroad was sold for $75,000 to Frank H. Goodyear, who planned to build through Arcade on the projected Buffalo extension of his Buffalo & Susquehanna Railway. Goodyear proposed to use the BA&A either for a segment of the Buffalo line or as part of a branch to Port Charlotte near Rochester for a coal port on Lake Ontario. The Buffalo extension was opened in 1906 without incorporating the BA&A into the line, although it may have used a portion of the abandoned grade between Arcade and Arcade Junction built by

the Buffalo, Arcade & Attica. Goodyear died in 1907, and the branch to Port Charlotte was never built. The Buffalo extension was highly unsuccessful, lasting only a decade. The B&S went bankrupt in 1910. The BA&A was returned to independent operation in 1913 and leased to W. L. Kann of Pittsburgh. The railroad, which was mainly a carrier of dairy products, went bankrupt in March 1917, and was reorganized on May 23 as the Arcade & Attica Railroad under local ownership. The A&A proved a moderately successful short line, dependent mainly on local originations on the south end of the railroad. Tonawanda Creek flooded on January 23, 1957, washing out several hundred feet of the railroad south of Attica. The directors decided to abandon the 13 miles from Attica to North Java. The remainder, from Arcade Junction to North Java, is in service at the present writing.

REFERENCES: C. F. H. Allen, "The Railroads of McKean County, Pa.," Railway & Locomotive Historical Society *Bulletin*, no. 76 (1949), pp. 52–56; Edward A. Lewis, *Arcade & Attica Railroad* (Arcade, N.Y.: The Baggage Car, 1966).

▼ ▼ ▼ ▼

The Bradford & Foster Brook Railway, a monorail, was organized under the Pennsylvania statute for chartering narrow gauge railroads on October 4, 1877, by Colonel A. I. Wilcox and W. E. Coddington of Bradford. The line was always considered part of the narrow gauge network in the oil field. The technology, which had been invented by General Roy Stone, entailed a line of 12″ × 12″ oak pilings rising four to ten feet above the ground. An oak beam of the same size ran horizontally, bearing a 25-pound rail. Wooden stabilizing rails ran three feet below the railhead along each side. Hinged sections were provided for road crossings and switches. The locomotives and rolling stock ran astride the beamway. The line, which was a common carrier of passengers and freight, was opened from Bradford to Gilmore (6 miles) in the summer of 1878. Initially it carried substantial traffic, but it was looked upon as less dependable than the Olean, Bradford & Warren, which closely paralleled it. The line's third locomotive exploded during its trials on January 29, 1879, killing six people. The disaster effectively ended the line's operation. It was seized by the sheriff on March 10, 1880, and removed on April 20.

REFERENCES: Lawrence W. Kilmer, *Bradford & Foster Brook Peg Leg Railroad* (Olean, N.Y.: Lawrence W. Kilmer, 1974); Mark Reinsberg, "General Stone's Elevated Railroad: Portrait of an Inventor," *Western Pennsylvania*

Historical Magazine, 49 (1966), pp. 186–95, 331–43, and 50 (1967), pp. 7–21.

South Carolina

All South Carolina narrow gauge railroads are shown on the map of North Carolina.

Branchville & Bowman Railroad

In 1891 Samuel Dibble bought the Smoak Tramway, a lumber tramway that ran nine miles northeast from Branchville, a junction between two predecessors of the Southern Railway. Dibble incorporated it as the Branchville & Bowman Railroad on April 11, 1891, and prepared to extend the line to Bowman, a town of some 300 about a mile and a half distant. The extension was built slowly in 1892 and 1893. E. T. R. Smoak became superintendent. The management bought a secondhand locomotive, No. 4 of the Augusta, Gibson & Sandersville, and a variety of rolling stock from 3′-0″ subsidiaries of the Southern Railway that had converted or were planning to do so. Although both freight and passenger services were operated, the railroad was mainly a lumbering facility. Ties for the Southern Railway were the principal traffic. In fiscal 1901 gross revenues were only $4,735. At that time the company was reported to have four miles of branches for lumbering operations. In the early twentieth century it was reportedly leased at various times to lumber operators at Bowman, Farris & Wise and Mittle & Schule. After 1918 the railroad was controlled by the Dukes family, also local lumber operators.*

---

* *Poor's Manual* reported the railroad's gauge as 3′-11″ from 1906 to 1919, but 3′-0″ both earlier and later. The 3′-11″ figure is apparently erroneous, to judge from what is known about the railroad's equipment, but it has been reproduced in various secondary sources. *Poor's* reported the line as having four locomotives in 1918, but this is apparently a confusion with the number of its only known locomotive. I am indebted to Wayne Lincoln for clarification of these points.

The railroad was frequently inactive after World War I and was reported abandoned in the spring of 1925.

Cheraw & Chester Railroad

Residents of Cheraw promoted this railroad as a connection to the Chester & Lenoir and the Charlotte, Columbia & Augusta, a standard gauge predecessor of the Southern Railway. The Cheraw & Chester was chartered on February 27, 1873, but could not immediately be financed. The promoters secured subscriptions from county governments and private parties, and let a bond issue in 1877. The railroad was opened 30.5 miles between Lancaster and Chester in 1880. The promoters' resources were exhausted with this construction, and the railroad was never built over the 55 miles between Lancaster and Cheraw.

The Charlotte, Columbia & Augusta leased the Cheraw & Chester on September 29, 1882, a week after leasing the Chester & Lenoir. The lease was abrogated on August 1, 1893, in the course of the reorganization of the CC&A's successor Richmond & Danville. A separate receiver was established for the Cheraw & Chester, and on December 1, 1893, it was returned to its owners. It was sold under foreclosure on June 1, 1896, and reorganized a month later as the Lancaster & Chester Railway, an identity it has maintained to the present.

The Lancaster & Chester converted the railroad, apparently early in 1902. As a standard gauge, it has been a prosperous short line serving a substantial number of cotton mills.

Chester & Lenoir Narrow Gauge Railroad

Not alone among the narrow gauges, the Chester & Lenoir was formed to make use of a right-of-way of a broad gauge railroad destroyed in the Civil War. The Kings Mountain Railroad had been built from Yorkville (York) to Chester, 23 miles, in the 1850s, but had not been restored after the war.

The Chester & Lenoir was separately incorporated in North Carolina as the Carolina Narrow Gauge Railroad on February 8, 1872, and in South Carolina as the Chester & Lenoir Narrow Gauge Railroad on February 26, 1873. The two were merged on April 3, 1874, along with the Kings Mountain Railroad. This arrangement proved to give predecessors of the Southern Railway an interest in the narrow gauge. The Charlotte & South Carolina Railroad had held

shares in the Kings Mountain, and the successor Charlotte, Columbia & Augusta asserted its claim to the equity.

Construction of the narrow gauge proceeded very slowly. Grading began in 1874, and the line was completed between Yorkville and Chester in 1874 or early 1875. Track reached Gastonia, North Carolina (45 miles), in mid-1876, and Dallas (49 miles) by the end of the year. By means of convict labor provided as an aid to the railroad by local officials, the grade reached Lincolnton in 1877, but the company was unable to lay track or otherwise finish the line. Dr. A. H. Davega of Chester, former president of the company, brought an action for recovery of $8,000 he had advanced to the railroad. Track was pushed to the Catawba River (53 miles) in 1880. After construction of a major bridge of three 110-foot Pratt-truss spans, track was pushed to Lincolnton (64 miles) in mid-1881, and to Maiden (73 miles) by the end of the year. The company had exhausted its resources and could not undertake the remaining 37 miles to Lenoir, even though some grading had been done. Since one of the main goals of the railroad was to transport lumber to the woodworking industry at Lenoir, the management's problem was severe. It arranged to lease the railroad to the Charlotte, Columbia & Augusta (which had become a part of the Richmond & Danville system) as of September 22, 1882, in return for the larger railroad's obligation to finish the narrow gauge in 18 months. With the proceeds of a bond issue of $100,000, the narrow gauge was completed to Lenoir on June 2, 1884. The ten miles between Newton and Hickory were built by laying third rail on the Western North Carolina Railroad. The finished railroad was a relatively large narrow gauge of 110 miles, with seven locomotives, 12 passenger cars, two head-end cars, and 111 freight cars.

The financial history of the railroad was part of the complicated process of formation of the Southern Railway. On May 1, 1886, the Richmond & Danville assumed operation of the Chester & Lenoir by leasing the CC&A. After the R&D went bankrupt, the lease of the C&L was abrogated in 1893. In the reorganization of the R&D system into the Southern Railway, the plan was originally to include the C&L, but because the narrow gauge was not covering its variable expenses, it was excluded. Neither the receivers for the R&D nor the CC&A wanted the railroad, and it was returned to its owners on December 1, 1893. A separate receiver was appointed, who operated the narrow gauge until 1897; it was then reorganized as the Carolina & Northwestern

Railway. In the following year, the management arranged for the Newton-Hickory mileage on the Western North Carolina to be relocated onto a new right-of-way immediately parallel. The C&NW began laying standard gauge ties in 1900, and converted the railroad late in 1902. The C&NW acquired the Caldwell & Northern narrow gauge in 1905, converted it in the following year, extended it to Edgemont, and operated it as an extension of the main line of 24 miles until 1938. The original line was operated by the C&NW as a separate railroad controlled by the Southern Railway until January 1, 1974, when its name was changed to the Norfolk Southern Railway, a wholly owned subsidiary of the Southern. The railroad was abandoned from York to Chester in 1972 and from Clover to York in 1981. The remaining 77 miles from Lenoir to Clover survive in the present Norfolk Southern system.

▼ ▼ ▼ ▼

The D. W. Taylor Lumber Co. built a private railroad in 1881 as a facility for its mill at Summerville on the South Carolina Railway. On December 22, 1886, the firm incorporated the line as the Summerville & Saint Johns Railroad, a nominal common carrier. The line ran 14 miles northwest from Summerville. In 1891 it was reported extended to 16 miles. The railroad had four locomotives, 20 or more cars for logs, and a caboose for passengers. The railroad served two stations in the Wassamassaw Swamp in Berkeley County, Appii Church and Deer Park. The Seaboard Air Line in 1889 showed some interest in acquiring the line as part of its projected secondary main line via Charleston to Savannah, but made other arrangements. The railroad was reported to the ICC as abandoned in fiscal 1896. It appears to have remained in existence either in private carriage or idle, and was sold to the J. F. Prettyman Lumber Co. in 1909 for use as a private carrier under the name of the Saint Johns Railroad. Prettyman was in operation as late as 1924.

REFERENCE: Collection of Tom Fetters.

South Dakota

Black Hills & Fort Pierre Railroad

At the time that gold was found in the Black Hills in 1874, no railroads served the area. When the mining boom occurred in 1876, the region had to be served by road drayage from the Northern Pacific or Union Pacific main lines or from steamboats at Fort Pierre on the Missouri River. The Homestake Mining Company, which had established itself as the dominant operator in the region, in 1881 advertised its intention to build a local railroad to haul timber, stone, and other supplies to its mine at Lead. On May 31, 1881, the line was incorporated as the Black Hills Railroad, but in 1882 the name was changed to Black Hills & Fort Pierre. The mining company may have had serious plans to build to the steamboat connection 162 miles away—approximately half the width of Dakota Territory—but the arrival of standard gauge railroads in the Black Hills in the late 1880s ended any such ambition.

A contract to build the narrow gauge was placed on April 29, 1881, and the first locomotive, a Porter 2-6-0, was brought in by mule team from Fort Pierre on November 29. In 1881 track was laid from Lead to Woodville, where Homestake had extensive timber holdings, and in 1886 to Bucks on Elk Creek to the southeast. The line had short branches both north and south of Lead. The arrival in the Black Hills of the standard gauge Fremont, Elkhorn & Missouri Valley Railway in 1887 caused Homestake to extend the narrow gauge up the Elk Creek Canyon in 1890 to a connection at Piedmont on the eastern edge of the Black Hills. The original line to Bucks was about 15 miles and the extension to Piedmont 21.5 miles. A major branch of about 14 miles was built up Box Elder Canyon from Bucks to Este in 1898. The canyons the railroad served were quite scenic, but the Black Hills had not yet been developed as a major tourist area. The railroad typically operated a single passenger train per day from Lead to Piedmont and a mixed train on the branch to Este.

Although the railroad remained mainly a facility of Homestake Mining's own activities, the company arranged on June 28, 1901, for the Burlington & Missouri River Railroad to operate it. For the rest of the narrow gauge's history it was operated as a minor branch of the Chicago, Burlington & Quincy system. As soon as the arrangement was made, third rail was laid on the narrow gauge's two short branches out of Lead, which aggregated only 2.5 miles, for standard gauge access to Homestake's facilities. In 1904 the B&MR was merged into the CB&Q. In 1906 a branch was built off the Box Elder Canyon line from Este to Merritt, somewhat over four miles, and extended in 1907 to serve newly worked timber lands. In the same year a cloudburst

A train of the Black Hills & Fort Pierre stops for its portrait in Elk Canyon. (W. A. Lucas collection, Railroad Museum of Pennsylvania.)

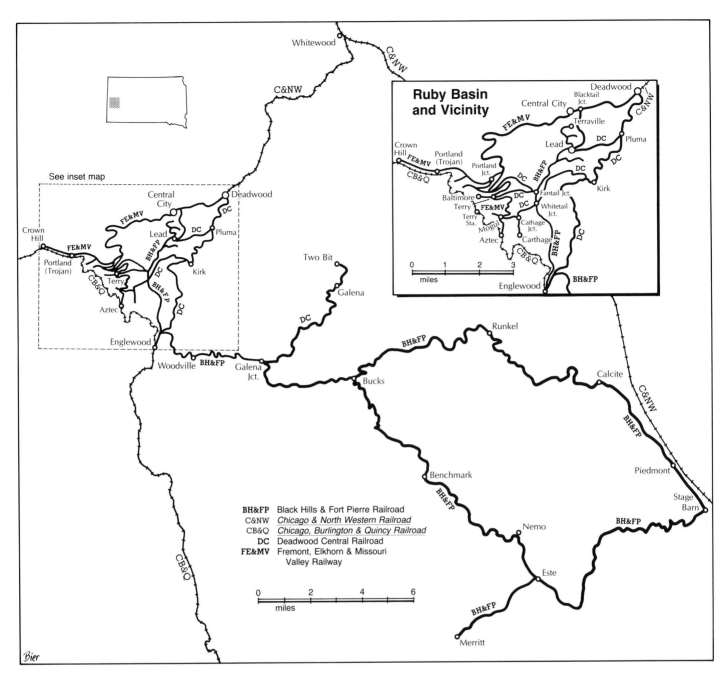

Ruby Basin
and Vicinity

BH&FP   Black Hills & Fort Pierre Railroad
C&NW   *Chicago & North Western Railroad*
CB&Q   *Chicago, Burlington & Quincy Railroad*
DC   Deadwood Central Railroad
FE&MV Fremont, Elkhorn & Missouri
           Valley Railway

produced a flood that ravaged the entire Black Hills area. The main line to Piedmont through Elk Creek Canyon was so badly damaged between Bucks and Calcite, about 15.5 miles, that although it was returned to service the management decided to replace it. The Burlington undertook to extend the south branch from Este farther up Box Elder Canyon and through Repass into Stage Barn Canyon to connect with the trackage between Stage Barn and Calcite. The new line of 11 miles was opened August 16, 1910, and the damaged portion of the former main line abandoned.

With the coming of motor transport in the 1920s, such general traffic as the narrow gauge had declined. Homestake planned to close the lime kiln and quarry at Calcite

that were the principal remaining sources of traffic on the line. The Black Hills & Fort Pierre and the Burlington jointly applied to abandon the line on October 25, 1929, and received permission from both federal and state commissions in December 14, 1929. The last train ran on March 20, 1930, and the railroad was dismantled in the spring. The CB&Q had laid third rail on the Englewood-Lead portion of the narrow gauge. Portions of this survived as a standard gauge branch of the Burlington Northern until 1984.

Deadwood Central Railroad

J. K. P. Miller of Deadwood and his associates incorporated the Deadwood Cen-

tral Railroad on August 15, 1888, in the expectation of building a large radial network of narrow gauge trackage to serve their mining enterprises in the Black Hills and even across the border into Wyoming Territory. They projected a network of 344 miles to haul coal out of Briar Hill, salt and oil from neighboring Wyoming, and various minerals from mines and quarries in the Black Hills themselves to their smelter at Deadwood. The actual attainments were less extensive. The first completed portion of the railroad was a mere three miles from Deadwood to Lead via Pluma, opened on February 26, 1889. Initially the company operated with a Porter 0-6-0 tank engine. As a direct communication between the two main towns of the Black Hills mining area, the railroad quickly became a major passenger carrier. By 1895 trains operated approximately hourly, taking only about 15 minutes for the trip.

Apparently to secure funding for further expansion, the management made an agreement with the Burlington system, which was expanding into the Black Hills. The Chicago, Burlington & Quincy, in the name of its local subsidiary, the Grand Island & Wyoming Central, in 1890 bought the trackage from Deadwood to Pluma, only 1.72 miles, and the unbuilt right-of-way of the Deadwood Central from Pluma to Englewood, where the DC could connect with the Black Hills & Fort Pierre. The DC retained the right to narrow gauge operation on the Burlington's track. With the proceeds of this transaction, the Deadwood Central's management in 1891 laid narrow gauge track down the Burlington right-of-way to Kirk and thence up Whitetail Creek into the Ruby Basin, in which it built four branches to mines. The new mileage was about 5.95 miles. In 1893 the CB&Q bought the stock of the Deadwood Central, but allowed the company to remain in existence and operated the property as an agent. After the CB&Q assumed operation of the Black Hills & Fort Pierre in 1901, the two properties constituted a single narrow gauge network in the area. They both served Lead and intersected at Fantail Junction in the Ruby Basin, but in 1905 the Burlington provided an additional connection by laying third rail from Kirk to Englewood.

Two major changes in the railroad were made in 1902. The Burlington decided on a branch into the silver-mining town of Galena, down Bear Butte Creek from the BH&FP main line. Because the Deadwood Central had extensive ore cars, and the BH&FP was mainly equipped to handle lumber, the CB&Q built the line of about seven miles in the name of the Deadwood Central, even though it connected with the BH&FP at Galena Junction and was isolated from the rest of the Central. The branch brought the DC's mileage to 17.68, far short of the promoters' original intention.

The other major change of 1902 was the electrification of the Deadwood-Lead mileage. The frequency of service between the two towns made the route an obvious candidate for conversion to an electric line during the first building boom of interurbans in the early twentieth century. The project had been discussed since 1893. The Burlington strung wire over just under four miles of track on the main line from Deadwood to Pluma and up the Lead branch to some newly built track on the stretch serving the upper portion of the town. The street run-

This famous photograph delineates the complexity of the railroad system in the mining area. In the tri-level crossing, the Deadwood Central is at the bottom, the Fremont, Elkhorn & Missouri Valley on the intermediate level, and private trackage of the Homestake Mining Co. on the high level. (Ed Bond collection.)

Locomotive No. 64 stands on unusual four-rail track on the Chicago & North Western's narrow gauge network in the Black Hills. (Ed Bond collection.)

ning included an 8-percent grade. Three narrow gauge combines were bought to provide the service. The electrification allowed an increase in frequency; in 1918 the interurban was scheduled for 14 trips per day in each direction. After 1902, the Burlington used the Pluma-Lead branch mainly for the electric cars, and brought most freight into Lead on the BH&FP line.

The narrow gauge network began to atrophy in 1910. The Burlington removed the third rail between Kirk and Englewood

in 1917. As elsewhere, the spread of the automobile had rendered the interurban obsolete, causing the Burlington to secure permission to abandon it on August 31, 1924. The track was removed in 1927. The Galena line, which had no traffic from mines after 1921, was abandoned in September 1928. In 1930 the CB&Q converted the line from Kirk to Fantail Junction to standard gauge and abandoned the branch from Fantail Junction. The successor Burlington Northern withdrew from the mining area in 1984.

South Dakota   515

Fremont, Elkhorn & Missouri Valley Railway

The Chicago & North Western Railway reached the Black Hills mining area by a subsidiary, the Fremont, Elkhorn & Missouri Valley. This carrier built north from Chadron, Nebraska, on what eventually became the North Western's line to Lander, Wyoming. The route skirted the Black Hills to the east, running through Rapid City and terminating in Belle Fourche to the north. Deadwood was reached on December 29, 1890, with a branch from Whitewood that required a tunnel of 1,300 feet. Although the FE&MV was a standard gauge railroad, and the North Western had already converted as much of its narrow gauge lines in Wisconsin as possible, president Marvin Hughitt resolved upon building a network of 3'-0" trackage to serve mines above Deadwood. In the summer of 1891 the FE&MV built 18.35 miles of 3'-0" trackage from Deadwood into the mining areas. The line ascended along Deadwood Creek through Central City to Portland Junction at the foot of Bald Mountain, where the line branched. One line proceeded south across the drainage pattern of the Ruby Basin to Aztec. The other proceeded west to Portland (Trojan); this line was extended toward Crown Hill in 1892 and completed in 1897, a total of about 1.7 miles.

The depression of the 1890s, coupled with the repeal of the Sherman Silver Purchase Act in 1893, greatly reduced traffic on the narrow gauge. At the end of the summer of 1893 regular passenger service between Deadwood and Central City was dropped. Mixed trains operated irregularly depending on mine output. As evidenced by the resumption of building in 1897, traffic revived with the economy after 1896. By the early twentieth century the railroad was quite prosperous. In 1902, in anticipation of a convention of the Grand Lodge of Odd Fellows, a dual gauge spur of about two miles was built to Lead, gaining about 200 feet in altitude. The railroad was operated with 4-8-0 locomotives, an unusual choice for a narrow gauge. On the Lead line it was customary to ascend and descend with the pilot toward Lead to assure that the crownsheet of the firebox would be covered with water. There were no turning facilities at Lead. The railroad operated hourly passenger service between Deadwood and Lead.

The North Western absorbed the FE&MV in 1903. The narrow gauge had a history similar to that of its counterparts in Colorado, but it declined severely after World War I. Passenger service between Deadwood and Lead was discontinued in 1924, and in 1928 the entire narrow gauge was abandoned.

REFERENCE: Mildred Fiedler, *Railroads of the Black Hills* (Seattle, Wash.: Superior Publishing Co., 1964).

Tennessee

Duck River Valley Narrow Gauge Railroad

In a state where most narrow gauges were nominal common carriers, the Duck River Valley Narrow Gauge Railroad was projected as a general transport facility. The company was chartered on November 4, 1870, to run from Johnsonville on the Nashville, Chattanooga & St. Louis at its crossing of the Tennessee River west of Nashville, southeast through Centerville, Columbia, Lewisburg, Petersburg, and Fayetteville to Huntsville, Alabama. Only the center portion from Columbia to Fayetteville was built. The valley of the Duck River, which gave the railroad its name, was between Johnsonville and Centerville on the western portion that was never undertaken. The promoters, led by J. H. Lewis of Columbia, also envisioned the line as part of a St. Louis–Atlanta narrow gauge trunk, which never took shape.

A contract for the first segment from Columbia to Lewisburg was awarded to Nestor & McCann of Nashville in 1874. The grading was completed and about six miles of track were laid in 1876. The line was opened to Lewisburg (20 miles) in March 1877. The first 1.75 miles from Columbia were third rail on the Nashville & Decatur (Louisville & Nashville) main line. Track was pushed onward to Petersburg (34 miles) in mid-1879, but the promoters had exhausted their resources. The shareholders voted on September 23 to lease the railroad to the NC&StL in return for financial assistance in pressing on to Fayetteville, where the narrow gauge would connect with an NC&StL branch. This arrangement allowed the railroad to be completed to Fayetteville (48 miles) on March 16, 1882. The railroad was now essentially a branch of the NC&StL into Columbia with a break-of-gauge at Fayetteville. The NC&StL was authorized by its shareholders on March 21, 1888, to buy the narrow gauge and to convert it. Actually, preparations for conversion had begun in February and the job was completed at the end of 1888. The NC&StL did a particularly thorough job, relocating three miles of line entirely, building nine cutoffs, easing the worst curve from 16° to 10°30', and reducing the ruling grade from 2.5 to 2 percent. The road was relaid with 52-pound rail. It was opened for standard gauge service on January 1, 1889.

The branch was abandoned, as it had been built, from the north. The NC&StL abandoned the original Columbia-Fayetteville trackage at the end of 1945, and the successor L&N abandoned the Fayetteville-Lewisburg portion in 1961, retaining several segments of the branch as switching tracks or spurs at the major towns.

REFERENCE: Elmer G. Sulzer, *Ghost Railroads of Tennessee* (Indianapolis: Vane A. Jones Co., 1975), pp. 52–60.

East Tennessee & Western North Carolina Railroad

Linville River Railway

For all this carrier's identification with bucolic Appalachia, it was an important hauler of iron ore and lumber. The ET&WNC was chartered on May 24, 1866, to build a 5'-0" line from Carter or Johnson's Depot (Johnson City), Tennessee, to the Cranberry Iron Works at Cranberry, about four miles east of the North Carolina border. The promoters managed to lay about five miles of track from Johnson City to Watauga Point, but never acquired either locomotives or rolling stock. The only reported operation was some stone removal in November 1872, with equipment from the connecting East Tennessee, Virginia & Georgia. The ET&WNC was declared delinquent in its obligations to the state and sold for $20,000 to John Hughes, one of the promoters. Hughes sold it on September 10, 1875, to General Robert F. Hoke, Ario Pardee, and their associates, who had formed the Cranberry Iron & Coal Co. in 1873, buying out the Cranberry Iron Works. Pardee was also interested in the East Broad Top Railroad & Coal Co.; this narrow gauge and the ET&WNC were to have a minority community of ownership throughout their history. The new owners offered for sale the

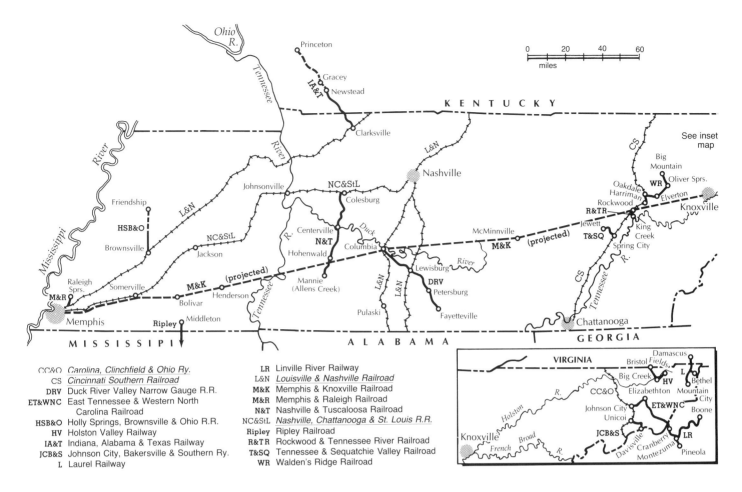

CC&O Carolina, Clinchfield & Ohio Ry.
CS   Cincinnati Southern Railroad
DRV   Duck River Valley Narrow Gauge R.R.
ET&WNC East Tennessee & Western North
       Carolina Railroad
HSB&O Holly Springs, Brownsville & Ohio R.R.
HV   Holston Valley Railway
IA&T Indiana, Alabama & Texas Railway
JCB&S Johnson City, Bakersville & Southern Ry.
L   Laurel Railway

LR   Linville River Railway
L&N   Louisville & Nashville Railroad
M&K   Memphis & Knoxville Railroad
M&R   Memphis & Raleigh Railroad
N&T   Nashville & Tuscaloosa Railroad
NC&StL Nashville, Chattanooga & St. Louis R.R.
Ripley Ripley Railroad
R&TR   Rockwood & Tennessee River Railroad
T&SQ   Tennessee & Sequatchie Valley Railroad
WR   Walden's Ridge Railroad

52-pound T-rail of the existing trackage and prepared to build the railroad as a narrow gauge. There was some difficulty in financing the project, such that title to the railroad was not transferred from Hughes to Pardee until May 22, 1879. The line was then built as quickly as the difficult terrain allowed. The route entailed an ascent of the Doe River Gorge with a prolonged 4-percent grade, four tunnels, and three large bridges; the railroad also had a tunnel approaching Hampton. The worst curve was 32°. The engineers chose 40-pound rail; partly because of the broad gauge origins, the line was relatively well built. It was opened to Hampton (14 miles) on August 11, 1881, and to Cranberry (34 miles) on July 3, 1882.

Traffic was mainly ore from the Cranberry mine, some of which was processed at the Cranberry Furnace, some of which was sent to a smelter of the Virginia Iron, Coal & Coke Co., at Johnson City. The ore was of high quality, used finally in tool steel. Especially after 1898, the line served mining and lumbering installations of other operators as well. The railroad typically operated a mail train and a mixed train daily.

Originally, the Linville River Railway was a lumber railroad, one of several such connections of the ET&WNC. As the Lin-

ville River Railroad, it was chartered by the Camp Brothers Lumber Co. on July 13, 1896, to serve a stand of white pine and a

Ario Pardee, one of the organizers of the East Broad Top, was among the largest coal operators in Pennsylvania. He also held an interest in the East Tennessee & Western North Carolina. (Ed Bond collection.)

mill at Saginaw (Pineola), North Carolina. Some grading was done, but the project was then abandoned. William T. Ritter and Isaac T. Mann, lumbermen of West Virginia, bought Camp Brothers's local properties for $12,000 at a public auction on June 6, 1898, and reincorporated the railroad as the Linville River Railway. They built the line from Cranberry to Pineola (12 miles) in 1899. Five logging lines were then built from Pineola; it was an orthodox operation of Shay and Climax locomotives. The track from Cranberry to Pineola, which handled a daily mixed train, was enrolled for common carriage from the outset.

Ritter had cut most of the timber in the area immediately tributary to Pineola by 1906; thus he built a new mill at Hampton in 1910. The ET&WNC had laid third rail on the 9.5 miles from Johnson City to Elizabethton between 1904 and 1906, and now extended it to the mill at Hampton. In 1903, in anticipation of the change, the ET&WNC had adopted the Janney coupler at standard gauge height, with a jointed shank on locomotives capable of coupling with either narrow or standard gauge equipment. In 1912 Ritter shut down the Pineola operation entirely, moving out the equipment by building a temporary connection east to the logging tracks serving the com-

The East Tennessee & Western North Carolina claimed with some justification that it ran the finest narrow gauge passenger train in the country. The rear view shows the parlor car *Azalea* on the train in 1914. The view from the front shows locomotive No. 9 on the train at Cranberry. The later scene shows a mixed train at the Elk Park station. (Ed Bond collection.)

pany's mill at Mortimer, North Carolina, on the Carolina & Northwestern. Having no further interest in the LR, Ritter sold it to the ET&WNC on August 1, 1913. The ET&WNC relaid the line with 50-pound rail, filled some trestles, and otherwise upgraded it for use by its rod engines. Lumberman William S. Whiting shortly bought 2,600 acres of timberland northeast of the railroad, and in May 1915 formed the Boone Fork Lumber Co. to develop them. This development prompted the ET&WNC to undertake an extension of 14 miles from Montezuma, two miles short of Pineola, to Whiting's plant at Shulls Mills. Completion of the extension on September 25, 1916, brought the track within eight miles of the historically isolated town of Boone, North Carolina, seat of Appalachian State Teachers College. Largely at the urging of the administration of the college, Boone voted a bond issue of $27,000, with the proceeds of which the LR was extended into Boone on October 24, 1918. Mail service began January 1, 1919, and regular passenger service on May 9. The ET&WNC regularly ran a daily round-trip from Johnson City to Boone (66 miles), including a parlor car, *Azalea*. Between 1917 and 1921 the railroad bought wooden, enclosed-platform coaches, combines, and a railway post office from Jackson & Sharp for the train; with some justification it claimed that the effort produced the most luxurious narrow gauge passenger train in the country. Owing to the decline in demand for passenger service in the Depression, most of this equipment was sold for service in Central America in 1936.

In 1906 CI&CCo. closed the furnace at Cranberry and bought the VIC&CCo. furnace at Johnson City, causing all of the ore from Cranberry to move the length of the ET&WNC. World War I stimulated this traffic, but the decline in demand after the war motivated the company to shut down the Cranberry mine in 1921. It was reopened in 1923, but closed permanently in 1929. Large-scale lumbering had also ended by this time, so that the railroad was left dependent on cordwood, general merchandise, and its mail contract. The company established a highway subsidiary in 1926, which ran buses between Bristol and Asheville via Johnson City and Elizabethton, and operated truck service, including the handling of some semitrailers on the railroad in a rare narrow gauge piggyback operation.

On August 13, 1940, a flood washed out much of the LR. The railroad applied to abandon it on September 4, and received permission from the ICC on March 22, 1941. The railroad dropped regular pas-

The East Tennessee & Western North Carolina upon taking over the Linville River began upgrading the former lumber railroad to its own standards. Here an ET&WNC crew fills in a trestle on the acquisition. (Ed Bond collection.)

senger service at that time, but on August 10, 1942, the management restored passenger trains from a war plant at Port Rayon, just west of Elizabethton, to Cranberry. This service, for which coaches were bought from the abandoned Boston, Revere Beach & Lynn, was discontinued at the end of the war. Freight service lasted another five years. The last freight train ran on October 16, 1950, and the narrow gauge was abandoned. The railroad survived as a standard gauge operation, however. Third rail between Elizabethton and Hampton had been removed in 1941 as a consequence of the abandonment of the Southern Railway's branch into Elizabethton, but the standard gauge remained between Johnson City and Elizabethton. This trackage is still in service. The railroad contracted its name to East Tennessee Railway at the end of 1983.

REFERENCES: Julian Scheer and Elizabeth Black, *Tweetsie: The Blue Ridge Stemwinder* (Charlotte, N.C.: Heritage House, 1958); Mallory Hope Ferrell, *Tweetsie Country: The East Tennessee & Western North Carolina Railroad* (Boulder, Colo.: Pruett Publishing Co., 1976).

Holston Valley Railway

The Willey Boom & Lumber Co. incorporated this railroad on September 10, 1892, and opened it from Bristol to Big Creek (8 miles) in March 1896. Although a logging railroad in purpose and operation, the line enjoyed a general freight and passenger traffic, especially in pleasure travelers from Bristol to points along the Holston River. It was extended to Fish Dam (11 miles) in 1903 and to Fields (13 miles) in 1904. The lumber company, which was rechartered as Morton, Lewis & Willey on July 6, 1896, cut the line back to Fish Dam in 1910, and reportedly closed its mill at Bristol in 1912. The rail line continued to operate in connection with the Bristol Traction Co., however. Bristol Traction acquired the line as far as Big Creek in 1915, converted it, electrified it, and operated it as part of the company's system until 1918, when the line was abandoned.

REFERENCE: Sulzer, *Ghost Railroads of Tennessee*, pp. 224–26.

Indiana, Alabama & Texas Railway

General John B. Gordon conceived of this railroad as a narrow gauge rival of the Louisville & Nashville, running from Evansville, Indiana, to Mobile, via Florence, Alabama. To this end, he formed separate corporations under the name of the Indiana, Alabama & Texas Railway in Kentucky, Tennessee, and Alabama in March 1882, but merged them later in the year. In November 1884 the company absorbed another unbuilt railroad, the Mobile, Clarksville & Evansville. Gordon chose to begin the line with the segment between Clarksville, Tennessee, and Princeton, Kentucky, about 57 miles. Both towns subscribed to the railroad, and at the south end an existing uncompleted grade could be utilized. Princeton was in the western Kentucky

coalfield on the Chesapeake & Ohio Southwestern, and Clarksville was on the L&N's Memphis line. Construction began from Clarksville late in 1884, and by the end of the year ten miles of track had been laid, with an additional 13 miles graded. By the end of 1885 track reached Newstead (30 miles), but even though an additional ten miles had been graded, no further rail was laid. The railroad reportedly had two locomotives and 75 cars, including passenger equipment.

In August 1886 the L&N bought stock control of the railroad. A minority of shareholders sought an injunction to prevent the transaction on the ground that the narrow gauge had secured its local subscriptions on the condition that the road would be an independent rival to the L&N. The L&N was victorious, but the legal action delayed absorption of the IA&T into the L&N until the following year. The L&N reported the line converted and extended to Princeton in December 1887. The conversion entailed abandonment of the southernmost six miles of the narrow gauge in favor of a new connection to the L&N from Elliott's Pond to Princeton Junction, three miles northeast of Clarksville, to avoid some tortuous trackage along the West Fork of the Red River. In 1892 the L&N leased the Gracey-Princeton portion of the extension to the Ohio Valley Railway (Illinois Central) for 99 years. The remainder of the branch, from Princeton Junction to Gracey, was abandoned on May 13, 1933.

REFERENCE: Elmer G. Sulzer, *Ghost Railroads of Kentucky* (Indianapolis: Vane A. Jones Co., 1967), pp. 116–17.

Johnson City, Bakersville & Southern Railway

William E. Uptegrove & Bros., engaged in lumbering on Clear Fork, began private carriage in September 1902. Uptegrove in 1903 sold his enterprise to the American Cigar Box Lumber Co., in which he retained an interest. On March 10, 1905, ACBL chartered the Johnson City, Bakersville & Southern Railway as a common carrier to operate the railroad. The line ran from Unicoi on the Carolina, Clinchfield & Ohio southeast to Davisville on the state line (7 miles). The railroad held 10.7 miles of track, including spurs; it sometimes cited Limestone Cove on one of these as its terminus. The line had two Shay locomotives, a passenger car, and a varying number of logging cars.

Uptegrove began liquidating his holdings in 1908. Lee F. Miller, a contractor, bought the railroad on September 10, 1909, and organized it as the Unicoi Railway. He substantially rebuilt the property and turned it over to the new management led by F. K. Bradshaw on January 1, 1910. The line was abandoned upon exhaustion of timber resources in 1918.

REFERENCE: Sulzer, *Ghost Railroads of Tennessee*, p. 125.

Laurel Railway

The T. W. Thayer Lumber Co. organized the Laurel Railway on March 21, 1905, mainly to serve its private interests, but the line was to serve at least three other lumber companies as well as operators of manganese mines in the area. It was built from Damascus, Virginia, on the Virginia-Carolina Railway south to Mountain City (16 miles), seat of Johnson County, Tennessee. The line had a branch of a mile from Laurel Bloomery east to Bethel, plus spurs to serve extractive enterprises. A Porter tank engine provided two passenger trips per day. The roster also contained a 2-6-0, two Climaxes, and three Shays. The operation was straightforwardly that of a lumber railroad. A branch of the Southern Railway served Mountain City, preventing the narrow gauge from satisfying much of the town's general transportation demands.

Exhaustion of timber and decline of the manganese mines caused the narrow gauge to cease regular operation in 1919 and to be removed in 1924.

REFERENCE: Sulzer, *Ghost Railroads of Tennessee*, pp. 227–30.

Nashville & Tuscaloosa Railroad

E. F. Falconnet of Nashville and his associates formed this railroad on June 6, 1877, to build a narrow gauge of about 200 miles from a point on the Hickman line of the Nashville, Chattanooga & St. Louis to Florence and Tuscaloosa, Alabama. After first considering Burns as the northern terminus, they decided to build from a point called N&T Junction, about two miles east of Dickson and immediately west of Colesburg; trains originated in Dickson and apparently used third rail to the junction. If the management had plans to build into Nashville, about 39 miles to the east, they were not reported.

In 1879 the promoters built the railroad to Graham (24 miles), but were unable to proceed farther. On July 20, 1880, they arranged a contract whereby the railroad would be conveyed to the NC&StL in return for the NC&StL's completing it to the north bank of the Duck River opposite Centerville. The NC&StL undertook construction immediately, reaching Goodrich (27 miles) in 1882 and the north bank of the river (33 miles) early in 1883; accordingly, the N&T was conveyed to the NC&StL on March 13, 1883. The NC&StL bridged the river into Centerville and extended the line to Kimmins (Lewis; 47 miles) in 1884. The railroad did not attempt further construction, but on September 24, 1892, it bought a 17-mile private carrier narrow gauge from its owner, the Southern Iron Co. The acquisition, which connected with the existing line a short distance above Kimmins, brought the line to Hohenwald (52 miles), seat of Lewis County, and to Mannie (Allens Creek; 63 miles), seat of the iron company's works. With the extension, and with seven locomotives and 94 freight cars, this was a fairly large narrow gauge. The line had one branch, a spur of two miles built in 1881 from Lyles to Warner to serve an iron furnace. For the $100,000 in cash and $25,000 in bonds that the Southern Iron Co. received for its railroad, it obligated itself to build two furnaces at Mannie and to ship the entire output over the NC&StL. With this assured source of traffic, the NC&StL proceeded to convert the line in June 1894. As a branch it remained relatively strong, with substantial traffic in phosphates as well as iron.

The line was cut back from Allens Creek to Hohenwald in 1942. The remainder survived within the NC&StL and its later entities until spun off to the South Central Tennessee Railroad, one of the several short lines of W. B. Kyle, in 1985. It remains in service.

REFERENCES: Sulzer, *Ghost Railroads of Tennessee*, pp. 141–44; Richard E. Prince, *The Nashville, Chattanooga and St. Louis Railway* (Green River, Wyo.: Richard E. Prince, 1967), p. 30.

Rockwood & Tennessee River Railroad

The Roane Iron Co. built this railroad as a 5'-0" mule tramway from its furnace at Rockwood 5.5 miles to King Creek, a landing on the Tennessee River. The line was converted to a 3'-0" railroad in 1877, partly for conformity with some private trackage the company was building to serve ore deposits from Long Island, 20 miles upstream. The cars moved to the furnace by a towboat-and-barge connection. The R&TR served a general common carrier function, connecting Rockwood with steamboats on the Tennessee. Three passenger trains per day were run. When the Cincinnati Southern Railway (completed between Cincinnati and Chattanooga in 1880) was built through Rockwood, the common carrier status of the narrow gauge became nominal; it was dropped in 1898. The line thereafter served as a facility for inbound ore movements to

Cars of the Laurel Railway, trucks and all, were carried on the flatcars of the Virginia-Carolina Railway to Abingdon, Virginia, where the logs were processed. (Ed Bond collection.)

the furnace. When the Cincinnati, New Orleans & Texas Pacific, lessee of the Cincinnati Southern, built a branch from Cardiff to Hood Landing in 1911, the iron company was able to reduce its river trip from 20 to 14 miles at the cost of instituting a ten-mile rail movement. This change in operations resulted in the narrow gauge's abandonment, also in 1911.

Tennessee & Sequatchie Valley Railroad

To serve the lumber installation of E. D. Albro & Co. and the mines of the Walden's Ridge Coal & Iron Co., this railroad was chartered as a common carrier on August 20, 1880. The intended route was from Spring City on the Cincinnati Southern up Walden's Ridge to Grand View, down to Jewett (12 miles), on about two miles to the headwaters of the Sequatchie River, and down its valley to Pikeville, seat of Bledsoe County. If completed, the line would have been about 42 miles. The railroad began operating two passenger trains per day between Spring City and Grand View on January 15, 1882. The line was opened to Jewett on August 31. Charles Clinton of New York bought a controlling interest in the property in mid-1882 and became its president and general manager, but he proved unable to extend the line.

In 1883 E. D. Albro obtained a judgment against the railroad for $52,740 and bought it on September 24. He reorganized it as the Tennessee Central Railroad with a charter to build west to Nashville via Sparta and east to Murphy, North Carolina, a total of about 175 miles. The route would have been to the south of the later Tennessee Central Railway, the standard gauge line between Harriman, Nashville, and Clarksville. Again, nothing further was built. The later history of the railroad is obscure. Beginning in 1890 it reported itself to the ICC as not in operation. Sulzer states that the burning of the Gum Gap trestle in 1891 brought an end to the operation. Clinton, who remained as general manager, sought to finance extensions to coal and iron mines in Cumberland County in 1892, but failed. In fiscal 1900 the railroad reported itself to the ICC as abandoned.

REFERENCE: Sulzer, *Ghost Railroads of Tennessee*, p. 215.

Walden's Ridge Railroad

The Oakdale Iron Works, seeking to connect its plant at Elverton with the Cincinnati Southern, secured a charter for the Oakdale & Cumberland Mountain Railroad on November 10, 1879. The route chosen was an extremely difficult one, from Oakdale on the CS east up Mud Lick Creek to Grassy Knob, across the Little Emory River and through De Armond's Gap in Walden's Ridge to the iron works. The ten-mile line was built in 1880–81. In order to build an extension northeast from Elverton, the parent company on October 23, 1882, merged the railroad into the unbuilt Walden's Ridge Railroad, which had been chartered in 1877 to run from a point on the CS to Winter's Gap (Oliver Springs) and east to Cumberland Gap. The extension of ten miles to Oliver Springs and Big Mountain was completed about the end of 1882. The railroad also had a varying mileage of mine spurs.

Before proceeding farther, the railroad was converted to 5'-0" late in 1884. In the course of conversion, the crossing of Walden's Ridge was abandoned in favor of a new connection with the CS at Harriman Junction, five miles southwest of Elverton. The line was converted to 4'-8½" in the massive conversion of the southern railroads from broad gauge to standard in 1886. The parent company arranged in 1887 to sell the railroad to the East Tennessee, Virginia & Georgia and transferred title on April 20, 1888. The ETV&G extended the line to Clinton, seat of Anderson County, before the end of the year. The line is still in service in the Norfolk Southern system.

REFERENCES: Fairfax Harrison, *A History of the Legal Development of the Railroad System of the Southern Railway Company* (Washington, D.C., 1901), vol. 2, pp. 903–7; Sulzer, *Ghost Railroads of Tennessee*, p. 282.

▼ ▼ ▼ ▼

Tennessee had three uncompleted projects that were to some degree interrelated. The Brownsville & Ohio Railroad was organized in 1870 by A. H. Bradford and others to build north from Brownsville, seat of Haywood County, on the Louisville & Nashville's Memphis line. Chief engineer W. D. Pickett advertised for the grading of 22.5 miles to Friendship in Dyer County. He apparently achieved this grade at least in part, but the project drops from the trade journals. In 1877 the project was revived as the Holly Springs, Brownsville & Ohio Railroad with the intention of building not only north to Friendship but south to Holly Springs, Mississippi. In 1878 the company laid ten miles of track to the north and reported the grade completed to Friendship.

The management of 1879 made an unsuccessful effort to interest the L&N in completing the line to Friendship. In 1876 the management had leased some equipment and 2.5 miles of rail from the Memphis & Raleigh, but when the terms of the lease were not complied with, contractors late in 1879 removed the iron and sold it to an unspecified narrow gauge in Arkansas, bringing the project to an end.

The Memphis & Raleigh was the smaller of two projects identified with Thomas H. Millington, one of the most prominent figures at the National Narrow-Gauge Railway Convention of 1872. The railroad was graded in 1873 from a junction with the Louisville & Nashville northeast of Memphis for about eight miles to Raleigh Springs. The line was said to be intended for suburban and pleasure travel in the fashion of steam dummy lines. The railroad reportedly was opened on July 20, 1873. Shelby County, which had advanced $50,000 in bonds toward the project, in 1874 began action to recover its contribution on the ground that the line had not been extended into Memphis as promised. This appears to have brought the operation to an end. Shelby County assented to the lease of equipment and rail to the Holly Springs, Brownsville & Ohio in 1876. Nothing further was reported of the project.

Millington's larger project was the Memphis & Knoxville Railroad, which was among the conspicuous projects discussed at the Convention of 1872. The line, of which Millington was chief engineer, was at that time projected on a relatively direct route from Memphis to Knoxville via Bolivar, Columbia, McMinnville, and Rockwood. By 1875 the company had graded most of the segment from Bolivar to Henderson, 28 miles. Failure to find financial support on the rest of the route caused the management to seek aid elsewhere. It found considerable interest in the southern tier of counties of the state, and secured a public subscription of $50,000 at Pulaski, seat of Giles County, and prepared to grade between Lawrenceburg, Pulaski, and Fayetteville. A Tennessee court in 1876 held the subscription void on the ground that the railroad was not legally chartered to build the proposed line. The adverse decision apparently ended any real prospect of the line's taking shape.

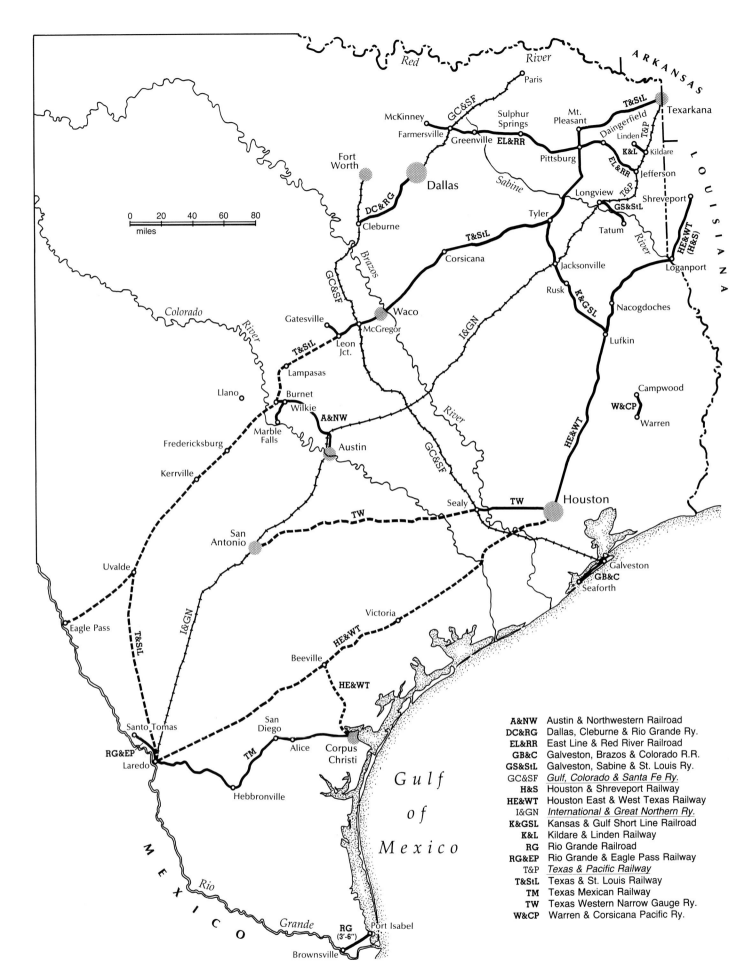

ARKANSAS

LOUISIANA

Red *River*

Paris

McKinney
GC&SF
Sulphur
Springs
Mt.
Pleasant
T&StL
Texarkana

Farmersville
Greenville
EL&RR
Daingerfield
T&P
Linden

Fort
Worth
Dallas
Pittsburg
K&L
Kildare

Sabine
EL&RR
Jefferson

DC&RG
Longview
T&P
Shreveport

Cleburne
Tyler
GS&StL

T&StL
Corsicana
Tatum
River

GC&SF
Jacksonville
HE&WT
(H&S)
Loganport

Colorado
River
Brazos
Gatesville
Waco
Rusk
K&GSL
Nacogdoches

McGregor
I&GN
Lufkin

T&StL
Leon
Jct.

Lampasas
Campwood
W&CP

Llano
Burnet
Wilkie
Warren

Fredericksburg
Marble
Falls
A&NW
Austin
River
HE&WT

Kerrville
GC&SF

Uvalde
Sealy
TW
Houston

TW
San
Antonio

Eagle Pass
Victoria
Galveston
GB&C
Seaforth

T&StL
I&GN
HE&WT
Beeville

HE&WT

Santo Tomas
San
Diego
Gulf

RG&EP
Laredo
TM
Alice
Corpus
Christi
of

Hebbronville
Mexico

MEXICO

Rio

Grande
RG
(3'-6")
Port Isabel

Brownsville

A&NW	Austin & Northwestern Railroad
DC&RG	Dallas, Cleburne & Rio Grande Ry.
EL&RR	East Line & Red River Railroad
GB&C	Galveston, Brazos & Colorado R.R.
GS&StL	Galveston, Sabine & St. Louis Ry.
GC&SF	*Gulf, Colorado & Santa Fe Ry.*
H&S	Houston & Shreveport Railway
HE&WT	Houston East & West Texas Railway
I&GN	*International & Great Northern Ry.*
K&GSL	Kansas & Gulf Short Line Railroad
K&L	Kildare & Linden Railway
RG	Rio Grande Railroad
RG&EP	Rio Grande & Eagle Pass Railway
T&P	*Texas & Pacific Railway*
T&StL	Texas & St. Louis Railway
TM	Texas Mexican Railway
TW	Texas Western Narrow Gauge Ry.
W&CP	Warren & Corsicana Pacific Ry.

0   20   40   60   80
miles

522   Texas

Texas

Austin & Northwestern Railroad

The promoters of this project, Rudolph Bertram, a merchant of Austin, and J. A. Rhomberg, a brewer of Dubuque, Iowa, envisioned it as a railroad of some 300 miles from Austin northwest to Abilene on the Texas & Pacific main line, with branches to the Rio Grande and elsewhere. The actual attainment was a local line from Austin to a quarrying area in Burnet County immediately to the northwest.

The railroad was chartered on April 20, 1881, and completed to Burnet (60 miles) on May 1, 1882. The last ten miles were laid in great haste to finish the railroad by the target date to qualify for a right-of-way through Austin, depot grounds, and $20,000. Service began on May 2. The railroad also received a state land grant of 600,000 acres. From the outset, the line had a heavy traffic of quarry products, but it was heavily mortgaged and chronically unprofitable. It gave some prospect of being part of an extensive network of narrow gauges in Texas, but this never materialized. The Austin & Southeastern was promoted in 1882 to build from Austin to Bastrop and La Grange on the proposed extension of the Texas Western, but the project was never finished. Similarly, the A&NW would have reached at Burnet the unbuilt extension of the Texas & St. Louis from Leon Junction to Laredo. The T&StL was reported early in 1883 to have purchased the A&NW in the intention of using it as a branch into Austin, but the T&StL's financial collapse later in the year prevented any such transaction from being implemented.

The A&NW was placed in receivership on October 13, 1883, with Rhomberg as receiver. Although the railroad had cost $1,197,000, its debts were so heavy that it could not be sold for the minimum bid of $200,000 set by the court. After several attempts, the railroad was sold on June 3, 1885, to W. B. Isham of New York on behalf of the bondholders. It was reorganized without change of name on April 21, 1888.

The State of Texas was in this period planning construction of its present capitol in Austin. The Capitol Commission's first plan was to use stone from the Oatmanville quarry, nine miles from Austin, but this source was rejected on the ground the stone was too variable in color and form. The alternative chosen was rock from Granite Mountain near Marble Falls in southern Burnet County. To move the rock, the A&NW undertook an extension of 16 miles from Wilkie, a half mile short of Burnet, to Marble Falls, with a spur to the quarry. By the time the extension was opened as a narrow gauge in May 1888, the directors had already decided to convert the railroad, but they made no progress before selling the line late in 1890 to C. W. Holloway. The new owner planned to extend the railroad to Llano, in an area of both stone and iron deposits. From a quarry at Ledbetter on the proposed extension, granite was expected to move at the rate of 75 to 100 cars per day to Galveston as fill for a jetty. Faced with this heavy flow of traffic, Holloway moved to convert the railroad during the summer of 1891. Standard gauge trains began running on October 1. The extension to Llano was undertaken from Fairland, ten miles beyond Wilkie, and completed on June 7, 1892.

The A&NW passed into the hands of the Houston & Texas Central in July 1891, but was separately operated until August 1901, when it became merely an extension of the H&TC's Austin branch. A subsequent extension was made from Burnet to Lampasas. Control by the H&TC brought the former narrow gauge into the network of the Southern Pacific's lines in Texas. The SP sold it in 1986 to the City of Austin for operation under the original name of the Austin & Northwestern Railroad.

REFERENCE: Joubert Greer, "Building of the Texas State Capitol" (M.A. thesis, University of Texas, Austin, 1932).

Brownsville & Gulf Railroad

This horse or mule tramway was chartered May 10, 1883, to span the mile between the Rio Grande Railroad station in Brownsville and the ferry landing. The line had a boxcar and three flatcars. No passenger operations were reported. Because of its 3'-0" gauge, it could not interchange equipment with the Rio Grande Railroad. The line was reported to have a locomotive in 1899. The Texas Railroad Commission considered it a common carrier, but in 1902 reduced it to the status of a tram road. The line came into the hands of the Mexican National Railway at approximately that time, but was sold on March 14, 1906, to the St. Louis, Brownsville & Mexico, ap-

An Austin & Northwestern train is shown at the railroad's principal source of traffic, the quarrying town of Marble Falls, Texas. (Smithsonian Institution.)

parently for conversion and incorporation into the larger railroad's local switching track.

Dallas, Cleburne & Rio Grande Railway

The Dallas & Cleburne Railroad was chartered on November 23, 1876, in the expectation of building southwest from Dallas to the major town of Cleburne, about 30 miles south of Fort Worth. When the project could not be financed, the railroad was reorganized on July 11, 1879, as the Dallas, Cleburne & Rio Grande Railway, with a charter providing for extension to the Mexican border. The promoters remained interested at least in the short run only in the Dallas-Cleburne route, and in 1879 managed to build it (53 miles). S. G. Reed, in his history of the Texas railroads, reports that they ran a single freight and a single passenger train to secure their franchise and to collect a bonus, but then gave up regular operation.

The right-of-way passed into the hands of the Chicago, Texas & Mexican Central Railway, which was formed on September 16, 1880. This enterprise, which included Scottish financing, proposed a standard gauge railroad from Chicago through Shreveport (Louisiana) and Dallas to a border crossing. Early in 1881 its construction company proposed to begin building on the Dallas-Cleburne grade. In June the directors proposed that the CT&MC build the Dallas-Cleburne line jointly with the Gulf, Colorado & Santa Fe, which was interested in the right-of-way as an entry into Dallas from the south. The GC&SF declined to make this arrangement, and instead bought the right-of-way in June 1882. It began converting the derelict narrow gauge in the following month, and quickly built the entry into Dallas, which at the present writing is still in service. The line was extended northeast from Dallas to Paris in 1887.

REFERENCE: W. T. Donoho to L. J. Cassell, "Historical Information on the Santa Fe Entry and Operation in Dallas County," typescript memorandum, Galveston, Texas, Feb. 9, 1954, photocopy in the collection of Russell Lee Crump; S. G. Reed, *A History of the Texas Railroads* (Houston, Tex.: St. Clair Publishing Co., 1941), p. 287.

East Line & Red River Railroad

Jefferson, at the head of navigation on Caddo Lake, a tributary of the Red River, was the principal port for freight movements to and from northern Texas. As railroads proliferated in northeastern Texas, the wagon trade to and from the port declined. William M. Harris, B. H. Epperson, and other local businessmen conceived of a narrow gauge railroad running west from Jefferson to deal with the problem. The East Line & Red River Railroad was chartered on March 22, 1871, but reorganized on May 11, 1876, in preparation for building. The promoters endeavored to finance the project by a lottery with $550,000 in prizes, but players who drew blanks were allowed to draw land from the railroad's state grant to the price of their tickets. Otherwise, the railroad was built by the shareholders out of their own funds without funded debt. The route was nebulous, being dependent on local subventions, but the promoters hoped to reach a point on the Red River near Sherman, about 150 miles away. They expected to haul cotton eastbound and lumber westbound.

The railroad was opened on December 5, 1876, from Jefferson to Hickory Hill (20 miles). On July 4, 1877, the line was opened to Daingerfield (30 miles), a town that had made a subscription of $13,000. Tracks reached Leesburg (52 miles) in 1878 and Sulphur Springs (92 miles) in 1879. Further extension required the promoters to mortgage the line for $7,000 per mile. Their proximate goal was Greenville (122 miles), where the town government had voted them a subsidy of $5,000 if the line arrived by October 1, 1880. The company missed the target date, but track reached Greenville shortly before the end of the year. Regular service began on March 14, 1881. The management planned to extend the line to McKinney, Denton, and Dallas.

Before any of the extensions was built Jay Gould bought control of EL&RR in June 1881, probably to prevent a takeover by the Texas & St. Louis. Although Gould was hostile to narrow gauge doctrine, he ordered the line completed to McKinney (155 miles) as a 3'-0" railroad. Tracklaying was finished in late May 1882. The EL&RR was absorbed into Gould's Missouri, Kansas & Texas in December 1881. In August 1882 the attorney general of Texas notified the MK&T that in his opinion the merger violated the Texas statute requiring railroads to be incorporated in the state and the officers domiciled there. He began action to revoke the EL&RR's franchises. The controversy on this matter was resolved by withdrawing the EL&RR from the MK&T on April 12, 1891. The line was put in receivership under William M. Giles, who on September 8 was authorized to make various improvements. The Green-ville-McKinney extension had been converted in 1887, and Giles was eager to convert the remainder. The railroad was sold on January 21, 1892, to Simon Sterne as attorney for Henry V. Poor, trustee for the bondholders. The court at Austin refused to confirm the sale, but instead directed Giles to remain in office and to issue $400,000 in receiver's certificates to convert the rest of the railroad. Giles did so, converting the remaining 122 miles on September 13, 1892—one of the largest one-day conversions in the industry. The court approved of Giles's actions and allowed the railroad to be reorganized as the Sherman, Shreveport & Southern Railway on February 28, 1893. All of the securities were held by the MK&T, and the line was operated as a nominally autonomous branch. It was extended 49 miles east to Shreveport, Louisiana, in 1900.

In a reorganization of the MK&T system, the SS&S was turned over on April 1, 1923, to William Edenborn, president of the Louisiana Railway & Navigation Co., who reorganized it as the LR&N's Texas subsidiary. Edenborn's widow sold the entire LR&N system to the Louisiana & Arkansas Railway on May 8, 1929. The Kansas City Southern took control of the L&A in 1939. Including trackage rights from Farmersville to Dallas on the Gulf, Colorado & Santa Fe, the former narrow gauge from Jefferson to Farmersville serves as part of the KCS-L&A system's Dallas branch. The 17 miles from Farmersville to McKinney were abandoned in 1940.

Galveston, Brazos & Colorado Railroad

C. W. Harley of Galveston and his associates projected this railroad as a line of about 150 miles from Galveston to Austin, paralleling the Colorado River of Texas for most of its distance. Their initial intention was to build southwest along Galveston Island, bridging Galveston Bay at the Caron-kaway Shoals. On the mainland, they planned to make use of the unbuilt grade of the Houston Tap & Brazoria. The first spike was driven at a ceremony on April 6, 1876.

When Harley proved unable to finance a bridge, he turned to the alternative of laying third rail on 30 miles of the Gulf, Colorado & Santa Fe as an exit from Galveston, but he also proved unable to make this arrangement. As a consequence, the actual attainments of the railroad were very limited. In 1876 it laid ten miles of track and in 1877 five more, reaching an end-of-track on Galveston Island called Seaforth. The railroad hauled sand in dump cars for fills in Galveston, but never achieved actual common carriage. The line was reportedly leased in 1878 to Drennan, Sullivan & Co., which held claims for construction expenses. The railroad went bankrupt and was sold for $5,000 on March 29, 1881, to Charles S. Hinchman of Philadelphia, who represented the bondholders. The railroad was sold later in 1881 for $60,000 to the Texas Mexican as an entry for a projected extension into Galveston. The Texas Mexican was unable to build to Galveston, and track on the local narrow gauge may have been removed.

In 1884 W. Hinchman and his associates revived the project by forming the Galveston & Western Railway to build from Galveston to Collins on the Texas Mexican 60 miles east of Laredo. The promoters' accomplishment was limited to rebuilding 13 miles of the narrow gauge from Galveston to Lafitte (Nottingham). The line was laid with 56-pound rail, probably in the expectation of early conversion. The management expressed an intention to convert as early as the spring of 1892, but could not do so. Efforts to sell the narrow gauge to the Galveston Terminal Co., the Rock Island, and the Gulf, Colorado & Santa Fe were all unsuccessful. The line ran two passenger trains per day and maintained a supply of flatcars for freight. Traffic was mainly passengers to the resort at the outer terminus.

On May 21, 1895, the management made an agreement with the Galveston, La Porte & Houston Railway whereby the latter would operate the narrow gauge and use it to enter Galveston. The Galveston & Western had begun laying third rail in the city in 1892, and had five miles of standard gauge track by the time the GLP&H arrived on May 12, 1896. The GLP&H, which was completing a Houston-Galveston line, used about a mile of the G&W approaching Galveston. In 1894 the G&W lost its right to run on Avenue N and 9th Street on the ground that the Texas Mexican had failed to fulfill its obligations under its franchise. An appellate court upheld this decision in 1896; as a result the company cut back its narrow gauge mileage to 7.8. The line was reported to the *Official Guide* as not regularly operated in February 1896 and as dropped at the end of 1897. The narrow gauge became a steam dummy line to the resort. Although the resort was largely obliterated by the Galveston hurricane of 1900, the Galveston & Western survived as a corporate entity until 1923, when its last four miles were sold to the Santa Fe for terminal facilities.

Galveston, Sabine & St. Louis Railway

Like many another, this was a railroad of grandiose plans but meager attainments. The Longview & Sabine Valley Railroad was organized by Brad Barner of Longview and chartered on January 4, 1877, to build a narrow gauge from Longview, the junction of the Texas & Pacific and the International & Great Northern, to Sabine Pass on the Gulf of Mexico, about 220 miles. Barner built four miles in 1877 and seven more in 1878, reaching Camden (Tallys), and serving a variety of sawmills and lumber camps. He planned to extend the mileage on the basis of demands of the lumber industry.

Instead, the L&SV was sold in January 1883 to the Galveston, Sabine & St. Louis Railway, which had been formed by John Durand of Rochester, New York, on December 18, 1882. Barner became vice-president. Durand's plan was to build from Galveston to a point on the Red River in Grayson County, with a branch from some point in Shelby County to the Louisiana state line. If built, such a line would have connected with the Houston East & West Texas in northern Shelby County and with the Texas & St. Louis, probably in the vicinity of Mount Pleasant, thereby becoming part of the collateral mileage of the Grand Narrow Gauge Trunk. Actually, all Durand accomplished was approximately doubling the size of the existing lumber railroad. He laid five miles in 1884 and six in 1885, reaching a point near Martin's Creek (Tatum), some twenty-two miles from Longview.

At this point, the Galveston & St. Louis Construction Co., which had built the extension, presented claims for $210,000, and sought receivership. The Construction Co. and the management each elected boards of directors for the railroad in 1886, and requested the federal court at Tyler to determine which should control the railroad. The two groups compromised out of court on a board of directors representing both groups. The new board favored conversion and extension, and immediately began preparations. The railroad was converted on May 23, 1887. The corporation was merged into the Texas, Sabine Valley & Northwestern later in 1887 and extended southward to a junction with the Houston East & West Texas at Timpson. The railroad was reorganized as the Texas & Gulf Railway in 1905, and was absorbed into the Atchison, Topeka & Santa Fe system in 1910. As the northern portion of the Santa Fe's Longview branch, the former narrow gauge mileage is still in service.

Houston East & West Texas Railway

The unusual name of this company was more descriptive of the intentions of its promoter, Paul Bremond, than of its attainments. Bremond, a wealthy Houston merchant, was the principal financier of the standard gauge Houston & Texas Central, the second railroad in Texas. He envisioned a line to the northeast through the softwood forest called the Piney Woods, and another parallel to the Gulf of Mexico into southern Texas. It is usually said that Bremond was converted to the narrow gauge philosophy by his observation of the intramural railway at the Centennial Exposition at Philadelphia in 1876, but to judge from press accounts, the decision to build the Houston East & West Texas as a narrow gauge had been made by the time the corporation was chartered on March 11, 1875. From the charter and the company's prospectus, it appears that the east line was intended to run from Houston to Texarkana, crossing the Sabine River at Logansport. Branches were planned from Nacogdoches to Tyler and from Goodrich to a point on the Sabine east of Newton. The west line was to run southwest from Houston via Richmond, Columbus, Victoria, and Goliad to Beeville, where it would split into a line southeast into Corpus Christi and a continuation through barely populated country to Laredo for a connection with the Mexican National Railway. After the building of the Texas Western Narrow Gauge, with which this company had a community of financial interest, Bremond and his associates envisioned the western line entering Houston over the Texas Western from a connection at some point west of the Brazos, probably Sealy. As it proved, no work was ever done on the west line.

The east line was, in fact, built, though with a change of terminus from Texarkana to Shreveport, Louisiana. Neither the Tyler nor the Newton branch was undertaken. Construction began at Houston with a patriotic ceremony on July 4, 1876. By April of 1877 about 20 miles of the railroad were completed. Bremond bought two of the locomotives, *Girard* and *Centennial*, that he had admired at Philadelphia. The railroad was opened to New Caney in the spring of 1878 and to Cleveland (43 miles) in the fall. By the spring of 1879 the line was open to Urbana, where the Trinity River had to be bridged. Rails reached Livingston (71 miles) in 1879 and Moscow (87.5 miles) in 1880. In the same year a depot was completed at Houston and physical connection was made with the Texas Western. Edward

Hulbert was engaged as superintendent in February 1880, but relieved of his duties in May. In 1881 track was pushed northward to a new town that Bremond and his associates founded, Lufkin (118 miles), named after Edwin P. Lufkin, chief engineer of the railroad. The next target was Nacogdoches, the principal established town of the area, but by the fall of 1882 track reached only Lewisburg, five miles to the south. Further construction was held up by litigation concerning the right-of-way. The railroad finally reached Nacogdoches (138 miles) on November 1, 1883.

In spite of the low speed with which the railroad had been built, its traffic developed nicely. Sawmills were established at several points along the route. The line was pressed on to Garrison in 1884. As the route approached the Sabine River the terrain became swampy, requiring several long wooden trestles of the sort common on narrow gauges. The company's funds had been exhausted by the time the line reached Nacogdoches, but Bremond arranged a second mortgage with the Union Trust Company of New York, which raised indebtedness to about $2 million, with fixed charges of $140,000 per year. Texas was at this time pursuing a policy of land grants upon completion of railroads, and the HE&WT had completed enough to qualify. Bremond sold 168,960 acres to J. M. Jamerson of New York for only $40,000 to secure additional funds for construction.

On June 9, 1883, Bremond and his associates chartered a subsidiary in Louisiana to build the portion of the railroad from the Sabine River to Shreveport. First called Gulf, Shreveport & Kansas City Railroad, the name was shortly changed to the Shreveport & Houston Railway. Under this name, construction began at Shreveport about May 1, 1884. The line was completed to the Sabine in the fall of 1885. By December, the HE&WT reached the west bank of the river. Meanwhile, Bremond had died at Galveston on May 8, 1885, at the age of 74. As far as is known, Bremond to the end remained committed to the narrow gauge principle. To facilitate dealing with Bremond's estate, the directors requested a receivership, which was granted. On July 8, 1885, M. G. Howe of Houston was appointed receiver.

The bridge over the Sabine had been under construction since 1884 by the King Iron Bridge & Manufacturing Co. The bridge was completed late in January 1886, with regular passenger service commencing on January 30. The railroad was a relatively long narrow gauge, 232 miles, and a major one, connecting two important southwest-

ern cities. The Piney Woods amounted to some 12 million acres of pine, for which the HE&WT was virtually the only rail outlet. The railroad also handled considerable traffic in cotton.

The railroad emerged from receivership in the early 1890s. The Louisiana mileage was sold to Joseph Richardson and Marcus G. Hawley of New York on July 15, 1891, and the Texas portion to Elbert S. Jemison, representing the Union Trust Company, for $1.2 million on August 2, 1892. The Louisiana segment was reorganized as the Houston & Shreveport Railway, but the Texas corporation was reorganized without change of name. Jemison became president of the new corporation. The new management had no residual enthusiasm for the narrow gauge and began immediate preparations for conversion. The Texas and Louisiana portions were converted simultaneously on July 29, 1894. The railroad remained in independent operation for five years before being acquired through stock purchase by the Southern Pacific Company in October 1899. The line retained its corporate identity, but was brought up to the physical standards of the Southern Pacific. The railroad achieved its most lasting fame as the protagonist of the Shreveport case, *Houston East & West Texas Ry. Co. v. U.S.*, 234 U.S. 342 (1914), whereby the U.S. Supreme Court gave the Interstate Commerce Commission power to raise intrastate rates to interstate levels to prevent discrimination against interstate commerce. The railroad operated under its own name until 1927, when it was leased to another Southern Pacific subsidiary, the Galveston, Harrisburg & San Antonio Railway. In 1934 the company was merged, along with its lessee, into the Texas & New Orleans Railroad, the SP's principal operating corporation in Texas and Louisiana. As such, the line remains a major secondary main line of the Southern Pacific.

REFERENCE: Robert S. Maxwell, *Whistle in the Piney Woods: Paul Bremond and the Houston, East and West Texas Railway*, Texas Gulf Coast Historical Association Publication Series, 7, no. 2 (Nov. 1963).

Kansas & Gulf
Short Line Railroad

Upon withdrawing from the presidency of the Texas & St. Louis Railway in 1880, Major James P. Douglas turned his attention to promoting a narrow gauge from Tyler to the south. The line was incorporated on February 18, 1880, under the name of the Kansas & Gulf Short Line Rail-

road. The charter provided for a route to Sabine Pass on the Gulf of Mexico below Beaumont. Plans for building to the north were never firm, but the company apparently did envision a line into Kansas to haul wheat to the Gulf. Initially, the promoters planned a route of 90 miles from Tyler on the Texas & St. Louis to Lufkin on the Houston East & West Texas. The area originated lumber and agricultural products, but the proposed connections gave the railroad the prospect, rare for a narrow gauge, of participating in long-distance interline movements. Notably, it could serve as a connection of the Grand Narrow Gauge Trunk to Houston. If either the Texas Western or the Houston East & West Texas had reached Corpus Christi, it might have served as an alternative route to Mexico for the Grand Narrow Gauge Trunk, though this was not among the intentions of the promoters.

The building of the railroad was facilitated by the existence of a narrow gauge tramway over a portion of the route. The Rusk Transportation Company, chartered in 1874, had laid 14 miles of wooden rail from Jacksonville on the International & Great Northern to Rusk. The line had been built by townspeople of Rusk in a successful effort to prevent the county seat from being removed to Jacksonville for greater accessibility. The K&GSL acquired the tramway at a foreclosure sale of January 22, 1881. The acquisition resulted in the K&GSL's beginning construction at Jacksonville rather than Tyler. In 1882 the tramway was upgraded to narrow gauge railroad standards, and Jacksonville was connected with Tyler. The corporation went bankrupt on December 18, 1882, but found it possible to push track on to Morrill, 62 miles from Tyler, by 1883. In order to secure money for completion to Lufkin, the company turned to the management of the Texas & St. Louis, which, in spite of its own troubles, was able to provide the funds. Lufkin (90 miles) was reached on November 1, 1885. There was some discussion of continuing the route to the south, but nothing further was done.

Samuel W. Fordyce of the Cotton Belt was eager to absorb the Kansas & Gulf, but the financial problems of the two companies prevented immediate merger. Fordyce's St. Louis, Arkansas & Texas bought the K&GSL on April 29, 1887, but the purchase was voided by a court order. As a consequence, the company was sold at foreclosure and reorganized as the Tyler Southeastern Railway on January 13, 1891. It was, however, operated as a branch of the Cotton Belt. The line was converted in

1895. The St. Louis Southwestern absorbed the Tyler Southestern on October 6, 1899. The line was abandoned from Rusk to Keltys on the outskirts of Lufkin in 1983, and from Tyler to Jacksonville in 1989. The remaining terminal trackage at Lufkin was sold to the Angelina & Neches River, and negotiations are in progress for sale of the segment from Dialville to Rusk to a local operator.

Kildare & Linden Railway

Although principally a facility for J. H. Bemis's Jefferson Lumber Co., this narrow gauge of 13 miles carried passengers and provided a general transportation service to Linden, seat of Cass County, from the Texas & Pacific main line at Kildare. The line was apparently not formally incorporated, but simply built by the lumber company in 1888. It was opened on February 1, 1889. Normal service was two mixed trains per day. The line initially had a single locomotive, but a second was reported in the last years of operation. The railroad was reported abandoned in 1900.

Rio Grande & Eagle Pass Railway

As the Rio Grande & Pecos Valley Railway, this carrier was organized on February 27, 1882, to build a standard gauge railroad from Brownsville through Laredo to Eagle Pass and to some point on or near the Pecos River. Some 500 miles of track were initially envisioned. The railroad was from the outset planned as an originating carrier for coal from several fields along the Rio Grande. The original management, led by A. B. Hunt of Laredo, was reportedly allied with the Texas Mexican. Accordingly, third rail was planned for the Laredo–Eagle Pass segment, and possibly also the Brownsville-Laredo portion, so that coal might move in narrow gauge cars directly to the line's 3'-0" connections, both in Texas and Mexico.

The most readily available coalfield was a deposit of cannel coal at Santo Tomas, 27 miles above Laredo. The coal had a high gas and oil content that lent itself to a variety of industrial processes, and well suited it to railroad use. Eighteen railroads burned it, and the Southern Pacific was envisioned as a possible buyer when tracks reached Eagle Pass. The Laredo–Santo Tomas line was opened as a standard gauge railroad on March 18, 1883, and third rail was laid in August. The railroad was put in receivership in May 1884, and sold on De-

cember 17 to Charles B. Wright, representing the bondholders. He reorganized it as the Rio Grande & Eagle Pass in 1885. The railroad was thereafter integral with the mining operations of the Cannel Coal Co. Extensions both northwest and southeast were projected, but never made. The narrow gauge rail was removed in 1895. The mines were closed in 1939 and the railroad abandoned about the end of 1946.

Rio Grande Railroad
Gauge: 3'-6"

Brownsville, the American city at the mouth of the Rio Grande, suffers from water so shallow as to be unsuitable for ocean shipping. Ships customarily unloaded at sea into barges or lighters, and the freight was transshipped at Port Isabel or other points on the Gulf Coast by wagon into Brownsville. Proposals for a railway dated from 1848. Mifflin Kenedy, Richard King, and their associates organized the Rio Grande Railway in 1866 to run from Port Isabel or Brazos de Santiago to Brownsville with the right of extension to Laredo. King, Kenedy & Co. simultaneously established a monopoly of local steamers on the Rio Grande. The railroad project was probably an effort to protect the monopoly, and no actual work on the enterprise was ever undertaken. Rather, on August 23, 1870, Simon Celaya, a local rival of the King, Kenedy interests, and his associates organized the Rio Grande Railroad. Celaya built the railroad for 22 miles from Jackson Street, Brownsville, to Port Isabel, beginning in February 1871. The company had an opening ceremony July 4, 1872, but only six miles were reportedly completed in the year. Hurricane damage to the uncompleted line in 1873 prevented its being fully operational until 1874. It was, nevertheless, among the earliest American narrow gauges, and shared 3'-6" with some of the other pioneer projects. The right-of-way was mainly straight on coastal lowlands, but had extensive trestlework. By narrow gauge standards, the line was fairly heavily built with 38-pound rail. Most of the traffic was inbound to Mexico off ships unloaded by the railroad's own lighters; the line had little traffic between ship arrivals. In 1873 the management bought a steamer, *S. J. Lee*, from King, Kenedy. The steamer was sunk in December 1873, but in May 1874, the railroad bought out King, Kenedy and gained a transport monopoly in the area. Rates were high enough to bring forth competition from teamsters by 1875. The rail-

road was operated by two 2-4-2 tank engines and two 4-4-0s.

Completion of the Texas Mexican and Mexican National diverted most of the traffic destined for Mexico after 1880, leaving the railroad mainly dependent on traffic for Brownsville and the other towns on the lower Rio Grande Valley. The railroad's proximity to the Gulf, combined with its extensive trestles, made it prone to destruction by hurricanes; it suffered serious damage in 1873, 1875, 1888, and 1906. The company defaulted on its bonds in 1909, allowing the St. Louis, Brownsville & Mexico Railway, a Missouri Pacific subsidiary, to acquire control. The corporation was reorganized as the Rio Grande Railway on February 1, 1911. To prevent the line from being scrapped, A. Albert Browne, mayor of Brownsville, and other local figures acquired control in 1914. They secured authority for an extension of 270 miles to San Antonio, plus branches to Falfurrias and Rio Grande City, but no work was undertaken. In 1917 D. A. O'Brien bought the railroad with the intention of converting it. In 1921–22 the line was largely relocated inland, the move increasing its length by four miles but reducing the trestles to one of 56 feet over a drainage ditch. Standard ties and heavier rail were laid at that time, and the railroad was converted on March 13, 1925. George S. Westerfield was appointed receiver in November 1925. He conveyed the property to W. T. Eldridge in February 1926. The railroad was reorganized as the Port Isabel & Rio Grande Valley in 1928 and abandoned in 1941. Terminal trackage survived in the Missouri Pacific system.

REFERENCES: J. Lee Stambaugh and Lillian J. Stambaugh, *The Lower Rio Grande Valley of Texas* (Austin, Tex.: Jenkins Publishing Co., 1974), pp. 162ff.; Le Roy P. Graf, "The Economic History of the Lower Rio Grande Valley of Texas" (Ph.D. diss., Harvard University, 1942), pp. 686–710; Anna Cora Petz, "History of the Rio Grande Railroad," *University of Texas Bulletin*, no. 2746 (1927), pp. 34–40.

Texas Mexican Railway

Since 1856 citizens of Corpus Christi had endeavored to promote a railroad through the grazing country of southern Texas to a crossing of the Rio Grande, partly to develop local agriculture, and partly to secure the entrepôt trade of goods bound for Mexico. None of the several projects was financed until completion of the Rio Grande Railroad in 1874 diverted much of the entrepôt to Brownsville. Colonel Uriah Lott, a successful merchant of

Corpus Christi, revived the local rail project in the form of the Corpus Christi, San Diego & Rio Grande Narrow Gauge Railroad, chartered on March 18, 1875. This was to be a relatively long narrow gauge, running 161 miles from Corpus Christi to Laredo. The first spike was driven on the Corpus Christi waterfront on Thanksgiving Day 1876, and five miles of track were laid by the end of the year. In the fall of 1877 the railroad reached Banquete (25 miles), and reportedly had about 17 miles being graded. Lott began to encounter financial troubles, and had to enlist the aid of Richard King and Mifflin Kenedy, two of the largest landowners in southern Texas, in order to proceed. Track reached Collins (40 miles) in 1878 and San Diego (52 miles) in September 1879.

Unable to proceed farther, Lott and Kenedy went to New York, where they arranged to sell the railroad to the syndicate of William J. Palmer and James Sullivan, who were interested in it as a connection to their Mexican National Railway at Laredo. The new owners rechartered the railroad in June 1881 as the Texas Mexican Railway. Palmer became president. The railroad was now amply funded, and was quickly brought to completion, reaching Laredo in September 1881 and inaugurating service in November. The management filed with the Secretary of State an application for authority to construct a very considerable additional mileage, notably a line of 390 miles from San Diego to Burr's Ferry on the Sabine River in Newton County above Beaumont on the eastern border of Texas. This line was to have branches to Tyler, where the track would have met the Texas & St. Louis, and to Galveston. Together with a projected line to El Paso, the additions would have brought the railroad to more than 1,400 miles. The management bought the Galveston, Brazos & Colorado for $60,000 as an entry into Galveston, but never undertook a connection. Apart from a spur of 4.67 miles built at Laredo in 1882, the start of an extension to Eagle Pass incorporated as the Texas Mexican Northern, nothing but the original Corpus Christi–Laredo mileage was ever built.

The railroad was successful from the outset. Wool, hides, tallow, live animals, and other agricultural products moved eastbound, along with cannel coal off the Rio Grande & Pecos Valley. Most westbound traffic was manufactures to the Mexican National, whose line from Mexico City to Nuevo Laredo was completed in 1888. Because of the compatibility of this connection, the line's narrow gauge was initially a minimal problem. The San Antonio &

Aransas Pass, being built south into the lower Rio Grande Valley, intersected the Texas Mexican at Alice in 1885. This connection, which was to become an outlet for the Southern Pacific system to Laredo, became progressively more important relative to the steamships at Corpus Christi. Accordingly, the management decided upon conversion as early as 1890, and voted to issue $1 million in bonds for the purpose. It began installing standard gauge ties, but did not, in fact, convert until July 17, 1902.

Subsequently, the railroad has been essentially a standard gauge extension of the National Railways of Mexico to Corpus Christi. Although nominally separate, the Texas Mexican's securities have typically been held or guaranteed by the National of Mexico. In 1939, under president R. W. Morrison, the railroad bought seven diesel-electric locomotives, becoming the first American Class I railroad to dieselize completely. The line is extant, one of the former narrow gauges with the least prospect of abandonment.

Texas Western Narrow Gauge Railway

Texas's first narrow gauge was organized as the Western Narrow Gauge Railway on August 4, 1870, by Dr. Ingham S. Roberts, T. W. House, R. O. Love, Eugene Pillot, W. D. Cleveland, S. K. McIllheny, Brown Botts, and other Houston businessmen. The company's original authority was for any gauge between 2'-0" and 5'-6". The name was changed on February 6, 1875, to the Texas Western Narrow Gauge Railway. Thereafter only a 3'-0" line was projected. The promoters' plans were nothing if not grandiose. By a statute of 1873 the projected route was from Houston through La Grange, Lockhart, San Marcos, and New Braunfels to San Antonio with a branch to Bastrop. This much of the project was actively promoted, but a statute of 1875 also gave the company the right to build west to Presidio with a branch from San Marcos to San Saba and on to some point on the northwest frontier of the state to connect with the Denver & Rio Grande or any other railroad of 3'-0" gauge. Presidio, on the Rio Grande some 635 miles from Houston, presented the prospect of traffic from a silver-mining area. There was also talk of extension through northern Mexico to Guaymas on the Gulf of California. Within Texas the promoters also spoke of serving Austin and of building a branch to Corpus Christi. If the line to Corpus Christi had been built,

the Texas Western could have served as part of an alternative route of the Grand Narrow Gauge Trunk, but this does not appear to have been a consideration of the promoters.

Relative to the projections, the Texas Western's actual attainments were meager. Construction began April 27, 1875, from a depot site at St. Emanuel and Commerce streets in Houston. The route ran out St. Emanuel Street and straight west into an agricultural area. At the end of the year about ten miles of track had been laid. By the end of 1876 the line had reached Wemberly, 30 miles. Three members of the family of James T. Pattison each gave 50 acres of land for right-of-way and terminal facilities in hopes of real estate development in an area that they dominated. The railroad reached this point on April 23, 1877, and established the town of Pattison as a terminus, 42 miles from Houston.

The promoters had, however, exhausted their resources, and could not support the railroad from the meager local traffic. The company went bankrupt, after which House and Peter Floeck arranged to transfer some of the securities to English financiers who had land interests in Texas. The company was to qualify for a state land grant upon reaching the Brazos River, but in 1878 the state declared this right forfeited for non-completion. In 1880 the railroad was reorganized as the Texas Western Railway. The new board of directors included no less than former president U. S. Grant and his son Frederick D. Grant. The new management was able to resume construction, bridge the Brazos, and reach Sealy on the Gulf, Colorado & Santa Fe's Galveston line in 1881. The extension brought the railroad to its final length, 57 miles. The new connection was a major source of traffic, but the line remained basically a rural narrow gauge dependent on local origination. Nothing could be done to build farther west.

Between 1890 and 1892 the Missouri, Kansas & Texas built its line to Houston through several of the towns projected for the Texas Western's route to San Antonio or Austin. The MK&T entered Houston through Sealy, thereby paralleling the Texas Western directly. From Sealy to Brookshire, the narrow gauge ran to the north of the MK&T, but for the rest of the way to Houston the narrow gauge ran to the south, mainly by about three miles. The MK&T was a full eight miles shorter and, obviously, was capable of much faster running. (A statement common in secondary sources that the MK&T entered Houston on the Texas Western's abandoned right-of-way is incorrect.)

It is remarkable that the Texas Western survived at all after the entry of the MK&T, but it struggled almost to the end of the 1890s. It passed into the hands of Col. Elijah Smith of Portland, Oregon, who abandoned it in 1899. The railroad's land in the vicinity of Pattison reverted to the Pattison family.

REFERENCES: Corrie Pattison Askew, *Historical Records of Austin and Waller Counties* (Houston, Tex.: Premier Printing and Letter Service, 1969); Reed, *A History of the Texas Railroads*, pp. 478–79.

Warren & Corsicana Pacific Railway

James I. Campbell, a lumber operator, and James N. Johnson of the Tyler County Land Co. organized this railroad on November 20, 1899, to run from Warren on the Southern Pacific to Corsicana, about 150 miles to the northwest. It was opened on January 6, 1900, from Warren, where Campbell operated a sawmill, to Campwood (18 miles). Although the railroad beginning in 1901 operated two mixed trains per day and participated in interline joint freight rates, the proprietors had difficulty in convincing the state railroad commission that it was a bona fide common carrier. Apart from an extension of a mile to "End of Track" in 1902, the main line was not built farther; and the railroad operated as a facility to Campbell's sawmill.

Along with the Campbell Lumber Co. and the Tyler County Land Co., the railroad was placed under receiver W. H. Morris on February 15, 1905. The *Official Guide of the Railways* began showing the line as 4'-8½" in October 1906, but this is probably an error; the railroad updated its entry in *Poor's Manual* annually and continued to report itself as 3'-0" through its last listing in 1909. The main line was cut back to Big Kimbel (15 miles) in March 1907. The state declared the railroad's charter forfeited in December 1907, and the line was operated thereafter as private carrier of the Tyler County Lumber Co. It was abandoned in fiscal 1915–16.

▼ ▼ ▼ ▼

Texas was notable for a large number of lumber railroads with ambiguous standing as between private and common carriers. The Lake Creek Railroad (8 miles; Montgomery–Hard Thicket), although incorporated and chartered on August 12, 1884, operated only as a private carrier of the Montgomery Mill & Lumber Co. The Railroad Commission of Texas upon its formation in 1891 listed the company as a common carrier. The management protested and the line was declared a private carrier in 1896. It had, however, been abandoned in 1895.

J. Lipsitz of Tyler operated two lumber railroads, the Durham Transportation Co. and the Pollok & Angelina Valley Transportation Co., both of which were organized in 1905 and dissolved in 1913. Both were tributary to the Lufkin branch of the St. Louis Southwestern, at Durham and Pollok respectively. The Interstate Commerce Commission listed both as independent Class III railroads, but the Texas commission never treated either as a common carrier.

The Jefferson & Northwestern Railway was projected by A. D. Clark, partly as a logging railroad for his mill at North Jefferson, partly as a common carrier to Linden, seat of Cass County, and to some point on the St. Louis Southwestern main line to the north. He incorporated the railroad in November 1899, and by 1903 it had reached a point called Cave Springs, 18 miles northwest. Track apparently had been extended to 22.5 miles before the railroad was converted about 1909. When Clark built the entry into Linden as a branch from Lanier in 1911, the Texas commission began treating the railroad as a common carrier. The main line reached Naples, a town on the Cotton Belt main line, in 1927. The railroad was abandoned from Lanier to Naples in 1933 and from Jefferson to Linden in 1941.

Similarly, the Angelina & Neches River Railroad had its origins in the purchase of an existing logging railroad of the Angelina County Lumber Co. in 1900. This railroad (10 miles) was converted in 1906 and extended. In 1911 the line reached Chireno, and the management arranged trackage rights over the Houston East & West Texas into Lufkin. The railroad became a common carrier at that time, although S. G. Reed, in his history of Texas railroads, states that it was party to some interstate rates as of 1900. The A&NR is still in existence.

The Elmina & Eastern Transportation Co., headed by Thomas S. Foster, was a ten-mile lumber railroad at Elmina on the International & Great Northern's Houston line. It was organized March 15, 1904, and was a common carrier to the extent of having small passenger revenues. Like some of the others, it was considered a Class III railroad by the ICC, but not a common carrier by the Texas commission. It was abandoned about March 1910.

Utah

American Fork Railroad

The Miller Mining Co. operated the Sultana Smelting Works northeast up American Fork Canyon from Lehi on the Utah Southern. The smelter mainly, though not exclusively, served the Miller Mine, which produced about $100 in silver bullion, $20 to $28 in gold, and a small amount of copper from a ton of ore. A mule tramway of about two miles connected the mine and smelter. Officers of the company formed the American Fork Railroad on April 3, 1872, to provide a rail connection to the Utah Southern at American Fork City, about three miles south of Lehi. Ground was broken on May 20. The six miles approaching the canyon were easy to construct, but the canyon itself was narrow, tortuous, and subject to flooding. The American Fork River had to be bridged 16 times in the first five miles. By the end of 1872 rails had reached an end-of-track called Deer Creek, about 16 miles from the projected Utah Southern connection. The actual connection had to be made temporarily at Lehi, for the standard gauge railroad did not reach American Fork City until 1873. The Miller management graded an additional four miles beyond Deer Creek to the Sultana plant, but this trackage would have entailed switchbacks with grades thought to be beyond the capacity of the line's early Mason Bogie locomotive. The existing line gained 1,900 feet, with a ruling grade of nearly 6 percent. The railroad was shut down for the winter, but in the spring of 1873 the management decided against laying rail on the extension. Mining in the area declined, and the railroad found itself dependent largely on tourist traffic. The canyon was spectacular, and a hotel was built at Deer Creek in 1877. The railroad was regularly closed for the winter, and opened for the last time in the spring of 1878. Ore movements proved very meager, and operations were shut down in May. Track was removed in June. (For map, see front endpaper.)

REFERENCE: Clarence A. Reeder, Jr., *The History of Utah's Railroads 1869–1883* (New York: Arno Press, 1981), pp. 193–208. This railroad was initially shown in *Poor's Manual* of 1873–74 as 3'-0", but thereafter as 3'-6". The latter is apparently in error. The *Railroad Gazette* uniformly reported the line as 3'-0". The builders' lists of Mason and Porter show the railroad's two locomotives as 3'-0", and they served on 3'-0" railroads following the American Fork's abandonment. Extensive newspaper research by George E. Pitchard brought forth evidence only of 3'-0" gauge. See his *A Utah Railroad Scrapbook* (Salt Lake City, Utah: George E. Pitchard, 1987), p. 24.

Denver & Rio Grande Western Railway

Unlike western Colorado, which was virgin territory when the Denver & Rio Grande entered it, Utah had over a decade's experience with standard gauge railroads when the D&RG's western line approached in the early 1880s. Following completion of the transcontinental railroad through Ogden in 1869, figures prominent in the Mormon Church built both the Utah Central between Ogden and Salt Lake City and the Utah Southern to develop the territory around Provo and Utah Lake. Narrow gauge was considered for the Utah Southern, but rejected in favor of compatibility with the Utah Central and Union Pacific. By 1879 the line had reached Frisco in southwestern Utah, and come into the Union Pacific's control. The existence of this railroad stimulated construction of three connecting narrow gauges, all of which came into the hands of the Denver & Rio Grande, and in part determined the route of the D&RG's entry. The three are described separately below. (For map, see front endpaper.)

Bingham Canyon & Camp Floyd Railroad

When the Utah Southern reached Sandy, 13 miles south of Salt Lake City, a connection into the Bingham Canyon mining area to the west became practicable. Hugh White and his associates chartered the Bingham Canyon & Camp Floyd on September 10, 1872. Their immediate target was the Bingham area, Utah's principal mining region for copper, silver, and other nonferrous metals. White began construction in October 1872, but by June 1873 had exhausted his resources and was forced to sell control of the railroad to a syndicate headed by Charles W. Scofield of New York, who had mining interests in the area. White agreed to remain with the railroad to superintend it to completion, which he accomplished on November 23, 1873. Several mine spurs were laid in 1874. A longer-range plan to extend over the Oquirrh Mountains to Tooele, Stockton, and Ophir in the Camp Floyd mining district was never executed.

Wasatch & Jordan Valley Railroad

Mormon Church leaders, plus Gentile businessmen in Salt Lake City, were interested in developing the mining area in Little Cottonwood Canyon to the east of Sandy. The Church wanted to draw upon a quarry at Wasatch for granite for the Mormon Temple, and silver had been found farther up the canyon to the east. William Jennings and associates formed the railroad on October 24, 1872. Construction began on November 4, utilizing three and a half miles of grade already laid by the Utah Southern for a projected branch. Rails were laid for eight miles to Wasatch in Fairfield Flat by mid-September 1873. Track was not pushed farther, partly because of the growing financial stringency, and partly because the grades up the canyon to Alta promised to be 3 percent to 6 percent.

The railroad, which was unprofitable, was sold in June 1875 to Charles W. Scofield of the Bingham Canyon & Camp Floyd, who agreed to complete the road to Alta. Scofield chose to build the extension of about seven miles as a horse or mule tramway, a technology he was already using on mine spurs in the Bingham area. The tramway was opened on September 12, 1875, for passenger and freight service. Snows in the area—Alta was, of course, to become a major ski resort—shortly closed the line, but in 1876 superintendent George Goss covered virtually the entire tramway with snowsheds. About 70 animals were required to work the line.

On April 29, 1879, Scofield merged the W&JV into the Bingham Canyon & Camp Floyd, the stronger of his two railroads. The combined railroad had a disappointing performance, mainly because of the declining output of the mines at Alta. It covered its variable expenses, but defaulted on its interest payments, precipitating a receivership in August 1881. The receivership was to separate the two companies briefly.

Utah & Pleasant Valley Railroad

Coal operators in the Pleasant Valley sought an outlet for their product to Salt Lake City, which was dependent on coal brought in over the Union Pacific at rates widely considered excessive. Their most direct route was a very difficult one, with two hard crossings of mountain barriers and a line along Soldier Creek to Springville and Provo. The Utah & Pleasant Valley was organized on December 10, 1875, by M. P. Crandall and other owners of coal land in the valley. They raised capital largely by selling bonds to Charles W. Scofield, who thereby became interested in all three of the Utah predecessors of the D&RG. Scofield gained stock control of the corporation in 1878 and became president. Tracklaying began at Springville in August 1878, and was completed to Scofield (55 miles) in the valley on November 5, 1879. An additional five miles from Springville to a junction with the Utah Southern at Provo were put in service in October 1880.

William J. Palmer's initial plan for the Denver & Rio Grande's entry into Utah was to cross the desert of eastern Utah via the town of Green River and the Castle Valley, and then traverse the Wasatch Plateau along Salina Creek into the Sevier Valley to a junction at Salina—the approximate route of the present I-70. There the railroad would have a north-south line up the valley into Provo and Salt Lake City and down the valley to a crossing into Arizona near Kanab. This route had the attraction of a penetration of Arizona, plus a possible route into Mexico not prohibited by the Tripartite Agreement of 1880. The D&RG, which was not itself empowered to build or operate in Utah Territory, incorporated the Sevier Valley Railway on December 7, 1880, to build the Utah mileage. Some surveying and a small amount of grading were undertaken in the Salina area, but the management changed its plan in favor of a more direct route from Green River to Provo and Salt Lake City via Soldier Summit. On July 21, 1881, Palmer organized the Denver & Rio Grande Western Railway to build the Utah mileage. The new company absorbed the Sevier Valley Railway, and more important, shortly absorbed C. W. Scofield's narrow gauges. The D&RG bought the bankrupt Bingham Canyon & Camp Floyd in September and the Wasatch & Jordan Valley in December. The Utah & Pleasant Valley was acquired on June 14, 1882.

With the three narrow gauge acquisitions in hand or in prospect, Palmer's forces quickly built the extension. By the time of the third acquisition, the D&RGW had built 45 miles from Salt Lake City to Provo, essentially parallel to the Utah Southern. The narrow gauge made use of the Jordan Narrows near Draper to avoid a crossing of a small plateau. The Utah & Pleasant Valley could be used for 38 miles southeast to Clear Creek (Tucker), whence the company built a difficult 14-mile crossing of Soldier Summit. The D&RG leased its Utah subsidiary, the D&RGW, on August 1, 1882, and undertook completion of the railroad. Its first major act was to abandon the U&PV's tortuous crossing of the Wasatch Mountains, which included switchbacks, in favor of a 13-mile line along Fish Creek to a junction with the main line at Pleasant Valley Junction (Colton). By the end of 1882 the main line had reached Price, the principal intermediate settlement, and been extended about ten miles east. D&RG crews reached the Utah line from Grand Junction on December 19. Construction was pushed from both directions, and the tracks from east and west met at Desert Switch, about 13 miles west of Green River, on March 30, 1883. The company then built an extension from Salt Lake City to Ogden, completing the east-west line on May 12, 1883. Initially, the terminal was made by laying third rail on Central Pacific tracks.

The heavy expenditure of recent construction taxed the D&RG's resources, producing some hostility to the management on the part of its foreign investors. Palmer, as a consequence, resigned the presidency of the D&RG in August 1883, but remained in control of the D&RGW. Frederick Lovejoy, a Pennsylvanian, became president of the D&RG, ready to effect economies at the behest of directors who had considered the Palmer management profligate. Palmer became convinced that Lovejoy was neglecting the D&RG's obligations under the lease of the D&RGW, as well as seeking to gain control of the Utah lines in violation of the terms of agreement. The dispute went into the courts in the spring of 1884. On July 2, before a definitive judgment had been delivered, Lovejoy ordered his men to seize the D&RGW equipment at Grand Junction, and on the following day had about a mile of track removed on the Colorado side of the state line, breaking the physical connection and severing the telegraph line between the two railroads. Temporarily, the D&RGW could reach Grand Junction only by wagon and stagecoach. On July 7 bondholders together with directors loyal to Palmer secured a receivership for the D&RG, with William S. Jackson, an associate of Palmer, as receiver. The track connection was restored on July 14. The episode soured the Burlington, the D&RG's principal connection at Denver, on the D&RG, causing the big granger to negotiate an agreement for western traffic with the AT&SF. As a consequence, the Denver-Ogden line was mainly reduced to a local facility, in spite of its obvious potential as a transcontinental route. The episode also created the prospect that the Burlington might itself build to Grand Junction. It never did so, but the possibility, along with the invasion of the Colorado Rockies by the Colorado Midland, gave the managements of the D&RG and D&RGW a powerful incentive to convert the Denver-Ogden main line.

In 1885 the D&RG's lease of the D&RGW was found by the courts to be valid, but the D&RGW was found to have been injured by the D&RG's arbitrary and capricious behavior. When the D&RG was reorganized in July 1886, it elected not to continue the lease. By way of compensation, the D&RG turned over 27 locomotives and considerable equipment to the D&RGW. The D&RGW came out of receivership in August 1886, with Palmer still in the presidency. Whether the D&RGW continued as a western connection for the D&RG or became allied with the Colorado Midland, it would have to be converted. Palmer had apparently come to that conclusion by 1887 and began firm plans for conversion by 1888. The project entailed building a new line from Crevasse, Colorado, to Whitehouse, Utah, which would replace the existing 53-mile route with another route, 8.5 miles shorter, through Ruby Canyon to the south. Transitionally, the D&RGW leased the portion of the D&RG from Grand Junction to the Utah state line, and organized and incorporated the State Line & Denver Railway to acquire the new right-of-way in Colorado. The SL&D had in its charter powers to build east to Denver via Glenwood Springs, a veiled threat to the D&RG. In June 1889 Palmer merged the D&RGW and the SL&D into the newly formed Rio Grande Western Railway, which effected the conversion. The 82 miles from Ogden to Provo were converted in 1889 and the remainder from Provo to Grand Junction by June 11, 1890. The narrow gauge line had been allowed to deteriorate badly, and in its last days was being operated in slovenly fashion; accordingly, the conversion was greeted with enthusiasm. The branch from Sandy to Bingham was converted effective June 2, 1890. The line from Sandy to Wasatch was converted in May and June 1891, and the long branch of 61 miles from Thistle to Manti, which had been built only in 1890, was converted in July 1891. The Manti line was unusual among the branches of the D&RG and its affiliates in being built to serve an agricultural area rather than a mining community. After conversion the line was pressed south down the Sevier Valley, and reached the gold-mining community of Marysvale in 1900.

The line to Salt Lake City remains the main line of the current D&RGW, one of the major transcontinental routes of the nation, and one of the most heavily utilized former narrow gauges. The Wasatch branch was abandoned in 1934, along with the mule tramway, which had never been converted. The tramway last operated regularly in the 1890s, but it was rebuilt in 1917 under lease by the Little Cottonwood Transportation Co., which operated it with Shay locomotives until 1925. The Thistle-Manti segment was abandoned with the rest of the Marysvale branch in 1983, but the Bingham branch remains in service. In a reciprocal arrangement with the Union Pacific the D&RGW line from North Salt Lake City to Ogden was closed in March 1986.

REFERENCES: Gordon Chappell and Cornelius W. Hauck, *Scenic Line of the World*, Colorado Rail Annual No. 8 (Golden: Colorado Railroad Museum, 1970); Robert A. LeMassena, *Rio Grande . . . to the Pacific!* (Denver, Colo.: Sundance, Ltd., 1974); Reeder, *The History of Utah's Railroads 1869–1883*; Donald B. Robertson, *Encyclopedia of Western Railroad History: The Desert States* (Caldwell, Idaho: Caxton Printers, 1986).

Salt Lake & Fort Douglas Railway
Salt Lake & Eastern Railway

The earlier of these related enterprises, the Salt Lake & Fort Douglas, was chartered in December 1884 and built mainly in 1887, principally to move sandstone from the Red Butte quarries into Salt Lake City. The railroad built ten miles of track originating at 4th West and 8th South in Salt Lake City. Grades ranged up to 10 percent, and curvature to 80°. The railroad was mainly operated with a small two-truck Shay, but it also owned several secondhand rod engines. Spurs served the Fort Douglas military installation, a brickworks, and a prison. (For map, see front endpaper.)

The same interests incorporated the Salt Lake & Eastern Railway in September 1888 to carry silver and lead ores from the Park City area to smelters southeast of Salt Lake City. The line was built in 1888–90 from Sugar House immediately southeast of Salt Lake City to Park City (32 miles). Grades ascending the Wasatch Mountains were as heavy as 6.25 percent, and the descent of 3.5 miles from Altus to Park City had grades up to 4.2 percent. The line was worked by rod engines and two Shays. On April 8, 1890, the management organized the Utah Central Railway, which built a

Salt Lake & Fort Douglas Shay No. 7 at the Wagener brewery at the mouth of Emigration Canyon about 1891. (George E. Pitchard collection.)

two-mile connection from Lincoln Park Junction on the SL&FD south to Sugar House to unite the two narrow gauges. The UC operated the SL&E and part of the SL&FD as a combined system, which was known popularly as the Utah Central. The management, which was headed by Joseph Collett of Terre Haute, Indiana, projected an extension to the Colorado state line, probably on the route later planned by the Denver & Salt Lake. The company reportedly graded 17.5 miles of the route east from Park City, and stated that it laid 7.5 miles of track.

The Utah Central failed in the depression of the early 1890s and was placed in receivership on November 27, 1893. The SL&FD was put under the same receiver separately in January 1894. The UC was reorganized as the Utah Central Railroad in December 1897. In January 1898 the Rio Grande Western agreed to lease the system in return for assuming its interest payments. It abandoned all but a mile of the former SL&FD, trackage that had apparently not operated after early 1894. In 1900 the RGW converted the Park City line, modifying its grades in the process. The Denver & Rio Grande assumed the lease in 1901 and absorbed the UC in its consolidation with the RGW in 1908. The Park City branch was abandoned in 1946 beyond Cement Quarry, approximately a fourth of the distance from Salt Lake City, when the right-of-way was condemned for highway construction. Some trackage at Park City was turned over to the Union Pacific. The remainder of the branch was abandoned in 1956 and 1957.

San Pete Valley Railroad

The Central Pacific Coal & Coke Co., Ltd., of London, chartered the San Pete Valley Railroad in 1873 to develop its mining properties in Utah. The company originally planned a 3'-6" line, but shifted to 3'-0" before building. Construction was undertaken in 1880 from Nephi on the Utah Southern 91 miles south of Salt Lake City through the San Pitch Mountains to the southeast. The line was opened on April 1, 1882, to Wales (30 miles), where the mining company had about 10,000 acres of coal land. An extension to Moroni (35 miles) was opened in 1884. Henry W. Tyler of London served as president, with Thomas Marshall of Salt Lake City as vice-president. Simon Bamberger, later governor of Utah and operator of the Bamberger Railroad, the interurban between Salt Lake City and Ogden, was managing director. The line was the first penetration of the middle Sevier Valley. The management from the outset planned on building farther south, but shortly encountered financial problems. The enterprise was reorganized in 1893 with the parent company becoming the Sterling Coal & Coke Co. and the railroad becoming the San Pete Valley Railway. Theodore Bruback, who replaced Bamberger as general manager, arranged financing for an extension to Manti (43 miles), and opened it at the end of 1893. In November 1894 he opened a difficult extension through Six-Mile Canyon to Morrison (51 miles), a coal installation on the east side of the valley named for a director of the firm in London. Bruback sought funds on the east coast and in Britain for a line north from Nephi to Salt Lake City and another south from Manti through the Sevier Valley to some point in southern Nevada, but he was unable to finance either.

Bruback decided upon conversion of the railroad about 1894; the extension to Morrison had been laid with standard gauge ties. The ascent of Salt Creek Canyon from Nephi had to be eased for standard gauge equipment. The line was converted from Nephi to Manti on July 9, 1896, and the remaining trackage to Morrison shortly thereafter. The narrow gauge rail was stockpiled for the southern extension, which was still projected. The Sevier Valley was by then traversed by the Denver & Rio Grande's Marysvale line, which directly paralleled the SPV from Ephraim to Manti, about seven miles. The SPV was not built farther south, although it did build a long spur to a brownstone quarry at Nebo in 1899.

The Denver and Rio Grande bought all of the securities of the SPV in October 1907, reducing the railroad to a pair of branches out of Manti. The Morrison branch was abandoned in 1923 and the duplicate track between Manti and Ephraim in 1926. The line was cut back from Nephi to Moroni in 1948. The remaining 11 miles from Ephraim to Moroni survived as a spur off the Marysvale branch until that line went out of service in 1983. Formal abandonment was approved at the end of 1986 and the rails were removed in 1987.

Summit County Railroad

The Mormon settlement at Salt Lake City, troubled by a lack of readily available fuel, sought to develop a bank of low-grade coal at Coalville. In September 1869 Mormon businessmen incorporated the Coalville & Echo Railroad to connect Coalville with the Union Pacific main line at Echo. They graded the line, but were unable to complete construction. On November 27, 1871, Joseph A. Young and other Mormon leaders formed the Summit County Railroad to take over the grade and franchise of the C&E. They undertook construction of the line as a narrow gauge from Echo in 1872 and began service to Coalville (6 miles) on July 1, 1873.

The narrow gauge served its function imperfectly, mainly because the Union Pacific charged rates from Echo that were considered exorbitant. The Mormon leaders shifted their interests to a direct line from Coalville to Salt Lake City, the Utah Eastern, and sold control of the SC to the UP in March 1877. The UP converted the railroad in 1880 and reorganized it on January 17, 1881, as the Echo & Park City Railroad. As a standard gauge line, the railroad was extended to Park City, a silver-mining area 21 miles to the south. The UP also built a spur of four miles off the original portion to serve a coal mine at Grassy Creek. The spur to Grassy Creek Mine was abandoned in 1947, but the remainder of the branch to Coalville and Park City remains in service.

Utah & Northern Railway

During the Civil War, gold mining was begun at Butte and other points in Montana Territory. At the outset, the mining camps were served by wagon freighting from Fort Benton, head of navigation on the Missouri River. Because of the seasonality of navigation on the Missouri, plus chronic problems of variable water level, mud banks, and strong winds, this form of transport was inherently unsatisfactory. When the transcontinental railroad was completed, western Montana was mainly served by wagon freighting from Corinne, Utah, a small community predominately of Gentile businessmen on the portion of the Union Pacific–Central Pacific line between Ogden and Promontory. The trip was nearly 500 miles across forbidding territory in eastern Idaho and southern Montana. A railroad along the route had obvious attractions to the hierarchy of the Mormon Church. Not only would it improve transportation to Montana, but it would open the intermediate country to Mormon colonization. Rivalry with the Gentile community of Corinne was presumably also part of the calculations.

John W. Young, William B. Preston, George W. Thatcher, and their associates began planning for the rail line, which they named the Utah Northern Railroad. They first considered two routes from the Union Pacific main line at Hams Fork, Wyoming, into Montana via Soda Springs, Idaho, and Monida Pass, but they rejected the connection with the UP in Wyoming as unlikely to benefit the Mormon settlements in Utah. They decided upon a route from Ogden north to Soda Springs via the Cache Valley, thence across rugged country to the South Fork of the Snake River, and finally into Montana through Monida Pass. The choice to use 3′-0″ gauge was made about the time of incorporation in August 1871 on the basis of the reported success of narrow gauge on the Denver & Rio Grande, which was, of course, barely undertaken. Colonel J. H. Martineau, who had surveyed the Utah Central and portions of the Union Pa-

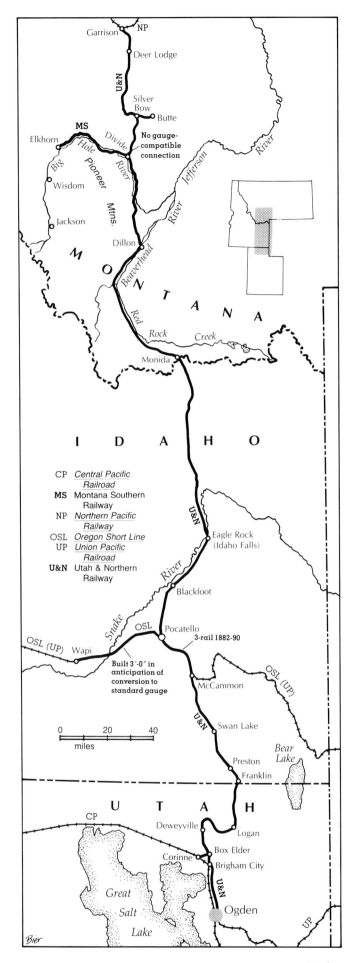

cific, was chosen chief surveyor of the railroad. Tracklaying began at Willard, just south of Brigham City, on March 25, 1872.

The projected line presented formidable difficulties in almost all areas, including the immediate exit from the populous area of northern Utah. Young and his associates were eager to serve the Cache Valley, in which Logan and other Mormon communities had already been established. Martineau proposed to do this by building through the Bear River Narrows, but the management overruled him and ordered a line over Mendon Divide, locally known as Cache Hill. This proved a difficult project, and rails did not reach Logan until January 31, 1873. Because the Utah Northern menaced Corinne's Montana trade, local businessmen formed a rival project, the Utah, Idaho & Montana Railroad. In a successful effort to abort this line, the management of the Utah Northern built a branch of four miles from Box Elder into Corinne. After a substantial bridge was completed over the Bear River, a project that caused some delay, the branch was opened on June 9, 1873. It proved unprofitable and was abandoned at the end of 1875; the rail was used for the extension of the main line. The next segment of the railroad was the south end of the main line, which was completed to Ogden on February 5, 1874. Rails were extended up the Cache Valley into Idaho, and reached Franklin on May 2, 1874. The main line now comprised some 78 miles. At Ogden it connected with another Mormon railroad, the standard gauge Utah Central, for access to Salt Lake City.

The Panic of 1873 had the usual dampening effect on the Utah Northern. The company graded 14 miles north from Franklin toward Soda Springs in 1874, but was unable to lay track or proceed farther into the mountains. The line had reached Franklin partly through the use of labor contributed by Mormon volunteers, but the area immediately to the north was largely unpopulated. The Mormon Church had little interest in developing the land beyond Soda Springs, but profitability depended on reaching the Montana mining region. Efforts at public aid were unsuccessful, particularly because Montana was more motivated by the Northern Pacific's project of entering the state from the east. As a consequence, Jay Gould was able to secure control of the Utah Northern between 1875 and 1878 for about 40 cents on the dollar. The change in control meant that the Utah Northern was to become permanently an appendage of the Union Pacific Railroad.

Union Pacific interests reorganized the railroad as the Utah & Northern Railway in

Two helper engines, Utah & Northern No. 85 and leased South Park Line No. 158, drift down the grade in Beaver Canyon, Idaho, after assisting a northbound freight. (Montana Historical Society.)

April 1878, and immediately began efforts to extend the line into Montana. In 1877 Gould had decided the projected route via Soda Springs was impractical, and ordered the extension to proceed via the Marsh Valley to the west. The Union Pacific's chief engineer, Washington Dunn, surveyed a route via the Portneuf Canyon, the Fort Hall Indian Reservation, and Eagle Rock (Idaho Falls), an existing community that served the wagon-freighting trade. Service to Eagle Rock was established on April 26, 1879, and the railroad made the town its division point. By March 9, 1880, track had reached the Montana state line at Monida Pass. Construction ended for the winter when track reached Dillon, 348 miles from Ogden. During the winter of 1880–81, shop facilities were built at Eagle Rock. Construction resumed in the summer of 1881, and track reached Silver Bow, seven miles west of

Butte, in October. Entering Butte was made difficult by a legal problem. The railroad's charter provided that it should run north via Deer Lodge to a point on the main line of the Northern Pacific. The NP had still not built into the area, but the projected junction point would later be known as Garrison. Because the Butte branch was not in the charter, the company had no legal right of condemnation, and its projected entry required the crossing of several mining claims. By threatening to bypass Butte and to build north from Silver Bow toward Garrison and Helena, the railroad brought about an agreement with the Butte municipal government whereby the holders of the mining claims were bought out with $3,400 of municipal funds and $5,000 spent by the UP. The railroad was completed into Butte on December 21, 1881.

The Utah & Northern proceeded with

Utah & Northern No. 11 is shown with its crew. The large headlight with prominent numerals was a Union Pacific characteristic. (California State Railroad Museum.)

Utah & Northern No. 85 was fitted with a snowplow for operating in the line's difficult winter weather. (California State Railroad Museum.)

the northward extension in 1882, reaching Garrison in November, 454 miles from Ogden. The management planned to lay a third rail from Garrison to Helena on the Northern Pacific, once that railroad had reached the area. By an agreement of February 1883 the NP was, in return, to lay a third rail on the Utah & Northern from Butte to the junction at Garrison. In October, however, the two companies had a falling out, such that the NP built its own line into Butte and the Utah & Northern never reached Helena. The company considered building its own branch to Helena that would leave the main line at Melrose,

bypass Butte to the east, and reach Helena via Radersburg. The company also considered extending the main line west along the Northern Pacific to Missoula, but never did so. An even more grandiose proposal was an Oregon Division, to leave the main line at Portneuf, Idaho, and run to the Pacific via Boise, presumably on the route actually built by the Union Pacific's Oregon Short Line.

The standard gauge Oregon Short Line was chartered by the Union Pacific in 1881 and built from Granger, Wyoming, to Huntington, Oregon, 541 miles. The line reached the Utah & Northern at McCammon, Idaho, in the fall of 1882, and entered

Pocatello (a newly established town that bore the local settlers' nickname for the local Shoshone chief), by 23 miles of third rail along a new dual gauge right-of-way that replaced the narrow gauge. Transitionally, while awaiting arrival of the standard gauge, Oregon Short Line crews laid about 45 miles of narrow gauge from Pocatello through American Falls to a point beyond Wapi. This line was operated essentially as a branch of the Utah & Northern only for part of 1882. The narrow gauge rails were then replaced with standard about October as the OSL built west.

The newly established junction caused Pocatello to become the operating center of the Union Pacific's subsidiaries in the area. The narrow gauge into the Montana mining region proved successful beyond anyone's expectations, but the traffic was now typically transshipped to standard gauge cars at Pocatello, rather than sent on to Ogden. The Union Pacific installed a Ramsey Transfer so as to move standard gauge cars north. The UP sent about 100 narrow gauge gondolas from its South Park Line to move coal from Wyoming to Butte via the Ramsey Transfer. This arrangement, as usual, proved a bottleneck. About 750 tons of freight were transshipped per day in November 1885. Plans for standard gauging the line north of Pocatello were made about that time. As on other narrow gauges, bridges were widened and standard gauge ties installed. The Union Pacific was no longer interested in destinations north of Butte, and arranged with the Northern Pacific to turn the line from Butte to Garrison over to a jointly owned subsidiary, the Montana Union Railway, on August 1, 1886. The Montana Union Railway was converted to standard gauge immediately and made part of the Northern Pacific's alternate main line via Butte. The Union Pacific retained trackage rights from Silver Bow into Butte even after the track was turned over to the Northern Pacific's exclusive ownership in 1898.

Upon completion of a new bridge across the Snake River in 1887 the Union Pacific was ready to convert the north end of the narrow gauge. The line had been relaid with 55-pound rail beginning in 1885, so placed that only one rail need be moved at any location. The entire 264 miles from Pocatello to Butte were converted between 2:00 A.M. and early afternoon on July 25, 1887.

Because the line south of Pocatello had been reduced mainly to a local service facility, the Union Pacific felt no urgency in converting it. There was the further matter that it required extensive relocation, both to avoid flooding in the Marsh Valley of Idaho and to circumvent the steep crossing of Cache Hill in Utah. In the Marsh Valley 27 miles of standard gauge at higher elevation were built south from McCammon to a point beyond Swan Lake. From that point a new line of 48 miles was constructed along the route originally proposed by Martineau west of the Bear River as far as Deweyville, 36 miles north of Ogden. A connection from Cache Junction to Mendon was built to tie the old trackage in the Cache Valley to the new route, and both the line between Deweyville and Mendon over Cache Hill and the original narrow gauge north of Preston were abandoned. The grade over Cache Hill was later used by the Utah-Idaho Central interurban. The changes reduced the distance from Ogden to Butte from 417 to 397 miles. The conversion of the main line was completed on October 1, 1890, and of the Cache Valley branch on October 26. The company had been merged into the Oregon Short Line in 1889, and was thereafter operated only as a major branch of the Union Pacific system. As such, it has always done well, and is still in operation. Remarkably, it retained passenger service until the establishment of Amtrak in 1971. The line from Silver Bow to Garrison turned over to the Northern Pacific in 1886 was conveyed to the Montana Western Railway in 1986, and is also still in service. The Montana Western also operates the trackage from Silver Bow to Butte.

REFERENCES: Merrill D. Beal, *Intermountain Railroads: Standard and Narrow Gauge* (Caldwell, Idaho: Caxton Printers, 1962); Robert L. Wrigley, Jr., "Utah & Northern Railway Co.: A Brief History," *Oregon Historical Quarterly*, 48 (1947), pp. 245–53; Robert G. Athearn, "Railroad to a Far Off Country: The Utah & Northern," *Montana: The Magazine of Western History*, 18 (1968), pp. 3–23; Mallory Hope Ferrell, *Utah & Northern: The Narrow Gauge That Opened a Frontier*, Colorado Rail Annual No. 15 (Golden: Colorado Railroad Museum, 1981), pp. 9–81; Pitchard, *A Utah Railroad Scrapbook*, pp. 2–13 and *passim*; collection of Cornelius W. Hauck.

Utah Eastern Railroad

Although never completed, the Utah Eastern was an endeavor of Mormon leaders to provide a direct route from Salt Lake City to the coalfield at Coalville, about 50 miles distant. Their first effort, the Summit County Railroad, was considered unsatisfactory because of its dependence on a Union Pacific connection. The Utah Eastern was chartered in January 1880 to run from Salt Lake City via Emigration Canyon or Parley's Canyon to the summit of the Wasatch Range, across Parley's Park to the head of East Canyon Creek, across a divide to East Silver Creek, down to Park City, and to Coalville. By November 1880 the line was built from Coalville to Kimball's Junction (16 miles), and on December 9 track reached Park City (23 miles), seat of a major silver-mining area. The management negotiated a contract with the Ontario Silver Mining Co. to bring in coal from Coalville. The Union Pacific in the following month, however, reached Park City with a standard gauge line that served the general transport demands of the area better. The UE management considered extension, either to Salt Lake City over the route later built by the Salt Lake & Eastern or to Alta to a connection with the Wasatch & Jordan Valley, but never built either.

The Union Pacific bought control of the Utah Eastern in the fall of 1883 and on November 20 announced its plan to shut the UE down a month hence. The traffic to the Ontario mine, which had sustained it, was diverted to the parallel UP line, and the narrow gauge was closed on December 20, 1883. The corporation was allowed to go into bankruptcy and to be sold at auction on February 21, 1887. P. L. Williams of the UP bought it for $25,000 and scrapped it. Most of the equipment went to the Utah & Northern.

REFERENCE: Leonard J. Arrington, "Utah's Coal Road in the Age of Unregulated Competition," *Utah Historical Quarterly*, 23 (1955), pp. 35–63.

Utah Western Railroad

H. S. Jacobs of Salt Lake City formed the Salt Lake, Sevier Valley & Pioche Railroad on May 2, 1872, with the financial support of several men in the local Gentile business community and John Leisenring, a prominent mine operator of Mauch Chunk, Pennsylvania. The railroad was to run southwest from Salt Lake City to the Tooele mining area, west of the dry Sevier Lake, through a second mining district in Beaver County and to a third at Pioche, Nevada. If completed, the line would have covered about 300 miles. Ground was broken near the Utah Central depot in Salt Lake City on April 14, 1873, and a locomotive, *Kate Connor*, was bought from Brooks. Jacobs arranged for the purchase of the sternwheel steamer *City of Corinne*, in operation on the Great Salt Lake, where the company planned a resort development at Lake Point. The projected line was located as far as Tintic, about 85 miles, and grading was done at several points on the 41 miles between Salt Lake City and Stockton. Jacobs ordered enough rail for 22 miles, and a small amount was laid leaving Salt Lake City. Jacobs became embroiled in a dispute with his directors about paying for the rail, and he resigned as president on August 1, 1873. In the course of the controversy, the corporation went bankrupt and the rail was sold at a loss.

Heber P. Kimball, who had been active in the company, interested John W. Young and other Mormon leaders in reviving the project under the name of the Utah Western Railroad. With Young as president, the new corporation was chartered on June 15, 1874. Young quickly contracted for enough rail to reach Lake Point (20 miles), and crews began to lay it in November. The railroad opened service over its first 11 miles on December 14. Trains began running to Half-Way House (25 miles) on April 1, 1875. Renamed *General Garfield*, the steamer operated excursions from Lake Point. The management was mainly interested in reaching the mining area around Stockton, but the terrain was difficult. The route chosen bypassed Tooele to the west to avoid gradients, but a station was established for the town about three miles to its north. In September 1877 rails reached an end-of-track unimaginatively named Terminus (37 miles). Completion to Stockton would have entailed a tunnel, which the company proved unable to finance, but a 2'-0" tramway built by local mine operators provided a connection to the mining district.

The Utah Western missed its interest payment in January 1878, and was placed in the hands of the trustees of its bond issue, Royal M. Bassett and E. F. Bishop, on April 16. The trustees brought about a sale of the property under foreclosure on November 3, 1880, for $36,000. The buyers, Bassett and W. W. Riter, organized the Utah & Nevada Railroad on February 16, 1881, intending to extend the line to Tintic. Before any extension could be undertaken, the Union Pacific on April 1, 1881, purchased 600 of the 700 bonds of the Utah Western and converted them into stock of the new corporation, gaining control on August 20. The UP, which was thought to be interested in the railroad as an exit from Salt Lake City for a line of its own to the San Francisco Bay Area rival to the Central Pacific, actually made no immediate change in the narrow gauge. The line remained an independently operated subsidiary until August 1, 1889, when it was merged with other UP subsidiaries in the area into the Oregon Short Line & Utah Northern Railway, which in turn became the Oregon Short Line in 1897. A spur of 2.5 miles was built to Saltair in 1888. A major resort was built there in 1893. The narrow gauge was converted by the OSL November 8–15, 1902. Actually, the UP made use of only three or four miles of the old right-of-way, otherwise building a new parallel railroad. The Saltair line was abandoned at the time of conversion. The UP made use of the line as the northern 37 miles of its San Pedro, Los Angeles & Salt Lake Railroad, the extension of its main line into Los Angeles. As such, the line remains a major part of the American railroad system.

REFERENCE: Reeder, *The History of Utah's Railroads 1869–1883*, pp. 257–99.

Vermont

Brattleboro & Whitehall Rail Road

The Green Mountains run the length of Vermont as a major natural barrier. Watercourses on the east escarpment of the mountains provide several possible approaches for crossings of the range. The Rutland Railroad and its predecessors crossed from Bellows Falls along the Williams River. Projects for a similar crossing up the valley of the West River from Brattleboro date from the 1840s. The West River Rail Road was organized in 1867 to build a standard gauge up the valley as far as Jamaica, but no work was done beyond surveying a route. In 1876 the company was reformed as the Brattleboro & Whitehall Rail Road, with a charter to build diagonally across the state to Whitehall, New York, on the Delaware & Hudson. The directors first considered a 3'-0" line, but their inspection of the Billerica & Bedford prompted them to change their plans to a 2'-0" installation. By the spring of 1878, some $2,000 was in hand from bond issues in the towns along the valley and from private sources. A survey was made of

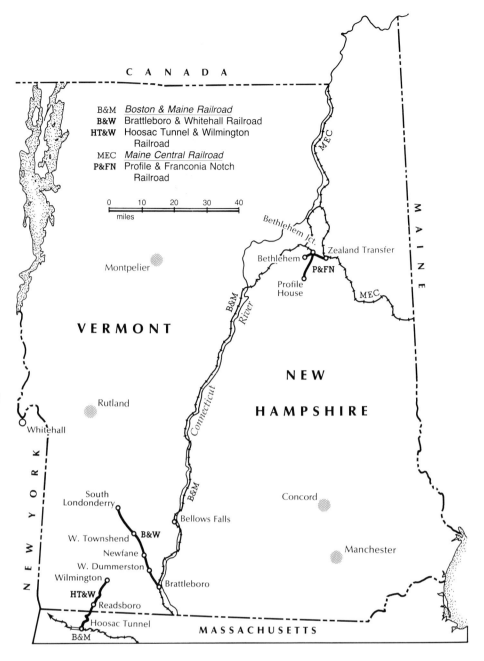

the route, and in October a contract for construction was let to Harris Brothers. Shortly before building, the plan was changed back to 3'-0", which, given the constraints of narrow gauge, was probably wise. The promoters seem mainly to have been interested in making a connection with the Erie Canal system in the Champlain Valley for shipments across New England, but they found financial support for no more than a local line up the West River valley.

Ground was broken on November 11, 1878, at Newfane, and the railroad was graded from Brattleboro to South Londonderry, 36 miles, in the summer of 1879. The company's resources were exhausted, and no rail had been laid. The management arranged in February 1880 for the railroad to be leased to the New London Northern,

predecessor of the Central Vermont Railway, for 99 years. The larger company agreed to complete the narrow gauge and to pay the Brattleboro & Whitehall $400 per year and half the profits of the railroad. In turn, the Central Vermont was obligated to operate two trains per day and maintain the line. Completion required about $150,000. Tracklaying was finished to South Londonderry on October 20, 1880, and service began on November 18. Nothing was done toward building a crossing of the mountains.

The narrow gauge never proved profitable enough for the Central Vermont to pay the Brattleboro & Whitehall more than the $400 contractual obligation. This was, however, enough for the corporation to hold an annual banquet for shareholders in Brattleboro, and to pay occasional small cash divi-

The last narrow gauge train on the Central Vermont's Brattleboro & Whitehall prepares to leave Brattleboro in 1905. (Ed Bond collection.)

dends. The lease was probably a more favorable arrangement for them than independent operation of the narrow gauge would have been. The Central Vermont was widely accused of neglecting the line's physical condition. The branch's location along a river resulted in frequent washouts in the spring. In 1886 the bridge across the mouth of the West River approaching Brattleboro collapsed under a mixed train, and two lives were lost. The bridge was replaced with an iron structure. Several smaller bridges were also replaced by iron spans before 1898. The physical condition of the railroad deteriorated after 1895, however. Ties rotted and derailments were frequent. Service was provided by a passenger train and a mixed train daily in each direction. The line served typical local transportation demands, but had a substantial source of traffic from the quarry of the Lyons Granite Co. at West Dummerston, seven miles from Brattleboro. Necessarily, the portion of the track from Brattleboro to West Dummerston was maintained better than the rest. The mixed train regularly doubled the grade up from the river valley from Newfane. The narrow gauge operated with four locomotives, three wood burners, and a coal burner.

Pressure for conversion came variously from shareholders, the granite company, and local residents who wanted higher standards of comfort and safety. Third rail was laid to the quarry about 1901, but the condition of the ties was so bad that many of the standard gauge cars derailed. In 1903 the Brattleboro & Whitehall corporation petitioned for receivership and abrogation of the lease. The directors alleged that the roadbed was unsafe, the rolling stock in poor repair, and the quality of service so low that traffic suffered. The Central Vermont responded with an action for foreclosure of the B&W's mortgage, on which it alleged that $150,000 in interest was un-

paid. The case was in the courts for two years until the two corporations agreed on a compromise. The B&W agreed to foreclosure of its mortage in return for $5,000, passes on the line for the directors, and free transportation of shareholders to the annual meeting for 20 years. The Central Vermont agreed to convert the railroad and improve its maintenance. The CV organized the West River Railroad to own the line. The entire branch except for one mile was converted on Sunday, July 30, 1905, by 350 men, almost all from regular Central Vermont track crews. The final mile was converted the following morning.

The line continued to be a minor branch, poorly maintained and subject to loss of traffic to trucks once roads in the area were improved. The track was wiped out by the flood of 1927, but rebuilt with state funds in 1930. The line was operated as an independent short line under the name of West River Railroad, mainly by James G. Ashley of Greenfield, Massachusetts, until 1936, when it was abandoned. The trackage from the quarry at West Dummerston to Brattleboro was retained as a private spur by the Vermont White Granite Co. until 1938, when the hurricane of that year wiped it out.

REFERENCE: Victor Morse, *36 Miles of Trouble: The Story of the West River Railroad* (Brattleboro, Ver.: The Book Cellar, 1959).

Hoosac Tunnel & Wilmington Railroad

The Deerfield River Pulp & Paper Corporation in 1885 opened an 11-mile line, which it called the Deerfield River Railroad, form the east portal of the Hoosac Tunnel in Massachusetts to Readsboro, Vermont, to connect its pulpwood mill at Readsboro with the Troy line of the Boston & Maine.

The line was a nominal common carrier, which mainly hauled pulpwood into and pulp out of the mill. Investment was estimated at $100,000. In 1886 the paper company organized the Hoosac Tunnel & Wilmington Railroad to own the eight miles in Massachusetts and to lease the remainder of the line in Vermont. Readsboro, a town of about 900, was an unlikely terminus, but there was considerable interest in a railroad in Wilmington, a community of 1,200, 13 miles to the north. The paper company organized another subsidiary, the Deerfield Valley Railroad, to build to Wilmington; the extension was opened on November 4, 1891. On January 4, 1892, all three railroads were consolidated into the Hoosac Tunnel & Wilmington. Headquarters were established at Wilmington.

The railroad regularly operated two passengers trains per day; the trip required about two hours. The railroad enjoyed a traffic of vacationers in the summer season. For a railroad of only 24 miles of main line, this was a rather large enterprise. The locomotive roster ran to ten engines, most of which were employed in services on non–common carrier branches into forest areas.

The Newton family of Holyoke, Massachusetts, which owned the Deerfield River company and the railroad, expanded into woodworking and other industrial activity along the railroad. The entire enterprise reached its peak in the first decade of the twentieth century. Consequently, it was considered surprising locally that the Newtons sold out their interests in 1904 to J. P. Kellas of Malone, New York, and his associates. Kellas paid $1.5 million for the railroad, 123,000 acres of forest land, and various manufacturing properties. Because the timber near the main line was exhausted, the Kellas management expanded the private carrier mileage considerably. Between 1908 and 1914, the railroad ran as much as 30 miles of such track.

In July 1912 the Kellas group announced its plan to convert the common carrier portion of the railroad. Work on conversion began with the spring thaw of the following year, and the railroad was changed to 4'-8½" on August 2, 1913. Two of the old locomotives were retained to work the remaining narrow gauge lumber spurs.

The railroad was purchased by the New England Power Company in 1922, apparently in the main to facilitate building of the Harriman Dam and Reservoir. The dam, which was at the time of completion the largest earth dam in the world, was built at Whittingham Station, about two miles north of Readsboro. The Wilmington extension of the railroad had to be relocated

The Hoosac Tunnel & Wilmington followed the Deerfield River for most of its distance, as shown in these two photos. In one, a freight passes a paper mill at Readsboro. (Ed Bond collection.)

to higher ground to the west. The power company sold the railroad to local merchants in 1926. A flood on November 3, 1926, inflicted heavy damage to the line, knocking out the trestle leading into Wilmington; as a result the railroad dropped passenger service permanently. The trestle was repaired, but was again destroyed on March 18, 1936. The local owners were unable to restore the railroad and sold it to Samuel L. Pinsly of Boston, for whom it was the first of several short-line acquisitions. Pinsly abandoned the line north of Readsboro in 1937. The remainder of the railroad survived into the 1960s, becoming the service facility to the Yankee Atomic

Power Station near Monroe Bridge, Massachusetts. The line from Hoosac Tunnel to Readsboro was abandoned in 1971.

REFERENCE: Bernard D. Carman, *Hoot Toot & Whistle: The Story of the Hoosac Tunnel & Wilmington Railroad* (Brattleboro, Ver.: Stephen Greene Press, 1963).

Virginia

Atlantic & Danville Railway

Both in date of opening and in survival, this was a relatively late narrow gauge. The company was chartered on April 21, 1882, to run from a point on the James River in Surry County to Danville via Waverly, Belfield, Lawrenceville, and Boydton. John M. Bailey of Waverly was chosen as the first president. Construction began at Claremont Wharf on the James on April 2, 1883. The railroad was opened to Belfield (Emporia) on the Petersburg Railroad, later the main line of the Atlantic Coast Line, in December 1885. By the time the track arrived in Belfield (54 miles) the management had decided to complete the railroad as a standard gauge from Portsmouth to Danville, reducing the narrow gauge to a branch mainly serving the local lumber industry. The branch had a spur, variously stated to be three or six miles, to a lumber mill at Savedge. The standard gauge line from Portsmouth reached Belfield on September 5, 1888, making use of four miles of the narrow gauge from James River Junction as a three-rail entry. The standard gauge reached Danville on February 15, 1890. The railroad was placed in receivership in January 1891, sold under foreclosure on April 3, 1894, and reorganized without change of name in 1895. The Southern Railway leased the A&D for 50 years as of September 1, 1899.

Remarkably, neither the A&D nor the Southern converted the Claremont branch, which became the last narrow gauge portion of the Southern Railway system. With the decline of lumbering in the area, the branch became a service facility for a lightly populated peanut- and cotton-growing area. The line survived until the Depression, when it was reduced to serving a single lumber mill at Waverly. Claremont was a town of only 434. The Southern applied to abandon operation of the line and received permis-

The narrow gauge line of the Atlantic & Danville made its principal connection with river steamers at Claremont Wharf. Here is the wharf in 1910 with the daily mixed train preparing to depart. (Ed Bond collection.)

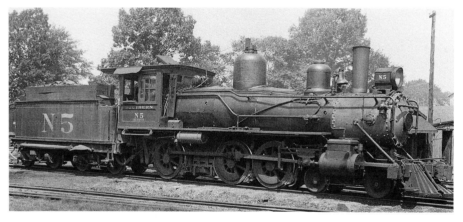

The Southern Railway identified the Atlantic & Danville's narrow gauge locomotives with the prefix "N." The engine is a Baldwin ten-wheeler of 1886. (Ed Bond collection.)

sion from the ICC on November 4, 1932, effective December 5. The Gray Lumber Co., which had used the branch for log trains, continued to operate the line for private carriage under lease until November 20, 1938, when it was finally abandoned.

The Southern gave up the lease on the Atlantic & Danville on its expiration in 1949. The A&D went bankrupt in 1960 and was acquired in 1962 by the Norfolk & Western, which reorganized it as the Norfolk, Franklin & Danville Railway. The N&W abandoned most of the west end of the line in 1982, and merged the NF&D into itself in 1983. The four miles of former narrow gauge from James River Junction to Emporia survive as part of a Norfolk Southern branch from Suffolk to South Hill.

REFERENCE: William E. Griffin, Jr., *The Atlantic & Danville Railway Company: The Railroad of Southside Virginia* (Richmond, Virg.: William E. Griffin, Jr., 1987).

Big Sandy & Cumberland Railroad

Gauge: 3'-6"

The W. M. Ritter Lumber Co. of Columbus, Ohio, secured a charter in Virginia for the Big Sandy & Cumberland Railroad on January 25, 1900, apparently to begin common carriage on some existing private trackage; the railroad leased the line from the lumber company. The route was from a connection with the Norfolk & Western main line at Devon, West Virginia, through the eastern tip of Kentucky into Buchanan County, Virginia, to mills of the company at Hurley (13 miles) and Blackey (17 miles). The 7.71 miles in Kentucky were separately incorporated as the Knox Creek Railway. The 2.4 miles south from Devon were laid with third rail. As with most such operations, the early history is obscure, but in 1910 the line was extended to Matney (24 miles) and in 1911 to Rife (26 miles). The mountain crossing between Blackey and Matney entailed a grade of 6 percent. With a curving route along Slate Creek, the line

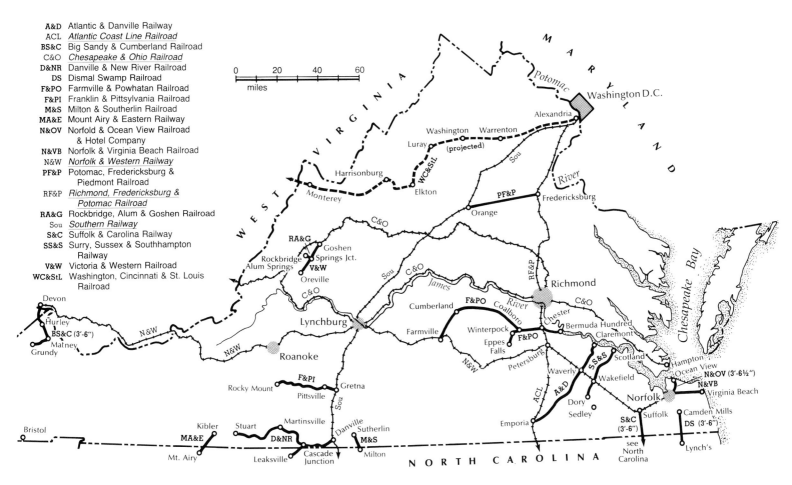

was brought into Grundy (33 miles), seat of Buchanan County, late in 1916. A daily mixed train provided a general transport service, but the line remained mainly a service facility for Ritter.

On October 12, 1923, the Norfolk & Western bought the entire stock of the railroad and prepared to convert it as part of the branch line mileage in the Appalachian coalfield. On October 27, 1927, the N&W applied to the ICC for permission to convert 13.46 miles of the existing line from Devon to Hurley, to build a new mountain crossing of 9.54 miles from Hurley to a point at the mouth of Home Creek (including a tunnel of 4,000 feet), and to convert 13.3 miles of private narrow gauge track of Ritter along the Levisa Fork of the Big Sandy River as a new entry into Grundy from the northwest. There would also be some line revision at Devon. The new line would be 36.3 miles, about three miles longer than the narrow gauge. The ICC approved the application, and the new line was opened in mid-1931. It remains part of the Norfolk Southern's extensive network of branches in the area.

REFERENCE: "Heavy Construction on the Norfolk & Western," *Railway Age*, 90 (1931), pp. 533–37.

General cargo on the Big Sandy & Cumberland was typically handled on mixed trains, but with the railroad's geared locomotives. (Ed Bond collection.)

Danville & New River Railroad

The project of a railroad from Danville to some point on the Bristol branch of the Norfolk & Western or its predecessors had existed since pre–Civil War times. Interested parties in the counties to the west secured a charter for the Danville & New River Railroad on March 29, 1873, but were unable to build because of the cost of bridging the Dan River leaving Danville. In an apparent effort to forestall an incursion into the area on the part of the Baltimore & Ohio, the Richmond & Danville agreed to assist construction of the D&NR by granting 250 tons of secondhand rail along with the right to lay third rail over the affiliated Piedmont Railroad from Danville to Stokesland (5 miles). This arrangement permitted the D&NR to leave Danville without building a bridge, and quickly brought the line into being. It was opened to Martinsville, 43 miles, on December 1, 1881. The D&NR made a second mortgage on the railroad to extend 32 miles to Patrick Court House (Stuart), the next county seat to the west. The extension opened on August 1, 1884. Proceeding farther would have entailed penetration of formidable mountains, and the line was not extended.

Rather, the company began operating a connecting narrow gauge, the Danville, Mocksville & Southwestern Railroad. This company had been organized by the Richmond & Danville on November 29, 1880, as part of its effort to prevent the B&O from entering the area. Construction began at Cascade Junction on the Danville & New River, 21 miles west of Danville. In April 1882 track reached the Smith River about a mile short of Leaksville, North Carolina. By an agreement of September 29, 1883, with the North Carolina Midland Railroad, the DM&SW secured $9,000 in local funds to bridge the river, but the Midland was given a half interest in the bridge. The arrangement brought the DM&SW's rails into Leaksville, eight miles from Cascade Junction, but it presented a conflict in the company's relations with larger railroads. Through its subsidiary, the Richmond Terminal Co., the Richmond & Danville owned 490 of the 502 shares of the DM&SW's stock. The DM&SW's management attempted to prevent a certificate for these shares from being registered. The dispute caused J. Turner Morehead to be appointed receiver on November 9, 1885. He leased the line to the Danville & New River effective March 1, 1886.

Also in 1886, the Danville & New River missed an interest payment on its bonds, causing it to be placed in the hands of receiver J. C. Wrenshall on January 12, 1887. The City of Danville pursued a claim against the company to the U.S. Supreme Court unsuccessfully. The railroad was sold to J. Willcox Brown for $300,000 on August 27, 1890, and reorganized as the Danville & Western Railway on January 8, 1891. The new company's mortgage of $1,052,000 was guaranteed by the Richmond & Danville. This arrangement brought the line into the Southern Railway system on formation on July 1, 1894. The line was one of several separately operated narrow gauges of the Southern.

The Southern merged the Danville, Mocksville & Southwestern into the Danville & Western on March 1, 1899. Because of industrial development in Eden, Leaksville, and neighboring towns, the former DM&SW presented the greater urgency for conversion. The Southern converted the branch and laid third rail from Cascade Junction to Stokesland, completing the job in 1900. Narrow gauge rail was removed from Danville to Cascade Junction and the main line converted as far as Martinsville in March 1902. The remainder, the

The Danville & New River's subsidiary, the Danville, Mocksville & Southwestern, had separately lettered equipment. Above is locomotive No. 1, a Baldwin Mogul with an extreme example of the extended smokeboxes in vogue in the 1880s. (Thomas T. Taber collection, Railroad Museum of Pennsylvania.)

lightly trafficked extension from Martinsville to Stuart, was converted during fiscal 1903–4, probably during the summer of 1903.

The Martinsville-Stuart trackage, which served a minor county seat of some 1,350 people, was abandoned in 1942. The remainder is in operation as a major branch of the Norfolk Southern serving the Miller brewery at Eden and a variety of textile mills.

Dismal Swamp Railroad
Gauge: 3'-6"

The Richmond Cedar Works was one of several lumber companies that operated in the Great Dismal Swamp of southern Virginia and northern North Carolina. In 1896 the company formed the Dismal Swamp Railroad to operate as a nominal common carrier from its plant at Camden Mills, near Great Bridge, Virginia, on the Chesapeake & Albemarle Canal to a point on Albemarle Sound in North Carolina. Portions of an existing lumber railroad were apparently used. The gauge was the 3'-6" customary among the local lumber railroads, considered the minimum feasible in the spongy terrain. The common carrier portion of the railroad extended from Camden Mills to Lynch's, a lumber camp about a half mile south of Lynch's Crossroads, North Carolina, approximately 26 miles. Track eventually was built about nine miles farther to a point in Perquimans County for use as a lumber spur. A daily round-trip for passengers was run from Camden Mills to Lynch's.

After a bankruptcy, the lumber company and the railroad were consolidated into the Dismal Swamp Corporation in 1941. The new corporation converted its operations to truck, and completed the dismantling of the railroad on November 27, 1941.

REFERENCE: H. T. Crittenden, "The Dismal Swamp Railroad Company," Railway & Locomotive Historical Society *Bulletin*, no. 64 (1944), pp. 61–68.

Farmville & Powhatan Railroad

One of the few narrow gauges to be converted from a standard gauge railroad, this enterprise had its origins in the Clover Hill Railroad, built in the pre–Civil War period from the Clover Hill Mine at Winterpock to Chester on the Richmond & Petersburg Railroad (18 miles). In 1867 the line was extended to the east three miles to Osborne's Landing on the James River. Throughout the

Tidewater & Western No. 1 is an unusual locomotive, a product of George W. Snyder of Pottsville, Pennsylvania. Snyder built industrial locomotives, but hardly any for common carriers. (Ed Bond collection.)

railroad's history it was integral with the coal-mining operation at Winterpock. The enterprise was placed in receivership in 1875 and was sold on April 25, 1877, to John W. Johnston as representative of the bondholders, who reorganized it as the Bright Hope Railway & Coal Co.

In May 1881 the Bright Hope management made the surprising announcement that it would convert the railroad to 3'-0" incidentally to extending it 11 miles from Chester to Bermuda Hundred at the confluence of the James and Appomattox rivers. The wharf at Bermuda Hundred could accommodate ships of 20-foot draft, allowing the railroad to load into coastal colliers. The line to Osborne's Landing was to be abandoned. The plan also entailed extension from Winterpock south 4.5 miles to Eppes Falls. The project was reported completed in October 1882.

To the west, Joseph Hobson of Rock Castle and several businessmen of Cumberland and Powhatan counties formed the Farmville & Powhatan Railroad on March 10, 1884, to build from Farmville on the Norfolk & Western main line to the towns of Cumberland and Powhatan. Tracklaying began on May 18, 1889. On July 23 Hobson bought the Bright Hope Railway for $200,000 and on October 1 merged it into the F&P. By the end of the year he had built 39 miles, and on March 3, 1890, he completed a connection to the Bright Hope mine at Coalboro, three miles short of Winterpock. The continuous line from Bermuda Hundred to Farmville was 89 miles. What was now the branch to Eppes Falls was cut back to Winterpock in 1892.

The railroad was chronically unprofitable, and was placed under receiver T. M. R.

Talcott on October 26, 1899. The property was sold under foreclosure on June 7, 1905, and reorganized as the Tidewater & Western Railroad. Talcott became general manager, and there was in the main a continuity in ownership. The new corporation had a favorable charter, empowering it to extend to the Kentucky or Tennessee borders, and to build branches within the state of up to 50 miles. The management considered extensions to Danville, Lynchburg, and elsewhere, but never undertook them. The line continued as a narrow gauge coal road, as before. Remarkably, the management did not report any intention to convert the railroad in the trade press. The line operated with seven or eight locomotives. There was one daily passenger train.

The line met an unusual end. It surrendered its charter on May 10, 1917. Langbourne M. Williams, who was appointed receiver four days later, arranged sale of the rails and equipment to the French government for use in World War I. The line was dismantled for shipment in June 1918. Reportedly the war ended before the equipment could be put to its intended use.

REFERENCE: C. F. H. Allen, "Tidewater and Western Railroad," Railway & Locomotive Historical Society *Bulletin*, no. 114 (1966), pp. 48–52.

Franklin & Pittsylvania Railroad

The owners of iron deposits at Pittsville persuaded the trustees of the bankrupt Washington City, Virginia Midland & Great Southern Railroad to provide them a narrow gauge branch of seven miles from Franklin Junction (Gretna). The line was built in

1878 under authority granted by the bankruptcy court on November 21, 1877. The branch was known as the Pittsylvania Railroad, although it appears to have had no separate incorporation.

The Franklin & Pittsylvania Railroad was chartered March 12, 1878, to run from Pittsville west through the two counties of its name to Rocky Mount, 30 miles. The line was leased from the day of completion, May 1, 1880, to the WCVM&GS and its successor, the Virginia Midland Railway. The Richmond & Danville came into control of the Virginia Midland on April 15, 1886, and quickly announced its intention to convert the narrow gauge. The line was converted near the end of August 1888.

Iron had ceased to be a major cargo, and the line existed on local lumber organizations. The Southern Railway, which succeeded to it in 1894, proposed to surrender the property to local operators in 1897, but encountered a legal action as a consequence of which it was ordered to continue operation under the lease of 1880. The lease was allowed to expire on May 1, 1914, when the railroad became a locally operated short line; it owned the Pittsville–Rocky Mount trackage and leased from the Southern the seven miles from Gretna to Pittsville. The company went into receivership in 1921, but was reorganized in 1922 as the Franklin & Pittsylvania Railway. In September 1923 the operators gave up the leased line and cut back operations to a mixed train from Rocky Mount to Penhook, 19 miles. An additional two miles to Angles were retained but not regularly worked. The railroad went into receivership again in May 1932, but the receivers on this occasion sought only to abandon it. They received permission of the courts and the ICC, and ceased operation in November. The Norfolk & Western bought the company's switching track in Rocky Mount for $1,000.

Milton & Sutherlin Railroad

Major William T. Sutherlin of Danville conceived of this narrow gauge to serve the local transport demands of Milton, a village in Caswell County, North Carolina, a short distance south of the Virginia state line. He incorporated it in 1876 and in the following year began building it from a point, which he named for himself, on the Richmond & Danville 11 miles east of Danville. The railroad was completed from Sutherlin to Milton (7 miles) in February 1878. It was a modest operation of a single locomotive, one combine, and two freight cars. Sutherlin considered an extension to reach the Deep River coal mines, but never undertook it.

To complete his railroad Sutherlin negotiated an agreement by which the R&D should grant him a rebate of 25 percent on all traffic from the narrow gauge up to $20,000, to be repaid to the R&D in stock of the M&S. This odd arrangement resulted in the R&D's rapidly gaining stock control of the M&S. On May 19, 1882, the R&D arranged to lease the M&S for 999 years in return for payment of interest on the narrow gauge's debt and guaranty of the principal. Sutherlin sold his interest in the road to M. M. Watkins and other local businessmen.

The usefulness of the narrow gauge declined greatly in 1889 when the Atlantic & Danville built its main line through Milton. When the Southern Railway succeeded to the properties of the R&D in 1894, it listed the M&S among the R&D's holdings "believed to be of no value." The Southern operated the narrow gauge for the R&D's receivers in July and August of 1894, but then shut it down. L. M. Warlick of Winston, North Carolina, bought it late in 1896, but proved unable to restore it to operation. The railroad was removed in the spring of 1898.

Norfolk & Ocean View Railroad & Hotel Co.
Gauge: 3'-6½"

W. H. Taylor opened this line in September 1879 as part of the development of Ocean View, a resort on Hampton Roads, eight miles almost due north of downtown Norfolk. It was a steam dummy operation of two locomotives, but for about the first

decade of its existence it handled freight, mainly produce of local truck farms. The management ceased reporting freight revenue in 1890. The line was converted and electrified with the Walker system on July 13, 1895. A receiver was appointed in April 1896, and the enterprise reorganized on March 4, 1898, as the Norfolk & Ocean View Railway. This corporation was consolidated with the Norfolk Street Railroad on November 2, 1899, into the Norfolk Railway & Light Co. Between September 24 and October 2, 1900, the line was converted to 5'-2" for conformity with the system generally. The line continued as part of the city's streetcar system, providing service to Ocean View via Fairmount Park. It was converted to bus on July 11, 1948.

Norfolk & Virginia Beach Railroad

In 1881 Marshall Parks of Norfolk and his associates bought a tract of oceanfront land six miles south of Cape Henry from the Seaside Hotel & Land Co. and prepared to build the Princess Anne Hotel, a pavilion, cottages, and other facilities for a resort to be called Virginia Beach. For access from Norfolk they incorporated the Norfolk & Virginia Beach Railroad & Improvement Co. on January 14, 1882. The terrain was flat and devoted to truck farming. Of the 18-mile line, 14 miles were on a tangent. The railroad was opened on July 28, 1883, although full service was not established until the 1884 summer session.

The financial history of the enterprise was very poor. Creditors from the construc-

This Forney locomotive was built by the Hinkley Locomotive Co. for the Norfolk & Virginia Beach. Consistent with the railroad's short-distance resort travel, the engine is equipped with double sand domes and pilots for operation in both directions. (Ed Bond collection.)

Potomac, Fredericksburg & Piedmont No. 1 prepares to take a mixed train out of the Fredericksburg yard. (Ed Bond collection.)

tion period secured a receivership late in 1884, but the receiver was discharged in 1885 when the company arranged a full discharge of its debts. This proved impossible, and a second receivership was established in November 1886. The line was sold under foreclosure on May 17, 1887, to Charles W. Mackey of Franklin, Pennsylvania, who reorganized it on July 1 as the Norfolk & Virginia Beach Railroad. Mackey immediately announced a bond issue of $200,000 to convert the railroad and to build a branch to Princess Anne, the county seat, nine miles to the south. The financial problems of the railroad were to delay this project for a decade. On March 2, 1891, the shareholders voted to merge with the unbuilt Danville & Seaboard Railroad into the Norfolk, Albemarle & Atlantic Railroad. The new management, headed by George S. Jones of New York, announced that it would convert the railroad during the summer of 1891, but was unable to do so. The enterprise was again put in receivership on May 25, 1893, and sold on April 26, 1896, to Alfred Skitt of New York, who on June 13 formed the Norfolk, Virginia Beach & Southern Railroad. Unlike his predecessors, Skitt found the funds for conversion. The work was done in April and May of 1897, and the railroad opened as a standard gauge line for the summer season on June 1. The long-projected branch was opened from Euclid to Princess Anne and to Munden at the head of Currituck Sound on April 23, 1898.

The NVB&S was absorbed into the Norfolk & Southern in 1900. The opening of the Chesapeake Transit Co. in 1902 as an electric line from Norfolk to Virginia Beach via Cape Henry caused the N&S to electrify the former narrow gauge in 1904 with standard interurban technology. Later in 1904 the N&S absorbed the CTCo., and oper-

ated both electric lines as a loop to the beach. Until 1919 the cars entered Norfolk by street-running, but they were then diverted into Terminal Station, which was already used by the Norfolk Southern's main-line trains. Electric operation was discontinued in 1935 in favor of gasoline rail cars, but passenger service was discontinued entirely in 1948. The line is in existence at the present writing as a branch of the successor Norfolk Southern Railway.

REFERENCE: Richard E. Prince, *Norfolk Southern Railroad, Old Dominion Line and Connections* (Millard, Nebr.: Richard E. Prince, 1972), pp. 10, 51–54.

Potomac, Fredericksburg & Piedmont Railroad

The project for a railroad west from Fredericksburg into Spotsylvania and Orange counties dated from before the Civil War. The Fredericksburg & Gordonsville Railroad undertook construction in 1872 and laid just under 18 miles of standard gauge track in 1873 from Fredericksburg to Parker. Early in 1876 the enterprise was reorganized as the Potomac, Fredericksburg & Piedmont Railroad, but in June it sold control of the property to the Royal Land Co., which was interested in building a narrow gauge line from the tidewater to the Shenandoah Mountains west of Harrisonburg, where it held about 200,000 acres of coal lands. After rejecting a route via the Rapidan River and Swift Run Gap, it decided upon a line of somewhat over 100 miles from Matthais Point on the Potomac River through Fredericksburg to Orange Court House (Orange), Standardsville, Elkton, and Harrisonburg to Rawley Springs. This route made use of the 18 miles of unused track and some additional grading

done by the F&G on the 14 miles west from Parker to Orange. Track crews respiked the F&G's 56-pound rail to 3'-0" and by the end of 1876 laid an additional ten miles of 30-pound rail west to Lafayette. In February 1877 Royal brought the track into Orange (38 miles). Regular operation began on April 14.

That, as it proved, was all Royal could accomplish. On May 13, 1878, the former PF&P management announced that it had regained control of the railroad. The owners, led by L. Harry Richards of Fredericksburg, showed some interest in extending the railroad, but actually ran it as a local narrow gauge until well into the twentieth century. Traffic was mainly lumber and cordwood, with a preponderance of traffic moving east to the Richmond, Fredericksburg & Potomac at Fredericksburg, rather than to the Southern or Chesapeake & Ohio at Orange. The railroad typically ran one scheduled train per day, and operated with two or three locomotives. Richards, remarkably, remained president until 1912.

Like many of the other long-surviving narrow gauges, the PF&P was badly hurt by automotive transportation after World War I. The corporation became insolvent and abandonment seemed imminent. Rather, Langbourne M. Williams of Richmond organized the Orange & Frederick Railroad on June 11, 1925, to buy the property after the Virginia commission had ordered the corporation dissolved. The O&F took over operation on June 15 and began preparations to convert the railroad. Standard gauge operation began on September 10, 1926. Oddly, seven of the intermediate stations were renamed at the time of conversion. On November 26, 1926, Williams changed the name to the Virginia Central Railway. In 1930 he secured a franchise for extension eastward to a point at the mouth of the Rappahannock River, but the Depression prevented building the line.

In 1937 Williams's heirs applied to abandon the entire railroad, which had largely been supplanted by highway carriers. Protests from firms on the line immediately west of Fredericksburg caused the management to amend the application to allow retention of about a mile of track at the east end. The ICC acquiesced to this arrangement on December 3, 1937. The VC, although reduced to a little over a mile of switching track, retained the legal status of a line-haul railroad, participating as such in interline tariffs. It was the shortest such railroad in the country. It survived until 1984.

REFERENCE: Ames W. Williams, "The Virginia Central Railway," *National Railway Bulletin*, 50, no. 1 (1985), pp. 4–15.

Rockbridge Alum & Goshen Railroad

Victoria & Western Railroad

These two connecting narrow gauges provided the dissimilar services of moving passengers to a spa and transporting iron ore to a smelter.

The Victoria & Western was opened in the spring of 1890 from Goshen on the main line of the Chesapeake & Ohio through Victoria to Oreville (18 miles). The line was a promotion of Chamberlain, Lee & Co., iron dealers of Columbus, Ohio, to provide a flow of ore from a pit at Oreville to their smelter at Victoria, two miles below the C&O interchange. The line was a common carrier, partly to participate in interline rates from the mill at Victoria and partly to carry passengers to Oreville.

James A. Frazier, manager of the resort at Rockbridge Alum Springs, saw the Victoria & Western as a means of rail access to his facilities. The line ran southwest from Goshen along Simpson's Creek, passing about two miles east of his spa. Late in 1889 he organized the Rockbridge Alum & Goshen Railroad, which opened its line of under two miles from the resort to the V&W at Springs Junction, ten miles below Goshen, for the 1891 season. In 1892 the two railroads ran two passenger trains a day from the C&O station at Goshen to the resort and the V&W ran two others from Victoria to Oreville for miners.

The V&W and the smelter at Victoria passed into the hands of the Virginia Iron & Railway Co., formed on March 1, 1892. This firm went into receivership in 1896 and was reorganized as the Victoria Furnace Co. The new owner gave up passenger service to Oreville, and leased the V&W to Frazier for a modest $600 per season, June 1 to November 1. This arrangement lasted until 1905, when both railroads were abandoned.

Suffolk & Carolina Railway
Gauge: 3'-6"

The Nansemond Land, Lumber & Narrow-Gauge Railway Co. was organized in 1873 in the expectation of carrying on the activities indicated by its corporate title. It may have engaged in private carriage, although evidence is lacking. The firm was acquired by the Gay Manufacturing Co. of Baltimore, which on February 26, 1884, rechartered it as the Suffolk & Carolina Railway with authority to build a common carrier south from Suffolk in the direction of

The Rockbridge, Alum & Goshen handled its passengers behind this Baldwin tank engine. (Ed Bond collection.)

Sunbury, North Carolina. The *Railroad Gazette* reported that the company acquired an unspecified amount of track from the Suffolk Lumber Co., an existing 3'-6" private carrier in the area; this would account for the extremely late choice of 3'-6" for the railroad. Mainly, the line was intended to connect Gay's lumber mills at Suffolk, Cypress Chapel, and Sunbury with the steamboat wharf on the east bank of the Nansemond River at Suffolk, but common carriage was envisioned from the outset. The Gay management planned to handle cotton, products of local truck farms, and fish from Albemarle Sound. A subsidiary, the Suffolk Steamboat Co., operated two daily steamers, *Olive* and *Pohatcong*, from Suffolk to Norfolk, and a weekly boat to Baltimore, the *Nansemond*. By reaching

some point on the Chowan River, the management hoped to deliver fish from Albemarle Sound to Baltimore a day faster than by existing routes.

The railroad was opened to Corapeake just south of the North Carolina border (15 miles) in 1884, Sunbury (22 miles) in 1885, Ryland (37 miles) in 1887, and Montrose Landing on the Chowan (40 miles) in 1888. The route skirted the western edge of the Great Dismal Swamp. (For map, see North Carolina.)

In 1897 the company began surveys to bypass Montrose Landing with an extension to Edenton, seat of Chowan County, at the confluence of the Chowan River and Albemarle Sound. The extension was built in 1902 as a 17-mile addition to the main line from Ryland, and the spur to Montrose

Suffolk & Carolina No. 5 was a rare example of a Porter 4-4-0 with a 3'-6" gauge. (Ed Bond collection.)

Suffolk & Carolina No. 10 illustrated the more ample dimensions possible with a 3'-6"
locomotive. (Munson Paddock collection, Railroad Museum of Pennsylvania.)

Landing was abandoned at the end of the year. The company also projected a branch from Beckford Junction diagonally southeast along the southern boundary of the swamp to Elizabeth City, but decided to convert the railroad before opening it. The main line was converted and the branch opened simultaneously on April 20, 1904.

The banking firm of Rudolph Kleybolte & Co. acquired the S&C in 1906 and reorganized it as the Virginia & Carolina Coast Railroad, preliminary to merging it into the Norfolk & Southern Railway—after 1910 the Norfolk Southern Railroad. As this railroad's Suffolk branch, the former narrow gauge operated until 1940, when it was abandoned along with the Elizabeth City branch. The terminal trackage in Suffolk was sold to the Virginian Railway.

REFERENCE: Prince, *Norfolk Southern Railroad*, pp. 13–14. The Railroad Commissioner of Virginia erroneously reported the Suffolk & Carolina as chartered on February 26, 1874, rather than 1884. See *Acts of Virginia, 1883–84*, Chap. 192, pp. 236–37.

Surry, Sussex & Southampton Railway

The Surry Lumber Co., the largest producer of yellow pine lumber in the eastern United States, chartered the Surry, Sussex & Southampton Railway on May 16, 1886, mainly as a facility for its mill at Dendron, but the railroad was a bona fide common carrier throughout its history. A predecessor, R. T. Waters & Co., had operated a private tramway with strap rails on wooden stringers, which connected with the Atlantic & Danville narrow gauge at Spring Grove. Richard T. Waters became president of the new corporation. The SS&S was opened from Scotland, a small port on the south shore of the James River opposite Jamestown, to Dendron (13 miles) in the fall of 1886. A pier at Scotland, on which track terminated, provided interchange with schooners and barges, with which most of the lumber was shipped. Steamers on the river, notably the triweekly boats between Richmond and Norfolk of the Virginia Navigation Co., handled passengers and general cargo. Seeking an outlet to the railroad system, the lumber company in the spring of 1887 undertook a southward extension to Wakefield (20 miles) on the Norfolk & Western main line, and finished it during the summer. The main line was extended south of the N&W, reaching Dory (28 miles) in 1894. The track as far as Dory was classified as a common carrier; the company had considerable additional mileage of branches, operated by the SS&S but at law in private carriage. The principal branch was a line, at its peak about 28 miles long, running west from Dendron. Called the West Hope branch, it crossed the narrow gauge line of the Atlantic & Danville at Griffin, but as far as is known the two railroads had no interchange facility there. The branch line mileage peaked at 51.5 miles in 1913. The railroad's practice was to ballast the main line and the West Hope branch with sand, but to use no ballast on the rest of the mileage. The branches were worked with 0-4-2 saddle tank engines and the main line with a variety of rod engines of orthodox wheel arrangements. Serving flat country, the railroad did not use geared locomotives. For most of the railroad's history, it dispatched a mixed train from Dendron at 6:00 A.M. to the wharf at Scotland, from which it ran a round-trip to a wye at Dory, and then returned from Scotland to Dendron. The trains served Surry, seat of Surry County—the railroad was named for the three counties in which it operated—and carried a substantial traffic in agricultural products, mainly peanuts.

The company maintained a rigorous separation of the private and common carriage of the railroad, even to carrying without charge the traffic of a local farmer so that the West Hope line could be maintained in private status. This policy was carried out to an odd extreme when the main line was extended first to a new camp at Vicksville in 1904 and then further to Sedley in 1906 in the expectation of establishing an interchange with the Virginian Railway. The lumber company built a second company town at Sedley and extended track into a timber stand south of the Virginian main line, but the trackage south of Dory was never put into common carriage, and the mixed train was not extended. The railroad also sought to avoid the status of interstate carrier in order to continue use of link-and-pin couplers and other nonstandard technology. Inbound interstate shipments were accepted by the station agent at Wakefield as agent for the consignee and reshipped at intrastate rates.

The railroad remained quite busy into the early 1920s, but thereafter declined rapidly as pine in the area was exhausted. After the mill at Dendron closed, the management applied to the ICC in August 1928 to convert the railroad and to extend it south eight miles from Sedley to Franklin and northwest 25 miles from Dendron to Hopewell. This proposal was strongly opposed by both the N&W and the Seaboard Air Line. The onset of the Depression made this project impractical; accordingly, the railroad requested that the ICC dismiss the application on June 23, 1930. The management had already petitioned Virginia authorities to discontinue service, and received permission on July 28. The last train ran on July 31, 1930, and the railroad from Sedley to Scotland was removed during the remainder of the year. The logging trackage had been taken up earlier.

REFERENCE: H. Temple Crittenden, *The Comp'ny: The Story of the Surry, Sussex & Southampton Railway and the Surry Lumber Company* (Parsons, W.Va.: McClain Printing Co., 1967). This book, though vague on chronology and inadequate in maps, is an excellent account of day-to-day operation of a lumber railroad.

▼ ▼ ▼ ▼

The Suffolk Lumber Co., which had been chartered on March 20, 1873, opened its 3′-6″ railroad in 1874 to connect the mill of the Jackson Lumber Co. at Whaleyville with the wharf at East Main Street in Suffolk. The line was at law a private carrier, although the management did handle occasional shipments from individuals as an accommodation, charging only the marginal cost of carriage. It did not regularly handle passengers. In 1877, when the line amounted to 10 miles from Suffolk to Summerton, about three miles north of the state line, a projected railroad, the Suffolk & Albemarle, proposed to use it as part of a common carrier from Edenton to Suffolk. Nothing came of the proposal. On March

15, 1884, the charter of the Suffolk Lumber Co. was amended to allow it to extend the railroad south toward Winton, seat of Hertford County, North Carolina. Had it achieved this goal, the line would probably have become a common carrier. It reached only a point in the woods in Gates County 12 miles south of the North Carolina border, about 27 miles from Suffolk. The company had the usual variable mileage of spurs. Building of the Atlantic Coast Line's extension into Norfolk on a route closely parallel caused the Jackson management to arrange for the ACL to handle both its logs and lumber, and to abandon the narrow gauge on March 31, 1894.

Washington

Cascades Railroad

The Cascades of the Columbia River 57 miles above Portland, Oregon, presented a natural barrier to steam navigation. The first railway around the Cascades was a mule tramway on wooden rails built by an

operator named Chenoweth in 1851. He sold the line to the Bradford family of steamboat operators, who incorporated the property as the Cascades Railroad on January 31, 1859. The installation was wiped out by a flood in 1861, but it was restored the next year by the Oregon Steam Navigation Co., which replaced the mules with the *Pony,* a 5′-0″ engine from the Oregon Portage Railway, the line's counterpart on the south bank of the river. The six-mile rail line was largely built on trestlework above high water. In 1880 it was converted to 4′-8½″ for compatibility with the railroad being built on the south bank by the successor Oregon Railway & Navigation Co., even though there was no physical connection between the two. In an effort to make use of equipment from the recently converted Blue Mountain branch, the OR&N changed the Cascades Railroad to 3′-0″ in 1883. In 1894 the line was washed out in a flood. About half the railroad was leased to a cannery for the movement of salmon to its plant, but the rest lay idle. By 1906 the cannery operation had ended and the line was entirely derelict. The Spokane, Portland & Seattle endeavored to condemn a right-of-way that crossed the narrow gauge at four points. A court order resulted in the narrow gauge's being rebuilt on a slightly altered route, with two crossings by the SP&S, but the line now served no useful purpose, being paralleled by standard gauge railroads on both sides of the river, and rivaled by locks through the dam at the Cascades. The Union Pacific as lessee abandoned it in 1908.

REFERENCE: Randall V. Mills, *Stern-Wheelers Up Columbia* (Palo Alto, Calif.: Bay Books, 1947), pp. 67–79.

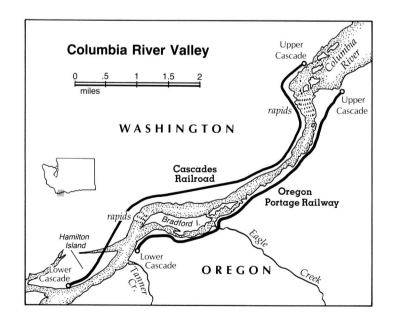

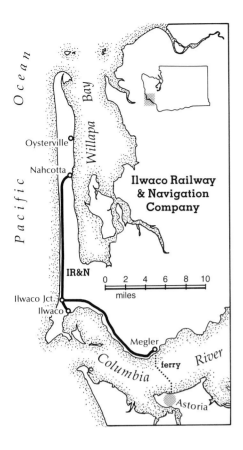

Ilwaco Railway & Navigation Co.

North Beach, a peninsula that separates Willapa Bay from the Pacific Ocean on the north bank of the mouth of the Columbia River, developed both as a site for resorts and as a harvesting area for seafood. Willapa Bay became one of the most important oyster-producing areas on the West Coast, and Ilwaco on Baker Bay at the base of the peninsula became a center of salmon packing. Regular steamer service to Astoria, Oregon's port at the mouth of the river, began in 1865, but local development was handicapped by the lack of a pier at Ilwaco. Lewis A. Loomis founded the Ilwaco Wharf Co. in 1874 to build a warehouse and pier into Baker Bay, which was afflicted with severe tidal problems. Loomis and his brother Edwin also acquired a stage line that ran up the peninsula to Oysterville, the northernmost town. When the existing steamer, *U. S. Grant*, was lost in a storm in December 1874, Lewis formed the Ilwaco Steam Navigation Co. to buy a replacement, *General Canby*, in 1875. The ISNCo. had a second steamer, *General Miles*, built at Astoria in 1882. Growth in passenger traffic to the seaside resorts warranted adding a third steamer, *Dolphin*, in 1886.

Loomis's efforts to build a railroad up the peninsula dated from 1883, when he in-

corporated the Ilwaco, Shoalwater Bay & Grays Harbor Railroad. On May 6, 1888, he rechartered the firm as the Ilwaco Railroad and on August 16 merged it with the steamboat company into the Ilwaco Railway & Navigation Co. Loomis's original plan was to terminate the line at New Saratoga, a half mile south of Oysterville, but the surveyors found a better terminus, closer to the channel and more sheltered from Pacific storms, at Nahcotta, about five miles to the south. Citizens of Oysterville proposed a northern extension, but were unable to finance it. No physical connection with another railroad was envisioned, or ever made. The 14-mile rail line was opened with a daily mixed train on May 29, 1889. The company's regular operation was a steamer departure from Astoria at 8:00 A.M. (to accommodate connecting passengers from the Oregon Railway & Navigation Company's night boat from Portland) connecting with the mixed train from Ilwaco at 10:00 A.M. Southbound the train left Nahcotta at 1:00 P.M. Unfortunately, the tidal problems in Baker Bay made rigorous adherence to this or any schedule difficult. The principal cargo was oysters in sacks, but the railroad also handled clams, crabs, and fish, much of it transshipped to coastal steamers for movement to California.

In 1891 the company decided to establish its own steamer service to Portland, and took delivery of the *Ocean Wave*, a sidewheeler that proved underpowered for the run of some 125 miles. The vessel was shortly leased and then sold in 1898. In 1894 the Northern Pacific attracted most of the line's traffic in oysters to its South Bend Branch, which provided a cheaper and more

direct route to the Portland and Seattle markets, leaving the railroad mainly a passenger facility.

The Oregon Railway & Navigation Co., which had been buying minority holdings in the company, bought out Loomis in August 1900, and took over operation of the railroad. The OR&N arranged a lumber traffic for the narrow gauge in logs from lumber camps along Willapa Bay, which were transshipped to Ilwaco for towing in rafts up the Columbia. The problem of silting at Ilwaco had worsened. By 1905 the railroad had to change its schedules every few days to allow the steamer from Astoria to call at high tide. The OR&N in 1906 authorized a rail line from Ilwaco Junction, somewhat less than a mile north of Ilwaco, east about 13 miles to Megler, approximately opposite Astoria. Construction, which entailed a tunnel of about 850 feet on federal property at Fort Columbia, was undertaken in 1907, and the line was opened on June 1, 1908. The extension was built to standard gauge clearances in the expectation of converting the narrow gauge and building a connection to Portland along the north bank. Because the NP acquired part of the intended right-of-way, this was never done. Rather, the OR&N ran its steamer *T. J. Potter* between Portland and Megler.

Together with other Union Pacific subsidiaries in the northwest, the OR&N was merged on December 23, 1910, into the Oregon-Washington Railroad & Navigation Co. Passenger traffic on the narrow gauge peaked in 1913, but then declined rapidly. The direct steamer to Portland was discontinued after the 1915 season, and the mile into Ilwaco was abandoned in 1916.

At Nahcotta the Ilwaco had this unusual gallows turntable with a double A-frame. (Paul Darrell, Frederic Shaw collection, California State Railroad Museum.)

Two trains of the Ilwaco make the connection at Megler with the steamer *Hassalo*. (Paul Darrell, Frederic Shaw collection, California State Railroad Museum.)

Fritz S. Elfving established a vehicular ferry from Astoria to McGowan, west of Megler, in 1921, facilitating automobile access to the beach resorts. The OWR&N brought out its own auto ferry, *North Beach*, in 1927, but the effort was unsuccessful. The railroad had lost most of its traffic, passengers, freight, and mail alike, to the highways. The ICC disapproved an arrangement for lease of the railroad to private parties in 1925. The UP filed for abandonment of the entire operation on October 8, 1929, and received permission on July 12, 1930. The final train ran on September 9, 1930. An employee, Captain Cal Stewart, bought the *North Beach* in 1931 and attempted to continue the ferry service, but was unsuccessful and sold the boat in 1932 to Elfving, who consolidated his operations at Megler. Elfving retired in 1946, and the ferry service was shortly absorbed by the Oregon Highway Department, which operated it until July 28, 1966. The present highway bridge was opened the following day.

REFERENCES: Frederic Shaw, Clement Fisher, Jr., and George H. Harlan, *Oil Lamps and Iron Ponies* (San Francisco: Bay Books, 1949), pp. 112–37; Raymond J. Feagans, *The Railroad That Ran by the Tide: Ilwaco Railroad & Navigation Co. of the State of Washington* (Berkeley, Calif.: Howell-North Books, 1972).

Mill Creek Flume & Manufacturing Co.

After selling his interest in the Walla Walla & Columbia River Railroad to Henry Villard in 1879, Dr. Dorsey S. Baker was active in promoting the Mill Creek Flume & Manufacturing Co. as a lumber railroad to the east of Walla Walla. The corporation was chartered on February 24, 1880, and in

1881 opened an eight-mile line from Walla Walla east to Dudley. The line ascended 600 feet along Mill Creek to a flume of the company that was the principal source of traffic. From the outset the carrier was expected to engage in the general business of a railroad. In 1882 a branch was opened from Dudley Junction, two miles east of Dudley, up Dry Creek five miles northeast to Dixie.

By 1890 a controlling interest in the railroad had been bought by the Oregon Railway & Navigation Co. In the reorganization of 1896 it emerged as owned 100 percent by the Union Pacific's Oregon Railroad & Navigation Co. The line operated as a minor branch of the UP system until sold on December 10, 1903, to an independent operator, the Mill Creek Railroad. This carrier reported itself to the Interstate Commerce Commission as not in operation. It sold the railroad on July 1, 1905, to the Northern Pacific, which merged it into its subsidiary, the Washington & Columbia River Railway. The NP abandoned the

branch to Dixie, and converted 7.4 miles of the Dudley line to Tracy. The line was restored to operation late in 1905. The UP had not provided scheduled passenger service, but the NP operated a weekly passenger train on Mondays.

The Tracy branch was abandoned by the Burlington Northern under an ICC order of November 2, 1970.

Olympia & Chehalis Valley Railroad

George S. Dodge of San Francisco promoted the Olympia Railroad & Mining Co. in 1873, partly to connect Olympia, capital of Washington Territory, with the Northern Pacific's Tacoma-Portland line at Tenino, partly to develop coal resources immediately to the south. He secured a subscription of $75,000 in bonds from Thurston County, along with 2,000 acres of land and 200 town lots in Olympia. He arranged for the line to be built by the Thurston County Construction Co., but was unable to finance the project. The construction company undertook to build the line in 1877 and completed it (15 miles) under the name of the Olympia & Tenino Railroad in August, 1878. President T. M. Reed, planning an extension southward to the Chehalis River, brought about a change of name to Olympia & Chehalis Valley Railroad in 1881. The Oregon Improvement Co. bought the railroad in April 1890 in the expectation of converting it and extending it south about six miles to develop coal resources at Cherry Hill. No extension was built, but the railroad was converted in the summer of 1890. On June 10, 1891, Oregon Improvement announced the sale of the O&CV to another of its subsidiaries, the Port Townsend Southern, which operated an isolated standard gauge line of 26 miles on the Olym-

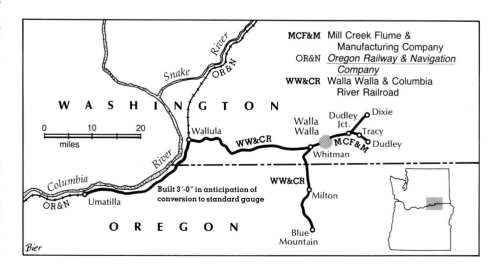

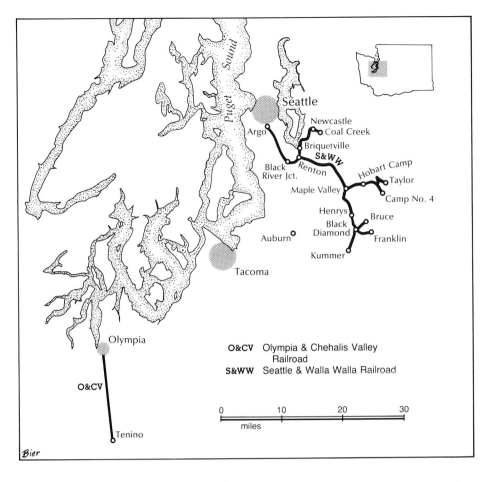

pic Peninsula from Port Townsend to Quilicene. The management proposed to connect the two lines, at first by extension of the northern line with a steamer through the Hood Canal, but later with a direct rail line along the west bank of the canal. A mile of track was laid south of Quilicene and three miles of grade were made north of Olympia, but the project was then abandoned.

Oregon Improvement was reorganized as the Pacific Coast Co. in 1897. In November 1902 the company sold the PTS to the Northern Pacific, which initially operated it as a separate, controlled line. On June 25, 1914, the NP bought the former narrow gauge from the PTS for $375,000 and leased the northern line, with which it had no physical connection, for 15 years to C. J. Erickson of Seattle, who operated it under the name of the Port Townsend & Puget Sound Railway. The NP made use of the southern seven miles of the former narrow gauge, from Plumb to Tenino, as part of an alternate main line south of Tacoma, opened in December 1914. The remainder, from Plumb to Olympia, was abandoned early in 1916 except for the two miles from Olympia to Tumwater, which became a switching spur at the capital.

REFERENCE: Gerald M. Best, *Ships and Narrow Gauge Rails: The Story of the Pacific Coast* *Company* (Berkeley, Calif.: Howell-North Books, 1964), pp. 131–42.

Seattle & Walla Walla Railroad

A. A. Denny, Bailey Gatzert, H. S. Yesler, and several other prominent early Seattle businessmen formed the Seattle & Walla Walla Railroad to build between the cities of its corporate title via Snoqualmie Pass and the valley of the Yakima River, about 280 miles. If built, the line would have provided an outlet to the Pacific for southeastern Washington alternative to the Columbia River, which was beset with serious rapids. It would also have been Seattle's first major railroad to inland points. Actually, the railroad attained only the status of a local short line serving a coal-mining area southeast of the city.

Grading for the railroad began early in 1874, but the financial stringency of the middle of the decade prevented putting any of the line into service until 1877. The first segment, to Renton (14 miles), built through swampy land largely on trestles, was opened on April 7. On October 15 an extension was opened to Newcastle and Coal Creek (21 miles), mainly to serve an installation of an affiliate, the Seattle Coal Co. The extension was on an almost uni-

form ascending grade of about 2 percent, with relatively heavy grading. The line had a cut 76 feet deep, a fill 50 feet high, and what the company claimed to be the largest trestle in the country, 800 feet long and 120 feet high. The coal company turned its locomotives over to the railroad and made some cash advances for construction of the extension in return for an agreement to haul the coal at fixed rates for 20 years. In the fall of 1877 the Washington territorial legislature petitioned Congress to declare the Northern Pacific's land grant invalid on grounds of non-completion and to turn it over to the S&WW. Because the S&WW's projected route along the Yakima River coincided with the NP's entry from Pasco, such a transfer would probably have brought the railroad to completion to Walla Walla, but Congress did not comply.

In November 1880 Henry Villard of the Oregon Railway & Navigation Co. bought the S&WW for $350,000, and reincorporated it as the Columbia & Puget Sound Railroad, which he made a subsidiary of his Oregon Improvement Co. Initially, he expressed an intention to build the full projected line to Walla Walla, but he in fact built only an extension to the coalfield between the Green and Cedar rivers southeast of the existing field. The extension of 20 miles from Renton to Franklin to serve mines of another affiliate, the Franklin Coal Co., was graded in 1884 and completed early in 1885. At the same time the management replaced some of the trestles on the Coal Creek line and expanded the marine terminal facilities at Seattle so that four ships might load coal simultaneously. The railroad also handled lumber, and in 1885 was reported to have a contract for moving 4,500 cedar telegraph poles from an on-line sawmill for the Postal Telegraph Co.

The country beyond either Coal Creek or Franklin was so difficult that extension of either line of the railroad was impractical, but the management built two additional branches. In 1885 it opened a three-mile spur from Black Diamond to Bruce, and in 1892–93 it built a ten-mile branch from Maple Valley east to Taylor to serve the coal mines in the Denny clay beds.

The Oregon Improvement Co. missed its interest payment of October 1, 1895, and was placed in receivership on October 4. Conversion was effected as part of the reorganization process in 1897. The court approved conversion early in June. Work began immediately and was completed in November. The railroad was sold along with Oregon Improvement's two other railroads, steamship lines, and coal subsidiaries on November 6. OI was reorganized as the

Pacific Coast Co. and the railroad as the Pacific Coast Railroad. It proved a prosperous short line, dependent partly on the coal mines and partly on origination and termination of freight in Seattle. The Milwaukee Road used trackage rights for 20.4 miles from Maple Valley for the entry into Seattle of its Pacific Coast extension, completed in 1909. The Coal Creek branch was cut back to Newcastle in 1919, and the Bruce branch was dropped in 1922. The Franklin line was cut back to Black Diamond in 1923 and to Maple Valley in 1947. The Newcastle branch ceased operation in 1933 and was formally abandoned in January 1935. The Taylor branch was abandoned in January 1945. The remainder, Seattle–Maple Valley, was absorbed by the Burlington Northern on March 2, 1970. The Milwaukee Road's use of the line ended with the abandonment of the Pacific Coast extension in 1980.

REFERENCE: Best, *Ships and Narrow Gauge Rails*, pp. 126–40.

Walla Walla & Columbia River Railroad

Dr. Dorsey S. Baker, a physician of Walla Walla who had also been active in steamboat operation on the Columbia River, sought relief from the high rates of wagon freight operators. On March 23, 1868, he formed the Walla Walla & Columbia River Railroad to provide access to the steamers of the Oregon Steam Navigation Co. at Wallula. After narrowly losing an election for local aid on September 18, 1871, he decided to build the railroad as a cheap narrow gauge with strap iron laid on wooden stringers. He opened ten miles east from Wallula in 1873 and began interchanging with wagon freighters at his railhead. In 1874 he built another six miles. In June 1875 he reached Touchet (19 miles), and began relaying his original track with 30-pound T-rail. The line was opened for full service to Walla Walla (32 miles) early in 1877. The railroad did quite well, mainly hauling wheat west to the river steamers.

On May 4, 1879, Baker sold his interest to Henry Villard of the Northern Pacific, who initially planned to build his Oregon Railway & Navigation Co. as a narrow gauge along the south bank of the river. Villard envisioned expanding the WW&CR into a network of narrow gauge mileage east of Walla Walla. In mid-1880 he built a branch off the WW&CR at Whitman southeast 19 miles to Blue Mountain, Oregon, but attempted no further extensions to the east. He had by this time decided to build the OR&N as a standard gauge railroad, but to avoid running his steamers through some difficult rapids, he extended the narrow gauge west 27 miles from Wallula to Umatilla, Oregon, in the summer of 1880. This was explicitly a temporary arrangement; Villard announced that the WW&CR would be converted as soon as the OR&N reached Umatilla from the west. The OR&N's standard gauge rails reached Umatilla in the spring of 1881 and the WW&CR was converted in May. The branch to Blue Mountain was initially allowed to remain narrow gauge because a portion of it was to be incorporated into a longer line. In the spring of 1883 the ten miles from Milton to Blue Mountain were converted as part of a line from Walla Walla to Pendleton, Oregon, and the segment from Whitman to Milton was abandoned.

The former narrow gauge mileage went with the OR&N into the Union Pacific system in 1906. This trackage is extant except for about ten miles immediately east of Umatilla that were replaced with a line diagonally to the southwest to Hinkle in 1951.

REFERENCES: W. W. Baker, "The Building of the Walla Walla & Columbia River Railroad," *Washington Historical Quarterly*, 14 (1923), pp. 3–13; Randall V. Mills, *Railroads Down the Valleys* (Palo Alto, Calif.: Pacific Books, 1950), pp. 7–13.

West Virginia

Cairo & Kanawha Valley Railroad

In 1852 an asphaltic hydrocarbon later called Grahamite—apparently of the same character as the Gilsonite of the Uintah Railway—was discovered on the north bank of Macfarlan Creek about two miles northeast of the town of Macfarlan. In 1864 mineral rights to the deposit were purchased by the Ritchie Coal Oil Co., which undertook a private narrow gauge railroad of 15 miles from the mines at Ritchie north to the Baltimore & Ohio at Cairo. In August 1865 the property, including the unfinished railroad, was conveyed to the Ritchie Mineral Resin & Oil Co. of Baltimore. The route was a tortuous one, built to lumber-railroad standards, and laid with iron strap rail on wooden stringers. The line was popularly known as the Calico Railroad, reportedly because a local hotel owner, James Merchant, made the casual observation at an organizational meeting that it was no wider than a bolt of calico. The line was worked by three small six-coupled locomotives. Standard practice was to doublehead a train of eight loaded gondolas up a severe grade of about two miles out of the Macfarlan Creek valley to Mellin. At the outset, local residents were allowed to ride on the narrow gauge gondolas without charge, but the railroad built passenger equipment and began charging fares. It also held a mail contract, but it did not otherwise hold itself out for common carriage. A series of explosions beginning in 1873, combined with exhaustion of the principal vein of Grahamite in the mine, brought an end to the operation, and caused the railroad to be offered for sale in Baltimore on June 18, 1875. The announcement of the sale stated the railroad to be 3'-10"; most secondary sources describe it as 3'-0".

The mine and the derelict railroad passed into the hands of Charles Edgar Appleby of New York in 1876, but he did not return the line to service. On March 2, 1888, Henry S. Wilson of Parkersburg bought the carrier and organized it on February 15, 1890, as the Cairo & Kanawha Valley Railroad. He was interested in the restoration of the mines and in lumbering around Mellin, but when oil was shortly discovered around Macfarlan, he extended the railroad into the valley. He opened the line as a 3'-0" common carrier from Cairo to Mellin (12 miles) in 1891, and down to Ritchie Mines (15 miles) in 1892. In 1894 he made the final extension into Macfarlan (17 miles), and completed relaying the entire line with T-rail of 20- to 40-pound weights. Wilson bought a secondhand 2-6-0, but shortly concluded that the line should be worked with ordinary lumber railroad technology; for the rest of its history it operated with two small Climax locomotives. The management ran a mixed train daily. It owned two combination cars, five boxcars for general cargo, two stockcars, and various flatcars for logs and lumber. Grahamite now moved at the rate of only about a boxcar per week. Wilson's charter provided for extension to Grantsville on the Kanawha River about 25 miles southeast, but no building was attempted.

The Cairo & Kanawha's mixed train is shown with its Climax geared locomotive at Macfarlan, the southern terminus. (Ben Kline collection.)

Wilson sold the railroad to a group headed by Charles F. Teter of Philippi, who reorganized it as the Cairo & Kanawha Railway on April 1, 1906. Teter planned to convert the railroad and to extend it into the coal areas in the southeast portion of the state, but he was never able to do so. The line operated in its traditional fashion until the late 1920s, when it suffered rapidly declining traffic. Operation was discontinued on November 22, 1929, and the railroad was scrapped. The two Climaxes were cut up in 1936.

REFERENCES: James Ankrom, "The Cairo & Kanawha Railway," *Railroad Model Craftsman*, May 1984, pp. 84–91; Brian Bond, "The Cairo & Kanawha Railway," *Narrow Gauge and Short Line Gazette*, July–Aug. 1986, pp. 18–23; collection of S. Dean Six, Harrisville, W.Va.

Clarksburg, Weston & Glenville Railroad
Weston & Buckhannon Railroad

In 1875 Henry Brannon of Weston formed the Weston & West Fork Railroad to connect his town, seat of Lewis County, with Clarksburg on the Baltimore & Ohio, 25 miles to the north. He solicited bids for grading a 3'-0" line in 1876, and let a contract in 1877. Some grading was done before the project failed. In 1878 J. N. Camden of Parkersburg and A. H. Kunst of Weston,

with several associates, formed the Clarksburg, Weston & Glenville Railroad to make use of the completed grade. The railroad was built quickly and opened in September 1879. It was a particularly orthodox narrow gauge, built for only $3,000 per mile, excluding equipment. The route followed Lost Creek, Hacker Creek, and the West Fork of the Monongahela River, with two heavy grades, one of 2.5 percent and the other of 2.7. It was initially equipped with two Porter locomotives and rolling stock from Billmeyer & Small. Later the railroad was said to operate with four locomotives. As the title indicates, the line was projected southwest for about 28 miles to Glenville, seat of Gilmer County, but the extension was never undertaken. The promoters also planned an extension of about 30 miles to Sutton, seat of Braxton County. The line to Weston enjoyed considerable coal and lumber origination, and was modestly successful.

Rather than make either of the originally planned extensions, the promoters in 1882 formed the Weston & Buckhannon Railroad to build a 15-mile line southeast to Buckhannon, seat of Upshur County. Although nominally independent, the W&B was operated with equipment of the CW&G, the directorates were interlocking, and Kunst served as general manager of both. The line was opened in 1884.

As late as 1887 the management appeared satisfied with the narrow gauge; it

planned to buy more rolling stock and to equip the line with air brakes. In March 1889, however, the promoters incorporated the Weston & Elk River Railroad to make the long-projected extension to Sutton. Having no desire to make it narrow gauge, they began immediate preparations for conversion of the two existing lines. They were unusual in entrusting the conversion to a contractor, A. M. Wisher. In anticipation of the conversion, the management merged the two narrow gauges and the W&ER into a new corporation, the Clarksburg, Weston & Midland Railroad, in April 1889. Also in 1889 the group formed the Buckhannon River Railroad to build from Buckhannon to Cherry River, about 80 miles. They merged this corporation with the CW&M on February 6, 1890, into the West Virginia & Pittsburgh Railroad with Camden as president and Kunst as vice-president. They arranged for the B&O to guarantee the line's bonds and to lease the railroad, an arrangement ratified by B&O shareholders on March 31, 1890. Wisher completed the conversion during the summer. The Clarksville-Weston segment was converted in July and the Weston-Buckhannon line on September 1. The line was separately operated until the B&O absorbed the WV&P in 1899. The Weston-Buckhannon branch was abandoned late in 1944, but the Clarksburg-Weston line is still in service in the CSX Corporation.

Clendennin & Spencer Railroad

Lumberman W. S. Lewis of Charleston secured a charter for this railroad in June 1894, planning to build from Clendennin on the Charleston, Clendennin & Sutton Railroad, in which he had an interest, to Spencer, seat of Roane County. He envisioned some overhead traffic, but he was mainly interested in development of coal and timber resources in southern Roane County, an almost wholly undeveloped area. In January 1895 he opened a segment of this line to Carlos (6 miles) and Hurricane (15 miles). In September he opened a branch from his camp at Carlos to Big Gap (10 miles) and another from Carlos to Colemans (6 miles). The line offered mixed train service on all three lines.

In December 1897 Lewis replaced this line with another of the same name on an entirely different route, presumably because of the exhaustion of timber on his original installation. The new line ran from Shelley Junction (Laurel), 15 miles northeast of Clendennin on the CC&S, north to Ash Camp (16 miles). It was extended to Odell

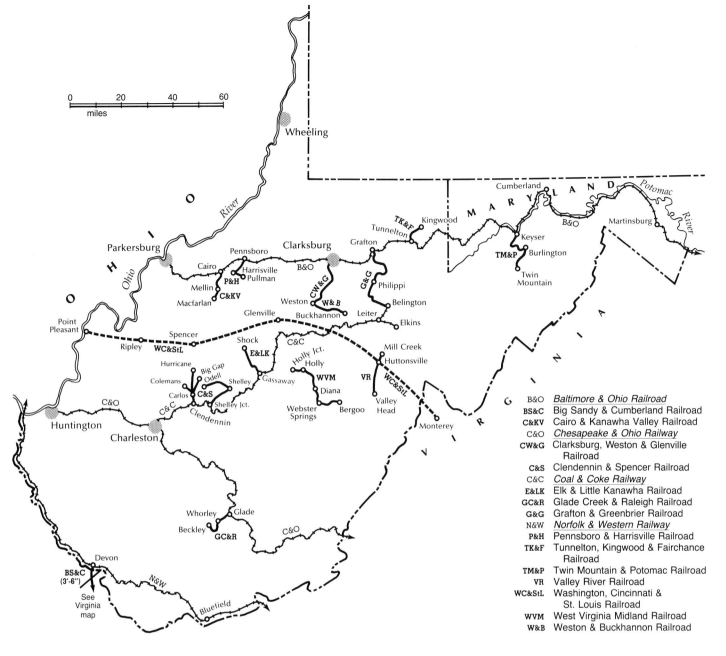

Scale: 0   20   40   60 miles

B&O	*Baltimore & Ohio Railroad*
BS&C	Big Sandy & Cumberland Railroad
C&KV	Cairo & Kanawha Valley Railroad
C&O	*Chesapeake & Ohio Railway*
CW&G	Clarksburg, Weston & Glenville Railroad
C&S	Clendennin & Spencer Railroad
C&C	*Coal & Coke Railway*
E&LK	Elk & Little Kanawha Railroad
GC&R	Glade Creek & Raleigh Railroad
G&G	Grafton & Greenbrier Railroad
N&W	*Norfolk & Western Railway*
P&H	Pennsboro & Harrisville Railroad
TK&F	Tunnelton, Kingwood & Fairchance Railroad
TM&P	Twin Mountain & Potomac Railroad
VR	Valley River Railroad
WC&StL	Washington, Cincinnati & St. Louis Railroad
WVM	West Virginia Midland Railroad
W&B	Weston & Buckhannon Railroad

(28 miles) in August 1898. The railroad mainly provided service out of a camp at Shelley in Clay County, seven miles from the Junction. The railroad began reporting itself to the ICC as a private carrier in 1900, but the *Official Guide* continued to carry the timetable of its mixed trains until April 1904. The railroad is believed to have ceased operation early in 1904 and to have been removed in fiscal 1904–5.

Elk & Little Kanawha Railroad

The Boggs Stave & Lumber Co. incorporated this nominal common carrier in 1909 to serve its operations in Braxton and Gilmer counties. The line was built between 1910 and 1913 from Gassaway on the Coal & Coke Railway to Shock (c. 29 miles). Beyond Shock, Boggs and its successor, the In-

terstate Cooperage Co., operated a private carrier, the Steer Creek Railroad, to a camp at Stumptown. Gassaway was a company town and site of the firm's mill for barrel staves, but the principal interchange point with the standard gauge connection was at Boggs, about three miles up the line. The railroad operated with Shay and Climax locomotives lettered both for the E&LK and for the Steer Creek. A daily passenger train was operated. In an unsuccessful effort to have the ICC declare it a common carrier so as to receive reimbursement for the period of federal operation of the railroads, the management claimed the line earned 65 percent of its revenues from its owner and the rest from common carriage. The line discontinued operation about April 1, 1919.

REFERENCES: Annie Harvey Dulaney, "The Elk & Little Kanawha Railroad," *The West Virginia Hillbilly*, June 25, 1983; Lee Rainey and

Brian Bond, "Elk & Little Kanawha Notes," *Light Iron & Short Ties*, 4, no. 3 (Sept. 1986), pp. 8–9.

Glade Creek & Raleigh Railroad

The Beatty Lumber Co. undertook the Glade Creek & Raleigh in 1896 as a common carrier from Glade on the Chesapeake & Ohio main line southwest to the company's main installation at Crow and on to Beckley, seat of Raleigh County. The history of the operation is obscure, but the line was apparently completed to Beckley (15 miles) in 1897. It was an orthodox lumber railroad, operated with Shay locomotives, notable only for a tunnel of about 100 feet approaching Crow. The Raleigh & Southwestern Railway, which was incorporated locally by C. H. Krise, H. Allen, and others in 1903 but never built, bought the GC&R

from the lumber company on October 25, 1906. The new owners apparently converted the five miles from Beckley to an interchange at Whorley with the Chesapeake & Ohio's Piney Creek branch; when the C&O bought the R&SW from the owners on March 21, 1907, it consisted of five miles of standard gauge and ten miles of narrow gauge. The C&O leased the remaining narrow gauge to the Raleigh Lumber Co., a subsidiary of the William Ritter Lumber Co., which used it as a facility for the mill at Crow. The line had some limited common carriage until July 1909. The mill at Crow was shut down in 1910, and the railway is thought to have ended operation at that time. It was removed by 1912. The C&O merged the R&SW into itself on February 28, 1910. The entry into Beckley from Whorley was abandoned in favor of other terminal arrangements, apparently also in 1912.

Grafton & Greenbrier Railroad

Local people formed the Grafton & Greenbrier for the immediate agricultural development of Barbour County, of which Philippi is the seat. In the longer run they envisioned it as a coal hauler with a route from Philippi southeast over the Rich Mountains to Beverly in Randolph County, thence over the Cheat Mountains into the valley of the Greenbrier River, and southward to a connection with the Chesapeake & Ohio near White Sulphur Springs. The route would have been a difficult one; it is not surprising that little of the project was executed.

The railroad was undertaken in 1883 and opened in January 1884, along the Tygarts Valley River from Grafton on the Baltimore & Ohio's Cincinnati line to Philippi (24 miles). The promoters received $70,000 in subscriptions from the Barbour County government. In mid-1884 the B&O bought control of the line and thereafter operated it as a subsidiary. Late in 1886 the B&O let contracts for extension along the projected route to Beverly as far as Belington, 17 miles southeast of Philippi. The extension, opened in 1887, was built on standard gauge ties in the expectation of early conversion. The line was pushed no farther, but Belington became an interchange with both the Western Maryland and the Coal & Coke Railway.

The B&O began intensive preparations for converting the line in 1891, but it also allowed the Grafton & Greenbrier to go bankrupt. The B&O bought the property at a foreclosure sale on January 30, 1892,

for $250,000. It converted the line in May 1892, and absorbed the corporation later in the year. The trackage became part of the B&O's extensive mileage of coal branches in northern West Virginia. The damming of the river to produce the Tygart Reservoir caused the northernmost 21.6 miles of the former narrow gauge to be abandoned in 1937 in favor of a 12.8-mile direct line from Grafton to Berryburg Junction. The new line and the remainder of the former narrow gauge mileage from Berryburg Junction to Belington are in service for the CSX Corporation at the present writing.

Pennsboro & Harrisville Railroad

Local figures promoted the Pennsboro & Harrisville in 1873 to serve the general transport demands of Harrisville, seat of Ritchie County. They opened the line in November 1874 as a horse tramway to Pennsboro on the Baltimore & Ohio (9 miles). The line was opened as a steam railroad on November 27, 1875. The property was among the most lightly built narrow gauges, with 12-pound rail laid on longitudinal wooden stringers, and ties at three-foot intervals. The route entailed a grade of nearly 6 percent for three-fourths of a mile, and extensive trestlework; the largest trestle was 220 feet long. The railroad, including equipment, was built for only about $3,000 per mile.

The railroad was sold on December 30, 1879, to M. P. Kimball of Pennsboro, who, on February 12, 1880, reorganized it under the unwieldy title of Pennsboro & Harrisville Ritchie County Railway. In May 1885 he rebuilt the line with 20-pound rail. In 1902 the railroad passed into the hands of M. K. Duty, who conceived of naming the line for his wife. On December 9, 1903, he formed the Lorama Railroad, and on June 12, 1905, transferred the property to the new corporation. In July 1910 he opened an extension of three miles from Harrisville east to Pullman. The extension was built to ordinary narrow gauge standards with 30-pound rail. The railroad remained a small operation, with two locomotives, three passenger cars, two boxcars, and five flatcars. Passenger service was discontinued in 1922, and the line was abandoned in 1924.

REFERENCE: *Railroad Magazine*, June 1945, pp. 60–61; S. Dean Six, "A Chronology of the Construction of the P&HRR as found in the pages of the *Ritchie Gazette*," unpublished typescript, in the possession of S. Dean Six, Harrisville, W.Va.

Tunnelton, Kingwood & Fairchance Railroad

A local group in Kingwood, seat of Preston County, undertook the Kingwood & Tunnelton Railway as a narrow gauge connection to the Cincinnati main line of the Baltimore & Ohio at Tunnelton (11 miles). They graded the route in 1885, but were unable to finance completion. The railroad was completed by a receiver on January 7, 1888. The property was sold on May 5, 1888, to a local syndicate composed of C. M. Bishop, William G. Brown, W. M. O. Dawson, George W. Whitesan, and others, who reorganized it as the Tunnelton, Kingwood & Fairchance Railroad. As the name indicates, they intended to extend it north to Fairchance, Pennsylvania, for access to the Pittsburgh area. In 1890 they also surveyed a route northwest to Morgantown through the Deckers Creek Valley.

Bishop's group proved unable to finance either extension, and in January 1895 sold their interest in the railroad for $30,000 to a syndicate headed by George C. Sturgiss and J. Ami Martin of Morgantown, who agreed to convert the line and to build the 30-mile extension to Morgantown within two years. The new group changed the name to the West Virginia Northern Railroad. The conversion proved fairly difficult, largely because a long cut leaving Tunnelton had to be widened. The conversion was reported complete in December 1895.

Sturgiss and Martin, after giving up their interest in the WVN, separately incorporated the proposed extension as the Morgantown & Kingwood Railroad in 1889. They completed it as a standard gauge line from Morgantown through Kingwood to M&K Junction on the B&O near Rowlesburg in 1907. It became a B&O branch in 1922.

The West Virginia Northern proved a prosperous short line with extensive origination of coal and lumber. It is in existence at the present writing.

Twin Mountain & Potomac Railroad

In a state where nearly all narrow gauges were dependent on coal mining or lumbering, the Twin Mountain & Potomac was owned by an orchard operator. Twin Mountain Orchards incorporated the railroad on May 24, 1911. H. L. Heintzelman was president. The line ran east from a connection with the Baltimore & Ohio's St. Louis main line at Keyser and then south up the valley of Patterson's Creek. It was opened to Burlington (16 miles) on August 6, 1912, and to Twin Mountain (27 miles) on March 2, 1913. The railroad operated with two locomotives, two passenger cars, and 18 freight cars.

The line is believed to have ceased operation about January 1919. John J. Baker was appointed receiver on November 13, and he abandoned the railroad in 1920.

REFERENCE: *Railroad Magazine*, Aug. 1949, p. 54.

Valley River Railroad

The lumber firm of Hence, Drumgold & Schull incorporated this railroad as a common carrier in July 1907. It was built from Mill Creek, 1.2 miles short of the terminus of the Huttonsville branch of the Western Maryland, south up the Tygarts Valley River to installations of the lumber company. Between Mill Creek and Huttonsville the narrow gauge was directly parallel to the WM. In the fashion of such railroads, it progressed slowly, opening when 6.5 miles were ready in January 1908. In 1909 2.5 miles were added. When the line reached Old Fort (10 miles) in March 1910, the company began placing the timetable of the daily mixed train in the *Official Guide*. In 1911 the firm sold the operation, including the railroad, to the Wilson Lumber Co. In the same year track was extended a mile to Elkwater (Spangler), which became the principal camp of the lumber company. In August 1919 passenger service was pressed farther out existing trackage to Valley Head (16 miles). The operation was integral with a private carrier, the Wilson Logging Railroad, which had the usual variable mileage of such lines; in 1915 it had 12 miles of track. The combined operation had five locomotives in 1913.

In February 1931 the Valley River dropped passenger service and announced its intention to abandon on July 1. Irregular operation appears to have continued until the end of the year, when the railroad was reported abandoned.

West Virginia Midland Railroad

In 1893 the Holly River Boom & Lumber Co. undertook a standard gauge private carrier, and opened it on November 1, 1894. Known simply as the Holly River Company's Railroad, the line ran from a connection with the West Virginia & Pittsburgh (B&O) at Palmer Junction (Holly Junction) to the company's mill at Holly and up the valley of the Elk River about 12 miles. The lumber company was placed in receivership on January 30, 1895, and reorganized as the Holly River Lumber Co., with the railroad separately incorporated on July 1, 1896, as the Holly River Railroad, still a private carrier.

John T. McGraw bought the railroad intending to use the four miles from Holly Junction to Holly as the north end of a narrow gauge from Holly Junction to Addison (Webster Springs). He incorporated it as the Holly River & Addison Railway on September 10, 1898, and absorbed the standard gauge on May 15, 1899. He built the narrow gauge in 1899 up the Holly River to Diana (18 miles) and Jumbo (22 miles). After considering two routes for his extension to Webster Springs, he undertook a line up Grassy Creek from Diana entailing a tunnel at the summit between the valleys of the Holly and Elk rivers. The 12-mile extension was begun in 1901 and put in service on May 26, 1902. Standard gauge track was retained from Holly Junction to Holly and also for about 2.5 miles to Marpleton on logging trackage to the east. The railroad served five lumber companies, in addition to serving the general transport demands of Webster Springs, seat of Webster County. Necessarily, the railroad had a varying mileage of logging branches.

The line was reorganized on April 6, 1906, as the West Virginia Midland Railroad. McGraw remained in control of the property. The corporation was placed in receivership on May 20, 1920, under George A. Hechmer, its longtime general manager. It was sold on July 24, 1924, to H. B. Curtin of the Pardee & Curtin Lumber Co., one of the on-line operators, who reorganized it as the West Virginia Midland Railway. In 1925 he secured the ICC's permission for an extension of 12 miles from Webster Springs to Bergoo for a connection with the Greenbrier, Cheat & Elk (Western Maryland). The extension was built as a three-rail line in 1927. This provided a preferable facility for Webster Springs, and the narrow gauge was shortly terminated. The extension to Bergoo was transferred in 1929 to the GC&E, which removed the narrow gauge rail. The ICC approved abandonment of the narrow gauge from Diana to Webster Springs in 1930 and from Holly Junction to Diana on November 7, 1931. The standard gauge track from Holly Junction to Holly was retained to serve the mill, but was reduced to the status of an intrastate switching line. The mileage of 1927 between Webster Springs and Bergoo remains in service in the CSX Corporation.

▼ ▼ ▼ ▼

In 1901–2 the Holly Lumber Co. built a private carrier, which it organized as the Pickens & Addison Railway on March 18, 1903. The line was put in common carrier status in the expectation that it would be built to Webster Springs, 28 miles southwest from Pickens. Actually, it proved to be a logging railroad, carrying only traffic incidental to the lumber company's business. The management never listed the line in the *Official Guide*, but it owned two combines and is believed to have carried passengers. The 13 miles with which the railroad started business grew slowly, in the fashion of such lines. Track reached Johnsonburg (15 miles),

A passenger train of the West Virginia Midland crosses a representative example of narrow gauge trestlework. (Ed Bond collection.)

a camp named for a vice-president of the company, in 1904 and Point Mountain Run (20 miles) in 1911. Holly Lumber wound up its operations in the following year and sold the line to George A. Hechmer of Grafton and his associates, who on October 23, 1912, organized the Pickens & Webster Springs Railroad in the apparent hope of building it to the original target. They ceased to report to the ICC or to *Poor's Manual* in 1915, and the line is presumed to have been abandoned at that time.

Lumberman Henry Spies of Pickens secured a charter for the Pickens & Hacker's Valley Railroad on September 11, 1899, as an adjunct to his logging operations, but he incorporated it as a common carrier. He opened it for seven miles almost straight west on May 1, 1900. About 1903 track reached Hacker's Valley (13 miles), a community of about 100 people that has survived. The line had a varying mileage of branches. C. D. Howard was appointed receiver on September 9, 1905, but Spies reorganized his lumber operations as the Mayton Lumber Co. and was able to lift the receivership without reorganizing the railroad. Mayton sold the property in 1920 to the Sun Lumber Co., which ceased operation of the railroad on September 18, 1921.

A nominal common carrier of the Clay Lumber Co. of Charleston, the Porter's Creek & Gauley Railroad was undertaken in 1896, and opened in January 1897 from Porter on the Charleston, Clendennin & Sutton southeast to Summit (10 miles). In addition to building a varying mileage of branches, the management in 1901 extended the main line to Abonijah (20 miles) and in 1902 to Middle Creek (30 miles; this was a lumber camp on the creek, not the town of that name on the CC&S). The railroad operated two mixed trains per day. The operation was abandoned, probably in 1904.

Wisconsin

Fond du Lac, Amboy & Peoria Railroad

This railroad, which was intended to build the route in its title, was incorporated separately as the Fond du Lac, Amboy & Peoria Railway in Illinois and as the Fond du Lac & Whitewater Railway in Wisconsin in 1874, but the two corporations were merged in 1875. The main line was to be 220 miles, but branches to Milwaukee and Chicago were envisioned. The route is a rather strange one, but the main line had the attraction of connecting the Great Lakes–St. Lawrence system at Fond du Lac with the Inland Rivers system at Peoria while bypassing Chicago. The corporation was headquartered in Fond du Lac, but it had some financial support in the area of Amboy, Illinois, where it would have originated agricultural products.

In the spring of 1876 the company let a contract for construction of the north 75 miles of the line to D. E. Davenport & Co. of New York, at a projected cost of $12,100 per mile. The intention was first to build into Milwaukee and later to complete the main line. Construction began, but was halted by summer, when the company failed to pay local subcontractors Lehman & McHugh. The company engaged in some internal refinancing, and was able to proceed with construction in 1877. By late fall the contractors had finished 30 miles of track to Iron Ridge on the Chicago, Milwaukee & St. Paul. As it proved, that was the limit of the company's attainments. The management by early 1878 had developed a factional controversy over control. President W. H. Boardman charged that the chairman of the board, Judge Alonzo Kenyon, was operating the railroad without authority from a valid shareholders' meeting. Boardman proceeded in state court, but secured control of the railroad through intervention of federal marshals. Kenyon's directors responded by securing an order in federal court for Boardman to show cause why he should not return the railroad to Kenyon. The U.S. Circuit Court appointed J. H. Brigham receiver to resolve the problem, and also to deal with various claims against the company from contractors. In 1879 the court found George H. Wellman to have a valid claim for $110,000 for construction expenses. The receiver was authorized to issue bonds of $120,000 in order to pay off Wellman and secure $10,000 for operating expenses. Also in 1879 the management arranged to handle standard gauge cars off the CM&StP at Iron Ridge on narrow gauge trucks to avoid breaking bulk. In 1880 the company built a mile of terminal trackage in Fond du Lac. Motive power was reportedly a Brooks 2-6-0.

There was no longer any chance of building to Oconomowoc, which had been the next target town, much less to Milwaukee or Peoria. The line's only real prospect was to become a branch of the CM&StP, which began efforts to acquire it in 1882. The CM&StP bought the line December 31, 1883, and converted it over the weekend of May 24–26, 1884. The line served as the Fond du Lac branch of the Milwaukee Road until 1980, when it was purchased by the State of Wisconsin. The southernmost eight miles, from Iron Ridge to Mayville, have been operated by the Wisconsin & Southern since July 1, 1980, and the rest is idle.

Galena & Southern Wisconsin Railroad
Chicago & Tomah Railroad

These two properties, though promoted independently, comprised a consistent network of 92 miles of 3'-0" trackage in the rugged, unglaciated Driftless Area of southwestern Wisconsin after their absorption by the Chicago & North Western Railway.

The Galena & Southern Wisconsin was promoted by businessmen in Galena, Illinois, to tap the lead-mining industry in the Driftless Area. The railroad was incorporated as early as March 2, 1857, but, as in many other instances, it could not be financed as a standard gauge. The promoters were able to finance it as a narrow gauge and began grading north from Galena in May 1872. By December they had graded 22 miles of line in the valley of the Galena River. The company's stock subscription was to pay for the roadbed, and a mortgage was to cover the track and equipment. The immediate target was Platteville, a well-established town in southeastern Grant County, Wisconsin. Because of the financial stringency of the mid-1870s there was a delay in construction, but the first nine miles of the line were put in service on October 2, 1874. The railroad was opened to Platteville (30 miles) on January 1, 1875. The management projected a line north to Muscoda on the south bank of the Wisconsin River, and also considered a long branch east to Madison. Construction was undertaken from a point about four miles east of Platteville variously known as Phillips' Corners, Ipswich, and Platteville Junction north toward Wingville (shortly to be renamed Montfort), an extension that would have amounted to 19 miles. In 1877 eight miles of track were laid as far as McCormick's, apparently an end-of-track of negligible population. The company planned to build on to Montfort in 1878, but it encountered financial difficulties early in the year. William H. Blewitt, the former superintendent of the railroad, attached its equipment for non-payment of notes he held. The bondholders prepared to seek control of the railroad. Operation was halted in June 1878, and the company was reported completely insolvent. The shareholders met, denounced the management, and elected a new board of directors. The Farmers Loan & Trust Company of New York brought an action in Federal Circuit Court in Chicago alleging fraud in the issuance of the company's mortgage. In 1879 a group formed the Illinois & Wisconsin Narrow Gauge to buy the line and extend it to Avoca, six miles east of Muscoda, but the transfer was never made. Rather, on May 15–16, 1879, the company was reorganized as the Galena & Wisconsin Railroad, which restored service to Platteville in the summer of the year and to McCormick's shortly thereafter. The new corporation wanted to build north, but was unable to do so. It operated the existing line with a 4-4-0 and a 2-6-0.

The Chicago & Tomah was a considerably more pretentious project. William Larrabee and D. R. W. Williams of Clermont, Iowa, together with associates in Wisconsin formed the railroad in 1872, planning a route from Chicago to Freeport, Illinois, and thence into Wisconsin via Mineral Point, Montfort, Fennimore, and Woodman. The line would have crossed the Wisconsin River between Woodman and Wauzeka, and proceeded up the Kickapoo River valley to the timbering center of Tomah. The line was mainly intended to carry lumber products from the Tomah area and agricultural products from intermediate points into Chicago. Construction began at Woodman on the

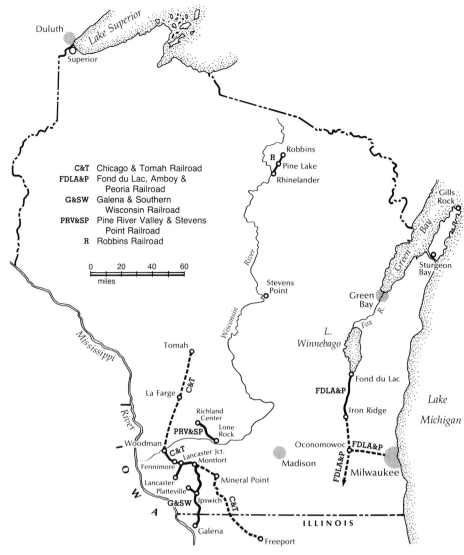

C&T   Chicago & Tomah Railroad
FDLA&P Fond du Lac, Amboy &
       Peoria Railroad
G&SW   Galena & Southern
       Wisconsin Railroad
PRV&SP Pine River Valley & Stevens
       Point Railroad
R   Robbins Railroad

Chicago, Milwaukee & St. Paul and proceeded south, apparently because of financial support in Grant County. In 1878 the company built the Woodman-Fennimore portion of the projected main line, and a branch from Fennimore to Lancaster, a total of 30 miles. In 1879 the company extended the projected main line by building east from Lancaster Junction, about two miles east of Fennimore, to Montfort. In the same year, the company graded some 20 to 30 miles up the Kickapoo Valley from Wauzeka to a point in the vicinity of Gays Mills, but it never was able to lay track, presumably because the cost of bridging the Wisconsin River was beyond the firm's resources. In 1889 the Kickapoo Valley & Northern Railway made use of the grade for its standard gauge line, which became the CM&StP's La Farge branch.

With both narrow gauges in a state of partial completion, the Chicago & North Western bought them in 1880 and merged them into a subsidiary, the Milwaukee & Madison Railway. The North Western in

the same year connected the two lines by laying track between McCormick's and Montfort. The narrow gauge network, however, was unconnected with the North Western. The management decided upon a connection from Madison, about 60 miles away. Originally, the company intended to make this connecting line narrow gauge from Montfort to Dodgeville and standard gauge to Madison, but before the grading was completed, the management decided to make the entire line 4'-8½". The North Western was eager to convert the network, and early in 1882 executed a mortgage of $920,000 on the narrow gauge mileage for conversion and improvement. With the proceeds, the trackage was converted in the summer of 1882 with the exception of the 16.4 miles between Woodman and Fennimore. This mileage was mainly on a prolonged 1.7-percent grade up the valley of the Green River, with one horseshoe curve only 250 feet in radius. It was impractical to modify the curve because of the narrowness of the valley, and as a consequence

The Chicago & Tomah achieved neither Chicago nor Tomah, but it served its limited mileage in the Driftless Area of Wisconsin with this small Baldwin Mogul. (Thomas T. Taber collection, Railroad Museum of Pennsylvania.)

By the time the Chicago & North Western's narrow gauge remnant between Fennimore and Woodman was abandoned in 1926, it had achieved considerable local fame. (Ed Bond collection.)

the North Western was forced to continue narrow gauge operation. The line hauled ordinary agricultural traffic, mainly cheese from a factory at Werley. This traffic went to trucks relatively early. The North Western applied to the Interstate Commerce Commission to abandon the line, and received permission late in 1925. The last train operated on January 30, 1926, and the track was removed during the spring and summer.

Of the converted mileage, the Galena line was cut back to Hazel Green Junction in 1939, to Benton in 1942, and to Cuba City in 1967. The remainder of the line and the rest of the former narrow gauge network were abandoned in 1980.

REFERENCES: Stanley H. Mailer, "The Ridge Runner," *Trains*, June 1971, pp. 24–28; "The Werley Train," *The Railway Gazette* (Mid-Continent Railway Society), Aug. 1970, pp. 7–14.

Pine River Valley & Stevens Point Railroad

The corporate title of this railroad is misleading relative to the actual attain- ments or the reported intentions of the pro- moters. Their immediate purpose was to connect Richland Center, seat of Richland County, with the Madison–Prairie du Chien line of the Chicago, Milwaukee & St. Paul at Lone Rock. The railroad was incorporated on August 5, 1872, and graded mainly in 1875. The line was opened for its full 16 miles in 1876. Although it pursued a tor- tuous route along the Pine River, the rail- road was built for only $4,375 per mile. The rails were maple stringers 3½″ × 5″ in cross section, with iron strap facing only on curves. Only about three miles of switches and sidings were laid with iron rail. The railroad had a single locomotive, one pas- senger car, one baggage car, and 12 freight cars. The office was in Richland Center, and the financing was apparently local. Presi- dent George Krouskop's reported intention was to build south from Lone Rock to Min- eral Point to meet the projected line of the Chicago & Tomah, rather than north to- ward Stevens Point. Nothing other than the original trackage was ever laid. The rail- road did relatively well hauling local prod- ucts to the CM&StP connection, and as late as 1879 was reported to be in the black. The management slowly replaced the wooden rail with iron, and by 1880 had only three miles of maple remaining.

The CM&StP, in the course of its nu- merous acquisitions of short lines, bought this one on May 26, 1880, completed the laying of iron rail, and converted the rail- road on the weekend of August 1, 1880. It remained the Richland Center branch until the Milwaukee Road's massive reduction in mileage of 1980, but was then conveyed to the Western Wisconsin Railroad, operator of the Madison–Prairie du Chien line. This trackage was taken over by the Wisconsin

& Calumet Railroad in January 1985, but the company has not operated the line. It remains intact but idle in the State of Wisconsin's rail bank.

Robbins Railroad

Rhinelander was a center of lumbering in northern Wisconsin, with eight sawmills located about Boom Lake, which had been formed north of the town by damming the Wisconsin River. The typical method of lumbering in the area was to cut timber in the winter months when logs could be moved by sledge, store them along the streams tributary to the lake, and then float them down in the spring freshets. As usual in lumber operations, Boom Lake provided storage for the mills. F. S. Robbins, who in partnership with H. S. Baird had established one of the eight sawmills in 1886, became dissatisfied with this technique because of its dependence on unpredictable water levels. In the spring of 1893 Baird & Robbins undertook a lumbering railroad from Boom Lake to a camp east of Pine Lake, about five miles to the northeast along what is now Wisconsin highway 17. In 1894 Baird withdrew from the partnership in favor of W. H. Brown. Apparently in 1895 the Brown-Robbins Lumber Co. extended the line seven miles to the south shore of Sugar Camp Lake, where the village of Robbins was established. The line was originally a private carrier, but in 1898, to secure the right of condemnation, the management incorporated it as a common carrier, the Brown & Robbins Railroad. Brown had left the enterprise by that time; his name was dropped from the lumber company in 1901, and the railroad was renamed the Robbins Railroad.

The line was a very nominal common carrier, although it did carry logs for other local lumber companies and occasionally hauled some local agricultural products. The railroad never operated passenger trains, but it ran mixed trains before 1919 and thereafter allowed lumberjacks to ride its freights. Its common carrier status made the railroad subject to the Wisconsin Public Service Commission's control of building and abandonment. In order to reach some timberland near Lake Julia, the lumber company, in its own name rather than that of the Robbins Railroad, built 15 miles of track from Robbins Junction to the northeast. Most of the traffic originated on this line, which was eventually pushed on to Kentuck Lake near the Michigan border.

In 1919 Robbins sold his interests to John D. Mylrea of Wausau and his associates, who formed the Thunder Lake Lumber Co. The name of the railroad was not changed. In 1920 Mylrea abandoned the common carrier line north of Robbins Junction. The southernmost six miles retained its common carrier status, but this became progressively more fictional. After handling some carloads of potatoes in 1924, the line carried only products of the lumber company. By 1929 the Thunder Lake Lumber Co. owned about 19,000 acres of land and had 900 employees. The company had 40 miles of railroad line, with six active locomotives. Nine of the ten locomotives in the railroad's history were rod engines; serving flat territory, the company used only one Shay geared locomotive as a switcher at Rhinelander.

Logging along the railroad ended in 1940. The railroad last operated in the spring of 1941. The Thunder Lake Lumber Co. secured the permission of the Public Service Commission to abandon the common carrier portion on June 19, 1941, and the entire line was dismantled later that year. This was the last common carrier narrow gauge in the Midwest.

REFERENCE: Harvey Huston, *Thunder Lake Narrow Gauge* (Winnetka, Ill.: Harvey Huston, 1961).

▼ ▼ ▼ ▼

A substantial number of narrow gauges were projected in Wisconsin but never brought to fruition; two of these are notable. The Milwaukee & Southern Wisconsin Narrow-Gauge Railroad was projected from Milwaukee to Beloit, and in 1874 reported itself partly graded. The promoters envisioned connecting with narrow gauges in northeastern Iowa and giving Milwaukee an outlet to whatever transcontinental narrow gauge trunk might take shape to connect with the Denver & Rio Grande.

The Wisconsin Peninsula Railroad was incorporated on January 8, 1881, to run from Green Bay via Sturgeon Bay to Liberty Grove township (Gills Rock) at the tip of the Door Peninsula. Had this railroad been built, it would have served the resorts and fruit-growing industry of Door County north of Sturgeon Bay, an area that never did have a railroad. In 1883 the charter was revised to provide for an extension from Green Bay to Fond du Lac via the east shore of Lake Winnebago.

Wisconsin had a large number of narrow gauge lumber railroads without common carrier status. Predecessors of the Wisconsin & Michigan Railway were 3'-0" but as far as is known, all had been converted before achieving common carrier standing.

Index

Index

Central Nevada RR, 443
Central New York & Western RR, 507
Central of Georgia Ry., 112, 373, 376
Central Ohio Division, B&O, 462
Central Pacific RR, 125, 245–46, 324, 326, 328, 337, 346, 440, 441, 442, 480, 531, 533
Central RR of New Jersey, 446, 449, 498
Central Valley RR, 272, 453
Central Vermont Ry., 187, 537–38
Ceres, NY, 507, 508
Cerro Summit, 218, 347, 348, 352
Chagrin Falls, OH, 464, 472
Chagrin Falls & Southern RR, 135, 464
Chama, NM, 218, 226, 291
Chanute, Octave, 250
Charleston, Clendennin & Sutton RR, 553, 557
Charleston, IL, 106, 477, 479
Charleston, SC, 28, 35, 393
Charlotte, Columbia & Augusta Ry., 182, 512
Charlotte & South Carolina RR, 75, 512
Charlottesville, VA, 85
Chartiers Valley RR, 502
Chase, H. J., 57
Chateaugay RR, 192, 196–97, 444, 453–54
Chateaugay & Lake Placid Ry., 454
Chattahoochee Terminal Ry., 303
Chattanooga, Rome & Columbus RR, 376
Chattanooga, TN, 57, 76
Cheap Transportation Movement, 90
Cheraw & Chester RR, 512
Cherokee RR, 76, 138, 139, 274, 303
Cherry Grove RR, 500
Cherryvale, KS, 401
Chesapeake, Ohio & Southwestern RR, 519
Chesapeake Bay, 25
Chesapeake Transit Co., 545
Chesapeake Western Ry., 87
Chesapeake & Ohio Ry., 24, 40, 84, 85, 242, 403, 404, 426, 427, 545, 546, 554–55
Chester, VA, 543
Chester & Lenoir Narrow Gauge RR, 111, 187, 459, 460, 512; relative costs, 182
Chewton, PA, 494
Chicago, Bellevue, Cascade & Western Ry., 240, 394; see Bellevue & Cascade RR
Chicago, Burlington & Quincy RR, 51, 344, 347, 348, 355, 358, 386, 387–89, 395, 397, 398, 431, 434, 531; narrow gauge lines in South Dakota, 513–15; see Colorado & Southern Ry. for Colorado lines
Chicago, Clinton, Dubuque & Minnesota RR, 394, 399, 428
Chicago, Danville & Vincennes Ry., 389
Chicago, Fort Madison & Des Moines Ry., 398
Chicago, IL, 26, 32, 33, 35, 40, 41, 42, 43, 56, 57, 58, 80, 82, 85, 101, 146, 148, 204, 244, 273, 281, 390, 392, 393, 400, 417, 426, 434, 475, 524, 557, 558; proposed site of narrow gauge convention in 1879, 98; narrow gauge from, 386–87
Chicago, Iowa & Kansas Ry., 386
Chicago, Millington & Western Ry., 51, 223, 386–87
Chicago, Milwaukee & St. Paul Ry., 41, 138, 185, 192, 215, 223, 240, 249, 277–78, 558; narrow gauge lines, 394, 397, 398, 399, 428, 429, 557, 559; entry into Seattle, 552; see also Bellevue & Cascade RR
Chicago, Rock Island & Pacific Ry., 314, 319, 344, 348, 386, 399, 525

Chicago, Southwestern & Pacific, 400
Chicago, St. Louis & New Orleans RR, 429
Chicago, St. Paul, Minneapolis & Omaha Ry., 438
Chicago, Texas & Mexican Central Ry., 524
Chicago & Alton RR, 385, 479
Chicago & Atlantic Ry., 281, 392
Chicago & Eastern Illinois RR, 387, 389
Chicago & Elgin RR, 26
Chicago & North Western Ry., 26, 177, 344, 398; narrow gauge lines, 396–97, 516, 557–59
Chicago & Ohio River Ry., 387
Chicago & South Atlantic Ry., 80, 393
Chicago & South Haven Steamship Co., 427
Chicago & Tomah RR, 557–59
Chicago & West Michigan Ry., 425, 427
Chicago & Western Indiana RR, 273, 393
Childers, H. C. E., 61–62
Chile, 61, 152
Chillicothe, OH, 475, 476
Chino Valley Ry., 323
Choctaw, Oklahoma & Gulf RR, 314
Church of Jesus Christ of the Latter Day Saints, 86, 530–36 passim
Cimarron, NM, 49
Cincinnati, Atlantic & Columbus Ry., 479
Cincinnati, Batavia & Williamsburg R-, 464
Cincinnati, Columbus & Hocking Valley Ry., 468
Cincinnati, Effingham & Quincy Construction Co., 390
Cincinnati, Flemingsburg & Southeastern RR, 231
Cincinnati, Georgetown RR, 467
Cincinnati, Georgetown & Portsmouth RR, 93, 214, 235, 292, 464, 466
Cincinnati, Hamilton & Dayton RR, 108, 387, 465, 466, 467, 478
Cincinnati, Indianapolis & Western RR, 387
Cincinnati, Jackson & Mackinaw RR, 464
Cincinnati, Lebanon & Northern Ry., 279, 465, 478
Cincinnati, Milford & Loveland Traction Co., 479
Cincinnati, New Orleans & Texas Pacific Ry., 521
Cincinnati, New Richmond & Ohio River RR, 465
Cincinnati, OH, 25, 32, 34, 37, 85, 104, 105, 107, 110, 149, 279, 293, 390, 391, 403, 464, 466, 477, 478, 479; site of National Narrow-Gauge Railway Convention of 1878, 92–98
Cincinnati, Portsmouth & Virginia RR, 465
Cincinnati, Van Wert & Michigan Common Carrier Co., 464
Cincinnati, Wabash & Michigan Ry., 475
Cincinnati Northern RR (NYC), 464
Cincinnati Northern Ry. (TC&StL), 214, 285, 464, 476, 477, 478
Cincinnati Northwestern Ry., 467
Cincinnati Southern Ry., 36, 173, 520, 521
Cincinnati Street Ry., 466
Cincinnati Traction Co., 467
Cincinnati & Columbus Traction Co., 479
Cincinnati & Eastern Ry., 92, 93, 214, 225, 231–33, 464–65
Cincinnati & Lake Erie RR, 468
Cincinnati & Portsmouth RR, 466
Cincinnati & Southeastern Ry., 402

Cincinnati & St. Louis RR, 93
Cincinnati & Westwood RR, 138, 214, 465–66
Citizens' Railway, St. Louis, MO, 435
Civil War, 32, 35, 51, 79, 285, 305, 313, 314, 383, 512, 533, 543
Claremont Wharf, VA, 249, 539
Clarendon, AR, 313–14, 318
Clarendon, PA, 240
Clarion River Ry., 500
Clark, W. A., 313
Clarkdale, AZ, 313
Clarksburg, Weston & Glenville RR, 489, 553
Clarksburg, Weston & Midland RR, 235, 553
Clarksdale, MS, 431
Clarksville, TN, 519
Clayton, GA, 77
Clearfield & Jefferson Ry., 485
Cleburne, TX, 524
Clendennin & Spencer RR, 553
Cleveland, Canton, Coshocton & Straitsville RR, 469
Cleveland, Canton & Southern RR, 464, 469
Cleveland, Chagrin Falls & Northern RR, 464
Cleveland, Delphos & St. Louis RR, 134, 467, 494
Cleveland, Grover, 286, 360
Cleveland, OH, 26, 33, 35, 37, 233, 274, 464, 467, 470, 471, 472; narrow gauge from, 468–69
Cleveland, Tuscarawas Valley & Wheeling Ry., 462
Cleveland, Youngstown & Pittsburgh Ry., 470
Cleveland & Canton RR, 464, 469
Cleveland & Pittsburgh RR, 479
Cleveland & Western RR, 467
Clifton, AZ, 309, 311
Clifton & Lordsburg Ry., 310
Clifton & Southern Pacific Ry., 309
Climax, CO, 283, 357
Climax locomotive, 305, 403, 404, 486, 490, 504, 517, 552–53, 554; described, 160–61
Clio, CA, 327
Clive, IA, 397, 398
Clover Hill RR, 542
Coal & Coke Ry., 554, 555
Coalbasin, CO, 339
Coalville, UT, 532, 533, 536
Coalville & Echo RR, 532
Coburg, OR, 480
Cockerill, John, 11, 61
Coeur d'Alene Ry. & Navigation Co., 382
Coeur d'Alene Steam Navigation & Transportation Co., 382
Coinage Act of 1873, 285
Colburn, Zerah, 17–18
Coleman, MI, 426
Colfax, CA, 328
College Hill RR, 214, 467–68
Collett, IA, 398
Collettsville, NC, 459
Collier, Henry L., 116
Collusive pricing, see Cartelization
Colorado, 79, 85, 92, 98–99, 111, 185, 213, 221, 267, 276, 287, 289, 291, 338–66, 440, 530; impact of Sherman Silver Purchase Act, 285–86; map on front endpaper
Colorado, Wyoming & Great Northern RR, 359
Colorado Central RR, 57, 159, 187, 190, 196, 214, 217, 222, 234, 240, 276, 287, 288, 338,

Des Moines, IA, 396–98 *passim*
Des Moines, Osceola & Southern RR, 397, 434
Des Moines Northern & Western Ry., 397, 398
Des Moines North-Western RR, 397, 398
Des Moines & Fort Dodge RR, 397
Des Moines & Kansas City Ry., 234, 235, 397
Des Moines & Minneapolis RR, 396–97, 398
Des Moines & Minnesota RR, 199, 396–97, 502
Des Moines & Northern RR, 397, 398
Des Moines & Northwestern Ry., 234, 235, 397, 398
Detroit, Bay City & Alpena RR, 420–21
Detroit, Grand Rapids & Western RR, 425
Detroit, MI, 108, 424, 426
Detroit, Toledo & Ironton RR, 468, 473, 478
Detroit Car Works, 204, 256
Detroit Southern RR, 473
Detroit & Mackinac Ry., 420, 421
Devon, WV, 540
Dexter, MO, 106
Diamond Springs, CA, 324
Diamond & Caldor Ry., 190, 217, 324
Dickens, Col. C. H., 19
Dickson, TN, 520
Dickson Mfg. Co., 140–44, 152, 452, 453
Diehl or Diehle, Wm. A., 95, 120
Diesel locomotives, 162, 164
Dillaye, Stephen D., 66, 68
Dillingham, Benjamin F., 379, 380, 381
Dillon, Sidney, 64, 400
Dismal Swamp RR, 543
Divide, MT, 437
Dixie, WA, 550
Dodge, Grenville M., 398
Dodgeville, WI, 558
Doe Run, MO, 433
Dolores, CO, 360, 361, 450
Donahue, Peter, 329, 335
Dougherty, PA, 484
Douglas, Maj. James P., 104, 109, 316, 317, 526
Downeyville, NV, 245
Dragon, UT, 364
Dredge, James, 173
Duck River Valley Narrow Gauge RR, 516
Dudley, WA, 550
Duff, John R., 64
Duluth, South Shore & Atlantic Ry., 423
Dumbarton Point, CA, 336
Duncan Mills, CA, 329–30
Dunkirk, NY, 31, 64
Dunn, F. W., 138–39
Dupont, OH, 109, 474
Durango, CO, 98, 201, 226, 287, 288, 289, 347, 350
Durango & Silverton Narrow Gauge RR, 155, 156, 291, 292, 353
Durant, Thomas C., 64
Durham Transportation Co., 529

Eagle Pass, TX, 105, 106, 317, 527
Eagles Mere RR, 486, 499
Eames vacuum brake, 153, 187–91, 453
East Broad Top RR & Coal Co., 155, 156, 174, 185–87, 206, 207, 287, 486–88, 501, 516; transfer arrangements, 258–62, 266, 267
East Line & Red River RR, 136, 262, 524
East New York & Canarsie RR, 60
East Palatka, FL, 370

East Saginaw, MI, 274, 283, 284, 424, 425, 426
East Saginaw & St. Clair RR, 424
East Smethport, PA, 256, 508
East St. Louis, Cahokia & Falling Springs R-, 384
East St. Louis, IL, 25, 82, 85, 104, 107, 108, 233, 252, 256, 273, 383–86, 477, 479
East St. Louis Connecting Ry., 105, 386
East Tennessee, Virginia & Georgia Ry., 516, 521
East Tennessee Ry., 519
East Tennessee & Western North Carolina RR, 159, 163, 184, 185, 201, 202–3, 234, 235, 263, 267, 289, 308, 516–19
East Waterford, PA, 501
East & West RR of Alabama, 99, 274, 293, 302–4, 376
Eastern Junction, Broad Sound Pier & Point Shirley RR, 417–18
Eastern Maine RR, 409
Eastern & Western Air Line Ry., 467
Eccles, David S., 481–83
Echo & Park City RR, 533
Eckley, Gen. E. R., 464, 468
Edaville RR, 291, 413
Edenton, NC, 546, 548
Edgartown, MA, 419
Edith, CO, 360
Edson, William D., 140
Effingham, IL, 93, 230, 233, 390, 391
El Paso, TX, 79, 80, 98, 275, 311, 344, 347, 528
El Paso & Southwestern RR, 310, 312
El Vado, NM, 450
Elberton Air Line RR, 373, 374
Eldred, PA, 507, 508, 509, 510
Electric streetcar, 272, 467, 494
Elizabethton, TN, 267, 517, 518, 519
Elk River, 84
Elk & Little Kanawha RR, 554
Elkader, IA, 398
Elkton, VA, 84
Ellijay RR, 375
Ellington, Mo, 433
Ellis, John, 12
Elmina & Eastern Transportation Co., 529
Elverton, TN, 521
Ely, Theodore N., 178
Embarras River, 229, 387
Emeryville, CA, 322–23, 336
Emlenton, Shippenville & Clarion RR, 494
Emlenton & Shippenville RR, 494, 495
Engineer, The, 17
Engineering, 17–18
Engineering Congress of 1893, 117
England, George, 13, 14
Englewood, SD, 514, 515
English, AR, 316
Ephraim, UT, 532
Eppes Falls, VA, 543
Erie, PA, 161
Erie Canal, 24, 25, 31, 537
Erie RR, 24, 25, 26, 27, 30, 31, 35, 36, 37, 38, 49, 64, 217, 259–60, 281, 450, 451, 470, 483, 496, 498, 504; narrow gauge lines, 392, 505–11; car transfer apparatus, 252–53, 254, 510
Espanola, NM, 344, 346, 347
Etherton, IL, 106
Eugene, IN, 103, 475, 477
Eureka, CA, 320

Eureka, NV, 247–48, 441–43
Eureka & Colorado River RR, 441
Eureka & Palisade RR, 89, 195, 233, 234, 235, 248, 312, 441–43
Eureka & Ruby Hill Narrow Gauge RR, 441
European & North American Ry., 407
Eustis RR, 411, 412
Evans, Dr. Carey A., 103, 467, 474, 475
Evans, John, 130, 353, 354
Evans, Walton W., 28, 61–63, 65, 68, 89, 115, 126, 295; portrait, 61
Evansville, IN, 519

Fair, James G., 335
Fairbanks, AK, 306
Fairfax, VA, 84
Fairlie, Robert F., 10–16, 19–20, 43, 48, 54, 76, 79, 123–25, 151, 170–71, 221; biography, 10; portrait, 11; "On the Gauge for the Railways of the Future," 16–17, 58; *Railways or No Railways*, 65; death, 274
Fairlie Engine & Steam Carriage Co., 14
Fairlie locomotive, 10–12, 14–17, 20, 61, 123–26, 175
Fairport, OH, 274, 464, 468, 469, 470, 471, 472
Fairview, IL, 387–89
Falkner, Col. W. C., 85, 432
Farmers Union RR, 223, 397
Farmersville, TX, 524
Farmington, ME, 242, 410, 412, 413
Farmington, NM, 236, 287, 290, 291, 350, 352
Farmville, VA, 543
Farmville & Powhatan RR, 543
Faulkner, William, 432
Fayetteville, TN, 516
Felton, CA, 336, 337
Fennimore, WI, 558
Ferries & Cliff House Ry., 324
Festiniog Ry., 12–18, 69, 70, 79, 91, 170, 416
Fink, Albert, 108
Finland, 28
Finleyville, PA, 498
Fish, George C., 61
Fishwick, John P., 293
Fitchburg RR, 177
Fitzgibbon, Abram, 10
Flagler, Henry M., 368, 370
Flaugh, CO, 360
Fleming, Howard, 50, 51, 54, 90, 92, 171, 174, 193–94, 195, 217, 223, 224, 301; *Narrow Gauge Railways in America* published, 91
Flemingsburg, KY, 231, 402, 403
Flemingsburg & Northern RR, 402
Flint & Pere Marquette RR, 172, 274, 283–84, 424–26
Flora, IL, 106
Florence & Cripple Creek RR, 145, 286, 358–59, 437
Florida, 28, 99, 366–71; land grant program, 99, 366; map, 367
Florida Central & Peninsular RR, 371
Florida Central & Western RR, 370
Florida East Coast Ry., 368, 369, 370
Florida Midland Ry., 369, 370
Florida Southern Ry., 366–68, 369, 370
Florida Transit RR, 370
Florida & Georgia Ry., 366
Fond du Lac, Amboy & Peoria RR, 386, 557
Fond du Lac, WI, 557, 560

Harbor Springs Ry., 223, 421
Harlan & Hollingsworth Co., 198
Harper, Charles R., 262
Harper, Dr. W., 262
Harriman, Edward H., 440
Harrison, ME, 407
Harrisonburg, VA, 84, 85, 86, 87, 90
Harrisville, WV, 555
Hartwell RR, 374–75
Hatcham Iron Works, 13, 14
Hauck, Cornelius W., 235
Havana, IL, 388, 389
Havana, Rantoul & Eastern RR, 56, 94, 99,
    104, 115, 135, 214, 387, 389, 475
Hawaii, 111, 302, 377–82; maps, 378, 379,
    380
Hawaii, Island of, 378, 379, 382
Hawaii Consolidated Ry., 378
Hawaii Ry., 378, 379
Hawaiian Agricultural Co., 382
Hawaiian RR., 378, 379
Hawkshaw, John, 19
Hawthorne, NV, 227, 439, 440
Hayes, A. C., 94
Hays, Milton D., 493, 498
Hayt's Corners, Ovid & Willard RR, 454–55
Hebron, AR, 316
Hecla & Torch Lake RR, 423
Heisler, Charles L., 161
Heisler locomotive, 161
Helen Thatcher White Foundation, 291
Helena, AR, 77, 313, 314, 315, 431
Helena, MT, 534, 535
Henderson, TN, 521
Herculaneum, excavations at, 28
Herkimer, Newport & Poland Ry., 455
Hetch Hetchy & Yosemite Valleys Ry., 161,
    190, 324
Hill, A. F., 94
Hill, James J., 37, 428
Hillboro Short Line, 465
Hillsboro, KY, 402
Hillsboro, OH, 465, 479
Hillsboro RR, 465
Hines, Edward, Lumber Co., 164
Hinkley Locomotive Works, 58, 134, 140, 142,
    144, 407, 409, 410, 416, 445
Hinkley & Williams, see Hinkley Locomotive
    Works
Hitler, Adolf, 37
Hoboken, NJ, 24, 25
Hoffmann, Walther, 272
Hohenwald, TN, 520
Holland, Charles M., 13
Holly Springs, Brownsville & Ohio RR, 521
Holly River RR, 556
Holly River & Addison Ry., 556
Holston Valley Ry., 519
Honesdale, PA, 27
Hooper, CO, 290
Hoosac Tunnel & Wilmington RR, 150, 285,
    538–39
Hope, AR, 319, 406
Horsehoe Curve, 218
Hoschton, GA, 373
Hot Springs, AR, 314, 318
Hot Springs Branch RR, 135, 184, 314
Houghton, MI, 423
Houston, TX, 109–10, 525–26, 528

Houston East & West Texas Ry., 91, 109, 115,
    137, 196–97, 235, 317, 406, 525–26, 529
Houston Tap & Brazoria Ry., 524
Houston & Shreveport Ry., 406, 526
Houston & Texas Central Ry., 115, 523, 525
Hower, H. C., 249, 501, 502
Hoxeyville, MI, 422
Hudson, OH, 80
Hudson, William S., 54, 60, 143, 149, 175
Hudson River, 25, 32, 43
Hudson River Day Line, 452–53
Hudson Valley Ry., 458
Hulbert, Col. Edward, 20, 56, 57, 77, 79, 84,
    85, 96–98, 111, 115, 116–17, 149–50, 151,
    174, 184, 198, 199, 225, 250, 303, 375, 470,
    476, 525–26; biography, 75–76; portrait,
    76; The Narrow Gauge Railway, 76; calls
    National Narrow-Gauge Railway Convention
    of 1872, 82–83; calls National Narrow-
    Gauge Railway Convention of 1878, 92–93;
    opinion on 2'-0" railroads, 289
Humphreys, Solon, 472, 496
Hunt, Joseph W., 103, 474, 475
Hunter, NY, 458, 459
Huntingdon & Broad Top Mountain RR, 486
Huntington, Collis P., 403, 440
Huntington, Henry E., 326
Huntington, IN, 281, 392
Huron, OH, 479
Huron & Eastern Ry., 426

Idaho, 99, 382–83; maps, 383, 533
Idaho Springs, CO, 341
Ignacio, CA, 335
Ihling, John, transfer device, 256, 257, 427
Illinois, 27, 42, 81, 85, 92, 99, 104, 106, 213–
    14, 383–91, 479; map, 384
Illinois Central RR, 27, 36, 41, 58, 105, 116,
    149, 236, 252, 256, 384, 386, 389, 390, 395,
    397, 405, 429–32, 519; ferries at Cairo, 268,
    318
Illinois & St. Louis Bridge Co., 385
Illinois & Wisconsin Narrow Gauge R-, 558
Ilwaco Ry. & Navigation Co., 215, 549–50
Imperial Livny Ry., 16
Independence, MO, 436
India, 6, 10, 16, 18, 19, 81, 294
Indiana, 27, 32, 75, 86, 92, 213–14, 216,
    391–94; map, 391
Indiana, Alabama & Texas Ry., 519
Indiana, Decatur & Western Ry., 387
Indiana Hi Rail Corp., 479
Indiana Rail Road, 390
Indiana Railroad, 404
Indiana & Illinois Southern Ry., 233, 283, 390
Indiana & Ohio Rail Corp., 478
Indianapolis, Bloomington & Western Ry., 389
Indianapolis, Delphi & Chicago Ry., 80, 93,
    101, 214, 263, 273, 284, 392–94, 398
Indianapolis, IN, 43, 80, 101, 263, 273, 390,
    392, 404
Indianapolis Southern RR, 392
Indianapolis Terminal Corp., 390
Indianapolis & Cincinnati Traction Co., 466
Indianapolis & Vincennes RR, 390
Indonesia, 157
Inland Rivers, 24, 39, 62, 82, 557
Inness, Thomas B., 285
Institution of Civil Engineers, 10, 18

Interchange of equipment, 32–35
International Rys. of Central America, 158, 483
International & Great Northern RR, 105, 316,
    317, 525, 526, 529
Interstate Commerce Commission, 24, 38, 234,
    287, 288, 290–91, 293, 301, 319, 504, 526,
    529, 550, 556; abandonment orders in Part
    II, passim
Interstate Public Service Co., 404
Interurban Electric Ry., 337
Interurbans, 83, 233, 236, 466, 471, 479, 515,
    532
Ione City, CA, 338
Iowa, 42, 55–56, 394–98; Board of Railroad
    Commissioners, 240, 244, 394; map, 395
Iowa Central Ry., 395
Iowa Eastern RR, 398, 399
Iowa Pool, 38, 40, 43
Iowa & Minnesota Ry., 396
Iowa & Northwestern Ry., 398
Ireland, 6
Iron Mountain Ry., 324
Iron Mountain & Helena RR, 314
Iron Ridge, WI, 557
Iron RR, 476, 477, 478
Ironton, OH, 104, 110, 476, 477
Isle of Man Ry., 9
Isthmus of Darien, ship railway, 263
Ivan, LA, 404

Jackson, MS, 431, 432
Jackson, William S., 124, 347, 531
Jackson & Sharp Co., 171, 175, 181, 193, 194,
    195, 200, 201
Jacksonport, AR, 314
Jacksonville, FL, 368, 371
Jacksonville, St. Augustine & Halifax River Ry.,
    368–69, 370
Jacksonville, St. Augustine & Indian River Ry.,
    369
Jacksonville, Tampa & Key West Ry., 366, 367,
    368, 369, 371
Jacksonville, TX, 526, 527
Jacksonville & Atlantic Ry., 196–97, 368
James River, 539, 543
Janney, Eli H., 36, 187
Janney coupler, 24, 36, 44, 187, 190, 268, 294,
    324
Japan, 19
Japanese National Rys., 294–95
Jefferson, GA, 373, 374
Jefferson, TX, 262, 524
Jefferson & Northwestern Ry., 529
Jeffery, Edward T., 350, 360
Jerome, AZ, 114, 313
Jersey Shore, Pine Creek & Buffalo Ry., 485
Jesup, Paton & Co., 185
Jewell, IA, 397
Jewett, TN, 521
John Ericsson, 12
Johnson, Lorenzo M., 66–71, 107, 110, 240,
    241, 250
Johnson, Lyndon B., 317
Johnson City, Bakersville & Southern Ry., 519
Johnson City, TN, 163, 202, 267, 516–19
Johnsonville, IL, 106
Johnsonville, MS, 429, 430
Johnsonville, TN, 516
Jones, CA, 333

Philadelphia & Atlantic City Ry., 91, 233, 273, 285, 446, 447–49
Philadelphia & Baltimore Central RR, 489
Philadelphia & Cape May Short Line, 446
Philadelphia & Erie RR, 500
Philadelphia & Reading RR, 285, 415, 446, 449, 485, 503
Phillips, Elijah B., 107, 116, 477
Phillips, ME, 410
Phillips & Rangeley RR, 411, 412
Phoenicia, NY, 253, 459
Phoenix, AZ, 114
Phoenix & Eastern RR, 311
Pickens & Addison Ry., 556
Pickens & Hacker's Valley RR, 557
Pickens & Webster Springs RR, 557
Piedmont RR, 542
Pierport, MI, 420
Piggybacking, 263
Pihl, Carl, 7–9, 16, 17, 18; portrait, 10
Pine Bluff, AR, 282, 293, 314, 318
Pine Bluff, Monroe & New Orleans Ry., 316
Pine Bluff Arkansas River Ry., 316
Pine Bluff & Eastern Ry., 316
Pine Bluff & Swan Lake Ry., 316
Pine River Valley & Stevens Point RR, 223, 278. 559–60
Pineola, NC, 517
Pinsley, Samuel L., 539
Pioche Pacific Transportation Co., 443
Pioche & Bullionville RR, 443
Pittsburg, Shawmut & Northern RR, 507, 509
Pittsburgh, Akron & Chicago, 467
Pittsburgh, Akron & Western Ry., 467
Pittsburgh, Bradford & Buffalo RR, 494, 495
Pittsburgh, Castle Shannon & Washington RR, 497
Pittsburgh, Chartiers & Youghiogheny Ry., 498
Pittsburgh, Cincinnati & St. Louis RR, 502
Pittsburgh, Fort Wayne & Chicago Ry., 35, 473
Pittsburgh, New Castle & Lake Erie RR, 97, 392, 494
Pittsburgh, PA, 25, 26, 35, 36, 60, 94, 99, 187, 467, 493, 494–97, 510; proposed for second convention of 1878, 96
Pittsburgh, Painesville & Fairport RR, 472
Pittsburgh Locomotive Works, 134, 138, 139, 140–44, 152, 374, 394, 428
Pittsburgh Rys., 494
Pittsburgh Southern RR, 94, 226, 257, 493, 497–98, 502
Pittsburgh & Castle Shannon RR, 493, 497, 498
Pittsburgh & Lake Erie RR, 497, 498, 503
Pittsburgh & Maumee, 467
Pittsburgh & McKeesport Car & Locomotive Co., 140–41, 144; advertisement, 169
Pittsburgh & Monongahela Valley RR, 498
Pittsburgh & Northwestern RR, 494
Pittsburgh & West Virginia Ry., 502, 507
Pittsburgh & Western RR, 98, 99, 217, 227, 276, 287, 467, 472, 488, 494–97, 498, 507, 508; map on rear endpaper
Pittsville, VA, 544
Pittsylvania RR, 254, 544
Placerville, CA, 324
Placerville, CO, 360
Plainfield, IL, 386
Plains, GA, 371
Plant, Henry B., 367, 370, 371

Plant System, 366–71 *passim*
Platt, Sen. T. C., 483, 509
Platteville, WI, 558
Plattsburgh & Dannemora RR, 453, 454
Pleasantville & Ocean City, 448–49
Plymouth, NC, 461
Pocatello, ID, 99, 256, 535
Point Pleasant, WV, 84, 93, 464, 479
Point Shirley Street Ry., 418
Poland, NY, 455
Pole, William, 18
Pollok & Angelina Valley Transportation Co., 529
Pompeii, excavations at, 28
Ponca, NE, 438
Poncha Junction, 290, 352
Pontotoc, MS, 432
Pools, *see* cartelization
Poor, Henry Varnum, 524
Poor, M. C., 190, 360
Poplar Bluff & Dan River Ry., 434
Port Allegany, PA, 485–86
Port Austin, MI, 284, 424–26
Port Gibson, MS, 431
Port Huron, MI, 192, 274, 283, 284, 424–26
Port Huron & Northwestern Ry., 99, 135, 136, 192, 216, 233, 274, 424–26; techniques of conversion, 283–84
Port Huron & South Western Ry., 424
Port Isabel, TX, 527
Port Isabel & Rio Grande Valley Ry., 527
Port Royal, PA, 249, 487, 501
Port San Luis Transportation Co., 332
Port Townsend Southern RR, 550
Port Townsend & Puget Sound Ry., 551
Porter, Bell & Co., advertisement, 151; *see* Porter, H. K. & Co.
Porter, H. K. & Co., 54, 60, 92, 131–37, 151, 163, 223, 225, 317, 323, 378, 419, 467, 513, 514, 520, 553; output, 140–44
Porter's Creek & Gauley RR, 557
Portland, ME, 6, 26, 30, 407, 413
Portland, OR, 326, 480, 481, 548, 549
Portland Consolidated Street Ry., 481
Portland Co., 407, 409
Portland & Ogdensburg RR, 407
Portland & Rumford Falls Ry., 410
Portland & Vancouver Ry., 481
Portland & Willamette Valley Ry., 285, 480
Portland & Yamhill RR, 480
Portsmouth, OH, 93, 464, 465, 466
Portsmouth, VA, 539
Portugal, 28
Portville, NY, 505, 507, 510
Potomac, Fredericksburg & Piedmont RR, 545
Potomac River, 25, 27, 84
Powellsville, NC, 461
Prairie City, OR, 482
Presidio, TX, 110
Presque Isle, ME, 407
Pressed Steel Car Co., 187
Preston, MN, 249–50, 428
Price, UT, 531
Princeton, IL, 386
Princeton, KY, 519
Profile & Franconia Notch RR, 445
Prospect, KY, 403
Provo, UT, 359, 530, 531
Pueblo, CO, 81, 267, 275, 344, 348, 352
Pulaski, TN, 521

Pullman, WV, 555
Pullman Co., 174, 204
Pulsifer, R. M., 370, 375
Punta Gorda, FL, 367, 370, 371
Purdue University, 165

Quarryville, PA, 207
Quebec, Montreal, Ottawa & Occidental Ry., 36
Quebec, North Shore & Labrador Ry., 295
Queensland Ry., 10, 12, 14, 61
Quincy, Payson & Southeastern Ry., 390
Quincy & Torch Lake RR, 423
Quirk, Robert, 117

Rabun Gap, 52, 77
Railroad Gazette, 17, 48, 58, 117, 172, 198, 274, 276, 457, 477, 546
Railroad Museum of Pennsylvania, 207, 490
Rails, 223–24
Railway Age, 48, 91, 99, 101, 111, 139, 223, 226; projected book on narrow gauge practice, 98
Railway Appliances Exposition of 1883, 146, 148, 150, 179
Railway Master Mechanics' Association, 175
Railway Reporter, 233, 495
Railway World, 91
Rainbow, UT, 365
Raleigh Springs, TN, 521
Raleigh & Southwestern Ry., 554–55
Ralston, CO, 341, 344
Ramsbottom, John, 7
Ramsey, IL, 256
Ramsey, Joseph O., 56, 57, 96, 224, 485
Ramsey, Robert H., 253–54
Ramsey Transfer, 108, 253–56, 258, 259, 427, 459, 476, 485, 490, 507, 535; advertisement, 271
Randolph, ME, 409
Rangeley, ME, 410, 411
Rangeley RR, 411
Rantoul RR, 389
Rate of return, narrow gauge railroads, 235
Readsboro, VT, 538, 539
Red Line Transit Co., 33
Red Mountain, CO, 221, 362–63
Red River, 104, 316, 318, 524, 525
Red River Valley RR, 404
Redstone, CO, 339
Reedsville, PA, 117
Rehor, John A., 227, 233
Rendel, A. M., 19
Rennie, Sir John, 4
Reno, MN, 250, 428
Reno, NV, 326–28
Rensselaer, IN, 42, 43, 80, 392, 393
Renton, WA, 551
Rew City, PA, 508
Rew City & Eldred RR, 508, 509–10
Reynolds, Joseph, 314
Rhinelander, WI, 560
Rhode Island Locomotive Works, 140–44, 152, 368
Rhomberg, J. A., 523
Richburg, NY, 505, 507, 508, 509
Richland Center, WI, 559
Richmond, Fredericksburg & Potomac RR, 545
Richmond, VA, 24, 28, 35, 85, 248
Richmond Consolidated Mining Co., 247, 441

Library of Congress Cataloging-in-Publication Data

Hilton, George Woodman.
    American narrow gauge railroads/George W.
Hilton.
        p.   cm.
    ISBN 0-8047-1731-1 (alk. paper):
    1. Railroads, Narrow-gauge—United
States.   I. Title.
TF23.H56   1990
385′.52′0973—dc20   89-21873
                                              CIP

  ⊗ This book is printed on acid-free paper.

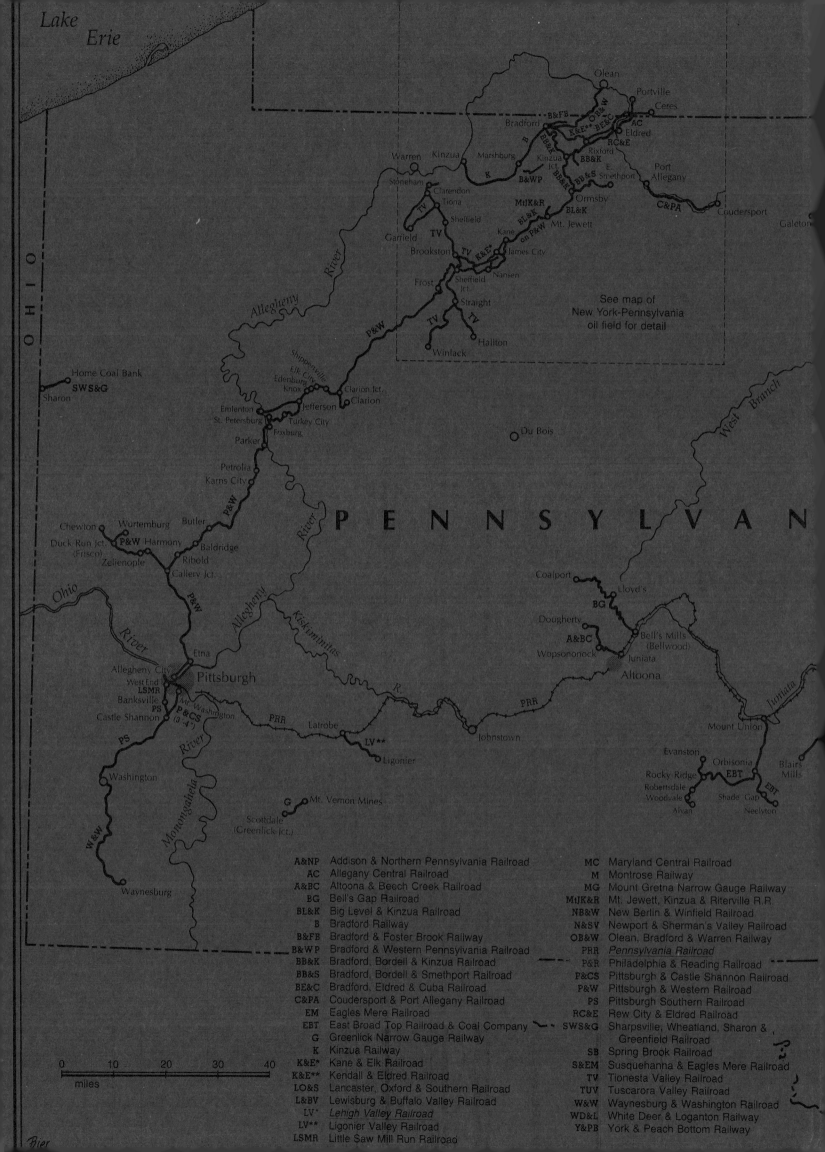

Lake Erie

OHIO

PENNSYLVAN[IA]

See map of New York-Pennsylvania oil field for detail

Scale:
0   10   20   30   40
miles

A&NP — Addison & Northern Pennsylvania Railroad
AC — Allegany Central Railroad
A&BC — Altoona & Beech Creek Railroad
BG — Bell's Gap Railroad
BL&K — Big Level & Kinzua Railroad
B — Bradford Railway
B&FB — Bradford & Foster Brook Railway
B&WP — Bradford & Western Pennsylvania Railroad
BB&K — Bradford, Bordell & Kinzua Railroad
BB&S — Bradford, Bordell & Smethport Railroad
BE&C — Bradford, Eldred & Cuba Railroad
C&PA — Coudersport & Port Allegany Railroad
EM — Eagles Mere Railroad
EBT — East Broad Top Railroad & Coal Company
G — Greenlick Narrow Gauge Railway
K — Kinzua Railway
K&E* — Kane & Elk Railroad
K&E** — Kendall & Eldred Railroad
LO&S — Lancaster, Oxford & Southern Railroad
L&BV — Lewisburg & Buffalo Valley Railroad
LV* — Lehigh Valley Railroad
LV** — Ligonier Valley Railroad
LSMR — Little Saw Mill Run Railroad

MC — Maryland Central Railroad
M — Montrose Railway
MG — Mount Gretna Narrow Gauge Railway
MtJK&R — Mt. Jewett, Kinzua & Riterville R.R.
NB&W — New Berlin & Winfield Railroad
N&SV — Newport & Sherman's Valley Railroad
OB&W — Olean, Bradford & Warren Railway
PRR — Pennsylvania Railroad
P&R — Philadelphia & Reading Railroad
P&CS — Pittsburgh & Castle Shannon Railroad
P&W — Pittsburgh & Western Railroad
PS — Pittsburgh Southern Railroad
RC&E — Rew City & Eldred Railroad
SWS&G — Sharpsville, Wheatland, Sharon & Greenfield Railroad
SB — Spring Brook Railroad
S&EM — Susquehanna & Eagles Mere Railroad
TV — Tionesta Valley Railroad
TUV — Tuscarora Valley Railroad
W&W — Waynesburg & Washington Railroad
WD&L — White Deer & Loganton Railway
Y&PB — York & Peach Bottom Railway